Palmyra:

The True Story of an Island Tragedy

Watch for the following books by Wesley Walker;

The New Martians

A Question of Chaos

The Piano Man

Email address
linfield@fastmail.com

Wesley Walker's

Palmyra:

The True Story of an Island Tragedy

Copyright Page

B&E Press

PO Box 75056
Honolulu, HI 96836

ISBN

10 digit ISBN: 0692569618

13 digit ISBN: 978-0692569610

ACKNOWLEDGMENTS

To Stephanie for her innocence and past belief; and also to those unnamed few who continue to believe;

Dedications for Kara, First Believer, constant with encouragement. And in remembrance of Gerald Rose, another long time friend and supporter; peace, brother; for Buster, may the inspiration and daring of your ventures bring the rewards you seek.

Let me not overlook Vincent Bugliosi and Bruce Henderson, without whose version I would have nothing to correct with truth.

Finally, for all those who disrespect truth and reality; may you eat the cake of your blissful ignorance and find comfort in your small-minded smugness.

Wesley Walker

Disclaimer

Every single word contained in the composition of the narration as found in Palmyra: The True Story of an Island Tragedy is entirely of my own choosing and thus I am solely responsible for any mistaken liability which may ensue, not to mention my readiness to stand firm in the face of all criticisms and castigations and defend the truth of these events.

Wesley Walker

FOREWORD

The bunk is my current mistress, lending all the comfort and consolation old loves cannot. She calls plaintively when I am too far away and squeaks like a virgin in the fevers of my longing during dark hours. In daylight, she is a desk in the fifty square feet of my cell-office, complete with sink and open toilet.

After many years and a life sentence for murder, I thought I had made a sort of bitter peace with myself. But one day in March, 1991, the journey back began with George Jones wailing his lonesome notes through the earphones of my tiny Panasonic: "I've had good luck and bad luck and no luck at all."

"Hey, Buck," a fellow convict called, leaning a grizzled head over the invisible line of my privacy at the doorway, "They're talking shit about you on the tube."

Out on the balcony rail of the cellblocks' second tier, I saw a vaguely familiar face, his mouth a smug cradle of ivory kernels beneath the obsidian snake-eyes I remember so well. We had met across a conference table in a courtroom six years before, each sizing the other up and concealing mutual antipathy. Vincent Bugliosi, a man whose first claim to fame was the prosecution of Charles Manson, had lately added another building block to his reputation with the publication of And The Sea Will Tell, the tale of his successful defense of Stephanie Stearns, my codefendant in a case charging the murder of Eleanor "Muff" Graham.

No one enjoys Bugliosi more than Bugliosi. He was on a roll, the dimensions of the cathode-ray tube almost too small to contain him. Four minus two does not leave two, he seemed to be saying. In this case it left one. There were four people, his analogy went. Two met mysterious deaths on a haunted hard luck atoll called Palmyra, a thousand miles south of Hawaii, and two survived. But only one was a murderer and he has been removed from the equation.

Me.

Then came the CBS mini-series. I saw only the first half, more than enough to prepare me for the book. I had always known the inevitability of being forced to assume the central role of villainy, but was still somehow strangely unprepared for the cruel inventiveness of my enemies.

Bugliosi thinks himself able to divine truth. He says of me, "lurking beneath his stoical CPA demeanor was an unmistakable malevolence that most people who came near him sensed in their very bones. I gazed at Buck Walker. Through it all, there he sat, taciturn and still, the only person on the face of the planet, in my view, who knew exactly what had happened. Yet there he sat like the rest of us, giving the impression he was being educated or tantalized along with everyone else. I wondered whether he could be thinking, 'What stupid jerks all of them are. That's not how I did it!'"

The story, a gospel according to Bugliosi, coupled to the tawdry sensationalism of the various forms of maniac I was portrayed to be, a gleeful murderer by poison, gun, knife, sledgehammer, acetylene torch and chainsaw, according to the pet fantasy, or merely a zombie slave to the evil will of the witch, Stephanie, would serve well in the pages of National Enquirer. Bugliosi, Bela Lugosi, close enough to Dracula, who licks blood from his fangs and compares me to Nazis, that towering figure of virtue who only defends the innocent. If you don't believe it, just ask him. The bigger the dragon, the more valorous the knight. Modesty is not one of his sins.

Without the crime of homicide and a murder, we would not have, in Bugliosi's own words, "unquestionably one of the most fascinating and enigmatic true murder mysteries of our times." Such a characterization, even if untrue, sells books.

I watched a depressing parade of small people with small minds, all closed like mousetraps, waving their theories about like banners in celebration of their precious moments of television fame, and was smug in my contempt for having resisted all suasions to appear with them. But it tortured me that they could speak and I could not.

Rub salt in the great wound of the insult, lift a sponge of vinegar to my lips. I am used to it, for life in prison is nothing less to me than an extended crucifixion. I look about me for the thief I will take with me into heaven, where I'm sure to find more dogs than people.

Yes, and I feel a dark rage, too, a madness rising up and threatening to consume me. Like the beast I have been painted to be, my quivering hand reaches for the nearest weapon and, with bloodlust in my cold killer's eyes, I charge forth to seek revenge...with my ballpoint pen and a pad of lined paper.

It's true, I am the only person on the planet Earth who knows exactly what happened on Palmyra, the fate of the Grahams. I am the only living eyewitness to events that transformed a tranquil paradise into a nightmare on a dying afternoon in late August, 1974. I have always believed my silence on the subject, my ability to lock it all within, was not only a necessary act of self-preservation but also a mercy granted to Stephanie and respect to the memory of Malcolm and Eleanor Graham.

You will see that there was a shame to be shared in diverse degrees among the three who instigated the choreography of death, and nothing but blissful ignorance for the excluded one. Truth is not always a thing of beauty. It is as often a makeshift framework upon which to display spectacles of the sordid and ugly.

Time has a habit of providing new perspectives on past events, not the least of which is my own ignominious position resulting therefrom. I languish in prison with only the grayness of my life's remainder and death to comfort me, death years hence or in the next hour, peaceful or violent, sudden or prolonged. There is little to please me, less to hope for.

If I am to be blamed, let it be for my concealment of truth by small deceits and a zipped lip, even if such concealment of the true account of how Mac and Muff died, and the disposal of their remains, constituted a firm belief in the rightness of my actions. Let me also be blamed, as I blame myself, for having served as an agent of instigation for those events. In the purview of an imperfect world, a society with its own thumb in one eye, if this was wrong, it must nevertheless stand for the proposition that I do not shed my beliefs at the first opportune moment -- especially since confession offered no relief from the situation. None of this, however, is to say that I did not wish to bare all and so free myself from the stubbornly exclusive intimacy of the secret.

You are going to learn a number of new facts, some shocking, some tawdry, and some embarrassing. Already I can hear the chorus of outraged denials, but we shall see what we shall see.

Before we get into the substance, I have a few more preliminary remarks to make. One is about Bugliosi. You may come to think that I hold him in contempt that I am overflowing with a particular vitriol. While I will call a spade a spade, the fact is I am deeply grateful to him for having saved Stephanie's ass. I could almost, but not quite, wish he'd been available to represent me. If he had, my trial would have been a far cry from the farcical mess it was. But since he and I come at each other from diametrically opposed poles -- the irresistible force meeting an immovable object -- serious personal conflict would doubtlessly have occurred. Never-the-less, he did a superb job with Stephanie's defense, even if he did get a few important things wrong. The fact remains that if I'd had a lawyer of Bugliosi's caliber, it is my firm belief that I would not have been convicted for murder. This mystery, and it is still a mystery except to a very few, would have been resolved long ago. For one thing, I would have testified and told everything that you are going to read here. The fundamental difference has been money, cold hard cash, and the resources to hire a skilled attorney rather than having to settle for whatever hacks the judge chose to appoint.

When considering the possible merit of the Bugliosi version of this case, remember that it is supposed to be a true story. It is not. Rather it is a sort of manmade monster of distortions careening between fact, error, and wishful thinking on the part of a few mean-minded participants whose objective considerations failed to overcome temptations to imagine the worst.

Then there are the outright lies and even some perjurers, including, alas, poor Stephanie, as well as those who suborned it. Winston Churchill liked to tell of the witty Irishman who said: "There are a terrible lot of lies going about in the world and the worst of it is that half of them are true." That's the problem with lies, they often seem true. Each of us has the responsibility to separate the wheat from the chaff, the burden of not jumping to the popular conclusion even though it sometimes seems to be the only one.

Beware those who sing their own praises, I tell myself – the best whores are the most shameless. Distrust those who love to punish. Two evils do not make a good.

The writer, George Orwell, took honesty to be a necessary ingredient of good writing, which he defined as "the power to face unpleasant facts." He had learned from his experiences in the civil war in Spain in 1937, the year I was born, that objective truth could cease to exist, that the people who controlled the means of communication could, and did, alter it at will. For this reason, his friend, Arthur Koestler, said that history was dead.

Bugliosi's book, since it purports to be true, may be considered a piece of history, a tiny fragment in the great mosaic of life. But when writers mix fiction with fact, they produce either art or propaganda, but not history. If the basic assumption, which lies at the heart of Bugliosi's book, is not true, then of what value are its 652 pages? Is murder proven or is it no more than a clever diatribe concealing a megalomaniacal motive to make mega-bucks?

"By waves and winds I'm tossed and driven," Joshua Slocum wrote in Sailing Alone Around the World, a favorite book of mine since my teen years. As I begin this tale, I like to think that I have something of his spirit when he continues, "Thus the voyage which I am now to relate was a natural outcome not only of my love of adventure, but of my lifelong experience."

BOOK I

A PASSAGE TO HELL

"There are many shades in the danger of adventures and gales, and it is only now and then that there appears on the face of facts a sinister violence of intention - that indefinable something which forces it upon the mind and the heart of a man, that this complication of accidents or these elemental furies are coming at him with a purpose of malice, with a strength beyond control, with an unbridled cruelty that means to tear out of him his hope and fear, the pain of his fatigue and the longing for rest: which means to smash, to destroy, to annihilate all he has ever seen, known, loved, enjoyed, or hated; all that is priceless and necessary - the sunshine, the memories, the future; which means to sweep the whole precious world utterly away from his sight by the simple and appalling act of taking his life."

Joseph Conrad,
Lord Jim

"Beware the Jabberwock, my son!
The jaws that bite, the claws that catch!
Beware the Jubjub' bird, and shun
The frumious Bandersnatch!"
    Lewis Carroll
    Through the Looking Glass

CHAPTER 1

After the awful dream of the night before, I awoke Friday morning to the heat of the day, staggering about the confines of the cabin tent in a fog to prepare tea. Cup in hand, I stepped out to greet sky, water, and earth, my eyes becoming dewy in the glare of light. I sucked deep breaths of pure unpolluted air, hoping to ease the throbbing after-effects of too much rum and too little sleep.

Stephanie called, a plaintive note in her voice. "Baby, will you wake your ass up? You've left me stranded again!"

Oh, shit. I'd forgotten she'd been left aboard Iola. I waded out calf-deep into the water of the lagoon until I could see the blue and white hull sitting fifty yards away like an ugly old duck with an amateur facelift, her new mast waving half-heartedly for reassurance from a sailorman that she was still desirable. I waved back, caught Steph's eye to let her know I was coming to the rescue, slipped into a pair of cutoffs, stepped around the snoozing hounds, and wended my way through the shadowy haven toward Iola.

"Sorry, babe," I said, untying the painter with one hand, then using a foot to push the dinghy her way.

"Well, I wanted to put Puffer ashore, get her out of the way so I can do some work. Gawd, I mean, we're leaving tomorrow and we've got to be ready."

She slid in a practiced motion into the yellow rowboat, and then handed down the sassy red mutt who resembled a fox but was twice as smart.

"There we go, Puffy-pie."

"Not much left to do, babe," I opined while watching her push the boat to glide back ashore. "We about got it knocked."

*****

I stumbled through the day, worrying my secrets, working and sweating, going through all the final motions necessary in preparing for our voyage to Fanning Island, two hundred and twenty-five miles southeast of Palmyra, a trip for which there had been no provision in the master plan.

Dickie had sent a radio message to Mac that he and Carlos would be delayed on their run from Hawaii, a thousand miles north, to re-supply us. Our food supply, already eked out with fish, coconuts, palm heart, tern eggs, and the occasional crab, was down to about ten days. The mutts were doing little better, although they loved the fish and coconut additives to their normal rations of dogfood.

Life was all about adaptation, improvising to make up for kinks or new developments in any plan or scheme, and so we would pop over to the plantation store on Fanning for interim supplies.

I say pop over, but it wasn't quite as simple as a run to the supermarket twelve blocks down the avenue. Since Iola had no engine, we were entirely dependent upon the often-fickle winds in the belt of ocean near the equator known as the doldrums. On top of that, the prevailing winds, when they blew, were dead out of the east, the very direction we had to go. The voyage, only about two days at five knots with an engine, would take us twice that if we were lucky, possibly six or more if we were not. We could get there all right, but it might require the patience of Job.

Finally, all the chores were done. Iola was ready. We had cleaned and scrubbed and stowed. The batteries for the running lights were charged, the gas-powered generator back ashore to power the refrigerator. I had promised to leave it for Mac and Muff's use while we were gone -- their shipboard refrigeration unit was on the blink. I had ferried all the fertilizers ashore to store them in the refrigerator house. After testing the redone forward hatchway for leaks, I had taken the old hatch cover ashore. Later I might add legs to it for a work table by our fireplace under the coconut trees at our adjacent campsite -- we wouldn't be needing it on the voyage because I'd permanently sealed the forward hatchway by gluing and nailing a piece of plywood over it and adding several layers of fiberglass cloth, resin, and paint. No more pesky leaks there.

I pulled out a butt, straightened, and lit it, puffed.

"Has Mac been over this morning?"

I gave her a sharp look. "No, why?"

"I was wondering where you got the cigarette. Thought he might have given you something for the trip."

"Oh, yeah, he did," I lied. "Some Bugler." Then, realizing the cigarette I was smoking had a Camel label printed on it, I added, "Plus, I found a couple of butts laying around."

"Where?"

The places I could find such valued items could be numbered on one finger, so I lied again. "Ah, over at Mac's workshop. Went over for a couple games of chess."

"Oh, are they home now?"

"Naw, I think they went fishing, " I suggested on the spur of the moment. "Didn't you hear them buzzing around the lagoon?"

"Oh, yeh."

"Probably having fish for dinner," I tried, hoping to plant the idea in her head.

She frowned.

"And coconut," I added. "Maybe tern-egg soufflé."

"Yek."

I went for a towel and soap, ready for some physical restoration at the communal bath -- the only bathtub on the island, which resided out in the open on old-fashioned iron legs next to the 12,000-gallon catchment tank of fresh cool water. I untied Sista and Popolo. "C'mon you lazy bums. Time to stretch 'em."

"Hey, Steph, c'mon," I yelled when we'd gathered back near Iola. "Bath time."

Her head popped up the main hatchway. "Give me another five or ten minutes. I gotta dig out something to wear."

"I'll meet you there," I replied, heading off with the mutts.

The path led along the end of the old WWII runway built by U.S. Army engineers when Palmyra had been a military outpost in the war with Japan, just along the edge of a small bay arcing into the shoreline of the lagoon. It curved around to the west past a corrugated metal equipment shed containing a roadgrader, a ten-wheel Army truck, an old corroded and useless sea-rescue launch, and a huge defunct stationary diesel engine, one of several, that had once supplied power to the island.

Through it at the other end was the Graham campsite, and to the left in a break in the reef sat moored their sleek and beautiful old character ketch, Sea Wind.

On past the ratty old house next door that had probably served as quarters for the commanding officer, where I had scavenged a couple of small tables and a still functional swivel-chair to furnish my tent. The large half-destroyed warehouse lay just ahead and, off to the right, the enlisted men's barracks, where I had scavenged my single bed -- head and footboards, springs, mattress and all for a cozy shore berth in my pasha's pavilion of a tent.

Swerving left onto the highest point of land on the island, a wharf area built by bulldozers scraping up coral against a telephone pole siding for the deep-water supply ships, the bathtub and adjacent water tank came into view.

The dogs scrambled about playing over the open area, showing some life in the cooling afternoon. I shed my shorts, grabbed up the hose, turned the taphandle, and stepped into the tub for a quick, refreshing shower. Ah, me bucko, and ain't that delicious now, I gasped to myself, reviving my numbed senses. I called the dogs, "Heya, Popolo, Sista, you, too, Puffhead, hele mai. C'mon now!" When they got close enough, Sista licking at the water running out of the tub's unconnected drain, I squirted them. Ah! Look at them prance and yelp, loving it as much as I did.

Then Steph came grinning to crouch between my knees while I sat on the rim of the tub to shampoo her hair.

"Oh, gawd, I love this bathtub," she shrieked.

"Enjoy it while you can, darlin'. It's back to saltwater buckets on the foredeck after tomorrow."

"Well, I wish someone would invent a saltwater shampoo that didn't leave my hair a mess."

"We could shave our heads, be Hare Krishnas, and not have to worry about it," I suggested.

"Yeh, right," she said with all the enthusiasm of a flea contemplating an elephant's ass with rape on its mind.

"You'd look sexy."

"I'd rather have a tit-lift, thank you all the same." We parted company back at Iola, she to board and change, me to do the same at the tent. I would wear long pants for the occasion, even sandals and a shirt.

"I wonder if I should wear a dress or skirt for a change."

"Sure, darlin', a short one -- show off your legs."

"You like my legs?"

"I love your legs, especially the meaty thighs and pigeon-toes."

"They're not meaty. Jeez, I'm getting downright skinny."

"No, you're not. You get skinny, I'm divorcing you."

"We're not married, sweetie-pie."

"Well, let that be a lesson to you then."

She didn't get it and neither did I, but a guy had to keep 'em guessing. Fifteen minutes later, I was back trying to whistle her up.

"In a minute awready!"

She'd opted for a sarong around her sumptuous hips, a yellow and black tiger-striped piece of cloth, a yellow halter, a kukui-nut necklace, and a pair of leather heelless clogs which she would leave ashore at the Graham campsite before boarding Sea Wind. She'd even made up her eyes and wore lipstick.

"Jeez, babe, you're beautiful!"

She simpered prettily. "Sorry, cowboy, this is for pleasure. I ain't working tonight."

I grinned stingily, trying to think of a comeback and failing. Now that it was time to answer the invitation to supper, my tongue and brain were seizing up. I said little as we made the stroll over, feeling queasy at the images trying to break past the dam of my denial.

"The Zodiac's gone," she noticed right away. "Mac, Muff? Anybody home?"

"Probably not back from fishing yet," I said.

She headed for the small bench fronting the lagoon. "Well, might as well enjoy the sunset. C'mon, we can smoke this doobie I brought."

She reached down into the halter to produce a fat joint.

"Got a light?"

I pulled out my old Zippo.

As the light of the day crept away into a hollow sunset, Steph speculated that perhaps they'd decided to do a bit of exploring. Or maybe they'd had engine trouble. I nodded.

She began to fret, slapping irritatedly at the occasional mosquito. "Maybe we should go aboard to turn on the masthead lights to serve as a beacon for them."

"Good idea. I'm sure they won't mind," I said, and then added, "Mac said we could make ourselves at home...if they were late."

I handed Steph down on to the main hatch ladder and the masthead lights came on a couple of seconds later.

"Are they on?"

"Yeah." I stepped down to follow her. Interior lights came on to illuminate the main cabin. "Oh, look," she said, seeing a tray of booze and munchies. "They left something out for us. Isn't that nice?"

"Thoughtful."

We sat across from each other at the dinette, where I began to set up the pieces on the ever-present chessboard, trying halfheartedly to interest her in a game.

No, she couldn't concentrate. Neither could I.

We wound up spending the night waiting for Mac and muff to return, me dozing and starting awake, Steph worrying herself sick. Once I awoke to find her gone. Up on deck, I found her at the bow waving her arms.

"What're you doing?"

"Maybe they can see us. I thought it might make 'em feel better."

"Oh," I said, and waved too, feeling like a hypocritical fool.

In the morning, Steph was impatient to begin searching. Mac and Muff might be stranded somewhere. They might be hurt. We have to do something.

"Okay, babe, keep calm. We'll go look for them."

I got Mac's 1-1/2 h.p. Seagull outboard from the equipment shed, filled the tank with gasoline from a larger container. When I had mounted it on the fiberglass dinghy and pulled myself back to Sea Wind, Steph had a pot of coffee going.

I sipped and lit a cigarette, feeling red-eyed and seedy. "D'ju get any sleep last night?"

"Not much."

I looked through the chart drawer and pulled out the one of Palmyra to spread out on the table. "Okay. We'll proceed in an orderly fashion. We go counterclockwise, catch the easy places first. They're probably not on Cooper or they could have walked here."

"Unless they're hurt."

"Okay. We'll deal with it as it comes. We'll work around to the southwest, then the other side of the lagoon. Get a pair of binoculars."

"You want something to eat?"

"No."

"Me neither."

We set out heading west, Steph trying out the binoculars along the shore. Puttering slowly, we passed the deepwater wharf area, the lagoon widening out in a gentle curve.

Steph pointed ahead to the right. "There's something over there."

I squinted. "Where?"

"Right over there. By those bushes along the beach."

I angled in over the shallows. We stepped out and waded in. It was the Zodiac leaning heavily against the greenery, all but upside-down, it's red gas tank in the sand a few yards away. I tied the painter to a branch.

"Let's turn it over. You get on the front." I took the aft end where the Evinrude was attached to the transom. We got it upright and dragged it to the water. Steph turned to walk about calling. "Mac! Muff! Hello!"

"They wouldn't be here, babe," I reminded her. "They could've walked back."

"Maybe it floated across the lagoon," she suggested, training the binoculars on the far shore.

"Yeah, maybe. You remember which direction the wind was blowing?"

She thought about it.

"No. From the south, maybe. Or the southwest, I don't know."

I handed in the gas tank, hooked the feedhose to the engine, and pushed into deeper water. I got in to squeeze the rubber bulb that pumped fuel to the engine while Steph steadied the craft, then began pulling the starter rope. After a dozen pulls, a few sputters and exhaust fumes, it finally started.

We towed the fiberglass dinghy back to Sea Wind. The search would go faster in the Zodiac. We made a brief stop at Iola to change into shorts. Taking a machete and a plastic jug of water, we set out to search until dark. We covered the small islets west and southwest, Steph calling out until her voice grew hoarse. We buzzed along the southern shore of the lagoon, pulling in to cross the palms over the narrow breadth of the islands to the ocean side.

Back aboard Iola toward evening, we fed the dogs and ourselves, sat around chewing our lips awhile, not saying much. In bed, I cuddled to Steph to comfort her, but probably taking more from her nearness than I gave -- until we crashed out.

In the next two days I submitted to Steph's insistence that we continue the search. We lifted the Zodiac over the causeway into the east lagoon and covered the remaining islets in the U-turn from east to north to west, the last a thickly overgrown clump that visitors bypassed as not worthy of exploration, its tangled intertwining of palm and shrub too thick for inland entrance without hours of hot labor with machetes. For that very reason, it was the one I had chosen as the first depository for our magical garden. I busied myself calculating how I would carve a narrow concealed trail into its center and clear a space in its interior with my trusty chainsaw to allow sun and rain unimpeded access. Ah, well, that was for later consideration.

In the meanwhile I watched hope fade from Stephanie's eyes, watched her, so somber and serious, fretting away. I was miserable for not being able to comfort and reassure her. She wanted to continue the search.

"We're not going to find them."

"We haven't searched along the north shore of Cooper yet," she stubbornly pointed out, her eyes growing moist.

"They couldn't be there. It's impossible."

"They might be. Maybe they're delirious or something."

"They're gone, babe."

She beseeched me with her eyes, tears starting down her cheeks. "Oh," she moaned. "I know, I know!"

I took her in my arms, the ineffectual clod who'd never learned how to soothe a weeping woman. "We have to figure out what to do," I said, trying to get her mind on something else.

That was a good one. I hadn't begun to figure out what to do. It had slowly been dawning on me that the situation at that point contained a number of complications not immediately apparent. Someone was going to miss Mac and Muff -- they would come looking.

"Let's go back to Sea Wind," Steph blurted suddenly.

"Huh? For what?

Baby, you need some rest." "No, let's go back," she insisted with a tinge of urgency.

"They might be there. Maybe they're back now."

I looked at her, an acid bile eating my heart. "Now!" "Okay, okay."

No one was there. She stood in the main cabin looking absently around -- as if some clue would reveal the mystery of their disappearance. She crawled up on the athwart ships bunk to open an access door to the foc'sle. She padded back to open the door to the head.

I grabbed her, wrapped my arms around her tight. "C'mon, babe, let it go. It'll be all right."

She trembled, her body heaving, gulping in air with hiccup sounds. I led her over to the settee and made her lie down. "You stay right there now, and try to relax. I'll get you a drink."

I looked into the cabinet holding bottles of liquor. I knew they had some apricot brandy, Steph's favorite. It had been offered to us before while on a visit. Muff had asked if we liked it. She and Steph had had some while Mac and I had stuck to the serious stuff. I figured she would keep sipping away until she was blotto. I held the bottle to her mouth for the first slug, left it in her hand.

"I'm going to feed the mutts. When I get back, I'll cook us up a good meal. Okay? I'll be right back."

"I have to feed Puffer," she said, who was curled up beside her taking strokes, quiet with the eerie vibes they shared. "I'll take care of it."

When I returned, I opened a can of tuna for Puffer and began fixing us up something to eat. Then we spent a few hours talking about Mac and Muff. The meal sat heavy in my stomach. It didn't seem right to be sitting there eating their food, drinking their liquor, even being aboard Sea Wind. Telling myself I had to be practical offered little consolation. The brandy had brought a glaze over Steph's eyes, but still she held on to consciousness. I figured a sleeping pill might lend the knockout punch and searched out a Placidyl from the medicine cabinet where I had once seen the bottle as I snooped while using the head.

"Muff was such a nice person," she said drowsily as I tucked her in.

"Yeah, she was." "And Mac was so vibrant."

"Go to sleep, babe."

"I love you, baby," she murmured. "Oh, Steph," I whispered. "I love you, too."

"How could it all turn to shit so fast?"

"It'll be better tomorrow."

*****

She was like a child, so innocent and vulnerable. I drank myself into oblivion, a tribute to the abrupt end of paradise, to our lost friends.

We did search along the north shore. There was nothing for it but to walk her through it. On Wednesday she insisted we try calling Curt Shoemaker, the ham radio operator in Hawaii with whom Mac had kept in touch, in fact had radioed messages back and forth with Dickie. I had already tried two days before, when we'd been trying to remember on what day of the week they were in regularly scheduled contact. I had no idea how to operate a ham radio. I tried to remember what Mac had told me when he'd once tried to explain the system. Was that the receiver, another console the transmitter? Wait now, wasn't one of them used to tune the antenna? There was a microphone with a button -- that had to be the transmitter. I clicked switches. Lights came on. We could hear static. Okay. Don't touch any of the dials. They could be tuned to the frequency Mac had last used to call Shoemaker.

"This is Sea Wind, calling Curt Shoemaker. Come in," I'd tried, exactly how they did it in movies.

Nothing but static. I repeated the phrases. Getting no response, I looked at Steph and shrugged.

"Try turning the dial."

I gave her the microphone. "Okay. You do the talking."

As the indicator moved along the scale, we caught a few voices here and there, a few words, but nothing that made any sense. Once we picked up a longer transmission that might have been Japanese or Korean.

"What do I say if I get him?"

"I don't know," I replied. I hadn't thought it through. "Just tell him who you are and what the situation is, I guess."

When it struck me just what the situation was, I got nervous. Shoemaker would surely notify the Coast Guard. Would they send a boat to investigate? Yes, for sure. And if they were through, they would find our secret plants, grown for their magical properties, those lovely little Christmas trees producing miraculous ingredients, those sawtooth-leafed little darlings upon which we hoped to get rich enough to continue our world voyage in grander style. Oh, Jesus!

I was relieved when we failed to raise anyone.

While Steph made herself comfortable on the settee, arranging pillows to lean back with her knees cocked up, having taken a Quaalude, smoking a joint, and sipping on the last of the apricot brandy, all in preparation to bringing Iola's logbook up to date -- in which she had made no entries since the previous Thursday, the day before Mac and Muff had disappeared -- I went up on deck to do some serous thinking.

Well, me bucko, you colossal asshole, I told myself, you'd better get your noodle limbered up. What the fuck are you going to do? You can't just sit here doing nothing. It's not the same as it was before. What if a boat comes in? What do you do? Well, we have to tell them what's what, meaning report the version I'd fiddled up. Maybe let Stephanie tell it -- she believed it. Either way, sooner or later, the Coast Guard or somebody would come to snoop around. They would check us out, want to see identification and boat papers. Would my ID stand up? Sure, if they didn't somehow learn that the real Roy Allen was a quadriplegic in a veteran's hospital. They could learn easily enough that Steph had once been busted for possession of hashish, that only recently the MDA charges against her had been dismissed. All they'd need was the mention of drugs to turn Iola inside out. We still had a small smoking stash aboard. Were there any seeds or debris caught in the nooks and crannies, any in the bilge?

The problem was sitting there minding two boats. Well, I suppose if I got rid of Sea Wind, we could just say they'd sailed away. Yeah, right, with Stephanie believing they'd had an accident and wanting to report it? Forget that!

. Maybe no boats would come for a while. No, one could sail in at any time. Dickie and Carlos would be down in October. What do I tell them? It always came back in a circle to the same problem -- sitting here with two boats and a story in which authorities would be very interested, indeed.

Well, there was always the obvious solution -- haul your ass aboard the sea-ready Iola and sail off for Samoa or somewhere, maybe Suvarov Atoll where that hermit, Tom Neale, had written a book back in the fifties. (An Island to Myself, Oxbow Press, 1955) Except for the junk left by the military, Suvarov sounded a lot like Palmyra -- there were numerous islets around a central lagoon, all thickly covered with coconut palms, other trees, and all but impenetrable brush and shrub. Plus there was brackish water well and none of the fish were reef-poisoned as all but two species and sharks were at Palmyra. Suvarov was only about 1100 miles almost due south and, like Palmyra, there were no permanent inhabitants. Once we crossed the equator, we would pick up the Southeast Tradewinds, which would make for windward slogging all the way. But if we took the trouble to make a few hundred miles easting, as we had been about to begin for the voyage to Fanning, it would be easy sailing on a reach.

Maybe I could impress upon Steph the necessity of not mentioning the current situation to anyone, the danger to me. No, get real. That just wasn't going to work. Stephanie was a laidback sociable person -- she loved to talk to people, went about wearing her heart on her sleeve, ready to be friendly to all comers.

How about going on to Fanning as planned, reporting Mac and Muff's disappearance, hang around there until it was all over? No way. The authorities would still want to question us.

They would come to Fanning, want us to accompany them to Palmyra. Some master plan this has turned out to be, me bucko.

In the meanwhile, the portside line anchoring Sea Wind to the reef parted from chafe. We hadn't been checking the mooring lines, five of them on Sea Wind, on a regular basis as good seamanship demanded. I had solved the problem on Iola by utilizing our anchor chain to keep us fast and worry free to mooring dolphins where Iola sat. Sea Wind was in danger of going aground to starboard.

I went out in the Zodiac, caught up the line with a gaffhook and knotted the two parts together, refixed it to Sea Wind after straining to reposition her further out. Without tending, Sea Wind could be lost -- she could grind on the coral and sink at her anchorage, leaving only her masts above water.

I returned to the problem. Sea Wind had a diesel engine. We could motor all the way to Fanning. Couldn't leave Iola behind -- if we got delayed, she would sink at her mooring with no one to pump out from the leak around the rudderpost. Can't leave Steph to perform that chore while I made the voyage alone -- no way. We could tow Iola -- deliver Sea Wind into the hands of British authorities, tell our story, get it over with. Then we could return to Palmyra and resume the original plan. We would have to uproot our beautiful little green babies, leave nothing of our secret plan to be discovered in case the authorities came for a looksee. Well, okay, I resentfully admitted, Dr. Buck, the illicit abortionist would do the dirty deed, then later reseed and incubate a new family. Okay. There was still some risk, but it had been cut to a minimum -- maybe it could work. What else was there? How about sailing Sea Wind out onto the open sea and scuttling her, I thought evilly, appalled at myself. My god, me boyo, how could you do that to such a beautiful thing while aspiring to become a Captain-Admiral of the Ocean Seas? Might as well burn all the poetry in the world! No, scratch that.

When I thought about it in the torturous way I was prone to, it occurred to me that the real problem was Stephanie, her attitude, her very being, what she was -- an open book full of love, ever ready to turn her compassion on any pain and seek to relieve it. She was already, in the name of love, doing what was most difficult for her -- closing off certain chapters with a seal of secrecy -- not to talk about certain subjects from the past, our personal situation, my true status in the world, the real reason we had sought out Palmyra, and our master plan. Well, she hadn't done so badly, all things considered, and to try to impose further censorship upon the character of what she was, was to tinker unwisely with the very essence of what I loved in her. No, the burden must remain all with me, to work around her, even manipulate her out of my own dire necessities, but not to seek to unduly impose upon or change what she was -- might as well go and do the unspeakable and molest children.

Obviously, immediate action was required. The longer we waited, the more questions there would be as to why we hadn't reported the matter sooner. Only I got very antsy at the thought of having to deal with the authorities. The Coast Guard wasn't the FBI or the DEA, but who's to say they wouldn't bring along a couple of representatives from Honolulu?

What else was there to do?

I destroyed all the babies, even the pre-pubescent children -- all except for five or six. With them, I climbed up and fixed them into the upper branches of trees, where sun and rain could nurture them to rise from the bags of nutrients, which fed their roots. We would have a nice little family going by the time we returned, teenagers ready to seek romance and repopulate new generations of an ancient familial line.

I had already ferried all the fertilizers ashore for storage in the refrigerator house. I had better load up the generator so it wouldn't come up missing with visitors while we were away.

I put the idea to Steph. She agreed. With little risk, we could motor out of the lagoon towing Iola. Someone would have to steer Iola while negotiating the channel out to the open sea. Then we would both get aboard Sea Wind to continue the tow to Fanning.

I began to familiarize myself with the procedures for starting and operating Sea Wind's diesel engine. I read a manufacturer's pamphlet, tried to remember all that Mac had taught me. There was a preheating element that took the place of sparkplugs. After it started, the internal explosions of fuel were maintained by the higher compressions of gases in the heated cylinders. The preheating element was activated by a button that created an irritating buzzing noise. Don't forget to open the valves to allow water to flow around the cooling jacket. Open the fuel lines.

After fiddling around for an hour or so, I finally got it started. Okay. The throttle and gear lever for engaging the prop were in the cockpit. Okay, we were in business.

Next, get Sea Wind ready. Take down the canopy. Load up all the tools, sailbags, lines, and miscellaneous stuff Mac had taken ashore. Stow everything away. Hoist the fiberglass dinghy onto the stern davits. Leave the Zodiac in the water for going back and forth between the two boats.

Get Iola in position. With Steph at the helm, I towed her over with the Zodiac to anchor a bit west of Sea Wind. We removed the dog-catcher netting strung around Iola's stanchions for re-rigging on Sea Wind.

We were ready.

With the engine running and Steph at the helm of Sea Wind, I set about freeing the starboard and port mooring lines, scooting from side to side in the Zodiac. Lastly, the stern lines. Back aboard, with the Zodiac secured alongside, I rushed to the bow to begin winching in the anchor chain as Sea Wind moved slowly forward out of her tiny cove.

The weather was fine and windless -- for the moment. Putting the prop into neutral, I handed Steph down into the Zodiac. Sea Wind would drift about unmanned until I got her aboard Iola and returned.

"I want Puffer for company," Steph said. Rather than waste time debating the point, I scooped up the mutt and passed her down, then leapt in myself.

"Jesus Christ, you and that dog!"

Getting them aboard, I dashed back. Putting the prop in gear, I began maneuvering toward Iola. I heaved the ready towline to 'Steph, who cinched it around the sampson post on the foredeck.

Next she had to haul up Iola's anchor. She couldn't get it to budge. The slight westward current in the lagoon had set the anchor firm, the nylon line leading to it from the bow taut.

"To hell with it," I yelled. "Cut it and let's go!"

She hopped down inside Iola for a knife as Sea Wind drifted by her. She dashed to the bow to saw furiously on the three-quarter inch nylon line. I put Sea Wind into reverse gear to hold position.

Suddenly Iola swung free, her bow beginning to veer around. Steph grinned and waved the knife in triumph and dashed back toward the cockpit. Jesus, I wanted to yell, be careful with that knife! But I held my tongue, afraid to distract her.

Under way, Steph steered Iola into the wake of Sea Wind. I got us lined up, making the course a gradually curving arc from west to southwest. As we entered the channel, I glanced back to make sure everything was all right, then increased the throttle a bit.

The channel made me nervous. We had gone aground on a nearby reef when we had tried to sail into the lagoon upon our arrival. We had spent a week anchored outside while awaiting a favorable wind. But the wind, when it had come, proved to be fickle and left us at the critical moment. Iola had drifted away from the entrance in a two-knot current, gently but definitely depositing Iola's iron keel to grind upon the reef. After two or three hours of backbreaking labor, we had managed to row out stern anchors and kedge ourselves off the reef into deeper water -- which is when two outboards had arrived to offer us a tow inside.

Better to get through it promptly, I thought. Midway into the critical part of the passage, the narrow path dredged through the reefs by the Army engineers so many years before, tense with all senses alert, I felt a slight yawing movement aft. Looking swiftly astern, I saw Iola veering out to starboard. Steph had abandoned the helm! She was leaned out over the cockpit coaming to port, grasping for a struggling Puffer, who was half overboard.

Oh, shit!

I reached out to shut the throttle down, to shift from forward through neutral into reverse. It was too late. Iola crunched up on the coral, heeling over to port, the mast shuddering. The forward momentum, not yet reversed, stretched the towline taut, causing Iola to heel even more. Running in reverse, Sea Wind slowly eased the strain, beginning to reverse direction. When the towline had slackened, I set her to idle in neutral. Stephanie stood frozen, clutching Puffer to her heart.

"Are you all right?"

She nodded dumbly.

"Hang on."

I pushed the gear into forward and goosed the throttle. There was little room to maneuver. Iola only heeled the more, her mast raking over to a 45° angle. It was no place to dawdle. When I had eased up and the towline had again become slack, I freed it from the cleat and heaved it away.

"Sit tight. I'll be right back."

I squared around to my original course and motored out to drop anchor offshore. Leaving Sea Wind idling, I jumped into the Zodiac to return for Steph. Iola was solid up on the reef to starboard. Standing up to hold on to a stanchion, I couldn't goddamn believe it.

"Christ," I bit out in exasperation. "I can't goddamn believe it!"

"I'm sorry," Steph said, bowing her head in contrition, on the verge of tears.

"C'mon, get in," I said, taking Puffer by the scruff in one hand and nobly ignoring an urge to fling her into the drink. "We can't leave Sea Wind out there untended."

When I'd gotten her back aboard, I left her with brief instructions. "Listen now, we can't afford any more mistakes. Mark your position, take some bearings. If the anchor slips or anything, you know, get it up and head further off. Just go around in circles or something if you have to. I'm going back to see what's what."

Once aboard Iola, I went below and pulled up floorboards. The bilges were filling. I checked under the bunks in the forecabin. Ribs and planks were ruptured inward from the force of the impact, the weight of Iola resting on a coralhead. Water was seeping in. I went topside, crawled headfirst under the lower lifeline at the starboard bow quarter, gripping the gunnels, and leaned down for a looksee. At the point of impact, Iola was resting solidly on a coral projection. I went all around the boat, even ducking my head under water in order to scope out the situation. The leading edge of the keel was wedged into the coral. When she'd struck, she'd scrunched up on it firmly, leaving the stern free and lower in the water.

I pumped out, then tried pulling Iola dead astern with the Zodiac. No go. Okay. Lighten the load. What was the state of the tide -- going out or coming in? I didn't know. There was nothing for it but to begin several hours of arduous labor, ferrying our belongings out to Sea Wind. I worked methodically, cleaning her out from stem to stern, even unshipping the stove, ferrying out a load, handing stuff up to Stephanie on Sea Wind's deck, returning empty to load again. Jesus, how did we ever get all this stuff into such a small boat! The large foc'sle in Sea Wind, which had served Mac as a workshop, was packed right up to the overhead hatch. Stuff was strewn about the decks. Steph worked at stowing it below. Between trips, I pumped out.

Some items, like shovels, rakes, and hoes, our dinghy and some sailbags, I ferried back inside. I stored the tools in the refrigerator house, left the dinghy, its mast, oars, and sails at the head of the seaplane ramp. The gasoline generator was a bitch, weighing about two hundred pounds. For that, as when moving it back and forth ashore from Iola, we had to swing out the boom on the mainmast, rig a hoist, and pull it aboard.

The wind was playing games, puffing this way and that, dying out and starting all over again. I hoisted the main and jib, back-winding them, looking for any help from westerlies that might decide to lend a hand. I pumped out again and tried towing astern with the Zodiac, waggling it back and forth, trying to play the pressures.

Suddenly, with a nerve-wracking rumble of coral scraping against hull, Iola slid back and floated free. I pulled her well out, then got aboard to free the backwinding sails. She sat motionless for a few moments before beginning a slow drift with the current. I worked the handpump located on the cabin roof near the main hatch to get the water out, keeping a tense eye toward the shallows. Out of nowhere, Iola's jib slapped taut with a gust of easterly wind. The boom swung around in a jibe, the mainsail catching the full force of it and slamming to starboard at the end of the mainsheet. To keep from being pushed toward the reef again, I quickly eased the jib a bit and hauled in the mainsheet. Iola began to move forward. I steered southwest to sail her on through the last bit of channel.

Lovely.

Without someone aboard Iola to pump constantly, she would never make it to Fanning. I tied the wheel to check below again -- the water was up over the cabin sole. I pumped out for the umpteenth time. Maybe I could get the shredder motor back aboard and try out my new pumping system. The trouble was that, while it might keep ahead of the incoming water, it only ran for about three hours on a tank of gas -- which meant someone would have to remain aboard to keep filling the gastank.

Who would do that? Me, while Steph drove Sea Wind? Steph, while I drove? No. What if we hit bad weather? Too dangerous.

Well, what? Think, me boyo! Haven't you always spouted the creed that the human mind was man's primary tool of survival?

Iola couldn't be repaired in the water. The damage extended over an area of about two feet square, only the resiliency of the fiberglass sheathing keeping the hole from opening up to catastrophic proportions.

I could tow her back in to try a grounding on the seaplane ramp. How deeply did it extend into the lagoon? I didn't know, but if it wasn't over five feet, Iola would never clear the end of it Even if I managed it, tide and wave would not allow her to rest there. Even with mooring lines fixed hard ashore, she would move and grind herself to pieces on rough concrete.

I could run her aground on a nearby reef. But for what? To salvage mast and rigging, two sails, some winches, cleats, and portholes? I might as well have left her where she'd gone aground in the first place. Between tide, wind, and coral, she would be ground to utter destruction.

What's the use? It was late afternoon by then. My thoughts ascatter as futile, my emotions in a turmoil, I fully understood that the loss of Iola meant the end of the master plan. We could not keep Sea Wind. Though I was sorely tempted to sail her south, just keep going, and take our chances, I knew it was impossible. With no papers and an alarm sent out about a missing vessel, she would be confiscated at the first port of call and hard, suspicious questions would be asked.

In the end, it seems I am a romantic by heart. Ah, Iola, my sweet, dumb, ugly little bitch, how could I have become so attached to you? You carried us off in our dream, were privy to all the details of our great plan, set us off to adventure and freedom. We attended you like parents, loved you with our hands and hearts, and now am I to leave your body exposed to rot, your bones lonely in the sun, your headstone no more than an inked symbol marking a wreck on some future chart?

Oh, you great motherfucker of fate, fuck you and all your bad-luck bastards! I found a stub of pencil, a piece of paper sack, and wrote a note to the gods of the sea: "Finders keepers!" I went topside to take command, the easterly now filling the sails stiffly, to by god enjoy our last sail together. I steered her to pass aport of Sea Wind.

Strangely, I remembered the previous owner, the sad lady who'd asked me to send her a photo. I never had. We had no pictures of Iola under sail. I yelled at Steph to fetch a camera. I steadied the course and tied the helm again, leaving her on a course to the southwest, consigning her to Father Neptune.

At last I left on the Zodiac to head back to Sea Wind. Once aboard, hauling up the anchor and getting Sea Wind headed east. I began to feel a nausea, whether from a return to seasickness or a combination of frustration and tension, I didn't know -- it was appropriate.

Our eyes were cast solemnly astern, a last sight of our brave Iola sailing her final voyage. Alas, even my last foolish notion was not to go unsullied. The fates had one last joke to play, a cruel mockery.

Iola's sails had grown slack, losing the wind, and she bobbed about like a lost child. She had slowly drifted around to point her bowsprit northward. The wind would fill her sails and drive her for a bit, then slack off to let her float aimlessly. By stops and starts of teasing winds, Iola slowly made her way toward the reefs off Palmyra. Our last sight of her was with her mast canted over at an angle, once more aground.

    While Steph slumped down, hugging Puffer, I was sick over the side.

#

CHAPTER 2

We chugged on into the darkness, beginning a routine of four hours on, four hours off, falling dead into our bunks off watch from the tensions of the day. It was not until the next morning that we began to emerge from our lassitude. Our course was still southeast, our destination still Fanning. By noon, making over eight knots, we had raised Washington Island, uninhabited and without a safe inner lagoon. We would have to begin conserving fuel.

We began to talk, to reassess the situation. What would be the consequences of reporting the Grahams missing, the loss of Iola? Would British authorities take possession of Sea Wind, leaving us stranded in a foreign jurisdiction? Without Iola, we were homeless. Sea Wind was no more than a temporary convenience.

Fanning now seemed like a dead end, especially for me -- a fugitive novice sailor marooned without an escape route. We suddenly found ourselves in a new movie. The hastily revised script left us with three choices: One, return to Palmyra, continue on with the original plan, allow the elusive fortune of chance to develop the future as it would; two, change our compass heading southeast to south or southwest and escape into the South Pacific; and three, return to Hawaii.

"What do you want to do?"

"I don't know," she replied. "What do you think?"

"I think we're fucked. We stay at Palmyra, sooner or later we'll have to deal with the authorities. The same thing if we head south. Even if we go back to Hawaii."

Really, there was no choice. We would have to go back, give up Sea Wind, and notify someone about the missing Grahams -- all of which increased the risk that my fugitive status would be discovered. If we were stopped and boarded by the Coast Guard anywhere along the way, it would probably mark the end of the ballgame.

Sick with defeat and apprehension, I began to plot a course for our return to Hawaii. Maybe we would not be stopped and boarded. We might make port as though we'd merely been out for a daysail. And if we succeeded, then what? Perhaps we would have some control over the circumstances of reporting and surrendering Sea Wind. Perhaps we could turn Sea Wind over to a middleman, a neutral party, and let him deal direct with the authorities. Or, the idea occurred to me, why not Stephanie, since she was not a fugitive subject to arrest. I could leave a written statement agreeing with the story she would tell -- the only one she knew. She could make excuses for my absence, perhaps an emergency that had recalled me to the mainland. Perhaps I could call them safely from a phone if they had any questions. And if there were any demands for my personal presence, why, Roy Allen would simply cease to exist.

We could disappear anywhere into thousands of square miles of rainforest. I still had remote marijuana camps where we could live, take up where we'd left off in our roles as grass farmers.

The whole episode could be counted as no more than a temporary setback in the plan. In a year or so, we could buy another boat and point her bow toward southern ports.

We would bypass Palmyra next time around, which had been transmuted in my own mind from a paradise into a congealing, aching sickness.

*****

We sailed almost lackadaisically, in no hurry to arrive, allowing plenty of time to gird ourselves with internal preparations for the pressures and problems ahead.

I fished along the way, catching several mahi-mahi and a nice tuna. About two weeks up from Palmyra, we were becalmed one day, cooking in the noon heat. I'd been tinkering with the refrigerator apparatus with intermittent success, and we had ice that day. The five of us were lolling about the cockpit area when Puffer began keening and ruffing over the side. Popolo and Sista joined her, poking their heads inquisitively into the netting to look below. I was curious enough to have a gander.

"Baby," I called to Steph. "C'mere and look at this!"

It was a huge swordfish, the first I'd ever seen. It's body was eight to ten feet long, the bill a rapier sword of at least four feet. It kept swimming back and forth under the hull as we followed from side to side.

"Wow! I wonder if I can catch him."

"Oh, baby, he's so big!"

I had no intention of trying to haul him aboard for eating. No, we would merely sport with each other, I, Ahab, he, Moby Dick, one-on-one, man against great fish. Jack Wheeler, who'd been at Palmyra when we'd arrived, had told us a story about a sick fisherman being impaled through the hull of the vessel as he lay in his bunk. They had put into the lagoon, seeking medical aid, but the man had died.

I remembered Melville had written of an incident in Moby Dick where a swordfish had punctured through several inches of hull wood to cause severe leaking in an old whaling ship.

Later I would learn that swordfish were territorial and were known to attack whales, plunging into them in a headlong charge, wriggling themselves free to charge again. (In 1882, during a Pacific crossing, a swordfish holed Bernard Gilbay's boat. After giving it a shaking, the fish was able to withdraw its bill. Gilbay stuffed the hole with wick and rags.

In 1901, under Captain Howard Blackburn, the ship Great Republic was attacked by several swordfish during an Atlantic crossing.)

The pelagic experts theorized that the swordfish sometimes mistook boats for whales.

But none of that was on my mind at the time. I got out my eighth-inch nylon line with the heavy wire leader, tied on a feather jig, and dangled it over the side.

When he ignored it, continuing to swim back and forth under the hull, I tried a plug lure, which didn't work either. I tried a bit of Canadian bacon on a hook, but neither was he having any of that.

We soon grew bored with his monotonous and incomprehensible ritual, and retired below for a cold drink, leaving the mutts to keep watch. Relaxing at the dinette, a loud thud echoed through the hull.

"What the hell was that?"

We rushed topside, suspecting the dogs as the source. They'd set up a furious barking. I looked over the side for a quick glimpse of a wriggling shadow disappearing into the depths. Looking around the deck, we found that nothing had fallen. Shrugging, we returned below, Puffer following us down to lie on the cabin sole. Eventually the faint sound of running water worked its way into our consciousness. It sounded like a faucet left running in another room. I checked the galley sink, then the head. Nothing.

"Could it be a through-hull fitting?"

Jesus. I didn't even know how many Sea Wind had, let alone where they were located. Let's see, there was the one for the seawater pump forward for hosing down the deck, then there was the one... "Puffer," Steph said, seeing she had jumped to her feet to begin sniffing around in a circle where she'd been lying. "Come here." In a moment, Puffer was beside her. "She's wet,"

Steph exclaimed, rubbing at her fur. "Puffer, how did you get wet?" She leaned to feel the carpet. "It's wet." "Is she pissing in here?" Steph shot me an accusing look. "No, she wouldn't do that... would you, Puffy-pie?"

I pulled back the carpet to lift one of the floor panels. The bilges, which were about three feet deep, were brimful of water.

"Holy shit! We're sinking!"

I lifted more panels. We were flooding. I rushed into the engine room, turned the valve on the outlet from the power pump, then started the engine. Pumping water out the side of the vessel at a prodigious rate, it took only minutes to empty the bilges. I checked the small automatic submersible pump. It was operable, but hadn't the capacity to keep ahead of the rising water. Where was it coming from?

I went through Sea Wind, trying to locate and check all the through-hull fittings, but failed to discover any leakage. It had to be a bad one. I could still hear that muffled faucet running. Scratching my head, I got down and leaned it into the bilge amidships. It was coming from portside, behind the watertank where I couldn't see. I crawled under the dinette to open a foot cabinet. The cloth goods inside were soaked. When I removed them, the problem revealed itself, eight or nine inches, perhaps a foot of swordfish bill protruding through the hull, water squirting in around the hole it had made.

"That fucking fish rammed us!"

I hurried topside to peer over the portside amidships. Nothing. The fish had apparently snapped off the end of his sword and fled. I knew enough not to immediately try to remove the bony protrusion because it was helping to stem the flow. If I pulled it out, we'd have water pouring through a two-inch hole under pressure.

I tried packing cotton around it, tamping carefully with a screwdriver and hammer. It was under control. We could keep ahead of it. Time to make a better patch.

I cut a foot square of five-sixteenths plywood, started some screws around the perimeter, with a bunch of nails crisscrossing the surface, then coated the other side with a caulking compound as a sealant.

Over the side I went in snorkel and mask, a rope tied around my waist, trying to get the plywood fixed in place. Steph stood ready to exchange screwdriver for hammer.

Ever tried hammering under water? A ten-minute job took over and hour, but it was done. Inside, I pried out the tip of the sword. There was still a bit of seepage, but the automatic submersible could handle it.

I vowed never to fish from the back of a whale.

*****

Stephanie had spent some time nosing into the nooks and crannies of Sea Wind, doubtless to see how the pros did things, as well as learn their interests and how they ordered their lives -- but probably from plain old snoopiness, too.

She discovered a few modestly interesting pieces of paper. First, Mac's wallet containing about a hundred bucks. Then another three hundred or so stuck between the pages of a book on emergency medical procedures. While she counted up the money, I browsed through the volume to learn how to perform an appendectomy, stitch a wound, and treat various maladies, wondering if I would have the nerve to remove my own appendix or amputate my foot should the necessity ever arise.

She also found a three-ring binder containing about a hundred typed pages, which recounted certain autobiographical incidents. There was the episode he'd regaled us with in person, where he'd drawn his gun to repel suspected pirates on an apparent collision course, as well as an occurrence where Sea Wind had been struck by lightning in Mexican waters. He had once or twice mentioned a desire to do some writing, perhaps some articles for boating magazines, or even a book.

Then there were the documents, the boat papers, a last will and testament, and a sort of codicil. Since I didn't think he'd left me anything in his will, I didn't bother to read through the dry legalese of it, but Stephanie insisted I read the related statement, which was unsigned and undated. It expressed his wishes concerning disposition of Sea Wind in the event of his death while at sea. It constituted a permission to whomever took possession of Sea Wind, that they could keep and maintain it for a period of two years, so long as the vessel was delivered to any port in the United States before the two years ended. There was a blank line to be filled in with the name of the party authorized to take possession. It didn't quite make sense to me. If he was dead, how could he authorize an unknown finder to take possession? If he were alive to fill in the blank with a name, by the time he died that person might not be around to take possession. Perhaps the finder was meant to fill in his own name.

"Why don't we just put our names there," Steph suggested. "You going to forge Mac's signature, too?"

She frowned. "Well, at least we know what he wanted."

The last things she came up with were Sea Wind's logbook and Muff's diaries, one wrapped in cloth and hidden in a sewing box. While I browsed through the logbook, reading an entry here and there, Steph paged cursorily through the diaries.

Some sailors make only the barest of entries in a logbook, mundane technical stuff relating to position and maintenance, the weather and states of the sea during a voyage, courses and speeds made good, landfalls, and notes of repairs to be made.

Others include more personal observations, thoughts and feelings. Like Stephanie and I, they transformed them into a diary of daily events.

Don Stevens, a visitor at Palmyra, had made long personal observations in the log of his vessel, Shearwater, which included personal feelings about the people he'd met along the way, and had even pasted in photographs. There was a poignant story about an intimate relationship with a Tongan girl.

Mac had also been numbered among the second type, the logbook containing enough of his emotions and thoughts about his experiences to convey a sense of his character.

I could not know then that there would come a time when I would kick myself for not having read it through very thoroughly. The same consideration held true for Muff's diaries, of which at the time I had not the slightest interest. I had in the past peeked into my sister's diary, as well as one kept for awhile by my wife, but had found them, against all expectations, entirely uninteresting. What might these volumes have revealed about the experiences and attitudes of their authors in the inquiry that lay unknown ahead of us?

But then there were also some letters, a few of which were from Mac's sister, Mary Muncey, complete with return addresses. He had mentioned her, his only kin as far as I knew.

Perhaps we could write her a letter, who more logical to inform of the circumstances than his closest living relative?

In my off hours, joint in hand, I began to labor over the details of a draft, one that would go through a number of revisions before it was finally completed. I could mail it upon our arrival in Hawaii, congratulate myself over a duty performed.

*****

The progress of dated dots marking our position marched steadily up the chart of the Pacific as we neared the Hawaiian Islands. Other than the incident with the swordfish, there wasn't much out of the ordinary to mark the days -- until the thirty-third day when we sighted Kauai. I kicked in the diesel and we stayed silently topside with mixed emotions, watching the huge green jewel growing up out of the ocean as the sun faded.

Strings of lights began sparkling in the darkness. We entered Nawiliwili Bay about eleven, a dangerous maneuver as all the books on sailing had warned us. But a new eagerness possessed us. After getting Sea Wind safely anchored, we rowed ashore to walk a half-mile up the road to the Oar House.

We sat at a table and ordered drinks. These were the first people we'd seen in six weeks and the air seemed heavy with voices, intriguing sounds, intermingling with the jukebox music. Our tongues were stuck to the roofs of our mouths as we became utterly fascinated in this new aura. Old familiarities seemed strangely novel. Sound and movement flowed about us with rich elegance. We were speechless, basking in the luxury of the all but decadent.

We stayed drinking, listening to new songs, until they closed. A waitress tried to engage us in a few minutes conversation, which brought us out of our trances. Steph looked at me, blinking her eyes, and smiled. I shrugged and grinned dumbly.

The next day, after awakening late, we hitched a ride into Lihue to buy dogfood. That evening we were invited aboard the nearby Vagabundo to meet the Mehaffeys from California, taking along a chilled bottle of wine, where we spent a couple of hours in pleasant talk of boats and sailing, recommending they visit Okoe Bay, a place where we had once camped out for an idyllic few days on the Kona Coast of the Big Island if they should get over that way.

The next day we lifted anchor and hoisted sail for Oahu to seek a haulout facility so that we could effect permanent repair to the damaged hull. The closer we drew to Oahu, the more nervous I became. I thought we had been lucky getting into the harbor at Nawiliwili unobserved by the Coast Guard. The difficulty was that we had no papers to prove we were lawful inhabitants of Sea Wind.

But we did have our papers to Iola, and thus I began an attempt to deceive. These papers contained the dimensions of Iola, her length, width, draft, and displacement, which was thirty feet on deck by nine feet at the beam by five feet of draft, and displaced about five or six tons.

Sea Wind, however, was 37' 5"x 11' 9" x 6' and displaced some twenty tons. If I could alter the zero in Iola's length to a six, perhaps add an eleven before the nine on the beam, and a one to the five or six tons of her displacement, it might pass muster. Sea Wind would become Iola. Would anyone notice the small discrepancies? Surely no one would pull out a tape to make measurements.

With a screwdriver, I removed the letters of Sea Wind's name and homeport attached to her stern. Then I lowered the fiberglass dinghy from the stern davits to provide a platform while I painted in Iola's name. I also painted Iola onto the running-light boards to either side.

We made Pokai Bay, along the southern coast of Oahu, by afternoon. Parading ourselves and dogs ashore to wash off the salt at the harbor park facilities, we met Lorrain Wollen and her husband, who lived aboard the small sloop, Juneau, anchored next to us. Then we dressed and wandered about the village of Waianae, shopping for a few things and dropping off some film to be developed.

On the way back to Sea Wind, I called Larry Seibert, our neighbor from Maalaea Harbor days on Maui when we had been rebuilding Iola. He drove out and we celebrated our reunion talking and drinking the night away, well-stoked on some good grass he'd brought along.

His very first questions, after getting a look at Sea Wind, now renamed Iola, related to how we'd acquired her. Steph looked at me to reply and I took a few long moments to think it over. Even though Larry had perjured himself on my behalf by signing a statement that he had known me for two years when I'd applied for a passport in the name of Roy Allen, and we had palled around for the six months we'd spent on Maui getting Iola ready for the sea, I really didn't know him all that well. I didn't want to test his friendship by telling him the story about the Graham's disappearance and our mishap with Iola, which would only invite more questions -- questions I didn't want to get into.

Finally, I said to him, "Look, Larry, there's more to this than meets the eye. You know I jumped bail on that MDA charge, and so I have to play things pretty cozy. We didn't plan on having to return to Hawaii, but sooner or later we're going to have to deal with the authorities and I know you don't want to get involved with that."

"No, man, I don't. How serious is this? Did you steal this fucking boat?"

"No, Larry, it's nothing like that," I said, trying to reassure him. "If it wasn't for the fact that I'm a fugitive, there wouldn't be any problem."

"You guys did go to Palmyra like you planned, right?" "Yeah, we just got back." "How was it?"

We told him a little about what it was like, the fishing and the thousands of coconut trees, about our grounding on the reef when we'd tried to enter the lagoon, the sharks. We told him about the swordfish attack, and I dug out the bony tip to show him, including the

hole it had made in the hull.

"We need to haul out to fix that," I remarked. "You know of a good place?"

"Gee, I don't know. I think they got one at Kaneohe." "Nothing closer?" Kaneohe would require sailing clear around the eastern tip of Oahu. "How about the Ala Wai?"

He told us he kept his own boat in a slip there. "Naw, I haven't seen one there. They only got a small-boat launching ramp, some fuel pumps, and public bathrooms with a laundromat."

"Maybe we can find one in the phonebook."

"Yeah, so how did you come by this boat? What happened to yours?"

I leaned forward to look him dead in the eye, very serious. "You really want to know, Larry, I'll tell you. But it's very important that you keep your mouth shut. You understand?"

"This is really serious shit, huh?"

"Yeah, man, it is. Somewhere along the line, the Coast Guard is going to be involved, maybe even the FBI."

"Okay, I take your word for it. So tell me a lie I can live with. What do I say if anybody should ask?"

I shrugged. "Hell, I don't know. Tell 'em I won it gambling in a chess game."

"Did you?"

"No. You know I didn't. You really want to know, I'll tell you."

"It's all right. You won it in a chess game. Fine by me." "I'll tell you about it later, okay? A couple of weeks. It's a long story."

"Sure, okay."

After he'd left in the morning, Lorraine came over to have coffee with us. We mentioned the need to haul out and she recommended Tuna Packers, a drydock facility in Honolulu at Kewalo Basin.

When Lorraine asked about how we'd acquired such a neat boat, it caught us both flatfooted. After a few moments of embarrassed silence, me thinking furiously to come up with a credible answer because I knew the lame story concocted with Larry wouldn't pass muster with any reasonably intelligent person, Stephanie took up the slack by telling her that we'd bought it from a rich yachtsman. She pointed out a photo on the wall of Mac and Muff aboard Sea Wind. At least Steph's answer served to head off further questions.

I called Tuna Packers and was told it would be a few weeks before they could accommodate us. I pled an emergency and told the swordfish story, that I needed to section out a plank below the waterline.

"Okay," he told me. "In a few days. I can give you a week, no more." He gave me a date. "Fine. We'll be there. Really appreciate it. Mahalo nui." " A swordfish, hah?"

When I told Steph, she suggested we'd better get some bottom paint, which was standard practice. Bottom paint contained mild toxins, which prevented algae and other marine life from collecting on the underwater portion of the hull. It was not supposed to be allowed to entirely dry. It was the last thing yachtsmen did before launching.

"Okay, right. And we'll need some caulking fiber." "We could give her some new paint topsides in a week."

"Yeah, what the hell, replacing the plank won't take long at all. Might as well spruce her up all around."

"We can use the four hundred bucks we found to pay for it," Steph pointed out. "That's okay, huh?"

"Sure, good idea."

We got busy preparing Sea Wind, making lists of items we'd need. We began sanding down the topsides. I removed the gold figurehead and the varnished bowboards, stripping and preparing the hull between waterline and rubrail, preparing the surface for another application of paint. I also sanded off the Iola appellation and painted over the name on the lightboards.

On October 18, 1974, I decided to try getting in touch with my lawyer on the MDA charge. Since my court appearance date for sentencing had been left up in the air the previous May, when I'd fled to Kauai to begin my escape to Palmyra, I wanted to make sure I was really wanted by the feds for jumping bail. His secretary told me he wasn't in when I called his office, that he was expected back in the afternoon. I decided to make a personal appearance.

If I wasn't actually on the FBI's wanted list yet, maybe we could delay the proceedings for a few more months, give me a little breathing space.

After waiting a half hour and getting antsier by the minute when he didn't show, I decided to beat it and call him later. Well, oh well, just down the street from his office lay Ala Moana Boulevard, across which was the state office for marine registrations.

I remembered how easy it had been, after purchasing the sloop, Margaret, and then reregistering her in my own name as Stephanie, then in a sly move later to sell her to myself as Roy Allen and again rename her Iola. My brain burning on the leftover fumes of the joint I'd smoked earlier, I hit upon what I thought was a clever idea.

I could reregister Sea Wind to Roy Allen, give her another name, something temporary -- which, aha, would provide me with all the proper paperwork to see us safely to the Big Island. So far we had been lucky, but we still had a couple of hundred miles to go – through waters patrolled by the Coast Guard. Rather than consider the matter more deeply, I acted on the impulse of the moment.

Inside the office of the Department of Transportation, Harbors Division, I filled out a form to register Sea Wind as a homebuilt vessel. Otherwise, I would have to provide a previous registration and title, along with a bill of sale to prove I'd bought it. I renamed her Lokahi, which meant unity or agreement, but also implied in its older meaning, "two souls with one mind" -- another of my romantic notions, to give Mac his due, that we were in accord with our love of the sea-going life.

When I told Stephanie, she blew her cork.

"How dumb!" she accused. "You had no right!"

I explained my reasoning.

"No, you fucked up," she insisted. "What if they find out? They'll think you're trying to steal it."

"Okay, okay. We won't use it."

"Really dumb."

What could I say? She was right.

The day before our haulout appointment, we upped anchor and sailed to Keehi Lagoon, our very first port of call after we'd left Maui on the refurbished Iola on our maiden voyage.

That evening we had a visitor. When I went topside to see who was calling, I found Ron grinning from ear to ear, waiting for me to invite him aboard. We had met Ron on Palmyra when the damaged catamaran, Bohilla Island, had anchored off the reef outside the lagoon to effect repairs in early July. Ron had wanted to jump ship and throw in his lot with us, but we'd encouraged him to rejoin his mates when the catamaran had sailed a few days later.

"Thought you'd be soaking up the rays in Samoa," I said. "Yeah, I was...for awhile. Didn't like it, flew back." "Deserted ship, huh?"

"Hey, man, that was a dangerous boat. We were lucky we made it to Samoa."

"So, what are you doing here?"

"Staying with these people next door," he replied, jerking a thumb at the Ferro cement boat. "Can I come aboard? We can smoke some grass."

"Ah, man, we're kind of tired. Maybe tomorrow."

"Got some good shit, man, relax you."

"Naw, thanks. We want to get some shuteye."

"So you came back, huh?" he asked, looking Sea Wind up and down. "Yeah, long trip. See you in the morning. We can go out for breakfast, talk story."

"Right, okay. See you."

Shit.

"Better set the alarm for early," I told Steph. "We don't need that hotdog hanging around asking questions."

"We better figure out what we're going to do. Have you thought about it?"

"I'm writing Mac's sister a letter," I reminded her. "Yeah, but what are we going to do with the boat?"

"I don't know. We could deliver it to Mac's sister in Seattle." "You mean sail it all the way up there?"

"Yeah."

"Gee, I dunno," she mulled. "We really should tell somebody." "I'm telling her in a letter."

"You know what I mean. We should report it to the authorities." "Well, I'm not going to do that in person. You know I can't take that chance."

"What then?"

"We'll just have tc leave Sea Wind someplace and call the Coast Guard."

"That won't look right."

"You can stay and face them if you want. You're not a fugitive." "What do I tell them?"
"The truth, the whole story, everything you know."
"What do I say about you?"
I shrugged. "Make up something...an emergency on the mainland. I had to fly to California."
"Geez, I dunno."
"You report it, tell them your story and let them have it. We can connect up later, get back to doing what we have to do." "What's that?"
"Growing grass. We can take up where we left off. Get it all together to buy another boat."
"Where would we live? Debbie's got our place."
"There's that place up in the hills outside Papaiako, the little camp. Or we can hike into Waimanu, set up a new operation." "Gawd, that would be nice -- it's beautiful. Remember when we stayed there?"
"Yeah." We'd parked Steph's old stepvan, which we called the Iron Butterfly, at the top of the entrance to Waimea Valley and hiked over several miles of mountains and valleys along the north coast. Waimanu was an unspoiled valley with no roads, no houses, and no people. It's only access had been by boat from the sea or an arduous hike in over little-used foot trails. It had several freshwater falls that fed a swampland at the center. I had often thought about building a permanent camp there, bringing in all the supplies by outboard, and adorning the mountain slopes surrounding three sides of the valley with pretty pakalolo.* Police helicopters never patrolled it because no one had ever been known to cultivate marijuana there. It was perfect.
"What about Dickie and Carlos?"
"No problem. We can track them down, tell them there's been a change of plan. We can still sell them all our grass. They can move it over here, deal it for the best prices, run it to California, whatever.
In the end, the question remained unsettled. At least we had plenty to think about. We went to bed. Talk of Waimanu had put Steph into another frame of mind.
"Why didn't we ever get married?"
"I don't know. We almost did."
It had been after the MDA bust, but before we'd gone to Maui to acquire Iola. All our experiences together, all the ups and downs, had only brought us closer.
I'd swore to myself never to marry again -- once was enough for me. But Steph had never
been hitched and was unable to entirely escape from society's custom. I was the only one, I'd swore to myself never to marry again -- once was enough for me. But Steph had never been married.
*Hawaiian word for marijuana.
She had never met a guy she'd ever considered as a possible husband. It was a part of the romantic tradition she'd never experienced. I'd actually considered it for the simple reason of pleasing her, the final proof of my commitment and love.
"Those yucky blood tests for nothing," Steph shuddered. She had a horror of needles.
"Hmp."
"You got any history of insanity or syphilis, anything like that?"
"Naw," I replied, getting a little antsy. "I don't think so. Maternal grandmother died in a catatonic trance is all. How about you?"
"Naw. My dad was an alcoholic."

"Um-hm."
"Yeh."
"You still want to do it, right?"
"Naw, it doesn't matter."
"What does? What do you want?"
"I was thinking of something else."
"Yeah?"
"Maybe having a baby."
"Oh."

A silence of wriggly thoughts beset us, a swirl of contradictory emotions, stilled us. Drive slow, me bucko, I told myself. This is serious biz.

"I think I'd sorta like having yours."

I sat up in shock to look at her. "Babe!"

"I don't know for sure yet," she continued. "Haven't made up my mind."

"It's a heavy subject, really."

"Yeh, I know."

"Marriage is one thing, kids are something else."

She was quiet, backing off I hoped. "We can't sail off around the world with a baby," I added.

"Why not?"

"Jesus, babe! They piss and shit and scream all the time!

They're always hungry. They need constant attention, doctors, schools, a whole bunch of stuff! Babies are a twenty-year responsibility!"

"You love your daughter, don't you?"

"Ah, Steph, c'mon! You know I do!" Which was maybe why I'd not sailed off into the blue before, because a child was my wife's way of squelching what she considered a juvenile dream? Maybe she was right to want something different, a stable, secure life, a home and family, roots. But, whether as a result of the forced stasis of prison life or a quality otherwise acquired, I had always been driven, and still was, by wanderlust. I also labored under a heavy guilt trip that I hadn't been much of a father to my daughter.

"I don't make a good father," I said.

"Oh, bull. I see how you go gaga over kids, Elena, and Laura's kid. They make a regular punk out of you."

"Yeah, but that's just short-term stuff. Kids are a lifelong commitment. You can't just boot them out and disown them if you decide you don't like it. I'm not ready for kids."

"So, okay, maybe it's premature. Right, put the idea of having a kid on hold."

"But we can get married if you want."

"Gee, last of the big spenders! Don't let me cramp yer style!" "You want to do it or not?"

"Gawd, those yucky blood tests," she grimaced, hugging herself in mock shudders.

"All right, okay. That's settled. We'll do it."

"I haven't said yes yet."

I got down on my knees. I knew the form. I'd done it before. Drama, romance, that's the ticket. A woman was a woman, and they all needed a little Romeo and Juliet.

"Will you honor me with your hand in marriage?"

Her face lit up in the most wonderful smile, her eyes sparkling with soft warmth. "I thought you'd never ask!"

"I'll even call your mom, fight a duel with your brother." "C'mere, you!"

We left before dawn to evade Ron's unwanted attentions and Sea Wind sat high in a drydock cradle before noon. I sectioned out the damaged plank and made a perfect textbook repair of the swordfish hole. We scrapped and sanded the bottom. The primary hull color was painted the original white. When it came to the bottom paint, which was blue, the yard had only two gallons. We needed four. Red was available, so I took two gallons of that, too. Painting half of the bottom blue and the other half red was not kosher -- what would the old salts say?

I mixed a little of each together to see how it would come out -- sort of a magenta color, lavender, whatever. Oh well, I thought, it'll be under water and nobody'll see it. But Steph liked it so well she wanted to use it to repaint the blue trimline around the gunnels.

"Jesus, they'll think faggots own it!"

"Naw, it's pretty. Different. Distinctive."

"No shit!"

So we mixed blue and red enamels for a purplish-pink blend which when applied gave Sea Wind the gay, striking air of a flower-float in the Rosebowl Parade.

I had laid out the bowboards and figurehead for reattachment, making the mistake of leaving them out overnight. In the morning, the figurehead was missing, along with a couple of my power tools. Well, maybe I could carve a tiki-head to replace it.

Larry had come by to kibitz and invited us to his boss' house for dinner one evening. Joseph Stewart was a congenial fellow, the owner of a sewing machine repair shop. Larry had told him the story about my having won Sea Wind in a game of chess, and he brought it up.

I hemmed and hawed, said yeh-yeh, and changed the subject. I knew he wasn't buying that poppycock and must have been wondering over the question with some suspicion. What was I to do? The fat was in the fire.

Steph asked if she could use his address for a yard sale. She thought it might be a good idea to sell our generator, the shredder, stove, anchor, and a few other things. He readily agreed, responding to Steph's peculiar charm, but I was uncomfortable, dreading that he would again raise the issue of how we'd acquired Sea Wind.

In the evenings, toking on a joint and sipping a gin and tonic, I worked on my letter to Mac's sister. (The complete text of this letter may be found in Appendix II.) I'd decided to tell her as much as possible without getting into chapter and verse. I gave her a basic account of the matter, but omitting certain crucial elements of the truth. I suggested accidental death. It would have to do. I had no intention of standing up and baring my soul, not to Mary Muncey or anyone else. With my criminal record, it would be like braiding my own noose.

Steph brought up the idea of an immediate plan.

"We can either do the deed here or go back to the Big Island and do it there. You understand that you're going to have to be the one up front on this, right?"

"Yeh," she gulped. "So where and when do we do it?"

"I'd prefer the Big Island. Home ground, more room to disappear." "Hilo?"

"No, that's all the way around the other side."

"Kailua Town?"

I thought about it. We both knew people there. We'd spent a couple of the summer months after the MDA bust hanging out there. But if anything weird happened, like the feds getting on to the real me, the fewer people who knew where I was, the better. "Maybe Kawaihae," I said. It was further north, a hop, skip, and a jump from the Kohala Mountains, among which lay Waimanu Valley. "Yeah, we can see Rick and his lady again."

Rick was Richard Schulz, an attorney and ex-judge. Steph had introduced me to them and we'd spent some lovely hours in their company. They lived just up the road from Kawaihae at Kamuela.

"The more I think about it, the better I like it."

Since Rick occupied a special position in Steph's life, as well as a peculiar one in mine, given the differences in the lifestyles of the three of us, this wasn't the first time mention of Rick had come up.

Steph had tried to call him from Pokai Bay. I had tried once or twice while Sea Wind was in haulout. Steph and I both agreed that Rick was the one person in the world who could be relied upon to give us good advice. He would have our welfare at heart, especially Steph's. We trusted him.

It had not always been so with me.

###

CHAPTER 3

Rick was Steph's friend. She had introduced me to so many of her friends. While most of them were nice enough, there were those who used her generosity for their own selfish ends and I was never trusting enough to take them on her recommendation alone, nor at face value.

As a man, I seemed to exist between a hope for paradise and a promise of hell. Because of those incidents in my own life, not the least of which had occurred in prison, I distrusted the facades people tended to construct around their personalities. I did not believe that the most important judgment we must make as human beings having to deal with other human beings could be made on the basis of a quick glance into their lives.

I had met enough individuals who were slick enough to piss on a chump's back and make him believe it was raining to prevent me from immediately taking Rick for the good and wise man that Steph believed him to be.

When she introduced me at the beach house in Puako, it was almost as if I were invisible. His handshake was light and ephemeral, his nod seemingly perfunctory, his eyes passing over me too quickly to see anything below the surface. Our first meeting had all the impact of a footprint on water.

In physical appearance, he reminded me of Timothy Leary, which was favorable since I found the "sixties guru of LSD" to be an amusing and stimulating personality. But there the resemblance ended, for Rick was perhaps the subtlest, most unobtrusive, and kindest man you can imagine. It would take time for me to discover his distinguishing traits and assimilate them into some semblance of a personality. He was well-read and thoughtful, educated in law, a familiar of politicians, an ex-judge in Honolulu, now a private attorney. Where I expected a tension of ambition to exist, I found only tranquility. Over the year or so of visits we had with him, most measured in hours but sometimes lasting several days, I had come to the conclusion that he had worked out all the major problems of living the good life for himself, accepting whatever was placed on his platter with equanimity. Without really knowing much about how he made his living or his financial resources, I came away with the distinct impression that, unlike most lawyers in my experience, he did not indulge himself in the adversarial viewpoint, but rather settled most of his representations out of court. Rather than look for dragons to slay for clients with gripes, he looked for agreements that could be made on the basis of human needs.

Because I was always busy studying him with what I fancied were X-ray eyes, drinking in his every little act, word, and mannerism like someone thirsty for a role model, I was more in my student mode than in trying to display myself for his approval. There was nothing I wanted from him except to observe and learn.

His wife was not cute or pretty. Being heavily freckled, streaked blond, and appearing as raw-boned and awkward, she nevertheless conveyed a sense of grace, a woman who was plain and quiet but beautiful. There was something between them that moved me, a love that was expressed and said more by implication than words ever could -- a look, a touch, a mutual consideration bordering on the telepathic. I had never seen two people more in harmony.

At first, I think he must have been a bit leery of me. What was a restless, energetic guy like me, driven by an inner flame, doing with a girl like Stephanie? It was obvious to all who knew us that we were polar opposites. Was I the tomcat who played with the mouse before consuming it, or was Steph a moth dashing her head against a hot bulb, attracted to a light that was also the fire of her destruction? Few saw us as complementary halves of a whole.

Once he asked me to relate an experience that had moved me. I was suspicious of his motives. I had learned in prison to conceal my emotions. To reveal a tender self was to reveal weakness, the favorite morsel of predators.

"What do you mean?"

"Nothing complicated," he said. "It's a question of values. If we know what moves a person, we know all we need to know. I'm curious to know what moves you, engages your emotions."

I thought about it. He was, not a predatory type.

"There was a deaf kid once, about five years old, who almost broke my heart."

"Tell me about him."

"He was born deaf. He had a voice, but couldn't talk -- because he'd never heard language, or music, or anything. He made awful noises, like screams. I used to try to imagine what it was like. Or to be born blind, you know? Never to see anything beautiful. Can you imagine how that must be?"

"Oh, I don't know. Can you miss what you've never had? It seems to me it would be worse to have gone blind or deaf later in life."

"Yeah, I see what you mean, but I've never been a millionaire either, but I think I know what I'm missing. You and I, we know what a person born with such handicaps is missing. Do you think there's any compensation?"

"They say a blind man hears much better than the rest of us. Who knows what sensitivities nature would grant a deaf boy in compensation?"

"Feeling," I said.

"Feeling?"

"I tried it once. I locked myself into my apartment and spent a whole day being blind and deaf. I put in earplugs and blindfolded myself. I had to go to the bathroom, fix things to eat, stumble about by feel, you know?"

"Hm. That's interesting."

"My tactile senses came into play. Touch and smell became intense experiences. Those nerves that are connected with sight and hearing seem to recircuit for the enhancement of the remaining senses. You're confined in a dark, soundless, narrower world."

"I can imagine."

"No, you can't, see, that's the thing, you really can't imagine. It's like being in prison, or being a nigger in the antebellum South, or the ugliest person alive. You can be horrified and even sympathetic, but only because you fear the loss of what you know. You can't know what it's really like until you experience it."

"Yes, I see."

"Did you know that if you cut off stimulation to all the senses, what they call sensory deprivation, you'll soon go nuts?"

"I've read that."

"It's as though your nerves turn upon your mind to tell it, since there are no messages being received through our senses, that there is no outside world. Nothing exists. Therefore, of what use is a mind that perceives? It begins to self-destruct."

"What about this deaf boy?"

"He found this dead bird in the backyard once. He liked birds. He watched them, pointed at them, made what I guess were ecstatic noises. He could grin, see, and laugh in a way. He'd learned to do that when he felt good. Anyway, he had no conception of death. How could he? He just marveled over this dead bird, trying to make it fly. He was so serious. He'd throw it up in the air, but it would only fall back again. He would leap about, flapping his arms, as if to tell it what it must do. He picked it up by the tips of its wings and ran down the driveway, making his awful gurgling noises, leaping and. cavorting about...as if he, himself, would fly and carry it with him into the sky. It was one of the saddest things I'd ever seen."

After a few moments of silence between us, in which I fancied he was imagining the scene -- I' described the boy as olive-skinned with white on white teeth and had mimicked his vocal noises and bodily gestures -- he asked me what it was, exactly, that I'd felt.

"In Greek legend," I told him. "There was a giant -- I forget his name -- who was invincible so long as he touched the earth. Hercules strangled him while holding him in the air. That's what I felt like. If all our strength comes from touching the ground, then my feet would never touch earth again -- sort of like dangling in space with a noose around your neck."

"I understand," Rick said, his voice quietly solemn.

I grinned to break the uncomfortable mood. "Ambrose Bierce," I said, quoting, "defined understanding as a cerebral secretion that enables one having it to know a house from a horse by the roof on the house. Its nature and laws have been exhaustively expounded by Locke, who rode a house, and Kant, who lived in a horse."

We laughed together, always a good indication.

"You like Bierce?"

"Yeah, the Devil's Dictionary. I haven't read much of his other stuff -- a few short stories."

"I do, too."

"I figured. I was browsing through your copy." I pointed to his bookshelves, always a point of interest with me, seeing what someone read. He had a lot of books. "Know what my favorite one is?"

"What?"

"'History is an account, mostly false,'" I quoted, "'of events, mostly unimportant, which are brought about by rulers, mostly knaves, and soldiers, mostly fools."

He smiled. "Isn't that a bit cynical?"

"Maybe. To me, it's a lot of truth in a nutshell. What's your favorite quotation?"

"In Bierce, you mean?"

"Anybody."

"Oh, let's see," he mused. "I like the one from Little Gidding, -- '"We shall not cease from exploration, and the end of all our exploring will be to arrive where we started, and know the place for the first time.'"

"T. S. Eliot. I like it. It's very Zen."

"You know Eliot?"

"No, not really. I've read some I like, but he's not my style. He's heavy and usually too obscure for me to figure out. But good if you're feeling contemplative -- like E.E. Cummings and Ezra Pound." "Do you meditate?"

"Doesn't everybody?"

"You surprise me, Buck."

"Why, because I'm not the stereotype you expect?"

"I'm beginning to think you do it on purpose."

"My grandfather taught me that. He said that when going against lesser men, I should be kind. If my opponent was equal, at least it would be a fair fight. But with your superiors, you can still come out all right if you can make them underestimate you. That's sort of a left-handed compliment."

"Well, thank you. Your grandfather sounds like a wise man."

"No, just a good old country boy. Used to be a cop. "What kind of music do you like?"

"Is this another trick question?"

"No, I'm interested to know. Why would you think that?"

"It reminds me of the tests psychologists give. You're not supposed to know you're revealing yourself."

"I suppose it is in a way. Are you afraid of that?"

"Depends on who I'm revealing myself to," I replied. "I like Janis Joplin, Jimmie Reed, blues music. I like the jazz of Miles Davis. I like Stravinsky's Rite of Spring."

"Is that another left-handed compliment?"

I laughed. "Sure, I guess so."

"Well, thank you again. You have nothing to fear from me." "I know, and despite your concerns, you don't have to worry about me. I've got no designs on anything you have."

He looked startled. "What do you mean?"

"You've seen me glaring, or scowling. You think I'm angry." "Are you?"

"Look, Rick," I said, taking off my glasses. "I want to show you something." "Yes?"

"That picture over there," I pointed. He glanced to a small-framed print, then looked back. Seeing the look on my face, his eyes widened momentarily, and he grinned. "I'm nearsighted. Screwing up my face helps me focus when I don't have my glasses on."

"It makes you look very grim," he said. "Do you do that on purpose, too?"

"Sometimes. You advised Steph to get rid of me, that I wasn't right for her."

"Yes, I did. Perhaps I was a bit hasty."

"She has poor judgment with men."

He frowned. "It's not that, really. She's one of the sweetest girls I've ever known. She's generous and loving. She sees only the good in people."

I grinned.

"All right, smart ass," he said.

"Just don't worry about her, okay? I happen to think very highly of her."

"Okay. I've enjoyed talking to you. We should try it again."

Once he read a poem he had written to a gathering of friends at his house. The occasion was learning that his wife was pregnant. His soft-spoken words flowed with restrained emotion. I was very moved. Stephanie became very romantic. It worked out.

Another day I sat and listened to him debating with an extremely intelligent and clever member of the Hare Krishna sect. The sandaled, robed, and head-shaven guy was very good, but. I thought if he persisted in trying to convert Rick to his views, he would soon begin growing his hair and wearing more conventional garb.

*****

Most of our conversations were short, having to do with no more than the most ordinary things, but often enough he sent me reeling away with questions like blunt instruments.

"What's the meaning of life?"

"Is that a serious question?"

"Let me be more specific -- what's the meaning of your life?" "Jesus, Rick, can't you ask some easy ones first, give me a chance to work up to the hard ones?"

Two months later, after consulting Ecclesiastes in the Bible, as well as a number of books on philosophy, psychology, anthropology, and so on, and coming away with a headache no closer to an answer than to live, want, and die, I returned to the question.

"Life is basically sad... because we die. And we're never ready to die. We're never sure human souls continue into a new life without the vessels of our bodies. And we're ignorant, so unknowing of what life and the universe is all about. And so the best cure, if it can be called that, is to learn.

Life is a lifelong process of learning, of trying to understand what the hell's going on -- especially with everything changing all the time. And that's the thing, see, learning never quite fails you -- you eternally believe that knowledge will somehow complete you, though, it never does -- and it leads you on as long as you're physically and mentally able to pursue it. You get old and arthritic and lay awake at nights wondering when the old ticker's going to give out. You are torn with lost loves, with speculating over what other choices might have meant. You see the world slowly being destroyed. Nuclear holocaust? Maybe. More likely we'll slowly poison ourselves to death. Have you ever considered that mankind might be a disease of planets? We come to know evil and wonder if there is any escape from it. Is there any honor left in the world? Values are transitory -- they are soon enough discarded and replaced with others, often as not less beneficial than the preceding ones -- the famous sliced salami analogy. Where will it all end? Who the fuck knows? All you can do is do your best to learn as much as you can. What the hell is going on with time and matter and movement in the universe? What has meaning to our tiny sparks of intelligence? Happiness? Is that it, whatever it is? Maybe. I'm happiest when I'm learning. When I am in pursuit of knowledge when I am acting to find an answer, perhaps only a small one in a chain that leads to another, that's when I feel most alive. That's when I feel like I'm functioning as I was designed to. Sometimes it tortures me, but it never alienates me from myself. Sometimes I fear what I will learn, and sometimes I distrust it, but I can never really, at bottom, regret what I've learned -- not as long as it seems to be true.

Learning and doing, loving and working, that's all I can say.

The next question he asked was even worse.

"What do you fear? What demons do you flee?"

"I can never get over the shame of having once spanked my daughter."

"What?"

"She didn't deserve it. She had done nothing wrong. Simply came between my wife and me during an argument. I took out my own anger on her. How can a father be the agent of injustice to his own child?"

"Buck, are you serious?"

I didn't have to remove my glasses for the glare I sent his way. "No, I mean, I didn't know you had any children."

"One. The most beautiful girl in the whole world." "Well..."

"Okay, sorry. I know you were asking something else."

And so, with hardly any thought, I told him about death, all I knew, the universal concern. I told him of when I had been a pallbearer as a boy and had unwittingly cracked a joke over my name, of all the ugly and senseless deaths I had witnessed in prison, of my grandmother's death, my father's recent death, of the humiliating interference of death into the realm of the living without warning.

When my father had died, the great torture and revelation had been how much I missed him, how unfair it was to cut him off from his dreams, and that I could never tell him how much I loved him.

With my grandmother, who'd died in a sanitarium in a catatonic coma when I had lived in San Francisco as a driving instructor, it had been a guilt-ridden thankfulness that she had been spared further indignities. As a teenager, she had seen her father kill her mother with a shotgun, then blow his own head off, and she had had to raise her brothers and sisters. She had worked hard all her life and, through all the ups and downs of it, there had always been an aura of sadness about her. She had raised her own beautiful, happy, but poor children in the farm country of Illinois and Kansas, my mother, my aunts and uncles. Her hair had always been long and indian black. Next to my mother, she'd been the kindest, forgivingest, most loving and loyal woman I'd ever known.

When I was in San Quentin, she'd begun to lose her mind, and had been placed in care of a private sanitarium. I had gone with my Aunt Josephine to visit her. I was stunned, hardly recognizing the white-haired old crone with sunken cheeks and deep, dark-circled eyes. They'd taken her dentures away so she wouldn't bite her tongue. She never spoke, only made mewling noises as my aunt and I fed her from a box of chocolates we'd brought, dabbing at the pink and brown drooling wound of her mouth with Kleenex. She kept her arms clasped about her ribcage in an embrace of self-comfort, her legs crossing and uncrossing in automatic spasms. There were scabbed calluses on her knees and ankles. Her eyes were the shallow button-eyes of a doll--you couldn't see very far into them and nothing looked out. I turned to my aunt helplessly, unbelieving.

"I've brought Bucky to see you, dear," she began bravely and from then on kept up a constant monologue of one-sided conversation as though to keep reality from intruding into pauses. "Remember what an ornery little scamp he used to be?"

Catatonic schizophrenia, or was it Alzheimer's? Nobody understood it, only that my grandmother had withdrawn from the world.

I would ever after imagine that the illumination that had been her self had left all the lights of heaven and hell to sit rocking in a dark cave lit by a tiny candle, crossing and uncrossing her legs and cooing like a child -- a place of safety where she could play with the toys of memory that pleased her, where nothing and no one could ever touch her again.

After an hour of my aunt's falsely cheerful and meaningless chatter mixing with the chicken-coop sounds of other old women in the home, we'd stood to leave. My Aunt Jo had kissed her on the forehead with a tenderness that shredded my heart and held her head to hers for a moment. I had kissed her, too, through a blur of unshed tears, and pressed my cheek to hers, closing my eyes, remembering the gentle and warm comforter she had been.

Then, holding her face in my hands, I had looked searchingly into the opaque glitter of her eyes. Suddenly, they focused, the irises changing shape, taking on depth, and way down a dark tunnel I could see something alive. She recognized me. She put the claws of her hands to my wrists.

"Little Bucky," she croaked with vocal cords unused to speech. "My lovely, darling boy. You're a good boy, son, always a good boy." She'd always called me son. The windows closed and she went back to her candlelight, leaving merely the remnants of bone and flesh in my grasp.

"She knows me, Aunt Jo! She recognized me!"

My aunt patted my shoulder and pulled gently at me. "She has moments like that, but she always goes back. Maybe it's a better place for her." I'd rather trust my fate to that last mad glint of recognition in my catatonic old grandmother's death-filled eyes, which were in that moment beautiful.

"Buck?"

"What?"

"If there's ever anything I can do for you, if you ever want to talk about anything, you let me know, will you? You're always welcome."

"Sure, Rick, thanks."

"I mean it."

When I would go up for my belated sentencing before Judge King in 1975 on the MDA charge, Stephanie would ask Rick to write a character recommendation for me.

Among other things, he would write these lines: "I have never had occasion to find any aspect of Buck's demeanor or personality objectionable. Whenever I have seen him in the company of others, he has always been courteous and respectful of their desires. Among this group, Buck has no reputation for violence that I am aware of." But that was all of the past and future. At the time, I only knew Rick was a friend who could be counted on to help us. I was thinking that we could lay it all in his lap, that he would help Steph through the rigmarole of dealing with the authorities. Besides, I wanted to broach the subject of filing a salvage claim.

My knowledge of Admiralty law was pretty sketchy, but I knew that if you saved a boat or cargo from destruction, you were entitled to some compensation. In the attempt to keep Sea Wind safe, we had lost Iola. I explained the idea to Steph.

"You mean we could wind up owning Sea Wind?"

"Well, I don't know. Maybe. That's up to the courts. But I'm pretty sure we'd be entitled to some compensation for our loss."

"Yeh, geez, it would help us out a lot."

"Rick would have to bring the suit in your name only," I said. "I'm not going anywhere near a courtroom."

"Okay. We should try to get hold of him again, let him know we're coming."

"Right. We can do that."

*****

The drydock manager was pushed for haulout space. We agreed to launch a day early, in six rather than seven. We had only a few touchups to make topsides. I would delay reattaching the letters of Sea Wind's name until we were on our way -- or maybe not until we'd reached Kawaihae, just in case. There was nothing left but to fuel up on diesel, which we would have to do at Ala Wai. Then we could make a fast passage by motoring the whole way.

Somewhere here during the week between Kewalo Basin and the Ala Wai Yacht Harbor, we had tracked down the thirty-two foot sloop belonging to Dickie and Carlos. While awaiting engine replacement, they had rafted together with several other boats. Making our way from vessel to vessel, we found them with a beautiful Japanese girl and were given a warm but surprised welcome.

"What the hell are you guys doing back here?"

"No choice. We got a problem. You got a cold beer I can wet my whistle?"

"Sure, c'mon in. What happened? Did you get our message? We sent a postcard to that guy, Shoemaker."

"Yeah, we got it."

"So, what's happening?"

"We got another boat," Stephanie said.

"Where's Iola?"

I shrugged. "Last seen under full sail."

Dickie looked blank, awaiting enlightenment. "You got another boat?"

"Yeah, a ketch. Nice one."

"Very nice," Steph added.

"Where? How? Christmas Island?"

Christmas was the largest island further down from Fanning in the chain of the northernmost Line Islands, which included. Palmyra.

"No. At Palmyra."

"Aren't you going to tell him how you won it in a chess game," Steph suggested with a hint of sarcasm, getting in a dig. Dickie was incredulous.

"You won a boat in a chess game?"

I grinned sheepishly. "Sure. Didn't you know I was the blind- fold champion of North America?"

"C'mon, really. What's going on?"

I sighed. I liked Dickie and Carlos. We'd done business and I trusted them. They were our partners. For two guys who'd never done any prison time, they were standup in my book. But I didn't know the Japanese girl from Sophia Loren.

"Let's take a walk," I said to Dickie.

"I want to show you something." We hopped back to the dock and strolled along.

"What's happening, Buck? We got a problem?"

I liked the pronoun, we. It was a declaration.

"Who's the chick?"

"We got a thing going. She's okay."

"Nice. You got good taste in. broads. She in on the business?"

He shrugged. "Ah, you know. She's probably figured out a few things. I was going to bring her down with us to Palmyra. Don't worry. She doesn't know about what we're doing down there -- not yet anyway."

"Okay. That's good."

"You going to take all day to tell me the problem?"

"We're going to have to change the plan."

"Why? It's a good idea, man. You said it could be done."

"It can, no question. The thing is, we can't keep this boat we have. It's not ours."

"Whose, then?"

"It belonged to a couple named Graham."

"Who're they? What's the deal?"

I shrugged. "They disappeared. We found their boat abandoned. We're headed over to the Big Island to see a lawyer about it, maybe file a salvage claim."

"You found it?"

"Yeah. We think they had an accident."

"What about Iola?"

"We lost her on the reef, trying to tow her out."

"You were going to tow it all the way back here?"

"No, to Fanning. After losing Iola, there wasn't much choice. We have to report this thing."

"You haven't reported it yet?"

"No, man, that's part of the problem. I jumped bail. I got a bogus passport. I can't go to the authorities."

"Yeah, I see what you mean."

"We're going to dump it on the lawyer. He's a good friend of the ol' lady's. Steph's going to get up front on the deal. Me, I'm going to disappear."

"What about our business?"

"Don't worry. I can set up again on the Big Island. I've still got a couple of camps. I can get back into operation in no time."

"You need money?"

"Naw, I'm okay for the time being."

Dickie stood there, trying to think it through. "Wow. You sure know how to throw a curveball."

"It'll be okay. You won't have so far to truck the grass."

"Yeah, that's a plus. But I liked the other idea better. A whole damned island to yourself. No cops. Tons and tons of good shit, man!"

I laughed. "Yeah, well...we can still do it. Something to look forward to. But in the meantime, I got to make a living, get some bread together for a new boat."

"Yeah," he sighed.

"Dickie," I reminded him. "This is all top secret stuff, huh?"

"I have to tell my brother."

"Yeah, that's okay," I nodded. "But not the chick." "She's going to wonder."

"Stick with the story I won it in a chess game."

"She's not going to believe that bullshit."

"Doesn't matter. It's only for a few days, a week maybe -- until I can get Steph hooked into the lawyer."

"Okay."

"We got to get. I just wanted to clue you in a little bit, save you a wasted trip to Palmyra."

"Ah, man," he grinned ruefully. "I was looking forward to it." "I'll be in touch, let you know what's what. Maybe we can meet in Kawaihae when you get your boat together."

"Yeah, right. You know how to get in touch."

"Yeah."

*****

We motored down the channel off the sea into the crowded yacht harbor at the Ala Wai. The fuel station was closed. We'd have to spend the night, top off the tanks in the morning before shoving off. We anchored in the turning basin between a couple of other boats, one of which we recognized -- the trimaran Ladybug, which we had once considered buying from its owner, Joel Peters, on the Big Island. He hailed us and we went for a visit.

"Nice boat."

Joel didn't know anything about Iola. "Yeah, we like it." We watched Robert Redford in The Candidate on his portable TV. Since Steph planned to do some laundry in the morning while I was getting Sea. Wind fueled up, she offered to do his.

Later, after feeding the dogs and putting them below so they wouldn't bark their heads off, we dressed and rowed ashore to pick up Larry. He was living just down the way in his homebuilt boat, which he called a cutter and I called a houseboat. I carried along the final draft of my letter to Mac's sister. My idea was to let Larry read it to fill him in.

He lived a disordered bachelor's existence. We arrived to find tools and materials scattered all over the garishly painted-in-red vessel. We rearranged things for a place to sit in the unfinished interior and smoked a couple of joints by lamplight.

I broached the subject of the letter, but between being stoned and hungry for supper, left it lying on his table.

"I'm too fucked up now," he said. "I'll read it tomorrow."

We had dinner and strolled down Kalakaua Avenue, fronting Waikiki, cruised over to Kuhio Street, hitting a few bars along the way looking for some good live music. With more grass and booze, the prime rib stoking us, we proceeded to dip from big buckets and paint the town red, hitting a joint here, one there, catching the shows, the music, dancing, talking and laughing with ourselves and any friendly looking strangers.

We closed out the night with coffee and fantastic pastries at King's Bakery, a 24-hour place. Larry dropped us out of the company van at our dinghy, then drove on around to park near his slip. We rowed across the silent water to crash through the slurping, jostling affection of our mutts.

*****

Unbeknownst to us, Lord Pollock, as we had dubbed him at Palmyra for his snooty ways, had had occasion to observe Sea Wind. Despite her gaudy new paint job and the lack of a name, he immediately recognized her distinctive lines. Just as immediately, without even going out to see if Mac and Muff were aboard, he assumed the very worst and called the Coast Guard and the FBI. I would later hear a story from one of my lawyers that he had even broken out a shotgun and was prepared to be deputized.

Lord Pollock just knew that the shoddy hippie couple had murdered his dear friends and stolen their yacht. He had read about smugglers pirating private vessels for illicit use in transporting narcotics, and had spread his lurid theories and suspicions far and wide, to anyone who would stand still for two minutes.

The FBI was apparently skeptical. Bureaucracies, after all, tend to be sluggish and move ponderously. Whether Sea Wind was kept under surveillance because of Lord Pollock's morally affronted sensibilities and his rabid demands that these maniacal slayers of innocents be immediately apprehended and clapped in irons, I do not know. In my experience the FBI tend to look upon the common citizenry with a certain patronizing contempt.

In the morning, however, all was made crystal clear.

#

CHAPTER 4

Stephanie had rowed over to Ladybug to fetch Joel's laundry. She was back in no time with the news that the Coast Guard had been by the night before to inquire.

Oh, shit!

Dressed in nothing more than cutoffs, I'd been gathering more appropriate garb to wear for breakfast. The immediate plan had been to go ashore for a shower, get our laundry started at the harbor facility, then pick up Larry for breakfast in a nearby restaurant -- after which we would say adios, refuel, and get in the wind for the Big Island.

I checked that our money was in my pocket, grabbed pants, shoes, shirt, and Steph, and headed for the dinghy.

"What?"

"Grab your stuff. We gotta get outa here. They'll be back." She caught the urgency in my voice. "Oh, my Gawd. Are you sure? There's no one around."

"Get in!"

"I gotta get Puffer."

She rushed back down the main hatchway. Puffer was lolling like Cleopatra on her divan below. She was right -- hardly anyone was astir in the harbor when I looked around. Except Joel.

I hailed him. "They say what they wanted?"

"Naw, just they wanted to speak to the owners." He shrugged. "They wanted to know why there was no name on the boat. I told them you'd just gotten out of drydock, that you probably hadn't got around to it yet."

We left him scratching his head as I began to row us ashore, doubtless too polite to inquire about his laundry. I headed for the nearest pier, a floating one anchored to concrete pillars driven into the bedrock beneath the water, a row of yachts lined down both its sides.

"Jeez, what's the rush? There's nobody even up yet."

Popolo and Sista would fix that -- they were both up baying their displeasure at being left behind.

"We should have put them down below," Steph said, our usual practice.

"They'll shut up once we're out of sight," I replied, stepping onto the pier. "C'mon, hurry up."

"No, they're going to wake everybody up and they'll all be pissed off at us."

"Goddamnit, we gotta get outa here!"

"Oh, hold your horses. We've got time." She pulled the painter out of my hand, repositioned herself at the oars, and began to maneuver around. "It'll only take a minute. Besides, I forgot the shampoo."

I stood torn between shouting an order at her, which she would not take too well, and telling her to bring Popolo and Sista back with her. I couldn't abandon my faithful hounds! But then I thought, what would I do with them -- leave them with Larry? Then I thought again.

Steph would take forever trying to load them into the dink from the high decks of Sea Wind -- if she could do it without capsizing and going into the drink. No, we could always get them back somehow, I thought, not knowing that it was the last time I would ever see them -- except for two live appearances on TV as celebrities.

I kept my mouth shut, fuming and dancing out my inner jitters. I watched as she got them below and came back up with the goddamned shampoo -- like we had all the time in the world. She turned to speak to someone on a neighboring boat who'd popped their head up -- probably to apologize. When she got back into the dink, she turned to have a few words with Joel -- probably discussing his fucking laundry.

Off to the left, moving lazily into the estuary leading into the harbor, I saw a launch. Did it look official? Suddenly, I felt vulnerable standing out on the end of that pier -- there was no avenue of escape, nowhere to run.

I motioned to Steph that I'd meet her at the bathhouse ashore and she began to head that way. I grabbed my clothes and shoes to begin the walk, but whoa, now, what's this, I asked myself as I spotted a guy studying me through a pair of binoculars. I hesitated, took time for another good looksee. I had on my prescription sunglasses. The launch, I could see as it drew closer, had the Coast Guard stripe painted down its side. I tried to wave at Steph to get a move on. But now another guy had joined the one with binoculars and he was pointing and waving my way, shouting something I couldn't hear.

There was nothing to do but simply stand there. Steph was well along the waterway between two rows of yachts as the launch passed yards away, turning to follow in her wake. It was loaded with men, some of whom weren't dressed for it, obvious landlubbers, and they clutched riot guns.

Ah, now, me boyo, ah, now, here we go. This is it.

I sat down the gear I was carrying. It wouldn't do to have my hands concealed.

When I stood up, the first two yahoos were running down the pier at me screaming. They had pistols in their hands. There was an infinitesimal moment when I hesitated between standing my ground, smiling and raising my hands, and doing what comes naturally to me in such situations.

My older, less civilized, instincts took possession of my motor nerves. I dove into the water between two yachts, went down under the keel, and made like a porpoise under a half dozen of them, coming up to gulp air between two more before diving down again, swimming in the direction from which they ran.

Under water, I could hear their feet pounding along the pier as we passed going opposite ways. I came up to seek air and dove again. When I came up the next time, it was in a brief airspace under the pier with just enough room to breathe. I heard feet and voices passing right overhead.

"I saw him over there!"

I'd lost my glasses. I ducked my head under. The only way they could find me was to send divers into the water, but it was a big harbor with hundreds of boats. At least they can't shoot me here, I thought. I hung on and waited.

"Try that other dock! He might have got across!"

"There he is!"

"Where?"

"Over there!"

Footsteps, fast movements.

"Get some men down there!"

"We've got him penned in. He can't get out of the harbor!"

Me in my little headspace, face pressed up into the few inches of air layered beneath the pier, I could hear very well, even see sky through narrow cracks in the boardwalk, could feel the feet moving overhead.

What I knew at that point was that the water was wet and it was time to practice the patience of Buddha. I remained in that position for hours, until my hands and feet were thoroughly wrinkled and a chill had seeped into my bones. I began to shiver uncontrollably, would have to make a move soon to get out of the water.

I felt footsteps coming along the boardwalk, heard the voices of several people, perhaps two men and a woman.

"What in the world has been going on around here today?"

"They're looking for somebody, an escaped convict or something." "No, a murderer."

"A murderer?"

"That's what I hear. Killed a man and his wife."

"My God! Did they catch him?"

"Dunno. Don't think so. Arrested his girlfriend, I hear."

"My God, I hope they get him. What next?"

My shivering increased. I'd been in the water for over six hours, the day well into the afternoon. I came up between two boats, eased my way to their sterns for a peek into the waterway. I could swim back across the turning basin where we'd anchored, but cops were probably all over Sea Wind. Besides, the shore on the other side was a bare rocky slope with no place to hide and nothing to impede any wandering eye. The people aboard neighboring boats had gotten a good look at me and were sure to report a sighting. No, that route would only be good well after dark.

The other way was hotels, shops, and people. I porpoised under a long line of yachts for a closer look. Across about a hundred yards of open water I could see a small-boat launching ramp inclining down into the harbor. It wasn't far from a hotel shop that I could enter from the harbor and exit on the street side, a. main artery, lots of people. Who'd notice another tourist in wet shorts fresh from a swim?

There was one guy working in the cockpit of his boat off to the side who would have a clear view of me merely by raising his eyes.

Swimming in the harbor was discouraged because of pollution, which had already killed all the marine life in the water. Only the hardiest mussels, stubborn algae, and the worst germs survived there. And me. So far.

I swam slowly, making no splashes. From childhood I had always taken to swimming like a fish. I treaded through the water in slow motion, only my nose and eyes, the top of my head, above the surface. A slow moving object is least likely to attract the eye. Once the man working in his cockpit seemed to look directly at me, but turned back to what he was doing.

I walked up the ramp, crossed the pavement, and entered the hotel tourist shop. I bought a pack of cigarettes and a book of matches with a soggy bill, grinning and shrugging when the clerk eyed me. I looked out the way I had come in, over the harbor. I saw nothing suspicious. Larry's boat, with its odd color and design, sat just down the way.

I took a last deep drag on the cigarette and stepped out to stride, not too fast and not too slow, directly down the pavement, out along the finger-pier, to leap nimbly aboard, and duck below.

Of course he wasn't there -- probably at work. Had he been aware of the hullabaloo? He must have wondered when we didn't show up for our breakfast date. My letter to Mac's sister lay where I'd left it the night before. I picked it up, wondering if Larry had read it. Should I stay and wait for him? My instincts said no. If the FBI hadn't already been by to see him, they soon would.

I was up and out, reentering the hotel shop to pass through and exit on the busy street side, where I strolled until I came to another tourist shop specializing in beach wear. Inside I bought a pair of sunglasses, a pair of thongs, and a colorful aloha shirt with matching trunks, which I changed into.

Continuing on down the way, I tried to improvise a plan. I should get rid of the new beard I'd let sprout on the return voyage from Palmyra. The bogus passport had my picture in a mustache. I needed to be clean-shaven. I needed clothes. I needed a place to hole up.

I stopped along the way to purchase a toilet kit, a pair of slacks, a hat, a pair of shoes. I headed for a small hotel I knew, a bit off the tourist path where a ring of prostitutes worked. For whatever reasons, cops rarely bothered them there. The management was discreet. There were no questions, no problems. I checked in without having to show any ID, which I didn't have anyway.

The six o'clock news was all about Steph's arrest and my escape. She had jumped out of the rowboat with Puffer clutched in her arms and ran. They'd found her trying to conceal herself behind some potted plants. It was the worst thing she could have done. The best would have been to wait and greet them with a smile. Perhaps a bit of my paranoia as a fugitive had rubbed off on her. They had booked her on suspicion of stealing Sea Wind.

The entire FBI complement in Honolulu was hot on my trail. My pictures were everywhere. The airports and harbors were watched. Viewers were urged to call the FBI or police if they had any information on my whereabouts.

I hung around for a day or two, never straying far from the hotel room, catching the latest reports on TV, and reading the fuller accounts in newspapers.

Stephanie was reported to have made a statement about dead people not being able to own things and that she thought Mac and Muff would have wanted us to have Sea Wind. I knew she had had the codicil to Mac's will in mind.

Popolo and Sista were also in the hoosegow. They had been shown on TV being booked into the local animal quarantine. Puffer had apparently eluded arrest like me. (The authorities had allowed Stephanie to hand over Puffer's safe-keeping to Joel Peters on Ladybug.)

The first order of business was to get Steph out of jail. I had to continue to evade capture so I could work at arranging bail. Then maybe I could figure a way to spring my mutts. I would have to make my way, somehow, out of the eye of the storm, return to the Big Island where I could lay low and begin working my schemes.

Boat or plane, the only two ways. If I hung around long enough, I could arrange a private trip by boat or small plane -- or I could go commercial more immediately. There was danger in delaying and danger in trying to go out through the Honolulu airport.

I studied myself in the mirror, now clean-shaven. In the straw hat with a camera around my neck, I could pass for any of a thousand tourists. The dark shades would hide my "bedroom eyes," as Steph described them. I needed a traveling companion, preferably a woman.

I went out to a payphone to call Larry. He was spooked by all the hoopla, but game to help me. He arrived in the company van, me ready to flee at the slightest suspicion. But all was quiet and ordinary. I told him what I wanted, a plane ticket, and the loan of a camera, and gave him some money.

"Okay. Anything else?"

"No, just make the ticket for the earliest flight tomorrow." It was too late for any more flights that evening. "Pick up a pizza and some beer on your way back."

When he returned an hour or so later as I had stood waiting in the shadows by a tree and a nearby alley watching the whores cajole their tricks in and out of the hotel, I took him up to the room. We munched the pizza, drank the beer, smoked a couple of joints, and switched channels

on the TV looking for the latest news.

"So now I know about the boat."

"Yeah."

"Did you guys murder those people?"

I looked at him, noticing his whole body tensed up. I had no idea that it would be the first of many, many times that question would be put to me in various forms. "What do you think, Larry? You think I'm chickenshit enough to do something like that?" He looked away.

"I know Steph couldn't harm a fly."

I waited.

"No, I don't think you'd do something like that."

"How does it feel?"

"Huh?"

"To be right."

He laughed nervously. "Jesus, what a mess."

Larry."

"What, man?"

"You're thinking maybe you could be wrong, right?"

He shrugged. "I've been burned before."

"I'm not a fucking skulking murderer, pal."

"Okay, okay."

"I'm not saying I couldn't kill somebody, man, you know, if I were sufficiently provoked. But not like that, just to steal a fucking boat."

"I'm sorry, Buck. I believe you."

I looked away and closed my eyes. "They just disappeared, maybe in an accident. We tried to take care of their boat. Iola was lost on a reef. We had to come back, to report it. You know my situation -- I couldn't get out front on this. We were headed over to see a lawyer friend of ours."

"What's going to happen now?"

"I gotta get Steph outa jail."

"What can I do?" Larry was enamored of Stephanie himself, having once or twice in his shy loneliness been favored with her sexual largesse.

"Just go visit her. Tell her everything'll be all right. Otherwise, keep your lip buttoned. You don't know anything. Okay?"

"Yeah, don't worry."

"I'll call you -- to see how things are going. You can be my go-between with Steph, messages and stuff."

"Okay."

We slumped on couch and chair, dozing the night away, and in the morning he drove me to the airport. I arrived about ten minutes before takeoff and spotted a nice big fat lady in a muumuu even more wildly colored than my shirt. She had four plastic shopping bags crammed full. I struck up small talk with her, discovered she was also going to Hilo, and offered to carry two of her bags -- the luck of the Irish.

On our approach to the boarding checkpoint, I saw a uniformed cop and a plainclothes guy, probably a fed. They were studying faces as they passed, looking down to compare them with the photos in their hands. Shit and Shinola, me bucko! I flexed up a grin and got to talking to big mama like I knew her intimately. She went right along oblivious to everything, doubtless enjoying the attentions of a handsome enough fellow.

As we passed the two flatfoots, I bent my head to lower the hat brim as though paying close attention to the lady's conversation. I got a good gander at myself staring up from the photos in their hands. Piece of cake.

*****

Back home in a milieu I knew well, I felt much safer. I caught a cab to a friend's house, where I had a couple of drinks, a couple of joints, and made some phone calls. I tried Rick Schulz again without success. Then I caught a jitney ride in one of the colorful character vehicles to Mountain View, about fifteen miles up Volcano Road -- the one that took tourists up to a view platform over the active Kilauea Crater -- and walked the final couple of miles into Hawaiian Fern Acres.

When I first saw the old homestead revealing itself through the foliage, I checked my stride on the gravel road, overcome with a whole wind-system of sighs. I had lived the happiest months of my life in this rustic little cabin, building it with my own two hands, working with Steph to make it livable. There was a two-seat outhouse set behind, the catchment tank, the old iron bathtub under the carport by the front door, and two mutts rushing out barking as I turned in at the driveway. Like Popolo and Sista from the same litter, they were barkers, not biters.

Debbie was home with her new boyfriend, a nice kid, and her exquisite daughter, Elena. When she saw me, her eyes got big as saucers before running out to hug me.

"Oh, Buck, we've been reading terrible things about you and Steph!"

I could hardly speak. Deb was a Hawaiian teenager, already a mother, and another on the way. I had always looked upon her as a younger version of Steph, she was so warmhearted and unassuming. She was like a baby sister to me and I had great affection for her.

"None of it's true. It's all bullshit."

"I know," she said, seeing my state. "I know."

Inside, she fixed me a cup of coffee while her boyfriend, a kid named Jason, passed me a lit joint. I looked around. Nothing much had changed. It was as though I'd never left.

"You want to talk about it?"

"Not now, Deb. I need you to help me out a little bit, not much."

"Anything. What can we do? You want to stay here?" "No, that wouldn't be good for you."

"Tell us and we'll do it."

I looked at Jason to see if she spoke for him. He nodded. "Give me a pencil and some paper."

The list I made contained a backpack, a sleeping bag, an air mattress, and a small camping tent. It included a one-burner Coleman stove and a can of fuel. "I'll also need some food. Use your own judgment, some canned and dry stuff, some coffee. Also, I'll need a pan or skillet, maybe a pot for coffee."

"We've got those. And some silverware."

"Better yet, pick me up one of those awful Korean knives, you. know, the cheap version of a Swiss Army Knife."

"That's a good idea."

"And some toilet paper."

She grinned.

"Couple of towels, a bar of soap."

"We've got those. How about shaving gear?"

"No, I've got that," I said, patting my little toilet kit.

"Anything else?"

"A machete."

"I've got an extra hunting knife you can take," Jason offered.

"Great, thanks."

"We'll have to hitch into Hilo."

"Okay, no problem. Take your time." I counted out some bills. "On your way in, stop at the airport and rent a car. I'll need you to give me a lift."

"How long should I rent it for?"

"Today and tomorrow."

They got ready, packed up Elena, and prepared to leave. Jason pointed to some ceiling panels. "Got some pakalolo curing in the rafters. Help yourself. I'll fix you up with a good stash to go."

I stood in the doorway, watching them heading out. "Hey," I called. "I haven't been here. You haven't seen me."

They nodded.

I opened a back window just in case a quick escape into the bush was needed. Knowing the dogs would warn me of anyone approaching, I lay down on the divan and fell asleep.

*****

The next day, Deb drove me clear across the island. I had her stop at the post office, where I mailed my letter to Mac's sister. On the way through Kamuela, I stopped in at Rick's house, but no one was home. Coming to the end of the road at Pololu, I got out, hoisted on the stuffed backpack, and prepared to hike down into the valley. I leaned in the window to kiss Deb goodbye.

"What about Steph?"

"Don't worry. She'll be out on bail soon."

"She can stay with us."

"That would be good. We'll see how it works out."

"I'll write her. You keep in touch."

I nodded. "Listen, Deb, it's important that you haven't seen me. The feds find out, they'll be all over your ass. You don't need that hassle. And tell Jason to take all the pakalolo out of the house for awhile, huh? Play it safe."

"I will."

"Mahalo, (Thanks) Deb."

"Po'maika'i." (Good Luck)

*****

That night, after reaching the floor of the valley, I cooked up a can of stew and some coffee. I smoked a fat joint and sat watching the waves roll with their foamy tips out of the darkness toward me. A soft wailing wind played the lonesome blues. I laid out my sleeping bag under the open sky, climbed in with my pensive mood, and let all the stars wink out at once.

When I awoke, it was gradually, naturally, and I lay listening to the sounds. There were birds, a distant snort of wild pigs, the breeze in the branches, the wash of the surf.

After coffee and a cigarette, I sat back to meditate, thinking about Steph. It was awful for me to imagine her in jail, the injustice of it, the enforced humiliation and depersonalization of the rigmaroles. Would a fat, ugly, crypto-nazi matron stick her sausage fingers up Steph's pussy and asshole looking for drugs, enjoying her resistance or submission, either way? Would the other inmates begin fucking over her because she wasn't conwise? Would she wind up being assaulted over the petty angers and resentments that run rampant in such places?

I grew restless with these thoughts and began to wander through the trees, moving for the sake of movement. I climbed a way up the far slope where I could look down across the golden beach, the sea dark at the horizon against a pale sky. The wide expanse of ocean had always symbolized the greatest freedom for me. Now it seemed to taunt me. My heart seemed to drop with a thud into my belly, sending a bubbling current of blood to pulse at my temple. Recognizing my helplessness, the uselessness of rage, I nevertheless railed against the invisible demons. Like a child, I jumped up and down, shook my fists at the sky, beat them against my thighs, gnashed my teeth, and snarled.

The great spaces, so full of nature's elements, were entirely unimpressed. Only the birds politely stilled their song for a few moments, as if they might consider some tune in my commotion, before returning to their former gaiety.

I began to move, packing up and trudging deeper into the wilderness, away from the sea. I came upon a wild sow with a litter of piglets, all snoozing in the sun. She came erect with a startled grunt and crashed off into the undergrowth, her babies squealing after, but I was too depressed to chase after them.

At the back junction of adjoining mountains, where the valley lay in mottled shadows, I came upon a pool filled by a waterfall so high the air was a spray of mist. I took off my clothes and jumped in. I caught my breath, the water was so cold. I washed, brushed my teeth, and shaved, my body a slew of goose bumps. After drying off and dressing, I pitched the tent in a tiny clearing away from the mist, and built a fireplace with rocks from the gully carrying the overflow to the sea. The arcs of rainbows rising in the mists did not cheer me.

When the light began to fade, I ate and drank coffee and smoked. Crawling into the tent, I lit the little lantern and rolled a couple of joints. Snug in the sleeping bag toking away, I dug out the three paperbacks I'd brought from the bookshelf at Deb's, and tried to read Carlos Castaneda's Don Juan: A Yaqui Way of Knowledge. The pakalolo was good and, in a pleasant state of euphoria, I drifted into another world.

In the morning I packed up to begin the arduous climb up the steep and trailless eastern slope. All day I fought through the thickly wooded crests and gullies of pristine forest adorning the Kohalas, until I came at last to another deep slope -- Waimanu- I slipped and slid, grasping at trees to break my momentum, to emerge on the flatland in the cool of early evening.

The middle of the valley was mostly swamp, fed by streams and waterfalls. A faint trail made by pigs and cattle, occasionally the hooves of horses carrying local hunters, curved around the U of the valley between swamp and solid ground rising into the lowermost slopes.

I turned north and marched to the sea. Along the way, I passed a thin trickle of water flowing into the swamp. Up above, I could see it running over rocks in a nice waterfall shower. After filling my canteen, I finished the trek in two hundred more yards to pitch the tent under a huge leafy tree by the shore.

I began the next day by running out through the surf to dive into the ocean. There is something about being in saltwater that makes me feel well and whole. Most of the Hawaiians I knew could never go for long without going down to the shore to immerse themselves in the sea.

*****

I was like a leaf blown in the wind. I sought distraction through the adventures of Don Juan and his callow biographer. I wandered around the entire circuit of the valley, only my own footprints disturbing the wet sand of the beach. I ceased for long periods to think with words, opening my senses outward. I tried to imitate birdcalls and the occasional snorts of unseen boars rooting in the damp earth. I would break into a run, wishing Popolo was loping at my heels, baying his deep, playful, pervasive call.

I took off my shoes, my bare soles seeking vibrations from the depths. Free to be a fool, I stood on my head like Don Juan and tried to force tears from my eyes, but no magic white deer appeared to whisper, "Why are you weeping?" I shrugged away the twinges of loneliness and feeling silly.

If only there had been a Don Juan in my life, a true man of knowledge, to teach me all the lessons I'd so desperately needed. If only I could draw mystical powers into myself from the earth and sky and sea, from the stars themselves, to become impeccable in spirit, to become as a natural warrior in protection against the evil and folly of the world.

Don Juan advised Casteneda to peer over his left shoulder and seek the image of his own death as guide and ally. When I looked, I saw nothing but my own fears comingling with the bright beauty of my surroundings. My troubled soul was, by turns, infused with a strange calmness and induced to tremble from so many extraordinary images, such an admixture of the strange and familiar.

We can speak of some days in long, gleeful speeches, retantalizing ourselves on the flavors of memories tasted anew, pleased and content as cows chewing their cuds in alfalfa fields. Other days inhibit our tongues, taciturn and thick with loathing -- they are as well forgotten though we know we are stuck with them forever. And there are the many unremarkable days, a gray crowd of them fading, with their boring routines, into invisibility, until our lives, only in moments of stingy clarity, appear as vast collections of the humdrum. We, all of us, may as well be convicts, we have so imprisoned ourselves in the drab clockworks of our lives. The rarest days of all are composed of infinite moments, one moving into the next, none with any boundary marking its passage, yet clear, lucid, and pure as diamond drops of water.

My days in Waimanu were lonesome and peaceful, my more chaotic thoughts contained behind a shaky dam in my mind. I was myself, a single, separate entity, a free man living in consonance with the elements of nature's gift. The sky made a light shower to wash me and freshen the air. The earth made a rivulet trickling down a rock face to slake my thirst. Birds made music to calm my spirit. The stark blue of the implacable sea faded to inscrutable gray at the horizon.

*****

Regardless of whatever anyone may say about my past, my present, and my future as a human being, I have never been a predatory beast preferring a solitary life, venturing among my own kind only when drawn by urges for sex, battle, or booty. I subscribed completely to what Pierre Teilhard de Chardin, the Jesuit philosopher, said when he wrote, "Love alone is capable of uniting living beings in such a way as to complete and fulfill them, for it alone takes them and joins them by what is deepest in themselves."

At the time, I considered the alluring idea of remaining in Waimanu forever. I knew

Stephanie would not remain in jail for long. Upon her release, perhaps she would go to stay with Debbie and Jason in our home. It would be easy enough to steal out to fetch her, but I fantasized that even if I did not, she would exhaust her mind and heart wondering where I was. She would search for me. The available clues would lead her to the answer, and one day I would wake up and she would be there, sweaty and tired, but bright-eyed and cheerful. "Hiya, baby. Whatcha been up to?"

And I would say, "Hey, babe, did you know that the stars are our oldest ancestors?"

*****

I read and smoked pakalolo and slept, trying to look at my hands in dreams, knowing that I would have to know, seek out the primal reason of my race. I would have to re-enter the world, rejoin the mad game, play by fixed rules against a house edge. I had to lose. How much was the question. I must assume a proper mood, become inaccessible, seek a worthy opponent, stop the world, and rearrange its lines.

One day I fasted, drinking only water. In the evening I gathered wood for a bonfire. Then I ate pakalolo and inhaled the smoke of its burning body, my own form of communion, beginning to feel the rhythms, to move nakedly like a primitive, intuitively chanting my Hawaiian mantra, "Kuokoa! Kuokoa!" (Freedom), raising my voice in the call of a colorful exotic bird winging ephemerally through the trees, chanting, "Ua mau ke ea o ka aina i ke pono!" (The life of the land is perpetuated in righteousness.)

Freedom in the Hawaiian language implied a sense of whimsy. If you could play, you could be free. In playing, you were free.

The branches of my fire burned to embers. What did romantic notions, or philosophy or poetry, have to do with real life? Nothing. Everything. Any human who has ever lived a reasonable number of years never got through life without making a fool of himself more than once. I fell asleep in the darkness, exhausted, knowing I had seen too much darkness.

When the sun had risen, I hiked out of my valley, up over the mountains and down through canefields to a road. It began to rain, soaking me, as I trudged down the cliffs overlooking the ocean. The sun returned and I sat smoking pakalolo in the downdrafts off the tradewinds, the sailor's friend. I climbed down to a rocky beach to wade in the surf.

A slim, dark figure strolled out of some bushes. He waved and grinned, called, "Aloha."

"Hey, aloha no."

Pehea 'oe?" (How are you?)

Oh, maika'i no. A'o'oe?" (Oh, fine, and you?)

"Ah, no more nothing to do."

"You know Hawi?"

"Why? You like go?"

"Bumbai," I nodded.

"My car oveh deh," he pointed.

"You like pakalolo?"

"Git?"

"Git."

"Shaka, braddah!"

We toked up together, then loaded my pack in the back seat of his car. I had him stop at a store on the way and bought two six-packs of beer. Arriving in Hawi, a small, peaceful town, I signed in at Luke's Hotel under the name, Joe Evans.

Carrying my pack inside, we sat and sipped beer, enjoyed the sociability of sharing a joint or two, grinning and talking. After a time, he said, "I go now."

"Hey, bra, here, I give you half da kine," I said, dividing up the remaining grass.

"Mahalo, bra. Mebbe I check you lateh."

"Aloha."

That evening I ate in a small cafe, reading through a newspaper for any word of Steph. It had turned into a serious matter, a real media event. The great hoopla of suspicion and innuendo was of murder most foul.

I asked myself how far that could go. What did they have to work with? A seemingly not quite kosher possession of Sea Wind. No bodies, no evidence of foul play, and no eyewitnesses other than Steph -- who, as far as I could tell, had told her story as straight as she knew it. And she had kept my real identity out of it, telling some white lie about having met me the previous April or May and sailing off with me for Kauai and then Palmyra. But with my photos all over the place, I knew it wouldn't be long before someone recognized me and made the connection for the feds.

I called Larry from a phone booth. It was a conversation that didn't last thirty seconds.

"Hi, it's me," I said when he answered.

"Yeah, uh, yeah," he acknowledged, a slight quaver in his voice.

"Did you go visit her? How is she?"

"Ah, uh, yeah I did. Listen, this line is bugged. The FBI is listening to every word."

"Oh."

I hung up and thought about it. Was Larry being overly paranoid? Maybe not. Which meant they probably knew about the passport, had found where he'd co-signed the application, and so could threaten to charge him with perjury. If so, he had been brave to warn me. I tried again to call Rick, again without success.

The next morning I discovered what a farce the old movie and TV bit was about the fuzz having to keep you on the line for so many minutes in order to trace a call.

I had entered the cafe to buy a paper. Through a connecting door into a bar area, I quickly spotted several strangers sitting around a table and knew they didn't fit. Whoa. Fear opened his mouth and bit at me for an instant, but I pinched his lip and pushed him away. I pretended to study the front page, peering at them through the sides of my wraparound shades. In hat and deep tan, perhaps they would mistake me for a local.

They were unaware of my presence. I walked out the door and strolled down the sidewalk away from them. At the corner, I crossed the street and was quickly out of sight behind a theater building that had seen better days.

My avenue of escape was clear and inviting. I could vanish back into the mountains and valleys. I stopped, slapping my thigh with the folded paper, considering, trying to decide. If I backed up Steph's story, which would also be the truth, as far as it went, maybe it would end the speculations that skullduggery had been done. Since I had left the new boat registration papers aboard Sea Wind, the feds might have a case for charging me with theft. But at least Steph would be off the hook. We were the only witnesses. Steph had no secrets to confess, while I felt no great desire to confess mine. If I was sent to prison, at least it would not be to Quentin or Folsom. I'd heard federal joints were easier to do time in.

Ah, me bucko, me boyo, me great buckaroo! One part of me said run -- the other part said stay and try to help Steph. The freedom of the mountains, valleys, and sea versus Steph, loyal and true-blue, full of love and committed. Her bail was in the works. Should I wait until I could talk to her? They'd probably expect that, have her under surveillance, but so what? I knew a trick or two.

Was I trying to convince myself to perform a noble act? Perhaps. But in retrospect -- not then having reached the now firm position that the government was an unalterably inimical entity to the likes of me, that the primary drive of the amoebic beast in its gargantuan sprawl was its own insidious aggrandizement and perpetuity in power, that the bureaucratic functions of its organs in its eternal eating and shitting habits composed a colossus that was all mouth and asshole, which parts were entirely interchangeable -it seems now as if I had been very naive to consider surrender at all.

But then, during those moments of critical consideration, and despite my background as a misfit in society, I still believed in democratic principles, yes, even in law and order, that justice would prevail. I had been tried on criminal offenses and found guilty as well as being acquitted. I had no bitches coming. When I was a kid, one of my favorite radio programs had been Gangbusters. I had, for awhile, wanted to grow up to be an FBI agent.

So, because of my ignorance then, the naive remnants of youthful idealism, but feeling, nevertheless, like Bach ought to be playing a grand and moving funeral dirge on his organ, I turned to go back, to deliver myself up to them. Besides, it might count in my favor.

I strolled around from behind the theater, coming out into a small park like grassy area directly across the street from the café and bar. I sat at a picnic table and laid the paper out before me. I took off my hat and sunglasses, and waited. It would not do to simply approach them with an insouciant wave and grin. They might think I had a gun concealed in the newspaper or a knife up my sleeve -- who knows? As far as they were concerned, they were hunting a murderer, and probably had me down as armed and dangerous. This way, they could study the situation, feel no threat, and hopefully everyone would keep calm.

After a bit, they came out of the bar. I smiled and waved a hand at them, an invitation. They all looked away except for a big local cop. One pulled out a walkie-talkie and two men, whom I'd already spotted surveilling the phone booth, got out of a nearby car.

One man was directed to go left down the sidewalk, to follow the same route I had, so he could get into position behind me. The two from the car went right and crossed the street.

I waved again at the three left standing there, beckoning to the one who seemed to be in charge. He wouldn't look directly at me or acknowledge my invitation. The big Hawaiian grinned. So, we would wait, while static crackled over their radios, to play it out according to some preordained form.

After a couple more minutes had passed, I wondered if they were stalking somebody else. I looked around. No, there was the agent who'd crept up behind me, now standing with gun in hand peeking from behind the scant cover of a tree. When I looked back, four of the others were running toward me, their guns out, too. Only the Hawaiian cop had elected to stand back and watch the Keystone Kops at work.

Careful now, me bucko, easy does it. I slowly raised my forearms, spread my fingers, and glued a sickly smile to my face, heard feet slapping up behind me.

"Don't move!"

"Freeze!"

All in proper movie style, their magnums all pointing at me. Their faces were flushed, eyes gleaming, bodies tense. They were just as hooked on the adrenaline rushes as most criminals. We held the tableau for a moment or two. Nobody twitched. The leader flashed his ID and badge with a nervous hand.

"Eh-eh-eh-FBI!" he stuttered. "Are you Bob Walker?"

"Buck," I corrected. The one in back handcuffed my wrists behind me. I stood up and stepped out with my legs spread so he could frisk me.

"You're under arrest!"

"No shit?"

The leader, FBI agent Henry Burns, (The media would report my "capture." Burns himself would never say that I had surrendered, but only that he had arrested or captured me.) eyed me, then blew his victory by saying, "You knew we were here!"

I nodded. "Wondered what was taking you so long."

###

CHAPTER 5

We quickly got through the next part of the script, the Miranda ritual. I gave them permission to search my room, even supplying the number. They put me in the back seat of a car. After a bit, two of the agents came out carrying my backpack and we began the drive to Hilo. One agent drove, across from him the impassive local cop who'd refused to become involved. Burns sat in the back with me.

Burns, who seemed to be one of those very sincere and earnest types, fit my own ideas of what an FBI agent should be, courteous and objective. He oozed sympathy, invited trust. I was impressed.

"Mind answering some questions?"

I shrugged. "Depends on the questions."

"Well, we'll take them one at a time."

"Why am I under arrest? You forgot that. Inspector Erskine wouldn't approve."

His jaw muscles tightened. "We've got a fugitive warrant. You're charged with failure to appear, jumping bail."

"Ah."

"I'd like to ask you some questions about the Grahams."

"What do they have to do with my jumping bail?"

"We're investigating their disappearance."

"Who said they disappeared?"

"Stephanie Stearns made some statements."

"Ask away." This was the reason I had turned myself in.

We began working into it. I began by giving him a factual account about arriving for the dinner invitation, finding the Grahams gone, and waiting for them to return, that we had spent the night aboard Sea Wind and commenced a search for them in the morning, about finding the overturned Zodiac on the beach, and continuing the search for several days without finding any other sign of them.

Burns kept interrupting with questions. When he learned about our campsites, he asked about them. "They were just ashore from your boats, right?"

"Yes, but we had also set up a tent, oh, fifty to a hundred yards east of Iola's moorage."

"And where was the Zodiac found?"

"I told you, about a half mile or so west of Sea Wind, along the shore of Cooper Island."

"Had you ever met the Grahams before?"

"No. We first met when they arrived early in July."

"Had you ever been under sail with the Grahams?"

"What do you mean? Our sailboats, our dinghies, what?"

"Your sailboats. Did you and Stephanie ever sail Iola alongside the Grahams on Sea Wind?"

"Oh. No, we never did."

"You never sailed alongside them in your boat?"

"No, definitely not. Once we were moored inside the lagoon, our vessels remained in place."

"Okay," he said, busy scribbling in his notebook.

As he wrote and busied himself flipping back through the pages of his notes, I looked out the window at the scenery over a route that I had taken many times. I was remembering where many of the roads to left and right led. There, that one led past the big public beach, then on down to Puako, where Rick Schulz used to live before building his own house at Kamuela. That one would lead along the west coast down to Kailua Town, where Steph and I had spent an interesting couple of months the summer of the year before. Oh, and this one would take us to whatisname's place, who grew some pretty good pakalolo, and that shaded one leading into high rainforest Steph and I had once explored while searching out sites to establish remote pakalolo camps.

"Now, let's see if I have this right," Burns began, bringing me back. "You say you discovered the Graham's overturned dingy fifty or a hundred yards west of Sea Wind? Couldn't you see it from the deck of Sea Wind that close?"

"No, I didn't say that. I said our tent was fifty to a hundred yards from our boat, Iola. East, not west. The Zodiac was found a half mile, maybe three-quarters of a mile west."

"Oh, so now you're changing your story?"

"No, you are."

"Well, I've got my notes right here."

"Then you've got your notes wrong."

"And you say you were never under sail alongside Sea Wind on the open sea?"

"I said I was never under sail alongside the Grahams." "You said..."

"I know what I said. I also know what you're up to, you little prick." Sooner or later, I thought, my brain starting to smoke from his slyness, everybody reveals themselves through their actions.

"You say you were friends with the Grahams?"

"That's right."

"Ed Pollock says hostility existed between you."

"Who said that?"

"Ed Pollock. You know him, right?"

"That asshole? He was a fucking joke to us all!"

"Why would he joke about something like that?"

"What?" I was beginning to wonder whether Burns and I were caught up in one of those weird science fiction movies, two alien creatures meeting in a magic window from separate but parallel universes, the one a step or two out of sync with the other -- or perhaps I had inadvertently done something that had caused the lines of existence as described in Don Juan's Yaqui world to warp out of alignment. But, for sure, the very clear picture dawned on me that this fine, upstanding FBI agent was weaving evidence into his own design.

"You murdered them, didn't you? Tell me about it."

"Kiss my ass. Nobody murdered anybody."

"I can help you. Get it off your chest. Tell me what happened."

"Ever tried pissing up a rope?"

"What? Listen, we can do this the hard way or the easy way. It's up to you. What did you do with their bodies?"

"Fuck you, agent Burns!"

"We'll see about that," he retorted, seething. "We'll see who fucks who!"

It was becoming pellucidly clear that no amount of the truth would serve me with this asshole. Burns' later testimony, delivered in his sincere and earnest mode, would constitute a neat little hatchet job. First mistake, I gave myself up. Second mistake, I talked to a fed. I learned the lesson.

*****

They lodged me in Hilo Jail. The local bail bondsman, the only one on the island, came to see me. I knew him slightly from when I had a few times wandered through his cattle pastures looking for the Hawaiian variety of psilocybin mushrooms, which only grew in cow dung. He was a greasy little guy who reminded me of certain anthropological reconstructions of what Neanderthal man looked like. He came on like we'd been friends for years.

"You like me go you bail?"

He dripped sincerity through the bars.

I laughed. "Sure, sure. When you can have me out? This afternoon?"

"You need anytings?"

"Cigarettes."

"I bring, bumbai," he promised, peering intently at me. He edged closer, licking spittle from his lips, swallowing. "You like tell me anytings?"

"Like what?"

"You kill da Grahams?"

"Get lost!"

"No, hey, I bring you smokes, eh?"

"Yeah, sure. A whole carton, huh? Looks like a long night." At least one vice to comfort me.

"You like come out talk to me in da oddah room?"

"Hah?"

"TV folks outside. Dey like see you."

So that was it. "Sure," I said. "They gonna throw me any peanuts?" It was his turn.

"Hah?"

I went out with him. Through the barred windows I could see a small crowd outside, a mobile TV unit parked nearby. People were peering in at me. A TV camera poked up close, a hand came through with a microphone. The Neanderthal became self-conscious, slicking his hair and trying out various grins. He sidled over to pat me on the shoulder, as if to say, "See, folks, I'm not afraid of him."

"Say sometings," he urged.

I knitted my brows, pursed my lips, struck a pose as though considering a profundity. Solemnly I turned to him. "Twas brillig and the slithy toves did gyre and gimble in the wabe. All mimsy were the borogroves and the mome raths outgrabe." (Lewis Carroll, Through the Looking Glass.)

"No, no," he cried, dumbfounded. "Mus spik English! No can unnastan' dat!"

*****

Later, a local newspaper reporter asked for an interview. I studied him, seeking some hint to his character. He seemed very young, hardly out of his teens, earnest, intelligent, but unassuming. Perhaps it was a part-time job with him, an extracurricular assignment in conjunction with journalism classes at the University of Hawaii. I wondered if they were still teaching what I had learned -- to keep facts separate from speculation. Because he seemed too young to have been corrupted by too much of the cynical, sensationalistic, issue-creating so-called journalism of the day -- as it was growing into the amoral beast it would become -- I decided to pass a half hour with him, which beat hell out of spending it in the cell.

I don't think he asked more than a half dozen questions, keeping himself busy with notes and nodding, as I gave him a straightforward sketch of events-- basically the same story I'd given to agent Burns.

"How do you feel about all this," he asked, making a vague hand motion.

"Like I imagine Prometheus felt," I said. "Not that I compare myself with him. Only what he must have felt when they chained him to a rock for vultures to feed upon his innards."

He managed a sardonic grin. "I know what you mean. Well, thanks for the interview. I wish you luck."

"Yeah, that would come in handy."

The Neanderthal sent me in one pack of cigarettes. The young reporter played it straight, reporting facts without innuendo.

*****

A day or two later, Burns showed up with an Assistant U. S. Attorney and some U. S. Marshals to fly with me to Honolulu. When we stepped off the plane and a TV camera and sound crew raced over, it became clear why I had such exalted company on the flight.

A guy in headphones pushed a mike at me, shouting questions. I said something to him.

"What? What? Speak a little louder," he demanded. "I'm not getting a reading!"

"You're undone," I repeated politely.

Shocked, he checked his fly. Then he saw that his microphone jack wasn't plugged in. He stopped to fumble with it as we continued on to the government car, then came chasing after us.

"Wait! Wait! Say something! How d'you feel about all this?"

I smiled. "Shitty."

He looked hurt, poor guy. He hadn't gotten a single usable word for the six o'clock news.

*****

At the Halawa High Security Facility, my fame had preceded me. "He da whacko wen kill dose folks, wen stole dere boat."

My social entree was not conditioned around the basic question of did I, but rather how. "Hay, bra, how you wen make (Hawaiian word, pronounced mah-kay, meaning kill.) dose folks. You wen make dem walk da plank, feed 'em to da sharks?"

The federal prisoner tank was a divided affair, a row of bars separating the dayroom, which contained five steel tables, a toilet, sink, and a shower stall, from the dormitory sleeping area, which contained ten double bunkbeds. The tables and bunks were all bolted to the cement floor. Outside the bars fronting a walkway was a TV set high on a metal shelf so it could be viewed by the inmates of two adjoining tanks, a concrete wall separating the two.

I began the process of sizing everybody up, trying to discover the pecking order, if any, whether any threats were apparent. I was a celebrity, a man involved in a big case, a man with an air of mystery about him. I hated it. First to be all but universally regarded as a murderer, and then to be fearfully esteemed for it. But, since it soon became evident that it wasn't going to go away -- the media continuing to foster the idea by its endless focus on every tiny aspect of the great mystery -- I decided to use it to make my way.

Perceiving no immediate threats to my well-being from those I had been tossed among, I aimed my mind toward getting myself through the long days. The choices were severely limited -- reading from a poor selection of discarded books donated to the jail, watching the tube, and gambling. We gambled night and day on everything from pitching pennies to betting on sports games, chess, checkers, backgammon, and must have played every card game known to man. Since cards were not permitted, we made our own from pieces of paper or cardboard.

On the tiny walled yards, the choice was basketball, volleyball, or handball. Having played for years at San Quentin, I played a fair game of handball and made a few bucks from guys who underrated me because of my size -- 6'1", 190 lbs. But I'd always had good reflexes and the necessary ball control to run opponents ragged.

It turned out the sergeant of the guard was the uncle of a friend of mine. After talking a few times and he having established my bona fides with his nephew (we'd done a few grass deals), I asked if it would be all right to start a dice game during recreation on the yard when we mingled with prisoners from other tanks.

"If no pilikia, (Trouble.) fine," he said after some thought. "First time pilikia, no more."

I got a more or less regular crap game going, which nicely supplemented my dwindling resources. I'd take a piece of chalk to mark out a table of sorts on the asphalt and a bag of coins for making change -- penny to a dollar, we were rolling. I'd explain the rule -- no pilikia or no more craps -- then break out the dice. Local people loved to gamble and if anyone made trouble, he would be going against everybody and not just me or some other guy. The sergeant had passed the word to the guards who would sit in the security tower. There was never any real trouble, other than minor bitching over losses, and it helped get us through the boring days.

Stephanie, out on bail a few days after my arrest, was not allowed to visit, so we wrote each other regularly -- getting to talk to each other only at court appearances. She was staying with some friends aboard their boat at Keehi Lagoon, friends we'd made when we'd spent a few weeks there before heading out to Kauai and Palmyra after a court appearance on the MDA charges.

The Grand Jury indictment was impressive. We had been charged with theft of Sea Wind, interstate transportation of stolen property -- to wit, Sea Wind and all her wares – smuggling marijuana, theft of $400 from Sea Wind, and illegal possession of firearms -- my pistol and rifle. I had two extra charges -- jumping bail and violation of U. S. passport laws.

The marijuana charge puzzled me. It was for 464 grams, over a pound. I knew we hadn't had any such amount aboard, and I wondered if a pound of grass had gone undiscovered by us aboard Sea Wind. Did Mac and Muff have secret vices? Had they managed to fake us out so completely? It turned out to be a bag of seeds I had somehow overlooked.

The smuggling, illegal possession of firearms, and bail-jumping charges would eventually be dismissed for reasons I am not sure and cannot remember. It may be that possession of marijuana seeds only, was not a crime and perhaps the prosecution could not prove ownership of the guns since they were not registered to me. The bail-jumping charge, which is really a failure to appear as ordered, was probably dismissed on the technicality that I had not actually been ordered to appear on a specific date (There had been some confusion in the court calendar during my appearance to plead guilty to one count of possessing MDA and the judge had told the lawyers they would be informed at a later time, which meant my lawyer would inform me – if he could get in touch with me, which he couldn't since I had already left for Kauai to put into effect my escape southerly).

When separate trials were granted, the charges of boat theft and interstate transportation would remain against us both. Of the remaining two charges, Steph would be charged with the theft of $400, while I would be charged with the passport violation.

Stephanie would be appointed Winston Mirikitani, a slender peacock of a dresser, but not much in the way of a criminal lawyer. I was appointed Jon Miho, who, so far as I could tell, had never tried a criminal case. Without consulting me, he entered pleas of not guilty and not guilty by reason of insanity. I jumped all over his ass on the second plea. There was no way I was going to play crazy or even sit still for some headshrinker to interview me, and insisted that he withdraw the plea. He did.

*****

In December, after having apprised myself of the heart of the case -- theft of Sea Wind -- I volunteered to take a lie-detector test. When I conveyed this news to Miho, he seemed a bit astonished but pleased to announce it -- perhaps it would save everybody the trouble and expense of a trial. A deal could be made.

Miho would inform Judge King that "Mr. Walker is willing to take a polygraph test with respect to the disappearance of Mr. and Mrs. Graham. We believe the results will be of assistance in our discussions with the Government."

Well, that was not exactly what I had in mind. I knew that I had never had any intention to steal Sea Wind -- despite the evidence of having re-registered her as a homebuilt vessel, which I would gladly explain in detail for the polygraph examiner so that he could test me on the question. I had not anticipated being questioned regarding Mac's and Muff's disappearances.

Miho would tell reporters, "While a polygraph is not admissible in court, results favorable to Mr. Walker could be used for plea-bargaining purposes."

I had no idea what was going through Miho's mind -- I only knew that I would never plead guilty to something I hadn't done. I thought that the polygraph would prove the truth about why we hadn't immediately reported the disappearance to authorities, as well as the reasons for the conflicting stories we'd given as to how we'd acquired Sea Wind -- the desire to conceal my fugitive status.

When I confronted Miho with what he had done, he told me the feds were concerned with one question and only one question: Had we, Steph and or myself murdered the Grahams. "If you didn't murder them, you've got nothing to worry about. Bill (William Eggers, Assistant U. S. Attorney prosecuting the case.) says if you can pass on that point, he's willing to drop the charges."

"What charges? I haven't been indicted for murder."

"No, the boat theft and stuff -- he'll drop those."

"Including the passport charge?"

"Well, I don't know. It's pretty cut and dried on that one."

"So he'd drop everything but that one and -- what? -- expect me to cop a plea to that one charge?"

"Yes, I think so, possibly so."

I thought about it. It seemed like a pretty good deal. I believed that not only could I pass the test on the question of theft, but also of murder. Furthermore, I believed Steph could pass on the same questions, and I suggested that she be polygraphed, too. Mirikitani soon announced that she had also volunteered.

I thought, somewhat naively, that things weren't looking so bad as they had at first. I had learned that my codefendants in the MDA case, ex-convicts all, had received very lenient sentences. Gilbert, who'd been arrested with me on the Big Island, and who'd actually pulled out a gun and leveled it at BNDD (Bureau of Narcotics and Dangerous Drugs, forerunner of Drug Enforcement Administration.) agents, had received straight probation with no time in prison.

Stewart, the suspected mainland source of the MDA in California, had received six months in prison (would serve only four months) and five years probation -- the only one of us who had a record of involvement in drugs.

I was kicking myself in the ass. How could I have received more than they? If I'd only known, I told myself, I'd never have jumped bail. I'd probably have never bought Iola and sailed to Palmyra. Ah, me dumb bucko, ain't life ironic!

So, one day shortly thereafter, three FBI agents showed up at Halawa Jail. As they were chaining and shackling me, I asked the occasion. They were taking me to FBI headquarters for the polygraph test.

"Does my lawyer know you're here?"

"He sent us," the agent in charge replied. "You volunteered, didn't you?"

"You don't mind if I call him, do you?"

"You going to take the test or not?"

"Sure, no problem. I just want to consult a little bit. Won't take a minute."

When the jailer had put through the call, I asked Miho if he'd sent the three agents.

"No, I didn't even know they were there. What's it all about?"

"They say they're here to take me for the polygraph test. They say you sent them."

"No, it's news to me."

"What do you advise?"

"Well, gee, I suppose you should just go take the test. That's what you wanted, isn't it?"

"Are you going to be there?"

"Why no. I hadn't thought about it. Where is it? What time?"

"They say the FBI building, as soon as we get there, I guess."

"Oh, dear. I'm really busy. You go ahead and I'll try to get over there."

"Have you seen the list of questions they're going to ask?"

"No, no, I haven't."

"Listen, I think we need to talk this over."

"Well, sure. When? What's the problem?"

"Well, gee, Jon, I just caught the FBI lying to me, for one. Also, I'd like to know what the questions are going to be, exactly what the deal is if I pass."

"Well, uh, golly, I'm pretty busy right now."

How about if we come by your office?"

"Ah, okay, sure, that'd be okay."

"Fine. You tell 'em, okay?" I said, handing the phone to the FBI man.

When we showed up, the FBI men grimly silent, I insisted upon a private consultation. After a bit of discussion, checking for possible routes of escape, and determining that it was long way down if I decided to jump out a window, they left us alone in Miho's office -- me still bearing the weight of chains and shackles.

"First of all, Jon," I began. "I think we should review the list of questions they're going to ask. I mean, just to insure we don't have a wide-open fishing expedition here."

"Right. Good idea."

He stepped out and returned with the list, which I quickly read over. There were only ten questions, a few of what are called control questions and some relevant questions.

The basic method of the polygraph is to compare certain bodily responses on a graph between control and relevant questions. A control question is relatively innocuous and to which the truth of the answer may be assumed, such as "Is your name so-and-so?" A relevant question goes directly to the crime you are under suspicion of having committed, such as "Did you commit the crime in question?"

As there were none relating to the question of stealing Sea Wind, it was obvious they were only concerned with whether murder had been done. I pointed this out to Miho, who seemed surprised, just as I was, by the brevity of the test.

"Is that all? Well, I'll just call Bill and make sure." After some discussion, Miho paused to tell me they were primarily concerned with the murder questions, that if I passed on that, all the other charges would be dropped.

"You mean everything?" I asked, incredulous. "The theft, the smuggling, the bail-jumping, the guns, even the passport? Everything?"

"Well, yes, that's what he says."

"What about the MDA thing?"

"Oh, you'd still have to answer to that, that's separate."

I didn't have to think about it. "Okay. Tell him it's a deal." He did.

"But I want you there," I added. "As an observer."

He told Bill, then nodded. "That's okay. I'll go with you." "And tell him to put it in writing."

He told Bill.

Miho frowned. "He says he can't do that."

"Why not? A deal's a deal. Put it in writing, what the fuck?"

"He says he can't. You'll have to take his word for it."

"Take his word!"

"I recommend you go ahead. Bill's a man of his word."

"Oh, you're vouching for him? You're going to make it good if he reneges?" That's the way it worked in prison when you vouched for someone.

"Well, uh..."

"Listen, I'll tell you what," I said, thinking fast to keep the deal on track, yet not quite willing to take anyone's word about anything. "How about this? Let's agree right now, before I take the test, that no matter how it turns out, the results are admissible in court. If I pass and he reneges, I've got an out. If I don't pass, my ass is grass." I knew this was the only way it was possible to get polygraph results admitted as evidence, that both prosecution and defense stipulate that they were acceptable.

He told Bill.

"He says if you pass, he's going to drop the charges, but if you don't pass, obviously he's not."

"That's fine with me. Now, get it in writing."

He told Bill.

"He says he can't do it."

"Can't put it in writing? Why not?"

"He says it's against government policy."

Whoa! What was this? Were they fucking serious? Trust your government? Ah, me dear boyo, a government representative was asking you to trust him! Well, maybe I would with my last nickel, but with my life? It was an FBI agent administering the test. It was the FBI who'd so recently lied to me with a straight face, the FBI who'd tried to trick me with his all-American sincerity. Whoa now, me bucko, trust an FBI agent, trust an Assistant U. S. Attorney, against whose word mine would count for nothing?

I made a last ditch effort. "How about if we go and put the deal on record in Judge King's courtroom? He'll drop the charges if I pass or everyone agrees we use the results in court, I don't care, either one -- just so it's on record."

He told Bill.

"No, he says. It's against government policy."

"It's a plea bargain, for chrissakes! The judge has to approve all plea bargains!"

"He says no. You'll just have to take his word for it."

"Ask him if he's got any Kapu property he wants to sell me!" (Joke, well-known to most Hawaiians. Property owners post Kapu signs, meaning "No Trespassing." Tourists, if they get out in the countryside, may see many of them. When they inquire, they may be told, "Oh, the Kapu family. They own a lot of property.")

"What?"

"No deal. The asshole won't go public with his word, it's worth jackshit to me!"

He told Bill -- in politer terms, of course.

*****

"Listen, Jon," I began when he'd hung up the phone, a last stab at salvaging something from the mess. "This case has already been tried in the news media and, so far, I'm on the losing end. Why don't you announce a press conference and just tell them about the government's refusal to honor its word on the record. I came into this deal in good faith and they want to play games. They tried to pull a fast one here today. They told me you'd sent them, but you didn't know anything about it. Just tell 'em what happened here today."

"Well, gee, I don't know..."

A phone call interrupted. Miho went into a long discussion about a divorce case. I fumed quietly until he'd hung up, a tentative agreement having been reached over a division of property, custody of children, and support payments.

"Jon, have you ever argued a serious criminal case all the way through trial in a federal court?"

"Well, no, but..."

"And you don't really want this case, right?"

"Well, I was appointed..."

"Yeah, yeah, but it's not really your cup of tea, right?" "Well..."

"You should think about removing yourself, Jon. I intend to fight this right down to the wire, tooth and nail all the way. You've either got to get into it all the way or get off it. I'm not easy to get along with, I admit. I don't want to embarrass you, but if necessary I'll go into that courtroom and plead my own case."

"I don't think Judge King would allow..."

"You've got to fish or cut bait, Jon."

*****

There was a brief newspaper article that I had refused the polygraph. Bill Eggers had issued a statement that I had been offered a chance to clear myself but had turned it down.

As a result, the feds refused to administer the test to Stephanie. (In a later year, when Bugliosi was fighting to introduce the results of Stephanie's subsequent polygraph test at her own expense, which she passed with flying colors, at her murder trial, Elliot Enoki, the new prosecutor, would say, "After reviewing the questions, Mr. Walker decided he didn't want to take the polygraph and refused to do so. After Mr. Walker's refusal, Miss Stearns also refused to submit to the test.")

On January 13, 1975, Judge King sentenced me to the maximum term of five years on the MDA charge. But also, no doubt because of the suggestion implicit in Miho's insanity plea, he added a 90-day psychiatric evaluation under Title 18, Section 4208(c). This meant that the sentence could later be modified to a lesser term depending upon the evaluation.

Accompanied by two U. S. Marshals on the flight to Los Angeles on the way to a federal prison facility at Terminal Island, I was not allowed any alcoholic beverages, nor money with which to purchase them.

"You can have a soda pop," I was told.

"Soda pop! Jeez, gimme a break, willya?"

They had allowed me to bring a small book of crossword puzzles to while away the hours. "Hey, you got a ballpoint I can borrow?"

"Yeah, sure. You any good at those things?"

"Well, I like to do them in ink because I never have to erase, if that tells you anything."

"Yeah., right."

An hour later I was ready with my fallback plan. I asked to use the bathroom. Inside the cubicle with a Marshal guarding the door outside, I pulled out a $20 bill from my secret stash and folded it around the note I'd surreptitiously written with the borrowed ballpoint on a piece of page torn from the crossword book. When I came out, I stopped to browse through the magazine rack and found an opportunity to flip it on a counter space where a stewardess was busy. When she looked at me, I smiled my best and winked, then returned briskly to my seat between the two Marshals.

The note inside the bill said, "Help! I am a famous international jewel thief on my way to prison. I'm innocent! I need a drink! If you could find it in your heart to bring me a double gin and tonic everytime I order a Seven Up, I'd be eternally in your debt. The gentlemen on either side of me are cops with no sense of humor. They monitor all my communications, but at least we can smile at each other over this little joke we're playing on them. Wish I had time to say more. You're beautiful."

A few minutes later, I caught sight of her going forward up the far aisle. When she came down our aisle, I thought I saw a mirthful gleam in her eyes. "Pardon me, ma'am. I've changed my mind. Could you please bring me a glass of Seven Up?"

She smiled. "Certainly, sir." She was beautiful.

"Thought you didn't like soda pop," said the Marshal.

I shrugged. "What else is there to do?"

After the fifth one, he commented on my thirst.

"Yeah," I replied, careful not to slur my words. "I think I'm dehydrated. Flying does that to me."

They could have poured me off at LAX, but were doubtless pleased to have such a compliant and well-behaved transportee in their charge. I was pleased that they were not half so repulsive without my glasses and that I would arrive free of malaria from the quinine in the tonic water.

At Terminal Island, a low security facility, I mostly cooperated and went along with the gag. I took all the psychological tests except for the Minnesota Multiphasic Personality Inventory, which I politely refused. I had over the years read negative studies of the value of the test in forming a picture of the personality. If you broke each of the 566 questions down into their multiple true and false choices and learned how each choice was related on a scale that purported to measure various aspects of personality, you would either weep or go insane trying to understand the rationale behind each question. How does a choice between George Washington and Abraham Lincoln apply to a masculine/feminine scale?

The MMPI, as it is abbreviated, is widely employed in institutional settings as a measure of personality. It was given to every inmate entering the California prison system when I had gone to San Quentin back in the fifties.

When I had first learned that I was suffering from a psychopathic personality disorder, antisocial type, it meant nothing to me. But later, when I had begun to read psychology and learn about various tests for measuring personality traits, I sort of went into a growing state of shock. I learned that this label would be with me for the rest of my life, purely as the result of testing in a clinical setting without any verification by field testing.

I remembered how several hundred of us had been going through medical and psychological testing during our two-month stay in the pre-prison classification procedure at Chino. We were always being herded off in groups for physicals, shots and immunizations, and whiling away the boring days taking even more boring psychological tests.

These included, in addition to the MMPI, the Rorschach Inkblot Test, the Thematic Apperception Test (TAT), the Stanford-Binet I.Q. Test, and some physical coordination tests.

It was all so much horseshit to us and so we played some games on the examiners, who were all college students majoring, presumably, in psychology. They didn't know any of us from Adam or each other. We would be called to these tests in groups by means of being issued passes with our names and numbers and destinations printed on them. On the basis of the pass alone, our names and numbers were transferred to the test sheets. What the examiners didn't know was that we often swapped passes among ourselves and went in to see who could outdo the other telling outrageous tales to them.

The TAT consists of a series of pictures that are shown one at a time. You have to make up a story about each one, from which, so the theory goes as propounded and developed by Dr. Henry A. Murray of the Harvard Psychological Clinic in the early 1940s, the trained interpreter may discover some of the dominant drives, emotions, sentiments, complexes, and conflicts existing in the individual personality'. The special value lies in its purported power to expose the underlying, inhibited tendencies which the subject is not willing to admit, or cannot admit because he is not conscious of them. The idea is that the subject will become so involved in the task by utilizing his interest and imagination to make up stories to fit the pictures that he will forget the necessity of defending his private self against such probes. Ideas he invents for his characters in the pictures may be applied to himself. Unaware that he is confessing, he provides what amounts to X-ray pictures of his inner self. Which is fine as far as it goes, but if Subject A takes the test posing as Subject B, then A's personality traits will be imposed upon B, which tells us nothing whatsoever about B's true nature.

"What'd you tell 'em on the one where the guy's got his hand over his face with the woman in bed?"

"Woman? That was a woman? I thought it was a cute fat-butt boy!"

"You rotten bastard!"

"What'd you tell 'em?"

"That the guy just learned the broad had gonorrhea!"

"Oh, you motherfucker! Get your mind out of the gutter!"

"I told 'em the guy was pissed because the broad wouldn't take a bath -- that she stunk!"

"You fucker! You had my pass!"

"You had mine! What'd you say?"

"That the guy couldn't get it up when he saw little critters jumping off her pussy-hairs!"

The same method of pass-swapping applied to the Rorschach, which is a series of cards containing multicolored symmetrical inkblots -- as though ink had been splashed on paper and then folded over for a mirror-image imposition. In describing what they remind you of, it is interpreted according to such determinants as color, texture, movement, shape and form. The theory is that certain mental states are associated with certain determinants. For instance, intellectualizers tend to see human movement. Emotion-laden people tend to respond to the colors. A greater tendency to respond to movement and form over color indicates that the emotions are not being effectively used. Tendencies to look at whole concepts as opposed to small, detailed aspects are also measured and compared. Concentrating on details over wholes is considered to be compulsive but organized.

"I told 'em it looked like a pink butterfly, drinking from a big wet pussy!"

On the MMPI, the results are presented in graph form. On it are three horizontal lines, with the middle line being considered the median, but within the upper and lower lines is considered as average or normal ranges. Below the lower line and above the upper line is considered pathological. A person without significant disturbances

or conflicts would score in a range between the upper and lower lines. Of the ten or so traits tested for, one is psychopathology.

"I put down that you liked flower-arranging over carpentry, dearie."

"Oh, you asshole! Well, I put down that you sometimes like to wear dresses!"

It was mind-boggling in retrospect to think of the hundreds, perhaps thousands, of men who were labeled with someone else's personality traits as derived from misapplied test scores, the linking of as many as three or four evaluations of three or four different subjects onto another. Whether some contradictory results seemed puzzling or were merely somehow averaged out is hard to say. The unforeseen danger ahead was that the prison administration tended to take these composite test scores seriously indeed, and woe betide the man who came out of this testing circus with indications of serious personality disorders. A mere neurotic might be seen as a dangerous psychotic. A first-termer might be confused with a career criminal, and therefore be considered a menace to society. The ones who got caught everytime they committed a crime were not considered as much of a problem, but the ones who were perceived to get away with a whole lot more than could be pinned on them were seen as too damned smart for early parole dates. A poor kid fresh off the farm, doing a nickel for joyriding, might be diagnosed as a malevolently intelligent psychopath of the worst sort, without conscience or pity, lusting after the immediate satisfaction of his own desires above all and ever-ready to do violence to that end -- and the poor kid would wonder why he was flattening out the whole five years while other first-termers on the same charge were being paroled after a year or so.

At Terminal Island, fortunately for me, I was diagnosed as a poor young man with a superior intelligence who'd temporarily lost his way, but who showed significant insight into his own behavior and was capable of learning from his errors. I was a sociable person with no tendencies toward violence and therefore posed no threat to the orderly operation of the institution or upon eventual release into the community. The chief psychiatrist had been impressed with my array of arguments against taking the MMPI. The good doctor had settled for personally administering the Rorschach in lieu thereof.

On May 25, 1975, I was back in Honolulu. By then, Jon Miho had withdrawn from the case and David Bettencourt had been appointed. My sentence on the MDA charge was reduced to three years. Less than a month later, on June 17, Stephanie's trial began. In addition to Mirikitani, James Wilcox from Los Angeles had joined in her defense.

In a sidelight to the main show, Eggers had offered a plea bargain to both Stephanie and I. If we would plead guilty to theft of Sea Wind, he would drop all other charges. It was not the first time. He had sent Miho out to visit me in Halawa Jail to convey a threat. If I did not agree to plead guilty, the prosecution would seek the application of Title 18, Section 3576, the "dangerous special offender" statute. Miho explained that it would subject me to an additional sentence, one most likely to be imposed consecutively, of as much as twenty-five years.

As you may imagine, sweat broke out on my forehead. I told him I'd think about it and let him know. When I looked up the statute in the U. S. Code, I found right away that the criteria for a defendant's eligibility under its provisions didn't even come close to applying to me. When next I saw Miho, I told him to tell Eggers to stick it up his ass, a message I'm sure was delivered in more euphemistic terms. That was the stick. Now came the carrot.

In a conference held in a holding cage apart from the courtroom, Eggers met with Stephanie, and me along with our attorneys, Bettencourt and Mirikitani. When Eggers presented the deal, it was on condition that we both accept it. It seems he had learned of my protective sensibilities when it came to Steph -- a little pressure to tell me that if I didn't take it, she would get no breaks. It wasn't bad as far as deals go. The maximum sentence was five years. The sentence on the interstate transportation charge was ten years. The sentences on Steph's alleged theft of $400 and on my passport charge was also five years. The lawyers assured us that all the sentences would be imposed concurrently, which meant a maximum of ten years. In effect, he was offering to cut it in half -- maybe less than half, depending on the mood of the judge when sentencing time rolled around.

The major problem for both of us to accepting this plea bargain was that we hadn't stolen Sea Wind, had never had any intention to steal her.

The way our system of law is set up, I'm sure there have been many thousands of defendants who have pled guilty to crimes they didn't commit. The process is scary. The government's tendency is to throw everything but the kitchen sink into an indictment that is meant to intimidate. The poor defendant, when he sees the large array of crimes against him, when he counts up all the sentences possible which may be imposed consecutively, yes, he may be ready to jump at a deal offering only a few years in prison -- guilty or not.

Such cases read easily and we may shrug such minor evils off as tiny defects in the system, but it's a different case altogether when you're actually confronted with such a choice. It is the most galling thing, the basic thought being "I have to say I did something I didn't do, confess to a crime that never happened, (When a defendant pleads guilty to any felony, the court requires a statement from him that it is being made of his own free well, without coercion or promise, that the guilty plea is entered because the defendant is, in fact, guilty. In other words, the court requires him in such cases to commit perjury.) if I'm to avoid spending umpteen years in some awful snakepit of a prison."

"How about if I plead guilty to something I'm actually guilty of," I offered. "The passport charge -- same sentence, what the hell?"

"No," Eggers replied. "I want something with a little more meat on the bone."

I shook my head. Stephanie, who had held her tongue during the negotiations, could no longer contain herself.

. "Jeez, yer hungry for meat, why'n'cha have a hamburger at MacDonald's! My treat!"

Eggers scowled and turned to leave.

"I'm not pleading guilty to anything," she stormed in outrage, turning to me. "Are you?"

"No, babe, you took the words right out of my mouth. I'm proud of you."

After Eggers had left, I looked at the lawyers. "Why don't you guys wait outside, give us a couple of minutes?"

When the door'd closed, Steph reached through the bars to touch me, kiss me. "Oh, baby," she wailed. "What're they trying to do to us?"

"Ah, you know. It's like in a whorehouse. They wanna fuck ya without a kiss."

She looked at me. "They don't kiss in whorehouses?"

"Nah, not much."

"Jeez, that's weird."

###

CHAPTER 6

In proving theft, the prosecution's theory of the case rested on several points:

1. The speculation that we had either purposely sunk Iola or abandoned her to an accident on the reef; the first assumption being buttressed by a search party's having found Iola's hatch cover lying ashore -- it having been purposely removed to facilitate sinking her.

2. The Graham's disappearance had not been timely reported to authorities.

3. The conflicting stories witnesses would report we had told regarding our acquisition of Sea Wind.

4. The haulout and repainting of Sea Wind was an attempt to disguise her.

5. The Zodiac could not have been capsized in an accident as implied by having been found in an overturned condition.

6. Flight from arrest indicated a consciousness of guilt.

Testimony by Ed Pollock and FBI agent Calvin Shishido would seem to indicate that Stephanie had told two conflicting versions about our departure from Palmyra. Pollock would say that Stephanie had told him that we'd tried to sail out in Iola, but that when she'd gone aground, we'd returned to take Sea Wind. Shishido would say that Stephanie had told him we'd originally tried to tow Iola with Sea Wind to Honolulu and had completed the voyage on Sea Wind alone after Iola had gone aground.

The prosecution would press the idea that Iola was unseaworthy and that we were low on supplies to the point of desperation -- which would serve as motives for wanting to steal Sea Wind.

Eggers would also try to show that Stephanie had been a party to my registration of Sea Wind -- if not by any overt act, at least by tacit approval. Shishido would testify that she had stated to him that "they" had registered Sea Wind.

Of course, Stephanie's attempted flight to avoid arrest with Puffer in arm was proof of "guilty knowledge."

The prosecution's major hard evidence, in addition to the hatch cover, was the introduction of several photos of Iola under full sail taken by Stephanie from the deck of Sea Wind. They were supposed to serve to make her out as a liar when she emphatically denied that Iola and Sea Wind were ever together "under full sail out in the blue water."

*****

Mary "Kit" Muncey was first. She established that Mac Graham was her brother and the owner of Sea Wind. She told of he and Muff's preparations for the trip to Palmyra. She read some excerpts from Muff's letters to her about having provided a few fish to us and about an incident concerning our dogs. She told of having gone to visit Stephanie at Halawa Jail in November, 1974.

On cross-examination Wilcox asked her:

Q: Do you recall saying to her: I believe you?

A: At what point?

Q: When she asked you if you believed her about what happened on the island?

A: I could not have said that.

Q: You don't recall?

A: I'm sure I did not say that.

However, in documents filed as Exhibits 17A and 17B, which established her as executrix to Mac's will, she had repeated Stephanie's story to her in some detail -- which served as the basis upon which a probate court in San Diego had declared Mac dead so that she could take immediate possession of not only Sea Wind but also a nice windfall of cash in his bank accounts and stocks inherited from his father.

In establishing her hostility, Muncey declared in outrage, "She has brought some sort of legal action claiming salvage."

Q: Which you are resisting?

A: Most decidedly.

Larry Seibert was next. He told about having received a manila envelope mailed to his boss, Joseph Stewart, which he attempted to deliver to Stephanie at the jail, leaving it with a jail matron. (They contained photos that Lorraine Wollen had picked up and mailed at Steph's request. The purpose of the testimony is to show the chain of possession to support the government's shaky claim that they were confiscated in accordance with due process of law.)

Seibert went on to say that he knew us previously from Maalaea Harbor on Maui and that he had met with us at Pokai Bay and at the haulout facility. He had seen the hole in Sea Wind's hull, as well as the tip of the swordfish bill. When asked to identify a photo of the hatch cover found on Palmyra, he would only say that it looked similar to one on Iola. When he went to visit Stephanie at the jail to deliver the photos, he said "Well, I told her the story that Buck had told me, and she said that's not true. What I told the newspapers is true."

Lawrence Briggs established that he was at Palmyra with a charter party of ham radio enthusiasts. He had sent his mate out with Jack Wheeler to help tow Iola into the lagoon. During our visit to his boat, he said he discussed our voyage down and "believe it was a 30-day trip. She said that they had not carried the mainsail and they had only sailed with the jibs."

He said he thought Iola looked in "very marginal condition" and she "looked kind of rough, like it had been a hard trip." The fiberglass looked like a "pretty rough job."

He said that he had become concerned when he learned "they were out of supplies or very nearly out of supplies." He thought "they had said that the boat leaked and that they pumped it fairly regularly."

In conversation with Stephanie, he said that she had told him the mainsail hadn't been used on Iola because "it was a question of not being able to steer the boat with the main up. I was under the impression that he was seasick. I believe she was the navigator, and he either got seasick for a period of time or -- that wasn't a big point with me because anyone that goes to sea gets seasick now and then."

Jack Wheeler was called to say he had spent fifteen months on Palmyra in 1957-58, and had returned for a month-long visit in 1970. In this case, he had arrived on June 16, 1974. In discussing Iola's arrival, he pointed out that Briggs "had hung up on the reefs three years before."

As to Iola, after having motored out for a looksee, he said, "They were at least a hundred feet off the channel on the north side ...so I asked them what their plan was, and got no response, so I says: Well, let's get those lines out (referring to anchor lines) and get out of here." He says we were "anchored with at least three anchors, (We only had two) but he was pounding on the reef, but it was quite calm and it was not sustaining any damage. He was just off the channel. He could have gotten out by kedging, maybe."

He remembered Roy giving him a letter to the owners asking permission to stay and offering to act as caretakers.

He said Mac's "intent was to have a nice, quiet place to write a book."

Our dogs were "friendly and nice, running around on deck, no problem." But later, "my boy was bitten by one of the dogs and we told them they had to get the dogs out of the area, and so they did. They moved them over and tied them up under some trees."

Jack related how he had shown us how "to take the palm heart," and that we could cut down all the young trees we pleased, but not any mature ones. He says he advised us that it was easier to leave through the lagoon channel than to enter since the wind generally prevailed from east to west and a slight current ran in the same direction. "I vividly recall telling them that they could never make it to Fanning. (We had never discussed sailing to Fanning with Jack Wheeler. Fanning would not become a factor in our planning until August, when we learned from Mac that Dickie and Carlos would be late in delivering our supplies.

They could get to Samoa or someplace faster." (Fanning was 225 miles, while Samoa was 1700 miles!)

Thomas Wolfe was next. He admitted that he and Norman Sanders had originally moored their boat, Toloa, in a bad place upon their arrival. "We took his advice and he helped us" to move to a space behind Iola.

He said Stephanie had told him, "I believe, on the second day... that they were running very low on food and that she was tired of eating coconuts and fish all the time and that she was yearning for some sugar."

He admitted that I had taken him fishing and that he had gone with me to the tent to fetch my .22 pistol. He told of us shooting mullet and trying to spear them.

Of Iola, he said, "The boat appeared in what I would consider a less than seaworthy condition in that I would not have attempted to sail from Palmyra in any direction whatsoever in that boat. The mast, to me, it appeared to be of less than adequate cross-section." The rigging wire "didn't appear to be in very good condition and it was rusted." (Iola's rigging was all stainless steel, which doesn't rust.)

He had never noticed whether it might have been 7/16-inches thick (suitable for yachts in the 60-80 foot range), and thought it was galvanized.

He didn't know anything about Iola leaking, but Stephanie had told him "she was worried as to how they were going to sail off the island because she was not sure their boat was seaworthy enough."

No, he had never actually been aboard Iola, but he had been aboard Sea Wind six to ten times and had been out riding around with Mac in the Zodiac "close to a dozen times." (All that in a four-day period between August 13 & 17!)

He said that in fishing with Mac out near the channel entrance "in about a half an hour we caught close to fifty pounds of fish."

He was "bitten severely in the stomach by the black dog."

He said Stephanie had given him some bread on the day they left.

Outside the hearing of the jury and not permitted to be entered as evidence, he said that Stephanie had "complained that Buck would plant marijuana plants every time she wished to plant vegetable plants."

Edwin Pollock got up to say that he had "never had a conversation of more than three or four words with Roy." Stephanie "told me about her navigation, told me about the boat leaking very badly and standing knee deep in water and pumping." (Quite a feat when you consider that our pump was mounted outside on the coach roof.) But he admitted, "I never saw them pump." Iola "was a very poor craft." His major observation was that planks were "cupped" under the fiberglass and so "there can't be a good bond, and it can't be too seaworthy." While he had never been aboard Iola, he was aboard Sea Wind "many times. I would say maybe twenty times." (During two weeks between July 2 & 16.)

He said Stephanie told him that "she wanted to buy food from us ...wanted to barter food from us.

They had said they had $10." Present during this alleged conversation were "Stephanie Stearns, Buck Walker, my wife, and myself."

He tried to describe the method I had used to net mullet with a light shining in the water.

He said that Frank Lange, a Coast Guard official, had first spotted Sea Wind at the Ala Wai and had called him to make an identification. He then rowed around Sea Wind, saw nobody, and called the Coast Guard and FBI. He claimed to have participated in the surveillance and search that he had chased after Coast Guardsman Wallisch in pursuit of Stephanie when she'd tried to run away. Pollock had escorted her back to the dinghy and rowed her out to the Coast Guard launch where a line was tossed to tow them out to Sea Wind. He claimed Stephanie told him that the Grahams had invited us to dinner aboard Sea Wind, but that they might be late because they had gone fishing and that we should make ourselves at home. When the Grahams did not return by dark, the spreader lights were turned on. We stayed aboard and began a search the next day. We found the Zodiac "capsized" on the beach at Paradise Island and conducted a search lasting several days. "They then attempted to sail out of the harbor in Iola at which time they lost Iola on the reef. They went back, boarded Sea Wind, and left the island."

Dr. Martin Vitousek, a research scientist at the Hawaii Institute of Geophysics at the University of Hawaii, described how he had been to Palmyra once a month for eighteen months during 1957-58. At Curt Shoemaker's request on October 11, 1974, he had flown a light plane from Fanning over Washington and Palmyra islands, including Kingman Reef some thirty-five miles northwest of Palmyra, searching for any signs of boats or people. After fifteen minutes over Palmyra, he had found nothing, not even any wreckage. A couple of weeks later he accompanied the FBI search party out of Honolulu, including Jack Wheeler, on a tugboat. He said the weather from August 27th through the 31st was mostly good with little cloud or rain.

Curtis Shoemaker said he'd met Mac at Radio Bay in Hilo in June, 1974, and that they'd agreed to maintain radio contact on Mondays and Wednesdays, although they missed some Mondays. Through July and up to August 27th, (A Tuesday) they'd contacted each other between 7-8 p.m.

Mac had "related his experiences on the island. What he was doing, what he found, and talked about everything from rain to birds, sharks in the lagoon, and everything. How to fish, and what fish were poisonous. I was trying to help him out as much as I could. Also, there were some other boats on the island, and I was relaying messages from some of these other boats to their parents, and I was acting, in other words, third party traffic. He didn't say too much about them.

There was a young fellow and a girl there. I think one of the dogs had almost attacked his wife, and he did mention that the dog had previously bitten some other people. There seemed to be a boat...he said it was unseaworthy and leaking badly, and the people on the boat were the ones with the dogs. The 27th was my last time that I heard from them...he said that the other boat...was leaving the next day."

Shoemaker added that he had tried to call the following Monday, then again on Wednesday, and continued calling for about three weeks. Since "there seemed to be a little anxiety between the situation with him and...them," he finally called Mac's sister. Then he called Vitousek at Fanning. After Vitousek reported nothing, he discussed everything with the Pollocks. Marilyn Pollock gave him Stephanie's mother's address and he called her. She claimed not to be aware that her daughter had left Hawaii.

Yes, Shoemaker did remember the message relayed from Dickie to Mac for us.

"Oh, it mentioned that the birds could be eaten. Something about -- there was, of course, a lot of birds down there and they apparently were hungry. However, they tasted fishy...and that we are trying to get together something in the way of supplies and bring them down to you." He gave the letter to an FBI agent named Lui. The only dinner he recalled Mac mentioning was a birthday party when several boats were there.

Milbur Roy Harrington, a marine control officer, testified that a Buck Walker had registered the sloop, Margaret, renamed Stephanie, on October 23, 1973, and that a Roy Allen had re-registered Stephanie as Iola on April 25, 1974. He also said, according to the records, that a Roy Alfred Allen had registered a homebuilt boat as Lokahi on October 18, 1974.

Lorraine Wollen said Stephanie told her she had come from the Big Island and was going to Kauai to hook up with a couple to sail south. She said Roy had left a glass ball and a note with $5 asking her to pick up some film at a Waianae drugstore. After learning of Stephanie's arrest, she took the photos to the Waianae Police Station. A policeman opened the envelope, looked at the photos, and told her he didn't think they were evidence, whereupon she mailed them to Larry Seibert. She remembered being told about the swordfish and the hole in the hull and discussing repairs. She had suggested Tuna Packers.

FBI agent Calvin Shishido had the longest and most important statement to make next to Stephanie. He had interviewed her soon after her arrest on October 29th. He said that Pollock had first sighted us and told him that we were not the owners. He saw Stephanie land the dinghy and run away with Puffer in her arms. He watched Wallisch and Pollock chase after her.

Aboard the Coast Guard launch, Shishido tried to advise her of her rights, but she kept interrupting to tell her story. She said that Sea Wind did not belong to her, but to the Grahams. She came into possession of it at Palmyra. She had met Roy Allen, whom she'd known for several years, at Keehi Lagoon in April, 1974, who was in possession of Iola. They sailed to Kauai, then to Palmyra, first raising the island on June 19th. They had some difficulty and were not able to get into the lagoon until "I believe, June 25th or June 26th, 1974."

On the way in, Iola got hung up on a reef. Jack Wheeler and others came to help them in. She mentioned that several boats had come and gone. She believed it was the last Friday in August when she was on Iola making preparations to leave the next day while Roy was ashore and that he returned to tell her they'd been invited to the Grahams for dinner aboard Iola (sic) that evening. He went to bathe. When he returned, he told her the dinner was for 6:30 p.m. and that the Grahams had told him they were going fishing for their dinner and they might be a little late, and if so, they could go aboard and make themselves at home. When they arrived, the Grahams were absent. They waited but the Grahams did not return. They slept on board Sea Wind and began a search in the morning. She said they found the Zodiac about a half-mile away on Cooper Island. "They found the outboard motor on the Zodiac overturned and the gas tank broken loose floating nearby." They put the tank on the Zodiac, attached it to the motor and used it to conduct further searches. "They continued searching until September 11," then left Palmyra.

She said "they rationalized that the Grahams' statement to make themselves at home meant that if anything should happen to them and they did not return, that they would like for Stephanie and Roy Allen to have their boat."

They tied a fifty-foot rope to Iola. She boarded Iola and Roy got on Sea Wind, towing Iola. "About a mile outside of the lagoon the Iola struck a reef." They untied it and sailed Sea Wind back to Hawaii. The last she saw of Iola, "it was hung up on the reef there as they sailed away."

She and Roy arrived at Nawiliwili sometime in October. They returned to Pokai Bay. From there they went next to Keehi Lagoon and then Tuna Packers. They repainted the boat. They did not report the Grahams missing at Palmyra because they couldn't operate the radio. They did not report them missing in Honolulu "because she loved the boat and she knew that if she reported this incident, the officials would take Sea Wind away from them."

She found $400 -- $300 in a surgery book and $100 in Mac's wallet. "She stated that on October 18, 1974, they registered the Sea Wind in Honolulu under the name Lokahi." She used the $400, or part of it, to paint Sea Wind. She assisted the Coast Guard to restrain the dogs. She was not under arrest at any time.

Roger T. Kent, another FBI agent, testified that "Miss Stearns had been arrested earlier that morning and I was with her throughout the rest of the day until she was taken to the Honolulu Jail. I was maintaining custody of her." As she was being booked, "I asked her if she didn't think she was taking a chance on allowing Sea Wind to be in the Ala Wai Harbor for fear it might be recognized, and she said: Yes, that she and Buck Allen -- was the name that we knew her associate to be at the time -- were very worried about that and they were only going to remain at Ala Wai just the one day and then sail out before -- hopefully before anybody recognized the boat."

Kenneth White, sales manager for McWayne Marine Supply, testified about his experience with Zodiacs and Avon inflatable boats. He had gotten together with Shishido to test the Zodiac. He found it to be a very stable boat, but admitted it was not impossible to overturn one. He also tested Mac's 9.5-h.p. Evinrude and found it in good working condition. It appeared to have been cleaned.

Ellabell Kaiama, a matron at Halawa Jail, testified that she had met Seibert when he came to visit Stephanie and took the envelope of photos from him. She first examined them and stated that some nude photos were not allowed and would be placed in the inmate's property. She kept the envelope at the gate and took it to the front office after Seibert's visit and turned it over to the FBI.

Peter Buisick, a Lt. Commander and assistant search and rescue officer in the Coast Guard, testified that he first heard of a report about the missing Sea Wind in October, 1974, as reported by Curt Shoemaker. He knew of no other reports.

The prosecution rested.

*****

Stephanie, the sole witness in her own defense, was called to the stand. She said that she had been arrested at nine o'clock in the morning. She told the court that on August 29th, (A

Thursday.) she had been preparing Iola for a trip to Fanning in order to obtain supplies. As to the reason why, she said that we had been expecting friends to arrive with supplies for us, but then the message had arrived from Dickie via Shoemaker and Mac. She believed the trip would take five days maximum. Mac had agreed, given the fickleness of the winds, that five days were more than enough. He had loaned her a chart of Fanning, which she traced, and Mac had told her he would assist with the Zodiac in getting Iola out the channel if the winds weren't right.

After obtaining supplies, "we were going to come back to Palmyra." She said that when our friends did arrive, experienced sailors, "we were going to try to kind of go with them" to the South Sea Islands.

She said that I had come by Iola about 9 a.m. and told her I'd just returned from Sea Wind and that Mac and Muff had invited him aboard for coffee where they tendered the dinner invitation for that night. (Thursday, August 29, 1974.) She hadn't seen the Grahams that day, but since they had provided the courtesy of bon voyage dinners to other parties, she didn't find it unusual. She had visited the Grahams many times and they had returned the visits, both aboard each other's boats and on land.

She said I was on and off Iola all day, stowing and getting the boat ready. She could not see Sea Wind from the deck of Iola. While she was baking bread in the late afternoon, she heard the sound of the Zodiac's motor. She hadn't paid any attention but thought it was going across the lagoon -- between, she guessed, 4 and 5 p.m. About a half hour before that, I had gone to bathe and she met me on the way back, herself on the way to the bathtub. She said I'd told her I had seen Mac, and that he and Muff were going fishing. If they were late, they had left some things out, and we could go aboard and make ourselves at home. She said I told her I would meet her at the Graham campsite.

She said we met there about 6:15 p.m. and sat and talked for fifteen or twenty minutes. She knew the Grahams weren't aboard because the Zodiac was missing. Then we went aboard because of the mosquitoes and because I'd told her it was all right. She had never previously been aboard in the Grahams' absence. She found the table set out with apricot brandy, vodka, peanuts, olives, and a box of cookies. We had drinks and went up on deck. After dark, she became concerned and found spreader lights to switch on. She didn't sleep much, but dozed off a little before dawn.

In the morning, I put the Seagull on the second dinghy and we began the search. She spotted the Zodiac "maybe between a quarter and a half mile away." It was on the beach parallel to the shoreline about five feet from the waterline, upside down. She saw the gas can about "20 yards" from the Zodiac. It started after many pulls -- "at least a dozen." We towed the other dinghy back to Sea Wind and continued the search all that day and two whole days after. She thought, in all, the search had lasted four days altogether.

She said that when we'd left Palmyra, we'd sailed to Kauai, then to Pokai Bay and Tuna Packers. She told about the swordfish piercing the hull. She said we had come into the Ala Wai in order to take on diesel fuel. "We were going to go back to the mainland, take the boat back to her," to Mary Muncey, to Seattle if possible, if not, San Diego. "We had found a will and it said that she was Mac's next of kin. I was going to tell her what happened to Mac and Muff and return the boat to her."

She had not communicated the Graham's disappearance because it would throw Roy "into connection with the authorities which he was afraid of." She knew about Walker and his past, that he was a fugitive on the MDA charge. She told a little about our legitimate jobs on the Big Island and Maui, that she had worked as a waitress and later as assistant manager of the Ginzo

Club on Maui.

On cross-examination by Eggers, the going got a little hotter. When he called her on Shishido's statement that she'd told him the gas can was floating in the lagoon nearby, she replied, "When we found the gas tank, it wasn't -- it wasn't still floating, but my assumption was that both the dinghy and the gas tank had floated to shore."

As to food, "We always had at least ten days worth of food. We never fell below seven to ten days worth of food."

As to Pollock's testimony. Eggers asked, "Do you recall telling him that you sailed Iola out of the channel and went aground on the reef?" She answered, "No, I didn't tell him that. I said Iola -I didn't tell him that I sailed the Iola. I told him that we had towed Iola out."

Q: Did you sail out of the canal there? The channel?

A: We didn't sail out of the island. We motored -- Buck was on board the Sea Wind and he motored out and towed the Iola. Judge King got into the act.

Q: What do you say happened to the Iola? You started off towing it out of Palmyra and what happened to it?

A: Yes. It seems to me as though we had gotten out of the channel or at least I got out of the channel somehow and I think he didn't stay in the channel and the Iola went aground.

Q: Went aground?

A: Yes.

Q: Where were you?

A: I was aboard Iola.

Q: How did you get off?

A: Buck came and got me with the -- after I went aground and -- I think at first he tried to pull the boat off -- well, I was attached to the Sea Wind with a rope and it was just -- the boat was tipping over even further. I got really scared, so he cut the rope and he took the Sea Wind out further beyond the reef and he anchored her and then he came back in the Zodiac dinghy which was still all set up.

Q: What were you going to do with the Iola? You were going to ride on the end of a rope being towed all the way back to Hawaii?

A: We were going to see how it worked out. We had never done anything like that before. We didn't know exactly what we would have to do to make it work. We knew it was going to be...

Q: (Interrupting) Did you have a set of supplies on the Iola to eat or were you going to row back and forth to the Sea Wind or...

A: No, we still had supplies -- we still had some supplies.

She went on to say that I had discussed with her the idea of turning myself in, but "he wasn't ready to turn himself in yet."

When asked at what point in time Sea Wind's name was removed, she replied, "Just outside the Hawaiian Islands," which I accomplished by unscrewing the letters.

She had gone with me to Palmyra, helped me flee, and tried to keep the FBI from learning my true identity because she loved me.

Q: (Wilcox) Did you want to marry him?

A: Yes. We had talked about it.

Q: Did he ask you to marry him?

A: At one time we had agreed to get married and we got as far as the blood test.

She was asked regarding her assumption that fish would be served at the bon voyage dinner on Friday evening. She replied, "I believe Muff was a Roman Catholic."

Muncey was recalled to the stand in rebuttal to testify that Mac was raised Episcopalian and that Muff was Seventh Day Adventist. (As Stephanie's answer on this question proved to be so damaging, it seems to be stupid on its face. While religion was never a subject discussed between we and the Grahams, I, too, had the vague notion that Muff was Catholic. The only evidence I could come up with in support thereof was a comment that Mac had once made, probably in jest, that Muff had been a good little girl at a convent school.)

According to Bugliosi, the big moment in Stephanie's trial, and the most damaging, was Eggers' cross-examination regarding five photos, enlarged to 8x10s, which were taken from the manila envelope sent to her via Wollen-Seibert-Kaiama-the FBI. (My friendly sergeant at Halawa Jail told me a quite different story regarding the chain of possession so important to potential evidence. Matron Kaiama told him that she had been cooperating with the FBI from the beginning, by order of the Captain. She knew ahead of time that Seibert would be delivering a manila envelope containing photos and had been warned that she was to intercept them, which she could legally do and then turn them over to the FBI, who had apparently seen them all while Seibert had them, but taking them from Seibert, or even looking at them without a warrant constituted an illegal search and the photos could thereby be excluded from the evidence.)

The photos in question had been taken by Stephanie from the deck of Sea Wind. The sequence begins showing Iola under full sail coming from portside astern of Sea Wind. The second and third photos show Iola abeam of Sea Wind. The fourth photo shows Iola ahead of Sea Wind. Photo five, which catches part of Sea Wind's rigging and thus identifies where they were taken from, shows Iola even further ahead of Sea Wind. Also the Zodiac can be clearly seen in the fifth photo, which shows more of Iola's stern, as being tied and towed from the aft port quarter. In all of them, Iola's forestaysail and slightly reefed main can be seen hoisted up the mast and full of wind -- she is sailing. I can be seen in all of them, four times in the cockpit and once on the foredeck to adjust a sail. No sails can be seen to be hoisted up the masts on Sea Wind. The sequence clearly suggests that Iola is approaching and passing a stationary Sea Wind.

Bugliosi reported that Eggers had asked the following question: "Would you explain, please, at what point in time when you and Mr. Walker were on the island of Palmyra were the Sea Wind and Iola together under full sail out in the ocean?"

Bugliosi reports that she said, "Never."

Bugliosi goes on to report that Shishido lowered his head to prevent the jury from seeing him smile. Jennifer Jenkins, as he calls Stephanie in his book, had lied. She had made the incredible mistake of denying what the photos conclusively proved -- that Sea Wind and Iola were at sea together and these five photos before the jury did not lie.

However, the question was not whether Sea Wind and Iola were together on the sea, but when Sea Wind and Iola had been together under full sail -- the question that Eggers had actually asked. Stephanie's answer was correct and true and Burns' attempt to distort my answer that Iola had never sailed alongside the Grahams into alongside Sea Wind finally revealed its significance -- he had already seen the photos and was trying to trick me into denying what the photos proved. (This distortion seems a very strange thing for a lawyer to write about his own client, but Bugliosi's purpose will become clear when we get to Stephanie's murder trial)

But Bugliosi also made another small distortion when he reported that Stephanie's answer had been the one word, "Never."

Her trial transcript reveals this:

A: Never. That --

But Eggers interrupts whatever she was going to say by quickly changing the subject and asking, "Do you deny giving these photographs to Mrs. Wollen?" No, she does not, but the subject was never returned to, not even by her own lawyers, and Eggers was allowed to pull a fast one.

On June 24, 1975, after summations by Eggers and Wilcox, the case was submitted to the jury. It didn't take long for them to find Stephanie guilty on all counts.

#

CHAPTER 7

The jury in Stephanie's trial had been troubled by one key question. In order to prove theft, Eggers had told the jury that he must ~ show the stolen property in question as "being the property of Mr. and Mrs. Graham or their heirs." He must prove Sea Wind "was the personal property of someone other than the thief."

Before allowing the jury to retire for their deliberations, Judge King had read them an instruction having to do with ownership and possession as related to stolen property. He defined stolen as "a word which is used in the statute --(and) means acquired, or possessed, as a result of some wrongful or dishonest taking, whereby a person willfully obtains or retains possession of property which belongs to another, without or beyond any permission given, and with intent to deprive the owner of the benefit of ownership."

Mary "Kit" Muncey had been established through a probate court in San Diego as his heir and executrix of his will. The implication was clear: She was the owner of Sea Wind. Yet, by what "wrongful or dishonest" act had we taken possession of Sea Wind at Palmyra? Whose permission could possibly be given? And if "intent to deprive the owner" was proven, who could determine the question of ownership at that time without the intercession and ruling of a court of law -- which did not exist on Palmyra?

Despite Eggers' statement, Muncey's proof, and Judge King's instruction, the jury had trouble over this point. They had sent in a note to the judge, which said:

Judge King, we are having trouble establishing ownership of the vessel Sea Wind after August 30, 1974. Is there anything in Section 661, (The section of Title 18, the criminal code, which charges theft.) U. S. Code or some other law that would help us decide ownership? We would like to be informed of such.

In reply, Judge King called the jury in to read this:

"The ownership of property of the deceased person passes automatically to his estate, subject to death or claims or ultimate distribution to the beneficiaries named in his will or to his statutory heir if there is no will."

What is so galling is that the case would rest upon the question of ownership and possession, especially when the law, itself, provided a far better answer --which, had it been read to the jury, would almost have certainly led to her acquittal.

*****

I had always felt that we had a valid salvage claim against Sea Wind. When we had boarded Sea Wind after Mac and Muff had failed to appear, she constituted an abandoned vessel, a derelict vessel.

If I hadn't acted to re-secure the mooring line that had parted, Sea Wind would certainly have gone aground and suffered damage sufficient to sink her where she sat. In attempting to care for both

Sea Wind and Iola in trying to leave Palmyra, we had lost Iola. Still, we had, at some cost to ourselves delivered Sea Wind to safety -- even after the swordfish attack. We had hauled her out and repaired the damage. We had considered sailing her all the way to Puget Sound in Washington in order to deliver her to Mac's sister. Stephanie's lawyers had filed a salvage claim against Sea Wind before her theft trial. I had filed one after mine.

Lawyers, like many professions, have specialties. Generally speaking, civil lawyers do not try criminal cases, and neither do criminal specialists invade the province of civil law.

Tax law specialists do not get involved in divorce cases, nor do business merger experts handle consumer complaint suits. And like many other professions, specialists in one area are incompetent in other areas. Such is the case when criminal trial lawyers come up against questions outside their specialties -- such questions as relate to maritime law for instance.

Most maritime questions arise under what has come to be known as Admiralty Law, and was not an area that I knew a great deal about. Sure, I had read tales about treasure-hunters diving to find old Spanish galleons and coming away rich. I had read about vessels found floating at sea with no one aboard. I had read feats of men having raised sunken ships from the ocean's bottom. In all such cases, the salvors had been rewarded for their efforts. All such cases came under the purview of special admiralty courts.

I had put my time in Terminal Island to good use by going to the law library to read up on this little known area of the law. I soon found it codified under Title 43 of the U. S. Code. In the federal law, the annotated version includes not only the relevant laws passed by Congress, but also the leading precedents as interpreted by federal courts.

I soon learned that salvage was the preservation of life or property from endangerment or loss at sea. Legal salvage occurs when some property is saved from some danger and the service is performed voluntarily.

A service performed in salvage must have four elements before it legally qualifies as marine salvage and the salvors are eligible to collect:

1. The object of property must be a recognized subject of salvage -- such as a ship in distress, one abandoned or derelict, and the remains of a vessel's wreckage, including its wares and cargo (a ship being defined as any vessel not principally propelled by oars and is used in navigation).

2. The salvors must enjoy some success (a service which saves or helps to save).

3. The object must have been in some danger (and in some cases, the danger may be future rather than instant).

4. The salvors must do their work voluntarily.

Under these definitions, our boarding Sea Wind, acting to save her from immediate and future danger by sailing her to Hawaii meets all the necessary criteria. The maritime law of salvage is based upon principles of equity. The legal rights of salvors to remuneration are absolute rights, independent of any contract.

But how does this answer the questions of ownership and possession, the very questions the jurors in Stephanie's trial wanted to know?

The common method of obtaining an award for salvage is to submit the claim for decision to a court of admiralty. The court will hear all the evidence, decide what the facts are, and suitably reward the salvors for their labors. But where does the award come from? Who pays it? In what form?

The law tells us that the salvor has many and quite stringent remedies if payment is not forthcoming from the owners or, presumably, their heirs. Almost always the salvor has the right of a maritime claim (a privileged claim) against the salved property itself -- in this case, Sea Wind and all her wares. This claim can be enforced by a proceeding in rem (the thing itself, the property in question) against the vessel -- which means the vessel can be seized and sold to satisfy the lien. And this claim takes precedence over all others in salvage cases.

The court in the case of the vessel, The Snow Maiden, D.C. Mass. 1959, 155 F. Supp. 518, had ruled: "A volunteer salvor has obligation to place it in a place of safety in which it would be available to owner, subject to libel in rem for salvage if desired."

In Petition of United States, D.C. Or. 1963, 229 F. Supp. 241, the court had ruled: "An award for loss or damage to a salving ship or for personal injuries, may be viewed as an item of recovery in addition to general award for salvage."

What was even more interesting to me, as well as most relevant to the question of the right of possession, were the following two cases, which, along with the previous two, are leading precedents in admiralty law:

Richard v. Pringle, D.C. N.Y., 1968, 293 F. Supp. 981: "Plaintiff who successfully prosecuted salvage operation and who did not abandon it at any time was entitled to rights of first salvor legally in possession (emphasis added)." The court also stated in this case that "When ship or property has been abandoned or when it has been temporarily left, and is in a disabled or damaged condition so as to require assistance, one who in good faith takes possession as a salvor is not an interloper or trespasser (emphasis added)."

The capper to this line of rulings came in Brady v. The African Queen, D.C. Va. 1960, 179 F. Supp. 321, when the court ruled that " One who has possession of the vessel, has begun salvage service, and is successfully prosecuting it, is entitled to sole possession of the property (emphasis added)."

In case these court rulings are not clear in showing that Stephanie and I were in legal possession of Sea Wind and therefore could not have stolen her, let me quote a leading expert in maritime salvage operations as well as the applicable law: (Marine Salvage, Joseph N. Gores) "With derelict property, a salvor can keep entire and absolute possession of it from the time he salves it until his services have been paid for. But because a salvor's rights are so rigidly protected, he is expected, except for derelicts, to surrender possession of salved property to the owner upon demand (emphasis added)."

And what is a derelict vessel? It is simply one that has been abandoned -- there was no hope that the Grahams would return to care for Sea Wind.

According to Admiralty Law, then, we were entitled to sole and permanent possession of Sea Wind. We did not have to surrender the vessel to owners or heirs, nor were we compelled under the law to submit a claim before the admiralty courts.

Plain and simple.

Ha!

*****

David Bettencourt was young, handsome, smug, and arrogant, a polar opposite of Jon Miho, but when all was said and done not much improvement. He had more time for the sport of hang-gliding than for his clients, who he tended to look upon as retarded -- people so handicapped they didn't know what was good for them. When I tried to explain the significance of admiralty law to the case at hand, he all but sneered at me, pointing out that the charges against me had been brought under the criminal code in Title 18, which had nothing to do with the admiralty law in Title 43.

But surely it could be introduced into a criminal trial under the circumstances as applied to my case in order to define legal possession?

"Doubtful, very doubtful."

Why not consult with an admiralty specialist? How about putting the question to a law professor?

"We'll see, we'll see. You have to keep in mind that this is a criminal case. You're basically charged with theft."

"That's the point. This is a salvage situation. We saved a derelict vessel from destruction, and according to admiralty law we're entitled to legal possession. There is no theft."

"Yeah, right. Try explaining to the court why you registered the Graham's vessel as a homebuilt boat!"

"To avoid apprehension on the bail-jumping charge."

"Now, why don't I believe that?"

"How about conveying the idea to Stephanie's lawyers?" Maybe they'd take the trouble to at least inquire into the question.

"Sure, maybe they're into chasing butterflies."

I wrote to Steph, laying it all out to her, imploring that she push the issue with Mirikitani and Wilcox, even asked her to show them my letter.

In the immediate aftermath of her trial, I had only TV and newspaper accounts to rely on, but later, when I'd acquired transcripts, nowhere did I find a single mention of admiralty or its application.

*****

Hardly a month after Stephanie's trial, Judge King having in I the interval reduced my sentence on the MDA charge from five years to three, the U. S. Marshals returned me to Terminal Island on July 11, 1975. The prison security was pretty loose. At that time, no prisoner was accepted there if he had longer than five years remaining to serve on his sentence. Since I had, by then, less than three, I was prime material, but I hated the place. Terminal Island, along with all the other federal prisons I would come to visit in the years ahead, was far worse than San Quentin had ever been.

Above all, prisons strip you of every last vestige of privacy.

At T. I., we all slept in dormitories and ate in a noisy, crowded cafeteria-style messhall. Even shitting, pissing, and bathing was done in full view in the communal facilities. Everywhere you turned, there was inmate or hack (Convict term for guard.) watching you.

In some prisons you can get into a cell alone and, in the dark hours, have some sense of privacy between the periods of flashlights shining in your face during the ubiquitous counts.

The thing about prisons, once you've learned firsthand what life is like in them, is that you can never entirely relax in such unchosen company. You never know for sure whether the guy next to you is a predatory type sizing you up for a meal. He may only want to rob you of a few packs of cigarettes, but maybe he's interested in you as a sexual object. He may not need a reason. He just may be nutso and the demons inside his head are telling him to kill you.

A convict, except among friends of longstanding where each has been studied and tested over the years, can never quite feel at ease unless he is alone and feels secure. Locked alone in a cell allows him that temporary feeling of security. I have known some men to purposely get themselves thrown into the hole for no more reason than a few days or weeks of feeling secure and alone.

In prisons where double occupancy of a cell occurs, which is the prevalent rule, you cannot even begin to relax your vigilance with your bunkmate until you've tried and tested him over a period of time. You sleep light, ever ready and alert to defend yourself if necessary against the anger and madness just below the surface of resentments that have been years building. If you were any kind of a man, there was no evading the issue; you had to accept and adapt to conditions as you found them, to deal with situations as they might arise at any moment -- be ready to defend yourself.

But for a man to maintain his self-respect, it also meant he could not abide the presence of that most loathsome of human creatures, the rat, the stoolie, the snitch, the informant. When I had served time in San Quentin, there had been few rats running around loose in the convict population of over four thousand. There were different attitudes in those days -- the lines were clearly drawn. A rat was rated on a level slightly below child molesters. I had been raised in a family of strong loyalties. You simply did not turn upon your own kind. It was a part of my character.

Mickey Cohen, a Los Angeles gangster in the 40s and 50s, who was known as a standup guy, put it like this: "It makes no difference if he gets hit with a thousand-year sentence or if he's facing the loss of his life a second later. He won't be a stoolpigeon. I believe a rotten cocksucker is either born a rotten cocksucker or he's not. Some, it may come out of them sooner or later, or vice versa. But it don't come out of you unless it's in you."

Nowadays it's a different world, not a brave new world but a cowardly one. The once clear lines wiggle and blur, disappear altogether. Betrayal is the in-thing. We live in the age of the rat. Everybody tells on everybody. Our national and state legislators have even institutionalized the practice by enacting laws, which serve to elevate rats into a specially protected status -- immunity laws.

You can be forgiven any crime, even murder, if you are only able to deliver up someone else to the insatiable hunger of the beast residing under the facade of the American system of justice. The

Fourteenth Amendment to the Constitution, which provided for equal protection of the law to all citizens, was dead and stinking. Clarence Darrow said that he would rather be dead than live in an America in which the lowliest of citizens can be convicted on the evidence of informers.

Someone like myself in this respect, to have to abide among informers-for-favors, has to exist like a dinosaur on the edge of extinction. My only hope was to seek and find other dinosaurs, those with old-fashioned values firmly fixed in their characters. There were a few in T.I., but we were surrounded by hordes of rats nibbling at our toes. Within a month or two, a busload of us was shipped out for the Jurassic Park of the penitentiary at McNeil Island. We celebrated the whole three days of the onerous journey by bus in our chains and shackles.

*****

It would have been easy to escape from T.I. The one guntower was at the front of the prison. Most prisons nowadays have not only numerous guntowers but also walls or rows of cyclone fences heavily enmeshed in razorwire to discourage those contemplating climbing over them.

T.I. had only one fence with a bit of barbwire strung along the top. It seemed like every other day someone was hitting the fence. Of course, most of them were caught right away. The enlistees manning a nearby Coast Guard station were paid fifty-dollar rewards for reporting and apprehending escapees, most of whom were emotionally hare-brained, who acted on impulse and had no real plan for getting themselves out of the area.

One time I actually watched a guy talking to his wife on the telephone, slam down the receiver with a curse and run for the back fence. He'd learned that Sancho was in his house taking care of his Ol' lady while he was away. The one serious escape I saw that was successful, the guy patiently sawed at a window in the third-floor hobby shop, which fronted the street below, and one night climbed down on a jerry-made rope, stepped into a waiting car, and was gone.

Don't think it didn't enter my mind. Every convict plays with the idea, including the short-termers, even if they never actually put it into effect. It's an irresistible fantasy. I looked to the ocean side of the prison. From our dorm windows we could see a nice little bay. Less than a quarter-mile away sat about a half dozen sail-boats at anchorage. In the several months I was there, not once did

I see anyone aboard them. I fantasized sawing my way out one night and ducking into the water below. I would take along a short piece of surgical tubing, one end tied to a piece of driftwood, for use as a breathing snorkel, and swim underwater to the anchored yachts. It was a move no one would expect. I could imagine hoisting sails at a late hour and heading out to sea -- Hawaii in a month's time. But, shit,

I only had three years to serve, could be out in two at worst. Besides, I had resolved to face it all down, get it behind me. Later, I would see this as a mistake, just as surrendering myself had been.

*****

McNeil was an old prison on an island several miles wide in the southern part of Puget Sound. But at least the customers were a better class than at T.I.

After a week or so spent orienting myself, I connived my way into an eight-man cell dominated by Hawaiians, of whom there were forty or fifty at McNeil. They had a formed a club, as ethnic minorities were allowed to do back then, and I immediately joined. I was assigned to work as a clerk in the inmate commissary, a job I would keep for over three years. After all, good work habits meant early release.

*****

I had no sooner gotten settled in than I was returned to Honolulu for trial. I came armed with sheets of paper quoting Title 43 of the U. S. Code, citations on every aspect of admiralty law pertaining to marine salvage that I thought might apply. If I could just convince Bettencourt that they constituted the perfect defense, were in fact the only defense, why, a trial and all the horseshit Steph had had to go through might be avoided altogether. Plus, if admiralty law was permitted in my case, it might also serve to overturn her conviction. Well, like they say, you can lead a horse to water, but...

Bettencourt didn't want to avoid trial. To him, just starting out in his career, it represented an opportunity to strut his stuff. If he could win a case that had already been lost, especially since mine was tougher than Stephanie's, it would be quite a feather in his cap. He was caught up in the game of it. Guilt or innocence made no difference to him -- win or lose, he'd still be paid and never have to serve a day in prison. The problem with strutting your stuff is you have to have something to strut.

Bettencourt would put up a half-assed fight, showing a bit of spirit here and there, even bring his drab passions into play for a bit of eloquence on rare occasions. But, alas, he was no

Bugliosi, a man meticulous in his study and preparation, one who knew every shred of evidence and applicable law intimately, who knew exactly what every single witness was going to say on the stand before he testified, and knew exactly what he was going to say in closely reasoned summation in putting it all persuasively together for a jury. By comparison, Bettencourt was a girl scout beside a career combat veteran, a mouse beside an elephant. Highly competent lawyers did not make their living dependent upon court appointments to represent indigent defendants. The trial began on December 9, 1975. With a few minor differences, it would be pretty much a rerun of Stephanie's trial, and with the same results. The prosecution, however, called twice as many witnesses against me. It seemed apparent that I had been settled upon as the real culprit -- with Stephanie no more than a poor unfortunate gullible enough to love me and get caught up in my shenanigans.

With the additions of evidence regarding my acquisition of a passport in a name other than my own, and the fact that I had been the one to register Sea Wind as a homebuilt boat, the body of the evidence was generally the same as against Steph. As in her case, the high point would come in the difference between my testimony and that of an FBI agent. Burns would say I told him one thing, while I would say it was something else. Of course, since I was forewarned about the five photographs of Iola sailing past Sea Wind, Eggers would not be able to repeat his courtroom trick against Stephanie.

Appraisers would be brought in to establish the value of certain of Sea Wind's wares, as well as the vessel itself. The several boat registrations between Iola and Sea Wind would be established. Our version of the hole made by the swordfish would receive additional support by the Tuna Packers boatyard manager testifying that he had seen a temporary patch below the waterline on Sea Wind's hull, which would cause Eggers and the FBI to abandon their attempt to show that the hole was caused by a bullet fired from inside the hull during the imaginary murder of Mac and Muff. Further testimony would be adduced on the movement of the photographic evidence from Lorraine Wollen's hands to Joseph Stewart to Larry Seibert to FBI Agent Hamilton back to Seibert to Matron Kaiama at Halawa Jail to her supervisor and back into Agent Hamilton's hot little hands -- a neat little trick enabling the FBI to circumvent the necessity of obtaining a search warrant to look inside the manila envelope and seize it as evidence -- all tidily approved by Judge King after a valiant effort by Bettencourt to have them excluded. I, myself, saw no harm in having them admitted.

There were some new faces. FBI Agent Henry Burns took Shishido's place at my trial. Donald Stevens, the captain of Shearwater, a yacht visiting Palmyra while we were there, did not testify at Stephanie's trial. Marilyn Pollock took her husband's place. Joseph Stewart, Larry Seibert's employer, showed up to say I had told him the story about winning Sea Wind gambling over a chess game. He created some confusion by saying he had the impression that the Grahams had sailed off in Iola. Robert Mehaffey, who had had us aboard his boat, Vagabundo, upon our return to Kauai, would add to the confusion by saying he thought we'd said we'd just come from the Big Island. He said we'd recommended an anchorage there, and he remembered the story about the swordfish attack but couldn't remember where we'd told hi-m it had' occurred. He also remembered some talk about Palmyra, but thought that had referred to a year before.

Finally, Barbara Allen was called to testify that she had married one Roy A. Allen in June, 1965, but for the past eight years he had been a patient in a VA hospital in Murfreesboro, Tennessee. She thought Frank Zieke, her live-in boyfriend at the time, had stolen the wallet containing her husband's ID. Since Zieke was a good friend of mine, the implication was clear.

Without any warning, Bettencourt pulled off a needless and shameful stunt. He asked Barbara with a sneer whether she'd told the FBI in November, 1974, that she hallucinated periodically while under emotional strain. Hadn't she received psychiatric treatment? Wasn't it true she'd told the FBI that she visualized people with horns who represented the devil?

Barbara had fled the stand with cheeks red and eyes cast down, taking time only to throw a glance of tearful sympathy my way. When Bettencourt sat down, smug look on his face, I leaned over to whisper to him. "Listen, you cocksucker, you ever pull a stunt like that again, I'm gonna knock you out of your socks right here in the court- room before God and everybody!" He was stunned. "Hey, pal, I'm on your side, remember?"

"You remember this, asshole. That girl lost her husband when she was twenty.

He's a quadriplegic vegetable in a VA hospital. She's the mother of two beautiful daughters, one of whom was born with physical deformities. Sure, she's hooked on speed and booze and sex and sees a headshrinker. She's got enough grief to bear without you humiliating her in public. You layoff that shit!"

"I'm sorry. I'm just doing my job."

"Isn't that what the Nazis said before they burned 'em?"

*****

Reading trial transcripts is about as boring as it gets and there is no way a non-participant can judge the credibility of witnesses since demeanor, gesture, reactions and tone of voice are necessary in most cases to determine whether they are sincere, confused, or lying.

Jack Wheeler said, upon coming to our assistance, that we had pulled up the anchor lines. "They'd already done all they could," he said, with respect to the situation and putting out anchors. He said visibility of the island from a yacht at sea was eight miles with the trees rising ninety feet. He would not allow his family to swim in the lagoon because of the sharks. He described how small sharks would attack the legs of waders in shallow water. He had instructed every- one that no guns were to be brought on to the island, and there was to be no cutting down of coconut trees except young ones. He believed Mac was there to write a book and he remembered carrying a letter from me to the owner of Palmyra. He identified a picture of the hatchcover he had found during the search in November, 1974. He observed that Iola was an older boat formerly known as Margaret, that she was a well-known class of boat, the original design being named after a bird.

Thomas Wolfe claimed employment as a chemical engineer for an agricultural chemical company. He recounted the entry of he and Norman Sanders on the boat Toloa into the lagoon and told of how I had helped them to their moorage. They had invited me aboard for brief chat. I would show them about, point out the freshwater and bathing situation, and take them fishing. In describing a fishing expedition I'd taken the two of them on, he told about our stopping at my tent to fetch a pistol. He told of how we had shot a fish and attempted to spear them. He said he had swam in the lagoon three or four times, once to wipe the bottom of Toloa and again to retrieve a dropped screwdriver, but had not seen any sharks. He did, however, see numerous small sharks along the island on the other side in water three or four feet deep. In recounting his claim that he was attacked and bitten by Popolo, he said the incident had happened when he'd gone to inquire about fishing. "When they heard my voice, they ran out and jumped on me and the black dog tore my shirt and bit me on the stomach here." He said it had left a scar. He said I had called the dogs off, cursed them, and stated, "We should kill the goddam dog and then we could have some steak around here." He said, "I told him I'd kill the dog if it ever came near me again" (According to the timing he claims here, he did go fishing with me again later on -- and where I went, my dogs went.)

He said I'd told him about the edibility of tern eggs and admitted he'd taken my broken buckknife and had given me a can of chili beans for it. As to my demeanor, he said that I "was not particularly bubbly," but admitted, "He was helpful to us, yes." He said he'd given some flour to Stephanie, "she baked us a couple different kinds of bread, and we had two or three different loaves of bread." He described one of them as six to eight inches in diameter and about an inch thick, while another was eight to twelve inches long like a regular loaf of bread.

Curtis Shoemaker said that he had continued twice weekly radio contact with Mac after he'd arrived, about fifteen conversations altogether, each about twenty minutes long. Dickie's letter to us had this message to my friend Roy Allen next time you are in contact with Mac Graham. Thank you for your assistance. Message: We have been delayed by unforeseen circumstances but hope to see you in October. We've enjoyed your letters very much.

Of interest is the fact that seagull eggs are considered superior eating to chicken eggs in many European countries, not only in nutrition but taste as well. Hopefully we will bring everything necessary to repair the engine, etc. Patty promises to bring turkey for Thanksgiving dinner. See you there.
Richard.

Shoemaker said that his last contact with Mac had been on August 28, 1974, (A Wednesday -- but in Stephanie's trial, he'd claimed his last contact was the day before, Tuesday, August 27, 1974.)

Larry Seibert spent some time explaining that his signing of the affidavit in my application for the Roy Allen passport was not really perjury since he claimed to have known me in Honolulu two years before. He said he knew me only as Buck and did not know my last name was Walker. On October 15, 1974, as a result of a call from me, he went to Pokai Bay and saw we had a different boat. He said I'd told him I'd won it gambling in a chess match from a "carefree millionaire." He said he also thought I had won $1000 and some provisions. He did not see the name, Iola, on Sea Wind's stern. He wasn't sure whether it was his boss or me who had told him the Grahams had left Palmyra on Iola. He also met me on October 30th in Waikiki. He said I appeared nervous, had shaved off my beard, and asked him to check on Stephanie. He had helped paint the bottom of Sea Wind at Tuna Packers and had noted the repair of the hole made by the swordfish, "a very good job." He had seen the broken-off tip of the swordfish bill as well as the temporary plywood patch over the hole. He said he saw no reason not to believe the gambling story, but did admit he had drunk alcohol and smoked grass when the story was told. He mentioned that he and I had watched a TV newscast on Stephanie. He said FBI agent Hamilton (the one who'd given the envelope of photos back to him to deliver to Stephanie) had threatened him if he helped me, and claimed not to have purchased the airline ticket for me.

Henry F. Burns, FBI, said he'd first become involved in the case when, acting on information received, he'd gone to Hawi. "We located Buck Walker who was on the street in the center of town. I walked up to Buck Walker and asked if he was Buck Walker." He said he'd displayed his ID and told me he had a warrant. "We took him from the table he was seated at" and put him in a car. He said I told him I was staying at Luke's Hotel under the name of Joe Evans, in room 19, and gave him permission to search. Hilton Lui, FBI, was present. FBI agent Kent drove us to Hilo. A Hawaiian police officer rode beside him. He said he asked if I had any objection to him asking questions and that I told him it depended on the questions. He said I told him I'd arrived on the Big Island on October 30th and at Hawi on November 7th. He said I told him I'd purchased Iola on Maui in the fall of 1973 for $2200 and had made substantial repairs of about $6000. On June 1, 1974, he said, Stephanie and I, with three dogs aboard, had set sail for Palmyra from Port Allen, Kauai, spending nineteen days at sea and had anchored for seven days outside the reef. When we attempted to sail up the channel, we got caught on a reef and two men came out in dinghies to assist getting us off the reef. I had met Wheeler and became friends with Mac. We played chess twice a week, half the time on Sea Wind and half the time at Mac's camp. At the end of August, Mac had invited us for supper "that night." I arrived at about 6 p.m. The Grahams were absent. I waited a half hour, then boarded Sea Wind to await their return. He said I told him that the Grahams had gone fishing that afternoon, that Mac had worn shorts and T-shirt, Muff a hat and bathing suit. He said I'd denied saying that in going over it later, that I'd said I hadn't seen them go fishing but rather imagined that's what they'd done because they often went fishing and were always dressed in that manner. He said I'd told him that after spending the night on Sea Wind, I had begun the search. He said I'd told him that Iola was about 200 yards east of Sea Wind, that I'd seen the Grahams' overturned dinghy 50-100 yards west of Sea Wind. "I asked him about this stating that he must have been able to see the dinghy from the Sea Wind if it were that close, and he said no, he couldn't see the dinghy from the Sea Wind and stated that he must be wrong in his figures, that it must have been a half to three-quarters of a mile away because it wasn't in his sight." I went to the dinghy and the motor was attached. It was overturned, up sideways on the beach. The gastank was there. The motor didn't start immediately, but after a few pulls it started. Only Walker, Stearns, and the Grahams were on the island.

There was a radio in Sea Wind and a radio in Iola. I searched for two-and-a-half or three days, then decided to sail from Palmyra to Fanning towing Iola with Sea Wind as it had an inboard diesel and two dinghies and two outboard engines. I put the dogs on Sea Wind and, with Iola in tow, proceeded out the channel. Iola got caught on a reef and I had to cut it free. I took Sea Wind beyond the reef and came back in the dinghy in an attempt to free Iola. I spent over an hour attempting to free it and had the sails up but was unable to get Iola off the reef. I took our belongings off Iola for transfer to Sea Wind. Burns said I told him I felt Iola was still in seaworthy condition at the time I abandoned it, that I'd told him it leaked but had never presented any great problem. When he asked me why I'd want to abandon a $6000 boat, he said I shrugged. He said I told him I'd gone from Palmyra to Nawiliwili on Kauai, spending thirty-three days at sea. I had stayed overnight, then sailed to Pokai Bay. I made arrangements to haul out at Tuna Packers. "I asked him why he wanted to have Sea Wind repainted and he told me because it needed paint." He said I'd told him I'd thought about telling somebody about the Grahams' disappearance but hadn't decided, although I'd thought about writing Graham's sister a letter. I told him lid never met the Grahams before Palmyra, nor seen Sea Wind, "and had never been at sea under sail alongside Sea Wind. He stated he was never under sail next to Sea Wind." I had told him a swordfish had punctured a hole on the side of Sea Wind and that I'd had to go over the side to repair it. "I asked him why he took the name Sea Wind off the boat and he shrugged and didn't reply."

On cross by Bettencourt, Burns said he'd made his report three days later on November 11th. At my arrest I was reading a newspaper. "I didn't notice him looking at me," he said. "I don't know if he recognized me or not." He said that, to his knowledge, I had not been in the restaurant when he was.

He admitted that I did not appear to be surprised at being arrested, and that I offered no resistance, no struggle. He'd made no recordings of the interview, only notes. He'd destroyed the notes.

Q: Wasn't the exact question you asked was he ever under sail alongside the Grahams?
A: No.
Q: Do you recall it?
A: No. I asked him a number of questions on that point. I asked him concerning the Grahams and I asked him concerning the Sea Wind.
Q: All right. Now, your FBI report didn't indicate that you asked him any questions. It simply says "Walker stated, Walker advised, Walker advised." Were you asking him questions?
A: I was asking him questions and he was responding. I didn't place my questions on that report. I placed his statements to me.
Q: So, would it be correct to say that his statement in your report paraphrased what went on in the car?
A: That is correct. There are very few things in quotes in that report. When I took a direct quote, I placed it in quotes.
Q: That was because of the difficulty in remembering his exact words?
A: Difficulty in writing down exact words and listening to his story at the same time.

He said the interview took practically the entire hour and forty-five minutes of the drive to Hilo.

Q: Now, in your direct examination, isn't it correct that you left out a portion of Mr. Walker's statement concerning the use of outboard motors to get Iola off the reef?
A: I asked him why he attempted to tow Iola out of Palmyra and why he didn't take Iola out of the channel at Palmyra under power, noting that there were two outboard motors on Sea Wind. He told me that the motor rack on the Iola was set up high and that he needed an outboard motor with a long shaft, and neither of the motors on Sea Wind had a long shaft so that it wouldn't push Iola.

Upon further questioning, Burns admitted he'd personally made no attempt to verify any portion of my story. He said I had stated that I'd talked to another individual about the possibility of writing a letter to Mary Muncey. He said I'd told him I'd fled to the Big Island because I "didn't want to get caught." He did not ask what offense I didn't want to get caught for. He said he was not sure he knew at the time of my arrest whether I was wanted for bail-jumping. (The records show that I was not indicted on the theft and related charges until November 15, 1974, one week after my surrender, but that the warrant for bail-jumping was executed on November 8th, the day of my arrest, and filed with the court on November 11th.)

No doubt believing he'd done very well in his testimony, having successfully withstood Bettencourt's cross-examination, Burns smirked at me as he left the stand. I managed to stifle an urge to shoot him a middle finger.

Then it was my turn to mix in a few lies with the truth. In admitting to using the name, Roy Allen, my first lie was only a small fib -- that Frank Zieke had given me the Roy Allen ID rather than Barbara herself. It was a small protection for her against a possible aiding and abetting charge.

My second small lie was inadvertent, a confusion on my part. I had said that I had $1200 on Kauai prior to our departure for Palmyra, when actually it was $1500. I had $1200 when we returned to Kauai from Palmyra.

I also said that Stephanie had $300-$400, plus $500 her mother had sent her, which was true. But I neglected to say we had spent the $500 on supplies prior to our departure for Palmyra.

Bettencourt began to lead me through the story. I told of how I had purchased Iola on Maui in October, 1973, for the purpose of fleeing the MDA charge and to "sail the seven seas." I told about leaks in the rudderpost and the forward hatch. I described Iola as packed about as full as she could get at Port Allen, that the entire forecastle was completely full of supplies, food, fertilizers, tools, and etc., that all stowage areas under the seats, the main bunk, and the seat lockers in the cockpit, as well as the storage area under the cockpit floor hatch, were all packed.

I told of breaking the handle off our pump and using the generator for the power tools to repair it. On going aground at Palmyra soon after our arrival, I said, "Well, the first thing I did was I took the sails down. The second thing I did was I unshipped our dinghy, put it in the water and rowed an anchor out. I dropped the anchor and had it hooked in good. I went back to the boat and got another anchor and rowed that out to the other side of the boat, and then we ran the anchor lines around the wenches and began to use the winches to pull ourselves back off the coral head. It took about two hours of really hard labor to do that and we did get it free. We got it off the coral head and we were kind of sitting there bobbing. And about that time is when Mr. Wheeler and his son, I believe, and a passenger -- I think it was the first mate on the Caroline -- came out in motored dinghies and offered to tow us in, and so they towed us in." I told of leaving the anchors in the water with red flotation cushions tied to their lines.

Then it was time to throw in another lie, a slight changing of dates regarding my last conversation with Mac on the 29th or 30th, not sure of the date, I said, but that it was a Friday. I said, "I saw Mac early in the morning, I guess eight or nine o'clock, and we passed the time of day. We smoked a cigarette or something like that. I went aboard his boat and we played a game of chess, a couple of games of chess, and he said he was going to help tow us out of the lagoon with his dinghy. So he invited us over for dinner that night. It was sort of a bon voyage thing. Then I went back over to our boat and Stephanie and I continued getting our boat ready to go the next day." I said I'd seen Mac again about one or two p.m., when he said he was going fishing that afternoon and, if he wasn't back at the appointed time, 6:30, to go ahead and board the boat and help ourselves to a drink and pupus (Snacks) he'd laid out, and "that's the last time I talked to him." After we'd gone aboard Sea Wind, I said, "They had a bottle of rum and a bottle of vodka set out and some cookies and something else to eat, I think nuts or something like that."

I told of continuing to work at preparing Iola for the voyage to Fanning, that because of leakage in the forward hatch I'd removed it and "nailed and glued a piece of plywood over the hatch hole and fiberglassed over that."

I told of us going to take a bath and then going to the Graham campsite to sit and talk awhile before going aboard Sea Wind as it was growing dark, of finding the rum and vodka, cookies and nuts.

I identified a photo of my tent and said that I'd set it up about seventy-five to a hundred yards east of Iola.

I told about turning on the mast lights and that we'd spent the night aboard and begun the search in the morning, of finding the Zodiac about a half mile down the lagoon. I told of righting it, launching, hooking up the gastank, starting the motor, towing the other dinghy back to Sea Wind, and continuing the search in the Zodiac for the next three days.

When the search was over, I told of discussing a number of alternate plans as to what we might do. We had considered sailing to Fanning in Iola, then in Sea Wind -- but had scotched that because we might wind up stranded in British jurisdiction. Finally, we had decided to motor the whole way to Fanning in Sea Wind towing Iola, where we would report the Grahams' disappearance. I told of our preparations of getting ready to get Sea Wind and Iola in tow and beginning the journey on September 11th.

"At one point, Iola swung a little wide -- and hit a coral head and went hard aground. (Since Stephanie had not mentioned her dog as being the cause of her abandoning the helm of Iola in order to save Puffer from falling overboard and thus causing the grounding, I refrained from mentioning that fact.)

I told of undoing the tow rope and continuing on to anchor outside the lagoon, then returning in the Zodiac to fetch Stephanie and Puffer, of how, after getting them aboard the anchored Sea Wind, I'd returned to Iola to set about trying to free her. I told of ferrying most of our stuff to Sea Wind, but of leaving a few things ashore, like our dinghy, its mast, rudder, centerboard, and a sailbag. I told of checking the damage on Iola. "A couple of the ribs were cracked, the planks were warped, and water was coming into the boat." After three hours of labor, I'd gotten her off the reef --"I got it to float, and I tried to tow it out. We were almost out of the channel area. Well, there was difficulty towing the boat with no one to steer it. So, after I had just got it out clear there --where I knew I was clear of the coral heads --I got aboard Iola and sailed out."

Upon being shown the five photographs Stephanie had taken, I identified the Zodiac tied alongside Iola and said that I thought we were a quarter mile to a half-mile distant from Palmyra when they were taken, which I thought was in the "early afternoon."

I told of pumping out a final time, leaving a note saying "Finders keepers," and returning to Sea Wind. At that point, I said, we changed the plan to go to Fanning and began the voyage back to Hawaii.

I described on a chart of the Pacific Ocean our return course according to our navigation, about where the swordfish had attacked Sea Wind, about the temporary repair, and that we arrived back at Nawiliwili after thirty-three days at sea.

At this point, Judge King interrupted, as he would do several times, to cut it short. "Just don't make it a long lecture...and bearing in mind that we already have this in evidence and nobody is object- ing to it, and we had an expert testify that that is what you have to do and why you have to do it."

Bettencourt: Your honor...
King: He may say that's why he did it, but, you know...
Bettencourt: Would you like to make other comments on the evidence?
King: Let's not have a lecture on sailing. Just ask him what he did.
Bettencourt: (Indicating Eggers) He spent three days trying to say this man...
King: That's my ruling. Proceed with the questions.

I described our method of navigation. After describing our return to Kauai, Bettencourt asked: Q: Prior to arriving at Nawiliwili, did you make any attempt to disguise Sea Wind?
A: No.
Q: Did you remove any items from it?
A: No.

Regarding the several discussions we'd had about what to do, I said, "Well, we were trying to decide exactly what we were going to do. I knew that if I came back to Hawaii and just hung around that sooner or later I would be arrested. So one of the things we discussed was sailing the boat to Washington to turn it over to Mac's sister, Mary Muncey."

Mac's will, two copies, one signed and one not, and the codicil were handed to me. I said I hadn't read the will, only the codicil. Over Eggers' objection, I was permitted to say what I understood of it. I said, "It said that in the event that anything happened to Mac, that whoever found the boat could keep it for an authorized period of two years on condition that after the two years it be returned to a port in the United States."

This codicil, though, was actually contained in the eleventh paragraph of Mac's signed will, and Bettencourt had me read it aloud. He apparently felt it was an important document, that it would some- how grant us a legal justification to be aboard Sea Wind, or perhaps to confuse the issue in the minds of jurors. I felt it was worthless in that respect, that my salvation lay in admiralty law.

Q: Why did you change the identity of the boat?

A: Because I was a fugitive. I didn't want to be arrested immediately. I wanted to work out the terms of my arrest -- if that's the way to put it --a little differently. (Stephanie had testified that I had told her I might one day turn myself in on the MDA charge. I had mentioned the possibility, but it was considered far into the future. Perhaps after several years when all the heat had died down, to walk in and surrender myself and show that I hadn't in the meanwhile been arrested on any other charges, might mean the court would be more lenient with me. But, although I paid lip service to the notion here, it wasn't a serious immediate consideration.)

Q: How were you going to work out the terms of your arrest?

A: Well, in our discussions as to what we were going to do with the boat, one of the things we discussed was writing to Mac's sister, writing her a letter and telling her about what happened, and sailing the boat to the Big Island, Hawaii, which is where we lived, and consulting with a friend of ours who is also an attorney, telling him the whole story and getting his aid before we went any further.

Q: And who was that person?

A: Richard Schulz.

Q: Did you ever make any attempts to contact him?

A: Yes, on several occasions.

Q: Where were you when you tried to contact him?

A: I think the first time was Pokai Bay. Stephanie might have called him from when we were at Tuna Packers.

Q: Do you have any personal knowledge of that?

A: No.

Q: Okay. When you called him what was his response? What did you get?

A: I got a recording.

Q: You got a recording?

A: That said he wasn't there.

Bettencourt returned to the swordfish and I related in some detail how that had come about. Then he jumped to the repairs and painting of Sea Wind and I described that. He had me describe what had happened on the day of Stephanie's arrest.

He inquired about registering Sea Wind and renaming her Lokahi, which I admitted and said, "Well, on the day that I registered it, I went down to Bishop Street to see Mr. Brook Hart, who was my attorney on the drug charge. I wanted to speak to him and he wasn't there. And just down the street from there is the Department of Transport with the Harbors Division and I guess it was an impulse. I went in there to register the boat." And here I got a little mealy-mouthed. "And also to establish some kind of paper claim for the boat because I felt I had a salvage claim to it."

Q: Why do you feel you had a salvage claim?

A: Because we had saved the boat from destruction.

Q: What destruction would have befallen the boat while it was anchored at Palmyra?

A: (Stretching from one to two, I replied) On two occasions the mooring lines became undone on Sea Wind.

Q: Now, was this before the 30th of August?

A: No, it was after the 30th.

Q: All right.

A: The mooring lines had parted. If I had done nothing -- I mean just let it go by its own business -- it would have drifted upon the reef and eventually have sunk there. So I secured the mooring lines and everyday checked it to make sure there was no further chafe.

Q: Did you speak to Brook about your problems?

A: No, he wasn't there on the day I went to see him.

Q: All right. Can you tell me why you registered the boat as homebuilt?

A: Well, because I didn't have the thing planned. I did not plan to go up there and register the boat. And when I was actually doing it, I was a little at a loss as to what to do. So I had to make up things there on the spur of the moment. I knew it was a mistake after I had done it.

I explained my reason for choosing the name Lokahi.

In describing my arrest by Burns, I said, "Well, there was a little restaurant and right next door to it is a kind of tavern, I guess, and they have connected doors in between. I walked into the restaurant area and I just happened to glance at the door and I saw Burns -- Agent Burns -- and a couple of other guys sitting there and I immediately knew that they were policemen of some kind. So I bought a paper and I walked outside and stood there for a minute and I walked down the street and I turned the corner and I thought, well, I had to take off running about now. I thought about it and I said, no, I'm not going to run any more. So I walked back to a little park area that was directly across the street from where they had been sitting, and I sat down. I spread out the paper and put my hands on the table and just waited for them to come and arrest me."

Q: How long did it take them?

A: It took them about ten or fifteen minutes. I was waiting there a long time.

Q: Was there any particular reason why you didn't run?

A: Yeah. I don't like being a fugitive. I don't like the feeling.

Q: After you were arrested, you gave a statement to Agent Burns?

A: Well, yes. I waited there and kept wondering what was taking them so long, and I guess it took them enough time to get me surrounded, you know, and they ran up with all their guns out and I kept my hands on the table. The first thing Agent Burns said was he was FBI and was I Buck Walker, and I said yes. And he said, "You knew were here, didn't you?" and I said, "Yeah, I wondered what took you so long."

I said Burns had informed me I was under arrest for bail - jumping. As to the interrogation,

I had this to say:

"Anyway, he started asking me questions and I answered several of them until I began to understand that he did not care for the facts or the truth. He was looking for evidence. He had already made up his mind that a crime had been committed, so at that point I stopped answering questions."

After a recess, it was Eggers turn. He began by taking me through my name and aliases. Yes, I was really Buck Walker and I'd used the names of Roy Allen and Joe Evans. When he asked if I'd ever used the name Angus Fairbarn, he surprised me, but I said, "Probably, yeah."

Eggers took me through the refurbishing of Iola, our shopping trip in Honolulu, and our food supply, trying to trip me up along the way and not succeeding. He tried to suggest that by the time we'd arrived at Palmyra we were all out of food - -in less than thirty days.

Stephanie had testified that she estimated we had a three-month supply when we had left Port Allen and that at no time did we ever fall below a ten-day supply. Eggers wanted me to specify the actual items, like fresh vegetables, no, except for a few onions and potatoes. Yes on canned meat and vegetables. Yes on rice. I affirmed Stephanie's estimate that by the first of September we had about ten days supplies remaining.

Then he attacked the leaking hatch, what I had done to fix it, his theory being that I had purposely left the hatch cover off to facilitate sinking Iola. He suggested we had had to pump Iola daily, but I corrected him to say it was about every third day.

Q: You heard the witnesses testify to the contrary. Are they mistaken?

Actually, I hadn't heard any of them say any such thing, but I replied, "They were never aboard my boat."

Bettencourt objected and asked that the question be stricken because it misstated the evidence. Judge King confirmed that he didn't recall any witnesses testify to a daily pumping.

When Eggers asked, I pointed out on a chart of Palmyra about where we'd found the Zodiac -- a half-mile or so west of Sea Wind.

Once again he suggested daily pumping of Iola, stating that was the reason I had chosen not to leave Stephanie on Palmyra while I de- parted to Fanning. I answered, "I didn't say anything about leaving Miss Stearns on the island while I departed for Fanning."

Q: Wasn't that one of your considerations that you had with respect to your removal of Sea Wind and Iola?

A: I never at any time contemplated separating from Stephanie down there.

He had to niggle.

Q: You were separated at least at the point in time when she was on Iola and you were on Sea Wind.

I wanted to begin a long sneering answer that began with, "No shit, Dick Tracy!", but only said, "That's right. We were about fifty feet apart."

He got back to Iola's grounding on departure.

Q: And you testified earlier this afternoon that, with repeated efforts, you were successful in floating Iola.

A: After three or four hours, yes.

Q: And you discovered that Iola not only floated but it had sustained some damage on that coral head?

A: I determined it sustained damage almost immediately, within the next fifteen minutes after it went aground.

Q: Why didn't you tell Special Agent Burns that?

A: He didn't ask me that.

Q: Nor did you offer it, did you?

A: No, I didn't.

He appeared to read from Burns' report, claiming that "Iola was not damaged," then continued, "and you indicated you felt you might be able to free it if you worked at it longer."

While I replied, "I didn't tell him it was undamaged, period," I wasn't sure whether this was a proper question. Burns had not testified at all on this point and, since I do not have a copy of his report, it may be simply that Eggers was getting cute again, playing fast and loose with the evidence. Bettencourt didn't object.

Q: But you did tell him you were unable to free it?

A: I told him initially I was unable to free it, yes.

Q: Did you tell him after your initial efforts that you were successful?

A: No. We stopped the questioning after that.

Q: Now, let me suggest to you that upon your exit, according to your story, when Iola went on the coral head, it was taking on water rapidly?

A: Rapidly? No. Q: Slowly? A: Slowly.

Q: Was there some haste with respect to your removing the personal possessions of yours and Stephanie's from Iola and putting them on Sea Wind?

A: Haste?

Q: Haste.

A: Well, not immediately, no. There wasn't any haste. The boat was hard aground. It wasn't going to sink or anything. It was going to stay right there. I tried to free it initially. I couldn't get it free. After I took all the belongings out it, it lightened it somewhat.

Q: Now, with respect to Iola's seaworthiness, at the time that you began to tow it out of the lagoon into the channel, was that sea- worthy? Was it a boat sufficiently equipped in order to make a sea voyage in some direction on the open ocean?

A: I would have been willing to continue sailing the boat around the world.

Q: Did you have plans to come back to Palmyra? A: At that point we did, yes.

Q: Even though you were going to Honolulu?

A: We weren't planning to go to Honolulu at that time.

Q: How much water was in Iola by the time you got it off the island as shown in these photographs?

A: There were six to eight inches of water in the bilges.

By this time, Eggers had become tiresome and I was losing patience with his tactics -- which may have been his aim. In the meanwhile, his questions seemed inane.

Q: How did you get back on Iola after Miss Stearns was on it? A: How many times do you want me to explain it to you?

Q: Try again, sir.

I gritted my teeth and told myself not to blowup at the asshole. A: We were towing the boat out the channel. I was aboard Sea Wind and Stephanie was aboard Iola. When the boat went aground, when Iola went aground, I Cut it loose. I continued outside the reef with Sea Wind and I anchored it. I got on the Zodiac. I came back. I got Stephanie and her dog, took her out to Sea Wind and left her with instructions as to what to do in case Sea Wind started dragging anchor. I then went back to Iola, checked the damage, began unloading it -- tried to tow it off first and then I unloaded it -- carried some of the stuff, most of the stuff, to Sea Wind. I carried some of the stuff back to shore and I went out and got Iola free and got it out through the rest of the pass. When I was out in the open ocean (and here I was inspired to insert another lie -- they wanted Sea Wind and Iola sailing alongside each other, as they all seemed to believe the photos showed, I would give it to them), I yelled to Stephanie, "Lift the anchor." The motor was already running. All she had to do was step on a button and the electric winch would lift the anchor. She sailed alongside me.

After having leaned forward in my seat on the witness stand to deliver this speech with some intensity, which had caught the jury's rapt attention, Eggers, seeming nonplussed that he had elicited this information, quickly turned to try catching me out on the damage to Iola.

Q: Once you discovered there was such a large hole in Iola, why did you sail it so far out to sea? What was the purpose of that?

A: In the first place, I did not discover there was a large hole in it.

Q: Who did?

A: A couple of the ribs were cracked. They were not busted all the way through. They were cracked and pushed in. Some of the planks were pushed in. The fiberglass was cracked over a fairly large area, I assume. I did not jump over to look. Water was seeping in through the cracks in the planks.

Eggers swerved again.

Q: And you had a generator on that boat, did you not? A: Yes, I did.

Q: And also the generator was hooked up to a bilge pump, was it not?

A: No, it was not.

Q: When you were tied up at the dolphin moorings, didn't you pump your bilges with an electric generator?

A: No, sir, we did not. Q: How did you pump it? A: With a hand pump.

He turned to the voyage back to Hawaii.

Q: How long did the trip take?

A: I think it was thirty-three days.

Q: Did you hear Mr. Wolfe say he made it in fifteen?

A: (Actually it was Stevens --Wolfe was going the other way) Yes, but they sailed differently from the way I sailed.

Q: Did you have any difficulties?

A: We had no difficulty whatever. To sail a course like that in seven days (most witnesses had claimed to have sailed from Hawaii to Palmyra in seven days) requires 24-hour sailing. We never sailed twenty- four hours a day.

Q: Do you have any recollection, sir, of not going to Nawiliwili, but perhaps you went to Hanamaulu Bay on the Big Island?

A: Absolutely no recollection. We did not go to the Big Island.

Q: Did you ever tell anybody you did?

I knew he was talking about the confused Mr. Mehaffey, who he would call in rebuttal against the answers he was now eliciting on the subject.

A: I had talked with someone about having lived on the Big Island, having sailed to the Big Island previously, but not on Sea Wind.

Q: Where was it that you removed the figurehead with greater exactitude?

A: I think it was between Nawiliwili and Pokai Bay.

Q: What did you do with it? You had it aboard the boat?

A: Yes. I had planned to put it back on. One time I was going to put a tiki there in place of it and I decided I didn't want to go to the trouble of making a tiki. So I was going to put the figurehead back on. One of the reasons it was taken off was because we planned to paint the boat. We took off the bowboards, the figurehead, and all the letters on it.

I explained that the figurehead had been stolen, along with a couple of my power tools, at Tuna Packers.

Eggers turned to the wills and the codicil. He asked if I'd read all of them. I pointed out I had read only the part Stephanie had shown me about Mack providing for someone to keep Sea Wind for two years in the event of his death. Finally, after nitpicking over what I'd read and not read, I said, "I wasn't interested in his will. I didn't feel he'd left me anything."

It was the single moment when the whole courtroom broke out laughing -- except for Eggers, who seemed quite annoyed.

Q: Now, your testimony, sir, on direct examination was that you changed the identity of the boat because you were a fugitive. Wouldn't it be more accurate to say you changed the identity of the boat because you stole it?

A: That is not true. I never at any time thought about stealing the boat. I felt from the very beginning that I had a valid salvage claim. Although I didn't know anything about admiralty law, I know if you save a boat from destruction that you have some claim to it.

Q: Is that what Mr. Bettencourt told you? A: I think that...No, I knew that much. Q: When?

A: I don't know how far back. I've known there are salvage laws in effect that, if you save some goods that are in peril, you have a right to them.

He brought up the fact that we hadn't notified the authorities about the Grahams' disappearance.

Q: Didn't it concern you that their family and friends were concerned about them?

A: It concerned me primarily to contact Mary Muncey.

Q: Did you contact Mary Muncey?

A: I wrote her a letter. I did not have any phone number. I wrote her a letter while we were in Tuna Packers haulout, and I explained everything that happened. It was an eight-page letter.

Q: When did you mail that letter?

A: I didn't mail it until November 2nd or 3rd.

Q: During your stay on Palmyra, Mr. Walker, did Mr. Graham ever give you permission to go aboard Sea Wind?

A: Yes, on numerous occasions.

When Bettencourt returned to the questioning, he honed in on the food supplies again. Then he took me through the eating of fish and the preparations of the many products derived from coconuts. I admitted I'd grown a little tired of the coconuts, but never of the fish.

He asked me why I'd left the tent behind and I replied it was because we'd originally intended to return to Palmyra.

Judge King interrupted to inquire about the letter from Dickie. I explained that it was in response to a letter I had sent him via the Pollocks. He wanted to know where Dickie was. So did the FBI. No, I didn't know where he was.

He also wanted to know whether I'd told Seibert and Stewart the story about winning Sea Wind in a chess game. Of course, he already knew this, but I think he wanted to help Eggers out by reminding the jury. I admitted I had. He wanted to know why.

A: Because I did not want to tell the true story to anybody at that time. When I told Larry about it, I made him understand that that was not the true story and that he would have to wait to hear that.

King: How about Stewart?

A: Well, I didn't even know Mr. Stewart except that I had just met him. Larry introduced me to him and I said, well, let's just say for the time being that I won it in a chess game.

Bettencourt, since he had introduced the idea in his opening statement that my trial for theft of Sea Wind also implied that I was being tried for murder, went directly to the question.

Q: Mr. Walker, did you kill Mac Graham?
A: No, I did not.
Q: Did you kill Mrs. Graham?
A: No, I did not.

King jumped back in to demand where I'd gotten the .22 pistol and I replied that I'd bought it from my brother.

To close out the case, Eggers called Robert Mehaffey to the stand in rebuttal. After eliciting the facts of our meeting at Nawiliwili, he said that he could not see a name on Sea Wind. He remembered my telling him about a trip from Palmyra but thought it had been in reference to a year earlier.

Q: Tell us where he went when he came back from Palmyra.
A: I don't think it was a specific statement about where he went on the trip back.
Q: What did he tell you?
A: Well, they talked about... They just said briefly that they had come back and we made the assumption that...
Q: Besides the assumption, where did he come back to?
A: Let me put it this way. We talked about his coming back and then there was a little harbor just below Hanamaulu Point on the Big Island of Hawaii and he said this is a good anchorage and I got out a chart and Roy showed me where the boat harbor was, and that was it.

He thought we had left there a few days previous and that the swordfish incident had occurred between the Big Island and Kauai and went on at length to describe the story told to him. After some con- fusion, he finally settled upon the idea that the swordfish incident had happened the night before we'd entered Nawiliwili, but he was sure I had told him it had happened on a trip between Hanamaulu and Nawiliwili. (The idea is patently ridiculous on its face. If the swordfish incident had occurred between the Big Island and Kauai, why go to Kauai? Oahu was closer.)

When Bettencourt returned to attack his testimony, he reminded Mehaffey that he'd given a statement to the FBI in November, 1974. Regarding that statement, he asked, "Is it not correct that this statement indicates you only had the impression that they had been to Palmyra a year before the date you spoke to them?

A: Yes.
Q: They didn't actually say that, did they? A: I can't remember.
Q: You don't recall that at all?
A: I have the impression also a year ago but I don't recall the statement, no.
Q: Now, your testimony is that Roy stated to you that he had just come from the Big Island?
A: Yes.
Q: But that the trip to Palmyra, your impression that that was a year ago?
A: Yes.
Q: Isn't it correct that you were discussing with Mr. Allen various anchorages on the Big Island?
A: Yes.
Q: Is it possible that you could be mistaken, that he did not say he had been on the Big Island within the last five days?

A: No.
Q: Well, did you refresh your recollection by reading your FBI statement?
A: No, I did not. As a matter of fact, I discussed it with Mr. Eggers before I ever saw that.
Q: Right, but did you read this statement prior to coming to court?
A: I did.

But couldn't he have been mistaken in confusing the sequence of islands we'd visited, the Big Island before and Palmyra most immediately? No.

To end it at last, Bettencourt called me back to the stand to rebut Mehaffey. I said we had met him upon our entry into Nawiliwili from Palmyra. They had invited us aboard their boat and we'd showed up with a bottle of wine for three or four hours of conversation.

I said that we had told the Mehaffeys that we were from the Big Island. "That's where we lived. Our home was there." We talked about sailing and storms. We had regaled them with the swordfish story.

Bettencourt asked if the conversation turned to a particular bay on the Big Island.

A: Yes. We're from the Big Island and they were talking about cruising over there, and one place Stephanie and I had camped before, called Okoe Bay, we recommended that to him. We got out a chart and showed them where it was. We told them it was a good anchorage there. And that was that.

*****

In a preliminary instruction to the jury, Judge King said: "I instruct you that the law as given by the Court constitutes the only law for your guidance, and it is your duty to accept and follow it. It is your duty to follow the law as I give it to you even though you may disagree with the law."

At the point of the case being submitted to the jury, this was the time for Bettencourt to pullout all the stops in arguing for instructions on relevant admiralty law as it pertained to the basic questions of salvage. It would be the key upon which the whole case turned.

The general rule in being entitled to have a particular instruction read to the jury is that it must have some relevance to evidence admitted or testimony adduced at trial. At two points in my testimony I had referred to my belief that I had a valid salvage claim against Sea Wind. By an easy construction, my testimony included all the essential elements germane to the subject.

Instructions are for the purpose of providing assistance to the jurors in reaching a verdict. They are basically rules for interpreting testimony and other evidence and should include all laws relevant thereto.

I suppose I expected Bettencourt to rival Shakespeare in a great speech of passionate oratory. I had been nagging him incessantly on the subject. But, alas, he was no Clarence Darrow.

Judge King, in turning to the instructions requested by the defense, gave Bettencourt the floor.

Bettencourt: Your honor, I also added one to that list.
King: Oh, you did? What did you add?
Eggers: It's a salvage instruction.
Bettencourt: Salvage and specific intent instruction.
King: Just one?
Bettencourt: Salvage and intent instruction.
King: And your next one about reasonable reliance upon an official statement of the law, I refuse that one.

Bettencourt: I withdraw that, your honor.

King: Huh?

Bettencourt: I'll withdraw it.

King: You withdrew it. Okay. And then there is only one more that you have and that's the...

Bettencourt: Right.

King: ...one I just got. You said about salvage and intent. (To Eggers) You object to that?

Eggers: I object.

King: I'll sustain the objection.

*****

After retiring to deliberate, the jury soon had questions and sent out a note to Judge King. It said:

"We would like clarification of a couple of points on the indictment. Our interpretation of Count I (Theft of Sea Wind) is that the defendant had to have the intent to steal and purloin the Sea Wind before leaving the Palmyra area. If we were to determine that the intent occurred at a later time on the trip to Hawaii, would that necessitate a not guilty verdict on Count I?

When I heard this question, my immediate impression was that it indicated that the jury believed my account of events at Palmyra up to and including our departure. They must believe that Iola had been sunk in an accident and that no intent existed at that time to steal Sea Wind. But it also seemed to clearly indicate their belief that somewhere along the way --probably by my registration of Sea Wind as a homebuilt vessel --I had formed the intention to convert Sea Wind entirely for my own use, which would mean theft. The issue of just where they considered my intent to have been formed became clear in the second question.

"Count II (Interstate transportation of stolen property). If property is considered stolen only from point in time at Kauai on return to Oahu, is it considered transported stolen property from Palmyra Island to Oahu?"

When I heard this question, I felt a momentary rush of elation. It told me that I would be convicted on the theft charge and acquitted on the interstate transportation charge. The maximum sentence I could receive would be five years, assuming that the terms of imprisonment on the passport and theft charges would be imposed concurrently, which I had been assured they would. So, at least I'd be no worse off than when I'd gone into the courtroom. Eggers had wasted the expense of a trial as to the penalty that might be imposed, which would be no greater than if he'd taken my offer in the plea-bargaining negotiations to plead guilty on the passport charge. If this was what he considered as meat on the bone -- an extra conviction with no time added -- he was welcome to it.

But Judge King would soon dispel any notion I had about an acquittal on Count II. While discussing what his reply would be in the presence of both counsel and myself, he said, "I will reread the instruction on time so that that is before the jury."

It was: "You will note that the indictment charges each offense was committed on or about a certain date (August 30, 1974). The proof need not establish with certainty the exact date of the alleged offense. It is sufficient, if the evidence in the case establishes beyond a reasonable doubt, that the offense, if you find there was an offense, was committed on a date reasonably near the date alleged." In other words, he was telling them that they could stretch the date of the alleged offense, August 30, to October 15, a period of 46 days.

King also read the other replies he would deliver to the jury. In answer to the first question, he said, "The offense defined in Count I must be committed 'within special maritime and territorial jurisdiction of the United States.' This term is defined in 18 USC 7 which reads in part insofar as it is pertinent here: 'The term maritime jurisdiction of the United States includes the high seas, any other waters within the admiralty and maritime jurisdiction of the United States and out of the jurisdiction of the United States.' And, for the purpose of this definition, with respect to the jurisdiction of the State of Hawaii, the boundaries of Hawaii extend three miles sea- ward from land." I interpreted this to mean that he was telling them that if I intended to steal Sea Wind at Palmyra, I was guilty, but if I formed the intention after returning to Hawaii, then they had to acquit me. My elation rose. They were going to have to find me not guilty of Count I, too!

But wait, suppose they decided I had formed the intent on the 80-mile voyage between Kauai and Oahu beyond the 3-mile limit? No, surely any property, stolen or not, moving between one island and another within the same state would not be considered to have left the state and entered the maritime jurisdiction of the high seas.

King's reply to come on the second question would seem, in its conclusion, to clarify the issue, but when taken with the first part of his answer, would seem to confuse it with ambiguity. It was this: "The offense defined in Count II requires a transportation in interstate or foreign commerce.

Interstate and foreign commerce is defined in 18 USC 10, which reads, 'the term interstate commerce includes commerce between one state, territory, possession, or the District of Columbia. The term foreign commerce includes commerce with a foreign country.' That's the send of that section. Transportation solely within the State of Hawaii is not in interstate or foreign commerce under this definition."

That, taken by itself, seemed clear enough to me. The federal court had no jurisdiction to hear the case if Sea Wind was stolen in the state of Hawaii and moved from one point to another solely within that state. The jury's question had said, "If property is considered stolen only from point in time at Kauai on return to Oahu..."

The only troubling point was the idea that the boundaries of Hawaii extended only three miles from land. There was no way I could get it into my head that traveling between the islands of the state could somehow be inferred as interstate commerce between one state and another, even if, in so doing, you passed over a portion of the high seas. If a thief in California, say, stole a boat and sailed it four miles out to sea only to return to the same place he'd stolen it, could that constitute interstate transportation? Whew! We were getting into gobbledygook here!

Bettencourt objected. "I don't think they are asking anything about the special maritime jurisdiction of the United States. I think they are asking about a variance from the indictment as far as point in time that the offense alleged occurred."

King would hear none of that. He read his replies to the two questions but failed to reinstruct on the "on or about" time element as he had said he would.

Bettencourt objected. "If I didn't hear you incorrectly, I thought you had indicated that you were going to reinstruct on the time frame element."

"No," said king. "I think I said I'll just leave it at that." "Well, may I register my objection?" "You may note your objection."

The jury would therefore not be reminded to consider whether over six weeks -- between August 30 and October 15 -- was "reasonably near" the date of the alleged offense.

The jury returned verdicts of guilty to all three counts. Bettencourt promised to appeal. In January, 1976, I was sentenced to terms of five years each on the theft and passport charges, and to ten years on the interstate transportation charge, which were all ordered to run concurrently with each other, but consecutively to the three-year term on the MDA charge -- the aggregate effect being that I had a thirteen-year sentence before me. According to federal laws then in effect, I would be eligible for release on parole after one-third of the sentence was served -- four years and four months. I was returned to McNeil Island.

*****

If for nothing else but nuisance value, I would provide paperwork for the system by filing a salvage claim. In my statement of facts, upon which the suit would be based, I recounted a simple story: Sea Wind was an abandoned or derelict vessel; the voluntary salvors had saved it from imminent peril of going aground on a reef and being sunk as a result of a swordfish attack; and that the salvors had lost their own vessel in the process.

What and where was an admiralty court? There was little in the way of guidelines. How did one serve a complaint against a thing (in rem)? Many of the precedents in the Annotated U. S. Code were district court decisions. I had just been tried by a district court. I followed civil procedure and filed with the court clerk in the federal district of Hawaii in Honolulu.

My filing went unacknowledged. All my inquiries and subsequent pleadings met a wall of silence. I had begun the suit within the required time limits. My request to proceed in forma pauperis (as a person unable to pay the otherwise required court fees), and filed a motion for appointment of counsel. All went unheeded. Did all my paperwork go straight into Judge King's trashbasket?

After a time, seeing the writing on the wall, I let it go. The experience helped to harden my conclusion that justice through the court system was only for the rich. For the poor, there was none.

*****

Other than the fact that I was thoroughly discouraged and pissed off, my first concern was with how much time I would have to spend in prison. Putting aside all arguments as to the benefits of imprisonment, such as whether punishment deters or rehabilitation is possible, the one point that everyone can accept is that the prisoner grows older. At that point, I figured the larger half of my life was over and the all-important question was what was I going to do with the meager half?

Ambrose Bierce defined prison as a place of punishments and rewards. "The poet assures us," he says, "that stone walls do not a prison make, but a combination of the stone wall, the political parasite, and the moral instructor is no garden of sweets."

Hm, thought I, nothing for it now but to look for those rewards. I would concern myself with getting through the punishment as best I could and do everything reasonable to make it as quickly as possible. Bettencourt was appealing, but his emphasis was on reversing the theft charge, which would make not a whit of difference in my overall sentence. But if the interstate transportation charge were overturned, it would reduce my sentence to eight years. As a result, my parole eligibility would be reduced to two years and eight months. Under the law in effect, the feds had to release me after two-thirds of my sentence had been served -- unless I was a fuckup. The difference, therefore, in the maximum time I might be forced to serve was between five years, four months, and eight years, eight months.

We went round and round, me sending Bettencourt passionate letters with closely reasoned arguments concentrated upon the interstate transportation charge. I had been delving into the law books. At one point, I was threatening to have him dismissed from handling the appeal. I would, by the sacred balls of Clarence Darrow and Vincent Hallinan, take it over myself.

The justices at the Ninth Circuit Court of Appeals were annoyed at receiving differing versions of appeal briefs -- I had been throwing in the kitchen sink of admiralty laws along with everything else -- and they ordered us to settle the issue between ourselves. After a long phone conversation, the both of us shouting and cursing at each other, we finally calmed down and agreed that he would proceed. I could only hope that he would argue as strongly for my issues as his.

In 1978, the appeals court reversed the conviction on theft and affirmed the conviction on interstate transportation. Bettencourt crowed over his victory. I did not. The supreme irony was that poor innocent Steph had stole Sea Wind all on her own; I had merely abetted her to move it in interstate commerce.

###
CHAPTER 8

The days passed at McNeil Island, the weeks, the months, and the years. There were mainly three activities that kept me busy: My job in the commissary, recreation, and my involvement in the Hawaiian club.

My job took eight hours a day, five days a week. Within a year, I had worked my way up to chief clerk. I did everything from ordering to inventory, from typing letters to preparing financial statements for the government auditors, from unloading delivery trucks to stocking shelves to bagging up store orders. The perks were a desk, an IBM Selectric typewriter, access to a copying machine, and lightweight pilfering privileges from store goods. At my peak, I was also paid $75.00 per month.

The various ethnic and other clubs sponsored teams in softball, basketball, volleyball, and football, and I usually had a spot on our club team. But my favorite physical activity was playing handball, one of the most effective exercises there is for keeping in overall shape. But, more important, I enjoy the game. I have never been particularly concerned about my physical fitness. My secret is simply to engage in those naturally healthy activities that I enjoy. For instance, I have never involved myself in weight-lifting because I find it so boring.

As to the Hawaiian club, which was called by the imposing title, the Aloha Polynesian Pacific Organization, mostly called simply the Aloha Club, I served in various elective positions. I made a number of very solid and interesting friends.

Twice a year we were permitted to put on banquets, very gala affairs held in the prison auditorium. Perhaps a hundred or so outside guests were invited from Hawaii and the local Hawaiian communities. Enough food was supplied for a real feast. Groups of entertainers performed and, for a few hours, we managed to forget we were in prison. We were allowed to conduct special sales to the inmate population in order to raise funds to pay for various activities. Our specialty was various styles and colors of tee-shirts with silk-screened Hawaiian design-motifs printed on them. We had in ten to twenty outside guests at our weekly meetings. The club brought a little bit of home into our lives.

I had acquired a small reputation as a jailhouse lawyer. Out of necessity, I had filed a number of petitions with the courts in my own behalf, almost all of which came to naught, and so in my own estimation my ability didn't amount to a hill of beans. For one thing, I hated it. When you begin to research an issue, you come into intimate contact with the gobbledygook of the law, the endless court decisions you have to read in searching for precedents that might apply to the case, the reasoning processes which often seem spurious, specious, and incomprehensible. I think I would almost prefer shock treatments in an insane asylum to being a lawyer. But, when guys would ask my advice or assistance, I gave freely of what I did know and charged nary a dime.

As always, I was a rabid reader. Like Jack London said, "I, for one, never have too many books; nor can my books cover too many subjects." My hero, Captain Joshua Slocum, stated the case even more succinctly: "I had already found that it was not good to be alone, and so I made companionship with what was around me, sometimes with the universe and sometimes with my own insignificant self; but my books were always my friends, let fail all else."

My tastes were eclectic; I was interested in practically everything: Novels, serious literature, poetry, non-fiction, self-help books, philosophy, psychology, moral and ethical systems, always tales of the sea and anything about boats and their designs, magazines galore, art books and biographies of famous people, plays, writing, and even bonsai, the art of plant miniaturization. I had browsed through various occult-type books but, contrary to a few screwball ideas making the rounds, soon rejected them as so much gobbledygook. I had no fascination for the occult, nor have I ever believed, as some ignoramuses have claimed, that, except for the life I live in my imagination, I could send my spirit to roam about the world without my body in tow. I am not stupid, exactly, and sometimes even fancy myself as smart as a whip, but whether my IQ ranges past 130 makes no difference -- it has not saved me from a catalogue of griefs in my life. For a while I was something of a prolific correspondent. Other than the usual mail exchanged with family members and a few friends, I had no abiding outside interests. But I longed for contact with people, especially women. An ascetic, celibate life, such as prison forces upon a man, only develops the Zorba in him, a muted, lustful longing. Being, therefore, not far from "the sort of man who would make love to a brass idol if nothing better presented itself," as C. S. Forester put it, I undertook to acquire some female correspondents.

Among my duties in the Aloha Club, I was also responsible for putting out a newsletter. We had a thousand or so names and addresses on our mailing list, mostly in the neighboring communities and Hawaii. I made some effort to make it interesting, something people would want to read. I wrote articles, stories, and a few poems, drew illustrations and cartoons, as well as edited others' contributions. The publication contained a lonely-hearts section for the guys looking for correspondents, and I decided to run an ad for myself. With a drawing of a hand with a finger pointed at the reader, this was the text of it:

ATTENTION WOMEN! THIS IS FOR YOU!
I sing and celebrate your necessity.
Nothing is worthy without you.
Indulge my conceit:
I have mastered the art of knowing
what is possible for me by seeing the beautiful in you.
I realize the exquisite notion of your beauty
by lending the magic of belief.
My secret is in leading your virtue
to hold itself as the central focus
of my experience.
As it is true,
I have but to share the moment with you
and we will both respond with passion,
in which nothing is so subtle
as the apparent.
I demand what you love in yourself,

the form of your erotic urges.
Total surrender to your pleasure
gives me possession of you as I wish.
My personal gift is a spell:
I come with rosebuds in my eyes.

Laugh if you want, but I received dozens of letters, including one from a famous star in pornographic movies -- young women, older women, women of every size, shape, and color. I was pleased and astounded. I wrote and exchanged photos with all of them. I couldn't help myself. I was not a particularly religious man, but beneath this windfall I believed as Tom Robbins wrote in Jitterbug Perfume, "A sense of humor, properly developed, is superior to any religion so far devised." Life sometimes seemed to me to be no more than a long epileptic seizure and we are lost if we can't make a dance of it.

Otherwise, my mates in prison, of course, were all bank robbers, burglars, drug smugglers, extortionists, kidnappers, sundry scam artists, and murderers, quite a few of whom I thought were upstanding fellows. Well, what choice did I have but to associate with those I had been thrown in with and make the best of it?

*****

One day, after about a year of watching her from afar at our club meetings, I got up the nerve to approach and talk to one of our regular women visitors.

Her name was Alice Edwards. She was divorced from her common laborer husband and had three children, only the youngest of whom, an eight-year old boy, still lived at home with her. She was not beautiful, I thought, but had good though delicate features, a pretty smile and eyes, and a fine nose. She was in her late thirties, had auburn hair, weighed ninety-eight pounds sopping wet on a thin five foot frame, and she had great legs. She was one of the shyest women I had ever met. For over a year, we simply talked and joked, taking a slow path of getting to know one another.

Seeing an opportunity, I once pulled her behind a rolling blackboard and kissed her. After that we began to hold hands when we could. We began exchanging letters. She lived in nearby Tacoma. It came to a bad end, but only temporarily.

Some lowlife spoilsport dropped a snitch-note on us. It accused us of forming an improper relationship. As a result, Alice was barred from any further visits to our club meetings.

Of course I was hot to find the lying rat sonofabitch. We were a close-knit club and it was hard to believe that one of our members would do such a thing. We discussed the issue at an open meeting, where everyone had their say. I made a small speech about the value of our club lying in the cohesiveness of its members, the mutual support that benefited us all. I closed by saying, rather forcefully, that whoever the traitor was, we didn't need or want him in our club.

After the meeting was over and we were all going to our respective cellblocks, a guy named Lennie approached me in the main corridor where a lot of hacks were standing around to supervise the movement. He had his shoes and shirt off. Lennie was reputed to be an expert in some form of martial arts. He was also reputed to have murdered a girl, stuck her body in the trunk of his car, and drove around until the smell attracted the attention of the police. In a belligerent tone, he demanded to know if I was accusing him of being a snitch.

I was flabbergasted. I'd had no idea who it was -- until that very moment.

When I realized that he was the guilty party and that we were having a confrontation, I backed off and tensed myself for an attack. But I had assessed his character over the years and I'd come to two conclusions: That he wasn't half as bad as he pretended to be and that he was a coward. He had been involved in a number of altercations and so I'd had opportunity to observe him in action. I noticed he always began the fights against weaker guys by sucker-punching them. He always made his attacks in full view of the hacks, who would run to break it up and separate the combatants -- which is why he'd made his approach to me in such a public place. He could be assured that in case his victim wasn't quite the easy victory he expected, the hacks would come running to save him.

"Was you calling me a rat, man?" he demanded, his legs spread and his fists clenched.

Before answering, I stepped back through the door into the cell-house where I lived, a single-cell unit that required a year's good behavior for eligibility. The unit hack was out in the corridor chinning with his buddies. If Lennie followed me in and we got into it, there would be no one to see it or interfere but other convicts who mostly tended to mind their own business.

"What if I am, punk? What you going to do about it?"

He looked around nervously. I grinned at him.

"C'mon out here and say that!"

"Naw, you come on in here and I'll say a few other things besides." "You scared, man?"

"I ain't scared of nothing that walks, talks, creeps or crawls," I replied, maintaining my grin. "I especially ain't, scared of sissy homosexuals."

"I ain't no punk, man!"

"Well, get your scared ass in here and let's do some dirty boogie, you cute little thing, you."

He glowered, muttered, trying to make himself do it, but cowardice won. "I'll be seeing you again, motherfucker," he promised, turning to walk away. "And you better have eyes in the back of your head!"

Lennie dropped out of the club and kept his distance. I considered whether to tell the other club members about the incident, but they might expect me to do something about it. I was short to being transferred to camp and I didn't want to do anything to screw that up. I had a plan for getting Alice approved as a personal visitor. It would only be a few weeks.

Devious sonofagun that I am, I decided to investigate the creep. I began quietly asking around. I talked to a couple of guys who'd served time with him at Oahu Prison, but didn't learn much except that he'd been transferred in a prison-exchange program with the feds and had a psycho rep. Finally, I approached a convict clerk in the Captain's Office. When I told him what I wanted, he said it would cost me three cartons of cigarettes. It was money well spent. He brought me a xeroxed copy of Lennie's entire security file, thirty or forty sheets of paper. It contained copies of disciplinary reports about numerous incidents of assault. It also contained a copy of an FBI memo to the effect that Lennie was a paid informant.

The jewel was an FBI 302 report marked, Confidential -- Heads of Department Only. It detailed the fact that he had been making reports to the FBI about certain figures reputed to be involved in organized crime in Hawaii.

Since the names had all been deleted, I had to speculate over the two or three men that might fit the description, all members of our club, of course. I xeroxed several copies of the FBI memo and 302 report and bided my time. On the day I was scheduled for transfer to camp, I went around to several particular cells and tossed a manila envelope on each bunk. The envelopes contained the four pages of the FBI memo and 302 report.

Later, through the grapevine, I heard that Lennie had run sniveling to the Captain demanding to be taken into protective custody. They locked him up in segregation for six months, where he refused to return to the mainline. Then they transferred him clear across the country to another federal prison. Many years later, I would hear that He'd been killed in an altercation. He'd been up to his old tricks, sucker-punching a guy in full view of the hacks. But his victim on that occasion had managed to brain him with a weighted ashtray stand before the hacks could save him.

*****

At camp, I had been assigned to the powerhouse, which was a building separate from the camp proper by about two hundred yards, where I tended boilers for the hot water supply. Only older, more stable convicts were assigned there, so it said something about how the prison officials viewed me.

Camp life had a certain flavor. It reminded me of the TV sitcom, Hogan's Heroes. We were all engaged in various antics to stymie Colonel Klinger's lump-headed guards.

There was plenty of grass around, for which I traded homemade hooch, called pruno. One day while chopping away wild blackberry vines growing out over the roadway in front of the powerhouse, I discovered a trap door that appeared not to have been opened in a long while. It was buried beneath a couple of inches of dirt. That evening, alone on the swing shift, I stole out after the 10 p.m. count to clear it away and lift the boards covering it. There was a set of rungs leading about ten feet down into a concrete room some eight-by-eight feet square. Through it ran several sewage and water mains. It was warm enough to keep the fermentation process of pruno cooking along nicely.

I told my friend, Gerry, about it. Later, we let another friend, Ollie, a guy I'd met at camp who was married to a Hawaiian girl, in on it. We began stowing five-gallon plastic buckets of pruno in the secret room for it to cook off, which was about five days to a week putting the buckets in and taking them out only at night. This hideaway was probably the most closely guarded secret at camp. As the pruno kings of camp, we not only traded for grass, but also for flats of eggs from the poultry farm and sides of fresh-smoked bacon from the piggery. There was nothing like a joint to stimulate the taste buds for bacon and eggs washed down with a cool pint of pruno.

*****

In February, 1979, after serving my requisite one-third term, I appeared before a panel of the U. S. Parole Commission. The thing I had going for me was a good record, no disciplinary problems and good work reports. I was granted a two-year presumptive parole date for February, 1981, which meant that if I could keep my nose clean until then, I was on my way. By that time, I would have served six years and three months. For a forty-one year old man who hadn't had a piece of ass in over four years, you can imagine the tortured thoughts Alice and I had for each other. I was hornier than a Texas horny toad. In accordance with the leitmotif of Hogan's Heroes and my self-conception as a jack-of-all-trades entrepreneur, I essayed to make me a plan to solve the problem.

My first plan failed. I requested permission to not only marry Alice, but to be granted a three- day furlough in order to do so. I intended to pack several months of honeymoon into three days even if I returned a broken man. Permission to marry was granted, but the furlough was denied. I argued my case for reconsideration. How could we tell our kids we'd been married in a prison? And besides, what kind of marriage was it if it wasn't consummated?

With an evil grin, the counselor informed me that if I wanted to consummate, they served three squares a day in the mess hall.

Back to the drawing boards where, finally, I came up with an audacious plan. Ollie's wife and kids had been coming with Alice to visit and we all visited together. From little stories he'd told me, his wife was a real animal in bed. They were as horny as Alice and me.

One afternoon as we strolled off our frustrations following a visit, when I'd worked out all the details, I put it to him. "How'd you like to have a good piece of ass, Ollie?"

"Yeah, right. I ain't into mahus, (Hawaiian word for homosexuals) man."

"I'm talking genuine double-barreled, cock-open broads."

"Sure."

"I'm serious, man. Your lady for you, Alice for me."

"Aw, man, I ain't into those quickies in the visiting room. Couldn't do that."

"I'm talking two or three days, time to fuck our brains out in private."

"I'm too short to escape."

"Me, too, pal."

"Then what?"

"Jeez, I thought you'd never ask. We'll build us a boat. We'll have the girls meet us at the back side of the island. We'll ferry them over the water. We'll keep 'em here for two or three days."

"Where?"

"We'll have to find a place, make us a campsite. We can stock it up, make it comfortable. When we're off shift during the days, we can sneak up and get it on. Whattaya think?"

A look grew upon his face that was not unlike that of a Basset Hound in a wienie factory. "Jesus Jumping Christ! Think we can do it?"

"Shit. Think we can't?"

Thereafter, every day when we were off shift and there were no body counts between 8 a.m. and 4 p.m., we violated the rule about trespassing outside the camp boundaries. We found a nice spot on a heavily wooded mountain slope that dropped down to a gravel road running beside a lake. We'd snuck away a few times to go fishing there. Slowly and carefully we began constructing the campsite. We purloined tools and materials, and patiently smuggled them up to our chosen spot, careful not to leave any obvious trails. We built a platform between several trees to keep out of the wet soil caused by frequent rains, and constructed a pole framework over which to drape clear plastic sheets. We camouflage-painted it in daubs of green and brown, then affixed bits of brush to it. This was old hat to me -- it was little different from the remote marijuana camps I had set up in Hawaii.

We brought up mattresses, blankets, pillows and sheets. We converted a gasoline blowtorch into a stove for cooking and making coffee. We laboriously carried up five-gallon milkcans full of water. We added magazines for the girls to while away the hours we couldn't be there. After a time, our little love hideaway was prepared. To celebrate the grand opening, I painted a sign in foot high letters with a spray can across the length of plastic flap. It said: PUTMAN'S FORNICATORIUM -- in honor of the current warden.

But we weren't done. Next came the careful construction of the rowboat, one of my own designs. We sawed and planed and fitted and nailed and glued. It was nine feet long and four feet wide, with an athwart ship seat for the rower, a stern seat for two people, and a bow seat for one. We built it out of three-quarter's inch plywood and I hand-carved and shaped the oars myself out of 2x6 fir planks. While Ollie painted it a flat black, I conned a guy in the diesel shop to weld me up a set of oarlocks. I told him they were to be used as stingers to heat water with electricity. We christened our good ship in tiny letters: The Love Boat.

By then, we were into June and we had the problem of moving our boat about a mile to the western side of the island where the waters of Puget Sound were at their narrowest to the mainland side. It was heavy.

It would take the two of us hours with many rest-stops along the way. The problem was that after the 10 p.m. count, subsequent counts were made every two hours until 6 a.m. We thought about letting a couple more guys in on the secret. With four of us to carry it, we might be able to sneak out between counts and accomplish the mission. We decided not to. If the secret got out and the boat were found, the authorities would surely assume it was to be used for escape, the furthest thing from our minds then.

Finally, we decided on a daring venture. Atop a hill a couple of hundred yards from the powerhouse sat the dairy, with several barns, offices, and equipment sheds. They had a perfectly good tractor and trailer used for hauling hay bales. As soon as it was dark, about 6:30 or 7:00, we snuck away so as to give us three whole hours to complete the task before the 10 p.m. count.

We hitched the trailer to the tractor. When I started the engine, it made a racket like a truck without mufflers. Jumping Jehosaphat on a pogostick! I shut it off.

"You think they can hear it at the camp?"

"I dunno."

"Go and watch. I'll start it up again. If you see any heads looking up this way, we'll forget it."

"Right."

I started it up. It was all I could do to keep sitting there. I wanted to break and run. I just knew everyone in camp could hear it. I imagined a couple of hacks speeding out in a pickup to investigate.

Ollie returned. "What," I said, unable to hear him over the engine's racket.

"It looks okay," he shouted.

"Fuck it, let's do it."

He hopped aboard and I drove down the hill away from camp, picking up the lake road. Some of the hacks went back and forth from their government-provided houses along this road. Just one vehicle was all it would take. A half-mile down the road, I went through the machinations of making a U-turn, then shut off the engine. The silence was startling, only crickets and a soft murmur of wind through the trees to let us know we weren't deaf.

We had already carried the boat most of the way down the mountain slope. With a few grunts and curses, we got it down the steepest part to the road and loaded it in the trailer. I climbed back up on the driver's seat.

"Listen, if a car comes or we see anybody, we both break for the trees, make our way back to camp fast as we can."

"Got'cha."

For the next fifteen minutes, it was grim-jawed tension. We passed back up over the dairy hill, heading down the road toward the water. We caught glimpses of convicts walking the camp perimeter road, clumps of men talking and smoking, some practicing their golf strokes. Not a one looked up our way. A scant hundred yards from the T-intersection at the shore road, we stopped to unload our boat, carry it into a thick copse of woods, and cover it over with shrubs and branches and leaves.

We got the tractor and trailer back to their proper places and made our way back past the powerhouse to a dark stretch on the camp road with time to spare.

Everything was ready. By then, we were well into June, and were ready to spring the idea on the girls. Would they have the nerve for it, to invade a prison island for a few days of frenetic lovemaking? Or would it seem too dangerous and tawdry?

*****

I had been receiving some disturbing news in the meantime. My mother was ill and required an operation and my daughter was sneaking out of the house at night, hanging out with undesirables, smoking grass, and getting into trouble with the police. She was twelve years old.

When problems arise in a family, we always want to be there to help out. We believe that our mere presence, if nothing else, will somehow make a difference. I went to the camp counselor to apprise him of these problems and to ask that I be granted emergency furlough. I would journey to see my mother, hold her hand and comfort her, see that she was in good hands, even rob a bank if necessary to pay her medical bills – but, of course I did not mention that part. Then I would go further south to see my daughter. I thought that I would be able to talk some sense to her, sway her on the basis of my own experience. The last thing I wanted was for her to ever see the inside of a jail as a prisoner.

My request was peremptorily denied.

I brooded.

*****

I called Alice to send a Canadian friend of mine a message to Vancouver, B.C. Fast Eddie came immediately to stay at Alice's house. When she next came to visit, I explained my requirements. My plan to smuggle her and Ollie's wife over for a vacation from the unsympathetic rules of the U. S. Bureau of Prisons was forgotten. Alice was suddenly afraid, but she was also brave. She agreed to convey my detailed message.

I had met Fast Eddie at Halawa Jail. I had accused him of stealing his name from Paul Newman's role in The Hustler. He claimed Hollywood had stolen it from him. He had been serving a short jail term for a credit card fraud. He was quite a few years older than me, a lifelong hustler and conman. He liked to gamble and we spent many an hour trying to outplay each other. In the process, we became good friends. He had a certain rough but humorous charm. He could regale you with the most funny and outrageous stories about the scams he had run over the years. When we parted company, we'd promised to keep in touch. He didn't owe me a thing, but he was the sort that if he liked you would give you the shirt off his back. He was the kind of true friend that we rarely find in our lifetimes, one who was ready to help a buddy in any circumstance. It would, take a few days to get things together. I didn't want Alice directly involved, since it was a little out of her line, but she had to know.

In the ensuing few days, I studied the tides and phases of the moon in the local papers. I wanted a dark night and a slack tide. About this time I became aware that Pablo, another friend of mine who was a Mexican national, was planning to escape. In contradiction to his usually lazy ways, he could lately be found jogging the perimeter road. One night I caught him out of bounds as I was heading up to Putman's Fornicatorium. He was practicing swimming in the frigid waters of the lake, preparing himself for the swim across to the mainland.

"Oh, amigo," he said. "This is going to be very hard for me. I don't swim so good. But I have to go. My family needs me."

"Why, hell yeah," I said. "I know exactly what you mean. But why swim when you can ride?"

"Hah?"

So, humble and unheralded, I contributed my part for better international relations between Mexico and the United States. At the shoreline, he tossed a pair of shoes that had his prison number stamped in them. Halfway across, he threw a prison shirt and a plastic bag containing letters and photographs.

"Maybe they believe I drowned and don't come looking for me, hah?"

"Good thinking."

When he stepped out on the far shore, where a lady on a motorcycle was waiting for him, he turned to shake my hand and embraced me. "Hey, my friend, you ever get to Tijuana, you look me up."

"Maybe sooner than you think, Pablo."

"Anytime. You welcome." He turned to the lady, said something in Spanish. She turned to the saddlebags and withdrew a six-pack of Dos Equis and a liter of clear tequila. As he handed them to me, he added, "That's a very nice boat you have, compadre."

"Gracias, man. Buena suerte."

He laughed. "A focking boat! You too focking much, gringo!"

For myself, I was pleased The Love Boat hadn't sunk on her maiden voyage. I felt like a boy scout who'd just done a good deed.

* * * *

There are several stories that had made the rounds about my own escape soon after. One had it that I'd hid out on the island for three days, successfully evading bloodhounds brought in to track me down. Another had it that a luxury yacht had picked me up and there had been beautiful young ladies and champagne to welcome me. The third story was the most bizarre: I had either swum the two miles to shore or been picked up in the water by a single-engine seaplane.

In later years, a rather gullible fellow wrote to say, "Can you give me any details on your departure from McNeil Island? Apparently, you're somewhat of a legend up there. My God, Buck, isn't the Sound frigid? Was the seaplane piloted by CIA-trained dudes?"

As much as it flattered me to have such connections, the truth is more prosaic. Although The Love Boat had passed her sea trials, I decided not to use it for my own escape. Ollie would have a real problem in trying to carry the boat back to its hiding place after I'd gotten across and he rowed back. I willed him my half. If he wanted to carry though on the original plan, everything would be in place. He could choose whom he liked to let in on the secret and have someone to help him carry it back and forth to the water after I'd left.

I went to Alternate Plan B. I had found an old tractor tire inner-tube, full of holes and without a valve-stem on the air-intake. I patiently patched all the holes, stealing over to the diesel shop to blow the inner-tube up for testing with a compressed air hose. The valve stem was easy. I simply removed one from a government truck and left it with a flat tire.

I found a piece of heavy-duty plastic tarp, which I cut and wove a line through. I would wrap it around one side of the inner-tube and tie it on top to provide a bottom for a makeshift life raft-style vessel. Then I carved out a double-bladed paddle and attached it to my new boat by a line so that if I dropped it, it wouldn't be lost.

Although I actually made my escape after the 10 p.m. count on July 9, 1979, that fact would not be discovered before the 4 p.m. count the next day -- which gave me a lead time of eighteen hours. By then I would be out of Washington and well into Oregon. Ollie would place a dummy in my bunk cubicle. They were a little loose about making the counts. The general rule is that the hack making the count must see some flesh or movement, but some of them were content to see the form of a body under blankets. My cubicle had a sign that said, QUIET PLEASE. Night-Worker -- Do Not Disturb. It would excuse my not standing for the 4 p.m. count. But, alas, an alert hack would discover the pillows and blankets stuffed into my bunk to resemble a sleeping form. Still, eighteen hours was nothing to sneeze at.

Seeing Fast Eddie's signal that he was waiting on the other side, a quick flash of headlights, I launched myself, pushed out my feet against the inner wall of my raft to shape a rough prow, and began paddling. Halfway across, the skies opened up to thunder and lightning. Hey, a little Rachmaninov, what the hell? But the downpour of rain it brought was so heavy it blanked out all sight of either shore. There was no point in paddling if I couldn't see where I was going, so I drifted about for what seemed like hours. I sat and drifted and froze, thoroughly soaked, waiting for it to pass. I imagined every swish of water was made by a killer whale coming to have me for a late snack. From the yard inside the main prison, I had often enough seen schools of them cavorting about.

When at last the rain let up, I couldn't recognize any landmarks. I had drifted along with the tide, but which way, north or south? I chose a point and paddled for shore, hoping it was the right one. In the shallows, I punctured the inner-tube and held it under until all the air had been replaced with water. Once ashore, I walked to the right perhaps a half-mile. I recognized nothing except that I was on the mainland side. Where was Fast Eddie? I'd told him if I hadn't showed up by midnight, that unforeseen circumstances meant it had been called off, and that he wasn't to wait. Was it after midnight?

I turned to trudge shivering back the way I'd come, envisioning being on my own, and having to hide out. I came to a dark house with a huge tree to the side of a road that dead-ended at the water. I heard a sound. It was like the snacker of a round being jacked into the firing chamber of a gun. I dropped the bag of personal belongings I was carrying and bolted like a jackrabbit at the sudden glare of light.

"Hey, old bean," I heard a voice call. "You're going the wrong way!"

Fast Eddie was standing under the tree grinning, beside a car with the interior light on. The sound I'd hear was the doorlatch. "Sonofabitch! You scared the shit out of me!"

"Not to worry. I've got a change of clothes for you."

"What time is it?"

"After one."

"You weren't supposed to wait."

"Yeah, well, ain't you glad I did?"

"Let's get the hell out of here."

I got in the back seat and tore off my cold, wet clothes, put on dry underwear, a pair of slacks, a shirt and shoes, all new. When I'd dried and combed my hair, I bagged all the wet stuff into a plastic bag and climbed into the front.

"Welcome to the free world, ol' buddy," Fast Eddie grinned, passing me a bottle of Bombay Gin.

"Shit, man," I exclaimed after a good swig. "How'd you know I liked this stuff?"

"Your lady told me. She's waiting to meet you."

I thought about that. I wanted to see her, but it wasn't part of the plan. I didn't want her involved any more than was absolutely necessary.

"C'mon, man. She deserves a little something. I can't figure out why, but she loves your ugly ol' ass. She's a good broad, lotta heart."

"Yeah, but she's straight, man. This kind of action's a little out of her line." Over the years of our conversations, she'd told me she'd hardly ever been out of Tacoma except once to visit an aunt in Sacramento. She'd married at sixteen because she'd gotten pregnant. Her ol' man had been a drunk and often beat her. All her hopes were pinned on me, an escaped convict. "I know. She was scared shitless, but she did what she had to do. Helped me find the spot where I waited, wanted to come with me. Got guts."

"Well, hell, let's go find her so's I can pin a medal on her petite little chest."

"I think she's got a different ceremony in mind."

"Yeah, I know. So do I."

After we'd crossed a bridge into Tacoma and met her, she almost broke my neck hugging me so hard. After smothering me in kisses, she insisted on going with me. I was adamant in my refusal. We were having our first argument. She was ready to cry. What was I to do? I was helpless before a crying woman.

"All right," I begrudged. "But only for tonight. In the morning you get on a bus to come back."

"I want to go with you!"

"No! Darlin', I can't take care of you. I got no money and no ID. I'm going to have to hide out, until I can get situated. When I do, we can hook up. You have to go visit me Saturday. You have to make them believe it's all news to you when they tell you I escaped. You're going to be one of the first persons they suspect. You've got to play it off and wait it out."

She was crying.

"C'mon, babe, don't cry. Hell, we've still got the rest of the night. C'mon now."

Fast Eddie drove us by secondary roads to a small town, where he went into an old, out-of-the-way motel and registered for two rooms. I ducked down in the back seat. No use leaving any clues.

Once inside, although I was exhausted, I sipped a gin and tonic, a great improvement over pruno, and we smoked a joint. Alice had never smoked grass before I came along to corrupt her. Then I did my duty and it wasn't at all onerous. The rickety, squeaking bed collapsed on us.

A knocking came through the wall of the next room over and Fast Eddie's voice mutedly called, "Everything all right over there?"

"Oh, yeah, man! Real fine. About as fine as it gets!"

###

CHAPTER 9

The next morning I kissed Alice goodbye and put her on a bus for home. The following Saturday, as I had insisted, she would go to visit me and pretend shock and bewilderment when the prison authorities informed her of my escape. I would call her every two weeks or so, but I would not see her again for almost two months.

In the meanwhile, Fast Eddie and I continued on a course southward, following Highway 1 at Crescent City, just across the Oregon border into California, on down toward San Francisco. I detoured long enough to check on my mother. Learning that the operation on her throat was not the major surgery I'd thought, I spent a couple of days with her before continuing on into the city.

We had to lay over a few days with Janey, an old girlfriend of mine. We were next door to flat broke. Fast Eddie had practiced some chicanery with credit cards to rent the car we were driving and keep the gastank full. After renewing old memories and being regaled with a certain improved sexual expertise, I borrowed $100 from Janey, hoping it would keep us in hamburgers and cheap motel rooms until we got where we were going.

In Los Angeles, I stopped to see my ex-wife. It was late when I called, but I could hear growing excitement waking my old flame from a lonely sleep. She didn't want to rouse our daughter, but she would certainly like to see me. Okay. I would have to put off the father-daughter talk for another time -- besides the situation was improved. The worst thing was that I worried so much about her, and felt so guilty that I hadn't been much of a daddy to her -- could hardly do more than tell her how much I loved her and missed her. I vowed to return as soon as I could with presents and spend some time together.

In the meanwhile, however, my old love and I renewed our intimacy in whispers and other muted sounds as we also renewed our old pleasure in each other while Fast Eddie tried to get some shuteye in the next bed over. We'd only been able to afford one room. What the hell, me, in all this renewal, I was like Zorba resurrected.

In Phoenix, we holed up at Gerry's studio apartment. We had to take turns sleeping on the foldout sofa. Gerry had just been released on parole from a halfway house. Without a car or any money - he had to walk two miles every night to his job as manager of a franchise hamburger joint. When he would return home from work in the early morning, he would bring a sack of hamburgers and frenchfries.

I was afraid to leave the apartment. I had no ID whatsoever. All a cop had to do was ask to see a drivers license and it was all over. After a week, I remembered an old buddy and called him. He sent me a thousand dollars. I rode a bus with broken air-conditioning downtown in the sweltering heat to a Western Union office with Fast Eddie. Sink he had ID, he had to go in to get the money order. After he'd cashed it, we stopped in a cheap bar frequented by sad and silent Indians for a cold beer. On the way back to the apartment, we bought groceries and beer to stock Gerry's bare refrigerator.

There we were, the Three Musketeers, poor as church mice -- no muskets, no rapiers, not even a horse. I had never robbed a bank and had no desire to, but the question came up. Gerry had served a term for bank robbery. He had stolen millions before getting caught and sentenced to prison, but he wasn't your usual run-of-the-mill criminal. He had been straight most of his life, a wife and kids in a suburban tract home and a job as a restaurant manager. After years of hard work, he'd finally saved enough to make a down payment on his own restaurant.

For a few years, he did well, expanding into a modest chain of restaurants. Then, during a repression and hard luck, he faced bleaker times. As he neared bankruptcy, he was unsuccessful in obtaining bank loans to see him through. Unable to face losing everything, he hit upon a simple but daring remedy. He robbed a bank of several hundred thousands of dollars. He put all the money into his business and expanded once again. But something had happened to Gerry. Robbing banks was more rewarding than the humdrum life he'd been leading for so many years. He'd acquired a sudden taste for the luxuries lots of greenbacks could bring. Life was more exciting. He acquired an expensive mistress. He went to the gambling meccas and racetracks and blew tens of thousands on the dice tables and nags. Robbing banks, the way he'd figured out to do it, which was to take every dollar held in the vault itself, and the new life it brought him, was much more exciting than anything that'd ever happened to him his whole life long.

So, Gerry explained to Fast Eddie, and me in soft, reasonable tones, how we could score maybe a half million, a million bucks, who knows. It would certainly ease the strain of our dire financial situation. He was so persuasive, it was hard to say no. He had once shown me a number of newspaper clippings describing his modus operandi and, while he had employed a pistol, no one had ever gotten hurt. He took pride in that fact. But there was just no way I ever wanted to point a gun at anybody for the sake of acquiring money.

Which is not to say I never had. I had been sent to San Quentin for a $40 robbery of a gas station in which I'd been afraid to load the gun. And in subsequent years, I had foolishly engaged in a few robberies and managed to make off with reasonable sums. But I had an experience that brought it all home to me just what a truly dangerous, stupid, and wrong undertaking it was.

I had attempted to rob a drive-in theater. I had cased the place and learned that all the money from the ticket booths was transferred to the manager's office at the snack bar building. Then, when the snack bar closed, all its receipts were added to the take. All the money would be in the manager's office. All I would have to do is wave the gun about and waltz away with the loot. I expected no resistance.

There were about a half dozen teenagers who worked in the snack bar. I had come in waving my pistol and told them all to lie down on the floor. They all did – except for one pretty girl about sixteen years old. She informed me in no uncertain terms that she wasn't about to lie on any dirty floor. In fact, she was going to walk out and summon the security guards and she hoped I shot my foot off!

So ended my career as an armed bandit. I ran out of the place laughing my ass off. Whenever I thought of that girl, I thought my sister, who had been just as full of spunk. Then, I thought of my daughter. How would I feel if some thug stuck a gun in her face? This simple thought became a bedrock tenet of my moral philosophy, as imperfect as it may be. Never steal from the working stiff – it's little different from robbing your own father. Which is why I liked the grass business so much – there were no victims to complain, only willing customers. If I had to have a victim, my favorite was the U.S. Government. I know there are those aplenty who will argue that to rob the government is to rob the taxpayer, but I see it as expropriating moneys already stolen from the common citizen. Even though I might quit stealing from the government. The government will never quit stealing from the citizenry, which includes my family and friends.

Therefore, I was not against robbing a bank per se – the FDIC, a government entity, would restore all the money stolen from a bank and individual workingman would suffer a loss – only that I would not point a gun at anyone to effect a robbery.

My fine principles, however,, did not make the problem go away. Men released from prison, let alone escapees like myself, are, for the most part, cast upon the lowest rungs of society's ladder. Me, what contacts did I have? Friends in the business community who would make me a loan or offer me a decent job?

It's true enough, and certainly understandable under the circumstances, that most of my real friends have all served, or are serving, time in prison. One makes the best of a bad situation. There are no pious monks available to associate with.

One of the friends I had made along the way was Lampong, a young, uneducated, and desperately poor lad from Thailand. I had met him at Halawa Jail. He and an older man, a Thai schoolteacher, had been arrested at Honolulu airport. They had each been strapped down with a kilo of pure Asian heroin. Lampong was no more than a mule, a courier trying to make some money to help support his family. He had never dealt or used any form of narcotics. He was paid simply for the dangerous business of delivering a package. He had never before been out of his own country. He spoke not a word of English.

Because he was slightly built and handsome to the point of prettiness, a couple of predatory types wanted to make him into a jail-house punk. I intervened and took both Lampong and his friend under my wing. I gave them chores to do so that they could earn a little money for necessities. They cleaned the jail tank and I taught them how to make coffee in metal bowls swung over toilet-paper donuts used for fuel. When I left Halawa for McNeil Island, I left them under the protection of a couple of friends, one of whom was Fast Eddie. Later, when they both showed up at McNeil, each had a five-year sentence. I gave them cigarettes, coffee, toiletries, and helped them get situated. Then I had them inducted into our Aloha Club, which therefore placed them under the aegis of our protection.

We had mostly communicated through sign-language and gestures. I had taught them a few English words. I also supplied the schoolteacher with a copy of a Thai-English Dictionary so they could get started learning a new language. Three years later, Lampong wound up as a tender on the poultry farm at the prison camp with me.

He was my egg connection. He was due to be released before I escaped, subject to immediate deportation. By then, he'd made great strides in his command of English and I used to sit and talk with him about his life in Thailand. He didn't have much to look forward to. Compared to some countries, Americans know nothing of truly abject poverty. The income of one welfare recipient in this country would take care of his entire family and he had a large one. When I asked him what he would do upon his return to his homeland, he sighed, shrugged, and opined as how he would have to go to the big city of Bangkok and involve himself in criminal activities.

Yes, of course you can see my mind was clicking. I was the man with a plan, and I had one working, but one that was still a few months away before I could bring it to the fruition of providing a regular monthly income.

But first things first. In the meantime, except for the $1000 I had borrowed, we three would-be musketeers still had our dire straits to deal with. It seemed my fortunes, unbeknownst to me at the time, were on the upswing.

The last time I had called Alice, she'd told me she was selling her house, which she owned free and clear as part of her divorce settlement. She couldn't wait any longer to be with me. I had kept putting her off, pleading a bad situation. Never mind, she would soon have enough money for both of us. When I cautiously inquired how much she expected to get from her house, she mentioned a sum over thirty thousand dollars. I didn't trust myself. "Bring only ten grand," I told her, but "What about your son?" It wasn't a good idea to get a kid involved.

"I'm leaving him with my ex-husband. I'll come back to visit as often as I can. Maybe he can come to stay with us later."

"You sure?"

"I'm sure."

She showed up in September with the ten grand, which she promptly gave to me. Well oh well. In addition to settling up my debts and spreading a little of my wealth to my friends, I bought a used pickup and an overhead camper. But the greatest benefit was yet to come. She provided me with her ex-husband's social security number, along with all the information I needed to acquire his birth certificate. I assumed his name, got me an Arizona driver's license and, in effect, became her husband.

With a few thousand dollars left over, we went on our long delayed honeymoon. For a month we traveled through Arizona to the Grand Canyon, then to Mount Zion National Park in Utah, and on to Death Valley in California, all by secondary roads. We camped out and cooked over an open fire. One night at a campground, we were startled to hear people cheering, whistling, and clapping their hands right in the midst of our trying desperately to make up for all the years of sexual frustration. Amused campers nearby had added their humorous approval -- our whole pickup had been rocking and rolling on its tender springs.

*****

You might think a guy in my situation, what with all the connections I'm reputed to have, would have no trouble at all acquiring phony ID. I had always heard talk in prison that for a couple of hundred bucks you could get a complete set made to order -- if you knew your way around. I had called around inquiring and got exactly nowhere. Well, I thought, if an enterprising mug like myself, for instance, could fill this gap he could make a nice piece of change -- what with knowing a few mugs who knew mugs who knew mugs and etc. Plus, it would be a great benefit to me, too.

So, I began to mull the problem over, to do some research, and try to figure out just what the requirements were for producing a good set of ID -- good enough to pass muster through the computers hooked into police cars nowadays. You get stopped by a cop for a traffic violation, he runs your drivers license through the National Driver Register (NDR) to check if your license is genuine. The NDR computer contains information on all the drivers licenses issued in the United States. It also contains outstanding warrants for unpaid traffic tickets. If the cop is the least suspicious, he may also query the National Crime Information Center (NCIC) to check for criminal records and warrants. They could also check your social security number to make sure it was actually issued to the name that's on the card.

What was required, therefore, was a set of documents that not only appeared genuine on their face, but would also come away clean on all the computer checks. Not an easy problem, but if you were properly motivated and had the ability to think the problem through every step of the way, the several methods to skin the cat would soon reveal themselves.

I had sent away for a number of semi-underground books that dealt with all aspects of the matter, including the more or less well-known publication, The Paper Trip, along with its several manifestations, written by an enterprising fellow. I went to public libraries to supplement my research. I bought some cheap equipment, a $20 Polaroid camera, a drawing board, some drafting tools, some paper stock, and numerous plastic sheets of press-on letters and numbers. Later, when my new sideline business would begin to pay for itself, I would acquire more sophisticated equipment. The end result was that I could provide a complete set of good, clean ID that would withstand all computer checks. All I needed from a customer was his photo, which for an extra fee I would myself provide.

As for myself, in order to combat the constant paranoia I felt as an escaped federal prisoner, at one time I had about thirty wallets, each of which contained a full set of good, clean ID, including credit cards. I could go in the door as John Doe and come out as Joe Blow. But mainly, I existed as Alice Edwards' husband. And I made $200 here, $300 there, sometimes $500 around the corner, selling ID to others in need.

By now, what with all my confessions here, you're probably telling yourself that I'm nothing more than a crook, a dyed-in-the-wool criminal, and that's true.

According to the law, that's what I was. But, like Rod Steiger once said in a movie, that doesn't make me a bad guy, does it? At the time, I had little choice. I suppose it could be argued that I've had little choice for most of my life, that once you've been relegated to the nether regions of society, there is no other way to rise out of your poverty, no other way to provide a decent living for yourself and your family -- but I won't. I'm responsible for my own behavior. I'll ride the beef. What have I got to lose at this point? On the other hand, I wasn't going around robbing my fellow citizens. I wasn't stealing from them, assaulting them, or murdering them for the sake of a few bucks. I've been called a violence-prone predator enough times to know the full meaning of the lie and I resent the insult, the unsubstantiated hollowness of the charge. I am what I am, but I'm not a cannibal -- I'd rather starve first.

*****

There are two basic kinds of criminal offenses, which law professors call malum en se (wrong in themselves) and malum prohibitum (wrong only because they are prohibited). The difference is this: The first, malum en se, constitute true crimes, those that involve morally reprehensible behavior and evil intentions, such as robbery, rape, assault, arson, and murder. We don't need anyone to tell us these acts are immoral and wrong.

For the second, however, malum prohibitum, which are variously called public welfare offenses, civil offenses, quasi-crimes, or regulatory offenses, we cannot tell whether these offenses are wrong unless we have a law that tells us so. They are not true crimes. There is no immorality to be attached to such offenses as, smoking grass (or for that matter, manufacturing, using, and dealing any other type of drug, as much as politicians and law enforcement types give us opera to the contrary), not paying taxes, and ignoring parking tickets. Doing or not doing acts in this category do not involve evil intentions, and since it's very difficult to find a true victim or a complaining party in these offenses, they are not wrong in themselves.

The most infamous example is the case of prohibition. One day it was perfectly legal to manufacture, sell, and imbibe whiskey and other alcoholic spirits. The next day, after the Volstead Act went into effect, all these things were illegal. Then, so many years later, when the act had been repealed, it was suddenly legal again. The problem was that making alcohol illegal created a black market, and thus the value of whisky and other spirits rose. There was a large public demand that repudiated the rightness of the law. As a consequence, organized crime elements burgeoned and grew fat on the profits, the effects of which we are still feeling after over seventy years.

The same may be said of criminalizing drug use. The problem, as well as the cost to the nation, has only grown since. Maybe one day we'll wise up and repeal all the drug laws, too, but I doubt it. The so-called war-on-drugs is so firmly entrenched in our state and national police bureaucracies that it is not in their interests to either win or end the war.

For myself, as a self-confessed criminal, I have to say that I favor crimes in the malum prohibitum category. (My thanks to Bugliosi for supplying the Latin terms. I stole them from his book, Drugs in America, a theft, by the way, that does not even reach the level of malum prohibitum. You might also want to note that, among other remedies he proposes for winning the war on drugs, he too advocates legalization – that is, after his first remedy to invade Columbia, murder or capture all the big traffickers and try them in specially constituted courts with life imprisonment or a death penalty in store, has failed. And it will fail because whenever big money is to be made in drugs, there is an endless line of would-be successors)

By October, we were back in the city, having rented ourselves some pleasant digs in an apartment complex. Our lifestyle was modest. I had never been particularly greedy, nor had I ever been rich -- if there is any connection between the two. But I had, from the point of view of relative poverty, rolled in dollars a few times in my life. Now, though, when I looked at my poke, I became alarmed at the rate of its Diminishment.

What would I do to keep the rent paid, the groceries on the table, when it ran out?

I considered whether I might have to get a job and work for a living, what that job might be. I'd done many kinds of work in my life and I wasn't afraid of it. Alice had never done a day's work in her life outside the drudgery of being a housewife and mother. Perhaps if we both worked, as frycook and waitress for example, we could make ends meet. I tried not to think about the $20,000 Alice still had coming from the sale of her house. After all, I wasn't a gigolo, who preyed on lonely women, was I?

Of course I did have my deal in the works to set up an import/export business with Lampong. He would export; I would import. Our product? Stone cold killer Thai sticks. After first going down and renting several private mailboxes at commercial post offices, I had written to Lampong, providing him with all the box numbers. He had told me that very high quality Thai grass was dirt-cheap in his country. I would pay him $500 for a kilo of grass that had cost him $10. In turn, I would sell it for about $1500 per pound, thus realizing a profit of $2500 on each kilo, plus I would have a few ounces left over for my friends and myself. He would send the grass through the regular mails, disguised of course, in kilo lots, and I would send him dolls and teddy bears stuffed with hundred dollar bills. Once we got the operation off the ground, Lampong would send me two kilos per month for the ensuing eighteen months, which would constitute a nice bit of regular income. The results of my initial labors in this area, however, had not quite yet begun to pay off.

In the meantime I worried, and while I awaited the first package from Lampong, mulling over the vile question of seeking tedious work at low pay, Lady Luck decided to pay me a visit.

One night, while making my way home from a visit with Gerry, I happened to pass a federal building. It was a late hour and the streets were deserted. While waiting for a red light to turn green, I idly watched a fellow emerge from this federal building carrying a duffle bag, which he deposited beside a mailbox on the corner. Then he went back inside. Hm. I cruised around the block and made another pass. No one around. I put my pickup in park, slid across the seat, opened the passenger door, reached out, pulled the bag inside, and drove away checking the large rearview mirrors to each side to see if anyone might have noticed.

In the parking lot before going in to crawl into bed with Alice, I went back into the overhead camper, lit a lamp, and dumped out the bag to see what I had. Well, well, weren't the feds busy with their mails? I began to open them. It was mostly uninteresting stuff, but there were some U. S. Treasury checks in a few of them. Ah, indeed, interesting. There was one for $25,000. A couple of hours later, when I had finished up, I'd decided to keep that one check. The next morning, I went to work with a stapler to seal up all the opened envelopes, then I drove to the nearest mailbox and deposited the bag beside it.

God must love me, even me, down amongst the least of His creatures, so fretful and needy. Else why would He send me 25 grand and direct me to the very spot He'd left it? Thanks be, I was not beyond redemption.

I made me up a fine-looking drivers license in the name that was printed on the check and drove to the nearest bank to open an account. I showed the lady my license and reeled off a fictitious social security number for the application. I deposited the check and waited for it to clear. The beauty of it was that it was a genuine check and nobody knew I had it, not even Alice. Of course, in time someone would become concerned when it didn't arrive as expected, but by then I would be long gone.

When it was discovered to have been cashed by a party other than the payee, some scoundrel who had forged his name, I knew the government would make it good to him.

Three days later, after I'd called the bank to inquire of my balance, I went down to transform it into handheld greenbacks. Rather than simply ask the teller to count the entire amount out in hundred dollar bills, which might seem a little suspicious and require filling out a government-mandated report for transactions over ten thousand dollars, I asked for several cashier's checks. They were as good as gold. I left a thousand in the account to allay any suspicion about opening and closing an account in three days. Then I drove to the next nearest banks along the way, cashing one check at each. Easy as pie. Present the check and ID to the teller, who calls the issuing bank and, voila, counts out thousands of dollars into my hot hands.

"Vegas, here I come," I told them with a smile.

The glove compartment was full of money. Before going home, I stuffed it all in a bag. I told Alice to sit down and close her eyes, that I had a surprise for her. I dumped the bag of money over her head, scattering bills all over the floor and her lap. I thereupon learned that money is an aphrodisiac.

But I hated having to leave that thousand dollars behind in the account. What had the government ever done for me? Oh well, at least we had enough to buy a TV and a stereo, maybe some new clothes, perhaps even a car so Alice could go shopping on her own. She was afraid to drive the pickup.

Hm, TV and stereo, no wonder I love my brain. It sometimes let me down, led me into trouble, but it was also all I had as a tool for survival. The more it knew, the better it functioned. Lately, it had been running on all eight cylinders. It told me how to get that thousand dollars.

I wasn't about to return to the bank for it, even though I thought it was too soon for a crime to have been discovered. But I did have a checkbook. I went to an electronics store and bought a TV and a stereo setup. The bill was just under a thousand dollars, which I had carefully calculated. I wrote out a check. The salesman called the bank it was issued on to verify I wasn't dropping a bum check on him. No problem.

But Lady Luck had already left for parts unknown. The salesman sent me around to the loading dock to receive the equipment nicely packaged in factory boxes. While the boy loaded them into the pickup, I scribbled a signature on the receipt. At the entrance to the street from the parking lot, thank God for my training as a driving instructor, I looked back in my rearview mirror and saw a horrible sight. The kid on the loading dock was writing down the pickup's license plate number!

I worried all the day, cursing myself for a fool. I'd better get out and sell the pickup while I could. Soon, it would be too hot to drive. I'd better begin the process of getting new ID together.

But, aha, you sly ol' brain, you! It came up with a cure for the problem. I rushed back to the store, gave them a hard luck story about having to leave town in an emergency, and told them I wanted to redeem my check for cash. Unthinkingly, I had withdrawn all the money in my account, but luckily I'd remembered my check. Being a conscientious citizen, I didn't want it to bounce.

"Very thoughtful of you, sir."

"Thank God for that," I agreed.

"We appreciate it."

"Don't mention it. After all, my reputation was at stake."

*****

It wasn't a week later that I got to see myself as a star on an evening show -- on the very TV set I'd purchased with purloined government dollars. Alice and I had been sitting back on the sofa, having just polished off a pizza with beer. As I was concentrating on planting a string of wet kisses up her neck, the show interrupted to demand my full attention.

It was a cop show, the local version of rat on a rat. It seems there are hidden cameras in banks that take pictures every sixty seconds whether a crime is being committed or not. There I was, in perfectly clear stills, shown smilingly accepting the cashier's checks.

"This crime was committed by a clever professional," the earnest narrator announced, which I took as a compliment.

After several more photos displayed a guy almost as handsome as Clark Gable, my trusty ol' brain experienced a convolution that was not unlike the epileptic seizure of a wino in the throes of delirium tremens. Viewers were urged to call a local snitch number to report whether they might recognize me or could provide any information on my whereabouts.

Great Googly-Moogly! I had managed to drive myself from a very nice city that I was growing very fond of. We hurriedly packed up our still meager belongings and slipped out of town that very night. Las Vegas, here we come after all. Do not crap where you live, the old saw has it. For the next eight months, the citizens and police of that glitter city, as well as the entire great state of Nevada, may be glad to know that I never committed a single crime there, unless trying to make yourself invisible was against the law.

*****

I had been missing my mother and daughter, although I had journeyed out into northern and southern California several times for brief, surreptitious visits. Visiting family and friends is where the most danger lies for a fugitive -- it's right up there with having no ID.

I had broached the subject with my ex-wife about having my daughter spend her summer vacation with me. She was against it for the very good reason that I was a fugitive. How would it be if I were to be arrested while in her company? While it was a good argument, it didn't relieve my need. I pointed out that it would also give her greater freedom to follow her own pursuits.

She would save on the expense of raising a child. Plus, I assured her, I was ensconced into a safe situation. Why, I wasn't even committing any crimes, scout's honor. No one even knew where I was.

Well...maybe she'd consider it if she was included in on the deal. She could use an all-expenses-paid vacation herself. Ah me, what was I to do, tell Alice, hey, babe, what do you say to separate vacations? I want to go off with my ex-dragon and our lovechild for a couple of months. Well, no, I guess not, I told the ex. Here's some money to help out. I'd have to stick to the sneaky-brief visits when circumstances permitted.

Aha and ahum and kiss my blisters, when next I talked to my mother over the phone, she told me my daughter was coming to spend the summer with her. "Mom," sez I, quick to grasp an opportunity. "How would you like an all-expenses-paid vacation?"

*****

When the time came, I called Fast Eddie. He had returned to British Columbia. I'd sent him some money.

"How you doing, ol' buddy?"

"Hard times. I hope you're not calling from jail."

"Nah, I'm doing okay."

"How's Alice? You still with her?"

"Yeah, fine. How'd you like to make a few grand?"

"How many's a few?"

"Three."

"Who I gotta kill?"

"Nobody. This is easy money. All you got to do is drive."

"What, a getaway car? You doing a job?"

"No, it's personal business."

"Gimme the skinny."

I told him. All he had to do was play backup to insure that my mother and daughter were safely delivered for their vacations. I would donate the entire proceeds from one of Lampong's grass packages.

The danger was this: If my mother was under federal surveillance when we met, that would be the end of the ballgame. The feds, of course, could not afford to keep her under 24-hour surveillance all the time, not for some small fry like me. But what they did do was send a couple of agents out from time to time to ask questions of the neighbors. The trick, if they happened to be around, was to know it and then...well, trick them.

I called my mom and told her to pack up and meet me at the Reno airport, only a few hours drive from where she lived in northern California. What she didn't know was that when she and my daughter began the trip, Fast Eddie and I, in two separate cars with CB radios were there to play the musical chairs of vehicular surveillance as cadged right out of the FBI manual. We kept trading places so no suspiciously interested parties would make us.

By the time my mother had pulled into a truck stop for gas and cold drinks up the road, sure enough, we had made two guys dressed like used car salesmen driving a drab sedan similar to those favored by the feds. Well, what could we do to make sure they weren't really used car salesmen? Go over and ask them for some ID?

No, but if they followed my mother along her exact route, right to the airport parking lot as I'd directed her, the wild coincidence would serve well enough to make a prima facie case to the contrary.

As we got closer and closer to Reno, the car maintained its pace a constant distance behind my mother's car. I radioed Fast Eddie to pass and catch up with me. We sped ahead in order to give us a few minutes to consult in private.

"What do you think?"

"Cops," Fast Eddie said.

"How do you know?"

"There's a stockyard smell in the air."

"Okay. Here's how we play it..."

As we came into Reno, I went on ahead to enter the airport parking lot. I put in my money, got a ticket from the machine, which caused a bar across the entrance to rise. I parked where I would have a good view of the entrance. In a few minutes I saw my mother's car stop at the ticket machine. The bar raised and she drove in. Directly behind her was Fast Eddie. At the ticket machine, with his car blocking the entrance, he stalled the engine. Directly behind him was the suspicious car that may or may not have contained used car salesmen.

I'd seen where my mother had gone to park, out of sight of the entrance. It was a big parking lot. I drove over a back lane to meet her.

"Hi, mom," I called. "Thought I'd meet you here and we could drive down and take in the scenery rather than flying. C'mon, I'll load your suitcases."

Mom and daughter may have wondered, so quickly did I have them seated in my car, what the hurry was. I was keeping a worried eye on the entrance to the parking lot.

Fast Eddie had the hood of his car raised, scratching his head. One of the salesmen was looking under the hood with him while the other was standing aside peering out over the cars in the lot. I drove out the exit.

At the nearest bar, I ordered a gin and tonic for myself, a Seagram's seven and soda for my mom, and a Shirley Temple for my daughter.

"What's the big rush," my perceptive young daughter asked.

"Ah, babe, I just needed to wet my whistle," I said. "It's hot out there. From here on we take it slow and easy and have some fun."

I drove to meet Alice at a hotel, introduced her, and left them to get acquainted while I went out to settle up with Fast Eddie. "They were cops, man. I know they were cops."

"What happened?"

"Nothing. After a while I got the car started, drove on in and parked."

"What'd they do?"

"Same thing. But they nosed around. I think they spotted your mom's car."

"That's okay. What then?"

"They went into the terminal. I sat around checking my watch and studying the boards, like I was waiting for a plane, you know?" "Yeah, good."

"They were going from counter to counter, probably asking about an old lady and a kid."

I laughed.

"They might stake out your mom's car."

"They got a long wait. What do you want to do?

I'm leaving in the morning."

"Ah, dinner, a few drinks, maybe try my luck at one of these clip-joints, head on out tomorrow myself."

"You take care, pal. Let's keep in touch."

"Oh, hell yeah. Easiest three grand I ever made. Call me anytime."

*****

Back in Vegas, I was having the time of my life. Alice was a hit with my mom and daughter. We took them out to nice restaurants, caught a few shows along the Strip, went out in the old pickup camper to spend the Fourth of July at Lake Mead. We took along a box of fireworks, fished, swam, and got sunburnt. I took my daughter shopping, bought her clothes and ice cream cones. She said she needed glasses and I bought her several pairs in different designer frames. It felt so damn good to play daddy to her.

I knew Alice missed her kids, especially her youngest. She had been up to Tacoma a time or two to visit them. She told me her daughter had asked if she had been staying in Arizona. She'd noticed the state tax stamps on the cigarettes Alice smoked. By such little things, I thought. You had to be paranoid even in the seemingly inconsequential stuff.

God, I thought, if I just had enough money to coast for a good long while, I would be tempted to take my daughter and Alice's son and go off somewhere and be a family. What a temptation! What a long old sense of longing and loss that fantasy engendered! I wasn't sure I was good daddy and husband material, but that made no difference to the ache I felt.

When it was over at last, we drove back to Reno with a stopover at Lake Tahoe. I had a friend living there, recently released from McNeil. After hooking my mom up with her car and saying goodbye, giving my daughter some Ben Franklins as a parting gift, Alice and I spent a few days with my friend, Patrick, and his lady in a cabin a short walk from the lakeshore.

*****

Through Patrick, I met a fellow that didn't know his ass from grass. He was an overgrown kid who'd inherited nineteen million dollars and had doubtless been deeply impressed by Francis Ford Coppola's classic movie saga, The Godfather. He thought there was some glamour playing the role and had retained a coterie of true amateurs as his supporting cast. He paid them a couple of hundred a week to hang around and honor him until such time as he sent them off on missions to buy and sell drugs. He was an abject failure in the business. Unlike the movie, his minions felt no loyalty at all -they were ripping him off left and right.

But it turned out he was sitting on two hundred kilos of bunk Columbian, for which he'd paid $500 a key and couldn't sell. I prevailed upon Patrick to show me. Maybe we could do some business. We went out to the storage place, a garage, and I sampled the stuff. Cheap shit. Patrick told me the guy had managed to sell twenty-five pounds at $200 per. At that rate, the guy wouldn't even break even. He also had two kilos of raw opium. Who knew from opium, Patrick told me. They couldn't hardly give the stuff away.

Me, I was figuring. In Hawaii, when I was in the grass business, I had once pulled off a cute little deal. I had learned, from a book in my grass library, how to make hashish, which is basically a concentrated and more potent form of grass. I had processed down about ten pounds

of primo cannabis into a black mud-like substance. I had shaped it into three-inch round cookies. Before the final process of drying them into hard biscuits, I had folded a matchbook cover around to use in stamping an oriental-appearing symbol on top of each. Then, to further dress them up, I had gone out and bought a bunch of Teruki brand rice cakes, which were imported from Japan. The only writing in English was the word Teruki, the rest being imprinted in Japanese characters. All I wanted were the cellophane wrappers. After carefully unwrapping the rice cakes, I folded and glued the wrappers around my little hash cookies. As a lark, I was injecting a bit of Madison Avenue into the grass business.

I mailed about two pounds of them to San Francisco, and then caught a commercial flight over behind them. When I'd picked them up, I took them to a grass and hash dealer I knew who lived on a houseboat in Sausalito.

"Hey, my man, " I said to him without uttering a word as to their origin. "What do you think about these little goodies?"

His eyes widened. He studied one of the cellophane packages "Teruki?"

I shrugged.

"Is this what I think it is?"

"What do you think it is?"

"Wait a minute. Let me test this stuff."

He tore the cellophane off one, broke the cookie and sniffed judiciously. "Oh, damn, smells good."

He broke off a tiny crumb and tasted it, closing his eyes. "Tastes good. I gotta smoke some of this."

He loaded a small pipe, toked a couple of times and passed it to me. When it was gone and we were both a bit glassy-eyed, I said, "Well?"

"You want a beer?"

"Sure, man, that'd go good."

When he'd served us and settled down, he asked, "Where you get this shit?"

"Aw, you know, just sort of fell into it. Pretty good, though, huh?"

"Oh, this is dynomite shit, no question." He grinned at me, preparing to enlighten the ignorant. "This, my man," he began with some glee. "Is Nepalese Temple Hash."

"No shit?"

"No shit. That symbol on the top?"

"Yeah?"

"That's the official temple stamp of the lamasery. The monks, high in the remotest regions of Nepal, cultivate and shape the stuff by hand. They're Buddhists, you know."

"Buddhists?"

"Yeah, they're poor, you know. They take vows, go around begging for food."

"Yeah?"

"Yeah, but still...they need money, right?" "Right."

"So they make this stuff for export. B-52 bomber pilots, stationed in Vietnam, Thailand, Asia, you know, they used to smuggle it back. Haven't seen any around for a few years."

"I wonder what Teruki means?"

"Probably a holy word."

"Yeah?"

"I want it, man. I'll buy all of it. I got a special clientele for stuff of this quality. I'll pay top dollar."

We made an easy deal. It wasn't really a money thing with me. It was an excuse to get over to the mainland to visit friends, to get out on my own and boogie a little. I'd left Stephanie at home to do her own boogying.

A week later, I was at a party. People were drinking, passing around joints, and the occasional line of coke was going up certain nostrils. This one guy, laden with gold chains and expensive clothes, began to grandstand. He pulled out a package of Teruki -- for connoisseurs only, please. He recounted the story of the Nepalese monks and the B-52 bomber pilots to a goggling audience full of ohs and ahs. No shit?

Really?

Wow!

*****

    I offered to buy fifty kilos at $400 per from the would-be godfather, but only if he agreed to throw in the two keys of opium. After a bit of showboating, he accepted. Forking over twenty grand to him, Paul and I loaded the fifty keys plus two into my pickup camper. Leaving Alice and Patrick's lady to guard the stuff, we hopped in his car for a quick trip to Reno.

    "What's up?"

    "My boy," sez I, turning my best imitation of W. C. Fields on him. "I'm gonna show you how to make a silk purse out of a sow's ear."

    In Reno, I go to the Yellow Pages, looking for Restaurant/Bakery and fiberglass supplies. I purchase several large metal dough bowls, which are about three feet wide and eighteen inches deep. I also buy several deep batter pots used in industrial-size dough-mixers. I buy a couple of wooden stirring paddles, a couple of blenders, some rubber gloves. At the fiberglass store, I purchase a ten-by-ten foot square of plastic tarp and fifty gallons of acetone.

    Back at the lake, Patrick's ol' lady donates a couple of bed sheets, which I forgot.

    I give them the skinny and divide the labor. We've got work to do. While Patrick and I break open the paper-wrapped grass packages and heap them on the tarp, the girls begin macerating it in the blenders and dumping the finely chopped debris into the pots and bowls. I have Patrick pour acetone in over the grass and begin stirring with a paddle. We have to open all the windows and get a couple of fans going. The smell of acetone is overpowering. Luckily, the cabin is isolated.

    I unwrap the two keys of opium and crumble them into a separate pot and liquidize it by adding acetone. Fifty kilos of grass works out to a hundred and ten pounds. The opium translates into almost four and a half pounds.

    After soaking and stirring the smelly brew of grass and acetone for an hour, we drape a sheet over an empty bowl and heft our potions to pour over it and strain out the grass debris, which we dump on the plastic tarp. After we've done the whole caboodle in a like manner, we are left with a dark brown liquid. To this I pour in the opium liquid, distributing it equally among the pots and bowls. Then I separate out about half of the debris and add that back into our brew pots. We stir again. Then, because we all have headaches from the acetone fumes, we repair to the pickup camper to relax and have a beer.

    Okay, what in hell are we doing? We are making, out of one hundred and ten pounds of grass, fifty-five pounds of hashish that is eight percent opium. The grass, now doubled in potency and with the opium kicker, ought to provide a decent smoke, with certain soporific qualities due to the opium, when we are done.

    After the acetone is almost evaporated, which it does fairly quickly, we will all don rubber gloves smeared with cooking oil and shape and pat out little cakes of the stuff, each of which will weigh roughly a pound -- round, square, oblong cakes, even heart shapes, what the hell, be creative. In the meantime, I am straightening out a wire coat hanger and reshaping one end to my own peculiar design with a pair of pliers. It is a stamping device that resembles a branding iron. In the final state, while the cakes are still damp, I will impress our trademark on the top of each cake. When the acetone has totally evaporated two days later, we have dark, gritty cakes with what appears to be an oriental symbol impressed on each. We place each cake in its own seal-lock bag. Voila! Temple hash containing a lamasery stamp by the Buddhist monks who have made it with their own sanctified mitts. What is the sound of one hand clapping?

    Out in Sausalito, I tell Patrick to let me handle the negotiations. My man is happy to see me. It's been awhile. He breaks out some Lebanese hash for us to smoke, but I tell him no, not yet. I want him to sample some stuff I've brought. I show him the cake. He gets excited.

"You sonofabitch! Where you getting this shit? What is it, some more of that temple hash again?"

"What do you think?"

"It's got the lamasery stamp, man. Jeez, I remember that Teruki shit you brought one time. Best fucking shit! And those Golden Buddha Sticks! Fucking primo! And that Bengali Beep! Oh, shit, man, you know I ain't seen nothing like that before or since?"

He goes into his ritual, first smelling it. "Oh man, what is this bouquet? It has that delicate pungency...but something else, reminiscent of...I want to say vanilla. I don't think I've come across this particular bouquet before."

He tastes it, chewing a piece, rolling it around in his mouth, savoring it, smacks his lips approvingly. He breaks out a pipe, lights a piece, inhales.

"Oh, say, rather mellow. Not harsh at all...just a bit of bite.

Well, let's see..." he mutters, toking away, drawing it deep into his lungs.

"What do you think?"

"Say, you guys want a beer?" He's sighing, speaking slowly and carefully, very relaxed. "Really mellow, laidback shit, my man, puts a buzz in your bones. What the fuck is it? Where you getting all this exotic stuff?"

I smile. "Hey, my lips are sealed. You're the expert. What do you think? Does it originate in Tibet or Nepal? Maybe Afghanistan? Definitely not Lebanese."

"No, no, hmmm."

"Turkey? Hm? No. Pakistan? India?"

"Has to be remote. The temple stamp. Probably Nepal, but maybe, just maybe, Tibet. They're neighboring countries, you know."

"Yeah?"

"Yeah, I think maybe Tibetan. I'm pretty sure. Yeah."

"I knew I came to the right guy, you bad motherfucker, you!"

"Hey, don't forget how many years I been in the business. Educated palate, all that, y'know?"

I marvel. "So what are you offering? One time shot, a little better than fifty pounds. I'm in a hurry to get on down the road."

"All like this?"

"The very same. I'm not gonna bend your ear the trouble I went through to deliver this stuff to your door."

"$700."

"I was thinking more like a grand." "Hey, it's good shit. Don't get me wrong. But we're talking quantity here, y'now? A little adjustment. $750."

"Just to shorten the haggling, I'll take $900."

"$775."

"$850."

"$800."

"Ah, what the hell. You're a good customer. Eight and a quarter, it's a deal. Round it out to the nearest thousand."

"Right on. Shake, pal."

We clasp hands, pump. We are both happy.

"When?"

"About three hours," he replies. "I gotta go out."

"Okay. We'll unload. You got a scale?"

"Superman got a cape?"

When he returns, we weigh it out. A little over fifty-five pounds. I'll keep the few ounces over for personal stash. He counts out forty-five grand.

"It's been great, man, but we gotta hit the road."

"I love ya, man, don't be a stranger."

As we are trucking on into San Francisco to look for a fine restaurant in which to celebrate, Patrick turns to me. "Teruki? Buddha Sticks? Bengali Beep, for chrissakes? D'ju make all that shit in the kitchen, too?"

"Old family recipes, my boy, legend in my own time, all that." I give Patrick five grand to split with his lady. Alice and I come out near twenty grand ahead, minus overhead -- not bad for a few days work. Patrick's ol lady is so grateful, she wants to strap a piece of ass on me. Patrick doesn't mind. Hell, he'll take care of Alice for me on the side. It is tempting, but I don't think Alice has reached that level of feminine liberation. We party for a few days, drop Patrick and his lady back in Tahoe, and head south for Vegas.

*****

Not long after, we had gone to the Western Union Office to collect a $5000 wire order, the repayment of a loan to a friend. Alice went in to get it while I waited out in the car. I noticed a couple of guys inside looking her over. When she came out, she said the lady inside had told her there'd be no trouble cashing it at the casino across the street. I drove across into the parking lot and we went inside. I noticed three men standing in front of the Western Union office looking over our way.

When Alice had cashed it and we were on our way back to the car, I felt an arm go around my neck and pull me backwards. Another guy stood in front of me wielding an icepick. The third guy was making a grab for Alice's purse, a heavy leather bag with a shoulder strap. She resisted, jerked the bag back and swung it around to slam the guy right on his ear. He went down. Alice carried, in addition to the five grand in cash and all the normal junk a woman needs, about ten rolls of quarter in her purse for me to make phone calls from a pay-booth. I was so paranoid I wouldn't have a phone in our apartment. I knew that sooner or later I'd be tempted to give the number out to a few friends.

The best policy during a robbery is just to cooperate and let the money go and hope you come away with your life intact. Sweet, timid little Alice, all ninety-eight pounds of her, had a different idea. Being a gentleman at heart, how could I let her fight the battle alone?

I stomped on the foot of the guy holding me. I was wearing cowboy boots. I swung an elbow back into his ribs. For my trouble, the guy in front of me stabbed the icepick a couple of inches into my shoulder. Alice swung her lethal purse again. The icepick went flying. I kicked out at the guy. Alice had been screaming bloody murder the whole time. People in the parking lot were looking our way. A couple of casino security guards came running. The three guys took off, but the guy Alice had let have it upside the head was a little wobbly. She let him have it again between the shoulder blades and he went down again. The guards collared him, but the other two got away.

The cops came. They took everybody's statements. We had to identify ourselves. They got our address. It made me very nervous. Investigators would be out to see us. Would we be willing to testify? Of course we would. We couldn't have these thugs running around our fair city. We ordinary citizens had to stand up and be counted.

We headed for a quiet bar we knew. Alice got the shakes. My shoulder hurt. By St. Elmo's flaming arse, one thing I knew! Alice was a brave girl and she loved me. At home, she poured disinfectant in my miniscule wound and put a Band-Aid over it. We cuddled together, half drunk. In the morning we would begin packing to move to another town, another state. There was no way I would appear in court and testify against any body. If the guy in jail was smart, he'd put off accepting a plea bargain until his lawyer could tell him the main witnesses against him would not be testifying -- for the simple reason that they had disappeared.

We went to Yuma, a sleepy little town on the Arizona border next to California. We rented a house twenty miles out in the desert. We were alone, it was peaceful, and we got a couple of Doberman pups to keep us company. It was a two-story, split-level affair. In the early evening, we could step out our bedroom door onto the roof over the living room to watch the sunsets. We would sit in lounge chairs, sip gins and tonic, and smoke a few joints, holding hands and talking quietly.

Life wasn't all it could be, but I had no complaints. "God, I've never seen such beautiful sunsets," Alice said. "Have you?"

I had, but there was some question as to whether I'd been quite so content with them.

"Shut up and kiss me," I said. "Now, kiss me again."

###

CHAPTER 10

I had been down to Tijuana to visit Pablo, who'd been my first passenger in The Love Boat, the fellow I'd rowed across McNeil Island's back passage to a waiting motorcycle. I was welcomed most cordially. After a good Mexican dinner, he expressed his sense of gratitude by offering me a quantity of grass at an attractive price. It seems he was involved in a business enterprise that transported marijuana up from the lower Mexican states for smuggling across the border. His part, since he owned a body and fender shop, was to build in special compartments in various types of motor vehicles, which would be filled with kilos of grass and driven over the international line at the very busy Tijuana/San Ysidro border station.

With a hundred kilos packed into a borrowed four-wheel drive vehicle, I'd made my first smuggling run over the border. It was so wild and full of adrenaline rushes that I vowed never to do such a thing again. I had simply had Pablo cut a ten-foot wide gap in the cyclone fence marking the border a few miles east of Tijuana. My plan was simply to bulldog my way through and hope to evade pursuit. Pablo told me it wasn't a new idea. Since it was very risky, he advised me against it. He explained that American border patrol agents tended to discover large holes in the fence rather quickly. He thought they might have pressure-sensitive electronic devices planted in the ground, which would quickly alert them to a vehicle passing over the adjacent land.

My finesse was to supply a diversion. Four of Pablo's employees, all experienced drivers, were on hand in their own cars to help out. When I had explained the ruse to them, I gave the signal one dark night that a section of the fence was to be cut out with bolt cutters. The four cars, with their headlights on, shot through the gap ahead of me onto American soil, two angling off to the right and two to the left. Then I shot through straight ahead with my lights out. Speeding over uneven terrain, I came bouncing out onto a paved road and screeched around to the left, looking for a dirt road that went off to the right. I didn't want to leave obvious wheel marks going into the open field on the other side of the road. As I tore along, an oncoming car honked and blinked its highbeams to tell me I had no lights on. I corrected the omission and slowed to make the turn as cars passed behind me on the highway, me praying that none of them were cops. I continued on a half-mile or so up a rising landscape and turned off into a stand of brush and trees.

I killed the engine, got out and spread an army camouflage tarp over the vehicle. Below me, across the road in the field, the four cars, with headlights cutting arcs through the night sky, were tearing all over the place, bouncing up and down. I could see the red lights of police cars, sirens screaming, speeding along the road to investigate. A helicopter with a searchlight playing below, whop-whopped into view. Three starburst rockets fired by Pablo streaked into the darkness from near the gap in the fence. The four cars, seeing the signal, all turned away from driving in zigzags and circles and fled back to the fence where they all passed safely back into Mexico. The whole show, driving antics and all, had taken only a few minutes.

I think the cops were somewhat bewildered. Hopefully, they would conclude it was all no more than a crazy stunt by drunken Mexicans. After a time, they all departed the scene, leaving one car behind to keep an eye on the fence gap. Early in the morning, after they were relieved, a truck and crew was out to repair the fence. Late in the afternoon, I took a leisurely drive toward Yuma. To avoid the agricultural inspection station at the Stateline, I drove north along a little traveled road on the California side of the Colorado River. After some twenty miles or so, I unloaded the hundred keys and hid them in a thickly overgrown marshy area near the river.

Then I drove back, crossed the Stateline into Yuma, turned north again, and drove another twenty miles home. That evening we watched a news report on TV about all the excitement along the Mexican border the night before. I was amused but pretended boredom.

"What say we rent a boat tomorrow," I suggested to Alice with a yawn. "And do a little fishing on the Colorado River?"

*****

While passing through San Diego, I had stopped in to visit another fine fellow I'd met at McNeil. Enrique was out on parole and doing well. He and his wife, Fae, operated a small but successful import business -- they bought various merchandise in Tijuana, rugs, blankets, furniture, baskets, leather goods, and sundry wares for resale from their shop in San Diego.

In the later half of 1980, he was arrested and incarcerated at the Metropolitan Correctional Center, a federal facility. It seems he had allowed another parolee to store some stolen goods in his garage. Somehow the police had got on to where the loot was hidden. Enrique, as you can imagine, was somewhat incensed. But, in the meanwhile, he sat in the hoosegow hoping his wife could come up with the twenty-five grand bail that had been set.

Fae owned another house and was willing to put it up, but it would take her a few days to get the $2500 cash the bail bondsman required. I had called Enrique from a phonebooth. When I heard the news, I rushed over to give his wife the cash. As he walked out that night, I was waiting for him. It hadn't been an easy wait. At the changing of the shift, I had recognized several hacks that used to work at McNeil. I put on my sunglasses and kept my hat tipped low.

I asked him why the parole authorities hadn't placed a hold on him, which would have prevented him making bail -- which idea I had retained from the California system so many years before.

"Nowadays, I think the parole agents have to have personal knowledge of a violation," he said. "Other than this bullshit, I haven't violated the conditions of my parole. They have to get a conviction before they violate me."

"How's it look?"

"Ah, man, they found that Crum bum's shit in my garage! The little fuck never even told me it was hot!"

"Guy rides his own beef, you should come out all right." "Yeah, only he claims not to know anything about it." "Uh-oh."

"Yeah, I can't rat on the little puke, but I get my hands on him, he's going to wish he'd ratted on himself!"

In the end, he had the choice of going back to prison or becoming a fugitive like me. He opted for the latter. To play it safe, he came to stay a couple of weeks with me and Alice -- just long enough for his wife to close out their business and sell everything that wasn't portable. He had been born in Mexico, but had acquired U. S. citizenship by serving in the American army in Vietnam. He decided to return to Mexico, far to the south.

"Well, hey, ol' buddy," I said to him in parting. "You take'er easy. Let me know if they got any good grass way down there. Maybe we can do a deal. Keep in touch. You got my box number."

He said he'd check it out and let me know.

*****

Ah me, the heart has its reasons, said Blaise Pascal, a 17th century mathematician and philosopher, which reason itself does not understand. I, Buck Duane Walker, a 43-year old man with enough experience to know better, fell in love with a 19-year old girl. I tried not to. I told myself it was foolish. Yet, it happened. It was madness, the most wonderful and horrible thing.

All my experiences with the romance and harsh reality of love for women had led me to the hard-learned proposition that reason must temper and rule over the heart's wild desires. Love, that wily coyote who had led me astray so often. I loved my family, I loved my friends, and with another love altogether I loved all the women I had ever loved. I had loved my wife, and each in different ways, Samantha, Stephanie, and Alice. To all of them, I had written a poem, trying my hand at the sonnet form.

THE PHOENIX TAKES FLIGHT
Tenderest woman who's largest eyes
arms my nakedness 'gainst the cages,
your purest mouth utters no goodbyes
and saves me from the lethal rages.
Your sweetest touch upon my urges
bears a nova sun from old starflight,
clarifying love's darkest splurges;
you shine alone in widest night.
Wisely blessing sensuous salvation,
awakening my longest lost child
(he dying a sleep of starvation),
you resurrect anew the pristine wild
Spreading of our galactic wings
through a void that dances and sings.

I knew of several experienced luminaries who taught that love was too powerful to be overcome by anything short of outright flight. But suddenly, for all my self-vaunted strength, I could not run.

"Thou blind fool, Love," Shakespeare accused, "what dost thou to mine eyes that they behold, and see not what they see?" (Sonnet #137)

Love was a punishment and a reward. Love was life itself. "What is this strange and bitter miracle of life," Thomas Wolfe asked. "Is it to feel, when furious day is done, the evening hush, the sorrow, the lost, fading light, far sounds and broken cries, and footsteps, voices, music, and all lost -- and something murmurous, immense and mighty in the air?" (Look Homeward, Angel)

Passionate love for a woman, like life itself, was a divine sort of madness, a grievous but pleasurable madness. No, all the poets, philosophers, and sundry observers of human folly, as well as my inmost deepest counsel, could not save me from falling in love.

I met her in a Los Angeles hotel room. I had gone to meet another friend from McNeil Island. David was reputed to be a bigtime conman, a manipulator from the more ethereal realms of finance. We had begun our relationship in casual conversation about books. Soon we were swapping paperbacks and discussing what we'd read. He was as charming and persuasive as all conmen must be. His great fascination was for schemes that would gain him dollar amounts with too many zeroes in them to ever seem more than the wildest fantasy to most of us.

He claimed to have owned a grand mansion in Miami, an 80-foot luxury yacht moored in the waterway behind his exquisitely landscaped back yard. He had a chauffeur for his limousine, maids and gardeners, yesmen all over the place. He owned a piece of a Florida bank, had investments in real estate. He hinted rather broadly of his connections to organized crime. He dropped the names of well-known mafia figures. He could charm a cobra out of its fangs.

But when a clique of prison extortionists approached him with physical threats, he was at a total loss. He must pay or get his bones broken.

Fretting, he came to me. "What should I do? What should I do? These guys got no respect at all!"

He told me who they were. Like Don Corleone, I thought reason might work best, an oblique approach in which the message would nevertheless be quite clear, low key and softspoken. With Dave in tow, I asked two very large Hawaiians, one of whom was my very best friend, to accompany us to the yard. We approached the three would-be extortionists.

"Hey, how you guys doing?" Dave stood silent while the Hawaiians grinned. "I've come to invite you guys to our club banquet. You interested?"

"Hey, yeah, man," one of them replied. "We've heard about your banquets."

"We like to invite a few outsiders, give them a taste of Hawaiian culture."

"We appreciate it, man."

"You guys were highly recommended to us," I went on. "We don't invite too many people."

"Well, we'll be there, man. Thanks."

"Have you met Dave? He's one of our newest members. He contributes a lot to our club."

Dave nodded. So did they.

"Okay, fellas," I concluded. "We'll see you there. Don't eat breakfast. We're gonna have a mountain of food."

"You guys really have hula girls coming in?"

"Oh, yeah, wait'll you see. Tahitian dancers, too. Hope you guys don't fall in love too easily."

And that was that.

Dave had told me about his family, his wife, son, and two daughters. His youngest, Lena, was a chubby, freckle-faced, frizzy-headed 15-year old. He had showed me a photo of her.

"Oh, yeah, Dave, a pretty girl," I said politely.

Little was I to know.

He had met Samerah X, his mistress, at the co-ed federal prison facility at Fort Worth, Texas, where they were both enrolled in a prerelease program. Samerah was an ex-cocaine addict. She had become a Muslim and taken the name Samerah in place of what Muslims called their slave names.

It seemed incredible -- a Jew and a Black Muslim.

I had met Samerah once before. She had been released before Dave and he'd sent her out to meet me in Vegas. She pleaded for money. Dave had lost everything after his conviction for fraud. The words she brought me, I knew, were not her own, but Dave's. He had coached her in every aspect of the ploy. In the name of free love and friendship, she was supposed to seduce me.

Rather than feel insulted, I was highly amused. What Samerah was offering was basically what a hooker offered -- a cold sexual expertise and an act designed to play upon the john's ego, a shallow, empty thing, an illusion for needy suckers.

I took her to see a show on the Strip, bought her dinner and drinks, rented her a hotel room, and politely bid her goodnight. I'd see her in the morning. After breakfast, I gave her a few thousand dollars and put her on a return flight to Atlanta.

But Lena, oh, Lord, had metamorphosed into a swan. She had long wavy dark hair, amber eyes, a perfect nose and mouth, a brilliant smile. She was slim and athletic in torn old baggy jeans and tee-shirt, her skin smooth and creamy. Her legs were long, her ass high, pooched out, and sassy. She bubbled over with enthusiasm.

I tried not to stare, but my eyes kept returning to her like confused magnets. My mouth was dry and there was a sweet nausea in my chest. I couldn't seem to take in enough air.

I was experienced enough to know that the thunderbolt had struck me and to resist its exquisite wound. I excused myself to change into something more comfortable.

When I came out of the bathroom, everyone laughed. I had changed into blue bib overalls, a green tee-shirt, and a raggedy straw hat, stuff I wore at home for comfort. Lena had a beautiful laugh. Already, unable to help myself, I was beginning to utilize my secrets with women. I took them for dinner in the hotel dining room, pretending to an aw-shucks-panache as though I were dressed in a tuxedo.

After I had ordered "one o' them thar fancy wines" and approved it to the waiter with an "'at's good enough, pardner," Lena was in hysterics. I had tied the napkin around my neck like a hayseed. I made a rude noise with my lips, pretending to fart. It was an old trick. I'd pulled it on my daughter once at a fancy restaurant. I'd looked at her sternly and said loudly, "Dear, how many times have I told you not to fart at the dinner table?" She was so embarrassed from giggling helplessly that she'd hidden her head under the tablecloth. When Alice had looked at me in shock, I'd accused her with a wrinkling nose and cocked eyebrow, "Why, you slut, you! Sit there and let me falsely accuse my daughter!" I'd had to throw money on the table as we all ran out holding our aching ribs.

There was a shocked lull in the hum of conversation among our fellow diners. "Whoops," I said, "musta been that musical fruit I et fer lunch."

"What?" Lena shrieked, tears glistening in her eyes.

"Ah, you know, Mexican strawberries. We call 'em beans up here. The more you eat the more you toot."

But on the plane to meet Alice in Vegas, I was not so much the clown. I strained at the making of a poor poem on a cocktail napkin, trying to draw some sense out of the jumble of my emotions.

>Exquisite samplings
>Allude to satiable feasts
>like preludes
>to great passages.

Our daily notions
never compare
with the ageless
dream.
A cruel premonition
reeks in the evening
of old betrayals
fevering the blood.
Completion always eludes us
an eternal moment too soon.

*****

When I had gone to meet Dave that first time in December, I had just returned from deep along the Pacific coast of Mexico. Enrique had sent me a postcard. "You ought to come down and see for yourself the beautiful things that grow here," it said.

I had flown to Acapulco, where he met me in his VW Beetle. From there, we had driven south all the rest of the day over a winding, potholed road, upon which cattle, pigs, and jackasses were wont to roam. Passing a small village, I had suggested we stop for a bite to eat.

"Don't expect any MacDonald's down here," he cautioned. "Hey, I like Mexican food."

The restaurant looked like somebody's home. It was, There were no signs advertising it, only two empty tables set out in the front yard, around which ran a low wall. A pig snoozed in the shade at one corner. A man came out and spoke with Enrique in Spanish.

"He says they only have shrimp soup, tortillas, and beer," he translated.

"Well, hell, let's order the whole damned menu."

Bottles of Bohemia came first, and then large steaming bowls of soup with tablespoons, a plate of tortillas. I tasted the soup cautiously. It was good. I ladled up a whole shrimp, with head, legs, and all. I'd never seen a whole shrimp before. So that's what they look like, I thought, as I spooned it into my mouth and began chewing. It was very crunchy.

When I looked up, I could see that Enrique was torn with some extreme emotion. Just then the man returned with an empty plate. With a haughty politeness only a peasant could muster for one even lower on the social scale, he said in passable English, "For the shells, senor, and of course the heads."

Enrique was afflicted with some sort of seizure. The hot Mexican sun felt warm on my cheeks.

*****

I was introduced to Jorge, a hustler type, a man who lived day to day on his wits. We rented a Jeep and drove half the day into the cool, winding roads of the mountains. At a certain point, engaging the four-wheel drive, we turned off on to a narrow, steep dirt trail. We came to a poor village by a river. I was introduced to the Jefe, a dark man in sandals, loose white peon trousers and shirt, a serape, and sombrero. He sported a great handlebar moustache. He reminded me of old photos I had seen in history books of Emiliano Zapata. He only needed a brace of pistols, bullet bandoliers crossing his shoulders, a rifle, and a horse.

The entire village lived in abject poverty. They grew mountain corn for subsistence, part of which they kept for themselves, with the rest being sold to the government. The villagers grew marijuana to supplement their all but non-existent income. El Jefe led us up along a jungly forest trail where he demonstrated what must have been tons of grass neatly wrapped into brown paper kilos. A boy, no older than fourteen, stood guard with a .22 single-shot rifle. With so much grass available, I couldn't understand the poverty.

Jorge and El Jefe explained, the former translating for the latter. It seemed that over the years the drug trade had moved further north so as to shorten the distance the product would have to be moved to the American border. Why would anyone buy grass here when they could get it a thousand miles closer to its destination? I was their first prospective customer in a year.

The grass was cheap. The problem would be to get it eighteen hundred miles to the border, then figure a way to smuggle it across. It was a complicated undertaking. I would have to think about it.

After demonstrating the method of switching off the fat, blood-swollen ticks, which covered our legs from ankle to knee, El Jefe broke out a jar of mescal while his wife cooked tamales wrapped in green leaves in an earthen oven on the ground. Jesus Christ, I thought, after we had shook hands and were winding down the mountain road in the chilly night, conditions were better in prison. These people were poor and uneducated. They might spend their whole lives in such circumstances, with little to hope for -- like convicts serving life sentences.

Enrique turned to me. "What do you think?"

"It's a long row to hoe," I replied.

"The grass is cheap enough."

"Yeah. Getting it up and over's the thing."

"Drive it up?"

"Who? You? Me? Man, no more of that stuff for me. My body's too old to handle the adrenaline."

"We could hire somebody to drive it up."

"Who? A Mexican? He can't cross the border. We'd need somebody else once we got the load up there. The more people we let in on it, the more it costs, the less security."

We were silent awhile, chewing it over.

268
"We'd have to do at least 250 keys, which is about all I could afford anyway. You got any money?"

"No. I may have to move up with El Jefe pretty soon." "We'd need transport."

"A truck?"

"Maybe. What about searches along the way? Any problem?"

"I'm told the federales often put up temporary roadblocks, search everything coming through."

"Oh, shit."

"But the worst of it is only between here and Mexico City. After that it's usually clear sailing to a border city."

"Maybe we could run a car ahead to scope out the roadblocks. Communicate over CB radios. Just wait until the roadblock lifts before going on."

"Yeah."

We chewed some more.

"What do you think?"

"Well, hell, ol' buddy. You need an income. So do those folks up in that village. Me, too, for that matter. Let's see what we can figure out."

*****

Back in Yuma once again, I began working it all over in the old noggin to come up with a Plan trying to imagine the entire process, along with alternatives, every step of the way. I made pages and pages of notes, adding and subtracting. Keep it as simple as possible, I told myself. Work out the contingencies, all the what-ifs, the fallbacks.

The nub of it all would depend upon deception, image, and distraction. I would have to draw upon my haphazard training in the theater. Illusion was everything.

What did I know of smuggling? I'd done a bit, but not much, although Pablo in Tijuana had given me a crash course in many of the methods used to get dope over the border, spending a long evening over a bottle of Sauza regaling me with stories. Pollos, which translated as chickens, or poor people, would be loaded with backpacks to make their way over selected border points on foot. Cars and trucks contained specially built compartments. Planes flew it over. Runs were made in boats up the California coast. Some fools went right through the fence in a make-or-break dash. But others were quite ingenious. Men wearing scuba diving gear swam around in the ocean towing packages weighted just enough to achieve a neutral buoyancy a few feet under water. Others employed radio-controlled model airplanes, zipping back and forth over the border all day long -- they were invisible to radar.

What could an amateur like me come up with against all the professionals? It was like a chess game, move and countermove, this attack against that defense, and vice versa. The stakes would be fair if I could win, but to lose would be disastrous.

Through a friend of a friend of a friend, I found two schoolteachers, a married couple. I hated doing business with people I didn't know personally, but they had come recommended. They needed money. The man had a beard and long hair. He balked when I asked him to shave and get a haircut.

"You kidding?"

"No, man."

I explained. Norte americanos with lots of hair and sloppy dress were considered lowlife scrounging hippies. They were favorites for rousting by the policia. I painted a picture of him as an actor playing a role. He and his wife would have to pass themselves off as quintessential middleclass vacationers. I told them how they would have to dress. They could not carry any personal stash of drugs on the trip down or balk. They would have to be smiling, dumb, and friendly all the way. They couldn't be too lavish with the minor bribes, called mordida, that would help to smooth the way, but neither could they be too tight.

I gave them money to rent a motorhome, a 27-foot Southwind, practically a bus. I showed them on a map where to go, what route they were to follow, a small town on the southern coast called Tehuantepec. I described an empty lot outside the town with a well where they could park the motorhome. They could make it a leisurely trip down, two weeks, have a real vacation on the way. Once at Tehuantepec, they were to wait for someone to contact them.

*****

I had a message from Dave to call him. He wanted to meet me in Vegas with a proposition. I took Alice along. Once again, I found Dave, Samerah, and Lena at a hotel. Dave tried to persuade me to throw in my lot with him. He had some scheme involving certificates of deposit, which I could never quite understand, which would make us rich. He was talking millions.

At the time, he was passing himself off as an operations manager for some feeder airline in Atlanta. He could flash his ID at almost any airline ticket counter and receive a courtesy discount.

I turned Dave down. First, I didn't quite understand exactly what he was talking about. Secondly, as a conman I knew he would try to use me as stooge and front man, the guy that takes the heat. I couldn't afford that. But then he wanted to know everything about what I was doing. Well, I mentioned smuggling a little grass, but I didn't go into any details. As much as I was an amateur in his line, so was he an amateur in mine. He suggested that I go to the hard narcotics like heroin and cocaine for the higher margins of profit, which, with his underworld connections in Florida, he could deal in wholesale amounts as much as I could get across. I politely declined. I could see that Dave was not so scrupulous as I when it came to using people. The almighty dollar came first with him. I could see he was a little put out, but he seemed to recover and roll with it well.

Business aside, we all got in a party mood and I recklessly invited them to stay a few days with us in our little hideaway outside Yuma. We drove down. When Dave and Samerah left on a flight to Phoenix to make connections for their return to Georgia, Lena stayed behind. She loved the desert country and my mutts. She would stay an extra week and follow on to Atlanta.

I was determined to steel myself and mind my manners. High on grass, gin and tonic in hand, I told her funny story after story, keeping her in stitches. All was well. The three of us were having a good time. My intentions were strictly honorable. I had no business fooling around with this girl, even if she did make me drunk on her beauty.

But one night Alice had a little too much to drink and went to bed early. I sat talking with Lena for awhile, speaking softly. Suddenly, Alice came barging in, angry.

"I know what you're talking about," she accused. "In here whispering behind my back!"

"Babe, please..."

"Don't think I don't know what's going on!"

"Good night, Lena," I said, standing abruptly. "Sorry about this."

I led Alice to our upstairs bedroom and turned on her when we were alone. "What the hell's the matter with you, carrying on like that?"

"Don't try to bullshit me! I can see the way you're looking at her, the little bitch!"

"Looking at her? How am I looking at her?"

"You want to fuck her!"

"Babe, I've wanted to fuck probably three out of every four of all the women I've ever seen in my entire life. It doesn't mean a thing."

"I want her out of here!"

"Fine, I'll put her on a plane in the morning."

"You'd fuck her right here in our home!"

"No. No, I wouldn't. I explained it to you before, babe, remember? This is our home, yours and mine, and it's sacrosanct. I admit I've got a roving eye. Every man does. It's not anything you have to worry about. I come home to you."

"Yeah, and everytime you go away on your little trips, you're probably fucking someone!"

"Jesus, you give me more credit than I deserve."

"Hah!"

"You just remember what I told you about that."

"What?"

"When home gets to feeling like a prison, I'm going to be leaving. I don't do too well in a choke-collar."

In the morning, I prepared to drive Lena to the airport. Alice was still in a bitchy mood. As I was loading Lena's suitcases into the trunk, Alice appeared.

"Where do you think you're going?"

"I'm taking Lena to the airport, dear."

"Good riddance," she spat and slammed the door.

"Just don't you forget about those choke-collars!" I yelled, totally exasperated.

Once we were on our way, I apologized.

"I'm sorry if I caused any trouble," she said. "I really didn't mean to."

"Aw, it's not your fault."

"What was that remark about choke-collars?"

I explained. "She's a good woman. She's got a good heart. Maybe it's my fault. Maybe I leave her alone too much."

"What do you do? Do you travel a lot?"

"Yeah, I do. Few days here, few days there. I try to take her with me when I can."

"You don't want to tell me what you do."

"You're a pretty sharp cookie," I evaded. "How about some breakfast?"

Over coffee, not willing to part company so quickly, though I was telling myself to keep playing the lovable old uncle, I asked her to do me a favor.

"What?"

"I need to rent an apartment here in town. Sometimes I have friends coming through and I need a place to put them up."

"What's wrong with the spare bedroom in your house."

"Well, ah, some of my business is none of Alice's business"

"And just what is your business?"

That was the question. I thought about it. This girl had started out in life with a silver spoon. Then she had known what being poor was like after her father had gone to prison and her mother had had to go on welfare. After high school, she'd gotten a job to help out. Did she know about her father, what a crooked sonofagun he really was? Anything about me?

"Basically, I'm a goddamn crook, I guess," I said at last. "I make my living by breaking the law."

"Doing what?"

"Oh, I buy and sell things," I stalled, but which was true enough. I had bought and sold cars, boats and motors, travel trailers, TVs, stereos, CB radios, and even furniture, all at a profit by exercising my wiles in the basic mechanics of capitalism -- buy cheap and sell dear. I was an inveterate bargain-hunter.

"What, exactly?"

"Um, ah...er," I stuttered. It was tough for me to confess. It was dangerous.

"C'mon, you old fart," she joshed, poking me on the arm. "Tell me."

"Old fart? I ain't old."

"Just a fart, huh?"

"Grass."

"You're a grass dealer?"

"Yeah."

"That's the last thing I would have guessed."

"Thanks. I smuggle it, too."

"Where from? Mexico?"

"Yeah."

"Wow. That sounds exciting. Is it?"

"Yeah, I think you could say that."

"Do you like it?"

"Beats robbing banks."

"So what do I have to do?"

We looked in the want ads. We looked at apartments. I chose one centrally located. It had a pool. Bedroom, bath, living room and kitchenette. I gave her money and sent her up with the manager to sign the papers. When she returned, we went shopping. Linens, dinnerware, a small TV, a clock radio, food and beer for the refrigerator. I had her call the phone company to install a phone. By then it was late in the afternoon. She wanted to shower before getting on the plane for Phoenix. She came out in a bathrobe with a towel wrapped around her hair.

Ah, me boyos, was she lovely, her skin so fresh and clean and young and glowing.

"Say," I said. "It's kinda late. Why don't you spend the night here? I'll come by in the morning to get you to the airport."

"All right."

"Well, I better be shoving off. Alice'll be wondering what happened to me."

"And suspect the worst, no doubt."

"Ah, well..."

"You want to shower before you go? It's been a long hot day."

"Yeah, I wouldn't mind. Thanks."

Like most women, as I am often surprised to learn, Lena had a mind of her own. When I came out of the bathroom, dressed except for my shoes and socks, she walked up to me, put her arms around my neck, and kissed me. It was not the kiss of a chaste virgin kissing a harmless old lovable uncle.

Our first kiss was cataclysmic, exploding us over the 25-year abyss of our experience. History rushed in a bold pulse of mere seconds as we unfolded convulsed in sheer excellence. It never happened quite like that again.

What was I to do but kiss her some more?

*****

Alice was pissed. I told her a lie about the car breaking down. It was too late. I was lost. I became devious. Enrique and Fae were in Tijuana. The schoolteacher couple was ready to head south. Ollie, my partner in The Love Boat scam, had escaped from a halfway house against all my advice to wait it out. He'd learned his wife was screwing a McNeil Island hack. She'd disappeared with his kids. He needed a place to hide out, money. Enrique and Fae were going to ride down with the schoolteachers in the motorhome. He could assess their suitability for driving back a load of grass.

The flashbulb of an idea went off in my head. I called Enrique. "Hey, you got room for two more?"

"Sure, I guess. What's up? Who?"

"Friend of mine. He can help us out down there."

"Who's the other one?"

"Alice."

"Alice?"

"Yeah, she needs a vacation."

I turned on the charm to convince her. "C'mon, babe. You deserve it. A month in Mexico. Ollie's going, too. Remember Ollie?" Of course she did, and she liked Fae and Enrique. She could have a ball.

"I don't want to go without you."

"I gotta stay here, babe. Business, pay the rent, all that."

"No, I want you to come, too."

"Can't, babe. I need you to help me out. I want you to study those schoolteachers, tell me what you think. Can I trust them? I want to know everything they say and do. You're my secret agent, okay? You're on a mission. But I want you to have fun, too. Buy yourself some new outfits. Okay?"

I pulled Ollie aside. "Hey, buddy, I know you're just out and all that -- ain't even had time to readjust, get your head right, your noodle straightened out. But this trip'll be good for you."

I'd given him some ID and money. I told him he could make some bucks if he wanted to get involved in the smuggling scam. He was game.

"Also," I added. "You gotta take care of Alice. You understand? You're her bodyguard. You look after her, take care of all her needs."

"Like what?"

"All her needs," I stressed. "I don't want her getting lonely. I'm counting on you, man."

He was a little stunned, but he got the message loud and clear. Hell, here he was, a man on the run, down and out, expecting desperate times, and he was going off on an all-expenses-paid vacation with some amiable people. Plus, he liked Alice. He was charged with not allowing her to get lonely, to fulfill all her needs. He was like a horse being led into an oat factory.

*****

> Methinks it true
> dear damsels are such
> that disorderly rhymes
> ne'er saying much
> doth in hard times
> win bards their due.

*****

Yeah, man, and ain't it true that love is also poetry! The trick is to abstract its essence into words. Sometimes the poet succeeds, but only for a moment here, to show a facet there. He is never able to catch the whole of it, the soul of it.

> O cloud-pale eyelids, dream-dimmed eyes,
> The poets laboring all their days
> To build a perfect beauty in rhyme
> Are overthrown by a woman's gaze. (William Butler Yeats)

No, the poet can only evoke emotions, formless things more numerous than the stars. Millions of words cannot quite recreate the feeling of love, for it is never the same two minutes running. It is in constant flux. But I, too, have tried to capture aspects of it.

> Oh, woman,
> you wound the wild heart
> with mad innocence

playing your fine part
to light my mind.
Oh, you,
who leaves me with a kiss
in nameless unease,
do you feel my dream
touching your thighs,
Demanding we sing or hush
the long sighs unheard
on an empty afternoon?
If not, I must bid all birds
 fold their wings forever.

*****

We drove to San Francisco, one of my favorite cities. We rented a room by the sea and walked barefoot in the sand at midnight. We stole through the foggy trees and walks of Golden Gate Park, kissing each other's cool lips. We tripped through the city buying her clothes, to dress her as she'd never quite been dressed before. I wanted to show her off and proudly displayed her to a number of my friends. Eat your hearts out. 01' Buck's still got something. I strutted my ego, my joy. I fancied I was her tutor, introducing her to the real world, teaching her, showing her, unfolding her. She wanted to do everything, be everything.

We sped down the coast confident we would catch up with the horizon. We wound up in a hotel in Tijuana, sick with the flu. I called the desk. A doctor came up and gave us shots, provided ampoules of sweet-tasting vitamins. For three days we remained inebriate on grass and booze, making love in the golden shafts of sunlight on the rug.

I phoned Gerry in Arizona, who had been taking messages from the people in the motorhome in Mexico. They were stuck at a trailer park in Guadalajara with two flat tires. They couldn't buy the right sizes to replace them. What should they do? The motorhome was loaded with 500 kilos of grass. El Jefe had fronted us the extra 250 keys.

I got the tire sizes, purchased them, and drove quickly to the old homestead to exchange the car for the pickup camper. Lena and I, with my two Dobies in the back, crossed the border at Sonoita, a quiet, sleepy little place which would serve as our first smuggling route into the U. S.

It took us three days to arrive in Guadalajara. I dropped Lena at a hotel before searching out the trailer park. Alice was ecstatic. Ollie looked tanned and tranquil, wearing a little smirk for a job well done. The schoolteachers were falling out drunk and arguing bitterly.

I spent the night with Alice. In the morning, we changed the tires. I counseled the feuding couple. I told them to drive to Sonoita and to wait on the Mexican side until they heard from me.

I would help them complete the run across the border. I kissed Alice goodbye. I noticed a new bloom in her cheeks. She wasn't nearly so resistant to continuing the trip without me as she had been. Perhaps she was learning the value of promiscuity. I clapped Ollie on the back.

"Good work, pal. Thanks."

"You got any more jobs like this, let me know."

Lena and I continued on to Mexico City, then Oaxaca. We went up over some high mountains on an unpaved road with almost no traffic, coming out at last to the sea. We spent three days moving into a two bedroom rented house with Enrique and Fae. Then I caught a small plane to Mexico City, transferred on a flight to Tijuana, where I walked across the border and caught a cab into San Diego. There I caught a flight for the hop over to Yuma. I went to Gerry's house and asked him to help me out. Since he would be handling the unloading and distribution of the grass, he was game. He and his girlfriend followed me to Sonoita in their car.

I put Alice and Ollie in the car with Gerry, but I borrowed his girlfriend, who was young, blond, and sassy. She was to be my daughter for the evening's work. The border gate closed at 8 p.m. At 7:45, the schoolteachers drove over onto American soil and stopped at the border station.

The customs agents came out to check the motorhome. I pulled in behind them to begin the distraction. I was to appear as drunk and fractious. I honked the horn, I yelled out the window for them to get a move on. I got out of the car, staggered up alongside the motorhome, accusing them of playing cutesy with rich tourists. My "daughter" tried to restrain me, but I became ever more abusive, really putting on an obnoxious show.

It worked. They lost their patience, waved the motorhome through and concentrated on me. They read me the riot act. They spent fifteen or twenty minutes on overtime tearing the car apart. I calmed down, became contrite. They threatened to have me booked for drunk driving.

"You're right, sir. And I'd deserve it, too. But my poor daughter'd be left all alone. We've been down here looking for her mother. She ran off with a fucking wetback. Goddamned bitch!"

All of a sudden it was something they could understand -- a domestic problem. I could go on home to Tucson, but only if I promised to let my daughter drive me.

*****

I spent a week with Alice. Like a drug addict, I wanted to hurry back to Lena for my next fix. But reality insisted upon its rude intrusion into the cloudland of my love. What was I to do about Alice? Could I simply tell her it was all over, that I'd found someone else, half her age at that, give her money and send her on her way? Not that I didn't love her, care what happened to her, the truth was that she loved me far more than I loved her. What was worse, she was dependant upon that love. I simply could not bring myself to break her heart. She had been a truly warm and caring person in my life when I most needed it. I could no more spurn her need for me than I could forsake my own for Lena. Thus, the question for me boiled down to how I might have my omelet without breaking any eggs.

Since I intended to return to southern Mexico, I worried about leaving Alice alone so far out in the country. I began to study the classifieds for a house to rent in town. About this time a package from Lampong came in.

I had rented half a dozen private mailboxes located in different cities in California, Nevada, and Arizona, not only to spread out the action on Lampong's packages, but also to send and receive personal communications -- all under different names.

These mailboxes were handy things for fugitives like myself. One, it kept my home address secret; two, it would be difficult to trace me if suspicion should attach to any one of them. Private postal services were usually operated out of storefronts in shopping areas, and many of them had 24-hour access. Using your own keys, you could enter at three in the morning to collect your mail. This meant that any police types would have to mount an around-the-clock surveillance to catch the boxholder on the premises. I often let my mail collect for some time, especially Lampong's packages, which might sit a month before being removed. Even then, just to play it safe, I always had someone else retrieve them for me.

On this particular occasion, my customer for the kilo of Thai lived in Mexicali. Since it was late, and I didn't like crossing the border at night, I checked into a hotel after having made delivery and collected payment. I called Gerry in Yuma to see how he was doing on unloading the Mexican grass.

"Where are you?"

"In Mexicali, why?"

"Read any newspapers lately?"

"No. What's happening?"

He proceeded to read me a brief article about a skull and some bones being discovered on a beach at Palmyra along with a nearby metal container.

It recounted the mysterious disappearance of Malcolm and Eleanor Graham and mentioned Stephanie's name and mine.

We had been indicted for murder.

The rush of sick memories all but overwhelmed me.

"You still there?"

"Yeah," I choked.

"Maybe you better think about staying in Mexico."

He was right. It was one thing to be pursued for what is called a walkaway escape from a minimum-security prison, but quite another to be wanted on a murder charge. A passive investigation, based upon the chance that I would be arrested on an unrelated charge and thus be discovered through a fingerprint check, would surely become an active one. It might involve the FBI, rather than the dregs of federal police who wound up as U. S. Marshals.

"Yeah," I repeated. "I think I'll stay down here permanently, but I need you to do something for me."

"Sure, man. Name it."

I wanted him to get Alice moved into town where he could look after her. I turned over my business with Lampong, providing him with a short list of trusted cash customers. Along with the Mexican grass business, he would serve to handle my end of the money, subtracting what was necessary to Alice's care and sending the rest on to me. I was grateful that I would be spared the necessity of informing Alice, but I knew he would make her understand the serious new ramifications.

In a state of depression, I returned to Mexico City to catch a feeder flight back to my new village home. For the first time in a long while, I thought about Stephanie, what she must be going through. At McNeil, our letters to each other had grown fewer and farther between until stopping altogether. I had received no replies to the last couple. She had moved from Hawaii to Southern California. She undoubtedly had a new life -- perhaps she'd even married and had children. Now the dreams we had once shared and had gone bad were all turning into a nightmare. The worst of it was that, short of turning myself in and confessing to murder, which I could never do, there was nothing I could do to help her. I arrived so drunk Lena had to take me home and put me to bed.

With less than twenty thousand souls, the village had little to offer by way of entertainment. There was no TV and all the radio programs were in Spanish. There were no theaters or fancy restaurants. There was no work, little in the way of business opportunity other than smuggling grass, which required only a few days a month, and not much more than idleness to occupy one's time.

We went to the beach near town almost daily, after which we would have a late breakfast or lunch at one of the modest hotels or restaurants. After siesta, we would take the dogs for a run. The evenings, often as not, found us in some bar getting soused. The days were hot and humid. I had had to bring down air-conditioners and fans to make our house livable.

A certain lassitude seemed to possess me and I became something of a drunk. But I had always handled liquor well, never becoming sloppy or out of control. One late night after leaving a restaurant three sheets to the wind, Lena and Fae suggested I was too drunk to drive and why didn't we walk the kilometer or so home. Just to prove I could handle my drink, I drove the pickup backward at full speed all the way. Still, I seemed to be beginning each day earlier and earlier with a drink and a joint.

Enrique had come up with a new plan to supplement our income -we would begin a smuggling operation into Mexico. At that time, American goods were in high demand, especially clothes. We decided that Fae and Lena could handle almost the entire enterprise on their own. We put them on a flight with connections to Tijuana. Enrique's mother and sisters would meet them and provide for a few days stay in their homes. They would all drive across the border into San Diego on a shopping trip, where they first bought entire sets of luggage. They would fill them with blouses, skirts, and dresses, along with lingerie and bathing suits. They would fill several suitcases with both men's and women's style blue jeans, which were much in demand. They would add various styles of men's shirts. It provided the girls with a bit of holiday from their lazy ol' men. When they returned, it was with over twenty pieces of luggage.

We spread the word the next morning. That afternoon, dozens of cars were parked around our house. The rush was on. We provided free beer. Before the day was over, we'd sold everything, including all the luggage, at handsome markups over cost. The mayor, the doctor, the local army commander, the chief of police, as well as sundry local businessmen, all began to come around with lists of items they wanted.

"Senores," they would ask. "Can you get me, the things on this little list?"

"Sure, no problem. Next time around."

"Ah, good, and when would that be?"

"Next month. Once a month."

"Oh, fine. By the way, do you play tennis? We have a fine private club."

We made enough profit to pay our rent, utilities, gas, and food bills for a month. The girls' three-day trips once a month provided, in effect, free living accommodations.

We were lucky, Enrique and I. Although we were fugitives, we lived safe and at peace. There was no crime to speak of and, thus, no real police presence. The police chief, a convivial gentleman, conducted us on a tour of his two-cell jail. He wondered if we might be able to supply an American-made prisoner transport van. I called a car thief I knew, who stole one from a police parking lot and drove it down. The chief was very pleased. We were citizens of some standing, good people to know.

And we both had a beautiful woman to love us. After a bit of bodysurfing, we would sit back in the golden sand with bottles of beer and a couple of joints just to feast our eyes on them. They'd both bought themselves designer bathing suits, which displayed their bodies to heart-wrenching effect. How could it get any better? We had conquered and been conquered perfectly.

*****

ON CONQUERING PERFECTLY

Pouting and strutting about proudly hands on hips, breasts aflower half the cheeks of her perfect ass immodestly displayed she said,

"Body-surfing's no fun!"

Dunked, tossed, crushed and mauled
by an inconsiderate sea
gamely contesting the waves

until sand was thoroughly housed in every crease and orifice she wailed
"It's no fun!"
Then she caught the perfect wave
in perfect form
and flew like a seabird o'er the froth
She screamed like a virgin in first flight
upsurging, soaring
in perfectly exquisite execution
Oh, there was no persuading her then
to quit the element
she was so fanatically enthralled But at last
drooping with the sweet weariness
of battles well-fought
she allowed me
to help her home to bed
"Next to fucking and of course you
I love body-surfing the most,"
she whispered through salty lips
ere sleeping the sleep
of an empress
who has conquered perfectly

*****

In July, 1981, after six months in Mexico, I received word that Gianmin, an old friend of mine, who lived in San Francisco, was dying. When I had called, his oldest daughter tearfully informed me that he was in the hospital. On the one hand, I received the news with great sorrow, but on the other it gave me an excuse to return to the United States. I was a bit tired of life in Mexico and I missed my family. Except for Lena, Enrique and Fae, my daily existence had become a sort of limbo. I had come to dread the treks up into the mountain village to visit El Jefe. No matter that I was welcomed like a king as their benefactor, the two or three days I would spend in the village giving lessons to teenage boys on how to grow a stonier marijuana plant, which would hopefully better their future economic situation, I always came away in a state of depression over the inescapable conditions of life there.

I had once ordered that the diesel-powered generator be removed from one of the big motorhomes used in transporting grass, so that for the first time in the life of the village they had electrical power. To celebrate, they had strung lines of lightbulbs around the village plaza, wired in radios, and staged a fiesta. There was something warm and wonderful to see couples dancing, girls flirting with boys, and the boys working up their nerve to begin courtship rituals, to feel the shared camaraderie of the men as homemade pulque and mescal were passed around in gourds and jars, to sense the emanations of strength and determination that had brought them together into a community, young women suckling babes in arms, the children laughing and playing as if there were no tomorrow -- and it was so sad it could break your heart.

"It's dangerous for you," Enrique had told me when I'd informed him of my plan to go north for a visit. "You should stay here." "Yeah, I know, but it's something I have to do." "You be careful."

"I'll be back, don't worry. A couple of weeks."

*****

In San Francisco, I left Lena alone at a motel for hours at a time while I went to the hospital to sit with Gianmin. He was a shadow of his once husky, ebullient self. He was old now, and wasted. I had known him since I was fifteen years old. He had been a fry cook at a Los Angeles diner and had given me my first joint. He was of mixed Chinese ancestry, born and raised to young manhood in Hawaii. He could hold me spellbound for hours telling me stories about life there, his exploits after journeying out into the world. He had sailed the seven seas as a boiler-tender in the Merchant Marine. He had once stolen some jewels and taken a luxury cruise to Amsterdam just ahead of the police. On the way, he met and married an English girl and lived in London for awhile. He had smuggled hashish from Holland, Beirut, and India. He had bought a few of Lampong's shipments of Thai grass and bragged of reselling them at $250 per ounce. He had always counseled me about the evils of heroin. But there was no longer any need -- I had lost my own friends to the seductive bitch. When he died, one of his hands in mine, the other in his oldest daughter's, I cried along with his three ex-wives and all his other children.

Lena had phoned her family, her father in Atlanta, her mother in Miami, and her sister in Phoenix, the latter down and out at a motel room. She was looking for a job after the traumatic breakup of her marriage. I had given her money to help out a little. I had spoken to Dave when Lena had him on the line. He was still pushing the partnership idea, trying to persuade me to front him a load of grass. He wanted me to deliver it in Atlanta; it would help him get back on his feet. I was feeling bummed out and became a little impatient with him.

"Hey, man," I said abruptly. "Everytime I see you, you're always talking big dollars. Now you tell me you can't even pay for a couple hundred keys of grass. Okay, I'll give you a little on front street, but quit ladling the bullshit on me. You don't hustle your friends, Dave."

"It's not like that, Buck," he protested. "Times are tough. I'm just trying to get something going, you know? I couldn't think of a better partner to have, that's all. I love you, man."

"All right. I'll front you fifty keys at a good price." "Now we're talking. How soon can you deliver?"

"No delivery, Dave. You'll have to pick the stuff up in Arizona, make your own arrangements."

"Okay. How do we set it up? What do I do?"

"Meet me in Tucson," I said, giving him the name of a hotel. "I'll contact you there."

"Right, okay. I'll be there."

"Dave," I added. "You sure you want to do this? It's out of your line, man. You sure you can handle it?"

"I can handle it. I just wish it was the hard stuff. I could move coke and gow all day long with the connections I got. More money in it. I could make us both rich."

"Forget it."

"Okay, okay."

"Just so you understand how it works, I front you, you owe me, right?"

"Yeah, no problem."

"You pay me when you say you're going to, I'll front you another load. You don't pay, you fuck me around just once..."

"Yeah, I know," he laughed. "You're gonna send some collectors to break my legs."

"No, Dave. I'll just take the loss. But we won't ever do business again. Never."

"You won't send no hitmen after me?"

"You think I'd knock off my kid's grandfather?"

"What? Are you serious? Lena's pregnant?"

"No, but she's been talking about it."

"You guys gonna get married?"

"Why complicate things?"

"Well, that's all right with me. You imagine what a kid would be like with your blood and mine mixed together?"

"Yeah, we'd have a smart, banana-nosed jackrabbit!"

After the laughter had died away, I promised to bring Lena to Tucson for a visit. Then I called Cheryl, his older daughter in Phoenix, to see how she was doing, to let her know we'd be by to visit her, too.

"Good," she said. "I'd like to talk to you."

"What about? What's the problem?"

"Well," she hesitated. "It's about you and my father."

"Yeah?"

"He's been calling here and asking a lot of questions.

" "What about?"

"It's a long story. I'd rather talk to you personally. You know, my father and I have never gotten along very well. We've hardly spoken to each other for years. Now, all of a sudden, he's calling me, very friendly, and he wants to know things."

"Yeah, so? Maybe he has a guilty conscience. Maybe he's just trying to make up for lost time, playing daddy and all that."

"I don't trust him. He wants to know about what you're doing."

"What'd you tell him?"

"Nothing. What do I know? I just think we should have a talk about it."

"Okay. We'll be down to see you in a few days."

When I'd hung up, nameless little demons were tugging at my instincts. I'd tentatively concluded that while Lena's sister was the smarter and more perceptive of the two, she was also more high-strung. A little uncomfortably, I shrugged off her warning as so much neurotic nonsense.

If I'd gone to see her in Phoenix first, I might have saved myself some trouble in Tucson.

*****

Because of my paranoia, which had been busy developing itself as a fugitive entity over the past two years, it had become all but an automatic habit never to just walk into a situation without first determining, as best I could, exactly what I was getting myself into. Because most of the people I dealt with lived on the outlaw fringe, it wouldn't do to simply enter into any surveillance they might be under because of their own activities.

Even though I had loved, admired, and respected Gianmin, and had trusted him totally, even with him, I had always put him through my evasive anti-surveillance tactics everytime I met with him. I would call out of the blue, tell him to meet me at some restaurant. I would never meet him there. Instead, I would be nearby so I could watch him arrive. Then I would call the restaurant and have him paged to the phone. I would tell him I couldn't make it, but could he meet me at another restaurant across town in an hour or so? I would tail him when he left, checking around to make sure nobody else was tailing him. If I was satisfied he'd arrived alone, I'd meet with him. If not, I'd put him through some more shenanigans. He'd caught on right away. It tickled him.

"Oh, you rascal, you! Run me all over town for a couple pounds of pakalolo."

"Gotta play it safe. Protects both of us."

"I don't mind. I never scold you for using your noodle."

"It don't bother you I put you through all these changes? I know you're getting kind of old..."

"Ah, you! You hush up! I can still kick you okole!" (Ass)

I laughed.

"No, is good what you do. Where you learn all this stuff?"

"From you. You always said I had to be careful doing serious business."

"Yeah, but you slow learner. Otherwise, you never go to prison." "You said never trust anybody unless I knew them a long time."

"Sure, sure, but where you learn all these tricks? I never teach you this huli-huli kulekana." (Round and round business.)

"Aw, I read spy novels."

"Spy books?" He laughed, incredulous, the roars coming up from deep in his considerable belly. "Oh, you scoundrel, you! Spy books! Hah!"

"Yeah."

"Fucking James Bond!"

*****

So, when I went to meet with Dave, rather than just stroll into the hotel and knock on his door, I sent Lena in with instructions. She was to bring him out onto the street and down a block or so to a convenience store, where they were to wait near a bank of public phones outside.

I was sitting across the street in a golf course parking lot two blocks away with a pair of binoculars. I watched Lena and her father walking down the sidewalk from the opposite direction. They stood near the phones and waited while I looked around. Finally, I got out of the car and went to a public phone at the golf course, where I called one of the phones at the convenience store. Lena answered. "Hi, babe. Everything all right?"

"Yes."

"Okay. You know what to do if anything happens, right?"

"Just stay with my father until I hear from you."

"Right. Put him on."

I told Dave to call a taxi and have it take them to a shopping mall about five miles away. I would meet him in a certain store. "What's going on?"

"Nothing, Dave, just playing it safe. I want to make sure you're not under surveillance."

"Me? I ain't done nothing. Why would anybody want to surveil me?"

"I don't know, Dave. You know a lot of big people, you know? Maybe someone wonders who you are, what you're doing."

"I ain't been seeing none of those people."

"Then we probably got nothing to worry about. I'll see you in a little while."

Back in my car, which had tinted glass all around except for the windshield, the kind you couldn't see through from outside, I took up my binoculars. Lena and her father stood waiting for the taxi. Everything looked okay so far, but the five mile trip to the shopping mall would tell the tale -- I could follow along behind to see if I could discover any other cars that might be following, too.

A car pulled up right beside me. I glanced over. It was a lone man dressed in slacks and polo shirt, probably going for a round of golf. I returned to my surveillance, carefully focusing upon all the parked cars along the street. Nothing.

When I glanced back at the car beside me, I noticed the man still sitting there. He was also looking down to where Dave and Lena stood waiting -- with a pair of binoculars. He was talking into the microphone of a radio.

Whoa! By the sacred balls of the golden minotaur, what a thrill it was, to be sitting no more than a few feet away -- I could see him, but he couldn't see me. He looked around, seemed to be staring right at me. I didn't move, hardly breathed.

The taxi had arrived. Dave and Lena got in and it moved down the street toward us. The guy beside me was glancing all about, speaking quickly into the microphone. I watched a car come out from a side street and turn in to follow after the taxi. Another turned in from the other side. They were both four-door sedans with blackwall tires, just like those favored by the feds in their carpools. There were two men in each.

The one beside me started up, backed out, and turned up the street toward the convenience store. He did a U-turn to stop at the curb, where another man came out from the store to get in. Then they sped past me.

Even though I already knew, I followed it to take up the tail end of the parade, watching them engage in the musical chairs of exchanging places in their vehicles. I'm sure neither Lena, Dave, nor the taxi-driver spotted them.

Oh boy, Dave really had some heat on him. Now, what was I going to do to get my ol' lady back?

*****

I left town. I drove to Phoenix. I called Lena's sister, Cheryl, at her motel from a restaurant across the street. I told her to meet me at a bar a few blocks down the way. I watched her walk out and start down the sidewalk. Nobody followed. In a while, I called the bar and told her I'd gotten hung up, that I'd see her tomorrow. I watched her walk back to the motel. After an hour or so of seeing nothing suspicious, I transferred myself to a bar a little further down the street, where I sat over a few drinks watching the motel entrance -- until it grew dark.

I wandered around to come in through a back entrance to the motel. I found Cheryl's room number and knocked.

"Oh, God," she blurted. "Am I ever glad to see you!" She threw herself into my arms and burst into tears.

"What's the matter, kid?"

"My father was here yesterday. He tried to fuck me!"

When I'd gotten her calmed down with a good shot of scotch and passing a joint back and forth, she told me about it. Dave had dropped by unexpectedly, effusive and full of fatherly hugs and kisses. He'd offered to take her out to dinner, all the while asking questions about me. Had she heard from me lately? Did she know my whereabouts? Did she know what I was doing? She'd told him nothing, suspicious of his motives.

She had fixed him a drink and gone into the bathroom to shower and dress for dinner. He'd come in behind her, where she wore only a towel wrapped around her. He'd tried to touch her, had pulled the towel away. She'd become enraged, slapped at him, and tried to push him out the door. He'd grabbed at her, trying to kiss her. He needed her with him. She could be his right arm. He would make her rich, the two of them working together. What was wrong with a little intimacy? They had to trust each other. They were above all the rules of society, all the false moral values. They were superior people. They had to depend on each other, please each other. In this day and age of contraceptives, what was so wrong about giving each other pleasure?

Cheryl became hysterical, screaming out all her hate and terror at him. She managed to shove him out and lock herself in. He kept talking through the door to her, his voice oily, trying to persuade her. She sat in the shower and clapped her hands over her ears.

"He's trying to set you up," she said, her voice hoarse, her eyes angry in their dark circles. "I know he is. He's going to betray you."

"He already has."

I told her what had happened.

"Oh, God, he's got Lena! You've got to get her away from him! She doesn't know what he's really like!"

Thoroughly sick, my heart sluggishly pumping vile juices into my system, polluting my mind, I swigged at the scotch and tried to reassure her. I would get Lena back, somehow or other.

*****

I called Fast Eddie, but couldn't get hold of him. I called Ollie, who'd went back up to Washington to hunt for his wife and kids. I told him to fly to Phoenix to meet me. I called Gerry in Yuma. Business was fine, Alice was fine. Told him the situation with Dave, whom he'd met once or twice. I called Alice. She missed me -- when was I coming home?

"I'll be there in a few hours," I told her.

I drove to Yuma, went to Alice's new house in a quiet middle-class neighborhood. I spent the night. In the morning, I told her a little of the story about Dave's treachery, omitting any mention of Lena. I couldn't stay. It was too dangerous for me. I had to go back to Mexico.

"I can't go on living like this," she said, her voice full of despair. "You've got to take me with you."

"Babe, I can't. Not right now."

"I haven't seen you in months. You pop in for an overnight quickie and then you're gone. I just can't keep going like this." "They're looking for me on a murder charge."

"Did you do it? Did you kill those people?"

"Oh, babe, I never thought I'd hear that from you."

"Did you?"

I looked at her, meeting her intense gaze. Everyone thinks they have a built-in lie detector. I suppose she could read the disappointment in my eyes, that she had failed some unnamed test. She turned away, biting her lip, her fists clinched.

All I could say was, "What do you think?"

"I'm sorry," she sobbed. "I'm sorry. I just love you so much and I can't bear to be alone anymore!"

"All right, babe," I consoled. "All right. I'll figure out something, I promise. Just give me a little more time to work it out. Okay?"

I questioned her closely about who knew where she lived. Only Gerry and his lady, who'd helped her move there.

"Your kids don't know? Your mom? No slips on the phone?"

"No. I've called them, but always from a phonebooth. No one knows but the few friends we trust."

"Okay, babe. Just pack up and be ready to go."

"When?"

"Soon. A couple of weeks."

"What about the grass?"

"What grass?"

She showed me, about thirty kilos in the spare bedroom. "Gerry's been storing some of it here."

"Okay. I'll talk to him about it. Right now, I need to take Han," I said, referring to one of our dogs. He'd grown into a beautiful, but playful, and thoroughly undisciplined and spoiled beast, a credit to his AKC champion forebearers.

"For what?"

"Got a job for him. Time he earned his Gravy Train."

"Wha-at?"

"Don't worry. I'll bring him back in a day or so. See you then." We kissed.

"Take care of yourself, baby."

"I'm trying, darlin'."

*****

Back in Phoenix, I hooked up with Ollie. I had him go rent a car and we installed a portable CB radio in that plugged into a cigarette lighter.

"So, what's the deal, bro? What's with the Dobie?"

"You're going to be a hotel security guard. Han here, is your highly trained assistant who can sniff out drugs, explosives, and unauthorized intruders. Attacks on command and will faithfully defend his handler to the death."

"Really?"

"Just keep him on the leash. He gets loose, you'll be chasing him all over the place. He'll think it's a game."

In Tucson at 3 a.m., Ollie made his way up the back fire stairs to the eleventh floor. If any of Dave's company was awake, after waiting for three days for something to happen, Ollie could just nod and keep going. If the coast was clear, he was to knock quietly on the door. If the wrong party answered, he was simply to ask if they'd called the desk for security and excuse himself for having made a mistake. If Dave or Lena appeared to open the door, he was to step in quietly and ask them to get dressed. Lena knew Ollie and would understand what was happening. He was to stay near the phone to make sure Dave made no calls.

It went without a hitch. He soon appeared with them in tow. They all got into his car and drove out of the parking lot. I waited a few minutes to see if anyone had followed them. Seeing nothing suspicious, I started up and began driving away, too.

I raised Ollie on the CB. "How we looking?"

"Okay so far." I gave him directions for a 24-hour restaurant and followed uneventfully through the all but deserted streets. I wasn't sure how to handle Dave. All I wanted was to get Lena away. Could I hide my knowledge of his treachery? I'd have to play it by ear.

The sonofabitch hugged me. I looked at Lena, quiet and reserved. "You okay?"

She nodded. I wondered if she knew what was going on.

Inside, after we'd ordered coffee, Dave, his face seeming no more than innocently curious, asked, "What the hell's been going on, Buck? Am I missing something?"

"Didn't Lena tell you?"

He shrugged. "Just that if you didn't show, it meant there was a problem, that you'd get in touch later. What's up?"

"You're under surveillance, Dave."

"Me? I don't believe it. It must be you."

"No, Dave. Nobody knew I was coming here but you and Lena."

I didn't mention Cheryl -- keep that in reserve. I told him exactly what had happened. "It has to be you."

"What do you mean? I don't have any heat. No way."

"I know what I see with my own eyes. Those guys were cops." "Maybe you made a mistake on your end somewhere. It doesn't make any sense they'd be tailing me. No one knows I'm here either."

How about Samerah?"

Well, sure…" he began, then his eyes widened. "you don't think…?"

He was so good that I almost believed him. I wanted to believe him. There must be some explanation that would absolve him. But I believed what Cheryl had told me. I looked away to hide the disgust in my eyes. Lena was uncharacteristically silent, almost somber. Ollie kept his head down. He showed his emotions too easily. If it had been up to him, he would have already kicked the shit out of Dave. It wasn't that I was without feelings – I wanted to reach out and slap that innocent look off his face, curse him for a traitorous piece of shit – but I couldn't do any such thing in front of Lena. I felt sick with impotent rage that I had to sit there and pretend not to be sick, keep my cool. That was the thing about evil I thought, looking at him. It appeared so complacent.

"Well," I muttered. "We've got to get on down the road. C'mon, I'll drop you back at your hotel."

When I'd gotten them seated in the car, I went up to speak to Ollie. "You stay here," I told him. "When I call you on the CB, I want you to get on the phone. Call Dave's hotel and ask to be put through to the rooms on either side of Dave's room. You got it?"

"Both of them?"

I nodded. "Whoever answers, you say, "Where's your informant?"

"Where's your informant?"

"Yeah. They might ask you who you are, or what you're talking about – you tell them, no matter what they say, "you better check on your informant."

Ollie grinned. "Okay. I got it."

"Don't hang up. Just keep listening for maybe fifteen seconds. Then hang up and call the other room. Same thing. I want you to tell me exactly what you hear. After that, head on back to Phoenix. I'll see you there."

"What about Dave?"

"He's my problem. I'm going to let slip we're headed for the Mexican border, see if I can lead 'em astray."

"See you, partner. Be careful."

On the way back, Dave asked about our grass deal.

"We're going to have to postpone that, Dave, until we find out what's going on. You go on back to Atlanta and let it lay for a couple of weeks. Check out Samerah. I'll check on my people." "You'll get in touch?"

"Yeah, we're going to head on down to Nogales just to play it safe. I'll call you from there."

"Right. Okay."

"Really weird shit happening, Dave."

"You're telling me. I can't get a handle on it."

After a bit of silence, he asked, "Say, this is a pretty nice car. What is it, a Buick?"

"Olds," I answered automatically.

I pulled over down the street from his hotel. "You take care, Dave. I'll be in touch."

Before I could react, the sonofabitch reached out to cup his hand around the back of my neck. He pulled me forward and leaned across Lena to plant a kiss on my mouth. I was shocked.

"I love you, man," he said, then released me. He kissed Lena. "I'll be seeing you soon, baby. It was a good visit we had."

He got out of the car. I was still trying to get hold of myself. I didn't know whether to vomit or bellow out my rage. The rotten sonofabitch had actually kissed me like...like the Judas motherfucker he was!

"Cheryl sends her love," was all I could think to say. "I talked to her earlier this evening."

I couldn't tell if he flinched. He closed the door and walked behind the car to cross the street. I saw him hesitate a moment, then continue on without looking back. My finely functioning brain was a little slow to pick up that he had paused just long enough to memorize the number on my license plate.

*****

I asked Lena to tell me everything that had happened to her over the three days she had been with her father. She seemed reluctant, speaking in a desultory manner. I questioned her. Had she been in his company the whole time? No, they hadn't gone to the bathroom together. Did he ever leave you alone in the room? Yes, a few times. Did he make any phone calls? Yes, a few. He called Samerah. Did you notice anything odd, out of place? No. Did you see him talking to anyone, any strange men? No, just the people in the hotel, waiters in the dining room, like that. Did you go out anywhere, to a restaurant, a movie? No, we were waiting for you to get in touch. What did you talk about? She shrugged -- just normal conversations. Did he ask where you'd been? Yes. What'd you tell him? That we were living in Mexico. He knew that. Did you tell him where? I don't remember. I might have. What else? I mentioned Gerry in Yuma. Did you tell him where he lived? No. He said he knew him, had met him before. Anything else? She hesitated, looking out the window. We talked about Alice. What about Alice? He doesn't think it's right that you're stringing us both along. He thinks you should make a choice. How do you feel? She shrugged and picked at her fingers.

"You've known all along how it is with me and Alice. I can't just discard her like an old shoe. She deserves better than that."

"I know. I'm not complaining. My father's just old-fashioned. He's concerned about me."

"Yeah."

"What's going on, Buck?"

I sighed. I didn't know what to say, so I sighed again. "Ah, I don't know. It looks like we've got problems. We're going to have to make some changes."

"What? What are we going to do?"

"I don't know yet. Where's your head at? You still committed? You want to keep trucking along with me?"

"I love you, Buck. I never knew what that was until I met you."

"Ugly old fart like me."

"You're not ugly. And you're not old."

"Just a fart, huh?"

"You said it, not me," she giggled.

Back in Phoenix, I stopped in for a few words in parting with Ollie. I gave him some money. "What happened when you called?"

"I did like you said. Guy asked me who I was. I gave him the second line."

"Then what?"

"He said, oh shit, then called to somebody, Bob or Bill or something, I can't remember."

"Then you called the other room?"

"Yeah. Nobody answered for a while. When they did, I asked where's his informant. He said, who the hell is this? Then I gave him the other line and shut my mouth and listened like you said. He kept saying hello, hello, are you there? Then I heard someone say, there he is, and they hung up."

I could imagine their panic upon finding Dave's room empty. Then for him to come strolling in minus Lena to enlighten them. I consoled myself thinking they would probably go off on a wild goose chase to check the border crossing into Nogales.

"What do you want to do?"

"Think I'll go back up Oregon way. I got a new lady up there.
I know these guys got a grass farm going up in the woods. Think I'll give that a try."

"You don't want to go back to Mexico?"

"Nah. Not enough action down there. Don't you get bored with that shit, man?"

"Yeah, I guess so. I'm thinking of making some changes myself."

"Come on up and show us how to grow grass."

"Nah, thanks. I'm thinking about going up to Canada, maybe get into something up there, settle down for awhile."

"Keep in touch, bro."

"Sure. You, too."

I couldn't resist the question that had been eating at me, even though I dreaded the answer. What would it mean one way or another? "When you went in Dave's hotel room, how many beds were there?" "Two, why?"

"They both messed up?"

He thought. "Hm. Now that you mention it, I think one was made up."

"Only one had been slept in?"

"Yeah. I'm not positive, but I think so. I watched them get dressed. Lena went into the bathroom."

"Okay. You take care, ol' buddy."

*****

Instead of going back to Yuma as I'd planned, to return Han, I turned north toward Flagstaff. I'd been there a couple of times before with Alice, once when we'd gone to the Grand Canyon and another time when we'd spent a few idyllic days beside a lake all alone and it had hailed -- days of enchantment. There seemed to be a lot of sad, drunken Indians there, but an otherwise quiet, laidback town. I thought about renting a house out in the boonies, with room to breathe and hike with the dogs. Maybe get some horses. Get into some business. What? I didn't know. Maybe a bar for sad, drunken Indians. My true love and me.

What about Alice? Well, why didn't I just take charge, move her and Lena in together, lay down the law, tell them how it was going to be? They loved me, I loved them, quod erat demonstrandum. Divide up the days of the week between them for my stud services, take Sundays off. I wasn't at all sure how well that would go over, but I didn't have a better plan. Charisma, me boyo, charm.

"Maybe Cheryl could come and stay with us."

"Yeah, why not?"

Boyohboy. If the Mormons could do it, why not me?

Reality intruded upon the fantasy. Something was missing from our relationship. The lightheartedness, the fun and ease, the excitement and enthusiasm whenever we touched each other. Our lovemaking seemed to be more of a desperate clinging to each other rather than the great laughing, crying release it had once been. We were awkward and uneasy. What dark forces were pulling us apart? What intuitions whispered wordlessly to me?

    I knew something drastic had happened, that something awful was interfering in the flow of my life. It was nothing I could name, just dumb feelings. I felt helpless and frustrated, nevertheless determined to struggle against whatever fate held in store. Perhaps it was only the subconscious settling of all the events that had happened over the past two years of fast freedom, a painful acceptance that love and loyalty can blind one to the truth. And I was so sad I couldn't speak.

    We had gotten into bed at a cheap motel one night without a word and switched out the light. It was so dark it was like being blind. Lena laid her head on my shoulder and cuddled up to me. I don't know what it was, an ache in my throat, burying eyes, life itself overwhelming me. Lena moved, felt a wetness on my chest, reached her hand up to my face.

    "Oh, baby, what is it? What's the matter?"

    I couldn't answer. She kissed me, drew my head to her breasts, trying to comfort me, whispering frantically, "Oh, baby, tell me what it is, please, what's wrong?"

    She tried to turn on the lamp beside the bed. I pulled her back, still unable to speak, and held her tight. She began to weep. What do you do with a crying woman? She clung to me in some awful dread, me, an anchor that had lost its hold on the bottom.

> My melancholy fancies no terrorist act
> more brutal to maidens than tears
> dreadfully squeezed from the marble faces
> of old lovers hoary with crimes.

#

CHAPTER 11

My daughter was again spending the summer with my mother and I couldn't resist going for a visit. Lena and I checked into a nearby motel, then went to a restaurant/lounge, where we got a table for four. After explaining the procedure, I got up to leave.

"How will I recognize them?"

"An old lady and a young girl, both blond."

I drove to a phonebooth to dial my mother's number. When she'd answered, I said, "Hi, Aunt Dotty, this is George." It was a simple code we'd worked out just in case the feds ever went so far as to put a wiretap on her line. George was a cousin of mine, but she could always recognize my voice in any case.

"How about we go out to dinner? I've got us a table reserved," I continued, telling her where. "Meet you there."

"What time, dear?"

"However long it takes to freshen your lipstick."

"Sounds good. We'll see you soon."

When she drove out to turn onto the road toward town, I was parked down the way, waiting with my lights out. There was hardly any traffic at all. I followed along behind. There were no tails. I parked and sat a few minutes just to make sure, then went in to join them.

314

Lena was at her charming and vivacious best. I danced with my mom, then my daughter, and finally Lena.

"Introducing me to your mother and daughter -- you must be serious," Lena said with a teasing smile.

"What do you think?"

"Your mom's a jewel -- she's so warm and friendly. I really like her. And your daughter's beautiful. You sure know how to make babies."

"I think my mom's wondering about you and me. You're only five years older than my daughter."

"Probably horrified her son's a cradle-robber."

"Nah, she thinks you like to molest old men."

"Only dirty old men."

We danced slow and close.

"I love you, baby," she said.

"I kinda go for you, too."

162

"Thanks for bringing me to meet them. Your daughter wants to know how long we're staying."

"Not long. We can't," I replied, biting my teeth. "Maybe a few days if we're careful."

"Let's be careful."

After dinner, Lena and my daughter excused themselves for the lady's room.

I asked my mom if anybody'd been around lately asking questions. She knew all her neighbors and they always told her when strangers came snooping about.

"No, not for awhile. Maybe they've given up on you."

"I doubt it."

"Well, you be careful, son."

We talked about family matters and she brought me up to date. Lena and my daughter came back to tell us they were going outside to look at the lake and talk. My darling bright-eyed girl seemed fascinated with Lena.

"She likes Lena," my mother observed, catching the warm glow in my eyes.

"You think so?"

"Oh, yes. You've always done well with girlfriends. They've always been so nice. It was only your daughter's mother who I had my doubts about."

"Well, nowadays I can only take her in small doses myself... and only because I have to. Let's not talk about her. How are you doing?"

"Oh, fine, fine." She could never bear to bring bad news to anyone. If she thought the truth would hurt, she'd ignore it. She changed the subject. "Lena's in love with you."

"Yeah, I think so. She just told me that."

"What happened to Alice?"

"She's around," I muttered uncomfortably.

"I liked her. Did you break up?"

"No, not exactly."

She looked at me but didn't ask. "Are you happy, son?" "Aw, sometimes. How happy can an escaped fugitive be?" "Well, you've had enough of the bad stuff."

"That's for sure. But it always seems to have a way of catching up to me." My turn to change the subject. "You got any boyfriends? Whatever happened to ol' Jack? I really liked that ornery old sonofagun. Remember the time we all smoked grass?"

We chuckled together, remembering. I'd been married then and still moonfaced in love with my wife. We'd taken my mom and Jack, who was close on to eighty years, out to dinner and dancing at a country and western place. We'd all gone out back for a breath of fresh night air. Leaning on a corral rail, calling softly to some horses, I'd lit up a joint. My wife and I had passed it back and forth, thinking my mom and Jack would never figure it out. Jack had sniffed loudly.

"Smells like that damned maryjewanna weed," he opined. "Used to go to my son's house down in the city. He smoked it. Could always smell it. Never said nothin'. Never let on I knew. What the hell, never seemed to do him no harm."

"You ever smoke it, Jack?"

"Nope, never did. Always wanted to. Curious, you know? Never had the opportunity."

"Now's your chance, Jack," I said, offering the joint to him. "Hell, looks like a Bull Durham home-rollie. This ain't gonna make me go crazy, is it?"

"No, Jack, I don't think so," I replied while my wife tittered away, squeezing my arm. "If you ain't gone crazy by now, this stuff sure won't do it."

"Well, okay, then. Just catch me if I fall down."

"I've got you, Jack," my mother assured him, her arm around his waist.

"Tastes like cornsilk and alfalfa," he said, after three or four tokes. "Used to smoke it when I was a shaver down on the farm." I lit another one and handed it to my mom. "You want to try it?" "Oh, no. Whiskey's good enough for me."

"Try it, Dot. Just so's you can say you did. Nothin' to worry about. Ain't done nothin' to me so far."

"Well, maybe a little bit."

I lit another one, then another, as we got to passing them hand to hand in a circle.

"It doesn't do anything," my mother complained. "I don't know why anyone would want to smoke it."

"Hell, look at the sky, Dottie. All them stars."

"Oh, my, it is pretty tonight, isn't it?"

We all leaned against the railings looking up at the stars. "Minds me a barn dances. Ever'body'd come with food and drink, all the neighbors from miles around. Have a high old fiddle in them days. You 'member barn dance's, Dot?"

"Oh, my God, yes. They'd spread sawdust all over the floor and just go sliding all over the place. Walker was a good dancer when he'd had a few and put his mind to it."

She always called my father Walker.

Well let's just get back in there and show these kids how it's done," Jack snortled with sudden animation. "Hell, I don't feel a day over sixty!"

"Reckon we can do that, Jack," my mother agreed in high good humor.

"You whippersnappers comin'?"

"In a minute. We want to say goodnight to the horses."

Jack neighed in his rusty imitation of an equine whinny. "That's how you do it!"

"Bye, horsies," my mother called, waving.

We cracked up after they'd gone back inside. Later, driving them home, they'd sat in the back seat whispering and giggling like kids.

"Oh, he passed on," my mother said. "He was a good man, but old age just caught up with him."

"Sorry to hear that. Old Jack. What a guy."

"Yes, I miss him."

"Me, too. I've missed you and my kid the most."

"We've missed you, too, son."

"I got up to see my ornery brother awhile back. And sis, too. God, their kids are almost all grown up."

"Oh, yes, and they've got such nice children, so beautiful, all of them. Matt and Tricia. Steve and Mike and David."

"I miss dad and Larry, too," I added and kicked myself for saying it. Mentioning my father and my youngest brother always made her teary-eyed. My father had died suddenly in his sleep, according to the story I'd heard. A piece of plywood had fallen on his head while working at a lumber processing company in Oregon. He'd gone home to bed with a headache and never woke up. My bother had died mysteriously by a gunshot wound to the head while I was at McNeil. I had never quite gotten the story straight, whether it had been an accident or suicide.

I had never been able to accept either version.

I patted my mother's hand while she dabbed at her eyes. "Let's go find the girls," I said.

"Get a breath of fresh air."

"Does Lena know you escaped from prison?"

"Yeah."

"How does she feel about it?"

"No big deal. All my best friends have done time. I trust her." "Your father was in jail once, too," she blurted. "Did you know that?"

"Dad? In jail? For what?"

"Oh, I'm not sure. I was only about fifteen when it happened. I think he and another boy stole a cow."

"A cow?"

She laughed at the look of disbelief on my face. "I don't think they really stole it. I mean, what can you do with a cow? We were all farm kids. None of us would steal a cow. It was just some kind of hi-jinks or something. But the farmer who owned the cow was a mean old cuss and he called the sheriff."

"So he went to jail for that? Stealing a cow?"

"Yes, they didn't take kindly to that back then. It was during the Depression. Everybody was poor back then."

"What happened?"

"Oh, the judge sent him off to a reform school, or maybe it was a work detention farm. Him and his friend."

"For how long?"

"Oh, a year or so, I think."

"No shit?" I was flabbergasted. If it hadn't been my own mother telling me, I would never have believed it. "Isn't that about when you met him? Where was it? Kansas?"

"Yes. That's when I fell in love with him. I wrote to him the whole time he was away in jail. I thought he was the most beautiful boy I'd ever seen. We got married after he came home."

"Jesus," I exclaimed. "My own dad was a cattle rustler and a jailbird!"

"Your father was a good man."

"I know, mom, I know. It's okay. I'm glad you told me." "I'm sorry he died like that, even if we did go our own ways after you kids all grew up. I never stopped loving him." "Me neither, mom."

"It was just so sad to die in mid-dream like that. He always followed after his dream -- just like you do, son, up and down all the time. You're more like your father than you know."

"Suits me just fine."

*****

Making love with Lena those few days took on new poignancy, deeper pains mixing with greater pleasures, our passions and needs almost driven frantic, leaving us dull and exhausted -- until we soon stirred and moved toward each other again.

*****

I called Enrique. I told him about Dave, whom he had known at McNeil, that he had likely figured out our scene in Mexico sufficiently so that the feds might come snooping around.

"They know where we're at?"

"Yeah, I think so. It's better we don't take any chances."

"Man, we're going to have to move somewhere else."

"Right. Maybe we should close down and find us a spot to coast for awhile. You got any ideas?"

"Maybe Vera Cruz. I've been there a couple of times. It's nice, out of the way, only two or three hours to Mexico City."

"Sounds good."

"When you coming back?"

"Week or ten days, long enough to tie up loose ends, I'm on my way. You better start packing up."

"Okay, my friend."

We drove to San Francisco, where I hoped to collect some money owed by two or three people. After parking Lena at our favorite hotel near the beach and Golden Gate Park, I went about collecting.

I couldn't find Janey, who owed me several thousand, so I left messages.

As I strolled hand in hand with Lena along the beach at midnight, wading in the cold water of the Pacific, my eyes full of the moon and stars, my heart sailing a tall ship over the sea, the dream returned. What was I doing, caught up in all this shit, all the demanding and contradictory complexities of civilization? I longed for a life that was slower and simpler. I remembered Palmyra and Stephanie. Samarang. We'd had a little blue boat called Iola, to life. We had been poised on the brink of the dream. It seemed to float like an invisible siren out in the darkness, whispering enchantments in my ear. The rising sun would bring a new light into my existence, and when it would sink over the horizon more beautiful than an acidhead's vision, I would sit a little weary, but relaxed and at peace, a gin and tonic in one hand, a joint in the other, speaking softly with... who? My friends, my mates, my loved ones?

For years, I had been designing the perfect sailing vessel, each facet of its layout and dimensions fixed in my mind. She would be a gaff-rigged schooner, fat and deep, heavy and strong, a double-ender with a bowsprit like a pirate's sword, not the fastest and most efficient, but roomy and comfortable in all seas and weathers, capable of getting there, anywhere in the world, lazily and surely. The sea would feed me, keep me, and rock me to sleep at night while the winds would call to me of new lands and people just over the horizon. Somewhere, somehow, the secret of my life would be revealed to me.

Well, why not? As long as I breathed and my mind was intact, the dream would be there, just ahead, beckoning. I could almost smell Samoa, Fiji, Tahiti, Tonga, and the Tuamotus.

Somewhere among the thousands of islands, I would find the Promised Land, an uninhabited one saying, I am yours. Take me and express your will on me. Bring me love and laughter and playing children, work and music and dancing, and let me drink of the sweat of your labor.

An escape, I knew, but why not? A running from was also a running toward. Why the hell not? Vera Cruz was a seaport. It must have shipyards, builders of boats. But what did it matter? I could build it myself, launch it, sail it away. My own design, my home.

"What are we going to do?"

"We're going to Vera Cruz," I said, as if nothing else need be explained. It was a new beginning. Vera Cruz.

"What about Cheryl?"

"We'll take her with us."

"What about Alice?"

"She goes, too."

Lena looked at me, than laughed. "Are you kidding?"

"No."

She studied me, playing it through in her mind.

"And Enrique and Fae will be there with us."

She looked out over the sea. It was so dark, she couldn't see very far.

"Maybe Ollie'll show up. And Fast Eddie."

"Who's that?"

"A friend, a brother. You'll like him."

"You think it'll work?"

"Why not? You and me, babe, we can make anything work." Suddenly I believed it. All hands turn to building boats. Quinn, you sly devil, I thought, you'll have nothing on me! (Quinn sailed off to the South Pacific with an all-girl crew in the sixties. His voyages, including social arrangements, were much publicized in newspapers and magazines.)

The next morning, after breakfast at the Cliffhouse, as we were on our way out of the city, I made one last call to Janey, caught her in, and went by her apartment.

"I don't have your money," she informed me right off the bat, looking restless and distracted.

"Ah, well, maybe next time. How you been? How's the Wildfire?" Wildfire was her kid, now a fourteen-year-old freckle-faced, smart-mouthed, and sharp little number.

I'd met Janey years before, when I'd begun a trip from San Francisco down to Los Angeles, while driving a big old stepvan. She'd been standing at the on-ramp to the freeway with a huge Harlequin Great Dane. I had gawked at her from across the street at a stoplight, knowing she would never hitch a ride with a dog like that. Well, what the hell, I had plenty of room for the beast and, besides, I liked dogs and girls. I pulled over and told her to hop in.

She was an earth-mother type, relaxed and warm and outgoing. We smoked a couple of joints and hit it off right away, swapping stories and information all the way down. After a soup and wine dinner, we made love on the ridged floor of the van as the Harlequin, a mere six months old puppy, drooled and whined and watched us.

After that, we became each other's escape valves. If one of us was blue, we'd call the other, get together and smoke it, drink it, talk it, and love it out. Her three-year-old son was called Wildfire because he was a fiercely independent holy terror.

Once, when I'd been having problems with Samantha and my estranged wife, who was divorcing me, I called her. She said the carnivals were meeting down in a small town in the southern desert, and why didn't we get away from it all for awhile. Janey had been raised in the carnivals. She knew everybody who was anybody in the business, had traveled all over the country on one circuit or another, and had worked a good part of her life hustling this carnival or that.

We journeyed down in my old Chevy van, in the back of which was a homebuilt bunk with just enough room to fit a light motorcycle. We had stopped off at an empty stretch of desert called Dirty Socks Hot Springs. You could tell by the smell of sulphur why they'd called it that. After bathing nakedly under the star-filled sky, we cooked up a meal over an open campfire. Janey tucked Wildfire into the front seat and kissed him goodnight.

"It's lovely out here," she said, lighting a joint.

"Want to go for a ride?"

"Now?"

"Sure."

"It'll wake Wildfire."

"Nah, we can push the bike down the road a ways before I crank it up."

"All right," she grinned. "On one condition."
"What's that?"
"We get naked first."

Ah, me boyos, if you haven't chased after wild jackasses through the desert at night on a motorcycle with a naked woman's thighs around your naked ass, all I can say is you've really missed something.

We had come out onto a two-lane paved road and were cruising lazily along in easy esses, the wind massaging our bodies, Janey's yard-long tresses streaming wildly in the flow, when all of a sudden a station wagon had pulled alongside us. An old man driving three old ladies were all goggling bug-eyed at us, their mouths hung open in shock.

I goosed the throttle and took off. Up the road aways, I hooked a U and tore back toward them, Janey waving madly, flashing a big tit at them as we roared off into the night laughing like lunatics.

At the carnival grounds, where a county fair was being held, we parked out among the workers' vehicles and went around meeting everybody. Janey was offered a job hustling a tent booth that featured a mechanical horse race. Left to my own devices during the day, I took Wildfire around to all the fair displays and we rode all the rides for free. In the evening, we went about among the crowds of people eating candied apples and cotton candy to see all the tent shows. One of them was the gorilla girl act. It was one of the most amazing things I'd ever seen.

Outside the tent, on a little raised walkway, the announcer, clad in a tophat, white bowtie and tails, a real class act, strode back and forth with a microphone in hand, hinting in exclamatory tones just what was in store for those who could afford a mere piddling fifty cents. To either side of him rose two mural-like signs painted on flats of wood and canvas. They depicted on the one a silhouette of a dark jungle with wild animal faces peering out. There was a figure of a Frank Buck bring-'em'-back-alive type under the words, Dr. Somebody's Amazing Gorilla Girl from Darkest Africa. The other sign showed a ferocious King Kong-sized gorilla with a scantily clad, terrorized woman clutched in his hand. The spielman told a wondrous tale of how mankind had descended from the great apes and how the good Dr. Somebody had proved it. He could hypnotize a human being, a girl, and put her into such a state of mystical dark forces that before your very eyes she reverted to her animal origins by changing into a gorilla.

Inside the tent with a crowd of curious and amused folk, Wildfire seated on my shoulders so he could see, the spielman had mounted a flatbed trailer on which sat a huge, steel-barred cage. Beside him stood a pretty girl dressed in a brief costume smiling, wriggling her hips and showing off her legs. With the words flowing in dramatic waves, he opened the door to the cage, walked the girl in to stand against the rear wall, locked her in, and began a show of hypnotizing her.

The girl closed her eyes and stood unmoving as the trance took hold. Then, before our awestruck eyes, she began to...change. We could see hair growing on her arms and legs as her body began to hunch forward. Her nails grew into black points. Her body shrank and widened, the shoulders and arms growing more massive. Her face slowly and horrifyingly took on the slope-browed, flat-nosed, wide-mouthed, hairy- awed ugliness of a gorilla.

In absolute silence, the gorilla, leaning on the knuckled pillars of its huge, muscular arms, stared evilly at us with mad, glittering eyes, red-rimmed with rage. When it leaped forward to slam against the bars, we all cringed and tightened our sphincters. The spielman leapt back, too. "Don't worry, folks," he reassured us in a breathless voice. "Those bars are made of pure tungsten steel and have been scientifically tested to withstand two thousand pounds of pressure per square inch. We're safe out here."

Just then, the enraged gorilla slammed its basketball-sized fists against the bars and, god almighty, the whole barred front of the cage crashed down to the floor! The beast leapt out with a bloodcurdling snarl! Fully half the onlookers broke and ran, the rest surely too petrified to move. A flap had been whipped aside, letting in the lights and raising the sounds from outside, so the tent wouldn't get torn down in the rush. I almost shit my pants. Wildfire was frozen into a solid ball of shock, my ears gripped in his tiny fists.

With barely concealed amusement, the spielman now cracked a whip, driving the gorilla defiantly back. He began to drone the words of the hypnotic trance that calmed the beast. Slowly, again before our very eyes, the gorilla changed back into a girl. She blinked her eyes and began to move, led out by the hand.

"What happened?" she said, oh so innocently.

Wildfire and I, after refreshing ourselves with snowcones, went back to see the amazing gorilla girl again and again. We couldn't figure out how it was done, but we were hooked.

In bed that night, I told Janey about it. She introduced me to the people who ran the show and they gladly demonstrated how the illusion was accomplished by the clever use of a movie projector and sliding black panels, which allowed the girl and the man in the gorilla costume to change places. As a former ham actor, I was fascinated.

It turned out they were trying to sell the show, truck, tent, props and all. Would I be interested in taking it on the road? Janey urged me, lent all the powers of her persuasion to convert me. I could wear the tophat and penguin suit, while she played the gorilla girl. We could get somebody to wear the gorilla costume. Wildfire could pull the tent flap back at the right moment so the scaredy-cats knew where to flee.

"C'mon, baby, you'll love it. It's perfect for you -- a whole new way of life. We can hustle our way across the country together."

I was sorely tempted, right on the verge of chucking it all for fifty cent-a-head entertainment. I had often looked back over my life and wondered, as we all must do, what would have happened if I'd taken a different turning at some point along the way. There were so many places where I could have turned right instead of left, detoured, back-tracked, found a new trail -- and this was one of them. I always ever after wondered how things would have turned out if I'd only taken the gorilla girl act on the road.

Somewhere along the way, in the ensuing ten years or so since I'd met her, Janey had picked up a heroin habit. She changed, became hard-eyed and calculating in the desperation that drove her from fix to fix. She had been in and out of jails, gone cold-turkey and joined methadone programs, been beaten up and robbed in drug deals gone awry, had even hooked her body to chumps down in the Tenderloin. She was lost to the opium demon and knew it, her only saving grace, a fiercely protective soft spot for her son, and perhaps an old friend or two.

Janey paid me off in beans, as the bootleg brand of cross-topped benzedrine pills are called, four bags of them, each containing 25,000 pills. She put them in a small suitcase and handed it to me. She hustled them to her carnie friends, who lived on them, needed them for getting through the long days and nights traveling the circuits.

"Are we square now?"

"What in hell am I going to do with these?"

"Oh, shit, man, you can stand on a sheet corner and sell them all day and night long, if nothing else. Hang around a few days and I can move them and have the cash for you."

"Nah, it's okay. We're square. I gotta get on the road. You take care of yourself, Janey."

I hugged her.

"Sure, nobody's gonna do it for me."

*****

Lena and I drove to Yuma, preparatory to crossing the border at San Luis Colorado, a mere twenty minutes from town. I met with Gerry to bring him up to date. We were out of business. I needed him to bring my IBM Selectric typewriter, with its dozens of ball-type heads, which I used in preparing bogus ID. Not that I needed any more ID, but that I had vague thoughts of once again trying my hand at writing. Vera Cruz, after all, was a place of romantic reputation.

He told me I'd have to wait until morning because the typewriter was in storage at a commercial facility. It would open at seven in the morning. Okay.

Lena and I checked into the Torchlite Motel on Fourth Street, the main drag of Yuma. We showered together and fell into bed to make love. Then I got up and dressed to go see Alice. I'd no sooner stepped in the door than she pulled me into the bedroom to satisfy her frantic need. I told her the plan. She was to pack up and get ready to travel. Gerry would put her on a plane to Los Angeles or San Diego, where she would transfer to a flight to Mexico City. I would be waiting for her.

I showered and dressed to return to Lena. When I had crawled in beside her, she rolled over and began kissing and caressing me. Lucky as I thought I was, was I really audacious enough to think I could handle three women under one roof, one of them not even tried out for size yet, and a sister to another to boot? Oh, me bucko, what a foolish web thou weavest!

Lena wanted to call her father about sending the rest of her clothes and personal belongings to her before we left for Mexico. I told her no. She wanted to know why. I broke the news to her about her father. She couldn't believe it. I explained in detail exactly what was going on. She didn't want to believe it. She was like a wounded puppy whose mother had just bitten off her tail. I hated Dave, wished I could hurt him somehow. I told her she could call and ask him herself once we were across the border, decide for herself.

In the morning, about nine, Gerry called and said he'd be right over. I got dressed while Lena went into the bathroom. I walked outside to meet him. He parked next to my car. I carried down the suitcase full of benzedrine tablets. We opened the trunks. He transferred the typewriter to mine and I put the suitcase in his.

"What the hell am I going to do with these?"

"Stand on a street corner and sell 'em day and night, I guess," I shrugged. "I can't take them with me -- coals to Newcastle and all that."

On that lighthearted note, just like that, I became aware of strange men, intent looks on their faces, moving in toward us from several directions.

"Oh, shit," I muttered and slammed the trunk.

Gerry saw them, too, and slammed his trunk.

"Wesley Walker," one of them announced, flashing badge and ID folder. "You're under arrest."

They all had guns in their hands. They didn't know who the hell Gerry was until they looked at his ID. Then, they informed him he was under arrest for harboring a fugitive, one Wesley Walker.

"Who?" I asked with a frown. "Just what the heck is this all about?"

"You're under arrest for escape from a federal prison, Walker." "My lawyer's going to love this. You've got the wrong man. My name's Bill Edwards."

He hesitated with the handcuffs, then took my wallet to study the name and picture on the drivers license.

"That's me, William Thomas Edwards," I explained with a forgiving grin. "Boy, you guys sure pulled a boner this time."

"It's probably a phony."

"Phony, hell. Check with the DMV. I've had that license for two years now, ever since I moved down here from Tacoma. Check the Tacoma DMV. That's where I had my last license from."

He pulled a photo, a prison mugshot, out of his shirt pocket and held it up to make a comparison.

I knew exactly what picture it was. Prison authorities always circulated the most recent photo they had of an escaped convict. It had been taken the day before I'd been transferred to camp on McNeil Island. I had known the convict who was assigned to take the mugshots. I had mussed my long hair out wildly, bugged out my eyes, and puffed my cheeks out in a mad Harpo Marx look. It made me look like a hyperthyroid maniac. It didn't look anything like the modest, unassuming good ol' boy dressed in country slacks and boots standing before them with a Stetson on his head.

I could see the doubt in his eyes, almost hear the "Oh, shit," in his head.

"Well, let's get the show on the road, boys," I smirked. "I'm eager to see what a judge is going to have to say about all this... to you!"

Oh, was it eating at him, the uncertainty. His mind was going ninety miles an hour -- just what he didn't need, a false arrest on his record.

Just as I was beginning to hope, maybe, just maybe...he reached over, pulled my shirtsleeve up and looked at the name tattooed on my upper arm: Buck.

He grinned. "Buck Walker, you're under arrest."

"Jesus Christ in a grocery store," I admitted. "I think you've got it right at last. You're smarter'n you look, you know that?" Two of them went up to grab Lena -- good duty if she was in the shower. They put us in cars and drove us to the police station. They said they were going to get warrants to search our cars. They'd already searched the motel room without a warrant.

I wasn't worried about them finding anything in my car, but Gerry's held the suitcase with the hundred thousand hits of speed. I was trying to figure how I could get him off the hook. Maybe I could say he didn't know what was in the suitcase, that I'd merely asked him to store it for me. If I'd known then what I found out later, I might have laughed instead. All those pills Janey had laid on me to square her debt, as the official laboratory police report would show, contained not a trace of any illegal drugs! Had Janey burned me, or had she been burned?

A certain comical chain of events was set into motion after our arrests. While the feds, a combined force of DEA agents and local police and detectives, set about obtaining search warrants for our cars, Gerry's ol' lady became worried when he didn't return right away as he'd told her he would. She drove over to the Torchlite Motel looking for him. She saw his car parked next to mine and heard the talk by onlookers about the arrest. She went over with her own keys and drove Gerry's car home. When she found $15,000 in a leather pouch on the seat and the suitcase full of pills, she got scared, just knowing they would come to arrest her too. So she drove to another motel and checked in.

Later, the cops would find her the same way they'd found me -- by driving around to all the not-so-many motels in town looking at license plates of cars in the parking lots. They had gotten Gerry's when they'd arrested us -- they needed it for the search warrant. They'd gotten mine from my old buddy, Dave, the traitorous stool-pigeon.

After standing around all day handcuffed in a holding pen, during which I ignored all attempts to question me, I broke my silence once to speak a few words to the guy who seemed to be in charge.

"Hey, man, that girl you got out there, she's a civilian. She doesn't know anything about anything, not even my name. Just a nice piece of ass along for a short ride, you know?"

"Yeah, I know. That was obvious. We turned her loose."

"Thanks, man. You did the right thing."

Only it didn't sound right coming from him. The usual procedure would have been to jail Lena, scare her, and try to pressure her into giving them information. It didn't set right that I'd run into the one good and decent DEA agent of the thousands of Crum bums wearing the badge. But it would all make sense when I lay upon a dirty jailhouse bunk trying to figure out what had happened. How had they gotten on to me? Who knew I would be at the Torchlite Motel, let alone Yuma? Gerry and Lena, as well as Gerry's girlfriend, knew about the Torchlight. Alice knew I was in Yuma. I couldn't believe any of them had betrayed me. But, what about Gerry? Had he been under surveillance and inadvertently led them to me? I hadn't utilized my anti-surveillance tactics when meeting him because he was as careful as me. No, it had to be something else, someone else.

*****

I had rarely used my Olds in border crossings. I didn't want its license number popping up too often in any computer for some sharp-eyed analyst to detect suspicious patterns of movement. The car was registered in Alice's name and, in order to insure her insulation from my activities, I had never used it to transport drugs -- with the single exception of the suitcase full of bogus benzedrine pills.

My bust was a simple and unimportant event, but of course the feds and reporters never liked things to be so. What excitement was there in such mundane events for anybody?

DEA agents like all federal agents and policemen in general, like to make themselves look good by exaggerating the circumstances surrounding a bust. They tend to see reporters as gullible souls wearing day-glo orange socks. It's an old hustle -- you see a sucker wearing his wants and needs on his sleeve, you make him believe you're giving him what he wants. Reporters want exciting stories, not lusterless reruns. They want good-against-evil stories where good wins. They want stereotypes -- clever cops against dumb crooks. After all, more than one generation has been raised on the exploits of TV characters from Joe Friday to Inspector Erskine to Starsky and Hutch to Don Johnson's Hollywood ideas of narcs on Miami Vice. Reporters want an exciting story; shameless cops give them one, no matter it's mostly fictional. Who cares? The bigger the dragon, the more valorous the knight and the shinier his armor.

The gullible lined up for their handouts. Buck and Gerry became international masterminds in narcotics trafficking. A huge task force of local lawmen and a federal narcotics team had been surveiling us off and on for months. Gerry brought in large shipments of Asian heroin, while Buck handled the plethora of drugs moving over the Mexican-American border. And were we ever clever. We had to be in order for the cops to be even cleverer.

The task force had had Gerry's home and business staked out for months. They had recorded dozens of my recent border crossings. They had Walker's gunmoll staked out, a woman who went under the alias of Luanne who could usually be observed in the mornings when she came out to set her garbage on the curb, a hardfaced doxie in a faded purple robe with her hair in curlers, always looking like she'd had a hard night. At forty, she was the oldest and most hardboiled of the molls in the Gerry-Buck Gang, and who the task force had dubbed the Den Mother.

It was known, too, that the aging villains at the head of this viper's nest preferred younger, more beautiful women. Gerry had a sexy eighteen year old, while Buck had lured a fetching nineteen year old into his lecherous clutches. While Gerry drove a Lincoln Continental, Buck was more discreet in his Oldsmobile. When the task force had discovered that Walker, the man with a thousand aliases, was an escaped convict, they decided to bust him, pressure him, knowing he would, as did all these vermin of few loyalties, turn on his associates like a rat deserting a sinking ship, concerned only for his own safety.

Then the task force got a break. Walker's Olds had rolled through the border checkpoint at San Luis Colorado, a mere twenty minutes drive from Yuma. Customs agents on duty had failed to make the vehicle as one on the Border Lookout List; but an alert city cop had spotted it at a local motel. A team of agents rushed to the scene to take up a sophisticated surveillance. Gerry was reported on the move. They watched him enter Buck's room and ten minutes later exit to crane their necks and peer about suspiciously in good cinematic fashion before both getting into Buck's car. The agents saw Buck pull a bag from under the seat, hand it to Gerry, who looked inside before passing over an envelope -- a deal going down.

The agents rushed in to yank Buck and Gerry from the car, spread-eagle them over the hood. The envelope was filled with hundred dollar bills, thousands of dollars. The bag contained a cornucopia of brightly colored capsules. A quick taste by an experienced agent determined they were barbiturates.

Ah, well, me boyos, a nice story played in several variations. The reporters were obviously too busy writing down the thrilling details to ask even the simplest questions -- like why was a search warrant needed when the miscreants had been arrested in the car, which circumstance would have permitted a perfectly constitutional search? How did you learn that the customs agent had missed the Olds on the Border Lookout List? Could we see the list? Were Buck and Gerry charged with the drug transaction that had been observed? What about all the other members of their organization? Were more arrests imminent?

Oh, well now, hah, hell no. It's good that the gullible remain gullible, which they are happily able to do with so little effort. Think how dull life would be without them.

But, getting back to facts, ladies and gentlemen, the sorry truth of my apprehension was the drab case of my old pal, David, rolling over to snitch me out so he could be forgiven his own crimes, whatever they were. He had tried to set me up for arrest in Tucson, but failed. And the feds were pissed off no end for having been made fools of. In the end, the best Dave could do is provide them with my license plate number.

All of which, after two years, one month, and three days of glorious freedom, I came to understand from inside the Yuma Jail, which was full of sad Indians with hangovers. I had been thinking furiously over everything that had occurred in the last week or ten days, poring over every detail of every event.

No drugs had been found in the motel room, nor any in our possession when arrested. The feds knew who I was only because Dave had told them, providing snippets of information as to my activities and whereabouts. They knew nothing of Gerry, except that he'd been present when they'd come to arrest me. They knew nothing of Alice's whereabouts. Dave had wheedled the news out of Lena that I would be visiting Gerry. They didn't know where Gerry lived, nor have him under surveillance. The feds had released Lena not because I'd tried to absolve her of any complicity or because the DEA agent happened to a decent guy, but only as favor to Dave.

They didn't know shit from Shinola. All the folderol for reporters could be taken as no more than smokescreen to cover Dave's slimy tracks.

But now that they had us in custody, they could learn more. They could learn about Gerry, his girlfriend, who was soon to become not only very interesting but frantically sought after. They could conceivably learn about Alice, her whereabouts, and she, by all the Irish saints, still had thirty keys of grass sitting in the spare bedroom of her rented digs!

I decided to take a chance. I knew that all calls off the jail phone might be monitored, but I also figured it would probably take them several hours to track the number to an address. Perhaps, since all the DEA agents had gone home, they wouldn't discover it until the next day, which would be too late. Talk about smokescreen, okay, they could chase after a bunch of names culled from the phonebook. I called about ten, muttered cryptic remarks, and hung up. On a couple I tried weird phrases in my newly learned Spanish, like el perro es un gato (the dog is a cat), along with a few choice Hawaiian phrases. Let their interpreters work at figuring that out. Let them do background checks on all the numbers I had called. Let them send out agents to question or surveil them.

Then I called Alice. When she answered, I said, "Listen very closely, babe. This is very important. You have to do exactly as I say. We got pilikia wit da makai. (Pilikia wit da makai in Hawaiian Pidgin means, "trouble with the police.") You understand?"

"Yes."

"First of all, as soon as I get through telling you what to do, I want you to lay the phone down and go do it. Right now. But don't hang up the phone. Okay?"

"Yes"

"Put on the rubber gloves you use to wash the dishes. Then get out some garbage bags. Put everything in them that doesn't belong in the house. You understand?"

"You mean the..." she began, but I cut her off.

"Don't say anything. Everything in the house that shouldn't be there. Okay?"

"I understand."

"Then take the bags down the alley and put them in somebody's garbage can. Got it?"

"Yes."

"Okay, now lay the phone down and go do it. I'll wait until you get back."

"Okay."

After about fifteen minutes, she picked up the phone again, breathless. "I'm back. Everything's gone. I went..."

"No, babe, don't say anything, just listen. I'm calling from jail. Gerry's here, too."

"Oh, no!"

"Yes, babe, I'm sorry. We knew it could happen. Now, the chips are down and everybody's got to play their hands. They're going to be by to arrest you sooner or later if you stay there." "What do I do?"

"In a minute, I'm going to hang up the phone. I'll call you back in about ten minutes. I want you to make two phone calls."

"All right. Who?"

"First, call Gerry's house, see if his girlfriend's there. If she is, you tell her what's what. Tell her to drive by and pick you up right away. No delay. Immediately. Then you two drive in her car to Phoenix and check into a hotel and wait until somebody contacts you. Got that?"

"Yes."

"Then call the Torchlite Motel," I said, and gave her the room number. "If nobody answers in the room, ask to speak to the manager. Ask him if the party in that room has checked out."

"That's all?"

"Yes. Do it now. I'll call you right back."

"What if somebody answers?"

"Tell them to stay right there, that you'll be by to pick them up in a few minutes."

"Okay. Oh, baby..."

"C'mon now, babe. This is when you have to be strong. I'm counting on you."

Then I called Cheryl in Phoenix to give her the news. She'd already received a call from Lena, who was on her way to Phoenix on a bus.

"How you fixed for money?"

"I've got some."

"Okay, Lena's got some, too. I don't know what to advise you, kid. Like they used to say in the movies, the jig's up." "It was my father, wasn't it?"

"Yeah, it was."

"The rotten sonofabitch!"

"Listen, Cheryl. Look after Lena, will you? I told her about your father, but she doesn't quite believe it. Keep her away from him, huh?"

"Don't worry."

"Why don't you two go on back to Miami? Your mother might like to see you."

"Okay. That's what we'll probably do. Are you going to be all right?"

"Ah, who knows? It doesn't look good right now. I just want to thank you for being a friend. You're a good broad, Cheryl. Sorry we didn't get to know each other better."

"You're the one that's been the friend, Buck. You take care of yourself."

"Goodbye, kid, and good luck."

"You, too. I'm sorry, Buck. I'm really sorry."

When I called Alice back, she told me no one had answered at the motel room and that the manager had told her the police had accompanied a woman back to get her belongings and now the room was sealed on police orders.

"It was Lena, wasn't it?"

"Yes, babe, but it's all academic now, so why rake it over?" "Were you really going to meet me in Mexico City?"

"Oh, yeah, babe. I don't abandon people I care about. I love you and you know it. What about Gerry's girlfriend?"

"She doesn't answer either."

"Okay. Look, you've got to get out of there immediately. When I hang up, you call a cab, go to a hotel and keep calling Gerry's girl until you get her. If you haven't got a hold of her by noon tomorrow, get on a bus for Phoenix, go to that hotel we stayed at one time. I'll try to call you there. You got enough money?"

"Yes."

"Well, that's it then. You take care of yourself, babe. I'll try to get some money sent to you."

"Oh, baby!"

"Listen, whatever you do, don't go back up to Tacoma right away. They'll be waiting on you."

"What do I do if they catch me?"

"Just keep your mouth shut like I've always told you and you'll be all right. They got nothing on you. But it's important that you don't say one word to them. They'll try to get you into a conversation in small stuff and lead you on to other things. They'll threaten you with all sorts of things, but just don't say anything. Only talk to a lawyer. You might be in jail a few days, but they'll have to let you go. Okay?"

"Yes. What about you?"

"I don't know, babe. Things aren't looking so rosy right now." "Can I write to you?"

"No, not right away. They'll be taking me back to Hawaii. You know how to send messages. Call and check every month or so to see if you've got any from me. You take care of yourself. I've got to go."

"Oh, baby, I love you so much!"

"I know, and it's meant more to me than I can ever say. I love you, too, Alice.

Be careful. You've been around me long enough to have picked up some of my tricks. I don't want to hear about you being in jail."

She was crying -- and what do you do with a crying woman? "Call the cab, babe. Goodbye."

*****

The next day, Gerry and I were taken to the country jail in Phoenix. We talked on the way. The only charge against him was for harboring a fugitive.

"Hell, don't worry about that. They have to prove you knew I was a fugitive. If it comes to trial, and I don't think it will, call me as a witness. I'll tell 'em I fed you some cock and bull story about how I got out on a writ or parole or something."

After being booked into the jail, I made a few calls on the phone in the cellblock and learned that Alice had managed to hook up with Gerry's girl. I called Lena's mother in Miami, who told me her daughters were on their way home. When she told me they planned to stop off in Atlanta so Lena could get her belongings before continuing on, my heart dropped.

I called Dave's number. When he answered, he was all compassion and commiseration, yo ho ho, and if there was anything he could do to help, why just let him know. He hadn't figured out that I knew was a rat.

"Lena and Cheryl there?"

"Sure, wait a minute."

Lena came on.

"Hi, babe, how are you?"

"I'm all right. How are you doing?"

"Just fucking awful without you."

She choked out a chuckle. "Me, too. God, I miss you so much." "Can we talk in private? Are you alone?"

"Wait a minute, I'll take the phone in the bathroom." When she came back on, I asked if Cheryl was there. "Yes, you want to talk to her?"

"In a minute. What are you doing there?"

"I just came to get my stuff. We're going on to Miami later tonight."

"Okay, good. It's really not a good idea for you to hang around there."

"I know."

I didn't know what to say. Parting was oh so much more than sweet sorrow, as Shakespeare would have it.

"You were right."

"Huh? About what?"

"My father."

"Oh."

"You were right all the way. He turned against you." "I know, babe."

"He worked with the feds to set you up."

"Yeah."

"I hate him."

"Just get out of there and go home. I'll call you at your mother's. Okay?"

"Yes. I love you, Buck."

"I love you, too. Now let me talk to Cheryl."

When she came on, I almost shouted at her. "What the hell are you doing there?"

"Don't worry. Everything's all right. We're catching a plane in two hours."

"Jesus."

"Lena wanted to get her stuff. We're leaving in a few minutes." "Okay. Sorry."

"The bastard tried to talk us into staying, said he could take care of us, put us into some money."

"Yeah, I'll bet."

"He just wants to use us. He doesn't care about anyone but himself."

"I know. Wish I'd figured that out a little sooner."

"Well, don't worry. We're leaving. He tries to put a hand on either of us, I'll cut his fucking heart out!"

"Just go home, kid. I'll be in touch with you one of these days. I owe you."

"You're a good man, Buck."

"Yeah, I know. That's what my mom says, and I always believe her. You take care.

Now put that lousy asshole of a father you're cursed to have back on the line."

"Buck, man, I love you. What can I say? What can I do?"

I knew it might come back to haunt me, but I didn't give a fuck -- I wanted to shake the puke up, strain his hemorrhoids. "Hey, don't worry about it, Dave, it ain't no big thing. There's more going on here than I can tell you about, you know?"

"Whattaya mean?"

"Hey, you're a sharp guy, Dave. I figure you at least got some inkling that I'm connected up a little higher than these local schmucks know about, right?"

"Uh, yeah, right."

"Yeah, legitimate people, you know what I mean. Only they're a little higher up in the food chain than the feebs and dykes." (Underworld slang for FBI and DEA) "You talking about...?"

"Don't say it, Dave. Don't say it on an open line. Just don't worry. I'll be seeing you in a few days, a week at the most."

"Oh, yeah?"

Did his voice change, go up an octave or so?

"You know me, Dave, all kinds of irons in the fire. But, listen, I might not be able to make it down in person. Don't worry. I'll have a couple of my guys come by to see you, deliver a personal message."

"Okay," he croaked.

"You okay, Dave?"

"Yeah, fine."
"You sure? You don't sound so good."
"I'm okay. I'm good."
"All these strange bugs going around. You gotta take care of yourself, Dave. We've got unfinished business, you know?"
"Right, sure, I will."
"I love you, Dave."

CHAPTER 12

In my feelings of abject failure during those first days, I consoled myself that no one ever connected to me and my devious schemes during the time of my status as a fugitive was ever charged with a crime, not even Gerry and me. No drugs were found in the motel room after an illegal search and none in my car after a legal one. No possession, no dealing, and no smuggling charges were to arise out of any of my activities, no cases whatsoever against anyone. Despite my personal failure, I had achieved a kind of success.

Within a week or so, a removal hearing would be held in the U. S. District Court and my return to Honolulu would be ordered for arraignment on a felony-murder indictment in the death of Eleanor Graham.

Now that I was in the custody of U. S. Marshals, it would begin a time of paybacks for having made fools of several branches of federal cops. The spiteful word had come down and the paybacks would be extensive. They would begin with the manner of my transportation to Honolulu, continue on into 1982 in Tacoma, Washington, when they would engineer a situation to land me in the toughest, highest security prison in the United States at Marion, Illinois, and would not end until they had created a variation of that same situation after my trial in 1985, which would again guarantee my return to Marion even though the U. S. Bureau of Prisons had ordered my transfer to the penitentiary at Lompoc, California.

*****

They began by shackling me up in the usual manner in wrist and ankle cuffs with enough chain to prevent any but small movements. If you itched in an awkward place, forget about scratching it. With more Marshals than was customary, they drove me in a caged van from the basement of the Maricopa County Jail to the Phoenix Airport, refusing to respond to my queries about our itinerary.

At the airport's non-commercial section, several Marshals drew pistols, sneering their malevolent looks my way as if daring me to try something, and took up guard stations. My goodness me, was their behavior meant to intimidate or did they expect some private army of gangsters to attempt a rescue of their beloved leader? They sure had a way of making a mug feel important.

After a nearby specially chartered twin-engined plane was warmed up, they rushed me inside, half carrying me, and shackled me to a seat. No parachute access or chance to escape if the plane went down, and still the steely-eyed silence.

"Say there, sir," I inquired politely of one of my grim-faced escorts. "Wonder if you could scratch my ass for me?" No grins, no smart retorts to my sally, only more hard glitter in the contemptuous eyes. These guys were pumped, ready for anything but nonsense.

We landed at a military airfield and were met by jeeploads of soldiers in black berets with automatic weapons, all of whom must have wondered just who in the hell this dangerous, evilly grinning white man dressed in civvies was. They escorted me to the brig and locked me in a cell. Fifteen minutes later, they all returned to drive us to a C-141 cargo plane with air force pilots. The Marshals and I were the only cargo.

We made a short hop to another military airfield in California to repeat the process. My only wish was that I had a free hand to salute our boys. When the Marshals came to take me from the cell to board another C-141, I requested an opportunity to take a piss.

Try it sometime, trying to relax the sphincter to your bladder with three maniacs standing over your chained and shackled ass with drawn pistols. Five hours later, we landed at Hickam Field in Honolulu. Under glaring lights, I was hustled to a waiting car and convoyed with a vehicle before and behind to Halawa Jail.

"You sure you ain't got me mixed up with someone else?" A little humor, what the hell. "Like maybe Idi Amin or Moammar Khadafy?"

The chief Marshal grinned at me. "We know who you are, Walker. You were second on our Most Wanted List."

"No shit? Who was first?"

"Kenneth Boyce, that fucking spy for the Russians."

"Damn. What'd he do?"

"Escaped from federal prison just like you."

"Ain't that the absolute pits. A fucking commie getting higher billing than a good patriotic American!"

*****

Halawa had changed in my absence. High security modules had been added to contain the badasses. No more dormitories where we could gamble all night, smoke a few smuggled joints, sleep the days away and watch TV between times. Now it was ten or twelve single cells in a double-tiered module where the inmates were under constant surveillance through a one-way bulletproof glass shield. We were let out for meals at steel tables and for showers during the day, when we could watch TV. No cards, no dice, no dope, and no money allowed in personal possession. The best we could do is play chess or checkers for cigarettes or candy from what we could order from commissary supplies once a week -- or portions of jailhouse food, which was pretty good.

I was overweight from the easy life in Mexico and so I went out every morning to the tiny walled recreation yard to play handball for an hour or so. Halawa would be my home for several months of meeting with lawyers and making court appearances. Every time I entered or exited the jail module, whether for recreation, a court appearance, or a visit with the lawyers, I was strip-searched coming and going. I was beginning to fancy I had a beautiful body that just had to be seen in all its glory to be appreciated -- again and again and again.

Still, for all that, I was able to send and receive private messages. Alice was safe with Gerry's girlfriend. Lena and Cheryl were safe in Miami. Enrique was safe with Fae in Mexico. Fast Eddie was doing what he does in Canada. Ollie was still on the loose, presumably growing grass up in Oregon.

The best news of all concerned Gerry. It seems he had been transferred to a prison facility in Florence, Arizona, on a charge that he had violated his parole. He hired a lawyer to file a writ of habeas corpus claiming that it could not be shown that he'd violated any condition of his parole until such time as a conviction was taken that he'd knowingly harbored a fugitive. The court had granted an evidentiary hearing on the matter and he was returned to the Maricopa County Jail in Phoenix. The judge had denied the writ, but the gods of fortune overruled him. When Gerry was taken from court back to jail to await transportation to prison, the computers told the jail administrators that the judge had granted the writ and ordered his release.

Gerry stepped out onto the streets fully realizing the mistake and promptly disappeared.

He connected up with his girlfriend and Alice, but they were low on money. He couldn't chance going to his bank and didn't even have a check or credit card he could use. I arranged for him to receive five grand that was tucked away in one of my private mailboxes for emergencies. I knew he would look after Alice. The feds would not catch up to them for two or three years.

In the meanwhile, I had been arraigned before my old friend, Judge King, and had entered a not guilty plea. Two lawyers had been appointed to represent me, Earle Partington and Ray Findlay, neither of whom I had ever seen or heard of before. Thus was to begin almost four years of legal maneuvering by defense and prosecution lawyers before I would finally come to trial in June, 1985.

After Muff's skull and a few bones had been discovered in January, 1981, by Sharon Jordon, with her husband on a yacht out of South Africa, the FBI had sent agent Shishido back to Palmyra on another search for evidence. They were accompanied by Assistant U. S. Attorney Elliot Enoki, who would prosecute the murder indictments. They found nothing of value.

When Shishido came to testify about the thoroughness of these searches, he was embarrassed to say he had never seen a huge green fuel tank located on the northeastern shore of the island, even though it was some three stories high.

The lawyers filed motions for dismissal of the charges on grounds of double jeopardy, collateral estoppel, and res judicata. The underlying claim was that we could not be tried for a crime, an element of which had already been adjudicated. Felony-murder required proving the underlying felony, the alleged theft of Sea Wind. The charge required proof of the allegation that a murder had occurred during the commission of a felony. In addition to the fact that my theft conviction had been overturned and the charge dismissed, the prosecution would have difficulty demonstrating that Muff Graham was actually killed while Sea Wind was being stolen since there were no witnesses or other hard evidence to support the allegation -- not to mention that the expert witnesses who had examined Muff's skull and bones could not establish any time or cause of death. If that was the case, I was ready to proceed to trial, take my chances, and get it over with.

Lawyers have an entirely different point of view. Their bread and butter is litigation. Why settle a case when it can be dragged out for a few years? Partington counseled me that the more time that passed the better it would be for me. It would take time to file all those motions on double jeopardy, collateral estoppel, and res judicata -- none of which would be granted. They also wanted to file a motion for a change of venue. I didn't stand a chance in Honolulu - the whole state thought we were guilty.

Okay, what the hell, I wasn't going anywhere anyway. I still had a few years to serve on my previous sentences. Also, I would probably receive another five-year term for my escape from McNeil. Okay, let's get the show on the road. Demand a speedy trial on the escape charge in Washington, let's get that over with. Partington thought it was a good idea and sent a letter to the Assistant U. S. Attorney who would prosecute the case in Tacoma.

In the meanwhile, I had a strange face-to-face meeting with Stephanie, whom I had not seen in six years. We were both scheduled for a court appearance together. Earle cautioned me that I should be very careful as to what I said to her. The lawyers and the Marshals had all agreed that we could sit next to each other and talk in the courtroom for a few minutes while awaiting Judge King's entrance.

In the courtroom, my shackles and chains were removed, but I was again searched to make sure I had no written secret messages to pass. Then Stephanie, who was out on bail, appeared in a dress and high heels, looking straighter than I've ever seen her. She was searched by a female Marshal to make sure she had no secret messages or weapons to assist in a desperate breakout. The Marshals sternly warned us that while we could speak to each other, if we so much as touched fingers we would immediately be restrained and searched again.

Stephanie had held out her arms for the search with a look of disgust on her face. "Just what is it you're afraid of, baby?" she sneered. With Partington and Findlay on my side and Weinglass and another lawyer sitting on her side, Enoki and his assistant looking on, a Marshall sitting three feet behind us, and another one to watch us from the front in the jury box, you can imagine we were somewhat inhibited. There was another lady sitting in the jury box with a stenographic notebook open and a pen in hand. She seemed very interested in staring at our faces. Unbelievable, a fucking lip-reader to take down everything we said!

We didn't have much to say to each other under the circumstances. After the hi-and-how-are-yous, it sort of sputtered out. But, since I hadn't requested this little tete-a-tete, I expected some message. Stephanie said her lawyers had asked her to ask me if I was willing to go to trial first since she had gone to trial first on the theft charges. I understood perfectly what she was asking. If I went first, her lawyers would get a free preview of the case against us and would have more time to prepare their defense. While I had no objection to that, the fact of the matter was that neither of us, exactly as had been the case in the theft trials, would have any choice in the matter. That was strictly between the judge and the prosecutor, no matter how much any defense lawyer might argue about who was to be tried first.

Bugliosi would later claim that Stephanie had told him that during this meeting she had asked that I consent to being tried first, that she claimed with some embarrassment that I had asked her to be tried first in the theft trials and that she thought it only fair that I now return the favor.

When Bugliosi inquired as to my reaction, he claims she said that I had told her I wasn't about to volunteer my neck for the chop-block.

Regardless of whoever created this nicely vilifying fiction, the simple fact of the matter was that my reply to her request began with a shrug. "It's okay with me," I said. "But I don't have any sayso in that. We'll just have to see how it works out."

Bugliosi went on to claim that Stephanie made a rather startling statement to him concerning this brief meeting. After stating that she had always believed Mac and Muff had gone fishing and died in an accident, she is depicted as going on to say I had told her that was my belief also.

Whether Stephanie actually told this lie or it represents another of Bugliosi's distortions isn't so important as what was really going on inside me.

Without including my lawyers, I had been coming to the personal conclusion that the complete story would have to come out. I had begun to imagine myself testifying in open court as to exactly what had really happened. It was not that I had lied in any crucial sense in the theft trial, but only that I had omitted to tell the full truth. As none of the lawyers in the theft trial had had the slightest clue as to that truth, they were unable to ask the particular questions that would have elicited it.

But, as I sat there those few minutes with Stephanie, I remember experiencing an all but overwhelming urge to tell her everything, a need to unburden myself of an awful knowledge that I alone of all the billions of human beings on the planet Earth knew. And the idea of that scared me -- it was something I did not understand about myself.

Poor innocent Steph, so unbelieving of evil in the world, so in need of protection, my old love, my noble mission, she sat there as faithful as ever in the basic goodness of the world as she saw it. Her brow was wrinkled, her eyes squinting in a frown with what she could not understand or believe about the forces now aligned against her. I wanted so much to take her hands in mine and tell her, make her see the truth of things, the reality of the tawdry and mean lives we lead, to explain to her, perhaps justify to myself, that I had not betrayed her by concealing the truth, but had only tried to protect her.

I couldn't do any such thing, of course. So many people, strangers without a drop of understanding or compassion, all straining to hear every word, to note every gesture and expression -- so many voyeurs. It was neither the time nor place.

*****

What Bugliosi did get right was about Stephanie zeroing in on the very heart of the case, the simple fact, which if proven, would be taken as the best evidence that murder had occurred.

"What I don't understand is that my lawyers are telling me that Muff's body was apparently placed in one of those metal containers out of that old rescue launch."

She was looking at me as hard as she could, trying to see into my secret depths, a pleading in her eyes for me to tell her it was all bullshit.

"I don't understand that," she said. I covered my mouth with my hand and leaned to whisper the words Bugliosi would claim Stephanie had told him, "Maybe Mac did it." It was an answer that told all and explained nothing. It was as close as I would ever be to telling her the truth.

She sat back in shock, her mouth open, eyes wide, her mind obviously areel. She looked away, closed her eyes tightly, focusing I sensed with all her being on that awful idea. Her head began to twist back and forth, shaking in denial. Such an idea did not fit with her conception of what kind of person Mac had been -- it went against the rosy grain of her experience.

I think it was from this point that she would begin a long and self-resistant withdrawal of her belief in me, the kind of man she had firmly filed away in her heart. The process would take years, even with all the people around her, from lawyers to family, picking at her with their firm suasions -- especially Bugliosi. He needed her to believe in the possibility that her beloved Buck was a murderer.

No, Stephanie would insist. They had an accident. Their dinghy overturned. They drowned or were eaten by sharks.

Wrong, Bugliosi would argue. If so, their bones would not appear seven years later in a metal box.

Wrong, wrong, Stephanie would insist. We don't know for sure any bones were ever in any box. The box was found nearby. So what? No one says any bones were in any box!

Bugliosi would insist, lending all the considerable power of his persuasion -- murder was done! Either you and Buck did it together or he did it alone! Murder was done!

No, no, Steph would resist. Buck is not a murderer. He cannot be. I knew him and loved him more than any man before or since. He simply could not do such a thing, commit such a horrible act!

Ah well, me boyos, it ain't what we don't know that hurts us, like Will Rogers said. It's what we know that ain't so.

*****

Who was right? Steph had lived with me for several years. We had eaten together, slept together, made love, argued, shouted, and cried together, had even shit and pissed together in our two-seater outhouse, had shared our hopes and dreams, the dangers of our adventures. Steph knew me as Bugliosi could never hope to do, but it was this very condition that I would meet constantly throughout the years to follow when it came to differentiating between believers and nonbelievers. Those who knew me could not believe I had committed murder under the circumstances. Those who did not know me were all too ready to believe it. And I have found no remedy for this failure in human nature to accept such a monstrous charge with so little evidence to support it.

Like an Agatha Christie mystery, most people prefer a murderer. Life is far more interesting when we can fit a crime into it -- and it makes better reading, as Bugliosi well knows.

In December, the Marshals came to give me another ride in another C-141 military cargo plane. After landing at a west coast airfield, we transferred to a specially chartered smaller plane to complete the trip to a rural airport outside Tacoma. I was taken to the jail in the township of Port Arthur, about ten miles south of Tacoma, with special instructions to the jailers that I was to be accorded the highest security housing.

Thereafter, a local lawyer was appointed to represent me and I began a routine shuttle back and forth to court. I pled not guilty for the sake of preserving my right to appeal.

There was no way I could win an acquittal. I submitted my case before the judge without any defense whatsoever. He would routinely find me guilty and I would appeal on the ground that I had not been granted a speedy trial as provided for in the Constitution. The prosecutor had delayed bringing me to trial within the required sixty days after my arrest and having been notified by Partington that I was available to be tried.

Everything had gone as expected. I was simply vegetating away on no recreation and the worst jail food I'd ever had the misfortune to be served. The feds were still into their paybacks and they got more serious about it on the day I went up before Maximum Jack Tanner, the federal judge in Tacoma who would routinely sentence me to the maximum term available -- five years, to run consecutive to all other sentences.

On that day, the routine changed.

The usual rigamarole called for two Marshals to arrive at the jail, where I had already been called out, allowed to change clothes, and waited in a holding cell. They would shackle and chain me as usual, lead me down into the garage to enter the backseat of a government car. They would get in the front and we would make the fifteen or twenty minute trip to the courthouse. There, I would be led up into a holding cell near their office and set free from the chains and shackles. I would usually consult with the lawyer before being handcuffed and led into the courtroom, where the cuffs were again removed. The hearing over, on went the cuffs and back to the holding cell I would go, escorted by the two Marshals.

I may have gotten to speak, with one of the great sleuthing brains who was painted in the Bugliosi book as my nemeses. A Marshal had come over grinning to say he just wanted to have a look at the guy he'd chased for so long.

"We finally got you," he crowed.

"Well, somebody got me all right," I replied. "But I don't remember you being in on it."

He had to brag about how close he'd come several times. He mentioned Reno, Tucson, and Lake Tahoe. For sure I knew about Tucson and Reno, but Lake Tahoe was a surprise.

"Oh yeah, we almost had you at the Cal-Neva gambling casino. You like to play craps, don't you?"

I smiled. I did not like the dice tables. I had never been in the Cal-Neva. Why ruin his pipedream by letting him know that my favorite form of gambling while on my escape had been the dog races, that I could have been found at the tracks at Black Canyon, Phoenix, Yuma, or Tijuana, when the Greyhounds were running.

"Yeah, we know you used a postoffice box there to receive mail. You were using the name of Howard Roark."

The idiot didn't even realize he was giving up one of his snitches when he told me that. When I traveled, I used different names for different places. Thus, when I learn of a particular alias popping up, I can not only put it to a particular place, but also know who knew me by the name. Patrick had had another girlfriend before the one involved in the grass-to-hash scheme from the would-be godfather, and I had used her postoffice box to receive a piece of mail. I would have to remember to warn Patrick about her. Howard Roark was the name of Ayn Rand's hero in The Fountainhead, a book and author I had long admired.

"Did you guys ever catch Boyce? I was kind of pissed you'd put him number one ahead of me on your Most Wanted List."

"Oh, yeah, we got him. We catch all you yo-yos sooner or later." "That must have been exciting. Were you actually in on busting him?"

He gave me an injured look. I smiled innocently. "Have you ever actually arrested anybody in your whole life?"

"We'll see what a smart ass you are when we get done breaking it off in you," he huffed and stormed away.

Yessiree, and on the day of my sentencing, did the routine ever change. No less than six Marshals showed up to double-shackle and chain me. They must have learned I hated weightlifting. They were armed with shotguns and automatic rifles. A four-wheel drive vehicle led the convoy with a third car bringing up the rear. The radio crackled with communications back and forth. A helicopter watched over us from the sky.

"What's the occasion, fellas?" To which question I received stony silence. They were too busy acting out their TV roles, glintyeyed and fondling their weapons.

At the courthouse, Marshals were stationed on the corners with shotguns and walkie-talkies. I could see men with rifles on a building across the street. I was hustled in, practically being dragged since leg shackles do not permit long strides, by a veritable phalanx of heavily armed men. At the holding cell, the chains and shackles were not removed.

My lawyer came in looking grim.

"What the hell's going on?"

"I'm not sure. I think they anticipate some emergency," he said.

"Well, why don't you run on out there and ask somebody? And see if you can get me unshackled while you're at it."

He came back to inform me that the courthouse had been cleared and that I would have to wear the chains into the courtroom. Maximum Jack had been informed and approved the procedure.

"What!"

"They say they have information that the Mexican Mafia is going to try to rescue you."

"What!"

"That's what they say. They're prepared for a breakout attempt."

Oh, brother! They were getting their paybacks with a vengeance, I thought. The bigger the dragon...

I tried, simply as an academic exercise, to recall if I had actually ever known any member of the Mexican Mafia. They had been around since the late forties or early fifties, I knew, and there had been enclaves of them in prison gangs. But I couldn't come up with a single name. All my recent dealings had been with Mexican nationals, a different kettle of fish altogether. The Mexican Mafia, or Eme, as it is called by those in the know, originated in Los Angeles by Chicanos, who were all born in the United States. By the eighties, the gang had spread to most prisons in California and members could be found throughout most of the states.

If my lawyer had told me some Mexicans were suspected to be planning my rescue, I might have been halfway convinced -- maybe Enrique or Pablo, egged on by Gerry, had gotten a plan together. But there was just no way it could happen without me being in on it. When the Mexican Mafia was mentioned, however, I understood immediately what was happening, the extent of the scam that was being run by the feds. I would be made into a very big and dangerous dragon and many knights would shine in the armor of their valor for having foiled me. I was led into the courtroom in chains by shotgun-wielding Marshals. Maximum Jack entered from stage left in his shirtsleeves, his judicial robe replaced by a purposeful look and an automatic pistol in a shoulder holster. By God, just let some of those two-bit taco-gobbling gangsters invade his courtroom!

It was short and sweet. Adios, amigo. I was dragged out and the film seemed to run in reverse to get me back to the jail, my head spinning. They were soon back to reburden me in the weight of stainless steel chains and bracelets and to fly me on another specially chartered plane to Vandenburg Air Force Base for a quick bus ride to the penitentiary at Lompoc. After a month locked in a cell there, the U. S. Bureau of Prisons, due to information provided by the U. S. Marshals Service and a so-called "usually reliable informant," regarding my alleged connections to organized crime through the Mexican Mafia and the recently foiled escape plot, designated me as a super-maximum security prisoner suitable for incarceration at the new Alcatraz, the U. S. Penitentiary at Marion, Illinois.

Whoa, me buckos! Fellows just can't take a joke.

So, for the awful crime of having walked away, or paddled, as the case may be, from a minimum-security facility and not having been charged with any other crimes while on escape, I came to see Marion as only insiders can see it. Some rather amazing events would occur there and I would meet and come to know some very interesting characters. On the downside, I was reminded, to paraphrase Mark Twain, that if you want to see the scum of the earth, go down to Marion prison at the changing of the guard.

###

CHAPTER 13

Marion Penitentiary was so-called for the nearest small town of Marion a few miles away in southern Illinois. Space was made for the prison's construction by the simple expedient of clearing a rectangle of virgin forest of about a hundred acres of trees. From the double cyclone fence line, adorned with layers of coiled razor-wire, lay two hundred yards of open ground to the tree line providing a clear field of fire for the riflemen in the gun towers at the corners of the rectangle. There was nothing to be seen of the outer world but the geometrically straight walls of these trees. It seemed like an insult to the ecology of the planet that so much of nature had been destroyed for the construction of such a canker sore.

Beyond the trees, farmlands had encroached upon every bit of land that wasn't swamp. The area was heavily surrounded by marshlands and was considered prime hunting grounds for ducks and geese. Winters were cold and snowy. Summers were hot, humid, and uncomfortable. There were, as I was to learn, about two months out of the year that brought beautiful, temperate days in the changing of the seasons between Spring and Summer, and between Autumn and Winter. The rest of the time you were chilled or boiled to the bone.

I entered Marion to march in my chains and shackles down the long, bare corridor into the prison proper, accompanied by a covey of guards whose faces were masks torn between a gleam of anticipatory glee that I might give them some excuse to beat the dogshit out of me and a sneering contempt that I was no more than a mobile pile of the pure form of that feces.

Anxious to get through the processing, I yessirred, nossirred, and maintained a polite, cooperative demeanor. Give me the company of convict losers any day, I thought to myself, where, though tortured a bit out of shape, I could find at least a semblance of humanity. Anything was better than feeling like a sheep among hungry jackals, these cold, alien creatures in the form of earthlings. Did they have wives and children like normal people? I tried to imagine what it would be like to have a father who had barely escaped being such a loser in life as to take up a career as a prison guard. I would rather be an orphan and take my chances living out of garbage cans. Well, perhaps that was why they had chosen such a livelihood -- they considered it less shameful than public welfare or waking up under a bridge with a bunch of hung over winos. What else were they good for? Not that it was a piece of luck as far as I was concerned, but by some quirk of social laws all the losers wound up in the same places -- we only wore different uniforms and some had a few privileges more than others. As I entered the cellblock to submit myself to the stony gaze of my fellows, all caught on the lowermost rung of life, I soon determined there were no familiar faces among them. Thus would begin the process of fitting myself into the society that had been chosen for me. We would all watch and test each other, ever alert for weaknesses and strengths to manifest themselves. Like it or not, I was now a member of a group of basically lonely outsiders who resisted all forms of authority, who were considered to be the most violent and predatory criminals in America.

Despite the singular fact that I had not a single act of violence on my record, it is a truism of social intercourse that traits of character seek out like traits in others. Biologists, anthropologists, and even sociologists, call it kind seeking kind, an inborn need to identify with others, perhaps in seeking assurance that we are not alone in the world. Most forms of life, if not all, are social by nature. We need others of our own kind to survive and give meaning to our existence. In any group of human beings, the caste system we seem fated to endure no matter our station in life, each individual will look upon all other life in a search to identify others with whom he can share his days, or at least some parts of them. And he will find assholes and fourteen-carat sonsofbitches as well as sterling characters. If it could be graphed, it would assume the common bell-jar shape so popular with scientists. On the narrow rims opposite each other would be what you considered assholes and sonsofbitches on the one end, and the sterling characters, among which you numbered yourself, on the other. The one group constituted a threat to your well being, while the other provided some degree of protection. In between, the great hump of the bell shape, were represented the larger statistical mass of men who posed neither threat or benefit, but served merely as neutral agents in the pot we all swam in. But the bell shapes of these relationships were never entirely static -- in a context of very strict social rules, especially when it came to stepping on others' toes, a constant alertness and diplomacy was required in order to maintain the relative positions. Here, what might be a social gaffe in politer society -- a wrong word, look, or physical gesture -- could lead to immediate violence. The bottom line behind the often polite rituals was that your life was on the line on a daily basis. It reminded me of the cowboy ethic -- where everybody wore a gun and so insults were few and far between unless you were ready to draw down, and you showed respect by doffing your hat with your gunhand.

One of the first sterling characters I came to know -- irony of ironies -- was a slim, intense man close to my own age, a vato de respeto (Man of respect – vato is a Chicano slang word equivalent to hombre in Spanish, meaning man.) in the Mexican Mafia, or as it is referred to among themselves, La Eme. (The letter M in the alphabet.) We began our relationship when he asked me if I played chess.

After a week of feeling each other out over the board in polite conversational skirmishes, each of us very cautious of revealing anything in the way of personal information, he about knocked me out of my socks one day by opining as how I looked the sort of man who might be a smuggler.

I laughed, trying to conceal my surprise, but admitted that I might have smuggled a thing or two over international borders. Over some of the toughest chess games I had ever played, he having the edge, we slowly revealed ourselves to each other.

When I had gotten to know him well enough so that a mutual friendship had developed, I began calling him Camaron, (Shrimp) which was an affectionate pun on his real moniker. In turn, he called me Fat Boy, which he sometimes translated into Spanish as El Largo Tripa and El Grande Panza. (Big Gut and Great Belly.)

"Are you the guy that got me here?"

"What you talking about, gavacho? (Chicano designation for a Caucasian.)

"So I told him the story of my last court appearance in Tacoma.

"I hola chinges su madre, (Hey, fuck your mother, a common expression – roughly equivalent to motherfucker.) they really set you up, my friend. You must have done something to make them mad at you. I wish I had been there to do that for you."

"Then they'd have really been pissed, probably enough to waste my raggedy ass."

"Hey, fuck 'em. It works both ways."

Another sterling character, among the half dozen or so I would meet during the next four years, was a fellow of Jewish extraction who'd been born and raised in New York City with close underworld contacts. He had, like Camaron, been down a good many years and would either die in prison or be an old, old man when he got out if the government had any sayso. They'd gotten him on the RICO statutes and railroaded him from the penitentiary at Lewisburg, Pennsylvania, much like me, on a phony conspiracy to engineer an escape. His forte, which drew us together in a common interest, was crossword puzzles. We were always asking each other's help on the tough ones.

"Hey, Buck, What's a five-letter word for bizarre?"

"How about weird?"

"Naw, it don't fit. Dat's what I thought wit da fourt letter R, but da second one's a U."

"Outre."

"00-tray? What da fuck kinda woid's dat?"

"French, I think."

"Dat's what I like about dese cocksuckers dey really help ta increase yer vocabalary."

"Yeah, me, too."

"Tomorra, we do da one outa da New Yawk Magazine."

"Yeah, that's a good one, Herb. Thanks."

Between these two genial rogues, I came across Dave's name. Both times he was connected to the name of Jimmie "The Weasel" Frattiano, an infamous stoolpigeon who'd gotten a yellow streak up his spine and began ratting on his own kind in order to save himself from some serious time for the crimes he'd committed, including murder. It seems, among other things, Frattiano was a hitman who would contract to murder anyone if the price was right.

"Oh, yeah, I know da name," Herb said around the ever-present cigar when I asked him about Dave. "Outa Miami. A real flake. Used ta hang out wit Frattiano, a fuckin' rat. Dis Dave's a real phony sonofabitch -- used ta drop names all over da place, like he knew everbody was anybody. I guess dere both eatin' da same cheese now." When I ran Dave's name by Camaron, he said, "Yeah, his name rings a bell. He used to hang out with a guy named Frattiano. I never met the rat cocksucker, but I remember Frattiano mentioning a connection in Miami. In fact, you can read about him in this book I got about Frattiano. I'll give it to you."

It was called The Last Mafioso, by Ovid Demaris. Two or three pages were devoted to Dave. It seems Frattiano had attended the bar mitzvah of his daughter, Lena, on her thirteenth birthday. There had been a falling out among fellow rodents, each of them accusing the other of holding out mob money, which, in the end, got them both into hot water. It appeared they had both rolled over a couple of years later. So Dave had been a rat when I'd met him. I was crestfallen to learn that my judgment of men, which I fancied was finely honed by then, had been so poor in Dave's case.

In another case to come, that of Noel Allen Ingman, I would find that my nose for rats had been right on the money. But that was three years down the road and it wouldn't make any difference. Rats not only tell what they know, they make up what they don't know.

*****

The feds began sending in pairs of agents, sometimes FBI, sometimes Marshals, sometimes DEA, more or less regularly every six months or so to interview me. Since they were all from a similar mold, I hardly paid attention to their ID. They wanted information on the whereabouts of Gerry and Alice.

"Who?"

"You know who we're talking about, asshole. Do yourself and them a favor. We're going to get them. It'd be too bad if we had to take them down the hard way."

"I can't imagine what you might want them for."

"Your old buddy's been robbing banks. We think Alice is helping him."

I laughed. "So that's what the world looks like when you've got your head up your asshole."

"We know all about your little smuggling operation in Mexico, the motorhomes, the whole ball of wax, pal."

"So why hasn't anyone been charged"

"You know your pal's fucking your ol' lady, don't you? How do you feel about that?"

"Oh, about as bad as I feel over your ol' lady fucking the garbage collectors while you're here interviewing me."

They came bright-eyed and bushy-tailed, eager to break me, turn me, and went away cursing me for a bad citizen with no social conscience, as if betrayal was the new coin of the realm.

"Give us Gerry and we'll do right by Alice," they said. "We'll give you a recommendation to the parole board, get you a transfer to an easier joint."

When that didn't work, they threatened to arrest my mother and other members of my family. "Oh, no! Has my mom been out robbing banks again?"

They kept coming, a half dozen visits in three years. "We can help you on your murder case," they said.

"How?" "You make a statement against Stearns and we can guarantee you a plea bargain to a reduced charge, second degree."

"Gee, that's awful tempting," I responded, knowing I could get a life sentence on second degree as well as first degree.

"You give us Gerry and Alice and full cooperation, we can get it down to voluntary manslaughter."

Feeling impish, I asked, "What can you do if I throw in an FBI agent, a U. S. Marshal, and two DEA agents?"

"What? What are you talking about?"

"Well, how do you think I lasted so long out there? How do you think I knew ahead of time the surveillance you had on my mother when she went to Reno, the setup you guys had waiting on me in Tucson? Think about it."

"Bullshit."

"I want a Presidential pardon."

"What!"

"Well, maybe I'd settle for a baseball card of Lou Gehrig."

"What!"

"Hey, you know what a Lou Gehrig is worth?"

"Smart sonofabitch! How'd you like a little taste of the hole? We can have you thrown in the hole shitbrain!"

They didn't understand that threats didn't work against someone already at the bottom of the barrel. Like Janis Joplin sang, when you ain't got nothing, you got nothing to lose.

"Good idea," I said. "Maybe I can get a breath of fresh air there." Even after Alice had been caught while visiting my mother, the two of them having hit it off from the first, and Gerry having been arrested out west, they kept coming. "Give us a case on Gerry," they said, "and we'll cut Alice loose."

I knew they had nothing on Alice but a case of malicious vindictiveness. Alice, for all her love and loyalty, simply was not a criminal. She had never been an active participant in my smuggling schemes. She'd never bought or sold grass. I knew she had certainly not helped Gerry to rob any banks. The last person a professional bank robber would want to assist him would be Alice. The best they could do was dick her around on aiding and abetting or harboring a fugitive, which would be very iffy charges when they had no witnesses other than myself, who was firmly committed to her defense. You know they're desperate when they get chickenshit enough to threaten your family. The right or wrong of it doesn't matter -- the feds, like psychopaths, want what they want when they want it.

"You got nothing against Alice," I pointed out. "You know fucking A well she's a civilian. What are you going to charge her with, giving her heart to the wrong guy?"

"You'll find out soon enough, asshole! We're not kidding around!"

No, they weren't. Noel Allen Ingman, their pet stooge on the federal witness protection program, his specialty being perjury in return for all the perks he was being given, provided the sole testimony that would convict Alice on a conspiracy to possess and distribute heroin. It was incredible. Alice, who wouldn't touch heroin with a ten-foot pole, was sentenced to three years as a first offender. Nothing was made of the fact that Ingman was a lifelong heroin addict and dealer, a type who would not dream of involving civilians in the trade other than to use and discard them -- they were basically decent citizens who could not be relied upon to maintain the strain of everyday immorality so rampant in modern day illegal drug business, the lying, cheating, and betrayal.

But poor Alice went to prison, and later, Ingman would make a similar case against Gerry, while Ingman, himself a lowlife of the worst sort who had done more damage to society than fifty Alices and Gerrys could ever hope to do over several lifetimes, would be rewarded with immunity for his own crimes, given false ID, money, and encouraged to go out and do it again.

Sitting it all out in Marion, I was thankful that I had had nothing to do with Ingman, a man whom I had met at McNeil Island, that from the first I had resolved, on the basis of an offer he had made to me early on and not trusting the set of his beady eyes, to have as little to do with as possible. I had warned all my friends against dealing with him, including Gerry. I felt a bit smug and superior, if very sad over what he had done to Alice and Gerry, that there was no way he could make a case against me, perjury or no perjury.

I had had nothing to do with him.

However, I had not taken into consideration the vindictive determination of the feds. By late 1984, I became aware that Ingman and others were being pressured by the FBI to make statements that I had confessed to murdering the Grahams. Ingman was the one who would come through for them. He would be primarily responsible for a new grand jury indictment in early 1985, charging premeditated murder of Muff Graham. I had failed to accord proper weight to the maxim I had heard restated in slight variations by many prisoners, which went like this: "If the feds have a hardon for you, even if you're Jesus Christ Himself, they're going to fuck you."

*****

In November, 1982, three months after my arrival, I was informed that a panel of the U.S. Parole Commission would hear my case and consider setting a parole date. I had just received an additional five-year term for the escape from McNeil and had a detainer on a murder charge. I looked upon the matter as an exercise in futility and declined to appear. The parole panel decided to hear my case anyway. By late January, 1983, I'd been informed as to the results of their deliberations. I had been granted a presumptive parole date, if I kept my nose clean, I would be released on parole on March 7, 1984. I didn't know whether to laugh or cry at the ludicrousness of it.

It turned out that the guidelines for the amount of time I should serve on an escape from a minimum-security facility was a maximum of one year. The paroling authorities had merely tacked twelve' months onto the nineteen months ahead of me when I'd escaped from McNeil. What did it matter? At best, I would simply be paroled to the detainer and transported to a jail to await trial. I forgot about it. But when I was within sixty days of the parole date, a prison counselor approached me to discuss an actual release plan. Did I wish to be paroled back to Hawaii?

"How about the detainer?"

"Detainer? What detainer? I didn't see any in your file."

"Oh," I gulped, biting my tongue, trying not to stutter. "R-right. Maybe it was dropped."

"I'll check again to make sure. In the meantime, you better start making a plan."

"Right, sir. I'll get right on it."

The next day he informed me that I had no detainers. Holy shit! And great earthshaking echoes of Gerry's good fortune in Phoenix a couple of years before! The unbearable beauty of the gods kissing me!

Because of the extensive publicity the case had received in Honolulu, I knew that my name had a high recognition factor attached to it, especially with the feds. If I submitted a parole plan for release to Hawaii, the parole papers and notification would be sent to the federal parole and probation office in Honolulu -- where they would immediately recognize that I was not entitled to be released. The general policy was to parole you to the same area from which you were sentenced.

I told the counselor I'd like to have my parole transferred to California.

"But why? Wouldn't it be easier to get a job and residence in your home area where you have friends and family?"

"Well, sir," said I with tongue in cheek. "Most of the people I know are ex-cons, drug dealers, or some other type of criminal. I want to begin a new life, become an asset to my community, and make new friends and associates among law-abiding citizens. I mean, even associating with ex-cons and people of ill repute would be a violation of my parole. By the saints of Ireland and the seven seas, the good Patrick and Elmo, I'm sincere about making a go of it out there."

I got an offer of employment from my brother's construction company in California. He also offered to provide residence until such time as I could get out on my own two feet. The plan was approved. No need to inform anyone that I had no intention of showing up for job, residence, or even reporting to the parole office. The minute I stepped out the front door, I was going to disappear. Within a few days, I would be in Vera Cruz to look up my old buddy, Enrique. The feds would discover soon enough that they had made a boo-boo and come looking for me. I crossed my fingers and hoped they wouldn't learn their mistake before March 7th.

On March 5, as I sat full of jitters before what appeared to be an incredible stroke of luck,

I was informed, alas, that my parole had been rescinded and a detainer had been lodged against me.

It seems that whenever a parole is transferred, the parole office from where you were sentenced is routinely informed of the matter. My name was belatedly recognized and a call was made to Elliot Enoki, the Asst. U. S. Attorney slated to prosecute the murder charge. Enoki got on the phone to the U. S. Parole Commission and the Bureau of Prisons to demand an explanation and to insist that I not be released.

"Hey, Buck, what? Ya gonna eat dat hamburger er what?"

"Huh? Nah, go ahead."

"'Bout time you went on a diet, Fat Boy. How about them french fries?"

"No, go ahead. Help yourself." "The pie?"

"No. Take it."

"Geez, whatsa matta? Ya sick er sumpin'?"

"Yeah," I sighed. "Just a bit. I'll get over it."

"Hey, I got jus da ting to help ya -- a New York Times super-crossword puzzle book. I'll let'cha do da foist one."

"Thanks, Herb."

"But are you tough enough to do 'em on yesca?" (Chicano slang term for grass.)

"You got yesca, Camaron?"

"I got."

"Shit, watch me."

"Little taste of crank in your coffee, man, you'll be up doing them all night."

I had to laugh. "Hoo, man! You know," I said to them. "I came here I thought it was the end of the line. But I gotta tell you, I wouldn't have missed it for the world. Otherwise I never woulda met all you grungy assholes."

Sometimes it was okay to call your best friends assholes -- if you grinned like I was doing.

A parole cannot be rescinded or revoked without proper cause. Had I violated a prison rule? Had I infringed against a condition of parole? No, not that I'd been caught at. The game's the game and the rules're the rules. The government named the game and laid down the rules.

The catch-22 in all this was that the government could get away with ignoring its own rules. The rules were only for the opponents of the government.

The reason given for the renege on my parole date was that new information had been received. What was that information? I was charged with the crime of murder and was awaiting trial.

Documents were sent to the Parole Commission describing Muff's skull and bones as having been found in a metal container. They described in grisly detail the speculation of FBI agent Calvin Shishido and Elliot Enoki the various possibilities of how death must have been inflicted, a blow to the jaw by a blunt instrument, the torturing by applying an acetylene torch to the head, dismembering the body, an attempt to destroy the evidence by further burning it in the metal container. I suppose I should have been relieved that they'd overlooked the possibility of cannibalism.

On the basis of this so-called evidence, I was taken in handcuffs before a special panel of the Parole Commission for a hearing on June 12, 1984. I was not allowed to have an attorney present. It took them all of five minutes to find me guilty of murdering Muff. They revoked my parole and continued my term of imprisonment to the expiration of my full sentence. No judge, no jury, no legal counsel, no trial as guaranteed by the Constitution -- merely a star chamber proceeding in which the result was a foregone conclusion.

It had been conclusively proven to me that when the feds have a hardon for you, they are indeed going to fuck you -- and they're not even going to fool around with a kiss to warm you up.

When I told Partington about the situation during an irate phone call, he was very blasé. What difference did it make? I was not legally entitled to a release on parole. When I pointed out that yes, I was entitled to a release on parole and that the accepted procedure was to release a parolee to the detaining authority for disposition of the outstanding charge, I could almost hear his shrug over the line.

"Sure, it's illegal," he replied. "But it doesn't make any difference. You can't be freed until after the murder charge is disposed of."

"Okay, disregarding the fact that I've just been found guilty of murder, if I'm acquitted after a proper trial, they still won't let me out because my parole's been revoked."

"Hm. Well, we can work on that problem when the time comes."

"How about working on it right now? You're paid to defend me against this murder charge. I've just been found guilty, for chrissakes!"

"I can only defend you in court."

"In that case, I want to demand a speedy trial."

"No, that's not a good idea. The more time passes, the better."

"Fuck that. It didn't matter while I was serving time anyway, but if I get acquitted like you keep telling me, then I can get out right away. It's a big difference to me, man. I'm doing the time."

"Listen, it takes six months just to exhaust administrative remedy, which is required by law before you can even bring the matter before a court."

"Well then, let's get on it while we're waiting."

"You can do that. It's just a matter of filling our forms and going through the motions."

"You're a big help, Earle."

"Sorry, but I'm not paid to take on the Parole Commission."

I would pursue the matter on my own. I would exhaust appealing the decision to the Parole Commission itself -- one of those built-in catch-22s. You are begging the party who wronged you to please undo the wrong but they, since they do not feel it is wrong, are not about to undo it -- they'd had their marching orders from on high; the word had come down through the Department of Justice.

But even in court, when I finally got the case there, relief would be denied and I would appeal the decision to a higher court -where it would again be denied. It cannot be said that the courts have no knowledge of the kangaroo process that goes on in prison parole hearings. It can be said that they approve of the process.

*****

In October 1983, two guards would be stabbed to death in Marion's Control Unit. As set up in the federal prison system, a Control Unit is a prison within a prison. It is reserved for inmates who have committed some act of violence in the mainline population. There are extraordinary security procedures in effect. Inmates may not have physical access to each other. They are kept locked down on single-cell status. Every time they are taken from their cells, whether for recreation, a shower, or a visit, they are handcuffed before the cell door is opened. They shower alone, recreate alone, and visit in a special bulletproof glass-enclosed facility where they may not touch their visitors and must communicate via a telephone system. The procedures are designed to incapacitate those deemed as violence-prone from having any opportunity to commit an act of violence against another.

Despite all these safeguards, one inmate would somehow slip free of the cuffs as he was being escorted to a recreational cage, acquire a knife and stab a guard to death in full view of other inmates and guards. A few days later, another inmate would do the same thing.

There was no question as to who the perpetrators were. There was no question of apprehending them. Even greater security precautions would be taken with regard to these two inmates. They would both be tried and convicted of murder. There was no question that they would die in prison -- the only question was when.

Warden Miller would take the opportunity, since there had been an obvious failure in security by his guards, to cover up the matter by proclaiming that there was a prison-wide conspiracy by inmates to take hostages and assume control of the institution. As a result, he would lock down the entire prison and convert it into one great Control Unit. He would call in special cadres of goon squads from all over the federal prison system to put his plan into effect by force and intimidation.

Warden Miller hated convicts. Before the lockdown, when we were still marched to the messhall for chow, he would stand behind the serving line glaring at each and every one of us. I had been told that he'd begun his career as a guard at Alcatraz. During an attempted escape, a group of convicts had gotten out of their cells, overpowered a few guards and gotten their hands on some firearms. Miller had been one of those taken hostage. It seems a horny old con had bent him over a bunk and cornholed him.

At first I didn't believe the story. Insulting rumors of this sort were a dime a dozen in prisons. It was a popular pastime to spread and embellish such rumors, only about ten percent of which had any truth to them, as though to console us that our keepers were no better than we and, in many cases, far worse -- the jaundiced but real enough perception as to the hypocrisy and injustice in our society. If true, it would go a long way toward explaining his seemingly pathological hatred. On the other hand, the ranks of prison personnel are riddled with assholes that had bad attitudes -- just like prisoners and society at large. Warden Miller's hostile behavior in the messhalls, the counselors explained, doing their toady PR work, was merely a case of making himself accessible to the inmate body in order to personally keep in touch with the general mood and morale, to hear any suggestions or complaints.

One day, an incident occurred in the messhall that would incline me to believe the rumor about Warden Miller was true, and his brutal methods in locking down the entire prison permanently would confirm the thesis that he hated convicts with a passion as a result of his degrading experience so many years ago.

*****

The Mouseman had acquired his moniker because of his eccentric relationship with mice. When they came out at night to roam the cellblocks looking for food, he would bait little homemade traps designed to catch them alive. He would feed and tend them and make pets of them. He always carried one around in his shirt pocket. He would let it run over his shoulders and incline his head so it could crawl up into his hair. Every couple of weeks, he would remind everyone of his nutso status by publicly biting the head off one of his pets, a gruesome and disgusting act. He always saved the heads. He would skin them and pick the skulls clean. He maintained a rather extensive collection of them, including an entire skeleton painstakingly reconstructed and glued back together like a miniature dinosaur. He would laboriously skin off the tiny pelts with a razorblade. After stretching and tanning, he would sew them together to form larger pieces. He was the only person I'd ever met who sported a hatband of mouse fur. He was working on a belt. He was very knowledgeable about the habits of mice, had studied their life cycles from birth to death. He knew all about their mating, eating, sleeping, and social characteristics. He also ate them, in fact had prepared some recipes. Since he lived in the cell next to mine, I couldn't help overhearing him giving lectures to an interested party in the cell on the other side of him. It seems his favorite recipe for baked mice was with peanut butter stuffing. When I heard it, I had been munching on a peanut butter cookie, which ended my late night snack rather abruptly.

For all that, the Mouseman was basically harmless. He never bothered anyone except to horrify new inmates with his head-biting-off demonstration. But heaven help you if you interfered in his relationship with the local mice population. I once saw him chase another convict around the cellblock with a knife, screaming he was going to cut his head off for having stolen one of his mouse skulls. The guy wanted to make a neck pendant with it. Another time he went off on a couple of hacks who'd been searching his cell -- they were going to confiscate his collection of skulls and pelts. When he got out of the hole for that, he confronted Warden Miller standing behind the breakfast line to complain about the interference with his hobby.

The Warden glared at Mouseman and told him to quit his sick screwing around with the mice. Mouseman made an impassioned and no doubt sincere plea about the benefits of his hobby. First, he couldn't afford hobby materials like others; second, he was working on a treatise that would further scientific knowledge in the field; and third, it kept him occupied and out of trouble.

"Trouble," the Warden snorted. "You've caused nothing but trouble since you came here!"

"Only because you keep sending those cocksucking hacks around to harass me! You leave me the fuck alone and let me do my hobby, there wouldn't be no trouble!"

"Get out of my face, you sick little bastard, or you're going right back to the hole!"

"Just because you got fucked in the ass by a convict, you don't have to take it out on me! I didn't fuck you!"

"You shut your filthy mouth right now!"

But Mouseman was not without understanding and sympathy. He abruptly changed his tactics. "Listen, I know you probably like it. That's okay. I've seen it happen before -- guy gets raped, he gets off, he likes it. Pretty soon he's switching around like a bitch. Hey, that doesn't make him a bad guy, does it? You should come on out of the closet, learn to live with your secret urges. You'll be happier."

By the time Mouseman had finished speaking, loudly and in full view of about fifty or sixty convicts, Warden Miller's face was beet red, the veins in his neck and forehead like ropes, his fists clenched.

"Just because a man is raped by an animal," he grated. "It doesn't mean he's any less a man! You fucking scumbag convicts are all alike!"

"Ah, you're just mad because he didn't romance you a little before fucking you."

"Guards! Guards!" Miller screamed, apoplectic. "Take this inmate to the hole!"

But even in the hole, Mouseman had soon captured more mice, was sharing his food with them, and whiling away the days cooing to them.

*****

After the second killing in the Control Unit, we remained locked in our cells for several days, not allowed to shower and subsisting on bag lunches, pieces of cheese or bologna between two stale pieces of bread. The Warden had been busy calling in selected hacks from federal prisons across the nation and forming them into squads of intimidating goons dressed in combat gear -- boots, jumpsuits, helmets with faceplates, and batons with steel rods down their centers. They wore no nameplates and could not be identified for the massive array of lawsuits that would ensue.

We knew it was happening one morning when we heard a celldoor rack open, then scuffling sounds, grunts, yells, and screams, as the first inmate was surprised by having four goons fall on him and forcibly tear his clothes off, after which his hands were cuffed behind him and he was dragged away.

All day it went on, one cell at a time. Some of the cons went down fighting, others tried to go along peacefully, and none got treated gently. Convicts began screaming out their fear and hatred, some preparing for battle, others doubtless praying as the goon squads marched inexorably down the tier, one cell at a time.

It would begin with an order. "Strip down, asshole!"

If the guy was cooperating, there would be a space of silence while he took off all his clothes. Then, "Turn around and put your hands behind you! Back up to the bars!"

We would hear the ratcheting sound of handcuffs being put on his wrists.

"Rack open cell six!" We would hear the door slam, then the movement of boots and bare feet slapping along the tier. There might come the sound of blows, grunts and groans, the sound of a body bumping down the metal tread of the stairs -- or only the sound of feet going down them. There was a suspense in all the sounds, how it would go with each convict removed from his cell.

If the guy said fuck it, he was going to do it the hard way, he might make some comment about their mothers, fold a pillow or mattress before him for protection, grab up his shiv if he had one, or anything that came to hand, even a rolled-up magazine, and invite them in. We'd hear the sounds, the clanks and thoks of wildly swinging batons against the bars and walls in their frenzy to strike flesh and bone, then the clumping down the staircase as they dragged his injured ass away.

One guy spread Vaseline all over his floor and when they all went sliding down on their asses as they rushed into the cell, he jumped on them from his bunk. Some of the guys got in a few licks, but mostly it all went the other way. There was no winning for us. Some got only a few bruises and a rush of adrenaline, but some got the holy shit beat out of them.

They had started on the upper tier and worked their way back, emptying out the cells. We wondered where they were being taken. Then they started on the lower tier. As luck would have it, I was housed in the last cell. The good news was that by the time they got to me, they were tired out from all the effort. The bad news was that their attitudes had degenerated into the worst possible.

If you refused the order to strip and back up to the bars for the handcuffs, they squirted teargas or mace in, then racked the door open and went in with clubs. It was tough to battle at least four thugs in boots, flak jackets, and visored helmets, all carrying clubs.

If you went along, there might just as well be some grunts and groans anyway as they pushed, pulled, and prodded you along. But, as they worked their way along into the afternoon,

I noticed the sounds of movement growing quieter and quieter. The goons were tired, over the first flush of excitement in being given their heads to get the job done any way they saw fit and fuck the American Civil Liberties Union and the bleeding-heart liberals who were into mollycoddling convicts. The two guys just before me had gone with hardly a grunt or groan, just rasped-out orders, the sound of handcuff ratcheting, boots, and bare feet padding away.

It was very quiet when they came for me, the last con in the cellblock. What are you going to do now, me boyo, I asked myself. It's fight, fuck, or hit-the-fence time.

When they got to my cell, I was already naked as the day I was born, a shit-eating grin on my face. "Hi, fellas," I said, lifting my hands palm up in a gesture of peace. "I'll bet I'm the first guy you didn't have to order to strip down. Hey, I believe in cooperation. You guys must be tired of this shit by now. I'm here to help you get it over with."

I backed up to the bars, lifted my wrists behind me for the cuffs. When the door racked open and I'd been pulled out and headed in the right direction, I kept my grin. "Wish I could buy you guys all a drink. I can see it's been a rough day for you."

I thought I detected a little smile behind the Plexiglas visor of the guy on my left. The guy on my right was short and I was always leery of them in authoritarian settings -- too many of them had little-man complexes and always seemed to take it out on the big guys. He elbowed me in the ribs and told me to shut the fuck up. Another guy behind me gripped the connecting links between the cuffs, applying an upward tension to keep me off balance and moving.

As we neared the shower area, the short guy to my right had been slapping his baton into his palm and occasionally nudging me in the ribs with his elbow. I had ignored him, having wiped the grin from my face in case he took it wrong, me, the epitome of cooperation, but keeping a peripheral eye on him all the same.

At the opening to the shower, which was about eight feet wide, he suddenly gripped the baton with one hand to each end, swung it out wide and prepared to drive a blow to my ribs. As his arms swung back to deliver it, I pushed backward off my leading foot, causing the guy on the left to hesitate and the one behind to rub up against me. The momentum of the little guy's swing, his target now out of position, all in a split second, went sailing right by me off balance. His feet caught the foot-high retaining wall at the base of the shower entrance, and he went sprawling headfirst across the tiled floor.

The guy behind immediately pushed forward and up on his grip between my wrists, slamming me face first against the wall. The baton in his other hand swung up between my legs, all in the fashion to which he'd been trained, to mash against my favorite testicle. As I began to sag, another blow came between my shoulder blades and I was held in that position while the little guy, madder than a wet banty rooster, picked himself up and drew his baton back like a baseball bat to hit a homerun with my head.

Don't ask me why, only that there is some humanity in the worst of people at the oddest times, but the guy who'd been walking on my left, the one who might have cracked a little smile at me, restrained the little guy.

"Knock it off," he said. "You brought that on yourself."

Then turning to the two who still had me pressed up against the wall, he said, "C'mon, let's get him around to the other side."

I felt the nightstick withdraw from my crotch, the pressure ease from between my shoulder blades, and we continued the march, me sucking wind and trying not to throw up. At the last cell, stumbling past a row of stripped cells all containing naked convicts, they shoved me in and took off the cuffs.

"You all right?" my savior asked.

"Yeah," I grunted. "If I can just get my nut down out of my chest cavity."

"Sorry about that, but you guys brought it down on yourselves. We don't take kindly to our fellow officers being killed."

"Hey, pal, I didn't kill them."

"Well, you guys were going to take over the joint, take hostages, and who knows what. We can't let you get away with that."

"That's pure bullshit!"

"That's not what the Warden says."

"Fuck the Warden!"

He looked at me and I wondered if I'd gone too far. "What'd you do to get yourself in Marion?"

"Would you believe I walked away from a minimum security joint?"

"No. You got to do more than that to get here. I can look it up in your record."

I wondered if it would do any good to dust off my halo and claim I was a model prisoner. Probably not. He'd probably never seen one before. So I just repeated myself. "I escaped from a fucking camp, the McNeil Island camp. Look it up yourself."

He shrugged and grinned in disbelief. "Whatever. Just remember, you can still fuck with only one nut."

"Thanks, man. You sure know how to cheer a guy up."

*****

When news had leaked out, the ACLU and many private lawyers were outraged. Many suits were initiated, both individual and class action. I began one myself, based upon Eighth Amendment rights, the cruel and unusual punishment clause to the Constitution. A magistrate named Meyers, who conducted quick and arbitrary hearings at the prison itself, heard them all. Each and every complaint was speedily denied. Most of them would continue on up through the appeals courts in that circuit to the Supreme Court, and all would come to naught. It was perfectly all right for prison authorities to take stern measures to protect against uprisings and it was too bad that some innocent parties got hurt along the way.

After two brief appearances before Magistrate Meyers in a severely shackled condition, wherein he informed me that I was not entitled to appointment of counsel -- there were only prosecuting attorneys defending against the complaint and prison officials, among which numbered a half dozen hacks smirking over the shiny black batons gripped in their hands -- I saw the writing on the wall and let my own suit slip into oblivion.

While being interviewed by a locally based attorney who was doing some pro bono work for some of the inmates, she told me that a relative of one of the guards who'd been killed in the Control Unit, a hack himself, had been caught trying to pour arsenic or cyanide into the Kool-Aid that was passed out along with the bag lunches to the locked down prisoners. Even though I never drank the stuff, I shuddered inwardly. The local denizens had dubbed the sickeningly sweet liquid as The Red Death.

I could only think of the Reverend Jim Jones and the mass deaths caused by cyanide in the Kool-Aid down in Guyana.

*****

The entire prison remained on permanent lockdown. At first, we got out of our cells only for showers, one by one, two times a week, or for medical emergencies. If we were taken out of the cellblock, it was with hands cuffed behind us and we were escorted by no less than four hacks, all sporting the black batons.

I was selected for orderly duties, which meant I was let out of my cell two or three times a day to sweep and mop the tiers and play errand boy for passing things like cigarettes, coffee, and books between cons.

Warden Miller, already promoted beyond the level of his competence according to the Peter Principle, was transferred to the penitentiary at Lewisburg, Pennsylvania, where the inmates almost immediately went on a food and work strike. With a new administrative head, conditions began to ease a bit at Marion. Every inmate was issued his own individual pacifier, a portable black and white TV with a 13-inch screen, and most of us became avid couch potatoes, if that isn't an oxymoron. In addition to sports, which have always been popular pastimes in prisons, we got into following all the soaps and game shows, as well as the regular network evening programs, mainly situation comedies and cop shows.

They began letting us out by twos to walk, visit, and exercise along the tiers -- then by fours. Soon we were taken by whole units about fifty inmates, to a small fenced-in exercise yard for recreation twice a week for two hours. Finally, they started up a cable factory employing about forty inmates, all of who were within six months of a transfer to another prison. They were all housed in B-Unit, where they were only locked down between 10 p.m. and 6 a.m. It was the only cellblock that was allowed to eat in the messhall or where an inmate could go out of the unit without handcuffs. Since Marion was a disciplinary prison, the individual theoretically had to earn the privilege of being housed in B-Unit by good behavior, but in reality the selection process was more or less arbitrary. Some guys were going to do many years between the Control Unit and the lockdown status of the rest of the institution before reaching B-Unit. So many were transferred in and so many had to be shipped out. In the spring of 1984, about six months after the lockdown, I was moved to B-Unit -- where I was to remain longer than anyone else.

A transfer to B-Unit usually meant, if you kept your nose clean, that you were within six months to a transfer. Except when I was out to court, I would remain for over two years.

*****

In April, prior to my appearance before a two-member panel of the U. S. Parole Commission in June for a rescission hearing, where I would be found guilty of murdering Muff Graham and my mandatory release date would be continued to the expiration of two-thirds of my full sentence of eighteen years, Earle Partington came to see me.

I was torn between two extremes in my feelings toward him. Because he was a mild mannered guy, soft-spoken and polite, I was inclined to like him. On the other hand, he wasn't the brightest lawyer around and I often had to go to some lengths to explain a question before he understood it. His legal pronouncements and advice all but drove me to pull my hair out by the fistful.

When he told me a change of venue was definitely going to be granted to either Oakland or San Francisco, since the question had already been considered on more than one occasion,

I asked him why. He said it was because Judge King wanted to attend the opera.

"Are you fucking kidding me?"

"No, he likes opera. So what? We got a change of venue. That's good for us. Who cares why?"

"You're telling me Judge King is going to be presiding at the trial?"

"Sure, he's chief judge now. He can do what he wants."

"That is not a good sign, Earle."

"What do you mean?"

I told him about my previous experiences with the man, especially a screwing he have given me on an evidentiary hearing in Honolulu when he wouldn't even allow me to be represented by my own privately retained counsel.

"Well, he won't be able to get away with anything in a trial as well publicized as this one. Don't worry. We've got this one in the bag."

"In the bag?" I was amazed. I had never heard of an attorney putting it so bluntly. They never, but never promised a particular outcome. "Buck," he grinned, so self-assured. "They can't make this felony-murder charge against you, no way."

"Explain it to me," I said, trying to control the hope that was trying to soar inside.

"There's just no way the government can prove a murder occurred during the course of a robbery."

"You mean the boat theft?"

"Yeah. They can't connect the allegation of murder to the theft. None of the forensics experts can determine the time of death, let alone the cause. To top it off, your theft conviction was reversed. Ray took it back into court and got it dismissed on speedy trial grounds."

"You're sure?"

"Listen, I had a talk with Judge King awhile back and he made the comment that he couldn't see how the prosecution could possibly make the connection. Believe me, it's in the bag. We probably won't even have to present a defense."

"Why not?"

"Because it will probably be dismissed after the government fails to make any connection between robbery and murder. They can't make a prima facie showing. We'll be presenting a motion to that end."

"You're telling me that the jury won't get to decide the case because Judge King will dismiss it before it gets that far?"

"Exactly."

When it had sunk in, I became angry. "Goddamn it, Earle, why the fuck are we dilly-dallying around? Why haven't we demanded a speedy trial?"

"No, no, it's better this way. The more time that passes, the better it is for us. It doesn't matter. You're doing time anyway." "Bullshit! If we'd already gone to trial and gotten the case dismissed, I wouldn't be in this stinking place! I had a fucking parole date for last month! Now, they're taking me up on a rescission hearing!"

"Well, that's all just a mistake on their part. It'll be rectified when the time comes."

"I could have been out right now, Earle!"

"Look, believe me, it's better this way. This case has been a media circus. The more time that goes by, the more distance we get, the better it will be."

"It's been ten years!"

"But only three since they found the bones."

"Jesus Christ, Earle, you ought to try doing some time in this shit-hole. I'll bet you wouldn't be so cavalier with your own life!"

"Look, we'll be going to trial soon, within the next few months. We won't do much better if we demand a speedy trial. The government would still have at least sixty days to play around with, not to mention excludable delays."

"That's what worries me, Earle," I said, drawing deep breaths and trying to calm down. "They've got all the time in the world to come up with something."

"What can they come up with? Is there something you haven't told me?"

I didn't know whether to laugh or cry. I hadn't told him anything. He'd never asked me. Early on I'd learned that lawyers never wanted to know anything, never appreciated answers to questions that had never been asked. They never asked you whether you committed the crime you were charged with. They didn't want to know, especially if you were guilty. If you couldn't tell them you were innocent, they didn't want to hear it -- and most of them were so cynical that if you professed to be innocent, they didn't believe you. Except for Bettencourt at the theft trial when he'd surprised me by asking the questions without any forewarning, never once had a lawyer asked whether I had murdered Mac and Muff.

"I haven't told you anything at all, Earle, not you or anyone else."

"That's good, that's good," he said, obviously relieved. But then he thought about it. "You never discuss your case with anybody in here? You never talk about it?"

"I tell people, when they ask me what I'm in for, what I was convicted of, that's all, how much time I'm doing."

"Nothing about the murder charge?"

"I've mentioned that I'm charged, that's it. I don't go into any details. There are a few guys around who remember reading about the case. Some guy once came and showed me an article in People Magazine. It had a picture of me."

"That's good. We don't need any jailhouse snitches coming out of the woodwork."

"Don't worry about that. I've got nothing to say to anybody."

"Keep it that way," he said, needlessly. "I mean, they can't even prove the bones were in the box."

"They can't? That isn't what I've read."

"No. I went to South Africa and interviewed Sharon Jordan, the lady who found the bones?"

"Yeah?"

"She told me there were no bones in the box, only in the sand. She said the metal container was stuck upright in some bushes. So, there's no way."

"What about all these scientific test reports on the waxy substance found inside? One of them said it was human protein."

"Yeah, but they can't specifically identify it. I was told it might not even be human -- it could have come from an animal, even certain types of vegetation. Even if it is human, one guy told me it could have come from vomit, shit, or even someone spitting in the container."

"How about all the other so-called evidence?"

"What?"

"They got Wolfe saying he saw me smoking grass, that I hit on him for some."

He grinned. "Did you?"

"No fucking way I'd hit on a perfect stranger for grass. Why should I? We had plenty."

"We don't have to worry about that. The judge won't let him bring it up. It's prejudicial. We could get a mistrial on that alone.'

"By the way, whatever happened to that grass charge they had against me?"

"What grass charge?"

I explained that when we'd originally been indicted on the theft charge, there had also been a count alleging we had smuggled in 464 grams, over a pound. But before trial, it had disappeared from the indictment, along with illegal possession of firearms.

"Probably because they couldn't prove it was yours. The grass could have belonged to the Grahams -- as long as you never confessed. The guns weren't registered to you, were they?"

"No."

"There you go. They couldn't prove they weren't Mac's guns.

" I nodded. "Well that answers that. I always wondered."

"By the way, you know they're scrutinizing all your mail and monitoring all your phone calls."

"Yeah, you told me already. I knew about the phones -- it's common knowledge. Don't worry, I only ever call my family, and we never discuss anything important."

"Just be careful. They're photocopying all your mail, incoming and outgoing. Don't write about it to anyone. They've got a stack that high." He indicated about a foot with his hands.

"Didn't think I'd written that many letters."

"Okay, just so you know. They're looking for anything and everything, whatever they can get. Any admissions from you would be the worst possible development."

"You think I'd tell anyone what I haven't even told you in a conversation that's protected by the attorney/client privilege?" He sighed. "Good. What did happen down there? They just disappeared in an accident, like you said?"

"Are you really asking, Earle, or you just want reassurance?"

"I'm really asking. Tell me about it. What happened?"

So I gave him the short, blunt version, which wasn't enough. He asked five or six questions for clarification on certain points. I answered them.

He was looking grim by then. "Listen, Buck," he began, pronouncing each word with an intensity that sat me back on my tailbone. "I'm going to give you my strongest advice. Don't ever -- you understand? -- Don't ever, ever repeat that story to anyone, and I mean anyone. You're not going to take the stand and testify anyway."

"I'm not?"

"No, that's the worst thing you could do -- is get up there and tell that story. We don't need it. We don't have to defend against a case that can't be made. No, that's definite. You're not testifying."

"My experience is that a judge and jury like to hear a defendant speak for himself."

"It doesn't matter. They can't make the case."

I was to be reminded of our entire conversation on this visit fourteen months later, and his final words would echo in mockery.

*****

By November, I had been approved for a transfer to Lompoc and was only waiting around to be scheduled for transportation. November also brought two letters from Ollie. Our paths had crossed in July 1982, in Lompoc, while I was awaiting transfer to Marion. He had turned himself in for having walked away from a halfway house, but had been given no more than a slap on the wrist. He was again on the verge of release on parole and planned to return home to his native Arkansas. He was discouraged that he hadn't been able to track his wife down after she had run off with a McNeil Island hack. He was worried about his four children, two beautiful girls and twin sons who used to visit together with Alice and I. He asked my advice.

I told him to wait until he got off parole because his ol' lady could have him thrown in jail with a phone call. I suggested he get a job or try going back to school -- he didn't have much time to do on parole. He wanted to know if I could put him onto some way to make some money.

"Ollie," I told him. "If you're thinking about pulling off a job or something, forget about it. You're not cut out to be a criminal. You know what it's like, man, you've had a taste of the shit. Get yourself straight, do your parole, make something for yourself and your kids. You'll find them sooner or later. Check with your ol' lady's relatives. She'll be in touch with them."

"That fucking bitch!"

"Forget her, man, she's water under the bridge."

"She's got my kids!"

"I know, but don't do anything dumb. It'll work out in time. Be patient."

"Shit, man, I'm going out flat broke and no prospects."

"How you going to Arkansas?"

"On a bus."

"Okay. You think you can detour through Reno?"

"I don't know. Yeah, probably. They're giving me a ticket to Little Rock and fifty bucks."

"All right. There's a little town outside Reno," I said, giving him the name. "If you can get yourself there for a couple of days, I can let you have a few grand."

"What do I got to do?"

There was a friend of mine who lived in a rural area and was holding twenty-five grand of my money. She was to keep five for herself and hold the other twenty for me. The trouble was, I had never been to her house and couldn't tell Ollie how to find it. All I could do was give him her name and post office box number. I would get a message to her to give him five grand. He would have to hang around the post office and wait for her to pick up her mail. I described the car she would be driving and what she looked like.

"Hey, bro, I really appreciate this. Is there anything I can do for you out there?"

"Just keep yourself free, man. Drop me a postcard once in a while."

"This broad," he said, hesitating. "She private preserve?"

"Nah," I said with a laugh, knowing what was coming. "Just a good friend. Why?"

"Well, man," he grinned. "I am just getting out, you know, and I'm hornier than a Texas fucking horny toad!"

"That's between you and her. Just treat her like a lady."

"Oh, hell yeah. You can count on it."

The lady went to her post office box six days a week, waiting for Ollie to show, but he never did. At Marion I had received a brief postcard from Little Rock saying he was doing okay and had enrolled in some college classes.

The next time I heard from him, he was serving two life sentences in the state prison at Huntsville, Texas. I never got the full story, but it seems he had hooked up with another ex-con and they'd kidnapped someone for ransom. When the plan went awry, his partner had promptly turned state's evidence and tried to blame it all on Ollie. The rat was rewarded by being sentenced to only twenty years.

Since the Texas Department of Corrections did not offer paying jobs to inmates, I arranged for him to receive a few bucks from time to time so he could purchase necessities from the commissary.

On November 1, 1984, I received two letters from him. The first was couched in guarded terms and said, "Uncle Joe and Uncle Sammy was here last week. They wanted me to go on vacation with them, either to California or Hawaii. But, regretfully, I can't get off for that long. They said Red's old man had been up their way and really interested in helping them out. Say, I understand that Earle is no longer on your side. Hope that doesn't hurt you too much."

Uncle Joe and Uncle Sammy translate as feds -- FBI. He was telling me that they wanted him to testify against me, as his second letter makes pellucidly clear, but that he had turned them down. Red referred to Cheryl. Her estranged husband, who had once tried to shoot me and rip off a load of grass down in Mexico, was doing his best to help the feds sew me up.

The bit about my lawyer, Earle Partington, I ignored as a piece of disinformation planted by the feds. But after the trial was over and I'd recovered from my initial shock and received further communications from Earle and an appeal attorney named Dennis Riordan, I would find myself battling bouts of paranoia and wonder if the traditional but informal and unspoken conspiracy by the feds to destroy evidence in my favor and create evidence against me did or did not include Earle Partington.

Ollie's second letter was addressed to my mother, who sent it along to me. It said, "I had a visit from the FBI from Honolulu. It appears that old friend of mine and Buck's, that turned snitch, had told the feds that Buck had told him and me about those two so-called murders that they are trying to pin on him. He may be called to testify at Buck's trial that Buck told him all about it. Of course we both know that that is not true, because Buck never did anything to those people. Well, evidently, they must have a weak case, because they offered me a real sweet deal if I would also testify that Buck told me he did it. They wanted to take me to Honolulu to talk to a U. S. Attorney there. I told them nothing, but told them I would think about it. Under no circumstances send this letter to him or write him about it. They are monitoring his mail closely. His last letter to me came with a Honolulu postmark on it. It would be to his advantage if they did not know that he knew they came to me."

This paragraph was more pregnant with meaning than I would recognize at the time. The snitch he was talking about was one Noel Allen Ingman, whom I had known at McNeil Island. Referring to Ingman as an old friend had to be read with a touch of tongue-in-cheek sarcasm. Neither Ollie nor I had liked this crumbum from the first time we'd laid eyes on him and had had as little to do with him as possible. Ollie's letter confirmed the point Partington had previously made, that all my incoming and outgoing mail was being photocopied. It appeared that my outgoing letters were simply forwarded to the FBI and federal prosecutor Enoki in Honolulu and then mailed on from there. It also told me that the feds were aware that Ollie had communicated this news to me -- a very important point that would become obvious in time.

Ollie also said that he was thinking about the possibility of running a scam on them. He would tell them whatever they wanted to hear in hopes that they would take him out of the very onerous Texas prison system and into a federal facility. But that he would never actually get up in court to testify against me. He wanted to know if it was all right for him to go ahead with his scam and that if he were subpoenaed into court to testify, he would simply tell the truth, that I had never made any incriminating statements to him and that he'd only said what the feds wanted him to say because they'd promised to get him out of Huntsville Prison.

With Partington's and Ollie's warnings in mind about the extraordinary surveillance given to my correspondence, I did not reply to Ollie's letter. I could not tell him to go ahead or not. To tell him he had my permission would have been helping to tie the noose around my own neck -- I could be charged with suborning perjury. I figured that unless he heard from me to the contrary, he would not proceed.

Instead, I copied out all the pertinent passages from both letters and sent them to Partington in order to warn him about what the feds were up to. Since he was my attorney of record, prison authorities were prohibited by law from reading or copying any communications between us -- which is not to say that they would not do it anyway. As for me, I played with the idea of notifying postal inspectors of this tampering with my mail by parties other than prison authorities. Prison authorities were allowed to check the contents of all letters for contraband, but I did not think that included the FBI or Assistant U. S. Attorneys who were required to obtain proper search warrants. Perhaps I could embarrass them by insisting that they be charged with some sort of federal offense. But it was only a mindfuck game for me. I knew they would somehow wiggle out of it.

*****

On January 10, 1985, I was flown out to San Francisco in a chartered plane by U. S. Marshals and booked into the city jail. I was placed in a high-security tank containing only three other prisoners. We were fed and tended by jail guards, never trustees, and were completely cut off from the rest of the jail population.

# # #

CHAPTER 14

Partington came to see me right away. He told me that I was about to be re-indicted on a charge of premeditated murder as a result of testimony taken by the grand jury on the basis of prosecutor Enoki's having hauled Ingman and Ollie in to testify as to the alleged incriminating statements I had made to them while under the influence of heroin and marijuana, bragging about how I'd murdered Mac and Muff.

"They're dropping the felony-murder count," I commented, never having quite convinced myself that it was going to be as easy as Earle had painted it.

"No, they're just adding the premeditated count."

"You mean I'm being charged with two counts of murder? Did they find Mac's remains?"

"No, they both relate to Mrs. Graham."

It took me a moment to digest that. "You're saying that I'm being accused of killing the same person twice?"

"They can only find you guilty of one or the other, not both." "So, what does it all mean?"

"It means those two snitches who testified before the grand jury are going to say that you made incriminating statements to them."

"Um, and when was I supposed to have made these statements?"

"At McNeil Island. Ingman's going to say that he knew you on the streets and was engaged in criminal activities with you."

"Me, engaged in criminal activities with Fairly Big?" I almost choked on the idea, caught between a laugh and outrage at the idea.

"What? Fairly Big? Who's that?"

*****

The unscrupulous, beady-eyed informant named Noel Allen Ingman, whom the feds had their cheese-baited hooks into, was a lifelong heroin addict and narcotics dealer who liked to be known as Big Al. After all, that was the very sobriquet applied to Al Capone by intimates, associates, and numberless awed members of the public at large. But, alas, in one of those quirks of irony so injurious to the egos of those who over-zealously stage-manage their own reputations, it was the grudgingly derisive consensus of his peers in the criminal milieu that he was ever after to be known as Fairly Big.

Fairly Big was never one to hold himself above corruption in the same way that his feet were not fixed above his head -- it was unnatural. Words like integrity and moral rectitude were related to implausible definitions, hardly susceptible to practical application in the real world.

Whenever he sensed the nearness of money, drugs, or advantage, he stood upon the rulebook to increase his reach.

Fairly Big hailed from Alaska. He was college educated, married who knows how many times, and begat an uncertain number of children. The information available indicates that he may have sold one or two of his children while yet infants, a suggestion he would indignantly deny on the stand. He claims he merely placed them up for adoption for their own good and nobody can ever prove he accepted money thereby. After all, a heroin addiction is pressing enough, but a dope addict wife doubled the problem and kids could be a real nuisance. Fairly Big claims he only did the Christian thing for these children.

Money was always in short supply -- heroin was expensive. It was only natural that his ol' lady hooked for a living while he stole, cheated, and connived as opportunity presented. The dope trail can be along one and there were other ol' ladies, children, and a variety of jails and prisons. He had once calculated that, considering the amount of heroin pumped into his veins over a lifetime, that his blood had to be more valuable than its carat weight in diamonds.

He saw the benefit of keeping the dope business in the family. As a logical consequence, he got his two sisters strung out and roped in, including two sons and various in-laws and hangers-on. Of this larger family, after all, he was the smartest, the cleverest, the most manipulative, and having them hooked on heroin meant that he controlled the short leashes he kept them on. Dare it be said that he was a budding godfather? Where was there a Mario Puzo to memorialize his exalted status?

Once though, during a slump period in his career he had sold his seventeen-year-old niece into white slavery to an acquaintance who was on the verge of investing some much needed capital into the family business and had expressed an interest in the girl. His niece had tipped the scale and Fairly Big was on a roll once again. But then one of his sons had been ungracious enough to die of an overdose supplied by the would-be godfather himself.

Fearing the authorities were on the verge of arresting him as a major trafficker in some of the purest China White to hit the Pacific Northwest in years, as well as chagrined by the growing disillusionment of his family, Fairly Big managed to turn impending defeat into a victory of sorts.

He went to the feds and made a deal to tell all, to testify against anybody and everybody, in exchange for immunity from prosecution for all his own crimes, some new ID, money, and favorable status on the witness protection program, called WITSEC in the acronym. A man in his position knew well the advantages of such a move. In the future, when he engaged in further criminal activities, dealing narcotics or whatever, all he would have to do to insure his continued immunity is to deliver up more bodies to the insatiable maw of the federal criminal justice system. After all, with immunity, he had what amounted to a license to commit criminal acts. It wasn't bad by way of a semi-retirement program -- it beat a life sentence in prison. He was a couple of hundred thousand dollars in debt and couldn't pay, thanks to his superior management abilities -- and his debtors were the sort whose collection method favored a sawed-off Louisville Slugger over the Chapter 11 bankruptcy process. Not only would he have an opportunity to put his debtors in prison, unable to collect their money, but if they should contract out the debt to special collectors, he would be safe in a secret location protected by the federal government no less.

*****

I first met Fairly Big inside the main prison at McNeil Island. For a few months we were housed in the Two Cellblock, which would have been about 1976 or '77 sometime. He was a known heroin dealer and user and was involved in scams to smuggle small amounts of heroin into prison for those purposes. I was introduced to Ingman by someone whom I can't remember, and had engaged in a few brief conversations with him. For a while he kept coming around to my cell in attempts to initiate friendly conversations, and a couple of times he offered me hits of heroin, which I declined.

On one side of me was housed a man reputed to be in the hierarchy of organized crime in Hawaii, while on the other side was a man reputed to work as an enforcer for Mafia elements in Nevada. There were a number of stories making the rounds about these two men. One was about the bodies of informants and other enemies being thrown into the active volcano crater, Kilauea, on the Big Island in Hawaii. Another had it that bodies were being fed to herds of pigs. Still another had achieved mythic proportions -- that when outside elements of criminal gangs had invaded Honolulu for the purpose of knocking off key members in the Hawaiian syndicate and taking over all criminal operations in the lucrative 50th State, their heads had all been shipped in one container back to their points of origin, and the bones of their skeletons had been shipped close behind with a note that said, "Delicious. Send more." The most prominent story about the reputed Mafia enforcer was that he delighted in pulling the tongues from stoolpigeon's mouths with a pair of pliers.

Well, who's to say if there's any truth to them? For my part, I saw only perfect gentlemen with impeccable manners who kept themselves clean and neat. Both, like myself, were model prisoners. But, because of my association with these two fine fellows, I was perceived as a comer in the criminal milieu with extensive underworld connections. All I can say is that I did not choose to be sent to McNeil, nor did I have any choice about which cell I would occupy, not to mention that my selection of friends and acquaintances was severely limited by the individuals made available to me by the Bureau of Prisons. Given the situation, I considered myself lucky to have the privilege of associating with these men, who at least were not child-molesters, informants, politicians, or psychotic serial murderers.

But it was because of the misperceptions about these friendships that Fairly Big was trying to suck up to me. He wanted to put out a contract on a former crime-partner who had beaten him out of some drugs and money.

He had first contemplated approaching the gentleman who had reputedly ripped the tongues from informant's mouths, but had demurred because the man had given him the willies with a look that could pierce stonewalls. Doubtless his own tongue froze in terror at the mere thought of it.

His second choice had been me, but I hadn't liked the weasly little bastard from the beginning. I called him an asshole and sent him on his way.

His third choice, the one he actually approached to put out his contract for a hit, was a Columbian fellow named Luis. After all, Columbians were reputed to be cheap, stupid, and ferocious. Luis liked to drink and Fairly Big invested some of his drug proceeds to provide him with pruno, a prison-made brew of fermented fruit juices. After mentioning that he knew the reputed Hawaiian and Mafia gangsters, he also dropped my name into the conversation, no doubt hoping to establish his bona fides. When Fairly Big finally got around to his contract, Luis looked at him like the fool he was and laughed in his face. Then, Luis, who was one of my convivial drinking buddies, came to tell me all about it.

When I learned that my friend, Gerry, was on friendly terms with Fairly Big, I warned him. Sorry to say, he ignored my representations that Fairly Big was untrustworthy and proceeded to expand their relationship. Once they were both released from prison, Gerry and

Fairly Big became involved in business ventures together. Gerry was invited to meet members of Fairly Big's family, his mother, his sisters, and his sons. When I learned of this, I warned him again, but by then Gerry had invested considerable sums with Fairly Big and had been charmed by his mother and sisters. When Fairly Big introduced him to his beautiful seventeen-year-old niece, Gerry fell in love. Fairly Big, seeing an opportunity to further bind Gerry to him, promptly "sold" his niece. He told her that if she would spend one night with Gerry in a motel, he would buy her a new car. The niece was susceptible to Gerry's charms and agreed. In no time, she was as much in love with him as he was with her. And so Gerry invested even more money in Fairly Big's losing propositions.

Gerry and the niece took up housekeeping in Yuma, where Alice and I were also living at the time. She was a delightful girl. Later, her grandmother, Fairly Big's mother, came to visit, and she was a lovely, down-home old gal.

Fairly Big would claim that he and I were such friends that when I escaped from McNeil, I came to visit him and he gave me money to assist in my getaway, but the fact is I only saw him twice after I had escaped and that was not one of those times.

The first time I saw him was at a motel, the Rodeway Inn, near the airport in Phoenix. There were six of us: Fairly Big, his niece, Gerry, Alice, myself, and Ollie. Fairly Big was ripped on heroin and kept trying to get all the rest of us to try it, but we were into no more than a few joints and drinks. When I had returned from a run to a liquor store, I caught him huddled up whispering urgently into Alice's ear. Reacting to her mute appeal for rescue, I intervened, saying rather bluntly, "Do me a favor and stay away my ol' lady, Al."

When I asked Alice what he wanted, she told me he had offered her a chance to make big money simply by delivering small packages and picking up payment for them. He had also tried to persuade her to let him shoot her up with heroin.

I got Gerry alone and told him about that and he confirmed that Fairly Big thought she would make a perfect drug courier because she looked so straight. About that time Fairly Big himself horned in with some very uncouth words to the effect that Alice was the perfect chump to be used as a mule and that I was a fool for not using her. At that point I had the little turd jacked up against a wall with my fists full of his shirt and told him in very certain terms he'd better stay away from me and Alice and keep his filthy mouth shut in the meantime. After which Alice and I left. Ollie didn't last long either, for he saw the same thing I saw in the little twerp. But somehow my friend Gerry was blinded to his faults -- just as I had been blinded to Dave's.

Then I met one of Fairly Big's sisters in passing. Alice and I had put her up overnight and drove her to the airport the next day after a night on the town seeing shows in Vegas. She was a nice lady, but unfortunately also hooked on heroin. I could only shake my head, at a loss to understand how his family could be so different from Fairly Big and yet accept being treated so poorly by him.

The second time I met him really pissed me off. Gerry had sent him down deep into Mexico to deliver some money I had coming from our grass operation. He was glassy-eyed on heroin and had been offering it to Lena and Fae, who were home alone when he arrived. When Enrique and I got in from a trip to the mountain village where we bought our grass, I found Fairly Big zonked out on my bed.

I could barely restrain myself. I was pissed that Gerry, knowing how I detested this little skunk, could send him down there in such a blatant violation of our security. Then the little cocksucker came up short on the money with a shrug.

"Hey, man," he said. "I heard they found a woman's body washed up in a box on that island down there."

"Shut the fuck up, Al."

"Hey, what the hell, man, I think it was pretty slick. Put her in a box, dump her in the ocean. Time'll take care of the rest."

"I didn't put her in a box, Al."

He shrugged. "Oh, yeah? Well, what do I know? You think your girlfriend will keep her mouth shut?"

I grabbed him and threw him against the door. Then I opened the door and shoved him outside. "Hey, man, what the hell!"

"You shut the fuck up, asshole," I said, pushing him down the walk. "Get in that Jeep and just shut the fuck up!"

I drove him the few miles to the primitive little airport where a dilapidated old DC-3 would deliver him to Mexico City for connections back to the States. He had a six-hour wait for the afternoon plane. I hoped the sun would cook what was left of his brains out while he waited. Or maybe the plane would crash. We had recently heard of one from this very airport crashing in the mountains with eighteen lives lost.

"You get on that plane, Al, and you get the fuck out of Mexico. You forget you been here and don't ever come back. You understand me?"

"Yeah, man, what the fuck! I do you a favor and you treat me like shit!"

"You are shit, motherfucker! I don't want your fucking favors! You just beat it, stay the fuck away from me, and keep your nose out of my business!" Then I called Gerry and read him the riot act. He said he was just getting what mileage he could out of Fairly Big because he was owed about eighty grand that he'd invested with him. I didn't ask in what. I didn't want to know.

*****

On January 8, 1985, two days before my arrival in San Francisco, on the basis of testimony by Ingman and Ollie, a grand jury issued superseding indictments against both Stephanie and myself. They charged not only that we had killed Muff during a robbery of the Sea Wind, the original felony-murder count, but also that we had murdered her by premeditation and malice aforethought.

As far as I was concerned, the rules of the game had been changed and Partinton's defense plan to offer no defense was dead. After he had delivered a copy of the new indictment, I put it to him.

"It's not so bad as you think," he said.

"Come again?"

"I don't think they can prove the body was in the box."

"What do you mean? They've got all those forensic reports that say it was."

"They're ambiguous. I've been talking to some private forensic specialists to discuss those reports. I don't think it can be proved conclusively. We'll have to get them to run independent tests and see what we come up with."

"You mean you haven't already?"

He shrugged. "There was no need under the old indictment."

In other words, he was totally surprised by this new development and would have to hustle to be ready. Feeling a depression creeping upon me, I put it to him with a bit of sarcasm.

"I knew about the possibility a few weeks ago, in December." "Why didn't you tell me?"

"I didn't think they'd be able to pull it off. Stephanie's lawyer, Bugliosi, is responsible for it."

"What? What the hell are you talking about?"

"Bugliosi sent a motion to Judge King asking that the indictment be changed to premeditated murder."

"And the judge granted the motion?" I knew it couldn't be done that simply. If King had actually granted such a crackpot motion, it would be easy enough to have it nullified by appeal to a higher court.

"No," Earle replied, confirming the point. "King hasn't the power to do that. It was a useless motion and Bugliosi knows it."

"Then why did he make it?"

"I'm not sure," he shrugged. "It's a matter of speculation."

"So, speculate. Why'd he do it?"

"To publicly communicate with Enoki."

"I don't get it."

"He's making a suggestion to Enoki, telling him that felony-murder won't fly, that the only chance he has to make a case is on a premeditated murder."

"Why not just tell him, pick up the phone, and call him."

"Because that's improper conduct. It smells of collusion. He's acting against his client."

"But he's doing it anyway!"

"Yeah, but he did it publicly, which leaves a smokescreen -- it's all out in the open. He's not sneaking around, engaged in some secret conspiracy. Besides, it makes perfect legal sense from the point of view of protecting his client's interests."

"You're saying Stephanie's and mine aren't the same?"

"Exactly. Your theft conviction was reversed, hers wasn't. Because of that, half their case is already made on her."

"I thought you said they couldn't show a connection between robbery and murder, that a killing occurred during the robbery."

"That's right."

I still didn't get it. If the prosecution couldn't make the connection of a killing as an intrinsic part of the alleged robbery, then it wouldn't make any difference whether the robbery, or theft, could be proved or not.

"Besides, now you've got two witnesses against you who are saying you admitted you murdered the Grahams."

Then I got it, or thought I did. "But these two witnesses -their statements can't be used against Stephanie, right? Only against me."

"Right."

"Jesus Fucking Christ! This cocksucker Bugliosi is worse than the prosecutor! He's trying to better Stephanie's position by fucking over me!"

"That's one way to look at it."

"What other way is there?"

"Forget Stephanie. Think of Bugliosi's position."

"What?"

"He's a big splash kind of guy. He writes books about his cases, makes millions of dollars. He smells a book in this case."

"Yeah? So?"

"With felony-murder, there's no real trial. Kaput! You and Stephanie walk. Where's the book in that? If there's no trial, he doesn't get to strut his stuff."

"Jesus, that's taking a hell of a chance with Stephanie's life." Partington didn't even bother to shrug, just lifted his eyebrows, and made a face.

*****

A trial date of February 4, 1985, had been set, but because Partington wasn't ready to proceed to trial, a continuance was granted until May. Over the almost four years since Partington had been appointed in the case, there had been a succession of second lawyers appointed to assist. It was explained to me that capital murder cases allowed the appointment of two lawyers. Findlay had initially been appointed, but then had withdrawn in order to enter practice in Germany. So a couple of others, neither of whom I ever met, got appointed for a bit of a free ride. Now, some months before, Chris Cannon, of the Federal Public Defenders Office in San Francisco, been appointed as second counsel. We had exchanged a few letters previous to my transfer from Marion to the SF Jail, and he came to see me.

I liked him. He was feisty, ready to fight the case. He spoke of tearing Ingman and Ollie new assholes when they got on the stand. He had read the 302 reports of their interviews with FBI agents and held a cynical view of the matter. He believed the FBI had suborned perjury.

"That's the way they work it. They go around offering these rats deals, plea-bargains, immunity, money, a place on the witness protection program, whatever it takes to get them to say what they want."

"Yeah, tell me about it."

"But they're slick about it. They don't just come right out and tell them what they want them to say. They ask leading questions, which are never included in these 302s. They show them statements other witnesses have made. It's a matter of emphasis. They get the message across, let these lowlifes know what they want. They never put their asses on the line."

"Makes sense. After all, they're dealing with people that would rat on their mothers."

"Yeah, right. But, technically they're not rats -- they're fucking liars."

"Yeah, I know."

"You didn't make any of these statements they say you did, did you?"

"Not in a million years."

"There you go."

"So what can be done?"

"We cast doubt. These are weak statements. I think we can tear them apart. If the jury doesn't believe them, they're useless."

"Think you can do that?"

"I think I can not only tear them new assholes, but I can embarrass those fucking feds, too."

"You sure?"

"Pretty sure."

I had been leading him on a little bit, enjoying his fighting spirit. But the time had come to spring an idea that was sure to sit well with him.

"What if," I began. "What if one of those witnesses got on the stand and repudiated the whole thing and told it like it really was?"

He looked at me, eyes wide. Chris was one of those guys that looked eternally young. Although he was probably over thirty, he looked like a gangly teenager. His complexion was all peaches and cream, and I wondered if he had to shave more than once a month.

"Would it be enough to get some charges against these fucking FBI agents, obstruction of justice, subornation of perjury, or something?"

"Probably not," he answered. "It would be his word against theirs. But it sure would be embarrassing. Is one of them going to do that?"

"I think so. I don't think he'll go through with it, actually come into court and testify against me."

"Which one?"

I told him.

"How do you know?"

"He wrote me a couple of letters to warn me they'd been around. He didn't tell them anything -- he didn't know anything. He also told me he was thinking of running a scam on them."

"What kind of scam?"

"You know, he'd tell them what they wanted to hear if they'd get him out of the Texas Department of Corrections. I hear it's pretty tough down there. I've been sending him money to help out."

"You sure he'll come clean on the stand?"

"Pretty sure, yeah."

"You got the letters he sent you?"

"Yep."

"I'll want to see them."

"No problem."

"They'll help when we get him on the stand. You're really sure about this guy?"

"I'm sure they'll be bringing him out here for the trial. You can always go ask him yourself."

"You can bet I will. Damn, this is good. It'll throw a monkey wrench in the works. I love the idea."

I changed the subject. "Is there any way we can speed things up? Four more months in this fucking jail isn't high on my list of things to do."

"Yeah, I know, but we need the time to get prepared. It's a whole new ballgame now."

"If I'd have known about it, I'd have preferred to stay in Marion."

"Maybe we can get you transferred to something better."

"Well, you know, the Bureau of Prisons had already approved my transfer to Lompoc. I was just waiting around for transportation. Why not see if you can get me sent on down there to wait out this delay?"

"I'll talk to Enoki and the judge about it. How they treating you here?"

"No complaints. It's just that I'm locked in a cell most of the time and there's not much to do."

"They let you out for exercise?"

"I get out fifteen minutes alone to shower and they let me out for an hour in the evening to use the phone -- that's it. Books are scarce and forget TV. I get to wait and watch the paint peel. It's a slow, boring process."

He laughed. "I understand what you mean. I once served fifteen days in the stockade when I was in the service. I thought I'd go nuts."

"I appreciate what you're saying, Chris, but you really don't understand. I would have been released on parole from prison last year -- on a mistake. They'd lost the detainer on this charge. If they'd let me out, I'd probably be down in Mexico right now. Instead, they learn their mistake at the last minute, take my date away, find me guilty of murder and continue me to the expiration of my term. Okay, bad break. I figure when I win the case out here, it'll all be straightened out and I'll go free. Earle's been telling me all along they can't make a felony-murder case. So I get out here, an old girlfriend comes to visit me and I tell her what's what, that I ought to be out in a month or two. Great, she says, I'll plan a homecoming party for you. Now this. All of a sudden, I can't see the end of it. I'm aware of minutes making up hours, hours becoming days, days going into weeks, weeks rolling into months, months stretching out to compose years, on and on and on. Normally, I wouldn't complain. I never stole that fucking boat, I never transported it in violation of interstate commerce laws, and I never murdered anybody. The MDA thing, the passport charge? Yeah, I did those. Together they mount up to eight years. I've served those eight years, every last month, day, hour, minute, and second. Then there was my escape. What the hell, if I were a prisoner of war, it would have been my duty to escape. But what about if you're in prison for something you didn't do? Okay, my tough luck. If I hadn't escaped, it would have been two years of freedom I'd have missed altogether, because that felony-murder indictment came down just when I was due to be paroled from McNeil. So how can I complain about that? I'm glad I fucking escaped. And now they're trying to stack a life sentence on top of it, and all those seconds, minutes, hours, days, weeks, months, years, and fucking decades are on the goddamned move and the fucking paint is peeling slow but sure, just about like my whole motherfucking life! You don't understand. You never will. You'll walk out of this rathole in a few minutes, go home, have a drink, and get some relief from it. You can't even begin to imagine what it's like to never have a break from it all. Only when you've done as much time as I have, can you understand...and I don't wish that on you."

He was a bit stunned at my tirade and I was a bit sorry I'd laid it on him but, like an irrepressible kid, he came up with the best reply possible. "Well, listen, Buck, in that case I don't want to know. But I did do those fifteen days in the stir and so I hope you'll at least admit they give me an inkling to understanding what you're going through.

I had to laugh. "Okay, Chris! Damn right! You've got an inkling!"

He grinned hugely.

*****

When next Earle came to visit, I told him what I had told Chris -- about my belief that Ollie would recant his testimony on the stand and tell the truth.

"You've got the letters? You only quoted parts of them."

"Yeah, right here."

"Let me have them. I want to read them with a fine tooth comb."

I handed them over. I didn't know it then, but that would be the last I would see of those letters. Earle would claim they'd disappeared. He would try to blame their loss on another attorney who'd be appointed to appeal my conviction. Still later, after I'd read Bugliosi's book and heard from Earle on the matter, I would begin to understand why they'd disappeared. "What do you think? Can it do us any good?"

"I don't know. This could backfire. It could hurt us."

"What do you mean? How?"

"Okay. What's he going to say on the stand?"

"Just the truth -- that the feds put the words in his mouth, told him what they wanted him to say."

"How do you know he'll say that?"

I shrugged. "I believe it. We can find out for sure before trial. You can go interview him."

"I will. But you've got to remember this guy testified before the grand jury. If he changes his testimony at trial, they can get him for perjury."

I looked at Earle. "What's that carry?"

"Five years."

"You think five years matters to a guy serving two life sentences?" "Maybe not. But I wouldn't count on him changing his story. What's he get out of it for helping the feds?"

"A transfer out of the Texas Department of Corrections into a federal joint."

"There you go. You think he'll jeopardize that? If he burns them, they won't deliver on their end."

"Ollie's not the type. I think he values my friendship more."

"Really?"

"Yeah."

He sighed. "I still don't like it."

"Why?"

"Because he's a liar right out of his own mouth! Which story does the jury believe, the first one he told the feds or the second one he tells in court?"

He had a point, but I still thought it could only help. Ollie was an uncomplicated, straightforward kind of guy. Simply telling the truth, knowing him as I did, could only lend credibility to why he was doing what he was doing. He would have nothing to hide. He would take pride in crossing the feds up, show that he was worthy of my respect. Best of all, they wouldn't be able to trip him up in any lies.

When I told all this to Earle, he shook his head as if he knew more about the human condition than I did.

"Im still not comfortable with the idea," he said. "How can you be so sure they won't trip him up in any lies?"

"Because, Earle, there won't be any lies."

He all but shouted, clearly exasperated with my apparent naiveté.

"How can you know that?"

"Goddamn it, Earle, I know for a fact that I never made any statements whatsoever to him about this case, let alone making any confessions. And Ingman? Forget it! He was right up there at the top of my shitlist! I wouldn't give that asshole a drink of water if he was dying of thirst! You think I'd sit down and brag to the little fuck about murdering someone?"

"Well...it's just something we've got to deal with, that's all." "So, let's deal with it. I want all the 302 reports on Ingman and Ollie regarding their statements. Maybe there's something in the statements themselves we can use."

"Okay. I'll get them to you."

*****

When Chris came again, I told him about Earle's reaction. He gave me a look that I couldn't quite interpret. "What's happening, Chris?"

"We may have a problem, Buck."

"What's that?"

He was thinking hard about it, whether to commit heresy. "Come on, Chris, what the hell? Are you working on my behalf or not?"

"Well," he began. "Partington and I don't agree on how to handle your defense, you know?"

"No. What do you mean?"

"Ah, well," he sighed. "Maybe it's just a matter of style. I'm very aggressive. I believe in going into a courtroom and kicking ass the best way I know how. Partington's different. He doesn't want to upset any applecarts."

"Can't you guys get together on this? Maybe if we all got together we could work it out."

"I've been trying to get him to turn over his files on the case so I can study them. I want to read the transcripts on your theft trial."

"That's a good idea. So what's the problem?"

"So far I've gotten exactly nothing."

"I don't get it. He's got all the transcripts, the trial, motion hearings, everything. I'll talk to him."

"He claims they're all back in Honolulu. Says he'll ship them to me."

"Okay, it'll work out. We've got four months to get it together."

"Sure, probably. In the meantime, I've got good news for you."

"What? They lowered my bail to fifty dollars?"

He laughed. "Not quite. They've agreed to ship you down to Lompoc for three months."

"No shit? Great." Then I had a thought. "On the mainline, right, out in the general population?"

"That's what they agreed to, yeah."

"Great, Chris, thanks. It'll beat the hell out of this hole. When?"

"Few days. You keep in touch, huh?"

"Bet on it. I'll write with all kinds of questions, ideas, and suggestions. I'll probably drive you up the wall."

"Don't worry about it."

"I'll call you, too. Can you take collect phone calls?"

"Yeah, feel free."

"I want to be involved in everything, all the way, okay? I don't waive anything. I don't stipulate to anything. Make 'em do it the hard way! Let's kick some ass!"

We laughed. We shook hands. I liked Chris. I think he liked me, too.

*****

Earle had informed me that one of the reasons for a four month delay in the trial date was because, now that the added charge of premeditated murder made it a whole new ballgame, he wanted to have the bones and box examined by forensic experts independent from government agencies and that Elliot Enoki, the Assistant U. S. Attorney prosecuting the case, was causing delays in turning those items of evidence over for examination.

On February 3, 1985, I wrote a letter to Earle, who had returned to his Honolulu office. In it I said, "As you probably know from Chris, I am very disappointed and displeased about the postponement of the trial here until May. I was on the verge of demanding a speedy trial. After four years, we should have been ready to proceed. I don't know how this prick, Enoki, can be allowed to play fuckaround games with the evidence at this stage. I have been made to understand that we should not displease Judge King because of his power to conduct matters to our detriment, but I see no guarantee that he will not follow that course anyway. From my viewpoint, he is not the most fair and objective Judge around. He handled the drug case, as well as the related boat case and had denied practically every motion put before him. Also, he gave me a screwing at an evidentiary hearing by refusing to allow private counsel to represent me and instead appointing counsel fresh out of law school who was more interested in playing along to get along than in vigorous representation of the issue there. He also refused to disqualify himself when he was one of the chief witnesses regarding the issue. Now, I'm told that if he is 'displeased,' he may take revenge in the courtroom. Can we make a case for changing judges?"

I told him that I was resigned to the May trial date, but that I wanted to put the time to good use that I wanted to be an active participant. I asked him to provide me with certain items of evidence, all the photos that might be used, copies of documents that would be in evidence, reports of any investigations, lists of witnesses, and answers to the many question that were occurring to me.

I had already told him that I was withdrawing my waiver of personally appearing at every hearing and asked whether it was necessary to personally write Judge King to so inform him.

"No. Don't bother. I can take care of that, no problem."

"I want to be present at all court proceedings from now on. I don't care if they have to shuffle me back and forth, I want to be there. Right?"

He shrugged. "Sure, but I don't anticipate that there'll be any formal hearings until May, when we're ready to proceed."

"Okay, good."

"There'll probably be some out-of-court things happening, having to deal with Enoki and Judge King -- like getting the box and bones released for independent examination -- but nothing you have to worry about. I can handle it informally."

"Okay, good. And you're going to get all the files and stuff to Chris? He's eager to get into it all."

"Maybe a little too eager."

"What do you mean?"

He thought about it, obviously looking for the words. "Put it down to different management styles, personalities, or experience, whatever, but we're not on the same wavelength. He's a very confrontational kind of guy, but sometimes it's better to tread softly, you know. He wants to mount an all out attack on the FBI for suborning perjury, mishandling evidence, you name it. They went to see one of your girlfriends who's doing time at the federal facility in Pleasanton, Alice. Who is she, by the way?"

"Like you said, an old girlfriend. We lived together for quite awhile when I was out on my escape."

"You know what she's doing time for?"

"Oh, yeah. One of Ingman's little stunts, working hand-in-glove with the feds. I don't think we've got anything to worry about there."

"You're sure? You didn't discuss this case with her?"

"A little bit," I admitted. "But not like you're thinking. I never made any great confessions -- except to tell her I loved her."

"That's not admissible evidence," he grinned. "Chris wants to go see her, find out what occurred at the FBI interview that's not in the 302 report, maybe call her as our witness."

"So? What's wrong with that? Sounds like a good idea to me."

"It's a matter of emphasis. She has nothing to add to the case one way or another -- unless she tells them you made incriminating statements to her, too."

"She won't."

"You're sure?"

"I'm sure. I've never made any such statements to anybody ever -- not that it makes any difference."

"Well, Chris visualizes possibly using her in a campaign against the FBI."

"What's wrong with that? I agree with him -- those sleaze balls are suborning perjury."

"The problem is that it's an exercise in futility. Do you really think he can catch them with their hands in the till?"

"It's the eight-point-five percent factor, Earle."

"What?"

"One juror is eight-point-five percent of the whole panel. Only one's got to believe it."

He shook his head. "I think it's a waste of time." "What else?"

"What?"

"The problem between you and Chris."

"Well, he also wants to call your friend, Ollie. You know my position on that."

"That it?"

"He thinks we should call you, too -- that you should get up there and tell that story in detail, get some counter testimony against some of these witnesses for the prosecution."

"I really don't see the problem with all that, Earle. What are your objections to fighting the assholes tooth and nail?"

He sighed. "Because it's unnecessary, it's all a sideline show. We need to focus on one thing and one thing only -- the issue of premeditation. Forget the felony-murder thing. That's out the window like I've told you all along. If the prosecution can't show premeditation, then they can't make the case."

"And premeditation boils down to whether they can make the jury believe that I put Muff's body in the box to burn her, destroy the evidence of the crime."

"Right, that's it in a nutshell."

"What about all these assholes that are saying we all hated each other?"

"You mean..."

"Wolfe and the Pollocks, that other asshole who was with Wolfe, Sanders."

"Little surprise there. We're going to call Sanders."

"Huh? I don't get it. From what I saw in the 302s, this guy's another one of those hindsight nitwits."

"Well, if I knew what a hindsight nitwit was..."

"Okay," I grinned. "Look, if you'd've interviewed any of these people before they were told that heinous murders had occurred and that Steph and I were the suspects, I'll bet every single one of them would have had nothing to say against us. Oh, the Pollocks might have said I was a bit standoffish, perhaps a bit crude in the social amenities. I thought they were a ridiculous pair and I probably let some of my attitude leak out around the edges. No, it's only after they've been psychologically prepped that we're villains -- dirty lowlife skulking murderers -- that they begin to lend significance to small things, which they exaggerate as time goes on, working up their outrage, letting us know about all their unacknowledged foresight, how they sensed something was horribly wrong -- my ominous looks to Marion Pollock, my lack of social graces to Ed Pollock, the whole hostility thing with Wolfe, that whole phony rat poison bit. The only guy who saw us interacting with the Grahams, the single eyewitness -- except maybe for the Wheelers who saw us together, and they have nothing negative to say about our relationship -- Larsen, all he can say is we had a very nice party. Sanders says he was surprised by the gun when Wolfe and I began shooting at fish -- he jumped behind a tree in fear of his life. Bullshit! Sanders and Wolfe both went to the tent with me when I got the gun. I carried it openly. I talked about what we were going to do -- a little sport. I'm letting them in on a unique, if maybe eccentric, little game. The guy's a nitwit."

"He's a college professor."

"He's still a nitwit and his hindsight's about as reliable as if he were using his asshole for a third eye."

Earle laughed. "Well, he's pissed off at the FBI and Enoki for ignoring him and now he's got a little story that might be helpful to us."

I was skeptical. "Yeah, like what?"

"We can get into that later. We've got the time now. Also, I got a letter from a friend of yours -- Gerry?"

"Sure, he's a good friend of mine, the best."

"You tell him to get in touch with me?"

"No, not exactly. He knows what's happening here. I've heard the FBI had gone to question him. He knows Ingman. I thought maybe he could provide some useful information to counter Ingman's testimony. You ought to go talk to him, see what he has to say."

"Okay, I probably will."

"Gerry worked at the powerhouse at the McNeil camp, too."

"Which means?"

"Well, I worked there. Ollie worked there. And Ingman did, too. Gerry and Ollie can both tell you what my attitude was toward Ingman."

"You and Ingman worked together, spent a lot of time together?"

"No, no. There was only one guy assigned to each shift. The only time I ever saw Ingman was in passing at the change of shifts. Next you're going to ask if we ever sat around getting high on dope together and telling each other lies about our exploits, right? No way."

"But Gerry did?"

"Gerry doesn't use drugs, not even grass. But yeah, he spent a lot of time with Ingman."

"What about Ollie?"

"Ah," I grunted, rolling my hand palm up and palm down. "A little. Not much. He didn't much like Fairly Big any more than I did."

###

CHAPTER 15

Two days later, I was sitting in solitary confinement in the segregation unit at Lompoc. The next day I was placed in a two-man cell with a friendly Guamanian who told me I'd just missed the weekly opportunity to make one collect phone call. With a stub of pencil, paper, and an envelope supplied by a hack, I wrote an angry letter to Chris. On February 8, I was able to borrow a stamp.

When I had explained the situation and calmed down a bit, I also wrote, "Just for the record, I withdraw any past waivers relevant to my personal appearance at any proceedings to which I am entitled. (During the previous couple of years or so at Marion, during which numerous motions were being made, Earle had asked me to waive my right to be present and, since I did not relish the conditions that went with the transportation by Marshals back and forth, I had agreed.)

If, after a reasonable time, you are unable to effect my transfer into the general population here, whether through negotiations with Bureau of Prisons personnel or, in the alternative, effect my return to the SF Jail, I will take it upon myself to write Judge King a letter to describe the situation and request a court order to have me returned to the jail there. I trust you will apprise Earle of all this as I have no carbon paper to send him a copy."

Being housed in segregation, if it was allowed to continue, would cause severe difficulties for me in trying to prepare for trial -- I would not be allowed to keep legal materials in my cell (those I had brought with me had been confiscated and placed in storage); I would have no access to the prison law library; neither would I be permitted to type letters or notes, nor even to make them with a ballpoint pen. (Ballpoint pens were not allowed since prison administrators considered them as possible weapons. Mere nubs of pencils were allowed, which could only be sharpened by chewing the wood away and honing the lead on the concrete floor.)

When the Guamanian was released, I asked him to call Chris and let him know. I had no faith that my letter to him would ever leave the hands of the authorities. When the rolling phone came around the following week, Chris wasn't available to take my call. I quickly placed another to a friend to ask that he convey the message. In the meanwhile, I sat and twiddled my thumbs, watched the paint peeling, and read a couple of western novels, fantasizing myself out onto the wide open prairies and mountains. The thing about cowboys was they could trust their horses not to stab them in the back. It was better than wasting my time, as I had already done, trying to gain an interview with anyone in authority who could do something about my complaints. The only thing I was able to learn was that I was classified as a special high-security prisoner in transit from Marion to Marion.

The following week, when the phone again came around, I managed to get hold of Chris.

"I got your letter a few days ago," he said. "I've talked to Enoki, the Marshal's office, and even Judge King."

"Yeah?"

"Those bastards! They told me a mistake had been made." "Right, sure."

"They say it'll be rectified."

"When? I've been in this shithole two weeks!"

"I don't know. Soon. They say they're working on it." "Listen, if I'm not out of here in a few days, put in a formal motion to have me returned to the jail there. We can't consult like this. At least in the jail, I'd have access to a phone everyday and you could visit."

"I'll do it. We have that right with the trial this close. I can begin preparing it today."

"Wait three days," I suggested. If I was put on the mainline at Lompoc, I would be able to call and let him know. "If you don't hear from me by then, go ahead and file it.

I demand to be present. I have that right."

"I've got your letter on that. Don't worry. We'll either get you into the general population or get you sent back here. I'll call Enoki again and make some waves." The next day an associate warden came to inform me that my transfer from Marion to Lompoc had been completed and I would be released into the general population that afternoon.

After getting situated in a cell, I showered, shaved, and called Chris to let him know. I thought to ask him if he'd received the case files from Earle.

"Not yet. I called to ask. He says he shipped them airfreight some time ago, says he's tracing the files with the airlines." "I'll try to call him. How's thing's going otherwise?"

"Not much I can do until I get those files."

According to a secretary, Earle wasn't in and she wouldn't accept the collect call.

*****

Freedom is relative. Going from Marion to the San Francisco Jail had been a step down. From there to the Lompoc slammer was still on the descent. But now I could move among a population of over a thousand men, all strangers except for a few familiar faces I'd met previously over the years. I could eat at a table with three other men in the noisy hubbub of the mess hall. Going to the yard was like going on safari to the African veldt. There were weight lifting equipment, baseball diamonds, tennis, handball, volleyball, and basketball courts, and a running track and strange creatures using all these things. The weather compared to the sweltering summers and freezing winters of Marion, was perfect, never too hot or cold. A fresh wind rose out of the west almost every day.

I could take in a movie on the weekends, go to a library for decent reading material. They had an education department that offered college-level classes. There was a gymnasium, a law library specializing in federal law. There were televisions and radios. The only thing missing was a beer, a joint, and a piece of ass.

In lieu of the beer, I renewed my taste for the prison-made pruno. The grass was real California-grown sinsemilla from Humboldt County. I forgot about the ass and spent some convivial afternoons with a couple of graying cons reminiscing about the good old days when robbing banks was an honorable trade.

The days began to pass and I got into a regular routine of spending as much time as I could in the law library. I wrote letters to Chris and Earle, made phone calls, and worked in the kitchen where I'd been assigned. I was already a bit overweight from languishing in Marion and the SF Jail, and I must have picked up another ten or fifteen pounds during the ninety days spent at Lompoc.

*****

By April, I had become more and more aware of the seriousness of the rift between Earle and Chris. It finally came to a head during one of my phone calls to Chris.

"The problem is, Buck, we have entirely different ways of approaching this case. Earle and I are butting heads every step of the way. He doesn't like disturbing the powers that be and I'm just the opposite."

"Give me an example, Chris. Maybe we can work it out. I want you on the case. I like your style. Judges, feds, prosecutors, they all shit like the rest of us and have to wipe with one hand or another."

"I agree," he chuckled, then grew serious. "I'll give you two instances, the most important ones as far as I'm concerned. The first is calling Ollie to testify. I've talked to him and think he'll make a good witness, especially after ripping holes in Ingman's testimony."

"You can do that?"

"Oh, yeah. I don't see a problem there. Ingman's mother, sisters, and a niece, are willing to testify for us. This guy's been a louse for a long time."

"What's the other one?"

"You. Your testimony. I don't know the full story there, but I'll want to sit down with you and go over it in detail. I understand from Earle that you made certain statements to him about what happened down there, that you claimed an unusual circumstance regarding the death of Mrs. Graham, and I think it's important to hear the whole story. If what I'm hearing is true, I'm sure it'll help with the jury -- they always want to hear from a defendant in his own words."

"I agree. I'm willing to tell you everything."

"Well, that's the problem, see. Earle is rather insistent that you don't take the stand."

"Yeah, I know. He's been telling me that for a long time and I agreed because he kept telling me they couldn't make the case on a felony-murder charge."

"That's right, but everything's changed with this new indictment."

"I know. Listen, this is no good. Let me see if I can talk to Earle."

"I don't think so, Buck. You know he's still stalling me on some of the files?"

"Damn, I thought you guys had that worked out."

"No, the conflict's more serious. It's not only outlook, ways and means, but also one of personalities. We're polar opposites. Somebody has to be in charge of the way things are going to be done. We can't go into court arguing over everything. I've tried to defer to him because he's been on the case for four years. And in all conscience, Buck, I can't sit back and accept the way he wants to do it."

"You're saying I've got to choose between you?"

"Well, you're the ultimate boss, it's true, but I'm not going to put you in that position. I think it's best that I withdraw from the case."

"Ah, shit, Chris, don't do that. Let me talk to Earle."

"I don't think it'll work out, Buck. Sooner or later the whole thing would come to a head and you'd have to choose one or the other of us. He tells me there's a Findlay, who worked on your case before, who's willing to take my place. How do you feel about that?"

"Ray's okay, but he's like Earle, very polite and soft-spoken. I like the sound of thunder."

He laughed. "He may be right, doing it his way. We can never be sure until the verdict's in."

"You think so?"

"Well, other than Ingman, it's very iffy that the government can prove the body was in the box. I've seen the results of the latest examinations of the bones and the box. It'll be one expert against another. Besides, he tells me he talked to Sharon Jordan, the woman who found them, and that she told him none of the bones were in the box -- they were all on the beach."

"Oh, yeah?"

"Yeah, according to Earle, she says she found the box in an upright position and that some branches of nearby bushes had grown down inside to hold it there. To prove the premeditation by inference, they have to show the body was placed in the box and burned to destroy the evidence. Otherwise the bones might have been burned on the beach."

"Yeah, he mentioned the possibility of showing that maybe somebody built a fire over them inadvertently."

"There you go."

"Listen, Chris, just hold off a few days and let me try talking to Earle."

"Okay, but I really don't see any other way. One of us has to go."

I called Earle without getting to speak to him, so I sat down and wrote him a long letter about it. I received a reply that settled the issue. It included a legal form for substituting Ray Findlay for Chris. Among other things, he said, "I can't tell you what a disaster it is that Ollie chose to make up that story as we cannot use him to impeach Ingman."

Unbeknownst to me, a hearing on this and other matters was held in the U.S. District Court in Honolulu before Judge King on April 2, 1985. I was not to know exactly what had occurred in that hearing until two or three years later when I received the transcripts of my trial and related hearings after an appeal lawyer had finished with them. To put it mildly, I was a bit amazed to learn of Earle's casual lies before the court.

*****

King: I guess the first thing we ought to take up is who is representing Walker.

Partington: Yes, your honor.

King: Tell me about it.

Partington: In regard to that matter, your honor, I'm finding a definite problem with having counsel split between here and San Francisco.

King: Yes, but I thought that one of the reasons we got counsel in San Francisco was because it was supposed to be more desirable.

Partington: Well, I think everyone presumed it would be but I had a discussion two days ago with Mr. Hewitt and Mr. Cannon about it, and it hasn't worked well. I can advise the court that it's creating problems for me in preparation of the case, because the material in the case is either there or here; and I'm finding that, particularly in view of recent developments in the case – Mr. Enoki has provided me with more discovery today – that it's making it very difficult for me to get ready.

King: Why did Mr. Findlay get out of the case in the first place?

Partington: Mr. Findlay went overseas, your honor, for six months.

King: Oh.

Partington: And Mr. Walker has consistently throughout this matter asked Mr. Findlay to come back; but that the other changes in counsel we've had, Mr. Findlay has been unavailable because of other trials in court; and the problem -- the other problem facing your honor is I'm so sick of airplanes. This -- I have been commuting, as you know, quite frequently to California to talk with the experts and meet Mr. Cannon. I'm just running into a problem, you know, in having...

King: Well, how does that help to have another local counsel?

Partington: Well, we can have all the material here, your honor, until the time of the trial, and work on it together. Unfortunately, and I have my practice here to worry about, so I have to spend a certain amount of time here.

In view of Mr. Walker's desire to have Mr. Findlay back on the case, and in view of the greater efficiency of having the co-counsel here to work with me while I'm here.

King: Are either of you licensed to practice in California?

Partington: I am, your honor; Mr. Findlay is not. In fact, I am a member of the bar in Northern Michigan, having been the Federal Public Defender there myself. And I'm asking to do this, your honor, really out of demeaness (sic). Right now all the material is in San Francisco. Mr. Enoki is going to be (making) more discovery, so I'd like to ask that the material be shipped back. As your honor was aware, Mr. Cannon was going to come over here to interview witnesses; that won't be necessary now.

King: Where is Walker's statement on this issue?

Partington: Walker is at Lompoc, your honor. I have not had a chance to get in touch with him directly. He previously authorized me to make the substitution when Mr. Findlay had become available.

King: And where is -- you know, I would like to hear from Hewitt and what's-his-name?

Partington: Mr. Hewitt asked me to represent to you that he had no objection.

King: Well, I would like to talk to him directly.

Partington: I have no objection to that. I will get a signed statement from defendant Walker, your honor.

King: And from your co-counsel, what's his name?

Partington: Mr. Cannon.

King: Cannon, yes.

Then King began to display something of his attitudes, which by the time trial had started would solidify into a more or less constant sneer.

King: You know, I had thought that in this case nothing new would come up; and it disturbs me that we have all these emergencies always being presented in the way of an emergency. We got Brother Cannon for this very purpose of having this thing move along expeditiously. Now Brother Findlay is going to get back in the case, why he's going to come back in a week and say: "My God, I didn't realize what was involved; I won't be able to go on May 28th..."

Partington: I can assure your honor...

King:"...I need another two months;" you know, et cetera, et cetera.

Partington: I can assure your honor there will be no delay in the trial calendar.

King: And then Brother Walker is going to say: "Well gee, my lawyer needed another two months, and they only agreed not to get it because your honor was putting pressure on;" you know. I can think of more horrible things than you could think of.

Partington: I can only assure the court that will not happen.

Mr. Findlay is familiar with the case.

King: Yes, I thought it was great to have Mr. Findlay in the case way back when he was in it. Or was it -- which one was he in? He was in this case, wasn't he?"

Partington: That's right, he was in the case for the first year.

King: Yes.

Partington: He was involved in all the pretrial motions, all the hearings we had on the matter.

King: Then he got out of it when we transferred it to San Francisco, on that grounds that he was unable to...

Partington: No, your honor.

King: ...participate.

Partington: Mr. Findlay got out of it prior to that; he went to Germany.

King: Well, somehow I guess I got the wrong impression; but there's a couple of storage shelves in my brain that stored the information that somebody wanted somebody in California, and Mr. Findlay got out.

Partington: No, that was another attorney, your honor. That was not Mr. Findlay.

King: Who was that?

Partington: Mr. Dzura.

King: Oh. Oh, all right. All right, I'll put another storage cell in there; that was Dzura.

Well, what do you say about this, Mr. Enoki? The government is going to have to live with this, if they get a conviction.

Enoki: I would point out, your honor that it's not required that Mr. Walker have two court-appointed attorneys in the first place. In the second place, you know, a lot of this has to do with information that I don't have access to, as to how they've arranged to handle the case, that is, Mr. Partington and Mr. Cannon; but it would seem to me that having counsel there would be more convenient, but then that's just a matter of my opinion looking at it from the outside.

King: Well, Mr. Findlay is sitting there. He's not making an appearance, he's only an observer, but maybe he'd like to...

Enoki: Well, I do know this, your honor, that in the event that a continuance is sought for whatever reason, whether one unexpectedly gets ill or something occurs in the interim, it will be more difficult, I think, to match a private litigant's trial schedule than it would be to match Mr. Cannon's, the Public Defender's Office, or any other lawyer, for that matter.

King: It was true that Mr. Findlay was in this case for about a year, or something like that?

Partington: Yes, your honor.

King: Well, what about it, Brother Findlay?

Findlay: Your honor, if the court please, I'm prepared to go ahead and commence trial assisting Mr. Partington on the 28th.

King: Have you had any communication with Mr. Walker?

Findlay: No, only through Mr. Partington.

Partington: Unfortunately, your honor, I cannot phone Walker at Lompoc, so I've -- we'll be getting in touch with him early next week; but I can advise the court...

King: Well, you go down and arrange it through the Marshal.

Partington: I'll be happy to.

King: And tell them to call me for approval; and tell the Marshal to call the warden up there. See if you can't get some communication; tell him it's a matter we have to decide right away.

Partington: That will be fine, your honor.

King: And I would like him to tell you that it's okay, and I want a written statement on the file. And you can start working; and I'll make it nunc pro tunc if you'd file those papers. And I want something from Cannon and I want something from Hewitt.

Partington: That will be fine. I'll prepare an omnibus statement, and file it.

King: Yes, and you're assuming that you get all of those, why, Mr. Findlay can go to work now.

"Now," the judge went on. With respect to whether or not he's entitled to two attorneys, as I understand the law, it is not required to; but I have given you two attorneys because it's a complicated case. As I read the CJA, the Criminal Justice Act, you don't have to have a capital case to have two attorneys; just one that has enough complications that the judge feels two attorneys are justified. I made that decision a long time ago. Okay?"

"That solves that problem, or does it?"

"I think it does, your honor," Partington agreed.

Then followed the motion that since the case was not a capital one, the statute of limitations had expired, and the charge should be dismissed, which received short thrift.

"That motion will be denied."

But then he went on to give the reason.

"As I understand it, the argument is whether this applies (the statute of limitations) to the nature of the offense or the nature of the penalty; and, for this purpose, I say it applies to the nature of the offense, and therefore it's still considered capital for purposes of the statute of limitations; and if I'm wrong, somebody will straighten me out eventually. So that motion is denied."

Earle might have argued that the statute of limitations itself defines a capital offense in terms of the penalty, that is, whether a death penalty may be imposed, but he did not. So far as I know, Judge King's decision was never appealed. Earle did not believe in the motion and only entered it at my insistence. Next, Earle presented a motion to force the government to allow him to interview Ingman and was demanding to know his whereabouts.

"Now we have someone who we have been advised is a witness," Earle argued, "and the government is saying we may not interview him. Now, the government has filed an affidavit from Mr. Ingman saying he doesn't want to talk to us."

"I would advise the court," he continued, "that another witness in a similar situation also gave such an affidavit. When I went to visit him at the Texas Penitentiary, he did indeed speak with me, in spite of the affidavit he had given to the government. And it's the position of the defense that we have the right to approach Mr. Ingman and ask him if he wants to tell us, face-to-face, or call, or something like that. Say he does not want to speak to us, that's fine; but I don't believe the government has the right to say: He's our witness and we're not telling you where he is, and we're not going to let you have any contact with him. We're not asking for his new name, or where he lives, or anything else. All we want is an opportunity to get in touch with this individual."

King: How could you not get the information of where he is if you don't -- I mean, you don't want to know where he is, you just want to get in touch with him.

Partington: Well, the government can present him at an FBI office somewhere, your honor, and we can go interview him. They don't have to give us his address.

King: They could put a hood over his head, and talk to you behind a gauze screen, or something?

Partington: Well, that's correct, whatever they want. We just want an opportunity to speak with him directly, particularly in view of this new discovery, your honor, in which he's made very damaging admissions.

King: And who else do you want to talk about?

Partington: Well, we did want to get in touch with Mr. Connor. We discovered on

Tuesday from our own investigation that Mr. Connor is in the federal penitentiary at Leavenworth. So we now know where he is.

King: And anybody else?

Partington: And we want to know if there was anyone else that the FBI spoke with.

King: You want a copy of their investigative report...

Partington: No, your honor. All we're asking for are the names and locations of any other inmates that they spoke to. The reason we're asking for this, is that the other witness when I interviewed him gave -- told me that he was offered very substantial inducements if he would make statements implicating Walker. Now, in view of that, now, Mr. Ingman and the other witness are being witnesses for the government, we have the right to challenge their testimony by showing that the FBI was making offers of inducements for inmates to come forward and testify, if they were. Now, Strickland v. Washington says the defense has the duty to investigate the case. There's no way in the world I can determine who the FBI talked to. They are in possession of that information. I don't want their reports.

King: I understand your problem. Let me hear from Mr. Enoki, and see why he doesn't grant your very reasonable request.

Enoki: I might add the court already denied this very reasonable request at the previous hearing.

King: You tell me why it's unreasonable.

Enoki: It's unreasonable because what in effect he's asking for is a list of nonwitnesses. That's basically what he's asking for; and there simply is no basis, you know, in the rules of evidence for discovery of this nature. We're not precluding him from conducting his own investigation; but I will point out that the representations that he has made in support of this are incorrect. For one thing, he never specifically asked me -- as far as I remember -- about Mr. Connor. Mr. Connor has not been interviewed. I'm not surprised his facts are all wrong. He thinks that Connor somehow was interviewed by the FBI anyway. So the premise, the very premise, in which he suggests he is entitled to this, is incorrect. I filed an affidavit from Agent Marshall indicating that this contention that the other witness was promised things to induce his statement is simply incorrect. It is not the case. There obviously was an agreement.

King: He was moved to a different prison after he gave the statement, or something like...

Enoki: Excuse me?

King: He was moved to a different prison after he was...

Enoki: There is an agreement that we would assist him, I believe -- I can't remember exactly...

King: Anyway, you gave him the agreement, whatever it was.

Enoki: Yes, it's in Agent Marshall's declaration. I believe I informed him of that.

King: And Mr. Partington has a copy.

Enoki: That agreement was made after he made the statements.

King: I understand that, all right, anything else?

Partington: Well, I'd just comment, your honor, that without discovery there's no way I can conduct an investigation. I wouldn't even know where to look.

King: Well, I have been led to believe over the years that criminal discovery is not the same as civil discovery; and your motions are denied.

Reading the transcript long after the fact of my conviction was almost like reading Kafka or having to deal with the paradox of Heller's Catch-22, and I was ever so thankful I'd never wished to become a lawyer.

Apart from a sort of belated preview of King's attitude that would only mimic itself to even more devastating effect at trial, it also confirmed my ever more cynical view of lawyers as all but total strangers to truth. Because of certain details I would later learn from Ollie, I knew that Enoki was not averse to playing fast and loose with the facts. Ollie would tell me that on one of the visits he received by FBI agents no less a personage than Eliott Enoki himself had attended; that Enoki himself had lent his weight to the inducements to get Ollie to tell the story they wanted to hear.

*****

By late April or early May, I was again adorned in the heavy chain and bracelet jewelry the Marshals so insisted I wear. They were going to drive me in a van back to San Francisco, show me the countryside. One of them was a tall, sunburned guy with a nicotine-stained blond mustache he was very proud of. He seemed to have modeled his deportment after Clint Eastwood's Dirty Harry character. His name was Roland Frink.

The first thing, after we'd gotten situated in the van, U. S. Marshal Frink gave me a flinty eye, pulled out a big, silver, pearl-handled .357 Magnum revolver, and said, "We got a file on you, Walker. I just want to let you know I don't like little sleazy sneakthief dope-peddling murderers. I hope you give me a chance to use this."

"Hey, pal," I quipped. "Maybe they didn't tell you, I'm a model prison. My moniker's Caspar Milquetoast. I think you got me mixed up with somebody else."

He glared at me.

"Plus," I added, pushing my belly out over the chain around my waist. "I ain't so little."

"Furthermore," I went on. "I know you're a big, brave, tough sonofagun, especially when I'm all chained up like this, locked back here in a cage, and you got John Wayne's six-shooter in your hands. But don't worry, I'm not gonna give you any problems."

"You better fucking not, you smart-mouthed asshole!"

"What's for lunch? I sure wouldn't mind a Big Mac and a milkshake."

Frink was a talker, the only thing that distracted me from the scenery. He told a long, rambling story to his fellow Marshal about being in on a raid of an Indian reservation or two.

He mentioned the names of Dennis Banks and Leonard Peltier. The latter was serving a life sentence for the alleged murder of an FBI agent. The case had became a cause celebre because the so-called evidence was circumstantial, questionable, and had created in other minds than the jury many doubts that he was guilty. I'd met him at Marion. Frink was telling about how he'd got to ride in a National Guard tank as they raided the reservation to teach the uppity redskins a thing or two about fucking with the federal government. It seems that one of the Indian leaders owned a brand new Pontiac and the tank had demolished it by running back and forth over it a few times.

They treated me to a Big Mac, a Coke, and some french fries. When I asked to be allowed to use the bathroom, Frink told me I'd have to tough it out until we got to the jail because they weren't making any more stops.

I tried, but two hours further on it became clear I didn't have the necessary fortitude. Ignominiously, I again requested a pit stop, pleading some urgency.

"Tie a knot in it, shitface," Frink suggested.

"Hey, come on, guys, huh?"

"I don't believe," Frink said in high form, laughing at his own joke. "That the Supreme Court has ever ruled that you have a constitutional right to take a piss!"

I leaned back, began trying to unzip my pants. "Well, pal, Supreme Court or not, you don't get me to a bathroom, I'm unloading right here."

Frink, who was driving, looked back to see what I was doing. When he saw my fingers disappearing into my fly, he jerked the wheel in shock and drove all over the highway. Horns were honking and tires were squealing.

"You degenerate sonofabitch! You piss back there, I'll..."

"I can't hold it much longer," I warned, wondering if I was going to get killed, either in a car crash or shot to death in outrage, over having to take a leak.

With his partner taking my side in the interests of not having to endure a drying urine smell all the way to SF, Frink jerked the wheel toward a gas station and screeched to a halt. Cursing and muttering, he opened the door and beckoned me out. I hobbled out and tried to keep from doing a little dance-step caused by my forced abstinence while waiting for the attendant to hand over the key.

As Frink steered me through the door, he drew his six-shooter, cocked it ostentatiously, and held it down along his pantleg.

"Get over there, asshole! You just try something, anything!"

Who was I to argue? I bellied up to the urinal and got a load off my mind. With the emergency over and the relief of feeling my dentures no longer floating, my innate flippancy returned.

"Hey, Frink," I said, turning to him with a lewd wink. "I can't get it back in. Can you give me an assist without getting too excited?"

With a flush of anger, he raised the pistol to my crotch. In no time at all I was zipped up and ready to go.

I started for the sink. "Mind if I wash my hands?"

He raised the pistol to sight at my head. "You do what the fuck I tell you, asshole, or I'll blow your fucking head off!" I paused for a moment, and then went on for the sink.

"Hold it! Just hold it right there!"

"Hey, listen..."

"Freeze, you bastard! Freeze!" He had both hands on the gun and had crouched into the officially approved shooter's stance, tense and shaking.

"You're going to have a hard time explaining it, Frink," I said with a dry mouth, pausing once again. "You think anybody's going to believe I tried to jump you while all chained up like a dog?"

I rattled the chains. "Maybe you'll see what it's like to be on trial for murder."

I waited a moment, then went on. "You think your partner's going to lie for you? Think about it."

I turned back to the sink. "In the meantime, I'm going to wash my hands."

I did. I looked at him in the mirror, giving him a broad target of my posterior. He lowered the gun. I couldn't reach up high enough for a paper towel to dry my hands.

"How about it, Frink? Can you give me a paper towel or two?"

"Fuck you. Get back out there and get your ass in that van."

"Thanks for nothing, pal," I said, taking my short steps by him as he backed away still breathing hard.

After that, a somewhat seething but subdued Frink did his duty and delivered me safely to the jail booking office.

I wound up right back in the very same cell I'd left three months ago.

Trial was still several weeks away, set for May 28.

*****

Earle came to tell me that Ollie had been brought from his Texas prison to the Oakland jail in order to be available to testify against me. He had already traveled down to Texas once to interview him, remarking only that Ollie was crazy and could say anything on the stand.

"I don't want to say I told you so, but…"he began.

"He's not going to testify against me, "I cut in.

"Buck, he's here. They didn't bring him out here for a change of scenery."

"You can talk to him, right? You have a right to interview prospective witnesses?"

"Of course."

"Go see him. Find out for yourself."

"I doubt if he'll talk to me again. The guy's a nutcase."

"He'll talk to you. I'll write a note for you to give him."

"You have to be careful what you say," Earle warded uneasily. "I can't be involved if you're cooking something up with him."

I handed it to him. "Read it, Earle."

He did, then looked at me. "That's it?"

"Is it ethical? Is it going to bother your conscience, cause you to lose sleep?"

He grinned sheepishly.

The note was short and sweet:

Aloha Blalah,

Earle is on my side. Just tell him the truth.

Buck

*****

When he returned, I just said, "Well?"

"Buck, we've got problems with this thing."

"What? He told you everything, didn't he?"

"Yeah, but..."

"But what? He's not going to testify against me, right?"

"Yeah. He told me how he'd made it all up, going on the leads they supplied him."

"And?"

"He's willing to get on the stand and make a clean breast of everything. I told him he'd be subjecting himself to possible perjury charges for lying to the grand jury."

"What was his reaction?"

He shrugged. "He didn't care."

"I don't see the problem, Earle. He's willing to tell how the feds suborned perjury. Didn't you read the 302 reports on him and Ingman? Did you catch the significance of that walk the plank phrase, how incredible it is? That phrase first popped up in the interview with Ingman. Ollie repeats it in his second interview, after deciding to try scamming them. Then when they go back to Ingman and feed him Ollie's statement, he uses the phrase a half dozen times."

"Yeah, but..."

"Walk the plank, Earle? Who's kidding who here?"

*****

FBI agents first interviewed Ollie on September 27, 1984, during which he told them nothing. He immediately wrote two letters to inform me. One was addressed directly to me at Marion and was couched in guarded terms because he suspected the mail between us was being read. The other, more direct, he sent to my mother, doubtless hoping she would visit me and reveal the contents in person. Instead, my mother mailed it to me. Both these letters were delivered to me on the same day, November 1st.

Of course Ollie had needlessly warned me that the FBI was reading our correspondence with each other and noted as proof that mail received from me bore a Honolulu postmark. I had noted that his letter direct to me also had a Honolulu postmark. When I called my mother to ask if she remembered the postmark on his letter, she did. Honolulu.

"I thought it was funny," she said. "Because most of them have a Texas postmark." She'd liked Ollie because when she'd sent him money at my request, he'd written back to thank her and they'd exchanged a few friendly letters.

Quod erat demonstrandum, the feds knew Ollie had communicated his intention to run a scam on them and had gone ahead anyway! They'd achieved their purpose in getting him to testify before a grand jury, along with Ingman, to the end of gaining the indictment for premeditated murder. A corollary of this argument is inescapable: They didn't care if he later repudiated his statements and testimony. They could get him for perjury and who would dare believe his word over that of FBI agents who would deny all?

On October 5, 1984, the feds went to Ingman, who had been cooperating with them on other cases. Ingman knew that his continued cooperation was necessary in order to maintain his privilege in the witness protection program. The problem was, he knew nothing that would help. He had made a vague statement saying that while I had never personally told him anything about the case, it was common knowledge that Stephanie and I had probably killed the Grahams, although he doesn't mention Stephanie or the Grahams by name -- since he didn't know them. But he remembered some story that I had made them walk the plank and that someone had made a comment about raw meat being thrown into the water to attract sharks.

With Ingman's not very helpful statement in hand, they returned to visit Ollie again on October 9. He began to run his attempted scam, which puzzled me for a while. I had not written to give him permission for the scam, in fact, could not have since I had not been informed by his letters, or even knew that the feds had been to interview him, until November 1. The FBI had delayed his letters until they'd gotten what they wanted.

I couldn't understand why Ollie had gone ahead with it before hearing from me. To all outward appearances, he was now an FBI informant. If that news were to become general knowledge, especially among convicts with whom he had to live, it could be very dangerous for him. But perhaps that was a part of the reverse scam the feds were running on him. The deal they'd offered him was that they would get him out of the onerous Huntsville Prison into a federal facility if he would tell them something they wanted to hear and would agree to testify.

Ollie then made a statement echoing Ingman about me making the Grahams walk the plank, but Ingman's raw meat to attract sharks became chicken guts. Getting into the spirit of things, he said that Stephanie and I were dressed up as pirates. He went on to embellish by adding the detail that I had tied their hands behind their backs and blindfolded them. He assumed I had thrown them into the shark-infested water in Stephanie's presence. Incongruously, he provides them with yet another version -- the Grahams were set adrift in a rubber raft without food or water.

With Ollie's statement in hand, the FBI agents, led by J. Harold Marshall, returned to Ingman. Begorrah, did they ever have something to refresh his memory with! Since they seemed fond of the walk the plank scenario, Fairly Big repeated it for them no less than six times -- only now it was definite, I had definitely made the statement to him. He even explained how he remembered that exact phrase -- because I had talked about a hassle with the Grahams and the man had begged for his life. He claimed Stephanie and I were aboard Sea Wind, having been invited to dinner, where we got into a disagreement, and I got violent. But then his memory began to falter -- he couldn't remember whether I'd said a gun was used or if I'd tied them up, but, ever helpful, he assumed one case or the other was true since I was in control when I made them walk the plank. The man, he said, was freaked out, sniveling and begging, and I laughed while telling how I'd made him shit all over himself. I had bragged of screwing with the guy's head and playing with him. But then he remembered specific comments I'd made, now translated into jailhouse terms -- that I'd knocked him out of the box or blew then away. After reflection, he believed I was telling him that I'd shot the Grahams. He repeated the bit he'd originated about throwing meat into the water to attract sharks. He reiterated that I had used the specific phrase, walk the plank, and that I got joy out of it.

In Ingman's first vague statement on October 5, there was no mention of Stephanie's name. She was simply referred to as the girl or my girlfriend.

In Ollie's second statement of October 9, Stephanie was again referred to only as my girlfriend. FBI agent J. Harold Marshall, no doubt belatedly realizing that new indictments were being sought against both of us, finally got Stephanie mentioned by her full name. Neither had Palmyra been named in Ingman's first statement, it being referred to only as an island somewhere distant from Hawaii. Ollie had followed suit, describing it as an island some distance from Hawaii.

But, by golly, the feds needed not only Stephanie to be mentioned by name, they needed a more exact location for the crime, and so they managed to let Ollie know the helpful points required of his statement. Accordingly, the 302 claimed Ollie had said that he assumed that all of the activities of Walker on the island of Palmyra regarding theft of the boat and the alleged death of the couple was done in the presence of Stephanie Stearns, who was with Walker during this incident, and that he could think of no further information linking Walker to the matter in Palmyra.

At Ingman's second interview, when the feds had carried Ollie's revised and assisted statement to him, Stephanie was mentioned by name no less than six times.

If it were not for the deadly intentions of the FBI, one could almost see elements of the Keystone Kops in their statement-gathering procedures. Ingman uses, so the feds say, the phrases walk the plank and raw meat. Feeding these phrases to Ollie, he repeats walk the plank but changes raw meat to chicken guts (Perhaps someone momentarily realized that raw meat was not readily available on Palmyra, but they seem to have overlooked the fact that Palmyra also had not a single chicken), and adds tied hands. Ingman repeats walk the plank and meat and parrots tied hands. Ingman, who did not know Stephanie's name, refers to her as the girl. Ollie, who also did not know Stephanie's name, has her full name inserted into his statement. After Ingman is shown her name in Ollie's statement, he then repeats it numerous times.

I can easily imagine a scenario that goes like this:

"Okay, we got walk the plank and tied hands firmed up," says J. Harold Marshall, who is more familiarly known to his fellow Kops as Hal. "Raw meat and chicken guts, well, what the hell, maybe by the time we get 'em before the grand jury, we'll have agreement there. But we gotta get Stearns' name in there, all this girl and girlfriend stuff, forget it!"

"Oh, yeah, Stearns," says Ollie in the imaginary scenario. "Howdaya spell it? Sterns? Oh, S-t-e-a-r-n-s, right? And what's da foist again? Right. Stephanie. Stephanie Stearns."

"Now, wait a minute," says Hal. "This distant island stuff ain't gonna play. We gotta have a name. It's called Palmyra."

"Palmyra? Oh, yeah. Howdaya spell it?"

Long after the trial was all over and the feds had no further interest in our correspondence, Ollie wrote to tell me that Enoki had straightened out all the inconsistencies in putting together the final version before the grand jury. Enoki had instructed him to reply only to the questions he would be asked and not to volunteer anything. Enoki then led him through the final edited version of his statement, no doubt so it would agree with Ingman's, by asking simple and leading questions.

You have to remember that words employed in an FBI 302 report are not those of the person interviewed, but those of the agent himself. There was no verbatim question and answer session recorded by a stenographer, nor were the interviews tape-recorded. The agent takes notes and then, apart from a directorial penchant for slanting statements into perjurious form, days or weeks later prepares the report from his notes and tying it all together in a way he may or may not correctly remember. Because the actual questions asked by agents are totally omitted, it is easy for them to suggest subject matter by asking the right questions.

We can imagine it going like this:
"Was the girl's name Stephanie Stearns?"
"Oh, yeah."
"And this distant island you're talking about, that was Palmyra?"
"Oh, yeah."
"Okay now, he made them walk the plank, is that right?"
"Right."
"And he threw meat in the water to attract sharks?"
"Oh, yeah? I thought it was chicken guts."
"But before that he tied their hands?"
"He did? I mean, yeah, right, he tied 'em up."

*****

"I don't like it," Earle repeated. "This guy can hurt us no matter what he says. Even if he comes clean and says he worked it all out with the FBI for a deal, that it's all lies, he's telling the jury in his own words that he's a liar. The jury's going to be asking themselves, yeah, he's a liar all right, but when was he lying, to the feds then or now to us? You see what I mean?"

"Jesus," I muttered, shaking my head.

"Besides he says you two cooked up this whole thing together."

"What!"

"It's all a put-up job. You told him to do it and then get on the stand and take it all back."

"He told you that? I don't believe it."

"He told me you told him to go ahead with the scam. You gave me the letters, Buck, where he was asking your permission. I'm not stupid. I can't get involved in this kind of stuff."

"Listen, Earle," I said, growing exasperated. "Get this straight. I didn't cook up anything with Ollie. How in the hell could I? He made his statement on October 9, and I didn't even receive his letters about it until November 1. You get it? All this was in the works, hell, it was all over with, before I knew anything about it. Besides, how in hell could I cook it up with him? You, yourself, told me they were photocopying all my mail long before that. Do you think I'm stupid? Are you stupid?"

"Okay, okay, I give you the benefit of the doubt. I'm just telling you what he told me."

"I don't understand that, but it doesn't matter, if he's willing to go whole hog on this, I think we should use him."

"Well, I don't. Maybe you can convince me, but I don't think so. I've explained to you what the dangers are. Now, just what do you think will be accomplished if we do use him?"

"If they're going to call him anyway, like you say, don't you think he's going to blurt out the truth while Enoki's questioning him? You think he's going to tell the bullshit story first and just wait for you to ask him the right questions to expose the duplicity? Hm?"

"I don't think Enoki's going to call him. If they're aware of what he wrote you in those letters, then Elliot would be a fool to take the chance of calling him:"

The anomaly struck me. First Earle had told me Ollie was going to be called by Enoki as evidenced by the fact that he'd been brought to California from Texas, and now he was telling me Enoki would be a fool to call him. But I only noted it without stopping to dwell on its possible significance.

"All the more reason why we should -- the defense calls a prosecution witness."

"I don't buy it. Tell me why you're sold on the idea." "Let me tell you a little story, Earle."

*****

It was a story derived from a series of related incidents that had occurred in 1966 when I had been charged with an armed robbery of a roadhouse in San Jose. Bugliosi had contrived for Stephanie's brother, Bob (called Ted in his book), to say that I had been committed to a mental hospital for the criminally insane, which fit neatly into his attempts to paint me as the worst of psychopaths.

So far as I know, I have never been insane, criminally or otherwise, unless you count the times I've been in love. But as to 1966, I recall having been fully functional and operating on all eight cylinders -- even if I was somewhat exasperated and pissed off.

Having been rudely tossed into the Santa Clara County Jail in San Jose, I was assigned a public defender to represent me. To put it plainly, this fellow was something of a callous fool. He didn't want to hear my protestations of innocence, the fact that I was an automatic suspect in every robbery ever committed because it was on my record from ten years before when I'd been convicted and sentenced at the age of eighteen.

No, his main concern, as it is for so many of these incompetent types who must feed from the public trough or starve, was to dispose of the problem by inducing me to cop a plea. It's the easiest way. I, along with millions of other miscreants, have done this. They've got your ass good, so go along and make it easy on yourself and everybody else. You know, and so does everybody else, that you're guilty. Given our system of justice, we absolutely need the process of plea-bargaining. If guilt had to be proved in every single case, the whole system would come to an abrupt halt.

But suppose, just suppose that the one in custody, the one charged with such a serious crime, was you. Yourself. Suppose further that you hadn't done it -- and who should know better than yourself? Would you go along, plead guilty, and guarantee yourself a sentence of X-amount of years in prison? Would you? Bugliosi, if you can believe him, would advise you not to.

But now, suppose you had this lawyer appointed by the court, a public defender, and he had no time for your protestations of innocence. Oh, of course, you'd get another lawyer -- if you could afford one. But if you could afford one, you wouldn't have some bozo out of the public defenders office representing you in the first place. When you're poor, you don't have any choice whatsoever. The judge says Mortimer Snerd is your lawyer, by all the gods of the judiciary, Mortimer Snerd it is!

So what do you do then?

Pray?

Dumb as I am, this is what I did: I informed him in no uncertain terms that I didn't want to see him ever again, that as far as I was concerned I was unrepresented by counsel, and that if he ever tried to speak to me again I would ignore him, pretend he was invisible.

When I appeared in court at one of the hearings along the way, I informed the judge that I refused to accept that particular asshole as counsel, and until competent legal assistance was appointed, an attorney who would listen to what I had to say and who would investigate the possibility that I hadn't committed the crime in question, well, faith and begorrah, I was going to exercise my constitutional right to remain silent.

What everyone failed to understand was that I meant exactly what I said -- literally. I shut my mouth and refused to speak until I was represented by competent counsel. As far as I know, this was an original idea with me. It wasn't a thing I had ever heard of anyone doing before. The judicial system didn't quite know how to handle it.

The public defender tried to visit me on several occasions after that, but I refused. At my next court appearance, where I was to enter a plea, I stood absolutely mute. The judge tried to question me, but I staunchly maintained my constitutional right to remain silent. The public defender could only shrug and enter a plea of not guilty by reason of insanity. It was all he could think to do since no lawyer may enter a plea of guilty without a statement by the defendant to the effect that he is pleading guilty because he is, in fact, guilty.

The judge ordered that I be examined by a psychiatrist. Since I was still maintaining my constitutional right, I refused to speak to him or cooperate in any way. Although I was in all ways a well-behaved prisoner in the jail, I refused to speak to anyone. If any snaky little jailhouse rats were going to get up in court and testify that I'd confessed to them, they were going to have to do it without a single word from me. How many people do you know who have truly exercised their right to remain silent? Proves I'm nuts, right? Yeah, like a fox.

Back in court, still silent as a fencepost, the psychiatrist shrugged his shoulders. How could he tell I was nutty when I wasn't actually doing or saying anything nutty? The judge decreed that I would be sent to a hospital for a 90-day observation period -- not a commitment as a criminally insane person.

Once at the hospital, seeing as I had ninety days in which I might finagle an attorney of my own choice, I broke my silence. When I informed the good doctors of the simple reason for my silence in the first place, they chuckled dutifully but I don't think they believed me -- there must be some more fascinating reason lying deep within my subconscious mind.

The point may be aptly illustrated by a true story. (Told by James Rachelson in his excellent though slim volume, The Elements of Moral Philosophy.)

It also may serve to underline a thesis relevant through this book. Some years ago, Dr. David Rosenham, professor of psychology and law at Stanford University, led a group of investigators to have themselves admitted as patients at several mental hospitals. The local staffs were unaware of their backgrounds; they were thought to be no more than patients. Their purpose was to learn by firsthand experience how they would be treated.

Although the investigators were "normal," their presence alone created an assumption that they were mentally disturbed. They behaved in their usual manner and did nothing to feign illness. But they soon discovered that every act of their normal behavior was being interpreted as some symptom of mental disturbance. When some made notes of their experiences, their hospital records reflected the patients were engaged in "writing behavior." One of the investigators confessed in an interview that he was closer to his mother as a child, but became more attached to his father as he grew older -- a perfectly normal turn of events. The staff, however, took his admission as evidence of "unstable relationships in childhood." Even telling the doctors they were normal was turned against them. It was called "flight into health." They were advised by real patients, who had caught onto the hoax, that they must admit they were sick, but feeling better, which the doctors would interpret as insight.

The investigators learned this central principle: Once a hypothesis is accepted, everything may be interpreted to support it. The hypothesis was that the pseudo-patients were mentally disturbed, and once that became the controlling assumption, it mattered little how they behaved. Every behavioral manifestation would be construed to fit the assumption.

As for myself, I ignored the doctors as much as I could and began trying to make my own arrangements for counsel. They tried to give me tests, they tried to get me to participate in group therapy sessions. I politely refused. I was not a behavior problem. They even tried to put me on Thorazine, but when I informed them they had no authority to impose chemical straightjackets since I was not committed as a patient and I would sue their asses for medical malpractice, they backed off.

Suffice it to say that when I returned to court for my jury trial, I had new counsel who was ready to fight the case. The insanity plea was withdrawn, and we went into the sacred chamber and impiously stuck the case right up their asses. The jury was out fifteen minutes and I was saved from the imposition of another five-years-to-life term of imprisonment.

However, I was not saved from imprisonment. My parole was deemed in violation on the ground that I had hoodwinked the jury. The parole board found me guilty of the robbery I had just been found not guilty of. This served as an early precursor to my experience with the parole panel so recently in Marion.

However, I did not relate any of this to Earle. The story I told him was the part about the trial itself.

The case in chief against me consisted of two main points. The first was the roadhouse manager's identification of photos of me supplied to him by police officers, followed by identification in a lineup. The second was a confession by my alleged partner in the crime to the effect that I had participated in the robbery. It was powerful evidence, but I knew it was all horseshit.

My young firebrand lawyer, a Mexican-American, believed in me. He first was able to cast doubt on the manager's positive identification by getting him to admit that the robbers had worn masks and hats. He and a barmaid had both described the two robbers thusly in their initial statements to investigating officers. He admitted that he had only seen their eyes, but he would recognize my cold-blooded, icy-blue killer's eyes anywhere. Then he admitted the cops had shown him photos of me before the lineup so he would have no trouble picking me out. In the end, after a masterful cross-examination, the manager admitted he wasn't at all sure it was me he had seen. He was just a good citizen trying to help the cops solve a crime.

The informant, who, like Ingman and Ollie, was not really an informant. He was a liar, a perjurer. He spun a long, seemingly credible tale about how he and I had pulled the robbery, made our getaway, and split up the loot. The fact that the local District Attorney had promised to write a letter of commendation to the parole board for him did not detract from the veracity of his testimony. And yes, of course, he had been allowed to plead guilty to a lesser charge and receive a one-to-ten year sentence rather than a five-to-life as robbery called for in the penal code. After all, he was guilty. He'd been caught with a quantity of cash that was hard to explain since he hadn't been gainfully employed for some time. And they had the manager positively identifying him even though he'd worn a mask. He'd seen the writing on the wall, but what the hell, he'd done the crime, and so he'd just have to do the time. But who's to say he couldn't try to pare it down a bit?

Alas, this so-called informant was caught in an irrefutable lie or two in the details. When my lawyer dramatically confronted him with the undeniable proof of his lies, the liar's smirk turned to one of chagrin. He had put himself in the position of being charged and sentenced to an additional five years for perjury. Conviction was a foregone conclusion. There was only one way he could save himself. He broke down and admitted the truth. No, I hadn't been his partner in the robbery -- that was another guy who hadn't been caught. He was only saying what the cops wanted him to say.

The members of the jury saw and heard with their own eyes and ears. They were back with a verdict of not guilty in a mere fifteen minutes. The jury foreman approached to hand me the ballots on the single vote they'd taken.

"Thought you might like to have them as keepsakes," he said. "We would have been out sooner but we had a cup of coffee first."

Not to let matters rest with my lawyer's brilliant cross-examination of these two witnesses, I had taken the stand to tell them I hadn't done it and submitted myself to an angry and sarcastic cross-examination by the prosecutor. I had seen for myself that a jury is capable of discerning real truth from the mere appearance of truth - when they've got both to work with.

*****

"You sonofabitch!" Earle exclaimed. "You cooked it all up! You knew that guy was lying! You knew he would have that phony breakdown and say you weren't the one after all! You're trying to do it again with Ollie!"

"Jesus Fucking Christ, Earle," I exploded. "You ought to be a chef! You've got fucking cooking on your mind all the time! Get it straight! I never cooked up anything, not then or now!

The fucking cops cooked it up then and the feds are cooking it up now!"

"Ollie said..."

"I don't give a fuck what Ollie said! Don't you understand? There's no way I could have cooked it up with him!"

"All right, okay," he said in a mollifying tone. "And you think it's going to work again? He gets up there and admits he's lying?"

"I think Oie will be more believable than Ingman, that's for sure. Ollie is not a devious sort of guy. He'll tell it as straight as he knows it. Let the jury decide."

"I still think it's taking a hell of a chance."

"Which is why I want to testify. Let the jury hear my story."

"They'll never go for it. It's preposterous. It's soap opera."

"That's right, and so is most of life -- fucking soap opera. Why do you think so many people watch it on TV, why those shows have been around so long? Because, as trite as it sometimes seems, people see truth in them."

"Real trials aren't like TV trials. This isn't just another episode of Perry Mason."

"How come you've never married, Earle?"

"Huh?" He blinked, startled by my question. "What?"

"Why is it a man your age has never married? I mean, are you normal or not? You fly the other way, maybe? You once mentioned meeting a psychiatrist on a plane. You implied it led to something. What'd you tell him?"

"It was a she!" he bit out, the flush of his cheeks working its way up his high forehead. In a few years, he would probably be completely bald. I wondered if he was vain enough to wear a toupee. "Besides, it's none of your business! My personal life's not an issue here!"

"Earle, Earle," I said, shaking my head. "Don't you get it? I don't care two cents worth about hearing any part of your personal life. I'm just making the point that everybody has something in their life that can be taken as soap opera. The relationship I had with my wife, jeez, we would have been good for a year's worth of episodes on One Life to Live."

"Yeah? And how's it going to play when Ollie tells them you and he cooked this whole thing up?"

"He actually said that?"

"He said you told him to go ahead with his scam on the feds. I can't begin to tell you what a disaster that will be if he says that on the stand. You gave me the note to give him telling him to tell the truth, Buck! So, why shouldn't I believe him when he tells me that?"

That stopped me. I didn't know what to say. It was unbelievable that Ollie would say that.

"And if you think the jury won't believe it, you're kidding yourself!"

*****

Somewhere along the way, during our meetings at the jail, we discussed other aspects of the case. Principal in my mind was why he didn't want me to take the stand. I believed that I would make a credible witness, that the jury would listen very closely to my every word. After all, I was the only eyewitness to the crux of the whole case. I wasn't stupid and Enoki wasn't going to rattle my cage in an attempt to confuse me. I would not be caught in any lies for a simple reason: There would be no lies.

"What about when they start going over your record? That's going to really impress them!"

"I'll own up. What else is there to do? But take a closer look, Earle. What is my record really saying? Does it show that eighteen years passed between the crime that sent me to prison at eighteen and the next one in 1974, the MDA charge?"

"They'll want to talk about that, too. Don't think they won't."

"What can I say? I did it. It was such a horrible crime, they gave me three whole years for it."

"Along with the grass, which you want to admit to, and the sophisticated hash lab," he stressed, "which they can call a DEA agent to testify to, you're going to come off as a professional drug dealer."

"Sophisticated hash lab, my ass! I did it all in the kitchen. Hell, anybody can do it. Nothing fancy about it."

"And what about your plans for starting up a marijuana plantation on Palmyra?"

A thought struck me. "Is all that relevant? I mean, what does it have to do with murder?"

"I don't know. State of mind, maybe. It has to do with your frame of mind, your intentions."

"How?"

"Well, it's all supposed to be secret, isn't it? You wouldn't want the Grahams to know, would you?"

"And so they discovered what I was up to and I killed them?" "The jury might well think that."

"Could we get it excluded?"

"I'm not sure. Ingman is going to say he was in on some drug and gun deals with you."

"Fuck Ingman. Didn't you tell me that Wolfe couldn't mention anything about grass because it would be prejudicial? What's your biggest objection to me taking the stand? Other than you think the jury won't buy any soap opera?"

He thought about it. "The real danger is this: From words right out of your own mouth, the jury is going to know you had criminal intentions. There's your convictions, your prison time. They're going to know you've been up to no good. What are they going to ask Ollie? Were you involved with him in any crimes? And, most important, they're going to know you had a fight with Mac. Did you kill him as a result? You, yourself, tell me you don't know. Don't you see, they can easily conclude that you're at least involved in his death."

"But that's not murder."

"It doesn't matter. If they believe you were involved in a bunch of other crimes, and that's a given, even if they don't quite accept a murder theory, they're not going to want to let you off."

"So, let them find me guilty of manslaughter. Maybe I did contribute to Mac's death. I was only trying to take care of myself and Stephanie."

"The jury won't have that option. They can only find you guilty or not guilty of first degree murder."

"Isn't manslaughter a lesser included offense of murder? Doesn't the judge have to inform them of that fact in his instructions?"

"Normally, yes, if there's evidence to justify it. The only evidence will be your testimony."

"Well then? All the more reason for me to take the stand."

"No. For one thing, the statute of limitations has expired on manslaughter. If you're convicted, you can't be sentenced."

"You're doing a good job of convincing me to get on that stand and tell my story, Earle."

"If you do, it'll be the biggest mistake you ever made. It can be argued that you can't be tried for manslaughter, let alone punished if you're convicted, and therefore you're not entitled to the instruction."

"No Shit?"

"No Shit."

Earle had made a strong case for me not testifying. He thought the best defense would be to prevent the government from making a prima facie case by casting doubt that Muff Graham's body had been in the box -- even if we both knew it had. He also thought he could cast doubt as to the burning and the alleged trauma to the bones and skull, that they could have been caused by other, more innocent means. I was inclined to believe he was right when it came to the jury having to choose between murder and murder, with no alternative of a lesser option. If the judge wouldn't read a manslaughter or self-defense instruction, it was better to leave them guessing. If I didn't take the stand, the prosecution also wouldn't be able to delve into my past record or activities -- except for what Ingman would say. He would mention having known me in prison and claim to have been involved in smuggling drugs and guns with me.

But Earle had failed to tell me the one thing that would guarantee Judge King reading instructions for lesser-included offenses, that I could waive the statute of limitations. I would not learn of this alternative until it was way too late.

While at Lompoc, I had begun to utilize the prison law library to reassure myself on a few points. Because I wanted to know whether my testimony, if I took the stand, would harm others, I looked up the statute of limitations. If I decided to tell the full truth, what with being subject to cross-examination and all, could any of my friends be prosecuted for what might be revealed in the process? Happily, the answer was no.

I had already read Title 18, Section 1111, under which the two alternative murder charges had been brought. The statute of limitations was to be found at sections 3281 and 3282. The first, 3281, informed me that there was no limitation on murder, a capital crime -- it could be charged at any time. She second, 3282, told me that after five years had passed, no one could be charged for a non-capital offense.

What, exactly, was a capital offense?

It was defined as "any offense punishable by death."

Did that mean I could be sentenced to death if convicted? No. In 1972, the U. S. Supreme Court had ruled in Furman v. Georgia that the death penalty, as it was written, was unconstitutional. This decision affected most of the states that had death penalties and also applied to Title 18, Section 1111.

The logic seemed elementary: If a murder conviction under Section 1111 could not be punished by death, then it was no longer a capital offense. Therefore, the statute of limitations as to non-capital offenses applied. Five years had long passed between the alleged murder in 1974 and the indictments in 1981 and 1985.

According to the strict letter of the law, I could not be tried or sentenced at all. I told Earle. He pooh-poohed the idea. Perhaps, like Bugliosi, he didn't want to be cheated out of his trial. But I insisted. He filed for a dismissal of the premeditated murder charge. Judge King, as we have already seen, denied it. It wasn't going to be that easy.

*****

During a standup appearance in court, I tried to size up the opposition. I had seen and listened to Enoki, a Japanese-American, argue before the court several times previously since 1981. Like many middle-class Japanese, I perceived him as securely ensconced within the authoritarian complex. He would follow the party line and prosecute me to the full extent of his ability. Before any other consideration, first and foremost would come his position within the pecking order of the Department of Justice. He was a cog in the machine.

I have no argument with anyone doing his job to the best of his ability -- an honest man doing an honest job, one he believed in. Thus, I harbored no ill feelings against Enoki at that time. It was only later, when I would learn that he was immune from any desire to be fair and had overstepped the boundaries of his position as a public servant in order to help insure a conviction without regard to truth that I came to hold him in some contempt. I would come to view him as no more than a sleazy ladder-climber without regard to ethical considerations, other than the public misconception, of his rise in the world. You can fool some of the people all the time and all the people some of the time...

But beside him in the courtroom was a new face, one to whom Enoki, nominally in charge of prosecuting the case, seemed to defer. "Walter Schroeder," Earle informed me when I had inquired. "Out of Washington, D.C. He adds a little extra power to the prosecution, some extra resources. It seems they have a special interest in your case."

"Why? Who am I? They think I'm some sort of bigtime criminal or something?"

"It's a high-profile case, good PR. They like to win those."

"Ah, I see. He going to run for office someday?"

Earle shrugged. "Who knows? They've offered a plea bargain."

"Oh, yeah? What?"

"They're offering to let you cop to a second-degree murder charge." "Big of them. What kind of sentence comes with it?" I already knew, but I sometimes liked to test Earle.

"Second degree gives the judge some discretion. It carries any term of years up to life imprisonment."

"Which means he could sentence me to one year on a good day and life on a bad day, right?"

"Yes, but if you accept the plea bargain, they've agreed to remain mute at sentencing."

"Big deal!"

With Judge King, I could easily predict that the sentence would be the maximum he could impose, and nothing Earle or I could say in mitigation would sway him. And what could I say anyway? There was no way I could stand up and admit, as the court requires with guilty pleas, that I had committed murder in any degree. Life for pleading guilty to a lesser charge, life for the greater...if I was convicted.

"Fuck that," I snorted. "Tell them I'll consider a plea to involuntary manslaughter...if I can make a comprehensive sworn statement for the record."

"Forget it. They won't go for that."

"I didn't think so. It's forgotten. Let's get on to other things. What's your defense strategy going to be?"

"We've already discussed that," he replied. "The idea is to create doubt that the body was in the box. I think we can do that."

"With this felony-murder charge, aren't they going to have to bring up the boat theft thing all over again?"

"Yes."

"How are we going to deal with that?"

"I think the best thing is to admit that you are a boat thief." "What!"

"I don't see any other way. We've tried to get all the evidence and testimony excluded on the grounds that your theft conviction was reversed and, when they didn't seek to retry you, it was dismissed on speedy trial grounds, but the judge denied the motion."

"Yeah, I remember. But it's not double jeopardy to retry the whole thing again?"

"No, because the reversal and dismissal has the effect of placing you in a position as if you had never been tried. They're going to rerun all the essential witnesses and evidence to prove boat theft.

They have to."

"Then I'll get up there again and tell them I didn't steal the fucking thing!"

"You already did that, Buck, and they convicted you. The court of appeals only reversed because of an ambiguous jury instruction."

"This time I'll explain the whole thing, get into all the nitty-gritty, which I wasn't able to do then."

"You mean about the grass-growing plan?"

"Yes. Now that the statute of limitations has run out on all that, I can tell it all without getting anybody in trouble. Plus, we can make a better push for the fact that I was in legal possession of Sea Wind under Admiralty law."

"A few days ago you were asking if all the drug evidence could be excluded. Besides, you're pushing the admiralty thing with the same judge who denied you the first time."

"Well, maybe we should rethink this whole thing."

"No, I think it would be a big mistake to get into a long discussion on drugs. They're going to think you're a drug dealer."

"So what? We're talking grass here. Hell, is there anybody above the age of twelve that hasn't tried grass?"

"MDA isn't grass. If you get on the stand, it's all going to come out. You'll be opening the door."

"That was no big deal. I got three years. One guy got six months and the other guy got probation, and charges were dismissed against two others, for chrissakes!"

"Ingman and Ollie are going to say you used heroin."

"That's bullshit."

"Ingman testified against your friend, Gerry, and your girlfriend, Alice. They were both convicted on conspiracy to distribute heroin. What's he going to say about you if we open that can of worms?"

"Earle, listen," I said in all earnestness. "I've tried out a few drugs along the way, you know, just to see what it was all about. But I'm not really into all that shit, the heavy drugs. I don't use them and I don't deal them. Grass and its by-products, sure, but that's less harmful than drinking alcohol. So, why can't we make a case for that? I'm not on trial for drugs. I mean, sure, Ingman can say anything his little worm-eaten imagination can come up with and I'll deny it all -- except for the grass."

"And the MDA."

"And the MDA. And that's that. It's my word against his. They're not going to be able to bring up one iota of evidence otherwise. Now are you going to tell me that the jury'll take his word over mine?"

"It doesn't matter. I can get all mention of drugs excluded, which is one reason why I don't want you on the stand."

"Give me another reason," I snapped, somewhat petulantly.

"I've given you all kinds of reasons, Buck. If you get on the stand, you'll be opening yourself up to letting the jury hear about all kinds of crimes."

"So what? I'm not on trial for any of that!"

"That's naive."

"Besides, the statute of limitations has run out on all that stuff."

"Not on murder-. If you tell that story on the stand that you told me, I'll predict, whether you're found guilty or acquitted, either way, that you'll be charged for the murder of Mac Graham."

"Mac wasn't murdered! And neither was Muff!"

"Well, you'd better give it some good, hard thought. I've given you my best advice."

*****

I did. It ate at me. I thought about it for day after day, night after night, torturously winding my thoughts around it all. In the chattering sounds of the day, the television sets and jailbird twittering through sixteen hours of the day and the relative quiet of the nights interrupted by cries and yelps and flushing toilets, I thought about it.

I made pages and pages of notes, going over every aspect of the evidence and witnesses. Hard evidence was very sparse, indeed. There was practically none. There was a box, a skull, and some bones. No one could say how and when Muff had died. It was all circumstantial. They would try to prove by inference that skullduggery was involved -the burns, the bones that were broken. Premeditation could be inferred if the prosecution could make the jury believe Muff's body had been placed in the box -- that she had been burned in an attempt to destroy the evidence and dumped in the lagoon to conceal the crime. It would all come down to the testimony of expert witnesses, forensic criminalists and scientists.

The prosecution witnesses would say, yes, in their opinion, based upon their tests and experience, the body was in the box. Defense witnesses would say, no, in their opinion, based upon their tests and experience, the body was not in the box. There were other possible explanations for everything.

And if the jury was inclined, even a little bit, to go along with the prosecution's theory, where would that leave me? Up shit creek without a paddle.

The jury would have to want to hear me say that I Wasn't a murderer, whatever else I might admit to. They would want to hear some explanation as to why Muff's body had been placed in the box, who had placed her there, why. It all came back to me, my testimony. But I couldn't just tell part of it, only what happened on that one crucial, ill-fated day. No, it was whole hog or nothing.

Whether to acquiesce to a lawyer's advice is to put a defendant between a rock and a hard place. From a viewpoint long in retrospect, I can see there were times when I could devoutly wish I had discarded Earle's advice, but in other cases with different lawyers, I am thankful I didn't. In a society that is at least quasi-legally conscious and oh so contentious, it is dangerous to reject a lawyer's advice. It is what lawyers would have us believe, and they are largely successful in that. In the case of a murder trial, it can be fatal. You are putting your feelings, which can never be objective as a defendant, about what constitutes a proper course above that of a supposedly experienced professional. We are all aware of the caveat about he who represents himself having a fool for a lawyer or a client, as the case may be. On the other hand, to go against the grain of one's own best instincts, especially when it all turns out bad, and when you think, in that long, tortured retrospect, that they would have served you better, is the worst.

There's also the all-important question of determining for oneself the quality of counsel. How can you tell a good lawyer from a bad one? By the amount of money he charges you? By his reputation? Or is the answer all contained in the results? Lawyers are the ones who always win, whether or not they win or lose cases. Unfortunately, poor people do not have the luxury of being permitted to make decisions about the quality of counsel, whether to consider fees or reputation. In our system, the judge has the prerogative of choosing your lawyer for you. He appoints a private attorney or refers your case to a public defenders office if the city in which you are being tried has one. Honolulu at that time did not, and thus Earle was appointed. San Francisco did, and thus Chris was elected. In such cases, you cannot judge a lawyer by what he is getting paid; he is getting the minimal fees the court will allow. Nor can you judge by what he might charge you if you were able to pay. As to reputation, well, what does anyone know of a lawyer he's never heard of before? But one thing is sure: Topnotch lawyers, the big guns, never get appointed by the courts to represent indigent defendants. Who has ever heard of F. Lee Bailey, Percy Foreman, Racehorse Haynes, Gerry Spence, or, God forbid, the big gun of all guns, Edward Bennet Williams, being appointed to represent a poor defendant? Has Louis Nizer or Vincent Hallinan or Bobby Lee Cook or Frank Rubino or Roy Black, or the current big gun in the national news of the last so many years, Alan Dershowitz, Professor of Law at Harvard University, ever been appointed by a judge to represent a poor person? Well, let's be fair. Surely some of these men, perhaps all of them at one time or another, have done pro bono work, volunteered for their own diver's reasons. Sure, and once there was a Clarence Darrow who often enough stepped forward to champion a cause without thought of remuneration. But not often, not often at all. The best lawyers simply do not appear on judge's lists of lawyers to be appointed. Only the names of young and desperate lawyers are on judge's lists, and if they remain there for long, it's a sure sign they are not in demand. It's the hack lawyer's last refuge before chasing ambulances or going on welfare and drink. Yes, of course there are exceptions, but they are as rare as dodos and dinosaurs, barely sufficient to prove the rule.

And has anyone ever heard of Vincent Bugliosi being appointed by a judge to represent a poor client? If we listen to him, he will only represent those he deems innocent.

So how's a poor boy to decide whether appointed counsel is an incompetent bum or a genius with naught bit good advice?

The truth may only be discovered in retrospect. Did he win the case or lose it? In two trials, Stephanie's, where most of the evidence and testimony was pretty much the same, and mine, it's easy enough to see. Earle Partington lost, while Vincent Bugliosi won. What would have happened to Stephanie if she'd been forced to accept Partington as defense counsel? What would have happened to me if I'd had the wherewithal to hire Bugliosi to defend me? In my imagination, I can see the looks of horror on the faces of Steph, her family and friends, Bugliosi and Leonard Weinglass. I can also see alternating looks of glee and chagrin upon losing one defendant and gaining another on the faces of Enoki, many FBI agents, the Pollocks, and even Judge King. Me acquitted, Stephanie found guilty. It is, it is as if Solomon's sword had cut the baby in half.

To this day, Steph stands convicted of having stolen Sea Wind. I do not. I was convicted of murder. Steph was acquitted. We both stand convicted of interstate transportation of stolen property. She is free, has been for many years. Where she has been free, I have not. Bugliosi, by his own admission, made five or six million dollars defending Stephanie, what with the book, movie, and all. Partington could have done better by learning a new trade and doing honest work for a living. And all for a murder that never was.

*****

Before proceeding to trial, my mother selected a suit of clothes out of what I had available to wear to court. I am a casual dresser and it has been more years than I can count when I owned a proper Sunday-go-to-meeting suit. She brought me a pair of dark shoes and slacks, a colorfully painted shirt and a tan, western-cut corduroy jacket that Alice had bought for me in Arizona. The jail authorities would not let her leave the shoes and so I appeared in all my finery, such as it was, barefooted.

Earle put in a motion for a court order directing jail authorities to allow me to have a pair of shoes for court. Judge King found the situation amusing and granted it. Later, when the Marshals were taking me back to the jail, we met Judge King in his civvies waiting for an elevator. He was a short guy and that worried me. Being over six feet tall, I'd met too many runts that were complexed over their diminutive size and their overcompensation almost always took the obsessive form of trying to cut those taller than them down to size. If he was that type, I thought, he must really hate basketball players.

"Hey, judge," I said, trying to feel him out. "I understand you're part Hawaiian, that right?"

He looked up at me, startled, his eyes magnified like fisheyes through his spectacles. Frink glared at me. The judge looked away without replying.

"Somewhere along the way," I explained, "I read a brief biography of your career. You hapa haole kamaaina, (Mixed blood old-timer.) eh?"

He ignored me even more and addressed Frink. "What's the problem with the jail letting inmates have shoes?"

"It's a security matter, your honor. They try to smuggle in drugs, money, and handcuff keys."

"I see." His eyes darted back to me.

I grinned. "Oh, don't mind me. I'm invisible."

He blinked and looked away.

"Tell you what, judge," I went on. "You come into court barefooted and you can rescind that order on the shoes. Me and you, we're probably the only two kanakas (Men, guys.) what get luau feets (A reference to toughness. Luau feets are tough, horny, and calloused, supposedly from walking on jagged reefs.) anyway, eh?"

I was throwing a little Hawaiian Pidgin at him in an attempt to make contact with him. I recalled him having employed it a bit with a couple of local jurors in my theft trial.

Still, he said nothing directly to me. Instead, his head rolled back and his eyes, big as oysters, were studying me like an insect through a magnifying glass. He was beginning to get to me. I wasn't quite sure whether he was on the verge of apoplexy over my effrontery at having addressed his august presence or was filled with horror and contempt at the nearness of the monster. Hell, maybe it was only gas or constipation. But whatever, it was rude and intimidating, which behavior only gets my dander up.

I closed the three middle fingers of both hands, sticking out the thumbs and pinkies in a Hawaiian handsign. Then, as best I was able with my wrists in handcuffs, I touched the protruding digits together and chanted out, "Ele ho'okalahupua. Oe a'ole akua. Oe hua ha'ule." (Black magic. You are not divine. You are fallen fruit. Fallen fruit is an idiomatic expression meaning variously friendless, an illegitimate child, or a fetus lost through miscarriage.)

He blinked again and croaked, "What?"

I doubted if he understood the words, but perhaps he was able to sense some broad meaning through the signs of my physical demeanor.

The elevator had arrived and Frink pulled me in and stood holding the door for the judge, who was back to staring at me.

The ever-deferential Frink asked, "You going down, judge?"

"Ah...uh...no," the judge stuttered softly. "You go ahead."

As the doors closed, I sneered at him and spoke my parting words sarcastically.

"Aloha, blalah! (Blalah is a special way of saying brother, but it implies a much closer relationship.)

"That was a real smooth move on your part, asshole," Frink commented.

"Didn't know we were in the same club, Rollie."

"Hey, you want to hang yourself, be my guest," he said, grinning evilly.

Anyone ever tell you you'd make a good hangman, Rollie?"

"In this case, I think you're right!"

I dismissed Frink and thought about the conclusion that was dawning on me. The venerable Judge King was basically spineless. Oh, he was a stern and self-righteous dictator in the courtroom, but I thought if it were brought back to him, he would buckle. The proof of my theory was made by no less a personage than Vincent Bugliosi himself. It had happened twice as far as I know, once politely and firsthand, and once not so politely and secondhand.

I had had the pleasure of witnessing it the first time when Bugliosi had made a motion, which King had all but denied. Undaunted, Bugliosi had continued on with his arguments, and lo and behold, the judge wound up reversing himself and granting the motion. It had occurred on January 11. I had only just arrived from Marion and was four weeks away from being transferred to Lompoc. Just before court convened, I had sat across a table facing Bugliosi. All counsel were present and they were discussing the motions to be made. Bugliosi had not joined in the legalese. Neither had I. We sat silent, sizing each other up.

The first moment our eyes locked, I knew we were enemies. I could feel not only a steely determination emanating from him, but also a haughty contempt. I must have had a curious, interested look on my face, hoping against hope, I suppose, that despite his being largely responsible for the superseding indictment, we might be on the same side. No, he had dismissed me as unworthy. I could sense it in his eyes -- I was an inferior, a hare-brained psychopath of little real intelligence. I had not had the wherewithal to hire his services in my own behalf.

He broke contact but the hint of his distaste remained in the tightening of his already compressed lips. I closed my eyes a moment, concentrated on one of my vision mantras, pictured an old man on a mountain and a shadowed bird in flight, the day forests had burned, and composed myself, sending out alpha waves. When I opened my eyes again to look at him, I knew there was no expression on my face. I was no more than a bland, chubby fellow with a slightly softened look in my eyes. Do not protest, do not react, I told myself. Let his ego comfort him in his supposed superiority. But in a tiny theater of my mind, a film-clip ran on, computing the possible reactions of a man like Bugliosi, so haughty and sure of himself in a courtroom, as he is confronted with dangerous situations outside his experience. It gave me a tiny sadistic pleasure to think that he would not hold up so well, that he would likely stain his shorts. I imagined his shame, the worst emotion a man can feel.

*****

In the courtroom, Earle had presented his motion first. He was attempting to prevent the prosecution from being allowed to introduce my testimony from the theft trial. Earle's soft-spoken arguments fell on deaf ears. Judge King denied the motion.

The government was also trying to introduce the testimony of an expert witness on small boats, notably inflatable-type crafts like the Zodiac. He had testified in my theft trial, but his present whereabouts were unknown. Now, the prosecution wanted to submit his testimony in transcript form. Earle argued to have it excluded. Judge King denied that motion, too.

Then it was Bugliosi's turn. He was arguing for the inclusion of Stephanie's polygraph results, or at least that she had offered that the results of new tests could be introduced by either side regardless of the results. However, when Enoki proposed that she be given the new test by an FBI agent, Bugliosi had quickly backed off and, instead, proposed an independent polygraph examiner who was acceptable to both prosecution and defense. Apparently, Bugliosi and Enoki believed in the ability of a machine to detect lies only if it was administered by someone they chose. Since it is very rare for testimony in any way relevant to polygraphy to be admitted in a federal court, Bugliosi surely knew he was merely going through the motions. It seems he sometimes did things like that -- just as he had made the motion before Judge King to have the felony-murder indictment changed to premeditated murder, knowing full well the judge had no such power. Still, he had nevertheless accomplished his mission. But now his motion was denied. Later, it would seem to bolster his self-styled image as a seeker after truth, a champion for the innocent, when he would write the passages later in his book.

His second argument, however, addressed a more serious question and I began to feel a certain awe over his powers of persuasion. The question was whether the prosecution could raise the matter of Stephanie's theft conviction to prove elements of the felony-murder charge. If they could, they would be well on their way to a conviction. Bugliosi argued that, since there was no evidence to show that the theft was identical to the robbery, it should not be allowed.

`The judge was obviously not inclined to grant the motion. Even Earle and Weinglass thought Bugliosi would not prevail, but, oh, how they failed to assess his preparation and tenaciousness. He was magnificent and from a viewpoint of having engaged myself in theater at

San Quentin for so many years, I would have voted him some special acting award.

He talked and talked and talked. He sneered at the prosecution, accused them of not acting in good faith and being deficient in knowledge of criminal law. He was himself a tough prosecutor in his day, by God, but never unfair! He thought this was one of the sneakiest tricks he'd ever seen attempted in a court of law! The judge, not yet getting the point, argued with him, beginning to lose his famous temper, sneering a bit himself, raising a voice tinged with incredulousness. But Bugliosi was not the type to back away from the judge's growing impatience. No, remaining calm, cool, and collected, courteous as ever in open court, he argued on, pointing out as to children the essential difference between his viewpoint and the government's. He provided at least two alternate theories to show possible circumstances that would make Enoki's argument not only unfair but also ridiculous. On and on he talked, a snake-oil salesman who at least appeared to believe in the cure he was selling, firm and undaunted, righteousness incarnate.

After a recess, Judge King granted Bugliosi's motion. It was as if he had walked on water or moved a mountain. Earle was in a state of pique, his envy showing. "How the hell does he win the argument when the law clearly states the contrary?"

The difference between Bugliosi and Partington was like that between night and day.

The end result was somewhat incredible. The prosecutor could try me all over again on the boat theft charge, even quote large portions from the trial transcripts, even though my conviction had been overturned, but he could not even allude to Stephanie's conviction, which still stood -- the great gobbledegook of the law.

Although I had long known it on some vague level never quite verbalized, later, when I had all the time in the world to contemplate the basic questions that would torture me, I would come to the firm conclusion that there was a vast difference between justice for the poor and for those who could afford it.

*****

The second time Judge King's spinelessness was proven, I read about in Bugliosi's account of a confrontation between the two just prior to Stephanie's trial. Bugliosi had been properly outraged at King's unconscionable treatment of Partington and Findlay throughout my trial, where they had been publicly humiliated by his contempt and sarcasm before God and everybody in open court -- thus letting the jury know that he favored the prosecution.

It was so bad that Earle came down with a severe case of shingles, which I understand to be a painful nerve condition. It seems Earle's nerves were not so reliable when the going got tough, later in the trial, when Sharon Jordan, the South African woman who'd found Muff's skull and bones, had told a different story from the one Earle had reported she'd told to him, he would appear to panic and be on the verge of nervous collapse.

It seems, though, rather than put up with King's onerous behavior, wringing his hands and whining about the judge's public slaps, as my lawyers had done, Bugliosi had confronted the matter head-on. According to his version, he put his foot down before King in chambers and told him in no uncertain terms that he, by God, was not going to put up with any such shenanigans in open court. Period. Bugliosi describes King as being somewhat shell-shocked from the encounter, but goes on to report that the judge not only minded his manners thereafter but even gave him some leeway.

Backbone -- it's presence or lack makes all the difference.

*****

On my way back to my cell in the jail after the process of jury selection had begun, I saw

Ollie. It was necessary on my return route to walk down a long, wide corridor to reach the special high-security tank. To each side were large dormitory-type tanks with barred fronts. I saw Ollie sitting at a stainless steel table watching a TV set. When he saw me, he rushed over to offer his hand through the bars. I knew we wouldn't have much time to talk, but for a couple of minutes there were no guards in sight.

"That fucking lawyer of yours doesn't want me to testify," he charged. "I told him the truth, the whole thing, but he said he wasn't going to call me."

"I know, Ollie."

"He said it would hurt your case. I don't get it. I wouldn't do anything to hurt you, blalah."

"I know, Ollie, it's okay."

"The fucking feds came to see me, too. They tried to pressure me. They threatened me with a perjury charge. I don't give a shit. Fuck them! You tell me what to do, I'll do it. I'm with you all the way."

"They know about the scam you tried to run on them, Ollie."

"Fuck 'em! They knew I was lying from the git. It's what they wanted to hear. Hell, they told me what they wanted me to say! I'm willing to get up in court and tell it like it is."

"Let me ask you a question, Ollie," I said, raising my hand to calm him. "I know what you're trying to do. I understand and I appreciate it. But what I want to know, Ollie, is why you didn't wait to hear from me before you went ahead with it. You asked my permission to run the scam and then you went ahead before I could tell you it was okay or not okay."

"What do you mean? You told me to go ahead!"

"When, Ollie? How?"

"In the letter you wrote! You told me it was all right to do it!"

"I didn't write you any letter, Ollie."

He looked at me, dumbfounded. "I got a letter from you, brother, I swear to God! I wouldn't bullshit you on something like this! I thought you wanted me to do it, that it would help you!"

"I believe you, Ollie," I reassured him. "But I didn't write you any letter. They were on my mail like flies on shit. I couldn't write and tell you to do that. They would have known. I didn't even get your letters telling me the feds had been to see you until November, three or four weeks after you started laying the bullshit on them."

"Those motherfuckers!" he shouted when it dawned on him. "They tricked me!"

A guard saw me and yelled for me to get moving.

"Listen, Ollie, do you still have that letter? We could get a handwriting analyst to prove I didn't write it. Maybe we could find out who did. It had to have been instigated by the feds. Maybe we could get them for suborning perjury. Its important evidence, Ollie."

"Ah, geez, man, I don't know! All my personal stuff's in Texas. I'd have to go through my letters and see. I don't know. I might have thrown it away."

"Well, think about it, think about it hard, bra. I got to go. How you doing? You need anything?"

"Ah, man, I got nothing. But don't worry about it. I can do without. Ah, shit, man, I really thought it was okay with you!"

"I'll send you some cigarettes and stuff, Ollie. I'll try to talk to you tomorrow when I go to court. I'll be going out everyday now. You let me know if you need anything else. Aloha."

I went along at the guard's urging, leaving him in anguish. He would begin sinking into a state of depression as the import of what he'd done crept over him.

*****

The whole question was how would Earle measure up? I had my doubts. I thought it better if I testified even with all the drawbacks Earle had pointed out. I thought Ollie should testify despite Earle's vehement protestations to the contrary. I was opposed to allowing him to paint me as a thief of the Sea Wind. He thought such an admission would be harmless, that since the felony-murder charge would almost certainly be dismissed after the prosecution's failure to prove a prima facie case, the jurors would be instructed to forget about it. I didn't see how they could, how they could separate one count of murder from another, and especially not if a defense lawyer himself was calling his client a thief. He told me he was planning to establish that in his opening statement.

"No, Earle," I argued. "I want to leave myself the option of whether I take the stand. You call me a thief and I do decide to testify, I'll say I had no intention, ever, of stealing Sea Wind. We'll both look like fools. What's the jury supposed to think, a defendant says he's not a thief while his lawyer says he is?"

"Buck, I don't want you on that stand. It'll be the worst mistake you ever made."

"Just leave me the option. You still think calling me a thief is a bright idea when all the evidence is in, we can discuss it then. You can always use it in your summation."

"Okay, but I still think it's better if we admit it first. It defuses all the evidence they'll adduce on that point."

"Earle," I bit out, becoming exasperated. "What the fuck difference does it make if the whole question related to theft, or robbery as the case may be, is going to be dismissed anyway?"

"Like you said, they won't be able to not think about it, no matter how they're instructed."

I wondered if Earle would drive me bonkers before the trial even started. Returning from the visit with Earle, I had a chance for a brief talk with Ollie.

"Hey, bra. Mahalo for the smokes."

"Okay. You need anything else? Toothpaste? Toilet articles? Anything?"

"Ah, man, I hate being on the bum."

"Don't worry about it. I can handle it. You let me know." Then I changed the subject. "How long before they take you back?"

"I don't know. Anytime."

"Are they going to transfer you to a federal joint?"

"Nah, I don't think so."

"How about your family? Did you get to visit with them when they took you back to Honolulu?"

"Nah, they fucked me there, too, the cocksuckers."

"Well, at least you got a couple of trips out of it, a change of scenery."

"Listen, Buck, I been thinking."

"Yeah?"

"Is Earle really on your side?"

I was taken aback. It was the second time Ollie had raised the point. The first time, in his letters informing me the feds had come to see him, I'd dismissed it as a piece of disinformation.

"Why do you ask, Ollie? What makes you think he's not?"

"Well, you know, your lawyer comes to see me and I give him the straight drawings on this whole business."

"Yeah."

"Then the feds come and threaten me," he explained with impeccable logic. "See? How'd they know I wasn't going to come through for them?"

"They knew from your first letters, Ollie. It took a month for me to receive them. You told me how a letter from me arrived with a Honolulu postmark. They've known all along what you were up to. They used you to get the indictment."

"Then why'd they bring me out here?"

No. They were going to see how it went. They thought I might follow through and testify against you. They came to see me over in the Oakland jail a few days after your lawyer came to see me."

"I don't know, Ollie."

"Somebody pulled their chain, man. Somebody told them what I was going to do in court if they called me to testify."

*****

"Earle," I said when next I saw him. "You did put my name on the list of prospective witnesses you had to submit, didn't you?"

"Yes, Buck, I did," he sighed. "But I wish you'd get it straight in your mind that you're not going to testify."

"How about Ollie? Is the government going to call him?"

"No, that's definite."

"And he's not on our list?"

"No. We've been over this, Buck."

"How do you know Enoki's not going to call him?"

"I discussed it with him. They took his name off the list. They know what he'd do if they called him."

"You discussed that, too, what he would really testify to?"

"Of course. It's no secret."

I hesitated. I wanted to believe in him. Yet, I knew he didn't believe me when I'd told him the abbreviated version about what had really happened on Palmyra. He had never asked me for any details, a step-by-step account. He was adamantly against me telling that story on the stand, had made no preparation to deal with it if I did decide to testify. Was he on my side or not? Could he make a case for Muff's body not being in the metal container? At the time, it was a proposition that I could only resolve by flipping a coin. How would he measure up against what I had seen of Bugliosi, where his single appearance in my presence had so impressed me? How would he measure up against Enoki and Shroeder? How would he measure up against Judge King?

###

CHAPTER 16
THE TRIAL
Tuesday, May 28, 1985

However loosely sketched, the lines were drawn and the trial was about to begin. There were many, many witnesses waiting to be called. Anyone who has sat through a lengthy, complicated trial knows they do not even begin to resemble those in the movies. Neither do they compare with trials in novels where the interaction between lawyers and witnesses so fascinate and engage our attention. No, anyone who has attended trials knows that they are mostly exercises in drudgery and boredom. It is as though the object of each side is to wear the other down in the weight of split hairs and non-sequiturs.

But there are always exceptions. Sometimes a witness will bring a certain infectious attitude to the stand. They are called in, deliver their testimony, and are gone. Sometimes they may shake us from our lethargy -- we may like them or laugh with them or hate them. Sometimes a rare one will enthrall us with dramatic tension.

Unless you are intimately involved in a trial, you will find it difficult to accept that almost all witnesses lie to a greater or lesser extent. Whoever can present his theory of a case in the best light, whether it be plaintive or defensive, wins. No matter whether the theory is simple truth or the most imaginative fairy tale, the task is merely to convince a jury by any means available that a particular theory, if only for right now, is most reasonable.

Whether to acquiesce to a lawyer's advice is to put a defendant between a rock and a hard place. From a viewpoint long in retrospect, there are times when I devoutly wished I had discarded Earle's advice, but in other cases with different lawyers, I am thankful I didn't.

In a society that is at least quasi-legally conscious and oh, so contentious, it is dangerous to reject a lawyer's advice. It is what lawyers would have us believe, and they are largely successful in that. In the case of a murder trial, it can be fatal. You are putting your feelings, which can never be objective as a defendant, about what constitutes a proper course, above that of an experienced professional. We are all aware of the caveat about he who represents himself having a fool for a lawyer. On the other hand, to go against the grain of one's own best instincts, especially when it turns out bad, is the worst.

There's also the all-important question of determining the quality of your counsel. How can you tell a good lawyer from a bad one? By the amount he charges you? By his reputation? Or is the answer contained in the results? Lawyers are the ones who win, whether or not they win cases. Unfortunately, poor people do not have the luxury of being permitted to make decisions about the quality of counsel, whether to consider fees or reputation. In our system, the judge has the prerogative of choosing your lawyer for you. He appoints a private attorney or refers your case to a public defender, if the city in which you are being tried has one. Honolulu at the time did not, and thus Earle was appointed. San Francisco did, and thus Chris was selected.

In such cases, you cannot judge a lawyer by what he is getting paid; he is getting the minimum fees allowed by the court. Nor can you judge by what he might charge if you were able to pay. As to reputation, well, what does anyone know about a lawyer he's never heard of? But one thing is sure, top-notch lawyers, the big guns, never get appointed by the courts to represent indigent defendants. To be fair, surely some of these men, perhaps all at one time or another, have done pro bono work, volunteered for their own reasons. The best lawyers do not appear on judges' lists of lawyers to be appointed, only the names of young and desperate attorneys. And if they remain there for too long, it's a sure sign they are not in demand elsewhere.

So how's a man to decide whether his appointed counsel is an incompetent bum or a genius with good advice? The truth may only be discovered in retrospect. Did he win the case or lose it? In two trials, mine and Stephanie's, where most of the evidence and testimony was pretty much the same, it's easy enough to see: Earle Partington lost mine while Vincent Bugliosi won hers. What would have happened to Stephanie if she'd been forced to accept Partington? What would have happened to me if I'd had the wherewithal to hire Bugliosi? I was convicted of murder; Stephanie was not. She has been free for many years; I have not.

*****

My mother selected the clothes I would wear to trial, bringing in a pair of slacks, a Hawaiian print shirt and a western-cut corduroy jacket. I did not own a formal suit of clothes. The jail authorities would not let her leave shoes, so I appeared at trial barefoot, clad in mismatched finery. Judge King, amused by my situation, finally granted a motion to allow me to wear shoes.

Just before court convened, counsel were seated at a table discussing motions to be made. Bugliosi, who attended my trial in preparation for Stephanie's, did not speak. Neither did I. We sat silently, sizing one another up. The first moment our eyes met, I knew we were enemies.

I could feel not only a steely determination emanating from him, but also a haughty contempt.

Earle presented two soft-spoken arguments to prevent the prosecution from bringing in testimony from my theft trial, and to exclude the previous testimony of a witness who couldn't be found. Both arguments fell on deaf ears and were denied.

When Bugliosi rose and moved to exclude the prosecution from raising Stephanie's theft conviction at her trial to prove elements of the felony-murder charge, he was magnificent. He talked and talked, although the judge obviously was not inclined to grant his motion. He provided at least two alternate theories to show the prosecutor's argument was not only unfair but ridiculous, and kept on talking until, after a recess, Judge King amazingly granted his motion. The contrast was no-contest; I came to realize there is a vast difference between justice for the poor and for those who could afford to pay for it.

For me, the whole question was how Earle would measure up. I had my doubts, strong ones. I wanted to believe in him, yet I knew he didn't believe me when I'd told him the abbreviated version of what really happened on Palmyra. He was adamantly against my telling that story on the stand and had made no preparation to deal with it. Was he on my side or not? How would he compare to what I had seen of Bugliosi, who had so impressed me with his single appearance? How would he measure up against Elliot Enoki and Walter Schroeder, who had all the resources of the FBI at their command? How would he stand up against Judge King?

*****

"Good afternoon, ladies and gentlemen," Elliot Enoki began in his opening statement for the prosecution. "Count one charges Mr. Walker with killing Eleanor Graham during the commission of a robbery. Count two charges the defendant with the premeditated killing of Eleanor Graham. Basically, that is an indictment alleging murder of the same victim under two conditions."

He displayed a large photo of Mac and Muff standing on the bow of Sea Wind. It looked suspiciously like the photo from the cabin of Sea Wind, which had mysteriously disappeared along with Sea Wind's logbook and Muff's diaries. Then, using charts of the ocean and Palmyra, Enoki painted a portrait of Mac and Muff's preparations and journey from San Diego to Hawaii to Palmyra.

"About the time the Grahams arrived, that is to say in the early part of July, 1974, a considerably different craft, the Iola, spelled I-O-L-A, occupied by the defendant, Mr. Walker, and his girlfriend, Stephanie Stearns, was also at Palmyra Island."

Like almost everyone, he mispronounced Iola.

He went on to paint a sharp contrast between the two vessels, depicting Iola as an unseaworthy tub, ill repaired, engineless, battered from her trip, and nearly out of food. The Sea Wind was Bristol and extremely well-maintained and stocked.

Enoki said that several witnesses would testify that the Grahams did not get along with Steph and I, and that Muff was afraid of me. Rather than suggest that they could have left the island at any time during the two months they were there, he implied that we should have left.

He mentioned Dickie's delay in delivering our expected supplies and said that we were so desperate that I, the inept fisherman -- who had grown up with a pole in one hand -- had to resort to trying to shoot fish. For coconuts, he said I sawed down whole trees with a chainsaw.

Enoki then established that the Grahams had maintained weekly radio contact with Curtis Shoemaker in Hawaii and that their last contact was on August 28, 1974, when the four of us were alone on the island.

Pausing to let the drama of the moment sink in, he went on to say, "In mid-October, 1974, the Sea Wind reappeared in Nawiliwili Harbor on Kauai" with only myself and Stephanie aboard. He noted that it was subsequently dry-docked and emerged repainted, renamed, and re-registered to me under the alias, Roy Allen, as a homebuilt vessel from Maui.

He described our respective arrests. He said that I had told FBI agent Henry Burns that I was not stealing Sea Wind and, in fact, had had nothing to do with the disappearance of the Grahams who, by this time, had not been heard from for approximately two months.

Enoki said I told Burns that we had been invited aboard Sea Wind for dinner and that the Grahams had apparently gone fishing in their Zodiac. Showing a picture of a Zodiac, he went on to say that Mac was an expert at operating such a vessel and that it was very stable.

"At any rate," Enoki continued. "Mr. Walker told Agent Burns that he saw the...that the Grahams went off fishing, that he and Ms. Stearns went to the Sea Wind to wait for dinner. They waited. No one arrived. They waited all night. No one arrived. And the next day, they commenced to search."

"The first part of their search, they found the Zodiac upside down, completely turned over in shallow water with the outboard still attached to it so that the motor was inverted in the water as well."

Repeating the confusion or deliberate deviousness of Burns from our single interview,

Enoki stated that I had first said the Zodiac was found 75 to a 100 yards away from Sea Wind, but on being told by Burns that it would have been close enough to have been seen, had changed the distance to 3/4 of a mile. He said I had started the engine "after a pull, a few pulls on the outboard motor." He said that an expert witness would show that starting such a motor after being submerged was a virtual impossibility.

Continuing to read and comment from Burns' version of my statement, Enoki went on to note that we had decided to sail Sea Wind to Fanning Island towing Iola. "He stated that on his way out of the channel from Palmyra, the Iola hung up on the reef," and unable to free it, abandoned it. "Now unbeknownst to Mr. Walker, Agent Burns had reviewed some pictures which were intercepted by the FBI enroute to being mailed to Stephanie Stearns, which showed the Iola photographed in the open seas, that is high seas, from the Sea Wind. It showed that a male figure appearing to be Mr. Walker was on the Iola, on the deck of Iola." When Agent Burns had asked me whether Iola had ever been on the open sea with Sea Wind, I had replied no.

He went on to mention that I had written a letter to Mac's sister in which I "denied stealing the boat" and that I was intending to file a salvage claim.

A search team was dispatched to Palmyra where no trace of the Grahams was found.

Continuing his rambling and disjointed statement, Enoki said that I had made some highly incriminating statements while I was in prison in the presence of several convicts. "The evidence," he said, "will not be a complete detailing of what happened on Palmyra if for no other reason than the defendant never gave a complete version of what happened. What he did say is that he made Mac Graham 'walk the plank' in toying with him, and had him plead for his life before disposing of the Grahams in an unspecified way. There will be little evidence to show whether Eleanor Graham was shot or strangled or drowned, poisoned. But in 1981, evidence was uncovered that confirmed her murder on Palmyra Island."

He detailed the discovery of Muff's bones near an aluminum box on the beach. An examination by the FBI laboratory revealed that a fire had taken place inside the box and there was a piece of cotton cloth and human protein found inside.

Then he got into the gruesome aspects to drive home the idea of brutality by implication. "Now, while the skeletal remains do not establish any form of dismemberment, some stabbing, some shooting, it did show a fracturing of both bones in the left forearm and a fracturing of both bones in the lower -- I am sorry -- bones in each leg, in the lower leg, below the knee, one in each leg. And the head of Mrs. Graham did provide some very telling facts. It was worn flat on the left side in particular, indicating abrasion against a flat surface for a lengthy period of time. It was also burned on the right lower jaw, and the top left head, but nowhere in between. The evidence will indicate that the burn on the top of the head occurred while the bone was still wet - for lack of a better word -- either through its own bone marrow or through external moisture such as water. The burns also will be shown to have occurred while a protective covering such as flesh was still on other parts of the head."

"There were also three teeth fractured when they found the remains, two on the upper left, one in the lower right. They were fractured by striking those teeth on each side of the face at right angles with blunt force, greater than that of a human fist. Now, although it's unknown if the fractures took place at the time of Mrs. Graham's death, they did take place prior to several years of abrasion which smoothed the fractures out. The fracture liens were smoothed out by abrasion."

"The lower left section of the jaw was also missing, fracturing off near the middle of the mandible, requiring also a great deal of force. There is also a hole in the skull, just above the left ear."

"Now, ladies and gentlemen, the prosecution is not going to promise you that it will be shown precisely how Eleanor Graham was killed, because I can tell you now that it will not be shown by any evidence in this case. What we will know at the end of this case, however, is that Eleanor Graham was, in fact, murdered by Buck Walker, the defendant in this case. You will notice without any doubt that the defendant wound up with the Sea Wind and all its food and valuables. The prosecution submits that it is confident that you will find the defendant to be precisely what we have charged him with being, and that is a murderer."

Despite his hesitancy, false starts, misstatements of fact and exaggerations, Elliot Enoki had managed to sketch in the fundamentals of his case and to show what he intended to prove.

It was time for the defense's opening statement. Judge King called upon Earle Partington, but much to my surprise it was Ray Findlay who rose to deliver the address. Ray was even more soft-spoken and timid than Earle. He further sketched in the setting of Palmyra and its surrounding areas, stressing the dolphins near the western end of the airstrip as being a place of much activity. All of the yachts, with the single exception of Sea Wind, had moored off them. In case the jury didn't understand what dolphins were, he explained them as groups of pilings used as supports to moor vessels.

He discussed the plan for Dickie to resupply us, and how we planned to celebrate Thanksgiving together. This led him into Enoki's suggestion that we were out of food. "They were desperate. They needed something to eat. They had to survive," he scoffed quietly. "I ask you, please, when you hear the testimony, you are going to be asked to listen to certain people who will testify concerning this island, Palmyra, what's on that island. I say, and I believe, and I respectfully submit, you are going to hear just about everybody say this: That island was plastered, literally plastered with tens of thousands, if not hundreds of thousands of coconut trees and there were coconuts lying all over that island."

Along with so many trees, full of coconuts and palmheart, the lagoon and outer shore was teeming with edible fish and various types of crab. The large bird population not only was edible, it also produced an all-but-endless supply of fresh eggs. "No one was going to be starving to death on this atoll," he concluded. "No one was going to be desperate from hunger, which has been suggested here."

After a brief videotape depicting the nature of the island, commented on by Earle, Ray began pointing out Strawn Island on the chart, as connected to Cooper Island by a narrow strip of land. It was an important area, he said, because it was where Sharon Jordan had discovered the skeletal remains of Muff Graham. He went on to say there would be testimony about the "morphology of the beach" and examination of the remains in the box. He mentioned a gentle current moving generally from east to west and emptying out through the entrance to the lagoon, then moved on to the arrival of Iola.

"When they came down here, they waited outside in this area just outside the channel, and after waiting a few days, they came in here, came into the channel, and attempted to get across the lagoon area where they intended to moor. They had some trouble here, and he ran aground. That's when Jack Wheeler and a gentleman who came off the yacht, Caroline, which was moored already here, came out with some smaller vessel some dinghies, and brought them back in and they moored over in this area here where the dolphins are located. Okay. In that area of the dolphins over here."

Ray seemed to be as rambling, confused and unprepared as Enoki had been. He was helping to establish that this trial would not resemble those we saw in movies, where lawyers' statements were succinct and delivered with style and drama.

He pointed out, in the same slow way, that we lacked the kind of abundance enjoyed by Sea Wind with regards to stores and equipment. "But, it's important to remember this: They weren't starving. They had supplies on that vessel. They had food in there...and they were bartering."

By this time Judge King began to establish the pattern of intercourse between the attitudes he would display to the lawyers for the prosecution as opposed to those for the defense.

He interrupted the opening statement of the defense with admonitions that would soon enough grow into a panoply of angry fits, sneers and insults. He had never once interfered with Enoki's statement, although he had addressed many of the same issues. Throughout trial, he rarely bothered the prosecutors, but rather saved the ammo of his verbal abuse for the defense attorneys. The difference was between night and day.

Ray rambled along about the seaworthiness of Iola, then abruptly changed course to ramble about Curt Shoemaker and the regular radio contacts he had with the Grahams. "He would relay messages to other people, including Buck, Buck Walker, passing radio traffic to him," he said, trying to get to the point. "In fact, that's why Richard Musick is so important. He sent a message down indicating to Buck Walker, 'I am going to be a little bit late. See you in October.' Short message, ladies and gentlemen. The proof will show that message came from Musick through Mr. Shoemaker, who is a ham radio operator on the Big Island, on the island of Hawaii, transferred down to Mr. Graham, to Mac, over to Buck Walker."

"And that transmission," he continued, his voice trying to rise above its own monotony as though the entire and irrefutable core of the case for the defense rested on the startling fact he was about to reveal. "The transmission of that message, the proof will show, came prior to any type of indication of any foul play whatsoever, if such there was, in this case. Long before any indication of any type of disappearance."

I half expected him to begin enumerating all the types of disappearances that were possible, but he fooled me. Segueing clumsily off in another direction, he said, "They didn't try to hide. Buck Walker wasn't trying to hide, didn't run off into the jungle and hide from these people, but had contact with them, went about his business, fished, gathered coconuts and generally took care of his own affairs on that island. He never attempted to conceal himself from anyone, never attempting to run away from anyone when he was there."

As if suspecting I might be about to fall asleep, he proceeded to make me want to pull my hair out by the roots and bang my head on the table. "Now it's important to remember this," he said, gazing with all the power and force of a burned-out light bulb at the jury. "When he was down there, he was fleeing from the authorities. There is no argument, there is no fight on that score. There is no fight and there is no argument that he is a boat thief."

It was all I could do to remain sitting there, clenching my jaw and making fists under the table. I wanted to jump up, shout at him to shutup, and sit down, to declare in a loud, angry voice in no uncertain terms that by God, I was not a fucking boat thief! In a furious whisper to Earle, I said, "What the fuck is this! I thought we'd settled this!"

Earle shrugged. "He must have forgot. It's okay."

"It's not fucking okay! I'm not going to get on that stand and say I'm a goddamn boat thief! How's it going to look with you guys calling me a boat thief and me denying it? Jesus Christ, Earle!"

"Try to control yourself, Buck. This is a courtroom."

"Where? In Kafkaland?"

"Just be cool. The judge is looking at us."

"Fuck the judge! What are you going to do about this? I want that remark withdrawn!"

"Buck, please. Don't get the judge mad at us. We can't withdraw the statement without looking foolish. It'll be all right. It'll be okay."

Meanwhile, Ray had continued blithely on. "But where the issue is joined is when it comes to the business of Mr. Walker and Stephanie Stearns killing of Muff Graham. That's the issue in this case. He stole the boat, yes."

I gritted my teeth, trying to grind my dentures to dust.

"You will hear specifically during the course of testimony, he made up a story to hide the theft of the Sea Wind. He took it, took the boat. He and Stephanie."

I sat there seething, breathing deep, trying to restore my equilibrium, to calm myself.

Ray meandered on through the trip back to the dry dock on Oahu where we had stopped to repair the damage caused by the swordfish. "Shortly after that," he said, "it was shortly after that, that they were apprehended. We don't deny that he was fleeing from the authorities at this time, that he was trying to steal this boat."

You have to give it to Ray. He certainly succeeded in making the jury remember that I was a boat thief, albeit an unconvicted one at that point. He was apparently unworried that he might have gone a long way toward helping the government to establish the predicate felony in the felony-murder charge. The real issue was whether there was proof beyond a reasonable doubt that his client had murdered Muff Graham.

Finally beginning to move into the heart of the matter, as he and Earle saw it, Ray pointed out that no one could be able to say "how specifically or even generally" Muff Graham had met her demise. They were out fishing. After all, Palmyra was known as a place of frequent vicious squalls. "There could have been a squall with winds which flipped the boat over after it was washed ashore."

"You will get a chance to argue the case," King interrupted.

Then Ray got to Ingman, the man responsible for the premeditated murder indictment. Ingman, he said, would be testifying to "certain admissions, statements by Buck Walker," but that the jury should wait before attaching any weight to his testimony.

"We have several people coming in who will tell you about Mr. Ingman, and one person who is in a very good position to tell you about Mr. Ingman's capacity for veracity and truthfulness, his reputation, his character for truthfulness, and that's his mother."

"Hear both sides, ladies and gentlemen, before you decide the case. Hear," he repeated, "hear all the evidence before you make up your mind, because there is a lot of evidence for you to consider in this case."

"Nobody knows how Muff Graham died. Nobody knows precisely when Muff Graham died, and nobody can point to any evidence, which proves beyond a reasonable doubt that the defendant, Buck Walker, committed the felony-murder or the premeditated murder. Evidence beyond a reasonable doubt is not there. Nobody knows what happened out at Palmyra at the time of the disappearance of Muff Graham. Nobody."

Wrong. I knew exactly what had happened.

*****

THE PROSECUTION
Larry Briggs

Briggs, skipper of the charter boat, Caroline, had spent two and a half days on Palmyra in June, 1974, arriving inside the lagoon just before we did, and leaving the day after we were towed in. He claimed to have known Iola previously as Margaret, an old boat used for day-sailing. When asked if she appeared seaworthy when he saw her at Palmyra, he replied, "Not by my standards. It was very rundown. The rigging was not in good condition. The engine didn't work." He said the hull looked pretty weather-beaten, and there was no way an experienced sailor would have sailed her down to Palmyra.

Briggs and I had rubbed each other wrong from the first, and it showed in his testimony. He claimed to have invited us to dinner. Actually he had given Steph an orange and I had eaten a couple of slices.

I had proudly regaled him with the story of our adventures down, laughing in triumph, which he reinterpreted to the court as whining and sniveling about a severely troubled voyage. He claimed we had told him things that were pure bullshit, and said that since he realized we had almost no provisions, he gave us the equivalent of half a dozen canned and packaged meals. Despite the fact that he claimed I was ungracious enough to ask for more, he said he gave us a few more things. The truth is, we had said nothing about being low on food and, other than the single orange for Stephanie, he had given us nothing, including the time of day.

The first contretemps with Judge King took place over this relatively petty but innocuous witness. This is where his prejudice toward the defense became manifest; as days passed, it was to become outstandingly clear.

Ray had asked Briggs if Jack Wheeler had been at dinner on the day of his arrival.
"Jack Wheeler?"
Findlay nodded. "For dinner."
"I'm not sure, he said it was the night of his arrival," King interjected. "In fact, I'm sure he didn't say it was then."
Findlay's eyes widened as he turned to the judge. "You can correct me then."
"Don't put wrong information into your question because it misleads the questions," the judge snapped.
"Judge, he can correct me."
King then turned to Briggs. "Was it the night you arrived that you had him to dinner?"
"I believe it was."
"The same day? The 25th?"
"As I recall," Briggs nodded.
Actually, it had been the 27th, the day Iola made it inside the lagoon.
There was a moment of silence as the judge fumbled about with papers. "May I continue now?" Findlay's voice was polite and quiet.
"Yes," grumped King, glaring at Briggs. "Earlier he said it was the 27th."
Findlay led Briggs on to admit that he had never been aboard Iola, let alone down inside to see the structure, then moved to Ferraro, one of the men aboard his charter. "Isn't it true that, in fact, Mr. Ferraro got along well with Roy?"
But before Briggs could respond, King jumped in with both feet. "Are you asking this man to say whether Mr. Ferraro got along well with the defendant?"
"Yes, your honor."
"I will sustain the objection," he ruled.
There had been no objection. Belatedly, Schroeder rose to say, "We will state an objection on that, your honor. It calls for a conclusion on the part of the witness."
"The objection is sustained!"
"But, your honor," Findlay tried, "the relationship between..." "Sustained," thundered

King.

"Your honor, I have got a lot of statements..."

"You have a lot of statements that are inadmissible," the judge spat. "If you want to get everything from anybody else in, then we will try a case that way. But just because somebody said something, you can't get it in evidence! You can call Mr. Ferraro!"

"He can observe them," Findlay replied, pointing to Briggs.

"Overruled! Overruled! Your question is objectionable!"

"I am sorry, your honor."

After taking a few moments to gather his wits over the judge's outburst, Findlay turned back to Briggs to try his pursuit on a slightly different tack. He was, perhaps, a bit addled and did not understand the thrust of King's ire.

"Do you recall making a statement to the Federal Bureau..." Findlay got out before being again interrupted.

"You are going to get into real trouble real soon if you are going to try to get around my ruling," King threatened.

"Judge..."

"We will take a 10-minute recess and you folks," he said, waving at the jury, "may step out of the courtroom."

Following their exit, he turned to Findlay. "Now, what are you trying to do?"

"Your honor, my question..."

King raised his voice, cutting him off. "What are you trying to do? Never mind what the question is! What are you trying to get in?"

"To have this gentleman give testimony concerning the interaction between Mr. Ferraro..."

"Tell me exactly what it is you want to get in" King demanded. "What is this statement you are talking about?"

"It isn't a statement, your honor."

King shook his head, furious. "You started to ask him, 'Didn't you make a statement?' What statement are you talking about?"

"Mr. Briggs' statement. He gave a statement to the Federal Bureau of Investigation on October 8, 1974, covering the events that occurred on Palmyra Island, which he is giving testimony about."

"Can we get to the statement you wanted to ask him about?"

"Your honor, he indicates in the statement that..."

"Can't you read it?"

"Yes."

"Well, read it!"

Findlay held up a copy of a report of Briggs' statement to the FBI. "He states that, 'Mr. Ferraro really seemed to get along well with Roy and Stephanie.'"

"Now, why is that admissible?"

"Your honor, it goes to show that he observed them interacting, that is, Mr. Ferraro."

"It doesn't make any difference."

"No, but it shows that he has knowledge of them interacting, that they were around each other."

"That doesn't make it admissible evidence from this witness!" "It's only his observation, your honor," Findlay pled, seemingly bewildered by King's attack. "It's not an assertion of any kind of statement. He observes people in the company..."

King stuck his jaw out like a bulldog toward Schroeder. "Do you object?"

"Yes, your honor," Schroeder muttered, seeming bewildered himself.

"Sustained!" King roared. "Now. Make your record and let's move on!"

"Your honor," Findlay persisted. "I think it's important to have..." "Sus-TAINED!" King shrieked. "Now, if it isn't important, you have a beautiful reversal!"

King drew a breath, not realizing he had stated the issue assbackwards regarding a possible reversal. "Please," he sneered, "do not argue with me over every ruling that comes into this case. Otherwise, you and I are going to have real trouble. You make your record. You want to ask this witness to make a statement similar to what you just read and I am sustaining the objection!"

Earle tried to come to Ray's defense. "Excuse me, your honor. There is going to be a lot of evidence about whether people were afraid..."

"Just a minute!" King shook his head in irritation. "Just a minute, Mr. Partington! One person at a time! Are you having trouble getting Mr. Ferraro, for example? Is he going to be a witness?"

"No, your honor," Earle answered. "We don't know where he is." "Well," huffed King, deflated.

The argument went on for some time with constant interruptions from King. In the end, Findlay missed the point that Caroline had arrived in the lagoon on June 25th, while Iola did not enter until the afternoon of the 27th, and Caroline departed again the morning of the 28th. We had spent perhaps 12 hours there at the same time. If Ray hadn't been in such a tizzy by King's angry and sarcastic attacks, he might have elicited the fact that Briggs had since been talking to other witnesses who were already firm in their hostility. If he had, he might have had the beginning of demonstrating some prejudice. But the tone of the whole trial had been established. King would continue throughout to interrupt Partington and Findlay, to berate them and rule against them. He would express anger, impatience, sarcasm, and generally frustrate them in humiliating ways. Never once would he address Enoki and Schroeder in such terms, remaining polite and respectful to the prosecutors.

Jack Wheeler

Wheeler had been to Palmyra four times, we learned under Schroeder's questioning, once having stayed for 15 months. He and his family had arrived in the ketch, Poseidon, on June 19th and left on July 6th. He had recognized the old Margaret when we'd arrived in Iola, and said that we had accepted a tow inside where we tied up between the dolphins in a line between Poseidon and Caroline.

Jack was getting on and managed to squint, turn about, and promptly point out a newspaper reporter when asked to identify the defendant. It got worse. He seemed to get confused and mixed up on the order of arrivals, incorrectly remembering dates and departures from Palmyra. He couldn't even remember the name of Sea Wind, which he called Sea Wolf. Jack said that he had told everyone that he represented Palmyra's owner and had informed them of the rules for staying on the island.

Going back over old ground, Schroeder asked, "Did you ever say anything to Roy Allen about the fact that you represented the owner?"

"Yes."

"And what was his response?"

"Positive. He recognized that and..."

But Schroeder cut him off. "Did he say or do anything when you told him that?"

"I'm not sure what he did. I think Stephanie wrote a letter requesting permission to stay," he replied, getting it backwards. I had written the letter.

"Was it necessary to get permission to stay on Palmyra?"

"Well," Jack shrugged, "if they were going to stay, I wasn't about to change it any, but they did write a letter."

"Well," King interjected, "you didn't refuse it? You didn't tell them they had to get out?"

"I wouldn't tell anybody they had to get out."

King seemed disappointed.

Schroeder went on. "Did you see this letter?"

"I saw the letter, but I didn't open it, of course -- it was sealed."

I remembered having shown Jack the letter and letting him read it to ask for his suggestions before sealing it up. He'd said it was a fine letter and he would personally see that Mr. Fullard-Leo received it.

Unable to ascertain that we had asked for or received food from anyone in Jack's family, he tried again. "Do you know the nearest point to Palmyra Island where one might have been able to come by some food?"

"Nearest food would have been Fanning Island."

"Would sailing to Fanning Island from Palmyra have been a difficult sail?"

Incredibly, Jack replied, "Impossible."

"Why is it impossible?"

"Because the ocean currents there are from east to west, at least two knots. Plus, it's also upwind."

I'm sure that Jack believed what he was saying, even though it would have been easy for anyone knowledgeable to discredit such testimony. Although difficult against current and wind, Jack's assertion that it would be an impossible sail is patently ridiculous. It could be done by the simple expedient of tacking a zigzag course at angles against the wind. Even Bugliosi, in Stephanie's trial, would point out that tacking was never explained to the jury during my trial.

Jack's testimony wandered and trickled down. It was lunchtime. Jack and the jury were excused. When he was recalled, Jack said he had not seen the Grahams aboard Iola or us aboard Sea Wind. He couldn't remember the Zodiac, but did recall that the Grahams planned to stay on the island for a long time. He collected mail to post in Honolulu and left Palmyra.

His next trip to Palmyra was made in November, 1974, on a search team, looking for the Grahams, one of about a dozen people, including the Assistant U. S. Attorney who would prosecute the theft trials, FBI agents and Coast Guard personnel, including divers. He described the fruitless search where no boats, wrecked or otherwise, were found, and no people.

In a brief backtrack, Schroeder got Jack to say he'd seen our forward hatch and that it was always closed. Actually, it was the first thing we'd opened to provide ventilation from the humidity.

"In your experience, what would happen if a boat sailed for open seas without the hatch cover being on," Shroeder began, making it obvious where he was going. "Or without the hatch being closed?"

"Take an awful lot of water in."

"What would the ultimate result of that be?"

"Well," Jack opined, "I don't think he would keep going into water to a point where he would sink, but you would have to do some bailing."

"When you searched the island, what was the first item that you found, if you recall?"

Schroeder wanted to hear about the hatch cover I'd left behind after I'd sealed it off to prevent any further leakage. The implication, as in the theft trial, was that we had purposely removed it to facilitate sinking Iola.

Jack said he had found some of our heavy-weather clothing inside the refrigerator house. Even if he had, how would he know it was ours? Then he claimed to have found the remains of clothing, glasses and earrings in a fire rubble at the Graham campsite, but that the fire hadn't done much damage. Although it seemed to be women's clothing, he couldn't remember much. "It just looked like they had thrown a drawerful of clothing into the fire," he said.

He was led to identify photos of Mac's workshop, saying that he had found our partially dismantled Mercury outboard and, finally, the missing hatchcover.

"Did you find anything else in the vicinity of the dolphins?"

"The Graham's mooring lines."

"How did you know they were the Graham's mooring lines?"

"They were brand spanking new dacron lines."

What he had actually found were the cut lines off Iola. We also had had brand new braided dacron lines. As Jack testified, it was where we had been moored -- where we had swung around later, with Mac's help, to take the place of Poseidon.

Then Schroeder got to the five photos of Iola taken by Stephanie from Sea Wind on our departure. They purported to show Iola heading for open sea with an open hatchway.

However, Iola's log clearly stated that I had sealed the hatch opening. Also, if you looked closely, you could see the sealed-over opening. How everyone missed that is beyond me, but I pointed it out to Earle.

Jack identified the aluminum rescue launch that had been stored in the equipment shed adjacent to the Graham campsite. He described the effects of squalls on lagoon waters, saying they created no more than a 6-inch chop inside the lagoon. And he claimed there were no obstructions to the navigable parts of the lagoon that might cause an accident, except for shallow water when parts of the reef were uncovered. Other photos would later show several dangerous obstructions to dinghy operation in the lagoon, none of which concerned me except to show Jack's poor memory.

When it came time for cross-examination, both Earle and Ray proved to be impressively unimpressive. Although Jack, with his poor memory, would have been easy to impeach, they missed every opportunity. There was one moment, however, when I thought Ray might be onto something -- the question of the fire rubble, the clothing, eyeglasses and earrings.

"During that time when you were down there with the search party and you saw the objects that you described in the area of the fire, was any of that, any of those objects recovered?"

"Yes."

"Who did that? Who recovered those objects, to your knowledge?"

"Shishido."

It was time for the judge to take a hand. "Well..."

"Actually," said Jack, "it was three or four."

"Do you want a stipulation from the government as to who recovered?" King asked Ray.

But Jack didn't like being interrupted. "The government..." he began.

Earle leapt into the breach. "I believe the problem of stipulation is that he asked it in the collective -- who recovered 'all of the objects.' "

"We shouldn't waste time on this," King admonished. "This is something that's known. In fact, you don't know it already...who picked up what and kept it as evidence and so forth?"

"Some of these items were kept as evidence," Enoki explained. "Some were not."

The whole subject was shortly shelved and I would not learn what or what not was saved as evidence and what significance it might have. I guessed it would have to wait until Shishido got on the stand -- if anyone remembered to ask. The fire rubble thing was a mystery to me. Neither Stephanie or I had built any fires to burn anything at all.

Much later, Bugliosi shed a small light on the incident by claiming that Eggers, the prosecutor in the theft cases, had discovered Mac's campfire site. He had poked around with a stick and eventually found several bits of cotton cloth, perhaps from a shirt, two eyeglass lenses -- one prescription and the other non-prescription. This was a somewhat different description than Jack's.

Under Ray's questioning, Jack confirmed the presence of sharks in the lagoon, but not the extent of them or that they posed a potential danger. When asked where the divers had searched, Jack said it was only in the shallow area of the cove where Sea Wind had been moored. A simple why or what-do-you-mean question might have elicited the fact that the divers had enough thrills without nosy and potentially hungry sharks making passes near them, but Ray missed the opportunity.

After a fruitless attempt to get Jack to admit he had read my letter, Ray gave up. "Your honor, I have no further questions of this witness."

But King wasn't through with Ray Findlay. "Before you do that," he shook his finger as at an arrant schoolboy, "you always consult with Mr. Partington."

Ray blushed. "I don't think, judge..."

"Always just say, 'could I have a second?'" King instructed as though explaining the ABCs, "and then turn around and look at Mr. Partington."

Ray threw his hands out in frustration and got as stubborn as he was ever going to get. "Your honor, there is a last area," he said.

"Mr. Wheeler, you mentioned something about the rescue boat on your trip down there in 1974." "Are you talking about the aluminum dropboat?"

"Yeah, the Air Force rescue boat."

"First time I saw it?"

"In '74."

Jack said he had last seen it sitting in the equipment shed adjacent to the Graham campsite in 1974. When asked how many boxes were contained in the rescue launch, he never gave a number, but only answered that they were all there as far as he knew -- he hadn't really checked.

"There are boxes that fit into the vessel? Is that correct, on this craft?"

"Actually, a part of the vessel. They're bolted in."

At that point, King took over and left Ray to twiddle his thumbs. "What kind of boxes?"

"Aluminum. They're not really a box. They're a storage area."

It slowly became clear that Jack believed the boxes were actually a part of the deck, a structural part of the boat. He hadn't really studied the matter but supposed they were storage boxes for supplies and stuff as it was a rescue boat.

"Okay, thank you," Ray concluded. His bravest moment was that he did not pause to ask King if he could just have a second and turn to look at Earle. No, he clenched his papers in hand

and strode back to his seat. King apparently failed to recognize Ray's teacup rebellion.

Schroeder dilly-dallied around with questions as to what Jack had said to us about sailing to Fanning, Samoa, and even back to Hawaii, but by then Jack had had enough and was balking. What emerged was that Jack thought he'd said a sail to Fanning would be difficult and a sail to Samoa would take about 15 days. As to Hawaii, he said, "I don't think that came up. See, they indicated also that they wanted to stay a lengthy period."

Schroeder returned to sharks. They were small and pesky, but would take a bite out of you. He'd already mentioned not allowing his family to swim in the lagoon.

At long last, Jack was excused. He dragged his weary bones away, rubbing his back and shaking his head in relief.

Edwin Pollock.

A retired math teacher, Pollock claimed to have lived aboard a sailboat for 16 years and sailed some 30,000 miles in the Pacific. He had arrived toward evening of the same day Sea Wind arrived. Both vessels had anchored outside the lagoon and proceeded inside the next day.

When it came to dates, Pollock was careless and imprecise, not at all mathematically inclined. When Schroeder asked him the date of his departure from Honolulu for Palmyra, he answered, "It would be about June 28th, somewhere thereabouts. We arrived on July 2nd. The 2nd is significant because it was two days before the 4th, is what we remember on a six-day trip."

Since he claimed to have anchored overnight outside the lagoon, where he watched Sea Wind arrive to do the same -- both vessels entering the lagoon on July 2nd -- then Lord Pollock, as I had dubbed him for his snooty ways, had made the 1000-mile voyage in an incredible 3 days -- under sail alone!

When asked about the condition of Iola, Pollock stroked his short white beard and said, "It was in poor condition. It was a carvel-planked boat. It had been glassed, which is really a death sound to a boat when it's carvel-planked. It means it can't be saved when you glass it. So the planks were all cupped and the glass was splitting underneath. It was unsatisfactory in my estimation."

The obvious thrust of trying to show Iola as unseaworthy was to provide motive -- a wholly specious one -- that we were afraid to sail any further on her and were desperate to acquire better transportation and thus began to covet Sea Wind. The related issue of trying to show we were low on food would thus indicate a corresponding covetousness for Sea Wind's ample stores. The weakness of these theories on motive was that if it could be contrarily shown that Iola was seaworthy and that replenishing our food supply was not much of a problem at all, then the prosecution's motives went out the window.

In his masterful summation at the close of Stephanie's murder trial in February, 1986, Bugliosi would state the true heart of the matter most succinctly, successfully laying these issues to rest. "The important point," he said, "is this: When Buck and Stephanie left Hawaii for Palmyra, although the Iola was certainly not a model boat, it obviously was seaworthy. How unseaworthy could the Iola be if it could make it a thousand miles on the high seas from Hawaii to Palmyra? Isn't that proof positive that the boat was seaworthy? And there's no evidence that either enroute to Palmyra, or while on Palmyra, the Iola sustained any major damage that would have made it unseaworthy and prevented it from making the trip from Palmyra to Fanning, a short trip. But whether or not the Iola was seaworthy is not the issue in this case. It's almost irrelevant. The real issue is whether Buck and Stephanie thought it was seaworthy. It's their state of mind that's relevant. The Iola could be the most unseaworthy boat ever to sail the seven seas, it could be as unseaworthy as a cement block, but if Buck and Stephanie thought it was seaworthy, they would not feel desperate and stranded, would they? Would they?"

Bugliosi also pointed out that Stephanie had made numerous entries in Iola's log regarding our plan and preparations to sail to Fanning. In addition, he noted that Tom Wolfe, a witness yet to come in my trial, had testified that Stephanie had apprised him of the possibility that we might sail to Fanning and, furthermore, that Mac, himself, who everyone agreed was the quintessential sailor, had obviously believed we could make Fanning because he had provided a chart of the island for us.

He would also point out that neither Jack Wheeler, the Pollocks, nor any of the other visitors to Palmyra, had ever attempted the "impossible" sail to Fanning -- except Don Stevens and Bill Larson on Shearwater. "We learned at this trial," Bugliosi explained, "that tacking against the wind is very common and easy. In fact, by tacking, a boat can proceed without a motor not only against the wind, but also against the current."

But Iola's logbook was not in evidence at my trial and Earle and Ray would fail to bring out such valuable information.

Pollock was asked if they had talked to either of us about our trip to Palmyra. "Yes, on the beach landing, Stephanie told me about her navigation."

"During this conversation with Stephanie, was Mr. Walker...was Mr. Allen present?"

"Yes."

"During this conversation, do you recall what you said to Roy Allen and Stephanie?"

"Just passing the time of day, probably asking him how their cruise was. Typical conversation when you first land some place, you want to know how other people did."

"Did either of them respond?"

"Stephanie responded."

Anticipating the possibility of hearsay at that point, Earle objected.

"What are you offering this for," King asked Schroeder.

"Your honor, we feel it's an adoptive admission."

It was a strange phrase, adoptive admission. He seemed to be saying that whatever statements Stephanie had made I would be liable for them if I did not immediately contradict her, that by my failure to correct her, I thereby adopted her statements as my own. Since it seemed a bizarre form of reasoning, I could only guess that it was related to the concept of guilt by association.

"Can we establish whether Roy Allen said anything or not first," King demanded, becoming peevish.

"Mr. Pollock," Schroeder said, "during this conversation, did Mr. Allen say anything?"

"No."

Incredibly, King overruled Earle's objection.

"Your honor!", Earle bit out, trying to contain his outrage. "Could we have an offer of proof made on a sidebar? I am not aware of any admissions."

"Well, we'll find out," King said. "If there aren't any, you are not hurt. If there are, they're admitted."

Earle couldn't believe his ears. "Excuse me, your honor. I think the rules of evidence excludes the government from placing evidence before the jury and then requiring the defense to object to it!"

"Overruled," King growled. "Go ahead."

The farce continued. Pollock was fabricating, I knew, when he claimed that Stephanie had told him she'd had to bail knee-deep water during the journey, because water inside Iola had never risen even six inches over the floorboards, not even when we'd taken the 90° knockdown. Nor had she asked if she could buy or barter food because we were low on supplies.

Yes, we had greeted them when they came ashore and introduced ourselves. And while Stephanie is sociable and garrulous, it is inconceivable that she would beg for food and spin an exaggerated yarn about being knee-deep in water.

He droned on and on about Sea Wind, his relationship with the Grahams, his knowledge of Zodiacs and so forth and so on. Then Schroeder led him back into pure fabrication. "Had you intended to stay only two weeks?"

"No. We planned to stay a month."

I remembered a meeting with Mac, a few words we'd exchanged, that let me recognize this lie. About a week after the Pollocks had arrived, I had asked him if he knew how long they were staying, and he'd said two weeks.

"Jesus," I'd muttered. "Another week of trying to avoid the assholes!"

Mac had laughed. "Couldn't have summed them up better myself," he'd said.

Lord Pollock's next lie was even more incredible; he said that Mac always locked Sea Wind when he left it, even for brief trips ashore. Pollock said he found that strange since he never locked his boat.

"How do you know that he locked the boat?"

"I watched. If I came over to get him to go some place, then it was always, 'Wait a minute, I'll lock up,,' so I saw him lock it many, many times."

Schroeder herded him willingly along to their last meeting with the Grahams. Mac had helped them get underway from the Zodiac, while Muff had come aboard to visit with Lady Pollock.

"Did you notice if Muff Graham was doing anything while she was talking to your wife?"

"She was crying, and she cried most of the time even after they got back aboard the dingy and left."

What I knew was that the Pollocks had left on Stephanie's birthday and that Mac and Muff had cheerfully accepted an invitation to attend. They had immediately zoomed over to Iola after handing up their mail to the Pollocks and we'd sat in the cockpit poking fun at their high faluting airs.

Pollock was irrepressible. He claimed to have noticed that Sea Wind had a new name, Lokahi, when he'd first seen her at the Ala Wai Yacht Harbor in Honolulu in October. When King had looked at the photos of Sea Wind as she appeared then before handing them down to Pollock, he asked, "Does the name show on it?"

The photos showed very clearly that no new name had been painted on Sea Wind. Pollock fidgeted about desperately searching through them, his cheeks growing redder and redder. He'd been inadvertently caught in an outright lie.

"No," he admitted so softly he could hardly be heard.

Later, his pomposity magically restored, he went on to imply by every means at his disposal that he had been instrumental in detecting the stolen yacht, coordinating clandestine surveillance, and in browbeating the FBI and Coast Guard into arresting the miscreants -- even to participating in Stephanie's capture.

Later, in Stephanie's trial, Bugliosi would make hash of both the Pollocks, getting them to agree that not only were we not starving, but that Lady Pollock had been friendly with Stephanie, including the fact that the Grahams were also friendly with both of us, and he would make it seem as easy as ordering toast and eggs to go with his hash.

But I was not to be so regaled of Lord Pollock's annihilation at my trial. Ray was to handle the cross-examination, a long, meandering foray of inept questions and mindlessly vicious answers. It was a frustrating exercise in watching him make a roundabout approach to Lord Pollock's ermine-lined balls only to back away before busting them.

The high point of Ray's cross was to allow Pollock to emphasize his lone and uncontradicted testimony about Mac locking up Sea Wind. And there would be no follow-up by asking other witnesses who had been aboard Sea Wind whether they had ever observed Mac to do so.

Good ol' Ray. After a pointless question about how soon a vessel could be seen entering the channel from the dolphin area, he was through. Instead of sending Pollock away with a headache, a nervously fibrillating heart, and painful hemorrhoids, as it would be so easy to do, Ray had sent him off smirking self-righteously with a polite smile and a "Thank you, Mr. Pollock."

Ol' painless Ray -- should have been a dentist.

Marilyn Pollock

"Did you ever see Mrs. Graham wearing glasses," asked Schroeder, a point he had missed with her husband, the point of the question seeming to be to connect glasses with the lenses found in the remains of a fire at the Graham campsite -- the implication being that evidence was being destroyed.

"Yes, she had to wear glasses," the mousy Lady Pollock replied.

"Glasses in frames as opposed to contact lenses?"

"She wore glasses with frames."

Other than sunglasses, I had never seen Muff wearing glasses. I argued with Earle, urging him to recall Pollock and check out the issue due to where it was leading. It might be a point on which the Lord and Lady hadn't gotten their story straight. He refused, saying it was a minor point.

From there, the testimony seemed to wander around until finally King took a recess and got the jury out of the room.

Schroeder said, "Mrs. Pollock is going to testify as to the activity of Mr. Walker in the form of repeatedly rowing by her boat in a dinghy, looking at her, watching her, and when she would speak to him, he would not answer her. This happened about 10 times."

I didn't quite get it. Was he saying that I was casing Tempest like a burglar, telegraphing my intentions? Or only trying to scare her? Of course I had rowed by their boat, ferrying furniture to my tent. Of course I had looked at their yacht, admiring the clean lines of her. But rowing by to glare and scowl and drive her to hysteria? Please!

Schroeder continued, "Mr. and Mrs. Pollock decided to leave. They communicated their anxiety to Mr. and Mrs. Graham. Mrs. Pollock said to Mrs. Graham that she was fearful that something was going to happen -- that's why they were leaving. It was at this point that Mrs. Graham began to cry and told Mrs. Pollock that she would never leave the island alive."

Fucking incredible! How fucking convenient! The idea of timid little Lady Pollock infecting Muff with hysteria was so ludicrous I could have laughed if I didn't know these people were deadly serious.

Earle spoke up. "Your honor, this is the first any of us have heard of this evidence."

"I told him about it this morning, your honor," Schroeder replied.

"No, not about this rowing by the boat and what-have-you. This is a first! Secondly, the only reason for offering this evidence is for the express purpose..."

"Well, all evidence introduced by the government is prejudicial evidence," King pronounced, reading Earle's mind. "That's what the government does. The purpose of the government's evidence is to prejudice." He looked about proudly, as if waiting for some sign of appreciation for his insight. "Well...", he said when no one applauded.

"I am not talking about prejudice," Earle demurred, apparently missing the relevance. "What I am talking about here is the government's attempting to, by a series of irrelevant events..."

"Well, let's take it one at a time," King interposed. "I suppose she could describe seeing Mr. Allen, whatever he was doing. Now, her reactions to what he was doing, that's where I have a little difficulty."

"Your honor," Schroeder interjected, "as to Mrs. Graham's declarations to Mrs. Pollock, the defendant has made a statement in which he maintained that on the day of the disappearance, the victim went out fishing with her husband. But before she left, she invited him and Stearns aboard their boat."

Earle was outraged. "That is not true, your honor!"

"And gave him," Schroeder continued, "carte blanche over their boat when they were out fishing!"

"Excuse me, that is not..."

King burst in. "Just a minute! She can certainly testify as to what he was doing, rowing about the boat. I am just thinking about the next step as to what her reaction to that was."

Schroeder wasn't about to let it go. He could see King beginning to roll around in his favor. "Well, your honor, we would argue that the jury might find that a woman who in this state of mind would not be inviting the defendant aboard her boat, more or less handing him the key to her boat, to her home and only possession."

"Excuse me, your honor," Earle said. "I charge the government with misconduct!

There is no evidence that Mrs. Graham ever invited the defendant to her boat! The evidence in this case is that Mr. Graham invited the defendant to the boat, and we have mentioned this to the government and the government's up here representing falsely that there is such evidence when there is no such evidence!"

Although I didn't guess it at the moment, that speech made in outrage at the government's tactics would be the high point of Earle's emotional expression. Thereafter, when King's hostility would become ever more apparent in his constant sarcasm and scolding of the two lightweights he, himself, had appointed to defend me, Earle would begin to draw back into himself like a whipped dog, and later even developed an acute case of shingles.

Lady Pollock, who had sat quietly during these and subsequent arguments and rulings, now understood it had all come out in her favor. She would be allowed to tell her little lie. She smirked at me before the jury returned.

As Schroeder began to question her about my rowing by her boat, she said, "He would row to another part of the lagoon, past our boat. Our boats were very close together, tied close together, and he would be looking at the boat. We have a beautiful boat. People do admire our boat."

King gave her a bit of the fisheye for beginning to wander, and she returned to the point.

"Mr. Allen would come close to the boat and look at it. And I would speak and he would never speak. And he had very hard eyes. Very upsetting."

Earle objected, moving to strike and the arguments went on. King gave hints to Schroeder on how to get the question and answer into the record, one way or another.

"Now," Schroeder said, taking the hint, "when you left Palmyra, did you meet with the Grahams before you left?"

"Yes. This is very upsetting."

Lady Pollock had turned on the waterworks, sniffling and sobbing into a hanky already in her hand. She looked at the jury and dabbed her eyes, then took a couple of deep breaths to show how bravely she was facing these awful memories. I was sick enough to throw up.

"Mac and Muff came over to say goodbye to us, and we had established a close friendship by that time. Particularly, I had established a close friendship with Muff. And Muff was terribly upset and I was upset, too. And Muff urged us not to go. And I said we had to go because I didn't feel we should stay. It was very uncomfortable. I wanted to get..." But then she paused to remember a phrase she'd rehearsed. "And I said, 'I wish you would come with us.' Muff was crying very hard and she said she knew she would never leave the island alive."

She glared at me. I returned her look with a stare.

She turned to the jury for support. "And it's hard to explain this for you to understand, but it's like a sixth sense. I think women have that. I said that I felt it was not a safe place and I wanted to leave. I urged her to please talk to Mac and see if they wouldn't leave. And I wish we had stayed. This maybe never would have happened!"

Earle was getting a lot of exercise, jumping up like popping corn to object to the many statements.

King turned to Lady Pollock. "Please don't add anything like that," he said in his kindest manner. "You are supposed to just answer."

"Can the jury be admonished," Earle reminded.

The jury was beginning to resent Earle. Who was he, anyway? Some self-appointed censor as to what they could hear? They'd already heard it and telling them to forget it was like telling children to spit out a piece of candy.

Ray began the cross-examination. If the Bible was right about the meek inheriting the earth, he stood at the front of the line to get a huge piece of real estate. He led her on a circuitous story about Tempest's approach to the channel, the weather and our respective mooring positions.

"Our stern," she said, "the back of our boat was to their stern, I think. I think then they turned around and came about."

That was true enough. We had swung around to get our bow into the wind to prevent rain blowing in the habitually open main hatchway. It was a perfect time to ask about Mac helping us, and to begin establishing that we were a long way from being on unfriendly, mutually exclusive terms, but he missed the opportunity.

He then spent an eternity in miniscule questions getting to the statement Lady Pollock and her husband gave the FBI back at the Ala Wai. "Mrs. Pollock, would it be fair to say that in the statement that you gave to the agents at this time, you made no mention whatsoever concerning this rowing by your vessel?"

"I wasn't asked that!"

"But you didn't tell anyone that you observed this, is that correct?"

"No. As I recall, all the agents wanted was identification of a photo of Roy Allen."

The questions went on and on. She claimed to have only answered what she was asked. However, in Stephanie's trial, Bugliosi managed to show that as she and her husband were on Palmyra, not the FBI, they couldn't know things to ask unless she told them.

Strangely, they "never asked" her about the most damaging things she had to say at either trial.

Don Stevens

A naval architect with some 25,000 miles of cruising experience, Stevens had been at Palmyra aboard Shearwater for 10 days between July 22 and August 1. I wanted to respect him because at my theft trial he had seemed the most objective of those who had visited Palmyra.

Schroeder began by inquiring what condition Iola appeared to be in.

"Old, but not too bad."

In Stephanie's trial, he would actually say that Iola was seaworthy.

Although he and Bill, his crew, had spent most of their time at Palmyra exploring, they had also spent time with both the Grahams and with Stephanie and me. He had seen the garden on the roof of the refrigerator house, and observed that we had cut down a tree and obtained the palm heart. But then his memory failed him. He didn't remember the thousands of coconuts on the island, and thought he had seen me wearing a holster.

There was no holster for the .22 pistol.

He remembered that I had shot fish and, although he had not witnessed it, he had later seen us cleaning them on the shore.

He said that Muff told him that neither of us had ever been aboard Sea Wind.

Incredible! Iola's log on July 9 said we had delivered coconut butter to Mac and Muff on our way to bathe and they had invited us aboard for "a very enjoyable evening with them, drinking wine, which tasted fine, and then some rum." On July 25, after the Grahams had been invited to supper at our tent, Mac arrived to ferry Steph to Sea Wind for coffee and chess. And on July 28, Stephanie wrote, "In afternoon and early evening, R went over and played chess with Mac while I engulfed myself more deeply in 1984." She didn't mention the constant chess games between Mac and me, sometimes aboard Sea Wind and sometimes at my tent, but she was, of course, not always present.

The point of Stevens' statement that Muff had told him we'd never been aboard Sea Wind is similar to the one made over several of the Pollocks' statements -- this was the first time it had ever been mentioned in the records in 11 years! It seems Don had gotten on the bandwagon to add his two cents worth of fictional testimony in aid of ridding the world of two monsters.

He went on to testify that Muff had expressed "some displeasure" when she learned that they'd invited Stephanie to join them on an afternoon trek, which testimony went unchallenged.

However, at Stephanie's trial, Larson was called. He was an important witness because he was the only one who would testify that he had been present at the party and had observed that the relationship between the Grahams and us seemed very cordial. Bugliosi had asked, "In your view, did it appear to be a friendly relationship between Buck and Mac?"

"Yes, it did," Larson replied.

"You watched Buck and Mac playing chess?"

"Yes."

"And when you saw Muff and Stephanie talking, did it appear, from where you were, to be a friendly conservation?"

"Yes, it did."

"Based on your observations of Stephanie with the Grahams, how would you describe this relationship?"

"It was friendly."

"Did you detect any animosity or hostility?"

"No, I didn't."

Ray, however, would elicit none of this at my trial.

Judge King asked Stevens to check Shearwater's log for the date of the trip that he, Larson, the Grahams and Stephanie had made. The entry, made on July 30, corresponded with Stephanie's log entry on the Iola: "I went with Bill and Don, Mac and Muff on an exploratory trip to Eastern and Barren Islands. Found some good shells and several bottles."

This was five days after our dinner party, and two since I'd spent a long afternoon aboard Sea Wind playing chess with Mac. Strange, then, that suddenly Muff would claim that we had never been aboard, that she didn't trust us and that she was unhappy that Stephanie had been invited along.

In asking Stevens about Iola's seaworthiness, he said, "I would say it was seaworthy with the exception of the pumping system." This he based on a pump that he claimed Stephanie had told him about. However, when asked if he had any knowledge as to other pumps that might have been aboard, he replied, "No, I don't."

Our main pump, manually operated, was in plain view on the cabin top beside the main hatch to starboard. It can be seen in at least two of the photos of Iola taken from Sea Wind upon our departure from Palmyra. Stevens had admitted to being in our cockpit and could hardly have missed the pump beside the main hatch, but Ray simply didn't ask the right questions to nudge his memory. It was becoming obvious to me that Ray was not only unprepared to ask hard, knowledgeable questions, but neither he nor Earle knew anything about sailing vessels or techniques.

Thomas Wolfe

A chemical engineer, Wolfe claimed to have extensive experience in sailing. He and Norman Sanders had moored just east of us. "The boat," he said, referring to Iola, "appeared extremely crude and rough, and was not what I would call seaworthy for a voyage of that duration."

He had come over to the refrigerator house to meet Steph and me to go fishing, which is when he said Popolo attacked and bit him on the stomach.

"After you were bitten by the dog," Schroeder asked, "did you say anything to Roy Allen?"

"I said to him, please keep the dog away from me or I would kill it. His answer was, 'That would be good because then we would have some meat around here.'"

"After you were bitten by the dog, what did you do?"

"Well, after I was bitten, we went back to the boat. I cleaned the bite with antiseptic. Then we went on a fishing expedition with Mr. Allen."

He said I had equipped him with a small hand spear, and was asked to stand in the water and spear the fish I shot. "And we did this for a while, but I couldn't spear any mullet." He thought I had shot one, probably two or three, but he wasn't sure.

He continued testifying, altering my gift to him of a broken Buck-knife somewhat later followed by his giving me a can of chili by claiming I'd specifically initiated a trade for the purpose of getting meat, because I was hungry for meat.

After I learned, over the years, the many theories as to how and why Steph and I had murdered the Grahams, I would, in a bitter moment, wonder how cannibalism had been overlooked as a motive.

Although Wolfe testified we were short of food, he did admit to receiving two loaves of bread from Stephanie after they gave her flour and sugar. Her entry in the log indicates that she also gave them a pan of cornbread and "split a coffee cake."

Wolfe went on to testify that he had been told, not once, but twice, by Muff that she was afraid of me and wished either we or they would leave.

According to Lady Pollock, Muff had been frightened of me on July 16, and by mid-August, according to Wolfe, she was still frightened and had no compunction as to whom she confessed. The prosecution was painting a false portrait of Muff as a hysteric. There was no way I could fit this idea in with the Muff I had known, a calm, cool, able and emotionally stable woman. Even assuming for the sake of argument that her alleged fears of me did exist, why would she tell them to a stranger she'd known for three days when only a few days later she submitted herself willingly to my romantic persuasions?

Apparently Muff had made a few disparaging remarks in letters to her family. That was understandable. She and Mac had come to Palmyra expecting to have the island to themselves. So had we. Our lifestyles were different; theirs reserved and traditionally middle class; ours liberal, freewheeling and laidback. But for all the differences, the cordiality of the relationship between the four of us had never been breached by harsh words or arguments. If she was afraid, it seems reasonable that she would have expressed her fears to her family and friends in her letters. Yet, there is not a single tinge of fear in any of them.

I wondered if Lady Pollock had passed that bit of poppycock on to Wolfe in the last few days.

The last point in Wolfe's testimony was something he had never mentioned before: rat poison.

"Do you recall what was kept in that shed in addition to the old fire truck?"

"There were quantities of rat poison in that shed."

I couldn't recall ever having seen any rat poison anywhere, although I'd seen a few rats. Not one other person recalled seeing rat poison on Palmyra. Wolfe had come up with a humdinger.

He was asked if he had had occasion to return to the shed where the poison was kept and replied, "Yes, we went in there either the night...the day before we left or the morning of the day we left."

Did he notice anything different?

"All the rat poison was gone," he pronounced in an ominous tone, glancing my way accusingly.

Findlay started well enough to impeach Wolfe's testimony on the statement's about Muff's fear and the rat poison, but he got caught up in more arguments with King and wandered off course again. He did manage to get in the facts of Mac's firearms, the revolver and a Derringer, both .357 magnums, although Wolfe thought the latter was a .22. And, miraculously, he did get to Muff's alleged fears.

"Mr. Wolfe, you had a conversation with Mrs. Graham concerning her general state of mind concerning sailing at the time that you were on Palmyra, is that correct?"

"That's correct, yes."

"And didn't she tell you at this time...did Mrs. Graham say that she was becoming afraid of sailing long distances and that all she wanted to do was get home and just keep sailing up and down the coast?"

"Yes, she did say something close to that."

"And did you not report that to Detective Alexander when you gave your statement in January, 1975?"

"It's in there. Yes."

But Ray never did get around to the big question: Well, why is it then you failed to mention Mrs. Graham's fear of Buck Walker before today? Nor did he ask a single question about the rat poison only Wolfe had seen.

Curt Shoemaker

A ham radio operator, Shoemaker had met the Grahams at Radio Bay, Hilo, Hawaii, where they moored along side him for a month prior to their trip to Palmyra. At his suggestion, the Grahams agreed to maintain a scheduled radio contact, which by August, was set to once a week.

According to a copy of his radio log, Shoemaker said he had been in regular contact with Mac, and mentioned dates slightly off from his testimony in Stephanie's theft trial. He also read the text of the message he had relayed through Mac:

"Dear Mr. Shoemaker,

Would you please relay this message to my friend, Roy Allen, the next time you are in radio contact with the Grahams? Thank you for your assistance.

Message:

We have been delayed by unforeseen circumstances, but hope to see you in October. We've enjoyed your letters very much. Of interest is the fact that Seagull eggs are considered superior eating to chicken eggs in many European countries, not only in nutrition, but in taste as well. Hopefully, we will bring everything to repair your engine and so forth. Patty promises to bring a turkey for Thanksgiving dinner. See you there.

Richard

Although a witness for the prosecution, Shoemaker proved my contention that we were receiving supplies in the near future.

When it came time to discuss the last few seconds of the final transmission, a flurry of objections erupted and was thoroughly discussed in a recess. Eventually, Shoemaker was asked, "Do you recall if the subject of the conversation ever turned to something that was taking place?"

"Well, toward the end of this contact, I could hear a voice in the distance. Then he said, 'Wait a minute. Something is going on. Let me go topside and see what's happening. There is a dinghy or something coming over to the boat.' And his comment was, 'I guess they've formed a truce,' or something like that, to that extent."

"Did he return to the telephone?"

"Yes, he did. He said there is -- something about their bringing a cake over -- and he said, 'I'd better find out what's happening.' And so I said, 'Okay, then I'll see you on the next scheduled contact.'"

"Did you schedule a next contact at that time?"

"Yes, we did."

"Did you hear anything in the background while Mac was telling you about these events?"

"I heard a woman's voice, some laughter, and I believe Muff was talking, too. There was some conversation going on there from a distance. It wasn't on the boat."

"Did you hear another voice in addition to Muff's?"

Incredibly, Shoemaker answered, "No."

Schroeder raised his eyebrows and tried again. "Well, did you hear anything else in the background aside from Muff?"

"Well, I heard -- it sounded like laughter and two females -- two female voices. There was some conversation going on. I couldn't tell."

Shoemaker then said he'd tried to reestablish contact on September 4, 11, and 18, with no success.

Findlay's cross-examination was, as usual, pathetic. He elicited that Shoemaker had heard "a woman somewhere in the distance, calling and laughing."

And that's about it. No setting him up with questions about him wanting to help the FBI bring the culprits to justice. No pointed questions about his memory. No devastating why questions about not having mentioned the "truce-cake" incident in the intervening 11 years.

Ray, through his questions, managed to emphasize the laughter of women that Shoemaker claimed he heard, thus showing a friendly relationship. He apparently thought that was sufficient.

I didn't understand all this testimony until I read Bugliosi's account in 1991. The link was between Wolfe and Shoemaker, between the missing rat poison and the cake! Enoki and Schroeder had managed to slip in the suggestion that we had murdered the Grahams by means of a poisoned cake!

*****

The next day, Friday, no less than seven witnesses testified for the government. Five were of little importance. The sixth, FBI Agent Henry Burns, would make serious points with the jury, which could be countered only if I testified. The last, Sharon Jordan, would be devastating if allowed to stand without an explanation from me.

*****

FBI Agent Henry Burns

Agent Burns had done a nice hatchet job on me at the theft trial by committing a few small perjuries. He and I both knew that he had succeeded and would succeed again. The knowledge passed between us, unspoken, invisible to others, whenever our eyes met. It was like he was mocking me, but there was nothing to be done. He was a practiced witness, and came across as earnest, honest, and well-spoken. Burns began by describing my arrest in Hawaii on November 8, 1974.

He went on to paraphrase what he said were my statements of the entire adventure. Although it had been 11 years and he had not maintained his notes, saying that it was not required at that time, he was amazingly able to quote both his questions and my replies.

"Now," said Earle when he took over on cross, "the reason there might be some concern in saving interview notes is to make sure there was no mistake in transcribing them, isn't that correct?"

"That's right."

"Now, you transcribed them onto what is known as an FBI Form 302?" "Yes, I did."

"And would it be correct to say that your transcribing them on to that 302, you were not attempting to quote verbatim, but to summarize the main point in the conversation?"

"Yes, I put some statements in there in quotes which indicated they were verbatim statements, but most of the statement was paraphrased."

"In fact," Earle asked, his voice rising as he honed in for what he doubtless considered the kill, "the overwhelming majority is paraphrased!"

"That's correct," Burns replied calmly.

Earle managed to punch some holes in his testimony by calling up statements made in

Burn's previous reports and getting varying responses. Finally, after supplying Burns with his own 302 report, Earle referred to the last paragraph on page 3:

"Isn't it true, in your 302, Mr. Burns, you stated that Mr. Walker told you that he had seen the dinghy 50 to 100 yards away, washed up on shore?"

"That's correct."

"So that when you testified on direct that it was on the water, you were mistaken?"

"That's correct. It was a misstatement."

The play went on, seemingly interminably. Regarding painting of Sea Wind -- if it was painted, if it should have been painted, if I had said it was painted -- until I realized these questions might have really been a smokescreen for Earle's real purpose. His next question and answer were right on point.

"Now, when you asked Mr. Walker about the two boats sailing together," he said, gliding into it as softly and unobtrusively as he could, "isn't it true that you asked the defendant if he ever sailed alongside the Grahams on the open seas?"

"Yes, I asked him that."

Which was true, and I had answered no. But later in the interview, Burns had referred back, his finger pointing to his notebook, and trying to be clever had said something like, "Now, let me get this straight, you say you've never been under sail alongside Sea Wind?" When I'd corrected him and restated that I'd said I'd never been under sail alongside the Grahams, he'd accused me of changing my story.

In a cheap shyster's trick, Earle quickly went on to other time-killing questions, stretching it out by pretending to search through his paperwork. The idea was to leave Burns' answer as it stood.

But Enoki, not quite so dumb as Earle hope, destroyed his accomplishment with his first questions on redirect.

"Mr. Partington asked you, Mr. Burns, whether you asked Mr. Walker if he had ever sailed alongside the Grahams on the open sea. Was that the only question you asked Mr. Walker about being on the open seas?"

"No, I asked him a series of questions," he grinned, casting his eye toward the defense table in mockery. "I was aware of that photograph. I asked him if he ever saw the Grahams before he got to Palmyra. He said he had not. I asked him if he had ever been on the open seas next to Sea Wind, and he said he had not. I asked him, in at least three or four questions, if at any time the Iola had ever been on the open sea next to the Sea Wind, and he told me it had not.

When they left Palmyra, he had the Iola caught up on the reef and he cut it free. The Iola, Mr. Walker told me, was never in the open sea next to Sea Wind at the time."

With that, he very effectively put the nails in the coffin on that subject -- even if he was probably lying about having seen the photos of Iola passing the anchored Sea Wind, which was an entirely new revelation.

I looked at Earle, who was grimly studying papers strewn before him. It was pathetic. He'd actually been hoping to get away with it, had figuratively crossed his fingers like an excited schoolboy hoping his mother wouldn't find he'd been in the cookie jar.

Enoki and Schroeder were whispering and snickering at each other, casting gleeful eyes toward a seething and embarrassed Earle.

After Burns had been excused and King had dismissed the jury for lunch, Burns made a detour by the defense table to rub it in. Some of the jurors, all up from their seats and beginning to move through the door near the witness stand, were looking our way. Burns had paused to shrug and smirk at me. I remembered his last statement to me when I'd cut off our interview so many years before with a heartfelt "Fuck you!" Just as sincerely, he'd said, "We'll see who fucks who!"

I beckoned him closer. He put his hands on the table and leaned toward me. Now that he was blocking the view from the jury, I lifted one hand off the table and gave him a stiff middle finger.

"Congratulations, asshole, you got away with it," I said.

For a split second, I saw anger glint in his eyes, but he caught himself, remembering he was in a courtroom. He drew back, shrugged, grinned again, knowing he'd won the encounter, and sauntered away.

"That son of a bitch!" muttered Earle.

*****

While Enoki and King discussed the order of witnesses for the afternoon session, Earle's resentments apparently ate at him. To everyone's surprise, he suddenly jumped up to but in.

"Your honor, at this time I would like to move for a mistrial in this case!"

"Move for a mistrial for what purpose?"

"Your honor, the government has offered the testimony from three witnesses concerning Mrs. Graham's fear on the repeated representations that Walker represented that Mrs. Graham invited Walker and Stearns to the Sea Wind for dinner!"

That wasn't quite true the way I had seen the testimony, although it did seem to be the implication. The fact was, Mac had made the actual invitation in Muff's presence. And, of course, she had no fear of me. Neither would she have thought of demurring. We were lovers, new enough to each other to retain the initial excitement in the affair. We were busy concealing the emotions over our secret, while desiring each other's company. There was a delicious danger in being together in company and maintaining the secret from Mac and Stephanie, letting the anticipation build for our next encounter.

King looked at Earle in disbelief. "Say that again!"

"The government..."

"I didn't hear any such representations!"

Enoki echoed. "I made no such representations."

Earle pointed. "Mr. Schroeder made the representation here yesterday afternoon in court, your honor. If I have a little time, I can find it on the transcript."

The argument went round and round, only to play itself out to its inevitable end. Earle kept trying, arguing into the wind. King waited to make sure he was through, and then looked to Enoki who shook his head in the negative. King looked back at Earle. "The motion is denied."

Earle slumped. Earle was nervous. Earle was worried.

I was too proud to slump in public, and probably too dumb to be nervous, but inside I was worried as hell. Primarily about my attorneys and whether they were going to show any more ability than they had so far, whether they had the spine to stand up to King. But mostly I was seriously beginning to worry about my own fate. All the first signs were ominous. Would they become the first symbols of the writing on the wall? Apparent enough to convey the dire message?

My lunchtime coffee was bitter, my sandwich tasted like sawdust. The cigarettes I chain-smoked while pacing the confines of the holding tank were acrid, leaving a foul taste in my mouth, a hacking cough in my throat. I was relieved when it was time to return to the courtroom.

*****

Just as Sharon Jordan was called, Earle announced to everyone's surprise that she and her husband were in possession of an 8mm film shot during their time on Palmyra and included photos of the bones they'd recovered.

"I am going to ask the Court, when the Jordans testify, that they be ordered to produce it. They wanted to sell it and I couldn't offer them enough money, your honor."

Enoki got in a disclaimer. "I might add we didn't learn of this from Mr. Partington until 11:30 this morning, so we are not in a position..."

"The government doesn't have it either," Earle confirmed, "and I just wanted to indicate to the court that I do want this film produced."

"Why didn't you ask for it before?"

"I wanted to wait until the film was in this country."

King was beginning to fume again. "Well, if they have some reason to protect it as private property, and if it isn't relevant, I am going to support them. If it is relevant..."

"It's very relevant, your honor," Earle said. "I have seen it."

But, as it would turn out, no one else would see it -- that is, except for about five seconds worth as a snippet was shown on the evening news.

Sharon Jordan

She was a beauty with long dark hair and a meticulously made-up face, her lipstick bright, glossy and perfectly applied. She was trim, well-built, and wearing a low-cut dress with high heels. The hem rose above her shapely knees. Even Judge King peered down for a sight of her thighs as she sat.

Schroeder brought out that she had sailed halfway around the world in a boat that her husband had built. He led her on to Palmyra. She, along with her husband and a friend, Ed Colin, had arrived in November, 1980, and stayed for three months. She had spent her time exploring and searching for Japanese jars, floats, and seashells while her husband preferred laying in his hammock and reading. On January 4, 1981, they discovered an old aluminum sea-rescue launch submerged in about 20-25 feet of water near the seaplane ramp, and within a week they had succeeded in raising it. They noticed it had a hole in it, the initials U.S.A.F. on it, and that it was missing two equipment lockers.

After that, Jordan began to explore toward Strawn Island further west, and on January 25, found a container, its lid, a wristwatch, some bones, and a skull, all in the same area. She first noticed the skull when the sun glinted off a gold tooth; she picked it up and took it to show her husband, wanting him to help her gather the rest because she "feared that the tide would come and then possibly wash away the bones."

Schroeder introduced the metal box and lid, which she identified. She pointed out that some of the holes had not been there when she found it, where pieces had been cut out for forensic tests. Schroeder had her move down from the witness stand where she situated the box and the lid next to each other, both upright, as the relative positions in which she' found them. She claimed not to have seen the box and lid when she first discovered the skull and bones because the "mangroves came over" or were "kind of hanging over" them. The box was about two feet from the roots of the mangrove, the lid about a foot. She marked a spot on the chart to indicate where she'd found them.

Then, still standing between the chart and the box, she turned to the box and lid placed before the jury enclosure. "The bones," she said, "were kind of in a crescent shape from this box, like this," and she spread her arm around in an arc, "but all in the immediate vicinity of the box. I would say about 90% of the bones were in the immediate vicinity."

Whether he knowingly assisted in the seemingly rehearsed demonstration or merely blundered in, King helped her out. "Which way were the thigh bones or whatever it is? The head was which way?"

"The skull was about over here," she said, pointing to the left.

"Pointing to the area of the lid," King said.

This cued her in to deliver her most dramatic gesture, one designed to fix the skull and bones irretrievably within the box, an idea Earle would never be able to dislodge.

"Can you imagine taking this box, if it were full of bones," she said, planting the idea, "and going like this," she continued, making a dumping motion with the box to indicate it spilling over onto its side, "and everything falling out?"

She made another sweeping gesture with her arm to create the imaginary crescent shape of the spill. "That's how it would look."

The courtroom was silent as the images she'd created sank in. It was simple and effective, so simple I couldn't believe it had occurred spontaneously.

When she returned with her husband to begin collecting the remaining bones, she found a wristwatch in the lid and her husband picked up a piece of wire. She said they'd placed everything in the box and put the lid on top before carrying it back to their camp. The next day, they returned with Ray and Betty Landrum, and Fern and Jean Prince and found a few more bones.

Since she had forgotten to describe the wire her husband had found, Schroeder asked her a leading question. "Did you notice if there was anything about the character or configuration or bend of the wire to indicate that it might have, at any time, been wrapped around the box?"

"Yes," she chirped brightly. "It was in the shape of a box. And at the time, we thought, well, this obviously was around the box."

Earle seemed too dispirited to object to the drawing of improper conclusions. But, of course, it was a perfectly correct conclusion. It was the length of electrical wire I had myself placed around it to secure the lid down.

Schroeder went on. "Before you sealed up the container, did you notice anything about the interior of it?"

"Yes, it was charred."

"Did you also notice anything about the skull?"

"It, too, was charred and it also had a hole in it."

There it was, the horror of it -- the charred skull and the charred box. The box had served as the instrument of cremation. The hole, what was it? A bashed skull, a bullet? Were some of the jurors casting surreptitious glances my way, the beginnings of disgust in them, or was that only my imagination?

Next Schroeder led her into the weather. There had been two severe storms before she had found the box and bones.

I missed the significance of this. Years later, after publication of Bugliosi's book, an astute friend would point out the obvious. One of these storms was supposedly the cause of the box being lifted from the bottom of the lagoon, wrenched open from its wire lock and spilled in a neat crescent for the strolling nude to discover. My friend also pointed out that, relevant to all known conditions, such an event defied all physical laws -- a storm could not have washed the box up on the beach.

According to Jordan, they contacted the authorities the following morning and they arrived on Palmyra on February 4, where they spent the next three days taking photographs, asking questions, and in general doing their thing.

Jordan swore to Earle when he took over the cross that she had maintained the integrity of the box during the ten days before the authorities arrived, that no one had gone into it. She identified photos of the area where they had been found and the photos were then moved into evidence.

She had plenty of time to observe the tidal action, high and low water marks and the set of the current within the lagoon before she left Palmyra in March. She knew that there was a westerly drift to the current because, "Roger, on the yacht, Romaur," had thrown a float overboard and she'd seen where it came to rest on the beach, the same area where she had found the bones.

So far, I had counted nine people, not including the Gilbertese Islanders, who had been on Palmyra during the time the Jordans were there. By the time she finished testifying, the number was up to thirteen. Jordan had been about to provide the names of the Gilbertese, but Earle glided right over the point before she could. I wondered how many of these people Earle had managed to interview. As far as I could tell, he had talked to only three of them. I wondered about the FBI. Had they been as sloppy as Earle?

On cross, Earle led her into talk about the natural life of the area, including the food supply. "And did you ever eat anything that you found on the island?"

"Yes, we did."

"Could you give me an example what that was?"

"We ate coconut, crabs. We ate land crabs. We ate Terns, Tern's eggs," she began, then hesitated. "Not really ate Terns. I am sorry. We ate Curlew."

"What is that?"

"It's a type of bird."

"Is there any difficulty in catching it?"

"You have to shoot them."

Earle continued to parade out nature's menu. More questions elicited the fact that, Wolfe's testimony to the contrary, there was lots of coconuts, both in the trees and on the ground.

"You wouldn't starve on Palmyra Island, would you?"

"I wouldn't, no."

She testified that she and her husband had dived around their boat using only snorkels. Neither of them had seen anything like the box she'd found except for the two in the rescue launch, even though the water was clear. She thought if a box -- Mac's box -- had been sitting off by itself, she would have seen it. But she hadn't.

The vegetation growing above the high-water mark, especially a plant called naupaka, was quite thick in places and could reach out as much as ten feet. Anything in, under, or behind it would be hard to see. In fact, Jordan had not even seen the box when she spotted the skull bones because it was mostly concealed under overhanging naupaka. The shelf area she'd been walking on that day was mostly coral and uncovered at low tide, while the naupaka marked the high tide line.

After her initial discovery, she'd rushed back to get her husband and returned over the water in a dinghy; the spot recognized by a concrete block with a mooring post. She admitted that the skull and most of the bones were found under the vegetation, yet the box had been about four feet down from the high water line. Still the naupaka growth had hung out over and down into the box. Yet, in response to Earle's specific question, she wouldn't admit that the naupaka was "growing" down into the box.

"Do you recall telling me, at the time you found the box, the vegetation was actually growing into the top of it?"

"I don't remember specifically saying the beach vegetation was growing into the box."

"Might you have told me that?"

She rolled her eyes and declared, "I might have."

"Now you indicated to me, as I believe you had to the FBI, that it appeared to you that the bones had tipped out of the box, is that correct?"

"Yes."

This went on for awhile, honing in on specifics of what she had said and when. Jordan was getting bored with the monosyllabic answers Earle was forcing on her.

"The statement wasn't exactly right, if you remember me telling you!"

Earle pounced. "Do you remember what was wrong with the statement?" "I don't remember what was wrong. It seemed to be something that wasn't quite as I remembered it."

Earle turned to King. "Your honor, may I give the witness a copy of that statement?"

"Are you impeaching her?"

"I don't know, your honor."

"Well, if you are not, then we don't need to go into it! I mean, you don't have to build up a strawman to knock him down if she hasn't said anything..."

"I'm trying to augment the testimony, your honor."

"Has she failed to augment it?"

"At this point, I am just..."

"It's always very interesting," Kind said, shaking his head at the ceiling. He sighed theatrically. "Go ahead. I assume it's going to be relevant?"

She finally stabbed her finger onto one of the pages after several minutes of silence and looked up. "My husband didn't see the bones directly. It says here, 'Her husband saw it. But underwater directly.' That's not correct."

Earle was nonplussed. King spoke into the pause. "Well, if you are not going to impeach her with the statement, why are we wasting time with it?"

"Refreshing her memory, your honor."

"About what?" The sarcasm, never far away, began creeping back into his voice.

"The incident."

"Well, you didn't ask her to refresh her memory," King stated, his tone rising in measurable decibels. "Now if that's what you want to do..." He turned to Jordan and lowered his voice. "Will you please read that to yourself and then..." turning back to Earle, "we will ask him what the question is!"

The farce continued between Earle, trying bravely to make his point, and King stopping him at every turn. Jordan began enjoying being the center of attention. Finally, Earle asked her, "In the course of our discussion, you said it looked like the bones just spilled out of the box, is that correct?"

Jordan, by then, couldn't quite suppress her grin. "Sorry, could you repeat that?"

Earle clenched his jaw and repeated the question, following up with, "And do you recall my asking you if there was any vegetation growing in the box and wedging the box in, how could the bones have just spilled out? To which you replied, well, you hadn't thought of that, the bones couldn't have just spilled out of the box?"

Jordan shrugged. "I don't remember."

The next confrontation was over the condition of the skull, which to Jordan appeared to have been charred, then back to the location.

They argued ad nauseum over a drawing of the location of the bones until Earle finally gave up and changed tack and asked about the 8mm film. Jordan said her husband had brought a lot of material with him, but she wasn't sure just what. It was obvious she was toying with him.

Earle was outraged. "Well, hasn't he offered the film for sale to the Channel 7 News?"

She could afford to be impish. King, Enoki, and Schroeder, her three knights, were standing by to ride to her aid. "He might have."

The arguments continued, but due to the many interruptions, Earle was unable to elicit much of anything concrete.

When finally excused, Jordan departed with poise and smiles for King, along with a warm thank you to the jury, Enoki, Schroeder, and even Findlay, who was eyeing her as appreciatively as every other male in the room. But she ignored Earle.

On her way back to the spectator section, our eyes met. Her brown eyes turned down in concentration I could only interpret as intense curiosity -- so this was the animal. I gave her a brief nod of approval -- yes, this was he, but what you get isn't what you see.

On a personal level, I had no problem with her testimony. Whether or not a storm had only recently washed up the metal container and spilled the bones for her to find in a neat crescent shape made no difference. I knew Muff had been in that box. But from a legal standpoint, relevant to Earle's strategy of trying to prove no body had been in the box, it was devastating.

*****

Earle was in crisis, his nerves frayed. Not much more than a quarter way through the 54 witnesses to be called, his dilemma now was whether he should testify in order to counter Jordan's testimony, to relate his own account as to what exactly was said or not said during his interview with her in South Africa. But in order to testify, he would have to remove himself from the case -- a point, when he stated it before the court, which seemed to fill Ray with trepidation that he would have to handle the remainder of the case on his own.

Earle was not shy about advertising the wearing of his hairshirt in the courtroom. He went into a long song and dance on the very question with King. He variously whined and sniveled with a stiff upper lip and hinted at his nobility over the possibility of abandoning his client in mid-trial, but truth was truth and duty was duty.

King rebuked him for having put himself into the position and said, "Well, you could also be duty-bound not to testify."

Earle, seemingly startled at this bizarre idea, replied, "Well, I really think that would put me in a terrible dilemma!"

"Well," King came back, weighing his words and casting a quick glance my way, doubtless to determine whether I was nodding off or looked intelligent enough to understand the import of what was being discussed, "you might evaluate in terms of what you would say in terms of what the probabilities are."

What the probabilities are. Translation: Nothing you say or do is going to make any difference; this case is lost.

They danced on, round and round, until King had had enough. "You are going to wrestle with the problem over the weekend."

"Yes," Earle agreed.

"And it will be solved by nine o'clock Monday morning."

"Yes, your honor, one way or another."

*****

The jury had long gone, the judge had just decamped, the prosecution table was hurriedly gathering folders and legal pads into briefcases, most of the spectators had made their exit, and Frink, along with another marshal, was standing and stretching in preparation for escorting me back along secret passages from the holding cell to their office.

Earle looked as though a gang of perverts had raped his best friend and were coming back for him. He was making motions with his hands as though he were washing them -- and well he should since he was contemplating a Pontius Pilate move on me.

"What should we do?" he all but babbled "What should we do?"

I looked at the yellow pad on which I had been making notes. I wondered what a psychiatrist would make of my doodles.

"Buck, we've got to make a decision! That lying bitch's testimony is devastating! We've got to do something!"

I glanced at Ray, who was making busy with his scattered paperwork. Could he handle it? I didn't think so. But then, my doubts about Earle had only grown -- so what difference did it make, really? Everyday, hour by hour, King continued to clarify the message. He was very polite and considerate to Enoki and Schroeder, contemptuous of Partington and Findlay. His preferences were apparent to all. Christ, he had appointed my lawyers! Were they on some shitlist of his? Was this their punishment? It was obvious they were in fear of him. I ran a brief fantasy through the theater of my imagination, of Earle rising angrily before the packed courtroom to declare in ringing tones that, by God, he wasn't going to take anymore! I imagined him like Albert Finney in the movie, Network, declaring his anger and frustration on national TV and causing thousands of viewers to fling open their windows and shout to the universe at large that they weren't going to take anymore! I even gave him a courage and dignity that he could only pretend to have.

"This trial is a farce!" he would shout to a shocked King, whose jowls would hang quivering below a gaping mouth. "Your honor's bias," he would sneer with great sarcasm, "against the defendant is apparent for all the world to see! Your unconscionable behavior in this courtroom has rendered the defense defenseless! And if this is what simple fairness and the law is all about, then I'm sorry to say that I'm ashamed to be a part of it! I will have no part in mocking what I have so long revered! I resign from this case!"

And he would storm out before King could say a word, and face the reporters, with lights and cameras aimed at him to elaborate some juicy sound-bites for the evening news. And Ray would rise with quiet dignity and say, "I concur, your honor," and also leave in the babbles between the hushed silences. And King would pump his mouth and cheeks like a blowfish out of water.

And then I would rise as the excited chattering stilled in anticipation, and I would remove my glasses and squint harshly in scorn and say something like, "Okay, you little cocksucker!" No, no cocksuckers -- this was in public and on the record. I would say, "Well, your honor," drawing it out most contemptuously. "It's just you and me now, and you'd better get it straight that I'm not going to take any shit...(no, substitute guff)...from you at all. You want to find me in contempt of court, good, because that would mean, by God, that there was some truth in this courtroom!"

Which is about as far as I got before pulling back from the temptation to explore it to the limits. It was futile.

"Buck, Buck!" Earle's voice came to me, his hand shaking at my sleeve.

"What?"

"What should I do?"

I refrained from telling him to go find a lake, and instead asked, "What about all those other people who were down there, the Landrums, the Princes, that guy Ed Colin, the other couple? And those Gilbertese -- she's got their names."

"I haven't been able to find any of them. It's too late for that." "You've had four years, Earle," I pointed out, twisting the blade. "You've had almost five months since the new indictment."

"We have to do something now," Earle cried. "I'll do whatever you say. If you want me to take the stand, I will. We have to counter that bitch's testimony!"

"But then you'd be off the case, right?"

"Yes, it's the law. I can't be a witness and represent you at the same time."

"You want off this case, Earle?"

He hesitated long enough for me to know the answer, but he denied it.

"No! But if I testify, I'll have to resign. What do you want me to do?"

I didn't say it, but I was really looking forward to getting back to my jail cell. "You decide, Earle," I said. "It's your case. You're in charge. You decide."

I turned to Frink and stuck my wrists out for the handcuffs. As we headed for the door, Earle was still washing his hands, but, like Lady MacBeth, perhaps he would find they didn't come clean so easily. Ray was still fussing with his paperwork.

"Couple of real pussies you got there, Walker," Frink said as we made our way down the dim, narrow corridor.

"Recognize a kindred spirit, do you, Rollie?" I sneered. From the likes of Rollie, the fink, I would even defend pussies.

Richard Musick

I hadn't seen Dickie in the eleven years since we'd hatched our Palmyra pakalolo scheme.

When he said he owned a small fixed-base operation dealing with aircraft charter, maintenance, and flights, I wondered if he had changed his ways or merely traded in his boat for planes in aid of speed and efficiency. Either way, I wished him well. In a brief exchange of glances, I knew he was telling me he was sorry to be there and I let him know it was okay -- I wouldn't hold it against him. If he'd left his old life behind and become more law abiding, he was still my pal and I'd have to do what I could to leave out his real involvement.

Schroeder led Dickie to our first meeting on Maui when we had talked about boats and boat building, then moved on to the correspondence about his coming down to meet us with supplies at Thanksgiving, somewhat later than originally planned. When he approached our return, Dickie's memory seemed to be faulty and then downright imaginative.

Finally, I figured out what was probably going on. In fact, I'd lay odds. I bet the Feds had tracked him down in the interval after my theft conviction for questioning without his knowledge that Muff's remains had been found. He, thinking he could do us no harm, made statements that would confirm the theft for which I'd already been convicted, but lead away from suspicions of murder. Stuck into a long question and answer session as Schroeder led him through it, lingering to emphasize the points he wanted to make, he now testified that when we returned with Sea Wind, we said that we had traded boats with another couple who were tired of sailing and they were going on to Fanning to fly home. Schroeder closed with a question about whether I had ever mentioned anyone capsizing or drowning on Palmyra.

"No, sir."

"Did he ever mention anyone disappearing on the island?"

"No, sir."

Dickie had done what he'd been stuck with doing, but then, like a metamorphosing butterfly, became a witness for the defense at the very moment Findlay rose to cross-examine him.

Dickie was led through his boating career, which was extensive, and his flying career, which amazed me; I'd known nothing about that aspect of his life. Then, Findlay began to talk to him about the seaworthiness of Iola.

"The boat was over-rigged," he said.

"How was that?"

"The cables that hold the mast up were of larger diameter than necessary." This was not only the truth, it was very contrary to Wolfe's niggardly remarks.

"Because a vessel has been glassed over, a wooden vessel has been glassed over, is there anything in and of itself, because of that fact, which would make the vessel unseaworthy simply because it was fiberglassed?"

"No, sir." This and testimony to come would counter Pollock's remarks.

When asked if it was necessary to look inside a vessel to determine its seaworthiness, he said, "Yes, sir, you probably would want to check the stringers inside the boat. You would want to check the turn of the hull at the keel to see that it was laid up sufficiently with the strength of fiberglass."

Asked to explain what he meant, Dickie responded, "As you went down towards the keel, you would lay up more glass -- you would make a thicker structure. Actually you are just using the form of the boat to actually rebuild or create a new hull."

For once, I was hearing basic truths about the structure and strengths of Iola! And when Dickie was asked about fixing the fictitious cracks Pollock and Wolfe had described above the waterline at Palmyra, he said they could be easily fixed: "Oh, above the water, absolutely."

After establishing that Dickie had been to Palmyra on at least two separate occasions, either in 1977 or 1978, it wasn't clear, Ray led him to availability of natural food resources. He concurred that it was abundant.

Following Ray's suggestion in aid of supporting the theory that Mac and muff had met with accidental death, Dickie acknowledged that a Zodiac, with which he was very familiar, could be flipped under certain circumstances despite their extraordinary stability.

About that time, King got into the act, asking if Dickie was testifying as an expert. This started a virtual firestorm of controversy. I think Ray was hoping to slide Dickie in as an expert of sorts, without going through the formal process. Dickie couldn't stay on to be recalled and qualified as an expert for the defense and Ray couldn't achieve it any other way.

Although the prosecution had not initiated any such objection, King was again objecting on their behalf, and as usual, had the last word. "You are opening up a whole barrel of fish that interferes with the government's case! When you get to your case, you can do whatever you want with respect to experts! Please, I object to your eliciting any testimony with respect to an expert now!"

Ray all but whined, "We just don't want to make him stay."

King glared. "I have done it! Now move on!"

Ray bowed to the inevitable. "Yes, yes, your honor."

"Mr. Musick, you have described that you had contact with Buck and Stephanie while you were in Hawaii. Could you fairly describe them as being persons who were, for want of a better phrase, hippy-like persons?"

And off we went again. Ray was trying to show that we were merely two of many people in those years living a free lifestyle and restoring boats as inexpensively as possible. But King was to have none of it, and after another diatribe, Ray returned to questions about seaworthiness. Dickie explained how a smaller boat is, in fact, safer than a larger one.

"If the Iola had been unseaworthy, in your opinion, would you have stated that to Buck and Stephanie before they set out anywhere?"

"Oh, yes, sir."

"And a boat like this, like the Iola, is capable of sailing, say from Palmyra down to Samoa, this kind of vessel?"

"Yes, sir."

These were good questions and I expected Ray to ask about Iola's ability to sail to Fanning, but he didn't. Instead he went in the opposite direction. For reasons known only to Ray, he asked a strange one. "Did you feel that Palmyra Island was somehow foreboding, a dangerous kind of place?"

"Absolutely, yes, sir. I had a feeling about that island."

"Can you say why?"

"It seemed to be an unfriendly place to be. Specifically why, I can't put my finger on it, but it was not an island that I enjoyed being on, particularly. I think other people have had difficulties on that island."

The obvious relevance to these questions -- which would be asked and answered again -- could only go to Muff's so-called state of mind; the weeping and fear of me that the Pollocks had claimed, as opposed to the fear of the island itself that she had expressed in a letter.

On redirect, Schroeder asked Dickie about Iola's first sinking, in Maalaea Harbor. "Now, when one fiberglasses over a wood hull," he asked, trying to nullify the points made about Iola's seaworthiness, "does that tend to indicate the wood hull is in rather poor shape?"

"It could indicate that, but not necessarily so."

Schroeder tried again. "Now, if fiberglass over a wooden hull was extensively cracked, would it tend to leak?"

"Yes, sir, if it is below the water."

No one had claimed to have seen any cracks below the waterline. How could they?

Schroeder leapt. "Now, if those cracks were below the waterline and one had no means of hauling the boat out, it would be difficult to repair it, would it not?"

Offhandedly, Dickie explained that so long as one had proper supplies, it would not be difficult to careen a boat. The rise and fall of tide on Palmyra would allow a boat, especially one with a shallow draft, like Iola, to be exposed to work on at low tide.

Schroeder made a last stab "If you had the fiberglass supplies?"

"That is correct, sir."

Of course I did have all the necessary supplies, the ample cloth, matte, resin and catalyst left over from my previous work on Iola at Maalaea. And it would have been easy to repair any cracks at low tide.

Calvin Shishido

An affable, easy-going sort of guy, husky and laidback, it was hard to imagine how Shishido had ever gotten into the FBI. Maybe because he looked like a local boy, someone who could move around in Hawaii without attracting much attention. At any rate, although he had since left the Bureau, Shishido had been the chief investigator in 1974.

He testified that he first saw Sea Wind at the Ala Wai on October 28, and he was responsible for inventorying the vessel. He had a list of the recovered items, which inventory was entered into evidence as Exhibit 16.

Enoki pre-empted a defense counsel question by inquiring about Sea Wind's logbook.

Shishido looked momentarily panicked. He obviously hadn't expected the question. "The ship's log of Malcolm Graham? I don't recall," he stammered. "I don't recall seeing..."

King asked if it was on the inventory sheet, a copy of which he was leafing through.

Enoki answered. "No, sir."

King looked puzzled. "Well, you are representing it is not there?"

"Well, I am asking if it is."

Shishido shook his head. "I don't recall seeing any logs, not by Malcolm Graham."

"Do you recall ever seeing a diary of Muff Graham?"

"No."

Had he seen either item at any time during the investigation?

"No, sir."

Later, I brought up the subject with Earle.

"Look, Buck, Sea Wind's log is gone and there is nothing we can do about it."

"Have you questioned those two FBI guys, Moroney and Tanaka? They might remember something." Their names had appeared on some of the inventory sheets.

"No, but it doesn't make any difference. The log is superfluous anyway. How can it help or hurt us?"

"The same way Muff's diary might help," I replied. "She might have written something in it about our affair, which would pretty well disprove this bullshit about her fear of me."

I went on. "You know, Earle, its possible Mac wrote in his log what really happened."

I thought he paled a little at the possibility, but after remaining silent for a few moments, he shrugged. "Doesn't matter. The log and diaries are gone. We can't get them. We have to go with what we've got."

Shishido's memory during Earle's cross-examination proved to be poor, as did, apparently, some of his thinking during his searches at Palmyra. He wasn't sure what he saw or didn't see, even large tanks. He was finally forced to admit that although he was on the island expressly to search in 1974, he had failed to wait for the water to recede from the brushline to look for bones in the area in which they had subsequently been found. And did he recognize in a subsequent search in 1981 what he had failed to do in 1974?

"No, sir," Shishido said. "At that time, in '81, my frame of mind was not that we missed it. My frame of mind was that somehow that container did somehow come ashore there and, you know, within a recent time.'

"Well, that is not my question, Mr. Shishido. What I am asking you is this: Did it occur to you during 1981, when you realized that low tide uncovered the shelf area, did it occur to you that you might have missed the fact in 1974 that the shelf might have been uncovered at low tide?"

"No, sir. I understood that the tides could go out and it could uncover, yes. I knew that, although I did not see it. I knew that it could at one time be in an uncovered state, or dry state."

"You didn't see any particular reason why you should delay the search until the shelf uncovered in 1974, is that correct?"

"That's right."

Earle swerved. "Now, in regard to the wire that was found, do you have any idea whether the size of the wire has been altered at all since you recovered it?"

"No, sir, the size appears to be the size as of when we got it."

"But you did not measure it, did you, before you turned it in?"

"Not measured in the sense of measuring feet. I measured some other measures, measured the way it went around the container. I put the wire, I slipped it over the container, and looked to see if it would fit, and it did."

"Do you remember how snugly it fit?"

"Snug enough."

I don't know how the jury saw the bumbling Shishido, or whether Earle was making any headway with his theories or alternative possibilities, but I knew Shishido had got that much right. I shivered in a brief flashback, feeling again the desperate dread I'd felt when putting the wire around the boxes, trying not to think what was inside them, what the situation was forcing me to do. I put my hand over my forehead and clenched my jaws, trying to still the acrid bite of rising nausea.

*****

After Shishido had been excused, King brought up the question of whether Earle was going to call Sharon Jordan's husband.

"At this point we don't think so," he said. "We don't think it will be necessary."

Earle had said to me, "The bitch has told her husband about what happened in court. He's pissed off about it and indicates he'll back up his wife's story. There's no point in calling him. It's not that important anyway. They still can't conclusively put the bones in the box. There'll be a lot of doubt when we get to the experts."

It seems Earle had changed his tune over the weekend, but I didn't bother to ask if he was going to testify in an effort to counter her devastating description of the bones having appeared to have been spilled from the box and scattered in a crescent shape. That would become obvious sooner or later.

William J. Eggers, III

Bouncy and eager, Eggers was a former Assistant U. S. Attorney dressed in clothes seemingly picked out in a thrift shop by a blind man. But they were attention-getting: from his puce-colored plaid jacket to his mismatched shoes and pants, he made a definite statement. Eggers, who had accompanied the search party, was questioned about the area he covered. But the real purpose of getting him to testify was to bring in my legal status. Enoki asked him about that as of October 1, 1974.

"To the best of my knowledge, he was a fugitive from justice."

As if that wasn't bad enough, Earle himself, who had previously fought to keep my history from this trial, asked on cross, "Now, you indicated, in October, 1974, defendant Walker was a fugitive. Isn't it true he was a fugitive from the charge of distributing a hallucinogenic drug?"

Unbelievable! He'd just told the jury that I was a drug dealer! Eggers, since the door had been opened, could have scored some points for the prosecution with his answer. Whether he simply missed it or merely showed some natural discretion, Eggers replied mildly, "Well, the sum and substance is that it was a drug charge, and I was sitting in court when he pled guilty, and I didn't pay much attention to it other than the fact that it involved pills."

Maybe Earle finally realized he'd put his foot in it, and tried to retrieve a little something. "Well, it wasn't for any violence, was it?"

"Not to my knowledge."

Enoki, on re-direct, had one question. What proceeding hadn't I shown up for? Earle shot to his feet and objected, offered to stipulate, tried everything he could, but got nowhere.

Enoki asked the question again, "Do you remember what proceeding he hadn't shown up for?

"Yes, I do," he answered.

"I will object," Earle insisted.

"Overruled!"

"Sentencing," said Eggers.

Dr. Oliver G. Harris

Harris, an assistant medical examiner-coroner for the City and County of San Francisco, was a forensic odontologist and dental anthropologist. As Earle had already stipulated regarding identification, it wasn't clear why he had been called until Enoki handed him a bag. Inside was Muff's oddly-splotched skull, exhibiting contrasting white and blackened areas, with empty eye-sockets, a nose-hole and the half-grin of the upper teeth. Her lower jaw was separate and broken.

It raised the planned-for gasp from the jurors.

Harris' testimony was that there had been blunt trauma to some teeth. "Because these, the roots of the lower molar tooth, #30, are deeply imbedded in bone and it would take considerable force in order to fracture the tips of these roots, and the crown of tooth #13 was fractured at the gumline. This would also take considerable force."

Regarding the broken jawbone, Enoki then asked, "Do you have any opinion as to what would have caused the mandible to fracture in the area that it did?"

"It would be more characteristic of a sledge-hammer, a ballpeen hammer, some heavy object or rock that would fracture out that section of the mandible."

The jurors were sober and wide-eyed at this gruesome revelation, some casting quick glances my way. Were they picturing me in their minds beating about Muff's head with a hammer in a mad frenzy to destroy her features?

After a suitable pause to let the implications sink in, Enoki asked if he had found any evidence of burning in either piece of the jawbone, and Harris talked about burn deposits, and then went on to say, "Well, it would take an intense fire over a long period of time to burn a tooth. These deposits I found on these cheekside surfaces of the tooth," he said, pointing out the areas. "I also found that the lower inferior border of that right side of the mandible was burned."

It was his opinion that these evidences of burning were similar to those found in the bodies of people who had died in a fire.

There were more horrified looks my way. My God, had he burnt her alive? Drenched her in gasoline and sent her into a screaming dance of agony? I felt humiliated and then outraged -- that anyone could think I would so torture another human being.

Enoki's next questions tempered this slightly, but only slightly, when it was brought out that these fractures had not occurred before death.

When Earle got up to begin the cross, he was fidgeting and moving gingerly. "May I ask the court to bear with me? I have a slight malady. Never get shingles. That's my only advice."

When he filed to get any sympathy, he turned to the dentist and began asking questions about his experience and knowledge of burning on skulls.

It appeared that Harris was not as confident or as knowledgeable of skulls as he was of teeth.

Finally, Earle asked him, "Would it help if you looked at it again?"

"Yes." The skull was passed to him, every eye following its progress. Harris eyed it, turned it, ran his fingers over it. "It appears to be raised," he said.

"That's not typical of a burn, is it?"

"I...I don't...I don't think you could really...because that might be a loss of calcium around those edges making it look a little bit raised," Harris began, stuttering slightly.

"Well, isn't it in fact raised?"

"It appears to be raised."

The questions went on, with Harris getting increasingly defensive, until King finally rescued him. "He has admitted that he is not a skull expert." He turned to Harris. "Is that right?"

"That's true."

He was fairly certain, however, that the fractures had occurred before the abrasions.

Earle pounced. "Can you definitely exclude, scientifically, that is, that there was an abrasion prior to the fracture?"

The difference was that if abrasion had occurred before, then the fracturing was caused by other means than those that might have contributed to her death.

"No," Harris admitted. "There might have been a repeat on the abrasion."

"That's what I was suggesting," Earle said, emphasizing the point. "Abrasion, a fracture, and then some kind of abrasion?"

Harris nodded. "That could happen."

Yes, and it was possible that the skull had been placed on a table and hit with a sledgehammer. "Or the sledgehammer could be in a vise and the skull could hit the sledgehammer, is that correct?"

"Yes."

"Or the skull could hit the coral reef, is that correct?" "I am not a marine biologist. I have no opinion on that." "You can't exclude that, can you?"

"I do not know the force of waves in marine biology, or the force of objects in the ocean. That is not my field."

"What I am saying," Earle persisted, "is that you cannot exclude the possibility that it was..."

"He says he doesn't know anything about it!" King shouted. "And naturally, he couldn't. He doesn't know whether it is possible or not! He just can't say!"

That about ended Harris. Earle had tried and hadn't done too badly with him. I found myself rooting for him in a sort of schizophrenic splintering of basic truths. After all, with the exception of Dickie, all the witnesses so far were out to help insure my conviction. But the fact was, most of the expert testimony was correct in interpreting the evidence in terms of Muff's body having been in the box, despite Earle's desperate attempts to keep her out of it.

John Bryden

Bryden, a native Scotsman with a bit of a burr in his accent, had transplanted himself to Christmas Island in 1969. He was on Palmyra from February, 1979, and remained until April, 1980. He had a lot to say about very little and a little to say about a lot. He claimed to have brought sixteen Gilbertese Islanders with him for work at developing a resort area for a private investor who'd leased the atoll from the Fullard-Leos and also for reestablishing the old copra plantation.

It was difficult to understand why the prosecution had called him. But, after colorful and accurate descriptions of the island and weather, it came out that it was he who had sunk the old rescue launch that the Jordans had raised. He couldn't remember any boxes on it and he'd never seen any like the one in the courtroom. To his knowledge, no human remains had been found by any of the Gilbertese because he believed they would have reported it to him since they were superstitious and would have been afraid.

He also pointed out most of the natural resources that could serve as food and opined there was no way an intelligent person could starve.

On cross, Earle wanted to make a point which King resisted. At a recess, Earle asked if he could make an offer of proof.

"Yes," King said, swinging around to him with a stern look. "You were going to go into class distinctions in the South Pacific," he accused.

Earle drove on. "Mr. Bryden would have testified from his experience in the Line Islands since 1969, he had noted that boating people are divided into two classes of people, those who tend to be well-prepared and you might call your upper class, and those who tend to be scrounging all the time, which you might call your lower or hippy class."

King looked at Earle like a bug over the top of his glasses.

"We have evidence," Earle continued, "from people that would support that they and the Grahams belonged to the well-to-do class, and quite obviously my client would belong to the latter class. We think we have a right to place that before the jury, to understand that within boating it is not an egalitarian society, that there are scroungers among the boating class and the upper class do not like these people."

King asked sarcastically if the relevance of such testimony was that the Grahams would never let me on their boat.

"No, so that the jury would understand that their class distinction exists, and my client was not unique, but rather one of a rather large class in the Pacific. The government is suggesting that my client is unique."

"As I recall it," King said, "the only person that has identified your client as a hippy is you!"

"Earle," I said, trying to contain my seething anger after Bryden was excused, King had departed, and the Marshals stood ready to handcuff me, "how do you define scrounger?"

He looked blank for a moment, then said offhandedly, "A beggar." "You've called me a boat thief and a beggar, neither of which is true and neither of which I appreciate!"

"C'mon, Buck..."

"How would you like it if I stood up and called you a faggot!

A flush of anger rushed to his cheeks. "I'm not a faggot!"

That's exactly the fucking point," I bit out. "I have never stolen a fucking boat in my fucking life and I have never fucking begged anything from anyfuckingbody -- especially not at Palmyra!"

"There's testimony says you did."

"Only from Briggs and he's full of shit! If I was so low on provisions that I had to beg on the first day, what the fuck did I live on for the next two months? It doesn't add up! And I don't appreciate you calling me a beggar. My mother and daughter have been sitting right out there," I pointed vaguely, "and I don't fucking appreciate your fucking insults and I better not fucking hear any fucking more!"

Earle's eyes were wide in shock. I had leaned over him, getting right in his face, and he had looked away. Frink was pulling at my arm in alarm.

"C'mon, Walker, chill out!"

I straightened up and turned to him, offering my wrists, the soul of cooperation. As he clicked on the cuffs, I spoke amiably with a stingy grin, "You ever tried pissing up a rope, Rollie?"

*****

Before the jury was called the next day, Earle once again plied a futile cause before Judge King, trying to exclude some of the more damaging allegations likely to come from the government's next witness, a self-convicted liar whom I'd known in prison. These included my escaping from McNeil Island, smuggling gems, guns, heroin, and so on. Though he argued valiantly, the end result was predictable: "The objection is noted and it is overruled. Call the jury."

Noel Allen Ingman

Ex-convict Al Ingman, wishing to be known as Big Al, but more popularly called Fairly Big by his less-than-respectful peers, was sworn in.

Under the witness protection program for testimony in other cases, Ingman was a known rat. Slight, stoop-shouldered, pale and fading, he promised to tell the truth, the whole truth, and nothing but with the unblushing self-assurance of one whose blood and bones are saturated with heroin. After so swearing, he had to be reminded by the judge that he could lower his right hand.

Ingman said that there had been a clique at McNeil Island camp in Spring, 1979, comprised of me, Gerry, Ollie, and himself, formed because we were all working various shifts at the powerhouse. He went on to describe each participant's role in subsequent drug activities. Imaginatively colored, he said they had been undertaken after his parole and my escape from McNeil and that Gerry had set himself up as the kingpin of a budding drug cartel.

When King offered Schroeder an opportunity to make a point, he explained that "the Witness Protection Program is administered by the United States Marshal's Service to take custody for a period of time of a witness who might be in danger of retaliation from someone he might be testifying against, and give him a new identity and move him to a new city where he will not be in danger of retaliation."

The implication was that he was in danger from me. The attorneys argued about how much of Ingman's past would be allowed before the jury. Although he had a rapsheet dating back to 1948, it was finally decided that he could be questioned only about convictions since 1964. There was also considerable discussion, out of the presence of the jury, about Ingman's drug addiction. Finally, Schroeder shook his head. "Your honor, the defense has, I would say, approximately six witnesses who are willing to appear for the defense to assassinate Mr. Ingman's character."

"I may not let him have six!" King grated, looking outraged. "I know they told me they were going to have a whole battery..."

Schroeder nodded eagerly. "They are going to testify to speculation, hearsay..."

"Your honor," Earle got in, "we are going to call his sister in." Earle was lying like a champ. It was actually two sisters, a stepmother, a niece, Gerry, and Alice Gilbert.

"Is there any reason why he can't ask him if he was addicted to heroin?" King asked Schroeder.

"No, I see no problem with that, your honor."

King studied the rapsheet. "Are there any arrests on that rapsheet that didn't turn up in the convictions? You are going to stick to convictions?"

Earle conceded defeat. "We are going to just stick with convictions."

"You may," King ruled.

"Back to 1964," Earle nodded. "We have one other thing."

"Mr. Partington, I will rule on each question you want to go into!"

"May I make a record, please?"

"On what? I haven't stopped you from doing anything yet!"

"May I make a record, please."

"What do you want to make a record of?" King was losing patience.

"In regard to the manner of this whole testimony."

"I haven't stopped you from anything yet!"

"If I can speak, your honor."

"Do you want to be allowed to do something?"

"I would like to be allowed to speak."

"What record do you want to make?"

"The government must prove..."

"Tell me what record you want to make!"

"Your honor," Earle persisted, "the government must prove, by clear and convincing evidence, that this activity that Mr. Ingman talked about took place. Now, we have a witness who is going to testify that it never took place."

"Do you have a motion pending before me to strike his testimony?"

"Yes."

"Denied!" King thundered. "Do you want to move for a mistrial?

" Denied!"

"May we have a hearing as to the foundation as to these so-called crimes he is testifying to?"

"Denied! Now, what else do you want to do?"

"I want to go into his relationship with his family and his narcotic addiction."

"When you say his relationship with his family..."

"Well, we understand he overdosed his 13-year old son and killed him in Mexico."

Between what King allowed or disallowed, and Earle failed to follow up on, we learned little about his son's death, but did establish that Fairly Big had fathered nine children along the way and eight were still living. Earle managed to elicit that two of Ingman's children were adopted by a family in Alaska, but not that Ingman had sold them, which we had both evidence and witnesses to back up. He did manage to get Ingman to testify that he had been extensively involved with drugs, running guns and other things, and that he hadn't been charged with any of it. With all of this, Earle managed to show the jury that Fairly Big was getting a lot more than money and protection from the federal government in spite of the government's claim that he had not been offered formal immunity. Ingman was not just a good citizen doing his duty, nor was he acting out of a newly acquired conscience; in fact, he admitted that were he to be convicted of the activities he hadn't been charged with, he would go away for a good long time.

With regard to my case, Ingman said that an agent had called him about me, but he had not told all he knew. However, when he turned up to testify before a grand jury about me, things changed. What few details of the Palmyra venture he had apparently gotten from his discussion with the Feds had now wended their way into his testimony.

As for the portion he made up entirely, it was so unbelievable I think even the prosecution had difficulty. In a nutshell, Ingman informed the shocked jury that, after being invited aboard Sea Wind for dinner, Stephanie and I had made Mac walk the plank! He said I had laughed while describing how the man had sniveled and shit all over himself.

It seemed incredible to me that the prosecution was sticking to this made-for-Hollywood scenario. Schroeder must have sensed how ridiculous it sounded in a somber courtroom, too, and proceeded to ask questions which the answers to would translate walk the plank into more realistic terms such as knocking out of the box, wasting, offing, and blowing away -- all of which he, Ingman, understood meant to kill.

In his turn, Earle managed to get Fairly Big to begin bumbling his way into it. He admitted that he had provided heroin for family members, including two sons. He admitted he had been addicted himself, although he fudged and mumbled many of his answers.

I waited for Earle to ask him if he had shot up that morning, but he didn't do it. Too bad. I'd been around addicts for years and had seen Fairly Big at close range both on and off the stuff. As subtle as addicts sometimes appear, it wasn't difficult to recognize the signs. Without a fix before court, Fairly Big wouldn't have been able to testify at all -- heroin helped steady his nerves and calm him down.

He, who had received over $28,000 from the government to "protect and support him," got a little foggy about exact amounts or why he got them. In reality, the perks he received were worth more than the actual dollar amount they gave him. For one thing, all warrants, as well as his criminal record, were removed from the NCIC (*National Crime Information Center) computer. This had the effect of making him a first offender if he should ever again be arrested for anything. Not that he would remain in jail long anyway before his FBI-DEA-Marshal Service sponsors came to his rescue. Not only did he have access to any amount of necessary false ID, but the fact that he had a veritable license to continue his criminal activities was best of all. The Feds did not simply relinquish a witness such as Fairly Big and allow him to go his merry way. No, they kept him on a short but mutually beneficial leash. Fairly Big was free to go out and involve himself in drug dealing activities, as he had done all his life, just so long as he gave up, every now and then, a few of his associates in criminal activities. In effect, he served as a roving undercover agent able, with his nose for drugs, to ferret out users and dealers anywhere. He could do whatever his natural talents allowed, buy and sell drugs, use them, steal and cheat to his heart's content, make as much money as he could on the side, right along with continuing to pick up cash payments from the Feds, just so long as he delivered up a sacrificial victim ever so often to the insatiable maw of the criminal justice beast. How could you beat that? There were thousands such as he, a criminal underclass that was protected by law from ever paying for their crimes.

"Well," Earle asked him, "if the government did not believe you were cooperating with them, you would not receive this money, isn't that correct?"

"I suppose so."

"And you were also providing information?"

"Yes."

And wasn't it true he had been trying to setup Gerry and Alice? Ingman nodded. Yes, he was trying to help the Feds with information on them.

In order to convict them?

"Yes."

Earle kept on, trying to winnow the chaff, succeeding here and there in showing Ingman for the liar and bumbler that he was. He inquired into Ingman's initial statement to the FBI, in the person of Hal Marshall, who sat before him to nod encouragement.

"I am not sure what I told them at that particular time," he answered nervously. "I told them a lot of things."

Hadn't he told the FBI that Walker never admitted killing the Grahams?

"He never did come out and say, 'I killed them.' There was a statement about blowing them away or offing them, or something like that.'

"Didn't you testify on direct that you understood that to mean killing?"

"I never said he didn't say that," Ingman protested, beginning to gibber. "I never told them that he had told me that he didn't say that he had never told me...or that I recall!"

"Didn't you tell the FBI in October, 1984," Earle persisted, looking up and down from papers in his hands, "that you believed, at least, that Walker and the girl had probably killed the couple, but that Walker had never come out and told you that?"

"I may have told them that! I don't know!"

"Wasn't the express purpose of this interview, as you understood it, to determine if Walker had made any admissions concerning this case?"

"Yes," he admitted. "Well, yes."

"And you lied to the FBI," Earle thundered as much as he could, rising up on his toes and pointing his finger accusingly, "isn't that your testimony?"

"Well,'" he stammered, "if that is...if I made the statement that he didn't...didn't kill them...then...I lied to them."

It went on and on in detail, Earle relentlessly pursuing into every nook and cranny of his out-of-court statements and his instant testimony. Ingman squirmed about, crossing and uncrossing his legs, pulling at his nose, rubbing his face, scratching, trying unsuccessfully between times to control his hands.

The jury had been swinging their baleful gaze between Earle and Ingman, from question to answer, and it was obvious their mood was one of contempt and outrage. The only question was, who was it directed at? Earle, for being so nasty to a witness, chivvying and bullying, or. Fairly Big, for being such a transparent liar, trying to con them with such a weak story?

I supposed their verdict would, in the end, tell the whole story. If they were to find me guilty, they must accept Ingman's story. After all, he was essentially the basic reason for a grand jury having rendered the premeditated murder indictment. How could they find me guilty and not believe him? Conversely, if they didn't believe him, how could they possibly find me guilty? I took heart from this seemingly irrefutable argument.

In and out, up and down, and round and round it wandered. Earle led him to the powerhouse at McNeil where I had supposedly told him the great story. Ingman allowed as how he had been stoned at the time, couldn't remember any details, and hadn't asked any questions.

Schroeder, in an attempt at rehabilitation, led Ingman through an all but maudlin account of what life was like on the witness protection program. Fairly Big lived on fear and permissions. He couldn't even go to a ballgame without permission. He couldn't even send his grandchildren gifts on their birthdays without having to go through the U. S. Marshals for security reasons, and Lord, wasn't it awful he was going to have to live in such a paranoid world for the rest of his life?

But at least he knew how to define himself when Schroeder asked him what a snitch was. "It means somebody who betrays his friends or associates and tells, informs," he replied.

What he left out was that a snitch's first duty is to please his masters, and what he doesn't know to tell can be made up -- with a little help.

And, of course, Schroeder clearly pointed out that Ingman could no longer be sent back to prison because of the danger of retaliation. The implication was that Ingman was a brave man for having stepped forward as a witness rather than it being the cowardly act of a weasel out to save his own ass.

Then it was Earle's turn again. One thing I can say about Earle was that he hated the little cocksucker. Throughout Schroeder's questioning, he had sat seething, his face ranging over a full panoply of disgusted looks. He knew Ingman was lying like a champ and righteously wanted to tear him apart on the stand. And I have to say that, throughout the trial, Earle's best effort was against Ingman. I thought he had effectively and totally destroyed Fairly Big's credibility. Only the jury's verdict against me could cause me to doubt this assessment.

"You have no real fear of going back to prison right now," Earle sneered, "do you?"

"No, not now," Fairly Big replied sweetly. "I am doing nothing to go back."

"You indicated, when you got strung out on heroin, you were the same as any other junkie on the street?"

"That's right."

"And junkies on the street are notorious liars, aren't they?" "They will do all sorts of things to get drugs."

"They will do about anything to get drugs?"

Ingman nodded. "When they are sick, they will do almost anything to get drugs."

"And you were like that once?"

"Yes, I was."

I leaned forward in anticipation that Earle was about to ask the question I had suggested. I had told him of my belief that Fairly Big was stoned on heroin when he'd first entered the courtroom.

"Are you sure?" His surprised eyes swung from me to Ingman.

Later on, seeing the effects of his experience wear upon him, I had said, "The motherfucker can hardly wait to get out of here so he can go shoot up again."

I had suggested that Earle ask him if he would be willing to submit himself to a blood or urine test to determine whether he had recently used heroin -- which he had claimed was all behind him -- and could detect traces of heroin residue up to three days ago. I thought it was a perfect question to close on.

Alas, Earle hadn't the balls to ask such a shocker.

When he was released from the witness stand, he was out the door in a flash and I would have laid odds the first question he asked the escorting Marshals was where the nearest bathroom was -- he would need a toilet stall for a new injection of backbone.

Dr. Douglas Henry Uberlaker

Curator of Anthropology at the Smithsonian, Uberlaker was a forensic anthropologist, his specialty being human skeletons. Although this was only his third trial, and his report had been written on a single page, I had an open mind until I learned he'd been an exclusive consultant for the FBI laboratories in 150 cases since 1977.

Enoki established that Uberlaker had examined Muff's bones in 1981, and had determined not only that the detached mandible belonged to the skull, but that the sex of the skeleton was female, 5'4" tall, and caucasion. He thought the white area on the skull had been caused by an exposure to extreme heat.

"Would an acetylene torch have that kind of heat capacity?"

"Yes."

Again, jurors were looking at me as if to consider whether I could have done such a thing. Earle objected to the leading question.

King shrugged. "Well, he has answered it already. But please," he lightly rebuked Enoki, "don't suggest the answers."

"Yes," Enoki said, satisfied that he'd gotten the reaction he wanted. He then went on to ask when the heat might have been applied.

Uberlaker's primary inclination was that the heat had been applied while the skull was covered with flesh which, beyond the burned area, had prevented the heat from radiating outwards.

His words lent a vividness to the horrible idea surely formed in the jurors' minds which, after a pause, he ameliorated by saying, "However, I must say it's conceivable that there would be other factors other than flesh which would give the same level of protection. If it were imbedded partially in wet sand or in a wet environment so that only that portion of the skull were exposed to extreme heat, it is conceivable that a similar effect would be derived."

An almost audible sigh of relief came from the jury. Was it possible someone had built a fire over her undiscovered skull in the sand to roast marshmallows?

"But," Uberlaker went on as if he were playing with the jury, "the most conservative interpretation, given my experience, is intense heat applied to a head while the flesh is still on."

"Could this intense heat be caused by sunlight, that is, direct sunlight?"

Uberlaker frowned. "I don't think so. At least theoretically, if this skull had been exposed over a large degree of time, say years, it is possible you might get that extent of calcination or bleaching with the sun, but with prolonged exposure, you would also get a type of erosion of the surface that we don't see here and it suggests that the heat source was something more intense, more direct than the sun."

The implication was clear: Muff's skull, at least, had not lain around exposed to the sun and thus confirmed the idea that it had only recently been washed up for Sharon Jordan to find.

And the rest of the bones?

They had shown a lesser degree of whitening, which could certainly be caused by sun-bleaching, Uberlaker explained. "And in my initial report, not knowing about the suggested scenarios in this case, I did find that compatible with the type of bleaching that occurs with sun exposure."

Not knowing about the suggested scenarios! The phrase rang in my mind. Someone had put ideas into his head to sway him from his scientific objectivity! Who could have done such a thing?

Since then, he said, he'd come to consider the salinity of salt water as a bleaching agent -- the immersion of a body in the sea over a period of time.

Had he noted any other wear or erosion by any other source?

"Yes. On the front left side of the skull, across the face, there is a very flat eroded area. It's fairly typical of what we term coffin-wear. If a skeleton has been in a coffin for many years, the slow movements with gyrations of the earth and freeze and thaw and these type of factors, subtle movements can actually cause abrasion of the bone against the flat surface that it's lying against and some of that is here."

The terms coffin and coffinwear had created a clear though gruesome picture in my imagination of Muff's body, her head, soon to become a fleshless skull, rocking and undulating back and forth in the box, moved about by currents, changes in pressure, the tides, and even the newly perceived "gyrations of the earth," over the long years of her immersion in the lagoon. I shook my head to dislodge the image and suddenly realized that Uberlaker had placed her in the box by his suggestive use of the coffin terminology. Earle did not object to the use of such words, whether from failing to recognize their significance in the all-but-mesmerizing effect that Uberlaker's words were having on everybody in the courtroom, or he had a plan to deal with it on cross.

Uberlaker went on to explain that there were several planes of abrasion on the skull. "The largest one is on the left side of the face at a slightly different angle. There also appears to be several smaller areas on the right side of the face."

I could not remember how Muff's body had been positioned in the box. I hadn't wanted to look. In putting the lid on to hide the grisly form, I had only glimpsed at a dark presence. But now Uberlaker's words were causing me to imagine that she had lain on her left side, necessarily curled into a fetal position, her head confined to a corner of the box. It seemed to explain the abrasions, the coffinwear. The left side was the worst, the side of her face lying against the bottom horizontal surface, the right side being less abraded from rubbing against the vertical side. I wasn't sure whether I was dredging up a long-buried memory or it was no more than a figment of my imagination suggested by Uberlaker's description. Throughout his testimony, I found myself resisting the images and the nausea they caused, and this would continue off and on whenever witnesses testified about the opinions as to what occurred relevant to the box sitting there before us. I hated that box, was sick with it, and try as I might, I could never quite banish my awareness of it.

Enoki continued. "Did you notice any abrasion on any other of the skeletal remains?"

Uberlaker frowned. "Not quite like that. Not the planal flat type of abrasion. Although several of the others, particularly the long bones do show erosion of their surfaces. In particular, the tibia, the large bone of the lower leg on the right side, seems to show a considerable amount of erosion."

The tibia was a bone between the knee and ankle, and I noticed the change in Uberlaker's choice of words from abrasion to erosion. So had Enoki, and he asked Uberlaker to explain.

"Erosion is a gradual process of rounding off the bone surfaces and smoothing out what are normally rough surfaces."

It was hardly a definition and certainly did not explain the differences between abrasion and erosion. Abrasion was caused by friction of one substance rubbing against another, the wearing away being caused by a harder substance against a softer, while erosion was a much slower process, which we normally think of as being caused by elements of nature like wind, water, and sand.

Uberlaker thought some erosion had occurred to all parts of the skeleton, but in differing degrees: By the bones more than the skull, and even more on the right tibia.

This would mean that the tibia had been subjected to erosive elements to a greater extent than the remainder of the skeleton. Had it been separated and exposed to more sun, wind, or water rolling it over sand? Had a dog carried it away? Were there teethmarks on it? How had it been returned to the rest of the bones for Sharon Jordan to find all in one area?

Enoki was not interested in pursuing the anomalies -- he was more concerned whether the good doctor knew anything about shark bites on human beings.

Yes, he did, but saw no evidence of them on the bones at hand.

What about other types of bites?

Yes, there was evidence of gnawing by carnivores, rats he thought. But a few had been made by a larger animal possessing canine teeth, perhaps made by a small dog or large cat. He described how rats, if gnawing on a body with flesh, are particularly fond of the ridged area above the eyes, as well as the large muscles on long bones.

While we were all shuddering at the idea, the question of whether the bones had been gnawed before or after the flesh had been removed became imminent. It made a big difference.

"It would be difficult for me to say exactly whether that was the case. My guess would be after. If there were a lot of rodents, and they had access to a fresh body rather than dry bones, one would expect there to be a lot more gnawing than there was."

Enoki veered to the hole in the skull. Uberlaker thought it had been enlarged since he had first seen it, but he thought that was consistent with another scientist having removed fragments for study. He had no firm opinion as to the cause of the hole, but noted that the bone in that area was very thin and could be easily damaged by a variety of phenomena.

When Earle's turn came, he immediately raised the subject of Uberlaker's bias through undue influence by others. Hadn't Uberlaker been advised to move out of a hotel where Earle was staying in order to keep' them from further discussions? Uberlaker said he thought it had to do with providing cheaper lodgings. Well, since his arrival, hadn't he met with other experts?

Yes, he had met briefly with Dr. Boyd Stephens.

And hadn't they discussed their findings?

Yes, and he had been given a copy of Stephens' report several weeks ago.

Was there any disagreement between them?

Only on the question of the extent of animal chewing. Dr. Stephens had used the word, extensive, while he wouldn't have.

And hadn't he also seen the reports of Dr. Hegler and Dr. Harris?

"Yes, I did."

Wasn't it true that intense heat on a skull that still contained a brain inside could cause fracturing of the skull as internal steam caused pressure within?

"Well, yes..."

And was there any sign of fracturing in Muff's skull?

"Not of that type, no."

Was there any evidence of burning material that did not come from the skull itself, but rather from the source of the burning?

Yes, there were residues of burning material evident in the blackish deposits on top of the skull that were superimposed over the white areas.

Earle reminded him of a conversation they'd had. "And in the course of that conversation, doctor, did you tell me that it appeared to you that the burning was years after death?"

"That is not quite right. No, it is not."

"I did note there was wear on different parts of the skeleton, but it wasn't directly beneath these black deposits. The point was -- the interesting point that we discussed -- was that the black deposits appeared to be not eroded, and that seemed to appear odd."

"Well, didn't you express the opinion to me at that time that the burning had taken place years after death?"

"The burning that resulted in the black deposits, yes."

And hadn't he concluded not only that the burning of the entire skull took place years after death, but that there was probably more than one burning?

"That is not quite right."

"In the course of that conversation that we had, didn't you tell me that it appeared to you that somebody had built a bonfire on the skull while it was nearly entirely buried in sand?"

Uberlaker, as cool as a cucumber, replied, "I don't recall saying that at all."

Earle was desperate. This wasn't going at all as he'd expected. Well, hadn't Uberlaker originally said that the bleaching of the bones had been caused by sunlight?

Yes, that was his initial determination.

And hadn't he voiced this opinion at the time of their visit? Yes.

And then he had received a visit from Enoki and Schroeder, who suggested that he was incorrect?

"No, they never suggested that I was incorrect. What did happen in the interim was that I learned additional facts in the case, and it suggested scenarios that included the possibility that there was a prolonged exposure to water, and I was asked if that would also produce a similar effect. I made that consideration, and I think the answer is yes."

As far as Uberlaker was concerned, either water or sun could account for the bleaching.

"But didn't you tell me on one of my subsequent -- the second or third visits -- that it was still your best opinion that this was sun-bleaching?"

"I don't recall saying that," Uberlaker replied blandly.

Earle fell back on an old lawyer's trick. "Could you have said it and you don't recall?"

"Mr. Partington!" King admonished, his temper rising.

Uberlaker shrugged. "I suppose anything is possible."

"Your honor, I am trying to find out if he doesn't remember."

King shook his head. "You should take an investigator along with you because you will wind up testifying most of the time!"

Earle threw his hands up. "This is my last trial! I am getting out of this business!"

King was seething. "Would you kindly not suggest that you are going to take the stand and testify to something else!"

"I do not want to testify!"

"Well, you are!" King thundered back. "Please don't do it!"

"Excuse me, your honor! This is proper impeachment!"

"Well, I am not sure about that! So let's not suggest that somewhere along the line you are going to say something that is contrary to what he said! If you are, then you shouldn't be in this case!"

"Well, I would agree with that, but I must finish cross-examining the witness and then discuss the matter with my client!"

"Would you finish cross-examining," King sneered, "and we will get more into this later!"

Earle dithered on into it, his concentration clearly disrupted. He began to argue with Uberlaker over the planed surfaces found on the skull, really niggling, and soon drew King back into it.

"I think," Uberlaker said disdainfully, "you are trying to extend what I mean by a plane to suggest something you would like me to say here."

Earle plowed doggedly on, mostly going nowhere. But he did get Uberlaker to admit, "I can think of a lot of different circumstances that would produce breakage of bone that are natural, that don't involve foul play or criminal activity."

Earle would not leave well enough alone. He was in a tizzy. He, himself, placed the bones in the box to ask what wear on them might be caused. He hypothesized them moving about in it from currents. Uberlaker helped him by adding sand, but waffled by saying the answer depended whether the box was full or not, what the extent of the movement might be, and that therefore, an exact answer was difficult.

He paused as if to give Earle a chance to intrude with another question, but Earle merely stood there with an expectant look on his face, Uberlaker continued.

"However, if there was movement, which I think you said, if ocean currents were moving the box, the bones were there, I would expect there would be some movement of bones against that box that could produce some semblance of the erosion similar to what we see on the skull."

It was incredible. Earle had set a trap for himself and proceeded to step into it. He had just helped Uberlaker to firmly place Muff's body into the box! Did he not know what he was doing? In the pause that followed, the whole courtroom had to know the magnitude of his foolishness. Earle had to know he had blundered. He tried to retrieve himself.

"Now, referring in particular to that tibia you found, isn't that a lot more worn than the other similar bones?"

"Yes, it is."

"Isn't that inconsistent with the other bones having been in a box?"

"Well, it is inconsistent with that as a general explanation for all of the phenomena that we have observed on the skeleton," Uberlaker allowed. "It certainly doesn't rule out the other bones being in the box, of it's own right. All it says that if, for some reason, that bone, to a greater extent than any of the others, was subjected to more and faster erosion -- if you ask me to try to imagine how it could happen in the box -- perhaps if there was sand also in the box, swirling around, and the box moved with the current, you could get some of that effect -- if for some reason the tibia were greater exposed to that element than the other bones."

Earle didn't know what to do with his hands. They flapped around like schizophrenic birds unable to decide where to take wing before being firmly grounded in a tight grip to the sides of the podium. He was desperate.

"In one of our prior conversations, didn't you indicate to me that you found that inconsistent with the idea of the bones being in the box?"

"I don't recall that statement at all."

Earle changed tack. "Dr. Uberlaker, if a complete humerus were found, could it have come from a skeleton that you have examined?"

"There are only two humeri in the human skeleton," Uberlaker smiled somewhat pedantically. "If the third one was present, it would have to represent a second person."

The implication was obvious -- it was a bone from Mac's body. It took me a while to recognize the significance of the idea. Earle had told me he'd found a girl who had found such a bone west of the seaplane ramp in 1980, almost a year before Jordan had made her find. It seems that Earle's reasoning was that if Mac's bones had been found on the beach a year before Muff's bones, then hers had to have been laying about all that time, too, however tenuous the logic of the connection.

Earle closed with a humdinger. He asked, after first emphasizing the burns to the skull and mandible, if there was any evidence of any burning on any of the other bones.

No, Uberlaker replied. Other than a low-level bleaching caused by sun or water exposure -- which he didn't consider to be in the category of burning.

The answer threw me for a loop. He was saying that only the skull had been burned, and none of the other bones! When I had digested that, I could only conclude that forensic science fell far short of what the powers that be would have us believe.

FBI Agent Chester Blythe

Blythe was employed as a microanalyst in the FBI laboratory where he specialized in comparison of hairs and textile fibers. His story was simple. A small bit of green cotton cloth had been found adhering to the inside bottom of the box. It was somewhat faded and, in his opinion, showed signs of having been burned. He said that had it been lying in the sun for some time, it would have lost all its color, implying thereby that it had not been in an exposed position. Exit Blythe.

FBI Agent Roger M. Martz

Martz was a specialist in forensic chemistry. He had analyzed a white substance found in the box. He had done solubility studies, infrared analyses, x-rays, as well as gas chromatography and thermotography. As a result he had found three different types of residues. One was calcium carbonate, which was consistent with the secretions of a marine serpulid worm. The second was aluminum hydroxide, which was characteristic of the decomposition of aluminum when subjected to water. The third substance was a wax like material containing fatty acids, along with calcium salts of such fatty acids. This last was consistent with the decomposition product of human fat -- it was called adipocere.

Under questioning, Martz said that adipocere is normally formed after death, when the body fat tissue is taken away from air -- an anaerobic condition -- such as under water.

It seemed on the face of it that Martz had placed a body in the box, but then with the next two questions and answers, he seemed to demolish the idea.

"Are calcium salts or fatty acids unique to adipocere?"

"No they are not."

"Are they unique even to a human being?"

"No."

He explained that other animals, as well as plants could also form calcium salts and fatty acids. Also, he did not detect cholesterol, which would have told him the salts and acids were definitely animal in origin.

On cross, Earle immediately established that the secretions of marine serpulid worms always grew on the bottoms of things in the water, the dark undersides. Martz had said that he'd found evidence of the serpulids only on the top of the lid to the box, indicating that it had rested upside-down in the water. The aluminum hydroxide could have been caused by humidity as well as immersion in water. Nor had he actually found adipocere, only the salts and acids that are consistent with it.

Why had Martz been called?

It seems someone had suggested a body might have decomposed in the box and he had been trying to confirm that.

Frank Ballentine

Ballentine, who had been operating and selling Zodiacs for 18 years, believed that it is the most stable boat you can find. He thought it would be difficult to capsize, having only ever heard of one doing so, and it in 30-foot seas at the time. He also thought it would take a 50 to 60-knot gust of wind to blow it over, if at all.

Earle's videotape of a Zodiac flipping over after its operator had fallen out backward would make Ballentine's statement seem ridiculous -- if King had allowed it into evidence, which he didn't.

FBI Agent Roy Tubergen

A serologist working in the FBI laboratory, Tubergen had received the box for the purpose of testing for the presence of human blood, and had run three different tests looking for it, the first positive, the second negative. Finally, Enoki asked him, "And did you conduct that third test?"

"Yes, I did."

"And was it positive or negative?"

Of course, I fully expected him to say positive. Why else had Enoki led him up to it?

"It was negative," he said.

Enoki moved on to the bit of green cloth, upon which Tubergen had performed the same tests. Again, a positive and a negative on the first two tests. On the third test, however, one called the ouchterlomy, which he described in great and loving but highly technical detail, using the blackboard to draw diagrams, he had managed another positive -- he had detected the presence of human protein!

Obviously preparing for contention from Earle, Enoki asked what had happened to the piece of cloth snipped away for the ouchterlomy test.

It was consumed in the examination, destroyed.

Had he photographed the test?

No, he had not. Nor had he made any notes. We were going to have to take his word for it.

Earle got him to admit that he had ran no tests to insure that the test-tubes were not contaminated. Then he asked if the crossover electrophoresis test, which Tubergen hadn't used, wasn't ten times more sensitive than the ouchterlomy test.

Not necessarily.

Did he know?

No.

Establishing that human protein was found in saliva and semen, as well as blood, Earle went on to other possibilities. Wasn't it also found in snot and urine?

Yes.

On the first test, the phenolphthalein test that had come up positive, what else besides blood will give a positive?

Well, corn, cabbage, and other vegetables, even bacteria -- many, many things.

Had he actually seen any blood, tissue, or cells, on the cloth under microscopic examination?

No.

And finally, had he tested the box itself?

Yes, with negative results all the way.

Dr. Boyd Stephens

Stephens was Chief Medical Examiner for the City and County of San Francisco; testifying 100-150 times a year. His testimony covered basically the same area as Uberlaker's, but got into more detail. He had the body rising from the bottom of the lagoon within ten days, and went on to speculate that the hole in the skull could have been a gunshot. Upon his examination of the bones, he immediately admitted to Enoki that he could not determine the cause of death. The radius and ulna bones in the forearms had transverse fractures, but the tibia bones in the lower legs had spiral fractures, which he described as breaks caused by rotation or twisting; kinds of fractures common in auto and skiing accidents. That kind of motion, he said, if done on a living body, would require great force -- hundreds of pounds per square inch. He could not determine when the bones were broken, whether before, near the time of death, or after. There was some animal gnawing on almost all of the bones, but not the skull, most done by rats.

One bone, however, could have been chewed by a dog.

Most of the bones were abraded. On the tibia, the abrasion that might have been caused by sand or coral came after the rat bites. There was no evidence of stabbing, gunshot, or dismemberment. The bones were bleached, which could have been caused by exposure to a marine environment as well as by sunlight.

Turning to the skull, which he took up in his hands to display to the jury, it was Stephens' opinion that the flat planes of abrasion on the left side had taken place after decomposition of the flesh. While he couldn't tell what specific object had caused the abrasion, it had to have been caused by rubbing against a flat surface.

Enoki directed Stephens' attention to the box. Could it, with its broad ridges, have caused such abrasion on the skull? Yes, he thought so.

After eliciting from Stephens that rats would normally gnaw at a skull, beginning around the eyes and nose, how did he explain the fact that this skull had no signs of animal gnawing?

"Well, the significance is that it suggests strongly that the skull simply was not available or exposed to the same situation as the long bones where animals could get to them."

He had separated the head from the body! But when had the separation occurred? Certainly long after death, since there were no signs of dismemberment. But if the bones had lain around for rats to gnaw on, where had the skull been? If they were separated, the skull removed from the rest of the bones, how had they all appeared together for Jordan to find?

Bones, after the flesh was removed, did not float. Thus, they could not have washed up from the bottom of the lagoon as a result of a storm, as Jordan's testimony implied. No, they had to have lain around for some time, long enough for rats to gnaw on over an extended period of time, long enough for the sun to cause bleaching, long enough for the elements to cause erosion after the rat bites.

Enoki turned to heat exposure. Had Stephens found any evidence of that?

Only on the skull and not on any of the bones!

"What type of heat was applied to the skull?"

"This is not the type of heat we see from sun exposure," Stephens replied. "We are talking about an accelerant or a gas that is burning. To calcine or burn something like that, something like 600° Celsius, which is about 1100° Fahrenheit or higher. If the bone had flesh on it or moisture in it, it takes a lot more heat to produce the effect, because you have to boil the water off to start burning of the bone."

He seemed to be saying that the head had been burned separately from the body. The accelerants could have been natural gas, propane, butane, or acetylene, although a charcoal or wood fire over a long period could have been the cause. He opined that there was flesh on the skull during burning, but could not determine whether it occurred immediately after death or at a later stage of decomposition.

Now, as to adipocere, how is it formed?

"Most commonly, it is in moist, cool conditions, without oxygen." "Is it always formed in human decomposition?"

"No, it is not."

"Is it unique to humans?"

"No."

"Is it unique to animals?"

"It is unique to animals," Stephens replied. He had never heard of it occurring from plants.

Were salts of fatty acids always adipocere?

No.

Do they occur in plants?

Yes.

After that exchange, Enoki's question as to whether Stephens had actually seen adipocere in the box seemed meaningless. Previous testimony established that no human adipocere had actually been found, only the salts and fatty acids that were consistent with it -- which were also consistent with non-human adipocere. But Stephens could see it, even now, with the naked eye, right there on the box in the courtroom, that whitish waxy-looking stuff!

"When adipocere is formed," said Enoki, getting to the heart of the testimony he was seeking, "assuming it is of decomposition, does it always form a pattern?"

Yes, it tends to hold the form of the limbs or body that formed it. But, alas, the whitish waxy stuff did not appear to make a human form on the bottom of the box!

Well then, Enoki went on, undaunted, why couldn't he eliminate that as a possibility?

"This material is kind of a soft waxy material that can touch or coat or be transferred to another surface," Stephens said, an answer far from being comprehensible. "It is for that reason that I can't say that it didn't come from decomposing human material."

Were both Enoki and Stephens punch-drunk? I was getting there from all the waffling, splitting of hairs, and trying to see every point made and unmade as both true and false. What was clear was that Enoki wanted a body in the box and that Stephens was bumblingly trying to put it there for him. Other than that, it seemed we were into absurdist theater.

Stephens believed that the burning occurred at or near the time of death, as he also believed of the hole in the skull.

And what was his opinion as to what had caused that hole. He had none.

Well, had he ruled out the possibility that the hole was caused by a gunshot?

No, he had not.

After an all but incomprehensible explanation of gas pressures from contact gunshots, as with the muzzle held against the head, coning and reverse coning effects of a projectile passing through bone in straight and tangential trajectories, he opined as how a high velocity bullet, even a .22 caliber one, could not have caused the hole because it would have continued on through the skull and there was no exit hole, nor was there any evidence, assuming the bullet hadn't the power to exit, that it had impacted anywhere against bone inside the skull.

Even Enoki had his face screwed up in a frown of concentration, trying to follow Stephens' explanations. "Just so it is clear," he said, "is it your opinion that that is a contact gunshot wound?"

"No, I can't tell you exactly what caused it."

Well, would the absence of evidence that a bullet had struck another part of the skull from inside, or an exit wound, exclude the possibility of a contact gunshot wound?

"No, it wouldn't. It is not at all uncommon with gunshot wounds to the head for the bullet not to strike the other side. The bullet used its energy in passing through the brain materials."

"What calibers?" King said, a glazed look in his eyes.

"All the way up to a .38 Special, your honor."

King was skeptical. "That still would not go out the other side?" Stephens shook his head. "Not the expanding ammunition. It can reduce all the energy going through the tough dura and other material."

Enoki handed him the .22 Bearcat revolver. Could this type of weapon inflict such a wound?

"Yes, it could."

"You are not saying that it did, you are saying that it could?"

"Yes, that is correct."

Enoki took the gun back and handed him a .22 caliber cartridge and asked if that type of ammo had any significance to the issue.

"No, it really doesn't. The reverse coning is caused by the gas pressure from the burning powder," Stephens replied. He explained that about a quart of gas was produced by each grain of gunpowder. "The gas produces the cone effect and the bullet initially makes the break in the bone."

Had he seen many such contact gunshot wounds?

Yes.

And did they exhibit the same characteristics as found on the skull?

Yes.

Mercifully, having more or less planted the seed of the idea that Muff might or might not have been shot in the head with my gun, Enoki passed Stephens over to Earle for cross.

There was abrasion after the fractures?

Yes.

Could he exclude the possibility, even the probability, that abrasion had occurred before the fractures?

No, he couldn't.

Could he determine what caused the fractures?

No.

But hadn't he said the gnawing by rats had come before the abrasions?

Yes.

Well then, if the bones were abraded in the box, the rats would have had to have gnawed them either in the box or prior to them being placed in the box?

That was true.

What effect did hermit crabs have on a dead body?

"They are scavengers, counselor. They will strip it very rapidly and, depending upon their population, rapidly can be one or two days." "If they number in the tens of thousands?"

"Then they can strip a body very, very rapidly."

The rats, would hey gnaw on a body without flesh as well as one with?

"Really both. They will eat flesh. If there is no flesh available, they go for the bones."

Wasn't the bleaching of the bones consistent with sun-bleaching? Yes.

"In fact, I think that your report said that the bleaching suggests intense sunlight, isn't that correct?"

"Yes, yes."

He had indicated that the inside of the box could have caused the planes of abrasion on the skull?

Yes.

Couldn't the outside have also caused that?

Yes.

Could he preclude the possibility that the skull abrasions occurred while the skull was imbedded in sand over coral?

No, he couldn't.

Wasn't it true that lead from bullets, when they penetrate bone, left traces on the bone?
Yes.
Had he found any traces of lead?
No.
Had the bullets he examined contained lead?
Yes.
And as to those bullets, were they the hollowpoint expanding type? No.
If the skull had been buried in wet sand, only partially exposed, with a campfire built over the top and burning for several hours, could that have caused the same effect as he had described to the irregular calcined portion at the top of the skull?
Yes.
Had he actually tested the box for adipocere?
No. He'd only seen the white spots.
"Now, you indicated that the hole in the skull was at or near the time of death. However, isn't it true that you cannot exclude the reasonable possibility that it was after death?"

"That is true. When I used that word...at or near death...I mean it could be either one. I can't tell if it was before or after."
"But it could have been a month...or two months after death?"
"That is true."
"It could have happened after all the flesh was removed from the skull?"
"Yes."
Hadn't the report of his associate, Dr. Hegler, indicated that the animal gnawing marks had been made at different times?
Yes, because some were abraded and some were not, so the gnawing occurred over several different periods of time.
"So we are talking about an extended period of time of gnawing?"
Yes, and in between there was abrasion adequate and long enough to wear down the surface of the bones.
Didn't some of the bones have rust on them?
Yes.
Was there anything in the box that could have caused rust on the bones?
No, there was nothing.
It ended on a humorous note. Stephens had been saying that he hadn't immediately gotten around to his examination and had found ant exoskeletons in the bones.
King asked, "Do you think those ants could have gotten there after they were recovered from Palmyra?"
"They could, your honor. I have not tried to make a species identification."

"They could be San Francisco ants or Hawaiian ants," King suggested.
Stephens shook his head. "They aren't San Francisco ants or Hawaiian ants or Washington ants."
Earle asked if he hadn't also found coral.
"Yes, inside the bones are coral. There is one little marine shell. There is some sandy-like debris as well."
"To your knowledge," Earle added, tongue in cheek, "there is no coral growing in the FBI

offices in Washington, D.C., San Francisco, or Honolulu, is there?"

Stephens, taking the cue, ended his testimony with, "I have suspected some coral growing in the FBI labs at times, but no, I have not proven it."

FBI Agent William Tobin

Tobin, a metallurgist, was able to use a great number of words to produce a greater number of variables, ending up that, outside of a fire in the box, apparently caused by a hydrocarbon accelerant, he wasn't positive about anything. Or if he was, it was presented with such detail and technicality, that virtually nobody in the courtroom knew what he was saying.

One example of his pseudo-scientific bureaucratese will give the essential flavor of Tobin. When Enoki had asked if he could determine how long the box might have been subjected to corrosion, he replied, "That in view of the extensive number of parameters and variables that must be known in an assessment of duration of exposure, that a conclusion cannot be reached to any reasonable scientific certainty regarding exposure of that trunk to the various elements, hostile elements in the natural environment."

When it got to Earle's turn, he asked about the hydrocarbon accelerant. "Did you put that in any of your reports?"

"No."

This went on for a few more minutes, then Earle asked him, "Did you find anything in this box inconsistent with it being used as a barbecue -- that is, without the lid on it?"

It was a dash of cold water and King didn't like it. "Well, did you look for that at all?"

"No, I didn't examine it as a barbecue grill, but I didn't find anything. I can't say that it wasn't used as a barbecue grill."

The farce continued, moving on to holes in the box, when and how they were caused and if they would cause the box to rise, assuming it was a body and not bones in the box. It ended, as it began, in confusion. No one really knew what Mr. Tobin was saying and I wondered if he did.

Herbert Daniels and Harry Steward

The prosecution wound up with brief testimony by some of Mac's old friends from the marina in San Diego. Daniels had been aboard Sea Wind many times but had never been invited when the Grahams were not aboard, and stated that the vessel was always kept locked.

This was to counter my claims that we had been invited aboard an unlocked boat. It was not brought out that no one locked their boats on Palmyra and that it was a far different situation than a busy San Diego marina.

More interesting to me was that he testified that Muff had looked up the answer to a question in her diary, thereby pointing to its existence. I whispered back and forth with Earle, trying to get him to question Daniels about it, but he said it was unimportant and there was no diary in evidence.

"Yeah," I said sarcastically, "just like Mac's logbook's not in evidence! That doesn't mean they don't exist!"

"Buck," Earle said obviously irritated, "There's no point." "There is a point," I insisted, repeating an old and useless refrain. "Muff might have written about our affair in that fucking diary!

Mac might have written in his log what really happened!"

"And how is that going to help us when we can't prove that they wrote anything at all?"

It was a good point, and shut me up, fuming. Even if neither Mac nor Muff had made entries regarding these crucial events, they had to contain something helpful to my defense or they wouldn't have disappeared. No, if either the diary or log had contained information harmful to me they would now be in evidence!

With Harry Steward, a former Assistant U. S. Attorney, who had only one point to add -- that Mac had had an acetylene torch aboard Sea Wind -- the prosecution closed the presentation of its case in chief.

The lawyers and the judge were involved in a long and boring discussion when Schroeder suddenly rose and asked to have a letter offered into evidence. I hadn't been paying much attention until I learned that it was my letter to Kit Muncey, Mac's sister. I was startled because King had rejected the same letter as self-serving in my theft trial. Then they went on to argue about technicalities. Bored, I waved and grinned at my mother and daughter, and even flashed a smile at my ex-wife. Startled, she forgot to maintain her stern observer status and smiled back, cheeks flushing. Then I began perusing the jury, drawing little boxes and making notes, wondering what they were thinking. The argument grew louder and my attention returned to the courtroom.

Earle's witnesses had not all been rounded up, and he couldn't produce a full day's worth of testimony on the spot. It turned out that Ingman's family hadn't gotten their subpoenas, and the Marshal's office wouldn't give them ticket money without them.

King was suspicious. "How long have you known that?"

"Known what, your honor?"

"Known they haven't gotten their subpoenas yet!" King roared.

"I was told two days ago."

"I am sitting over here! All I need do is pick up the phone and order it!"

"I called the Marshal."

"I don't want to hear any more excuses!"

King called the jury back to excuse them until the next day. When they were gone, Earle moved for a judgment of acquittal on the felony-murder count. He argued for and Enoki against. Finally, King put into words the attitude Earle had been telling me about for years. "I have real difficulties with that first charge," he said. After yet more argument all around, King closed the matter by saying, "I am going to grant the motion."

"Hey," I said to Earle, "you were right all along. Good argument; you won."

"I knew all along they didn't have a case on that charge," he crowed. I waved at three of the ladies in my life; the Marshals wouldn't let me approach the railing for any hugs and kisses.

Something was nagging for recognition in my consciousness, but it wasn't until I got back in the holding cell, lit a cigarette, and began pacing that it hit me.

One, the felony-murder charge had been dismissed, but not all the evidence and testimony in support of it! A large part of the charge was the alleged underlying theft or robbery. Even if King instructed the jury to put aside evidence regarding stealing Sea Wind, could the jurors do it? Would the judge so instruct them? How? Even if he did, what good would it do with my own lawyers calling me a thief?

The only way to get all that out of the juror's minds would be to start over with a new jury, but I knew King would never do that.

Two, the letter to Kit Muncey. Earle had had no objection to its introduction into evidence and, normally, neither would I. It was sincere, as far as it went, and I thought it conveyed legitimate concerns and information. But as my own lawyers had told them I was a boat thief, how would such a letter from the thief go over? Was he merely trying to cover his tracks? It was hard to separate myself from the vantage point of having written the letter to how the jurors might view it. There was no way the jurors could know unless I took the stand. And if

I did, it was me against my own lawyers, and how was that going to go over? What bothered me most was that Enoki, rather than Earle, had introduced the letter into evidence. Why?

By the time I returned to my jail cell, I was in a foul mood, depressed and pessimistic. "How's it going?" a relatively new inmate asked as I walked by his cell. "They were talking about you on TV."

He had only been in there a week or so and had been designated as under protective custody. He was always trying to strike up conversations, but I had noticed that he always shrank back out of reach whenever anyone neared him from the other side of the bars.

Being suspicious, I had spoken hardly a word to him. For all I knew he was another potential witness like Ingman, who would volunteer to testify that I had also confessed to him.

I growled, "None of your fucking business, asshole!"

CHAPTER 17
The Defense
Thursday, June 6, 1985

Having finally obtained a copy of the Jordan film, which at one point showed Sharon Jordan holding up the skull for display before tossing it into the box, he tried without success to have it shown to the jury. King took the occasion to castigate Earle some more for delaying to inform anyone of the film's existence.

Then Earle tried to get in a film-clip showing sharks in a feeding frenzy over a dead manta ray, which was also denied. He went on to read a stipulation into the record. If a Mrs. Jamieson were called, she would state that Muff had told her she thought she was not going to come back from her trip alive.

He was stipulating all over the place without consulting me. I was in no mood to agree on anything with the government. Besides that, I failed to see the value of Jamieson's testimony. Was Earle trying to show Muff as a hysterical type and her so-called fear therefore of no importance?

He had once asked if I knew Muff was into occult stuff. "No," I'd said. "What are you talking about?"

"Palm-reading, Tarot cards, astrology, all that bullshit."

"It's news to me," I said, frowning. Muff hadn't seemed the type at all.

"Yeah, apparently she read omens into all kinds of stuff." "Who says so?"

"Her friends. I talked to her friends."

"Who exactly? How many?"

"Well, Marie Jamieson for one. She's some kind of kook herself.

I don't know if we want to call her or not, get into that stuff. She'll have us riding UFOs into outer space."

It had seemed inconsequential to me, one of those weird little anomalies. I didn't believe it and I didn't care, but if Earle wanted to show Muff in that light, why not call Jamieson and let her take us all into fantasy-land? It seemed but a short step from where we were already.

Samuel Lawrence Seibert

Larry, looking younger than his years, was slim and naive-looking with blond curls and smooth skin. He had been our friend and acquaintance at Maalaea Harbor on Maui. The crux of his testimony was that he had not only seen the swordfish bill pulled from the bottom of Sea Wind and the plywood patch over the hole when it had been hauled out into drydock, but also the damaged area after I had repaired it. That was it, short and sweet.

Schroeder managed on cross to bring out that we had not only helped each other, but Larry had signed an affidavit swearing I was Roy Allen at the passport office, although he knew me as Buck. He also elicited that Sea Wind was not the same boat we had left Maui in.

"And tell me if this is what he told you," he said. "He won it gambling in a series of chess matches with a carefree millionaire and he said he also won provisions and $1,000 in cash, didn't he?"

The overall suggestion was that Larry was trying to help a friend, but had been caught out. If he would commit perjury on a sworn affidavit, then why not lie on the stand about a swordfish hole?

He would be recalled after the next witness to identify a photo taken during Iola's launching. It showed Larry on deck with Stephanie holding a bottle of champagne.

I didn't get the point. I still don't.

FBI Agent Hilton Lui

Lui and another FBI agent, Leslie Amann, had interviewed the Pollocks on October 29, 1974. Had Mrs. Pollock told them that Muff had expressed fear to her?

"Not that I recall."

If she had, would he have put it in his report?

"I would have."

Schroeder wanted to know if he or the other agent had asked whether Muff had expressed fear.

No, they hadn't.

It was an exercise in nonsense. How could they ask about fear if it had never been mentioned to them?

Charles Morton

A criminalist and forensic scientist, Morton had been asked to examine the white residues in the box and to determine whether there had been a body inside it.

Earle was still doggedly trying to keep the body out of the box.

"I found no direct evidence that would make me conclude there was a body in there. Whether or not there would be -- some of these materials that would be compatible with that -- I can't...I can't say there is anything that would exclude that possibility."

"So, in other words, you can't exclude it, but didn't find any evidence that would definitely establish it."

"That's correct."

At the mention of adipocere, King got into the act by scolding Earle over the fact that Morton had not been qualified as an expert on the subject. Round and round they went until King finally took off his bifocals and pinched at the bridge of his nose. "How you could have possibly been preparing this case for so many years and not have gotten this information in this case is beyond me!"

But, having split all the hairs, King would allow Earle some leeway to develop his line of questions in trying to separate the body from the box. If a body had been in the box and the lid had been on it, there would have been some evidence of the residue there as well -- especially since the box had apparently rested upside-down in the lagoon as evidenced by the serpulid worms on it. Without a lid, of course, the box was not a proper container -- a body would float away or the bones spill out onto the floor of the lagoon.

Had Morton found any evidence of body-patterning in the box or lid with regard to the waxy material?

"No, I did not."

On cross, Enoki tried to diminish Morton's expertise. After establishing what Morton was not: A chemist, an anthropologist, a metallurgist, a pathologist, a medical doctor, he went on to say, "Would it be fair to say that anyone who studies a lot of crimes and becomes generally familiar with tracing evidence would have the same experience as you?"

Morton narrowed his eyes at the insult, but kept his cool.

If a patterning did occur, there's nothing to say it would be washed away?

"That's correct."

There were times like this when a sort of emotional fugue overcame me, that logic had been tainted by the surreal. Threads of logic would slip away, leaving a kind of vertiginous vacuum in my reasoning processes. Enoki seemed to be trying to show that an absence of evidence was proof of the thing alleged. I couldn't retain such evanescent thoughts for long, let alone try explaining them to anyone. They came and went, leaving little behind but unease.

When Enoki was done, King looked at Earle. "I thought you said you were going to examine the wires."

"Yes, your honor."

Another dose of King's sarcasm.

"Would you?"

It seems the wire was around the box as it contained traces of a yellowish paint similar to that found on the box.

Gary Alan Sims

Sims was also a criminalist, an expert in serology, the study of blood, semen, and other bodily fluids. His purpose was to refute the FBI serologist's claim of human protein on the piece of green cloth.

His first task had been to examine the cloth, note the areas of stain, photograph, and document the findings. This was a dig at FBI Agent Tubergen, who had not documented his tests at all.

Next he removed a few tiny threads to check for blood. That test, like the FBI test, was positive. The next test, the same as the FBI test, was to determine if blood was human or animal. This time, it was negative.

Tubergen's had also been negative, but on the third, called an ouchterlomy, he had gotten a positive, which was the basis for his opinion that human protein, not blood itself, had been present.

Sims, however, had gotten a negative. But he went on to a fourth test, called the crossed-over electrophoresis, one approximately ten times more sensitive than the previous one. It, too, was negative. Even then, he had not stopped. His final test, an ammonia extraction technique substituted for the usual saline solution, indicated to him that it was not possible to state if there was evidence of human protein.

The jury would have to choose between the contrary findings of the two experts. Whether adipocere, blood, or protein from a human source had been found in the box -- each point contested by contradictory interpretations of the evidence -- would have to serve for the up-in-the-air inference that a human body had left it.

Matthew M. Jones

An expert on inflatable boats, Jones had been a professional sailboat race manager for ten years. He thought that a Zodiac with motor could be flipped by a wind of over 20 knots. To counter the testimony of a prosecution expert on the same subject, Ray asked him if such an event would leave scratch marks or damage to the wood transom, which held the outboard in place.

"I don't believe so," Jones replied.

Gerry

My old pal came in the same side door as Ingman. Unlike Ingman, I knew that cuffs, chains and shackles had been removed only moments before.

Earle quickly established that he was 41, and presently serving time at Leavenworth Penitentiary for bank robbery and a drug conspiracy conviction involving heroin. Gerry had met Ingman at McNeil Island in 1978.

"What was the defendant's attitude toward Ingman?"

"He didn't trust him very well."

"And how did he manifest this?"

"By telling me...that the man has a bad reputation on the inside, that I should be careful of him."

"Did Walker get on with Ingman?"

"Not at all, no."

"Was that a mutual feeling at the time?"

"Yes."

"How did Ingman manifest his attitude toward Walker in McNeil?"

"He...he just," Gerry began, searching for words, "I don't know exactly how to put that. Ingman is small and he doesn't like big people, and he...he always had, you know, he was always taking shots at him, you know."

"Verbal shots?"

"Yes, yes. Like, 'He thinks he is a tough guy...because he is big.' And I said, 'Well, he doesn't come across to me that way at all,' and I was always trying to mediate between the two. I liked them both at that point."

When asked when his opinion of Ingman had changed, he replied, "Well, it took place over a period of time, but of course when he testified against me at a trial in Portland, Oregon, and I had to listen to him lie for three hours..."

King turned to Gerry, skeptical. "You thought he was lying. You say he was lying for three hours?"

"Yes. Well, there is no doubt in my mind. I know my situation. I was on trial for conspiracy to distribute drugs." He went on to point out that he was a bankrobber who didn't know anything about drugs. Ingman had been into drugs all his life and had taught him everything he knew. "He got me involved...because he knew I was struggling, trying to get back in the restaurant business."

It was Ingman who'd set up a heroin operation and gotten Gerry involved in it for the money. Though he didn't say it, I knew the connection also had to do with Gerry having fallen in love with Ingman's niece, Tamee, a teenage girl at the time who'd survived in a family of heroin addicts to become an intelligent and lovely young lady.

Earle put it to him. "Were you guilty of the charge in Portland?"

"Oh, yes."

"That was bank robbery?" King asked.

"No, conspiracy to distribute heroin. I was guilty of letting Ingman talk me into getting into drugs, yes."

When Ingman had rolled over to become an official rat in order to save himself from the noose he'd felt tightening around his own neck, Ingman had reversed their roles, claiming that Gerry was the kingpin and brains of the operation.

"Have you ever been into drugs?"

"No, I have never taken any drugs or so ld an ounce or anything,"

Gerry said with a straight face. I knew his answer was partly true and partly false. I had never known him to use any type of drugs. He didn't even smoke cigarettes. He liked an occasional beer or mixed drink, but I had never seen him even begin to get shitfaced. Of course there had been our grass-smuggling enterprise, but even in that he had served only as a waypoint, a kind of middleman. He had occasionally taken possession of the grass I was procuring in Mexico and smuggling over the border, but only until customers, all of whom were my contacts, would take delivery and pay him the money I completely trusted him to handle.

Gerry's ignorance of the drug business was abysmal and he could never have gone into any drug business on his own. I had led him into the grass business, from which he had benefited. Ingman had led him into the heroin business, mainly by taking Gerry's money and promising fantastic profits, which had led him to disaster.

After mentioning that he'd been paroled to Arizona from McNeil in 1979, where he again knew me, Earle asked him where I was living.

"In Yuma for awhile; he lived in Las Vegas for awhile; various places."

"Did he live in Mexico?"

"Yes."

"Now, was defendant Walker involved in any way with this heroin conspiracy you were engaged in with Mr. Ingman?"

"No."

Earle hadn't the sense to establish when the conspiracy had begun, which was after our arrest in Yuma in 1981 -- after he had been released by mistake.

"To your knowledge, was Mr. Walker engaged in any gun-running in Mexico?"

"No. No, absolutely not."

"Were you?"

"No."

"Were you engaged in any business dealings with Mr. Walker during this period?"

"Yes, I was. I did send goods to Mexico, but they were consumer goods."

"Would you give me an example?"

"Designer clothing, cameras, video recorders, video cassettes, especially adult movies, things like that. They have a markup down there three to five times over retail value and we had a friend down there that would sell these items for us."

"And what was Walker's role in this?"

"He would see to it that the goods got down there and that I got my money back. In other words, I purchased the items, I would take them in a motorhome across, he would take them down to our friend, our friend would sell them, he would bring me back my money and we would start the process again."

All of which was true enough. After my friend, Enrique, and I had worked the deal a couple of times, using his wife, Fae, and Lena to fly to Tijuana, go shopping in San Diego, and return with suitcases full of highly salable goods, I had told Gerry about it. He began sending down similar goods with the drivers of the motorhomes. Of course he was not going to admit that these same motorhomes would return to the U. S. packed with hundreds of kilos of marijuana. Neither was I. That would be self-incriminating and the feds had no hard evidence that we had done such a thing. If they had, we would both have certainly been charged with it.

Earle asked how many times Gerry had been a criminal defendant.

"Four."

"Four. Have you ever testified at any of those trials?"

"No."

"Why not?"

"I was guilty and my attorney told me not to testify."

"Because you would have to tell the jury you were guilty?"

What a question! I could have laughed, except I had learned that the federal prosecutors had refused to make any plea bargain with Gerry. The usual deal in exchange for a guilty plea is to reduce the charge in some degree which would allow a break in sentencing. But since the prosecutors would only allow him to plead guilty to the maximum charge, he had nothing whatsoever to lose by insisting upon the full jury trial route.

"Yes, yes," Gerry replied with a straight face. After all, his answer was for the jury. "I would just as soon not add perjury to it."

Had Gerry formed an opinion as to what kind of person Walker is?

"Yes, I have. I feel he has always been a man of his word; high principles. To me, he has a lot of personal integrity."

"Is he a violent person?"

"No."

Earle nodded. "Now, going back to McNeil Island, was there ever a discussion about what defendant Walker was in prison for?"

"Yes."

"And, during that time period, did defendant Walker ever make any admissions to your direct knowledge, that he had done anything to the people whose boat he had taken?"

"No, to the contrary. He said to the contrary that he hadn't, that he had been accused of it indirectly, and that he hadn't. He said he admired and respected those people and he felt bad about that, that he was even accused of it."

"During this time period, do you find it reasonable that Walker might have made..."

King interrupted. "No, no!"

"During this time period," Earle began again.

King raged. "I have never heard of such a question!"

"I haven't asked it yet, your honor," Earle pointed out.

"You are asking for his opinion if he finds somebody else's testimony reasonable,"

King charged, stabbing a finger at Earle. "Please don't do that! If you want to make an offer of proof, ask for it out of the presence of the jury! But don't try that! Not with me!"

Earle didn't have the balls to tell King to try saving his sarcasm, sneers, and tantrums for when the jury wasn't present. No, he only said, meek as a mouse, "Very well, your honor."

He changed the subject. "Who is Tamee Cyphers?"

"My girlfriend."

"Do you have a child by her?"

"Yes, we do."

"Who is Judy Dudley?"

"Her mother."

"And who is Iris Gage?"

"That's Tamee's aunt, Judy's sister."

"And who is Winona Ingman?"

"That's Tamee's grandmother."

After a few more sneering inquiries by King as to everyone's relationship to Fairly Big, Earle established that Gerry also knew Alice Gilbert and that she was my girlfriend in the period '78-'81. Was there an incident at a get-together in Phoenix between Walker and Ingman?

"Yes. Ingman had come to Phoenix and rented a two-bedroom suite at the Rodeway Inn and we all joined him there. It was kind of like a party. And at that gathering there was six or eight people. Ingman tried to introduce Alice to heroin, tried to tell her how good a high it was and everything. And, in fact, he offered it to everybody."

Gerry paused in thought. "I think there was one other guy there that he brought with him...that they were doing heroin...and he offered it to everyone and everyone declined. And later, he cornered Alice and tried to talk her into doing heroin."

"And what happened?"

King butted in again, making Earle establish who else was there: Me, Gerry, Ingman, Ollie, Tamee, and Alice, and perhaps one or two unnamed others.

"Walker saw Ingman talking to Alice and walked over and discovered that he was trying to...talk her into shooting heroin."

"Then what happened?"

"They had a few words. He told him to keep that away from Alice, that he didn't want her fooling with it."

King was unbelieving. "Walker told Ingman?"

Gerry looked at King, stared at him for a few moments, then repeated like Mr. Rogers, emphasizing every word as though giving a lesson to a slightly retarded child. "Walker told Ingman that he didn't want Alice fooling with anything like that."

"Then what happened?" Earle asked.

"Alice walked away and Walker and Ingman had a slight argument and..."

"After the argument, what happened?"

"Well, Walker left, but the argument consisted of Walker telling Ingman to leave her alone and Ingman telling him..."

It was a long story, but the short of it was that I was a fool for not using Alice as a drug mule -- a naive person I could get on drugs and manipulate. Fairly Big thought I was a chump and a punk, a softhearted fool, and said as much. Gerry omitted the part where I had snatched the would-be godfather up by his lapels, slammed him against a wall, and stated my wishes in the matter in no uncertain terms.

"And finally Walker took Gilbert and left."

"And then what happened?"

Fairly Big had called me several more chumps and punks in my absence, went so far as to say, "One of these days I will get him! I am not going to let anybody like that talk down to me just because he is big!"

"Do you have an opinion as to whether Mr. Ingman is a truthful person under oath?"

"Yes, I do," he replied, turning to look directly at the jury. "He is absolutely a liar and a perjurer. He perjured himself at my trial, and I had to listen to it for three hours, and it is inconceivable that Walker would trust him with any type of information."

So far, Gerry had been a good witness, the polar opposite of the shifty-eyed Fairly Big.

But now it was Enoki's turn, and he was intent on doing a good job on cross. He pretty well succeeded; if I had known what was coming, I would have been sorely tempted to excuse myself from the room.

Enoki started by asking Gerry about a half dozen aliases, most of which he freely admitted to. Then he focused on two of the names Gerry didn't cop to. "I don't ever recall using that ID. I am trying to be honest...if you want to put it down there..."

"You don't remember?"

"No, I don't...I don't remember using either of those names."

That could well have been true. While the Feds might have found all those IDs, Gerry might not have gotten around to actually using some of them. That was the point, to have some unused ones in reserve in case there was a sudden need to change ID in a hurry.

Gerry was thinking. "Joe Valentine," he blurted. "You don't have that one there. I have used that one."

That was the first of only two instances when the entire courtroom unexpectedly broke out in laughter.

Enoki moved to convictions, and got Gerry to admit to armed robbery and kidnapping in Arizona in 1982, bank robbery in Utah the same year, and another bank robbery in Oklahoma in 1984. Finally, Enoki said, "And did each of those bank robberies involve taking hostages?"

"No!" Gerry said, a bit outraged. "It involved taking the bank manager to the bank and emptying the vault out."

Unlike the usual run-of-the-mill bankrobber who hit a teller's window for a few thousand dollars, Gerry took all the money in the vault -- which amounts might be in the hundreds of thousands or even over a million dollars. Technically, taking the manager to a bank in the morning before it was open was kidnapping, but it was astonishing how few of his victims had anything bad to say. One time he had sat down with Fast Eddie and me, when we were desperate for money, and explained his method of robbing a bank. The gun and kidnapping had turned me off.

"No, no," Gerry had said. "I've never hurt anyone! These guys are intelligent. They don't resist. It's no money out of their pockets. I never point a gun at them. Usually I just point to it in my waistband. I don't even have to draw it out. You want to know something? It's all a bluff! Hell, I'm not going to shoot the guy! I'm very polite to them!"

It was true. I'd read perhaps a half-dozen newspaper accounts and the victims always said how polite, considerate, and soft-spoken, how very reasonable, Gerry had been. One newspaper had dubbed him The Gentleman Bandit. Another had referred to him as Prince Charming.

Enoki veered to the crew at the powerhouse where I had supposedly bragged of murder. Hadn't an inmate known as Ollie also been there?

"Yes."

What was this? Were they going to call Ollie as a rebuttal witness? Had the Feds in the meanwhile gone to threaten him with more charges and time if he didn't come through for them? I couldn't see that he would cave in under threats or promises and began to hope that they would be foolish enough to call him. Earle would be forced to deal with what he had so ardently wished to avoid -- it would be in his lap.

Enoki changed course again, returning to the get-together in Phoenix. Didn't he know that I had escaped from McNeil Island? Gerry admitted only to suspecting it, but not asking.

And hadn't Gerry himself been an escapee at the time?

He hadn't, but he recounted an incident that occurred later.

"In 1982, they let me out of jail by mistake. I didn't escape ...it was some type of booking error or something. They still think I planned it."

He had called his lawyer the same day he was released and learned that the attorney hadn't gotten him out on a writ or bail.

"So," Enoki said, pouncing. "You knew your were supposed to be in jail during that time?"

"Yes, he told me he had not acquired my release," Gerry said, grinning. "So I thanked him."

Everybody laughed again, including me.

Then Enoki got into discussing heroin trafficking that Gerry had been picked up for after he was no longer associated with Ingman. Gerry said he hadn't actually sold any, but yes, the material in the trunk of the car was used for cutting heroin, something Ingman had taught him how to do.

Enoki kept scoring a point here, another there, some minor, others major. I sat there torn between embarrassment for Gerry and anger at Earle, who should have known all this, been prepared for it. Pathetically, he had spent a mere 15 or 20 minutes interviewing Gerry during the lunch-break.

Enoki went on to nail Gerry for the false IDs. Gerry had testified in Portland, at Alice's trial, that I had made them when he was trying to protect Alice without incriminating himself. Now the testimony was coming back to haunt him. He was trying to help me and didn't want to say I had provided the licenses, so he said he'd made them himself. There was no way out; Gerry either lied in Portland or was lying now. King, mercifully for once, told Gerry to stop talking. Gerry just sat there abjectly staring at the excerpts of his Portland testimony.

"Do you know what he is looking at, Mr. Partington?" King asked.

"Yes."

Earle had known about the problem and had not gone over it with Gerry before his testimony!

Enoki had severely damaged Gerry's credibility, but he had one last bit to add. "Isn't it true that you asked the defendant, Mr. Walker, to get you out of Leavenworth, Kansas, to testify here today?"

It wasn't true, I knew. Earle had asked me if there was anyone who could refute Ingman's testimony about my alleged statements at the McNeil powerhouse. There was only Ollie and Gerry. Since he hadn't wanted to call Ollie, Gerry was elected.

"Isn't it true you wanted to use this opportunity to escape?"

Gerry grinned. "I wish."

They sparred around. Gerry admitted nothing, but allowed as how he would make use of any opportunity presenting itself. Finally, Enoki let it go. He was not unhappy to say, "No further questions."

Galatea Eatinger

An attractive woman, Eatinger had found what she believed to be a human thigh bone on Palmyra in 1980, the year before Sharon Jordan had made her discovery. She had come to Palmyra in a group of four boats, containing eleven other people. Strolling the beach in a search for crabs one afternoon, she found a rather large bone. Very dry and clean except for a green tinge of algae, she described as about as thick in diameter as a golf ball, except for the ends, which swelled out to a little less than the diameter of a tennis ball. Remembering the case in which a couple had disappeared, she wondered if she should report this find to the Coast Guard or the FBI. Not only had all the members of the group known of her find, Eatinger had also entered it in her diary. But, not really wanting to be involved, she had later tossed the bone overboard. Eventually, she mentioned it to Dr. Richard Grigg, a marine biologist at the University of Hawaii. Grigg had accompanied Partington to Palmyra in August, 1984, and advised her to report the find to Partington. She did.

Later asked to try and identify the bone, she finally related it to a human thigh bone, the humerus, possibly the left one and described having found it approximately 300 yards east of the place where Sharon Jordan had made her discovery the next year.

Schroeder, a bit nasty, asked, "So knowing that this bone might be evidence in a murder case, you pitched it overboard?"

"That's right," she replied, undaunted. It had been a grisly thing and in the way.

"Did you go to any authority?"

Eatinger gave him a look, taking the opportunity to return the sneer, and replied, "I talked to people that I respected."

Schroeder tried to make something out of Eatinger having reported it to a defense attorney, but Earle would later call FBI Agent Harold Marshall to the stand to show that proper notification had been made and that Marshall had chosen not to pursue the matter.

*****

King excused the jury, but decided to have a little discussion with the attorneys. "I got this note from you, Mr. Partington, in which you say to me Ingman's relatives have arrived, but the hotel won't let them check in without money."

"Yes, your honor."

"This is incredible! Don't you have any knowledge about these things?"

"Well, your honor, I am living on credit cards. I don't have the money."

"Well, put them on a credit card!"

"I am not there," Earle pointed out.

King clinched his jaw muscles; his jowls were quivering. "What hotel are they staying at?"

"Holiday Inn, where we are all staying."

"You didn't make arrangements?"

"Yes, the reservations were made. I checked with the United States Attorneys and was told that the Marshals should issue them vouchers."

"Don't bother me about this!"

"I was told to ask you to order the U. S. Marshals to issue the vouchers."

"Well! I'm sure I am not getting into something that I should have a two or three day hearing on this thing! I don't know how many thousands of dollars we are spending on this case! This is ridiculous! Can't you advance them the money, or talk to the hotel people?"

"If the court will release me, I can go to the hotel."

This absurd interrogation continued until finally King, head in his hands, said, "Well, call them! I could make reservations in Paris over the phone for the Holiday Inn!

Give them your charge card number and we will settle all this business later!"

Alice Elizabeth Gilbert

I didn't really understand why Earle wanted my old sweetheart, but I think he felt she could counter Ingman's claims that he, Gerry, and myself had conspired to form a criminal organization to smuggle hard narcotics and guns over the Mexican border.

Of course I had conspired with Gerry to smuggle grass, and only grass, from Mexico.

And he had been peripherally involved in bringing American consumer goods into Mexico, but I couldn't understand how anyone could think I would engage in anything more risky than a game of tidily-winks with Fairly Big. Gerry had been indiscrete in telling him too much about our activities, had, for chrissakes, once used him to deliver money to me in Mexico.

The problem with Alice was that she had been convicted of conspiracy to distribute heroin, thanks to Fairly Big and his need to throw victims to his FBI and DEA controllers to keep his witness protection status. Knowing Alice, if she had actually delivered any heroin between Gerry and Ingman after I was gone, she couldn't have known what she was doing. I had told Alice stories about the horrors of heroin and had instilled a great fear in her. No way would she ever let anyone give her such poison.

I was glad to see her again, even under these circumstances, but I felt a deep pang of guilt. I was responsible for her situation. I'd tried to protect her, had warned her to get away from Yuma after I'd been arrested, and even arranged for $5,000 to help out. But, although she'd managed, with Gerry's assistance, to stay free for almost three years, she was finally arrested visiting my mother in California.

Alice spoke softly, having to be admonished to raise her voice. Yes, she had met me at McNeil Island in 1977 while visiting a prison cultural club. Yes, she had lived with me for two years, but had no knowledge of my running guns into Mexico or of any involvement with heroin.

Her opinion of Ingman?

"He's a liar."

"Do you like Mr. Ingman?"

"No, I don't."

Did she see anyone in the courtroom who'd visited her in prison? She pointed out FBI Agent Marshall. "He told me that he wanted to talk to me about this case. He asked me if we had ever talked about it, or if he had ever said anything to me, and I told him no." And what did she understand that to mean?

"That if I would testify to what he wanted me to testify, that he could help me out of prison."

Schroeder gave her a bad time on cross; I was sorry she had been called. The upshot was, as I had already known, she didn't know anything about drug running or guns or Palmyra.

Had she met Ingman here? There? Because her case was still on appeal, Alice took the Fifth when it came to questions on drugs and Ingman over and over again, as she had been strongly advised by lawyers and even King. Earle complained that Schroeder, through his futile questions, was testifying, and even King was becoming impatient. Finally, Schroeder made his parting shot. "Now, Miss Gilbert, once upon a time, you were friends with Ingman, weren't you?"

"No, sir." Alice was adamant.

King looked at her. "Never?"

"No, sir."

Finally excused, Alice grinned and waved. I returned her wave.

The jury was excused and the inevitable, interminable, discussions about the next witnesses began. It was finally determined that the defense would have six witnesses the next day and two late arrivals on Monday, then maybe or maybe not myself. Earle told King, "That we decide this weekend. We are still talking about it, your honor."

Earle had just lied to King. Rather than discuss the possible pros and cons of my taking the stand, we merely re-argued the contrary positions we had taken early on. Always in the back of my mind was the idea that Earle knew better than me what he was doing. That idea, however, resided right next door to the fear that he didn't.

*****

Rodney A. West

Friday began with an Air Force major with thirteen years of experience in meteorology. Assigned to Hickam Air Force Base in Hawaii, his mission was to provide accurate forecasts for military air traffic throughout the Pacific Basin.

He testified that thunderstorm activity had occurred directly over Palmyra on August 27, 1974, but had subsided and moved on by the next day. On August 30, 1974, according to his reading of satellite photos, Palmyra was subjected to light to moderate showers, which by September 1, had become a low overcast with occasional showers.

Earle got him to describe squalls as sudden gusts of wind associated with heavy showers, which could last from a few to twenty minutes. Vest said there was a good chance squalls occurred over Palmyra on the days of August 26th, 27th, and 28th, but fading by the 29th and 30th. The winds in these squalls probably reached 30 knots, or 35 miles per hour.

Earle's purpose was twofold; that there was thunderstorm activity and squalls present on Palmyra during the time-span when Mac and Muff disappeared, thus strengthening the possibility that they died in an accident -- perhaps a capsize caused, by the winds -- and also to counter testimony of the prosecution's meteorologist, Dr. Ramage.

Earle asked him about the differences between their conclusions.

"I think the most significant one...as I read his testimony...is that there were no thunderstorms in the area."

"For what day?" King asked.

"I think he talked about all of the days."

"And I assume it's your responsibility to make sure the Air Force gets the correct weather?"

"It's my job. I am going to lose it if I am not right."

Enoki, on cross, tried to pin West to absolutes, then to probabilities. The discussion went round and round until everyone, including Enoki, was confused, and King irritated.

West got through it all right and even poked a bit of fun at King and Enoki by saying, "Let me clarify...again. I'll go slowly this time."

Stuart Hilt

Earle had hired Hilt, a private investigator, in 1981. Having accompanied the defense team on their visit to Palmyra, he was able to talk about the sharks in the lagoon, and described the pieces of missing flesh and bite marks in the foolhardy dogs he had watched try, and often succeed to catch them. He had also been in an aluminum skiff out in the lagoon when a squall hit.

"We were shipping water! Very sudden, quite violent, and we didn't know if we were going to get back!"

"How many people were in the boat?"

"Five, and three dogs."

King took the opportunity to get in a dig. "Any lawyers?"

"Some lawyers," Hilt grinned. "Two lawyers, your honor."

"You were in no danger," King said.

Hilt testified to having met Galatea Eatinger and notifying FBI Agent Hal Marshall of her find.

On cross, Schroeder reprised the squall, making the point that they had not overturned their boat.

Scott Rice

A Ph.D. oceanographer, Rice testified about his findings on two samples of white powder, known to the prosecution as "wax-like white substance." He had worked on several samples from different areas inside the box, stating that they were composed mostly of salts or fatty acids.

The FBI chemist, Roger Martz, had said the substance was not inconsistent with human fat. Rice said the substance could be derived either from plant or animal cells -- there was no way to differentiate which. As is always true of professionals, and especially expert witnesses, they agree or they disagree, but the layperson, most especially the juror, seldom really understands what the argument is all about, much less knows whom to believe.

Tamee Cyphers

Tamee, 22, and a sophomore at the University of Portland, was short, blond, and compact. She was one of those rare females who exude extraordinary sex appeal. Although not beautiful, only pretty, her presence sent all the males in the room into rut. Ray was in love, all rosy-cheeked. "I asked her to dinner," he said.

"Yeah? What happened?"

"I was about the twentieth to ask since she's been here. She turned them all down."

"No shit?"

"Except for the Air Force major, that guy West. He hit on her out in the hall."

"Yeah?"

"I think she liked the uniform," he said disgustedly.

The first questions established her relationship with Gerry and Ingman. Tamee was Gerry's girlfriend and the mother of his child. She was also Ingman's niece. She knew me from Arizona.

The next batch of questions was to discuss the heroin addiction rampant in her family.

"My mother was a junkie, my aunt was a junkie, my uncle was a junkie, my step-father was a junkie, my other uncle was a junkie, and my cousin was a junkie."

"What do you mean by junkie?"

"A heroin addict."

"And do you know where this heroin came from?"

"I know it came from Al Ingman."

At 16, she had met Gerry through her Uncle Al, who offered to buy her a car if she would sleep with his friend. Although she had initially refused, she had been talk into at least having dinner. It culminated in a two year relationship and a child, a real love match.

"Miss Cyphers," asked Earle, "do you feel that you know Mr. Ingman well enough to have an opinion as to whether he is a truthful person under oath?"

"Yes, I do."

"And what is that opinion?"

"I think he is a very untruthful person."

In trying to impeach Tamee's testimony, Enoki was reduced to taking cheapshots. Wasn't she acting as an intermediary for Walker and Gerry? Wasn't she biased?

"Are you calling me a liar?" she'd demanded.

Enoki backed off. On redirect, Earle asked only whether Tamee's mother had been a heroin addict for years.

"Yes."

Judy Dudley

Tamee's mother and Ingman's half-sister wasn't a bad looking woman at 38; there was a distinct family resemblance between mother and daughter. Earle put her through the paces.

No, she did not know me; we had never met. She had been introduced to heroin by Fairly Big while in her early 20s, and had been convicted three times for possession. She said her sister, her brother-in-law, and two nephews -- Ingman's sons' -were all heroin addicts and the heroin came from Ingman. She thought Ingman would lie any time it would benefit him.

Schroeder's attempts to impeach her didn't work, but he tried valiantly to show that she had feelings for Gerry, and had banished Ingman from the family for testifying against him. I wondered how the jury was reacting to this soap opera.

Iris Gage

Judy's sister testified that she had been a heroin addict for ten or twelve years, introduced by her brother, Al Ingman.

"Are you afraid of Al?"

"Yes, I am afraid of him."

"Why?"

"Because he's very vindictive. He doesn't...if you do something to him, he doesn't like it. He's vindictive."

Asked about Ingman's veracity, she replied, "I don't really think the truth has a lot of meaning to him. He is more concerned of the benefit for him and he will stretch the truth or lie to benefit himself."

"Would he lie under oath?"

"I believe he would."

Schroeder hit on her addiction, and asked her about being a dealer. "No," Iris replied firmly, but freely acknowledged using.

Winona Ingman

Fairly Big's step-mother was 72, but still spry and alert, with a country twang that reminded me of my grandmother. She had married Ingman's father when Al was five, and although he had sometimes lived with his birth mother, Winona had mostly brought him up. She was asked about his entrance into the Witness Protection Program.

"He said that he was going to jump parole. He was going to... that he had signed up for the Witness Protection Program, but he wasn't going on it. He was getting so much money, I guess, to travel on, the way I understood it, and was going to just disappear on his own, skip out, he and his ex-wife."

Winona was emphatic about having no connection with heroin, and was outraged at being asked about convictions.

"No way! No!"

Yes, she had remained more or less close to Al throughout his life; he had treated her well. She knew about the heroin, but would not tolerate any doings like that around her.

"I guess you know your stepson well enough to know whether he is a truthful person, is that right?"

"Yes."

"What is your opinion?"

"He has never been truthful. He has more or less lived in a fantasy world, Al did. He seemed to fantasize what things should be, and lied about what they really were."

"Is he the kind of person who would listen to a story without asking questions?"

"No, no. He is really inquisitive. He wants details of everything. Why? How come? What for? And so forth. If he would listen to a story, he would want the details."

Schroeder tried to impeach her with little success; even King didn't go for some of his questions. By the time she was through, I thought even the jury looked a little put out over Schroeder's treatment of her.

*****

I spent the rest of the afternoon in my jail cell with four pints of fermented orange juice torturing myself over whether I was winning or losing. The crux of the matter was based on two points that were required to prove premeditated murder: 1. Had Muff's body been in the box? 2. Did the jury believe Fairly Big's cockeyed story that I had bragged to him about murdering the Grahams?

On the first part, I knew Muff's body was in the box, but had the prosecution been able to prove it beyond a reasonable doubt? As to the second, premeditation was fore planning. Even if the jury believed the Grahams had met their deaths by foul means, there was no real evidence that they had resulted from premeditation on my part. When it came to doubt, what was reasonable?

If I took the stand, what would I say? The truth would create confusion between Earle's chosen defense and my own. Of course, by the time it occurred to me that by not insisting on testifying from the beginning, I had basically been hoist by my own petard. My own lawyers were calling me a thief, but I would certainly refute that on the stand. They were trying to show that Muff's body had not been in the box, but it had. And the questions I anticipated from Schroeder and Enoki, well, they had to be licking their chops hoping I would testify.

Logic told me there should be strong doubt in the minds of the jurors, but what were their feelings? How could I know? Had that young girl turned a baleful accusing eye toward me? Had one of the older ladies cast a look of sympathy? That cold-looking man, had he made his mind up? Did the jury interpret my unfocused squint as an attempt to see them clearly, or merely as the scowl of an arrogant psychopath?

Well, fuck it, I said to myself, well along by then on the effects of alcohol, when in doubt, sing! "Goodnight, Ire-e-ene, goodnight, Iree-ene, I'll see you-u-u in my-eye dreams!"

"Nice song, Buck," someone called out. "But you can't sing worth a fuck!"

*****

On Monday, June 10, King excused the jury while we viewed Earle's 30-second video of a Zodiac, just like Mac's, cruising along at around 15 mph. When the driver rolled out, the Zodiac's nose rose up out of the water. The boat did a backflip and ended upside-down. So much for the testimony about the Zodiac's so-called stability.

Enoki questioned whether the Zodiac and motor were comparable, and Earle emphasized, "The same size motor and the same size Zodiac."

But King sustained the objection. That figured. He didn't want the jury getting the idea that Muff's death might have been accidental.

Earle tried again. This time to introduce another video, this one showing, in part, hermit crabs eating a fish. He lost that round, too.

"This case is not about crabs eating dead fish!" King roared.

Richard W. Grigg, PhD

An oceanographer from Scripps was next. He had been to Palmyra in August, 1984, as part of the defense search team and had spent nine hours in scuba gear going over the deeper parts of the lagoon, and another six or seven hours snorkeling. Much debris had been seen -- drums, scrapmetal, wire, pipe -- but no container from the rescue launch. He said the bottom was very stable and that there was not enough current energy to move anything, not even a box like the one in question, once the depth went beyond fifteen feet. He and his fellow diver had been down as far as ninety feet.

Enoki's cross was short and somewhat desultory, as though he were merely going through the motions.

*****

Norman K. Sanders, PhD

Bouncing in with a self-important air, Sanders appeared imposing and distinguished at first glance. He was tall and slim, with a neatly trimmed gray beard. However, his demeanor slipped almost immediately into the less attractive mien of the politician he was. He early on boastfully announced that he had been elected to the Australian Parliament, a position equivalent to a United States Senator. He had been trained, however, as a geomorphologist, one who studies the coast and the forces acting upon it. That he had been on Palmyra in 1974, and met Mac, Muff, Steph, and myself, had brought him here on this day.

Sanders claimed to have explored Palmyra extensively during his four days there, and to have gone fishing with Mac in the Zodiac several times. He said we were low on food, and he and Wolfe, his sailing partner, had traded Stephanie flour for bread, and myself canned fruit for a Buck knife. He said he thought Iola was seaworthy enough for the area.

When asked about Mac and the Zodiac, he said, "Well, Mac really was proud of his Zodiac and the speed it would attain, and we generally would go places as fast as it would go."

"Were there obstructions to boating in the lagoon?"

"It is full of junk, steel spikes that stick up. It is full of concrete blocks. At one time they had quite a large installation there, and there is a lot of underpinnings. At low tide, you can see them and avoid them, but at high tide, they would be a hazard to a small boat."

He said Mac saw Palmyra as an adventure, one of the last uninhabited islands in the

Pacific, but Muff felt it was a hostile place, as did he. He wrote in his logbook, "Palmyra, the place where even vinyl rots." He talked about the disrepair, the poisonous fish, and the sharks in the lagoon.

Sanders confirmed that, although unusual, swordfish have been known to strike sailboats.

After learning of Muff's death, he had contacted the District Attorney in Honolulu, offering his assistance, and his letter was passed on to the Feds. Eventually, he was signed on as a defense witness. When Earle asked what had been said to him in a phone conversation, Sanders replied, "A voice sounding like Mr. Schroeder's said, like, 'Well, these are nasty people. They are killers. These are nasty people, you know. Why are you working for the defense? These are nasty people.' And I said, 'Look, as far as I am concerned, they are not killers until proven guilty. I am just trying to help the investigation.'"

Earle asked, "Did you feel there was an attempt to influence you improperly?"

"Yes."

"To alter your opinions?"

"Yes."

As a geomorphologist, Sanders then testified about Palmyra, showing photographs and discussing his findings. The bottom line, in his opinion, was that Palmyra was subject to extremely rapid fluctuations in the amount of sand found along the beaches.

Getting to the heart of the matter, Earle asked Sanders, "In view of the sand movement you have testified to, what would happen to a skeleton on that beach over a period of time?"

"Well, it would be buried in the sand...it would just lay there until some action dug it out again."

That ended Earle's direct and re-exposed his theory that Muff's skull could have been buried in the sand for years until someone came along and built a bonfire on it.

Schroeder concentrated on sand movement on cross, and established that the beach where the bones had been found dropped approximately a foot and a half due to accretion, thus exposing the bones.

"I gather, doctor," he said, "that you are not saying that this did happen with respect to the accretion of the beach covering the skeletal remains, only that it possibly could have?"

"Yes," answered Sanders, "I say it as a distinct possibility, far more than a box floating to the surface and somehow spilling the bones."

"Your honor, I move to strike that as being non-responsive."

And King did. Then, speaking to Sanders, he asked, "What would be the minimum time it would take for that beach accretion to cover over skeletal remains if, in fact, it did?"

Sanders wouldn't commit himself. He said it could have been weeks, months, or years. "There is no way to tell. There really isn't."

Schroeder and Sanders droned on. They talked about the Grahams and the inhospitability Sanders felt about Palmyra, then got to threats.

"You didn't feel frightened, the least bit apprehensive, of the defendant?"

"Only his dog."

"But not the defendant?"

"No."

"Do you recall an occasion where you hid behind a palm tree because you thought Buck was going to kill Tom Wolfe or yourself?"

"Yes, I do, and that was a very frightening experience."

Schroeder then managed to elicit a fantastical tale out of Sanders, who said I had pulled out a gun while on the reef fishing with Tom and waved it around. He had been so terrified he jumped behind a palm with his machete. Then I had started shooting at fish and it was obvious that Tom had known about this the whole time.

He had conveniently forgotten that both he and Tom had come with me to the tent for the express purpose of getting the gun to shoot the fish. It had been stuck in the back pocket of my shorts, the only clothes I was wearing. It was impossible that he hadn't known I'd had it.

Schroeder had made his point, to leave the jury with the idea of a maniac wildly waving a gun around, and kept on going. Sanders had turned into a witness for the prosecution.

"If Mr. Wolfe had testified that both of you were on board that evening and that Muff had said, during the conversation, that she was frightened of Buck, would you dispute that?"

"Oh, no. I wouldn't dispute that. I couldn't dispute that."

It was time for lunch, but the inevitable arguments ensued. I mulled a question. Sanders had mentioned a tension between the two couples there, we and the Grahams, but admitted he had never once observed us in social interaction. His sense of this tension, since Steph and I had never bad-mouthed the Grahams, had to have come solely from Mac and Muff. Had the tension existed between Mac and Muff, themselves, and been mistaken as between them and us? I could never really know for certain, but from personal details I knew, I thought it possible, even probable. No matter the public facade of a marriage, there were always internal tensions that displayed themselves to the perceptive eye and, of course, I knew things about the Grahams that would never be in evidence.

Duane Spencer, M.D.

Spencer was not a professional witness, but as a Navy doctor he had dealt with considerable trauma through his years in military service. He had examined the skull and part of the mandible as well as a photograph of another piece. After a long, farcical, and incredible altercation about the presence of the other piece of mandible, and the photograph of it -- which was in Earle's hotel room -- the jury was finally recalled.

Basically, after discussing his observations in this case, Earle asked Spencer if he'd found any evidence of burning on the lower mandible.

No, he had not. Earle wanted to emphasize this point. If there was no evidence of burning other than the top of the skull, as the evidence seemed to indicate, then the prosecution theory that I had burned the entire body to destroy evidence was on very shaky ground. None of the prosecution forensic witnesses had found any signs of skeletal bones having been burned. "Did you find anything," he asked, "on the teeth that would indicate there had been any burning?"

"When we looked at that tooth, we saw nothing that led us to think that there had been burning,"

Spencer elaborated on his experience with burn victims from fires -- the Caldecott Tunnel fire, a train fire, Vietnam, auto accidents, and so on -- explaining the differences in bodies being burned both antemortem and postmortem. Grisly. Too grisly for me. Everyone was squirming uncomfortably at the detail.

Going on to discuss the abrasions on the skull and mandible, Spencer gave an example of a body in the deadman's float position -- face downward -- that washed up on shore and became abraded on the sand.

Asked if he had any disagreements with the testimony of Dr. Harris, the forensic dentist who testified for the prosecution, he replied, "In general I agreed with much of what he said, but there are some points that I disagree with."

He pointed out that after death, bone and teeth dry out and become brittle, and as to so-called blunt trauma in that state, it didn't take much force to fracture them. Therefore, he disagreed with Harris' theorizing that it had been caused by blows from a sledgehammer or ballpeen hammer, or rocks.

After Spencer was excused, along with the jury, I drifted into never-never land while the attorneys argued about the exhibits in evidence until I heard King ask if both sides rested. They did.

King wanted to be sure I understood it was my decision not to testify and that I did not necessarily have to take the advice of my counsel. Earle assured him I did. The silence lengthened as everyone waited for my response to King's next question. "That is correct, Mr. Walker?"

I met his gaze, drawing my delay out for long seconds -- my little bit of defiance. It would not be until I had read how Bugliosi had so brilliantly defended Stephanie that I fully understood Earle's incompetence, that Earle would never be in the big leagues, simply did not possess the necessary qualities. During my trial, though, even with the evidence unrolling before my eyes on a daily basis, I was unable to exorcise the fearful hope sustaining me from my own objectivity. Judgment of our fellows is all. If I could not accurately assess a man's character, I had to lose in my dealings with him. There was no way I could testify under the circumstances.

"Yes," I said, sighing inwardly. "That is correct."

At least I didn't address him by the honorific.

*****

Back at the jail, with no more fermented Vin de L'Orange to console me, I went into a deep funk of thought, black and depressive. Had the prosecution convinced the jury or had Earle and Ray managed to create enough doubt to preclude a guilty verdict?

As far as the forensic evidence went, that soft and malleable stuff, there was no way I could conceive that a reasonable person could find me guilty of premeditated murder. For every point scored by prosecution witnesses in support of a theory for murder, the defense witnesses, by going 180° in the opposite direction, not only diminished the prosecution theory but also provided alternative hypotheses for interpreting the hazy evidence toward conclusions that did not include murder.

The test was whether the jurors could conclude that premeditated murder had been committed beyond a reasonable doubt, which conclusion must exclude every other reasonable hypothesis. And, since there was no hard, incontrovertible evidence, it all boiled down to questions of inference.

On this point alone, I thought the jury, since there was no hard evidence upon which to base an easy decision of guilt, would quickly return a verdict of not guilty because of the obvious doubts arising as a matter of inferential logic. Or, they would spend a very long time arguing and trying to resolve their differences.

My greatest unease came over the question of Ingman's testimony. Jurors were admonished to observe the image each witness presented and to determine in each the degree of veracity they would accept. They could believe or disbelieve any portion of testimony, could accept or reject it totally. Would they believe Fairly Big in any important way, or would they believe his family that he was a liar and a manipulator for his own gain? If they chose to believe Ingman, I was clearly doomed. If not, how could they possibly render any verdict but acquittal?

Then there was King's insufferable behavior throughout the trial. There was no question in anyone's mind as to where his sympathies were. How much influence would his conduct have upon the jurors?

The bottom line, by all the precepts of human reason, was that the case for the prosecution was insufficient to support a guilty verdict. At best, given the eccentric differences among individuals, I thought the jury would not be able to reach a unanimous verdict -- which was fine by me. The government would almost certainly retry the case. Only next time it would be an entirely different story. First, since I had already been acquitted of felony-murder, there would be no evidence relating to boat theft, the conviction for which had been reversed by the appeals court anyway. Second, Partington and Findlay would not participate in any way. In any retrial, if I were to have my say, there would be little cross-examination of the prosecution's forensic witnesses. After all, they were basically correct in their findings, that Muff's body had been in that metal box and there had been an attempt at cremation. It was only in certain cockeyed conclusions that some of them had gone astray -- in trying to prove the prosecution theory that sadistic torture and murderous violence had occurred.

I tried to put myself in the jury's place, although I knew doing so was nigh onto impossible. There was no way I could remove all my experience of lawyers and judges, of court systems, and of prisons. There was no way I could free myself of my experience and come with an innocent and naive eye to sit in judgment in a trial. They were not my peers. There was no way they could understand my experience, no way I could teach them in their fearfully smug little worlds of hypocrisy and self-delusion.

Ah well, and was I any better? Suffering does not necessarily ennoble or enlighten. Blandness without ugliness is often mistaken for beauty. The jury would probably decide on gut feeling, plain and simple, and forget all the fancy talk.

The Verdict
Tuesday, June 11, 1985

Back in court with the jury present, King began by reading a preliminary instruction to the jury.

"At the beginning of this case," he said, "I read you a count one, which we call the felony-murder count. Count one is removed from your consideration, is no longer of concern to you, and you should not speculate for its removal. The fact it was removed from your consideration should not influence your verdict with reference to the remaining count and you must base your verdict on that count solely on the evidence in the case. So, we have one count for you, count two."

The jurors looked perplexed, blinking their eyes and looking around at each other. So they weren't to be told that the government's case on the felony-murder had been insufficient and that I had, in effect, been acquitted of that charge. No, of course not -- it might cause them to wonder about the rest of the case.

I looked at Earle, waiting for him to rise and argue that the jury should also be instructed to disregard all evidence that applied to the felony-murder charge, all the evidence that had been submitted in support of boat theft, but it was a vain wait. I did not know, although it should have been obvious, that all jury instructions had been gone over and agreed to in chambers -- in my absence, thanks to Earle.

It was time for the summations. When Enoki wasn't meandering down a trail of boredom, Partington was; each for fifty pages or so as they would turn out in the trial transcript, before Enoki closed out with an additional thirty pages. Neither was prepared as Bugliosi understands the term. They had made lists of points, in no particularly coherent or progressive manner, and went ambling about over their wimpish paths of speech. Rhetoricians and logicians would have wept.

Enoki said I was obviously guilty of murder on the evidence; Partington said no, there was a reasonable doubt.

Enoki closed on drugs and theft -- that I was fleeing a drug charge and had murdered in order to steal. "But even guilty boat thieves and fugitives don't have to make up stories about how someone disappeared if they really, in fact, disappear."

"But they didn't just disappear," he went on. "They were murdered, and when you kill somebody to steal their property, you do have to make up a story about that disappearance in order to explain how you end up with the property. And I submit to you that his story is simply not good enough because the facts and circumstances in this case show that they are simply not true. I would therefore ask you to return a verdict that does reflect the true circumstances of this case, that is that the defendant, Buck Walker, in fact, murdered Eleanor Graham."

Partington focused, albeit with a somewhat astigmatic lens, upon reasonable doubt. When he came to calling me a boat thief, I clenched my jaw to get through it.

"Please understand," he said, "that merely because he is a boat thief doesn't mean he is a murderer. It is a giant step from stealing a boat to killing someone. In fact, a very giant step. And contrary to some of the government's assertions in this case, if you steal a boat you better come up with a story where you got it. If you are a boat thief, you are not going to sail into Pokai Bay and say, 'How do you like my boat? I just stole it down in Palmyra Island.' It is not unexpected or unusual for a thief to lie about where he got the stolen property. But that is not evidence of murder. And if you could conclude that people who steal also kill who they steal from, theft would obviously be every bit as serious as murder and it is not."

Whether or not there was any identity between theft and murder, Partington had certainly managed to conclusively establish me as a thief and to provide an adequate motive for murder.

His best argument was directed toward Ingman. "You notice how Al Ingman ties it all together and he points the finger at Walker and he provides the premeditation."

He said, "If you believe Al Ingman is telling the truth, most certainly you must convict the defendant. But if you doubt that he is telling the truth, the government's case comes apart like a house of cards."

As for myself, the point upon which all my hopes were pinned, since a positive defense had not been entered, was in the fine line of logic delineating the options regarding circumstantial evidence.

Earle said, "This case is one of circumstantial evidence. Circumstantial evidence is not invalid evidence. It can be good evidence. However, Judge King will give you the following instruction: 'If the jury views the evidence in this case as reasonably permitting either of two conclusions, one of innocence and the other of guilt, the jury should, of course, adopt the conclusion of innocence.

"Note that this instruction does not say that the conclusion of innocence has to be more reasonable, or even as reasonable, as the conclusion of guilt. It simply says that if the evidence reasonably permits a conclusion of innocence, you should reject the conclusion of guilt. That's the law."

He played upon theories explaining death that precluded murder, other possible interpretations of circumstantial evidence. He contended that the prosecution had presented four possibilities relevant to Muff's death: gunshot, rat poison, walking the plank, and blunt trauma. Why, he asked, did she have to die in one of these ways?

"Now, it gets really bizarre," he said, giving his nth degree of significance to his words, "if you want to think into this. Why do they have to have a double murder? Why can't they have an accident and a single murder? Why can't it be a double accident?

"Why can't there be any number of possibilities," he asked and that was what reasonable doubt was all about.

In the end, he summed up, the government's case came down to four minus two equals murder. "Ladies and gentlemen," he remonstrated, "we all learned in elementary school that 4 - 2 = 2! If the government wants to prove murder, they are going to have to do a lot better than they have done here in the last two weeks!"

"Brilliant! Simply brilliant!" Ray ecstatically whispered to me as Earle concluded. I came out of my stuporous funk long enough to wonder if I could talk him into passing me a little of the potent stuff he'd obviously been smoking.

Enoki's rebuttal, his second chance at summation and the final words that would close out the case contained, among his rambling presentation, two clever and perhaps persuasive points.

One was about the wristwatch Sharon Jordan claimed to have found in the separated lid of the box. Although no one could identify it as belonging to Muff, it was a woman's wristwatch with a silver-colored metallic watchband; and if you looked at the photo of the Grahams "you will see that on her left wrist appears to be a silverish colored band remarkably like a silver watchband."

It was a sly point, there being no hard evidence the watch was even connected to the case other than it was found in the same area as the bones. Enoki, suggesting the significance of the watch for the first time, was hinting to the jury that they could draw any inference they pleased.

Earle was up to complain. "Your honor, I must object to this! This is not rebuttal and I have had no opportunity to address this!"

"Your understanding is that you have had no chance to answer," King said, brushing him off by saying somewhat facetiously he would tell the jury that.

But Enoki's best point had been made a few minutes before. "When the defense talks about what one scientist can say and what that scientist can't say, it is isolating one scientist's view. You don't have to take an isolated view. You can use all of the circumstances in the case."

Was he telling them that since the prosecution had called more scientists to the witness stand that the balance should therefore shift in their favor? But that was only an introduction to the real heart of what he wished to stress.

"A scientist can't use Sharon Jordan's unrefuted and, for that matter, unforgettable testimony about how it looked to her – like the box had tipped over and spilled the contents...out where the bones were found."

It being bad enough that he had to look up to the jury, Enoki rose up on his toes to lift his short stature to deliver his most telling point.

"I would submit to you that her testimony alone was worth at least ten other experts coming in and saying I found this and I found that in that box, because she saw it there, and she told you what she saw -- it looked exactly like the bones came out of the box!"

After Enoki had finished, King lullabyed us all in the final glut of words by droning out the instructions.

U. S. Marshal Roland Frink, otherwise known to me as Rollie, the fink, was appointed to supervise the jury.

Within a couple of hours or so I was back at the jail. I hadn't even had time to change from my court clothes into the wrinkled garish orange overalls comprising penal garb before the Marshals were back to inform me a verdict had been reached.

In my personal experience, a quick verdict had twice previously told me that I had been acquitted. But all a quick verdict really meant was that the jury had their minds made up before they retired to deliberate. I thought, and would believe for several years, that Earle had, for once, hit the nail on its head when he stated that if the jury believed Fairly Big, they must find me guilty, and if they didn't believe him, they must find me not guilty. The rest of the case against me simply had too many loopholes to remove all reasonable doubt.

I had braced myself like a gambler that needs a particular card to win a hand. Or perhaps it was more like a loser who hopes against hope that the system he is caught up in really does work in the interests of justice. But a quick glance at Rollie's eyes told me I was not to be disillusioned.

"How do you find?"

"Guilty."

Bugliosi reported that I was tight-jawed and grimacing, as though steeling myself, and that after the verdict had been rendered, I raised my gaze to glare murderously at the jury. My only memory was that I was trying my damnedest to show absolutely nothing. To show emotion was to show weakness. I would not provide a show for anyone's sadistic pleasure. But poor young and gullible Robyn Shaffer saw something else. She reported that if she lived to be a hundred, she would never forget the stone-cold anger directed at her.

As I was led out of the courtroom, thankful that my mother and daughter were no longer present for me to see their eyes spilling over with tears, Rollie said, "If you ask me, your lawyers were the best thing the prosecution had going."

"Nobody asked," I muttered.

To me, it was the height of irony that it would be Judge King, during his all-but-constant castigations of my lawyers, who had inadvertently stated the essence of the trial when he said, "Maybe I'm operating in never-never land where rational thought is irrelevant."

No maybes about it.

###

CHAPTER 18

My only consolation -- an empty one -- was the inescapable conclusion that, as crooked as I was, I was more honest than the time in which I lived.

Sentencing had been set for three weeks down the road. I endured the commiserations of my jail mates and had a good drunk on some jail-brewed fermented orange juice. The hardest chore was rising up out of the lethargy of my shock to call friends and family with the news. There wasn't much to talk about but love.

It was while talking to someone on the phone that a nearby TV got my attention with an item on the news and I learned that Gerry had escaped.

It seems that following his court appearance for me, he had been shipped to the federal pen in El Reno, Oklahoma, along with a Joe Dougherty whom I'd never met, to await court appearances on a bank robbery indictment. They had somehow managed to get out of their handcuffs, overpower the two marshals, and relieve them of their weapons. They took their clothes and left them in their birthday suits to play ring-around-the-rosy handcuffed about a tree.

I broke out into laughter. I couldn't help it. But my laughter was cut short when I heard the announcer say: "Federal authorities are reported to be in possession of information which leads them to believe that the fugitives are heading to San Francisco in order to break out recently convicted murderer, Buck Walker, a member of their gang."

Shades of the Tacoma scam! The cocksuckers were going to do it all over again! It had worked like a charm three years before when I'd been going back and forth to court on my prison escape, and now some sly fed had dusted it off for a rerun. Goodbye Lompoc, hello Marion.

Sophisticated criminals like me, who could call in favors from the Mexican Mafia and who commanded his own gang of bank robbers, could expect no less than the highest and most onerous security considerations.

The parameters of the sorry joke began to enlarge the very next day when two serious young marshals showed up to lend their best efforts to stymie the plans of the bankrobbers. They would not be able to break me out of the SF jail if I weren't there, ha-ha. They would take me over to the Oakland jail, throw me into solitary confinement, and hold me incommunicado.

As in Tacoma, there went the lead car and there came the chase car, all loaded with serious men armed with automatic weapons, me chained in the backseat of the middle car. If that weren't enough, the earnest young marshal literally riding shotgun in the front passenger seat reversed himself so he sat with back against the dashboard where he could level his sawed-off 12-gauge shotgun at my face.

"You make one fucking funny move," he snarled in a fair imitation of Clint Eastwood in a Dirty Harry movie, "you even breathe too hard, I'll blow your fucking head off!"

Who was I? Houdini? I sat very still for so many eternal seconds, feeling a kind of madman rising up inside, a heady sense of freedom emerging from all chains of fear. Found guilty of murder, a sentence of life to come, and a cruel vision of years of rotting away, what did I have to lose? What else could they take from me? It must have been that sneering smug look in his eyes, eyes that glittered with perverted lust, that did it, the attempt to intimidate.

I suddenly leaned forward to put my chin on the backrest, pressing my forehead against the barrel-end of the shotgun. "Go ahead, you cowardly piece of shit," I breathed in a very quiet, calm, and reasonable tone. "Blow my fucking head off."

I don't know which came closest, me getting my head blown off or him shitting his pants. It was a tossup. My consolation was seeing, sensing, a sudden stark fear rising up in him. Of course he'd like to shoot somebody. It would put him into a special category -- a combat-experienced cop who'd downed a bad guy or, in the mafia vernacular, made his bones -- a fantasy I'd bet he'd played with more than once.

Only it wasn't like the movies in real, close-up life. His Dirty Harry snarl hadn't instilled the cringing fear of cinematic portrayals. No, he was feeling the fear, the sudden, sickening rush of adrenaline. What the hell, it was how so many of these assholes became adrenaline junkies. Only now he'd unexpectedly overdosed himself.

He actually pulled the shotgun away from my grinning face and feebly tried to push me back with his free hand. When the gun swung toward his partner, the driver ducked and tried to push it away.

"Hey, what are you, crazy or something!" the would-be killer cried.

"Get that fucking thing out of my face," the driver shouted, swerving over the lanes of the Oakland Bay Bridge.

He pointed the shotgun at the ceiling and shoved me back in the seat. I started laughing. I couldn't help it.

"What are you, nuts," he screamed, panting in deep gulps of air, his voice quavering with tension. "You wanna die, you crazy motherfucker!"

"Hey," I grinned. "You want to shoot someone and I got nothing to live for. Maybe we can work something out. I don't give a fuck."

"You sick fuck! You try something like that again, I'll blow your fucking head off!"

"Boo!" I cried, lunging forward again. He flinched and pulled the gun back again. I went into hysterics. I just couldn't help it. I really didn't give a fuck if he blew my head off. It was the most comical thing to imagine this idiot trying to explain a double-handcuffed, double-leg-manacled prisoner in the backseat with his head blown off. "Well, he tried to escape! He tried to jump me!" I could imagine him stuttering self-righteously to a bevy of raised eyebrows.

I only half-recognized the moment as a type of satori I'd never quite experienced before and for the next ten days I more or less remained in a fetal ball contemplating the lint in my navel and trying to fit it all into a proper Buddhistic perspective.

Soon enough they were pulling me out into bright light, people moving, the sun and fresh air, me in now wrinkled and smelly court clothes, for the drive back to SF to get my prescribed dose of medicine.

When Earle asked me how I was, I didn't deign to answer. A silence had taken hold of my innards and I hadn't spoken a word since my arrival at the Oakland jail. Nobody really needed words from me -- except perhaps for reassurance. I only followed orders, did as directed, and kept my mouth shut.

Earle spoke to King. King said the matter before him represented "a particularly heinous crime," before sentencing me to life imprisonment.

I meditated. King, in all his long career, had never had the pleasure of sentencing anyone to death. If he only knew how much more sadistic it is to make a man spend forever in the narrow confines of a prison cut off from all the pursuits that made him human, he, and others like him, would not bemoan the lack of a death penalty. I almost felt sorry for us both that he couldn't sentence me to be hung and to shit on the floor below as he watched. Would he have the nerve to watch? If so, would he toss his breakfast?

The courtroom drone went on while I treasured, tried to touch, that perfect ball of silence within. Under the laws then in effect, I would be eligible for parole -- not that I would ever get it -- in ten years and so therefore let us run this little sentence consecutive to all others.

But gee, said Earle, the mandatory release time is thirty years and the defendant would be around eighty by then, so why go overboard? Apparently there are too many dangerous 80-year olds about already. Did the defendant have anything to say?

I considered suggesting an exercise to the judge and all officers of the court that involved sexual congress with rolling donuts, but was too innately polite, as my reputation well advertised, to offer such crudities. For the sexy court reporter, I smiled and winked, but I could see she didn't know how to handle that.

Being blessed without the ability to communicate by speech and symbols except in the most primitive way, animals had a lot going for them. They had no knowledge of the curse of Babel, which caused such sickness in men.

In silence, chained like a wild animal, I rode in the armed caravan to some small airport on a military base and was put on a plane and, in time, arrived at the small airport at Marion, Illinois, where a caged van was waiting to take me home.

I was conducted straight to the segregation unit and placed in a cell by myself, as usual, much refreshed after a shower and an issue of fresh prison garb. The word went around. I had a few friends who had had the news before I arrived. They sent down coffee and cigarettes. Since I hadn't had any coffee for almost two weeks, that first cup was delicious.

A couple of guys were calling down their sympathies.

"Hey, what the hell," I called back in the time-honored bravado of the convict who refused to wear his hurt in public. "Ain't nothin' for a stepper! I'll do this bit hopping around on one leg!"

"Shit happens," someone called.

"Nah," someone else replied. "Shit doesn't just happen! It's created by assholes!"

Sounded right to me. I thought of a little refrain a friend of mine had written during our amateurish attempts at establishing a poetry workshop, the words having somehow become indelibly impressed upon my mnemonic neurons from twenty-five years before:

Fuck the world
An' all 'at's in it.
If'n any's good,
I'm agin it.

The next day, my case having been considered by the powers that be, since I was one of the few model prisoners at Marion, I was restored to my status in B-Unit, the same I had enjoyed before being taken out to court some seven months before -- except I was no longer approved for transfer. I would spend another year before again being considered for transfer.

I read, I watched TV, following all the soaps and game shows, catching old movies late night. I played chess and poker with guys who, though congenial enough, took games seriously. Since I was the best chess player in the unit at that time, and the second or third best poker player, the other two being secret teammates when we'd get a game up to relieve the suckers of their money, it provided a few extra amenities.

Then one day, returning from picking up trash in the new miniscule exercise yards constructed since the lockdown, one of my duties, I found myself sweating and out of breath. I had let myself go, preferring the life of the mind to the physical. Why give a fuck? I wasn't going anywhere that appearance counted. I wouldn't be going to any shindigs requiring a tuxedo. I got on the scales and saw numbers attached to my weight that established some sort of new record. Keep this up, I thought, and a heart attack would let me cheat the government out of a lot of time. It was comforting in a way, but too easy. I was stubborn and contrary. I did not want to die in prison and I would not make it easy for the government or myself.

I set up a system of exercise and began jogging in place. I quit smoking cigarettes and went to three cigars a day. In six months, I was doing 500 sit-ups at a whack and running several miles a day. I lost 60 lbs. and felt great.

*****

It was February, 1986, and Steph's trial was about to begin. I had written to Earle to convey an offer to Bugliosi of my willingness to be called as a witness at her trial. I had a plan to help Steph. If Bugliosi called me, he would have first stab at questioning me and could structure them so that the answers would be helpful to her. Of course, I had no intention of confessing. But, under cross by Enoki and Schroeder, the fact that I had already been convicted of the alleged crime would surely be brought out. Yes, of course, her jury could believe a murderer sat before them. If anyone was so direct and impolite to ask whether I had, in fact, committed murder, I would answer truthfully, no, of course not -- but with an evil sneer and maybe a bit of maniacal laughter. I would draw upon all my acting ability acquired so many years ago in the

San Quentin Drama Workshop, to hesitate, gulp, and shift my eyes about uncomfortably, to make the jury disbelieve me. I would disguise my innocence as guilt. I would go in without having shaved in several days, getting dark bags under eyes all red-rimmed from lack of sleep (perhaps an all night poker game), and I would look seedy and disreputable. I would not wear my glasses so that I had to squint to see, appear to be glaring. I would pull a sort of reverse sting like Marlene Dietrich had done in Witness for the Prosecution. And if there were any questions I didn't wish to answer, why, I wouldn't. I could either mockingly take the 5th Amendment or, if King wouldn't permit that and ordered me to answer, I could tell him in open court to go fuck himself. What could he do? Give me a bunch of chickenshit little sentences for contempt of court?

If handled right, and Bugliosi was certainly capable of milking it for all it was worth, it could have been played to an award-winning performance. The jury could be made to believe, without me ever having to actually say so, that I was a cruel, vicious murderer who had only kept the innocent Stephanie in the dark and used her gullibility toward my own evil aims, used her goodness as camouflage.

But it was not to be. Perhaps he distrusted me, perhaps he wanted all the glory to himself. A few months before, federal cops had begun showing up again trying to intimidate me into helping them recapture Gerry. But there were no threats or promises they could make.

Bugliosi got wind of these visits and worried that I was making a deal to testify against Steph for some remission of sentence. There was nothing the feds could offer, short of a Presidential pardon or a transfer to camp where I could escape again, that could lighten my burden. For the great psychologist he touts himself to be, the discerning judge of character, he somehow managed to misread me at every turn.

But Steph was acquitted and I experienced some sense of relief. At long last, she could get on with her life. I imagined she would make a nice bundle of money out of the book Bugliosi would write trumpeting his singular accomplishment.

* * * * *

A couple of months later, on May 1, 1986, Bruce Henderson wrote me a letter to introduce himself and to say that he was collaborating with his co-author, Bugliosi, and Stephanie to write a book about the case. He had attended both my trial and Steph's.

He said that since major sections of the story would be told through "the eyes and mind and character of Stephanie," he had been spending, and would spend a great deal more, time in her company.

I wondered offhandedly if Steph would suck and fuck his brains out. Why not? It would assure her a great role in the book.

He went on to say that he had never counted on being able to interview me. I would doubtless have an appeal working and been advised not to talk about the case. But Stephanie had strongly suggested he write and try to visit. He said, and it warmed my heart, that she had always spoke well of me and was still struggling against accepting the prosecution's theory of the case. But could I, perhaps, provide background and things from my childhood to "aid in fleshing out your character in the book and depicting you both honestly and accurately." We could avoid any topics I didn't like, but the book would be written whether I provided input or not.

"What I find myself writing," he said, the words rising up eloquently, "is more than a tale about two mysterious deaths on a deserted isle. It is predominantly a love story. There is the love that Mac and Muff shared, strong enough to cause Muff to do something she didn't want to do (sail) and be somewhere she didn't want to be (Palmyra). There is the love that you and Stephanie shared, which, given the adversities you endured during your years together, might have been an even stronger bond."

He wrote: "Steph says I should be sure and find out from you what conditions were like in San Quentin when you were there. (I can see SQ from the deck of my home.) To this day, she gets chills when she tries to recall your vivid descriptions. Come on, Buck, don't hold back. I want the readers to be shocked and appalled as Stephanie was when she first heard about life there."

"Your writing is a treat to read," he wrote back on June 24th, after I had responded in a small way with 20 pages or so about life at San Quentin. "You are informative and entertaining, a balance that some professional writers find difficult to achieve. The content was right on target in providing me with the sort of material I need in order to paint your character as a breathing, feeling and thinking human being."

He sent me one hundred dollars and promised to send a further thousand for another hundred pages. "I would love," he said, "to see some material from you about the trip from Hawaii to Palmyra. Was it really as bad as some accounts?"

Of course, I was pleased by the compliments, believing them genuine, but the bit about our voyage to Palmyra in Iola threw me for a loop. Bad by some accounts? Whose? Who was there besides me and Steph? I didn't recall it like that at all. A few hardships, sure, but also some thrills. Most of all, I remembered the adventure of it. What was Steph telling him? Did she have some agenda I knew nothing about?

Yes, I would provide my perspective of our voyage to Palmyra, and would he care to hear my account of my first meeting with Steph, which I thought he might find amusing? Before going further, however, I required a personal note from Stephanie.

I had hopes she would write me privately and provide a return address. I was curious to see how all this had affected her. Perhaps we could correspond a bit and she could provide some idea of the angle she was playing. I was more than willing to go along with whatever it was. Lurking like a restless fugitive hiding in a cave was the idea that somewhere along the way, if it seemed a good thing to do, I would tell her the truth. I would let her know not only to reassure her if she needed it, but that I had loved her by my actions more than I had ever stated in words.

Henderson wrote again in July with no mention of Steph. "By the way," he said, "the jury gave no weight to Ingman's testimony; several jurors told me they cancelled Ingman against Gerry (as one inmate against another)."

Needless to say, I was stunned. The foundation of my logic as to why the jury had found me guilty, the assumption that they had believed his lies, began to quake and crumble. I floated about for days wracking my brain in search of an anchor for my reasoning processes.

I couldn't get a handle on it. I wrote back to ask him to please provide "A report of all you know as to the jury's reasoning processes in reaching their verdict. What were the deciding factors in their conclusions? At least they didn't believe that lying little asshole, but knowing that now it's beyond me how they came to their verdict in view of the circumstantiality of the case. For instance, how did they conclude murder had occurred, let alone that I did it? I didn't think that had been proved by the evidence. Did my not taking the stand have anything to do with it? I've heard very little about the jury's thinking and I'd appreciate your input."

Before receiving a reply, I was transferred from Marion to Lompoc. I wrote to inform him of my change of address. In his response, he said, "Regarding your interest in my observations at your trial, I think that will be best done when we meet in person."

Attached was a note from Steph:

Dear Buck,

It isn't easy to write after all these years. Bruce wanted me to let you know that it's OK for you to discuss our relationship with him. Bruce is really a nice guy and I'm glad you're talking with him and providing information for our book. I'm busy in my career selling business phone systems and getting on with the rest of my life.

Puffer sends wags and licks.

Stephanie

No return address. Okay. Either she didn't want any contact -- so she could get on with her life -- or, more likely, she'd been strongly advised by all and sundry to maintain a separation. Her career? Business phones? Stephanie? My dope-taking, grass-dealing, eternal-free-love-hippy-seeing-the-world-through-Parest-capsule-colored-glasses taking up a career in the straight world? It was hard to imagine.

"Our book," she'd said, identifying with Henderson and Bugliosi, but excluding me. It was her story. Okay, I got the message. I would play along. I would leave off her complicity in my crimes. She would not be my partner in the pakalolo business. I would omit the raw sexuality of our relationship, the open-ended arrangements. I would not badmouth her in any way. I would say only good things about her, which wouldn't be difficult at all. I would let Henderson's questions serve as clues to what she may or may not have told him.

I got busy writing. I saw no harm in relating the story of how Steph and I had met. The bit about her dealing grass and me helping her so I could get a date would probably be omitted anyway. I wrote of acquiring Iola, rebuilding her, and the voyage from Maui to

Honolulu to Kauai to Palmyra -- even a little about the island and the people there, including Mac and Muff.

On October 2, Henderson wrote to inquire of progress.

On October 8, I sent him the hundred pages I'd promised. I was done with it. I had other things on my mind. I had the beginning and ending of a novel. All I had to do was fill in the space between them.

On October 31, he wrote to acknowledge receipt. "You've done well, Buck," he said. "I particularly like the description of your early life and your relationship with your father. Some of the other scenes you've written overlap what my narrative will be covering from Stephanie's perspective (naturally). So, that material is less usable for the book."

Then he tried to stiff me on payment. "Questions will surely arise," he wrote, "as I integrate portions of your material into the book, and your answers to them are part of the work I've hired you to do."

There are two areas you didn't address yourself to that I would like to ask you about. 1) Can you give me any details on your departure from McNeil Island? Apparently, you're somewhat of a legend up there. My God, Buck, isn't the Sound frigid? Was the seaplane piloted by CIA-trained dudes? 2) How should I portray your activities and life during the years from mid-1979 to mid-1981?"

He had ruined my prison supper of fried liver. "We had," I fired back, "a simple and straightforward contract that even a microcephalic couldn't misconstrue." To let him know I wasn't anyone's hireling, I reminded him of our deal in McGuffey Reader terms:

1. Bruce will ask questions (done);
2. Buck may select the questions he wishes to answer (done);
3. Buck's answers shall run to 100 pages (done);
4. Bruce will pay $250 upon Buck's acceptance of the above agreement (done);
5. Bruce will pay $250 upon receipt of the 100 pages (not done);
6. Bruce will pay $500 when his book is published (who knows?).

"I have discharged my obligation. You want to welsh, that's on you, only let's not call a screwing anything but. If your attention is still with me at this point, I'm going to chance saying this just once: You deal straight, I pick up the cards, I play straight. I conduct myself according to a personal code of honor, however trite that may sound. I know honor is a word that is disappearing from the rat mentality so popular in today's society. Be that as it may, when I have the choice I deal only with those who are, in the argot of my current milieu, standup. Your niggling copout failure to pay the amount owed endangers the position of trust I have so courteously bestowed upon you."

Good old Brucey was restrained in his reply. He hoped I'd found my outburst therapeutic, but nevertheless, from his viewpoint, "I found your letter to be juvenile and insulting." He had waffled around the terms of our contract but he hadn't expected me to feel cheated -- he was sorry for that. And he was going to pay me, "because I too am a man of my word."

Things were never quite the same between us after that and I would remember that last comment with some bitter irony some years down the road when his and Bugliosi's book was finally published.

I returned to my own pursuits. As an autodidact, I would become even more so by a voracious tendency to read everything in sight -- magazines, newspapers, and books of every stripe and fancy. I would be as much a scholar as circumstances permitted, the sublimation of the Zorba in me for his Appollonian boss. And I would continue to write, exhausting hundreds of ballpoint pens in millions of words. Pedantic, pedagogic? No, not at all. Let me conform my works to my basic character -- to be entertaining rather than pretentious. Give a good read, be amusing, startle the reader every now and then. Try to remain sane in an environment that drove you toward insanity. My imprisonment, if nothing else, presented me with a great opportunity to discover and develop at last any latent writing talent.

The Last Dinosaur was about a man of principle who had orchestrated a daring and spectacular robbery, an explanation of character and the changes in people resulting from their association. I was working on filling the space between my beginning and ending, a self-defined potboiler of all potboilers, a Mickey Spillane in the guise of a Thomas Wolfe, my twist that my hero would escape his enemies in the end, the elaboration of a pipedream.

In 1987, by then a few hundred pages into it, I experienced another of my rare satoris. Prison life being what it is, it occurred to me, then 50 years of age and healthy as a good workhorse, that I might nevertheless be living on borrowed time. Given the randomness of circumstance so pervading our lives at any given moment, we are all susceptible to instant and unexpected death. Even more so in prison.

How many dozens and dozens of men had I seen or known of who had met sudden and violent death over the years of my imprisonment, most times for the most trite reasons imaginable? I had seen men killed by mistake, for chrissakes, assailants, acting as hit men for a third party bearing a grievance, attacking the wrong victim. Once, at McNeil Island, while a crowd of convicts exited a movie in the auditorium, I noted several ahead of me in a drunk and boisterous state. One of them, a particularly vicious and stupid thug, said, "Aw, shit, I just feel like stabbing some punk!" His pals urged him on -- it had been a dull movie and they could use a little excitement. But who, they wondered, considering the crowd around them. They saw no enemies nearby, no one they had a grudge against.

"How about him," one suggested, pointing out a quiet, retiring type, a bookworm who kept to himself.

"Who?"

"That lop with the glasses. The one with the funny haircut, looks like a fucking rooster."

"Yeah, an asshole if I ever saw one!"

"Fuckin' faggot-lookin' motherfucker!"

Two quick stabs with a homemade shank coming out of a sleeve and the guy was down and dead in no time, the crowd parting to walk around him with only a sidewise glance, not wanting to be involved, minding their own business. Death, silent and creeping unawares, giving no reason anyone could understand -- just one of those weird things that happen.

In the frame of mind that such thoughts engendered, the idea confronted me in all its stark simplicity that should I meet a similar fate, the truth of what had happened at Palmyra would never be known. I had never told the full story to anyone. Oh, I had told Earle, when he'd finally surprised me by asking, an abbreviated version consisting of no more than the barest facts. I really didn't have to explain to family and friends, and those who believed the worst of me weren't likely to be persuaded otherwise.

So why the desire to tell the story? Ah well, me boyo, that was the question, wasn't it?

First, because, as anyone knows who has been wronged, who has experienced false accusations, there is instilled a burning sense of injustice and, even though justice is a concept all but impossible to define, we all believe in it and seek it. It burned my ass no end that I had been placed into a category of human garbage which I held in the utmost contempt -- men like Ted Bundy, Lawrence Singleton, Wayne Gacy, Son of Sam, Charlie Manson, etc. ad nauseum.

Second, my family and friends deserved an explanation, if for nothing more than to confirm their beliefs in me. Especially my daughter, who was too young and inexperienced to really understand everything that was happening to her father. I loved her dearly, and it killed me to see that love returned tinged with tentativeness, doubt, and questions glistening in her eyes, needing some affirmation that she had not been born of a monster. And I being unable to sit her down and explain, only able to say, "No, sweetie-pie, it's all bullshit, and someday I'll be able to explain it to you."

"But why," she asked so earnestly, "why are they doing this to you?"

How could I tell my darling child, growing so quickly through puberty and becoming a woman that the why of it was the most difficult part of her education as an adult human being and that it was a process that lasted forever? The young are little concerned with things very far in the past or future.

So I decided to write it out, mainly those crucial events at the heart of it all. It would, once I had started, become a bit more, a condensed version of the case itself, a repository of my emotional reactions as well as the plain truth. Perhaps, now that I fancied myself as having some latent talent for stringing words together, I could impress upon it a certain style, even a bit of old frustrated poetic license, make it an arresting, enlightening, and shocking document.

I labored away for a month or so to turn out 60 or so pages, which I entitled A Mystery of the Sea, a phrase taken from Bettencourt, the lawyer who'd represented me in the theft trial.

I showed it to a close friend, a guy who'd been around the pike a time or two, who, under the quintessential conman's cloak of complexity, had a very down-to-earth, no-nonsense approach to things. He, too, aspired to be a writer. He would go on to publish a book of essays that had been printed over a period of several years in a major California newspaper. We had read each other's stuff and talked endlessly about writing, our ideas for stories, situations, and characters.

"Wal," he opined in a country-boy twang originating out of Fresno and not-very-distant ancestors migrating out of the South. "It's about what I expected, I guess, you lettin' your dick get you in trouble."

When I thought about it, I realized it was a very succinct observation -- even if it did make me feel foolish.

"How's it read?"

"Overall," he said, pulling at the shaggy handlebar mustache, "it's a damn fine piece of writing. You got a way of making phrases Thomas Wolfe would envy, sonorous, rolling, poetic."

He was just the opposite, simple and straightforward, using adjectives with great economy, the next best thing to Ernest Hemingway, only a thousand times more funny.

"So, it's okay?"

"For what? You going to try publishing it?"

"Nah, fuck, who would be interested? Just a memorial to the truth, you know. File and forget." I shrugged, then as an afterthought "Maybe I'll send it to a couple of people."

"Yeah," he smacked. "I do have one criticism."

"What?"

"When you get to tellin' those things at the heart of the whole damn thing."

"Yeah?"

"You're tryin' too hard. You're tryin' to be literary, for chrissake!"

"Literary!" I cried, embarrassed. It showed my pretensions.

"Yeah, fuckin' literary! Just cut out all the fancy language. You're trying to put too much meaning into it. It's basically goddamned soap opera! Just tell it straightforward, like you'd tell it to me when we're walkin' and talkin' on the yard. Forget all those fuckin' literature and poetry professors!"

It was the best advice I ever received, but I would ignore it at the time. I sent away to Washington, D.C. for the papers to have it duly copyrighted. It was now on file with an official government agency.

The next year, 1988, I'd re-established contact with my ol' pal, Rick Cluchey, from San Quentin days. I had seen a movie called, Weeds, starring Nick Nolte, which was a fictional takeoff on Rick's prison experiences as an actor/director/producer in a company he had formed called Barbwire Theater.

My old pal said he was writing a book about the San Quentin Drama Workshop. He was getting in touch with some of the fellas seeking their reminiscences and would I care to contribute?

I promptly sat down and wrote a 50-page piece called The Q-Factor, trying to rein in my literary pretensions to pen something stark and hard-hitting. I only succeeded in places, other times letting it all roll up over me like a festering sore. If my truths were awkwardly attired, strutting, and sometimes full of anger or grief, then fuck it, by God, because even then an irrepressible humor poked through the cracks and that was just the way it fucking was. I was no Jean-Paul Sartre, or even a Truman Capote, with a detached clinical eye. Neither did I have their genius. I was a by-God-Buck-fucking-Walker and I was going to write Buck-fucking-Walker no matter how many influences were working at me from all those writers I admired.

Rick was stunned.

I pushed my broom and swung my mop in my lowly duties as cellblock janitor, and worked my Walter Mitty dreams into my novel.

In May, 1990, I heard from Henderson. He wanted to quote from a letter and poem I had written to Stephanie from McNeil Island in 1978, and thoughtfully included copies of them. I found it interesting that Stephanie had saved them.

"Your letter of May 5," I wrote, "caught me at a critical point in the final pages of my novel, The Last Dinosaur, where all loose and devious strings of plot and character must be tied together into a neat bow. So, although it was a surprise to hear from you, I can't say it was welcome. You've succeeded in distracting me with a letter and poem from a dozen years past.

"The first was an illumination, the lighting of a dim room where an old self sat collecting in the dust of memory. I see, even then, the glaring little jewel of my impulse to write, its facets of ambition uncut, the polish of confidence unapplied.

I gave him permission. Sure, quote away. Since he claimed for about the half-dozenth time to be near publication, I rethought a proposition I had flirted with several times since writing A Mystery of the Sea. Would he and Bugliosi be interested in including a statement from me in their book, one going to the very heart of matters? Perhaps I would include The Q-Factor. But on condition -- if they were interested, they were to be included as is, word for word. If not, they could make no reference to them.

I sent the proposal.

Sure, he replied. He'd like to see the material and agreed to my terms.

I sent the two pieces.

"I must say, Buck," he wrote, returning them, "your scenario of events on Palmyra reads rather well; engaging, exciting, even sexy. Our book, however, is not the proper forum for you to tell this story. (If you had testified to it, that would have been different, of course).

"I do have a problem with your version. I can't see you (or anyone) remaining mute at trial to protect the virtue of a long-dead casual lover. And I can't see you doing so for the added motivation of keeping the painful truth from Kit and Stephanie. It doesn't add up."

I quickly reread A Mystery of the Sea to see how he could have arrived at such a trite conclusion regarding my silence. Well, I could see where he might have leapt to such a simplistic conclusion based upon there being no mention of the long battle with Earle over whether I would testify. Henderson had assumed that the initial and subsidiary considerations in concealing knowledge from Steph, and thereby in some incredible stretch of his rubbery reasoning saving Muff's reputation from the soap opera odor of promiscuity, were primary reasons.

File and forget.

*****

Over the several yeas since my trial, the meaning of a life sentence had finally sunk in, which, when it happens, is a time of utter depression and hopelessness. I had had an appeal pending and a new lawyer to handle it, a guy named Riordan in California.

After an exchange of letters over the two or three year course of the appeal, I was not deluding myself that it would do much good. When I read the brief, which seemed well-written considering it was quite limited as to the issues it addressed, I was disappointed. When I brought up the question of King refusing to read instructions as to lesser included offenses, he sent me a couple of pages of transcript which he said had rendered the issue moot because I had refused to waive the statute of limitations as to lesser included offenses. In addition to reading the two pages differently than he interpreted them, I knew fucking-A-well I had never been offered the opportunity to waive them.

I dug out my copy of the transcripts and had to read them in their entirety -- in itself a study in tribulation -- to find where in the trial they had occurred, and when I did it outraged me all over again.

Once again I was asking myself whether Ollie's suspicions were correct. Had Earle been on my side, however ineptly, or had he been a planned disaster planted by King? Or did the feds have their hooks in him to insure he would take a losing course while putting on a show of advocacy? It was easy enough to consider every paranoid idea.

One of the issues on appeal was King's allowing Ingman to testify as to our alleged partnership in smuggling drugs and guns. Riordan assured me that were the issue to be presented before a California State court of appeal, he could guarantee a reversal, but he was not at all sure how it would go over in the federal system.

I tried to convince him that I had never been offered, or even discussed with Earle, the opportunity to waive the statute of limitations, hadn't even been aware that it was possible to do so. I even researched the question and came up with a leading federal case holding that the proper procedure was that a defendant must be offered the opportunity. Riordan said Earle had refused for me. I pointed out that he had no right to do that without consulting with me and, besides, I hadn't even been present at the hearing and, besides further, I had not waived my right to be present (although Earle had). I was incensed.

The only obvious recourse to enter the issue on appeal was by making a claim of ineffective assistance of counsel. Lawyers are reluctant to proceed against their brethren on matters of competency. Riordan made it clear he would not do so. The only alternative was to try it on my own. But it had been my experience that inmate-generated appeals find little favor with the courts.

 File and forget.

*****

 By 1990, after almost four years at it, I completed The Last Dinosaur. I had been sending letters to publishers, including an outline and two or three chapters. Nothing. I had written to dozens of literary agents. Nothing.

 I tried to console myself with the fact that the modern classic, The Fountainhead, by Ayn Rand, was rejected by twelve publishing houses before one took a chance and the book went into reprintings for the next 25 years. Wasn't that the story of every tortured author writing his heart out who was worth a damn anyway? Hadn't Jack London in his Martin Eden clearly delineated the process? I ignored Mark Twain's advice to write for three years without pay until someone offered to pay, but if no one did, the would-be writer should take that fact as a sign that he was intended for sawing wood. I preferred Jessamyn West's advice to aspiring writers to take chances, to risk making a fool of oneself -- even risk revealing the fact that he is a fool. Was I in for the long haul or the short term? Who was I to bemoan a lack of instant success? What was three years to a lifer? So far as I was concerned, I would continue to push broom and swing mop rather than saw wood. I would patiently await incontrovertible proof of West's final proposition while waiting to die of old age -- if not surprisingly sooner -- in prison.

 Buck, me fine ol' boyo, I said to myself, you've got plenty of time, nothing but, to establish yourself as a writer. Quit'cher ferking around and jump in both feet first. Ask yerself the question 10 years from now.

 Being into the "terrible lizards" by way of analogy for certain disappearing values, I wrote another novel which I called A Dream of Dinosaurs, a bittersweet little story, somewhat roman-a-clef, about a couple of escaped convicts establishing a grass-smuggling enterprise with their womenfolk, a kind of love story.

 By early 1991, I was done with it and working on a plotline and characters for my next novel. But a number of inquiries began to pour in, the beginning of a 3-year long distraction. There was one from Inside Edition, another from Hard Copy, and more. They all wanted on-camera interviews. It seems And The Sea Will Tell, Bugliosi's and Henderson's book, had finally hit the bookstores. A two-part miniseries movie was due to be aired in March. A media blitz was on.

 I considered it. I had seen a few segments on both Inside Edition and Hard Copy and thought there was too much sleaze involved. It was Globe, Star, and National Enquirer on the air.

 I could imagine what they'd do to me. I had never been treated kindly, not to mention fairly, by the media, and distrusted them. I declined all offers to appear on-camera.

 Then I read the great hoax of a book by two sleaze-artists of a different order, allowing the full import of the insult to my intelligence to sink in. Overflowing with self-righteous anger, I spent the next three years transferring furious words to some 2500 pages of a reply. My trial alone covered 820 pages.

 Even though in places it rose up to the demands of difficult arias, overall I know it was a bad job. I had wasted three years of my life on it. Well, not entirely wasted. After all, it had provided three years and 2500 pages of writing experience.

 But enough of the insanity, me boyo, file and forget. Return yer pristine self to the saner pursuit of another novel. By 1997, I had finished The Piano Man, my most purely fictional work to date and rollicking good therapy for my recovery from the disaster of my foray into non-fiction.

I pushed my broom, swung my mop, and plotted a fourth novel. But then circumstance, time, and a gossamer thread tied to an old friend drew me back to unfinished business. A relationship and correspondence reaching back almost forty years through the near and intimate, the far and dispassionate, the tapestry rich with color to threadbare and faded -- a woman, wouldn't you know, reached out to me and said, "Let's settle the hash of those clowns, finish the unfinished business of the past. We're near our rocking chairs on the front porch and we need tranquil minds to enjoy the view."

And so I returned for a last visit, to relive it all, retell it yet again. To remember.

BOOK II
THE VOYAGE OUTWARD

"So long as he kept moving he would be all right. For men like himself the ends of the earth had this great allure: that one was never asked about a past or future but could live as freely as an animal, close to the gut, and day by day by day."
--Peter Matthiessen
At Play in the Fields of the Lord

"I went to the woods because I wished to live deliberately, to confront only the essential facts of life, and see if I could not learn what it had to teach, and not, when I came to die, discover that I had not lived."
--Henry David Thoreau
Walden

"You are what you do. A man is defined by his actions."
--Kuato
Total Recall

"Alas for he who never sings, but dies with all his music in him."
--Oliver Wendell Holmes

CHAPTER 1

Who is Buck Walker? I am tempted to answer in the words of Lewis Carroll, "I can't explain myself, I'm afraid, sir, because I'm not myself, you see." I have had many names, as well as many selves, over the years and a story for each, but most of those are my secrets because they are not relevant here. You will hear about Roy Allen and a few others.

My true name is Buck Duane Walker. Most people think Back is a nickname and I've taken a lot of kidding over it. Buck Rogers to Buck Owens to Bucky Bug, a comic strip character out of the thirties. Just plain Buck, not a nickname or a diminutive for Buckley, Buck- Minster, or Buckingham. Just Buck, as in you're out of luck, Buck, go fuck a duck. People pass the buck. That's because I ain't built for speed. You've heard the phrase, buck it up to the top? Yep, always figured that was where I was headed. The buck stops here? Sure, baby, but only because you got a nice smile. What does a wild bronc do? That's right, buck. Buck is masculine, the male of the species. A young buck is bold, brave, and vigorous. Buck the system? That's me. You got enough bucks, you're rich. Buck up, kid, 'cause without me, things are gonna get worse.

Although I've answered to many names, including numbers and epithets, it was my impressionable young mother who, through some naturally pregnant whim, caused the named Buck Duane to be entered on my birth certificate in September, 1937, when she named me after Zane Grey's hero in <u>The Lone Star Ranger</u>. She told me this at a fairly early age, including the observation that since his life, after trial and tribulation was satisfactorily resolved in the final chapter, why, so would be my own, and I should always believe in that. However, I never got around to actually reading the book until 1983, when I chanced upon it in a library at the U. S. Penitentiary at Marion, Illinois, which in that same year would be transformed into the ultimate prison in America, the replacement for Alcatraz..

So who is Buck Walker? Is the Buck Walker of, say, 1945 related to the one who was sentenced to San Quentin in 1956? Is the Buck Walker who went in the same one who came out? Is the man of 1974, a critical year in this account, anything like the one in 1991, or the more mature one of 1998? There are genetic theories and social theories, but in the end "a permanent self is nowhere to be found." (Open Secrets, Walter Truett.) It seems that every explanation for character must fall short for the information not available for inclusion. Nevertheless, we must assume that some pieces to the puzzle are better than none, and so continue the quest to find and fit them together.

As a boy, I was a wiseass whose mother noted in his babybook: "If you ask me, Bucky Duane, I'd say you were a smart aleck." And I replied, "Who asked?"

At age nine, when selected to help carry the coffin of an infant son of family friends at my first funeral, I couldn't resist the bald gentleman who approached me to ask if I was a pallbearer.

"No, sir," I said. "I'm a Buck Walker."

Adventurous and enterprising, I always had something going on. I learned to read early when my mother taught me words off cereal boxes and cans of food, and soon enough could read street signs, billboards, and neon signs, keeping my siblings informed about all the signs they would meet during a car ride. From there to the regular devouring of The Saturday Evening Post, Popular Mechanics, and National Geographic was merely a hop in the skip and jump of a lifelong love of words, feeding my fertile imagination. Like so many children of the age of magazines and radio, I believed that the motion picture reels turning on the screen of my inner vision could be made to come true. And some did.

Sitting on the high seat of a hole-in-the-wall sidewalk shoeshine stand with my dad, I watched the old black man popping his rag and got the idea to go into business for myself. Only I would bring the shine to the man rather than making him come to me -- and deliver it with a sunny smile. After constructing my custom-made box from old fruit crates and a web belt from my sailor uncle, and borrowing money from my dad for supplies, I'd spend every weekend it didn't rain and most of the summer tramping the streets looking for the dull footwear I would shine for five cents a shoe. Before long I was the richest kid in my neighborhood, always good for a candy bar or a soda pop, and welcoming my pals into the business, training them and assigning territories. We were, after all, a group of independent businessmen, and all we needed was an office building -- which wasn't long in coming. We all got together to build a clubhouse from lumber scraps, which we called the Nickel-A-Shoe Club.

The war years and war movies at the local Roxy brought dreams of becoming a pilot. From zooming model airplanes through the air by hand in dogfights with Messerschmitts and Zeros in the movies in my mind, I was right there in the cockpit, flying through space with a joystick between my legs, a machine gun firing button under my thumb. I sped across the skies like a comet, ace pilot with twenty-three kills painted in iron crosses and rising suns on the fuselage.

It wasn't long before I had to build my own plane, one I could actually sit in, my very own next-best-to-the-real-thing out of wood, nuts and bolts, pieces of glass and bicycle parts. I'd flown a few times with my dad, who had a pilot's license, the great thrill of my life then, and knew all about flaps and rudders and ailerons.

I built it in the empty lot next door to our house, a mono-wing modeled after a Mustang with sliding canopy and featuring fore-and-aft seats. I hooked up a bicycle sprocket and chain so the prop would turn when I pumped the pedals, and the ailerons on the main wings would move when I shunted the joystick, the rudder turn when I pushed old automobile brake pedals hooked to strings from the tail. I got an imitation leather helmet and goggles from Kress' five and dime, made a scarf from an old bedsheet and soared through the skies of my imagination.

My sailor uncle had given me a government-issue survival knife, along with three Japanese cigarettes he'd brought back, which I wore strapped to my leg so I could free myself when I crash-Landed and had to cut the harness straps -- then I would pretend to smoke an enemy cigarette after a hard day in the sky saving my country.

When I gave rides in the passenger seat, I'd describe the flight from start-to-finish, filling their minds -- and my own -- with word-pictures, sound effects, and shouted warnings of attacks.

I had friends who lived in the military housing near the airport, and we would sometimes play around the planes and hangars there. There was one plane in particular that attracted me, a yellow and black beauty owned by an old codger who would carry me to the prepubescent orgasmic limits of my dreams of being a pilot.

He was more vintage than his two-seat open cockpit biplane, who called modern day small plane pilots pissants. He was a WWI veteran who affected shiny boots, jodpurs, an old leather flight jacket, and the requisite leather helmet and goggles from bygone days. With the de rigeur long white scarf dramatically wrapped around his neck, he was soon to become my real live, breathing pilot hero of the skies.

The plane itself, with its grease-gasoline-cold-metal-leatherseat mustiness, the joy of a real, honest-to-god joystick, was heaven. No matter I could barely see over the rim of the cockpit and couldn't reach the rudder pedals, I was in a real plane. I could hear the roar of the motor in my mind, feel the backwash of wind through my hair and gravity pulling at my body as I left the ground and began to soar...

"What the hell you doing up there, you little sonofabitch?"

"Oh, is this your plane, sir?"

"You're goddamned right it's my plane! Get the hell out of it!"

"Yes, sir," I said, scrambling out onto the wing and hopping to the ground. "Sorry, sir."

"You belong out here, boy?"

"Just came out to watch the planes, sir. I'm going to be a pilot."

"Is that right?"

"Yes, sir. I build models. I have a Messerschmitt 109, a Junkers JU-88, Spitfires, Navy Hellcats, Zeros, and Mustangs."

"Oh, yeah? Got any like this baby?"

"No, sir, not exactly. I have a Spad, a Sopwith Camel, and a tri-wing Fokker. The Red Baron flew a Fokker. Eddie Rickenbacker flew a Spad before the Camels came out."

"You know what this one is? Ever seen a rotary engine like that?"

"Only in pictures, sir. I've heard they're more reliable than the Spads and Camels and Fokkers, because it's a newer design." "Smart little bastard, ain't you?"

"Yes, sir."

"You forgot to tell me what kind of plane this baby is. You Know?"

I didn't, but I had an answer. "That's the most beautiful plane I ever saw, sir."

"Yeah?" the old pilot muttered, standing back to cast his gaze over it as if the idea of beauty were new to him.

"Yep. I'd give anything to have a plane like that."

"How much you got? Maybe I'll sell it to you."

"I've only got a dime. I was going to buy some soda and candy."

"Yeah? What kind do you like?"

"Dr. Pepper and Butterfingers, sir."

"Well, here's two dimes," the pilot said, fishing in his pocket. "Go on over there and get us our lunch."

Having descended from the glories of an air war in Europe to the ignominy of dusting crops for farmers, the pilot stood contemptuously watching the Piper Cubs, Luscombes, Aroncas, and Ercoupes gliding down the runway on routine flights. "Goddamned sissies," he would sneer. "Can't a one of 'em fly worth a good Saturday night fuck! Look at 'em! Ain't a pair of balls between a baker's dozen of the goddamned pissants! Need the whole fucking runway to work up enough nerve to get 'em up."

I kept coming around, helping out the old pilot when he worked on his baby, handing him tools and listening to him cuss, admiring him and the plane, standing forlorn with the longest longing in my heart as he left me and I stood to witness how flying was really done.

He'd fire up the engine, go quickly through a pre-flight check in his head while she warmed up, push the throttle up, release the brakes, and go bouncing out to the runway.

Onlookers would stop to watch the old character, shaking their heads and grinning.

With nose to the wind, he would pause, throttle down, a small sneering grin surely on his mouth, then rev her up to full throttle, the engine screaming, the wood and fabric trembling in the blast, release the brakes, and begin to roll. The tail would lift and, in hardly more than a hundred yards, he would shoot up at a forty-five degree angle, do a barrel-roll and fan off to the side with wings vertical to the Ground.

I imagined him laughing all the way. And one day, one magic day, he said, "Might as well see what it's really like. You got the balls, kid?"

"Yes, sir," I gulped " Yes, sir."

"You ain't scared?"

"No, sir."

"Okay, kid, good. You just hang on. I'm gonna give you a ride you'll never forget."

He started with a ground loop, one of the most dangerous maneuvers that can be done in a plane. It had no other use but to show off a pilot's daring and skill. No sooner had the wheels left the ground than it climbed in an arc upside down going in the opposite direction, then without pause followed the loop into what seemed to be a suicidal dive into the asphalt runway. But it completed the circle, leveling out a few feet above the ground -- and I began to breathe again and blink my saucer eyes.

He must have shown me every trick he knew. Upside down, I felt the seatbelt biting into my groin, clutching for handholds to quell the feeling that I would fall straight down out of the plane. The power dive made it look as if we were going to crash into the ground, the engine sound winding into a crescendo, but at the last finely tuned moment would pull up and barrel-roll a few times for good measure. Flying barely over treetops, he would work the rudder pedals in such a way that the plane glided sideways, waggling one way and another, scaring cows and horses in the pastures scudding by below.

Then, gaining altitude, came the stall and the spinning dive. He cut the engine, leaving the prop to freewheel as we spiraled down in relative quiet, the awful blast of sound returning just in time to prevent a crash.

I had not pissed or shit my pants. I had not heaved up my breakfast. I had not screamed from fear, but from great excitement and joy. I had become one with the plane in the sky, the crazy old pilot.

When we had gotten back on the ground in a three-point landing smooth as pudding, and rolled to the hangar, the prop whop-whopping to a stop, I was exhausted in the eerie silence, deaf and limp, all the vibrations now a numbing buzz in my body.

"You still back there, boy?"

"Yes, sir," I croaked, my mouth drier than desert sand. "Well, what do you think?"

"Jesus Christ, sir!"

I moved from airplanes to bicycles when I got a Schwinn from my dad one Christmas, learning all the boyish tricks to show off while riding it. It wasn't long before I was creating my own -two-seater tandems with three wheels, others with the frame turned upside down, the front forks reversed, handlebars and seat extensions rising six feet from the ground (tricky to mount, but what a ride!), and once, a riding platform welded between two bikes side by side so we could take a load of little kids riding.

In the onset of my lifelong entrepreneurship, I had the usual job and business experiences -- a paper route, mowing lawns, and serving as dishwasher, waiter, and frycook in the restaurants my mother and Aunt Blanche would lease and operate from time to time over the years. During summers, beginning at the age of fifteen, I worked for my father in the several of his various construction companies.

I knew my father's education beyond high school was entirely self-acquired. With his intensely curious mind and continuous quest for knowledge, he had developed an understanding of engineering principles approaching the professional. The man could build anything--buildings, houseboats with Cadillac engines, machines for paving roads, gravel separators, even an advertising apparatus mounted on top of a company van featuring four-by-six foot screens fore and aft which displayed changing ads, interspersed with jokes and gag pictures to catch the eye, reflected from photo-slide machines inside. He was the eccentric and occasionally sensational inventor and showman of the county.

As I got older, we wound up in Los Angeles, and I came to like going to school less and less, often playing hooky and wandering the city riding trolley cars and going to movies. Why go to school? My dad hadn't and look at him. But my father was adamant. If I didn't at least attend long enough to graduate high school, then by god I could find my own damn job and begin looking after myself -I couldn't work for him or my mother and aunt.

I was supposed to fall on my face and learn my lesson. I had a car, a 1941 Nash, and had learned enough from my dad to get a job as a lathe operator in a small tool company making wing-tip tanks for jet airplanes. I was on my own and soon moved into an apartment near the Coliseum.

Then, nearing my eighteenth birthday, I ran headlong into the adult criminal justice system.

My buddy, Tommy, was a streetwise orphan who'd scuffled about on his own for a few years. We were inseparable, running the streets and hanging around looking for fun or mischief or ass or whatever.

Tommy had an aunt, an over-the-hill actress in a fine Hollywood home. Though she was an alcoholic, usually greeting us three sheets to the wind, dressed in no more than slip, negligee, or bathrobe, her long and beautiful black hair a tousled mane, I found her fascinating. She allowed us to drink with her, as she'd grow increasingly sentimental and regale us with juicy Hollywood stories mixed into aching views of past glories.

When the booze ran short, as it often did, she'd hand Tommy a twenty, sometimes a fifty, to go out for another bottle. He never gave her the change, and sometimes even poured liquor down the drain so he'd be sent out again. The one time I was sent for booze, I brought back the change and Tommy rebuked me. "She's got so much, she'll never miss it."

Once, in what I thought was an effort to assuage her loneliness, she sent Tommy way across town in my car to fetch back a niece, leaving me alone with her. Whoa! Tommy was no sooner gone than she came on to me like Delilah to Samson, and me, in my horny youthful exuberance, I leaped at the opportunity.

Suddenly all the allure of the actress came out in her and I was her leading man. The disappointment of the quickie on her bed only stimulated more posing, gesturing, and dramatic speech.

"Oh, Bobby, dearest, what wounds of long lost idyls do you bear me? Sweet youth and memory's bane hath wrought a witch's cauldron in my soul, I fear."

Or somesuch.

She couldn't get my name right, but she knew what she was doing and soon had the next love scene orchestrated for her own needs. Ah, me, please! So this is how completely shocking, how utterly fascinating the secrets of a sophisticated woman really are! What a great leap in my education!

Then she threw up and began to moan and weep. I cleaned up the mess, helped her into the bathroom, and was running a tub when Tommy and his cousin came in. In outrage, he chased me out of the bathroom for a confrontation while I was trying to dress as fast as I could. I had taken advantage, he accused.

"You kidding me, asshole? She practically raped me!"

"You fucked my aunt! How'd you like me to fuck your sister?"

"You lay a hand on my sister, I'll kick your ass up over your shoulders!"

"You and who else? You can't even fight off being raped by an old lady!"

It was our first fight and, after being driven from the house by his irate cousin, we drove around aimlessly arguing and passing a bottle of vodka back and forth until around 3 a.m., when Tommy asked me to pull over so he could take a leak.

While I sat in a drunken stupor, Tommy got out a tire iron from the trunk and broke out the display window of a music store. I was startled awake at the great crashing of glass to see him grabbing a trumpet and a saxophone. Running to toss them in the backseat, he jumped in while I put the car in gear to speed away.

"You fucking asshole! Are you fucking crazy?"

Tommy laughed. "Fuck it. You don't like the way I make my money, we can sell the horns at a pawnshop."

"You fucking asshole, you, somebody could have gotten my license number!"

"Naw, shit, everybody's asleep. Don't worry."

"Shit," I spit out, tromping on the brakes. "Get out and close the fucking trunk before a cop stops us!"

The next day, with our girlfriends, Tommy wanted to pawn the horns, saying he knew a guy who didn't care if they were hot. But the guy only offered fifteen bucks, so we drove to another one and sent the girls in on the theory they could get more. All four of us were busted.

At the stationhouse, Tommy confessed so his girl could get off. Mine said we were just along for the ride and didn't know anything. Then the cops said they were going to arrest Tommy and his girl, so he told them I was in on it, not his girlfriend, that I had driven the getaway car. We were booked; the girls were let go.

Tommy knew the ropes and quickly copped a plea for a short jail term. I pled not guilty and went for a jury trial. Tommy was back out on the streets before my trial even began. When he visited me in jail, I asked him if he was going to testify and get me off the hook, but he wouldn't answer.

"Ah, what are you doing here, you bum," I said, disgusted. "Hit the road!"

During the months of waiting for my trial, I had plenty of opportunity to work on my fighting skills. In that vast zoo of predatory creatures paling away in the artificial light of the myriad passageways of the L. A. County Jail, I quickly learned that in order to survive it was best to bust a guy in the mouth whenever in doubt of his intentions. I also learned that survival had a price when I ended up with five days in the Hole as a result of visiting a little justice on a deserving asshole.

The Hole was a bare concrete and steel cubicle with no light whatsoever. I was given a pair of long johns, a thin blanket, and sufficient time to contemplate my sins without the distraction of sight. I whiled away the maddening hours singing every song I knew and when I became hoarse, would toss a button from my long johns and search for it in the darkness. After a hundred and twenty timeless hours, with kidneys and joints aching from lying on the cold cement, even the poor jail light celebrating my release caused painful tears.

My lawyer talked me into waiving a jury trial, saying it was so cut and dried I'd be found innocent by the judge. I wasn't. Then the lawyer told me the judge was going to throw the book at me, that my only chance was to admit I was in on the burglary and apologize for wasting the court's time. Choking on the humiliating irony of it, I did it. After several months in jail, I was granted probation.

By the time I got out, my family had moved further out in the suburbs. I was bummed out with no money, no friends, and my family riding me all the time. I couldn't find a job, but I'd heard plenty of stories in jail about how easy it was to get money -- all I had to do was take it away from somebody else.

I sawed off a .22 rifle so I could hold it like a pistol. Even though I felt desperate, needing enough cash to be able to get out on my own, I didn't want to point a loaded gun at anybody, take a chance on hurting someone in an accident, and so I left the bullets home. Then I stole a car and looked for a place to rob. Pulling into a gas station, I told the attendant my battery was low and I couldn't turn off the engine. I kept the car in gear, ready to pop the clutch. After the tank was full, the attendant came over to my window and I waved the gun at him.

"This is a robbery."

"Yeah, I know. I've been robbed before," he said, memorizing my face. "Hang on a second and I'll give you the money." He went around to the front, opened the cashbox near the pumps and returned to shove a wad of bills through the window.

"Thanks."

"Don't mention it."

My take was forty dollars, mostly in ones.

A few days later, it having been so easy, I tried again, stole another car but before I could repeat the process, a cop car began to chase me. I tromped on the gas, screeched around a corner, looked back to see how I was doing, and crashed into a parked car. I jumped out and ran, cutting across a lawn to run behind a house.

"Halt or I'll shoot!"

I looked back to see if they had a clear shot at me and ran headon into the corner of the house, knocking myself silly. The cops picked up the empty gun and the guy from the gas station identified me. That was that -- teach my ass to look back!

Not yet nineteen, I felt a hundred when I was sentenced for ten-years-to-life. I could see no hope at all. My life was at an end.

# # #

CHAPTER 2

In prison, there are criminals and there are criminals. The most dangerous are those ill-humored types who possess a streak of vicious misanthropy, who seek the violent thrills leading to self-destruction. They are nihilists, anarchists, and terrorists. They are true thugs who are generally lacking in conscience or insight. Although unpredictably rabid, some are quite intelligent in a sterile way. Others are merely stupid.

Another portion of the outlaw milieu, however, comprises men with all the likable attributes of folk heroes without the element of being overly earnest, obsessive, or arrogant. They are witty, generous, fun-loving characters who would rather be clever than violent, have a good time, and live well. Although they usually love stolen money, they mean no harm. After all, as spendthrifts and wastrels, they fully intend on redistributing it back into the economy at the earliest possible moment. They possess a decent, if somewhat imperfect morality, and cling to an anachronistic code of conduct.

In between these extremes are many mixtures. Perhaps your next door neighbor who went on a toot out of need, greed, whim, or injury. Perhaps even you, tomorrow or the day after. In a land with a million laws, where practically every activity has been defined and condemned, where we need constant advice in the spiraling complexities of our times by batteries of other crooks, the ones with briefcases, who can ever be certain?

However, to subject any human being to a prison environment such as existed in San Quentin in 1956, is to demonstrate society's own brand of perversity. As we have exigently bent ourselves as a country more and more upon the path of so-called law-and-order, building more and meaner prisons, that environment has only degenerated. Prisons now are largely factories producing human time bombs packed with defective fuses of rage and frustration, liable to explode without warning, immediately or years hence. They serve to regenerate all the worst elements we are seeking to escape.

Because the law does not apply equally to all, the abiding lesson to be learned in prison is that the greatest crime was in being caught for our transgressions, proving ineptness, outright stupidity, or plain bad luck. In being punished, we in turn become victims to a grand array of permissible tortures. What do we learn but that justice, a largely blind, angry, and perjurious subversion of spite and revenge, is so much gobbledegook?

Having said all that, it will be easy for you to understand that I hated San Quentin with every last morsel of my passionate but compromised youth. I hated it for the ever-prowling fear, the incipient violence, the inescapable mind-deadening routines, the microcephalic thuggery of our keepers, and knowing that at the end of every social interaction lay crouched, patient and inexorable, the ultimate resolution of all disputes by physical force, the threat of death.

You will doubtless be astounded to learn that, in retrospect, I find a certain poignant nostalgia coloring my remembrance of those awful years. I have a quiet pride at having survived as abler, tougher, and immensely more confidant. As others my age were matriculating college and finding their careers, I would be receiving a rainbow education among a wide spectrum of rascals and misfits, both good and bad. I would graduate from the ghetto of San Quentin with honor -- meaning my luck did not entirely desert me and I did not succumb to cowardice, suicide, murder, madness, or punkism.

I have come to realize that it was within those gray, fog-enshrouded walls of San Quentin that I came to clutch my own bootstraps and begin a great existential leap into a new self. Besides catapulting my seventh grade education well into the college level, I acquired a realistic degree in self-discipline and surprisingly considerable inner resources -- I thought myself somewhat better armed to confront and endure the crueler epidemics of a hostile world.

*****

I had met my friend, Rick Cluchey, in jail while we both awaited transport to Q. Swapping paperbacks had led us into discussions over what we had read, then telling each other stories, playing games, and indulging in the endless varieties of bullshit that jail offers. We began to recognize each other, becoming warily allied in our rejection from society, fellow desperadoes quasi-resolute in our headlong flight from the sinister, ludicrous, and oh-so-dear fantasies of remembered freedoms. We ruled so little, hardly even the tiny spaces of our immediate existence, but we had our dukes, our feet, and our street-sly wits and reflexes in defense of bodily harm, while our secret, more sensitive selves began the slow piecework of weaving gossamer ladders sufficient to carry us up out of the pits into some unknown, wildly imagined future time.

We were both assigned to the South Block, where newcomers were housed. It was the largest cellblock in the world, containing a thousand cans with two sardines each. It was like sharing a bathroom at home, with a bunkbed in place of a tub. Showers were three times per week, when a hundred men -- a tier-section -- were herded through ten showerheads in ten minutes. You had to be polite about bodies coming into contact with other bodies and if you dropped your bit of lye soap, you definitely didn't bend to pick it up.

Rick, who had arrived before me, helped me connive my way into the vocational dental lab, and thus I escaped the dreaded Cotton Textile Mill where I was slowly going gaga from the cacophony of Rube Goldberg-type machinery, the endless cotton strands in my eyes, mouth, nose, ears, and clothes. I would learn a trade and, at the same time, be able to avail myself of the separate shower facilities.

He'd laughed and slapped my back to jolly me out of my grim mood when I'd arrived, my shoulders hunched, hands in pockets, looking like death barely escaped from a gunny sack when we had met the next day on the yard.

A rotten old convict in the jail had told me the day before riding the prison transport that I was too young and pretty to last long in Q. He'd told me I would be approached by armed perverts who would say, "Shit on my dick or blood on my knife, punk"

I'd stolen a spoon from the messhall at my first meal and sharpened one end on the concrete floor. I clutched it with a tight fist in my pocket. The first motherfucker that said those words to me was going to have his blood on my knife.

Rick had convinced me that things weren't quite so bad and that I should get rid of the shank. "Use your noodle. Keep your mouth shut and step light. You'll learn the ropes okay."

*****

Once he stood before me to read a single paragraph from Schopenhauer. "You understand that?"

"Let me see it," I replied, snatching it from him. It was written in English, but I hadn't the faintest idea what it was about. "No, do you?"

"No. But it serves to point up a deficiency. We should understand our own fucking language. The more I read and think, the more I see things ain't so simple."

"Yeah."

"We've got our work cut out for us, bub. How can we ever learn to get by if we don't even know what's going on, what's being thought and said?"

"Right."

"There's millions of books in the world, probably everything we'd ever need to know, if we could just find and understand them."

"Yeah?"

"Yeah, but what do we read? Westerns and private eye shoot-'em-ups, adventure thrillers, smut, and the fucking comics!"

"What's wrong with comics," I enquired, defensive over my years of collecting and reading them. "What's wrong with any of it?"

"Nothing. They reflect our sillier side, which ain't bad, mind you. We gotta keep a sense of humor about the whole mess. But we're missing something important. We ain't so fucking smart at all, pal.

We don't even understand that one paragraph, let alone the whole book."

"So what? You think it's about cracking safes or robbing banks?"

"Don't be funny. We gotta do something."

"What?"

"I got this book, 30 Days to a More Powerful Vocabulary."

*****

Herman Spector was a stern little librarian, a lonely old Jew who loved books and was determined to have the best library in the penal system in his corrugated iron quonset hut. Books were stacked in every nook and cranny, over twenty thousand of them, and Spector managed to find -- in time -- nearly anything you could ask for.

It became the first of my several haunts. I read hundreds upon hundreds of books and came to treat each volume as a precious jewel. I came to believe that everything I ever wanted to know really was contained in a book somewhere, and I had only to discover its whereabouts. I began with fiction of every stripe and fancy, but moved on in time to philosophy, history, psychology, anthropology... got a good dictionary and a Thesaurus, which became portable extensions of my mind.

Then one day in the yard, I overheard two old cons talking. They were discussing philosophy, ranging far and wide in terms I'd never heard. They were speaking English, but it might as well have been in Bantu for all I understood. It was a rerun of Cluchey's paragraph from Schopenhauer. He was right. I had a serious deficiency!

Climaxing weeks of heavy thought, I imperilled my rehabilitation by dropping out of the dental lab after almost a year and enrolling in school, the second of my favorite haunts, where I spent the next two years in class -- six hours of day school and four hours at night, eating my way through every course they had offer.

Working unsung in the cramped prison schoolhouse, teaching English and American literature, grammar, composition, and journalism, was the best teacher I ever knew. He was also a jewel of a man. I took every class he taught. His name was Stanley Jacobs. Everyone called him Jake, but after we had become friends, I called him "Stanley Steamer."

He had an easy loose-jointed way about him, and he was fond of gestures, moving about as he read us passages from the great works, his deep-timbered voice now soft and lulling, then outraged and thundering -- a passionate man.

I have fixed in my mind forever a vision of him pacing back and forth across the wooden floor at the front of the classroom.

He had served as an army major in the Pacific campaign and had been wounded in one leg. As a result he wore a metal brace from knee to foot and walked in a clumping limp.

We were studying Moby Dick, I having fixed whales, the sea, the ship Pequod, and all the vivid characters into my mind. And as Jake read a passage for us, pacing and shouting, swinging about to drive his fist into the open book for emphasis, there he stood before our very eyes, Captain Ahab, an indomitable figure of a man, clumping o'er the canted quarterdeck on his pegleg, ranting, "Why, man, I'd spit on the sun if it insulted me!"

During my third go-round in his journalism class, having worked my way up to editor and feature writer for the 4-page school newspaper, we became closer. Sometimes we were alone in the classroom working on the layout, drinking coffee and smoking -- he a pipe, me a cigarette -- and sometimes our conversations would take a personal turn.

It was during such an intimate moment that I was privileged -nay, honored -- to hear the story of his great burden. American troops had effected a costly landing in terms of killed and wounded on some island, and fierce battles were being fought. He had been ordered on an intelligence mission -- to take a small squad of men, make their way into the jungle and spy out concentrations of Japanese troops, munitions, HQs, and gun emplacements, to supply Naval ordinance with targets to be bombarded.

Well into the mission, they'd captured a Japanese sentry, which placed Major Jacobs in a dilemma -- he couldn't spare the men to return the prisoner to American lines, nor could he be taken with them since he would pose a danger of discovery. He ordered his sergeant to shoot the enemy soldier, but he refused.

At this point a lull occurred, Jake contemplatively puffing on his pipe, his eyes peering through the desk, the floor, the foundation, and the underlying bedrock, seeing what only he could see.

"So what happened? A court-martial for the sergeant?"

"No. It was an illegal order. He was not obliged to follow it."

"What'd you do?"

"Well," he sighed. "You know what they say, never issue an order you're not willing to carry out yourself."

"So you..."

"I thought about it, but there really wasn't time to give it the attention it deserved. I believed it was important to get the information we'd been sent for -- it might save American lives. On the other hand, shooting the prisoner seemed tantamount to murder -even if he was the enemy. He was a man, a frightened man...probably with a family. He didn't make the war any more than I did."

"You called it off and took him back."

"No...I shot him and completed the mission."

I could find nothing to say. The silence between us seemed to contain an exquisite noise, a rush of dark wings, the air taking on weight and bearing me down.

"Was I right or wrong? Huh! Six of one, half dozen of the other. How many times have I been over it? Millions of words have been written about morality, for thousands of years. In the end, it comes down to a very personal choice, usually a quick decision. We can't take a poll, seek advice, or decide -- and yet, we have to. Was I right or was I wrong? Does the good of the many outweigh the rights of the few? Can we commit immoral acts for a moral end? I live with it -- there's a certain resignation -- but I'll probably wrestle with it forever."

His smile seemed sad, a bit sheepish, as he rose to break the trance. He took my arm to steer me from the classroom, he clumping, Ahab, pursuing the great whale.

When I finally graduated from high school, my appetite was only whetted. Curiosity is more addictive than drugs; there is no high more euphorious than knowledge. I wrangled a job clerking to the Supervisor of Academic Instruction and, using my flimflam skills, parlayed my need for college correspondence courses I couldn't afford into maintaining the high. More well-off convicts, wanting to improve their chances with the parole board, would sign up, I would do all the lessons, take the exam, and see that they got the credit. They got the fame of the facade; I took the unsung quiet of the substance.

*****

I was paroled at twenty-three. Having lived like a monk for over five years, my appetite for real-life experiences could all be boiled down and summed up into a prime need for pussy.

Young men deprived of female companionship for so many years of forced celibacy have a certain naiveté -- a tendency to fall in love with every female they lay eyes upon. I fell in love with fourteen year old girls and sixty year old women, with none of whom I'd exchanged so much as a word. Once, walking down the street, I fell madly in love with a gorgeous transvestite...until she got close enough for me to see the five o'clock shadow. Love was easy, but it was mostly all one way in my mush-mouthed fantasies and stalking the wild pussy was tougher than pissing up a rope.

I had been paroled to work in my father's TV business, one he started when the family moved to Stockton after I went to San Quentin. I saw my opportunity in erecting antennas, something he didn't want to do. I told him I would handle that part of the work. I sold his antennas, took a commission, and filled my days with hot summer labor doing installations. The money rolled in. In four months, I had a down payment for a new car, bought a new wardrobe, and was ready for some action that would relieve the nights restless with frustration.

In the same four months I had only managed to rectify my dire need three times with a kindly black prostitute I'd picked up on a downtown street. The first time I was a few bucks short and she'd let me slide with a quickie. I made it up in a hefty tip the next time when I went for the more elaborate double-fuck. Sex with whores is not quality ass, but at the time I was more interested in quantity.

I soon set off in my new car for Tijuana, the sin city of renown in those days, my goal nothing less than to visit every whorehouse and dive to be found, to sample pussy in every nuance, to touch it, smell it, taste it, and verily to bathe in every stratum of its magical properties. From two dollars to fifty, I did my best. I had come to conquer.

Having nearly accomplished my goal, I fooled myself into thinking I had also acquired some experience of female psychology, and went looking to plumb the profounder depths of that glorious creature, woman. Then, God curse me, I saw one sunbathing in the nude and was smitten with the awful and delirious first of a thousand small deaths. I fell madly, sickeningly, hopelessly in love with the most beautiful spirit ever blessed to reside in the shape of woman. In the stunning glory of her perfection, I promptly went blind and lost all reason.

Having lived so long out of books, life at second hand, I had romanticized reality into ideal forms. I had left the hyperbolic fantasies of prison life expecting to attain perfection in short order. After all, I was fundamentally self-enlightened and if you can't trust yourself, who can you?

She was intelligent, versed in the arts, and liberal. Descended from Connecticut Scots, she was kind to animals, children, and the underprivileged. Hell, I was all three and more, but she thought I was a jerk.

I became a tortured soul, an obsessive artist painting my beloved from jealously guarded glimpses of memory, a poet pouring out his impotent heart. I lived in a menagerie, hiking into the mountains with an old coyote-chasing hound, collecting trapdoor tarantulas, feeding Charlie, the giant rooster, coffee and worrying that he would kill all the cats in the neighborhood, and feeding the crazy guinea pig tranquilizers to counteract his epileptic seizures. I photographed birds in flight and bemoaned my earthbound fate. I listened to Dvorak, Stravinsky, Beethoven, and Miles Davis, and sought God in clouds under the influence of Peyote.

Then one mad night I mistook a eucalyptus tree for my erect penis and somehow wormed my fevered way into my beloved's arms, her beauteous breasts pressed close upon my cheeks, where I uttered all the unutterable poetry in me. The dizzy bitch heard and believed, but in the morning with a strange man demanding entrance, she sent me on my way. All magic in the world had died an unremarkable death.

Unrequited, unsettled, and disillusioned, it was almost a relief when I returned to Q on a parole violation. I fell into a routine and began a humbler search for the obviously missing pieces of myself.

*****

Our choice was to beat our heads against stone walls before a blind and deaf audience; to discipline rampant passions and learn to become professional criminals rather than remaining amateur hobbyists, dilettantes, and emotionally hare-brained yoyos; or to take arms against the odds in an attempt to remedy certain apparent character defects sufficient to permit a bit of hamming and flimflamming about a richer geography -- to pursue our eccentric and sundry inclinations with the least hindrance. In an absurd world, we had to become as responsible for our own fates as the unreason and lottery of life would permit.

Thus it was that I wound up a hardcore member of the San Quentin Drama Workshop, where others, like me, came seeking to create, out of whatever material was available, sustenance for their curious appetites. It was one of the few places in prison where the soul could revel in millions while the body lived on dimes. After all, what was real life to us? It was a tease, a torment, a daily bearing of our crosses. Easy to realize our despair, we could neither overly indulge it and survive, nor could we escape. There was no way around, over, or under the absurdities. They would not vanish. They formed a wall that dared us to try bursting through.

Persistence was the key, artifice all. The stage reflected our need. A role was a strawman passing into defective memory. Ah, but whilst one wore the glittery robe of his role upon that stage, it was to shed the drab meanness of life, a time to be more than we were, if only in pretense. The straw quickened and breathed, provided other views of existence, suggested possibilities, raised up hidden parts of ourselves. After all, who is so sure of his position that he does not assume or pretend? Were we to close ourselves off in sadomasochistic loneliness or open ourselves to the communion of exquisite wounds?

It is good to be curious. To be curious is to seek. To seek is to find. To find is to express a long gamut of responses from chagrin to indifference to happiness. To find is also to laugh. It is best to laugh. All-consuming laughter is the highest signpost of civilization, the foremost symbol of reason, and the epitome of evolution. When did man begin to laugh in his elevation from his animal origins? Why, at the very moment he began to free himself by his reason from the drudgery of his automatic survival behavior which so enthralled him to his environment. Good humor, laughter, the delight, the great luxury -- ah, me buckos, at the Workshop, at home among the scalawags, this third of my favorite haunts, I was alive and laughing.

*****

The first play I ever saw was Samuel Beckett's **Waiting for Godot** in San Quentin. My old pal, Rick Cluchey had a leading role. The stage was set in the old North Messhall, a high-ceilinged warehouse type building with a guard's catwalk above. It was filled with long narrow tables with attached benchboards, all arrayed in three sections with aisles between -- everyone ate facing the same direction. It was our theater. Every weekend we queued up in rowdy fat lines to attend a movie.

I knew Rick had involved himself in the newly formed Drama Workshop, but a play filled with inept convicts seemed like silly shit to me in comparison to the escapism provided by movies. The living stage seemed so limited and I felt a bit cheated at first that I had been sucker enough to attend when I could have better spent my time digging for jewels in Spector's library.

I didn't understand much through the first act, but I enjoyed watching Rick's histrionics. Then something began to happen. It had to do with the relationship between the pairs of characters, first Didi and Gogo, and then Lucky and Pozzo. I had had some experience as a rider of freight trains and remembered the living in hobo jungles, eating Mulligan stews, and listening to the pretentious stories of hopeless, homeless men, the waiting for the next train that would take us somewhere, anywhere, nowhere. Waiting.

All our lives we were plagued by waiting for something, though it usually seemed only an inconvenience in the flow of our lives. We were fixed on goals, one after another, hoping that the attainment of each would somehow make a difference. A first this or a first that, a memorable loss of virginity -- love, money, acclaim -- always a first something. But then the less memorable seconds, the first blush of enthusiasm wearing away in jaded repeats, an infinity of reruns, only the details changed -- donkeys chasing carrots, convicts serving terms of imprisonment.

It dawned upon me that waiting was a palpable nausea, an indeterminate wait broken into thousands of smaller intervals. News of an escape was more cheering than the gospel caught on the last shred of a sinner's belief.

And the characters were hardly bizarre. Like the characters on the stage, a stark and sterile setting, we all waited and clowned and picked at ourselves and each other. Our hopes were all concentrated upon the illusions of tomorrow. Resolution was on the way, meaning around the next corner. We believed it was possible to wrest a pattern of personal fulfillment from the rabid maniac of the world, "who from the heights of divine apathia divine athambia divine aphasia loves us dearly with some exceptions for reasons unknown but time will tell." (Waiting for Godot, Samuel Beckett)

The play was depressing and hopeless, a poetry of madness. We were all blind twits, hearing the babble and shouting the babble, reeling in a macabre dance round and round. But I had laughed, too. It seemed trite and stupid. It rambled. It also flew on baby wings of poetry, brief flights of song.

I obtained a copy of Godot to read and reread at leisure. Beyond the obvious that Godot, a mystery figure who never appears, seemed to represent change, that Didi and Gogo were awaiting a savior who would make their lives better, more meaningful, no answer appeared in the course of my torturous attempt to analyze the play. I saw only the presentation of a vast human problem, a universal riddle.

How could it be resolved with the ineffective instruments of my understanding? The mind itself can be more of a prison than concrete and steel. Yet, what else did I have to work with? Our only hope seemed to be that we could become greater than we were. Within the absurd world of Beckett's play, freedom was a difficult burden to bear. It was easier to flee involvement than face endless choices of living, but to where? We had only the world. Could we not accept our conditions of servitude and become as Lucky, bound to our keepers from mutual need? There was something definite about slavery, and therefore comforting.

We didn't have to be responsible. Pozzo, the master, and Lucky, the slave, could as well switch positions, so reversible were the differences in their relationship. Convicts and guards could change uniforms with little apparent effect.

Why bother to make an effort? Why not accept life on the soap-bubble rim of existence, seek a comfortable niche on surface tensions -- which compose our illusions of dignity, power, and possession -- as the world directed? Worse, where could our dissatisfactions with the superficialities of life lead us if we fought through the illusions that sustain it only to find naked and unadorned emptiness lying beneath? There lies despair.

I despaired. It seemed that I could compress the whole of my life into Godot, and where did that leave me? Was there any choice other than suicide or a stoical resignation that might deliver me from the pain of all my unsatisfied desires? This question would lead me to examine Buddhism, to attempt to relate to the Four Noble Truths and the Eightfold Path, a personal inner journey to seek understanding of myself in relation to the world that would hold my interest for the next forty years.

But at the time, the only answer seemed to be to wait. When Pozzo has become blind and Lucky dumb, they fall down before Didi and Gogo, who attempt to help them up, and they all wind up scrambling helplessly upon the ground. Didi asks Pozzo, "What do you do when you fall far from help?" Pozzo replies, "We wait till we can get up. Then we go on." In waiting, there was hope. Despair itself, upon more than cursory examination, seemed meaningless and boring. Life is not static; it marches on, however blindly. Enthusiasm is a Phoenix, constantly renewing itself. Despair was an expedient that might serve as a source of direction. To where? Ah, well, me buckos, who the hell knows? There are more possibilities than stars. Let me search and explore in the changing shapes of my abilities and perceptions. Let natural good humor reassert itself. Let me be surprised. Godot constitutes a dialogue between inner parts of the self in composing the riddle; it is inevitable; it is our dilemma.

*****

It was that scoundrel, Cluchey, who hooked me in. He accosted me to read for a small part in Time Limit. He explained that only bodies were needed and I could hide in the crowd. I would be an extra. No, I wouldn't have to speak. Well, maybe a few lines, what the hell.

I read my eight lines, trying desperately to stifle the quaver in my voice. I got the part. We rehearsed. We made costumes. We built the set. We tried makeup on each other. Damn, I thought, envying the key players, maybe I could get into this, to strut about mesmerizing the masses with my wonderfully projecting voice, to remain titillatingly humble in the standing ovations, to be a star, somebody.

The Workshop had been allotted unused space on the second floor of the old gym building, where they created their own little theater -- a stage, dressing and makeup room, and enough salvaged seating from the old chapel for an audience of about a hundred -- and a certain intimacy was found in narrowing the distance between players and audience.

It was rumored that those dark, musty quarters once housed the old gallows back in the days before hanging gave way to cyanide as the favored method of inflicting state-imposed death penalties. It was a creaky old building where ghosts of penal dead seemed to sigh from the rafters.

The Workshop served for the presentation of training vehicles, the one and two acters, while we took the fewer three act plays to the stage in the North Messhall.

One of our leading players, Manny, a basketball-tall, dark and handsome fellow with a voice as powerful as Orson Welles, James Earl Jones, or Richard Burton, belonged to the Screen Actors Guild -- he was a serious actor. While he might have been an undiscovered incarnation of Omar Shariff, I was definitely the bastard son of Marlon Brando in my own heart.

On opening night, I took one peek from behind the curtain at a thousand hardened, unforgiving convicts, and went catatonic. I was sick with fear and shame. No fucking way I could step out there and say anything! But it was Manny who blew his lines, who went dumb in the pregnant silence. From some magic of self-possession, I whispered cues to him. It was easy when you'd memorized half the play in order to anchor your own eight lines. His gratitude was more sustaining than the applause after the final curtain. I was hooked.

To be involved in the Workshop meant necessarily to be involved totally. One could not merely be an actor, a director, a set designer, or a lighting technician. If you weren't directing, you acted. If you weren't acting, you turned a hand at building the set and props. You played with makeup. You studied your Stanislavsky. You swept the floor. You pulled curtains. Sooner or later you tried your hand at every little activity out of the dozens or hundreds that go into the production of a play. You discovered your talents if they existed. If you could, you did. If you couldn't, you did something else.

For me and a few others, particularly Cluchey, the Workshop was a stairwell to be climbed one step at a time, testing at every riser the ability acquired, the wherewithal to take the next step. I learned stagecraft, took on bigger roles, even leading ones, until, eventually, I had done everything except write and direct.

In my late-learned literacy, I began to imagine myself authoring a play. After all, I had taken journalism and writing classes, had formed a small poetry workshop, penned a few short stories, and hammered out a short western novel. It didn't work. Cluchey kindly suggested that I try adapting an existing play and my version of One Day in the Life of Ivan Denisovitch was performed with moderate success.

Meanwhile, my pal of ten years had been quietly busy writing The Cage. When he brought it to me, I was stunned. It was a street brawl of a play, set in prison with three psychotic murderers and a handsome young man, possibly innocent. Cluchey had wrenched the essence of the prison experience from his guts and abstracted it into something ominous, horrible, and magical. He offered to let me direct it.

To me, The Cage represented nothing less than a kind of psychoanalytical feat of astounding proportions, as though in order to be redeemed from the prison of one's self it was first necessary to reveal the darkest dungeons where the worst criminals dwelt in a mad twilight zone of death, where the light of life no more than flickered, an underground of the soul's evil urges.

A play is a malleable thing in the hands of a director, being whittled and reglued to conform with his conception. Cluchey and I talked, made changes, worked out the moves. The one affectation that grated on me was that the prison was in France and the actors were required to speak English with French accents. But this fact also presented a challenge to our abilities and I could understand it as a method of distancing oneself, including our audience, from the grosser realities of the author's vision. A play about convicts, presented by convicts to convicts, under the circumstances would have been like giving a glass of hot sand to a man dying of thirst.

The Cage was gloomy and depressing without relief. The entrance of the new inmate brought a contrasting note of sanity into the gutter madness. But reason cannot prevail as a point of light in the dark psychosis of a zombie tomb -- a point, of course, that the author was making. The new man is tried and condemned to death in a Kafkaesque kangaroo trial, his guilt or innocence beside the point. As judges and jury, prosecution and defense, they no more than reflected the essential aspects of the outer world's system of justice as seen through convict eyes. However, the play is less hypocritical by its portrayal of depravity as the central reality, an existential position where even a facade of morality is not allowed to function except as a token dramatic device. To be innocent is to be a victim. Innocence, that quality we profess to adore in children and find so contemptible in adults, cannot exist in such extreme situations.

We all become what we are by choice, according to our nature and circumstance. How free the choices are is another matter entirely. How many choices are made from inherent weaknesses of character? How many options are the unavoidable lesser of evils in a given situation? The Lucky part of us has a rope tied around his neck, held by the Pozzo part of us. Lucky must keep going because Pozzo is driving him. Pozzo must keep going because Lucky is pulling him. Humanity, with all its baggage, can neither remove the noose, nor let go the rope. It is the perpetual motion machine of our predicament.

Neither Beckett nor Cluchey solve the problem, but they do provide a certain impact upon our sensibilities by the dramatic forms of their respective statements, an impulse to think. The circle of life is a spiral reaching out into all unoccupied space. We cannot endure vacuum; let us fill it.

In the premier performance, I got into my bag of tricks, my penchant for mischief. I wanted to create a bit of liveliness by staging a particular segment as a sort of pseudo-religious revival scene. If we are all mad, all our gods are mad. Hatchet, a mass murderer who rules his cellmates by force and fear, stands raving upon a stool, seeming to draw his bizarre visions from the audience, to suck them across the distance between actor and observer. He has his enraptured cellmates straining to see his vision -- a manifestation of his insane resolve to wear a hole through the stone walls with his fingers -- they peering, even leering, at individuals in the audience. The idea was that the observer not be permitted, in this instance, to maintain his remove from the situation.

Cluchey played Hatchet, while I could not resist the prerogative of assigning myself the role of a necrophiliac undertaker. The first outside audience was stunned. No doubt they came prepared to be charitable, but went away, hopefully, with their smug underpinnings shaken from their certainties.

What is certain, however, is that a strange tranquility had taken hold of me. I somehow understood, in a most pellucid illumination, that this experience marked a change in our respective cycles, the gooseflesh on my arms and neck presaging a point of passage. We had been through so much together, two street sly, conwise buddies, having begun our parallel voyages through the great seas of submarine shit a decade before. I had been paroled twice and twice returned to regale him with sad and funny tales, which in retrospect must have been a torture to him. At that time he had no hope of parole, only the wild lottery chance of a legal loophole, commutation, or escape. But The Cage brought an impetus of outside interest in the author, which eventually led to the Governor's commutation of his life-without-parole sentence.

It was my turn to bid him farewell, to escort him for the short walk between two gates that would lead him outside the walls. Dressed in civilian clothes, he shook hands like a politician, dozens of friends clapping him on the back, wishing him luck. Like the actor he was, he strode out upon a new stage, another play, with perfect aplomb. On TV that night, we saw him leave San Quentin Prison in a Rolls Royce, a beautiful woman pulling him into the car. It was a worthy exit, a worthy entrance, an end, a beginning.

*****

The ironies are too much for me, too sad for comment. In our own prison parlance, suffice it to say he quit the tired old bitch and I was unlucky enough to be present at her revival. I remember the nightlights bejeweling San Francisco. I had a wife, children, and a cat in a flat. He had a wife and a dog in a house. I taught young ladies and old women how to drive automobiles. He had begun the Barbwire Theater, never forgetting, never forgiving, never allowing his wounds to incapacitate him.

We had gone with Ken Whelan, an old prison buddy and fellow alumnus of the Workshop, to a restaurant. Between these two genial rogues, Rick invited me to joint Barbwire Theater and Ken urged me. They were going on the road with a troupe to storm the Big Apple. I went to Rick's house to meet his wife and dog. I sat on the exquisite furniture. We became inebriated into the late hour of the night, the early hour of a new day. He had a well-stuffed study, a typewriter, large tables of working space, and a window that opened down onto the street. I remembered all the times we had laughed from deep in our bellies, until we cried, until we became sick.

*****

Although it was a phantom presence never far from our respective realities, a lurking vapor to envelope and choke us, a fearsome, omnipotent figure awaiting his cue to enter upon the ongoing play, I have hesitated to launch upon the subject of death. With all due respect to the situation, no one could be more responsible than in the paranoid alertness necessary for the survival of oneself. To leave it unsaid is to leave it undone. Yet it is a vision so gruesome and grotesque that one can only devoutly wish it could evanesce into the dimensions of a bad dream and be forgotten.

We were immersed in the idea of death, constantly inhaling its daily breath. Only soldiers in the heat of war, of hand to hand combat, or perhaps medical people, could have been more aware of the immediate perceptions of coldness creeping into warm bodies, the malodorous exudations from the onset of putrefaction. We witnessed the dozens of instances of mayhem and murder. From the vantage point of a few yards or feet, sometimes inches, we witnessed the more or less regular parade of stabbings and clubbings, the sweet cloy of blood deep in quivering nostrils, the half-shit gore oozing from ruptured intestines, the gray brain tissue, the jagged white of bone pushing through torn flesh, the dark, sticky, congealing red of the heart's fluid.

Some seemed to become inured, indifferent, callous, others fearful and angry, but all jumpy in its presence, our animal reflexes taking over to raise our hackles. There were the mad mutilations of self, as though pain and disfigurement could drive the enemy from within. There was the silly and complacent character who had castrated himself so as to no longer suffer the frustration of sexual desire, thus erasing the fear of where it might lead him. We watched his beard quit sprouting and his skin grow plump and pink as a baby's. We heard the screams of a man with a cruel enemy who had been caught locked in his cell when a Molotov cocktail smashed against the bars to convert it into a barbecue chamber. We saw a man hang out over the fifth tier babbling frightfully, threatening to jump. We saw his need for comfort, his cries for help, turn back upon him in shocked consummation from the spectators.

"Jump, you chickenshit motherfucker!"

And he did, covering his eyes and consigning his despair to space and gravity, only to escape the clutch of death by cruelly converting himself into a paraplegic cripple for the remainder of his stunted life.

The general tendency was that if you had not become blasé in the presence of death, you at least pretended it, for always there were the eyes of others upon you in the aftermath, studying you, seeking a weakness. To be weak was to perish.

There was a glass display case containing a bulletin board attached to the wall at the end of the North Cellblock near the entrance to the upper yard. For a time it contained dozens of candid photos of living and dead bodies that had suffered injury. They showed all the details of leaking skulls fractured by various crude instruments of local warfare, bellies slit to permit the exit of intestinal snakes, faces smashed beyond recognition, an occasional eyeball popped from its socket, limbs hacked from torsos, leaving cracked bone and grisly hanging stuff, a severed head in a rictus of horrible surprise as though it were conscious throughout its own decapitation. At the top of this sordid attraction was a neatly hand-lettered sign reading:

THIS IS YOUR HOME. MAKE OF IT WHAT YOU WILL.

Through some compulsively morbid fascination over the brief period of its existence, it was a daily magnet drawing all to its basic inelegance. You could not help but study every detail with bile rising, a taste in your gums that was cousin to the smell of old piss, all the while trying to remain cool because one of the attractions was watching others watch it. No one could look at it without being looked at, some feral eye seeing every nuance of expression. Only at night in your bunk alone with the searing images burnt into your mind forever could you safely wonder the ominous wonder of whether you, your own precious self, might wind up in such humiliation, such defilement, a spectacle of the macabre.

After so many years of uncountable deaths in all their candid modes, you could raise your eyes from the book you lay reading upon your bunk, interrupted by the thud of a body so rudely brought to rest upon the concrete apron before your cell and, without expression, note the widening pool of blood edging up to your doorsill, the slaughterhouse smell entering the shallow pumping of your lungs. You could react with all equanimity to the sight of a ghoul quickly rifling the body for drugs or money, perhaps a wristwatch, before the guards arrived. Whatever you felt for having heard that he had been seized by epilepsy or was set upon for an unpaid debt and catapulted out into infinity, you never displayed that emotion. You could even be cool enough to ask a guard to unlock your cell for lunch call and to track through the blood with all the appearances of being irritated at the inconvenience.

You could permit yourself a slight grimace at the news of a young man you knew, full of life and humor and talent, hanging himself. He had murdered from extreme provocation, knew it, but nevertheless refused to excuse himself. He had no hope of ever getting out of prison before he was an old, old man.

You could sit on the toilet in your cell, hidden behind a blanket draped from the upper bunk, weeping silently at the death of a childhood friend. He hadn't a very long sentence remaining to serve, but he was going blind from the ravages of diabetes and they would not give him compassionate parole. To be blind in prison, totally helpless and dependant was too horrible to contemplate. With all due deliberation, he had wired his door shut to prevent any quick succor in the event he was discovered too soon, then wound it around his neck from the upper bunk and splayed his legs out. By the time they'd found him, gotten tools to cut the wire job on his door, his head was all but severed, and there was no piece of his cell floor not covered in the jugular flood of his blood.

There were times when the yard would grow still, the murmur of a thousand voices, the shuffle of aimless feet, caught in the quietudinous aftermath of a guard shouting, "Dead man on the line! Dead man on the line!" All eyes would follow a condemned prisoner being escorted across the yard. You stood the silent vigils as men on death row were ritualistically executed. You grimly watched the stovepipe exhaust leading from the gas chamber over the North Cellblock as white steamy wisps of cyanide gas were vented to dissipate into thin air.

For years the name of Caryl Chessman was a sickness eating at you. You had read his first book, Cell 2455, Death Row, where you saw too much of yourself. You admired his fighting spirit. Everyday he survived was a triumph for all of you. Murderers walked the yard while he had never killed anyone.

The first time you were crudely slammed into the silent-by-rule Shelf, you rode up the elevator to the sixth floor over the North Cellblock, listening to the guards cracking jokes about stopping in the gas chamber for a bit of fun, trying to intimidate you. How long could you sit strapped into the chair with a hood over your face before screaming for mercy?

The Shelf operated on the silent system. You weren't allowed to speak except in response to the authority of sarcastic guards. You spent sixteen hours per day on a concrete slab without a mattress, which was taken out every morning after a regulation eight hours sleep and rolled tantalizingly across the walkway from your cell. The only reading material permitted was a Gideon Bible, the true educational value of the experience for otherwise you may never have read that amazing book from cover to cover several times over.

You stood naked under the snickering leers of those same guards waiting apprehensively for the sergeant to read you the rules in less than thirty seconds. You saw Caryl Chessman, his arms through the bars at the entrance to death row, resting on his elbows, nodding and grinning sympathetically to the nineteen year old that you were.

"How you doing, pal?" you inquired.
"No complaints. How you doing?"
"Ah, hanging in. You know."
"Yeah, what else is there to do?"

You were led before a sergeant in all your youthful glory, to smirk at him, stronger then, when he had finished his sarcastic instruction to keep your fucking mouth shut unless spoken to by the proper authority.

"You understand that, asshole?"
"Yeah, man."
Bam, a nice little slap to your head from behind.
"You see something funny? You say yessir! You understand that, asshole?"
"Yep."
Bam, bam. Another attention-getting slap to the head, a little jolt to the kidney.
"What, asshole? What?"
"Yeah, I understand fine...asshole!"

What the hell, a few slaps, jabs, and kicks got the circulation going. The satisfaction of refusing to say sir would have to hold you for the next thirty days. You could read your Gideon Bible; Daniel in the lion's den, the tribulations of Job.

So many times you saw him crossing the yard, seeming to stroll, to look about grinning that sad-eyed grin, denying the call of "Dead man on the line! Dead man on the line!", bravely mocking.

When his time had come finally, there was apparently no regular executioner. Interested guards could put in their names for selection by lot when it came time to do the dirty deed. The guard assigned to the security of the schoolhouse had tendered his request for the honor. The guards hated Chessman with a passion, as though he were a symbol of resistance to the full exercise of their power, the ultimate legality of being permitted to kill. This particular guard had a lust to kill Chessman, as though his continued existence were a personal insult. He fidgeted and paced, awaiting word that he had been selected. He was not. For weeks before the execution, we all steered around his rage.

On the great day, he brought a radio to work with him. From across the entrance foyer, I peered surreptitiously at him through the open door of his post, making busy behind the counter of the college correspondence section. He was agitated, sweating. I swear he drooled. He turned the volume up. Surely reprieve would come as it had so often before. No, at so many minutes past 10:00 a.m., Caryl Chessman was pronounced dead. The guard slapped his knee, stood to stretch and breathe deep, then turned his gleeful and gloating malevolence upon us all. Q was silent, only a susurrus of whispers wafting about like soft breezes disturbed by an unspeakable passage of omens.

I could imagine nothing more horrible than to have been in Caryl Chessman's place, to be led to the Green Room, as they called it, to be strapped into that hard chair, to have noted the acid vat into which would drop the cyanide eggs held under the seat, to be keenly aware of an audience come to witness his straining at his bonds, choking on the fumes, his eyes bulging under the cloth hood, the doctor listening to the pulse of his heart wired into electronic sound as it came to a stop, to silence.

An awful ravenous beast was loose in the land.

*****

Leaving Rick's house, remembering our laughter, my memory told me there were places in my history – from the vantage of traveling full speed, at capacity, upon that fine edge that separates life from death – where there were no questions. Thus, no answers were required. There were no complaints, thus nothing to be resolved. Everything was in its place, functioning according to its grand design. There were no surprises except the perception in distant retrospect that nothing was needed – no changes were necessary or desirable. All that was flowed naturally into being all that was possible – those perfect points in the space-time continuum that was Buck Walker. As a human being, I seemed to have occasionally existed at the apex of my humanity.

But, ah, me buckos, there are criminals and there are criminals. The most dangerous are those who come with fetters – to bind you, to keep you from the world. I could not bear stasis, the boredom of inactivity, of remaining in any place for very long. Perhaps my itinerant nature was born in prison, perhaps before. There was never any but the most temporary surcease from restlessness. I was forever going on to the next dance. The call of the wild was upon me. The Bacchanalian world awaited my exploration. Living is moving. I could not follow anyone, nor lead. Is life a treasure hunt on April Fool's Day? Where and what were my talents, if I had any? What was worth pursuit? What was possible? Am I the maniac of Gadara who could not be fettered, only saved? Who could cast my demons into a herd of swine and drive them into a lake to drown? (The two versions of the biblical story of the Gadarene may be found in Mark 5:1 and Luke 8:26.)

###

CHAPTER 3

So there I was, a thirty-four year old driving instructor, living in an upstairs flat in San Francisco with a beautiful wife who worked at the Museum of Art, a bright fourteen year old stepson, an adorable five year old daughter, a Siamese cat, and responsibilities galore.

That sunbathing-in-the-nude woman of the long legs and finest ass-ever, transplanted-to-Southern-California-from-Connecticut with her long dark and wavy mane, who'd stolen my heart so many years before, had lost the dream of the sea -- if she had ever truly had it.

After my reimprisonment on a parole violation, I had from time to time wrote her letters, pestering her with my attempts to impress her with my not-readily-apparent qualities, enthusiastic if a bit callow plunges into demonstrating my intellectual, poetic, and humorous capacities, searching for the chink in her armor that would allow me to prove not only that I wasn't a jerk, but that of all the men she'd ever known, I loved her most -- and she began to reply to them.

Concealing the hugest fantasies arising out of direst needs and sternly leashing the wildest passions, I had once included the semi-humorous, semi-nonchalant line: "If you're ever in the neighborhood, please feel free to drop in for tea."

One day I was called for an unexpected visit. Hurrying to spruce up a bit so as not to keep whichever member(s) of the family waiting, I strolled without any warning or preparation into a dream that was pure poetry.

From that frozen point in time when the realization hit me like an internal hurricane, blinking at last, drawing my jaw up from the record-setting drop-point, she said -- the most perfect smile on her most perfect mouth, her large to-die-for eyes aglitter with amusement, rising, from the seat across the table with her perfectly succulent body -- she said, "Well, you said I could drop in for a spot of tea!"

The day was suddenly a different day, bright with promise and possibility, a day full of deathless moments, a day where nothing existed but we two inside a golden sphere of electricity, an eternal day, one that ended all too soon but would add to my substance forever.

I have no idea what words were spoken after that, only that she had moved to nearby San Francisco, that she might visit again anytime, and that somehow our fingers touched -- and touched again, one hand courting the other, touched with hints of great messages requiring no words, fingers playing, dancing, kissing, caressing, all but making love right there on the tabletop before God and everybody.

One thing led to another in the chain of cause and effect, the sought-after but never-quite-as-we-expected path to gardens never-quite-fully-conceived, and so we took up living together in an idyl where the hide-and-seek child in each of us sometimes disturbed the peace with startling reports of firecrackers.

But the parole officer informed me that living in sin with an impure woman constituted a definite violation of the rules of my parole, even though I was unable to find the clause in my copy.

And so we married in a hasty but solemn, if somewhat comical in the backward glance, traditional ceremony at the Eastside Presbyterian Church in Stockton.

Soon enough we fled the rules for our own and found an aerie as storekeepers on a two-mile high mountain in New Mexico. And what's heaven without a little journey through hell for some fun? New Orleans, Texas, in the hot, humid heat of summer, working on the railroad every other night and every other day, working for the baby my baby was going to have entirely against my express wishes, knowing I, with my eternal wanderlust, was not good daddy material, but loving the lump in her belly anyway.

Jail then and the news that I was, gasp, a father carried with me back to Q for -- guess what? -- Numerous violations of all those tiny irksome rules of parole that I wore like a plastic bag over my head. More visits, now with a sun-haired, sky-eyed baby girl in arm, and my own old dream of the sea wavering.

*****

Reading of faraway places made me dream of faraway places. I, the ever-stymied international traveler, would-be citizen of the world, I had my dreams and I had to make them come true. Beyond the trick bicyclist, fighter plane pilot, and a few other false starts, lay a more abiding dream, a dream of the seas.

I don't know how old I was when my fascination with watercraft began, but it must have begun in the baby bath with my duck and boat toys when I would dip my head under the water, hold my breath, make like a fish, and come up laughing. At five, however, my mother almost died of fright when I jumped off a bridge into a moderately deep and moving stream. My dad had been brave but pissed when he'd jumped in after me, to wade ashore a couple of hundred feet downstream fully clothed with the soggy bundle of myself in one hand. He whacked me, hugged me, and told me never to do that again. My mom had hugged me, and then shook me, demanding to know why I'd done such a thing.

"Fun," said I.

"Little dickens was laughing all the dang way," said my father, shaking his head and trying out a stingy grin.

By seven I was a swimming fool and essaying to build my first boat, a box-like affair that promptly sank halfway across Whiskey Slough.

At about the age of ten, me and two friends, ahem, borrowed an outrigger canoe from Sea Scout headquarters, which we managed to sail after a fashion, spending about as much time in the water as in that tricky-to-sail vessel. Every time me and my pals got together a few dollars, we would rent an outboard river skiff to fish and explore the San Joaquin River and its many tributaries and islands. At Lodi Lake on family outings, we rented canoes and pretended to be Indians.

My dad and mom, all us kids, grandparents, the whole tribe of aunts, uncles, and cousins, as far as I could tell, were always avid fishers. My dad had begun building houseboats, one with a captain's pilothouse and a Cadillac engine, for weekends spent fishing and swimming on the river. Once I had spent many days of a summer puttering about by myself in one of his smaller ones, finding hidden little coves and uninhabited islands, and building fires ashore to cook the fish I'd caught, dreaming that I was a modern-day Huck Finn who would one day voyage after the cargo freighters all the way to San Francisco Bay.

One day in prison while working my educational scams, a sterling opportunity appeared before me in the form of a fellow whose parents had plopped down hundreds of dollars for a course of instruction by correspondence from the Westlawn School of Yacht Design. Lord have mercy, I loved this fool who was tired of it before he could complete the first lesson!

"Ah, me boyo," sez I. "For a small consideration, I will not only do the lessons for you, but I will also take the exams, and guaran-fucking-tee that no grades less than Bs will be duly recorded in your education records. The parole board will love you for this."

"Gee, great. How much?"

"It's a long course," I pointed out.

"Yeah?"

"Probably as long as two years. Designing boats requires not only mathematical ability, but also mechanical drawing, both of which I can assure you of my proficiency. Drop in and I'll show you on my records."

"How much, man?"

"A mere pint of ice cream per week, which works out to one measly dollar a month, more or less."

"Deal."

And so for over a year, well stoked on ice cream and Skene's Elements of Yacht Design, I immersed myself in the mystery of making boats that wouldn't sink or capsize.

I got halfway through the course before the guy was transferred to camp. Ah, well now, I had not only a seriously stimulated interest, but also resources for acquiring books on the subject, not only of designing them, but building them from various materials, as well as learning how to make them go where you wanted them to go -- faraway places.

There was an old guy whom I never met but wished I had. I read about him in local newspapers. He had the dream of the sea and finding himself all alone, finally decided to go for it. He lived beside the river and was a welder. Using what he knew, he designed and built a trimaran -- out of steel sewer pipe! The main hull was six foot in diameter and had a submarine-like turret hatch on it. Three-foot diameter pipes made up the outer hulls, all connected together with a system of welded girders and trusses. It was the damnedest boat you ever saw, but he stuck a mast on it, hoisted sails, and took that sucker down the river into San Francisco Bay -- right on out under the Golden Gate Bridge for parts unknown -- my kind of man!

*****

My wife's family had owned the same large and comfortable house in Pasadena since her childhood. It had been an anchor in her life, a place she could always go and be welcome. My family had been a moving one, from Colorado to Kansas to Idaho and Nevada, and all up and down California, making temporary homes wherever we were -- and so I had done a lot of traveling in my youthful years, perhaps picked up the habit then.

My wife liked to travel, sure, but she tended to stay fixed in place for years at a time, preferring to establish a home nest from which to make sorties. Me, I liked to keep moving. If I found a place I liked, I'd want to stay awhile, keep possessions to a minimum and maintain my traveling trim.

My ultimate dream, therefore, could best be expressed by having a home that traveled with me -- sort of like the Indians packing up their tepees when it came time to move on to new hunting grounds. Nowadays like-minded folks can accomplish this by owning motorhomes and travel trailers. Still though, their reach is limited. But the oceans now, they reach around the globe, capable of carrying me to just about any exotic place I'd want to go. On the seas, a boat is a self-contained equivalent of a motorhome or travel trailer, the ideal vehicle for a man of moderate means who has a deep and abiding wanderlust. And so that was my dream, a dream of the seas, a permanent and long-term way of life for a quick-study jack-of-all-trades to earn his way as he goes.

People in love, of course, tend to share their dreams, hoping mightily they are the same or that each may at least accommodate the other. But what if the dreams conflict?

At first, it didn't seem as if they did. Her eyes would sparkle, her flashing teeth, too, whenever I would go off into my flight of ideas, painting pictures of my desires and spreading them all over the world's geography -- I'd read tons of magazines and books from National Geographic to tales by all the great travelers and world explorers, accounts of sea voyages by the hundreds.

"God," she said. "Wouldn't that be great!"

"I can't think of anything better."

But it may have been my enthusiasm that attracted her more than the dream itself -- or else the realities of life as she perceived them may have changed her priorities. Who knows? Love, romantic love, can be a form of madness. It blinds us to facts that even fools can see. Love tends to be a form of idealizing relationships in order to weave them into the patterns of our fantasies. Looking back, it seems obvious. If I hadn't been possessed with the demons of love, I would have seen a lot sooner than I did that it wasn't going to work out.

But things weren't so clear then. There was a marriage, children, a living to make, and I was still in love -- but beginning to become disillusioned, less enamored with the situation as time passed. Life was becoming static. Living on the edge, both us working and barely making ends meet, life, as much as we both enjoyed what San Francisco had to offer -- interesting people, restaurants, entertainment, events -- life was fast becoming a rut.

Take restaurants as a single instance. We both enjoyed eating out at all the great dining places the city offered. She'd mention a new one we just had to try. I'd suggest we stay home and save the money. But this one is Greek -- or French or Indonesian or German or Thai or Russian -- a nice little family restaurant run by immigrants with the most exquisite whatever. And of course I couldn't resist. So off we'd go to these expensive little places and enjoy the food, the people, and the atmosphere -- become very romantic. The problem was an uneasy reservation I would carry with me that, sure, it's great, but there goes our money and we're never going to be able to save up enough to go into business for ourselves, never going to provide us a chance to get ahead of the game, acquire the where-with-all to make the dream come true -- that we would forever exist in similar circumstances, in a flat, working nine to five, aging, the kids growing up, life passing.

"What kind of business," she would ask.

"I don't know. Something we can do together, make some real money, be our own bosses. Maybe a boutique. You design, you're good at that. I'll do the renovations, get together a labor force, supervise. We can both hustle the goods."

"That takes money -- a lease, a good location, equipment, all kinds of stuff we probably haven't thought of."

"I know that. We need to save money. We need to get together a startup nut. I know a little about it I watched my dad start up a dozen businesses from scratch. We can do it."

"Well, it's going to take awhile."

"So? We live on grilled cheese sandwiches instead of blowing our dough in restaurants. We watch TV instead of going to the movies, maybe read a book, which we haven't been doing too much of lately. We drink at home instead of nightclubs. We need a plan, one we can follow."

The kids needed clothes, the car needed fixing, the rent was due -- the list was endless, went on forever. I liked some of her friends, she liked hardly any of mine -- mostly ex-convicts. She didn't appreciate me inviting them into our home, didn't want me hanging out with them -- and I resented it. She resented it when I didn't like some of her friends, thought they were phonier than a three-dollar bill, and sometimes made crude cracks to their faces. So many years in prison hadn't exactly prepared me for a smooth blending into society.

"How are we ever going to have what it takes to get a boat and sail off into the blue?"

"Buck, we have responsibilities now. The kids need a home, schools, doctors. We can't just drop everything and take off in a rowboat."

"We're in a fucking rut! We're not doing anything to improve the situation. Twenty years from now we'll still be working at some job or other."

"Well, I've got a good job and I like it. Why don't you try for a better-paying job?"

"Why don't we move somewhere it's not so expensive to live?"

"Where?"

"A smaller town, out in the country maybe."

"Ugh, please." She hadn't cared for Stockton all that much, hadn't cared much for life on the road with me.

"Well then maybe you can tell me how we get the boat? Hell, if I had to, I'd go out in the woods, chop down trees to build the fucking thing."

"Do a Thor Heyerdahl, huh?"

"Damn right!" Thor Heyerdahl was one of my heroes -- the life he'd lived, I could see myself doing a lot worse than following his lead. He'd once gone with his new bride on a shoestring to live like natives on an island in the Marquesas, a great adventure.

Then the raft Kon Tiki, later the reed boat. Hell, how could he not be my kind of man? "We got so many hooks in us, this life we live here, we'll never get free!"

"You might try using your imagination for something a little less juvenile than sailing off around the world!"

I was shocked. "Juvenile?"

"You're a grown man. You have a family and all the responsibilities that go with it. You can't just decide, like some eighteen year old kid, to join the Merchant Marine so you can see the world."

"I wonder what they pay?"

"What?"

"The Merchant Marine."

"Oh, grow up"

"Families go to sea all the time. They teach their own kids -- they have special courses. Think how it'd be growing up like that. I'd've given my left nut for a life like that."

"Yeah, well, just make sure you don't give them both up"

"Maybe I'd grow a new set!"

*****

Then along came Samantha, who was immediately attracted to that streak of wildness in me. She hailed from Alabama, had married young, raised four kids, divorced, then married a Chicago attorney, had another kid, then eight years old, bright and possessing a wild streak like me, divorced again at age forty, but still a well-put-together 100% female with a fetching accent and smoky promises in her eyes.

The friend traveling with her had come out to be closer to a friend of mine in San Quentin, another jailhouse romance. He'd asked me to help her get situated, and she'd stayed with her obnoxious brat of a ten year old neo-Nazi for awhile -- a huge mistake. After three days, we all hated them both, she a strident, militant, self-defined feminist futurist.

Samantha had what few women in my experience did, one of those rare, intuitive women who possessed an instinct about men, one who understood the essential sexual nature at the root of all masculine behavior, and accepted the limitations that those qualities impose on romantic relationships. In other words, she was a swinger of vast experience with both men and women -- she could not only go either way, but also in-between and beyond.

It took me a good six months before realizing that she was in control of our relationship, so subtle and unobtrusive were her manipulations. Although in bed -- and on staircases, in bathrooms, on beaches under the stars, standing up in an alley, in cars, and once even in a restaurant where she jacked me off without anyone the wiser -- we did everything her way, new and exciting things, shameless things, she somehow managing to make me believe that I, the ever-inventive and considerate lover, was in charge, the process nevertheless transforming me into a more sophisticated lover, furthering my education in the ways of women, and teaching me to discipline and direct my blatant enthusiasms.

My marriage, if it could be called that, began to come unglued at the seams as I sampled from both the old and new relationships, inevitably comparing them. It was not that I did not love my wife, for I did, but a new love, which I resisted, had entered into competition. And it was not that Samantha wished to help break up the marriage -- she would have been perfectly content for it to continue so long as it didn't interfere with her getting as much of me as her liberated needs required. She was not jealously possessive, willing, to let a good thing go around just as she herself liked to go around.

I, myself, was not so liberated -- as yet -- and neither was my wife. Our relationship thinned, the rift widening with every passing day, growing more bitter and vicious.

Not yet having committed to taking up with Samantha, I had moved out of our flat. But one night when I had a particular need for her peculiar comfort, she had turned me away, already having committed herself to another man's company for the evening. Bereft, I went home kissing up to my wife, with whom the sexual aspects were becoming less and less satisfactory -- which is when I committed a really crude and stupid act.

We lay upon the bed, both of us restless and in different worlds, only our bodies having come together in some desperate act that the more frantic it became the less it fed our needs, and I asked her the unforgivable question which could never be taken back or otherwise excused.

"Do you think it's possible for a man to love two women at once?"

Her screaming reaction, her utter revilement, drove me out in shame and shock. But it was hard to cut the ties, to be sane. Something drew me back, something drove me away. Was I running toward something or away from something?

Once, shod in a pair of heavy boots, I called her from ten blocks away in a hot phone booth. She informed me that she and my daughter had just swallowed a bottle of sleeping pills. I dropped the phone and began to run full tilt, my feet thudding down the sidewalk faster than if I'd been running from the cops. A stitch up my ribs, out of breath, and my legs as heavy as logs, I arrived just in time to see her bundling my daughter and herself into a waiting cab, her face uglified by a vicious grin as she looked back through the rear window.

No, she hadn't had a change of heart, horrified at feeding herself and our daughter sleeping pills, and heading out for a hospital to have their stomachs pumped. It had all been a dirty trick.

The phone calls became fewer as my attentions turned more toward Samantha, a perfect consolation, but one I initially balked at in my penurious condition. I had quit my job, bought an old station wagon, and had moved over to Marin County across the Golden Gate Bridge, where I had begun to draw unemployment.

As I had often done, I sought to escape and begin a new life from scratch. Feeling somewhat misogynistic, I left California, driving up through Oregon and Washington, headed for a job or, a crab-fishing boat that plied Alaskan waters out of Seattle. Signing on meant four months living and working aboard the crab boat, four months during which I could save almost all my pay for a stake, and four months without the company of women -- which I damned sure didn't need anyway!

Ah, me boyos, how well a man knoweth himself not! Before I could arrive at the docks the ships sailed from, I turned around, drove all the way back, straight to the beach cottage where Samantha stayed with her son in Stinson Beach. When she answered my knock, I planned to be nonchalant, just-happened-to-be-in-the-neighborhood-and-thought-I'd-drop-by, hoping a man wouldn't open the door to give me a knowing smirk. When she appeared, she said simply, "Oh, Buck," then pulled me inside and led me straight to bed.

We made a pretty good team, she good at dealing with people, me with ideas. She was living in a house too big for us, so we sublet two rooms to allay expenses. Then I found an eight-bedroom place in nearby Bolinas and, suddenly, ideas going off like proverbial lightbulbs in my head, we were soon into a strange but innovative new business for ourselves.

We leased houses all over Marin County, big expensive houses, estates, really nice fancy homes, which at the time were a glut on a depressed real estate market. Then we would carefully sublet them room-by-room, transforming each into a quality communal living situation, attracting upperclass wannabes, and doing very well financially. We called it between ourselves Quality Commune Services (QCS), which, after a time, became abbreviated as Quacks -- - because the work and headache of keeping it all together out of a notebook and our heads, the necessity of playing mommy and daddy to over a hundred rent-paying tenants who brought every disagreement to the ultimate authority -- us, we two -- it would all soon enough begin to pall. How could I be a father to a hundred grownups when I couldn't even be one to my seven year old daughter?

But, whoa, let us not forget the fringe benefits! Opportunities abounded, connections begging to be made. The benefits include, frequent sexual and business encounters. In addition to orgiastic possibilities in coupling, we often managed to turn an extra buck where no one else could see the profit. I not only turned small grass and pill deals from time to time, but practically had my own whorehouse to sample freely from, the self-liberating independence energies of the sixties still rampant.

Once I wound up with twenty thousand decks of pre-WWII, really funky porno playing cards, which I hustled as connoisseur collectors' items through mail order. People short at rent collection time found creative ways to come up with it. I wound up with an old Chevy van and a light Honda motorcycle, even a couple of horses for one of our country properties. Once Samantha and I were offered starring roles in a porno film, the business of a loving couple in one of our houses. There went my chance at stardom, I being too shy!

After a year and a half or so, it all became too much for me. Quacks was driving me looney trying to cope with all the shit that occurs when diverse elements of the human species attempt to live together in harmony. How far can the Bacchanalian call carry a man anyway?

A man without purpose is a man who's restless. The old dream of the sea began to reassert itself, dreams of sailing to faraway places. I had, along the way, acquired two round-the-world airline tickets, good for a year, which I had tucked away for the time Samantha and I could make a lull in the hectic day-to-day scheme of things -- London, Paris, Berlin, Madrid, Rome, Greece, India, Japan -- and promptly forgot them.

I had taken to reading my favorite book in the Bible, Ecclesiastes. "Vanity of vanities," sayeth the Preacher. "All is vanity. I communed with mine own heart, saying, Lo, I am come to great estate." But "that which is crooked cannot be made straight: and that which is wanting cannot be numbered."

"And I gave my heart to know wisdom, and to know madness and folly: I perceived that this also is vexation of spirit."

"For in much wisdom is much grief: and he that increaseth knowledge increaseth sorrow."

"I said in my heart, Go to now, I will prove thee with mirth, therefore enjoy pleasure: and behold, this also is vanity."

"I said of laughter, It is mad: and mirth, what doeth it?"

"I sought in my heart to give myself unto wine, yet acquainting my heart with wisdom: and to lay hold on folly, till I might see what was good for the sons of men, which they should do under heaven all the days of their life.

These passages struck chords and I wondered if the Preacher had not been influenced by Buddha.

Hawaii, it occurred to me, sat like a string of emerald jewels surrounded by the greatest sea of all, a place where zillions of sailboats arrived and departed for other destinations, other faraway lands and people. I asked Samantha if she would be willing to close out the business and go with me to Hawaii. She said no, she liked it where she was, thank you, in her perfect element.

Samantha's world did not extend much beyond the immediate reach of her senses. Other than intense sexual passion and an enduring fondness -- she somehow managed to remain friends with all her old lovers -- as normal people have for their pets, ordinary emotions like envy or jealousy, ambition or anger, and God forbid, political fervor, were all but complete strangers to her own nature. When she encountered them in others, she controlled her astonishment and became an intuitive parrot of sorts, a mirror reflecting her conversants to good effect, a sounding board, a good and patient listener.

When I kissed her goodbye to continue the search for my destiny, she said only, "Be good to yourself Buck."

A few months later, when I had begun to establish myself on the Big Island, postcards began to arrive from London -- and Paris and Berlin and Madrid and Rome and Greece and India and Japan -- all from Samantha. She had a new beau and they were both enjoying the tickets I had left behind, thank you very much.

Having been through the worst, the best, and all the grayness in between, I got off the plane in Hilo and began to look around.

###

CHAPTER 4

I took to Hawaii like the fish in me took to water. The laid-back lifestyle, the varieties of beautiful people, and the landscape -- the mountainous interiors, the rainforested slopes, right down to the fine beaches at the shoreline, the villages and towns sprinkled along the two-lane roads, mostly lovely weather year round -- all bade me aloha, Buck, welcome.

Stepping off the plane in Hilo for my first deep breath of sweet tropical air, I was on a natural high with two suitcases, a few thousand bucks in my pocket, the challenge of a new life before me, and a definite feeling that I was in my natural state of existence.

The taxi took me on a one-minute ride along the hotel loop fronting Hilo Bay between the airport and the major city, population some thirty thousand souls. I rented a bungalow in a fifteen unit motel formed in a U-shape around a swimming pool, the bay only a matter of yards away. The camelhair overcoat was the first to go, then the necktie, those suitable accouterments of life in the Bay Area, in favor of cotton drill pants and a short-sleeved shirt.

After changing, I meandered out to the road and saw a bar up the way toward the airport fronting another bungalow-style motel. Because it had a curious number of peaked and curving lines painted along one side, I went for a closer look. They were waveforms showing how high the last three tidal waves, called tsunamis, had risen up over the land!

I went in to inquire further over a drink. It was quiet, only a few customers scattered about, with a dark smiling bartender and a waitress.

"Aloha, sah, what I can serve you, please?"

"Gin and tonic, I guess."

"Ah, easy, no pro'lum."

"How're you on margaritas?"

"I fix fine, only no mo'ah Mekikoni limes. 'Melican only. Is okay?"

"Whoa. What's that? No more what kind of limes?"

"Mekiko. Is country down from 'Melica."

"Ah, Mexico. No more Mexican limes -- only American ones?" "Yes, so sorry. You like?"

"No, no, my man. You can't make a proper margarita without Mexican limones. Tell me this, what's popular with the tourists?"

"Oh, they like maitais an' chi-chis."

"Good?"

"Oh, yes. I make wit okolehao."

"Okole-who?"

373

"Okolehau. Is Hawaiian booze. Very strong. Okolehau mean hot ass, only we tell tourists it mean hot pants."

I grinned. "Sounds good to me. Fix me up something with okolehau."

It had coconut and pineapple flavors mixed with something earthy -- like tequila or mescal. Then he told me about the tsunamis, relating anecdotes about dumb tourists wading out in the shallows to pick up fish flapping about when the water receded before the wave struck and being carried a half-mile inshore. It was not really a crashing wave as I'd always imagined, but more a rising swell of sea that moved up and over its usual boundary -- nevertheless of such force from the pressure of its mass to do extensive damage coming and going.

"No worry. Only happen every ten, fifteen, twenty year."

I made a note to myself to check the date of the last one painted on the side of the building. I ordered up another of the same. "Double up on the okolehau, my friend. That's pretty good stuff."

"Right'chu ah, sah." He turned to speak to the waitress. "Mele, bring pupus fo'ah dis gennulman, wiki-wiki."

I wondered if I'd heard right, hoping it wasn't something in a diaper. Sitting up my drink, Mele came close behind with little dishes of food and a pair of chopsticks.

"We need more chicken," she told the bartender.

"I fix," he responded, disappearing.

The waitress grinned, tall, very tall, blond, and skinny as a rail, but otherwise not bad looking, nose like a windvane. "You know how to use these?" she said, indicating the chopsticks. "I can get you a fork."

"No, that's okay. Mele, pretty name."

"It's Pidgin for Mary."

"Pidgin?"

"It's a mixture of English and Hawaiian, with the odd Chinese, Japanese, Filipino, and Portuguese, thrown in, the English having its own peculiar pronunciation."

"The Rs are silent and dragged out like broad As."

"Yeah, you've got a good ear."

"You're not local, right?"

"Hardly. I'm from California -- Santa Cruz."

"No kidding? I'm from San Francisco, Marin County."

"Oh, yeah? I know a lot of people there. I graduated from UC Berkeley."

"Hey, I roomed with a dance instructor there for a couple of weeks. So, what brought you over here?"

"Summer break. Couldn't afford Europe."

"Ah."

"Liked it, decided to stick around awhile."

"You been to Honolulu? What's that like?"

"Ugh. Big city, tourists, lot's of bullshit."

"Right. I just left all that."

"You got a job lined up?"

"Nah, I can afford to coast for a couple of months, give me a chance to look around. How far to town?"

"Easy walk. Try the Kaukau Place. It's nice and laid back. All the haoles go there."

"What's that?"

"A pizza place, vegetarian dishes. Sometimes they've got a band. Imported beers."

"No, what's a haole?"

"You and me, baby -- caucasions. It really means foreigner, anybody who's not Hawaiian, but now it stands mostly for whites."

"What time you get off work? Maybe you could be my guide for awhile, show me this Kaukau Place."

"Sure. I'm off at six. Where you staying?"

"Just a stroll down the road. What am I eating, by the way? Tastes like chicken. It's good."

"It is. Deep-fried chicken-bits. The other stuff's squid. You dip it in the yellow stuff -- miso sauce."

"Good," I said, trying it. "Kinda chewy."

"Yeah."

"What's pupus mean?"

"Snacks. Serving pupus is a custom here. They serve them everywhere, some simple, others more elaborate."

"So I could just about live in a bar?"

She laughed. Great overbite.

"Yeah, I guess. And a lot of them stay open until four-thirty in the morning."

"Enough time to wander down to the beach for the sunrise." "Yeah. I might be a little late. Give me your room number and I'll come by."

I did. It was early yet, so I wandered about, stopping in at a couple of other bars, found Ken's Pancake House, which I was to learn was the only twenty-four hour eating establishment on the island. Walking along the side of the road toward Hilo, I saw an island of a couple of acres that could be accessed by a footbridge. It had lawns, bathrooms, benches, and picnic tables -- a park. It was called Coconut Island. A couple of old guys were trying their luck fishing from the bridge.

Continuing on to Kilauea Avenue, which turned out to be the main street, I turned right to look down off an arched bridge above a river rushing over a rocky bed to the sea. I turned back for the busyness the other way, shops, restaurants, grocery and department stores. I bought a pair of thick-soled rubber thongs, which seemed to be the preferred footwear, and a couple of colorful tanktops.

I stopped a trio of hippy-types, two guys and a girl, asking for directions to the Kaukau Place, which was only a pretext. The girl had lived in Marin County, so we swapped tidbits trying to establish whether we knew anyone in common. I offered to buy them all a beer, but they were on a mission, so I popped the question.

"Hey, maybe you can help me out. I'm looking to score a little stash of weed."

"Nah, man, can't help you. We're health freaks, don't do no drugs."

"Can't point me in the right direction?"

"Nah, man, we don't mess around, ya know?"

"Yeah, I can dig it. Peace."

As we parted company, I heard one mutter, "Fucking makai." I bought a six-pack of Bud and strolled back to my new digs, sat with an open can and a Camel watching two local guys with two foxy haole girls playing around the pool. One of the guys struck me, a well-muscled and proportioned body, longish coal-black hair, brown skin, and a face movie-star handsome. He had a great smile and moved with an appealing dignity, a sense of confidence and self-possession. I didn't know it then but in a few months we would meet and he would become not only best friend, but introduce me to the first course of an extensive education in the business which would be my principal source of income for the next couple of years.

*****

The light of the day was fading. Since Hilo was located on the eastern half of the Big Island, it was perfect for sunrises, but the high elevations of the interior brought late afternoon shadow.

Mele showed up with an overnight bag and a request to use the shower and change.

"Sure. Care for a beer first?"

"Please. You want to smoke a doobie with me?"

"Pretty please."

I sat beside her on the couch. She was almost as tall as me. Sipping and passing the joint back and forth, I asked what makai meant.

"Oh, see, they don't use directions here, you know, like north, south, east, and west. Everything is either toward the mountains or toward the shore. Mauka is toward the mountains. Makai is toward the ocean." It didn't make sense so I told her how the hippy-type had used the word.

"Oh, shit, they thought you were a cop. Makai also refers to the police."

I laughed.

"Are you?"

"Me? Oh, darlin', if you only knew! To me, that's very insulting."

"Why? Are you a crook or an ex-con?"

I looked at her. "You think we might try a kiss or two before getting into true confessions?"

Without waiting for an answer, I had my lips on hers, my tongue exploring her overbite. The kiss-count went way beyond two, each growing longer and more interesting as our bodies got closer and closer, our hands moving, feeling, pulses shifting to a higher gear.

"Whew, man, wait! I'm all sticky from work. I want to shower first."

"Mm, okay, feel free."

"Why don't you roll us up a couple more numbers," she suggested, pushing over the sandwich baggie with a half ounce or so of grass and a packet of papers.

"Sure. You know where I can get some of this stuff? It's pretty good."

"Oh, yeah, no problem."

I twisted up a couple, heard the shower, took stock and decided. I took off my clothes and stepped into the bathroom, knocking on the open door. "Hey, Mele."

Her head popped around the curtain, hair all wet. "Yeah?" "I'm all sticky, too."

Although I preferred women with some meat on their bones, I never-the-less discovered that in some cases there is, indeed, some truth to the claim that the closer the meat to the bone, the sweeter it is.

*****

The pizza was excellent, with a whole-wheat crust, and so was the beer, a Heineken for Mele, a San Miguel dark for me. The place was crowded, mostly with haole hippy-types, a lot of long hair, beards, and unconventional dress. The entertainment was, well, interesting, a small stage allowing amateurs to try out their stuff. The place reminded me of certain bohemian or beatnik coffeehouses in North Beach in San Francisco. I liked it, an open corner place with two double-door entrances and big plate-glass windows, down-to-earth tables, benches, and chairs. The musicians were a guitar, a banjo, and a harmonica, their interpretation of Dylan songs -- not bad.

"Oh, there's Jeff," Mele said, nodding toward a blond long-haired, bearded figure. "He's my connection. Give me fifteen dollars and I'll get you a lid."

"Can you introduce me?"

"He won't sell to you. He only deals with people he knows personally."

I gave her the money. "Listen, just introduce me. I'll buy him a beer. Then you can whisper in his ear, whatever, go take care of business. But tell him it's for me. See, I want to get to know him, let him see he can trust me so we can deal direct. Okay?"

"Sure, c'mon."

Mele did the honors and we joined Jeff and a plump, freckled red-haired girl. Fresh beers on hand, the whispering started and Jeff soon sent the red-haired girl out. When she returned a few minutes later it was to pass a rolled and taped baggie of grass under the table to Mele, who slipped it to me. I peeked down at it in my lap, nice, fat, and green.

"Great. Why don't you stick it in your purse for now?"

She did.

"Stuff looks fresh, not brown like Mexican or Columbian," I said to Jeff. "If it's anything like Mele's, it'll be a good toke. I appreciate it."

"Oh, yeah, good shit. Better than Mele's. She's got Kona-side. This is Puna-side."

"Oh, yeah? What's the difference?"

"Kona-side, see, that's the other side of the inland, the dry side. See, there's a windward and leeward side. Kona's on the leeward. Over here, the Puna-side, we get all the rain. What she's got is Kona Gold. It's good stuff. But Puna's the best in the whole fucking world."

"No shit? Ever tried Michoacan," I asked, naming a small state in Mexico that had put out some pretty mean smoke.

"Oh, yeah, I've smoked it all. Panama Red, Columbian, Hindu Kush, Thai, all good shit when you get the primo grade. But this beats 'em all, the best. They call it Puna Butter."

"Weird name."

"Yeah, the name comes from a butter that Hawaiians make out of grass."

"Really?"

"Yeah, it's green -- because they use fresh grass, it's still got the chlorophyll in it, see?"

I nodded. "How they make it? You mean like butter you can put on your toast? They eat it?"

"Yeah, yeah, that's it, right."

He explained that it was made by macerating freshly harvested pakalolo, (Hawaiian word for marijuana.) and saturating it in butter melted over a low heat. Since the stony THC (Tetrahydracannibinol, the atomic combination of four hydrogen atoms that helps make up the intoxicating element in marijuana.) in grass is oil-soluble, the ingredients of the high are precipitated in to the butter, which soon turns green from the chlorophyll. After straining out the leafy debris, the butter is refrigerated back into firm cakes ready for spreading on toast, bagels, English Muffins, whatever, a nice way to start the day.

"Amazing," said I, who knew no more about grass than how high it made me.

"Yeah, the locals got a few tricks makes the stuff kickass. You hang around long enough, you'll see what I mean."

"Things are looking better and better." Now if I could just get used to walking around in thongs. If I ever had to run, I thought, the first thing would be to kick out of them.

Back at the bungalow with two six-packs of San Miguel, Mele and I were soon shed of our clothes, two fresh bottles before us, as she twisted up a couple of fat ones from the stash I'd bought.

There are two basic kinds of high delivered by grass, downers and uppers. The down-high slows you down, lays you back, and makes you lazy. It's nice and cozy. The up-high is just the opposite --it stimulates, makes you active, feeling good to be alive, manic. The down-high is common; the up-high is very rare. The Michoacan I'd mentioned had been an up-high the few times I'd smoked it from a small stash scored in San Francisco -- in fact it had surprised me. The name or origin had nothing to do with whether it was an upper or downer; it was just a special difference that nature seemed to provide from time to time for mysterious reasons.

Luck is mysterious, but there it was. My first day in Hawaii I had a Puna Butter up-high, a cold bottle of San Miguel washing down over a great pizza, and ready for my second go-around with a long-tall-Sally hot to fuck. Amen.

*****

When I awoke late into the light of the next morning bathed in a fine sheen of sweat, Mele was gone. After a shower, a shave, a cold beer and a thin joint, I strolled down to Ken's Pancake House for a waffle with strawberries and whipped cream and a cup of coffee. Good business, cheerful employees and customers. Meandering back to my digs, I thought about renting a car, going sightseeing. They'd probably want a credit card, which I didn't have. The sun was hot. Maybe I'd buy a hat. Might as well get some groceries, stock the shelves and refrigerator with a few basics. Better have another beer and another mini-rollie while I thought about it some more. Refreshed and with a few joints tucked into the cut seam of my pants at the waist, covered by my belt, I put on my shoes for some serious walking. Up front, near the entrance of the hotel next door, I found four marines in a good mood piling into a rental car.

"You guys heading into town?"

"Yeah, man, if that's where the pussy is."

"Can I hitch a ride? You got room for one more?"

"Hop in."

The driver was a sergeant closer to my own age. The other three were kids riding out of their teen years, exuberant kids with not enough action to expend their energy on.

"You know where there's a liquor store?"

"Sure, just down the way here."

"You a hippy? You a drug-crazed hippy?"

"Nope. I'm a psycho-ninja-killer in disguise."

"Right on!"

"We like hippies, especially the girls! They like you, they put out, just strap that old pussy right on your arm!"

"It ain't your arm you fuck with, dickhead!"

"We like hippies cuz they got drugs! Drugs and pussy and good hooch, what else is there?"

"Why the fuck'd you join the fuckin' marines, you asshole?" "Semper fi, gash-face! I'm in Hawahya, ain't I?"

Whew! I'd hooked up with a lively crew. I'd noticed the sergeant sizing me up in the rearview mirror. "Can you put us on to some smoke, man?"

"I'm new around here myself, pal, sorry. Met a guy last night but I don't know where he hangs out."

"Shit. Sure would like to score a few lids."

"However," I decided, "I got a few joints I'd be happy to share."

"Right fuckin' on!"

"There's a liquor store! Stop the car!"

The two kids in the back with me were out. "Okay, whattaya want, Sarge? Taking orders. Whattaya like, dude?"

"Whatever you guys are drinking's fine with me," I said.

"Get me one of them little bottles of 151 rum," Sarge ordered.

While they were out I undid my belt and pants and let the two in the front seat watch me pull out a cellophane-wrapped packet containing five joints. I handed the Sarge one. "Here, you guys can get that one going. But maybe we should take a little drive while we're smoking, you know?"

"Yeah, good idea. Thanks, man, really appreciate it."

"Hey, what the fuck, brothers under the skin, right? I like you guys."

"Right on, brother."

"Cept when it comes to pussy. I don't do seconds or thirds. I fight for first fuck or go without."

"Man after my own heart! Get down, you bad motherfucker!"

The two kids returned with the rum for Sarge and two bottles of Boone's Farm strawberry wine, which turned out to be some nasty shit. Through the first two joints while cruising down the rim road highway after a few slugs, I laid it on the kids. "Ugh! You guys actually like that shit?"

"Hey, what the fuck! It's better than Tokay or Muscatel!"

"What do you have against Cabernet Sauvignon?"

"Ooh, fancy!"

"Even burgundy. Only thing stops me from throwing up is I'd have to taste that shit again!"

"Try some of this," Sarge offered. "Put a little hair on your chest."

"Yeah," quipped one of the kids. "Dissolves pubic hairs stuck in your teeth, too!"

We rollicked around town all day, hitting bars, making noise, and laughing our asses off. By late afternoon, the kids needed steadying when it came time to walk, but Sarge was like a rock, a tolerant, easy-going rock, able to ambulate and drive under all circumstances.

"Good kids," I muttered to him in a bar while they were arguing over what buttons to push at the jukebox.

"Yeah," he grinned. "But who the fuck likes good kids?"

"I do."

"Yeah, me, too."

"Where you guys out of?"

"Kaneohe."

"Where's that?"

"Oahu."

"You get over here often?"

"Ah, every month or two for a few days. Beats Honolulu."

"You stay the same place every time?"

"Yeah, usually. We get special rates."

"Maybe I'll see you next time around, try to do you a little better on the grass side."

"Hey, that'd be great. We like to take some back, sell it to the guys in the barracks, supplement the stingy pay, you know?" "How much you take back?"

He shrugged. "Whatever. Usually only a few ounces, but we could handle a couple of pounds or so, maybe more."

"I'll see what I can do," I said, thinking I'd see Mele and get hooked into Jeff. "When you leaving?"

"We're out of here at 0600."

"Don't know if I can move that fast. I'm just off the plane here myself. But I'll give you a few joints' worth out of my personal stash. Next time you're over, maybe I can do better."

"Right on, man. That's some really good shit you got."

"Yeah, ain't it."

By eight o'clock, we were all dragging ass toward our beds. I thought about tottering on down to the bar where Mele worked. No, shit, it was too late. She was off shift. Had she come by? Just as well we'd missed connections I was exhausted and it was tough sleeping with a cooing broad trying to sit in your face.

*****

It was about a week before I saw Mele again, but not from choice. I'd been down to her place of work to inquire and been told she'd quit. When next I saw her it was at Kaukau Place and she was with a local guy an inch or two shorter than her, but wide and husky, a guy with an attitude as evidenced by the hard look on his face. I had stood and started to wave, but she turned away, sat down at a table with the guy. I knew she'd seen me but was making like I didn't exist. Ten minutes later two other local guys came in to join them, and Mele excused herself for the bathroom. I waited a bit, then made my way to the short hallway where the facilities were, picked up the receiver to a payphone and pretended to make a call.

"Mele," I said when she opened the door to come out. "Hey, what's happening?"

"Oh, listen," she reacted, backing in out of sight. "I'm here with my ol' man, you know, and he's kind of possessive."

"Your husband?"

"My boyfriend."

"Oh. I went by looking for you -- they told me you'd quit your job."

"Yeah, we're moving over to Maui."

"Oh."

"Listen, do me a favor, huh? Act like we don't know each other. Otherwise there might be pilikia, you know?"

"What? Pilikia? What's that?"

"Trouble. He's the jealous type."

"Oh. Well. No problem. I wish you luck."

"Mahalo. Oh, sorry. That means thanks."

"Oh, hey, I should be thanking you. It was a great welcome to Hawaii, you know? Mahalo." She smiled, that great overbite, her thin long nose a real cutwater, mascaraed blue eyes like pale sapphires. "It was nice, Buck. I hope we meet again sometime. I gotta go. Bye."

"Bye."

Well, me restless boyo, I counseled myself as I returned to my lonely beer, time to quit ferking around and get to work.

*****

A week later I was operating a D-8 Caterpillar clearing spaces on residential lots for house construction in an undeveloped subdivision called Hawaiian Fern Acres. It was all virgin rainforest-type growth over a vast flow of black lava that had erupted and run down the way a hundred and fifty years before -- or thereabouts.

The topsoil could be measured in inches, the ferns and trees and vines sending their roots through the crust below. It was amazing to me that such profuse plant growth could exist in such conditions, an all-but-impenetrable jungle of more new varieties than I was used to -- even wild orchids.

Like Jeff had said, we were on the wet side as I soon learned, the skies suddenly clouding over and dropping a torrent of rain. But never too cold; more refreshing than anything. Then it would be gone, leaving the jungle steaming in the hot sun. Sometimes it would pour down for several days and nights, but the land soaked it up and I was somewhat nonplussed that there were no creeks or streams to handle runoff, only dwindling pools caught in hollows.

I worked the Cat maybe two days a week, then spent another couple of days working with the boss and another guy doing construction work.

The boss was an entrepreneurial type, a favorite of mine, who was trying to drum up interest in the long neglected subdivision. Hawaiian Fern Acres had been laid out into two-acre lots with a rough grid of road scraped out by bulldozers. It was roughly a half-mile wide and a mile or so long, situated a quarter mile off the main road from Hilo, fifteen miles down, up to the Volcano National Park where the active Kilauea Crater bubbled away. The highway, called Volcano Road, passed through a village called Mountain View. A turnoff just before Mountain View led through sugar cane fields to Hawaiian Fern Acres, where there was maybe a dozen small residential abodes scattered about, mostly occupied by hippy-types in self-built structures, with maybe two or three locals -- one a pig farmer, the other a small orchid grower. No two houses or cabins were alike.

Curious, Mountain View. I'd been born in a town called Monte Vista, which translates as Mountain View.

Most of the owners of the lots were absentee-owners living on the Mainland, their properties likely purchased for future vacation or retirement homes. Most of the lots had been ignored for years.

The boss had conceived the idea of contacting the hundreds of lot owners and taking up 10% options to buy -- which meant he would come to some agreement on the total sale price of the lot, then pay 10% down with the balance due in two or three years. This gave him the right to improve the property, develop it by building a house, installing a septic tank, supplying utilities, and selling it all at a profit. The problem was that no utilities extended into the area -- no water and sewer lines, no electricity. Hey, no problem. You start small, drum up interest, create a demand -- by and by you had all utilities flowing in, a serious residential tract under way.

In the meantime, there were those twelve or so abodes where maybe thirty people were getting along very well, thank you. The answer to the water problem was to build a catchment tank that would be kept full from the roof runoff under a hundred and sixty inches of annual rainfall. The sewer problem was answered by installing underground septic tanks -- or an outhouse in a pinch. Electrical power could be supplied by an on-site generator -- in a pinch there were kerosene lamps, stoves, and even refrigerators. Central heating or air-conditioning? Forget it -- this was high ground, mild weather, never too hot or too cold. Lots of rain, but it kept your surroundings pretty, made your garden grow, and provided plenty of sweet water. Double-wall construction with endless bureaucratic codes? Forget it -- this was Hawaii. Single-wall construction and a corrugated metal roof was standard. Forget cement foundations -- set the houses up on poles to keep them above the pooling when the rain really poured.

My work was sporadic and variable. One day I might be out driving the Cat, the next throwing up a shed, a warehouse or a small house -- a cabin really -- of only six hundred and twenty square feet of floor space, a one-roomer with possibilities of adding on. The boss might have me down to the land records office going over the subdivision plat and copying down owners' addresses. Then he'd have me typing letters with propositions to them.

The warehouse we'd thrown up was for the purpose of storing building supplies, which had been purchased and shipped from Mainland U. S. ports -- buying them locally meant much higher prices. The boss' girlfriend lived at the same place I did, she having a more expensive bungalow with a nice little veranda that opened to the pool and the bayview beyond. She was a nice old gal and often enough invited me to join them for a grilled steak.

In my off hours, I was out on the town looking to boogey -- pussy, drugs, drink, interesting characters, and, as always, for an angle. In my couple of months on the scene, I had popped over to Honolulu for three days of taking in the city and all its tourists, the sights -- Waikiki and Diamond Head -- all the hustle and bustle. I'd also made a jaunt back to San Francisco and over the Golden Gate to Marin County to visit friends and party. But for business, too.

My stake was dwindling and I had to come up with a way to replenish it soon or I'd have to find a cheaper place to live and a regular job, change my free-wheeling lifestyle, which was depressing to even think about.

After a renewed acquaintance with Samantha, she still percolating along in the quality commune business, I went to see my old buddy, Gianmin, who lived with an Afghan right across from the old Kezar Stadium. I had an idea, but needed a small loan to pull it off properly.

I had naturally noticed, particularly when poring over the classified ads in newspapers, that many things cost more in Hawaii, especially stuff that had to be imported -- which was probably 90% of all goods available, the shipping costs raising the prices.

In San Francisco, I had made some comparisons. When I came across a warehouse sale in Oakland for household appliances, the lightbulb in my head went off. Medium-sized refrigerators were selling for $169.50. I thought maybe fifty of them would fit into a Seatrain or Matson Line shipping container. Calling them, I made a tentative deal for that many at a discount price of $149.50. Since I didn't have enough to pay for them and no credit, I went to Gianmin to borrow four grand on a short-term loan. The old bastard told me, sure, two-for-three, the exact rate that was charged in San Quentin. I calculated. Six grand back to him off what I could make when I sold them in Hawaii. Okay -- if I could get my price. If not, I was going to be out-of-pocket when it was all over. Well, risk was always a factor in capitalism -- put your money where your mind is.

I had a semi-truck driver come out and we loaded them into a trailer for delivery at the Matson dock in Oakland, where the container was hoisted aboard the ship for Hilo.

Back on the Big Island, the process was reversed and I had the trailer delivered to park out front of my boss' warehouse. After running an ad in the local newspaper, it didn't take me a week to sell them all at $349.50. What with all my overhead and repaying Gianmin, my poke had been increased to about ten grand.

Shit, I told myself, ain't nothing for a stepper. But alas, with money in my pocket, I am a profligate. Greenbacks flow through my fingers faster than greased sardines. I put in a few days labor and drew my wages on the one hand, and lived licentiously and extravagantly on the other.

When I learned I didn't need a credit card to rent a car, only cash, I was soon touring around the ring road that all but encircled the coast of the island. The break in the ring was at Waimea Valley on the eastern side at the north point and at Pololu Valley on the western side -- only a few miles as the crow flies from Waimea Valley, fingers of mountain ridges spread with beautiful valleys in between. I drove over the Saddle Road, which was a more direct link between the windward and leeward sides, up over the central highlands, stopping in for dinner at Kamuela on the downside western slope, hitting little villages and fine beaches along the way -- from coal-black sand to golden -- and boogying in Kailua Town on the Kona-side for a long weekend, the ol' dollaroos dribbling away. I'd even spent a couple of days sailing about with a couple of local boys in an outrigger canoe, fishing and cooking out on deserted beaches, chugalugging beer, sucking on fat joints, and eating our catch.

I had a fuzzy plan of sorts.

From day two of my arrival on the Big Island, I had been growing three or four pakalolo plants in styrofoam coffee cups from the few seeds I'd found in Mele's stash -- seeds I popped into an ashtray when I'd rolled us a couple of joints. I had simply scooped up a bit of dirt from outside and planted them. They had grown a straggly six inches or so and one day, in a moment of lack, I'd dried them in the oven for a couple of joints. Now I had more seeds picked from three pounds of grass I'd bought and sold to Sarge when he'd come over again with some of his boys, increasing my poke by a few hundred on the transaction. I'd gone out to Hawaiian Fern Acres one day and wandered off into the bush to clear a little plot to plant them, expecting in short order to find them shooting up like the lush surrounding foliage.

No such luck. Still, if I could somehow learn to grow the lovely Puna Butter in sufficient quantities to support myself, well... In the meantime, I had no complaints about my luck even though, unbeknownst to me, there was good news and bad news just over the horizon. The good news immediately affected my social life while the bad news dribbled in over the next few months -- my fuck-you money began dribbling away without much in the way of replenishment. The good news also made for a severe change in my lifestyle, a process of simplifying, and since it was ten times cheaper than the one I was growing accustomed to, it also stemmed the outlay of my hard-earned bucks.

I met Stephanie, an entirely new experience with an entirely different kind of woman than I'd ever previously known.

*****

I'd met this college student who was whiling away to the end of semester. We'd spent some drinking and toking time together, and I'd hit on him several times to put me on to his grass connection.

One late afternoon the boss' girlfriend had invited me over for a steak and some good wine. Sitting out on the veranda eating and talking in a relaxed way, I saw this female figure coming out of a bungalow just down the way -- sashaying our way. She wore a long green granny dress in heavy clogs, clip-clopping in short pigeon-toed steps with hips wiggling like a hootchy-kootchy dancer. A frizzy-headed hippy, I thought, but with serious tits and ass, a wide and beautiful dimpled grin pasted on her face -- a sight to see.

All the Zorba welled up in me, a quivery sort of anticipation. I'd brought a copy of Nikos Kazantzakis' novel with me, rereading it for the third or fourth time -- never having lost my fascination for his metaphor of two different characters interacting, each affecting the other, those parts of the self that are usually dichotomized as Appolonian and Bachanalian.

She passed, looking back over her shoulder at me before disappearing into the bungalow where the personification of a Hawaiian god lived. I wet my dry tonsils with a good slug of Claret, determined that I would speak to her when she returned, which was in a few minutes. This time I noticed a large carpetbag-type purse slung from a shoulder strap. She sashayed by again to return to the first bungalow, the spirits of our grins toward each other all but striking sparks in a friendly testing of blades. My ol' quickwitted self couldn't think of a thing to say, but right then and there I realized a favorite truth from Zorba, where he tells his bookish intellectual boss "...he who can sleep with a woman and doesn't commits a great sin. My boy, if a woman calls you to share her bed and you don't go, your\soul will be destroyed! That woman will sigh before God on judgment day, and that woman's sigh, whoever you may be and whatever your fine deeds, will cast you into Hell!"

Thus, fearing for the damnation of my soul, I lost all interest in meat or drink, rising clumsily from the table, stumbling, preparing to march myself to the bungalow, demand entrance -- kick down the door if necessary -- confront her to announce that by all the gods her soul's essential exudations were thick in my nostrils.

The boss and his girlfriend were snickering.

Just then the college student came rushing out the same door she'd entered. "Buck, Buck, Buck," he called and waved. "C'mon, c'mon, c'mon."

I moved toward him in a trance. "C'mon, Buck. Geez, the connection's here. You wanna score or not?"

He led me in. There she sat at a table apart from a loud crowded party in full swing. I sat across from her -- again that marvelous smile pulling at the strings in my own face. Out with a baggie, rolling a joint, lighting it, passing it to me. "See how ya like this."

I liked it, passing it back and forth, sharing saliva, and bought a bag for fifteen bucks. We talked, who knows saying what. Her big eyes, her dimpled smile, the reddish-gold mass of frizzy-curled hair, the Manhattan accent that I'd never liked now enamoring me.

"There's an outdoor concert at Coconut Island," I said. "Wanna go with me?"

"Ah, gee. I'd like to, but I can't."

"Why not?"

She opened the almost full carpetbag, showed me the baggie-rolls of grass. "I gotta sell all these. I promised the guy. He fronted them to me. I need the money."

Shit.

Hm.

"How many you got in there?"

"Fifteen more."

"If you can sell them in time for the concert, will you go with me?"

"Yeh, but..." I grabbed her bag. "Don't go away. I'll be right back," I said, and strode away out the door. Sarge and a dozen of his boys were next door.

"Hey, Sarge, ol' buddy," I began as soon as he opened the door, me barging in. "Best I could do. $20 a bag, but fat ones. Good shit."

"Nice purse you got there, dearie," said the smart mouthed kid with him.

"Thanks. Wait'll I change into my miniskirt, we can go dancing, sweetie-pie. I'm hot to trot."

Sarge took a look and told the kid to go round up the boys. I walked out with three hundred bucks, gave Stephanie her purse with two hundred and twenty-five in it. Hey, what the hell -- fun is fun and biz is biz. She counted it.

"Gee!"

"No time to waste, darlin', and it's passing by the minute."

"C'mon, I gotta make one stop then I'm free for the evening."

She had a 1954 International Metro stepvan with a pink butterfly painted over the grill, an auctioned off old mail truck. I noted a duffle bag and a sleeping bag in the back, a couple of inches of fat votive candle stuck to the floor, as she fired up, shifted the long floor-lever, and banged and rattled us away. Since there was only a single seat for the driver, I stood and held on.

It was simple, quaint, and charming. I dubbed her chariot the Iron Butterfly as we chugged over to pay off her connection, running in and out, yelling, "Roll us up some fat ones, baby, for the music! They got a good band there tonight!"

I did, then bade her stop at a liquor store where I popped for three bottles of Cabernet. Open bottle in hand, another in her purse, and one in reserve, we huffed and puffed and wet our whistles, parked, and strolled over the bridge. In no time at all we were kissing as if locked into a style about to pass us by.

High and full of exuberance, we danced on the lawn, kissing, kissing, and kissing, laughing and twirling about, a kiss near the bandstand turning into one of total abandonment as we reeled in a cyclone to fall back upon the raised stage, bodies and lips locked -- until a cheer from the onlookers brought us back.

In the Iron Butterfly again, having firmly arrived at the moment of silent commitment to further explore the developing situation, I studied her as she drove, asking questions, giving answers. She was 25, had been in Hawaii for several years, visited all the inhabited islands except for Niihau, worked occasionally for wages, and sold grass to get by. Of Jewish descent out of New York, she had never married, had no children, a free spirit searching for love and whatever.

"Where do you live?"

"Wherever I am."

"You know."

"You're looking at it. You're in it. Aloha, baby."

"Can I use the bathroom?"

"Wait, I'll find a tree."

"Where's the kitchen?" "Ken's is open."

"What about a bath, a shower?"

"We can go for a swim, hit the cold freshwater shower at a public beach."

"That's it?"

"Wait'll you see my bedroom."

I didn't relish it -- a thin pad rolled out over the corrugated metal floor, no place to piss in the middle of the night, no bathroom to wash up in the morning, no stove for coffee, no refrigerator for beer.

"Where are we going?"

"Just looking for a place to park."

She found it along the hotel loop not far from my bungalow. With the motor off, it was quiet. She lit the candle and rolled out the sleeping bag. We laid down next to each other to kiss and touch. As our breathing grew heavier in prelude to taking off our clothes, we were rudely interrupted by a pounding on the passenger-side door, a rather large young bumpkin demanding to be let in.

I sat up as she went to open the door and the guy half fell inside, clutching at her.

"C'mon, babe," he slurred. "I gotta hardon won't wait."

"Hey, listen, man, I've got company, you know?"

He looked at me. "Fuck 'im. I'm better company."

"Hey, c'mon, be nice."

A conversation of sorts ensued over the next few minutes with Stephanie trying to persuade him to leave, but he only became more insistent, spewing out lewd and leering references to his superior penis and her outstanding oral abilities, leading himself right up the ladder to outright belligerence. Throughout, his hands were busy at clumsy fondles, which she resisted. I could see that she was embarrassed, at a loss as to what to do.

"Hey, man," I said, standing. "Why don't you take the hint and buzz off?"

"Why don't you eat shit, asshole?"

I started forward. He backed away. "C'mon, c'mon, asshole, let's see what'cha got!" She grabbed my arm. "No, don't do anything. I don't want any trouble. We can just drive away, find another place. Please."

"Don't worry, darlin'. I took a course in how to win friends and influence people."

But she didn't believe me, hid her face in her hands and turned away from the door so she wouldn't have to watch.

Well, gee, here was an opportunity to show my stuff, all the jail fighting skills I'd learned, the boxing skills at Q, none of which in this case would require any Queensbury Rules. This was my chance to vanquish the rude foe, claim the lady's hand, and ride off in triumph.

Let's see now. He was bigger than me, younger, too -- actually a nice looking kid. But he was drunk and his reflexes were off. Plus, he'd probably never had to deal with a madman. I'd decided on a variation of the "crazy man act", which I'd seen performed now and again on inexperienced inmates in jail to relieve them of their money, scare the shit out of them, and make them compliant.

And of course I did fancy myself as something of an actor. After all, I had played a madman in my pal Rick's play, had directed the madness of my cellmates in The Cage. I took a couple of deep breaths and stepped out.

"Here, man," I began while moving toward him, sticking my hand in my pocket. "I don't want any trouble. Here's all my money, eight hundred dollars."

His eyes were on my right hand when I pulled it out of my pocket.

"You can have it all."

I reached out with my left hand, grabbed his right wrist and pulled him toward me, spinning him around. With his back to me, I put my right arm around his waist, hooked my left forearm around his corresponding elbow, then began stepping backwards, kicking at his heels. Just like that, he was plopped down on his ass, my grip transferred to his head. Quickly stepping my legs over his shoulders and hooking them back below his armpits, I pressed down with the weight of my body. He was immobilized. I grabbed his nose in one hand, his lower lip in the other, then went into my spiel, my voice harsh and terrorizing.

"You goddamn motherfucking cocksucking sonofabitch, don't make me kill you! I just got out of jail for shooting a goddamn mother-fucking cocksucking sonofabitch for messing with my wife and I've only got four goddamn motherfucking bullets left for my gun and I don't want to goddamn waste them on you! BUT I WILL IF YOU EVER PUT YOUR FILTHY GODDAMN MOTHERFUCKING COCKSUCKING HANDS ON MY WOMAN AGAIN! You understand me, motherfucker?"

He could only make glugging noises between the shocked gasps. I let him go and stepped back. "Four bullets or not, you're here when I get my gun loaded, I'm blowing you a new asshole, you goddamned motherfucking cocksucking sonofabitch! I don't care!"

I'd let my voice drop to a muttering of gibberish, moving toward the van, my eyes hyperthyroidally glaring. "Honey, get my gun I hate having to eat those fucking cockroaches in jail I like 'em too much honey get my gun where's my bullets in your purse this motherfucking goddamn...", but the rush of his feet padding along the pavement told me there was no longer any need and I started laughing.

"Oh, gawd, what'd you do to him? What'd you do?"

I got hold of myself. "Nothing, darlin'. He's fine. I just told him a little secret that he doesn't understand."

"Why's he running?"

"He's just in a hurry to work on that secret, that's all." She looked at me. "What secret?"

"Whether I'm crazy or not. C'mon," I said, taking her hand. "Let's go to my place. We'll be more comfortable." Actually I was also thinking that maybe the young lout might go shore up his courage with some buddies, perhaps arm himself, and return for another go-round.

Inside, I held her and kissed her ears, her eyes, her cheeks. "C'mon, sit down. Open that last bottle of wine. We can sit here and smoke some of this very fine grass. Here, take off your shoes."

"What'd you do? You sounded like a maniac." "Well, that was the idea. Ever heard of method-acting?"

"Yeh."

"See, method-actors, the really good ones, they go down inside themselves for the emotional content in their words, expressions, and gestures. I was playing crazy to scare the guy, that's all. I held my breath and strained -- that makes my veins stand out, my face red. Then I growl out horrible words, trying to dredge up personal pain and rage from past experience, whether my own or others'. Sometimes I just mimic a role I've seen played in some movie. In this case, the idea was to come off like an insane psychotic killer, which scares the shit out of just about everybody. It's all bluff, really, suggestion, the guy's own fear working against him."

"Why did you call me your wife?"

"Because that usually puts a guy in the wrong right away. You don't mess with a guy's wife when her husband is standing right there." "Are you sure you're not crazy?"

She had a stingy grin on her face. I pretended to think about it. "No," I answered. "I'm not sure."

Whereupon we both burst out laughing, and one thing led to another and we were both naked on the floor doing what we'd wanted to do from the first.

I was thinking in the quiet aftermath that if I hadn't been there in her van, she would likely have let the guy in, sedated and comforted him in his urgent need. But what cared I, the horny and newly liberated man? What was good for the gander was good for the goose. You couldn't wear it out, only improve its function. Like the Eskimos said, loan a man your boat and it might come back broken, but loan him your woman and she comes back good as new. And really, wasn't I the lucky one? I'd ricocheted from the champion piece of ass of all time in Samantha to a more youthful runnerup making a determined challenge for the title.

Later in the bathtub together, silly grins on our faces, I asked her, "Was it true, what he said?"

"What?"

"You give the best head in Hilo."

She was pleased, if a bit embarrassed, rather than insulted, and one of those playfully mysterious looks came over her face which only women can ever successfully manage -- a look that said "That's my secret, but I may let you in on it someday."

The future seemed filled with all sorts of somedays.

CHAPTER 5

When the rent was up on my bungalow a week or so later, I moved kit and caboodle into Stephanie's van. The first thing I did was build in a few amenities, the principal of which was a double-bed frame complete with mattress. I bought a two-person puptent, two backpacks, a Coleman one-burner stove, a sleeping bag, and pillows and linens for the bed, a few cooking and eating utensils. To top it off, in under the bed with the rest of the stuff went two diving masks with snorkels and a fiberglass sling-spear for fishing.

We had our own motorhome, jerrybuilt and ugly as it was. We hit the road carefree and full of enthusiasms, joined together in the excited anticipation of discovering new pieces of ourselves and each other, new places, people, and experiences. We hit the road looking to do some serious trucking, exploring the island and ourselves, our feelings for each other, browning like heathens in the sun, smoking all the varieties of pakalolo we came across and making love always. When we played music in a portable tapedeck-radio combination, I sometimes whipped out my kazoo to add my own riffs. We traded tastes in music, her contemporary ones against mine mostly locked in the past, Janis Joplin, my goddess of rock'n'roll and long old favorite blues.

All along the way, we were sizing each other up, building a sense of mutual trust. I was a go-it-aloner and do-it-yourselfer, while Steph was game to try anything. We were good trucking partners, I the planner and nuts-and-bolts half, she the socializer and smoother-outer -- taking up each other's slack.

Stephanie, I was somewhat dumbfounded to learn, had friends all over the island. Damn near anyplace we came to that contained people, she soon located someone she knew. Many, but not all, of them were people with whom she had joined in passing sexual liaison, most of them retaining a fondness -- but not all. Some were takers without much giving, users who considered her easy prey. Whenever I met them, whenever I came to the conclusions about their one-way attitudes, I altered my aura in subtle and sometimes not-so-subtle ways to let them know that I was a dog who would bite back in protection of my sweet little road-bitch.

Our first idyl was Southpoint, the southernmost tip of the island. On the way along the turnoff from the main road, we passed a ranch house or two and what I took to be a seemingly deserted radar station. Then the pavement ended and we continued along a barely visible dirt track over the empty treeless down-sloping plains. Well, nearly empty. There was lots of grass and feeding cows with half-mad looks about them. It was the wind, I reckoned, always blowing, only changing direction let you know it was everywhere always. Then the faint trail disappeared and we laid our own wheeltracks over the little hills and dales to park with the Iron Butterfly's rear doors to the sea.

The beach just below a six-foot dropoff of earth, was completely covered in seashells to a foot or so deep. We collected hundreds, maybe thousands. There were many varieties, but the most common was a type of black-and-white speckled one containing a natural stringing hole. Soon we had bracelets, anklets, and necklaces of them. Then I thought we could probably sell them, so we began stringing dozens of necklaces.

Fifty yards away lay a golden sand beach smooth and free of shells. We had already been down to Kalapana where the sand was coal-black. And now, a few hundred yards further along lay a beach of jade-green sand. The water generally ran out in shallows in eddying currents over endless coral formations and we would swim lazily along the surface taking in the wonders of form and color, sometimes losing ourselves in pakalolo-induced fixations until our hands and feet were wrinkled from being in the water so long, a chill invading our bodies which the sun soon cured.

Stephanie had scored some LSD and we decided in our great isolation with only the looney rolling-eyed cows for company to take a trip. Sipping on cold beers from our ice cooler and having heated a bit of Dinty Moore's beef stew on our trusty little one-burner, we lay nude on our stomachs next to each other, chins on pillows, watching the changing effects of the fading light upon the seascape through the open rear doors, listening to Papa John Creach fiddle his way up the heights while the magic lysergic amines of the acid worked its way over our senses.

There was too much energy flowing through us to lie still for long. The breezes over our naked bodies outside under a million stars were exquisite, as though dozens of cool lips were kissing us.

Stephanie began to run about, her arms outspread, head thrown back, twirling and leaping. "Oh, gawd, I feel so great! Baby, isn't it beautiful!"   l

"Oh, yes, oh, yes, my sweet darlin' girl," I chanted, joining her, dancing about. "This, right here and now, is what it's all about!"

We danced and played and kissed and touched and laughed, Papa John stroking his horsehair bow over our heartstrings, shivering up goosebumps from inside, sending thrills of sensations twanging through our bodies and minds.

Oh, me bucko, you have to run, run like you could run for miles and miles as a boy along the levee banks, run free and untamed, run for the sake of running, run, run, run -- and I began running over the grassy knolls, with every step a ha! leaping from my throat, step, ha!, step, ha! Ha...ha...ha...ha... Stephanie trilling behind, giggling and screeching and ahing and oohing.

My vision was a few yards ahead, my mind seemingly there, too, spying out the path, never stumbling or hesitating, extra-sensory-perception in action, and we ran on and on gulping great gobs of air into ourselves like manna from the heavens.

Until.

There was a darkness, an emptiness ahead, a danger, a cold and lonely death. And I stopped, heaving, alertness pouring from me like needles, turning to grab Steph. She tried to dance around but I stopped her, held her until her senses tuned into mine.

Panting and sucking air, she cried, "What, baby, what?"

"Sh."

We quieted ourselves, calmed our bodies, peering off into the darkness.

"What?"

"There's something missing."

"What?"

"I don't know. There's space and coldness and... and something." Her tense mood matched mine. "Oh," she breathed.

Holding hands, we edged forward. Suddenly it was there, a great black hole in the earth, like a mouth or a cave or a hole. We crept closer, looked down toward the center of the earth, a dark mysterious giant wormhole to infinity.

And suddenly we saw shimmering stars, a more or less round circle of them as big as a barn, little points of light blinking.

"Water, fucking water," I said as it came to me. Twenty feet below us was a smooth mirror of water and we were seeing the reflections of stars in the sky.

"Oh, my gawd, baby, we could have fallen into that! What is it? What's it doing here?"

The walls of the watery pit were straight up and down. Once in, there was no way out without help from above. How deep was it? A drowning hole for the unwary, none to hear your cries for help but the dumb looney-eyed cows, the only witnesses besides theoretical angels, spirits, and gods.

"Let's go back. I don't like it here."

"No, let's stay. I think we can learn to fly here."

"What?"

"Jump on my back, c'mon, piggyback."

She lifted a leg over my hip, pushed up to put her arms around my neck, her other leg clamping me, my forearms under her knees. "Like this?"

"Yeah."

"What now?"

Her pussy was warm against the top of my ass where it blended into my spine, her tits warm and wet with the sweat between us. "I run, I leap, we fly off into the darkness for the stars."

"Are you fucking crazy!"

I laughed. I shrugged her off, knelt and pulled her down, kissing, licking, and sucking, wanting to ingest her inside me, be consumed, feed her, satiate her.

"Oh, oh, baby, oh, yes!"

There are endless ways to fly.

*****

After a dip in the shallows, splashing and giggling like two kids, we dried off, we lay on top of our bed to squirm and toss, turn and roll, our bodies coming into contact for awhile, then pulling away to allow the breezes to evaporate the recently merged areas of skin sticky with sweat, unable to sleep, the energies still dissipating, dozing a bit, then waking and moving to new positions in our sprawl.

And my mind clicked along in consonance with my senses, seeing part's of myself, examining them, trying to connect them to other parts, adding pieces to pieces, making bigger ones and fewer, aiming for an integrated whole, but never succeeding, the puzzle too vast and shapeless on the edges to contain the perceptions as a whole entity.

In the kaleidoscopic swirl of the whole of myself at any given moment passed pieces that I cherished, having over time discovered the seeds of their substance and, with ever-renewed awareness, watched them grow, all relatives forming the extended family of my character.

There was the idea that my mind served as the primary tool of my survival in any given circumstance, that rich but subtle thing that differentiates a human being from all the other animals and raises him to supremacy. Reason, thought, the ability to look inward and outward and merge the two views into a driving force of some considered control.

Then there was my physical self with needs that often seemed beyond understanding and control, vague urges rising up to put their toes on the accelerator. Beyond reading, thinking about what I read, and my general and specific experience in the world over a lifespan so far achieved, there had been two primary role models to serve as teacher and guide by assimilation -- my father and a high school teacher at Q. The first had taught me by example the value of the mind in providing life's necessities -- food, shelter, and security -- through a process of benign competition in the opportunities presenting themselves out of the seemingly random chaos of the universe. I had also absorbed a certain basic morality -- that lying, stealing, and violence were mostly but not always wrong -- a certain rough code of honor, unrefined and inarticulate as it was. The second role model had proceeded to complicate matters; he showed me down a path leading to a larger world than I had known existed. He taught lessons in ethical behavior, that one's moral worth was essential in negotiating one's way through the inescapable social matrix -- a subject vastly more complex than my lazy notions had theretofore conceived, the one pellucidly clear need for self-respect paramount. Life required one's constant attention – to shutoff that higher part of the self, that essential core of character, to suspend reason and knowledge, was to invite disaster.

And I had done exactly that more than once, on some few occasions skating right out on the rim that divides life from death. And always in the aftermath of events gone wrong came the retrospective examination for the cause, which sometimes I seemed to detect with surety, but other times remained in the shadows of uncertainty.

Boiling down the fundamental proposition meant that with the fact of life came a corresponding desire to live it that fluctuated like a ship negotiating passage among reef-strewn seas. Some days were clear and sunny, not a reef in sight; others were storm-tossed and dark, the sound of surf pounding reefs lost in the foggy turmoil; then shipwreck, a marooning on some inhospitable isle. Even then, therefore, to continue with all inborn and acquired skills to make the best of it, to improve my vicissitudes. Unlike lesser animals, we must rely upon our minds rather than physical prowess; one comes before the other.

I had survived the narrow world of prison, the severely limited stimuli, making do with what was available and not doing so badly after all -- except for the constant awareness of what I was missing, all those unfulfilled yearnings for life swelling up in me. I had survived the violence-prone prison environment for so many years, not through being the baddest ass around, and not by instilling fear and preying upon weaker souls, but by some blessed ability to avoid violence. Violence is basically mindless and force never prevails for long in shaping human behavior. People will always resist force in the long run because it represents the essence of slavery -- which is not a natural condition. Physical force is morally defensible only as a last resort to protect against violence. This was a belief I had come to embrace completely.

In the Los Angeles County Jail before being sent to San Quentin, it had been necessary to physically defend myself against certain predatory types from whom there was no escape. I was lucky to have grown big and healthy, with a decent set of reflexes. These incidents, however, amounted to no more than fistfights.

In Q, the violence was potentially more serious with the availability of weapons. You could get yourself killed for the most ridiculous of reasons. Cluchey, having trained for Golden Gloves competition in Chicago, had taught me the rudiments of boxing. I continued my lessons in the ring at Q, where an excellent boxing program had been in existence for years. Boxing, of course, no matter how good you are, is of little use against two or three assailants armed with knives and clubs. The trick was to avoid them altogether, which was where the mind came into play -- the ability to foresee situations likely to lead to violence and to step out of their way or to exert an influence directing them away from you -- and all at the same time building an image of yourself that deflected rather than invited violence. It was a precarious balance, one requiring constant attention, but I had successfully managed it.

I had also firmly arrived at the philosophical position that free enterprise was the best system ever devised for human beings to better their positions. The capitalist ethic first posits the freedom of individuals to compete in the business of producing goods and services and trading them to others for mutual profit.

Enter my latest venture idea, the cultivation, harvesting, packaging, and sale of pakalolo -- pertaining to which I was presently engaged in a process of making contacts through the lines of Stephanie's friends and acquaintances who would serve me well in the enterprise when the time came.

It was simple. The best marijuana in the world was grown in Hawaii -- Kona Gold, Maui Wowee, and Puna Butter, as well as several other popular brand names emanating from the other islands. Hawaiian Fern Acres was located in the Puna District on the Big Island. Weather-wise, it was ideal -- plenty of water and sunshine and a sub-tropical climate which could produce two crops per year, unlike most Mainland conditions which permitted only one crop per annum in the six months it took marijuana to mature.

Already I had begun to acquire knowledge of the subject -- a slim paperback manual entitled The Cannabis Cultivator's Handbook, the first publication of over fifty that I would gather and consume in what some would describe as an obsession, but which I preferred to call an affaire de coeur. In time, I would become an expert, self-styled as the case may be, in the cultivation and preparation of pakalolo and its several by-products. And my conceptions of the venture would grow, schemes abounding -- from nothing to Madison Avenue in 3,687 not-so-easy steps with headaches galore.

In the cooling early morning hour, I sighed, and rolled over to snuggle against a nice set of cantaloupes.

*****

The sun well up in the sky, we went out to find our hole, found several of them. We speculated that they had been created by giant gas-bubbles trapped in the original lava flow -- which idea had been scientifically documented. There were tourist attractions to several of these phenomena, one called the Thurston Lava Tube, which appeared as a tunnel-like cave. It had been formed by an elongated tube-like bubble of trapped gas with the ends later knocked out. Some of the bubbles formed near the surface, with only thin layers of lava crust over them. When the crust broke, cavities appeared. The water in the ones we found may have been from an underground aquifer or seawater seepage. In one lay the skeleton of a cow shining up through the crystal clear water.

I had heard stories by locals when I'd been driving Cat about bulldozers breaking through the upper crusts of such gas bubbles and plummeting eighty feet to the bottom. They enjoyed the wariness in me that the stories produced, and once when the Cat had broken through such a crust and began tipping forward, I had leapt away in a great thrill of fear. Fortunately it was only about six feet deep and I had been able to back the tractor out and fill it with debris.

*****

We turned off every road, knowing only that it was mauka or makai, would go up or down, exploring every byway, from mountain hideaways to pristine little beaches and bays.

We met people, shared food, grass, booze, music, and even sex when it seemed appropriate.

Once, with a hitchhiker named George in tow, a handsome and insouciant Irish lad who thought highly of himself, we stopped in to visit a short but curvy Italian lass with long black tresses who lived with another girl in a bare-bones pioneer-like cabin, which was very cozy.

It's sleeping arrangement was a king-sized bed in a loft requiring a climb up a ladder.

The four of us were sitting around a table smoking grass, drinking wine, and carrying on in flirtatious conversation. George and the lady of the house were exchanging looks, sizing each other up. The idea before us was not that a free-for-all orgy was in the offing, but that we two couples would share the bed as a place to get it on, two couples each able to watch the other in action, which excited us all.

Stephanie pulled out a bottle of Parest 400s, which was the largest dose of pharmaceutical methaqualone available. They were originally intended as sleeping pills and provided a warm, relaxing feeling. Steph loved taking them before sex, claiming they were conducive to long, lazy fucks. I had tried them, finding that she was definitely onto something. Plus, unlike a lot of downers, methaqualone left you refreshed and alert the next day rather than depositing you in dragassed drug hangovers.

She parcelled out one apiece. George had never taken them. The girls explained. George was typical of most people who wound up misusing drugs -- he figured if one was good, two must be twice as good, an idea that had very definite limitations in most cases, dangers that could lead to overdosing and death. But George was insistent, bragging of his high tolerance -- which had begun to get to me. "No, only one," Steph said. "That's all it takes."

"C'mon," George wheedled. "One little cap ain't gonna do me."

Steph looked to me for help. I was feeling mischievous. Hotshot George wanted to strut his stuff, fine, let's see what he's got to strut, if anything.

"Sure," I said. "One more won't hurt him. Worst he can do is sleep like a log for twelve hours."

"Sleep, shit. What I been hearing, this is a performance drug. I'm gonna show youse how a real man performs."

"Here, George," I offered. "Have another glass of wine, help you wash 'em down."

What we all knew, but George didn't, was that alcohol acted like a kicker to the drug, making its effects more immediate and profound. "Sure, man, hey, that's good wine."

A half hour later, with three of us all warm and cozy and ready for the climb to the loft, I shook the all-but-comatose George. "C'mon, George. It's time to feast our eyes on all this gorgeous female flesh and et cetera."

"Yeah, yeah, umma way."

The ladies went up giggling, reaching the bed and beginning to take their clothes off.

George had managed to stagger to the ladder where he was barely holding himself upright.

"Need some help, George?"

"Nanana, uhcanduut," he muttered, sliding to the floor.

"Well, if you're sure," I grinned and climbed on up.

"Yayayaaaa..."

I disrobed and aimed myself for a spot between the girls, bejesus, the dream of every man, all fantasies to the fore as to just exactly what I was going to do with two of them at once.

But they had their own ideas.

"George, c'mon, I need help!"

Only silence from below as George spent the night curled around the foot of the ladder on a hard floor in a coma. Only ohs and ahs and sighs and wows from above.

*****

At Kailua Town, where we sold our necklaces from a seawall fronting the bay to passing tourists, tried a few clubs for food and music, we continued up to Puako, where I met Rick Schulz and his wife living in a beach house. From there it was on up to the end of the road at the entrance to Pololu Valley, where we to loaded up backpacks to hike down in and around.

At the backend of Pololu, we found a waterfall so high that only sprinkles and mist reached the cold clear pool below. We bathed, frolicked, toked up, and pitched our tent.

What a perfect place to grow pakalolo, I was thinking. No roads in and no tourists -- it was privately owned and used as a pig farm. Stephanie told me that she'd heard there were several more valleys on the way to Waimea Valley to the east, where the road started up again, that a number of farmers lived in Waimea, but that there was one she'd heard about halfway between there and here called Waimanu, pristine, uninhabited, and calling to us.

"Sounds great. We'll have to do it one day."

"Why not now?"

"Well, babe, we got to start thinking about putting money in the poke. It's been beautiful going the way we've been going, but if we keep it up long enough we're going to be flat broke -- no gas and oil money, no food and drink money, no grass money. We'll be like those guys on the beach I told you about, living on coconuts, bananas, guavas, and whatever fish they can catch."

I'd once left Steph with friends and walked a mile or so to this little crescent of beach for the purpose of spear-fishing along the reef for our supper. I'd taken along a few joints and had sat myself under a tree to get my head right before beginning.

Two naked guys had appeared from one end of the beach, one carrying some unhusked coconuts, the other a green stalk of bananas. We'd exchanged looks and waves as they'd passed, disappearing out of sight at the other end. An hour later, I was sitting with three fish under the tree toking up another joint in preparation to dressing them out and heading home to the Iron Butterfly and supper. The two guys, having donned shorts, strolled over.

"Hey, man, how's it?"

"Fine, how you guys?"

"We were wondering if maybe we could trade you something for some pakalolo."

"Ain't got but a couple of joints with me."

"Hey, that's better than nothing. We ain't had none in a while." "Don't see why not. It's all over the place."

"Well, we ain't got no money."

"Oh, yeah? How you getting by?"

As boys back to nature, barely, as it turned out. But they had some magic mushroom honey they'd trade me for the two joints.

"What's that?"

"You never heard of magic mushrooms?"

"Nah, what're they?"

They were nature's way of providing mankind with psilocybin, tiny psychotropic mushrooms that grew in old cowshit. The macerated tops would dissolve in honey over several weeks' time -- very stony stuff, they assured me, better than LSD. Well, I'd tried some stuff called psilocybin, whether organic or synthetic I didn't know, while once hitchhiking with a fine freckled piece of choice ass down to Santa Barbara to visit an old prison buddy who'd married into money. I'd like the psilocybin but not the crabs she'd given me.

"Sure, let's see what you got."

They soon returned with a 12 oz. jar about half full of golden honey. I handed over the joints, one of which they lit up. "Just a tablespoon, two at most, will do you, man."

"Oh, yeah?"

"We brought you a spoon."

I stuck a spoonful in my mouth and sucked on it, nice sweet honey was all I could tell. But a half hour later, as we sat shooting the shit, their skin began taking on a luminescent glow, pulsing, their voices containing an echo.

"Primo grass, man, thanks. Really nice looking fish you got there."

"Mm, yeah."

"Stuff's coming on, right?"

"Mm."

"Okay, man, we'll leave you to it. Be seeing you."

"Ah!"

"Huh?"

I pointed to the fish. Shit, I had a half dozen twilight zone highs left in the jar for two measly joints. It was only fair. "You want us to take the fish?"

Mm.

"Right on, right on."

Right on, right om, om mani padme hum-m-m-m. I had a whole ocean of fish. All I had to do was spear them. Om mani padme hum, fishies, ready or not here I come. But the coral formations were so fascinating that I skimmed over the surface for three hours studying them, forgetting all about diving down to invade the fishes' pretty cities like a murderous alien monster -- they were my friends.

Wrinkled hands and feet, a chill, the warmth of the sun blissful. Forget fishes, darlin', I will feed thee honey.

"You mean like work, get a job, all that?"

"Yeah, maybe a house to live in, too."

"A house?"

"Yeah, you remember what those are?"

"Yeh, vaguely."

*****

Steph told me she had once worked with a guy painting the stripes in a parking lot. We went to see him. Frank, who was an all-around guy when it came to any kind of construction work, was loafing along three sheets to the wind -- a tall, distinguished looking older guy with salt-and-pepper hair and a swashbuckling mustache, an abrupt but friendly manner.

"Nah, hell, I ain't got nothing going right now," he said. "Odd jobs here and there. What can you do?"

"He's like me and you, Frank," Steph put in. "He can do anything."

"Oh, yeah? Small fucking club -- ain't but three of us in the whole fucking world."

"Seems construction work's scarce around here," I contributed. "Yeah. Do better in Honolulu, 'cept it's all union stuff. Fuck unions!"

"I hear you."

"Can you roof?"

"Yeah, I've laid a few."

"Might be some work in a coupla months. They're putting up fifty houses in a tract on the way to Pahoa, Hawaiian Fucking Gardens or something. I think I got the roof part sewed up on a subcontract deal. I'll pay you ten bucks an hour, cash, no checks, no withholding -- off the books."

"Sounds good. Two months, you say?"

"Yeah. You make it 'til then?"

"Oh, yeah."

"There's a little demolition job I been offered, but I said fuck it. Only a day's work. Pays five hundred, but the job's all on you. You got tools?"

"Yeah."

"Know how to operate a mobile crane?"

I didn't, but I said, "Oh, sure, no problem."

"Okay, I'll call the guy, he's in Honolulu."

"What's the job?"

"They did a remodeling thing on a department store in Hilo -- new ownership. You only gotta take down a coupla signs. Nothin' to it."

"Sure, okay, we can handle that, no problem.

*****

The signs, one in front and one on the side at a central corner location, were made of metal, about five-by-ten feet in area and six inches thick, and were attached to two steel beams protruding from the side of the brick building at the second story level. Okay, rent an electric hacksaw and a mobile crane. We needed a truck to haul the signs away to the dump.

"Know anybody's got a truck?"

"Hm, yeh. How about a Ford flatbed?"

"Good. Call the guy, offer him twenty-five bucks for an hour or so's work. Tell him to come here."

She called. "Okay. He's on the way."

"Okay. He gets here, have 'im drive you up to that tool rental place for the electric hacksaw. I'll meet you back here."

"Where you going?"

"For the crane, darlin'."

Only trouble was, I had never operated a mobile crane in my life. Well, how hard could it be? Drive one piece of heavy equipment, drive another.

It rented for twenty-five dollars an hour. When the yardman took me out to show me the contraption, rather than display my ignorance -- in which case he might not want to rent it to me -- I slyly asked him to check it out for me to make sure it was in good operating condition. As he climbed aboard, started it up, and tested all the hydraulic levers, I watched very closely, trying to memorize everything.

"Fine, thanks," I said, hopped aboard, put it in gear, and drove off just like I knew what I was doing.

At the jobsite, with plenty of onlookers to witness any booboos I might make, Steph introduced me to her friend. His truck was a pickup flatbed.

"Think it'll handle those signs?"

"Oh, yeah, sure, little overhang is all."

I turned to Steph. "Babe, you see that window up there? Go ask for the manager, have him lead you to it. You go with her," I told the guy. "Help her wrap and connect the cable, then start sawing the connecting beams. I'll get situated down here."

I lowered and fixed the hydraulic pads, which provided a secure operating base, pulled levers that would untelescope the crane-arm, positioned it, payed out the cable with a hook on the end.

Once the cable was wrapped and hooked, I gave them the highsign. One operated the saw while the other squirted oil. Soon it swung free and I moved levers to swing it out over the truckbed, which is when I found out just how heavy the sign was. For the weight, I was over-extended and the entire crane began to tip over on its mounts. Great jumping Jesus on a trampoline!

I hit what I hoped was the cable release lever and prepared to jump. The sign dropped with a crash...neatly onto the truckbed below ...and the crane righted itself with another spine-jarring crash.

I grinned sickly at the onlookers. Nothing to it, folks.

I'd learned my lesson. We moved around the corner to repeat the process, this time with no crashes. Signs to the dump, rental equipment returned. We'd made over four hundred dollars for an hour's work.

We used it to rent a split-level four-bedroom, two-bath house, completely furnished, with washer and dryer, a nice screened sunroom to the side, and a two-car garage, all on a nice sloping lot between Olu Street and Volcano Road, nice lawn, trees, shrubs and flowers -- in a staid middleclass neighborhood just beyond central Hilo. The amount paid included a hundred and fifty dollar security deposit.

"Gee, what are we going to do with such a big house?"

"Never you mind. We're gonna live rent free, maybe make a few bucks profit."

"Yeh? How?"

"Nice sunroom. Put up some bamboo shades and a bed, we got another bedroom."

"Baby, what?"

Well, of course the ol' gray matter was bubbling. Drawing upon my late experience with Quacks in Marin County, we had soon rented out the other bedrooms for more than enough to pay the rent and utilities -- taking the largest, where the washer and dryer were located on the lower level, for ourselves, which had sliding glass doors into the backyard for a separate entrance.

I threw together a waterbed frame, bought a mattress and liner for our room, then transformed the sunroom into another bedroom with the addition of furniture and blinds, and we set about looking for the perfect tenants.

"See, babe, the secret is, we gotta get people who are mellow, can live with others without too much fuss, people who can pay the rent every month. Now, who do you know fills the bill?"

"Gee, lemme think."

Two young guys in the upstairs bedrooms, one a student with money from home, the other with a regular job, easy-going both of them. Hundred bucks apiece, couldn't beat it.

Then came Carol, a Filipino girl with large black eyes, long raven hair, bee-stung lips, and a set of buns that had their own laws of physical motion. I had to watch my jaw -- that it didn't gape and dribble. She took the upstairs sunroom for seventy-five smackeroos.

Linda, a skinny little blond with glasses and contacts, troubled by zits, but a sweet forlorn girl working as a waitress while waiting for romance to enter her life, took the small bottom room next to ours.

Lord have mercy, all friends of Steph and a partying crew if I ever saw one. Carol was soon hopping between beds upstairs, with poor desperate Linda occasionally taking the odd man out. We cooked and ate together, partied and fucked without too much concern for privacy.

"Baby," said Steph with a brow furrowed from thinking. "We could rent a few more houses and make a business out of this."

"Hush your mouth, darlin', don't even think it!"

Sweet pakalolo, I was thinking. There were hundreds of square miles of all but trackless rainforest simply sitting there waiting to provide a secure environment for my sought-after enterprise. Surveillance helicopters, which were few and rare, simply could not cover all the wild areas of the island. Pakalolo plants, properly dispersed, could only with the greatest difficulty and luck be discovered hidden in the profuse natural growth -- so my thinking went. Steph and I would have to begin trucking about searching out those perfect places, a few of which we had already found.

Fortune smiled. We were invited to a birthday party for Don, who happened to be the personification of a local god -- the one I'd seen cavorting about the pool on my first day on the Big Island. He was of mixed Hawaiian and Portuguese descent and still lived in the bungalow across from the one I had lived in.

About a dozen people attended, with sarong-wrapped local girls serving delicious Hawaiian dishes. Don had a striking auburn-haired little Oklahoma live-in girlfriend who he was about to marry. We hit it off right away, Don and I, me advising him on the construction of a home on a lot he owned up in a portion of rainforest.

We would drive out to survey it, discussing ideas. It was one of those areas zoned for residential lots much like Hawaiian Fern Acres, where almost no construction had occurred and neither were there any utilities.

Smoking grass over a couple of cold beers, I told him "When you're ready to begin construction, give me a call, I'll be out to give you a hand. The two of us could knock up the foundation mounts for the poles, pour and set them in a few hours. You got a floor plan?"

"Yeah, something small, maybe an A-frame with a loft, you know?"

"Oh, yeah, easy. Shit, we could put up the basic structure in a few days, a week at most. You could move in, finish the rest as you go." "Maybe a building party. Invite guys who have some building experience, our wahines (Women) cooking up some steaks or something, lots of cold beer."

"Sounds good, man. Hey, you know this is some really dynomite pakalolo you got."

"Yeah," he grinned. "Grow it myself."

"No shit? That's what I'm looking to do."

"Oh, yeah? I been growing it a long time. I got a collection of seeds from all over the world."

"Really?"

A week later, Don called me, asked if I was doing anything. "Naw, what you got in mind?"

"I want to show you something. I'll be by in a few minutes."

With an ice-cooler full of beer in the back of his pickup, a half dozen full gunnysacks, and a pocketful of joints, we set out. Rolling down a rough dirt road through rainforest country, he pulled into a little hideaway cleared just for the pickup. We each hoisted a gunnysack, which were all full of dirt, and began a trek of a mile or so along a winding path into the shadowy jungle.

"What's this for?"

"Topsoil. Wait. Soon you'll see."

Oh, my sweet honeydewed nuts! We came into a nice clearing that allowed the sun clear passage to at least a hundred pakalolo plants in various stages of growth, from potted little seedlings to Christmas trees eight feet high.

"This is my nursery," he explained. "I also grow some personal stash here. You're the first person I've ever brought out here."

I felt honored. He took me on a tour, pointing out things of interest, from babies to adults, the changing characteristics marking stages of growth, the differences in types of cannabis varieties, and how to distinguish the sex of a plant. He explained the method of producing sinsemilla, a Spanish word meaning without seeds, the most prized for its stonier qualities. The energy normally stimulating a female plant, the only gender providing a high, to produce seeds was redirected into THCs -- the elements that got you high. Therefore, when a male plant first distinguished itself, it had to be removed before its flower pods opened to spread pollen to the female plant. Set off some distance by itself, he showed me a hermaphroditic plant, one that had sexual characteristics of both genders.

"It's a genetic survival technique," he explained. "The plant can't reproduce without the interaction between the sexes -- the male plant pollinating the female. Seeds are like babies. Some female plants, if isolated from male plants, will produce a branch that is male and pollinate itself. Sort of like virgin birth, you see. The seeds from such a plant are valuable because they produce a higher percentage of female plants and so I set them aside to replenish my seed supply."

"Amazing." Since I found all this fascinating to the nth degree, I hung on to his every word.

"If you're interested," he said. "I thought we might try a fifty-fifty partnership. I'll teach you everything I know."

"You've got a partner. I appreciate the opportunity."

"What we need to do," he said, leading me to a table upon which were a hundred or so soil-filled paper cups, each containing seedling plants about eight inches high. "Is find a good spot to transplant about a hundred of these children. It's a lot of work. We have to carry them out to my pickup, drive them to the spot, then carry them all back into the forest and get them situated. For now, we need to carry in the other bags of soil."

As we hurried back over the trail, Don pushing a wheelbarrow, I was thinking. I had seen that Don's method was to haul in topsoil, which was purchased from a local fertilizer and nursery store, and laboriously transfer it to the selected site. Then he would build little mounds and transplant the seedlings into them. There had to be an easier, more efficient way.

I had leaned that commercial orchid growers used a durable plastic bag filled with their own pre-fertilized mixture of soil for rooting their plants. They held five to seven gallons of soil and had holes punched in the bottoms to allow drainage. I thought if we used such bags we might not only lose less soil to erosion from heavy rainfall, but also have the advantage of being easier to handle and making each plant fully portable. We could shift them around to more advantageous parts of the landscape.

When I mentioned this idea to Don, he grinned and said, "I think you're going to do all right in this business."

*****

Over the next couple of weeks working together, we had filled a hundred of the growbags and set them out in a place I had selected in Hawaiian Fern Acres. Then we transported out a hundred babies in cups for transplanting.

Over the next couple of months, we would go out to check on them every two weeks and Don taught me a trade secret that I hadn't found in any of the volumes in my growing library of literature on the subject. It was called pinching.

When the plant was very young, but had begun its secondary growth of leafage, the topmost bud was pinched off between the nails of forefinger and thumb. In addition to providing a few joints of interim smoke, the process accomplished these things:

1. It created a "threat" to the plant, which caused it to respond by producing more of the stony resins;

2. The pinched-off portion was replaced by two new branch-shoots growing laterally, which meant it would not grow in the Christmas tree configuration that might attain a height of eight, ten, or twelve feet, but rather become more bushier horizontally and reach a mature height of only four or five feet -- an aid to camouflaging them in the forests.

3. Since developing node branches located further down the main plant stalk were also pinched, thus creating new double-branching, the harvest of stony buds would increase in quantity and quality.

Thus had I begun my budding career as a grass farmer, a cannabis cultivator, and a totally sane lay-scientist in my kitchen laboratory.

*****

My old boss, the entrepreneur, had decided that Hawaii wasn't for him. Progress in the construction business moved too slowly for his liking. Building materials were expensive and had to be shipped from Honolulu or Mainland sources and experienced workers were hard to come by. There was no great land or building boom on the Big Island. In Honolulu, there was more opportunity, but also more competition and a different set of conditions. He had decided to liquidate everything and return to the Mainland.

I bought his old uninsured Ford work car for seventy-five bucks and agreed to sell off some remaining lumber and metal roofing. "What about all the property you got optioned?"

"Aw, hell, I'll just have to let it go. I'm going to keep the warehouse property -- I own that outright."

"What about the land with the cabin?"

"I'm buying that one on time. It's actually two adjoining lots, but I don't know if it's worth it. Probably won't be able to resell it without a watertank and plumbing system."

"How about if I take over the payments, reimburse you for what you have in it?"

"What have you got in mind?"

"Thinking about moving in and living there," I said. It would be closer to my new business. "I can put in whatever's necessary to make it habitable. What're the payments?"

"Would you believe fifty bucks?"

"Jesus, that's good. What's the total price?"

"Five thousand -- that's for both lots, four acres."

"Even better."

"That what you want to do?"

"Yeah, I'm planning on hanging around. I like it here."

"I'll let you take it off my hands for five thousand."

"Five? You got a few hundred in the land, maybe a couple grand in the materials."

"Don't forget labor and equipment costs."

"Call it four grand."

He grinned. "Never get rich this way. Okay, it's a deal. How you going to pay me?"

"Five hundred now, the balance in cash within six months."

"That's six months without interest."

"Make the five hundred the interest, four grand in cash in six months, you tight-assed old bastard. I want a fifteen percent commission on all the leftover materials I sell for you."

He laughed. "Okay, deal."

"We'll need to go to the bank to sign over the papers."

"Nah, I've got a purchase agreement direct with the owner. I'll give you a bill of sale and drop him a letter you're taking over payments."

*****

Don and I set out another hundred plants at a location not far from the cabin and property I'd purchased. It wasn't quite as good as the first place, but it had the advantage of being nearby and not so far off into the bush.

*****

"Darlin," said I to my sweet patootie. "Let's get our shit together and do a little truckin', a little campin' out."

"Where?"

"It's a surprise."

"Oh, yeah? How long we gonna be gone?"

"Maybe a month or so, maybe longer."

"Frank needs a place for awhile. We can let him have our room."

"Yeah, that's fine."

We packed up the Iron Butterfly and left the Ford in the garage -- a two vehicle family and still operating on beans. On the way in to Hawaiian Fern Acres, I detoured to show her the recent emplacement of pakalolo plants.

"Oh, gawd, they're beautiful."

"Yeah, we're going to set up a serious operation, really get into it. Next on the agenda is a nursery of our own, me and you."

"You serious?"

"Oh, yeah. Think you can get your head into all that?"

"Yeh, it might be fun. Whatever you wanna do, baby, I'm with ya all the way."

"Okay, partner, shake."

"Shake, shit. Gimme a kiss."

*****

At the property, she went from being pleased to stunned.

"What's this?"

"C'mon, I'll show you," I said, parking the Butterfly beside the carport attached to the white washed, silver-roofed abode and leading her inside.

"It's empty."

"Yeah, it's brand new. No one's ever lived here. We'll have to fix it up, build in some stuff, get some furniture, erect a watertank, figure out a bathroom plan."

"For what?"

I put my arm around her. "Babe, this is going to be our new home."

"Yeh?"

"Yeah."

"I never had a home of my own."

"Me neither. You gotta help me figure out how we want to do it -- like kitchen, closets, where the furniture goes, a whole bunch of stuff. It's gonna be a lot of work."

"Oh shit."

"What?"

She had tears in her eyes. "Oh, baby, it's so beautiful, the whole idea -- our own home."

I kissed her. "Yeah, it'll be great. We can use the Iron Butterfly as a spare bedroom -- in case we have overnight guests."

"Oh, shit!"

"What?"

"There's no place to make love."

"Don't worry. We'll move our waterbed in -- soon's we figure out where it goes."

"No, I mean now. Right now."

"Oh."

# # #

CHAPTER 6

Living out of the Iron Butterfly, we set to work. The first items on the agenda were to provide for necessities -- a bathroom and a water source. Steph right beside me wielding saw, hammer and nails, we threw up a two-seater outhouse, acquiring a couple of barrels for strategic placement and removal through a rear compartment, which saved us the chore of digging a hole in the lava. It was set out behind the cabin and since it faced mauka -- a beautiful view of Mauna Loa -- we purposely neglected to install a door at the entrance. It was a true throne room, the seats mounted high to accommodate the barrels beneath.

A bag of hydrated lime and a cup served in place of flushing to control odors. Steph painted the inside royal purple.

Next a low level watertank beside the carport, rising only to the level of its eaves, where gutters had been added to direct the flow of rainfall from the roof and provided us with over a thousand gallons of soft sweet water. A hose with a showerhead provided an outdoor bath.

We built in closet space and bookshelves, added windows, a raised kitchen with a three-stool bar counter, sinks and cabinets. We added a layer of cedar siding both outside and inside, transforming it from a single-walled construction to triple-walled. In addition to being well-insulated, we both preferred natural woods to painted surfaces.

In time, when Frank had moved out of our bedroom in the Olu house and we had returned to close it out, we transferred our waterbed to our new home, which was becoming very cozy. Our furnishings were all cheap and catch-as-catch-can make-do, an L-shaped divan in a corner by the bar composed of secondhand stacked single-sized innersprings and mattresses in tie-dyed covers and pillows, which Steph had made. We picked up a large cable spool to serve us as a round dinette table, acquiring a miscellany of chairs from the county dumpgrounds for repair and restoration, another table to serve as a desk, some bedside night-stands, some area rugs to embellish the bare pressed-sawdust flooring -- for which later we would come into a load of fine Koa hardwood for refinishing when we got to it. And we hung a ceiling of two-by-four foot fiberboard tiles from the rafters to provide an attic and dampen the sound of rain on the metal roof. We also built in clever hiding places for valuables.

I had acquired a gas-driven generator to power the electrical tools being gradually added to my collection, but we considered it a nuisance as a source of house power. Instead, we came into an old three-burner kerosene stove, one that was originally designed for use in Third World countries and had to scour the small country stores on the Big Island for a supply of the curious circular wicks. A stovetop Dutch Oven served for Stephanie's growing fascination for baking breads, cakes, and pies.

Gracefully styled glass lamps provided a soft glow of light in the evening. For lack of refrigeration other than an ice-cooler mostly used for beer, I constructed an old-fashioned evaporator cooler for vegetables mounted outside a kitchen window for easy access. It was a device once used by farm wives in the days before iceboxes and then refrigeration came into widespread use. It consisted of a covered cage with a wood base, over which hung a fitted shroud of cotton canvas. Fixed atop was a drip-bottle of water to keep the canvas wet. Natural evaporation provided a heat transfer to keep the inside cool.

We had worked ourselves into a pioneering spirit, pursuing ideas that would take advantage of the slightly primitive circumstances, and so we decided we needed a garden for fresh vegetables. For this, since there was not much available in the way of suitable ground, we gathered large chunks of broken lava and stacked them into a wall like the old heiaus (Holy places built by the Hawaiians in the old days.) and formed into a circle with about a twenty foot diameter as a container for the topsoil hauled in by the pickup load. Then a half dozen chickens to provide fresh eggs. We planted Bougainvillea along the sides of the driveway.

Cold-water showers, of course, could not long suffice. One day when we had gone further up Volcano Road a few miles to Glenwood to visit Laura, who was Stephanie's very best friend, an opportunity presented itself to improve our bathing facility.

Laura lived with her five-year old daughter and an in-and-out boyfriend named Leonard, a local boy. Laura had taken us across an unused cow pasture to a copse of trees to show us her almost-ready-for-harvest stash of pakalolo plants, which she would soon be wanting to sell to supplement her inadequate income from welfare. We agreed to help her turn it into cash when the time came.

Near one of the barbed wire fences we had been climbing over, I spied an old iron bathtub setting up on little curved legs which had been used as a watering trough for cows. It was an heirloom, fully eight feet long, of a type not manufactured since the 30s or 40s.

"Laura, who owns that bathtub?"

"Gee, I don't know. It's been there forever."

"Do they still run cows or horses to pasture here?"

"Not in the last couple of years."

"Would you mind terribly if I stole it?"

Steph gave me a look. "What, baby?"

"Darlin', that's our new furo (Japanese word for hot-tub, popular in Hawaii.) you're looking at. Think hot steamy baths."

She eyed it. "Hm, yeh, it's big enough to fuck in, too." The four of us dumped it over to empty out the water, then with one to a leg, we hoisted the heavy bastard up and staggered back to load it into the Iron Butterfly.

Back home, Steph and I manhandled it into place under the carport between the entry and the watertank. I built in a cedar bottom to sit on and a hinged cedar top with neckholes at each end which gave us, after filling it and sticking a two-burner campstove under it to heat up the water, a two-person family bath -- no waiting.

*****

Nor had we neglected our new business enterprise. I had set up a large table by placing a full sheet of plywood over three sawhorses to act as legs, with a structure over it to provide a tent-like affair of clear plastic sheeting, which went out beyond the outhouse into concealment on the adjoining property. It was to serve as our nursery for starting pakalolo plants and would contain a couple of hundred sixteen ounce paper soft drink cups with holes punched in their bottoms.

Into the cups went our own mixture of potting soil with plenty of nitrogen to promote initial growth. We had established a system, first by sprouting a batch of seeds in a jar of water containing Rootone, which eliminated all dead seeds that would not sprout. Then, when the seeds displayed a tiny white lump on one end, the sprout breaking out of its husk, we would transfer them sandwiched between paper towels kept wet on a plate. A few days later, when the inch-long roots with a tiny pair of green primary leaves had shed their encasement, we would carefully lift them with a chopstick for transfer to a hole poked in the soil in a paper cup. From there the cups would go into the nursery table for tending the next month or so. If the day was sunny, we would open the plastic flap of the tent protecting them from the damaging effects of heavy rainfall.

In the meanwhile, we had been hauling out loads of topsoil in Don's borrowed pickup, mixing in loads of old chickenshit that were free for the taking from a chicken farm. When the shit got so deep in a commercial coop, the farmers would move out all the chickens and allow all comers to come scrape out free loads -- a cheap way to clean them. Sometimes we would throw in a nice light mix of cinders gathered from acres of spew near an old once-erupting volcanic vent, which helped aerate the soil and provide better drainage. Then we'd test the whole batch for the PH factor, which is an acid-alkaline measure, and if it came out on the acidic side, we would add lime and sometimes bone meal to render it slightly alkaline, which the plants favored.

We were beginning to get off into it, studying the tracts of our new religion, ordering what we had learned, comparing and evaluating bits and pieces, fitting them together into a comprehensive whole on the subject, beginning to initiate proper experiments with control groups and maintain records.

*****

Then one day we returned home from an outing to place a group of sixty plants in a hideaway only Steph and I knew about, our first independent undertaking, to find a message written on a piece of scrap-wood propped on our front steps. It was from Don to inform me that the second planting had been ripped off, the one I had shown to Stephanie.

We rushed immediately over to see for ourselves. All the plants, only three to four months old, had all been coming along nicely, beginning to bush out in their lovely greenery of sawtoothed leafage, the five, seven, and nine-fingered leaves -- and all had been chopped, leaving only a forlorn few inches of stalk, some of the bags maliciously kicked, torn, and scattered. It was not just a theft, but also an act of contempt, the equivalent of a burglar trashing a house after he has stolen what he values and then shitting on the floor as a sign of his respect.

I was stunned. I could only remember having been the victim of a crime twice in my entire life -- once when a whore had picked my pocket for thirty dollars and again, back when I was married and living in a remote farmhouse, having had our home invaded by burglars. As to the first, I had been chagrined and humiliated, angry with myself for having allowed a whore to put one over on me, and finally laughing it off. As to the second, I thought I could almost relate to what a woman feels upon being raped. Cocksuckers had violated our happy home! And I had been outraged. My wife had called the cops before I could forbid her. She had talked to the investigating officers while I seethed. A month later, when the cops had made absolutely no progress in solving the crime, I had by then tracked down the culprits on my own, found our stuff stored in a garage in a nearby town, and repossessed it.

Well, there would be no cops on this case, only private eye Buck, smoke pouring from his ears, his tongue cramping over the invective rushing from his mouth -- the goddamned motherfucking cocksucking sonsofbitches! All that fucking work, busting my ass, and they'd deprived me of the fruits of my labors, disrupted my plans for the use of the expected income! And it's a damned good thing Steph and I hadn't made any babies or I'd have claimed the goddamned motherfucking cocksucking sonsofbitches had stolen food from our children's mouths!

"Calm down, baby," Steph tried to soothe, cooing sympathetically when I'd collapsed on the bed in the Iron Butterfly gnashing my teeth, my fists clenched in frustration for lack of a target to use as a punching bag. "Just mellow out now, sweetie-pie."

"Argh!"

"Here, take a good toke on this," she cooed, stroking my brow and holding a joint to my mouth. I smoked it, then another, Steph helping me, trying to get myself unagitated. Then she had my dick in her mouth, and when it was hard, had mounted me, rolling her hips with some determination -- and what man could keep his mind on the goddamned something-or-others with all that going on?

"Feel better?" She snuggled against me, kissing my neck.

"Yeah, thanks."

"Any time, baby, no problem."

"Darlin', anybody ever told you you're one peach of a girl?"

"Nah," she said, closing her eyes and hugging me. "Kinda guys I fool around with, they ain't much into mush talk, ya know?"

"Thy beauty is to me like those Nicean barks of yore that gently o'er a perfumed sea the weary wayworn wanderer bore," said I from the warmth of my heart, most likely misquoting a line from a poem by Poe.

"Oh, baby, I love you."

"I love you, too, babe."

*****

"Hey, it happens," Don said as we sat at his kitchen table over cold beers. "They got these thieves, all they do is drive up and down roads in the country looking for pathways into the rainforest. That tells them somebody has been going back and forth, walking a regular route -- and they stop and explore all of them looking to find somebody's stash and rip it off."

"Goddamned motherfucking..."

"Now, now, baby," Steph shushed. "That's all behind us."

"Look at it this way, if you'd have been there when they showed up, you could have gotten hurt, man. Most of these okolepukas (Assholes.) go armed."

"Oh, yeah?"

"Yeah. The problem isn't with the cops. Most of them don't care. Most of the local makai smoke pakalolo themselves, you know? It's only the BNDD (Bureau of Narcotics and Dangerous Drugs: forerunner of DEA.) you have to watch out for -- they're okolepukas but not hard to beat. There's only a few of them operating over here anyway -- mostly they're in Honolulu. No, the biggest problem is these pilau'aihues (Stinking thieves.) You'll see them, maybe two or three guys in a pickup just cruising around, drinking beer and smoking pakalolo, looking to rip somebody off."

"Jeez, Don, cruising around in a pickup, beer and pakalolo -- sounds just like us. You got any idea who any of these assholes are?"

He shrugged. "I've got my suspicions on a few of them, but no hard evidence. You ever see a guy hanging on to a rope while standing on top of a pickup cab moving slowly down the road, you'll know."

"Hah? Standing on top of a pickup?"

"Yeah, so he can better see pathways running off from the side of the road."

I shook my head. "Goddamn."

"Yeah, and let me give you a little piece of advice. You're way out there in the boonies, no phone. These fucks sometimes bulldog their way right into your house with guns looking to rob you. They think you're in the business, they'll hit your house sooner or later thinking you've got a stash inside."

"Whoa!"

"You want, I can let you borrow one of mine."

"What have you got?"

"Oh, no, baby, let's not have any guns around."

"What do you mean? What do we do if some thugs come barging into our home?"

"Just let 'em have whatever they want. Your life's more important than any fucking grass."

"And if we ain't got no money or grass in the house, ain't they gonna be pissed off! Fuck that!"

Don gave me a .22 H&R, nine-shot revolver.

Steph was mad, keeping silent during the twenty minute drive back home. "What, babe, how long you gonna break my balls over this?"

"I don't like guns. They can kill people."

"You think I'm just gonna let some assholes break in our home, beat us up, pistol-whip us or whatever, and not do anything?" She kept quiet.

"A gun's only a tool. It's who's behind it you gotta worry about." "You get pretty pissed off sometimes."

"Yeah, well, that's just blowing off steam. I'm not gonna do something dumb."

"I still don't like guns."

"Jesus, babe, it ain't a question of liking or disliking them! I wanna fondle something, I'll fondle you! It's a question of taking care of ourselves! Think about it! We gotta look out for ourselves -- ain't nobody else gonna do it!"

"Calm down."

"I am fucking calm! I ain't gonna stand by and let no goddamned motherfucking..."

"Cocksucking sonsofbitches!" Steph concluded in a shout, having by then learned that song.

"What, babe? Who? Where? Hand me my pistol!"

"You idiot!"

"Calm down, babe. Roll us a joint -- gotta mellow you out."

*****

"Laura wants to sell off her pakalolo," Steph told me.

"How much has she got?"

"Fifteen pounds."

"Let's go see her."

Over cups of coffee, we sampled the fruit of Laura's efforts. It was pretty good. "How much you want for the whole caboodle?"

"Well, I don't know. As much as I can get. I'm keeping a pound for myself, and I gave Leonard one, too. He's out selling it to his friends by the lid."

"How much a lid?"

"Fifteen, I think."

"That's comes to $240 a pound. You got thirteen left to sell, you sell 'em by the lid it comes out to...let's see...$3120."

"Well, I don't want to sell them by the lid. I don't like Leonard out dealing them either."

"Would you take two grand?"

"Well, I was hoping for more than that."

"I gotta make a profit, too, you know."

"I know, I understand that."

"Tell you what, I got an idea. Would you take three grand? That's close to what you'd make if you sold it by the lid."

"But how would you make anything?"

"Don't worry, I'll still make my end, and then some."

Steph was frowning. "How ya gonna do that, baby?"

"Simple. We sell it for $25 an ounce. This is good grass, right?"

"Yeah, but why would anybody pay $25 when they can get it for $15?"

"Simple. Go where they're people who'll pay $25."

"Where's that?"

"Honolulu."

"Oh, wow, yeah," Steph grinned. "We can go by and see my doctor friend so I can get my Parest prescription refilled. We can have some fun."

"Oh, God," Laura said. "I wish I could go with you."

"Why not? Let Leonard babysit." Steph grabbed Laura's hand.

"Come with us, Laura. You need to get out and around a little, you know?"

"How long would we be gone?"

"Few days," I said.

"No, let's stay at least a week. We can rent a camper and do some trucking."

"The thing is getting the grass over to Honolulu. Think carrying a suitcase through on the airplane would be safe?"

"Don't worry," Steph said. "I know a guy'll fly us over in his own plane. Lemme call 'im."

As Steph went into another room to call, I looked at Laura. To me, she looked as though she were caught between dread and excitement. "This your first time?"

"Yes, but I see a lot of people doing the same thing and it doesn't seem to be that big a deal."

"Yeah, the biggest risk comes in the dealing. Even that doesn't seem to be too big a thing over here, but still you could wind up in jail for a few days."

"Oh, God, that's what scares me. That's why I don't like Leonard to do it."

"Where you grew it out there, that's not a part of the property this house is on, is it?"

"No, see, that was the thing. I figured if the cops or anybody found it, you know, well, it could be anybody's."

"Yeah, that's smart."

Steph returned to peek her head around the door. "Tomorrow about noon sound okay?"

I looked at Laura, who hesitated.

"C'mon, Laura, you're going with us."

"Okay. If Leonard's back tonight. I have to tell him."
*****

After helping Laura weigh and bag up the ounces for twelve pounds, leaving one whole, we hit the road for home.

"This guy with the plane, where you know him from?"

"Oh, around. You know."

"He smoke grass?"

"Yeh."

"He knows there's three of us?"

"Yeh."

"So what's he get out of it?"

She squirmed.

"He's expecting a little action from you, right?"

"I didn't promise him anything. He's just a nice guy, all right?" "Sure, right, but you ain't paying him in pussy."

"It's my pussy."

"That's right, and you can do whatever you want with it, but I ain't no pimp and there ain't no broad gonna pay my way with her pussy."

"I ain't no broad."

"From me, that's a compliment. I mean it, Steph. I'll take care of your boyfriend."

"He ain't my boyfriend. You are. How you gonna take care of him?"

She was eyeing me suspiciously. "You ain't gonna do that crazy man thing again, are you?"

I laughed. "Nah, not this time. I'm gonna give him something he'll like better than pussy."

"What?"

*****

At the private plane section of Hilo Airport the next day after loading our suitcases into the luggage compartment of an aluminum four-passenger Luscombe, having noted the nice kissy little greeting between Steph and the pilot, not to mention the look in his eye, I stepped forward to assert myself without too much folderol -- had to get this guy's head screwed on right. I grabbed Laura's arm, "C'mon, Laura, you're the guest of honor so you get to ride up front." I helped her in, then turned to Steph, "C'mon, babe, me and you get the smooching section." I handed her into the rear, taking the gift-wrapped package out of her hands.

"Hey, man," I said, turning to the guy. "I really appreciate you running me and my ol' lady over to Honolulu. Her and Laura are really excited about this trip."

He was eyeing me, getting the message. Time to drop it on him. "Here, this is for you, a small token of my appreciation." He looked at it. "What is it?"

"Pound of primo smoke, man. Figured maybe you and I could do a little deal. Sometimes I need to get a few suitcases over to Honolulu," I pointed to the luggage door. "I could make it worth your while."

He grinned. "What'd you say your name was?"

*****

The first thing we did was rent a VW poptop camper and hit the beach at Ala Moana. We swam, we sunned, we drank beer and snuck a couple of tokes. Since I had never sold grass on the streets to perfect strangers and didn't want to start, my whole plan consisted of getting in contact with Sarge and the boys at Kaneohe. He had told me that ounces of pakalolo, depending on the quality, were going from $25 for so, on up to $40 or more for the primo stuff. Laura's stash which, with Leonard's help and expertise, was organically grown, using only natural fertilizers -- mainly fish emulsion and cow dung -- definitely qualified as primo, and I'm figuring $25 a crack all day for my old pals and their buddies.

I called him. He couldn't get off base. But, when he learned what it was all about, he told me to come on out, that he'd arrange a pass for me at the gate.

"Hey, I got two ladies with me. Can you get us all in?"

"Sure, no problem. You selling them, too?"

I laughed. "No, man, not hardly."

"You could, man. I could get you a line of swinging dick gyrenes with cash in hand. Pussy and pakalolo! Combination like that, you could break this base in one day!"

"I might have a little problem talking them into it, Sarge. It's my ol'lady and her best friend."

"Oops, sorry."

"Hey, see you in a while, huh?"

Returning to the VW, I couldn't resist. "You ladies into turning about a hundred tricks this evening?"

I got looks.

"The boys want pussy and pakalolo! We can break the whole fucking base!"

Laura was shocked. Steph frowned, then asked, "How much they pay for the pussy?"

Laura and I almost fainted, she from more shock, her face going red, me from laughing so hard.

*****

We sold a hundred lids or so, Sarge sending his boys around to take orders and collect money so as not to draw attention to a crowd of weedheads mobbing the camper. The Sarge and the boys were very polite with the girls.

"Hey, Sarge," I said while speaking to him on the side. "I need a coupla pieces. Can you do me any good?"

"Yeah. M-1 all right?"

"Yeah, that'd be okay, but I was thinking more along the lines of pistols, you know?"

".45 do you?"

"Yeah, that'd be fine."

"I'll ship 'em both to you. The M-1 will be disassembled."

"That's okay. Can I ship you a package in return?"

"Yeah, but make sure it's wrapped securely."

*****

Well, we still had about ninety more to go. We went to the doctor's house, a pediatrician and family man with a lovely wife and three kids. After a bit of social chitchat, Steph finally said the code words. "I need to consult with you, Doc."

He led her back to an office, from which she emerged in a few minutes with a grin. After we left, I asked her about it.

"I got a prescription that's good for three issues of Parest," she said. "I gave 'im two ounces. He wants to know can we get him a pound."

"Oh, yeah, I don't see why not. Next time around. He gonna pay for it in prescriptions?"

"I don't see why not."

Hm.

"What's next on the agenda, baby?"

"I wanna go see this guy named Henry who Don put me onto. See if we can move any more pakalolo."

Henry, also Portuguese-Hawaiian, was stoned but functional. "Hey, man, aloha. I talked to Don. He says you're a good man to do business with."

"Mahalo, man. Don speaks very highly of you, too."

"He better," Henry grinned. "We been blalahs a long time. So what can I do for you?"

"Well, I'm kinda on a sight-seeing tour, you know, getting to know people, figuring out what's what, handing out samples of product," I said, tossing him a lid. "Here, try some of that. I think you'll like it."

"Oh, yeah, I'm pretty sure I will if Don's involved. He always turns out primo stuff. Problem is, he doesn't produce a whole lot."

"Well, he's got a partner now and we're gonna branch out. Gotta work our way into building up."

"Yeah, I know how it is. When you got at least a hundred pounds together, let me know, we can do a deal."

"Can you come pick it up or would I have to deliver it over here?"

"We can go either way, depending on the circumstances. It's no big thing to send over a haole sampan (Popular style local fishing boat.). But remember this, Buck -- shortest possible route -- don't expect us to come all the way around to the Hilo side."

I thought about it, trying to visualize a chart of the islands in my head, the most direct route between Honolulu and the Big Island. I put it at the northeast sector, anywhere from Kailua Town on up to Pololu Valley. Pololu would be ideal except for having to truck the product down by backpack. "Okay, I'll remember that."

"You know where Milolii is?"

"No, sorry, I don't."

"It's a coastal village on the Kona side. A volcano eruption sent down a lava flow to the sea way back -- missed Milolii, but left miles of barren black lava. There's a little crescent of beach that it missed, too -- just stopped and flowed around it into the sea -- about two miles from Milolii. Almost nobody goes there, maybe the occasional fisherman or some kids camping out for a few days of privacy. It's a nice secluded spot. You should check it out."

"I will. In the meantime, I've got five pounds or so all broken down into lids if you're interested."

"At what price?"

"Four hundred, twenty-five a lid."

"Ah, that's higher than I'm used to paying."

"Hey, no problem. The markup's so I can make my expense money out of the trip over here. I'm moving it for somebody else."

"Yeah, I understand. Tell you what," he said, digging into his pocket to retrieve a wad of C-notes. "Here's a grand. I'll take half of it off your hands. Just remember I did you a favor."

"Don't worry. I've got a memory like an elephant for things like that."

He grinned. "That's good. The latest buzzword going around for pakalolo is Elephant Ear."

"No shit?"

"Yeah, everyone wants Elephant Ear. Whattayou call this stuff?" "Glenwood Green." We had named it for the lone store on Volcano Road that marked the so-called township in the area where Laura lived. "Well, it's Elephant Ear now."

*****

At the northshore of a fine long and wide beach, we sat and watched surfers riding big ones. We were by then four or five days into our trip, usually spending nights parked at one beach or another. Laura had the single berth in the poptop above, while Steph and I took the lower double. Laura, it turned out was somewhat on the straight side, possessing a tolerant but more or less conventional set of middleclass morals -- which tended to inhibit the free-for-all-like sexual antics Steph and I had been busy accommodating ourselves to. Other than tearing off a quick piece during a late night public shower and once in the early morning hour as I quietly cuddled to Steph's buns through Laura's snore from above, we were practicing a bit of abstemiousness. It was obvious, watching them together, that they were close friends, Laura tolerating Steph's licentiousness as long as it didn't become too blatant and Steph trying to conform herself to Laura's limitations.

Well, we still had forty or so lids to sell. "So what do you think," I asked, consulting them. "We just run around asking people they want to buy some?"

"How could we tell if they were cops?" Laura had the same reservation I had. Ex-cons tended to fancy they had a nose for smelling out cops, but I wasn't at all sure it could be done with no more than a glance or two.

"Nah," Steph said. "That ain't the way you do it. See, the trick is to get a prospective customer to smoke a doobie with you. Narcs ain't supposed to indulge. Besides, simple possession of a few joints is a misdemeanor, a twenty-five dollar fine. Cops ain't got time for petty shit like that."

"Yeah, and then what?"

"Well, usually they'll ask you, see, can they score some of the same stuff, and so you sell 'em one."

"So we gotta pack around a half dozen ounces or so and keep all the money on us?"

"Well, yeah."

"How about you girls go out and about with a pocketful of joints, you know, talk to people, light one up, pass it on. If they hit on you, send them to me at the VW. That way we at least get two or three judgments whether it's all right to deal with 'em."

Steph looked at Laura. "I'm game."

"Okay."

"Also, I want to try a little experiment. If they ask you how much, just say affordable or worth the price. If they press you, tell 'em you're not sure because your ol'man bought it."

"What's that do? What kind of experiment?"

"Well, they're going to know it's good shit, right? I want to see what the market is. They ask me the price, I'm gonna say whatever you think it's worth, maybe smoke another doobie with 'em, get 'em snockered."

"What if they offer you ten dollars?"

"Then they'll get it for ten dollars. Look, we've already made Laura's money and all our expenses, including airfare home. What we make on this last batch is gravy."

They liked the idea, and off they went with sunny smiles in their fetching bikinis. Not a single customer offered less than twenty-five, many going to thirty or thirty-five, a few as high as forty, and one tourist clear to sixty. Our lids were full fat ounces and not the short ones that were so often the case.

We decided to celebrate by renting a hotel room in Waikiki for a hot bath and a night on the town.

"Oh, gawd, a hot bath," Steph yelped.

"Who's first?"

"As the leader of this expedition, naturally I get first dibs," claimed I.

"No, Laura's first."

"No, you go first, Steph."

"Let's flip for it. Odd man goes first."

Steph won.

Laura turned on the TV and we sat watching for a few minutes, could hear Steph running water, splashing, and making vocal sounds of pleasure.

"I love the way Steph approaches everything," I said.

"Hm?"

"Her enthusiasm, her sense of humor. Even in things she doesn't enjoy doing, you know, she makes up her mind to do it and goes right at it."

"Oh, yes, I know what you mean. She's got the warmest heart of anyone I've ever met, can get very determined."

"She was dealing grass, we met, you know."

"Yeah, she told me all about it."

"I think it was her smile, the way she walked that first attracted me. She has this sort of aura that just exudes from her." "Sometimes it blows my mind how you two got together."

I sat up on the single bed against the wall separating the bathroom, assumed a lotus position. "What do you mean?"

"You know, it's like a case of opposites attracting, I guess."

"Yeah, that's what a lot of people think, but we've got more in common than appears on the surface."

"Like what?"

"Well, you know, what I just said, making up your mind to do something and hen getting fully behind it, getting the job done. Other ways, too."

"You know what most people see, don't you?"

"What?"

"An aggressive-passive thing. Opposites. You're aggressive, you push, you want to take charge."

"Only if I think I can do something better."

"And Steph's the passive one, just following wherever you lead."

"Yeah, maybe, but it's more than that. We're pretty much in tune on most things. I don't think its just ego, you know, like I want to be king shit or something. I don't think I'm really the leader type. I'm too much of a loner. But, you know, if I find somebody worth following, shit, boss, just give me an order."

"That's not the way it seems."

I bounced my head back against the wall. "Well, what can I say? A lot of people jump to conclusions on the basis of shallow perceptions. They might come to a different conclusion if they lived with us, saw all the little interactions that aren't so obvious."

"I'm not criticizing. I'm happy for Steph. She loves you, you know."

"I love her, too."

"Do you really? You're not just using her like all the other guys in her life?"

"Yeah, I know about that. I've met a few of those assholes. I resist love, you know. Had some bad experiences. But I also think it's probably useless to resist. Because my natural propensity, it seems to me after some deliberation on the matter, is to love. Inside, without love, I'm sad and lonely, just like Steph is, probably everybody. I guess it's just that I can cover it up better -- I'm not so obvious as Steph."

"So tell me about what you two have in common."

"Long list, Laura, really."

"C'mon, now, give me a for instance."

I thought about it, discarded sex right off the bat. Laura was a little straitlaced, even if she was sexy and attractive. I pushed off the wall, got up to turn the TV off, retrieved our portable tape-deck, searched out a Jimmy Reed Tape, punched it in, turned, grabbed her hand and pulled her up. "Okay, c'mon, now. This is something we're both into."

Laura laughed, tried to pull away, me going into all those moves undignified to the point of comedy, me in my cutoffs and nothing else, playing the fool a bit, but dancing, too, like Jimmy Reed always made me want to do with that seductive rhythm he had, was master of, the guitar dooba-dooba-doobaing up and down a short scale, the harmonica honking and screeching right up my nerve-edges.

"Nah, nah, c'mon, now, Laura, can't dance alone."

She tried, kept laughing, embarrassed but game, me grinning, doing my silly-serious thing. Jimmy Reed was my favorite mood-improver. "Hey, what'cha doin' out there!" came Steph's muffled voice. "Having fun! C'mon, babe, hurry up before Laura quits on me!" Laura was staggering and giggling, off balance, and I grabbed for her. We both fell on the bed laughing and blowing.

"Laura, you gotta get out and dance more!"

"I'm not very good at it."

"No, you do all right. You just need practice. You'll get some tonight. Doesn't Leonard ever take you to a boogey joint?"

"Oh, he's worse than I am."

"One of these days we're gonna come and take you both out to the Polynesian Room. Good live bands. You ever been there?"

"No, where is it?"

"On the hotel loop in Hilo, right by the water. They got a nice back veranda so you can sneak a couple of joints while getting your breath back."

"I'm done," Steph yelled. "Who's next?"

*****

After disembarking at Hilo and driving Laura home, we found an anxious Leonard awaiting us.

"I was worried about you guys. The BNDD and some local cops have been running all over the area looking for pakalolo stashes. I figured you were busted."

Why Glenwood, a sparsely populated one-store blip on Volcano Road, a couple of side roads containing maybe a dozen widely separated homes, a quiet, laidback community of mostly farmers and ranchers?

Ah.

Glenwood Green. Talk of good grass gets around. The narcs had only to consult maps to find where the only Glenwood in the islands was located.

Hm.

No more Glenwood Green. No more Puna Butter. From now on, people, we get creative. Henceforth, we would name our product, no matter it's point of origin, Bengali Beep, Calcutta Cooze, Thai Bhang, Hongkong Horse, and many other honorifics based on foreign locations. Let the narcs investigate the world. Let them chase flies. No more inadvertent telling on ourselves.

* * * * *

A month or so later, after Don and I had harvested our first planting, a hundred and ten pounds or so, we sent it all over to Henry via Steph's pilot friend and his plane, who was very happy to keep ten pounds for himself. Henry had been impressed by our method of delivery, necessitating no more than driving out to Honolulu Airport in a van to receive the load -- which made Don and I each fifteen grand richer.

All debts paid off, we improved our household -- and added to the family population. Steph had been suckered into accepting two black kittens, which we named after 60s' radicals -- Stokely and Eldridge -- who would grow into sleek and beautiful miniature black panthers. Me, I had taken a half-wild bitch of a dog off Don's hands.

"She belonged to a friend of mind lived mauka, but he moved over to Oahu on a job," Don explained. "I can't keep her where I live. She needs to be out in the country. She'd be a good watchdog for you."

I looked her over, a big mutt, a wiry, shaggy coat of gray and black fur, a big head and alert eyes. "What the hell is she, some kind of setter?"

"Ah, who knows? I think she's got some Shepard somewhere along the way and some Staffordshire Terrier, who knows what else?"

"Staffordshire Terrier? Isn't that what they call a Pit Bull?"

"You mean the American breed they call a Pit Bull? No, not exactly, but I think the Staffordshire is one of the breeds that went into making the American version. Staffordshires are good, loyal dogs, good with children."

"Oh, yeah?"

"Yeah, I been around dogs all my life. Lot of people have them over here. Had some myself. Great dogs."

"Don't they use Pit Bulls in dogfights?"

"Oh, yeah, man, you'll see it once and awhile around here -- just like cockfights, gambling, all that. But, man, the way they treat those dogs to make them mean, it's awful -- makes you wonder about fucking human beings."

"What, Don?"

"This guy I know, he's into dogfights. He puts them in wooden boxes, completely dark, starves them, and beats on the box all the time to drive them crazy. And he beats them. They come out really vicious, dangerous dogs. They'll attack anything that comes near them."

"Jesus, that's awful!"

"Yeah. Everytime I see that pua'a, (Pig.) I feel like shooting him, feeding him to his own dogs."

"I don't blame you. Man, that is really chickenshit, treat a dog that way. Who is this asshole?"

"You'll meet him sooner or later. He lives in Mountain View."

My new mutt's name was Duchess and she turned out to be a great dog for us -- even if she was a bit wild and sometimes disappeared into the bush to chase wild pigs or the stray impious mongoose. She had obviously been trained as a watchdog, maybe even for hunting, letting us know whenever people approached, whether on foot, which was rare, or in vehicles long before we saw them. I felt a little safer that we would always be alerted to the approach of strangers, among which might be those armed rip-off artists.

Don taught me the Hawaiian words that had been used by her previous owner. Hele mai for come here. Noho for sit. Hina moe for lay down. Kuleana for business, which was used to alert her that work was in store and would cause her to become frisky and wag her tail with excitement. The last command word was lele, which meant attack -- which I had tried once while alone with her. It caused her to crouch and snarl, very seriously looking for something to tear apart. I only had occasion to use it once in all seriousness -- when one of those rip-off artists was making off with thirty or forty pounds of our grass -- but the armed and fleeing asshole had been lucky enough to escape.

I also learned to say kapu, which meant forbidden, when I didn't want her doing something -- like chewing up one of our pakalolo plants. But the words I used more than any others were maika'i ilio – good dog. Duchess was a maika'i ilio.

Chickens, cats, a dog, later many dogs after a birthing by Duchess, another black cat we called Angela, in keeping with our custom of naming them -- some pussy to distract Stokely and Eldridge from eyeing each other with lust in their little lubricious hearts -- and, for a time, a wild little bore piglet of whom I had visions of turning into a 500-1b. watchhog to help guard the many of our babies and children who could not defend themselves against molesters and killers -- our pakalolo plants. We were all a family, all living together in peace with each other, and into it with a will -- being a family.

Even though Laura's five-year old daughter made me gaga with love everytime we went to visit and play, the expression of what I was deprived of with my own daughter, when all was said and done I thought it was probably better for us, Steph and I both, that we had no children and none on the horizon to devote ourselves to, that there was therefore less heartbreak in store for us.

###

CHAPTER 7

With an M-1 and an Army Colt .45, I returned Don's .22. I bought ammo and tried them out in the rainforest and was pleased to see that Duchess leaped to full alertness rather than cringing away. I hid the M-1 under the raised kitchen flooring and the .45 in a hidden nook behind a removable panel in the barfront for quick and easy access in an emergency.

I also bought a 1949 Ford pickup-sized flatbed with stake sides. I was amazed that the rusty old wreck ran, but it had no seat in the cab and almost no brakes. Neither was it registered. Since I had no plans to ever drive it out of Hawaiian Fern Acres, I felt no need to have it licensed. I would put in new brake shoes and use it for hauling our filled grow-bags to sites within the subdivision. It cost me all of $50 to a hippy in need.

Life went on. We worked, we played, we trucked about on business and pleasure. We visited a growing number of friends, often staying with the Iron Butterfly parked nearby for several days, all the while searching out places to park a stash of pakalolo plants. Once we halfway explored a site I liked the looks of. Later Don and I hiked with backpacks several miles into the hills off the coast road running north out of Hilo, through canefields on up into untracked rainforest. On a hilltop near a stream, we built a permanent camp, having to make several trips in to supply it.

With machete and a roll of wire, we chopped small trees and the limbs and branches of larger trees to wire together a platform off the ground with a simple structure overhead to drape a large segment of nylon-reinforced plastic sheeting, which was purchased by the roll -- when unfolded from it's 3-foot roll size, it stretched out to some twenty feet. All put together, it gave us a tent with a rough wooden floor of about 12x12 feet. It served as our nursery and supply shed for tools, fertilizers, paper cups, and grow-bags. We had found a place where there was plenty of red loam-like soil, which saved us the onerous chore of hauling in our own. We would spend a couple of days at a time there, bringing our sleeping bags and food enough to hold us. With only a hundred plants or so, it would prove to be the best of our stashes.

Stephanie and I might situate only thirty grow-bags one place, fifty another, and then suffer through the anger and frustration when we discovered thieves had made off with a batch. Still, we blundered on, doggedly worrying over our mistakes, busting our asses in the labor involved, ever-endeavoring to improve our knowledge and methods.

A year or so into it, I had come up with a way to stymie the thieves, a beautiful 20-foot long 2x12-inch plank. Loading a couple of dozen grow-bags on to the flatbed, each containing a foot-high pakalolo seedling, we would tie the plank slanted up from the truckbed over the cab, we two sitting on wooden crates inside. When we had reached our site, we would stand the plank straight up from the truck-bed, its foot secured by a rope, and let it fall off to the side. Behold, a ramp that allowed us to begin our pathway fifteen feet into the brush lining the sides of the road. Then, upon stepping off the end of the ramp, we would begin the path on a slant parallel with the road rather than running at easily discernible right angles to it -- a mere piddling solution involving perception and plane geometry. There were no paths going off from the road itself and none apparent in the slanting parallels running in zigzags. To improve on our ability to carry only one bag apiece at a time, I nailed together two poles with a fruitbox between, which would hold four bags -- a laborsaving device. One of us to an end, we stretchered our babies into their new homes. We called our humanitarian device the Coolie Wagon.

*****

By dint of patience and gritted pearly whites, by time carrying us on with our curious minds, delving ever deeper into pakalolo lore, trying and failing, trying again and succeeding, failures and successes a part of the stride of our progress, we leafed and dreamed on, our ambitions beginning to grow right along with the ever more elaborate dreams, entrenched dwellers in Pakalolo Land.

We had constructed an experimental station on the back part of the property that abutted our own rear perimeter, a sizable tentlike structure that would keep the rain off. It would eventually contain seventy plants. One experiment was water -- how much did pakalolo require? Were there minimums and maximums? We had read that pakalolo roots needed well-drained soil, that too much standing water could drown them. We would keep records, each plant identified with a numbered tag, and note the controlled but differing amounts of water hand-carried to them, try to determine whether more or less water made a difference in their stoniness.

We had read an article in a horticultural magazine about the growth-inducing properties of gybberillic acid -- marketed as Gybberillin -- used by rose-growers. We sent away to the Mainland for a quantity of aerosol cans containing it -- another few tagged plants for that experiment, more records.

Then, when we had read an article written by a Catholic nun, a research scientist, on the case of inducing polyploidism in diploidal plants, including marijuana, we had to try that one, too. Marijuana, a diploid -- meaning it contained two chromosomes in its genetic makeup -- could be induced to become ployploidal, having more than two chromosomes. The good sister had written that when odd-numbered counts of chromosomes occurred -- sometimes mutating naturally -- it would also increase the stoniness of marijuana by exponential quantities. With visions of producing a new breed of supergrass, we flew off to Honolulu with a pound of our best for another visit with Steph's pediatrician friend.

Appreciative to the point of rewriting Steph's Parest prescription and an amphetamine one for me in what were called Black Beauties in street vernacular, we sat down with his family for a backyard barbecue where I explained our special need for a pharmaceutical substance called colchicine, which was a deadly poison that was nevertheless prescribed in judiciously minute doses as a treatment for gout and rheumatism. The good doctor was intrigued and wrote me out a prescription.

Back home, I dissolved the pills in a quart jar of water with Rootone and dumped in about a thousand seeds. Only about thirty of them would survive the trauma of the colchicine, plenty enough for a seed crop since the first generation would be poisonous to smoke anyway.

Well then there was the claim right there in black and white that hops plants could be grafted onto marijuana roots -- the idea being that the root, which produced THC, would transfer it's stoniness to the hops plant -- the resulting plant appearing quite different from marijuana.

Hops were, as everyone knows, used in the manufacture of beer and grew on vines that reached thirty feet in length, requiring a lattice to support them. There was nothing for it but to send away for some hops root cuttings, which were preferred over seeds by hops farmers. We would sprout them along with some pakalolo sees and, at a certain point, graft the hops tops onto marijuana roots -- which hybrid we could grow openly right out in front of God and everybody since only God, who didn't seem to mind, would be the only one to recognize it for what it was.

My thought processes being constituted in such a way as to lead from one to another into a hierarchy of ideas, naturally I contemplated one of my favorite brews -- beer. I had occasionally produced a homemade brew from the several varieties of guava growing wild all over the place. Sugar, yeast, and water added to a guava mash in a five gallon bucket would produce in a week's time a very tasty drink with an alcoholic content similar to wine. But a beer brewed with stony hybrid hops-marijuana plants, hey, we were talking about a new way to enjoy the magical properties of THC!

And...

Since grass is oil-soluble, which means the stony ingredients can be leeched out by oil, fat, alcohol, and other non-water-based catalysts, a true marijuana beer or wine ought to be possible using macerated pakalolo as the mash. When the sugar, yeast, and mash began to ferment, thus converting the sugar to alcohol, it should also be imbued with the taste and stony qualities of the grass.

We had upon occasion ingested pakalolo, whether by a dose of the original Puna Butter on our morning bagels or by eating the fresh green top buds we had pinched from our baby and teenage plants -- a pinch to grow an inch --either straight off the bush or prepared in foods, salads, cookies, brownies, turkey-dressing, what have you -- Steph was thinking about writing a pakalolo cookbook -- and had found that in the proper amount it kept your head in the ozone all fucking day.

By then, my fantasies were leading me to Madison Avenue. With the beer, for instance, perhaps utilizing our new hops plant, I envisioned bottling it with a proper label -- maybe call it Buck's Boogey Beer or Steph's Stony Stagger Ale.

And why not other unique products?

Why not regular packages of machine-rolled joints, take away the bother of cleaning and rolling your own, create a proper mood in the packaging, make it colorful and amusing, real collector's items, label them with all the names -- Panama Red, Kona Gold, Maui Wowee, Matanuska Thunderfuck -- you name it, all the popular names that had been coined over the years? Why not create new labels, as we were discovering we had a penchant for? Tricky Dick's Special Mix, with a label containing a picture of a smiling Richard Nixon -- improve his glum public image. Mao Tse Tung's Magic Goat Dung, a label with Mao and Chinese ideograms. Inside I would place a small printed notice: If you bought this product out of some vague notion of supporting the so-called dictatorship of the proletariat in the People's Republic of China, or out of Marxist-Leninist socialist sympathies, you've been burned, you commie cocksucker, because this is a pure example of laissez-faire, capitalistic imperialism!

I could design a special built-in extension for the machine-rolled joints to resemble a filtertip for use as a roachclip. We could produce not only one-ounce lids but also pound-sizes in vacuum-packed cans, even poptops, all with colorful, humorous labels, convey a proper fun mood for weedheads. We could, from the A-to-Z recipes derived from our literature on the subject, extract a hashoil and encapsulate a proper dose into gelatin capsules -- just like health nuts did with goldenseal and other natural vitamins and minerals and herbal remedies with their own little hand-operated encapsulating machines -- sell it as, say, Dr. Feelgood's Flagitious Febrifuge, (Flagitious means wickedly shameful; Febrifuge is a medicine to relieve fevers.) one cap for an all-day high. We could design and establish a whole line of marijuana based products, cigarettes, beer, maybe a decently aged wine and other alcohol-grass liquors, food enhancers, spices, pills and capsules, all with marvelously designed packaging.

We knew a weedhead named David, the gorgeous Filipino Carol's current boyfriend, whose family owned a bookstore and printshop in town. David was skilled in all phases of the printing processes. Steph and I could draft up a whole slew of packaging designs to the proper dimensions and get with David in secret for some late-night extracurricular press and cutting runs.

From various catalogs I had collected we found almost everything necessary to the enterprise was available by mail-order purchase: All the chemicals, materials, glassware, condensers, isomerizers, and vacuum-pumps for a small lab setup to extract hashoil and concoct new hash creations; sophisticated cigarette-rolling machines; can-sealing devices; whole truckloads of cans in every size and shape imaginable from the American Can Company.

Holy Guacamole! I was envisioning a veritable industry! The very finest pakalolo products, no seeds, stems, or bother, and lots of funny packaging -- when they hit the market and swept the country, nay, the world, by storm, providing a new standard for dreamy-eyed entrepreneurs, everyone who took a chance and imbibed, suicidal depressives hearing the wakeup call, they would all want it, demand it! And they'd pay premium prices for such quality products!

But wait now, me boyo, un momentito. When something like these hit the market, they would naturally create a lot of publicity and consequently bring bigtime heat -- every narc in the country would be hot to nail your ass! Once that happened, I wouldn't last long as the Madison Avenue Grass Tycoon -- no, my ass would be grass. Remember the heat engendered by Glenwood Green.

No, no, no.

But.

What about one mediocre splash in the great ocean of grass-and-freedom-lovers in the world, an exciting little ripple in the oppressive scheme of things, a one-time do-it-and-get-out deal? Stockpile a bit to make it worthwhile, say a ton or two, convert it all into the various lines of products, hit the market like a hot issue of stocks or bonds, take my profits and retire from the business -display a bit of flamboyance for the thrill-seekers, then disappear into the unsung substance of my small fortune, go anonymously on to other pastures.

Hm. Sigh. Well. I certainly wasn't ready to accomplish such a visionary scheme at the time, but who's to know or care if I filed it away for future reference, when and if good fortune and the vicissitudes of life happened to place me in a position to pull it off?

*****

In the meantime I practiced on short runs of hashcakes, like the Teruki brand of Nepalese Temple Hash, for trial runs and a chance to see old friends in San Francisco. This time it was Buddha Sticks. I had built a hydraulic press composed of a quarter-inch welded steel box six inches on a side. An angle-iron framework held a hydraulic carjack that served to contain a steel lid that was jacked down into the box. With it, I would place six-inch long sprigs of primo pakalolo in cross-laid alternating layers, compress and congeal it all down into an inch-thick brick -- a grass-cum-hash slab of Buddha Sticks.

While turning the few pounds of them into quick cash to pay for the trip, I ran across an old prison buddy. Kieth was a kind of kook, leaning to racist rightwing political crackbrained ideas, which I'd never held against him because they'd always seemed like hot air rather than something to actually practice in real life. I had sometimes taken amusement in baiting him into long arguments and making fun of his positions.

Kieth was the fellow who's prison-caught girlfriend had come out from Chicago with Samantha, she who had been put up in our apartment with her storm trooper kid in order to be close to San Quentin's visiting room. Talk about opposites, a futuristic-liberal-militant-feminist, and a reactionary neanderthall! The relationship lasted only a few months after Kieth's release on parole. When I went by to see him, he was with a pale Nordic blond named Mary, both of whom were involved in a communal-teaching-social-philosophy-practicing thing called Moore House or Morehouse, a radical sort of touchy-feelie thing that I never did quite understand or care to. But Kieth seemed to have mellowed out, talking about establishing what he called the Restored Church of Jesus Christ International, which I took to be a scam, and he didn't get overly excited when Mary tried to crawl in bed with me early one morning as I slept on a sofa in their living room.

Me, I had tales to tell of Hawaii and the cultivation of maryjewwanna. He did not use any drugs that were not legitimately prescribed by a doctor, but he was asthmatic with plenty of pills and inhalers around. He was fascinated with the possibilities of making more in the grass business than he'd ever had in his life, as well as bringing a dim light of salvation to the heathen in Hawaii.

I left him with a mind aboil in new schemes and went to visit another old prison buddy, Royal. After I'd sketched out my situation, inquiring whether he might be interested in receiving shipments of grass in the future, he said, "Sure, man, but how're you going to get it over here, on the airlines?"

"No, I don't feel too confident with that method, even though flights from Hawaii are considered domestic flights and not subject to customs. I've got a better way."

"What?"

"I'll let you know when the time comes."

"Okay. Listen, maybe we can do a two-way thing. I'm hooked into these guys who're manufacturing MDA."

"Oh, yeah? What's that?"

"You never heard of MDA, the Love Drug?"

"The Love Drug? You shitting me?"

"No, man it's a really groovy high. It's a little like LSD or psilocybin and a little like speed, but neither really. It's basically a feelgood thing, makes you feel just fucking great."

"Oh, yeah? Never heard of it."

"It's popular here in California and spreading. It's good to fuck on, which is why they call it the Love Drug. Broads really like it."

"Oh, yeah? So how'd you get into that?"

He shrugged. "Met these guys. The honcho's a graduate in chemistry at UC Berkeley. He's kind of a purist, you know, a guy with vision -- wants to turn on the whole world. MDA is good shit. No addiction and no side effects -- except maybe a little wear and tear on the old genitalia. You gotta try it. See, things work out right, you could be our sole Hawaii outlet."

"Hm, well, I don't know..."

"These guys just shipped about a half million dollars worth of MDA down south, man, in peach cans -- really slick, man. These guys are on top of it."

"Peach cans?"

"Yeah, and dig this. Their laboratory? I mean a complete fucking chemical lab, man, it's all set up inside an Airstream travel trailer. You get it? A movable lab, man. They keep moving it around, you know, so they can keep ahead of the heat. They go in somewhere, maybe a lot up in the north woods, do a manufacturing run, then move the whole operation somewhere else. They got regular connections for moving the shit in New York City."

I was impressed. "Yeah?"

"C'mon, I want to show you something -- blow your mind."

Royal drove us in his Camaro from San Rafael into San Francisco to an empty house in a residential area. Once inside, he led me down into the basement to show me a machine. It was big, about five feet high with a like diameter, a motor-driven device of curious metal rods running in a circle and sitting atop a heavy cast-iron base. "What the fuck is that?"

"My baby, a pill-making machine. All those rods, see, they're dies for compressing powder into pills. All the big companies have them, aspirins, drugs, whatever. Sucker weighs a ton -- have to use a forklift to move it. Here, let me show you."

He dumped a bag of powder into a feed-chute. "This is just a placebo compound. See, the chute feeds it down to the rotating dies, thirty-six of them. They go around, compressing the compound into a pill, then pop 'em out the exit chute. Watch."

The fucking thing rumbled, causing vibrations in the floor, made a loud clattering noise, the die-rods moving around in their circular track, jumping up and down like pistons. Pills began pouring out the delivery chute into a pan. He shut it down.

"See, my job, since I'm a machinist, is to make new casting dies. They want a heart-shaped one. We're going to add a red food coloring to the MDA, make red, heart-shaped pills -- the Love Drug."

"Fucking amazing." I was thinking about the possibilities of running grass or hash pills through it. Fuck MDA -- a little jar of Cannabis pills, one a day'll do ya!

"Sucker cost twenty grand, used."

"Yeah, so when can I try this stuff?"

"How about I come over for a little vacation? I'll bring a few ounces, you can show me your grass operation. We can party down." "Yeah, sure. Sounds good. When?"

"I don't know. Soon's I can find a week to get away. You gonna fix me up with one of those sloe-eyed island girls?"

"I'll see what I can do."

* * * * *

One morning Duchess roused me from my snuggle-to-Steph-waterbed comfort. I slipped into a pair of shorts and looked out the window. She was standing there, her nose in the air toward the road, sniffing, listening, and throwing out timed barks. There was nothing to be seen -- probably a car still coming down the road. When it got closer, I would hear the crunch of tires in the gravel. I fired up the kerosene stove, got a pot of coffee going, then stepping out to wash up at the tap on the watertank.

"Duchess, hey, c'mon, girl, give it a break."

She ran over, flapping her tongue, grinning and growling happily. "Good girl. What? Somebody's coming?"

She yipped, a good watchdog, alert. Soon I could hear the tires in the gravel, a slow-moving vehicle. When it came by, a pickup with two guys in the front and one sitting in the back, I got a couple of grins and waves. I waved back. When it had passed, I walked with

Duchess out to the road for a looksee -- they were traveling awfully slow. Now the guy in back was standing up, climbing onto the cab roof, steadying himself with a loop of rope coming out the cab-windows, looking off to one side of the road.

Cocksuckers! Pilau 'aihues, as Don would say. I thought about it. The guy on top was only looking down one side of the road. Sure, they'd cruise slowly back so he could study the other side of the road. Oh, man, oh, man, they would be coming back! I could get the M-1, the .45, confront them, put the fear of God in them! Oh, man, the idea!

Whoa, now, wait a minute, me bucko. What if they're armed? Well, shit, I had twenty shots of .30 caliber and eight shots of .45. Yeah, right, a shootout right in front of your house -- what a wakeup call for Steph who'd go bonkers. And even if you buffaloed them, you'd be tipping your hand -- they'd know where you lived. Well, what then, the goddamned motherfucking cocksucking sonsofbitches!

I went for a cup of coffee, fired up a joint. It would be awhile before they came back, time for me to think. Forget the firearms -- they were a last resort, when somebody brought the shit to me and I fed it to them. Hadn't Don once mentioned a relative, a cousin or something, who was a makai, a cop? Maybe we could find out who these assholes were, where they lived, then figure out something.

When they returned twenty minutes later, the guy on top moving to sit when they passed, I was off further along into the bush. I could hear Duchess barking. By the time they passed my position, the guy in back had climbed on top again, all of them looking off to the other side of the road. I wrote down their license number.

*****

Two things happened. The first thing was Don got married and I didn't go to the wedding, but promised to attend the reception.

"C'mon, baby, why don't'cha wanta go? Don's your best friend."

"That's why. I can't watch him do it. Weddings are depressing. Marriages never last. I'm gonna sit home, smoke some hash, drink some hooch, and feel sorry for my buddy. Somebody's gotta do it."

"Jeez, I heard everything now! Drive me up to Laura's. I'll go with them."

"Sure, I gotta get some ice and beer anyway."

"Do me a favor, huh?"

"What's that, babe?"

"Don't ever ask me to marry you. I wouldn't wanna be stood up at the altar!"

"Okay, sure, but if you should change your mind, keep it to yourself, huh?"

"Anybody ever told you, you can be a big okolepuka sometimes?"

I was shocked, "Never. And I wouldn't believe them if they did."

"Jeez!"

"I'll see you at the reception. Save me a piece of cake."

The second thing was I met a cop on my return from dropping Steph off. He was sitting in a parked car just off the road at the entrance to Hawaiian Fern Acres, just through the canefields a quarter mile off Volcano Road.

I didn't know he was a cop at first. He was a tall nearly bald guy with a fringe of prematurely white hair, an older guy but not so old, a lieutenant with the Hilo Police Department I was to learn. It seemed a bit suspicious him sitting there, not out with his hood up like he had car trouble or something. I stopped for a closer look.

"Hi, how you doing? You need any help?"

He smiled. "No, I'm fine."

"Mind if I ask what you're doing here?" "Minding my own business."

"Ah, and just what is your business?"

He was amiable enough, smiling all the while. "It would be better if you minded your own business."

"Hey, you know, normally I'd agree with you, but I live here and sometimes the wrong people come out here."

"Like who?"

"Oh, thieves, people looking for trouble. It's very quiet and peaceable out here, you know. Nobody wants trouble."

"Well, my friend, you don't have to worry about me. I'm here to make sure there's no trouble. Whereabouts you live?"

"First house on Lehua."

"You know the Filipino pig-farmer on Pikake?"

"Oh, sure, I met him a couple of times. Nice fellow." His eyes widened. "You like chickenfights?"

"Nah, not much. I been to a few, though, you know, just so I could see what it's all about."

"Well, you know they're illegal."

"Sure, but so're a lot of other little things. No big deal, huh?"

"Yeah, that's one way to look at it."

"Well, say, if you're ever in the neighborhood, drop in for a beer. Don't mind the dog -- she barks a lot, but she won't bite you."

"Mahalo. I might do that sometime. First house on Lehua, huh?"

"Yeah. Here, you better have one right now," I said, grabbing a cold bottle out of the ice-cooler. "It'll probably get a little warmer in the afternoon."

"Mahalo nui. I'll be seeing you."

"Name's Buck." I stuck out my hand.

He shook it. "Lopaka. Most folks call me Lo."

Lopaka, Lopaka, I thought to myself while driving away. That was the Hawaiian form of Robert. So Lo must be the same as Bob. Friendly enough, but a little strange. I went on past the turnoff at Lehua and on to Pikake. When I neared the Filipino pig-farmer's place, sure enough, there were about fifty cars parked all up and down the road. There were festivities in progress, a cookout, beer, and most likely cockfights to come. I pulled in, parked, and wandered on in looking for the owner.

"Buck, my aikane, (Friend) pehea 'oe?" (How are you)

"Oh, maika'i no, (Fine) my friend. Hey, you know there's a guy up at the entry road looks like makai?"

"Oh, yeah, no problem. He's on lookout in case any other cops show up. He lets us know on a radio, you know, so the chickens can disappear into the rainforest."

"Ah, I see. Good idea."

"Get yourself a plate. We got kalua pua'a." (Pig cooked underground with hot rocks, a luau feast)

*****

A week later, Lo stopped in, smiling but a bit leery of Duchess. "Duchess, hele mai. Kapu now. Maika'i ilio. C'mon up, my friend. It's okay. She just likes to announce visitors."

After getting him seated with a beer in hand, he looked around. "This is very cozy. You do it yourself?"

"Sure, me and the wahine," I replied, referring to Steph.

"You need a floor."

"Yeah, we'll get around to it one of these days."

"I might know where you can pick up a load of koa wood -- make a nice floor."

"Oh, yeah? I might be interested if the price is right."

"Lot of people out here grow pakalolo."

"They do?" Steph and I, both eyes wide, innocent.

He grinned. "It's kind of like the chicken fights, you know, one of those little things that're against the law -- no big deal."

"Yeah, right, no big thing."

"This is Hawaii. We're more relaxed over here -- not like the Mainland. We live at a different speed."

"You been to the Mainland?"

"Oh, yeah. Las Vegas, crazy town. Go over on gambling junkets once in a while. Hawaiians like to gamble."

"Ever been to San Francisco?"

"Yeah, a couple of times. Fine restaurants, beautiful wahines from all over the world."

"My favorite city -- next to Hilo, that is."

°You want to do a little pakalolo, don't let me inhibit you. I like a good toke once in a while myself."

Hm. Well. Gee. We didn't have any in the house right at the moment and I didn't want to go out and let him see where we kept our little smoking stash. And I wasn't about to lead him out along the paths into the bush to show off our nursery and experimental station, pick a sprig or two to smoke. Still, I'd like to smoke a joint or two with him, to reassure myself.

"Let me show you something, my friend," I said, going to the open front door where a potted plant grew. I hefted it and brought it in to sit between us. "What do you think about this little beauty?"

It was a weird plant, a thick stalk six inches up from the potting soil. Then it branched into two shoots straight up about two feet, one a bit higher than the other. It was covered with a profuse growth of tiny single-bladed leaves of dark earth-green and very shiny, as though coated with wax. If you looked close, you could see tiny black seed bracts and a golden fuzz of plant cilia. The bracts were empty and cracked open with none of the white pulp found in viable seeds.

"What is it?"

"You know what pakalolo looks like?"

"Sure. That's not pakalolo."

This baby was the lone survivor of the second planting Don and I had set out, the one ripped off. A few days afterward, days of rain, Steph and I had gone to load up the remaining bags for use in replanting. One single chopped plant, out of the hundred that had begun there, had sprouted two little green shoots just below where the machete had chopped it. The two shoots grew straight up. When I had seen the mutated nature of the leaves, the absence of sawtooth edges, I had tried to pollinate it by shaking the golden dust from male plants over it, which didn't work -- though the plant was clearly female as evidenced, by the seed bracts. I had left it on our front steps for months with none of our visitors ever recognizing it for what it was -- many of whom were experienced grass growers. My theory was that the plant was a more exaggerated version of a reaction against the pinching process we practiced. In this case, the plant had responded to severe injury by disguising itself and producing more resins. The two arms of it were very sticky to the touch, almost as if someone had poured syrup on it. The reason one arm was shorter than the other was because I had cut off a few inches of bud on one side. I had gotten so snockered over smoking half a joint, which I'd let go out, that I'd asked Steph to drive us into Hilo -- where exactly we were going and why is forever lost in the fumes. At Volcano Road on the turn for the fifteen mile drive to town, I gave the other half to Steph. When we came to, we were forty miles the other side of Hilo, winding lazily along the coast road.

"Babe, where the fuck are we?"
"On the way into Hilo, baby, what'd'ju think?"
"Hilo, shit! We'll be at Naalehu pretty soon!"
"You sure?"

Lord have mercy! This was stay-at-home pakalolo. We parked off the road, walked down to bath\in an icy-cold rivulet flowing from the mountains, tried to make love, but were chased away by tiny stinging mosquitoes that left red itchy bumps all over us.

"This, my friend," I said to Lo. "Is a very special plant, blessed by the gods who have bestowed magical properties on it. Ua mau ke ea o ka aina i ke pono."

He grinned at me, thought I was putting him on. "Hey, I'm Hawaiian remember? I know what that means."

"Right. The life of the land is perpetuated in righteousness. This plant, this gift of the gods, will make you truly appreciate the meaning of those words."

"Oh, yeah?"

I cut off the top of the higher arm, tossed it to Steph. "Flash dry that, babe, roll us up a couple."

She shredded it in her fingers, licking the stickiness off, tossed it in a small frying pan, lit the stove, and shook it over the heat long enough to dry it out enough to smoke, then rolled us up a couple, I lit only one, passed it to Lo.

"Mm, nice bouquet," he said, taking a toke and holding it, smacking his lips, tasting. "Nice spicy taste."

We passed it around having to relight it a couple of time because it was so thick with resin.

Soon we were all silent, feeling the spirit rise up in us, laughing, taking over, transporting us to a place especially made for contemplating the essence of infinity, putting wings to our backs, haloes to our heads. Years later, I looked at Lo, my friend, my very beautiful friend, and I grinned and Steph grinned, and we waited for our friend to grin, but he couldn't quite manage it until much later.

*****

"Whew! Shit!" he blew as we were drinking coffee and eating to moderate the transmogrification. "I ain't ever been that fucking high in my life!"

A week later, Lo and I drove by his directions to a site where a home was being built and, together, we loaded a stack of koa onto a flatbed trailer rented in town. It was after midnight.

"Cheapest wood you'll ever get. Now, you'll have a really nice floor."
"Who's the guy owns it?"
"Don't worry -- an okolepuka, a fucking politician."

*****

One morning just at the break of dawn, I was awakened by Duchess' furious growling, her serious barks. I got out of bed for a looksee. Duchess' nose was pointing toward our experimental patch out the back way. As I walked out to climb a small rise, she took off running. I pursued, quickly becoming alert. Catching up to where she waited, I found that all our lovely children had been devastated by a mass murderer -- they'd all been machete-chopped six inches up their main stalks.

Oh, Jesus! These we visited almost daily, tending and caring for them, spoiling them with love, humming gay tunes as we lovingly fed and pruned them, concerned for their health. I had read an article about plants responding favorably to music and had often enough sat stoned among them tootling riffs on my kazoo, bringing to them the irrepressible mirth to be found in the roots of blues music. And now they were all gone while I stood in shock.

Duchess ran around in circles barking up a storm of outrage that echoed in my heart. Then she picked up the scent and tore off into the brush, leading the way. "Lele, lele, lele!" I sang in grunts as I chased after her. "Kuleana! Lele, lele, lele!" Bastard dickhead! Goddamned motherfucking cocksucking sonofabitch!

Coming over a hillock, I caught a glimpse of a man with a fat round green sack slung over his shoulder. "Sonofabitch!" I screamed.

He turned around and fired a pistol at me. I hit the ground. When I chanced a peek, he was gone. Knowing the lowlife would shoot Duchess if she caught up to him, I called her back. "Duchess! Hele mai! Hele, hele, hele mai!"

When I saw her tearing back toward me, I turned to run back to our cabin to find Steph sitting up all sleepy-eyed. Without a word, I grabbed the Colt and ran out to the '49 Ford, which was the last vehicle in the drive. I jumped in to sit on the wooden crate, twisted two wires together, and fired her up. Duchess leapt into the back, full of the excitement of the chase. Steph, alarmed to see me run in and snatch up the pistol, came out to inquire as to what in hell was going on.

"I'm going after the motherfucker who chopped all our babies!"

"What?"

"He stole all our babies from the experimental plot," I yelled, blasting down the driveway without mufflers.

I knew he had to be heading for Pikake, the next road over on the far side of the street-grid laid out in the tract. By making three right turns, I might be able to catch up to him. The first turn out of the driveway was okay, but on the second at the crossroad, when I had picked up speed and forgot about the brakes which I hadn't got around to fixing, the door flew open and only my elbow clamped over the windowsill kept me from flying out of the cab. For the third turn, I eased up on the gas pedal, gearing down, then tromped it again. As I tore clattering, squeaking, steaming and blasting down the road, it dawned on me that I'd forgotten to put any clothes on.

It made no difference, I was so pissed off. I was going to blast that goddamned motherfucking cocksucking sonofabitch to kingdom come! And there he was, a light green pickup coming toward me in the distance. Eat shit and die, you donkey-dick-sucking bastard! You should have gone the other way!

Belatedly, I began thinking about my options. Just what in the hell was I going to do? Well, I could broadside the old Ford in the road to block him, jump out behind it as cover. Duchess would leap out barking. What then? A shootout? Jesus, I was buck-naked! What if he had a partner-in-crime and they were both armed? I'd be outgunned! Well, Duchess would help surely, go tearing into them, send chunks of flesh flying. With no brakes, I could see myself crashing off the road into the brush and trees as the green pickup sped by me. No, fuck that. No use taking the chance of getting us both shot over a few pounds of grass. More like thirty or forty pounds!

Okay, I'd blast him or them as we passed each other. They couldn't know I was the irate owner driving toward them. I'd have the element of surprise. Sure, but -- the thought sobered me -- shoot them? A couple of two-bit grass thieves? Well, goddamnit, they'd ripped off five months of my labors -- all that effort for nothing! Damn right, shoot them!

Okay, maybe that was a little extreme. I could shoot out one of their tires. Yeah, then maybe yell out that I was going to get some of my friends and come back and settle their hash. Maybe they'd abandon their vehicle and take to the woods. Maybe I'd get my grass back and maybe I wouldn't. But at least I could return to shoot out the rest of the tires and burn up their fucking truck if nothing else.

Wait a minute. What if the culprits had gone in the other direction? What if the truck coming toward me was driven by an innocent party? Christ, the old Filipino pig-farmer who lived further up this road, didn't he have a light green pickup? What if it was him? Okay, I'd just let it pass. If it was the old Filipino, I'd grin and wave. If it was somebody else, I'd hope my instincts could tell me something.

The truck passed. It was a stranger and he looked guilty. Duchess began barking. The pickup bed was loaded with fat green bags. The sonofabitch! I hit the brakes...and kept right on rolling. Finally the tired old Ford rolled to a steaming stop as I watched the thief disappearing in the rearview mirror. Delicately shifting gears and working the clutch, I got turned around and took up the trail. It was too late -- he was long gone.

But somehow I'd been possessed of enough sense to memorize his license number.

Once back home, after coffee, a couple of joints, working out my frustration by regaling Steph with the story, I kidded her out of her fears and she began laughing over the ludicrous aspects of a naked grass farmer pursuing the bad guy in a barely functioning old rattletrap Ford.

"But, gawd, baby, you could have been hurt," she pointed out, giggling. "You could have been shot. I mean, with your ule (Penis) hanging out and all."

"Now that would really have made me mad," I retorted, which sent us into new gales of laughter. (*An allusion to a story coming out of World War II when the Japanese attacked Pearl Harbor. An enemy plane was purported to have crash-landed on Niihau. The pilot had gone strutting about proclaiming victory in the name of the Emperor and that the entire population of native Hawaiians were prisoners. One rather large local boy didn't move fast enough for the pilot in following orders and he shot him. Well, that wasn't so bad -- it was only a flesh wound in the leg. But when the pilot shot him again, in the stomach this time, that was too much. The Hawaiian grabbed the pilot by his ankle, swung him around and dashed his brains out against a wall. This incident, true or not, gave rise to the saying that if you shoot a Hawaiian more than once, you're sure to make him mad at you.)

A thief never appreciates the ramifications of his crimes until he, himself, has become a victim. Let him lose some cherished property to a thief and his outrage knows no bounds -- as is the practice in some Islamic countries, he is ready to implement the policy of cutting the hands off thieves.

So it was with me, something of a hypocrite that I was, whenever a patch of lovingly tended pakalolo plants was lost to thieves.

Along with a pound of my finest dried and manicured buds, I passed over to Lo the two license numbers of pakalolo thieves I had secured. A few days later he gave me addresses, along with a brief character summary.

"I did a record check on these bums," Lo said. "They've both been in and out of several jails on burglary and theft charges. One guy's on probation and the other served a couple of years in O.P. (Oahu Prison, the state penitentiary, located in Honolulu.)

They both like to beat their wives and kids -- a half dozen domestic disturbance beefs. This one guy ratted his way out of a drug robbery case with the BNDD."

"Nice fellas."

"Yeah, you be careful with these guys, Buck."

"Ah, hell, Lo, I'm not gonna invite 'em into my home or anything."

"What're you going to do?"

"It's better you don't know, right? You'll find out soon enough."

"No pilikia, huh?"

"No, my friend, don't worry."

Late on a dark and stormy night, to steal a phrase from Snoopy, Don and I paid a visit to these bums. The first guy had a pickup in his drive and a motorcycle in a detached garage. We doused both in gasoline, the pickup inside and out. Tossing matches and running down the road to Don's pickup, we heard explosions that sounded like rifle-shots, which kicked up our adrenaline levels. A few minutes later, while sipping from hot cups of coffee as we headed for the other jerk's address, we figured out it was exploding tires.

The second guy had a pickup and a brand new car. We poured two bottles of syrup into the pickup's gas tank. The car had a lock on the gascap. Well, we could siphon some gas out of Don's tank for another vehicle barbecue or...while I kept watch, Don jimmied the hood, removed the sparkplugs and dumped handfuls of fine roadside gravel into the cylinders.

For our night's work, one pickup and motorcycle were total losses, and the roof of the cinderblock garage collapsed. Only the engines in the other two vehicles were destroyed.

When Lo found out, he popped for a bottle of whiskey. "I like your brand of justice. Nobody's got a clue!"

"Yeah, but the cocksuckers are still around."

"Maybe you should've left a message."

"Damn, Lo, that's a hell of an idea."

*****

Two months later we did it again, only differently -- without destroying their recently purchased replacement vehicles. This time it was psychological warfare.

Fireworks are popular in Hawaii. There is a practical joke device that, when wired into a single sparkplug and taking less than a minute to install, goes off when the car is started. It first emits a long wheeeoh-sound before exploding in a good cherrybomb crack and blowing a nice cloud of black smoke, but does no damage except to the nerves.

Especially when a phonecall follows to his house and a menacing gravel voice says, "Da liddle pro'lum wit yer car today, dat coulda been six sticksa dynamite, ya know. Ya should prolly move to anodder island. Next time ya might not be so lucky, hah?"

Invisible enemies are the worst.

The Big Island soon numbered two less pakalolo thieves.

*****

Royal sent an ounce of the gray powder that was MDA to my postoffice box in Mountain View.

Among drug-users, there are two basic types; one uses drugs and the other allows drugs to use him. Even fools can overdose on aspirin. My first experience with MDA, wouldn't you know, was an overdose.

We had gone up to visit Laura and Leonard. Two other laidback couples were present to enjoy the Sunday get-together. With beer, grass, food, and amiable people about, I broke out the MDA. It was the awfullest-tasting shit I'd ever been dumb enough to stick a wetted finger into. The question was not only cutting out a proper dose of the powder, but how to ingest it.

I remembered a method taught me when I first tried swallowing half a tube of foul-tasting cotton from a Wyamine inhaler for a legal dose of benzedrine. The trick was to chew up a couple pieces of gum, then spread out the sticky wet stuff to enfold the cotton -- and swallow the gum.

Somebody dashed down to the Glenwood store for a couple of packs of Juicy Fruit. Everything went fine in my cautious divvying out of doses -- except when it came to myself. Figuring I had a higher tolerance -- just like good ol' George on the Parest 400s -- as evidenced by years of experience at handling all sorts of drugs without going crazy, dying or suffering any ill effects other than an occasional hangover, I cut out about three or four times more for myself.

Everyone except Leonard and I had wandered on down the road to visit the folks in the next house a half mile away -- a nice day for a walk in the country.

Sitting across a table from Leonard, I broke into a sweat, began to feel nauseous. Leonard's voice droned in and out as I lay over on the bench I was sitting on, feeling a gust of wind lifting me in a swirl towards the eye of the hurricane.

"Hey, bra, mebbe take too much, hah?"

Whoa now, me bucko, time to steel yourself and resist! I managed to rush all areel into the bathroom where I stuck my finger down my throat and threw up.

Then it got good, my mind pellucid with the natural beauty and order of things, my body energized and light as a spirit. It was an absolutely marvelous day outside. MDA was merely reminiscent of acid or psilocybin or mescaline in that it tuned up your perceptions. What looked good, or smelled or tasted or felt good, became even better -- everything amped up. When Leonard and I heard music wafting in from outside, it turned out to be Steph and Laura and the others returning, their voices a tinkling melody in the air.

Steph, her eyes aglitter, pulled at my hand. We climbed a fence and skipped through a copse of woods to a grassy pasture beyond.

"Oh, baby," she purred. "I feel so good!"

"Um-hmmm."

We kissed so softly, so tenderly, so totally with sweet warmth. I picked daisies to put in her hair and went to gather more for a bed of flowers.

"Baby," she crooned.

"Hm?"

"Come back." She lifted her arms to me, wet lips aglisten, eyes sultry.

I felt like the Cheshire Cat in Wonderland, grinning so widely.

"What, babe?"

"Let's get naked."

"Ah."

"I wanna fuck."

"Oh." "Now."

Whereupon I discovered that MDA is an elixir of eroticism, that expert writers were either ignorant or lying when they told us there were no true aphrodisiacs.

*****

Not knowing his price, I shipped Royal a nice teddy bear from which all the stuffing had been replaced by a couple of pounds of lightly osterized pakalolo so I could keep his fine nasty powder for myself and Steph and friends.

Then I figured out that a proper dose fit nicely into a #4 capsule and converted the remaining portion to a large handful of honey-hued gelatin-encased hits.

*****

Kieth wrote to say a poor young hippy couple would be arriving and could we help them get situated? J.D., at eighteen, was an aspiring rock guitarist whose head was otherwise empty except for the residues of any available drug. Debbie was seventeen, pregnant, and a very lovely girl of Chinese-Hawaiian ancestry. She played flute. Of the two, Debbie had all the brains.

We met them at Hilo Airport, welcoming them with traditional plumeria leis, stocked up on beer and food, and took them home as members in good standing of the menagerie of our family.

Soon enough we would initiate them into the pakalolo-growing business in order that they could make enough to keep their shit together since neither had any job skills worth mentioning.

There was an abandoned cabin set back out of sight from the road on Pikake that we knew about. We all went in and began to fix the place up, gathering furniture and all the homemaking accouterments necessary to making a go of it in the rainforest, cleaning out the watertank and fixing the roof gutters, and all the while as they lived with us, sleeping on the corner divan made into a double, teaching them the rudiments of grass cultivation, even transporting a load of bagged and ready plants to hide in the jungle for them to practice on.

As Debbie was close to term, I gave J.D. a pistol as a signaling device. The two places were within gunshot distance. When Deb thought it was time, he was to walk down to the road and fire it a couple of times and we would come running to get her to the hospital.

I had to give him some basic lessons in the use of firearms in hopes that he would not shoot himself in the foot. "It's not a toy, J.D.," I told him. "You only go for this when you need it. I don't want to hear you taking potshots at birds and stuff. You keep it hidden away and don't let anyone know you have it. Okay?"

"Yeah, sure, but can I practice with it some more? First time I ever shot a gun. It's a real kick."

###

CHAPTER 8

Duchess must have taken on the promiscuous habits of her owners. The few days she came into heat, she must have joined in sexual congress with a half dozen mutts. When she gave birth to eleven pups, one of which died, it became obvious that her litter was the result of several sires, hardly were any two alike.

Expecting the additions to our family, we had built a simple birthing and nursing pen just inside the door, padding it with old blankets, to contain the pups until they'd been weaned. Steph's mothering instincts had taken over to the extent that she insisted on buying baby bottles and stocking powdered and evaporated milk -- just in case.

Debbie's call came first. J.D. had fired two shots to alert us. We had driven over in the car to carry them off to the hospital in Hilo, where she gave birth to Elena, a perfectly beautiful little doll of a baby.

By the time we got back in the rain, Duchess was gone. Hours later, she was pawing on the door for super, a much thinner beast than the bloated one we had left. We fed and watered her, then followed her out into the bush where her feral instincts had led her. Well, it was raining and so we ferried them all inside. There were two short-haired fawn-colored beauties with dark snouts and legs, a pure black one, a brindle, some shaggies, one with a large dome-like skull, and a ragtag remainder.

We cooed at them, babying all, showing them off, and tested the waters for prospective owners. A couple of months later, when they could all run around yapping and playing and feeding outside, we added a wild piglet I had caught while on an outing with some local boys boar hunting in the rainforest. We called him Boss because he bullied the others at feeding time, taking over the bowls of dogfood and not letting them eat until he'd had his fill.

I studied the ones I wanted to keep, settling more and more on the black one, the strongest and healthiest, but I liked the brindle for her unique coloring, her beauty. Don took the two fawn-colored ones, J.D. and Deb took two, and four went to other suckers for puppies.

The black, a half Labrador, I called Popolo, meaning black in a slightly impolite sense. Since the brindle, who had a congenital hip weakness, was his sister, we pronounced her name in the Hawaiian way, Sista.

Then Boss disappeared into the bush one day and Duchess soon followed, perhaps the two off into an eternal chase-and-elude game. But Duchess had done her duty in teaching all her offspring to bark at the approach of strangers and we handed on the Hawaiian command words.

Steph, already a proven sucker for puppy love, just had to have a cute little reddish-colored foxy-looking mutt, who, after much agonized consulting with all the auguries, she decided to call Goldenberry. But the mutt soon came into her more popular name by the fact of her mischievous instigations of the other two into chase games, all agrin with pink wagging tongue and puffing away. She was the Puffer. The relationship forming between Steph and Puffer was proof enough for me that humans and canines are perfectly capable of indulging in extra-sensory perceptions between species -- they read each other's minds and moods.

"Put on your miniskirt, babe," I ordered. "And pull your panties up tight so some cheek hangs out. Time to teach the peasants how not to play pool."

"Oh, gee, the Smile Inn. You must be hungry."

"Yeah, thirsty, too. Besides, I enjoy watching you make absolute fools of grown men."

She grinned, leaping to get ready. "Gawd, and you don't even have to be all that good."

"You're pretty good," I owned. "You manage to beat me often enough."

"I been known to fondle a cuestick or two."

"I know you have, darlin."

The Smile Inn was an odd little place that had become one of our favorites when going into town. It provided a game or two of pool for me -- just enough to set up the suckers among the mostly male patrons -- and a couple of hours of great pupus and free drinks as Steph took on and beat all comers at eightball -- beautiful to watch.

The Smile Inn was nothing fancy -- an oiled wooden floor, seven or eight tables with chairs, a small four-seater bar, and two pool tables. It was owned by a middle-aged Japanese woman with a thirty-year old overly plump simple-minded daughter who served as waitress, a sweet smiling girl eager to please. It had once been a shop with attached living quarters, the main showroom having been converted to tavern use. The patrons were overwhelmingly local people, mostly workingmen.

I ordered two drinks, paid for them, and put a quarter in the pool table to release the balls -- the only money I would spend for the next two or three hours as I ate a more or less continuous flow of pupus served in little dishes and bowls, getting slowly snockered in the like flow of drinks Steph won on pool bets with the locals.

After the first game, which was desultory on my part -- it being necessary for Steph to win--I retired to a nearby table with a shrug and a grin, holding out the cuestick to anyone who would take it.

The challenger had to supply a quarter for the game. Steph would smile her sexy emanations at him, then proceed to make the most pornographically suggestive shots in history -- walking around the table to study the shot, bending over to allow the poor besotted chump a peek at her nether parts. With sex on his mind, arousal heavy in the air, how could he concentrate on making a shot?

Steph was pretty good, but she could even beat those better than her by the seemingly ingenuous display of her body. She assumed a whole array of suggestive positions, positions sure to fire up masculine imaginations -- perhaps by stretching out a leg upon a rail and bending over to position herself for an awkward shot. I could see the glaze working down over their eyes, the need for more booze to wet a dry mouth. She would pat their cheeks, squeeze their arms in sympathy when they inevitably lost, play with the stick and balls in innuendo. When Steph was on the table, alcohol sales went up and the Japanese lady soon recognized that fact and treated us as honored guests.

Steph would take little breaks to sit and munch on the inventively delicious range of pupus arriving at the table, to try to allay the effects of the alcohol she, too, was consuming -- a drink every game, although she would skip some and have them sent my way.

Steph grew inventive as time passed and the alcohol slowed and cozied her. She might open her blouse for a view of deep cleavage, fanning herself, commenting that wasn't it warm and too bad she couldn't play in her underwear. The men tried to wear her down, hoping she would become too plastered and weary over the hours, all fantasizing they would be the one to beat her, each trying to entice her into a more exciting bet, she declining with a look that said, "Well, you know, maybe if my ol' man wasn't here."

There was a game down to two balls, Steph's color and the eight-ball, and it was the other guy's turn -- a long table shot to a corner pocket would win the game for him.

"Wait," Steph said. "I like to live dangerously. What say to a little extra wager to liven things up around this joint?"

You could almost hear the communal intake of breath, feel the pulse of testosterone-enriched blood pushing the temperature up a degree or two. There she stood, hand on cocked hip, one foot out of her clogs, the instep rubbing up her calf, the back of her knee, lipstick aglisten, a sultry glitter in her eyes.

"What?" A croak, a quick gulp of his drink. "What?"

"That'cha can't make this shot, baby."

"What? What's the bet?"

"Hm, lemme see," she teased. "I'll hold your ule the next time you go mimi. (Peepee); Urinate. If you lose, you tip the waitress five bucks."

I could see a dozen grown men trying to crowd into the miniscule bathroom in order to be able to witness the payoff, the proud but quivering winner gamely hoping his weenie wouldn't embarrass him.

"And I'll even help ya," she added, handing her cue to an overheated onlooker, stretching one smooth fleshy leg upon one rail, the other at a right angle along the other rail, leaning forward to balance herself, placing her pussy right over the corner pocket.

"Just aim for my kohe," (Vagina) she grinned with a wink.

Collective breaths were held, including mine. She was getting a little over-confident of her power, too sassy. It was I who would lose face if she had to pay off. What could I do? Put on a show of anger, pick a fight? They would mock me, hold me in contempt if I allowed her to pay. If she had to pay.

The guy took his time -- too much time, really, for such an easy straight-in shot -- trying to work his nervous system into the perfect shot. It had to be hard-driven, a masculine shot, the stick snaking forward in a power-stroke, the ball banging into the pocket.

If.

"Right there, baby," Steph coaxed, stroking the target in a lewd gesture. "I know you can do it."

The nervous nellie miscued, sending the cueball spinning impotently away, a moan of disappointment from all except me. Beautiful.

"Oh, poor baby," Steph commiserated, taking her stick back and going over to plant a quick kiss on his cheek. "Maybe next time."

She easily sank the last two balls.

"Baby, you had enough? Let's go for a swim. I wanna cool off."

"Sure, babe. Can you still drive?"

*****

Scrimshaw came by one day with a tale of woe. He was a personable guy with a ready smile and a flattering word, a local hustler about town trying to live by his wits -- which meant he was sometimes up but more often down on his luck. He had a lovely wife and two attractive kids on welfare. I had done a few small grass deals with him -- he claimed to know everybody who was anybody, often bragging of organized crime connections in Honolulu.

Awhile back he had approached me at the Kaukau Place to help him out on a dope scam. It seems he sometimes sold bogus dope to a sucker when he could find one dumb enough.

Needless to say, I'd turned him down. "Damn, Scrimshaw, you looking to get yourself shot?"

"Aw, these lames! They don't know real coke from cocaine-laced baking soda -- time they figure it out it's too late. Fucking tourists, what're they gonna do?"

Well, it seems the two prospective customers weren't quite dumb enough and when they complained, Scrimshaw had pulled out a pistol and robbed them. To his chagrin, he found that they both had I.D. as agents of the BNDD, whereupon he took a fall for armed robbery and was now out on bail, trying, so he claimed, to raise enough money to repay his "people" in Honolulu for putting up bond. No problem, the fix was in -- the ohana hui (Family organization.) had judges in their pockets.

Scrimshaw was broke and needed money. Could I see my way to fronting him a few pounds of pakalolo, which he could sell by the lid and make a few hundred bucks?

My few experiences with Scrimshaw had taught me that he was shaky when it came to trusting him. He always had a plausible story, delivered in his most charming manner, as to the reasons he came up short on his end -- an endless tale of bad luck. But, gee, who could blame him if he was the sad sack of conmen, a comic fatalist upon whom fortune was heaping more than enough punishment? He meant well, didn't he? And he was a man, wasn't he? And he had a family to support, didn't he?

While Steph entertained him for fifteen minutes, I drove to one of our nearby stashes to remove two entire pakalolo plants hanging upsidedown from a line strung between trees -- the natural air-dry curing process that took several days after harvesting. Stuffing them into a garbage bag, I returned to present them to him.

"There should be close to two pounds there time you get done stripping it down."

"Hey, bra, mahalo," he said, displaying a nice set of ivories. "You're a lifesaver."

"Only I'm not fronting it to you, Scrimshaw."

"What, man? I'm stone broke. I can't pay you until I sell the stuff."

"Don't worry about that. This is a gift. You did me some favors, you know? So I'm doing you a favor."

"Aw, aikane. I don't know what to say."

I wondered if he could actually make his eyes all dewy on command or whether it was a sincere emotion. I suspected he'd make a pretty good actor if he could be taught not to overdo it.

"Three days from now, I'm gonna call your wife and ask her if you gave her two hundred and fifty dollars. I find out you didn't, I'm gonna be very disappointed, man."

"Hey, what do you think I am? I love Rita and my kids. I'd do anything for them." He gestured at the bag, properly indignant now. "Who do you think this is for anyway?"

I grinned. "Have a beer, Scrimshaw. Get your shit together. I'm still gonna call Rita in three days."

He grinned back. Oh, you sly rascal, you! I don't know why you don't trust me. I made money for you, didn't I? All the time I'm running all over the place for everybody, doing things for them, making connections for them, spending all my money on gas, busting my ass, and nobody appreciates it."

As he had been speaking, he'd stood to pat his pockets and turn for the door, leaving his beer unfinished.

"Don't forget the bag."

"Hah? No, no, I'm not leaving. I just want to get something out of my car."

He returned with a six-inch length of bamboo. He pulled out a pocketknife, sat down, and split it in half lengthwise. Then he took up one piece and began carefully splitting off narrow sticks. He turned his charm on Steph.

"Stephie, sweetie-pie, you got any black thread?"

She dug him out a spool from her sewing kit.

"What the hell are you doing, Scrimshaw?"

"Wait, I'll show you, teach you a little trick I know."

After he'd split the other half of the bamboo, leaving a pile of oversized toothpicks, he pulled the trash bag over to reach in and break off a branch. Then he cut off buds and began winding them around the bamboo slivers, attaching them by spiraling winds of thread.

"Thai Stick," he explained with a leer, proud of himself. "I can make more kala (Money) this way. These little sticks imported from Thailand, I can sell them ten dollars apiece to the tourists and other lames."

"You amaze me, Scrimshaw," I said, laughing.

"Live and learn, man," he replied, smug as a dung beetle in a fresh cow pie. "Live and learn."

Before he left, I gave him a dozen caps of MDA, explaining what it was, suggesting he ought to treat Rita to a night at home after the kids were put to bed. "Maybe you can pass them around, see how they go over, see what the business possibilities are. Might be something you can make some money at in the future."

*****

One day, with Steph gone somewhere, I was feeling at loose ends and bored, so I went to visit Frank, who was always upbeat and entertaining. Plus, I would get to feast my eyes on Barbara and exchange secret little looks of longing.

When Steph and I had returned to the Olu Street house to close it out and move our waterbed into our new home, we'd found Frank in his usual state of inebriated high spirits sprawled out with this beautiful smooth-bodied peaches-and-cream female who was maybe twenty years younger than him. They were necking and giggling, both naked as jaybirds.

"Buck, Steph, hey, c'mon in," Frank greeted cheerily. "Fix yourselves a drink, try some of this special imported Bengali weed I got." He pointed to an open baggie of pakalolo, stuff we had sent out to market.

"This is Barbara," he went on, introducing the naked wench, who smiled prettily. "Barb, Buck and Steph."

We all waved and nodded. "Sorry to dispossess you, Frank, but we need our bed. We're moving into a new place."

"You got a new place? Shit, so do I. Moving into one of those cooperative apartments at the Palm Terrace. Barb and me are gonna try a little unwedded connubial bliss. She's got two kids. Guess I gotta play daddy, too."

"Hey, great. Congratulations."

Steph had been busy rolling a couple of joints from Frank's stash, lit them, passed one to Barbara, while we shared the other.

"What do you guys got going? The country? Where?"

436

"Hawaiian Fern Acres, up Mountain View way, regular fucking mansion."

"Oh, yeah, great. What? Are they doing any building up that way?"

"Nah, nothing happening. Just us in the boonies."

I had recently spent a few weeks with Frank roofing fifty houses at Hawaiian Gardens on the way to Pahoa, a small tract of identical houses, boxes beside other boxes. We'd gotten pretty tight busting our asses and knocking off a case of beer and a few joints every working day. We appreciated each other's willingness and ability to get the job done. He'd made out like a bandit and I'd been happy with the hundred bucks a day I'd been pulling down in cash wages.

"Good grass, Frank," Steph said. "What'd ya call it? Bengali?" She was being coyly playful, knowing full well from the name that it was some of our own stuff.

"Yeah, shit's from India. You know, where they got all those Bengal tigers fucking English used to shoot? Stuff makes its way to Indonesia, the Philippines, Korea, Japan. Then the Koreans and Japanese smuggle it over in fishing boats."

"No shit? Good smoke, Frank. "

"Yeah, but a little more expensive, twenty, twenty-five a bag, but worth it, you know?"

"Yeah, whew, mean toke, Frank."

He grinned, an old boar in hog heaven. "You know me, my connections, only the best."

I'd never forgotten the sight of Barbara, Lord have mercy, a succulent wench if I ever saw one. Now I was headed over for a visit, few drinks, little pakalolo, some jokes and laughs, do some magic tricks for Barb's beautiful daughters, one about ten, the other seven or so, exchange soulful looks of unfulfilled longing with my ol' buddy's ol' lady.

I wanted to kiss Barb all over, maybe even suck her toes if that turned her on, fuck her silly and recite mushy love-poems -- but I never would as long as she was with Frank. As licentious as I was, as free-wheeling in my opportunistic sexual morels, ever ready to do my own fucking and allow everyone else the same freedom, I nevertheless drew the line at fucking a buddy's ol' lady unless he made it clear it was all right -- which I had done with a few of my buddies who had eyes for Steph, and vice versa.

"Buck, you nail-driving sonofabitch," Frank greeted, three sheets to the wind. "C'mon in. Where's Steph? You guys in to hit the sauna?"

Frank had given me a key to the Palm Terrace workout room by the pool, which contained a shower area and sauna. Steph and I, sometimes with J.D. and Deb in tow, took advantage of the facilities now and again late in the night when we were in for a night of dancing at the Poly Room -- where we sweated out all the accumulated poisons, showered, and drove down to a beach to catch the sunrise before going on to Ken's Pancake House for breakfast on our way home.

"Nah, Steph's off somewhere. Just at loose ends looking for good company."

They had visitors, three building contractors from Honolulu. We were introduced. They were talking about another subdivision project, this time a hundred houses, of which Frank had the subcontract for the roofing. They were all drunk, in a raucous party mood, but with an undercurrent I didn't understand. But which soon became apparent when Barbara came speeding in from a bedroom attired only in bra and underpants, obviously zonked on booze and the pharmaceutical amphetamines she was fond of, her speech like a speeded up record she was talking so fast.

"That's all I'm worth, huh, Frank, you asshole? Fifty fucking dollars a throw? Okay, Frank, cash in advance! I'll suck 'em and fuck 'em, wanna go up my ass, that's okay, too, fifty bucks worth, no dawdling, show me your money, assholes!" She held out her hand to the three leering guys.

"Barb, what the hell?"

She turned on me. "What, you wanna get in line, too? Fifty bucks, sucker, cash on the barrelhead! Hips, lips, or armpits, baby, fifty fucks!"

"Barb, what?"

"On second thought, you can go first, free of charge, warm me up for these other assholes!"

"Barb."

"Frank wants to sell my pussy to his buddies, fifty bucks a throw! The cheap sonofabitch is too stupid to ask for a hundred! Fucking whores in Waikiki make a hundred for a quickie fuck and he wants to peddle my ass for fifty!"

"Ah, shit," Frank growled. "It was jush a fuckin' joke! Go get'cher fuckin' clothes on, you dumb bitch!"

"Dumb, huh? Dumb, huh? I'll show you dumb, you fucking idiot! Fifty fucks! C'mon, put it in my hand!" She was dancing around in front of the three guys, her hand out, demanding. "I'll give you something to remember boys! You can take it home to your wives, teach the old dogs some new tricks! C'mon, c'mon! What's the matter? You can't get 'em up, huh?"

"Give 'er fifty! Give 'er fifty!" Frank roared. "Go ahead an' fuck the bitch! She like's gangbangin'! Go ahead! I wanna watch!"

The assholes were pulling out their wallets, trying to count out the money.

"Yah, c'mon, let's party! Fifty chickenshit dollars for the tightest, most educated pussy on the Big Island! Show you some tricks you never seen in all your miserable lives! Fifty bucks! All three of you at once! C'mon!"

She tore her bra off, freeing a really nice set of mammaries.

The assholes were all hot, slopping their drinks, fondling themselves, leering, and one guy working at undoing his pants. "Take off the pants! Take off the pants!" another croaked, getting to his feet.

Mm-mm, I had to admit, I'd have that for breakfast anytime. Then she was off for the bedroom, rolling a set of buns that'd make a dead man sit up.

Everyone, including Frank, was lurching to follow. Barbara was jumping up and down on the bed. "C'mon, c'mon, I only fuck on top of money! Lay them fifties down, my boys, and let's see what you got!"

"Fuckin' bitch! Fuckin' bish! Fuckin' bish! Go 'head, fuck um, ya fu'in bish!" Frank was staggering about, crashing back on the bureau, knocking bottles and tins and jars flying.

One of the three was in, had his pants off, looking ridiculous in jockey shorts, shirttails, and his shoes and socks. The other two held up an unsteady doorway.

"Gi'me a money," Frank was muttering. "Pimp ge's alla money!"

Ah, well, me bucko, this crazy man sure's shit been getting a workout lately, I thought, taking a deep breath, holding it, getting the veins popped out, my face red, looking at Barbara as a dumb little girl taunting three child-molesters. I grabbed the nearest. "Get the fuck out of here, you piece of shit, or I'm gonna stomp your miserable ass flat!"

I pushed him backwards where he stumbled and fell, turned to grab the next, glaring madly. "You, too, cocksucker! Get your shit and get the fuck outa here, you GODDAMNED MOTHERFUCKING COCKSUCKING SONOFABITCH!"

The guy backed off in shock. My insane gaze sought out the third one, who was stumbling around trying to get a foot in his trousers. "Your mother know what you're doing?

Huh? Your wife and kids know what you're doing? Huh? You know what the fuck you're doing, you GODDAMNED MOTHERFUCKING COCKSUCKING SONOFABITCH? Huh? Huh? Huh? Get the fuck outa here!

They fled.

Frank was speechless, his mouth and eyes both wide. I grabbed him, pulled him up, fighting off an urge to hug him, pulled him toward the bed, pushed him to plop back on it. Barb leapt away, speechless too.

"Wha'a'shi' ya shink ya doon?"

"Shut up, Frank. I don't much like you right now!"

His eyes rolled and he passed out.

"Barb, get your clothes on."

"Don't tell me what to do in my own house!"

"Yeah, right." I turned to go.

"Wait! Take me with you!"

"Where's your kids?"

"At school. Take us with you. We can pick them up at the school. I don't want to stay here anymore. Frank's an asshole!"

"What would I do with you and two kids?"

"Make love to me then."

"Nah, not today, Barb."

She burst into tears, threw her arms around me. "Please don't leave me here, Buck! Please don't!"

Well, me bucko, here you are with a naked dame in your arms and, jeez, don't she feel good! "Barb, please! Either put some clothes on or go to bed." I tried to push her toward where Frank lay snoring.

"I'm not getting in the same bed with that asshole!"

"Then get some clothes on or I'm leaving."

"No, don't go! I'll get in Tiffany's bed." She turned to head for her daughters' bedroom, and me being what I am couldn't help but admire the view. Someday, I sighed.

I tucked her in, kissed her on the forehead. She grabbed me, smeared saliva all across my face, and stuck her tongue in my mouth, spreading her desperation.

"No, Barb, c'mon. Try to get some sleep."

"I can't fucking sleep! Jesus Christ, it's only noon! Besides, I took some speed."

"When?"

"Before breakfast."

"Shit. You got any downers?"

"Some nembutal in the bathroom."

"Stay in bed. I'll get you a couple."

I brought two back with a glass of water, helped her take them, admiring her tits all over again as she sat up. She laid back down. "Oh, shit, I have to be up for the kids when they come home!"

"No, no, stay down. I'll pick 'em up, take them home with me. They'll have a good time in the country. Tomorrow's Saturday. I'll bring 'em home tomorrow sometime. You two ought to get it together. You carry on like this in front of your kids?"

"No." She began crying again. "I don't want to. He's such a jerk sometimes. I think he only wants me around because I'm so much younger -- he likes to show me off, prove he's still got what it takes."

"He loves you, Barb. He just ain't into all the mushy talk. He takes good care of you and your kids. You both really ought to work on getting along."

"Oh, shit, I know. It's pretty good most of the time. He dotes on the kids, spoils them rotten. It's just sometimes...you know?"

"Yeah. I gotta go."

"You'll pick up the girls?"

"Yeah, don't worry."

"Kiss me before you go."

I was perfectly prepared to kiss her on the cheek, but no, she insisted on a real kiss, just one. We'd never shared a real one. Ah, man, how strong can you be?

Oh, and it was sweet and nice and tender and full of passions promised and so sweet, even if she was full of toxins, her mouth a honey factory. I tore myself away, got out of the building and ran through the parking lot to the arched concrete bridge over the river winding among the rocks below to the sea, breathing deep, trying to calm myself.

Right above on the four-foot wide upper surface of the arch, Steph and I had once climbed in drug-induced bravado to make reckless love, plunging at each other in the night as cars whished by below, the idea that a miscalculation in our orgasmic throes could send us plummeting hundreds of feet to become one with rushing water and still rocks adding to the exultancy of the moment.

I distracted myself with beers in bars, chatting up anyone who'd hold still for it, sneaking off for a quick joint, killing time until three o'clock.

"C'mon, kids," I yelled. "It's safari time. Your mom sent me. We're off to the wildest deepest jungles of darkest Africa!" "This is Hawaii, Buck," Tiffany giggled.

"Doesn't matter. We're going where wild dogs chase panthers, and panthers chase killer-chickens, and killer-chickens chase wild dogs! And crazy people chase everything, even butterflies!"

"You're funny, Buck!"

That was true. Very funny.

*****

It is written that for everything there is a season and, as we have seen, into each life some soap opera must fall. So it was one day when Steph went off to visit Laura and returned in a strange, faraway mood, her eyes following an inner image.

I figured she was stoned and was more concerned with going into Hilo for some pizza and beer at Kaukau Place. Into the Iron Butterfly and away. Steph livened up and came out of herself. We went to the Poly Room to dance to live music until the predawn drove us down to the beach for the sunrise -- a quiet time, each lost in our own thoughts, passing joints back and forth. Soon enough to Ken's for breakfast, enough energy for the cool morning drive home.

We were cuddled back on the bed waiting for the dark to lighten. I asked about Laura and her daughter, how were they? They hadn't been home.

"Oh. So what'd you do all afternoon?"

"Leonard was there."

"Mm."

"So, like, we got it on, ya know?"

"What about Laura?"

"What about her?"

"Don't you think she's going to be upset when she finds out?"

"Why should she? I'm not trying to steal him away."

"Steph, Laura's your friend and you know what she's like. She doesn't have the same understanding that we do. Don't you think she's going to be hurt when she learns her best friend has been screwing her ol' man?"

"Why should she? She fucked you when we were in Honolulu." "What? What are you talking about?"

"You and Laura got it on in that hotel room we stayed at -- while I was in the bathtub."

"Steph, I've never fucked Laura. But even if I had, what's that got to do with it? Obviously you wouldn't mind if I had. But, you know, Laura's in love with Leonard and I think she has very traditional attitudes about that."

"I know you fucked her. Don't lie to me."

"No, Steph, I didn't. If I had, I'd tell you."

"I heard you."

"You heard us dancing, kidding around, talking."

She was silent.

"Do you think Laura would lie to you?"

"No."

"Then why don't you ask her since you don't believe me. It's just not happening between Laura and me, babe."

"Okay. I'm sorry."

But I could tell she wasn't -- it was bothering her.

"Remember when Wade came to visit us?" "Your buddy from California?"

"Yeah, you wanted to ball him."

"Yeah, he was a real nice guy."

"Remember what happened?"

"What? We fucked. It was nice. No big deal."

"No, babe, now listen."

"What?"

"Wade's like me. He doesn't believe in fucking around with a pal's ol' lady."

"Whaddaya mean? We fucked a coupla hours – three times."

"Yeah, I know, babe, but not until I told him it was all right.

You came on to him and he backed off. Remember? When I saw the mutual attraction, I told him it was cool. I took a walk."

"Down at South Point."

"Yeah, I sat on the beach making necklaces out of seashells."

"I remember."

"The point is, I made it okay. He had my permission. You should have made sure it was okay with Laura. How do you think she's going to take you fucking Leonard? In her own house yet?"

"Why should she care? I'm not trying to break up their relationship."

"Everybody's not like us, babe. Some folks are possessive. They get jealous. They get upset and hurt when their mates screw around. I know. I used to be that way myself."

I knew I was wasting my breath. Steph did not understand. She'd only ever been involved in quickie affairs, like as not with men who went for the easy lay and then dropped her. She'd never, so far as I knew, been in love with a man, never had a man return her love and be willing, like me, to get involved in a longterm affair. When it came to love and sex, Steph came from outer space so far as most of the world was concerned. She was a flowerchild from the sixties, unable to conceive of any wrong she might do by spreading love, which perhaps she equated with sex, around so indiscriminately. When it came to sex, Steph was not immoral, she was perfectly amoral -- the usual standards of the world simply didn't apply.

This trait, or attitude, in her often exasperated me, that sometimes I had to explain matters of common knowledge as if to a child. It isn't that she wasn't intelligent, for she was, but more that malice and all the attendant negative feelings most of us are subject to simply weren't in her makeup. Very straight, usually smug people are generally baffled when it comes to understanding her character. Their habit is to shrug off her behavior, her apparent lack of concern for what is happening to her, and relegating it to some simpleminded categorization -- "Oh, she's just a slut, an airhead, what can you expect?" -- and failing to see that it has to do with her basic innocence, her goodness. Evil was not a concept she could truly get her mind around -- it was something that did not exist, a yawning gap in her personality. If there was no evil, what was there to fear? Oh, she was sometimes petulant, but never malicious; often hurt, but never allowing it to matter. She had forgiveness and excuses for every asshole who'd ever mistreated her. She was the most unique person I had ever known and, for all her sociability and friends, also the loneliest.

Well, who am I to preach? I could learn lessons from her as well as teach them. When I become exasperated, I suppose I have a tendency to become cruel. I have little patience with morons and so when she just didn't understand the wrongness of fucking the guy her best friend was madly in love with, I blew it.

I had never struck Stephanie, never would, had never even grabbed her shoulders to give her a good shaking. I had never committed any act of violence in her presence -- except for the showtime of my crazy man act and throwing rocks at the Iron Butterfly.

"Besides," she said. "She never asked me if she could fuck you." I stormed out, turned in my agitation to shout, "Are you fucking retarded?"

Silence from the van. No movement, no speech. I picked up a rock, threw it, heard it thock against the broadside of the Iron Butterfly. "Do you hear me? Are you fucking stupid?"

I looked for another rock, a bigger one. It made a more satisfying clunk. What? Did I hear a squeak, a reaction? No. Bigger rocks, lots of them. Clunk, clank, thwang, thwack. Ah, yes, now I heard them, the sounds she made.

"Oh! Oh! Oh!"

More rocks, shot-putting the bastards now, bam, thud, boom! More noise. "Stop it! Stop it! Stop it!"

Oh, now stop it! Just when I'm into it! A rain of rocks bamity-blimity-blam!

"Please stop it! Please! Please! Please!"

Oh, God, me bucko, what the fuck are you doing? I don't know! I'm the stupid one! What the fuck am I doing? Crawling with bitter shame, boiled with self-loathing, I returned to find her sobbing, frightened, alone in her pain. Oh, God, you colossal asshole! How fucking could you?

I took her in my arms, tried to comfort her, tell her I was sorry, trying not to sob myself. What to do with a weeping woman, let alone a weeping self? I had never known. Just let it go until it stopped. What else?

"I'm sorry, babe. I'm really sorry."

"I thought you loved me," she hiccupped through the ebbing flow.

"I do, Steph. I do love you."

"Then how can you throw rocks at my van?"

"Well, babe, believe it or not, that was a sign of my love." "Gawd, you must have thrown a hundred rocks."

"Goes to show. I love you a hundred rocks worth."

Yes, you can imagine, we began to laugh, the sun coming up at last, teasing away the tomfoolery of the late darkness, leaving us exhausted. We skipped breakfast. I drove home with her kneeling on the bed behind, her arms around me all the way. She was so taken with my statement that it became a solid future reference between us. Who else in the entire world had ever loved her a hundred rocks worth?

*****

Royal showed up with three ounces of MDA. I could see that he looked upon our property and household with a certain disdain, even though he tried to conceal it. He believed in image, that the flash of it revealed the man. He dressed stylishly, drove a new Camaro, had a beautiful girlfriend, was tall at three inches over six feet, blond, slim, and handsome. Charming and debonair, women generally adored his smile, his manner, and his attention. He was possessed of a sly intelligence which, through the conman in him, could make you believe it was greater than it was. He was highly manipulative and valued his own ass above all. The chinks in the facade of his image simply did not exist in his estimation of himself. Although he was neither, he fancied himself a great lover and master of psychology. He would not admit to handicaps, the first step in overcoming them, and his greatest weakness, which he doubtless considered a sign of his innate superiority, was his fondness for heroin.

When I showed him a hidden plot of a hundred pakalolo plants nearing maturity, he was more impressed.

"Beautiful. How much will you harvest here?"

"Oh, a hundred pounds more or less."

"Is that it, all you got going?"

"Nope."

"How much altogether?"

"Secret information, Royal. Question is, how much can you handle?"

"I don't know. Let's talk money."

"Hundred pound lots, three hundred per."

"Thirty grand."

"Yelp."

"What about delivery?"

"I'll throw that in -- delivery right to your doorstep if you want."

"How?"

"My business."

"What about the MDA thing?"

"It's nice, but I'm not really interested in being a sales rep for people I don't even know."

"How about if I bring them over, introduce you? You can take a look, make up your mind then."

"Okay, sure."

"In the meantime, can you help me sell the three ounces I brought -- help pay the cost of this trip?"

"How much you want?"

"A grand will do."

"I'll let you know."
"Soon?"
"Couple of days."
"All right. How's a guy get a vacation around here?"
"You want city shit, or you want to get out in the country?" "Little of both. Where they got those dusky almond-eyed native girls?"

*****

Scrimshaw brought out a guy called Tony, who he claimed was connected up to the mob in Honolulu. Tony looked like a mafia button-man right out of the movies, a black pinstriped suit, Florsheims, dark glasses, curly black hair and a pencil-line mustache.

Scrimshaw introduced Tony to me out in the driveway and I introduced him to Royal. I had suggested that he let Scrimshaw handle the sale, but after a short go-round about Scrimshaw's character, Royal had insisted that he handle it himself.

"What's this Scrimshaw like?"
"A two-bit hustler, flaky."
"You vouch for him?"
"No way."
"Why you bringing him into this?"
"Only show in town, Royal. Since I've been here, I've never seen any heroin, cocaine only once, psychedelics here and there, almost no uppers or downers except prescription stuff, but grass up the yingyang. You get the picture?"
"What about this guy he's bringing?"
"Never met him. My only connections are for grass. I gave Scrimshaw a dozen hits. He claims he sold ten of them at five bucks each. I've been asking around -- nobody's ever heard of MDA."
"Fucking bunch of lames."
"What do you want to do?"
"I don't know. What do you think?"
"Give them to Scrimshaw, tell him you want fifteen hundred. Even if he gets out and hustles them by the hit, he'll see he make money at five bucks a hit. That way, you'll probably get a grand back and a long story for the rest."
"I gotta front the stuff?"
"Oh, yeah."
"And when would I see any cash?"
"Couple of weeks probably."
"I need some now."
I could make you a loan. You don't gotta worry about money while you're here. I'm doing okay."
"Nah, shit. Have 'im bring the guy. I want to get a feel for myself."

Tony knew the talk, appeared to know drugs, was neat about dropping references to his people. Of course he knew MDA, the great Love Drug. Sure, they could do business, but quantity, you know, man. "Three ounces is nothing. I only buy it so my people can sample the quality. What can you do on an order for a hundred pounds?"
"No problem. You got the cash, I got the product."
"Tell me where you want the money. When?"
"I'll be in touch through my man, Buck, here. Everything goes through him."

"Hey, that's okay for a few preliminary deals, you know, give everybody a chance to look each other over, but when we get to serious business, we like to deal with the source. You understand? Maybe you could come over to Honolulu. I'll introduce you around, comp you all the way. You can bring some of your people. We can all have a good time, man. Honolulu's where it's all happening."

Royal was impressed. Tony brought out a wad of C-notes that would choke a horse and nonchalantly peeled off ten.

"Okay, good to meet you, look forward to doing business with you. But no more of this ounce shit, huh? Pounds, okay? What numbers we looking at on a pound?"

"Just one?"

"Yeah, to start with."

"Thirty-five hundred."

"Yeah, that sounds okay. Now, what about ten pounds? What kid of discount on quantity, man?"

"We can talk about it. I gotta touch base with my people, but I'm sure we can work something out that we can all live with."

"Okay, then, I got a plane to catch. I can send word through Buck here, huh?"

"Yeah, maybe you can leave him a number where he can call you."

"No problem." He took out a hotel union business card, wrote a phone number on the back. "Just ask for Tony Cool. You got a number you can give me?"

Royal looked at me. I shrugged. "No phones out here."

"Okay. I'll send a message through our man over here, Scrimshaw."

That last one made me think. Scrimshaw was connected into a slick number like Tony Cool? Well, he'd showed up with the guy, hadn't he?

Still.

*****

Steph was in shorts and halter, Royal and I in bathing trunks and tanktops, trucking in the Iron Butterfly to Hilo to pick up Royal's almond-eyed local beauty.

"Hey, this is kind of cozy."

"Yeah, lotta trucking, lotta good memories."

"So where we headed?"

"Other side of the island, place called Milolii," I said, figuring this was a good time to check out Henry's suggestion. I'd found it on a map, a little cove a couple of miles south called Okoe Bay.

When our passenger stepped in with her large Keenesian eyes, bee-stung rosebud lips, long raven tresses reaching down over smooth dusky skin to a set of globular buns that 'd make a blind man cry, I said with a smirk, "Royal, this is Carol. Carol, my friend from California, Royal."

Watching them size each other up made me thankful we weren't out in the sun where the glint off their teeth could become laser beams. I lit up a joint, passed it to Steph, lit another for Carol.

"Tell me, Carol, were you born with too many teeth or did a dentist do that for you?"

Her grin went wider. Royal laughed.

"How about you, dude? That a congenital thing or what?"

*****

Two days later, after a night spent at South Point and another at Kailua Town, we arrived in the coastal village of Milolii, a small wooden church, a general store, maybe thirty houses and other buildings, a beach with a half dozen outriggers, and a softspoken mayor who recommended we leave the Iron Butterfly on the road in front of his house for the hike into Okoe Bay.

With extra jugs of water, plenty of food for three days, grass and a dozen hits of MDA, all contained in backpacks, we trudged over the hot, barren black lava to our oasis, a nice golden sand beach, a few coconut trees, an offshore reef with plenty of fish for my sling-spear. I trudged on bemoaning the fact that I was leader of the expedition and couldn't walk behind Carol, whose ass was driving me crazy. She and Steph had disrobed near the campfire and run down to bathe in the sea before bedtime at South Point. From that moment on, the first time I'd ever seen her bare buttocks, they had been taunting me in my fantasies and driving me to outdo myself with a very pleased Steph.

We set up the tent, enough room inside for four sleeping bags. Steph and I had thrown down outside at South Point and Kailua Town, leaving the decadent comfort of the Iron Butterfly for Carol and Royal. But now I was thinking orgy, a little mate-swapping in the dark, everybody well-motivated on MDA and grass. I knew Steph was game from the way she looked at Royal. And I was sure Royal could accommodate himself to playing switcheroo with two sexy women -- after all, he was an ex-con like me with too many years of unfulfilled fantasies. It was only Carol I wasn't sure about, just how liberated she was. So far as I had seen, if she liked the cut of a bloke's jib, she rolled with it -- but only one guy at a time and nothing kinky.

Well, that wasn't counting on the effects of the MDA, which I had found was definitely an aphrodisiac, especially on the female sex. Once at the Poly Room, I'd wound up dancing with a pretty, slightly overweight redhead with a million freckles who barely reached five feet in height. The excess weight seemed to be all in her buns and I found myself wondering if white women could be steatopygic. Steph had been at a table with friends, dancing with other guys, the joint really jumping.

"Hey, Red, you like to get high?"

"Yeah, man. What you got in mind?"

I'd pulled out two caps of MDA and said, "Open your mouth." I tossed one in and swallowed the other.

"What is it?"

"Good stuff, darlin', you'll see."

Twenty minutes later, feeling so-oo good and noting a lustful glitter in the redhead's eyes, I asked, "Hey, you wanna see my motor-home?"

We didn't even get our clothes off during the first go-around, our best being jeans to our ankles, and jeez, me boyo, have you ever in your life seen so many freckles -- was it possible to count them? -- and have you ever in your life heard sounds like that from human vocal cords! Then we got naked. She liked my Jimmy Reed. "Yuh got me runnin', hidin', run an' hide uh anyway yuh want uh let the good times roll, yeh-yeh-ye-eh! Yuh got me doin' wha'cha want, baby, wha' cha want me to do?"

Amen. The Love Drug.

"I declare this beach a nudist colony," proclaimed the clever Steph. "No more clothes until we leave!"

And so it was. The afternoon was spent swimming, sunbathing, necking, copping feels, everybody looking over everybody else's body, me mostly fixed on Carol, Steph on Royal, me and Royal comparing female bodies, Steph's big tits, Carol's petit ones, both with succulent nipples, nice asses both, Steph's bigger, but Carol's fixed on well-oiled bearings, proud and sassy, light-skinned and dark, both smooth as satin, big wide mouth on Steph, pouty little fat one on Carol, both unself-conscious about their bodies, Carol studying me and Royal, comparing, Steph, too, but more on Royal because she was familiar enough with me -- an entire afternoon's worth of foreplay, enough heat in the arousal to melt the nylon of our tent.

After a light fish supper as the sun went down in a technicolor Hollywood production, chased with canned litchi fruit and cowboy coffee, Steph and Carol rolled a supply of fat joints while I dug into the backpack for four caps of the wonder drug.

Sitting around the low-burning fire waiting for it to come on, whoa, me bucko, control yourself! But no, betrayed as usual, my lesser brain became dominant, took control.

"Oh, baby," Steph gushed. "Isn't that beautiful'?"

She took it in her hands. "My gawd, so engorged with good red American blood, so-o hard!"

"I do feel faint," I tried with the last of my wit. "And my feet are cold."

"Let me blow some hot air into you, poor thing," she cooed, her mouth moving down.

Carol and Royal watched and, since I was basically a shy lad, having felt uncomfortable with Samantha's friends in spontaneous nude situations, I leapt up to pull Steph toward the tent. Inside, except for a faint glow from the dying fire outside against one wall, it was darker than a midnight with no moon or stars. The energy spent on sight transferred itself into intensifying all the other senses. A half hour later I was so full of pussy, satiated in its taste, smell, feel, and sound effects, I felt like meowing.

Then Carol and Royal came in and I thought, aha, now Steph and I can get turned on all over again with a porno sound show, letting our imaginations work overtime and who knows what then?

Quiet, only the sound of breathing, small movements. What the hell? Had they tricked us, expended themselves outside before coming in?

"What say to a joint, babe?"

"Yeh. I left 'em outside. Back in a minute."

Then I heard Carol say, "Execuse me, nature call," and I felt her leaving, too.

"So, what do you think, man, Carol a fox or what?"

"Yeah."

"I've been wanting to tear off some of that forever, never worked out."

No response.

"So how was it, man? You gonna tell me what I been missing, or what?"

"Nice."

Nice? That was it? Nice?

Steph calling, "Baby, I can't find 'em. Where ya got the stash?" "Uh, shit," I grunted, getting up, going out to where she knelt by the last embers of the fire. "Jeez, babe, where'd you put them?

They were right there."

She put a finger to her pursed lips in a shushing gesture, beckoned me down beside her.

I whispered, "What?"

"Carol's bummed out."

"What's the matter?"

"C'mon, let's take a little walk."

We strode off aways.

"What?"

"Your friend, Royal, can't get it up."

"What!"

"Sh. He hasn't fucked her not even once."

I was shocked. "No shit?"

"Yeah, she's really pissed. She liked 'im, ya know, and he ate her out a little the first night, but he stopped too soon. She's gone down on him three times in the last three days, tryna get 'im up -nothing. What's wrong with him?"

"Jesus, I don't know."

"Go talk to her. She feels like she's being used."

"Used?"

"Well, you know, baby, she's hot to trot and ain't getting no action."

"That's awful. I don't see what the problem is."

"Go talk to her."

"Okay, okay, where'd she go?"

"Down that way."

"Okay. Jeez."

"Take you time. I'll handle Royal."

"Hah?"

"C'mon, baby, don't go dumb on me. Now's yer chance to do a nice boy scout deed."

"You want me...?"

"Yeh, I know you been hot to try her out from the first day you laid eyes on her. These are our friends, right?"

"Right."

"Okay. You take care of Carol. I'll see what I can do with Royal."

"Right." What a dream ol' lady Steph was, I never ceased to marvel.

"Kiss me first."

I did, a nice long one, then hugging each other.

"Have fun. I'll see ya later."

I hitched up my nonexistent trousers and went off to do my duty. She was standing there in the shallows, hair and body wet under the stars, hands on hips, legs wide.

"Carol."

Only the upper half of her body moved to look at me over her shoulder, then turned back to the sea and stars, an island goddess if ever I saw one. I came closer.

"I don't know what to say. I'm sorry."

"For what?"

"For putting you in this position."

"There's something wrong with your friend, and I don't mean just in his limp dick."

"What? What do you mean?"

"Something inside him. I don't know. It's like he's dead. He gives me the creeps."

What in hell did I say to that? I was stunned.

"Put your arms around me, Buck."

I did, from behind. She sighed, leaned back into me, that great ass in the perfect spot, but I felt a weird lack of arousal. Her words were going around in my head -- something inside him -- like he's dead -- gives me the creeps.

"I need you to make love to me, Buck."

There was something in the way she said it that made me sad, kindled a spark of anger at

Royal. She turned to put her arms around my neck and kiss me, oh, so softly and sweetly at first, then a deeper, longer one, our tongues exploring.

She drew back. "You taste and smell like sex."

I started to pull away. "Lemme take a quick dip."

"No, it's okay. I like it."

We kissed some me, my head spinning, but not enough to keep my hands from going down for handfuls of ripe cantaloupes, her words somehow electrifying me.

"I know Stephanie sent you down here to fuck me, but I really need you to make love to me, Buck."

So strange. Despite the self-induced gratitude of a boy scout having done a good deed, I would ever after always feel that I owed something to Carol.

*****

The next morning, after Carol and I had returned to the tent to cuddle ourselves to sleep, Royal was dressed and wanted to leave.

"Hey, it's nice, you know, getting back to nature, but it gets old fast. I need some action. I mean, man, there ain't even any music here."

Action, music, hm. Did my old pal have a heart? Did he not have ears for the susurrus of wind through palm fronds, the mysteriously wondrous tempo and timbre of expression in a passionate woman's voice?

"Ever read Shakespeare, Royal?"

"What're you, kidding me? Let's get outa here. I need to get back home, start taking care of business."

"Yeah, okay." Thou blind fool, I thought, what dost thou to thine eyes that they behold and see not what they see? They know what beauty is, see where it lies, yet what the best is take the worst to be.

Royal and Carol had nothing to say to each other. Steph was in some kind of funk. The Kona Airport near Kailua Town was nearest. Royal could hop over to Honolulu for a connection to San Francisco. The hour or so's drive was very quiet.

"Maybe I'll see you in a couple of weeks or so, bring over my main man, Lenny, some of his boys. You been thinking about the MDA thing?"

"Yeah, sure, but you know I'm not real enthused. You can see for yourself there's not much action for quantities -- this is all small town and country, man."

"Yeah, but with the connection to Tony Cool in Honolulu, man -- you heard what he said."

"Yeah, well, we'll see how it works out. How about the grass thing, you interested?"

"Sure, man. I can move your stuff all day long, especially if it's the same quality I've smoked since I've been over here." "It will be, guaranteed."

"Okay. Let's keep in touch, work something out."

"For sure. Sorry about Carol, man. I really thought she was someone you'd go for."

"Hey, forget it, one of those things. She's kind of a cold bitch, you know, got some real kinky stuff inside her. No big deal -- broads are dime a dozen. Your ol'lady's nice, but I figured, hey, she's your ol' lady, you know?"

"Yeah, right." I think my effort to keep a straight face succeeded.

*****

Heading back toward Kailua Town, I pulled down toward a tiny cove where I had seen several sailboats. There was a haulout ramp inclining down into the water. I parked to smoke a joint with the girls, to ask them what they wanted to do, my wandering eye taking in the lines of the boats. There was one small one in drydock, a ladder going up to the cockpit. I watched a one-legged man in a bathing suit hop down the rungs. He ignored the crutches leaning there to begin hopping fifty yards down to a small floating dock connected to the shore by a ramp. Straight on down he went, as well as a one-legged running man could go, right on out to the end where he dove into the water, came up blowing to utter a great roar of pleasure. Had to grin at a guy like that. Little did I know that in not so very long at all I would get to know this interesting character very well.

Steph and Carol thought a hotel room for a hot bath as a prelude to dinner and a search for some live music would be the thing.

Somewhere along the way in our foray through the evening, Carol picked up a jolly tubby little fellow who called himself Spanky, one of those irrepressibly cheerful types who knew his wooing talent lay in getting women to laugh. Plus, the little bastard could put on a hell of a show on the dance floor. We all took to him right away, took him away with us. He and Carol got the hotel room while Steph and I mooned away in the Iron Butterfly, rear doors open to the warm breezes of darkness and the sea as Papa John Creach sang of teaching us how to make our gardens grow.

"So, how'd it go with Royal?" I thought to ask.

She made a face. "Limpdickitis all the way. He claimed it was caused by tension and too much drug use."

"What kind? He say? Not MDA and grass."

"No, but you know he's got an outfit for shooting up, huh?"

"No shit?"

"Yeah."

Ah, Royal, you fucking idiot, I thought. I might as well introduce you to Janey. You can stick your nose up her ass and follow her to total and everlasting enslavement.

A morning bath by all, joints and cold beers enhancing the general lively mood, then breakfast and on the road, Spanky aboard and ready for anything. Steph and Carol said South Point again, the lonely rolling plain, the looney cows, the great wormholes to infinity, sun and wind, the intimate sense of freedom and beneficence for all mankind -- as long as they didn't come crowding around with their long noses out.

It was mid-afternoon and Steph and Carol took some acid. Spanky had never tried it, was afraid to, and said no, thanks, he was fine when it was offered. So did I. They wandered away to look for seashells as Spanky and I searched out bits of scarce wood, made a fireplace, and dumped in a bag of charcoal briquettes over which to cook our supper, but I was feeling too lazy to go spear-fishing.

We lolled about, toking and valiantly working on the beer before the ice melted -- and talked of this and that.

"Hoo, man, I really got lucky this time."

"Hah?"

"Carol. Is she beautiful or what?"

"Indeed."

"Must be my innate character."

"No doubt. She's strong on character."

"Jeez, man, this is a great place."

"Yeah, no fucking tourists to ruin it so far."

"Yeah, I know what you mean. Give me nature over so-called civilization any day."

"Amen."

"Nature's not crazy or evil -- only people."

"I can dig it, Spanky. It's the element of the unpredictable. You never know where madness is hiding. Give me a sudden earthquake, a volcanic eruption, tidal wave, storm, whatever, I feel safer than riding a bus with wary-eyed strangers who look at you if you laugh too loud."

"I hear that, Buck. Imagine Nixon with his finger on the nuclear trigger. People scare the shit out of me."

"Yeah, me, too. But fear's a teacher, you know."

"Huh. I guess."

"I mean, fear's just a dumb feeling, right?"

"Well, not always. Sometimes it's pretty smart, I'd say."

"Right. Fear says run, get the hell out."

"Sure."

"But, you know, sometimes it's unreasonable, and when it is, see, then you can learn from it. I mean, you know, you can't just give in everytime, make a run for it, live like a scaredy-cat."

"Oh, yeah, I understand that, sure, not letting the assholes bamboozle you."

"Right, the fucking busybodies, the fucking moralizers, the fucking thought police."

"Authority figures, right. I've been running from them all my life. They're the ones scare the shit out of me most. Nietzsche, I think, said it -- beware those who love to punish."

"Oh, yeah?"

"No sense of humor, you know, serious about everything."

"Oh, yeah, I know all about that."

"I mean, they spend all their time trying to make everybody ashamed, and you know why?"

"Well, sure, shame's a part of your conscience. It's the worst thing a human being can feel."

"Control. They're fucking control freaks. They're ashamed of their own cowardly lives, want to get you into the boat with them." "Fuck that."

"Fucking A, listen to those sick assholes, you'd be ashamed every-time you turned around."

"Ugh, man, don't make he barf."

"Oh, man, no, don't shame yourself now!"

"Well, I can arrive at my own shame without any help, thank you all the same."

"Yeah, and what do you learn from it?"

"That it's fucking awful!"

"You probably got a conscience, Buck. That's good."

"Thanks. You probably do, too."

"Oh, hey, flattery, you know, you silver-tongued devil!" "Lemme tell you something, Spanky."

"What, man?"

"I ain't got one drop of making pity for your jolly little ass."

"Really?"

"Really."

"That's good, right?"

"You know, Spanky, you ain't half as dumb as you look."

"Hey, you're a lot smarter'n you look, too."

"Self-pity's the worst."

"I defy you to find a single drop in me, my man!"

"That's good, that's good, cuz you know what that teaches, don't you?"

"What, man, gimme a hint!"

"Nothing more than self-pity."

"I knew that -- just wanted to see if you did."

"You're not only a philosopher and a psychologist of some immodest means, my friend, but you're also one hell of a dancer. How the fuck you learn moves like that? You take lessons or something?"

"Hey, man, please with the insults already! Where's the creativity in that? I'm a fucking artist, Buck!"

"So what's the secret of your creativity?"

"You wouldn't believe me."

"I might."

"Fun."

"Fun?"

"Yeah, as in enjoyment, you know? All life's a dance and the secret is to have fun."

I looked at him. "You are one profound motherfucker, Spanky."

"I have never knowingly fucked anybody's mother in my life... but I have great expectations!"

"So, how do you feel about cunnilingus?"

"Makes me hungry. We got any more potato chips?"

I laughed. "You're all right, Spanky. You ever wanna fuck my ol' lady, feel free."

"You serious?"

"Well, you gotta interest her in wanting you to fuck her."

"Oh. Well, if Carol wants to fuck you, then please feel free." "Thanks, but I already have."

"Pretty nice piece, ain't she?"

"Very nice, a lovely girl."

"Fucking beautiful! How'd I get so lucky?"

"Charm, Spanky. You're charming. You made her laugh, cheered her up. She was down in the dumps."

"I knew that. Oh, I see, in a roundabout way you're trying to tell me you're charming, too."

"Well, ain't I?"

"Only thing I can't stand is fishermen -- they always got their lines in the water!"

*****

After dark, when we'd gotten the fire going, the charcoal smoldering nicely, cooking up sausages in garlic, onions, and bell peppers Carol headed off to the Iron Butterfly claiming she wasn't feeling so good. Steph looked after her, seemingly in a quiet, pensive mood. Spanky and I worked the food, getting everything laid out, fritos and cheese dip, plates and utensils, slicing good dark rye bread.

Soon Steph followed after Carol. A half hour passed. Supper was ready.

"Spanky, go call the girls."

He returned alone. "They're coming."

I shrugged. "Let's eat."

We dug in. Another ten minutes passed.

"What the hell? Hey, Steph, Carol," I called. "C'mon, you're missing out"

Nothing.

"There a problem, Spanky?"

"I dunno. They were talking."

I sat down my plate, got up to stride over to the van. They were lying close together on their stomachs, heads together, Steph's arm around Carol's shoulders, Steph in a long granny dress, Carol in shorts and shirt, their legs kicking around like kids -- whispering away.

"Hey, you guys gonna eat?"

"Yeh, we'll be there in a minute, babe."

"Food's getting cold."

I turned to walk back. Steph caught up. "Carol's not feeling so well."

"What's the matter?"

"I'm not sure."

"She sick?"

"Uh-uh."

"She's not tweaking out on the acid, is she?"

"No, it's her mood,"

"Her mood?"

"She's in a very strange mood. She keeps talking about being used."

"Hah?"

"We've been talking."

"I noticed."

She took a breath, looked at me, then Spanky, then back to me. "She wants to spend the night with me." Then she looked down, fidgeting with her hands.

Somewhat taken aback, I said nothing.

"Is it all right?"

It was dawning on me, a nice little unexpected shock.

"She needs a friend."

I found my tongue. "Sure, babe, that's fine. That's what friends are for. Me and Spanky will bed down out here, guard the herd, see if we can think up some cowboy trail songs."

She sighed, kissed me on the cheek. "Okay, I'll see you in the morning. Goodnight, Spanky."

"Night."

"Sure you don't want to take some of this food? It's really ono."(Delicious)

"No, that's okay. If we get hungry, there's plenty of stuff for pupus."

We watched her return to the Iron Butterfly. Soon the flickering dim light of one of her votive candles gave a glow through the windshield and I could see that the curtain hung on a wire behind the driver's seat had been pulled.

Spanky and I exchanged a long, wide-eyed look.

"Better have a joint, my friend. Looks like we're stuck with eating all this stuff."

"Yeah."

Well, well, well. It wasn't as if our tongues had been stolen or maimed. Hell, there were no serious predators in Hawaii except human beings and they were miles away, oblivious to we two stooges who were indeed talking between pregnant silences, talking about this and that, a new subject every few minutes, following up on none, talking to make noise, noise to mask our thoughts, talking about everything but what was foremost in our prurient minds.

Stuffed on all the food we'd polished off, still working on the beer and continually passing joints back and forth, it was Spanky who first worked up the nerve to approach the subject.

"What do you think's wrong?"
I shook my head. "Too deep for me."
"What do you think they're talking about?"
I shrugged. "Who knows? Girl talk, I guess."
"About us, you think?"
"Maybe. Could be philosophy, you know. They're not dumb. They read a lot of books."
"Solving all the key questions of the universe, you think?"
"Yeah, maybe even the curvature equations of the space-time continuum."
"What the hell's that?"
"I dunno -- never could understand it myself."
"The light's still on."
I looked. "Yep, I believe you're right, Spanky -- vision like an owl."
"I wonder what they're doing?"
"You know, I'm kind of curious about that myself."

A long silence. We looked at each other, at the van, peering closely for the minutest tremor. What the hell were they talking about? What the hell were they doing?

"Well, think I'll make room for some more beer."
"Good thinking. Mind if I join you?"
"Plenty of bathroom out there."

Whew, what a relief, watering the hungry earth, studying the configurations of stars, none of which blinked out so far as I could see. Well, if they had, it would take a million years for the news to reach me. Same conclusion for novae -- they might explode and make new stars, but what in hell did I know right now?

I drew a breath, my mind made up, turned to whisper to my fellow conspirator. "You take the little window on one side," I said, referring to the narrow grilled slots on each side of the Iron Butterfly. "I'll take the other."

"Okay," he whispered back, barely able to suppress his excitement. "Okay."
"Sh, quiet now, very quiet."
"Like a fucking Indian, don't worry."

We crept out around slowly and carefully in bare feet, coming with dry throats and bated breath to our respective viewing apertures. We looked down inside to the bed, then looked at each other across the narrow space, wide eyes seeing wide eyes. They were beautifully and starkly naked, their bodies soft and glazed in the candlelight, the richly lewd dreamy quality of masculine fantasy, the profound poetry of arousal, privileged to view a secret ritual, each of us trying to control his breathing, each of us wishing, surely, that we'd thought to carry along another bottle of beer.

So that was what they were doing.

Much later, back in our lotus positions before the glow of charcoal embers as though contemplating the great Tantric mysteries, having popped two more beers, our tongues locked into the silence of exhausting awe, it began to rain. Rather than rush to the van as even fools are supposed to have enough sense to do, we draped ourselves in sleeping bags and suffered through the night -- Proud ascetics not daring to disturb the sacred visions every man seeks but few find.

###

CHAPTER 9

Royal sent a pound of MDA to my postoffice box. I called the number Tony Cool had left. Fine, good. Tony Cool would send his man, Sid, over with cash. Scrimshaw would bring him out to Hawaiian Fern Acres.

Sid, a short plump Japanese with a Fu Manchu mustache, left Scrimshaw in the car at the road as he walked up the drive. He wore high-heeled cowboy boots.

"Hey, you Buck? I'm Sidney Hayakawa. Tony sent me. You want to call your dogs off?"

I yelled at Popolo and Sista. "C'mon in."

Seating him across the table, I offered him a beer.

"Yeah, sure."

When Steph had served us, she said, "Care for a joint?"

"No, thanks. Not while I'm on business."

"Good stuff."

Sid grinned, a leering, sinister grin. "Maybe next time around, doll."

"Hayakawa," I mused. "Hey, you related to S. I. Hayakawa in Berkeley?" S. I. Hayakawa had been an English professor at UC who was now a U. S. Senator from California. He'd written an interesting book on semantics.

"Huh? Nah. It's a common name in Japanese -- sort of like Smith or Johnson."

"Too bad. I was hoping you could tell me whether he suffered from narcolepsy."

"Huh? Nah, I don't know."

"Just wondering. Once knew a woman had the ailment. Scared the shit out of me everytime I got in a car with her."

"Oh, yeah?"

"She'd fall asleep at the wheel. Had more accidents than anyone I ever knew. Survived 'em all. Always complained about high insurance rates. I see in the papers he's always dropping out for a snooze in the Senate."

"Yeah, well, can we get down to business? I got a plane to catch."

"Sure." I went over to the open window behind the kitchen bar, dug behind a cushion on the divan to retrieve a sack. Steph had stood ready to heave it out across the path leading to the outhouse -- a mere ten feet into dense grass and bush. I put it on the table.

He took out the ziploc bag, opened it, wetted his pinky, and dipped it for a taste. When the utter bitterness had got into his taste buds, he made a face.

"Um, good shit." He took a swallow of beer. "This a pound?"

"Sure, you want to weigh it?"

"Nah, that's okay." He tried not to frown, smacking his lips, the bitter taste seizing him, I knew. He drank more beer, squishing it like mouthwash before swallowing, trying to disguise his reaction to the awful taste that would not go away for fifteen or twenty minutes. "Here, here's the bread."

He tossed a folded-over stack of thirty-five C-notes across the table. "Three and a half big ones, right?"

"Right."

"Okay, listen, we want to deal, get a regular thing going, you know. Tell Royal we liked the sample. If this is as good as the last, we're definitely interested."

"Sure, okay."

"But we're going to want to get into quantity, you know? Money's not a problem. You say when and where, we'll be there."

"Sure, sounds good." I'd been thinking about it. "Listen, save you some trouble next time around -- you send the money with Scrimshaw, let him pick up and deliver the stuff."

"Nah, no good. He's small potatoes, a fucking gofer. We don't use him for this. He's too flaky."

I shrugged. "Hey, he's your man."

"Yeah, well, only because he's got relatives with a little clout, you know. He's smalltime. We throw him a bone once in a while. He owes us for pulling him out of a dumb deal a while back. Nah, he's out of this. From now on, it's me and you."

"Um."

He'd finished the beer, still working against the vileness in his mouth, me trying not to laugh and succeeding.

"Okay," he said, putting the ziploc back in the paper sack. "I gotta go. Couple of weeks or so, gimme a call at that same number. Sometimes a broad answers, okay? I ain't in, just leave a message when you'll call back. I'll be there when you call again. But Scrimshaw's out of it. I'll deliver the message to him loud and clear."

"Um."

"Be seeing you."

"Hey, Sid."

"Yeah."

"Next time leave the piece at home, huh? Guns make me nervous."

He tried to grin, but only grimaced. "Sure. First time meeting you and all, just being careful, you know?"

"Yeah."

I walked him out to the driveway, nodded toward Scrimshaw, who waved from the car at the road.

"Your ol' lady, she in on this?"

"No, man, she's got nothing to do with it."

"We don't have to worry about her running off her mouth, right?"

"Yeah, don't worry."

"Hey, broads, you know, they're good for fucking, cooking, housekeeping, but business..."

"Um."

"Next time, just me and you. We keep it private, you know?"

"Sure, good idea."

*****

I pulled out a grand and sent the rest to Royal, then called to let him know.

"Hey, great," he said after I'd run it all down to him. "So, what's this Sid like?"

"Pure snake. I don't feel comfortable around him."

"What's the problem?"

"I don't know, just instinct. You meet some people, they rub you wrong, maybe chemistry or something. How about I hook him into you, you deal with him, save you my commission?"

"What, man, you don't want in on this? I smell serious business just around the corner."

"I'm doing okay, Royal. I don't like the vibes."

"Vibes? What're you, a fucking hippy? Get real. We're looking at big money here we get this thing developed. The whole state can be yours -- you'll have a franchise monopoly."

"Would I have to do promos, sign autographs, shake hands, kiss babies, Royal?"

He laughed. "Hey, man, hang in. I'm gonna bring Lenny and the crew over, let you see for yourself what's happening."

"When?"

"Soon. When you gonna ship me a good load of that fine grass?"

"Soon."

*****

I shipped Gianmin a hundred pounds and tested out my idea for moving larger amounts of pakalolo to the Mainland. All I did was reverse the process with the container on a Matson Line carrier. The hundred pounds went into an old refrigerator scavenged from the Hilo dump, which went in first. Then I loaded in other old refrigerators, stoves, washers and dryers, junk furniture, snapped on a good padlock and sent the key to Gianmin. He knew what to do -- I'd explained.

It all went smooth as fudge and a month later he sent me thirty grand, half of which I gave to Don.

But not before Royal showed up with Lenny and three other guys and a couple of broads.

*****

Royal and Lenny showed up in Hilo. Steph and I were at the Hilo Airport in the Iron Butterfly to meet them.

"Our version of a limousine," I explained. "You get by your first impression, it's actually more comfortable than your mainland versions."

"Oh, charming," said Lenny with a significant look toward Royal. "And a lovely lady chauffeur," he added with a dazzling flash of considerate ivories for Steph. "How quaint."

Our happy home, God's little four acres in the boonies, almost drew out the sneer waiting in reserve. I noted him noting the old iron tub converted to furo with its cedar covers, the neckholes, studying the outhouse as though he'd never seen one before -- probably hadn't -- the lack of appliances except for the primitive kerosene stove, the lamps, the sawdust-board floor, the unmatched array of furnishings. I mused whether he was going to ask if we, in bare feet after having slipped out of our thongs at the door, were the Hatfields or the McCoys.

It was something to think about, the contrast in styles. There I slouched in jeans and comfortable loose cotton shirt that Steph had made for me with her own two hands, she in one of her long granny dresses and no makeup, neither of us wearing jewelry, not even watches. There they sat in expensive slacks and shirts, Italian shoes, watches, rings and gold chains, faces perfectly shaved and hair styled, fingernails manicured, both brushing at imaginary dust on the chair seats before sitting, Lenny maintaining a poker face but cataloguing everything, while

Royal tried to hide his embarrassment.

I had tried their style and found it pretentious, the wannabe ultimate consumers of everything expensive and showy, their would-be declaration to the world in the very standards the mainstream of society demanded -- to prove that all the proper buttons had been pushed on the elevator to the top -- but I had a feeling they'd never voluntarily tried mine or want to, a return to bare necessities, simpler, Less complicated life.

"No TV. What do you do for music?"

"We hum, tap our feet, clap our hands. Sometimes I play my kazoo." I pulled it out of my pocket, the twenty-five cent piece of painted tin, gave it a couple of demonstrative tootles.

"You serious?"

"We got a battery-operated turntable, a radio with a tapedeck. What do you like?"

"Jazz, you got any jazz?"

"Not much. Might have a Dave Brubeck." I searched through the LPs. "Yeah, Take Five, that all right?" Soon the progressively intricate chords and fingerings of the piano filled the room, the light whiskering of drum and cymbal, the old upright bass viol.

"Care for a beer?"

"Couldn't get a martini, I suppose?"

"Nope. Might be a little Red Mountain in the jug if you like cheap wine."

"No, thanks. You got Heineken?"

Why was I not surprised? Heineken, the in-beer that year. "Nope, sorry. San Miguel, if you like imported. Otherwise plenty of Bud." "San Miguel? What's that, Mexican?"

"Filipino."

It was dark, heavy and rich in taste. I could see he didn't like it, but politely sipped at it.

"Quit fucking around and break out some of that dynamite grass, Buck."

"Sure, c'mon, let's take a little walk. You can pick your own, guaranteed fresh off the bush."

I led them past the outhouse to the narrow hidden path onto the adjacent property, meandering up and down and around into the bush to a stash of fifty or sixty nearly mature pakalolo plants scattered over a depression in the landscape.

Lenny gaped. "Jesus, I've never seen a marijuana plant that looked like that. Aren't they supposed to look like Christmas trees, like ten feet high?"

"If I let them grow naturally, sure. But then they could be seen from the road, too. We do that intentionally." I explained the pinching process, the theory behind it, the several benefits.

"This sinsemilla?"

"Sure 'nough. Pick yourself out a nice bud. You, too, Royal."

I cut them off with a pocketknife. "Thank you, darlin'," I said to the plant. "I certainly appreciate it. You're beautiful. I'll bring you a nice shot of rock phosphate when I return."

In my peripheral vision, I caught Lenny eyeing Royal with another of those raised-eyebrow looks, then smirking to me, "You think they understand?"

I grinned sweetly. "I think the communication between me and my babies is superior to what I have with most people. We never have misunderstandings now that I've learned their language." What neither of them knew was that rock phosphate a month or so before maturity made them even stonier, that these were special, each and every one having been sampled and when found exceptional in quality, had been moved to form this elite group.

"Ha, right!"

After Steph had flashdried the buds and rolled up a few, Lenny began to come down with a case of glassy eyes, Royal close behind. "'Nother beer, you guys?"

"Yeah, hey, that's pretty good beer, you know, sure."

Their speech sputtered out, intelligent enough to know, the both of them, in the reserve they held, that their words could come out jumbled, sound silly, that some small thing could make them giggle, laugh like maniacs over nothing, and so they held themselves, striving for self-control amid the growing confusion of electrical connections in their brains, their bodies showing the tension of the effort to remain blasé.

"So, what do you think?"

"Not. Bad," said Lenny.

"Whew," said Royal.

I winked at Steph, nodded. We had games. "Pusillanimous, I think," I began.

"Perhaps a bit of the sonorous, some little echoes," Steph responded.

"A lulling susurrus. Or is it a snoring?"

"Tediously Sisyphean."

"Sometimes succinct."

"Others, sententiously succulent." "Yes, with oh-so-sensitive succubi."

"Ah, psychosexual serendipity!"

All delivered with a judicious air, they hadn't a clue, had tried to follow in a serious contemplative demeanor through their now syrupy intellectual processes.

"What do you think, Lenny?"

"Hm? Oh. Sure. Undoubedly Stood guff."

Steph turned away to keep from cracking up.

"So, what, you guys want to stay here? Shitting's a little primitive, but hey, great view."

"Ah. No. We. Got. A. Room."

"Yeah. A. Hotel. You. Got. Us. A. Hotel?"

"Sure, I made you reservations in a nice hotel."

"Mm."

"Um-mm."

We ferried them to the hotel, led them in, got them through the check-in, escorted them to the room, left one collapsed on the bed, the other nodding vague thanks.

*****

When we called upon them the next day, they wanted to rent a car and see Hilo and Kailua Town, the two major cities that, by Mainland standards, were no more than large villages. Tooling along the way in a station wagon, Lenny asked if all the roads were like this -- two lanes.

"Yeh," Steph replied. "Except for the unpaved ones, which sometimes get down to one lane."

"Primitive, really primitive," Lenny muttered. "Is it like this on all the islands -- everywhere in Hawaii?"

"Well, there's always Honolulu if you miss the freeways. It's, like, a city with tall buildings and everything."

"I should hope so," Lenny said, flashing his great smile. "I've got tickets to a Rolling Stones concert and I can't see myself sitting on a rock in the hot sun."

After overwhelming them with the provincial delights of Kailua Town, we headed for the Kona Airport. I caught a glimpse of the one-legged man leaning on crutches apparently supervising two other guys up ladders sanding the hull of his boat.

Airborne for the big city, now snockered on good pakalolo, Lenny's cranial impulses connected through certain synapses to inquire, "Hey, don't they have an active volcano over here?"

"Yeh. Kilauea Crater. Got a nice old colonial style hotel up near the active vent. It's got a landscape that reminds you of the moon...or maybe one of the levels of Dante's Hell."

"Oh, yeah? I'd like to see that, the unimaginable power with the potential of a nuclear bomb. I love displays of power."

"Maybe next time, Lenny."

"No, no. We'll go back after the Rolling Stones."

"We should have called ahead," I offered. "Made hotel reservations."

"No, I've got that covered. I talked to my partner last night -- he's rented us a place on the beach out by Diamond Head, the Dillingham Mansion, got it for a whole week. He says it's great, plenty of room for everybody."

"Gee, really?"

"Yeah, you know it?"

"Mm, ve-ery nice. Must cost an arm and a leg."

"Nah, only a few grand. He's got a limo lined up for the concert."

"Fancy."

Lenny flashbulbed us with the charm of his smile. "Hey, if you can fly high, why not? Only the best when I'm trying to attract franchise partners, give them a view from farther up the mountain, you know?"

*****

At the Dillingham Mansion, which had a walled front and a great iron gate, we toured the two-story place admiring the furnishings, which were elegant. Out the back over lawn and well-tended gardens over a low wall and privet hedges lay a fine golden beach. An artful tree to the side, a beautifully gnarled trunk that had been patiently shaped into a flat canopy of tangled interwoven branches by several generations of bonsai masters provided a spot of shade for viewing the near-naked beauties on the beach during cold-drink respites, times to contemplate one's blessings. It was reputed by the caretaker to be near two hundred years old.

We were introduced to the tall bearded Saul who looked like a biblical patriarch in expensive casual clothes, two New York boys who often broke out in spontaneous duets on harmonicas, and two babes of unexpected dimensions. One was tall and skinny, but very graceful in her movements, with a long tangled mane of hair and a million freckles. The other was a conventionally pretty auburn-haired wench with an openly lustful eye who seemed to be the result of two different women joined at the waist. Her top half was that of a normally endowed female of smooth and creamy complexion, while the bottom half was downright rubinesque, having stout muscular legs, thunder thighs, and basketball buttocks.

Hilaria, the lean, balletic, and polka-dotted, and Rachel of the full and rounded nethers, they roused competing lusts in me. Every minute henceforth would be spent in plotting to bed them, singly or together -- the mind boggles! -- to in them and out them, up them and down them, to wipe my tallywhacker and walk off singing God Save the King.

Steph was smitten by Saul in her semitic genes, and he by her, a renewal of the Samson and Delilah legend, Saul who, in an account from his own mouth, had three days before sat at a Hollywood party with Ali McGraw and immediately called Lenny from a table phone to prove it. Ali was delightfully reported to have said, "Hi, this is Ali McGraw from Hollywood and I hope your friend can fuck better than Steve McQueen."

And Lenny, so handsome and debonair, had replied, "If he doesn't, call me back, our policy is to leave no beautiful dames improperly fucked," to which we all had cheered.

*****

Lenny opened a briefcase filled with C-notes, carelessly grabbed a bunch, and handed them to me. "Buck," he said. "You know this town. Take Royal, go out and rent us a couple of cars, fill them with beautiful women, bring them here. It's party time. I mean seriously Dionysian party time. I've got the money, Saul brought the Love Drug, you got that kickass grass -- a houseful of beautiful people. What more do we need?"

"A sackful of hardons," Royal quipped.

"Bring back one or two of those beautiful island girls I've been hearing so much about."

"You got it," I said.

We rented a Lincoln with Lenny's cash, then filled the back-seat with three hookers enticed off Kalakaua Boulevard in Waikiki by waving hundred-dollar bills at them. After delivering them to the mansion, we returned to rent a Mercury Cougar to repeat the process.

"Hey, man," Royal asked. "You got any connections for gow in this town?"

"No, not really. I could call a couple of guys I know, ask around."

"Appreciate it. It's nice to wind down on from the MDA."

Me, I hadn't seen any need whatsoever. "Sure, man. All those other people into that, too?"

"Just Lenny and Saul. The New York guys and the broads don't fuck around. You ought to try it with us. We get into some long and interesting conversations. You could learn a lot about what's happening."

"I'm doing okay, thanks anyway."

I called Henry. "Sure, I can get you a spoon or two, whatever you want. Didn't know you were into that shit."

"I'm not, Henry. I'm catering to a bunch of nui alii (Big shots, royalty from the Mainland.) You ought to come on out, take a look. There might be some kuleana (Business) in it."

"Where?"

I told him. He whistled. "Shu, man, they got nui kala, (Big shots, royalty.) Huh?"

"Yeah, looks like it."

"Okay. I'll drop by later this evening, see what's happening. You mind if I bring my wahine?"

"No, that's fine, Henry, but there'll probably be a lot of loose women running around -- in case you want to join the party. I think it's going to be pretty wild."

He laughed. "Okay. I'll see you later."

*****

When Henry showed up late that night, the bacchanal was in full swing. The two New York guys were sitting naked on a couch trying to outriff each other on harmonicas with me still clothed throwing in wrenches off my kazoo. Two naked whores sat rolling joints on a coffee table. People were running in and out in various stages of dress or undress as the case might be, chasing around in shouts and laughter through the garden, down onto the beach for a midnight dip, all inspired on varying amounts and mixtures of drugs and booze.

I called Royal out to introduce him and pay for two fat balloon marbles of heroin. "Hey, right on, man."

"Royal, I thought maybe you could leave a sample of MDA with Henry here, let him see for himself just what it is you're selling."

"Sure, man, no problem. Let me go find Saul -- he's got the bag."

While waiting, we smoked a couple of joints and I took the time to explain the situation, the effects and dosages of MDA, as well as the pound price. No need to explain the money that could be made -- he'd figure that out all on his own. Before he left with a half ounce, I thought to ask if he knew a Tony Cool or Sidney Hayakawa. No, he didn't. He'd ask around.

"Be careful of the Iapana, (Japanese) man. If he's hooked into the Yakuza, (Japanese organized crime.) okay, but otherwise you got to be careful."

I wandered upstairs looking for Steph, whom I hadn't seen in several hours. I found her in a room with Saul, fully clothed, their heads together over a table in soft smiles and whispers.

"Oh, babe, there you are," she said. "I been looking for you."

"Here I am. Hi, Saul. How you two doing?"

"Uh, fine, uh, okay, uh, just having a little chat. You know us Jews, we always got something to talk about."

"Well, hey, don't let me disturb you. I was looking for Rachel. You seen her?"

Steph grinned. "She was running up and down the hall in something gauzy a few minutes ago."

"Oh, yeah? See you later."

Outside, I met Royal coming up the stairs. "Jesus, that Rachel is hot to fuck! She almost sucked my ear off with what she was going to do with me!"

"You lucky fuck! I was hot to try some of that myself!"

He grinned, one up on me. "Tough. I'll let you know how it is. I got to find an empty bed."

He rushed off.

Steph came out to pull at my arm. "Sweetie, will you please come in here and tell Saul it's all right? He's afraid you might beat the shit out of him."

"Sure, babe. Have you seen Hilaria?"

"Nah, not lately."

Back inside, I said, "Hey, Saul, what the fuck, you thinking about mistreating my ol' lady?"

"No, no, man, I wouldn't think of it!"

"Then why's she complaining to me. I'm on a mission, Saul. I ain't got time for this!"

"Uh, well, uh..."

"Saul, listen, let me be brief. Next time I see Steph, she better have a big fat grin of satisfaction on her face. You hear me?"

I gave him a wink and a twitch of my lips.

"Oh, sure, man, wow, thanks, I really appreciate that."

At the turn in the staircase, I ran into the gauzy Rachel. It looked like she'd torn down one of the sheer muslin curtains I'd seen dancing in the breeze of an open window.

"Oh, there you are," she gushed, pinning me to a wall, one arm around my neck, the other hand groping my crotch. "I need you, baby, oh, how I need you! I need you to eat me! I need you in me! I want to eat you up! I need your rod up in me, all up in me, everywhere!"

"Oh, god, yes, baby," I gushed back, the words disappearing into her hot sucking mouth, my hands like magnets to the malleable steel of her watermelon ass.

"Hurry, hurry!" She turned to leap like an Amazon up the steps to disappear down the long hallway.

I began to tuck myself away, glorying in the hot spots her fingers had fondled, to button myself up. There was Hilaria in a wide skirt, barefoot and nude from the waist up, her delicate mounds peaked with pink buttons.

"Oh," she said, taking a long appraising look, one of those Mona Lisa enigmas shaping her wide mouth. "Excuse me."

I was flustered. "No, wait!" But she was gone. Which way to go, up or down? What a decision! I wavered, left foot wanting to go down, right foot up. I got my feet in agreement and went up, opting for the larger portion of already steaming flesh.

Down the hallway I sped, opening doors. Empty, empty. Oops, Royal and one of the New York guys on two beds with four whores, all naked. At least Royal hadn't beat me to Rachel. On down I went to the master bedroom, where I heard animal cries. "Oh! Yes! Oh! Yes! Oh! Ah! Ye-aaaasss!" and "Ugh! Oof! Uh! Un-uunnh!"

I opened the door. Ten toes up to the ceiling, ten toes down to the rug, two big asses going round and round, and if that ain't fucking, fine me ten dollars, too! Rachel and Lenny.

Shit! He who hesitates.

I turned to run downstairs after Hilaria, was in time to see her skipping out the back door hand-in-hand with the other New York guy.

Double shit!

I paused in the crushing blow to take a count. There were six of us guys. There was Steph, Rachel, Hilaria, and six prostitutes, which meant there were two loose females just waiting to perform a professional service on my needy ass. But I couldn't find them anywhere. Maybe they'd decided to stroll the beach with their free C-notes for some active tricks.

Back at the room with Royal and the New York guy. I blush to describe what was going on, but one inviting pale plump white ass of a blond on her knees between Royal's legs seemed to invite me. Poking clumsily away, I couldn't help but notice the blond wasn't succeeding in her determined ministrations over the limp flesh before her, which she interrupted with an annoyed look over her shoulder at me.

"Hey, cowboy, I'm busy here, you know! Take a number and wait in line!"

Triple shit!

Stumbling dejectedly back to my own room to collapse in frustration, I noted Lenny's briefcase. What was this, a test? I sat up, opened it, and began counting. I had six hundred-banknote stacks of Ben Franklins before me when Steph came in wearing a snit.

"Fucking limpdicks! I can't figure it out!"

"What, babe?"

"Saul can't get it up! I like to sucked his asshole through the head of his dick and he can't get it up! Says it's because of the heroin!"

"What an eloquent way you have with words, babe. Royal's the same. Hooker's gonna cave his head in, she's sucking so hard."

"Not bad yerself, dude. You didn't take any, did you?"

"No way, babe, no way."

"You up for a little exercise? I'm all hot and bothered, I can tell you!"

"Sure, babe, me too. Go brush your teeth, take a shower. I'll be in in a minute."

She was on her way, shedding clothes. What the fuck was I doing counting money when my honey was in need? I put it all back, shut the case, began shedding my own clothes.

"Mm, you taste like Pepsodent," I remarked after joining her in the shower.

"What?"

"Nothing. I like Pepsodent."

*****

There we were, sitting high up in the tiers behind the stage as if we were the guiding spirits of the concert, able to see the reacting faces of the crowd come to boogie with Mick and the boys. There we lolled, full of benevolence for all rock'n'rollers, the vibes of our snockered souls reaching out to belie the Stones' plaint about not getting no satisfaction, the double negative expressing our high good humor with plenty of satisfaction.

Mellow with leftover exuberance from the music and the lingering fumes of, ahem, Antarctic Ashram Hash concocted by a contingent of Urbuc Hindu scientists to relieve the boredom of seismic studies of volcanic activity deep in the southern pole, we dashed out the rear entrance to our midnight black limo in a protective enclosure -- the entrance-exit of the stars -- and when the gates opened we were beset with a crowd of fans screaming out their love for the Rolling Stones, we, the half-snockered souls pressing vee-signs with our fingers against the smoky windows -- peace be unto thee, rockers of the world.

Steph directed the chauffeur to the Pali, a steep incline up the central mountains of Oahu where the sea air blew up channels to seventy miles per hour, and we all stood in the winds of the gods with arms outstretched as wings to guide our soaring over the jeweled lights of the city below.

*****

We were soaring on a chartered plane, Lenny, Royal, and I, Steph, Rachel, and Hilaria, all staring out the TV screens of our windows at the varigated beauty of island coastline, the blacks and golds, the deep blue and luminescent greens over shallows, the greens running to deep earthy tints in the jungled interiors, the smoke from Kilauea Crater, the blackened crust over the lava lake shot through with fiery veins, the landing in Hilo. Earthbound then, rolling up Volcano Road in a rented stationwagon to a reserved suite of rooms at the elegant Volcano House perched on the rim of a vast desolate caldera cracked by vents of steam, we rested then, restored ourselves on food and drink.

Rachel, alas, clung to Lenny. Hilaria, foolish girl, allied herself with Royal. Good. Perhaps she would turn away from his apparently continuing impotence for someone, well, like me, to relieve her itchiness. In the meanwhile, Steph and I held hands, affectionate and at ease with each other. We all prepared ourselves for the evening's mission as proposed by Lenny, the Great -- we were not mere tourists after all, but a special breed of discoverers seeking unique views in our explorations. We would not trudge upon Pele's slopes in the canned and guided tour to the platform overlooking the active crater. No, we would gather in a secret enclave at night with flashlights, wend our way up the perilous slopes fuzzy with Pele's hair to grip fingers and faces over the rim itself, a line of Kilroys -- we would be there with our noses up the Devil's Asshole. We had a supply of the purest LSD to enhance our perceptions during the pilgrimage.

Enter a touch of soap opera, the vagaries of dynamic relationships. At the appointed hour, Steph was ready for bed, surrendering to some lassitude, desiring only a Parest and some snuggling. We had broken ranks in order that I, the official guide, might reconnoiter the way by joining the daily guided tour with park rangers shepherding the flock. I was busy memorizing the route, which if strayed from, could be dangerous. There were chaotic formations from previous eruptions, jagged depressions, holes and lumps, vents spewing sulfurous breaths, soft and crumbly places around the rim itself. But the experts had plotted a safe pathway to a raised platform set back from the rim and all I had to do was tag along and remember.

The slopes were fuzzy with long black hairs. Steph stopped to gather strands in a hotel envelope. "They're supposed to be lucky, Pele's protection for those who come to her altar."

"What are they?"

"They're caused by smoke and heat. Tiny molecules lump together on the surface, then gather more in long fine strings like hair."

"Amazing."

"Some folks put them in amulets for personal protection. Others fix them into their houses. The mayor at Milolii told me that the beach at Okoe Bay was made because a fisherman was trapped there -- he had a bit of Pele's hair in a locket on a chain, so Pele went around him."

I was naturally doubtful. Escaping molten lava on a beach is easy -- you merely swim into the protection of Neptune, or whoever the Hawaiian equivalent was, one god's realm to the next, all competitors for the faithful. "And all the people in Milolii had Pele's hair over their doorways, right?"

She smiled. "You have to believe."

"Do you?"

She shrugged. "Why not? It's cheap enough for peace of mind."

*****

Steph slept with her envelope of hair beneath her pillow. Royal was in a heroin stupor. Lenny and Hilaria had come together on the Love Drug. Rachel was pissed; she was scornful. She and I, the only supplicants before Lucy in the Sky with Diamonds.

Unable to remain cuddled to Steph, I'd gone to the hotel lounge to imbibe the essence of cognac, to look for my friend, Luminous Loki, the jolly resident musician who played guitar and piano. I'd met him some months before when Steph and I had stopped in at Volcano House on our return from a visit to Waimea Valley, from where we'd hiked into the Shangri-La of Waimanu.

It had been a lovely trip and we had played with the idea of moving in permanently, not so impractical at all. The sands of its beach rarely felt the imprint of human footsteps. There was so much of the jungly green and brown foliage of tree and bush and vine that we could hide ourselves away in a camouflaged shelter -- come in with nylon-reinforced plastic sheeting, a roll of wire, a machete, all our camping accouterments, our pakalolo farming supplies, we could grow acres of beautiful children, add to the positive in life, subtract from the negative, live like Adam and Eve in the Garden. Rather than arduously pack all our necessities in on our backs, we could buy an inflatable boat, a small motor, ferry it in, seriously situate ourselves for a year or whatever, dedicate ourselves to cementing together the parts of our whole, the apotheosizing growth of life and love without the debilitating effects of so-called civilization, live simply and purely.

In the sparsely populated hotel lounge we'd met Luminous Loki, which was our affectionate nickname for the musician. He drank with us, played sentimental songs we requested, and invited me up to accompany him with my amplified kazoo. We had fun, playing and singing blues songs, Steph leading the applause of startled and amused guests. We had invited him to visit us at Hawaiian Fern Acres, drawing him a map of how to get there -- and he'd showed up to present us with a hand-carved pakalolo pipe with a tiki representing the god, Loki. We had utilized Loki to draw illumination into ourselves and had played all our favorite records and tapes, talking music, eating, drinking, and laughing the day away. Thereafter, we always called our friend Luminous Loki.

I thought, if I found him on duty, we might step out for a little toke of the Antarctic Ashram Hash, and together could ad lib our way through the blues riffs inspired by my muse, Lucy.

Instead, I found Rachel.

"Are you a man or a fucking mouse, Buck?"

I thought about it, and answered, "I'm a fucking maniac who masquerades as a mouse."

She thought about that.

"Good."

"Good?"

"You ever try to imagine what the ultimate fuck might be like?" "The ultimate fuck?"

"The fuck after which all else pales by comparison."

"Doesn't it change, the idea? Once you've achieved it, the idea grows. The ultimate fuck is always tomorrow, around the next corner."

"Bullshit. There is an ultimate fuck that sets the standard for all time."

"I don't know. I think I've had it more than once already, a contradiction in terms. And you know what? They were all totally unlike each other, each unique in its own way."

"Oh, yeah? Which was the best, the most memorable of all?"

Heavy shit. "I can't say. I think when I was in love."

"Love, shit! That's illusion. The ultimate fuck lies in transcendence of all illusion."

"It does?"

"It brings together all the past and future into a single illuminating point, an orgasm at the meeting point of life and death, all the history contained in our genes all the way back to the big bang, baby, encompassing all the eons of eternity -- birth and destruction and rebirth in a flash!"

"No shit?"

"Let's go."

"Where?"

"To the great asshole. That was the plan, wasn't it? You going to wimp out on me, too?"

"The crater?"

"Well bugger the whole world together. Come on."

"Wait. We'll need the flashlights."

"We don't need shit. Only ourselves."

At the kickoff point, a deadend road that marked the bus stop for the foot-trail, there was nothing for it but to follow her example -- I took off my clothes. I was excited by then, my mind photographing Rachel's magnificent physique, a sibyl from ancient times, the most voluptuous temptress of all time, a seeress and revealer of arcane knowledge just before she destroyed you in a final illumination -- or, perhaps, provided you with the ultimate fuck.

I followed after her exaggerated ass, those great swollen orbs of her buns, those primordial gluteous maximi drawing me on into the darkness, panting in dread and desire, ready to risk life and limb to feel those herculean thighs wrapped around me, to hold me impaled in the curly-haired steaming mound of her own fat little volcano, from whence the fire of her fury would consume me, inflame me, electrify me, enlighten me -- the ultimate fuck, the ultimate satori that would fling me like a beachball kicked by her contemptuous feet into a nirvana that surpasseth all understanding, imprint me forever upon the substance and meaning of the universe. I would follow the hidden little rosebud of her asshole to the Devil's Asshole itself.

"Wait! Wait!"

"Wait, shit!"

I pushed harder, caught her. "No, Rachel. This way."

"What?"

"This way, come this way."

She embraced me, kissed me, frantic with lust, feeling me, groping me, drinking me into her pores. And I clutched at her, sucked at her mouth, wanting to leap up and fuck her in mid air.

"I love you, Buck! I love you!"

"I love you, Rachel!" But privately in the untouched center of myself I knew, as she surely must, that this was illusion, that what drove us was too primitive for words or concepts.

"Fuck me! Fuck me! Fuck me!"

No, not yet. The heat was higher, we had to go higher, where the fire from the center of the Earth broke out to laugh at the coldness of space.

"This way, this way," I chanted, drawing her after me, the maniac out of his guise as a mouse, I led her up the trail by intuition, my hidden intelligence remembering the way.

There was a glow, clouds of fumes rising, a tremble in the ground transmitting up through the soles of our feet, a sensing of heat. I led her on, stumbling into a shallow ravine to one side of the platform, pulling up a handful of Pele's hair. Nowhere to put it, unable to discard it, perhaps sublimally superstitious, and needing my hand, I stuck it into my mouth, chewed it, ate it. It tasted gritty, like sand or glass. But I was safe now, protected from inside by Pele's hair -- at least until I shit it out.

We lay pressed together into the hard vee, our heads out over the rim, breathing sulfur, feeling the heat from below sucking at our bodily liquors, entranced, holding our breaths until we had to draw back for wisps of air. Below, a vast flat black iris shot through with reddish-gold veins. It seemed to pulse, the disk rising and falling, breathing.

Whether the ultimate fuck was near, I didn't know, but it seemed as if the ultimate arousal was upon me. My hardon lay between groin and rough lava and even the pain and discomfort felt good. My hand crawled down her spine to the nether cleft of her, digging into her apex, a finger up her pussy, a thumb up her asshole, and she never flinched or let me know she knew what I had done.

The black disk sank, the crust breaking here and there, spouts of molten flame shooting up several feet, only to fall and form pools that cooled and dimmed.

"Look," she gasped.

To the far side a stream of red molten lava gushed up, spreading over the black crust, then sank again as the crust rose -- and it kept rising, up and up it came, closer and closer, the fiery veins fading out, only the upper cooling black surface rising higher and higher.

"Fuck me," she growled in a deep voice right out of The Exorcist. "Fuck me! FUCK ME!"

I was over and in her like a shot, she humping up her ass to accommodate me, my eyes wide and unblinking on the rising black disk, only a rosy glow around its rim to mark its level, my penis safe in the warm, clutching wetness of her, plunging, wondering if my orgasm would end in a great scream of fiery death if Pele or the Devil had a spasm of mirth or irritability.

It was too hot and we drew back to suck breaths, plunging, panting, and grunting all the while, writhing and struggling, full of fear and desire. After trembling and muttering, the surface began to sink again, the crust cracking again, the red veins streaking like lightning bolts over the dark iris. It sank and erupted in great fiery geysers, bloody golden fountains of the heart's excruciation.

I fucked and fucked and fucked, my whole body awash in sweaty exudation, my whole inner being rushing up the arch of climax. And Rachel knew! The clever, instinctive bitch knew!

"No! Don't come! Not yet! Not yet!"

She struggled, rolled, uncoupling us, beating and kicking at me. I fell aside, pushing at her. She drew away, then pounced on top of me, her thighs wide, skootching up, grabbing me with both hands, slotting us back together again, the backside of my body pressed, every square inch of it, into the rough torn embrace of unforgiving, scrapey hardness beneath -- all except for my head, which stuck out over the lake of magma. And she fucked me like a terrible demanding goddess, rolling those iron-girded hips, flexing those marvelous buns and thighs, straining at her own speed over the beggarly supplicant of my agonizing self.

She grabbed my wrists, pulled my hands to her breasts. "Squeeze them, squeeze them! Harder, you bastard, harder!"

I followed orders, caught up in her intentions, raising my head from the heat, gasping for air, crushing her breasts with my clenching fingers, pinching her nipples.

"Suck them! Bite them!"

I sucked and bit.

She screamed. "Now fuck me! Fuck me!"

I slammed up and down, rocking her, she gripped to the rim, her wet face pressed against the side of mine -- was it raining? -- peering, I knew, into the Devil's Asshole, sniffing his flatulence, her spiritually straining body trying to become one with the fiery cracks, the molten fountains, squirming and trembling and gasping and trying to scream.

"Fuck me! Fug me! Fu' me! Fu'm! Fuu-uuuu-uh-uh-unh!"

Then the chunk of rim we lay upon broke with an ominous crack and gave way, hurling us out into space, falling to crash through the crust hundreds of feet below to be consumed. Ashes to ashes, dust to dust, orgasmic organisms into inorganic matter, round trip complete.

A billion years later, the eons regenerating us in the pool of life from simple one-celled animals into lungfish crawling upon land to quadripeds and bipeds to complex if slightly malfunctioning systems of organization, our wits grew into semblances of our former selves. We broke apart, pushed and pulled, struggled to inch ourselves away, to crawl and depend on each other, standing, stumbling, leaning against each other, descending to cool air, our bodies drying, the relative chill gently shocking us back toward our old ways.

At the road, exhausted, we lay upon our lately discarded clothes and rested, trying to summon up strength to make it to our beds. We spoke not a word, only sighed and moaned little moans, grunted little grunts, managed to get half-dressed and wend our way back clutching at each other in support.

At her bed, gentleman that I am, she pulled away as I pushed her to collapse facedown. Numbly I sought my own, sat beside an oblivious Steph, slid to the floor into the red-veined all-consuming black eye inside me.

*****

"Jesus Christ, babe, I woke up and almost freaked," Steph exclaimed. "I thought you were dead!"

After helping me to the bathroom, stiff and sore, I got a look at myself in the mirror and almost freaked myself. I was black as a coal miner, dried blood over my mouth and chin, my tanktop stiff with it. Apparently I'd developed a nosebleed on the way back. When Steph had got a look at my body, she went off again.

"Jesus Fucking Christ, baby, what happened?"

My elbows and knees were scraped raw. I had scratches and bruises on my back and ass, even on the underside of my dick, a big toe nail torn into the quick, most of which was discovered as I stood wincing under a hot shower, washing away the sooty grime, Steph helping me with tender ministrations of washcloth, helping to discover the extent of the damage as it was revealed.

"My God, sweetie, what happened?"

I grunted. "You oughta see the other guy."

"What? You got into a fight?"

At that point, I wasn't sure there was a difference between fighting and fucking.

"Nah. We went up to the crater last night, fell down a couple of times, crawling around in the dark, all that. We forgot the flashlights."

"Jee-sus. You guys actually went after all."

"Yeah, some of us."

"So how was it? At night?"

"Something."

In long-sleeved shirt and full-length pants, a bandaid on my toe, we met for a late breakfast in the dining room. We were one missing.

"Where's Rachel?"

"In the bath," said Hilaria. "She'll be a little late."

She gave me a look, kept sneaking peeks at me, but said nothing.

The breakfast was buffet style and I heaped my plate, began shoveling it away like I hadn't eaten in a week. I couldn't get enough grapefruit juice, then coffee. I was definitely dehydrated.

Rachel showed up in pants suit and dark sunglasses, attacking her food like a Sumo wrestler. The meal was subdued for conversation, only a few polite murmurs making the rounds.

I was ready for a fat joint or two to complete the process of starting my engine. Steph and I strolled along the road in front of the hotel, passing one back and forth.

"So, what do you think?"

"Kinda hectic."

"You having fun?"

She shrugged, rolled her head. "Mm, yeh, but I think I'm ready to go home, get a little peace and quiet."

"It's like being on speed the last few days, don't even have time to relax and think about things."

"Yeh, and you notice how everybody seems to talk so fast?"

"Yeah, like speedfreaks. Those New York guys, I couldn't hardly understand a word they said."

"Well, New Yorkers talk fast on the natch. I think I used to talk like that."

"Weird the way you change without noticing."

"Yeh."

"So, what, you ready to go home, huh?"

"Yeh. You?"

"Yeah. Fuck this."

"Buck, Steph," Lenny called. "C'mon, we're going to the beach!" We stopped, turned, and waved. "We can have them drop us off at Mountain View on the way down."

"We gotta pick up my van in Hilo."

"Oh, yeah, I forgot. We could take the car in tomorrow to pick it up."

"Yeh, if it'll start."

The Ford workcar I'd bought from my boss was into the last few clicks on its odometer. "Hell, we can always hitch in."

"Yeh."

Getting our stuff together, the last of the group, Lenny honking the horn out front, I said, "So what, you wanna go on in and pick it up today?"

"Yeh. Let's go to the beach. I could use a swim, lay in the sun. You, too, it'll do you good. Then we'll go home."

"Okay, good. You're in charge today. I'm just along for the ride."

"Don't worry, babe, I'll take care of everything. You just rest up, get yourself right."

*****

At the beach, a small deserted one, Steph reran her trick of declaring it nude, and the secret of the night before was soon revealed to all. Rachel's body was in worse shape than mine, the difference being that she proudly displayed hers, a veteran with a story for every wound, while I slunk away in disgust for a swim. Talk about post-coital withdrawal. Her body the morning after was about as appealing as a Twinkie at a full-blown luau -- disgusting.

The water took me, held me in its cool, healing amniotic womb, beginning to renew me, work out the kinks, ease the stiffness, peel away the scabs, wash me clean for the extra-curative rays of the sun. I poked around the reef, diving down to play scatter with the finned beauties below, saw a large barracuda almost invisible except for its eyes, marking time, watching me. Then it was gone and the huge, ugly head of a moray eel poked its head from a burrow to grin at me. All these terrible beasts of which I'd read countless fright stories, I'd met them all, including sharks, and nary a one had taken a bite out of me. Then from below looking up at the light coming down, there swam the graceful Hilaria, long, slim, and balletic, a sight to see, an experience of pure aesthetics for me, now free -- for the moment -- of all carnal fantasy.

I came up to tread water beside her, lifting my mask, spitting out the snorkel. "Oh, hi," she said. "Thought I'd see the reef. I've heard they teem with all sorts of marine creatures. Can you show me?"

"Sure."

"California, the water's all murky along the beaches. You can't see anything. Here it's so clear and beautiful."

"Yeah, different worlds."

"Rachel's got quite a story about last night. Is it true?"

"I don't know. What'd she say?"

"You two went up to the crater last night. How was it?"

"Something."

"I wish I'd gone now. I'd like to have had that experience."

She was studying me closely, grinning fetchingly, but I was unmoved -- except for her aesthetic appeal, the appreciation in my intellectual processes remaining above my neckline, a sort of dumb exultation over the natural order and beauty of things in the universe, nothing to fear or be rudely surprised by in its mathematical purity.

"I saw a barracuda."

Her smile was gone, her eyes and attitude changed in a flash of fear. She looked around uneasily.

"He's gone."

"Oh."

"Want to see a moray eel?"

Another little shock, more unease. "Aren't they dangerous?"

"Nah. You don't bother them, they won't bother you -- live and let live, you know? Just float along the top and watch."

We adjusted our masks and snorkels. I dove down, searching for the moray hole, found it, swam over behind it in a wide arc to pause before the opening. He'd already begun to stick his head out before he could possibly have seen me, sensing my approach somehow in the mystery of his powers. His whole head came out, the terrible beaked jaws moving, twisting and wafting about sinuously on its long flat neck, probably studying me with the same curiosity that I studied him, neither of us quite daring to pass over the invisible line between us. What a strange creature, we both must have thought, each in the peculiar manner we were able.

I blew bubbles and he undulated in reaction, we two in a kind of dance. I'd seen documentary films of divers swimming close enough to reach out and stroke them, feed them, actually doing it. But not me. Who knew when a moray's tolerance ended and human fear took over?

Out of air, I surfaced.

"Oh, my God! I thought he was going to attack you!"

"Nah. I think he finds you more appetizing." I grinned. She wasn't amused. "Let's head back. Go that way around the reef, lot of pretty fishies."

She paddled away and I followed, both of us for the view -- she the particolored fish safely from above, me occasionally diving to look up at her, change my perspective, a truly exquisite sight to see.

*****

Hilaria disappeared into a thick grove of palms while I walked to the towels Steph and I had spread out. She was gone and so was everybody else. I plopped down to dry my head, grabbed a beer from the cooler, lit a joint from the few Steph had brought. Where the hell was everybody? Was I missing something? Fuck it.

Fifteen minutes later, when I rolled over, I saw Steph a few hundred yards down the beach running toward me full blast. As she got near enough to make out the expression on her face, I got up in alarm. Her features were grim. At the end of her strength, she was starting to stumble, lose control. I ran out to meet her, grab her, hold her.

"Babe, what? What's the matter?"

She collapsed against me, heaving, clutching at me.

"What, baby? C'mon, sit down, catch your breath." I helped her over to the towels. She fell back, eyes closed, arms out-stretched, knees raised, huffing and puffing. I popped another bottle of beer, knelt beside her, waited. When she'd recovered enough, I sat her up, held the cold bottle to her mouth. She grabbed it and chugalugged, stopped to gasp.

"Oh, gawd, that's good!"

"You okay?"

"Yeh."

"Where's everybody?"

"Probably watching Lenny fuck Rachel."

"No shit?"

"Well, Royal was when I left, limp dick and all."

I made a face, shrugged -- yeah, so what else was new?

"Jeez, what'd you guys do up thee last night? Wrestle like on TV, slamming each other around? She looks awful, worse than you." "How come you left?"

"Ah!" She shook her head irritably.

"You had a look on your face. What happened?"

"Nothing. I just felt like running -- get a good breath of fresh air, you know?"

"C'mon, babe."

She pouted a few moments, her brows knit. "Rachel was talking about my tits, said I ought to put on a bra, that I was obscene."

I tried not to smile. "She's got some nerve! You should have said something about the obscenity of a woman displaying her hairy balls in public!"

She broke with a chuckle, but wasn't ready to let it go. "You think my tits are too big, too long?"

"I love your tits, babe. Besides, it ain't the tits that count. Inside, you're twice the woman Rachel will ever be -- and I think she knows it, too."

"Yeh?"

"I think she's jealous. I think she knows you've got something she can never attain."

"Oh, yeh? What?"

"Character. Plus, as wild as last night was, you're a better piece of ass."

"Yeh?" She was simpering now, the grin working out fully over her mouth, making her twice as pretty.

"Yeah. You don't see me packing my bags to run off with her, do you?"

"Yer a peach."

"I'll kiss yer arse, it's a peach. So, what say we get out of here, go home?"

"Yeh, I've had enough of this shit."

We stood, hopping around to get into our bathing suits.

"I was thinking maybe to try out Lenny, you know? I heard he was a pretty hot fuck."

"Seems to be doing better than others I'm too polite to name."

'Yeh, so anyway, we take a little stroll in the palms, holding hands, ya know, just talking. We get off alone and start fooling around a little, getting into it...and here comes Rachel like a riot and Royal smirking close behind."

"Yeah?"

"Yeh, and so that was the end of that. Lenny's fucking Rachel over a leaning coconut tree, Royal's drooling on himself, and I'm off for a run."

"No class at all. I'm gonna go let 'em know we're outa here. I gotta have a word with Royal anyway."

What I found was Lenny gone, Rachel on her knees sobbing and screaming how much she hated men, Hilaria embracing her, patting her back and trying to calm her, with Royal the gleefully cynical observer.

"Hey, man, c'mon, let's talk."

He fell in beside me. "Yeah, man, what's happening? Is that bitch a crazy fucking nymphomaniac or what?"

I thought maybe sad and hurting, maybe desperate, surely frustrated, but not crazy. I had an urge to go over to Rachel and tell her she was the hottest fuck I'd ever had, which was true, and that I'd remember the night with her as long as I lived, which was probably true, but I only said, "We're outa here. C'mon and give us a ride into Hilo."

He stopped, turned. "Wait. I gotta go find Lenny."

"Nah, man, c'mon. Won't take you ten minutes to drive us in. Besides, we gotta talk. Okay?"

"Sure, lemme get some clothes on, see if I can find the keys."

Steph between us in the car, I told him. "Hey, man, I gotta tell you, I'm not interested in the MDA thing. You wanna hook up with Tony Cool and Sid in Honolulu, you got their number, but I'm out of it. Okay?"

"Sure, man, but I don't understand your attitude. There's gonna be big bucks in this thing."

"Hey, I wish you luck, man. No hard feelings."

As Steph headed toward the Iron Butterfly, fishing out her keys to unlock it, I turned to shake hands, say goodbye.

"Hey, listen, bro," he said. "I'm in a little bit of a bind and maybe you can at least do me a favor."

"What's that?"

"See, I'm sitting on about fifteen pounds, well, that's all my own, you know. So like, I'd appreciate it if you'd keep this just between us. I'm just trying to look out for myself, you know."

He was telling me he'd ripped Lenny and the crew off somehow, probably by adding cut to the product before running it through the pill machine, filching aside a few pounds at a time.

"Maybe you could move a few more pounds for me, just so's I can get a little bread in my pocket, you know, see me through."

"Hey, man, you can wait another month, I'll be shipping you over a hundred pounds of grass, you can make at least as much as I do you handle it right."

"I need bread now, man, besides I ain't into welfare."

"It ain't welfare, pal. You better pay me every dime I got coming."

"Hey, don't worry. Whaddayou, think I'm bum pay or something?"

Me, I really couldn't say at that point -- we'd never done any but chickenshit deals between us, no problem.

"Look, man, let me send you four pounds, that'll give me ten grand my end, tide me over, you know?"

"Okay, man, but after that you're on your own as far as the MDA goes. I'm gonna stick to my grass business."

"Sure, man, if that's what you want -- I'd appreciate it."

"Okay, man. You be careful. You really ought to lay off the gow, Royal. You're missing a lot with that shit."

"Hey, don't worry. For me, it's just a little vacation, you know?"

"Yeah." No use sighing -- it was wasted breath. I could see the calculation in his eyes, the hint of contempt, but shrugged it off as no more meaningful than a lack of need on my part for his approval.

###

CHAPTER 10

Royal shipped the four pounds, two of which were sold to Sid, one in Hilo, the other in Honolulu. I sent it all to Royal, seven grand, figuring that when I sold the third to send the final three grand he had coming and hold out five hundred for myself. The last pound I'd keep buried in the hermetically sealed military ammo box in the rainforest after selling the third to Sid.

Kieth and Mary arrived to follow in our footsteps to homestead and work with us in the pakalolo business. They arrived with not much more than personal belongings, a few pieces of furniture, and a fiberglass French Army jeep, all shipped in a Matson Line container. They came also next door to broke and expecting our help to get situated. We put them up in the spare bedroom of the Iron Butterfly, which was no longer operable because Steph had run it off the road during a visit to Laura.

Kieth and Mary arrived to follow in our footsteps to homestead and work with us in the pakalolo business. They arrived with not much more than personal belongings, a few pieces of furniture, and a fiberglass French Arm jeep, all shipped in a Matson Line container. They came also next door to broke and expecting our help to get situated. We put them up in the spare bedroom of the Iron Butterfly, which was no longer operable because Steph had run it off the road during a visit to Laura.

*****

A tow truck had shown up late in the afternoon hauling the Iron Butterfly behind, its front wheels cocked way out of alignment, the frame twisted, radiator broke, a headlight shattered, and grill and pink butterfly mashed in.

Steph alighted from the cab beside the driver, chewing on a finger and looking sheepish. "I had a wreck," she said.

"Jeez, babe, you all right?"

"Yeh."

"What happened?"

"I tried to miss a dog running in front of me and swerved off the road."

"D'ju miss the dog?"

"Yeh."

"Nobody else hurt?"

"Naw, just my van."

"Go inside, have a beer, smoke a joint, relax, while I help the driver get 'er situated."

"Where ya want it?"

"Pull 'er on up the driveway, hold to the right, then make a sharp left at the watertank. We can drop her right there."

"Can I get turned around and back outa there?"

"Yeah, no problem. You can go right around in a circle back out the driveway."

"You got it."

After we'd done the deed, I paid the guy and went inside. She was sitting slumped at the table, an open bottle before her, toking, at a joint. I paused to grab myself a beer and found that my hands were shaking. I'd inspected the van and come to the conclusion that it hadn't been traveling too fast or Steph would have gone through the windshield what with the high seat, large glass front, and no seatbelt, although it was possible she might have broken her legs over the big steering wheel on the way out, or even had her chest crushed against it -- me imagining the worst all the while.

As a former ace driving instructor, I had naturally given Steph the benefit of points along the way, correcting mistakes she made. She had paid attention and learned them all -- except for the lessons that couldn't be practiced until certain dire incidents came to pass. One of the most difficult to impress upon all, but particularly women, was the concept of not swerving off the road to avoid collisions with stray animals, especially at high rates of speed, especially if you had a vehicle full of people, your family for example, your spouse and kids, maybe grampa and gramma. To swerve for a dog or cat, a rabbit or roadrunner, even a larger animal like a deer, is to endanger the lives of yourself and your loved ones. It sounds a bit calloused when you counsel them to apply the brakes only and not to swerve -- in this case, to put it bluntly, fuck the animal and save the human. All very nice in theory, but unless it can be internalized as an ironclad habit like us cold-blooded killers can do, almost everyone allows their instinct to make the swerve and suffer the consequences.

I sat down and looked at her, trying desperately to quell the anger that had arisen in me. She looked guiltily back. "I know. I fucked up. I wasn't supposed to swerve, only hit the brakes. Well, I got it half right -- I hit the brakes."

"How fast were you going?"

"Not fast. Twenty-five or thirty. You know that little road to Laura's place."

"On the highway, you would have been going fifty, right?" No need to exaggerate. We both knew the Iron Butterfly's top speed was about fifty-five.

"Yeh, probably."

"And if you'd swerved off the road going that fast," I said, pausing to let her imagine Volcano Road with its deeper ditches and trees beyond. "It would have been a different story, right? You would have totalled the van and yourself."

"Yeh, I know. Jeez, everything in the back flew forward. It's a good thing the bed's down low. I think I bruised my tits on the steering wheel."

She tried a shaky laugh, but I wasn't letting her off so easy. "And if Laura and her kid had been with you, they'd have been a pile of wrecked bodies right on top of yours."

"Yeh, I know. I'm sorry. It all happened so fast, I didn't have time to think. I just did what I did."

"I love dogs, darlin', you know I do. But I love you more. And I don't want to lose you over something stupid like that."

"I know."

She began sobbing. Well, there, I'd done it -- controlled my anger, stifled the need to rant and rave, and now here I had her weeping again and what does a man do about that? Feel guilty and take her into my arms, grateful that I could.

After awhile she said, "I think it was Popolo's and Sista's daddy. I couldn't run over him, could I?"

We both broke out into choking fits of laughter. Then we inspected the damage to her tits.

*****

As a consequence, we push-started the old Ford and made it into a used car lot in Hilo where we got a hundred and fifty dollars in trade on a year-old Datsun pickup.

I missed the convenience of the Iron Butterfly, so I plotted to make a replacement. I built a big plywood box that slid up over the sidewalls of the pickup bed, the roof a foot or so above the cab top, with little grilled windows on all four sides for ventilation, a rear door that lifted to provide a sun and rain shelter. There was enough room inside for a double mattress, a dufflebag or two, a jug of water, and our trusty one-burner Coleman -- not to mention a small rack for one of Steph's votive candles. Underneath between the bottom and the pickup bed was plenty of stowage space. It needed only four people, one to a corner, to pick it up and fit it over the sidewalls, anchor it to metal hooks with eye-wire cables and turnbuckles. It only needed painting and we were ready for trucking again.

*****

In the meanwhile, to business, both social and financial. Mary was a giddy, happy-go-lucky broad full of enthusiasms and I liked her -- even when I discovered that under the facade of the outer image beat a steely and determined intelligence. She liked to dance; Kieth didn't, and therefore...

Kieth could be weird and obnoxious, fully seventy-five percent of all his ideas crackpotted and harebrained, yet he, too, possessed a burning intelligence and steely resolve.

Giving them a brief guided tour of our special stash on the next property over and a crash course in the art of cannabis cultivation, Kieth refused to indulge in the vile weed and clucked disapprovingly when Mary joined us in our daily communion with the pakalolo gods.

I worked his ass on the coolie wagon, hunting out new stashes, teaching him about the twenty-foot long plank and pathways, shoveling shit and soil and filling bags, getting him into shape with serious labor. He suggested the manufacture of deadly boobytraps to be placed strategically around each stash, having learned in an army demolition squad all about various explosives and clever Viet Cong boobytraps.

The small holes with a cardboard cover laid over with a disguise of clumps of grass to conceal a shit-smeared bamboo stake sharpened to a penetrating point on the business end, called a pungi-stick, was simple enough and would probably prove effective in injuring intruders. But what if they were kids or pets out playing around? I nixed that idea.

His next boobytrap idea was clever, too, and he would demonstrate it by building one for me. It consisted of a rather large rattrap with a solid wooden base. Where the wire spring slammed over from one side to the other when tripped, he drilled a hole and fitted a metal sleeve cut from a length of pipe, the inside diameter of which was perfect for slotting in a .410 gauge shotgun shell. A thumbtack was fixed to the wire spring so that when it was tripped, the point slammed into contact with the fulminate of mercury cap on the bottom of the cartridge, causing it to discharge. The devices were to be camouflage-painted and hidden in bushes and trees with undetectable green fishing line strung in a perimeter. When someone tripped the green string, a nearby bush would explode to pepper the intruder's ass -- or blow half his face off.

I put the kebotch on that idea, too, for the same reasons as the pungi-sticks. I wasn't willing to injure or kill someone, even if they were the despised thieves, over some pakalolo plants -- as much as I loved and depended upon them. No, I'd rather creep around in the night and destroy their motor vehicles, wage psychological warfare. Wasn't there some karma in it all -- what ye sow so shall ye reap?

But soon enough I had cause to rethink the whole idea. I had found some limbs torn from my babies, some culprit's hastily discarded thong. Somebody had discovered our special plot. Shit, we would have to move them all to another place, and quickly, too. They were a week or so from full maturity and represented a good fifty pounds of exceptional product. Downwind of the dogs and quietly, the thieves could return that very night to plunder them. Harvest early or move them immediately that was the question.

"No, let's catch the assholes," Kieth suggested. "We'll set an ambush and put the fear of God in them."

"How?"

"We'll set up puptents, disguise them, one on each side near the footpaths. You take one, I'll take the other. We'll stand guard though the night. You take one dog with you, I'll take one with me. We'll catch the cocksuckers in the act."

Whoa! The entire repressed guerilla fighter was coming out of Kieth, the irregular warfare tactician, and he was issuing orders like a Special Forces colonel.

"What if they come armed? We don't want any shootouts, Kieth." "Not even if they shoot first?"

"Well..."

"Don't worry. I'll send an automatic burst at the sky to warn 'em. They hear that, they'll shit their pants."

*****

Kieth had taken over my M-1, which I'd never fired again after that first time to make sure it worked. Among other things, he was an expert gunsmith, having once owned a gun shop prior to his incarceration, and was a secret numbered member of the rightwing Minutemen. After first informing me that it had a defective gasplug -- whatever that was -- he'd sent away for a replacement part, along with a flash suppressor, a bipod barrel mounting, a new folding stock, and an M-2 trigger housing.

When he'd put it all together and taken me out to demonstrate it, I'd about shit my pants. It seems an M-2 trigger housing allowed the weapon to go from semi-automatic to fully automatic, and the damage to a foliage of small trees, shrubs, and fern plants had been awesome, as well as the sound effects, when he'd loosed a full 30-round clip.

"Jesus Christ, man, this ain't fucking Vietnam!"

"My name's Kieth, but don't worry, Jesus is on his way, and until he gets here, we gotta take care of our own."

Why did his words echo in my mind? Hadn't I used a similar justification when Steph had protested against keeping guns in the house? "Isn't that thing against the law?"

"Hey, man, any fucking gun is against the law for us."

He had a point, still though...

He'd slapped in another clip, slammed the loading bolt, and held it out to me. "Want to try it?"

I wish I could report that I said no, that there was a crossing of the line and then there was a crossing of the line, but no, I was a red-blooded American male raised as a hunter with gun in hand, a non-military type who'd nevertheless fantasized firing a machinegun from the time I was a kid in grammar school and the Army had sent uniformed squads of GIs with tanks and machine guns in gratefulness for having purchased twenty-five dollar savings bonds in great patriotic displays during WWII.

So I grabbed that sonofabitch, bit my teeth, and prepared to annihilate some rainforest.

"Hold it down! It's gonna wanna go up and to the side!"

Somebody was lying to somebody. It wasn't near as good as sex and it didn't feel a bit like my dick. I told Kieth he could keep it, that it was all his.

He wanted to give me a Walther P-38, 9 mm handgun, but I said no, I had my Army Colt .45.

"One of the finest handguns ever made, the Walther P-38, better than the Luger. All the Wehrmacht officers carried them."

Lot of good it did them, I didn't say.

"This baby'll do," he said, patting the M-2. "Until I can afford an AR-180."

*****

The next to come out were the two-way handheld radios. "Communications are necessary in all military operations for backup support and intelligence in the field," he said. "We communicate every hour on the hour, step outside our bivouacs for a looksee, otherwise depend on the canine sentries. Whoever makes contact calls up the other for fire support."

I wanted to salute, say, "Yes, sir!"

For three nights we kept the watch, two of them filled with heavy rain, the days spent sleeping and replacing batter in the walkie- talkies.

"Fuck this, pal! I'm ready to harvest!"

"No, wait! Here's what we'll do -- put out some of my .410 gauge boobytraps. We'll hear 'em go off -- we can grab our shit and go running."

"Okay," I said finally after having thought about it -- the idea had some merit. "Only we place them up high and point 'em at the sky." I didn't want to blow some kid, or anybody else, away. I thought that by the time we got there, whoever it was would be long gone, flying away home in fear to wash out their shorts.

Well, a week later, no alarms had gone off, so we went out and harvested those badass kids, replanted month-old babies in their place -- not so valuable a crop to lose, only aggravating.

"Baby," Steph wheedled. "I think maybe we ought not to keep any close by like that anymore."

"Hah?"

"Too much strain. You realize how tense everybody is? Jeez, I spend all my time worrying something awful is gonna happen! I may have to get a Valium prescription."

"Hm." I thought about it. She was right. "Okay. We've already replanted, but we'll make plans to move them somewhere else."

"You think maybe we could find Mary and Kieth a place of their own? I'm a little tired of listening to that asshole's raving every waking hour. You shoulda never got him smoking grass!"

My sweetie-pie was right again, but by golly for once I had a humane reason -- to cure Kieth of his asthma. Amongst all our literature so assiduously gathered on the subject there was one on old herbal remedies for any number of ailments, first published in the previous century before the miracles of modern medicine, and one section had to do with the various treatments offered by marijuana, which included stomach problems, high blood pressure, glaucoma, gonorrhea, and, marvel of marvels, chronic bronchitis and asthma!

When I pointed this out to Kieth, providing a loophole, as it were, from his vehement loathing against all illegal drug use -- he believing the propaganda he'd been fed that one drug necessarily led to another until one was left with a lobotomizing and morally deleterious drug addiction -- the three of us persuaded him to try it. Three days passed without the use of inhaler, pill, panic attacks from shortness of breath, or breathing into a paper bag. A week later, he threw out all his medicines and became a diehard proselytizer for the miracle of cannabis sativa, cannabis indica, and all its derivatives. Alas, it also gave him a case of verbal diarrhea! The man had an endless encyclopedia of weird subjects over which to pontificate. He could spew out drivel by the hour without ever quite repeating him-self.

"Just think if Hitler had been a weedhead, it might have curbed all his excesses and mistakes -- we'd have a whole different ballgame. He had severe intestinal ailments, too, you know, and lung problems, which is why he didn't smoke and neither do I. Grass might have given him whole new perspectives."

Yeah, I said to myself, we might not even have had a world war if Hitler had only been a weedhead. Otherwise, there was no arguing with Kieth, his positions once taken poured in concrete and those who dared debate an issue like wielders of wet noodles as chisels.

"Right, baby," I said. "Exceptionally astute thinking on your part. Let's go get Deb and J.D. to help in the manicure, weighing, and bagging. I wanna show you this place I found."

It was a deserted, if miniscule, homestead set up ten feet off the ground on poles, so weatherbeaten it blended into the surrounding foliage from back off the road aways. It was so cramped, maybe 12x12 feet, with a wing elling off barely large enough to contain a twin-sized bed, from the side of which ran a wide porch across the front, a staircase that was more a slanted ladder than proper steps. It only needed a watertank and some gutters off the roof to keep it full. It would be up high enough we could make a proper overhead shower. The best was a long, well-camouflaged depression out back that I had paced off to estimate the square-footage of it -- roughly a hundred feet long and fifty-five feet wide. We could put in six hundred plants, the biggest single plot we had. Since it was off the last road over in the subdivision, we could flee out a back path and disappear into square miles of the Olaa Forest Preserve in the event of invading narcs, abandon it and leave nothing to identify us, since there were no roads beyond to cut off retreat. Steph and I would be on hand to minister to our babies sanely, curb our forays out to boogie in Hilo, utilize Kieth, Mary, Deb, and J.D. to do our shopping for us, keep us supplied. We could have one couple or the other housesit for one hour a week while we went over for a hot bath in our furo, put forth a serious effort to get our finances together, sit back and start looking for a sailboat to buy, plan an itinerary. What the fuck, time was passing, the dream was passing. I had a woman, a friend and lover of surpassing abilities, a partner who'd become truly infected with a case of hull and rig designs, a fascination for admiralty charts of the Pacific Ocean, a wanderlust that matched my own, game to go anywhere and do anything with me.

"Kinda cozy," she said. "Needs a little fixing up. Think we can fit together on that iddy-biddy bed?"

"Sure, babe, we only use half the one we got anyhow." She smiled that smile I loved. "Well, then..."

"Mm?"

"Yeh, let's do it."

*****

Returning home after picking up Deb, J.D., and two girls down the road from us, our nearest neighbors, we got to work. First laying out a large sheet of plastic, we began bringing in the pakalolo plants. Everyone began breaking off the branches from the main stalks, and piling stacks beside themselves. Then they would take up one branch at a time, hold it at its base and strip off the buds by running forefinger and thumb along it firmly. The stalks and stems would be discarded.

After a few minutes, everyone's thumbs and forefingers would be dark with an accumulation of resin. I would go around the circle scraping it off with the curved blade of a linoleum knife. This resin, later formed into balls, constituted the finest natural essence of the plant, the purest, stoniest high, and we kept them as treats for ourselves and friends.

Kieth and I had put together some drying kilns by gutting old refrigerators and gluing in strips of wood to hold stacks of screened trays. After filling the trays with the green buds and packing the refrigerator full, we would light a one-burner Coleman to stick beneath a hole cut in the bottom. The heat would rise through the screened trays to exit at a hole in the top. Thus, we accomplished in hours what usually took days -- the curing by dehydration.

Then we would bag and weigh them into one-pound ziplocs. Our product, unlike many others, had no throwaway -- seeds and stems. Our pounds were pounds of pure smoke and a customer was not left with thirteen or fourteen ounces after picking out all the stems and seeds.

We took pride in our product, giving good value, and leaving no customer unsatisfied.

These processing sessions were occasions to party. We would provide ice-coolers full of beer, plenty of pupus to snack on, and all the grass you could ingest. They were fun times, we all moving around chatting, flirting, and joking our way through the several routines -- and everybody took home a good stash of our finest.

*****

We began moving into our hideaway, fixing it up and resituating ourselves. We brought our dogs over, began setting out our crop, bagging up the soil-mix at the old digs, hauling them over in pickup and coolie wagon, transplanting from our stock of babies.

We became seriously intimate with each other, totally in accord, with no distractions of others, no wandering eyes or loose and careless fantasies. We brought all our experience to bear on each other, allowed our hearts and minds and bodies to intertwine, rosy and relaxed in our own company, the two parts of our whole barely distinguishable but growing, taking deep root in a single substance.

*****

I sent a hundred pounds to Royal via the Matson Lines container trick. Kieth and I drove another hundred pounds over to Milolii, his jeep able to carry us over the lava to Okoe Bay, where it would be ferried out by rowboat to the Haole Sampan with Henry aboard. He said he was interested in a pound of MDA.

I paid Kieth a share out of the proceeds from Henry. He bought a Colt Woodsman .22 caliber pistol, an AR-180, and an expensive purebred Weimaraner. On the drive back, he was happy, excited, seeing a new future before him.

"You know, Mary thinks she's pregnant. We've been trying to make a kid since we met and took up together over a year ago. I swear, I thought we were never going to make it. We had a bunch of tests -found out I have a low sperm-count. Man, I've always wanted kids, lots of kids, especially sons."

"Hey, man, congratulations." Inside, I didn't know what to think. Poor kids, having a crypto-fascist father, the stern regimentation I could imagine, a quasi-fundamentalist upbringing. On the other hand, Kieth had mellowed out, seemed to become more human, more tolerant. He'd even quit teasing Steph about her untermenschen Jewishness, Deb about the mongrel miscegenation of her racial mixture. He even laughed at some of my awful jokes. Maybe love for a child, his own, would hit him, complete the transformation. Maybe the kid would inherit his asthma and he'd get it started right on pakalolo. Who knows? The future seemed rosy and wide open to possibility.

"You know, you're the best friend I've got in the whole world, Buck. We were on the verge, Mary and I, of asking you to contribute your seed."

"What!"

"Hey, man, what the hell? I think you got good genes, you know? You're Irish, I'm Scotch -- it's in the ballpark. We don't know any Germans."

"You wanted me to fuck Mary, knock her up, so you guys could have a kid?" I was aghast. Fucking Mary would have been okay, but knocking her up? Whoa!

"Sure, she's always liked you. We were in that Morehouse thing, you know, learned a lot. No big thing, the sex bit. It's just a question of making a kid from good stock, you know?"

"Yeah, well, it's all academic now, right? You did it all on your own."

"Yeah, but you were the only one we could think of we'd want to contribute the seed."

I looked away, he doubtless thinking I was moved by his confession, but really to all but shred my lips to keep from being seized by hilarity.

"It's an honor, Kieth," I managed. "I feel really honored, bro."

"Hey, thick and thin, right?"

*****

One morning as Steph was fixing a light breakfast in bra and panties, while I sat in cutoffs over a cup of coffee, the whole house, small as it was, suddenly lurched to one side, then whipped to the other on the resilient reaction of the tree-poles it sat upon. We both wound up on the floor, everything on shelves, counters, and tabletops crashing around us.

"What the fuck!" I blurted, looking at Steph with eyes as wide as hers.

Then we heard a rumble and the whole house began shaking as if seized by a fit of DTs, all the stuff on the floor in a rattle-dance.

"What the fuck!"

"Earthquake, I think," Steph uttered in a soft, breathless voice.

"Shit! Let's get outa here!" I crouched on two legs and one hand as I pulled Steph crawling on her knees out onto the porch. I noticed the dogs had fled from their usual resting place under the house, were both belly-flat to the ground, legs splayed. We made it down the trembling ladder and lurched to join them. We saw the house lurch to the side and whip back again, then stand there trembling. Jesus Christ, I was thinking, any more of that and the whole house is going to be flung off its mounts to crash below. The rumbling sounds and tremors moved up through our prone bodies, me wondering if the earth would split open, swallow us, and close again.

Then it was over, hardly a minute into it, the stillness eerie for a few moments before the dogs were up and barking.

"Oh, now you bark," I accused, put out that they hadn't warned us. Weren't animals supposed to be able to sense these things coming? No, they thought it was a new game we had initiated, grinning and leaping about, waiting for the next move. "Fucking no good lolo ilios!" (Stupid dogs.)

"Jee-zus!" Steph exhaled, half-standing, ready to go down again. "You think it's over?"

"I dunno. I guess." I checked myself. "Well, at least I didn't piss my pants."

"My hero."

Kieth and Mary came by to regale us with their experience, and for several days that was the game -- How it was with me when the earthquake struck, whew!

It seems Kieth and Mary had been in bed, our waterbed, and Mary had just expressed her boredom of the moment, exhorting Kieth to do something to bring a little excitement into their lives -- when the ceiling tiles began falling on them, the bed undulating in waves.

"Gosh, it was better than those vibrating beds you put a quarter in at cheap motels," Mary exclaimed.

"When the ceiling started falling, I thought the whole roof was caving in. All I could think of was Mary and our baby, so I threw myself over her."

"My hero! I thought for a minute it was going to be the wildest sex we ever had!"

And we told them our experience, and then Deb and J.D. came by with Elena to tell us theirs, and we got to tell ours a second time.

"God must have heard me asking you for a little excitement," Mary said.

"Well, yes, I've been known to channel messages both ways."

We were all drinking coffee, passing doobies around, grinning and joking like survivors when I hit the floor with a shout, "Look out! Here it comes again!" Eyes, wide, mouths agape, legs spreading, but nobody hitting the floor, all staring blankly at me lying there like a fool.

"Lucky for you I was joking or we'd all be sitting in the middle of the road now!"

They either had slow reaction times or poor senses of humor...or I hadn't fooled anyone with my foolishness. So I settled down to enjoy myself in the uncommon cheer and affections we were all feeling in the crowded little house.

*****

Kieth was hungrier than I, more ambitious. I had told him about the MDA situation, had seen his eyes light up. He and Royal knew each other. Although he didn't say it in so many words, I could see that Kieth thought I was a fool for dragging my feet on such an opportunity -- which was fine with me. I could see he was eager for a piece of the action and so when I said, "Hey, man, why don't I introduce you into the deal? You can take over my spot, become the Hawaiian King of the Love Drug," it was all he could do to control himself. Kieth was not the type to lose control, to behave spontaneously -- everything had to be considered and planned. He hated surprises.

"Right, okay. What kind of percentage are you going to keep?"

"Nothing. You know the arrangement I have. Anything else is between you and Royal. I'll give you half of my commission on the next sale and introduce you to Sid, let him know. After that, it's all yours."

He nodded. "How does the deal go down?"

"Nothing to it. He'll send word by Scrimshaw -- you've already met him. You call, arrange to meet in Hilo. You deliver the package, collect the money, send Royal his end. That's it."

"Why Hilo?"

I shrugged. "Why not?"

"You should control the meeting ground. What are your security arrangements? What if Sid decides to rip you off?"

"Kieth, c'mon. Sid's a vicious little bastard, but he's not stupid. Why kill the goose that lays golden eggs for him?"

"That's another thing. What if he's setting you up, just waiting for a bigger deal, like a hundred pounds, before making his move? What's to stop him from wasting you?"

"In a public place? That's not too smart."

"You need backup, insurance."

"However you want to do it when it's all yours, that's up to you, Kieth."

"How're you going to work it this time?"

"I'm gonna meet him in the Penny's parking lot around noon, walk over, get in the car with him, make the exchange, get out and walk away."

"Sweet suffering Jesus! That's no good!" Kieth went into his song and dance. The meeting had to be in a remote spot not subject to prearranged surveillance or ambush, which meant we selected it, were first on site to control all approaches. If everything looked kosher, I would go in to make the exchange while he covered me. Anything went wrong, he'd sniperscope the asshole's head right off his shoulders.

"There's a decent scope I can pick up, only eighty dollars. All I got to do is sight it in on the AR-180."

"Forget it. We got an agreement -- no guns. This is business, Kieth, not warfare."

"All business is warfare. These little nigger bastards want to take over the world."

"He's Japanese."

"Same thing. They all want to take the white man's place, make us their slaves, fuck our women, dilute the purity of our superior gene pool, make us degenerate and Godless like them."

"Fuck, Kieth, this is a simple drug deal, not a moral crusade. It's a profit thing, a demand and supply thing, for which you can thank our degenerate government for passing the laws that create black-markets -- all in the name of two-bit morality."

"I know that! Fucking government is going to wind up giving the whole country to the heathen!"

"Hey, what the hell? It's all stolen property anyway. What, you want to save a nation of thieves?"

*****

My pal, Don, my kahuna pakalolo, (Kahuna is a priest or teacher; adept in a certain area. Thus, kahuna pakalolo becomes a master, expert, or teacher, on the subject of marijuana.) was going to Alaska for a high-paying job on the oil pipeline, an adventure from mild climes to the cold of the North. I briefly considered going with him, sure I could find employment with my welding or other construction skills, but my head and heart were firmly fixed on southern isles.

When he told me about it, he informed me that I was his sole inheritor of his share of our joint camps, including the first he'd taken me to for my first lesson, and that in return he sure wouldn't mind taking a supply of MDA along for personal use. I brought him a hundred caps. "For those cold nights in polar bear country," I told him.

"Mahalo, blalah. People keep kidding me about fucking an Eskimo and shooting a polar bear."

"Nah, Don. They got it backwards. You shoot the Eskimo and fuck the polar bear."

"Whatever. Forget the shooting; I'm into the fucking."

"If you can get the bear to take a few of those caps, you'll have no problem."

I also gave him an envelope half an inch thick.

"What's this?"

"Little cushion -- ten grand. I hear things are expensive up there."

"Ah, man, I'm doing all right. We'll make it okay."

"Hey, ol' buddy, you got it coming. Consider it your share from the Papaiiko camp."

"That's still got a couple of more months to go before harvest."

"Well, that takes care of your half right now."

"Ah-ha, okay, aikane. Aloha nui."

"Aloha nui loa, blalah."

*****

Kieth came by in his French jeep to tell me Scrimshaw had brought a message for me to call Sid, and took me out to a payphone in Mountain View. Sid said he and his people were ready for a bigger deal. "How big?"

"Ten."

"Ain't got that much, Sid, not right now. I gotta get in touch with people on the mainland."

"Hey, fuck this, man. We're ready to up the ante and you can't deliver?"

"Not up to me, Sid. I'm just a go-between."

"Well, fuck it. Let's go over and see Royal, you and me. I'll bring bread enough for ten, comp you the whole way. He can introduce me to his partners -- we can work out the details for bigger shipments. This goes good, we'll do fifty next time."

"Let me make a call and see if that's okay."

"Okay. Tell 'im we got cash in hand."

"Right."

"You gonna talk to the man, right?"

"Well, Royal, you know."

"Hey, talk to the man. At least pass the message up the line. No more of this penny ante go-between shit. We're ready for some serious business, okay?"

"Yeah, sure, I'll pass it on."

When I hung up and called Royal, he said, "Wow, sounds good. Only right now's not a good time. I ain't got ten on hand and Lenny's out of town."

"How about Saul?"

"Nah, they both went together -- back to the Big Apple. Be a week or so before they return."

"So, what do you want to do?"

"Put 'em on hold -- nothing else to do."

Sid was pissed. "Fuck, man, the motherfucker told us he could take care of business!"

"Hey, I just pass messages. You guys gotta work it out."

"How the fuck we gonna work it out, we can't even talk face to face?"

He had a point.

"Gimme his fucking phone number, lemme call 'im myself. We gotta get moving on this thing."

"Ah, can't do that, Sid. Let me call him back and ask if that's okay."

"Fuck, man, tell him to call this number! We gotta get this straightened out!"

But when I called back, Royal was out, his girlfriend of the moment sounding abrupt and put out. When I asked when she expected him, she said, "I don't know and I don't give a shit!"

I let Sid rant and rave over the news until he asked how much I had on hand for a quick interim deal. I had a couple ounces short of two pounds and briefly considered throwing in some cut to pad it out. They'd probably never figure out the difference. But fuck that -- I wasn't going to move from a resolve not to sink to the nickel-and-diming, squeezing and padding, petty scuffling shit that too many dealers got into, the short-scamming that sooner or later led to hard feelings, more betrayal, and even violence, a subversion of the true principles of free enterprise, the constant whittling away of the ethics of the trade.

Therefore, knowing Sid was not interested in fractions, I somewhat nobly told him I had only a pound.

"Fuck, shit! Awright, meet me in Hilo tomorrow at noon! Fucking shit! You're gonna keep calling Royal, right, get the fucking message across?"

"Sure, Sid. Same place?"

"Yeah, man, fuck, shit, yeah!"

*****

I turned to Kieth. "You ready for this, man?"

"I'm ready."

"Okay. Tomorrow I'm going to hook you into Sid, give you his number in Honolulu. You already got Royal's. After that, it's all yours, right?"

"Right. How're we going to do the deal tomorrow?"

"You come by an pick me up about eleven. Leave Mary at home. Bring your walkie-talkies. You'll hold the shit while I go meet with Sid in his rental car. When I signal you, drive over and park next to us, pass the bag, and you two can get a look at each other. I'll make the introductions, let him know what's what. Okay?"

"You going to be armed?"

"No, Kieth, I told you -- no guns."

"I don't like it. What if he tries something?"

"Then he gets a free pound."

"He ain't getting no free pounds off me!"

"Fine, Kieth. When you're in charge, run it any way you want. Tomorrow we do it my way -- no guns."

"Okay," he begrudged. "But I still don't like it. I take over, there's going to be some changes."

"Fine, Kieth. You'll be the boss."

*****

When I informed Steph, she wanted to go with me. "No, you're not in on this business. This is the last deal and then I'm out of it."

"I wanna go into town, do some shopping, see some of our friends. We ain't been nowhere in a coupla months. Jeez, lighten up and let's splurge a little. We can spend the whole day in town, go to a restaurant, maybe get in some dancing, ya know?"

"Okay, okay. Make us a plan for tomorrow. I gotta go dig up a pound for that asshole, Sid."

"Good. I'm glad you're out of it. Those two assholes deserve each other."

"Hah? Who?"

"Sid and Kieth. Maybe they'll get married and run off together."

*****

In the morning I gave the pound to Kieth in a paper sack. He put it into a briefcase he'd brought.

"A little less conspicuous," he said with a superior air.

He didn't know that I usually bought a big bag of chips, emptied it out, put the MDA in and added chips over the top, then went to meet Sid like a lummox stumbling around munching on the chips.

"Sure, good thinking. I'm gonna ride in with Steph, meet her later -- we got a few errands."

"Okay. I'll follow you in."

At the mall, Steph parked just off Kilauea Avenue. "You stay here. I'm gonna go in and come out through Penny's to meet Sid. I'll see you in awhile."

"Okay. Be careful."

I kissed her. "You know what to do just in case, right?" "Yeh, yeh, jeez, I don't like to think of that."

"Just in case, babe, you never know."

"Yeh, yeh, I just drive away, wait it out."

"But you don't go home."

"I know, I know. I go stay with Laura or somebody a few days."

"Right -- even over the Kona side would be good."

"What about the dogs?"

"Send somebody else to pick them up. Send a message to Deb and J.D. -- they can walk down and get them."

"Okay, okay, jeez."

Sid was parked way off around the other side near a street running off from Kilauea. He was pacing around alongside the car. When I waved, he nodded and got in to wait for me. "Where's the shit? You got the shit?"

"Yeah, Sid, no sweat," I told him after getting seated next to him.

"Where's it at? Where's it at?"

Was he nervous or still agitated -- in a snit from yesterday?

"Don't sweat it, Sid. First, we gotta talk."

"What? What? You got hold of Royal?"

"No, man, sorry."

"What? Man, what's with those bozos? I'm ready to fly over right now. I'll pay your roundtrip fare. We'll go see 'em, take money."

"Yeah, that's fine, Sid. I think it's all gonna work out. You just gotta be patient."

"Patient, shit! What's the deal?"

"I got this guy. He's hooked into Royal. You're gonna be dealing with him from now on."

"What? Who? What the shit?"

"He'll be here in a minute or two. He's bringing the bag. I'll introduce you."

"What? He came over from the Mainland? From Royal?"

"Yeah, he's gonna live here, be your regular connection. You can work out whatever deal you want with him."

"Okay, okay. Where's he at?"

I pulled out the walkie-talkie, began extending the antenna out the window.

"What's this? What's this?"

"Okay, come on," I said into the handset.

"What the fuck's this?"

"Chill out, Sid. I'm just letting him know. Okay?"

Kieth appeared beside the car on my side, parked the little four-banger jeep, stepped out and handed the briefcase through the window, then leaned down to look in.

"Sid, this is Kieth. Kieth, Sid."

Sid started to reach out a hand, but changed his mind, nodded instead. "Yeah, awright."

Kieth didn't even make the gesture, merely stared. He'd probably have refused to shake had Sid held out his hand, try to intimidate him from the start.

"Get a good look. You guys'll be dealing with each other from now on. I gave Kieth your phone number, Sid. He's in touch with Royal. He knows the setup."

"Yeah, yeah, okay, good."

I waved Kieth away. He got in, drove a hundred feet away, copped a U-turn to park facing us, then very ostentatiously brought a pair of binoculars to his eyes, looking right at us -- another message to Sid. Jeez.

"What the fuck's he doing? What the fuck's he think he's doing?"

"Forget it, Sid. Let's do business." I picked up the briefcase, put it on my knees to open it, clicked the catch.

"Who the fuck's he? What the fuck's he doing?"

I turned my head for a look -- Kieth was still sitting there, his binoculars on us.

"Nothing, man. It's okay."

The briefcase slipped sideways toward the floor, spilling out the paper bag with the MDA in a ziploc and Kieth's Walther P-38. If a Japanese could blanch, Sid blanched.

Oh, shit. Fucking Kieth.

"What the fuck's this! What the fuck's this! I thought we had a deal! No guns! What the fuck!"

I reached down, grabbed the gun by its barrel, stuck it back in the briefcase, snapped it shut, set it on the floor by the door, then picked up the bag to hand him.

"Nothing, Sid. Forget it. It's a mistake."

"Man! Shit, man! This sucks! What's that motherfucker think he's doing?"

"Jesus Christ, Sid! Can we get the show on the road? You want this shit or not?"

"Awright! Awright! I gotta get the bread outa the trunk," he said, quickly stepping out, slamming the door, and walking to the rear. The trunk? That didn't sound right.

The next thing I know, a pimply-faced little asshole is right next to me pointing a gun at my head, screaming, "All right, hold it, you motherfucker, or I'll blow your head off!"

A small army came out of nowhere, shotguns pointing at me through the driver's window and from the windshield in front. The door opened and hands pulled me out, bearing me to the pavement on my back. A shotgun barrel pressed into my stomach and the pimplehead was screaming, "Go ahead, you cocksucker, try something, just try something!" I wondered how he'd take it if I asked him for a hanky to wipe the spray of spittle off my face.

I heard feet running, somebody shouting, "Hey, watch out! He's gonna shoot!"

The guys hovering over me were turning their heads in Kieth's direction, reflexively cowering down. I looked, too. Kieth, doubtlessly believing a ripoff was going down, had leapt out of his jeep trying to get a pistol out of its holster concealed under a windbreaker. He got it out -- the .22 Colt Woodsman -- took aim...and froze. Probably at the police uniforms that some of them wore, and no doubt because of a dozen pistols and shotguns all pointed at him.

In some cases, hesitation is good, but I'll never understand why the cops hesitated. Here they had perfectly good legal cause to blow Kieth to shreds -- which I was sure they were going to do. But they didn't, and after a frozen tableau of a thousand years, Kieth finally relaxed his hand and let the gun fall. Then a guy with a shotgun ran up, drove the stock into Kieth's chest and knocked him down. Another guy kicked and then they were all over him, pulling, pushing, slipping in the odd punch, and handcuffing him.

In a flash, all the excitement over, I was pushed, pulled, cuffed, and in the backseat of a car heading for Hilo Police Station, where we were slammed into a holding cell, both stunned, in shock.

"Jesus Christ," Kieth blurted. "What happened?"

Duh. It was too obvious to deserve a reply. Sid and the pimplehead had both identified themselves as agents of the BNDD. They soon arrived to separate us for interrogation.

"You got one chance, and only one," Sid began with a chickenshit little grin. "You give us Royal and his partners. You help us, we help you."

"Sid, jeez, you really had me fooled. You were such a slimy little cocksucker, I figured there was no way you could be a cop."

"Hey, pal, you better wise up. You're dead and stinking. We got you on film -- you're sewed up, twenty-five or thirty years. Like I said, you work with us, we work with you."

"Tony Cool BNDD, too?"

"He's a Honolulu police officer works with us on loan."

"Tell him he had me fooled. I thought sure he was a pimp."

"You better wise up, asshole."

"Hey, you know as much as I do. You've been in on it from the git."

"Royal's been arrested on the Mainland."

"So, gee, Sid, whaddayou need me for? You got the whole gang."

"Don't try to bullshit me! We know about Lenny and Saul."

"Who?"

"Leonard Bickers and Saul Manowitz. You're one dumb motherfucker, Buck, you know that?"

"Aw, man, just because I didn't graduate high school until I was twenty-one."

"No, you don't get it. We've been after Bickers and Manowitz for over a year. They led us, along with your friend, Royal, to you. We followed the whole crew over here when they came over to party. We got you all on film, the New York guys, the broads, you and your ol' lady. Does she know you were down in Waikiki hiring hookers off the streets?"

Whoa! What the fuck had I stepped into? "Next you're gonna tell me that geek, Scrimshaw's BNDD, too."

"Oh, no. He's just one of our snitches. He tried to sell me and my partner some bogus cocaine. When that didn't work, he tried to rob us. He's got a lot of shit to work off."

Holy fucking hummingbird turds! Talk about revelation! Well, I thought about it -- and I would be doing just that in the next week or so, it made sense, crossed all the Ts and dotted all the Is.

"We know about your grass dealing, too, and your little hash-making operation. We know about your smuggling grass and hash from India and Japan. We know it all, pal."

I noticed he didn't mention my shipping grass to California in Matson Line containers. As to India and Japan, well, that only told me that our creative names and stories were working well.

"We know about your postoffice box in the name of Angus Fairbarn."

"But you didn't find out about my Green Hornet decoder ring, right?"

"We've got a combined task force working this case, FBI, BNDD, and local police, here, California, and New York. We got a raid going on in Hawaiian Fern Acres with search and arrest warrants."

"You mean I been living right in the midst of a bunch of criminals?"

"Yeah, be funny. Stephanie Stearns and Mary Gilbert are two of the names we got on arrest warrants."

"What, don't tell me they been robbing banks again!"

"Aiding and abetting. Your ol' lady was present during two drug sales of MDA."

"You know fucking-a well she's not in on any of this shit."

"Yeah, well, she can tell it to the judge."

I waited.

"Unless you want to get your priorities right. You help us out, she's got a pass. You help us get Lenny and Saul in the bag, we'll go to bat for you."

I thought about it for all of .03 seconds.

"Sid, you gotta quit eating those shit sandwiches. They're what's ruining your chances with the girls -- that is, if you like girls."

Sid looked at his partner when he'd returned from Kieth, who shook his head in the negative.

My cracks didn't bother him at all. He shrugged, gave me another shiteating grin and said, "Yeah, well, think about it while you're sitting in the slam. You want to talk, you got my number. A broad answers, don't worry, she's BNDD, too."

Hello, Hilo Jail.

Kieth was put in a cell on the second floor, while I got the last one on the outer wing of the ground floor. No TV, no radio, nobody to shoot the shit with -- only a barred window without glass to let in the mosquitoes at night. The place even had two fences around the outside with a couple of dozen confiscated pit bulls running loose in between.

That night, by pressing my face to the bars, I could see deputies entering the corridor and carrying many fat green plastic garbage bags, turning to go to the opposite end where they stowed them in an empty cell.

I read about it all in the next day's newspaper. They had found and confiscated hundreds of pounds of pakalolo, a few guns, and arrested a few people. Mary had been arrested. Deb and J.D. had escaped arrest. So had Steph, although they were looking for her. They found her a couple of days later with her hair dyed red.

*****

When a guard brought me a tray of food the next afternoon, he looked me over with a grin.

"Hey, you know a guy named Don?"

"Yeah, he's a good friend of mine."

"Yeah, I know. He told me all about you. I'm his nephew."

"Oh, yeah? Hey, how's it going, bra? You hear from Don? How's he doing?"

"Good. He likes Alaska. Says he's been trying to fuck a polar bear, but they run too fast."

"Probably hell on foreplay, too."

He laughed. "Hey, man, I'm sorry to hear all this bad kuleana you got. Anything I can do? You need anything? Want me to pass any messages, call anyone for you?"

"I could use some cigarettes. I got kala in my property envelope up front."

"No problem. I bring you some in a little while. What brand you like?"

I told him. "What's with all those green bags they were carrying in last night?"

"Oh, that's all the pakalolo they've confiscated. Whole fucking cell's clear full."

"No shit?"

"Yeah. Some of it's premature, you know, but a lot of it is right there, looking good. Hope you don't mind, but I'm going to help myself to a couple of pounds."

"No, hell, feel free."

"I'll bring you a nice top bud, help you pass the time."

"Hey, appreciate that, bra. I could use a few magazines, too, you got anything laying around."

"Sure, no problem."

"You know what's next on the agenda? They going to take me to court or what?"

"Nah, there's no federal court here. They'll probably be taking you over to Halawa Jail in Honolulu in a few days."

"Ah."

"Hey, say hello to my other uncle when you get over there," he said, giving me a name. "He's a sergeant."

"For sure."

"Also, Henry called. He wants to know if there's anything he can do."

"You know Henry, too?"

"Yeah, we're cousins. We Portagees got to stick together, you know?"

"Right on. Tell him to come visit me when I get over there. How'd he know I was in jail?"

"Aw, man, you were on all the TV news last night. The feds are getting a lot of mileage out of this. PR, you know."

"No shit?"

"Yeah, and now they got the BATF (Bureau of Alcohol, Tobacco, and Firearms.) in on it, too."

"Oh, yeah? What the hell for?"

"They found a submachinegun or something, I think. Plus the boobytraps. They're kinda pissed about those."

The M-2 conversion and Kieth's AR-180, which I understood could also be converted to automatic fire. Well, those were on him -- except the guns he'd purchased had been registered to Mary, who had no criminal record. I doubted if they'd found my .45. Then the kid -- he was in his early twenties -- told me a story that had us both laughing.

It seems that one of the narcs, while generally searching the property roundabout our home where Kieth and Mary were living, had tripped the green fishline causing a nearby tree to explode in the skyward blast of a .410 shotgun cartridge. He'd hit the ground believing someone had fired at him and, with leaves and twigs raining down on him, had begun firing wildly into the bushy shadows. Hearing the gunfire, other narcs across the way began firing toward the sounds. It had taken them awhile, all crawling cautiously about, sending and receiving panic messages on their handheld radios, to discover that they'd all been shooting at each other. Then another trip line had been stumbled into and another treetop exploded before they'd figured it all out and called in the BATF who'd found a few more of the untripped gizmos.

Yeah, I could see why they were pissed off. Whoa! I was just glad nobody'd shot anybody or the hot water we were in would have begun boiling.

*****

Fitfully sleeping cocooned in a blanket with my nose through a slit for air in defense of mosquito hordes homing in on fresh food from the open window, some noise awoke me a couple of hours before dawn. I could hear murmurs, sounds of movement. Slapping at the winged pests, I pressed my face to the bars to see figures in aloha shirts and straw hats toting out the fat green sacks of pakalolo.

When I asked my new friend about it, he winked and said, "Aw, probably going to burn it, you know."

"At three in the morning?"

"Hey, no good to waste time, ah?" He grinned before adding, "Or anything else."

Ah, indeed. The pakalolo would be burned, all right, long and slowly -- in thousands of brief flits of flame and ember, all rolled in wee bits of tiny paper oblongs. Unnamed men were filling their pockets on the products of my labors.

"Besides, they left a couple of bags for evidence."

Evidence of what? Against who? Only a few had been charged with marijuana offenses, minor possession of personal stashes, none of the bulk of the grass being legally attributable to anyone.

"How much they get altogether?"

"Gee, about five hundred pounds, I think."

Well, that was fresh grass weight. When it was cured, it would come out to less than half that. Still. Bastards were worse than thieves! Smarter, too!

*****

Steph, Mary, Kieth, and I were all transported over to Honolulu and booked into Halawa Jail. When we appeared on arraignment before a federal magistrate, we were handed indictments and informed that our bail was set for each at ten thousand dollars. My indictment, of course, was the lengthiest, containing seven or eight charges, including using a telephone to facilitate the commission of a felony. When I added up all the sentences it was possible to receive, it came out to thirty-seven years.

*****

Bail was my first thought, of course. I could get us all out for ten percent of the total bail amount deposited in cash with the clerk of the court -- which meant I had to consider who I trusted enough to go dig up one of my hermetically sealed ammo boxes. I had about settled on Frank or Barbara or both in the few days spent considering those who had phone numbers and were relatively close to my stashes. Following my directions, they could dig up one, take out the necessary funds with enough to fly it over to Honolulu.

"See, just go to our house and head out toward the outhouse, but when you pass the backside pace off about ten steps, then go left to a mound about five feet high, the other side of which contains a crack in the lava filled over with dirt. Or, go up Pikake from the entrance road to the third rise in the road, park and go right to a triangle formed by three Ohia trees a few feet into the bush where a mound of baseball-sized lava chunks..."

With Ohia trees, loose chunks of lava, cracks in the ground all over the place, the roads all undulating up and down, it might take months to find my little treasures!

Well, maybe I could talk Frank into putting up a grand to get me out, and then I could go do the necessaries to get the others out. Henry sent me an ounce of pakalolo delivered by a friendly sergeant in a hollowed-out book to raise me out of the doldrums of my long, long thoughts. It was a history of Hawaii. Except for a few pages in its opening and closing, it was all a mystery to me.

Then, suddenly, we were all standing outside the courthouse, Stephanie the only one grinning, we other three with startled, half-believing looks on our faces.

"My Aunt Momi," Steph explained. "She gave me ten grand, got us all out. I still got six grand left in my purse. You up for a pizza and beer? My treat."

Munching and sipping away, I asked why.

Steph shrugged. "She read about us, saw it all on TV. You know Momi. She thinks all drug laws are insane. She likes me, you too. I was a favorite of my uncle's before he passed away. Besides, he left her a lot of money."

Momi had a house in Honolulu, a big one with a swimming pool, another in Toronto, a very hip and rich lady of Hawaiian-Chinese ancestry who'd been the love of a man who'd done very well for himself, including building a polynesian village center that was a great commercial success and popular tourist attraction.

We had visited her a couple of times when she'd been in residence in Honolulu. She'd even come to visit us once, but had been permanently cured by the necessity of having to use our primitive bathroom facilities. We had enjoyed a few hours of humor-filled conversation with her paele mahu (Black homosexual.) traveling companion.

"She figured we might need the rest for a lawyer. She gave me a name -- Brook Hart."

After renting a hotel suite, bathing off the patina of jail, getting our sex lives up to date, we went to see Mr. Hart. He was sharp, a fixer type, dressed expensive, a long sharp-nosed face, thinning on top, handsome, personable.

The five of us talking it over in his office, he cut to the bone. "Okay, here's what I can do. First, the charges against the ladies are dismissed, but only if you two guys cop a plea to one substantive count."

"What's the max?"

"Five years."

"What if we fight it?"

"Then you all go to trial and it costs you a whole lot more.

I can get the ladies off, no problem, but you and Kieth are dead in the water -- no way out, technical or otherwise. They got you and Kieth in the act, both armed. You're lucky you're not dead. Plus, they got you on film and tape-recorded phone calls, Buck."

"You can guarantee the charges against Steph and Mary will be dismissed?"

"Yeah. They only brought them to put pressure on you guys to turn snitch."

"Okay. How much?"

"Eleven thousand, and I need some earnest money."

"Two grand do?"

"That's fine."

Steph?"

She counted out twenty C-notes.

"Oh," he said. "One more thing. This MDA, what is it? I've never heard of it."

I rattled off the chemical name I'd gotten from Lenny, and told him the essentials.

"Can you get me a sample? I want to have it analyzed, make sure it's actually illegal and all."

"Sure. You mean it might not be?"

"It's a longshot. MDA is definitely proscribed in the drug laws. But, from what you tell me about this mysterious chemist, maybe he changed a few molecules around. Who knows?"

"I'll get a sample to you."

"Way you describe it, the stuff sounds good. Any bad side effects?

"No. Only if you take too much."

"How much is too much?"

"I'll send it in individually measured doses -- capsules."

"How about addiction potential?"

"Maybe psychological. Otherwise, none."

"Okay, fine. Let's get the ball rolling."

Hm, I was thinking, he seemed very interested in the Love Drug itself. Well, perhaps I should send over plenty of sample.

"One question," I said, turning to him as he was ushering us out. "Can you drag this thing out as long as possible, postponements, all that?"

"Sure, no problem. A year or so do you?"

"Fine. Nice meeting you."

"Keep in touch."

*****

Back on the Big Island, we surveyed the damage. Our 600-plant plot was devastated, but our baby-planter, containing a hundred or so cups with newly planted seedlings had survived discovery. The little house Steph and I had shared was a mess. So was our house on Lehua, the one Kieth and Mary had been living in. Only my Colt .45 and the Papaiiko plot, which was outside of Hawaiian Fern Acres, had made it through. As to my ammo boxes, I hadn't yet gone to dig them up -- only checking that there was no hole dug up near the house. Kieth and Mary knew nothing about them and I wanted to wait for an opportunity when they were absent.

In a few days, while I contemplated starting over from scratch, was considering all the pluses and minuses of the situation, Kieth informed me that he and Mary were moving over to Honolulu.

"They got a Morehouse over there. With our experience, we can fit right in to the system. We've already made arrangements. Brook got my jeep released, so we'll have wheels."

"Sure, man, whatever you want."

"Problem is we're hurting on the money side. Think you can make us a loan to see us through?"

"Yeah, sure. When you leaving?"

"Soon's we can get it altogether. What're you going to do?"

If he was out of it, no use explaining -- gonna have to play the cards a little closer from now on. "I dunno. Gonna have to look around, check things out."

"You know it's no good out here in the Acres, huh? They've got it scoped."

"Yeah, probably. You wanna gimme a hand loading our camper onto the pickup? We're gonna do a little trucking."

"Sure, man. Boy, that fucking Royal sure fucked up a good thing with that MDA."

Royal had been arrested in California and made bail. I figured what with his getting himself a lawyer and Lenny and Saul probably cutting him loose from the MDA connection, it was going to be a long cold day in hell before I saw any of the thirty grand he owed me on the pakalolo shipment.

"What, babe," Steph asked. "What're we gonna do?"

"First, give a grand to Kieth and Mary. They're outa here."

"Yeh?"

"Then we pack up our trucking gear and the mutts, hit the road."

"Where we going?"

"Find a spot for the babies we got left."

"Oh, yeh, where?"

"Anywhere out of the Acres."

"Then what?"

"You wanna quit, too?"

"Naw, baby, I'm in for the long haul."

"Maybe we go over the Kona side, visit Rick and some other people, help 'em with their new house in Kamuela."

"Yeh, that'd be nice."

"Relax a little, start making a new plan."

"What?"

"Think sailing. Maybe it's time to start looking for a boat."

"Yeh? Gee. What about all this shit we're in?"

"We'll work on that, too. Only one thing, babe."

"Yeh?"

"I ain't gonna stand up and take no five years in prison. Okay?"

"Yeh, right," she said with a frown, working on it. "But how're we gonna...?"

"We'll work on it. First things first. We got some time to figure something out."

"Whew, yeh! What a fucked up coupla weeks this's been. Can it get any worse?"

"You know what they say -- when you touch bottom, there's only one way to go."

###

CHAPTER 11

After Keith and Mary had left for Honolulu, we spent the next week or so putting out our babies in a remote section of virgin rainforest, dividing them into two separate plots. We would abandon them to the mercies of mother nature and hope for the best.

Deb and J.D. were moved into the Iron Butterfly with Elena for a few days until they could replace Steph and I in our house when we departed. We were about to become gypsy wanderers again and had been working at packing up our Datsun camper. I had bought a secondhand cabin tent of ten-by-twelve feet for the purpose of being able to take up squatter's rights more comfortably. Steph had gone into Hilo with Deb, J.D., and Elena, for a last shopping run. We would be on our way the next morning.

Lo stopped by, a rueful grin on his face and a bottle of okolehao in his hand.

"Buck, my friend, you fucked up."

"Yeah, Lo, hey, tell me about it."

Seated across from each other over the cable-spool table, sipping and toking, he said, "Buck, Buck, I thought you were an akamai kanaka, (Smart man) but it turns out you're another lolo okolepuka. (Dumb asshole.) You got this beautiful property, this nice cozy house, a good woman, even these fine ilios. (Dogs) You got, well, you had, a nice pakalolo business. Everybody knows you likes you...well, except for a few okolepukas and they don't count. You had it made, my friend, and you fucked it off."

"That's okay, Lo, rub my nose in it."

"You deserve it! Oh, you made me so huhu (angry) when I hear all this kaka (shit) going down!"

"Yeah, I know, it's okay, Lo. I deserve it. I fucked up."

"You fucked up big time! You got the fucking feds on your ass! You got all those assholes coming over here, snooping around, making pilikia (trouble) for everybody! Nobody likes the feds. As long as you stuck to the pakalolo, nobody cared. That's local business. We understand. We tolerate. A little gambling, a little grass, a few pills here and there, who cares? But this MDA shit, you know, bringing all those Mainland people over here, getting involved in a sophisticated multistate drug operation, getting the feds on your ass, are you fucking lolo?"

"I'm fucking lolo," I admitted contritely.

He threw up his hands. "Ah, my friend, what the fuck you going to do? There's too much heat now. We can't even have the cockfights no more until things quiet down."

"Yeah, I'm sorry, Lo. I know I fucked up bad."

"Well, two or three months, things will get back to normal."

"You think?"

"Yeah, as long as you don't make no more waves. Those fucking boobytraps, man! You got some people pissed off at you."

I rolled my eyes, accepted it.

"That fucking haole okolepuka you had out here, he was a mistake, really bad news."

"Well, he's gone now."

"Yeah, I know. Good fucking riddance. The guy was pupule, (crazy) a real nutcase. I got his rapsheet. How the fuck you get involved with him?"

I hesitated, then decided. Lo wasn't dumb. He probably had my rapsheet, too. "Met him in prison."

"Where? California?"

"Yeah, San Quentin."

"What were you in for?"

"A chickenshit robbery."

"I already knew that. But, you know, you haven't had any more convictions for almost twenty years. I figured you'd smartened up, learned to slip and slide, not get too greedy. You're a good guy, Buck. I like you. You're my friend. I really liked the way you handled those fucking grass thieves. That was a class act. Most guys would have done something a whole lot cruder. You were being very smart then."

"Yeah. I seem to have my ups and downs."

"Well, get your ass up and stay up! What are your plans?"

"Gonna get on the road, disappear for a while, keep a low profile."

"Where?"

I shrugged. "Somewhere along the Kona side probably."

"Okay, that's good. It's quiet over there. I'll give you a couple of names, some good people. I'll let them know you're coming."

"Thanks, Lo, I appreciate it."

"Also, spread the word that you're going to Maui or Molokai or Kauai. That'll relieve some folks, mislead others, it'll work out better, yeah?"

"Yeah, sounds good."

"You got another name you can use? Buck, you know, everybody knows that name."

"Yeah, maybe I can come up with something." I was remembering that I used to kid around with Don, my kahuna, and I'd taken to calling him the Great Kahu, taking the first two syllables of the word rather than the second two as was usual in forming the diminutive. Some locale pronounced my last name as Waka, which mean sharp, protruding, a bright flash -- yeah, man! I would become Kahu Waka, but to further confuse the issue, I would spell my last name Oaka, which was pretty close to the same in pronunciation. Kahu Oaka.

"Okay, good. When you leaving?"

"Tomorrow."

"You take care of yourself, Buck, and that fine wahine you got."

"For sure, Lo. Listen, hang on a minute, huh? I gotta go get something."

"Okay, sure."

I wended my way on unsteady feet into the bush, retrieved one of my ammo boxes ready for last minute loading, brought it back into the house. Lo watched me open it. I took out one of the two pounds of primo pakalolo and handed it to him, quickly closing and sealing the box. Underneath the second pound lay almost a pound of MDA, a baggie full of dried magic mushrooms, another full of peyote buttons, some Parest 400s and Black Beauties. Last but not least, almost eighteen grand in C-notes.

"Little personal stash, Lo. The assholes didn't get it all."

"Hey, all right. Everytime I smoke this stuff, I'll think of you."

"One more thing."

"Hah?"

I went over to the bar counter, let him watch me pull out a wooden peg from the bottom of a picture frame, then swing it up to reveal my hidey-hole for the Colt .45. I took out the clip, cocked and locked the breech open, handed them to him.

"Hey, nice serious piece of work, Buck."

"Yeah, got it from a Marine buddy. I don't want to pack it around with me. Don't want to leave it behind either. The kid who's going to be living here, he's kinda lolo, you know -- probably shoot his foot off."

"You ever use it?"

"Nah, just to make sure it worked. Only kept it for any assholes might wanna bust in, kick my ol' lady and fuck my dogs, you know?"

He grinned. "Yeah. You know that hippy couple lives in that little shack way down toward the end of Pikake?"

"Oh, yeah. Space cadets, but harmless."

"Yeah. Couple of assholes broke in on them looking for drugs and money. All they had was pocket-change and a few joints."

"Yeah?"

"They're nice kids. I felt sorry for them, used to take by a bag of groceries once in a while, you know?"

"Yeah. They're all right."

"Fucking assholes pistol-whipped them, fucked them up. They made it down to the Filipino's place, he gave them a ride into Hilo Hospital."

"Goddamned motherfucking cocksucking sonsofbitches! You know who they are?"

"No, not yet. But we got good descriptions. The wahine's an artist. She drew us some nice pictures."

"You find out who they are, send me word, Lo. You and me, we'll go fix their hash."

"No, my friend. I'll take care of this one, don't worry." "Maybe I oughta leave the piece for J.D., give him a few more lessons."

"No, no, Buck. The kid's a dipshit. I'll look in on them from time to time."

"Anybody ever hurts Deb or Elena, all bets a re off, Lo -- I'm gonna fuck 'em up!"

"Just calm down, Buck. Let me handle it. You keep your head down, don't make no pilikia. I can fuck them up legally, you know? Resisting arrest or something. I'll look after your people here. I'm going to get those two assholes, too -- bet on it."

"Okay, Lo. I trust you. Aloha."

We embraced. "Aloha nui, aikane."

*****

The next morning, we loaded Popolo and Sista into the camper, along with an ice-cooler of beer and food. We were ready to hit the road. Puffer, the specially privileged mutt, would ride in front with us. We kissed and embraced, said goodbye, then whizzed down the gravel road. I had a million things on my mind -- where we were going, what we were going to do, the MDA I was going to unload, a return trip to harvest the Papaiiko pakalolo camp, whether our two new hidden stashes would survive on their own, looking around for a boat, the legal situation, and berating myself for all my mistakes, getting involved with Royal and Kieth and all the shit they'd brought, having to leave my home, the uncertainty ahead. Asshole, asshole, asshole, I muttered inwardly to an image of myself with one foot in his mouth, the other up his ass.

"It's sad to be leaving," Steph said.

"Yeah."

Then she brightened. "What say to one last fuck before we go?"

"Hah?"

"You know, get the aloha spirit -- make love."

"Here? Now? In the front seat?"

"Nah. Stop somewhere. We'll find a nice spot."

I looked around. "Where?"

"Anywhere. Right here. It's all nice."

I parked. We got out, leaving Puffer in the cab. Popolo and Sista were up sniffing and wruffing out the side grill. We held hands to make our way through some woods, found a grassy clearing, sat to cuddle, kiss, and smoke a joint.

"How ya feel, baby?"

"Ah, okay, I guess."

"Bummed, huh?"

"Yeah."

"C'mon, let me make you feel better."

I was game. I tried. Then I tried harder, beginning to feel a bit desperate. It was no use. John Thomas was off duty until further notice. I was crestfallen, ashamed.

"What's the matter, babe?"

"I dunno. Fucking thing don't wanna cooperate!"

"Lemme help."

But it was no use. Jesus! Become a priest, live in a womanless monastery?

"It'll be all right, baby. Don't worry. It happens, ya know?"

"Yeah."

We made our way back to the Datsun, me dejected, Steph commiserating.

"Hell of a way to start a new life."

"Nah, we ain't started yet. We're still ending the old one, ya know?"

"Fucking limpdickitus!"

"Ain't it the pits!"

We got in, started up, began moving. "Okay," I said. "You're right. We hit the highway, we start our new lives. I got a new name."

"What?"

"Kahu."

"Kahu? The Great Kahu?"

I tried to grin. "Yeah."

"So who'm I? I got a new name, too?"

"Yeah. You're Kekepania."

"Kekepania?"

"Yeah," I said, ad-libbing it. "Alii Kekepania."

"Alii, I know that word. Royalty, right? The kings and queens, the princes and princesses. What's Kekepania?"

"Your name, Stephanie. The Great Fucking Stephanie, queen of my heart."
"How about a little Credence Clearwater, babe? Get off on the right foot? "
"Yeah."
Workin' ever' night an' ever' day, big wheel keeps on turnin'.

*****

In Kailua Town we met one of Steph's girlfriends who rented a house a half mile or so out along the main road, across from which lay a lovely beach. After beer and buds with she and her boyfriend, a light supper, music and conversation into a late hour, they invited us to spend the night in their driveway. We couldn't miss the party they were throwing the following evening.

Most of the next day we spent at the beach, frolicking with the mutts. Popolo was a true water dog. He followed me everywhere. When I went bodysurfing, he was right beside me. We played. In deep water, I would dive down out of his sight while he paddled in circles above baying for my return. Sometimes he would stick his head under the water to look for me, and would follow along the surface if he saw me swimming away. The longer I was out of sight the greater the intensity of his anxious harooing.

That evening at the party, which had spilled out into the spacious backyard, we met a girl whose father owned the centrally located Kona Steakhouse, the classiest dinnerhouse with bar and lounge in town. She told us the liquor license had been suspended for six months and so it remained closed down.

Ah, did my nostrils detect the faint aroma of opportunity? I remembered the private bottle club Samantha and I had opened in Marin County for the exclusive use of our QCS tenants. In this case, while there was no existing private membership, mightn't a case be made for a public bottle club? Instead of selling liquor, the customers could bring their own bottles and we could sell them setups, glasses, ice, and mixers, much as I had seen in Texas so many years before when I'd passed through. We could still operate the restaurant end of the business. But why should customers come to the Kona Steakhouse to be so inconvenienced when it came to ordering beer or wine with their food, have to bring their own bottle for a drink in the lounge? Well, there had to be some attraction that would cause them to overlook the inconvenience.

What?

There were a lot of young people in Kailua Town, all looking to party and have fun. We still existed in the age of rock'n'roll. Could we find a really good earthshaking getdown boogie band?

A great keyboard guy named Teddy Ginn, whom we'd met here and there and got our heads right together, was at loose ends looking for some action. He knew other musicians. Why not?

The problem was that in order to put it together properly, I would have to assume the center of attention, which I was loath to do. I not only had to keep my head low, but I also didn't want to get stuck into an enterprise that required my management, which could be a real headache. I had previously managed restaurants and had no desire for a reprise. My primary mission was to find a proper boat that would carry me away from the islands. Still. Why let the idea go entirely to waste?

I channeled it through Steph, who ran it by her girlfriend, the two of them sitting down to try it out on the owner's daughter. After a week of playing with the idea, discussing it up one side and down the other, and sounding out Teddy Ginn for a commitment, the girl approached her father. He said okay, she could play around with it until the liquor license was restored -- but she had to change the name of the place.

Steph came up with the idea that it be called Boogie Hawaii, and we built a gaudily painted sign to hang over the old name above the entrance. By then, it was a more or less communal enterprise, attracting the interest of friends, and the project had assumed a momentum of its own. I merely offered suggestions through Steph when they ran into problems.

We had erected our cabin tent in the backyard and had settled in to join in the fun. Steph and I, along with Fat Charlie Chieu, a jolly fellow who had connections at the nearby harbor for fresh fish, would run the lunch operation, mainly sandwiches and salads, which we would serve in a beautiful outdoor setting. The Kona Steakhouse had a lovely garden out back in a fenced-off area, flagstone steps around landscaped fishponds, and gazebo-like covered seating areas with wrought-iron and raffia-laced chairs and tables. We might even offer a joint to certain customers in aid of tuning up their taste buds.

The lunch trade was quiet and lazy. The supper trade had been cancelled altogether as too complicated. It would be replaced by the serving of pupus when our party-goers got the munchies. Even with a cover charge no one would make very much money, but that wasn't the point. Boogie Hawaii would be a hangout, a few bucks to get by for participants, and a great way to spend the summer. We were going to provide a place to boogie, baby, the in-place to be.

We all made psychedelically colored posters announcing the grand opening, which was not up to snuff. People didn't quite understand the idea of a bring-your-own-bottle joint. Okay, a few would act as runners to take a customer's money for a quick jot to the nearby liquor store -- where I had already made a deal for some kickback. We had shills passing out our handbills. Teddy had put together a great and versatile band. Still, movement was slow and discouragement began to mark the faces of our group.

The place had heavy wide shutters over large screened but pane-less openings along one side. I got a couple of guys to go open them while I stopped to have a word with Teddy.

"Also open the front door, the back door, the emergency fire exit, and every fucking window you can find."

I turned to Teddy, who was beginning to droop. "Little snort of coke would go good about now," he opined.

"Open your mouth, Teddy."

"What?"

"Open, man, open." I threw in a cap of MDA. "That'll get your ass in gear, Teddy, trust me. Now crank up the amps, man. We want bigtime sound, you dig? Go to the floor with it, man. We gotta get some people in here, get this joint to jumping."

I took a walk to see how far away the music could be heard. It was a fine sound with a heavy beat, a good rhythm. It could be heard two blocks away. I watched heads turning, curious and interested, looking for the source. What was happening? By the time I got back, Boogie Hawaii was jam-packed. People were waiting in line. They were in the street, clapping in time to the music. Some were dancing. The aroma of good grass wafted about. A few local cops were looking things over, but they'd caught the mood, too. We hired one of them as our off-duty bouncer in case any trouble popped up. It never did. Sweet duty if you could get it. Inside, the dance floor was packed with wildly gyrating couples. We were a hit.

I gave Fat Charlie a pocketful of MDA caps to hustle. We would split the money. Fat Charlie was the most upbeat, funny, sociable, dancingest fool of a four hundred pound man I'd ever met. He knew everybody and they all loved him. He could roll up to a table of unattached tourist girls, con them into a tequila-drinking contest, get them guiltily passing joints around, toss

MDA caps in their mouths, dance the legs off them all, and leave them laughing. Fat Charlie was a happily married family man. We became great friends, getting our heads together to work deals, turn a few bucks.

"Da love drug good, blalah, but need moah pakalolo," he said with a grin you could fit a canoe into. "Can move da kine all night long."

"Don't worry, aikane," I assured him. "Bumbai, I git one little paka patch ready foah harvest."

"No shit? Git?" "No shit. Git."

*****

"Time to hit the Hilo side, babe. Gotta check on the Papaiiko patch," I told Steph.

"Good. I wanna check those babies we put out."

"No, babe. You gotta stay and run the lunch thing with Fat Charlie. He'll come by in his van to get you to work and back."

"Aw, baby."

"I'll check the other stash, too. Plus, I gotta see about putting some new ID together."

"How ya gonna do that?"

"I dunno. I'm gonna see Frank, a couple of other people, ask around."

"You going to the Acres?"

"Not if I can help it. Why?"

"I thought maybe you could get J.D. and Deb to work on sprouting another hundred cups. We could put them out someplace, too, ya know?"

"Good idea. I'll swing by, see how they're doing."

"I'll miss ya, baby."

"Keep checking the boat ads. We gotta get something going."

"Yeh, okay."

Since Papaiiko was on the way, I did that first, parked on a back lane of the canefield and made the hike up the little mountain. Shit, only about forty plants had survived and they were looking ragged. Must have had a mean storm early on to do that much damage, I thought. I harvested, hung them up to dry in the hot sun, and spent the rest of the day and night beerless, teasing my thought processes with no more than coffee and pakalolo fumes.

Tomorrow, I would pack the twenty-five or thirty surviving pounds down to the Datsun, stop in to see Frank, then hit the airport for what I hadn't told Steph. Momi's gift of ten grand was eating at me. It had been very decent of her to do that, but I had to pay her back, let her know I appreciated it. Steph would only argue. She had no problem accepting family money, but her family wasn't mine and there was no way I'd play poor stepchild.

Frank was out but Barb was home with her daughters. We spent a couple of hours playing Monopoly. Then, while the girls were out in the patio feeding their cat, I put it to Barb to ask Frank about ID.

"You want ID?"

"Yeah, I'm hotter than a firecracker right now. I need a new name, some ID to go with it, maybe a passport."

"I've got my husband's old ID, drivers license, Social Security card, birth certificate, his old military ID, the works. He'll never need it."

"Let me see it."

She showed me. "He got any kind of a criminal record?"

"No, not really. A few misdemeanors."

"That's okay. Driver's license is no good, but I could use the birth certificate and Social Security card."

"Take them. Does this mean you're going to be my husband?"

I grinned. "We can pretend if you want, but I'm really not too much into wedded bliss. I look forward to playing house with you someday, though."

She sighed. "Me, too."

"How's things with you and Frank?"

"Oh, okay, I guess. Same old same old. We're restrained from screaming and throwing things at each other by the kids. Why bum them out?"

"I gotta go. Tell Frank I said hi."

"Yeah. Thanks for the pound. Where'd you import it from this time?"

"Africa. It's called Kilamanjaro Kickapoo."

"I love you."

"Me, too."

"If this is what they call platonic love, it sucks."

"Ain't nothing platonic about it. Too much lust involved."

I headed for the airport with the kisses of three lovely ladies drying on my cheeks.

*****

"Hi, Momi."

"Buck, come in, come in. Where's Stephanie? Is everything all right?"

"Yeah, fine. She stayed behind this time. Private business between me and you."

"What?"

"I wanted to say thanks for the ten grand. It got us all out of jail in a hurry. I appreciate it. Also, thanks for putting us on to Brook Hart. He's doing a good job. Steph's going to come out clean on that one."

"What about you?"

"I'm going to cop to one count. It's the best I could do. It's not so bad."

"You came all the way over here just to say this?"

"No. I came to repay you the loan." I slid an envelope across the coffee table.

"It wasn't a loan. You don't have to pay it back. It was a gift."

"For Steph, it was a gift. For me, it has to be a loan. I don't mean to insult you. If Steph had stuck it in her bank account or something, no problem. But she spent it on getting us all out of trouble, which I was responsible for. You see what I mean?"

She studied me. "Yes, I think so. You're talking about independence and self-respect, aren't you?"

I nodded. "Your husband, he must have been a hell of a guy. Steph's told me a lot about him."

"He was. Life's not the same without him."

"I brought you a little interest, too," I added, taking out a pound package and sliding it across. "Token of my appreciation." She smiled. "Mahalo."

"I gotta go."

"You know, we all used to worry about Stephanie. I think You're the first decent relationship she's had with a man."

"Well, I happen to think highly of her. She's got the biggest heart of any woman I've ever known. We're a team."

"Don't be a stranger. You're always welcome."

"Thanks, Momi." We embraced and kissed.

She held me, looked up at me. "You're ever in trouble, you ever need help, you know you can come to me, don't you?"

"Yeah, Momi, I'm grateful. You're a real peach."

Deb and J.D. weren't in so I left them a note.

The two plots of our secret stash of babies hadn't survived. They'd all succumbed to a lack of water, naught left but the wilted and dried remains of their poor bodies. It hadn't rained for something like six weeks on the Hilo side. Well, the bags were still in place. Maybe we could replant them.

*****

Fat Charlie was ecstatic over the pakalolo.

"It needs a couple more days of curing in the sun."

"No pro'lum. I take care a dat. I need some moah da love drug."

"Okay, we'll get together, cap some up."

*****

Sundays were slow.

"Steph, darlin'," I whispered in my honey's ear. "Pass the word. Sundays we let down our hair. We open all the doors and windows for a free-for-all jam session. Forget cover charges. This is for fun, for the salvation of our souls. Everybody gets their head right. Everybody boogies down. This is Hawaii and it's a boogie kind of summer. Forget the food part. Everybody lives on booze, grass, and music all the livelong fucking day, sunrise to sunset."

"Baby, people go to church here. We don't wanna make 'em mad at us."

"Oh, right," I amended. "Okay, we go from noon to midnight, after church's over."

"Yeh, that's better."

Sundays became monsters, the joint jam-packed and spilling into the back garden, in the alley, the street in front, on the seawall just across the street fronting the bay and boat harbor. Musicians, singers, and bands lined up so long we had to put together an ad hoc scheduling committee. The word was getting out. Several big names were flying over from Honolulu nightclubs to join in the action -- George Benson, Harmonica Red, some local stars, some slumming moneyed people, fine fucking women. Boogie Hawaii was the place to be on Sundays, where the action was, and it would go on through the summer.

Fat Charlie was hustling the Love Drug and ounces of specially imported Bogata Buds, secret compliments of yours truly, the undercover man.

*****

Days found Steph and I, if we didn't go to the beach in the mornings before opening the lunch operation, down at the small boat harbor on the way to the airport, lending a spontaneous hand to haulouts and launchings via the ramp descending into the water, getting into conversations with sailors, checking sailboat ads and following leads.

Jim Leatherman, the eccentric old one-legged character, regaled us with tales of his worldly adventures. He had lost his leg while attempting to row from Bombay, India, to Mogadishu, Somalia.

"Heard them black girls could fuck your foreskin off." "So, what happened?"

"Fucking boat got swamped in a storm, had to swim for it. Took me three days to reach land. Fed the fishes my fucking leg!"

"What, a shark?"

"Naw, fucking infection when I banged it up on the reef. Sucker swelled so big it looked like a fat pig ready for roasting! Fucking doctor was a witch-doctor, couldn't read or write a lick! He sawed it off and tossed it in a river that ran to the sea."

"Well, Jim," I pointed out the obvious, the nineteen-foot beautifully proportioned deep-keel, high-aspect rigged sloop he'd been working on for months. "You got a nice little boat there ought to get you anywhere you want to go."

"Damn right. I made a fucking poodle into a bulldog, thickened the hull, added ballast, beefed up the rigging on the mast."

"How'd you thicken the hull?"

"Got a good ol' boy out here with a fiber-resin gun, laid me a quarter-inch over the original pussy stuff. Fucking boat was made for Sunday fair-weather sailors! I made her into a trucker, magicopresto!"

"Where you headed with her?"

"Was going to Palmyra, but that's still fucking America. Changed my plan for Suvarov. It's an atoll. Got coconut trees, all the fucking fish you can eat just waiting to leap into a frying pan. Even got a vegetable garden and a shack left by an old hermit. I'm staking her out and taking over! King James, the First, of Suvarov!"

"Where the hell's it at?"

"'Bout eight hundred miles south of the equator. Here, here's a book you can read all about it -- last guy was there so many years."

<u>An Island to Myself</u>, by Tom Neale. "They got people there? Villages?"

"Nope. Occasional yachties passing through, just enough rich suckers to hustle when times are slack and slow."

"Protected anchorage?"

"Oh, hell yeah. Whole fucking lagoon, surrounded by reefs, nice passages through though."

"Fresh water?"

"Brackish water in a well in a pinch. Otherwise, ought to be plenty of rainfall."

"Sounds good."

"Well, say there, young fella, you look young and strong. You handle a belt-sander?"

I grinned, knowing what was coming. "Sure. I been known to work in the construction trades."

"How about a few hours work on that hull? Fiber-resin composition left 'er kind of rough."

"What's the pay?"

"Pay? I'm a poor one-legged cripple hand-to-mouthing it on a minuscule disability pension, barely getting by on my charm and good looks!"

"I ain't no fucking communist and I don't believe in welfare. Now, make me a serious offer, I'll help prettify your toy boat there."

"Toy boat? Why, you big asshole, that boat'll take me anywhere I want to go, even Ant-fucking-arctica!"

"That don't sound like no offer I ever heard."

"All right. I'll tell you the biggest fucking lies you ever heard in your chickenshit humdrum life! I'll supervise and give you some champion fucking lies the whole time you're working. I'll even hold the electrical cord and give you some expert advice. I oughta charge you! I keep lying, you keep working. You catch me in a dull lie or running the same one by you twice, you can quit."

"Hm," I pondered, considering. Guy knew how to make an offer.

"I'll even throw in a tour of the world through my sailing directions, smarten your ignorant ass up."

"Your what?"

"World Sailing Directions, boy. Better than a Monkey Wards catalog. Show you Palmyra. Show you Suvarov. Show you Tahiti. Every fucking island and harbor in the whole fucking world. You want to be a sailorman, boy? You came to the right fucking man!"

I worked four hours in the hot sun listening to a line of bullshit nine miles long, Steph the while supplying us with cold beers. Then we smoked a couple of joints and engulfed a large bag of Fritos with dill pickles.

"C'mon, I'll give you your first lesson."

"Tomorrow. We gotta go to work now, a job in town."

"What the hell you do?"

"Get yourself down to Boogie Hawaii, there's a free sandwich and beer for you."

"Boogie Hawaii? What the fuck's that?"

"Ask anyone, they'll point you the way. Food for the stomach, food for the soul."

"You ain't trying to trick me into church, are you?"

"Can you dance on those fucking crutches?"

"Dance? I got a wooden leg for that, not that I fucking need it!"

"Yeah, well, bathe and shave yourself, iron the wrinkles outa them wino's pants, and pay us a call."

"Ain't nothing worth all that!"

"Lot's of pretty girls there."

"Yeah? Well, maybe I can reschedule my appointments."

*****

We missed one Sunday to drive up the coast to the harbor at Kawaihae to check out a boat ad. We met Joel Peters, who was trying to sell a thirty-four foot trimaran called Ladybug. I recognized it right away as a Piver design. I had read a book by Arthur Piver, the father of the trimaran in the 60s, but was a little suspicious when he disappeared at sea while testing his theory that he could surf a thousand miles on the open ocean faster than any other sailboat ever made. Catch the downside of a wave, set your sails just right to keep ahead of the crest, and away you go. Trouble was, they capsized there was no righting them -- you went from a saucy yacht to a raft in one little flip. Still, they were great shallow water craft, fast, and provided a nice platform with high initial stability, great for getting over reefs at high tide into lagoons that had no ship's passage through them. They were light enough, you could winch them up on a beach where there were otherwise no safe harbors nearby.

We passed a pleasant afternoon, the four of us -- Joel with a fine long-legged blond in sexy shorts -- in grass, beer, pupus, and tales of sailing the Tuamotus after building his boat in Costa Rica. We returned several times in our vacillating considerations, stopping along the way to visit Rick Schulz in Kamuela lending a hand in the building of his new house.

We kept looking.

*****

Jim had introduced me to World Sailing Directions, which were similar to coastal pilot books. They were loose-leaf binders that could be updated with the insertion of new information sheets, and contained charts of islands and harbors and anchorages the world over, all kinds of sundry local knowledge. I lost myself in them when I could get away from the constant hum of

Jim's con. He could fill the local layabouts' heads with dreams sufficient to get them to help him with the work on his boat.

He had a plan to colonize Suvarov with a new society in search of freedoms dying out in America, a commune of self-sufficient people establishing a new paradise on earth. He invited us to join him in sailing down in his boat. However, my latest count toted up four, maybe a half dozen, young guys and gals that he'd invited to sail down with him. His boat could realistically contain only two exceedingly tolerant people on long voyages, and I predicted that when the time came the old fart would wind up as a solo navigator. But, whee-oh, did he ever make me think about stealing a page from his plan for myself, modify it to fit the dreams Steph and I had been slowly a-building.

A boat, a plan, a destination, in any order but all together in a neat package, that was the ticket. After acquiring my own set of World Sailing Directions, I began with a plan, a recent growing dream of the past couple of years. The Great Pakalolo Escape Plan. Like Tom Neale, I would find me an island for myself, a Garden of Eden, where King Kahu would reign with Queen Kekepania in lonely splendor, a place where we could raise a large pakalolo family without the nuisance of meddlesome interlopers. And the plan itself would serve to further facilitate escape. A running away is also a running toward.

The South Seas, the South Pacific, the old magic fables of magnetic dreams. But why south? Why not north? Hawaii was in the northern hemisphere, its eight major islands themselves the southernmost of a chain of smaller and mostly uninhabited islands stretching thirteen hundred miles northwest from Kauai.

My first inclination was to begin a quick implementation of my plan at Nihoa, a volcanic island a mere 150 miles from Kauai, which comprised some 155 acres. The fact that twelve of them were fertile and once intensely cultivated was part of its allure. Twelve acres of pakalolo represented almost 60,000 individual plants. My mind boggled. No way two people with no more than hand tools could handle such a labor. Maybe one acre, a couple of tons or so. Nihoa's drawback was the lack of a safe anchorage in all weathers. Thus, we had considered the utility of Joel's lightly built trimaran. We would winch it up on the beach, live ashore, and relaunch when a harvest was ready for market a day or two's sail away.

No, too close. We needed a more remote place. There was French Frigate Shoals, almost 500 miles from Honolulu, a crescent-shaped atoll consisting of thirteen islets. During World War II, it had been the site of a Navy airfield installation. The problem was that it contained an active Coast Guard base for the purpose of manning a Loran station, which transmitted radio signals to aid in navigation.

The low islands, the atolls, which were formed by the growth of coral reefs on the tops of underwater seamounts, unlike the high islands, which were formed by active volcanoes, began to fascinate me. I had only seen them in picture books.

Further out lay Laysan, 790 miles from Honolulu, a sand island one by two miles in size, known for its numerous birds. Guano had once been mined there, and thus it would provide all the natural fertilizers necessary for the plan. Further still, at over a thousand miles, lay Pearl and Hermes Reef, an oblong atoll made up of seven sand islets, also formerly worked for guano. But by then you're only about a hundred miles from Midway, an active U. S. Navy base, too close to an American government facility for a soon-to-be fugitive.

Well, then, south it is. There was Johnson Island westerly, but it too, was a military base. And further south at almost a thousand miles, lay the northern portion of the Line Islands, composed of a bare reef that uncovered at low tide -- Kingman's Reef -- four atolls, two inhabited, two not. The northwestern most, the only one under American jurisdiction, was old Jim's island, Palmyra. Washington, the next island over, had no safe anchorage. Fanning, a working copra plantation, was inhabited. Christmas, the largest in the group, was really inhabited. Of the southern portion of the Line Islands, those lying from the equator south, Jarvis, Malden, Starbuck, Caroline, Vostock, and Flint, upon close study none were so providential and appealing as Palmyra, a privately owned island with no permanent population -- only the occasional yacht passing through. All coral and sand, thousands of coconut trees and miscellaneous vegetation.

During World War II an important U.S. naval air transport base had been developed. An airstrip had been constructed, a ship's passage had been blasted through the surrounding reefs, a wharf area had been built up for unloading supply ships. Warehouse, barracks buildings, bunkers, radio towers, and other structures had been erected, even a hotel operated by Pan American, a sea plane landing area and ramp, fortifications and roads, causeways connecting all the islands in a circular perimeter, the housing of six thousand military personnel, all now in a state of rot and decay, rusting machinery, nature's elements working their patient way, helped by occasional fires, the remorseless sea washing away the causeways to recreate separation between the dozens of islands around the central lagoons. Decades of torrential rains working their demolitions in slow motion for nature's inexorable regrowth. Thousands of Sooty Terns had taken over the airstrip for their seasonal mating and nesting activities.

Discovered in 1802 by Captain Sawle, an American, and named after his ship, Palmyra, which displaced the older name of Samarang, it was claimed by King Kamehameha IV for the Kingdom of Hawaii in 1862, then by Britain in 1889, but was wrested away for inclusion in the Hawaiian Islands by the United States in 1898. Judge Cooper, after whom the largest islet is named, acquired sole title in 1911, and used it for a copra plantation. He later sold all but two islets to the FullardLeos, who kept it in the family. When Judge Cooper died in 1929, his two islets, Home Islands, passed to his heirs.

Palmyra was looking better and better. With a thousand miles of ocean separating us from the next nearest bit of U. S. property and all its attendant evils, especially narcs and thieves, we would grow grass to our heart's content. The climate and rainfall were ideal. And a thousand miles was not so far for the necessity every six or eight months to sail our crop to market -- although returning to Hawaii would be taking a chance, the one risk in the developing plan.

But, unbeknownst to me then, a resolution to that problem lay just over the horizon.

Hm. No soil as such, only sand and coral, which, while we could make use of it, was so deficient in all the nutrients required for the nurture of healthy children. But there was plenty of vegetation which, with our recent experience and learning abilities, could be mulched up to make a compost. We could add fish offal for nitrogen, take along all the necessary fertilizers and trace minerals, a supply of paper-cups and gro-bags. We would need a garden-shredder for reducing vegetation, shovels, hoes, rakes, trowels, machetes, and a chainsaw to clear jungle.

We would have our tent for a land camp, a roll of nylon-reinforced plastic sheeting, odds and ends of metal, wood, and fiber-glass supplies. The tools for constructing baby nurseries, wire and cord to stretch between trees for sun-curing harvested adults and an electrical generator for my power tools.

Destination selected, plan well along, we began the making of lists, endlessly discussed and revised, but continued the longing search for a proper vessel to carry us away.

*****

Our summer of fun with Boogie Hawaii was over. We packed up our cabin tent, along with the mutts, into the Datsun. Three months had passed since our ignominious arrests. Time was a wasting. We had no more secret stashes of pakalolo, no other source of income except for the occasional middleman deals I managed between cultivators and the marketplace.

Well, Brook had promised us a year, time enough to get in another crop from start to finish. We snuck into the acres, set up temporary housekeeping in our tiny little earthquake-proof digs, now left with the devastation of 600 gro-bags. No, we would not attempt to replant them, but only stay long enough to nurse a hundred babies sufficient for transplanting into our more remote two-part stash, maybe retruck into Waimanu to establish another planting.

In October, however, responding to a newspaper ad, I flew to Maui, deplaned in Wailuku and caught a cab to Maalaea Harbor to look over a sailboat hull in drydock. Mastless and painted a sickly yellow, she, the good sloop Margaret, looked forlorn, but there was something about her lines, the graceful sheer, the bowsprit, the stern bumpkin that had all but disappeared on modern designs, that gave her an air of character.

After a couple of hours spent going over the inside and counting up the gear that was included, then walking around the outside and realizing she would need lots of work to get her ready for a voyage, the price was right and I flew to Honolulu to make the deal.

On the way I mused. Inside, Margaret had been beautifully refinished in Robusta wood, all the vinyl cushions newly custom-made, but the engine had been removed leaving only a propshaft and propeller. The bronze portholes were all available but needed bedding and sealing in place. Most of the rigging and mast-fittings were present in a jumbled mess. The wire rigging was stainless steel, seven-sixteenths- inches in diameter, more appropriate for a yacht in the 80-foot range, the forestay, backstay, and upper shrouds. We would have to supply new lower shrouds. There were six stainless steel chainplates for anchoring the shrouds to the hull. There was an antique bronze bilge-pump that would need overhauling. There was no toilet or sinks, but several through-hull fittings for them. Five bronze winches were available for overhaul and mounting, two heavy-duty ones for the cockpit and three smaller ones for the mast. There were bags of sails needing repairs, a length of anchor-chain and a Danforth anchor. Could we do it all in, say, eight months before a judge tried to ship me off to prison?

Charlie, the harbor master and part-time U. S. Customs agent in Wailuku, who had given me a key and led me to her, a crusty old curmudgeon, had told me the Margaret had been neglected by a previous owner who had allowed her to sink at her moorings from a slow leak. A crane had raised her out of the harbor, breaking her mast in the process, to deposit her propped up on struts and blocks of wood. Abandoned, she had been auctioned off for $10 to a man who quickly resold her for $400 to a dreamy-eyed young couple. They in turn had begun the work of restoring her. While the girl worked on the inside, the man had overlaid the entire hull, including deck and doghouse, with a heavy layer of fiberglass, using heavy matte and roving and finish with lighter glass clothes. She was a bit rough, some of the underlying planks limned in outline. But she was solid, basically two hulls in one, a fiberglass hull running from a quarter-inch thick at the gunnels to three-eighths inches on the keel, a solid wooden hull with planks one-and-three-quarters-inches thick fitted inside the newer glass hull. Somewhere along the way, extra ballast had been added by bolting to the bottom edge of the keel two oblong, round hunks of steel that resembled an eight-foot long torpedo. When I thought about it, I realized that this torpedo provided a Scheel-type keel configuration that the inventor claimed assisted the sailing characteristic in going to windward by preventing leeway without increasing depth. Her displacement was about six long tons on a twenty-six foot waterline, while her deck was thirty feet from stem to stern. The five-foot long bowsprit and the four-foot long bumpkin, for the purpose of lengthening the sailbase, brought her to thirty-nine feet overall. Her length-displacement ratio was close to 350, which is fairly heavy, meaning she would have a good motion in seas and could carry more stores than lighter displacement vessels of the same length. Not being sure of the amount of original lead ballast and the added weight of the torpedo-like appendage, her ballast-displacement was only guessable, but the torpedo had to add initial stability and righting moment, and thus increase the safety factor.

Somewhere during my inspection, alone with my survey, the old dream of the sea had begun to seize me as I had never quite been seized before. An impatience overcame me, a restlessness, at the nearness of it, the reality, for I could envision commissioning myself somewhere along in my labors as a Captain-Admiral of the Ocean-Seas, sense in the marrow of my bones the beginning of the First Great Voyage of Circumnavigation before me.

The present owner, the young lady before me, related the dissolution of she and her husband's dream. He'd been busted on a dope beef and they needed money. They were asking $2500. She settled for $2260, a bargain for a million dollars worth of dreams.

When we had completed the deal, exchanging money for paperwork, I had caught a strange intensity in her eyes. As we were saying goodbye, she reached out to squeeze my forearm.

"Would you do me one favor, please?"

It was one of those moments, all the fragments of a shattered dream saddening her eyes. "Yes. Yes, I will," I said.

"When she's in the water again, when she's a proper yacht, will you send me a photo of her?"

I promised.

I swung by the Harbors Division of the Department of Transportation to re-register the Margaret in my name, re-naming her Stephanie in honor of my true love, my sweet patootie.

Our last act before departing for Maui was to transplant a hundred babies in the two fifty-bag stashes still undiscovered in a remote old rainforest. Hopefully, this time they would serve to hedge the bet in future finances.

We shipped the Datsun packed with everything we could manage. The dogs went into cages for the trip.

"I don't like Puffy being in a cage," Steph complained.

"Baby, it's only for less than an hour."

"Less than an hour's too long for anyone to be in a cage!"

I thought about it, which was easy for a man with my past. "You're right, babe. You're fucking-A right."

"I don't see why they can't sit with us if we buy tickets for them!"

Deplaned and all together again, the five of us caught a cab with an uneasy driver for the Wailuku pier where our Datsun, shipped ahead of us, waited. Soon we were in Maalaea, Steph and I holding hands, Popolo pissing his claim upon the keel.

"That's it, huh?"

"Her."

"Huh?"

"Her. All ships are female. Ain't she beautiful?"

"Well," she shrugged with an impish frown. "I always knew ya had great taste in broads, baby, but I can't say I'm flattered to be in the same class as...that!"

We moved in, climbing up and down the ladder, Steph and Puffer and I inside, Popolo and Sista to guard the approaches from below.

We christened our undertaking with an act of love on the narrow settees. My first task was to build in a double bunk.

We went at it with a will, day in and day out for five months, sometimes so caught up in it that the workday was fourteen hours long. There were many problems to be solved and, while it's true I know how to find and use a book -- we were regular customers at the public library in Wailuku -- and figured I'd studied myself into some expertise in the construction of boats, not a single one of them would remain unsolved by the time we set sail for Palmyra.

First, to make the inside livable. I built in a double berth just aport of the companionway ladder, extending it back into the area under the cockpit locker. Adjacent to that went a small dinette sufficient for two. To starboard went a kitchen counter with a sink and a gimbaled propane stove, figuring two five-gallon tanks would serve us for six months if we were careful. For backup we had Coleman two-burner and one-burner campstoves. I bolted two metal footlockers above the vee-berths in the foc'sle, which would serve entirely for stowage. I reseated the portholes, reworked the main and forward hatches. We bought a missing helm-wheel, mounted it, and overhauled the cable-and-pulley steerage to the rudderpost. We looked at several gasoline and diesel engines, but finally said fuck it, we'd be pure sailors. Robin Knox, and several other circumnavigators could do it, so could we. Tom Colvin, a great designer of serious sea-going vessels, often enough left no room for an engine. Before the invention of the steam engine and the internal combustion engine, nary a boat in the world had missed them.

I plugged all the through-hull fittings. The purpose of through-hull fittings is to take in seawater and to pump it out, as through a toilet in order to flush it, or through the cooling jacket of a water-cooled engine. Some boats had seawater inlets and outlets attached to their galley in order to conserve freshwater in washing dishes. Most boats had outlets leading from bilge pumps to remove water from inside the hull, usually from leaks. Through-hulls almost always have emergency stopcocks for use in the event that hoses leading to and from pumps are ruptured. All were plugged and sealed, thus removing one more worry. We would take on seawater the old-fashioned way by tossing a pail overboard attached to a rope for hauling it back aboard.

The antique bilge pump, after much frustrated tinkering, was deemed unreliable. I bought a new teflon and rubber heavy-duty pump, which I mounted on the coachroof next to the main hatch in order that it could be operated from the cockpit. A long detachable inlet hose ran down beside the companionway ladder directly into the deepest part of the bilge area. All water inside a boat drained to the lowest portion of the hull inside -- the bilge. The outlet hose ran directly over the side of the boat topside.

To top off the main hull construction, I laid another couple of layers of heavy roving over the portion of the hull that would ride beneath the water when afloat, and a couple more layers of lighter cloth over the entire hull for the purpose of making the surface less rough. Endless sanding, the godawful itches from fiberglass grit bedding itself upon my sweating body.

While I was at it, I saturated all the planking and ribs inside from about a foot above the waterline down to where the vee of the bilge joins the keel. This was perfectly proper since the wood was thoroughly dried after over two years in drydock.

Then we painted her a lovely seawitch blue to the gunnels, over which the topsides were painted white. On all areas of the deck we sprinkled fine washed beach sand over the freshly applied paint in order to remove all slick areas and provide a nonskid surface.

By all the saints of the Sandwich Islands, I thought, employing the name Captain Cook had used to name Hawaii in honor of Lord Sandwich, upon standing back to admire Stephanie's hull, that's one lovely little bitch, tighter than a virgin's nether parts!

Now but to rig her out and think about launching. Whoa now, me bucko, a mast had to be perfect and, although I'd done considerable study on the subject, I'd never actually built one -- and here I was confronted with the task of making a sturdy pole forty feet long.

In olden times, a mast was no more than a tall, straight tree with the limbs chopped off and debarked. Some of the older, larger vessels used solid wood masts that were not much different from telephone poles, stayed and guyed to remain in place. Later still, along with developing physical sciences and the invention of waterproof glues, hollow masts were conceived and constructed. Properly designed, they proved to be just as strong as the solid ones, but saved on undesirable weight aloft.

Spruce has always been the wood of choice, that is, before extruded aluminum, because of its long grain and flexibility, but it was not available in Hawaii and the costs of shipping it from a Mainland port would have been more than if I'd gone out and bought a ready-made one. However, no less an authority than L. Francis Herreshoff, one of the leading yacht designers in the earlier part of this century, highly recommended the plentiful Douglas Fir as an alternative.

I had selected choice grade two-by-six-inch planks, all to be laminated with resorcinal glue, all properly scarfed in staggered joints. I made my own clamps from plywood slats and carriage bolts, laid the planks over sawhorses, using wood chips to adjust the lay as needed, which I judged by eye and a carpenter's level since the floor in my building space wasn't exactly level. I'd decided to forego the greater complexity and time required in a hollow mast for a solid one three boards thick. After gluing it all together, I shaped it by hand, rounding off the sharp corners and lending a taper to the top half so I could utilize the masthead fitting that had come with the hull. I fashioned tangs and spreaders, rigged her out with fore-guy, backstay, and upper shrouds. The lower shrouds, running from just beneath the spreaders, were of new five-sixteenths-inch stainless steel wire bought at an auction of naval supplies. With all the proper fittings for attaching the shrouds to the chainplates, foreguy, and backstay, all with turnbuckles for fine-tuning the adjustments, we were ready to mount her.

Originally, Margaret's mast had been eight or nine feet longer because it had been mounted through a hole in the coachroof and slid down inside to slot into a part of the keel. Since the former owners had filled in the coachroof, and the old-fashioned mounting of such a mast would be a bitch, I opted to mount it on top. To compensate for the strain this would place on the coachroof, I had fixed directly below the mounting spot a four-inch steel pipe running from the underside of the ceiling down to the maststep in the keel.

The next problem was to erect the sonofagun. With all its hardware attached, that sucker had to weigh in excess of three hundred pounds, and it was long and unwieldly. With a little help, we got it aboard, the foot of the mast slotted into the base of the new maststep, its top laid out to extend beyond the bumpkin. I attached the backstay and the aft most lower shrouds to the chainplates. Then, running a rope from the end of the forestay, which passed through a pulley mounted on a temporary vee-shaped framework mounted just ahead of the foreward lower shrouds in order to provide a proper initial lifting angle, the other end of the rope attached to the bumper of our Datsun, a friend drove it slowly forward, the mast lifting, steadied by Steph and I on deck. At a certain angle, we removed the vee-frame and pulley. The Datsun went forward again, the mast continuing to lift. We began attaching the upper shrouds and remaining lower shrouds, tightening the turnbuckles sufficient to hold the mast in place. Then we eased off the tension provided by the Datsun, connected the foreguy to the end of the bowsprit. Lovely the laws of physics for accomplishing labor beyond the strength of mere muscle!

The Margaret-Stephanie had originally been rigged as a sloop, meaning she carried two triangular sails, the main aft and a jib forward. I had added another forestay from the top of the mast down to a point on deck some six feet aft of the stay affixed to the end of the bowsprit, thus providing another headsail -- called the forestay-sail -- and converting the rig to a cutter configuration. It would prove to be a fortuitous idea, for we would later discover that it was advantageous when it came to rigging for self-steering.

Next came a boom to complete the rigging, and so I fashioned another pole from my fir planks and glue eighteen feet long. We had no gooseneck fitting, which is a universal joint necessary to fixing the boom to the mast (so that the boom can move up and down and side-ways). I threw one together of my own design from scratch by cutting and welding pieces of three-eighths-inch plate steel. Worked like a charm. Our little boat had taken on a jaunty air with her mast and rigging, beginning to look like a creature longing for the water. My hands-on experience, besides encouraging my sea fever, told me that before mast, spar, and rigging failed, the entire deck from stem to stern would have to be ripped off.

*****

We had naturally acquired new friends. First, there was Larry, a sewing machine mechanic who had taken leave of absence from his job in Honolulu to build a fort foot yacht of his own design. When I'd first laid eyes on it, I'd complimented him on his houseboat, but he'd stiffly informed me it was to be a double-ended cutter with a high-aspect rig. Oops.

But Steph had employed her inimitable charms upon him and we were soon helping each other out, eating together, smoking together, and drinking together, talking shit about things nautical. When the comet Kahoutek was lighting up our skies, we all journeyed up in Larry's car to the two mile high peak of Haleakala, an extinct volcano, to spend a chilly night toking, sipping, and bullshitting after studying the phenomenon in the sky with binoculars.

"In olden times people believed that comets were presagers of fortunes to come, whether good or bad. Astrologers were out in force to make their predictions," I tried idly.

"Yeah? No shit?" Larry was snockered, a dumb look on his face as he tried to consider this information.

"Aw, gawd," Steph said. "Let it be good times. We've had enough shit this year!"

"I'll vote for that."

"Yeah, me, too," Larry managed. "Next year we go sailing!" "Yeh, you hear that, Mr. Kahoutek-in-the-sky? Give us a good year cuz we're going sailing!"

*****

Larry and I became closer. One day a Pake (Chinese) showed up in an old pickup.

"Damn, that old eyesore's looking a lot better," he commented, studying our good little ship. "You do that?"

"Yeah," I grinned. "Me and my wahine, with a little help from our friend, Larry, here."

"Didn't know dumb haoles could do work like that."

"Duh, me and Larry might be dumb, but Steph's a fucking genius and she's our boss."

"Oh, yeah? Hey, lady, these too lolos ever do any net-fishing?"

"Hey, my ol' man can do anything! And Larry's pretty good at figuring things out, too!"

"Oh, yeah? You two dummies know anything about akule fishing?"

"Duh, what's an akule?"

"A fucking fish, 'bout yay long," he said, gesturing a foot or so in length with his hands. "They swim in schools on the outer reefs."

"Never heard of them."

"Well, you're gonna damn well learn plenty! That is, if you wanna make a few bucks from time to time."

"Oh, yeah?"

"Yeah, so just get'cher asses in my pickup, and let's get the show on the road! Fucking akule are running!"

Tooling along the coast road around Kihei Bay, he began his spiel. "See, the way it works is, I go fly my Piper Cub out over the water to find where the akule schools are. We communicate over walkie-talkies. I tell you guys where to drive the pickup, where to launch the boat, where to make the surround. You know what a surround is? Never mind, I'll tell you. One guys rows in a big circle while the other guy pays out the gillnets. We surround the school inside, see? Then you scare 'em into swimming into the nets, see?"

"How do we scare 'em? No, wait, I know. Larry ducks his face under the water."

"Don't worry, I'll show you. Then we got these nets full of akule stuck in them, see? And all you gotta do is haul 'em into the boat. By that time, I'll be back from the airport to help you take the fish outa the nets. Okay?"

"Okay."

He left us with a rowboat full of gillnets loaded into the pickup bed. Soon we could hear the Piper buzzing overhead and his voice crackling over the radio. He directed us to drive along the road to a certain spot, where we manhandled the boat down to the beach for launching. I rowed while Larry handled the radio.

"Okay, okay," I could hear the Pake. "Go to port. We'll make a left-hand surround."

Since I was facing backward, my left was to starboard and I unthinkingly went that way.

"No, no!" the radio screamed. "The other way, you dumb asshole! To port, to port!"

Okay, I got it right, bending at the oars.

"Faster, faster! In a circle! In a circle! The circle's got to be a hundred yards wide! Faster!"

I rowed in the circle as Larry payed out the neatly coiled nets over the transom, and soon completed it.

"Now, tie 'em together and row to the center of the circle and scare 'em!"

The scare device was a tank of compressed air with a long hose to drop into the water, a piece of chain attached as a weight. When the valve was cracked, a great explosion of air bubbles burst forth and the fish fled in all directions -- headlong into the nets surrounding them.

"Okay, okay! Good! Now start hauling them in! You might have to untie 'em, bring one at a time! Looks like we got a good catch. I'll meet you on the beach!"

There were three lengths of net, each about a hundred yards long, all tied together. The nets were about twelve feet in depth, made of nylon monofilament, cork floats along the top and lead weights along the bottom to they would form an invisible wall in the water.

Jesus Jumping Jackanapes! Hauling in one net full of wriggling fish left us with only a few inches of freeboard. Carefully I headed for shore, the both of us holding our breaths for balance so the damned boat wouldn't swamp.

The Pake waited with washtubs full of ice, showed us how to remove each fish with a deft twist from the net. A few local people wandered down to help us. In a couple of hours we had the other two nets in, cleared, rolled, and tucked back in the boat, loaded up and ready to go.

He paid the locals in portions of the catch for their help, then turned to us. "Okay, let's get these tubs loaded. You boys did a fair job today. Looks like we got eight-nine hundred pounds. I'll drop you off, take'em to market, meet you back at Maalaea."

We left the pickup with the boat at his place and got in with him. "You boys grab you some of those akule. They're ono. Get your wahine to fry you up a mess. She know how to cook?"

"Oh, yeah."

"Well, get cleaning them fish, boys. I expect dinner when I get back -- an hour or so."

When he returned to join us inside for fried fish and beer, he paid us a hundred and fifty apiece. "Akule goes for seventy-nine cents a pound," he said. "Made seven hundred. That do you?"

"Oh, hell yeah," I said. "Darlin', lean over there and kiss that ugly old goat, ask him when we're going fishing again."

*****

Larry drove me to the postoffice, where I filled out an application for a passport. Two pieces of ID were required. I displayed my new birth certificate and Social Security card."

"Need something with a picture on it," the man said. "You got a drivers license?"

"Nah, I don't know how to drive. My friend here's been giving me lessons."

"Okay. He can sign an affidavit he's known you for two years, we can process it. You know this guy as Roy Alfred Allen for two years?"

Larry, quick and game and sober, said, "Sure, but I didn't know his middle name was Alfred."

"Good enough. Sign there."

In a few weeks I had a passport. Roy, you devil!

*****

There was an old bearded guy called German John that came by one day looking like a hermit with long tangled hair and beard.

"Gott in Himmel," he exclaimed. "Zee old Margaret, her looking pretty again! I knew her before she sink, a shame! A famous design! Many boats made from her design! Zay call zem Seabirds!"

"Oh, yeah?"

"Sure, she's a sweet boat, a fine sailer! You see! Mower, Huntington, and Day, zay conceive, make ze first drawings! Copied many time! Check old Rudder magazines, you see!"

I studied her with new eyes, trying to see what German John saw. He was an old salt, having messed about boats all his life, building and sailing them. The design was more or less conventional to my eye for an older type vessel, the hard chine allowing for easier construction than the traditional wineglass cross-sections.

At the Wailuku library, I looked up old issues of Rudder. Sure enough, there she was, a design dating back to the turn of the century, a twenty-five-and-a-half-foot yawl called Seabird. A yawl is basically a sloop with a tiny mast added most sternward as a steadying sail.

Several people had had a hand in the original design, including C. D. Mower, L. D. Huntington, and Thomas Fleming Day, the editor of Rudder, the leading publisher at the time of boating articles and small sailboat design.

Seabird was expressly designed for Rudder and called for a good all-around sailing vessel, capable of being easily and inexpensively built. It was such a successful design that a number of requests began pouring in from others who wanted a similar yacht. The plans were expanded to twenty-seven feet, then thirty, and even larger. As Day would proudly boast in his magazine, "I am not a designer, but I claim to be the author of this craft!"

In early June, 1911, Thomas Fleming Day, along with two friends to serve as crew, set sail from Rhode Island for the Azores. Many observers at the time felt that Seabird was too small and frail for the rigors of such a trans-Atlantic passage and feared for their safety. In mid-Atlantic, Seabird was caught in fierce seas, the wind blowing at a gale force of forty knots and gusting to fifty.

Day describes in detail, and even some elation, the manner in which Seabird carried he and his companions through several days and nights of the storm to safety in the Azores.

My own and Steph's attitude in taking to sea aboard the future Iola reflects after his attitude in setting sail aboard Seabird, and I quote: "In a large vessel a man is on the sea, but in a small one he is with the sea. The aim of the owners of a passenger steamer is to surround the voyager with objects that will cause him to forget that he is at sea; they create as much as possible a land environment. He is roofed over and barricaded in so that he cannot see the sky overhead or the sea beneath except by craning his neck over the rail. The ship is made as nearly as possible to resemble a hotel, and the foremost boast of the owners is that she resembles a land tavern. In a few years they will do away with what little deck is left, and the passengers will voyage to Europe completely under cover, the only view they have of the ocean being through stained glass port-lights."

Prophetic words, as anyone who has seen modern luxury liners with their swimming pools, spas, sports events, fancy balls, and chandeliered dining rooms may attest. But then Day waxed more poetic, when he added, "What can such cooped beings know of the sea? Of its beauty, its grandeur, its loneliness? They never see it as we do, sleeping under the stars, or laughing and romping under the sun. Have they joined the moon in a watch, when the wind and wave are dancing the dance of silver?"

Unbeknownst to me at the time, there would come a day in the future when I would remember those words while listening to ignorant critics maligning Iola's seaworthiness and I would say silently to myself, although I wished to proclaim it to all, "Kiss it where the sun doesn't shine!"

###

CHAPTER 12

A rental car stopped as I was heading for the bathroom/shower house provided by the county as a harbor amenity, and a head popped out a window to ask, "Hey, do you know what time Buzz's Steakhouse opens?"

Buzz's was a two-story building set near an inner bend of the tiny bay, the top half being a fine restaurant specializing in prime rib, while the bottom half was open on one end and was reserved for banquets. The proprietors, a young, amiable Tahitian couple, had graciously given me permission to use the banquet space for the construction of our mast.

The inquirer was a short, intelligent looking guy somewhere around thirty and sported a neatly trimmed beard. His eyes gleamed with humor and curiosity. A taller, younger fellow with a scraggly mustache sat beside him.

"Sure. About 6:30, an hour or so," I replied.

"How's the food?"

"Superb. You can't go wrong eating at Buzz's."

"They serve cocktails?"

"The lady's an expert, and a treat for the eyes, too. Even got a wine list."

"Sounds like our lucky day. You know, we've driven by on the road above a dozen times and never even knew they had a yacht harbor here."

"Where you guys from?"

"Up the coast at Lahaina."

"Interested in sailboats?"

"Yeah, man. We live on a 32-foot Islander. Sailed her down from Mexico."

"Oh, yeah? That's interesting. I'd like to hear about it. Tell you what, give me ten minutes or so to shower and change, you can come aboard my boat for a drink or two while you're waiting."

"Sure. Where you located?"

I pointed to the blue and white hull sitting on a slight rise next to the ocean shore. "Right there. Don't mind the dogs. They bark a lot but are very friendly you get to know them."

He craned his neck for a looksee. "Oh, yeah, looking good. What kind of work you doing on her?"

"Rebuilt the old tub from the hull up. She's an older design."

"Yeah, I can see."

"I'm Buck."

"I'm Dickie. This is my brother, Carlos."

I shook with Dickie, nodded to Carlos. "Listen, you think you can brave the dogs, go on over and climb aboard. I'll see you in a few minutes."

When I returned, they were sitting in the cockpit watching a few diehard surfing kids riding the waves further along. I climbed up. "You guys into surfing?"

"Oh, yeah. We just came from the northshore of Oahu. Awesome."

"Come on down. Welcome aboard, such as it is."

After breaking out cold beers and making a quick judgment, I offered them a smoke from my stash -- the better stuff.

"Wow, good shit. You know where we can cop an ounce or two?"

"Sure." I got out a jewelry box from the stowage space below the double berth, popped the lid. There were about a dozen ounce baggie-rolls inside. "Take your pick."

"Wow, those are fat," Carlos noted.

"Yeah, sinsemilla. No seeds, no stems. What you see is what you smoke."

"How much?"

"Twenty."

"Good deal." Dickie laid out enough bills for two. "Shit's more expensive in Honolulu."

"Yeah."

One thing led to another, the feeling-out process of getting to know each other. They invited me to dine with them.

*****

Steph was away at her new job. After four months or so, with all the major work done, she'd decided to look for a job in order to pass the time and provide more income.

"How we doing moneywise," she'd asked one day out of the blue.

Me, I was secretive about finances, never getting into the dollars and cents of it with her. I did the worrying, she did the soothing. I shrugged. "Ah, okay, I guess. We could always use more. Fucking boat's eating us alive."

"Well, you're bringing in the fish money from the Pake. I figure I should get a job and put some in the pot."

"Nah, you don't have to. We're not that bad off."

"I want to. I'm getting bored. I need to meet some new people."

"What've you got in mind?"

"I dunno. I been looking in the help-wanted ads."

Her first effort was an experience. She'd seen an ad for an outcall masseuse. Me, I'm thinking massage parlor stuff. "Babe, I don't think you want to get into this."

"Why not? It's legit. I talked to the guy on the phone. He says it's mostly older people. You give 'em a little rub, talk to 'em, provide company. Old people, ya know, he says they get lonely, they got their aches and pains. Says they're nice and generous, always tip if they like you and call in to request you by name.

"Oh, yeah?"

"Yeh, plus I think I'd be good at it -- all that practice we've had on each other."

"Yeah, there's that, all right."

"I'm gonna go by and see 'im. He lives in Wailuku."

"When? I gotta go into town today, buy some stuff for our stanchions and lifelines, start figuring out how I'm gonna do it."

"That's all right. You can drop me off on the way, pick me up later."

"Sure, okay."

When I picked her up, she seemed subdued, her face frowning in thought. I passed her a beer, lit a joint.

"So, how'd it go, babe?"

After a long swallow and a deep hit, she shook her head. "Whew! I don't know what to think!"

"What, it's a hustle?"

"No, I dunno."

"Well, what?"

"The guy likes me, says he wants to hire me, that I can make two-three hundred a week once I get lined up with some regular customers."

"Yeah?"

"Gawd, it's kind of incredible, ya know?"

"What?"

"Well, see, he had me take my clothes off so he could, like, demonstrate how his customers liked their rubdowns, ya know, so he could show me different techniques. That was okay, kinda like when we do each other, right? But the next thing I know, the dude's nekkid and things got sort of mutually oral. Okay, no big thing. Only then he took me in the bathroom to show me another service he provided. He had me squat up on the toilet seat, see, and he stuck this plastic thing in my okole -- an enema, can you imagine! Called it a colonic. Well, by then I'm beginning to wonder, ya know? He wanted me to come back for another lesson, but I ain't into that kinko stuff, right? Plus, he never paid me the fifty bucks he said he would."

I pulled off the road, biting my teeth. I didn't know whether to cry, laugh, or go back and beat the shit out of that motherfucker.

"What, baby?"

"Jesus Christ, Steph! Goddamn it, babe! That really takes the fucking cake! That GODDAMNED MOTHERFUCKING COCKSUCKING SONOFABITCH! I'm gonna kick that slimeball's ass clear up Haleakala and down the other side!"

"Oh, no, now, baby! Just calm down! It's no big deal! I already figured out he's an asshole! Now just chill out and forget it! Here, take a nice big toke, nice and deep now, and hold it. That's good. Now take another. It's okay, baby, it's okay. Forget about it, awright?"

Her next effort got her on as a waitress and soon thereafter as assistant manager at the Ginzo Club. She worked from five p.m. to one a.m. I'd been in to check it out. The manager was a nice, friendly little guy, the customers mostly working class people. Everything looked okay, on the up and up. They all liked Steph, naturally. Plus, they serve ono pupus.

*****

I accepted Dickie's invitation. It was also a chance to get a doggie-bag full of prime-rib bones from the proprietors with whom we'd made friends. Steph and I ate there once or twice a week with Larry. It soon become obvious that both Dickie and Carlos were experienced sailors, Dickie especially being very knowledgeable in navigation, seamanship, boat construction and maintenance.

"Where's your sails?"

"Got to dig them out, do a little patch work before I bend 'em on."

"Oh, yeah? We're getting a new set. Maybe you could find a use for our old ones. They're still in fair shape."

"Sure, I'll take a look at 'em."

"Might have to trim the foot, maybe not. We're pretty close to the same size."

"Maybe just put in some low reefing points. Be easier."

"Yeah, that's an idea."

"Where you at in Lahaina? Maybe me and the ol' lady'll drop by for a visit one day, see how real sailors do it."

"Sure, we can go for a little daysail, do some fishing, whatever."

Later on we did, went for a sail and I got seasick. But it was the beginning of a developing friendship and the trust that went with it.

It wasn't long before they had told me about having smuggled a couple hundred pounds of Mexican grass to Hawaii, which is about the equivalent of carrying pea-coals to an anthracite mine.

"From Mexico, man?"

"Yeah," Dickie grinned ruefully. "Didn't make much. Shit's selling for ten bucks a bag in Honolulu -- last gasp backup when the local stuff dries up."

I laughed.

"We're looking to supplement our income, Buck -- if you should happen to know where we can get some decent stuff for a good price and turn a profit in Honolulu."

"Well, let me think on it. I've been mostly out of contact for the past few months."

I'd told them a little about being a grass farmer. "Maybe I can put you in touch with some people on the Big Island -- if you don't mind sailing over to pick it up."

"Nah, hell no."

"You got an outlet in Honolulu?"

"Well...sort of."

"Don't worry. I can help you out there, too."

"When?"

"Ha, man, well, I dunno. Lemme see. I'm kinda busy trying to get my boat launched, you know?"

"Hey, here to the Big Island's a one day sail. We could pop over and back in three days. We'll help with the work on your boat."

"Okay, lemme think about it, figure out a plan." I was thinking about the two little stashes Steph and I had left behind. How were they doing? Had they survived? Only one way to find out. But it was too early yet. They needed a month at least, maybe two, to reach maturity.

*****

By early March, 1974, the good little ship, Stephanie, was ready for launching. With Larry, Dickie, and Carlos on hand, plus a few locals we'd become friendly with over the months, we'd gotten her jacked up out of her blocks and transferred to a steel-frame launching trailer.

Everyone helped push her over to the head of the launching ramp, where the trailer would be hooked to a steel cable wound around a diesel-powered winch-drum.

Gruff old Charlie ambled over. He leaned back, his belly pushing out the front of Bermuda shorts, through which stuck spindly legs. He had never been long on conversation, but Steph and I had developed an affection for the old character.

"Damn, never thought I'd see the day," he barked in his abrupt manner, a twinkle hidden in his eye. "Don't look like the same boat. Kinda purty."

What a great speech, I thought, grinning and raising my beer can to our little sapphire of the sea.

"Yep. You ready to do her?"

I nodded. Steph was on the foredeck with the champagne, waiting with a face full of smiles to lean over and crack the bottle.

Charlie pulled a lever, releasing the brake in a controlled run and the trailer rolled sternwise down the ramp. Suddenly there was a little jerk, probably due to an overbinding wind of cable on the drum. Such a little lurch, a little shudder, and a deafening silence as supporting blocks on the portside fell out with a crash.

"Steph, grab something," I yelled, as the several tons of our new baby, not yet properly named, not yet having reached the baptismal waters of a new life, screamed and crashed heavily over onto her side the mast quivering at twenty-five degrees from the horizontal. Steph was sprawled across the deck, clutching at the starboard gunnel. I leapt up on font of the trailer and hauled her off. She was trembling, face drawn in shock.

Our baby lay still now, all onlookers stunned to silence. Two steel support beams, curving up from the trailer frame, had pierced into her body like blunt knives, leaving gaping holes in her underbody.

Blood boiled through my heart and mind like acid. All my dreams and determination in that moment turned to bitter ash in my mouth, a black humiliation of disaster. Anger and frustration welled up, suffusing me with rage. I hadn't truly realized how involved I had become, gradually binding my own fate with the object of my growing affection, giving something of myself in every touch, lending all the tears of my sweating labor into a tower of pride, an inner and barely suspected tension growing the while.

Whether I would implode or explode was the question, or merely go berserk. Mad thoughts rose up, images of sloshing gasoline over her and sending her to Valhalla in a Viking funeral pyre...or, flickering peripherally the absurd, a grand wienie-roast.

I bit my teeth, clenched my fists, my body jumping with spastic motions. When is an Irish lad ever caught speechless?

I couldn't handle it. I grabbed Steph, marched her to our pickup parked a few yards away, the ice-coolers in back full of beer for the launching party, pushed her in, started up, and roared away in scorched rubber, my eyes averted from all those other eyes, our hero leaving the stage in disgrace.

I couldn't seem to breathe. I pulled off the main road into a secluded bit of woods overlooking Kihei Bay, leapt out cursing in loud capital letters, and began beating my fists against our poor innocent Datsun, steam all the while hissing from my ears.

I sat down utterly exhausted and thoroughly depressed, the warrior beaten on the verge of winning. Steph hugged me, crying, "Naw, c'mon, baby, it'll be all right."

I lit a cigarette. She pulled it out of my mouth, threw it away and stuck a joint in its place, lit it, and fetched me a beer. Gal knew what her whipped dude needed.

"How ya feel, baby?"

"Lower'n a snake's ass in a wagon rut."

"C'mon," she said. "I'm driving. Where we going?"

"Guess you better find us a hotel -- unless you wanna sleep in a corner on top of each other."

"Yeh, well, it's only temporary, what the hell. Tomorrow night we'll be back in our own bed."

Damn! Woman was smarter than she looked! I began thinking about what had to be done as we slowly got drunk together and quietly crashed into a healing oblivion.

*****

Larry advised that we ought to sue old Charlie because the obvious fault was his careless operation of the winch. It seems he had spread this idea to every listening ear in the aftermath.

And word had apparently reached Charlie.

As I was squatting over our injured baby, considering all the precise ways and means of righting her, Charlie drove up, got out and walked over, his mouth pulled down in a mean bulldog curve.

"What'cha gonna do?"

"Well, Charlie, I'm going sailing in that boat. She's the only one I've got. So I aim to fix her up."

"Ya gonna sue me?"

"Nope. Forget the loose talk. It was my fault. I shoulda had her braced up better."

"Well, I'm real sorry it happened."

"Yeah, me too. I apologize for acting like a kid yesterday, running away and all. I was just feeling bad."

"Aw, hell, son, I know. I fed your dogs last night, took 'em for a walk. What'cha wanta do with her?"

"I figure it like this..."

We got her upright by drilling a hole through the keel just above the torpedo ballast in order to anchor her with cable attached to the trailer frame, and then patiently and laboriously using hydraulic jacks and blocks to inch her up. I had learned my lesson. For the second attempt at launching, I had so blocked and strutted and secured her with nylon and dacron lines and even anchor chain that she looked like a bandaged and trussed little pig. She tipped over again, the whole trailer had to go with her.

In ten days, sometimes working eighteen-hour days, Steph returning from work at one-thirty or two in the morning to find me still at it. I replaced two ribs by partnering the sectioned ones to new ones and laying in two thicknesses of three-quarter-inch plywood to replace the sectioned out planks, then re-fiberglassed over the patch. A little refixing damaged portions inside and we were ready to try again.

Inviting no one, only Charlie, Larry, Dickie and Carlos, Steph and I on hand, she went dancing a little jig into the water. We tied her along a nearby pier. Steph broke the bottle of champagne and we all cheered.

While she went below, the rest of us bent to gathering up the blocks and lines and getting the trailer back up out of the water. I was feeling pretty smug to have overcome all difficulties in restoring our saucy little yacht to her natural habitat when Steph's rude shout punctured the mood.

"Baby, come quick! We're sinking!"

*****

Inside, the bilges were filling. I thought furiously. It couldn't be coming from the hull -- that was tight as a drum -- and not from through-hull fittings. Wait a minute! There'd been two through-hull fittings that hadn't been pluggable. I lifted out the companionway ladder, pulled up another floor-panel. There it was -- the logshaft stuffing box. Our boat, when she had an engine, had had it connected to a driveshaft direct to a three-bladed prop. I'd considered removing it and plugging up the shaft hole, but had left it for an undeveloped idea of using the driveshaft, which would turn when we moved through the water, to power a small trickle-charging generator for our batteries.

I grabbed a handful of the puttylike bedding compound and jumped into the water off the stern. Underneath, I packed it around the propshaft opening. Back aboard, I rigged up a faucet pump, which is a device connected to waterhoses and a Y-section so that the force of water running through a hose connected to a faucet created a vacuum and suction. Soon enough the waterline in the bilges lowered.

Might as well check the other one -- the rudderpost. Sure enough, a little seepage but not much.

Later I would remove the prop and its shaft and plug it permanently and thoroughly. I fitted it with a wooden plug in one end and by filling the five or six foot length of it with epoxy resin poured from inside.

Get to work on the stanchions and lifelines. Popolo and Sista moved aboard. We'd need to rig some netting to keep them from falling overboard at sea. We were getting close. We had to make a court appearance in Honolulu in May.

*****

It was April and we were moored near the tiny entrance to Maalaea Harbor, two sternlines ashore and an anchor from the bow into the mud below. Next to us was an older cabin cruiser of narrow beam and a straight up-and-down bow, a character boat. We'd never seen anyone aboard her.

One early evening as I was feeding the dogs on the foredeck after a day's work and a shower, I heard a faintly familiar voice hail me.

"Buck! Jesus Christ! Come over and drink a beer with me!"

I looked up, the first girl I'd met in Hawaii. "Mele! Damn, girl, how you doing? Figured you'd come to your senses and returned to the Mainland."

"Not yet, but I'm getting there. C'mon over. Let's catch up."

Talking and toking the hours away, watching the sky change colors in the sunset, sipping away on cold beers, dried squid, cold shrimp, cheese, and soy crackers for pupus, we exchanged stories.

Mele had been having an on-and-off affair with a local guy, the husky one I'd seen in the Kaukau Place. He'd declared himself and asked her to come live with him and be his love -- which is when she'd moved to Maui. She lived Hana-side, which was higher ground and less populated.

"It was great for a long time. I really fell in love with the guy, and he treated me right, you know? But then I found out he's a gangster, hooked into the Honolulu mob. Okay, so what? That doesn't necessarily make him a bad guy, right? Mostly he makes his money off gambling and grass. Who cares? But now he's got a piece of a prostitution business and the drugs are a little more serious -- like Asian heroin. Plus, there's something going on, some kind of contention. He's gotten paranoid, packs a gun, has a bodyguard. What's worse, he won't talk to me, only tells me to shut up. We hardly even speak any more. Only now we've got a kid."

"What, a boy or girl?"

"A girl. Oh, God, Buck, she's the most adorable thing! I named her Malia, after my mother, Marie. Kailani after his mother. Malia Kailani."

"Pretty name."

"How about you?"

"Got a really great ol' lady. We're fixing to sail off to some island paradise further south."

"Where? Tahiti?"

"Tahiti's on our itinerary."

"Where's she now?"

"Works at a club in town."

"What's its name?"

"The Ginzo. Why?"

"Oh, that's okay -- a laidback place. My ol' man's got a club in town. You don't want to hang out there."

"What's it called?"

She told me. "I read where you got busted about six months ago."

"Oh, yeah?"

"You must 'really have gotten into the pakalolo thing."

"Yeah. You could definitely say that."

"And that MDA stuff. What's that? They really call it the Love Drug?"

"Yeah. It's the aphrodisiac we're not supposed to know about."

"Really? You have any more?"

"Sure, I'll give you a handful -- for you and your ol' man." "How about me and you? Right now?"

"Hm. What time is it?"

"Eleven-thirty, why?"

"My ol' lady gets in around one-thirty. I like to be home when she arrives."

"Two hours, what the hell? It sure beats what I've been getting. "Be right back. How you fixed on beer?"

"Still got half a case left."

*****

Sometime later I asked the time again. Mele's long slim body illuminated in the moonlight as she stood to peer at her watch by the high deckhouse windows.

"Two-thirty."

"Damn. She should have been home by now."

"You care for her, don't you?"

"Yeah, I do. We've been through a lot together. She's a real trucker."

"What's she like?"

"I don't know how to describe her. It's a long song and dance. How do you describe a woman who fits right in on almost any level you can name, all the little things you can imagine. We're interested in the same things mostly. We read all the same books. We talk about them. Where I'm weak, she's strong, and vice versa. We take up each other's slack, you know? Sometimes she seems so laidback and blasé, accepting everything that comes around the pike, you'd think she didn't have a brain in her head. But then she lets you know she's not only got a brain but a serious mind to go with it. And when she makes up her mind, whoa, that girl's got serious fucking determination. What I could never understand is why no one ever saw all these qualities in her. She's been around, you know, trucking all over the islands for years before I met her. She's game for just about anything. She's loyal. She gets on the bus, she's riding it to the end of the line. We're like pieces in a jigsaw puzzle. She's one half of the picture and I'm the other, and all our pieces fit together. Plus, she has this inner serenity most times, and she helps keep me serene, too."

"Sounds like quite a girl. Is she beautiful?"

"Nah, not in the sense you mean. More like the punkin-cheeked girl next door -- cute, I guess. But outer appearance, that's only the frame that contains the real art. Inside, she's very beautiful -- a beacon of light in the fog."

"Shit, Buck!"

"What?"

"Nothing. If it wasn't for my daughter, I could almost wish I'd grabbed your ass when I had the chance."

"Aw, who's to say it would have worked out? You might not have liked some of the shit I've put Steph through."

"Yeah, maybe. It just makes me sad to listen to you talk -- the way things have turned out with the guy I fell for."

"Things'll get better. You gotta hang in."

"Yeah, sure."

"The guy like to travel?"

"We've been on a few gambling junkets to Vegas, that's about it."

"He's got money, right?"

"Yeah."

"Try to get him interested in going somewhere. You know, where he's out of it, where he can relax and forget about the pressure. Ever wanted to go to Paris or Rome?"

"Oh, man, are you kidding?"

"No, Mele. I guarantee you, if I was rich, for the next ten years, maybe forever, I'd be a traveling man, a real world traveler. My best subject in school was geography. I could name you all the states and their capital cities. I could give you the capital of any country you named and tell you where it was. My favorite toy was a globe of the world. I read about all these places, how the people live, the clothes they wear, their customs, religions, forms of government -- all I want to do is go see them all, meet all those people. Paris? Yeah, one day. I'll be moored on the Left Bank of the Ile de Paris -- where the artists and poets hang out, you know? -- a wine-colored beret, a beard, a deep fucking book by Jean-Paul Sartre in the original French -- just a prop, see? -- and Steph will be out shushing the tourists from disturbing the great man at work and hustling his delightful essays and tales about his travels, all the women he's loved, the occasional insightful poem."

"Oh, Buck, shit, how did I miss you?"

"Nah, c'mon, Mele. You could wrap that unappreciative lummox you got around your finger, you took a notion. You're a bright girl, you got a college education."

"Yeah, right, and I can buy a cup of coffee with it -- if I have any change in my purse, right?"

"Gee, where have I heard that before?"

"Paris, hm? I don't think he'd ever go for it."

"He loves his kid, right?"

"Yeah, he dotes on her."

"And he's worried about something, right?"

"Yeah."

"Well, you know, if some guys showed up to, like, rub him out, and they showed up at your house, say, you and the kid would be in danger, right?"

She gave me a long, strange look.

"So maybe if he understood that, he'd see the sense of at least protecting his wife and kid. You married?"

She shook her head no.

"Maybe he'd send you away for a few months. Then maybe he'd miss you."

"Okay, I see what you're saying." She leaned over the dinette we were sitting at to kiss me.

"Ah, by the way, Mele, where's your ol' man right now? Does he know where you are? Is he going to come looking for you?"

"Sooner or later he'll think to come by here. We had a fight. He went off to his club. I came here to do some thinking. You worried?"

"I confess I am. I'm also worried about my ol' lady. What time is it?"

"Almost four."

"Shit. I'm gonna walk down to the payphone, call the Ginzo."

"There's a car coming."

Oh, shit. I ducked down, got dressed as fast as I could. If it was her ol' man, I just hoped I could sneak out and slip over the side before he or his bodyguard could see me. Who would hear any gunshots out here? Steph and I were the only ones living aboard. Well, there was Larry, but what could he do? Alas, poor Buck! I knew him well!

"It's a pickup with a big box or something in the back."

Whew. I got up for a peek. Steph was just getting out, taking off her shoes in preparation for getting into the little yellow fiberglass dinghy I'd built. The dogs were up making happy little noises, tails and tongues wagging. She pulled herself over, got aboard talking baby talk to them, picked up Puffer and went below.

"I gotta go. It's been great, Mele, seeing you again." I leaned down to kiss her. She stood up, still naked, and kissed me one long, last time.

"Whew! You deserve the best of everything, Mele. I wish you luck. There's ever anything I can do, let me know, you got it."

"You take care, Buck. Maybe I'll see you in Paris someday."

"Listen, one more thing. Talk to the guy's mother. Get her on your side. Guy can't tell his mom to shut up."

She smiled, that great overbite.

*****

"Where the hell were you," I demanded right off the bat. "It's late. I was worried."

"Oh, there you are. I wondered."

"Why are you so late?"

"Nothing important."

"I was gonna call the club when I saw you drive up."

"Sorry."

"Steph."

"What?"

"C'mon."

"I was out with a guy. He paid me two hundred dollars to fuck me."

"What!"

"Hey, it's no big deal, ya know?"

"What, you're hooking out of that fucking club and it's no big deal?"

"Just a little. Only two or three guys. They're lonely. They wanna pay to fuck me, no big deal. Everybody comes out ahead."

I plopped down on the settee across from the minuscule dinette before I forgot in my agitation that the ceiling was only five feet, nine inches from the floor. "How in the fuck!"

"Calm down." She lit a joint, handed it to me. "You want a beer?"

"Yeah! What the fuck, Steph! You're selling your ass out of that joint?"

"Only a little. I'm thinking about taking on a few more customers. It pays pretty good, ya know?"

"So does robbing banks!"

"It's not the same. Nobody's hurt, nobody loses. It's not like I planned it or anything. It just happened. See, there was this old Oriental guy, really a nice man. But he's lonely, ya know? If we're not too busy, I sit and talk with him. He says his wife's kinda cold, that she's not interested in sex. Well, he sits in the bar all night, and when we close he's kissing my hand and telling me how sweet I am."

"Yeah, I'll bet!"

"No, really, babe. So, finally, after a month or so, ya know, this sad old guy, he hits on me, says he'll pay me a hundred dollars just to eat my pussy. What the hell? I took pity on the poor guy. Gawd, he ate me out for, like, an hour! He said it was like being in church and he was praying before an altar. I mean, he was so reverent. He said my cunt was like a shiny pink butterfly, ya know, caressing its wings and licking the nectar off it. He was really nice, such a gentleman. I mean, my heart really went out to the guy. I gave him a nice little blowjob he said he'd never forget. He had a cute little dick and there was hardly any come at all. Jeez, he was even crying!"

"Ah, Steph, Jesus! I don't want to hear this!"

"What, we can't talk anymore?"

"We can talk, but does it have to be about this shit?"

"It's not shit. You oughta try a little understanding. You're thinking I'm some kinda whore or something."

"That's exactly what they call broads who sell their asses! Talking's about owning up, too!"

"You're making a judgment without knowing anything about it!"

"I know all I need to know!"

She had tears in her eyes. I toked and drank and it wasn't helping at all. I'd probably never get any sleep. The MDA was still working its energy through my body. Sometimes there's too many sighs inside and there's nothing for it but to wait them out.

"Okay. Don't cry. So why were you late? You out with this poor old guy again and his little pink butterfly had magically transformed into one of Heaven's own angels freshly born of the seas? He found wet feathers in your pussy, right?"

She broke with a laugh, wiped at her eyes.

"Naw, it was this fat Portagee. He's been hitting on me offering money. So I finally said okay. We drove down by McHenna Point. First he fucked me doggy fashion. Okay, no big deal, it was all over in a coupla minutes. Except he stunk so bad. I guess he came to the Ginzo from work without going home to bathe. So he pays me a hundred bucks. But then he says he wants some head. Well, I didn't wanna, so he offers me another hundred bucks, so what the hell? Only he stunk so bad down there and he kept trying to deepthroat me. I gagged and almost threw up when he came. He gave me another twenty dollars cash and an eighty-dollar check."

Listening to all this shit and feeling like I was about to throw up myself, I nevertheless realized that Stephanie had some weird need to not only confess, but to confess in every tiny detail, as though words themselves could exorcise the acts they described. She was not ashamed of what she'd done, but only troubled by the misery in the world, about what she and others had to suffer in getting a little relief. I tried to relate her behavior to myself. What if, I asked, Mele had paid me two hundred bucks for a fuck that she needed far more than I did? Ha, I'd probably be flattered, might even go into business myself if there was any market. It all boiled down to a male point of view versus a female point of view, and the twain weren't even close to meeting. How could I condemn her? How many times had I whored myself in life when there wasn't a dollar in sight to be made?

"Babe," I said, loving her through my anger and frustration, and drawing upon the wisest, deepest philosophy of which I was capable, as righteous and straight as I could put it. "You can't save the whole fucking world. It's enough if we can save ourselves and maybe help a few others along the way. If you don't want to wind up with a lot of worthless paper, you'll demand cash in every transaction. Not checks, not credit cards, not IOUs. Cash. It's the coin of the realm."

*****

It was time to check our two little Big Island stashes, time to test Dickie and Carlos. I had told them that it was a hit-or-miss proposition, but they were game to check it out.

Steph drove me up to Lahaina, kissed me goodbye, and said she'd be on the lookout for when we sailed by Maalaea on our way to Kawaihae.

I was seasick again only a couple of hours into it. They kept giving me chores to do -- make a sailorman out of you yet -- so I'd be too busy for dumping over the side. Out in the strait between Maui and the Big Island, the wind picked up and the waves went higher. I was on the helm, Dickie giving me little steerage pointers, how it was better to steer to a point on land or a star than to keep your eyes glued to the compass for a course. He showed me by examples how to tell when the sails were sheeted right for best advantage in the wind, talking and talking and talking to keep my attention away from being sick, trying to instill as much knowledge as possible in the time available.

It got dark and a million stars appeared. The murmuring sea was right there a few feet away and miles deep -- a huge valley between two underwater mountains -- and I knew full well what Thomas Fleming Day had meant with his printed words. Wind and wave, moon and star, a white little boat with white sails, three men in a tub rub-a-dub-dub all dancing the dance of silvery flashings in the night.

After making harbor and anchoring, Dickie having conned his Islander in by chart and depth-finder, Carlos at the bow as extra eyes, we rented a car the next morning and I gave directions to guide us over the complicated grid of gravel roads and back trails to the first of our hidden plots. About twenty-five or thirty plants had survived.

"Not bad, not bad," I opined.

"What happened to the other ones? Why'd they die?"

"'Most of those were probably male plants. Their only purpose is to pollinate the females. Not much in the way of sinsemilla, I'm afraid."

We harvested, cutting the branches off the main stalks, placing them in plastic garbage bags, then drove on to the other plot. About the same, the plants taller and heavier from their burden of seed than our usual pinched variety, but producing less useable and less stony product. Well, something was better than nothing. I was wishing we'd taken the time to plant more, but the excitement of finding a boat at last had taken our attention away.

By nightfall, we were back at Kawaihae, where we ferried the load aboard in a little inflatable dink before crashing out. We were up and away early the next morning.

On the way, I heaved over the side regularly. "Try eating something," they said. I did -- and heaved it all over the side.

"Jesus, boys, I sure wish you'd get to work making me a sailor-man!"

"Ever think about driving trucks," Carlos quipped.

Instead of spending the extra hours sailing on up to Lahaina, I had them drop me at Maalaea, where Dickie lowered sails and motored in. It made me rethink our engineless status. It would be a bitch getting in and out of small harbors on sail alone. Hm.

Steph was in, surprised to see us, inviting Dickie and Carlos to stay and visit awhile.

"Nah, babe, they got work to do." I'd told Dickie that he and Carlos had to cure the pakalolo before weighing and bagging it up for the trip to Honolulu. In a few days I would fly over to get with Henry and he would be on hand to meet them at the quiet and laidback Keehi Lagoon harbor.

*****

The reason for my trip to Honolulu was to re-register our boat into my new name, Roy Allen. I thought we might also come up with a more permanent name. Stephanie had been a whim to please Steph, my own decision, but she hadn't been particularly thrilled, and our sweet baby had sat around with no name on her transom. So I thought we might come up with one that was meaningful and pleasing to us both.

We went round and round trying out different ones, letting our fancies run free. Nothing was working until Steph said, "L'Chaim," like she was trying to cough up some phlegm.

"That means 'to life', right?"

"Yeh, like a toast."

"I like it. But maybe we should translate it into Hawaiian. Whattayou think?"

"Yeh, geez, see how it sounds. We gotta find out the words."

Easy enough. We had it the next day. I meant to, ola meant life. I ola. We married the two words, made them one. Iola. To life. It was a done deal. Our dancing little boat had a name, was ready to spread the wings of her sails and fly through the sea.

*****

One day while on a trip into town, we passed the place that Mele's guy owned. The entire front was opened and it sort of reminded me of a sidewalk cafe. There were only three people in it that could be seen, a bartender, a waiter, and Mele's ol' man in gold slacks and a dark Hawaiian shirt sitting at a table reading a newspaper over coffee.

"Hey, babe, you up for lunch, a sandwich maybe?"

When I'd parked and we'd made our way to the place, I paused with a sunny grin to ask, "Are you open for business?" He paused to look up from his paper. "Sure, c'mon in," he grinned back. As we started forward, he added, "Why don't you join me? I always like to meet new people. I'm the owner. You're welcome. Please sit down."

"Hi, pleased to meet you. My name's Roy Allen, and this is my wahine, Stephanie. We're staying aboard our sailboat at Maalaea."

"I'm Kama, short for Kamahoahoa, too much of a mouthful for most haoles. I've got my own boat there. Maybe you've seen her," he said, giving her name.

"Oh, yeah, that great old character boat! They don't make them like that anymore."

"Yeah. I don't get out as much as I'd like." He turned his head, raised his voice. "Waiter! Bring these folks menus, wiki-wiki!' The waiter rushed over to comply. We ordered.

Suddenly Steph had a grip on my arm, leaning against me, her head downturned, doubtless admiring the muscular sculpture of my forearm, my artist's delicate hands.

"What, babe?"

She shook her head without raising her eyes. I ignored her -- probably the onset of one of those strange female moods, the vapors or something.

"You know, Kama, I had a boat like that I'd be going places," I said, feeling like a boyscout trying to do a good deed. Maybe I could plant traveling ideas in his head. "You ever take her on a long voyage?"

"Nah, just between the islands. I lived aboard her in Hilo Bay for awhile, but business, you know, it takes up a lot of my time."

"What's her range? What, she's about sixty feet on deck?"

"Yeah. I'm not sure her range. Load up enough barrels of diesel, probably go anywhere."

"What kind of engine?"

"Oh, one of those big old, slow-running Listers. Good engine. Never give me any pilikia."

"Oh, yeah. I almost bought a small one for our boat, but it was too complicated for me. Hilo Bay, hey? We're from the Big Island. I lived a few months I first got over here from California in a motel right up near where Volcano Road starts."

"Oh, yeah, the loop, sure. Vacationing, just cruising, what?"

"Nah. We bought our boat here, rebuilt her. Heading over to Oahu, then Kauai, then, well, southern parts here we come!"

"Ah, man, that must be nice, just pack up and go. I always wanted to go to Tahiti, see where my ancestors came from."

"Lemme tell you something, Kama. All my life I've dreamed of sailing away, never quite got it together, one excuse or another, family, business, circumstance, always something. Now, man, I'm nearing forty years old, I finally made up my mind, committed myself.

You got a wahine, kids?"

"Yeah."

"How old's your kid?"

"She's just a baby. Can't go running off to sea with a kid."

"A girl? Hey, great. I got a daughter, too, most beautiful kid in the whole world."

He grinned. "Nah, mine is."

"Well, you know, if I had my kid here with me -- she's only nine years old -- she'd be on that boat with me. Think about it, how it would be growing up on a boat, man. Hawaiians, Tahitians, all island peoples, they're all water people, boat people. You could take your daughter to Moorea, Rarotonga, the Tuamotus, Samoa, go down and see the Maoris in New Zealand, give her a real taste of history, how the Polynesians live. Here, man, the whole culture is being lost. It's all city shit, haole ways. You're younger than me, man, but don't wait too late. There's a whole fucking planet out there! Kuleana, kaka! You're dying here by the inch, man! Life is out there! Adventure! You ever heard of Atlas?"

"Hah? Oh, yeah. He the guy got the world on his shoulders, right?"

"That's him. One of the Greek gods. Lotta work carrying around the world on your neck, you know? What's Atlas gotta do to have any fun, enjoy life?"

He looked at me blankly.

"I'll tell you. He's gotta shrug."

"Shrug?"

"Yeah. He's gotta dump that load. Get himself free. You free, Kama, you really free, man?"

Thank you, Ayn Rand, for that little homily.

"You make it sound good, Roy."

"It ain't really so hard once you make up your mind."

I bit into the sandwich the waiter had brought, ignoring Steph's deathgrip on my arm, sipped the draft beer. I don't know why, but I was getting to like this guy. We kept shooting it back and forth, meandering all over the conversational field. There was something about the guy, a kind of charm, an attractiveness, an intelligence, beneath the stockiness of his build, a strength. I had noticed the bartender, a local, keeping an eye on us and the street. He was probably the bodyguard. The waiter, a haole, was all over the place, picking up, sweeping, mopping, polishing, keeping himself busy. I thought about dropping Henry's name on Kama, see what happened, but decided against it. No use letting him know where I was coming from. I'd probably never see him again.

A phone rang. The bartender answered, waved at his boss. "Would you excuse me, please?"

When he'd turned away, Steph whispered, "That guy!"

"What guy?"

"Sh! The waiter!"

"What about him?"

"He's the guy!"

"What guy?"

"The massage guy, the one that owes me fifty bucks."

I looked at a pasty guy who did a fair job of hiding from the sun. What was he, a cat burglar from northern Wisconsin? But big and muscular. I suddenly realized that Steph had decided to leave her personal feminine liberation behind in favor of traditional male chauvinistic stereotyping -- she expects me to do something about her problem. Oh, me bucko, how much mileage can you get from your crazy-man act before someone breaks your nose?

As if I didn't get it, she petulantly reminded me by repeating herself. "He still owes me fifty dollars!" Me and my boyscout tendencies!

When Kama had returned, I got right to it, fool or brave soul that I am. "Your waiter, Kama, he been with you long?"

"Hah? Nah, a month or so. Why?"

I decided to go native on him. "I get one little hehia wit him."

"A problem? What?"

"He wen' ho'o'ino (insult) my wahine in one iki kuleana aelike. (small business deal)

"Him?"

"Ae."

"My waiter?"

"Ae."

"Waiter! Hele mai, wiki-wiki!"

The mutt rushed over, obviously anxious. He knew something about his boss, his reputation. "Yes, boss, what can I do? What do you need?"

"You wen' insult this woman here?"

"No, sir! Absolutely not, sir! I wouldn't thing of it!"

Kama looked at me. Steph was studying her lap, blushing -- whether from pleasure or embarrassment, who knows? Okay. My role. Something icy, steely, but exceedingly polite to emphasize a bloodthirsty viciousness waiting to step from its insubstantial confines.

Cagney? Bogart? No, more modern, more realistic. De Niro? Olivier? Harvey Keitel? Pacino? Yeah, Al Pacino, when he tells his brother Freddy to never go against the family again.

"I believe you owe my wife one hundred dollars," I began. Give her the indefensible legitimacy of a wife, that always worked. Double the amount, what the heck. Would he dare protest?

"As mutually agreed," I continued, pausing in order to quietly stress the phrase, to allow him to shiver at the possible consequences of breaking a sacred contract.

"When she participated in an exoteric demonstration of the more, ah, arcane elements of elevated colonics," I went blithely on, betting that he, like Mele and so many other young people, was a college joe who'd stayed to work and hustle his way in the sunny fields of opportunity that the islands offered. I was pretty sure Kama had no idea of what I was saying -- at least he didn't burst out laughing.

I concluded. "Is that not correct?"

He gaped at me, gulped, and blinked. He knew I knew. "Ah, yes, sir, that is correct," he replied, obviously desperate not to get his ass caught between a door and the jamb. "And I apologize most profusely. I inadvertently misplaced the lady's address and was prevented from mailing the check. I was about to approach with full payment, sir, as soon as I realized who she was. I was only waiting until you'd finished your meal, sir. Madam."

Had to give it to the guy -- he was thinking on his feet. Kama broke in. "You owe dis wahine one hundred dollah?"

"Yes, sir, I do."

"You pay her now."

"Yes, of course," he said, quickly fishing out his wallet to count with trembling hands seventy-one dollars upon the table. "Ah, I'm afraid I'm a little short, sir. Would you take a check for the balance?"

Kama whipped out his wallet, threw down a fifty and retrieved a twenty. "Here! I deduct it from you pay!"

Going for the Oscar, I ostentatiously drew a one-dollar bill aside. "Thank you. Let this be the tip for your services today."

"Now then, my friend," I said, turning back to Kama. "Where were we?"

"I tink I fire dat haole," Kama said, glaring at his retreating back.

"Oh, no, please. At least not until he's worked off the advance on his wages."

He grinned at my wink.

When we left an hour later, our tab was on the house.

*****

Nimble little Puffer wasn't nimble enough when a rusty old rattletrap of a pickup came tearing through at ten miles per hour over the speed limit of fifteen on the turnout road into Maalaea. It whacked her head over teacups and, as the old flivver screeched to a stop, she ran off ki-yiing on three legs into a strand of nearby forest.

Steph immediately went into hysterical mode, chasing off after her little alter ego crying, "Puffer! Oh, Puffy-pie, come to mama! C'mon, Puffy-wuffy, poor baby," until she, too, disappeared.

I approached a tall old duffer half-whiffled and shaken from the experience. "Say, bud, you can't read that big sign says 15MPH? We got children and dogs running around down here and you come tootling through on prayers and wine fumes? You just ran over my wife's pooch, and she loves that dog more than kids because we can't have kids."

"Jesus, mister, I'm sorry as hell! I didn't mean to hit that poor animal! I got dogs myself, and nine grandchildren! I wouldn't harm a fly!"

"Well, all right, I believe you, damned if I don't. But you gotta get them big feet of yours off that gas pedal. You were going just a little too fast."

"Yes, sir, I know that, sir, and I'm damned sorry. You bring that little dog up here, we'll run him into the vet. I'll pay all the bills. Damn, I'm sure sorry!"

"Nah, forget it. You seem like a decent guy. You go on, now. We'll handle it. But you watch your speed next time you're passing through here."

"'I sure will, mister, you can count on it."

I walked toward the strand of trees, Popolo and Sista up and alert, taking it all in. "Steph! Steph!"

No answer. Better just wait for her. A half hour later, she came out weeping pitifully. "I can't find her! I can't find her anywhere!" "Don't worry, babe, we'll find her. She's probably laid up somewhere licking her wound. She's gonna be all right. You go on inside. I'll go find her."

"No, I'm coming with you! She's hurt! She may be dying!"

I didn't walk twenty feet into the woods, but casting back and forth across the footpath, before I found her curled up at the foot of a tree looking as cool as if nothing had happened.

"Here, Steph."

"Oh, Puffy-pie! There you are! My poor Puffy-wuffy! Mommy's been looking all over for you!"

She bent to pick her up, which sent Puffer into a new set of high-pitched yips.

"No, babe, don't touch her."

"What's wrong with her? Is my widdle sweetsie-weetsie okay?" "You go on ahead, babe. I'll carry her."

I had a way with dogs, had been around them plenty, knew what to do -- old hat for me. I got her cupped under my forearms and carried her back, not a whimper out of her -- up the ladder and inside. Her left hind leg was broken in two places down low.

"Don't worry, babe, I know what to do. See, I cut out a piece of plywood for the underside of her leg. It runs up high to her belly. We pad that end a bit. The bottom runs a little below her foot. We slip it under her leg, wrap it carefully, then tape it up. She'll lay around a day or two and then be up clumping around so she can go to the bathroom. She'll be fine."

"No, my gawd! We gotta get her to the pet hospital, the vet so he can X-ray her, give her shots for the pain, antibiotics, put her to sleep so he can put a cast on it!"

"No, babe, we don't need none of that shit. I'm telling you..."

But Steph would have none of my home remedies. If I didn't drive her and Puffer to the vet, she was going to call an ambulance, by-gawd-and-don't-mess-with-me-where-my-Puffy-wuffy's-concerned!

I knew when to fold 'em. I carried the mutt down to the Datsun, laid her in the seat between us, and had to quietly, most politely, and in my kindest voice, insist that she not try to pick her up and cuddle her.

At the vet's clear up Hana-side, I carried her in. The doggie doc first noted that Puffer's leg seemed to be broken. Then he X-rayed her to confirm that it was broken in two places. Then he proceeded to cut out a piece of plywood on a jigsaw, pad the high end, slip it under the leg gently, wrap it with gauze, and tape over it.

Gentleman that I am, I remained silent.

"There you go, ma'am. Six weeks or so, she'll be good as new."

"That's it?"

"That's it."

"Aren't you going to give her a shot for the pain?"

"She doesn't need it. By now, she's got her own internal painkillers working. She'll lay around and sleep for a couple of days. Don't worry, that's natural."

"Will she be able to walk in that thing?"

"Oh, yes. She'll adapt to it, go to the bathroom and everything. "I think she should have a shot for the pain. I know she's in pain. I can feel her pain."

He looked at me. I rolled my eyes and nodded. Give the mutt a nice little high, what the hell.

"She'll have to stay overnight if I do. I'll need to monitor her."

Okay. Fine. Maybe we could give her a CAT-scan, too, test for hemorrhoids, allergies, and pre-menstrual stress. Guy probably only charged an arm and a leg, two fingers and three toes down, five years on the balance at an affordable APR.

Steph had to get drunk, cry into her cups, and tell saccharine, ultra-cutesy love stories about her little pootsie-wootsie that would make a catatonic beg for mercy.

I filled her cup, lit her joint, rubbed her neck and brow, suggested she take a Parest and played How Much Is That Doggy In The Window softly on my kazoo in lonesome blues riffs until she zonked out.

I kept my outrage over the bill to myself.

*****

Not three days later the old duffer in his rattletrap came through again, this time creeping along at five miles an hour. Good, guy had learned his lesson.

We were situated near a curve in the road. It was just after supper and I had come down to take Popolo and Sista for a run out along the promontory enclosing the bay.

At the moment, the pickup was coming toward us. As much as I get along with animals and however much I fancy an understanding of their behavior, I would never in a million years try to explain Popolo's motivation for what happened next.

I had just unclasped his collar from the long chain that kept he and Sista near the boat, when he growled a serious growl and broke into a full charge straight for the pickup. It was so sudden and so unexpected and over with so fast that neither I nor the old guy had a chance to react. Popolo ran head-on into the pickup. Which brought him up short rather abruptly. Ouch! Suddenly the front part of his body was going backwards, while his nether end was still catching up. He slid sideways under the vehicle and a rear wheel bounced over his hindquarters.

The pickup lurched to a stop. I ran to Popolo, peripherally aware of the old guy ducking to the side and screaming, "Jesus, mister, I wasn't speeding!"

Popolo was picking himself up, trying to shake the stars from his head. I was on my knees, touching and examining him, muttering, "Popolo, Popolo! What the hell you think you're doing, boy?"

He shook his head, a stunned look in his eye as he warily considered the tailgate -- as if he couldn't believe a mere inanimate mechanical device had rang his bell. He was bleeding from a cut above one eye, had raw abrasions and pieces of missing fur in several places -- but he was on his feet, shaking his head, a baleful look growing in his eye, the spunk of a renewed growl. I grabbed his collar to lead him back to the boat before he decided to try tearing the bumper or the exhaust pipe off.

Sista, still tethered, was barking up a storm." C'mon, boy, c'mon now. Get yourself over here where we can fix you up," I coaxed. He was limping on a hind leg.

By then the driver, sober as a judge, was out. "Jesus, mister, it wasn't my fault! I was going slower than a baby can crawl! He charged right at me! What's the matter with that dog?"

I waved a hand in annoyance. "I don't know. Maybe he doesn't like your pickup."

"Don't like my pickup? What's wrong with my pickup?"
"Burns too much oil."

Off to the vet for X-rays and the application of antiseptics and salves. Doggie doc was going to get rich off us.

Popolo had a hairline fracture in his upper thighbone. Nothing to be done but let him lay around and snooze it off.

I'd always thought Popolo was a little on the dumb side, for all his slaphappy disposition, but he'd clearly demonstrated his ability to learn. He never attacked a pickup again.

Steph's theory was that he was like me. He got pissed off whenever anyone messed with his womenfolk.

*****

Dickie and Carlos showed up with my share of the proceeds, eight grand, a half and half deal. He'd gotten three-fifty each for the fifty pounds from Henry, a slightly lower price due to its slightly inferior quality. He also brought me a big bag of seeds I'd asked him to shake out for me. The extra five hundred I cavalierly wrote off to expenses. Dickie popped for prime rib and an evening of celebration at Buzz's.

We were preparing for our maiden voyage and made plans to get together in Honolulu. They wanted to do some work on their own boat.

We would finalize our plans. I had let them in on my secret plan for Palmyra and they were excited.

*****

Our eyes and hearts were turned seaward, anticipating our first voyage. So one fine day as the wind rose in a steady breeze, we started the 20-h.p. Mercury outboard I'd bought from a Korean acquaintance for fifteen dollars, having only to replace the water pump and mount a hinged outboard rack on Iola's stern, freed ourselves from the sternlines ashore, and motored out to hoist the anchor over the bow.

The damn thing was stuck in the mud. I dove down, trying to free it while Steph zipped this way and that to maintain position.

When I'd surface for air, I'd swallow my heart to see her on the verge of one imminent collision or another with piers, boats, bank, or reef area in the very small harbor that Maalaea was. The dogs were crazy with excitement, leaping all over, barking up a storm. Larry, Dickie, and Carlos, were all shouting advice from shore. I had the distinct notion that we'd all somehow gotten caught up in a Laurel and Hardy comedy.

By all the saints of the misty isles of ancient kings, it was time for the Captain-Admiral to take command. I climbed back aboard, ordered the mutts below. Larry swam out, dived, and freed the anchor. As I hauled it up, Steph got us headed in the right direction.

Putt-putting out beyond the waving and yelling of our well-wishers, I hoisted the main, set the jib, shut off and hauled up the outboard. We trimmed sail. Ah, me fine old buckeroos, here we were! This was it. We were asail, all alone, for the first time in our lives. I called the dogs up, going below to carry up the peg-legged Puffer and having to assist Sista up the ladder, for the momentous occasion.

It was glorious. For a couple of hours or so. Until we ran out of wind. We started the motor and switched on the running lights as it was full dark by the time we passed Lahaina on the starboard beam. By ten we began picking up the winds as we approached Kalohi Channel, the often rambunctious sea lane between Molokai to the north and Maui and Lanai to the south.

So far all we had done is steered north, but now, as we came to make our first navigational decision of a left turn, we studied our charts and took bearings to triangulate our position just as the books had taught us.

The five of us sat crowded into the cockpit. Since I had not yet strung netting in a perimeter along the lifelines, we were keeping the mutts close. Already they had assumed various snoozing slouches, bored with it all. We put them below.

Taking turns at the helm, neither of us able to sleep, I was thankful of not so far having suffered a return of seasickness. Lolling with my back against the doghouse looking at faint trails of phosphorescence in our wake, Stephanie's face in the red glow of the compass light seemed more beautiful than I'd ever seen it. I was excited, exultant, and I could see that she was, too. We were alive, focused, forgetful of our troubles. I was born for this, I was thinking. This is what it's all about, freedom, independence, the taking of fate in my own hands. The starry constellations moved in their courses, we in ours.

By dawn we were well down the strait with our port gunnel awash and the seas heaving. So was my stomach by then, but even the occasional retching over the side while Steph took the helm didn't dim my exhilaration. I'd rinse my mouth with seawater, splash some over my head, and get right back to it. The wind had to be over thirty knots, the spray flying. We were heeled hard over, sailing flat out, wrestling the helm on a rollercoaster ride. It was sort of like a first piece of ass, the one you're never supposed to forget.

Steph's eyebrows were raised. "Shouldn't we shorten sail?"

"No. Later if it gets any worse. Let's keep on trucking awhile, okay?"

"Okay!"

"Yahoo!"

By then we were well into the strait between Molokai and Oahu. Fifty yards off the starboard beam, a great white and black killer whale leapt clean out of the sea, wriggling a curious grin at us before splashing back out of sight. We'd read reports in newspapers about these behemoths sinking a yacht near the Galapagos. It was easy enough to imagine one belly-flopping playfully across our midsection, but we saw no more of him.

In the lee of Oahu, wind and wave abated. Poking leisurely along, we bypassed the Ala Wai Yacht Harbor in favor of a quieter, less crowded mooring at Keehi Lagoon. The voyage of a hundred and ten miles or so had taken us twenty-six hours, our average speed slightly better than four knots. We were weary but happy. Getting Iola moored, we took the dogs for a romp, had a shower at the harbor facility, and served up a cockpit supper for all hands. As the colors of the day changed into the magic of twilight, we left the mutts lolling on deck as Steph and I fell tiredly but cozily into our bunk, rocked gently to sleep by the gods of the sea.

I thought sleepily of my late father and of the many who had told him "it won't work" or "it can't be done," of how he had ignored them and proceeded to do what he had to do. I had inherited his belief in himself. Like him, I was wont to "plan something that everyone says is impossible, then jump in with both feet and do it."

I've only just begun, I thought, and there were many miles to go. But we had taken our first test and not been found wanting. I rolled to spoon against Steph with a last sigh of satisfaction.

###

CHAPTER 13

We had shipped the Datsun by barge and soon had wheels to get us all over Honolulu in our forays for all the supplies still needed. We broke out all our lists and went on a spending spree. Charts, sextant, binoculars, an extra compass, and star-guides at a nautical store; a gasoline-powered generator, a powered garden mower and shredder, a chainsaw, and tools at a department store; a multiband shortwave receiver and a supply of batteries at an electronics store; nylon and dacron lines, extra gastanks and containers for more freshwater storage to implement our built-in thirty-gallon tank at a marine store; personal toiletries, enough to last two people for a year, soap, toothpaste, toothbrushes, shampoo, paper towels and toilet paper; a case of a thousand soft-drink cups, a case of a thousand gro-bags, three hundred pounds of Osmocote 18-6-12, our favorite main-fertilizer in time-release beads, enough for six hundred babies, miscellaneous fertilizers and trace elements, a soil-test kit -- all the accouterments required for raising large families of pakalolo; garden seeds for fruits and vegetables -- what Palmyra lacked, we would plant; a visit to Steph's favorite doctor for a renewal of her favorite prescriptions; fishing supplies, lines, hooks, a heavy-duty deepsea pole and reel, an assortment of leaders, sinkers, and lures, a hoop-net, all added to our masks, snorkels, and sling-spear; a visit to Henry, where I traded the last of the MDA for a nice hunk of hashish to add to the two pounds of primo pakalolo; five-gallon jugs of gasoline to be lashed on deck; refilled butane bottles; and all the etceteras of preparing for a 1000-mile voyage to a remote, uninhabited atoll.

We spent, we bought, we toted, and we stowed, labeling and packing away into every nook and cranny. We prepared a map-list of where everything was located so as not to make retrieval of an item a wide-open treasure hunt in case we forgot where a thing was. We bought only enough food to get us through from day to day, trying to save enough stowage space for our final spree -- a three month supply of food.

"Gawd, baby," Steph said, wiping her brow. "It's a good thing we're not rich. Spending money is so exhausting!"

Dickie and Carlos had arrived for enlistment into our service. We spent evenings aboard our boat or theirs working out the final details of our plan. We would leave for Palmyra in June; they would voyage down to resupply us in September, and stay a few weeks in case we needed extra hands in our labors. They would return to Hawaii to wait until December or January before coming again to resupply us. By then, we should have a load of pakalolo for a run to market. Henry would take everything at premium prices in cash. The cycle would continue until we said stop, at least one year, perhaps two.

Larry, not privy to the plan, had arrived in his houseboat-cum-cutter painted fire-engine red, and settled into a slip at Ala Wai. He was chagrined to learn that despite his high-aspect rig, for which I had employed my late experience in helping him to build and install the mast -- would not point even a single degree into the wind. He had to have Maui Made towed to Honolulu.

Conversely, when Dickie had lent his expertise in correcting Iola's compass, we had found that she would tack a course within an arc of 100 degrees to windward, which meant she could sail a course of 50 degrees off the wind. Windjammers and clipperships of old could only achieve about 75 degrees off a direct heading into the wind. The most modern sailboats of the time could go just a bit better at 45 degrees, and later some specially designed and finely tuned racing hulls and rigs would be reputed to achieve as little as 35 degrees. We of course, were quite satisfied with Iola's sailing characteristics.

*****

As our court date approached, we were awakened one early morning by a rapping above, someone calling Steph's name. She got up, made some noise of surprise, and announced that it was her brother. After hurriedly throwing something on to go above and greet him, he and Steph sat in the cockpit while I blundered about to wash up and make coffee. After a brief introduction, he invited us out to breakfast.

Bob was a very different person from Steph, very straight and conventional, probably a Republican, but likable nonetheless. He was witty and charming, but I could sense that he was at something of a loss as to how to deal with me. Of course I immediately understood that his purpose was to save his dear sister from the Svengalic sway of a vile drug dealer. I thought he might be having trouble reconciling his firsthand impressions, drawn from a handsome, polite, and amiable fellow, with his preconceived notions of evil incarnate. He was trying desperately to size me up in order to work out an approach. It wasn't difficult to feel sympathy for him. I would have done the same in his place, though perhaps with less tact.

Dropping me back at Keehi, Steph went off with him for the day. Generous soul that I am, I would give Bob every opportunity to work his suasions on his sister. I felt confident enough that the relationship Steph and I had established was strong enough to withstand any and all assaults. And I was willing to test the proposition by allowing him a free hand to try rending us asunder. Perhaps he had come expecting to be met by a drug-torn maniac hyped to rant, rave, and threaten violence. Poor fellow, no wonder he was confused. He had no idea that I had learned a hard lesson over the years, that it is better to let a relationship go by the boards than to try prolonging it through desperate and artificial means. The real truth of love, which few seem to discover, is that you allow a loved one to find fulfillment through someone other than yourself. You do not attempt to possess or own, and you do not manipulate to a selfish end. This is the recognition of true freedom. What you would have for yourself, you must not begrudge others. If Steph could be talked into leaving me, it was better she do so. Either way she chose, it would tell me everything I needed to know.

Over dinner at Honolulu's Chuck Wagon, a buffet-type place that featured prime rib, I gave him my version of the legal situation and informed him of the plea-bargain which would result in all charges against his sister being dismissed.

When Steph had excused herself for the lady's room, Bob said, "My sister tells me that you two are going to flee Hawaii after your court appearance. Is that true?"

"Steph must really trust you -- to tell you something like that," I replied noncommittally.

"You needn't worry. I'm not going to betray that trust by calling the FBI on you."

"I appreciate that, Bob. What else has she told you?"

"Do you really think that this relationship you have, your plans and all, is good for my sister? I mean, do you love her enough to do what's good for her?"

"You mean assume all the meddlesome qualities of a do-gooder, Bob? First, I don't assume in the least that Stephanie is retarded. I know for a fact that she is an intelligent adult woman fully capable of making all the decisions that affect her own life. Second, our relationship is entirely voluntary on both our parts -- she is free to leave at anytime. Third, what you're asking, although you don't seem to realize it, is that I inflict pain upon Stephanie, which is what would result if I suddenly kicked her out of my life. With all due respect, you're talking to the wrong guy. You have carte blanche to try to persuade her. You should spend your efforts on her and not waste your time on me."

Bob was stunned, I could see, his normally loquacious tongue in a knot from shock. But he seemed to recover nicely and could smile with me in meeting Steph's benevolent gaze at us both when she returned.

As we were leaving the restaurant, me stuffed and happy on the two ribs I'd managed, the second bottle of wine, Bob held back to let Steph go on ahead. I knew he was about to take another stab at it.

"Listen, Bob," I got in first, trying to not only save him the trouble but also to reassure him if I could. "I want you to know this much. I care about Steph more than I can say. I've always tried to take care of her, as well as protect her, and I'm going to continue to do that."

"I appreciate that, Buck, but I still have my doubts."

"Well, Bob, that's a personal problem, isn't it? But since you're Stephanie's beloved brother, please feel free to call on me if you think you need my help. In the meantime, thanks for the dinner and I wish you luck."

*****

"Steph, babe, what exactly did you tell your brother about us sailing off into the blue?"
"Hah? Not much."
"You mention Palmyra, what our plans are?"
"Nah, c'mon, ya kiddin'?"
"How about my new name?"
"Nah."
"So what'd you talk about? I mean, you've gone off with him for two or three days now."
"Aw, just catching up, ya know. We ain't seen each other in a while."
"Steph."
"He's tryna talk me into dumping you."
"I knew that."
"He thinks you're criminally insane."
"What!"
"Well, he had your rapsheet, ya know – got it from somebody he knows in the feds -- and claims you were committed to an institution for the criminally insane."
"What!"
"Don't worry, baby. I told him how you'd told me all about it, that you were only faking it."
"I wasn't faking it! I was exercising my constitutional right to remain silent in the face of false accusations! Besides, it was only for ninety days and I was found to be perfectly sane!"
"Now just calm down. Let's smoke some of that hash you got from Henry. Bobby's only tryna help me because he's concerned."

"Well, he oughta try getting in touch with reality – laying all that boogaloo scare shit on you!"

"Here, babe, take a nice deep toke. Mellow out. Jeez, nothing's changed."

"Royal's here."

"That idiot? What's he want?"

"Nothing. He's gotta put in an appearance, too, enter a plea."

"What, he's gonna cop, too?"

"Yeah, to one count."

"Kieth and Mary'll be there, too, right?"

"Yeah."

"Jeez, we're not gonna get into a long song and dance with them, are we?"

"Not if I can help it."

"Ya think they're ever gonna pay us the money they owe?"

"I ain't counting on it."

"Creeps."

"Take a deep toke, babe."

*****

Everyone was there, Royal, Kieth and Mary -- she with new little baby Joseph in her arms -- Bob to make sure I didn't pull any tricks, and Brook Hart.

We three guys entered our pleas of guilty to one count and the charges against Steph and Mary were dismissed. Brook wanted to talk about money.

We talked. He wasn't satisfied.

"Well, look," I said with a straight face, knowing full well what I was about to do, only wanting to get out of there. "You're also going to get all the money we got deposited with the court for our bail -- four thousand, right? We can sign that over, too."

"Okay."

Kieth and Mary were situated in their Morehouse setting. They claimed to have participated in a nude group birth in a giant heated bathtub when their son was born. Royal hovered, silent and barely able to contain a sneer.

"I've been painting Brook's house," Kieth told me. "Trying to help pay off our debt. I don't know when I'll be able to pay you back that thousand, man."

"Don't worry about it." I wasn't going to be around to collect anyway.

When Kieth and Mary had left, she kissed me and said with an impish twinkle, "Just think, little Joseph was almost yours."

The only joy that averted calamity brought was that they'd also told me the kid had inherited Kieth's asthma and that, with any luck at all, he'd grow up to be a weedhead.

Seeing Steph off alone with Bob, he speaking earnestly, she smilingly patient and serene, nodding her head, I walked down the corridor a ways with Royal.

"So, you fuck, when you gonna pay me that thirty grand you owe me?"

"Ah, man, thing's are kind of tight, you know -- all these lawyer bills."

"You're bum pay, Royal. You got more excuses than a cat's got licks for his own asshole."

"Aw, man, gimme a break! I'll pay you your fucking money! It's just a matter of a little time for me to get back on my feet."

"So how's Lenny and Saul?"

"Keeping a low profile. I don't see much of them anymore."

"I don't wonder." It hadn't been long ago Royal'd been singing their praises, swearing up and down they'd be there with money and support if any trouble came down.

"Hey, why don't you and your ol' lady come on over to my hotel? I got a nice room. We can go out to dinner, have some fun, my treat. My return flight's not until tomorrow."

"Nah, man, I don't think so."

"Don't be like that, Buck. Hey, man, we did hard time together, survived all that fucking shit. This ain't nothing but a little glitch for a couple of steppers like us. C'mon over and take a load off. I brought some good gow."

"Nah, I got a date with my ol' lady. We're going dancing. You know how to dance, Royal?"

"Yeah, I know how to dance."

"You oughta do it more often. It beats the hell out of gow."

*****

It was our last celebration before heading out for Kauai to wait for June, the traditional beginning of good sailing weather for the North Pacific when the northeasterly tradewinds steadied and storms were rare.

Dickie and Carlos were on hand.

"Here," Dickie said, pulling out a handful of silver-dollar-sized wooden wafers about a half-inch thick.

"What, wooden nickels?"

"No, for lashing your mainsail to the boom. Those brass hooks you got are going to lead to torn sails."

I looked at them. They had holes in the centers and a rounded groove in one side.

"I carved 'em myself -- with a pocketknife, sanded 'em down smooth. You screw 'em in staggered along both sides of the boom. Get rid of those hooks. You crisscross the bungi-cord over the reefed sail, just like you're doing. Only no snags with these. I'll put 'em on for you in the morning."

"Wow, Dickie, thanks, man," I said, moved by the gesture. "That's a great idea."

He was modest. "Hey."

"Well, Dickie, I'll tell you what those little wooden jinguses are gonna buy you," I said, relishing seeing the look on his face when I handed him the keys and announced, "These are for the Datsun, camper, kit, and kaboodle. She's all yours."

"What!"

"Yeah, man. We ain't gonna need her where we're going."

"You can sell it, man. Must be worth a grand or two -- pay for all that food you have to buy yet."

"Nah, we got enough for that and then some. You guys need wheels, right? You can load your boards in the back for the north-shore when the surf's up. Consider it a contribution toward expenses for all those supplies you're going to bring us."

"Just as long as it doesn't include your hounds," he grinned. "Nah, we're all gonna become salty dogs together."

*****

That night when they dropped us off, my little brother Larry and his buddy Cal were waiting. Talk about surprise.

"What the hell are you doing here?"

"Is that anyway to greet your favorite bro," he cracked, hugging me. Kid was strong, grown up. "Came over to see your ugly mug, see what all the song and dance is about."

"How the hell'd you find us?"

"Called all the boat harbors, asked if they had a blue boat called Iola."

"Oh." I'd written him, joking that I could use a hand in the rebuilding. "Why didn't you come when there was work to be done?"

"Hey, I'm the smart one in the family, remember?"

We sat late into the night in the cozy closeness below, drinking beer and toking. "Hey, Cal," Larry said to the friend he'd grown up with. "We might as well dump that Mexican stuff we brought overboard. Leave it to my brother to have the real stuff."

"What, you guys carried some grass with you on the plane?"

"Yeah, but hey, don't worry. We brought our guns, too, just in case the fuzz got onto us and we had to shoot our way out."

"At thirty thousand feet!" Steph got in.

"No problem. We had parachutes. You did remember the parachutes, right, Cal?"

"Parachutes?" Cal was trying valiantly to keep his eyes from crossing.

"You guys really brought guns?"

"Hey, you keep telling me about these six hundred pound wild boars you got running around. Figured we'd go bag a few, you know, live on pork chops."

"Goddamn, kid," I blew. "That's a serious federal offense!"

"Nah, we did it all legal, declared 'em. They flew over in the cargo hold. Wouldn't let us bring any ammo, though."

"Fucking cab driver thought we were gonna rob him," Cal cackled. "We hadda put 'em in a suitcase, carry it in the trunk."

"So where's all the hogs, bro? Point us the way, we'll fill your freezer."

I had to laugh at his teasing, the merry insouciant look of him, loving him. "Ah, gee, kid, I guess I forgot to tell you. The local folks don't use guns for hunting wild boars. It ain't sporting."

"What? Don't tell me spears."

Some local boys had once come by to take me pig-hunting with them. When I offered my M-1 and .45, they'd said no, they went only with dogs and pocket knives.

Of course I was incredulous.

They explained that they chased after the baying of the hounds, that when they'd tired an old boar out and he'd turned to confront them, keeping him lunging about in a circle of nipping, barking dogs, one brave hunter would await his chance to send its soul off to Hog Heaven, which was accomplished by jumping on his back and slitting his throat before he could throw and gore him with foot-long tusks.

I thought they were having their fun with me. It wasn't until the next day when I discovered they were dead serious.

We'd chased for hours through the rainforest following the yip and haroo of the hounds until coming finally upon the great beast himself, big and black at four or five hundred pounds, tusks like scimitars cutting the air, pissed off and ready to take on all comers. Two dogs had already been torn by those tusks, one mutt trampled, all to survive for the white thread, needle, and mercurochrome they would be sewed up with in the field by the boys.

The dogs were noisy rushing blurs circling around him, growling and barking, rushing in to nip him. When the boar would turn toward one tormentor, others would leap in from the rear. He spun, squealing his rage.

The boys had their pocketknives out. Me, too. One guy jumped, landed on the boar's back, but went flying when he spun. He was lucky, only getting a few hoofprints on his body before the hounds distracted the beast. The sonofabitch charged right at me, looking as big as a rhinoceros and twice as ugly. Fuck you! I went up a tree!

The valiant old porcine warrior had taken a few superficial slashes, a few toothmarks, before busting out of the ring and into the bush. While the remainder of the hounds kept after him, we all stopped to tend and carry the wounded ones back to the pickup where the cold beer was. Out came the pakalolo and then, when it got dark, we built a fire, cooked up some food, waited for the rest of the hounds to tire and show up, and said to hell with it.

Now, I'd decided to have a little fun with my wisecracking brother. "Nope, no spears. It ain't sporting. You gotta give the pig a fair chance, okay? I mean, running out and plugging a boar long distance with a high-powered firearm, how's that gonna increase the size of your nuts?"

"Nah, see," I continued, getting into it. "What we do first is get us all a pair of those fancy brown and white wingtip shoes golfers wear."

"Yeah?"

"They help you maintain your footing in the rainforests, which can be very treacherous -- those little spikes on the soles?"

"Yeah?"

"Uh-huh, you don't wanna lose your footing one of those five hundred pound fuckers comes after you, right?"

"Uh-huh."

"So when you run up on one of these terrible hairy black beasts with red eyes full of rage and bloodlust..."

"Yeah?"

"You just jump up on him and do a tap dance, you stomp him into puredy fucking hamburger. I mean, you boys got any balls or not?"

*****

They spent the night on deck in sleeping bags with Popolo and Sista. After breakfast served up in the cockpit, we told them we were headed over to Kauai. They were game. Dickie and Carlos came by, Dickie to replace the sail-cord snaps while Carlos hit it off with Larry and Cal, who were about the same age.

We got cleared away and motored out toward the exit to the open sea with snappy winds coming down off the mountains to the north.

I hoisted the main and pulled up the Merc. We went nowhere, just flapped and tossed. Dickie and Carlos were shouting from shore, but I couldn't make out what they were trying to tell us. "You guys hear what they're saying?"

We all listened. They were both pointing and making gestures, but the lines were slapping and the sail clapping in the wind like firecrackers, and their message just wasn't getting across. What was this, some kind of semaphore signaling? I'd have to dig out one of our volumes on sea lore to interpret their arm signals.

Suddenly it quilted and I could faintly hear their voices. "You make out what they're saying?"

"Raise the jib," Steph said.

The jib? Oh, Jesus on a jukeball, me boyo, raise the fucking jib! I ran for the halyard, hauled her up. Steph sheeted it in, spun the helm, and away we went.

"How long you say you been studying up on how to sail, bro?"
My beloved little brother, the smart-mouthed runt of the litter.

*****

Unlike the novelty and excitement of the zippy wind and wave of our maiden voyage from Maui to Oahu, the overnight sail to Kauai was easy and laidback. The winds were light and variable, allowing us to experiment with different combinations of sails. We ran up an overlapping genoa for a time, then tried wing-and-wing by poling out the forestaysail to the opposite side of the jib. All the while Steph and I practiced nautical language which is largely unintelligible to landlubbers, Larry and Cal scratching their head, raising their eyebrows, and watching curiously from their lolling positions my dance about the foredeck to effect changes in the sailplan.

"Yo-ho-ho and where's the blinking rum?" Cal said, trying to get in the spirit of it.

"Wal, shiver me timbers! Let's splice the mainbrace!" snorted my brother.

Entering the harbor at Nawiliwili Bay on the southeastern side on lowered sails with the Merc driving us, we made a right turn and then a left to get around a manmade seawall composed of great chunks of cement dumped in a long, wide row.

Sailing past a luxury hotel with a golden beach, a Hobie Cat came whipping past us with one hull raised from the water. Two beauties with their breasts freed from their bikini bras stood laughing and waving at Larry and Cal who had risen from their torpor to hang out over the lifelines clutching with one hand to the shrouds, the other stuck out with thumb up like hitchhikers, faces alight in silly grins.

"D'ju see that?"

"Did I see that?"

"I told you it was a good idea, coming to Hawaii!"

"You told me? It was my idea!"

What had pleased me was that I'd hardly felt any seasickness -- only a touch of queasiness -- and that Larry and Cal were looking greener than me.

While the boys set off to explore, the tiny township of Lihue up the ringroad a few miles, Steph and I renewed our habit of making lists and working toward getting all the items checked off.

We began to tell them something of our plans, showing them Palmyra on our charts, describing it, and mentioning how long we planned to stay -- leaving out only the pakalolo part. We invited them to come along.

"What, a weird time warp, right? This is a Swiss Family Robinson movie?"

"No girls there? Could you drop us off in Australia on the way?"

They began to look at us askance. Nice little overnight sail, hardly out of sight of land, was one thing, but being stranded at sea with a captain who was still basically a landlubber and to wind up on a desert isle where there was no action in which to engage their youthful energies -- no taverns or hootchy-kootch girls in sight -- well!

After whispered consultations, they decided to return to Honolulu.

"Listen," I told them. "You get tired of all the neon lights there, try the Big Island. Hilo. I'll put you on to some of our friends. They'll help you get situated." I told them to stop in and see Deb, that she could point out a couple empty homesteads in the Acres where they could take up squatter's rights.

"Hey, bro," Larry asked. "You couldn't take these guns off our hands, huh? We'll probably be sleeping on the beaches. Besides, we could use the extra bucks."

I gave them a hundred and fifty dollars for the lever-action rifle, a Marlin .30 caliber, and the Ruger .22 caliber single-action revolver. Would I have any use for them? All I'd ever needed guns for in Hawaii was for personal protection against thieves, but there'd never arisen any necessity to actually use them. Still, they'd made me feel better about my ability to defend home and hearth in the event any emergency situation came flying at us out of the blue. Would we have to contend with thieves on Palmyra? Unlikely. How about pirates? We'd read enough tales of small vessel piracy on the high seas, but most of those were in the Caribbean, and along certain parts of Africa, and in Asian waters.

I cleaned, oiled, and greased them, wrapping and packing them away, along with a couple of boxes of ammo.

I rented a car and we drove up to Hanalei Bay at the northwestern point to kill a few hours until delivering Larry and Cal to the airport in Lihue for their flight to Honolulu. Then we used it to begin buying and hauling food supplies. The foc'sle was packed, the two metal footlockers, the stowage spaces under the vee-berths, stuff stacked and secured atop their cushions by bungi-cord. Bungi-cord was such a handy item, we'd bought an entire roll of it, along with a box of the pointed metal hooks that attached to the ends of a length for securing. Soon enough we ran out of things to do. We were only killing time, waiting to turn over the page of our calendar.

*****

One day we loaded the mutts into our little yellow dink while I rowed our precariously balanced vessel up a river a mile or so. It reminded me of pictures I'd seen in National Geographic of impenetrable green foliage falling into the river from both banks. But we managed to find a nice spot for a picnic where the dogs ran happily off to explore and chase about.

A lovely day was upon us as we lolled cuddling upon a blanket, the crinkles of blue sky through dark leafage, sunlight sparkling on the lazy stream. Steph felt good lying in the nook of my arm, her face like that of a Renoir girl in an expression of thought.

"Baby?"

"Hm?"

"How did we ever get together?"

"I dunno. You came, I saw, we conquered."

"No, really. Why did you choose me out of all the girls you could have chosen?"

"I'm attracted only to the best, darlin'. It's my innate good taste in broads."

"The best? The best at what?"

"Well, you can drive a nail and saw a piece of wood better'n any girl I ever knew."

"C'mon. You didn't fall in love with me for that."

"Best head in Hilo," I tried.

"Really, baby, just be serious for a minute. I mean, I look in a mirror, I don't understand what you see, what turns you on -- plain old Jane personified. Why not Carol, or Barbara, or Laura? They're beautiful."

"Sure, but they don't eclipse the vessel of their keeping."

"What?"

"They're only pretty on the outside, a feast for the eyes, but not near as much as you're a supper for the soul. It's what you have inside that makes all the difference."

She gave me a look. A woman arching an eyebrow at me was always a stimulus, an invitation, and so I launched upon my theory of feminine beauty.

"See, babe, there's basically two kinds of beauty that women have, the inner and the outer. The outer beauty is physical, that odd and ineffable series of fleshy features that -- who knows how? -- Causes us to call her beautiful. But all those attributes are no more than an accident of nature -- it's in the genes. Nobody has any choice in the matter. You're born beautiful, you're born plain, or you're born ugly. There's nothing anyone can do but make the best of it.

"Inner beauty, now, is different. There, we've got a choice. We can make ourselves beautiful on the inside. Oh, it would be nice to have beautiful parents, to be born physically perfect, paragons of beauty. Unfortunately, only about two percent of people are born to be physically beautiful. The rest of us gotta make do. But lemme tell you, of these two kinds of beauty, I favor the self-created.

"We've both known examples of these physically beautiful types who are absolute assholes, so egotistically stuck on themselves they figure they're entitled to everything without any effort. They're ugly inside, unfuckingbearable -- sadists, child-molesters, BNDD pukes, fucking politicians, all those cruel and vicious haters of everyone but themselves. But no matter how ugly a person is outside, if there's an inner beauty we can love them.

"Remember that book we read, The Elephant Man? How he had something inside that raised him to the level of poetry? Sad as hell, but fucking beautiful. And The Hunchback of Notre Dame, he had something inside his deformed body that makes us want to reach out to him his hopeless love for Esmeralda. It's what's inside that counts. You, babe, you're fucking beautiful inside, which is why I love you so much."

Plain Steph was melting, beautiful eyes all misty.

"Plus," I added, inspired. "You not only got a great ass, but I was always a sucker for pigeon-toed broads!"

She kissed me. I kissed her.

"Feel up for a quickie, darlin'?"

"How about a longie?"

"Could we compromise on an inbetweenie?"

"Yeh, anytime. Quickie, longie, inbetweenie, I'm always ready for you, baby."

"One of the things I like about you."

"Only you."

"Yeah?"

"Yeh. You wake up in the middle of the night with a hardon, go right ahead, but slow to start, huh? 'Til I get slippery. You want, like they say, hips, lips, or armpits, any time, lemme know. Front, back, upside down, top or bottom. Anytime at all, day or night, rain or shine, I'm ready. Like, right now."

During this short but fine speech, her words as winged as any found in poetry, she had slipped off her underpants, adjusted the saddle, grabbed the horn, and climbed on for a ride. Joined in the roots of our carnal pleasure, but the day, the place, the time, the words, and our juicy lips, all such as to lead our pleasures in each other up a spiritual plane in a fundamental act of mutual exaltation.

In the aftermath, as they say, as we lay in the afternoon shade drying and cooling our bodies, pleasantly lethargic, I was moved to thank her.

"Thanks, babe. What you said, I appreciate that. I feel honored. Anyone ever tell you you have a succinct way of putting things?"

"Suc-cinct," she pronounced. "Oh, yeh, that reminds me. Anytime you wanna sink down and suck my pussy, the same goes, right? I love the way you suck pussy!"

*****

June but days away, we decided to sail around to Port Allen on the southern shore where, unlike the enclosed Nawiliwili, we could at least see the sea. Setting out in the afternoon, we arrived well after dark. None of the flashing lights seemed to match up with those on our chart. All the books had told us never to attempt entering an unfamiliar harbor at night. We proceeded slowly and, after a near miss with a seawall, entered the tiny harbor without mishap and were feeling smug about it.

What a convenience our secondhand Merc had been in assisting us in and out of harbors, I was thinking, beginning to regret not making more effort to install an inboard engine. Oh, we could have gotten in and out of all of them without an engine, but only by long patience and effort. Well, too late now. We had only one more to leave and one more to enter, and months or years before we'd have to do it again.

Last minute shopping, not so much now. We were packed and ready. We had time to go to the nearby beach to swim, sun, snorkel and bodysurf. We made up picnic lunches and went hiking about the beautiful countryside.

The days were growing longer as we sat out upon the seawall gazing longingly to the south, girding ourselves for the leap outward. The sun was warm, the spray cooled us, and we could see Niihau rising like a great pristine jewel out of the ocean.

*****

Since San Quentin, where I had developed a sporadic but abiding interest in the various disciplines of Yoga and Buddhism, I had rarely debated my attraction to the subject with others.

In 1962, when I had first truly fallen into the state of divine madness of love for the woman who would become my wife and mother of my only child, I had tortured myself through several obsessive episodes in aid of plumbing my own depths -- painting, writing poetry, stories, and strange little plays, spending all my money on film and cameras -- artistic pursuits.

I had been staying with an old prison buddy in Sierra Madre Canyon, near Pasadena, after having returned from my mission to visit every whorehouse in Tijuana. I spent my days suffering in the anguish of my unrequited love, making eccentric companionship with the animals we lived with, a big, fierce white rooster, an epileptic guinea pig, and a scarred old coyote-chasing hound. I traipsed with groups of local kids on expeditions to dig up trapdoor tarantula and photograph them with close-up billows lenses. Other days I photographed birds in flight, enamored of their ability to escape, to fly above it all. I smoked grass, ate peyote buttons, and felt like howling at the moon.

A forest fire had broken out in the mountains above. Firefighters were brought in to contain it and airplanes dove down to bomb the flames with loads of chemicals. I decided to hike up with my camera to see if I could capture some of those dramatic events on film.

I had climbed up and around the steel and concrete dam that kept the winter rains from flooding out the denizens in the canyon below, on up over steep ridges beside a bone-dry arroyo and into the hills, then into the mountains, several hours of the most strenuous effort. Tired and sweating but excited nevertheless to be so close to the action, I got photos of firefighters in hot movement and the silhouettes of bombers caught against the sun as they dropped their red fans of chemical dust to suppress the flames.

In the late afternoon, thirsty and exhausted, I began the trek back down the mountain, hills, and arroyo, thinking only of bath and beer. Along the way I met an old man, about seventy or so, white-haired, wearing a proper dark suit, tie, and felt hat. He was standing under an oak tree, leaning on a walking stick as though waiting for a cab or limousine to arrive. He was neat as a pin, not mussed or disheveled in the least.

"Hello there, young fella," he greeted me. "Quite a grand view, don't you think?"

I was flabbergasted. How had he gotten there? There were no trails or roads nearby. He had to have been delivered by a helicopter or I was hallucinating, neither of which was the case.

"Taking pictures of the fire, are you?"

"Yeah, got some great shots," I replied. "What're you doing up here?"

"Oh, just strolled up for a looksee. How's the fire? They about got it under control?"

"Yeah, I think so. How the hell'd you get up here?"

He shrugged. "Walked up. Nice day for it -- except for the fire. Shame about that. Forests are so beautiful. Hundreds of years to grow a proper forest."

He had just strolled up for a looksee, an old man out for his daily constitutional, not a hair out of place, not a drop of sweat, just meandering up out of curiosity. Jesus jumping jars of jawbreakers, I had a hard time accepting his presence!

"Live there?" He gestured with his cane down the steep slope of the arroyo toward the dam and the shaded community below. "Nice view from here. Pretty."

"Yeah. Hot bath, cold drink, and a soft bed's what I want. You need help getting down? You can follow me if you like." "Oh, good heavens, no. I'm going over that way. Car's parked a few miles yonder. Thank you kindly all the same."

Uneasily, I waved a hand and turned away. "Nice meeting you. Goodbye."

"Yes. Guess I'll be on my way, too. Goodbye."

He turned and sauntered away, disappearing slowly from view as we made our way down opposite sides. After a bit, I stopped to sit, rest, and smoke a bitter cigarette in a dry mouth. Something about the old man got to me. I had expended every effort to get up to the fire and he hardly any. There was about fifty years difference in our ages. How was it possible?

Still, there was something humorous in the situation and I felt cheered. I began to feel a certain new invigoration, a strange sense of the here and now, a reveling in the immediate moment of myself. It was so absurd, the old man being there like that, so nonchalant.

Energy and attitude magically restored, I found a new bounce in my step. I plunged into a gallop and, by leaps and bounds, I flew down a steep grade of the arroyo scattered with loose gravel, rocks, and small boulders, sliding and recoiling in dangerous springs, managing to maintain a perfect if precarious balance, any stumble from which could have done my flesh and bone serious damage, until I came up against the wall of the dam. I rested a few minutes, exhilarated, high on some mysterious source of energy. I climbed up the ridge on one side to descend beyond the dam to a footpath that led along a row of Eucalyptus trees, the sweet, spicy scent rich in my nostrils, then over a footbridge to the paved road. Along the way, feeling so glad to be alive, I glanced up, saw a bird about to leave a branch, and quickly, almost instinctively, raised the camera and clicked the shutter.

When that last photo was developed, it somehow contained and eclipsed all the drama and danger of the men and machines battling the forest fire. It was a perfectly composed shot of a dark bird in flight, the wings and tail-feathers defined in chiaroscuro against a sky fractured by the silhouettes of branches. It was the soul of the day, the old man, and myself.

That day, the old man, the bird in flight, all coalesced into an image upon which, over ensuing years, I would focus my attention and concentration in assuming an efficacious mood for meditation -- my mantra, a day of deathless moments.

Years later, when I would tell of this event to a Tibetan monk, my tutor for a time, he said he thought I had perhaps accidentally achieved a variation of what Buddhists called lung-gom, a trance-walk. Tibetan monks, when traveling long, arduous distances on foot between villages in the Himalayas, may, when a blizzard threatens, put themselves in a transcendent state of lung-gom, and begin to cover distances not normally thought possible for human beings.

It represents the most efficient use of one's physical and mental resources in order to save one's ass for another day.

Lung-gom is related to dumo, which translates as mystic heat. Initiates into the discipline are trained by taking them to a frozen lake, where they shed all their clothes. Their gurus chop a hole in the ice, immerse sheets into the frigid waters, then drape them around their bodies until they are frozen solid. The ability to control one's metabolism may generate enough heat to keep from freezing to death. The number of wet sheets they are able to withstand freezing on their bodies serves as an indicator of the degree of their success.

*****

I have been true to my rinpoche, the Buddhist adept who guided me to the beginning of my unique path, the steps I would take in the way of accepting the Four Noble Truths and seeking enlightenment through the Eightfold Path, the basic tenets of Buddhism.

Buddhism, strictly speaking, is not a religion, although many consider it so. This erroneous connection is made because wherever Buddhism has established itself the regional religions, whatever they are and whoever their gods, have attached themselves to the practice. The religion and deities are different in different countries; those of Tibet are not those of India are not those of Japan. In the United States there are Christian Buddhists.

Buddha was only a man, an extraordinary one to be sure, who essayed to teach and not assume to godhood. Many of his followers, however, have apotheosized him. All the tantras, the texts of Buddhist literature, are about the ins and outs of achieving not only enlightenment but also an end from suffering through means of the Eightfold Path.

Buddha's insight, some five hundred years before Jesus Christ, was first the formulation of the Four Noble Truths, which were such that anyone could understand. 1. Existence is unhappiness; 2. Unhappiness is caused by selfishness (want, desire, greed); 3. Unhappiness ends when selfishness ends; and 4. Selfishness ends through the Eightfold Path.

The Eightfold Path is a prescription for living. It has to do with teaching and learning right behavior in the areas of: 1.Understanding; 2.Purpose; 3.Speech; 4.Conduct; 5.Vocation;

6. Effort; 7.Alertness; and 8.Concentration in a manner mindful of the Four Noble Truths.

Each and every human being is different from all others; each is unique, and therefore each pursues a unique path toward salvation or enlightenment. Individuals must get each of the eight parts of the path right for himself. The teacher merely assists the neophyte in leading him to find his own answers, which may not be right for others.

The Eightfold Path, therefore, is a basic method of attaining freedom from the extremes of self-indulgence and self-torture. Buddha's teachings included a set of concepts about how the mind works -- the oldest psychology of which the world has any record, and it has become the basis of a sophisticated system of thought. Its main propositions are that ordinary human existence is an unsatisfactory state in which people make themselves miserable through a fundamental misunderstanding of their own nature.

Since I have myself experienced enough misery to last several lifetimes, you may understand my interest in the subject.

Buddhist teachings up to about the time of Christ were called Hinayana, also known as the lesser vehicle. With the help of scholars and practitioners over the centuries, Hinayana transformed into a more vigorous form called Mahayana, or the greater vehicle. Hinayana established itself in Ceylon and Burma, while Mahayana spread throughout the Orient, including Tibet, China, and Japan. In China, one school increasingly focused on meditation -- called djana in Sanskrit -- and became identified by a version known as ch'an. Translated into Japanese, it became Zen Buddhism, Zen being a very pure form of Mahayana.

Tibetan monasteries became centers of Buddhist scholarship, and included both Hinayana and Mahayana -- but also a mysterious third force called vajrayana, the diamond vehicle, which is more widely known as Tantric Buddhism.

The origins of Tantric Buddhism are lost, but it seems to have involved an absorption of teachings from non-Buddhistic sources: Hindu philosophies, Indian Yogas, and probably at a later date, the Sufis, the holy men of Islam. Tantrism was a major force in Indian Buddhism by the seventh century and Tibetans trace the history of vajrayana in their country from the eighth century.

The word vajra is sometimes translated as lightning bolt, which conjures up images of great power, such as the psychic energy the yogis believe to be available within the human body. It also suggests an instantaneous burst of enlightenment, called satori. Vajrayana also means the short path. Since vajra may also be translated as diamond, we thus arrive at the diamond vehicle. The diamond image is used in many ways in Tibetan Buddhist literature to describe the universe and the basic quality of mind -- clear, brilliant, indestructible, and many-faceted. Vajrayana teachings stress self-acceptance, self-study, and the naturalness of enlightenment.

The vajrayana tradition is a heritage of tantras, or texts, and of practices, which may include chants, body movements, rituals, and images to be held in the mind as visual meditations. In a way, it is an elitist form of Buddhism, since much of its lore is kept secret and transmitted only to students judged ready to handle it. Although it may be a short path to enlightenment, it is not an easy one. Its more advanced practices are both strenuous and dangerous, involving long hours of concentration and frightening journeys into the depths of the unconscious. It also requires relentless honesty with oneself and insists on valuing every experience in order to unite spiritual growth with the reality of one's life.

I ride the diamond vehicle like a Hell's Angel rides a Harley. I have kept the secrets my tutor entrusted with me, the promise not to add a buddyseat for hitchhikers.

Which means?

Simply this.

I am a man, neither much worse nor better than other men, who seeks to understand himself, others, and the world he lives in, to be a good man and have some worth. Most people, including myself, have at one time or another been afflicted by what Buddhists call samsara, or going around in circles. The mind goes around within the narrow confines of social reality, stuck in socially programmed habits and behavior patterns and ways of thinking. The waking-up process called enlightenment, to which we all yearn, is a breakthrough to a fresher appreciation of reality, one less fettered by social values and beliefs.

The monastic life, which countless Buddhists have chosen and in a way is what prison life has forced upon me, is a path of renunciation, celibate, vegetarian in most countries, spartan and plain. The Buddhist monk is required to live under conditions considerably more severe than those imposed upon the general public because it is believed, to be the most efficient way to become enlightened, to break free of the attachment and the narrow view of the unenlightened samsaric mind. A monk's behavior should be above ordinary morality.

Most Buddhists choose to live like ordinary people, to get married and obey laws and make no effort to be different. The element these lifestyles have in common is that they take ordinary social morality to be nothing more than a reference point, never an ultimate code of behavior. The question, in choosing a way of behaving, is: What works best for me? Different strokes for different folks.

Others, like myself, having borne too much of the enforced monastic life of prisons, the madness, cruelty, injury and death, the going around in circles on a single sadomasochistic level, wild tantric outcasts, like me, who seek to ride the diamond vehicle, have sometimes taken precisely the opposite path from that chosen by monastics -- to live below or above the level of ordinary social morality and thus become free of lust through satisfying it, and to steer clear of the subtle egotism of being more virtuous than others.

As one who seeks enlightenment in the larger sense, I have so far largely failed, even though I have attained many insights into my own character and others, as well as how the world works. But in failure, if one is to survive, a man must have all the nerve of a blind gunfighter. If he does not know whether to shit or go blind, he must squint one eye and fart, then get on with the business of living in the world he finds himself in.

The mind lusts after the great abstractions, the mighty insight, the next moment, the vivid memory of the past -- anything but the homely reality of the present. We believe devoutly that life is something other than what is happening now, and we will search anywhere but right in front of our noses for its mystery.

The most difficult undertaking of all is to arrive at some understanding of oneself. If I follow a fool in myself, let my feet bleed on the sharp blades of my wayward path. In my seeking through the thorny byways, looking for the parts of the whole, I often become obsessive, focusing my concentration in order to plumb the depths as well as I am able.

When I grew grass, I pursued the subject through books and experience right up to the point beyond which I could not go without microscope and a knowledge of plant genes and chromosomes, perhaps leading me even to molecular levels of truth relative to cannabis sativa and indica. Pakalolo, in a way, composed all the elements of my eightfold path -- my viewpoint, aim, speech, action, livelihood, effort, mindfulness, and concentration. Changes would occur for the better when I became what I was, a grass grower, smoker, and a midnight toker, and everything that rode its coattails. But not as a player in others games.

This same focus, obsession, and fascination, has driven me to learn about boats, their design and construction, to sail and navigate, to be with the sea. It is, in a way, the basic motive force of what I had learned from my father -- if you're afraid, or curious, to walk down a dark alley, why, walk down that dark alley.

Compassion, called karuna in its Sanskrit form, is a necessary element in all things, and Buddhism teaches that when the nature of human experience is accurately perceived, one not only enters an enlightened state, but that compassion is naturally present. Compassion is as inherent to enlightenment as the conditions of craving and dissatisfaction are to the samsaric mind. And since the enlightened state is held to be always latently present in ordinary experience, it follows that the feeling of compassion is also latently present. It is not something outside yourself that you should acquire in order to be a good person, but a quality already there, if not quite yet noticed.

In Buddhism, this focus or obsession is called samadhi. It sometimes occurs to us naturally and easily. It is the state of artistic creation, of productive work, of the best moments of athletic activity. It is the experience of being lost in what you are doing, so that the distinction between it and yourself seems to disappear. You are what you do. In true samadhi, whether accidental or induced, inner mental processes come into harmony. There is rapport, positive feeling tone, clear conceptionalization, attraction with a sense of purpose, and the ability to keep the attention fixed.

These elements of the mental processes are called dharmas. They are used like a ladder in order to get to a place where you can throw away the ladder and perhaps see that it was not absolutely necessary to begin with.

Who you are becomes much less important than what you are and how you are right now. Since all truths are manifestations of mind, the way to judge any concept is by its value to a given mind at a given level of development.

Just as the ego futilely attempts to tie a rope around the wind, to make fixed and permanent what is by nature always changing, so do our emotional miseries attempt to rigidify our experience into safe programs. The mind becomes like the demented computer, HAL, in the film 2001: A Space Odyssey, which began to sabotage the great cosmic mission for which it was created.

The idea that the way to become free of binding passions, by means of the diamond vehicle, which is to go into the act desired rather than retreat from it, is found in the Tantric text: "So the wise man renders himself free of impurity by means of the impurity itself."

There are three primary Tantric approaches to problems presented by forms of behavior we can't seem to control, such as, for example, drug or alcohol abuse or some recurrent pattern of sexual misconduct, and they are: Vanquishing, ennobling, and yielding.

Vanquishing means going cold turkey, overcoming the problem by an act of will. But it may not work. It may be worse than the problem. Removing a symptom does not remove the problem.

Ennobling is transferring the emotional drive toward a more appropriate object, a sublimation, as when frustrated sexual energies are displaced into artistic creation. Buddhism does not indulge the prisoner-of-desire image so popular in Occidental romantic traditions. It insists you are also the prison builder, warden, guard, and gatekeeper.

Yielding leads to such practices as the ritualized sexual act that is sometimes taken to be the whole of Tantrism. Yielding basically has to do with paying attention, being mindful, alert to what is happening. Mindfulness practice is at the center of The Buddhistic way of experiencing life and deals with discovering independently that our adventures in hedonism, the pleasures we try so hard to obtain, the ecstatic experiences we try so hard to recreate exactly as they once were, often turn out to be rather flat, if not downright unpleasant. It all has to do with not being here, now, cluttering our minds with fantasies, expectations, intellectualizations, self-images, and disappointments. Go ahead and do it, whatever it is, if you think you must and it doesn't harm anybody else. Welcome surprises and don't be greedy. Pay attention to what changes. It is based upon the principle best enunciated by Arthur Koestler in The Art of Creation: "Step back to get ahead." (I am indebted to Walter Truett Anderson for his book, Open Secrets, for much of the clear language in setting out this short course in Buddhism.)

It's a matter of going one's own way. Buddha himself says in one of his sutras, or discourses, "Do not put faith in traditions, even if they have been accepted for long generations and in many countries. Do not believe a thing because many repeat it. Do not accept a thing on the authority of one or another of the sages of old, nor on the ground that a statement is found in the books. Never believe that which you have yourselves imagined, thinking that a god inspired it. Believe nothing merely on the authority of your teachers or of priests. After examination, believe that which you have tested for yourselves and found reasonable, which is in conformity with your well-being and that of others."

Which is pretty much what Jesus of Nazareth said more briefly in Luke 12:57, St. James Version: "Yea, and why even of yourselves judge not what is right?" Or even more clearly in the New International Version: "Why don't you judge for yourselves what is right?"

As to myself in the lifelong quest, I had always sought to discover talents, whether they existed inside me, what they were, and how I might develop them. I had tried poetry and prose and found myself lacking. Despite my great love of music, especially the blues, I had to discard any idea of becoming a musician when a true friend, a musician himself, was cruelly kind enough to point out my partial tone-deafness. I thought I had some talent as an artist, but nothing exceptional it turned out. After years of study and practice, I had given up drawing, oil painting, and photography as professional pursuits.

Failure? Well, the game's not over until it's over. Whatever's left after all is said and done, that's what we work with. We take it and do the best we can. What else is there to do? Everything is true and everything is false, a running away is a running toward, the message is in the movement. Does the boat have a hole in it or does the hole have a boat around it? You can lead a horse to water but a pencil must be lead.

With all due consideration for all things considered, it was with the image of that day, that old man, my trancewalk, and the photo of the bird in flight, that I approached sailing off into the mysteries lying over the horizon of a dark ocean.

Steph wore a short sundress, her legs and feet bare. She wore no makeup, her hair wind-tossed, her hand warm in mine, our arms warm where they touched. She was a plain and natural girl, a beauty within, artless without, and on that day I felt a great spiritual affinity with her. It occurred to me in a sort of shocked satori of realization -- the simplest truth -- that she was the best friend I'd ever had. I knew that her commitment to me and our venture together was total, as was mine to her. We had started out having fun, living from moment to moment with a consideration only now and again for tomorrow, and somehow love had snuck up on both of us. Beneath what seemed casual to others, the substance underlying surface characteristics of an unconventional relationship, existed a deep shared bedrock from which we had emerged as two parts of a single creation.

We sat together like god-stunned heathen upon the seawall staring moodily to the south, the sun warming us, the spray cooling us, and the days growing longer. And so it came to us at last, this dream of the sea, as we freed ourselves from land on the first day of June and motored out of the harbor, hoisted all sail, heading south-by-southwest, destination Palmyra, or, as we preferred to call it by an older, more romantic name, Samarang.

###

CHAPTER 14

We were away by nine o'clock, the sailing fine for a couple of hours. We kept turning our eyes toward Niihau to starboard, the sole purely Hawaiian island. Haoles were purportedly discouraged if not banned from visiting, a place where there were no airports, motor vehicles, or tall buildings, a place where the locals could still speak their own language and live in their own old ways. Perhaps we looked at it, too, because it would be the last bit of real estate we would see for the next thousand miles.

When we were becalmed a couple of hours later, we had plenty of time to study it through binoculars, but could see no sign of habitation at all.

As the wind picked up again in the early afternoon, we settled down to sailing. By six, we lowered all sail in order to maintain an upright Iola long enough to prepare supper. While Steph whipped up something on the stove below, I filled doggie-bowls on the foredeck, then poured them a ration of water.

When it came time for them to go potty, we would have to begin teaching them to do their business on the foredeck, no more taking them for an evening run ashore. A bucket or two of seawater would flush the decks clear. There I was, after all those years, my duties torn between positions as Captain-Admiral of the Ocean-Seas and Chief Flusher of the Canine Latrine.

Since the wind had picked up a bit and Steph was taking the first watch of the night, I hoisted only the jib. I went below to lay up and try to quell the queasiness. At ten, I took the wheel while Steph went below to snuggle into the warm place I'd left her. At one a.m., hearing me dump over the side, she was back to relieve me.

It was worse below and I was soon up for another fine spasm of retching. Although I'd known for years that I was subject to motion sickness whenever I rode in the back of a car or bus, never once in all my years of imagining a life on the sea had I conceived of the ignominy of constant nausea. What if it was going to be like this all the time? Life as a truck driver suddenly seemed very sensible.

My seasickness was like a sine wave. It rode me up to the peak of dumping, then let me coast down into the valley of relative relief before the next ride up to stomach spasms. I tried everything -- eating small snacks, imagining myself as a baby rocked in my mommy's arms, that I was a kid having fun on a rollercoaster, by deep meditation and trying to convince my inner ear that all this motion was normal after all, trying to call up any zillion-year-old traces in my genes from any fish forebears lurking in my ancestry, by doing yoga breathing exercises, and by cursing in capital letters in the voice of my crazy-man act for my brain to quit sending sadistic messages to my stomach. I wondered if sex would work, get me focused into something more pleasant. Logically speaking, vomiting and orgasm could not exist in the same time in the same place -- only I didn't much feel like trying.

*****

By morning it was hot and humid. I pulled up a bucket of seawater and dumped it over my head. It felt good, so I did it again. Hey now, maybe I'm on to something. Might as well cheer up the crew, too. Steph got a bucket for which she paid with a nice little eek of shock. Then the mutts got it. They were running about trying to evade me, yapping up a storm, shaking bursts of water-beads from their fur. Nobody escaped.

Then, still under forestaysail alone, which Steph mistakenly calls a jib in the log, so we could use the boom for a ridgepole, we tied a canopy over the cockpit where we all lazed and dried in the shade. During all this, Steph had tied the helm in position and discovered that Iola would self-steer. My addition of the second forestay proved to be a boon. We could keep under way throughout the night without constant attendance on the helm -- albeit at a reduced rate of speed, maybe two knots. When we had studied the situation enough to know that when the wind veered, Iola would simply change her course a bit and keep on trucking with a proper relationship to the breeze, we turned on the running lights, went below, and crashed out.

Something deep inside must have told us that this was not good practice, a boat, however small and slow, sailing blind, for every hour or so I would rise up out of the black, dreamless oblivion, roll out, take two steps up the ladder for an all-round view, then leap right back into the sinkhole of sleep.

In the morning, I learned Steph had been doing the same thing all night long, each of us unaware of the other doing it. Well, if I was hitting it on the hour and she on the half-hour, it wasn't a bad way to keep watch while we both snoozed the night away. I consoled myself that we were not traveling in a busy sea lane and that, therefore, risk of collision was low.

I had no sooner told myself that when, in the rougher sea and some rain, where the circle of visibility shrank, we saw the lights of a big ship steaming across our bow on a heading of WSW -- probably a Navy ship heading for Johnston Island.

"Baby, we're leaking from the forehatch. Can you take a look at it?"

I soon discovered that it only leaked when we took a wave over the bow -- when it rushed back over the foredeck, the force of the water causing it to squirt up inside the inner rim. The weather-stripping was shot. I packed it all around with the claylike bedding compound, which proved to be only a temporary solution. Rough weather and consequent bow waves soon had it leaking again. Repeat the bedding compound remedy until it leaked again -- put on future fixit list.

I tried trolling but no luck. No land in sight, it was a good time to perfect our navigational skills. Our first effort brought us out to 17° N, which did not accord with our deadreckoning estimation.

The wind got a little crazy and we simply steered the way that seemed least uncomfortable, which was between 120°-210°. At this rate we would travel two or three thousand miles to cover one thousand.

*****

It took two days for the mutts to learn a new Hawaiian word. When they would whine and pace about the deck in a circle from aft to fore to aft, a longing look outward for a sight of land, I would lead them to the foredeck and say, "Kaka!" But they would only give me a look and strut huffily away. After two days, I was beginning to wonder if they were on strike.

It was Puffer who got it first, but not from minding me when I ordered, "Kaka!" Puffer was somewhat handicapped by the plywood cast affixed to her hind leg. She could clump around like a canine Ahab, but squatting at sea was a chancy business. Steph, of course, was leading the assist with her own version of doggie-talk. "Widdle Puffy-wuffy do doggie-doo for mumsy-wumsy, ooh, and her feel better-wetter, mn-hm!"

The Puff pissed. The Puff shit. Halleluiah! We both praised her. Popolo and Sista were jealous. They trotted forward to investigate, their noses working over what Puffer had left. Popolo lifted a leg in precarious balance and tried a shot at one of the butane tanks lashed against the forward edge of the doghouse. Not bad for three or four tries. I complimented him. Sista, needing a dose of affection, got the message and began unloading. I patted and hugged and praised her. "Maika'i ilio! What a good shit! A beautiful shit, baby. I'm proud of you!"

Then, after more olfactory investigation, Popolo squatted to outdo both Puffer and Sista, squeezing off some serious turd. He had that look -- "Well, okay, boss, you want turd on the deck, you got turd."

"Popolo," I whooped. "Maika'i ilio! Oh, my boy, you are the champeen shitting dog of all time! Maika'i ilio! You get a milkbone for this!"

It took several buckets of water from over the side to flush their toilet.

*****

On the third day, magico-presto, my mal-de-mer left me standing on my sea-legs. By god, I was a sailorman at last! I felt so good, I invited the whole crew forward for a bath with Dr. Bonner's peppermint soap. Steph and I lathered up, then lathered up the mutts, me hauling bucket after bucket up to rinse us all off.

Ah now, me fine buckeroos and all the sea gods of all the lands of all the peoples who'd ever had the genius to invent watercraft, which was fucking-A plenty, the Captain-Admiral was in command!

"All hands prepare to sail wing-and-wing," I ordered, me of course to hoist and set them while Steph steered, the mutts to admire this fine division of labor. By my great uncle Seamus, we were moving! Speed enough for trolling. I broke out the deep-sea fishing gear, the stuff for the big ones. Paying out the line with a feather-jig, I set the haft into a pole-holder fixed to a stanchion. I was ready for some fish. We would all have fish for supper. Maybe while I was waiting for a bite, I'd take another peek at those books on navigation.

I'd no sooner stepped below than the call came. "Baby, you've got a bite! Hurry!"

Rushing back up, I heard the humming of line leaving the reel at an alarming rate. I grabbed the pole, began putting on the brakes. Holy Komoley! I damned near lost the rod before levering it back in a big cee of an arc, then staggered backwards when the line broke. Whoa! There were some serious fucking fish swimming around down there!

*****

Back to navigation with serious intent now. We'd been out of sight of land for five days without any clear idea, give or take a hundred miles or so, of our position. Sooner or later, a piece of land was going to be there for us to bump into.

We began a routine that would become a regular one. Steph had no aptitude for taking good pictures with a camera, often cutting off people's heads or feet or getting everything lopsided. Her technique with a sextant was about the same. She got altitudes of a noonday sun that placed it all over the sky, even as late as twilight. So, while she tuned in WWV on our shortwave receiver for the GMT (Greenwich Mean Time) time-ticks, noting the exact time and starting a stopwatch, I would hook an arm around a shroud to steady myself, find the sun, adjust the vernier screws on the sextant and call out "Mark!" when I had it focused down to kiss the horizon. She would hit the button stopping the watch which, when the minutes and seconds were added to the time from the radio, would give us the exact time of the sight -- a necessary element in computing longitude.

So far, as of June 6th, we had estimated our latitude as 14°17' N, which, when we finally got our shit together, would turn out to be wrong by about 120 miles. This was not good. But clouds obscured the sun, and the wind and waves had picked up to further stymie us, and finally rain. Forget about it. I got on foul weather gear, sent Steph below with the hounds, and ran before the 30+ knot winds on jib alone steering a loose course between 225°-240°. What the hell, it was in the general direction we wanted to go.

Six or seven hours later, at two or three in the morning, wind and wave and rain eased up. By dawn, Steph was up brewing coffee and complaining about the stuffiness below. I went forward to check and adjust an air-vent. I knew the safe practice was to run a line or two from bow to stern, attaching yourself to it with a shackle from your safety-harness. This setup would prevent you in the event of an accident from falling overboard and being washed away in the night.

Perhaps I was over-confident now that I'd come through our first little blow at sea. After adjusting the vent, I stood for a few moments on the coachroof hanging on to the boom, casting my gaze all around the horizon. Some movement caught my attention and I swung my eyes back -- just as the sea heaved, Iola pitched, and the boom swung in a short, swift arc out of my grasp and back like a baseball bat into my chest. Stumbling back, my foot caught the handrail along the side of the coach-roof and I went somersaulting toward the sea.

The blunt end of a starboard stanchion post was rather rudely introduced to the small space between my nose and left cheekbone, a meeting full of shock as my vision was filled with a great flash of light Steph heard the sound of a hundred and ninety pounds of flesh and bone hitting the deck between cockpit coaming and gunnel, where she found me totally unconscious. When I came to a few moments later, I mumbled "Umph!" and struggled to sit up, Steph pulling at me, a look of fright on her face.

"Geez, baby! What happened? Oh, uck, gawd!"

My hands came away from my face dripping red. I stared dumbly, then began feeling my head for the obviously mortal wound.

"Geez, I hope ya didn't knock yer brains out," Steph grimaced. She hated the sight of blood. "Ya can't afford to lose any!"

"Ith my noth," I gushed, testing it tenderly.

She bade me lay back while she leapt below to fetch a wet towel, soon got the nosebleed stopped and cleaned me up. I was eyeing that stanchion, thinking a mere four inches to the other side and I'd have went out cold into the drink. Women's lib would doubtless have hailed Steph as the first single-handing female Captain-Admiral of the Ocean-Seas. Whoa!

*****

Another overcast day. Trying to work out an average speed over almost a week at sea, I came up with a latitude of 16°15" N, which meant we'd progressed over a hundred miles backwards from our estimate of the day before!

Toward evening, winds, sea, and rain were back with us stronger and heavier than ever. We tossed and pitched, yawed and scudded the whole miserable night long, bilge-water sloshing everywhere.

On the morning of June 8th, the rains stopped, the winds moderated, and the seas began to calm. In compensation, the gods had left us one miserable flying fish on deck. I pumped out for the third or fourth time, an average of once every two days. In port it had been once every three days. We took in fifty percent more water while underway. The faster we went, the faster the water came in through the rudderpost leak. Still, faster is a relative term. Instead of pumping out ten gallons, I pumped fifteen -- or more often -- no big deal.

When the sun came out, we got a decent fix, which we considered fairly trustworthy At 159°30' W, 15°28' N, at one minute before one p.m., after seven days at sea, and five after beginning to worry about it, we figured out we were three hundred and eighty-four nautical miles almost dead south from Port Allen.

That night, remembering a simple trick of navigation I'd read about, I shot the North Star with the sextant for a latitude check. Latitude, a position on a north-south line, is the same number of degrees the sextant marks the North Star above the horizon. This secret had been discovered some time before Columbus set sail for Japan and found the Americas. It was close enough to give us confidence we were on the right track.

The real trick of navigation was in finding longitude, a position on an east-west line, which required accurate time.

We had been studying our books like mad, both of us working independent solutions, which rarely agreed. Who was right? Who wrong?

We had three books that taught the art-science of navigation, the first written by a sea captain. The second was Bowditch, a classic work on navigation and seamanship, for many years the seaman's bible.

Bowditch was hard-going, having first been published in the early 1800s by Nathaniel Bowditch, an American mathematician and astronomer. It was among the earliest authorities for captains of U. S. ships and naval cadets. The third was the most helpful, Kittredge's Simplified Navigation, a parting gift from Dickie, which focused mainly on sun-sights.

When I finally got it, I taught it to Steph, who was still scratching her head. We'd go mostly by the sun and dead-reckon between the times it showed its face. The rest, after getting our sights -- always trying for two to make what is called a running fix -- was all about looking up certain figures in the Nautical Almanac and H.O. 249, both books of tables published by the U. S. Hydrographic Office, and then performing a few arithmetical operations -- addition and subtraction -- and thereby arriving at LOPs (lines of position).

A few days later, we were into our routine. Steph on the time, me on the sextant, she working out the figures and LOPs, me reviewing. We were beginning to note regular fixes in our logbook, our progress marked by dated dots on our chart.

*****

By the tenth day out, just as I was beginning to suspect that deepwater fish were smarter than me, that they spent all the day below laughing at me, I snagged a five-foot long Mahimahi, the most delicious fried fish in the whole world. Hot damn, the first one I'd ever caught!

I knew what they looked like from a picture in our fish book, but was totally unprepared for the stunningly colorful ritual it would display in dying and offering itself to our frying pan. It was green, then purple, then blue, then yellow, all in eyegrabbing iridescent day-glo colors! Bleeding bloody boobless bobbysoxers, if I could go out like that all my mourners wouldn't know whether to shit or go blind!

I filleted it up while Steph went below to prepare the frying pan and a batter. I fed the mutts little tidbits of scraps as appetizers.

After cleaning up, I sent out the fishline again and fiddled about as mouth-watering aromas wafted up through the hatch. When Steph called me to dine, I hurriedly reeled in the line, careless enough to entangle the end of it on the Merc's propeller. Shit! I bent down to free it but instead caught myself in the thumb, the hook gouging deep. Nice move, me dumbo! Got yerself in a nice half-overboard position, don't'cher?

"Steph!"

"What, awready? Come and eat. It's ono."

"Bring me the wire-cutting pliers!"

"Hah?" She popped her head up for a fine view of my nether parts. "Oh, gee, baby, very nice, but I don't think it'll fit in the pan." "I'm hooked, goddamnit! Bring me the fucking pliers!"

"Don't you swear at me! You take a kick in the ass about now, sweetie?"

She ducked below and was back in a flash. "Here!"

If I let go with the free hand that held me, I would go overboard. "Lay them on the deck, darlin', please. Then grab hold of me so I don't go overboard."

She wrapped her arms around my hips, her hands feeling about. "Where? Here?"

"No, not there! You want me singing soprano?" I levered my legs out straight on the deck. "Grab my feet."

Lefthandedly, I let go my grip, grabbed the pliers and snipped the wire leader to the hook. I hauled myself up and sat looking at it. The hook was firmly embedded. There was no pain -- my thumb was numb.

"Yuk," Steph cringed. "Pull it out!"

"No, you can't. There's barb. You want to wind up amputating my thumb?"

"Well, do something!"

I knew what to do. I grabbed the hook and bent it around so the barbed point came out a new hole. I thought Steph was going to faint, but the mutts never blinked an eye.

"Now, take the wire-cutters and snip off the barb."

Steph was squeamish. I guided the pliers into position and told her to cut it. She gripped the handles with both hands, closed her eyes and squeezed. For some dumb reason, she also twisted.

"Yargh!"

"Oh, baby, did I hurt ya?"

"Well, it was numb, but you fixed that!" "I can't do it! I'm not strong enough!"

"Get a file."

"Oh, gawd!"

It was hard for her, but she was game. In the process, she filed away half my thumbnail.

"Steph, darlin'," I said in my kindest, most patient tone. "Try it with your eyes open."

Then it was done and I slipped the hook out. She poured on an antiseptic and bandaged me up. Whole thing had made me hungry.

"Fine, darlin'. Now I'm ready to eat."

"Oh, gawd, I think I've lost my appetite!"

Not for long, though. Damn, that was some really good fish. We ate until we were stuffed. We fed the dogs until they were stuffed. We still had enough left over for another go-round. Whoa, and I was worried whether we'd brought enough dogfood!

*****

Our route proved to be a good fishing run. I caught a couple more Mahamahi and one twenty-pound Tuna, which, after looking it up in our fish book proved to be yellowfin. We sashimied that sucker, Steph substituting hot mustard powder for the wasabi the Japanese used in the soy sauce and we ate it raw -- we and the mutts in ecstasy the whole time.

We even caught fish when we weren't trying. We'd come up on deck in the morning to find a dozen or two flying fish lying on the foredeck. They weren't bad eating either when fried up, but it was a nuisance cleaning and preparing them -- they were so small, maybe six to eight inches. They would fly into the forestaysail in the dark and plop down on deck.

In the daylight, when we would sometimes see whole schools of them lift out of the sea in a coordinated glide in an arc of two or three hundred feet, they were a sight to see. The fact that they lifted from water to air meant that predator fish were pursuing them -- it was their way of evading becoming a meal for bigger fish.

*****

Late in the afternoon on the eleventh day, after getting a good running fix with two sunsights, I began to think I was seeing something absolutely astounding -- a huge sea serpent miles off coming toward us. I could see it undulating through the sea. We were under full sail and the monster was coming closer.

"Steph, you see that?"

She looked, shading her eyes, which suddenly grew wider. "Oh, yeh! Geez, what is it?"

"Get the binoculars."

She did, standing on the ladder and bracing herself over the hatchway for a look.

"What is it?"

"Gee, I dunno. It's really big, whatever it is."

"Lemme see." I could see its head and long spine undulating up and down out of the water as it continued its course straight at us. No, this can't be, I told myself. Sea serpents do not exist -- regardless of all the crackpot reports of the Loch Ness monster. But wait! What about a giant squid? I tended to believe that they existed in the depths of the ocean, that marine biologists thought whales dove thousands of feet down to munch on them -- and received wounds when the giant beasts resisted. Only they had lots of tentacles, more than an octopus.

In awe I continued to look. My God, we've found a sea serpent and can't even report it! We'd never gotten around to hooking up our VHF radio, which was very short range anyway. And since it was headed straight for us, probably to gobble us up, we'd never become famous as discoverers of the giant Stearns-Walker Sea Worm.

But then, aha, beginning to breathe again, I could see, as it came ever closer, that the great long wave of it was beginning to fragment like a pointillist painting viewed too closely. My God, it was hundreds, maybe thousands of fish, all cooperating in a synchronous swimming exercise, individuals in the lead soaring and diving, a whole train behind emulating the leaders. Closer and closer they came, until I could see their funny-shaped noses.

"Porpoise!" I cried. "A school of porpoise!"

Soon enough they arrived, leaping all around Iola, grinning and snickering at us. The dogs going crazy, Steph and I laughing. When they'd passed us by, the mutts throwing their last triumphant barks after them, Popolo, Sista, and Puffer, all came to us to be rewarded with hugs and pats and exclamations of "Maika'i ilio!" for having saved Iola from attack and driving the intruders away.

*****

On the thirteenth day, after a good running fix, we figured we were within 120 miles of our destination. I worked out a few calculations. We had been averaging a miserly 64 nautical miles per day, which meant an average speed of 2.66 knots. Oh, some days we went faster. Between June 11 and 12, we had recorded 106 miles, which meant an average speed of 4.4 knots over a 24-hour period. But in days to come, running into the doldrums, we would do even less.

The trouble with being "pure" sailors -- not having an engine -- meant no wind, no sailing. Little wind, little movement.

I knew that most sailboats, with all-out sailing 24 hours per day, and thus averaging over a hundred miles per day, could make the 1000-mile trip in a week, more or less. Such sailing was exhausting, taking helm watches four hours on and four off the entire voyage. Plus, where other boats would start their engines and continue making speed through those days that offered little wind, pure sailboats like Iola had to loaf along and wait for wind to come.

Only three days before, on an overcast and all but windless day, we had discovered that our Merc had died a quiet death. Knowing we would have a use for it once we arrived to assist entering the narrow passage through the reefs into the lagoon against contrary prevailing winds, I had made a practice of starting it every few days and letting it run for five or ten minutes. But three days ago, on my last try, no amount of pulling on the starter rope or fiddling would get it to fire up, not even pulling off the protective casing and pouring gasoline down the carburetor. We were truly pure sailboat sailors now.

Well, no big deal. We'd get into the lagoon sooner or later -all it required was patience. Oy vay, you schlemiel, you can be so cavalier now! Soon enough, patience indeed would be required!

In the philosophical meantime, though, I idly mused over the difference in sailing technique and outlook between Steph and I, pure sailors, who were beginning to feel at home with the sea, and...well, all the others.

There were two maxims that differentiate the two types. The first is: Fast passages are safe passages. Sailors in this group apparently feel that all time spent under sail upon the open sea represents danger. Therefore, the least time spent, the better. They sail all out from port to port, then spend much time in harbor bragging over their elapsed times and what great sailors they are to have survived the self-imposed hardships of such intense and stressful voyages. The mentality of this type would seem to be related to that of racing sailors who constantly spend themselves in fine-turning their vessels and gear in order to wring every last ounce of speed from them for the purpose of knocking minutes and seconds off their elapsed times. But, this is one thing for racing sailors, quite another for cruising sailors.

The second type, the group to which we belonged, is illustrated by the maxim: Sailboats should have destinations, not ETAs (estimated times of arrival -- The original quotation from which I draw this maxim, "Puffboats have destinations, not ETAs," is derived from the log of Donald Crowhurst, who had attempted to perpetrate a hoax while participating in a single-handed race of circumnavigation out of England. He had simply remained in the Atlantic and radioed reports that he was making record times in his trimaran. He mysteriously disappeared, his yacht found floating derelict by a freighter.) This group of sailors is in no hurry, quite happy to spend as much time as possible at sea -- and surely includes all the great singlehanders beginning with Joshua Slocum. Their home is their boat, the boat's home the sea. They respect the ocean, the wind, all the elements, but they do not fear them. All the necessary principles for sailormen to deal with forces of nature have been known for many years. After all, those forces give the sailor his life. They are to be understood and accommodated. What kind of sailor's life is it that's spent in brief voyages and long stays in port? We were in no hurry; our appointment schedule was quite flexible. One goes to sea not only to get somewhere, but to be at sea.

*****

There was a nagging question of fear that had rose up to pick at me ever since the time of my somersault into unconsciousness on the fifth day of our voyage. In the ensuing ten days, I had found myself being very cautious and careful, psyching myself out imagining the endless possibilities of disaster. The sea had become scary.

Well, there came a day, June 16, while drifting about on our worst day in terms of forward progress, firmly in the doldrums, sky gray with overcast, the occasional rainsquall to excite us for fifteen minutes -- until they passed to leave us bobbing like a cork on the lazy swells. It was boring, hot and still, and I had taken all the sails down to remove the irritation of their monotonous flapping and banging about. I was brooding over my close call, thinking about the four-inch difference of my fall that had made all the difference.

Steph was below trying to relax and read, Puffer and Sista with her to escape the heat. Faithful Popolo dogged my footsteps as I padded quietly about in bare feet. I was feeling fearful little pangs, beginning to sense danger lurking from every quarter. I thought and paced and dripped sweat. Popolo had stopped to sit and watch, wagging his tongue to cool off. A bucket of water would be nice, I thought. Better yet, a swim. I hadn't immersed myself into the sea since the beginning, a long time. But I was afraid. I just knew a great white shark was waiting to gobble me up.

Well, me bucko, when you're afraid of a dark alley, what do you do?

Tasting bitter morsels, I silently stepped over the bow and began easing down the chainlinks of the bobstay. I lowered myself into the water as Popolo came over to crane his quizzical head down at me.

"Sh," I admonished.

Then I pushed off and dog-paddled away. Out a ways where I was sure Steph couldn't hear, I began to swim, knifing through the water. Ah, it felt good, coolly kissing and caressing my entire body. About a hundred yards off, I turned to tread water, wafting up and down in the gentle swells. Iola drifted lazily, Popolo standing alert now, never taking his eyes from me. I ducked my head under the water and looked down. I could see a school of small fish. It was surprisingly bright and clear, beautiful and dreamlike. Further down, as the penetrating light hazed into darkness, I could barely make out vaguely moving larger shadows.

When I looked up, the sun had peeked through the grayness. I looked all around. There was the sea and a bowl of sky over me. I was alone, totally alone, with the creatures of the deep. I looked down again, beneath me further than I could see lay the inkblack depths. How much freer can you be, me fine old boyo, I asked myself, than this, the one place in the world you've elected with all due deliberation to be with nary a single restraint other than your own limitations? What was I, a mere speck on this vast ocean, trying to prove? I shrugged, having offered myself to the voracious leviathan of the deeps, destiny demanding something else of me, unknown. I swam back leisurely, pulled myself up the bobstay, heaved silent and dripping onto the foredeck. Popolo sniffed me, took an exploratory lick. I ruffled his neck, calm, serene. The sun was out.

As Jake, my old teacher, was fond of saying, "A thousand years from now, it won't make any difference."

"Steph, babe," I called. "Get the sextant and the time. I think we might get a fix."

We had managed all of six or seven miles in the past twenty-four hours.

*****

Two days before that, on the day we'd figured we were 120 miles from Palmyra, and an average clocking of sixty miles a day would have us there, I had had evidence of a big and hungry fish below. On that day, we had had some wind and had cooked along under main and jib for some six hours.

Making good speed, I had decided to try trolling a lure, getting it out, setting the reel with some drag, and the haft in the pole-holder.

Whip-whip, the pole bent to inform me of a bite, then bent again. A humming of line spinning off the reel at an incredible rate had the pole arched into a severely squeezed cee. Before I could fix a loop of rope over the helm-handle to hold course, the line on the reel ran out. The pole-holder was wrenched loose, bending the stanchion, and the expensive pole, big reel and all, went sailing like a spear over the water in our wake to disappear forever.

"Geez, babe," Steph asked, poking her head up the hatch at the sudden screech and slam of noise. "What was that?"

"The second big sonofabitch that got away," I managed, flabbergasted. There were some serious fucking fish out here! I wondered if I'd hooked a huge Blue Marlin or a passing whale.

"We need to pump out, too, babe."

"Okay. I'll do that first," I said, digging out the overboard hose and attaching it to the outlet valve of the pump mounted to starboard of the hatchway. Working the handle vigorously up and down, it busted off in my hand. Oh, shit, what next?

"Babe, we gotta get the generator topside. I need to use my power tools to make a new handle."

"Yeh, good idea. Guess we'd better if we don't wanna be passing buckets up and down."

It was heavy, maybe two hundred pounds, but we managed, me lifting and pushing from below, she pulling from above, to manhandle it out into the cockpit. The problem with running it below was carbon monoxide from the exhaust and gasoline fumes. The first was no real problem, just opening all the portholes and hatches to air out. But gas fumes would sink into the bilges awaiting a spark that would blow us to hell. Thus the generator rode below with an empty gastank, while all the gasoline rode lashed on deck.

I replaced the original plastic handle with a length of bronze genoa track, which turned out to be better than the original, necessitating only cutting a length and drilling a couple of holes. All fixed and pumped out, I decided to hook up the battery-charger. I'd noticed our running lights at night growing dimmer. Then I turned to the stanchion post, removing the remains of the pole-holder and hammering and levering the stanchion back to some semblance of its former self with a monkey wrench.

"How about some popcorn, babe?"

"Yeah, sounds good."

We'd stocked an ample supply, Steph cooking up a big bowl of it every couple of days. She'd discovered a way to make it greasy without butter, which we didn't have because of no refrigeration to keep it. She'd heat a few tablespoons of cooking oil and add a couple of drops of something called butter-flavor extract -- which was included in a very extensive spicerack. We couldn't tell the difference from the real thing.

*****

By the 17th, still making very little progress -- although we'd gotten enough wind to raise main and genoa to milk it for all we could -- it became time to be doubly patient. I had smoked my last cigarette. Steph cooked cornbread while I fed pakalolo to my nicotine habit.

Brilliant me, I'd figured to kick the tobacco habit by a simple and logical process. I'd take one carton of cigarettes and when they ran out that would be it. There'd be no getting weak and running down to the corner grocery for a pack.

We got a fix -- some consolation.

*****

Squalls are interesting and unusual weather patterns in miniature. They are sudden bursts of wind, often quite violent and carrying heavy downpours of rain, but they are usually of short duration and may last no more than fifteen or twenty minutes before passing on. Our first experience with them came within days after embarking on our voyage. They can often be seen on bright, sunny days as a distant dark line miles off toward the horizon. If the wind is blowing them toward you, the dark line thickens as it approaches until it seems to be a black wall. It strikes suddenly and the wind may increase by a factor of two or three times. Sailors are warned to head up or to reduce sail. If it is a warm day, the rain is refreshing. Then it soon passes on, the black wall receding in a dark line toward the horizon.

But sometimes, especially when their approach is missed or the speed of their approach misjudged, they can hit a boat under sail like a gale-force storm -- one minute all is quiet and well, the wind ten or fifteen knots, and the next whipping you madly at forty knots.

Some who have not heeded their approach, especially under full sail, have been dismasted and capsized. Our one bad experience was a humdinger.

Under full sail on a nice day, I had seen the dark line on the horizon. No problem. When it got closer as a black wall and the winds began to rise, the raindrops fall, I would simply head up -which means steering directly into the wind. The sails would slap excitedly at the elements rushing by before the headsail would fill and the vessel pick up speed on a close-hauled course -- as near as it will sail into the wind, in our case fifty degrees. With speed comes steerage and you soon head up again to let the sails billow uselessly before falling off to repeat the process.

Since it is easy to misjudge the strength of these miniature storm systems, the safer course is to lower sail, perhaps only retaining a small jib in order to maintain steerage.

My experience until then had been with relatively mild squalls, the wind perhaps going from ten or fifteen knots up to twenty-five or thirty knots -- no big deal. Seeing as I had plenty of time before it struck, I had tied off the wheel -- Iola would steer under full sail for a short length of time before veering off course -- and slipped below to remove my sunglasses and to clap a sou'easter rainhat on my head and to take up a windbreaker in case it lasted for awhile and became chilly.

Steph was stretched out on our berth reading.

"We'd better close the portholes, babe. We got a squall on the way."

"Okeh, right."

She'd no sooner stood then Iola heeled violently over in a great explosion of sound, tipping us ninety degrees to port. Suddenly water was pouring through the portside portholes in great gushes. I leapt to muscle one down to close and lock it, while Steph struggled with the other. The left side of our boat was now the bottom. Water was pouring in through the open main hatch.

Jesus jumping jackrabbits! I levered myself out into a cockpit half-filled with water just in time to see the tip of our mast lifting from the sea. As the mast continued to lift the sails filling, Iola shot forward from a dead stop. I wrestled the helm, trying desperately to get her headed dead into the wind and upright. With the sound of cherrybombs going off in a furious flapping of the sails as Iola slowly came up, I rushed forward to unship the main halyard and pull the mainsail down. Leaving it a great ruffling mass, I went on forward to work at hauling down the jib. Crawling out prone on the bowsprit, my legs wide to encompass the spritstays to either side, I held one arm to the sprit and one for pulling down the jib, plunging all the while up in the air and down into the sea as Iola bucked away.

When finally I made my way back to the main hatch, Steph was wading in shock in water almost up to her knees. She'd gotten all the portholes secured, but we were almost swamped.

"Babe, use a bucket to bail. Throw it into the cockpit."

The cockpit was self-draining. While she searched for a bucket, I began working the pump for all I was worth, switching arms when one tired. Gallons of water flew by me as Steph heaved it by the bucketful from inside. An hour later, the pump was sucking at the last inches in the bilge.

The squall had long passed and the sun was out. We hauled out bedding and clothes to hang everywhere to air-dry. Four hours later, we'd restored order below. The mutts were lolling on the foredeck.

Finally, coffee and a joint to relax and restore ourselves.

"You believe that shit?"

"Whew, babe, that was scary."

"Motherfucker!"

"Yeh."

*****

The next day, sunny, lazy, and no wind, we repeated the laborious process of hauling up the generator again. Something was wrong -- the batteries weren't holding their charges. Well, what could you expect from secondhand car batteries, which all three were, especially when they'd all just been rescued from drowning?

We got another running fix and I tried rolling up and smoking a tea bag. Not very satisfactory at all. A little pakalolo, a little meditation, a bucket bath of saltwater, a freshwater wipedown to avoid stickiness, rolling sex on the high seas -- then read a book. Keep busy, keep distracted. What was patience but the ability to wait it out? I'd had plenty of practice.

*****

The next day, going into our nineteenth day, at 4:15 p.m., we spotted Palmyra. Only the day before, after getting our positional fix, which placed us about thirty miles away, Steph had asked how far away the island could be seen.

On the basis of reading in World Sailing Directions that coconut trees were described as growing as high as ninety feet, I'd made a rough calculation and opined as how we might see it eight to ten miles away.

The next day, after another running fix, the last sunsight about 2:00 p.m., Steph repeated my estimation. "Eight to ten miles, huh?"

"Yeah, about."

"In that case," she said, frowning over the chart and pacing off distances with dividers. "We ought to raise Palmyra in about two hours."

"Yeah?"

"Right over there," she said, sighting off the compass and pointing over the bow to port.

"You sure?"

"If we've got our shit together on navigation, fifteen, sixteen miles. Put on more sail."

I did. Two hours. Sure enough. It was. Dead ahead. Slightly aport. Palmyra.

"Thar she blows!" I cried excitedly. "Thar she blows!"

"That's for whales, baby."

"Hah? Oh, yeah. Land ho! Land ho! Avast, ye swabs, break out the rum! A ration of grog for every mother's son! Land ho!" We were sailing-assed navigating fucking fools!

Steph brought up the drink, the last bottle of beer saved for the occasion. The whole crew was on deck, peering toward the dark, bushy brillo pad growing in the distance, our noses twitching at a warm, sweet aroma in the air. We spilt a little to the gods of the sea, as was the custom among old salts.

"To Samarang."

"Iola."

We drank, feeling fucking-A great. Shipwrights, sailors, and navigators, just as we had promised ourselves.

"Goddamn, you're good, baby!"

"Not bad yerself, dude."

We'd found our island -- and then we lost it.

We made a course to come around well west, seeking the channel through the reefs that lay at a point southwest in the circular chain of islands that composed the atoll. Through binoculars, we picked out the surf breaking over the offshore reefs toward an enticing white sand beach on the northshore. Soon we could discern with the naked eye that the bushiness was composed of a profuse growth of thousands of coconut trees.

As we made our way south around the western end, we spotted the wreck of an old dredging barge and compared its location as marked on our chart. We picked out the old radio towers, bearings off which gave us a fair orientation. Easing around to the southwest, we studied the lagoon shore area along Cooper Island, the major land mass. There were numerous buildings to be seen, the most prominent being a large barn-like structure set back from a built-up wharf area, the highest ground point on the island. Further east was moored a single yacht -- at the dolphins shown on the charts adjacent to the western end of the airstrip, we guessed.

By then we were headed due east in light winds and the weather began to close in, a light, misty rain enshrouding the islands in grayness. Anxious to keep clear of the extensive outlying reef areas, we bore off east-by-southeast. The winds began to pick up and the sea grew rough.

At a certain point, judging that we had cleared the eastern end of the island, we veered northeast. Later, after full darkness had enclosed us, I lowered the sails to reset the forestaysail for self-steering on a course to the northeast. After tying off the wheel, we went below to dry out.

The weather worsened, the wind howling through the rigging and the tossing of our little drunken boat prevented any of us from sleeping. We kept our eyes on the belowdecks compass, fearful of any deviation that would indicate we were being driven west or south toward the reefs of Palmyra. Popping our heads up for a looksee was wasted effort.

About 2:00 a.m., I went topside to change our course for the northwest. By 5:00 a.m. the wind had died altogether and we were becalmed. The full light of dawn told us Palmyra had disappeared.

Three or four hours later, we found it again lying dead west. The winds rose lightly from the southeast, chased by enough squalls to drive us back to where we were the day before at the same time -- northwest, but becalmed. It was frustrating to be so near and not be able to regain a position off the southwest corner in order to anchor near the entrance into the lagoon. By nightfall, we had attained a position dead west, but with no moon or starlight to guide us were effectively blind. Therefore, we altered course again heading northwest under self-steering forestaysail.

Though the winds were light through the night, they had driven us out of sight of Palmyra once again. Later, they picked up briskly from the southeast, the very direction we wished to go, and so we tacked widely east to south-by-southwest, hunting through the intermittent rains, the sun peeking out for a single quick sight.

By darkness, nothing. The wind died altogether and we lowered all sails and let ourselves drift. All the next day we were becalmed, spending the day reading and peering outward. We managed two sunsights for a good fix. We were a bit too far north and west to see Palmyra.

On June 23, however, four days after first raising the atoll, fair northeastern tradewinds arrived, allowing us to hoist all sails in pursuit of our lost island. By lunch, we had found her and had ample time to seek out an anchorage near the entrance.

The winds were dead against us and the passage through the reefs too narrow to attempt tacking. We would wait and hope for a more favorable wind. No sooner had we gotten situated than we saw another sail north of us. Through the binoculars it proved to be a shallow-draft catamaran which had anchored on the northwest part of the reef about a mile or so away. We thought about rowing over for a visit, but no, we couldn't chance leaving Iola unmanned in the fickleness of wind and weather. That night we saw a light along the south shore of Cooper Island inside the lagoon, a bonfire -- a signal sent by those inside to guide us in? They couldn't know we were engineless. We took it as a cheery greeting.

We passed two more days reading and messing about as the northeast trades held steady. In the afternoon, the motorsailer Caroline passed us twice at a good clip, too far away to hail. It entered my mind to try hitching a tow, but they were already heading into the passage.

*****

Having now ample time to rest, relax, and recreate, meaning catching up on sleep, sitting back in the sun with a joint and a good book, and catching up on sexual activities which the exigencies of our new routines had somewhat curtailed, there was of course plenty of opportunity to think and discuss our thoughts, indulge in the easy intimacy we had become accustomed to.

By then we had discovered firsthand a number of likes and dislikes about sailboats. For my own part, I had taken a fancy to bowsprits.

Although they were not really necessary on modern yachts since their original purpose had been to spread more sail lower down when masts were much heavier and shorter, they lent a rakish air. But on my ideal boat, which I was constantly designing and redesigning in my head and in sketches, it would include a platform and pulpit for ease and security in handling headsails.

We both disliked not having a toilet and shower. We both disliked rationing supplies of fresh water. You could get clean enough on saltwater baths, but if you didn't wipe down with a cloth dipped in fresh water, you wound up with a residue of salt on your skin and feeling sticky.

Laundry, oh! Our method had consisted of stuffing dirty laundry into a meshbag, tying it to a rope, and tossing it overboard for a few hours -- which worked well enough. But if you didn't rinse them in freshwater, which we often didn't, except for bed linens, we had to vigorously shake out the dried residues of salt and plankton. The good news was that we had rarely worn many clothes -- when not buck naked, a bathing suit or shorts at most.

The leaks through Iola's rudderpost and foreward hatch were irritating, but not really so bad since a few minutes of pumping by hand every few days would empty out the bilges. Still, an automatic electric pump with a float-switch in a naturally dryer boat would be better.

I had already learned the value of having an engine and an onboard generator, which would provide an electrical system. A refrigerator and freezer would be nice for keeping all those perishables we'd learned to live without -- even a simple thing like a cold drink on a hot day. But more importantly so that we would be able to get in and out of harbors rather than having to await favorable vagaries of weather -- as we were now doing. And of course our fancies played with other luxuries, too, like air-conditioning or even a fan. A ham radio setup or a single sideband would certainly facilitate long distance communication. We could call around to various operators in order to send and receive messages. We could talk to Dickie.

More storage space would be nice, which meant a bigger boat. We could have brought a year's worth of food supplies and other stuff besides. Along the way we had compared the spartan accommodations of Iola with other boats -- for instance, Dickie's Islander 32. In addition to being aboard Joel Peter's trimaran, we had helped to launch a 45-foot trimaran at the small harbor outside Kailua Town. By comparison, the accommodations were sinfully generous, enough deck-space to have a dance party.

But there were also the diehard dream-chasers in vessels even more spartan than ours. Old Jim Leatherman's 19-footer, which only had sitting headroom and couldn't carry much in the way of supplies. There was the long-haired and bearded old beatnik in a 26-foot converted coastguard open lifeboat -- to which he'd added keel, deck, and sail-rigging, and a thousand serious books, not a fiction title among them. He'd boiled his existence, a sailing life of many years, down to its simplest terms -- want not, need not. He made me ashamed of my ambitions.

In my studies of yacht designs over the years, I had come to appreciate the seaworthiness, lines, rigs, and interior arrangements of certain long-distance cruisers like the Westsail designs in 32 and 42-foot lengths. I admired the sturdiness and sea-keeping abilities of their designs carried over from the basic hull configurations of Norse fishing boats called redningsskoites after Colin Archer, John Atkins, and W. I. B. Crealock, including the Ingrid designs, all older boats. Unlike Iola, I was sold on the value of double-ended boats, which took stern waves with greater ease. In this respect, I had always admired the Tahiti Ketch and Dreadnought designs of John Hanna. Then I'd discovered the beauty of Robert Perry's canoe sterns. Last but not least, I'd become enamored of the Native American hullform called pinky, which originally served as hardy fishing schooners. For a long time I thought ketch rigs with jib-headed masts were best until I took a short sail around Kihei Bay in a 32-foot gaff-rigged cutter -- a boat that was for sale and I regretted not having found it before the forlorn Margaret -- and so had come around to the old-fashioned gaff-rigged schooner configuration.

I liked wood on a boat, the warmth and beauty of it, but had gone by it and fiberglass, aluminum, ferro-cement and ferralite as hull materials in favor of corten steel as the way to go in my dreamboat. Everything else would be wood.

I was constantly sketching out hullforms, playing with keel, bowsprit, and stern designs, laboriously drafting out sail rigs and interior arrangements to scale, all the while explaining to Steph my reasoning, whether from esthetic, utilitarian, or romantic notions. I loved sheer-lines and bowsprits.

"How's the sheerline look to you, babe?" I would ask Steph, standing to stretch and invariably bumping my noggin on Iola's ceiling.

"Oh, that's beautiful," she would coo. "Especially with that clipper bow."

"How about the raised bulwarks aft? I cribbed that from Herreshoff. Guy had a genius for sheerlines."

"Most of his sterns were heart-shaped, weren't they?"

"Yeah, but I think it adapts well to the cruiser-canoe shape."

"Oh, good. It's pretty."

"But one thing I can guaranfuckingtee you!"

"What's that?"

"We're gonna have enough headroom for a basketball team," I replied, rubbing the crown of my skull.

"And a proper bathroom."

Bathrooms. Well, the subject led to matters scatalogical. There was, of course, the question of bathroom custom, which has only received passing mention in regard to our mutts, but a serious question when you consider that Iola had no toilet.

In harbor, we'd made do with facilities provided ashore. Iola had had a sorry toilet in the bow when we'd purchased her, but it had been so ancient and dilapidated, having ruptured hoses and a hand-operated waterpump that didn't work, that I had torn it out and plugged the through-hull fittings. On the high seas, however, the question loomed large. For me, taking a whizzer was no problem long as I remembered to aim downwind.

Our dogs, of course, had adapted themselves to the foredeck, but in rough weather it could be hilarious. We had to assist in helping them to maintain the proper posture in order to keep them from sliding all over the deck. Steph or I would take a poor beast by the collar and help it forward. Then we would have to squat, brace ourselves and the mutt, and try to hold he or she steady while performing the necessities -- which took some doing with the boat heaving and tossing and splashes of cold water coming over the bow.

For Steph, since the female of the species have their own necessities, a different problem presented itself. The same problem became apparent for the male of the species when it came to making doo-doo. This undignified position taken aboard a ship is not a late phenomenon, for even the ancient mariners had to deal with it. But the solution, too, has long been known. The Japanese of old, who fertilized their crops with human excreta, called it the honeybucket.

A sailor had to find himself a bucket and a maintainable if not comfortable position in the boat, brace himself and do his thing. If he were fastidious, he would immediately take it to dump overboard. This was usually accomplished by heaving the entire bucket into the sea -- again, never upwind! -- Attached to a rope so it could be rinsed out.

The method works as we can attest, especially Steph. There is one inherent danger, however. When the sea was rough, the most auspicious time to employ the honeybucket, the best place in the boat was the lowest amidships, which meant down inside the cabin. The users could brace their feet to either side, grasp the mast support, and hope for the best. The peril came in negotiating the ladder up out the hatch where, in rough seas, two hands were better than one. Getting the bucket up into the cockpit for a heave over the side was a decidedly chancy business. One slip and oo-whee! In practice, though, it wasn't so bad -- you simply handed it up to your partner on deck.

Me now, I had discovered a way that lent some exhilarating variation to the tired old method to which a large portion of mankind had come to consider an absolute necessity. Shitting is boring, which is why we get so much reading and thinking done on the commode.

Iola's old-fashioned bumpkin, which comprised two heavy timbers running out in a triangle from the stern deck, formed an apex located four feet beyond the transom. The backstay from the top of the mast attached to the apex of the bumpkin and, to provide a counter-force, a chain ran from the apex down to a point below the transom where it was sturdily anchored into the hull. This configuration formed a kind of four-sided pyramid of lines, and provided a natural platform for assuming the position.

You simply had to grasp the backstay, step out on one of the timbers, seat yourself, place your feet on the chain for good bracing, and do all your heavy thinking in the fresh air. Stripping down buck-naked was advisable to save yourself the necessity of dropping whatever lower garment you wore under the more challenging circumstance. Donning a safety-harness, attached to a rope firmly hooked to the boat, was also a good idea in case you fell overboard.

Stephanie usually employed this method, too. In rough, steep seas, however, the ever-bountiful ocean could also provide an automatic wiper and bidet. Riding the bumpkin in rough seas was like riding a rollercoaster. When Iola lifted her stern over the peak of a wave just before sliding into the trough, your nether parts could be as high as ten feet from the surface of the water, but in the trough as a succeeding wave rose behind the bumpkin you could dip under water up to your waist. This, of course, can be either shocking or refreshing, depending upon the mood of the throne-user. In these circumstances, it is only by the purest will power that one is able to control his sphincter to good effect.

When I had first watched Steph's mouth drop open in shock, wide in a soundless gasp, her eyes big as fried eggs, as she crashed down from the upswing of the bumpkin into water above her navel, and then seeing her well-rounded, but tightly-clenched buns again lift to the sky, I couldn't help it, I almost died laughing. But my darling girl was brave and, oh, how she tried to see it through, bouncing up and down on her teeter-totter. But at last, alas, having no Buddhist training except for traces of the sexual aspects of Tantric practices, she gave up, climbed in, and slunk off for the honeybucket below.

Some images drawn from life's vicissitudes forever fix themselves in our minds and, for me, this was one of indelible imprint. I tried to be a gentleman, of course. To maintain some polite discretion, but on one of those days as we lay about awaiting a wind with our names written on it, the image struck me full force and my sober, contemplative mood was suddenly burst asunder with belly-shaking laughter.

Steph raised an eyebrow and frowned.

"I was thinking about the last time you tried to take a shit out on the bumpkin!"

"Not funny, you asshole," she said, but grinned with a certain rosiness in her cheeks.

I shrieked out my hilarity to the seabirds winging about overhead.

"Yeh, well, I seem to remember that you were so shrunk up in yer privates that they looked like an albino beetle trying to follow a little worm into a tiny two-peanut bag, baby!"

Whoa! No wonder I loved my honey! She joined me and we both shook like dogs shitting bones, she making noises like a Pekinese being fucked by a Saint Bernard, me like a donkey buggered by an elephant.

The next day, tired of watching all the fish sneering at me from six or seven fathoms of crystal clear water over the reef, I broke out my handline and soon snagged two giants. According to our fish book they were Ulua. Alas, we had read in World Sailing Directions that they were reef-poisoned, a thing called ciguatera -- something to do with the composition of the coral. I cut them up in strips, soaked them in brine, and hung them out to dry. I thought we might use it as bait when we went out beyond the reef to fish. It was a real downer to learn that none of the reef fish caught in and around Palmyra could be eaten because they were poisonous.

Several huge manta rays with wingspans of twenty feet glided gracefully by as we read our books and magazines while awaiting a change in wind direction.

*****

We removed Puffer's cast. We bathed her leg in seawater and she licked it and lay out to let the sun work its healing magic. She was soon bounding up and down the hatchway ladder on her own.

*****

On June 27, we awoke to light winds from the southeast. Perfect. We pulled up the anchor and hoisted all sail, heading east, quickly taking bearings to line us up for the entrance running southwest to northeast. Off to the north, we saw the catamaran also hoisting sail. Perhaps they would try to follow us in.

Reaching far enough east, we lined up one of the radio towers on a proper bearing and turned our bow to the northeast, the wind now abeam from starboard. We could see the channel clear and open. Nearing the mouth of the passage, the wind became erratic, pausing and puffing, getting into a suspense story. Unbeknownst to us, there was a slight current of about two knots running from east to west across the channel entrance, which began to carry us out of alignment. Then the wind died altogether and left us bobbing about.

A sudden bump and a gentle shudder snapped us out of our frustration. Our keel was bumping upon the reef! Bump-bumpity-bump, and we were hard upon it. I quickly lowered the sails, thoughts rushing through my mind on little panic feet. Keep calm, I told myself, figure out what needs to be done. There's no immediate danger. One of the small islets lay within a hundred yards rowing distance.

First to check for damage. "Babe, check the bilge for water. I'm gonna check underneath."

I dove over the side to see what I could see. Iola was resting upon the solid iron part of her keel, no discernible damage. I swam around to the other side and dove again and looked a shark right in the eye. He was only about five or six feet long and not looking particularly hungry, but I must say he gave me a bit of a thrill.

Only a Browntip, I told myself, not a Mako, Tiger, or Great White. But then I saw his pal nearby and a third out of the corner of my eye, the second making a streamlined turn toward me. I can't say that they seemed unfriendly -- more curious, perhaps -- but I nevertheless preferred my sharks in groups small enough to keep my eyes on. Where had that third shark gone off to? As simply as that, I suddenly found myself standing upright on the foredeck of Iola, dripping water, my feet firmly planted, and no memory of how I'd gotten there. I'd simply had the desire to be aboard and there I was.

"Oh, there you are," Steph said. "The bilge is okay." Then she eyed me with a funny look as I wondered if her affidavit would be enough to document a telekinetic feat.

"What?"

"Nothing. Friendly sharks."

"Yeh? They invite ya to dinner?"

"Ha-ha."

"So, geez, whatta we do?"

"Get our anchors out into deeper water, kedge off."

We unshipped the dink, loaded an anchor and line, and I rowed out off the aft port quarter. I repeated the effort to set our second anchor off the aft starboard quarter. We cinched the lines in wraps around our two heavy-duty cockpit winches, got out the handles, and began, one to a side, to belabor them.

Slowly, with hair-raising sounds of grinding over the next couple of hours of sweat and backstrain, we inched ourselves into deeper water.

We were floating free. Naught but to move our anchors further out and crab our way into deeper water for a new anchorage and begin the wait for another favorable and, next time, more dependable wind.

The catamaran north of us had dropped sail.

"Hey, we got company," Steph said.

Two dinghies were motoring toward us from the passage, an older man and a boy in one, and two guys in the other.

"Hello," the older man called, pulling at the brim of a Panama hat. "Thought you might be in a little trouble. Need any help?"

"Nah, we're doing okay. She's floating free now."

"Engine trouble?"

"Nope. No engine."

"Wondered why you was anchored out so long. We can probably tow you in, you like."

"Well, ah, uh," I began, thinking about getting our anchors in.

"Yes, please. That would be very nice," Steph said.

"Name's Jack Wheeler. Throw a line and we'll get started."

"Okay. Thanks."

The anchors were stuck fast. I cursed under my breath trying to free one. The two guys in the other dink had motored over above the other trying to pull it in.

Jack was becoming impatient. "Don't like to stay outside the lagoon in a small boat," he warned. "We need to get started in."

I grabbed up two red flotation cushions, threw one to the other two working at the second anchor. "Tie it on the end of the line. I'll retrieve them later."

I quickly tied the other to the line I had been working on and tossed it overboard. The red cushions would serve as highly visible markers for later on. Then I tossed another bowline to the second dinghy and they towed us in.

The lagoon was sapphire blue in the deep center areas, blending into varying shades of green where the coral formations could begin to be seen, becoming quite clear as it lapped over the shallows onto white sand beaches. The taller coconut trees were enormous, all growing in profuse strands over wild jungly undergrowth. Our heads were filled with odors of syrupy sweetness as we entered a humid atmosphere inside, the rich growth and decay of vegetation.

We curved around in an arc eastward, both of us taking in the southern shoreline of Cooper Island. To the far west sat a two-story concrete building all but invisible in the surrounding foliage. We passed rickety old wooden piers, one of the two radio towers behind. They were constructed of steel girders and rose up above the tops of the trees. A large rusting barn-like structure of corrugated metal -- an old military warehouse half demolished on the northern unseen side -- sat beyond a built-up wharf area braced by fat wood logs driven into the dredged out coral below, an unloading dock for Navy supply ships. Beside the half-collapsed warehouse stood a 12000-gallon steel freshwater tank, its supply coming from rainfall off the roof of the good side. A great rusting heap of empty 50-gallon metal fuel drums formed a crumbling wall off to the side. Near the shore past the drum-pile stood a spindly lean-to of poles and palm fronds. Looking back, we could see a long two-story building beyond the old warehouse, which would prove to be a barracks. Then we were passing a cement ramp inclining down into the water -- for launching and hauling out small craft and seaplanes, as Jack would later explain. Behind it sat a long low building open all along one side -- perhaps a vehicle park or garage. Near a tiny cove was a dilapidated old house with another long corrugated metal building adjacent. Inside the dark confines of a wide opening could be seen an aluminum motor-launch set up on several 50-gallon drums, and behind, the vague outlines of large wheeled vehicles. Ahead we could see the mile-long remains of the old airstrip, its pavement fractured through here and there with shrub-like growths of vegetation. Just to the right were a series of perhaps a half-dozen dolphins, which were islands of concrete, steel, and timber sunk down into the coral to provide mooring points.

Between the first two dolphins, moored fore and aft, sat Jack Wheeler's steel ketch,

Poseidon. Between the third and fourth dolphins was the motorsailer, Caroline, a charter boat out of Honolulu with a party of teenaged ham-radio enthusiasts -- the one that'd passed us twice with a wave and no word two days before.

Jack, his son, Steve, and the other two guys, helped get us situated between the two vessels, the shore but fifteen or twenty feet away. The mutts were wagging their tails and throwing out friendly barks, Popolo no doubt anxious to get started marking out all the trees with his peculiar brand of ownership.

In all, it was a strange composite of impressions, foreign and familiar, beautiful and exciting despite the rot and ruin, the dreary dilapidation. There was a sense of unspoiled prestineness laid over with a patina of war history. It was a glimpse of the garden of paradise consuming the invasion of tropical slums at a snail-like geologic pace, an illusion of lushness disguising the plainness of a hard and poor environment.

Thus humbly we came, the far-wanderers to Samarang.

# # #

CHAPTER 15

After twenty-six days at sea, the ground at first seemed to be shifting slightly under our feet. Jack eyed us oddly as we staggered a bit on rubbery legs. We had silly grins on our faces.

"Ah," I grinned as Steph looked on the verge of a giggle. "Takes a while to get your landlegs back, what?"

"Well," Jack said. "Welcome to Palmyra. Being a representative of the owners, I like to introduce myself as the unofficial mayor of Palmyra. If you'll follow me, I'll take you on a brief tour to acquaint you with our local amenities."

We left the dogs somewhat reluctantly, promising ourselves to return to free them for a romp over dry land as soon as we got the lay of things. They were leaping about barking, tails all aswitch, mauling each other in play. They knew they were about to be paroled from the tiny doghouse of their prison.

"This here's our shore camp," Jack began with a wave of his arm at the scrubby point of land adjacent to his boat. The brush had been, cleared away and there were a couple of tables and benches set out under the shade of the trees. "Nice fireplace there if you want to do any outdoor cooking. You'll have to try some of my wife's smoked fish."

"Oh, you can eat the fish here? We'd read they were all poisonous."

"Well, there's two or three varieties that are edible. We used to keep a cat," Jack explained. "This was back on previous trips. Spent fifteen months here once. Anyway, we'd feed the cat some fish, then watch her very closely. If she threw up the fish after awhile, we'd know it wasn't fit to eat. But if she kept it down, why we figured it was all right for us, too."

This was good news. I related how I'd caught the giant Ulua outside the lagoon but hadn't dared to eat them.

"You did right there," Jack nodded. "They're not good for eating that big. But the smaller ones, Papio, same fish, only not growed up, are excellent eating. You won't want for that kind. There's also plenty of Mullet. You'll see them swimming around the surface in schools. But leave the Red Snapper alone. Fine catches and good eating back home, but here you'll get mighty sick, maybe even die of 'em."

"How about sharks? I saw some just outside."

"There's plenty of them around. I'd be careful taking a dip.

It's usually okay in shallow water, but keep a sharp eye out. No resident doctor here."

He motioned us to follow him across the leading edge of the asphalt airstrip, which was about as wide as a football field is long. Suddenly there was a great cacophony of chirping and flapping of wings. Literally thousands of black and white Terns had risen in protest at our intrusion. There were eggs and baby chicks in various stages of growth all over the place.

"This is the old Army airstrip, built back in the forties, thereabouts. It's about a mile long, although you can't see the other end from here because of that large area of vegetation that's taken over down there. Birds nest all the way down though."

We were stepping gingerly to keep off the eggs and babies. Occasionally a mad mama would divebomb our heads, brushing across our hair.

We made it across without mishap and began following a footpath leading in a westerly direction through the brush and soon came to another clearing. The path wound past the second largest building we'd seen on the way in, sandwiched between two old houses, with garage-like openings at each end. Inside were a roadgrader with blade intact, an Army ten-wheeler truck, and, damn my eyes, an old red firetruck, beside which sat the corroded aluminum shell of what had once been a rescue-type launch. To the side was a greasy clump of machinery Jack identified as an old diesel generator once utilized to supply electricity to the island. The approaches to the houses on either side were overgrown with wild vegetation.

Continuing on around, we came to the other long building open all along one side facing the lagoon, nearby the concrete ramp sliding into the water. A couple of Caroline's passengers, nerdy-looking teenagers, were making busy operating the radio equipment they'd set up inside the building. Jack had set up several fifty-gallon drums to catch rainfall off the corrugated metal roof.

"Use this for washing clothes and dishes. Wouldn't advise drinking it. Might catch dysentery from the bird poop on top," he cautioned.

Then we followed him around a huge pile of empty drums to pick up the pathway again. Lea and Sharon, his wife and teenage daughter, were waiting to join us. We passed one of the tall steel-girder radio towers in coming to the large, half-collapsed barnlike structure. He told us he thought it had once served as a supply depot. The landward side to the north was half burnt out, a mass of twisted and blackened metal and wood.

Around to the lagoon side lay the wharf area, an area of high flat ground obviously built up by the industrious use of Army bulldozers. Just beside the remaining half of the warehouse stood the galvanized steel watertank in fair condition, which Jack said was usually kept full from the plentiful rainfall. Gutters hung under the eaves of the slanted corrugated iron of the roof to direct the flow of runoff toward the tank's intake. Someone had set up an old bathtub beside it with a hose running off a tap from the tank.

Sharon demonstrated by turning it on and we stuck our hands out to feel the surprising cold and clear gush of water.

"Wouldn't advise drinking the water here either," Jack admonished, jerking a thumb at the roof. "Bird poop and dysentery."

"That's about it for the tour," Jack concluded. "Over there," he added, pointing north to a long, two-story building, "that's the enlisted men's barracks. Still has odds and ends of furniture and stuff. There's a path through the trees takes you out on the north shore. There's old buildings, concrete ammo dumps, gun battery housings, and miscellaneous machinery all over the place. I'd be careful around the junk areas if I was you."

"Any points of interest you'd care to recommend for tourists?"

"Well, lessee," he mused. "Further to the west you'll find a concrete building all but hidden in the jungle. Twenty, thirty drums of old aviation gasoline there. Octane rating's probably dropped quite a bit due to age, but it works fine in small gas engines. You can help yourself."

"Great, thanks. We've got a small generator."

"Ah, well, you'll want to know about the ice cream parlor then. It's back beyond the way we came."

We all treaded our way back over the airstrip, bypassing Jack's lagoon-front resort area, where Lea and Sharon left us with an invitation to visit, and wound back east, turning off to the right after fifty yards or so. There he led us to a flat-roofed concrete building, about ten-by-twenty feet in size, nestled in the brush and trees. It had little barred slots along the top of the walls under the eaves, one door and no windows. Along one wall outside sat a portable gasoline generator with a wire running inside through one of the barred slots.

"Not sure what they used this place for -- maybe an ammo dump. Keep my generator there so's we can use this refrigerator. Cools your beer, keeps your fish. Make ice cubes, ice cream, and what-have-you. Very useful down here. Gas is free. I guess you'll inherit it when we leave. How about that?"

"That'll be just fine as a matter of fact. Thank you."

"Well, feel free to use it any time. You folks make yourselves at home. I've got some chores waiting aboard my boat."

I was preoccupied with thoughts about the bathtub with the fresh water hose. We were going on four weeks of saltwater baths with the odd brisk shower thrown in by squalls. We returned to Iola only long enough to collect soap and towels and set off to get it done.

It was great. The water was breathtaking. We squirted and splashed each other like kids on a hot summer day. We lathered up in liquid peppermint soap, washing each other's hard-to-get places, and came away between cool kisses feeling clean and bright and rosy.

"We ought to bring the mutts over for a bath," Steph suggested. "They're pretty salty, too."

"Righto. Maybe tomorrow. Good thinking, matey."

We returned to bail out the mutts. They went crazy rushing all over the place, trying to wear out their tail joints. They immediately set up a great howling competition with the Tern colony. We kapu-ed them from that and led them rushing off to the west where they could run and romp about. Popolo set out in a hopeless venture to mark all the trees with his personal brand.

*****

Back aboard with Puff, leaving Popolo and Sista ashore to lay about in the shade, we began to reorder Iola for a life in port. While Steph sorted clothes for washing and rearranged things below, I got the deck shipshape.

Since the day was sunny and warm, I opened the forward hatch to half-cock and readjusted the vents. With the breeze now coming dead out of the east against our stern, the air would flow through the open main hatch and out the forward hatch.

Next to secure the mainsail into neat reefing, set up the boom crutch to keep the boom from bouncing around, and bag up the headsails and stow them below. Coil, bind, and hang all lines -- the halyards and sheeting lines. Set up anti-chafing gear on our mooring lines fore and aft, scrub the deck, fix up our little sun canopy over the cockpit.

Finally, fill the dog dishes with food and water for Popolo and Sista and ferry them ashore.

"How we doing on water, babe?"

"We're down to ten gallons. We need to resupply."

"Guy off the Caroline, the one chaperoning the kids, says he heard it rains almost everyday. Next time it does, we can set up our catchment and fill up."

"Oh, good. Well, tomorrow we do laundry, okay? We can take it over to that tub, do it there."

"Yeah, sounds good."

We looked at each other, then grinned and came together in a hug. "Whew," she said. "We did it."

"What? Think we wouldn't?"

"Sometimes I thought we might be sailing around out there forever."

"Ahoy, Iola."

It was Tony, the mate on Caroline, one of the guys who'd come out to tow us in, to invite us over for a visit.

We stood around in the large covered cockpit eating oranges, complements of the captain, and engaged in idle conversation.

"Must have been rough, nineteen days to get here," the captain commented.

"Nah, it was okay. We took it easy."

"Except for the capsize," Steph threw in.

"Yeah, that brought a bit of excitement."

"How'd it happen?"

We took turns relating the story from different perspectives, making a big joke of it and laughing, admitting our fear but shrugging it off into the realms of humor now that it was past and we were alive to tell about it.

"The watches must have been exhausting -- only two of you."

"Nah," Steph said. "Iola self-steers under the jib. We just tied the wheel every night and went below to sleep."

"You sailed under a jib all the way here?" The captain was in credulous, beginning to lift himself into a superior position, keep some distance from these rash airhead hippies.

"Only at night. But it was a forestaysail, not a jib."

"And the leaks. Gawd, I hated the leaks, water sloshing in the bilges all the time," Steph added.

"You don't have automatic bilge pumps?"

From the tone of his sneer-tinged question, I wondered what sort of panic attack he would go through upon discovering a serious leak in his own vessel with his electrical system down. "Handpump and a bucket works pretty well," I said, mocking him. "We only use our batteries for the running lights. It's a lot of hassle charging them up."

"Hassle? Just start your engine. It's automatic."

I grinned. "If we'd have had an engine, we wouldn't have needed a tow. Besides, we got no engine except for that outboard you see on the back there, but it went kaput on the way down. What can you expect for fifteen dollars?"

"You sailed down here without an engine?" It was clear that he was beginning to suspect we'd escaped from the boobyhatch.

"Hey, what the hell, it was done all the time before the steam-turbine was invented. Columbus didn't discover America in a luxury yacht."

This guy, the captain, was basically a Sunday sailor. He took tourists on day outings. A charter to Palmyra was probably his longest cruise, a serious case of backup-radio-and-backup-lifeboats in case he began leaking and his pumps were down, a fast-passages-are-safe- passages type. I felt like sneering myself, but managed to refrain. After all, he'd been good enough to treat us to an orange apiece. It was harder not to inquire about some vodka to complete the Screwdriver, but I was afraid he might hand me a potato. We weren't paying customers.

Tony rowed us back to Iola grinning. I'd noticed he'd made some effort to keep a straight face in front of his boss. "Don't mind him. He's one of those guys goes to the toilet with a bottle of lavender water so he can claim his shit doesn't stink."

"Nah, hell, he ain't bad," I admitted. "As long as visits are kept short."

"You guys want to take a little stroll later, we can share a couple of joints. I brought some personal stash along."

"Really appreciate the offer, Tony, but no thanks. We're gonna try for an uninterrupted night's sleep."

"Okay, sure, I understand. We got here, I was out on my feet standing so many watches. Offer's open any time, but private, you know." He emphasized by placing a vertical finger to his lips. "These people are all straight, the Wheelers, too."

"Right. Thanks, Tony. Goodnight."

"No, wait, Tony, hey," Steph cut in. "We forgot the letters to Dickie and my mom. Can you mail a couple of letters for us when you get back to Honolulu? They were leaving within a day or two for the pop over to Kingman Reef.

I'd taken an hour to regale Dickie with our trip down and to let him know we'd arrived, while Steph worked on a message to her mother in California.

"Oh, yeah, sure, no problem."

"Yer a peach, Tony, mahalo."

"Hey, could you write a note to my girlfriend, tell her that?"

*****

A little lazy sex was better than a sleeping pill. We woke up ten hours later all caught up on sleep and full of energy. While Steph hung clothes out to air, I fiddled with the batteries trying to figure out what was wrong.

"Help me get the generator topsides, babe. I wanna try putting some more charge in 'em."

"What for? We ain't gonna be needing 'em anytime soon."

"We'll need to haul it up anyway when the Wheelers leave, for the refrigerator. We can leave it topsides until they go." "Oh, yeah. I'm gonna bake some bread today."

"Yeah, great. Maybe figure out something we can use for an ice-tray, have something cold to drink later on."

"Good idea. I can make up some iced tea."

Seeing the sound of the generator running was drawing frowns of irritation my way, I soon desisted. Instead, we went to do laundry, the mutts traversing and circling us all the way, noses and tails busy.

We saw Jack standing off from the teenagers messing about with their radios. "Hi, Jack, how you doing?"

"Darn kids are using Morse code," he said. "Didn't know anyone still knew that."

"Oh, yeah?"

"They're going to Kingman Reef next so they can claim to be the first to broadcast from there. Babysitter says they're going to write it up in some amateur radio magazine."

"Oh, yeah? That's interesting. Where they from?"

"Aw heck, who knows? Rich kids from the Mainland somewhere." He eyed the baskets and detergent. "Off to do laundry?"

"Yeah. Figured to use the bathtub as a washing machine, if that's all right."

"Sure, but shoot, you can use that water right there," he said, pointing at a nearby full 50-gallon drum. "Save you the trip. It's what I collect it for anyway."

"Gee, thanks, Jack," Steph grinned her prettiest. "Stuff'll be three times as heavy on the return trip."

Jack doffed his Panama and strode away.

I meandered down to watch the kids. Maybe I could learn something about ham radios, how to set up and use them, their cost and durability. Their chaperone, a big, easygoing guy, gregarious and talkative as the salesman he was, offered me a small cigar. Just like that, without even token resistance, I accepted -- not even two weeks into my non-smoking program.

He talked and I nodded, all his words going in one ear and out the other. Cigar was so good and I was inhaling so deep -- like pakalolo when you're down to your last joint and you want to wring every last bit of mileage out of it -- that I got high. Then dizzy and a bit nauseous. I broke out into a sweat.

The guy eyed me. "You okay?"

"Yeah. Cigar's getting me high. Ran out of tobacco on the way down. Trying to quit, you know. Whew!"

"Oh, I know. Thing about quitting, you know, is it's easy if you know you're going to start again. Me, I've quit dozens of times. Nothing to it."

I grinned sickly.

"But permanent, well, that's different. Here, you better take a couple more of these," he offered, moving the soggy end of his own from one side of his mouth to the other. "I brought plenty, believe me. This trip's mostly boring for me. Nothing like a Playboy, a cocktail, and a cigar to relax. I'll give you some more before we go."

I took two and put them in the pocket of my cutoffs. "Thanks, my friend, I appreciate it. Well, I better get over and help with the laundry."

"Looks like Jack's getting ready to help," he noted, as we both turned toward Stephanie. "Or at least supervise. Guy's a tower of advice for everybody, likes to hear himself talk. If he could just improve his grumpy attitude, I could put him to work as a salesman."

I headed over, the guy strolling casually behind to stand off and take it all in. Jack was reading Steph a whiney-voiced form of the riot act.

"See now, you've ruined the whole dang thing so nobody else can use it!"

Steph had simply stuffed all our laundry into the full drum, spilling the excess out on the ground. Then she'd poured in detergent and reached a hand in to the armpit to swirl it all around.

"What's the problem?"

"Well, she's using the whole barrel for a washing machine, and it's a waste of water. You can't waste fresh water down here. Now nobody else can use it until we can collect more and it hasn't rained in a good five days. Now, you're welcome to use it, but you've got to use some sense, too -- show a little consideration for others."

"Sorry, Jack, you're right," I offered, speaking up for Steph who was speechless with embarrassment. "We should have figured that out for ourselves. Won't happen again. You want I should bring another drum over for the next rain?"

"Oh, heck, that's all right. Just dump that one out when you're done. But now you don't have any to rinse your clothes out. You're going to have to carry them all over to the bathtub anyway. See, young lady? Now you've got even more work in store all because you didn't stop to think."

He stomped away self-righteously muttering to himself. The chaperone sent a rolling-eyed smirk and a shrug my way. Steph was on the verge of tears.

"Don't worry about it, babe. It ain't that big a deal. Fucking watertank's got thousands of gallons, more than anybody can use since they can't drink it."

"Gawd, he made me feel so stupid."

"Forget it. What Jack needs is someone like you to mellow him out with a joint and a soft word when he gets pissed off."

"You think?"

"Yeah. Only it ain't gonna be you. We don't mention pakalolo around anybody. That's why I turned Tony's offer down. This is a secret mission, babe. Mum's the word. We're dropouts on a back-to-the-land health trip. Okay?"

"Yeh, right."

*****

I made a point to meander over and jaw with Jack, who seemed fond of Popolo and Sista. I'd seen him petting and talking to them, feeding them some little tidbit from his pocket.

"Nice hounds you got here. That a Lab?"

"Half. They're both from the same litter. Your guess is as good as mine on the rest."

"Brindle's got pretty coloring. But the black, he's a real hound -- strong and quick."

"Yeah, we're probably nuts for bringing 'em along, but we just couldn't leave 'em behind."

"I'm kind of amazed they aren't out wreaking havoc with the birds."

"Oh, there won't be any problem there. We told 'em not to bother the birds."

"How you do that?"

"Just yell kapu at 'em. They know. We brought 'em up on Hawaiian words. You see 'em doing something you don't like, just yell kapu at 'em."

"Sure, I know that word. Well, I'll be darned. What do you do if they don't mind, kick 'em?"

"Nope. I figure a guy who kicks a dog probably beats his wife and kids, too."

"Well now, you might have something there. But you got to have some kind of discipline, too."

"We do. We don't hug and kiss them. These are very friendly dogs -- they need their hugging and kissing."

"Hmp, well, whatever works, I guess. The kids like 'em. Tried to get them to accompany them on a fishing trip to the northshore. There's a nice spot. I'll have my boy show you. Anyway, the dogs wouldn't go with them."

"Yeah, they stick pretty close to home. We used to live way out in the country -- trained 'em as watchdogs."

"Is that right? Sure ain't heard 'em barking much."

"Well, I think they're a little confused about property lines, don't know what to guard and what not. On Maui, they had a leash law and we kept them tied below our boat in drydock. On board, they'll bark if fish or birds get too close."

"Now, ain't that a toot," Jack said, managing a snort passing for a chuckle.

I changed the subject. "Whatever induced you to spend fifteen months here, Jack?"

"Oh, scientists come here every now and then, study the atmosphere, ocean, tides, marine life, weather patterns, stuff like that. Back then I was the official caretaker, riding herd on those people, keeping them out of trouble. That's where all the gasoline came from -- stuff that was left over."

"Government-funded probably. They always seem very cavalier when it comes to wasting the taxpayer's money."

"Ain't that the truth."

"So what, you know the owner pretty well?"

"Yep. He likes to keep an eye on things, worries about people trying to sue him. You planning to stay awhile?"

"Yeah. We're kinda fed up with civilization, you know? Thought we'd find an uninhabited island for ourselves, kinda get back to nature and live quiet and simple. Like that guy, Tom Neale, on Suvarov. You ever read that book -- An Island to Myself?"

"I did. It was interesting."

"We brought down all kinds of seeds and tools. Hoping to get a vegetable garden going."

"Might have a little problem there."

"What, the birds?"

"No, they're no problem. They only eat what they can catch out of the sea. It's rats, for one thing. They're mostly vegetarians out of necessity -- climb trees and gnaw into the coconuts. Maybe bust a few eggs, eat a few baby chicks. Not many, though. Nighttimes, mama birds are nesting along the runway. They gang up on the rats, who're mostly nocturnal anyway. No, it's those danged hermit crabs. You seen any of them yet?"

"Nope, don't believe I have."

"They're scavengers, eat darn near anything. They live inside seashells -- drag 'em along everywhere they go. They got a soft body and need the seashells for protection. They get into your garden, they'll eat all the shoots coming up. You need to put a screen or something around your plot. Even then, you might need to grease it up some. Little boogers can climb!"

"Hm. Guess we'll have to work at figuring something out. What about on top of a flat roof, like where the refrigerator is?"

"Well, shoot, that might work. Now, why the heck didn't I think of that?"

"I was wondering, Jack -- maybe you could advise me -- if maybe I couldn't write a letter to the owner and offer to serve as caretaker in your absence."

"Hm, that might not be a bad idea. People come here, I dunno, they sometimes act crazy. They set fires to the buildings. That's what happened to the warehouse. You'll see some other places burned to the ground. Just plumb loco."

"Figured someone keeping an eye out and they knew it, might inhibit 'em." I was trying to pattern my speech after Jack's, who was kind of country. I was guessing he'd originally come from somewhere like Missouri or thereabouts. Talk a man's lingo, he listens, which is one of the reasons I'd done so well in Hawaii -- I'd taken the trouble to learn Pidgin and a few hundred local words.

"Sure, good idea. You write him a letter, I'll deliver it, give you a recommendation."

"Why, shoot, that's right kind of you, Jack."

"Owner don't like guns on the island. You got guns?" "Yes, I do, Jack. Doesn't everybody?"

"Well, I reckon so, but it's a sorry state of affairs when sailing folk all have to go armed."

"Sure can't argue with that."

"Just so you keep 'em aboard your boat. We don't need no accidents down here. Had some yahoos potshotting at the birds one time, whatever took their fancy."

"No problem. Ain't got much ammo for 'em anyway."

"You should probably put in a paragraph about not holding the owner liable whatever happens."

"Sure, I can do that. I'll let you look it over, make sure I got it right."

"Be glad to."

A little later in the day, as we set out with the dogs to explore the northshore, we met Jack and his son, Steve, coming down the south edge of the runway pulling a wagon. It was loaded with a chainsaw, axe, hoe, and machete. The wagon was red, a kid's playwagon.

"That's quite a wagon you got there, Jack," I grinned. "Need to hitch one of my mutts up to haul it for you."

"That'd sure be handy. Hot working the afternoons. Gonna have to stick to the cool of early mornings, looks like."

"What're you doing?"

"Oh, I promised to do some work on clearing the runway. Guess the owner plans to fly down, think about doing something with the place."

"Dad," Steve interrupted. "Can I go? We're going fishing, remember?"

Jack nodded. "You go ahead. Try to catch us some supper."

I got back on the birds. "How's he going to land with all those birds there?"

"Well, I guess they'll just get rid of them."

"Huh? How?"

"Poison 'em, shoot 'em. Durned if I know. Maybe just go around stepping on all the eggs. That's why they come here, the birds."

I could feel Steph chilling up, the idea of killing thousands of the graceful winged creatures bordering on blasphemy to both of us. I tried to cover for the feelings she wore on her sleeve, distract Jack from noticing the look of horror in her eyes.

"First bird I ever saw didn't build a nest," I gestured. All the unhatched eggs lay bare upon the pavement.

"Yep. I reckon the sun keeps 'em warm enough of a day, and the mamas sit on them nights."

"Well, we're off for a little hike. Next time you head out to do some work, gimme a call. I've got a chainsaw, too. Be glad to help you out."

"Aw, shoot, Roy, that's mighty neighborly of you. I'll do that -- probably early while it's still cool."

When we were out of sight, heading along the path leading to the wharf area, Steph began to vent her feelings. "Geez, I can't be-live it! Just murder all those pretty birds so a plane can land! For what? Probably so they can put in a golf course, a restaurant, and oh, a hotel or two for white-legged tourists!"

"Yeah."

"Who'll probably never leave their air-conditioned rooms except to go to junk stores for gewgaws!"

"Yeah," I agreed. "And put up signs saying keep off the grass."

"Probably sell fishing licenses and boating permits, open a tax office, bring the cops down! Conform to the rules! Put'cher clothes on! No singing above so many decibels! How's yer credit? Can ya pay for all this?"

"You got it, babe, fucking-A rights! The destruction of nature's always been called progress."

"Yeah, the more they kill and wreck in the world, the more money they got to waste their lives away counting it!"

"We could paint some signs, have a demonstration."

"Yeh, right!"

"Except it's private property."

"So what? They got no right to destroy the whole planet! We can have a sit-in on the runway so they can't land!"

"In all that bird poop?"

"Don't laugh," she ordered, laughing.

"Who's laughing," I said, laughing. "Give me bird poop or give me death!"

We kidded each other out of the downers, like a game, a running dialogue of the ridiculous. It channeled frustration into laughter, transformed the outrages of life into forms less intolerable. There's serious and there's serious and fuck it if you can't take a joke.

I kissed her. "You're beautiful when you're mad," I said, pulling her to angle off around the barracks building. We peeked inside, saw rows of cots and mattresses, a dormitory, before tripping on through to a fine white sand beach with a nice cooling breeze.

Looking both ways, we could see that the trees and undergrowth were like a wall, leaving only so many feet of jagged coastline where the sea washed up. The dogs had run into the shallows to prance and chase around, wanting to play. We joined them in screaming, barking, splashing and carousing about, giving ourselves over to the dancing immediacy of the moment.

"Shine, sun," Steph called, her arms to the sky.

"Kiss me, breeze!" I chorused.

It was an absolutely beautiful day and we shrugged out of our skimpy clothes. Palmyra became Samarang, the difference between the two lying in the realm of magic. After awhile, we all lay to soak in the sun, drowsy in the warmth, puffs of wind tickling our bodies. There was no past, no future, only being. Here and now. Layers of shells armoring our selves seemed to fall away, the veneers grown for civilization's sake, now so far away. We were free and full of sighs of relief, holding hands, surrendering and accepting our own natural presence, our place between earth, water, and sky.

"Oh, baby! Oh, baby!"

"Yeah."

"I love you."

"Me, too."

"What?"

"I love me, too."

"You big jerk. C'mere and kiss me."

"Yes, ma'am."

We drifted away for a thousand years or so, until the sound of the dogs' wruffing and pointing their noses to the east as we emerged from the growing enthusiasm for the honey hiding in our mouths. Distant figures. We slipped back into the modesty of our shorts to go and meet them. It was Steve, Sharon, and another young girl, a friend from school who'd been invited along.

Steve carried a pole and a string of Papio. After a ritual greeting, they all petting and talking to the dogs, who were lavish with the wet affection of their tongues, they directed us along to the good fishing spot.

"It's a cement wall, about eight or ten feet high, right along the beach. The water comes right up against it."

We left them in their pubescent blushes, their oh-so-knowing mirth, all on the verge of giggling over having espied two naked adults doing what they were oh-so-interested in. Teenagers are natural voyeurs and they'd gotten their eyes full.

We found a glass ball, a fishnet float that had probably come from a Japanese or Korean fishing boat, and speculated that it might have drifted for thousands of miles. We would keep it, pretend it was a magical crystal ball containing messages from the future.

Arriving at the wall a mile or so eastward, we stood looking down into a pool formed by the retaining cement and rebar on one side and nearby reef formations. We could see Papio darting about and a school of Mullet meandered lazily by playing follow the leader. Papio have a tense fierce expression, full of energy, now quivering in one spot, then streaking to another quicker than the eye could follow. The Mullet were more whimsical, waggling gracefully near the surface. Then a six-foot long shark glided smoothly around with a certain insolence, obviously the boss.

"Oh," Steph grimaced. "I don't like him."

Sista didn't either. Her hackles rising, she backed away, a natural coward, and began to whine and bark. Popolo, who had no fear of anything smaller than a pickup, tossed a few offhand barks for Sista's sake. Puffer was silent except for a few high-pitched yips, enough to let everyone know whose side she was on.

"Awright, you guys, cool it. C'mon, let's have a coconut."

I selected one from the ground, shredded the husk off by pounding it on a sharp edge of the wall, broke a hole in the top with the machete I'd carried along, and offered it to Steph for the first sip.

It was sweet and cool. I drank and then whacked it open to dig out the meat, feeding bits to the mutts who gnawed with obvious relish. It was so good, we had another. Then another before continuing on.

Traipsing into the jungle, we found a huge steel tank rising in a squat bubble of cancerous green paint and scabrous rust, probably a fuel tank dating back to the war. We traipsed on, me whacking with the machete through the underbrush until we came out to a clearing where there stood two old houses shaky and sagging with rot and bugs. The remains of a third were no more than a blackened mound of charcoal over a cement foundation -- one of the burned down buildings Jack had mentioned. A few rats were spotted scurrying in the dark rafters of the two still standing.

It was a short walk from there to the easternmost end of the runway. Strolling along the northern edge, heading back west, we came upon a large building that contained defunct refrigerated walk-in lockers, obviously the main food storage depot. Outside sat a scaly forklift that hadn't moved from it's resting spot in years, perhaps decades.

We were walking light and carefully now through the thousands of Terns. Mama birds blew up in explosions of wings and angry scolding. Baby chicks scampered away. Eggs were everywhere.

"I wonder what they taste like."

"What, the birds?"

"No, the eggs," I said. They were only slightly smaller than chicken eggs, an off-white with dark speckles. Without refrigeration on Iola, a small stock of eggs hadn't lasted long.

"Popolo!" Steph suddenly shouted. "Kapu!"

Popolo was snuffling inquisitively after the tailfeathers of a panicked, cheeping, and running chick. But it was too late. He'd gobbled the whole chick into his mouth.

"Oh, Popolo!" Steph shrieked in horror. "Kapu! Kapu!" "Popolo!" I called. "Hele mai!"

He came to me, dropped his head and bellied down before me, opened his mouth and deposited the chick, unharmed, between his paws, almost as if he were offering a gift. We were flabbergasted. The fat little creature, now sticky with dog saliva, ran off cheeping wildly as Popolo's tongue flapped pinkly in the breeze. He had a smug look on his face.

"I'll be a sonofabitch!"

"Oh, you didn't eat the little baby," Steph cooed, hugging him. "Good Popolo! Maika'i ilio!" He loved it.

*****

It was late afternoon by the time we returned, tired now and hot, but full of cheer. We stopped by the refrigerator house to chugalug Steph's ice tea made the day before. We decided to take another go at the bathtub, washing down all the dogs and picking over them for ticks. All of us by then were feeling so good we practically strutted back to Iola. I fed Popolo and Sista ashore, mixing canned dogfood with the dry as a treat while Steph fed Puffer aboard. I husked a few coconuts, broke the shells open, and dug the meat out. Steph made up some treat for the refrigerator. Then we sat down to eat, taking our tea in the cockpit with the sunset.

Jack gave us a hulloa and invited us over to their camp for fresh smoked Papio and quiet conversation. While Steve and the girls played with the dogs, feeding them bits of the fish, Steph ran her coconut concoction to the refrigerator. The fish was delicious. Lea had smoked it over smoldering coconut husks after marinating it in soya.

Back aboard, we lit a lamp and an incense stick to disguise the aroma of pakalolo, our first and last joint of the day. Cozied up in bed, we turned to our books. I had pulled out Euell Gibbons' Beachcombing in Hawaii, which contained an entire section devoted to all the things you could do with coconuts. I read avidly, soaking it up to the strains of Hawaiian music coming over our radio from a Honolulu station as it comingled with the rustling of palm fronds, the lap of water gently rocking the hull, and the intermittent rush of wings and birdcalls in the night.

*****

In the morning, Jack woke me from sawing logs and I rushed about washing up, making a quick cup of coffee, and digging out our chain saw and a cane machete.

Along with Steve, we put in a couple of hours working at clearing a large overgrown clump of high bush dug stubbornly into the runway, their roots like hardwood. Few days of this, I thought, and I'll have to re-hone the cutting blades. But the exercise was good, soon getting me into a sweat.

Removing his hat and wiping his brow with a handkerchief, Jack measured the height of the sun. "Reckon that's enough for today. She's gonna be warming up soon."

Steve, anxious to be away, loaded up their tools into the wagon and disappeared, while Jack and I shared a seat on a fallen palm tree in the shade.

"How long you fixing to stay here, Roy?"

"Oh, six months or so. Maybe longer. See how it works out."

"You got enough supplies last you that long?"

"No, we brought about three months worth of food, but we've made arrangements to be resupplied in September. We ought to have a garden going by then."

"Ever done anything like this before?"

"No, not really. Had a piece of raw land on the Big Island -- rainforest. We had a cabin, garden, some chickens -- kind of pioneer-style living."

"Been around much in your boat?"

"Nope. Only Maui, Oahu, and Kauai. This is our first big voyage. Sort of learning as we go."

"How you like it so far?"

"Like they say down on the farm, Jack, hog heaven. I'm really enjoying it."

"How was your trip down?"

"Slow and easy mostly. We didn't push it. Had a little excitement along the way. Thing about not having an engine is you gotta have long patience. Our Merc hadn't a conked out, we'd a been in here ten days ago. Hardest thing was trying to figure out a three-month food supply."

"Yep, that's a tough one when you're used to going week to week. How you doing?"

"Okay so far. Probably miscalculated on a few things, but I don't figure that to be much of a problem with all these coconuts.

I was just reading up on all the things you can do with them. Milk, ice-cream, butter, oil, even hooch I ever work up enough nerve to climb one of those suckers."

"Well, you can sure help yourself there. You can cut down all the young trees you want, but the owner wants the mature ones left alone. You know about palm heart?"

"Only what I read. It's the pulp inside, right?"

"Yeah, but only about the top three or four feet of the tree. You peel away the outer layers, come away with a nice log of it. You cut it in hunks, goes good in salads, but you can cook it, too. You dice it up, salt it, and bake it, you got something tastes kind of like peanuts."

"What about these sprouting ones I see laying all over the place?"

"Oh now, those are good you get 'em about a foot high. The meat inside's all made itself into a bread-like stuff, sweet and juicy, but there's no water. You can cook 'em up, they taste kind of like yams."

"Papio and Mullet, they the only fish not poisoned here?"

"Well, there's the sharks, but they got a funny taste unless you know how to prepare it. They got some mussels you can eat if you can find them. Lots of Coconut Crabs. You can even eat the hind-ends of the Hermit Crab you take a notion. There's another, too, a big blue crab, but they're kind of rare. Haven't seen one in a good spell."

"How about the Tern eggs? They any good?"

"Some people like 'em. They got a fishy smell when you break 'em open, got a different colored yolk, more orange than yellow. I don't much care for 'em myself, but some of those scientists way back sure did."

I figured we could do all right once we got a garden going. Fresh vegetables would be a real treat over the canned variety, and it looked like we had a yearlong growing season. Pakalolo ought to do well too, once we figured out a growing medium for them to take root in. It was too bad we couldn't get some banana trees going. They'd do well here. Back in the Acres we'd kept stalks of several varieties of bananas hanging from the carport beams. And how would guavas, orange trees, and avocados do here, I wondered.

*****

Steph had baked an extra loaf of bread for the Wheelers and had a treat of what she called coconut grated ice milk, which I thought was more like a coconut popsicle -- first I'd ever had. Yummy.

We went out on a short sojourn to gather and husk more, enough to provide a meal for the mutts, who loved it, and a milkshake for us pureed in the blender. We took home some of the miniature football-shaped sprouts for baking. I was thinking about Gibbons' recipes for milk, cream, and butter. Then, there were the Tern eggs. I had to figure out a way to determine the freshness of an egg so that we didn't crack the half-formed fetus of a chick into the frying pan.

Hm.

*****

After another morning spent working at what I now conceived as a hopeless task of clearing the runway in the way we were going about it, I hooked up with two of the four guys on the catamaran, Bohilla Island, still anchored out over the western reef. They'd eaten one of the Ulua and all gotten sick with severe stomach cramps, fever, and vomiting. They were headed for Samoa from California in the home-built craft, but the hulls were working apart from their cross-bracing members and they were scavenging about for whatever bolts and wire they could find.

Talking to the young captain-owner, who was a personable guy, I got the impression they were having a hard time. I helped them remove some long bolts from the roadgrader and then went about helping them collect a supply of coconuts. Then I took them to the bathtub in case they wanted to clean up.

"Maybe later. Be nice to get a freshwater bath."

As they rowed out toward their boat, I waved. The young captain called, "I'll see you in awhile. We'll go get your anchors."

"Okay. Meet you at my boat. It's the blue one."

Back aboard, I told Steph about them. "How about we invite them to supper tonight? They look like they could use a good meal."

"Hm. Okay. I'll make up a big pot of spaghetti, maybe a pie."

"You all right? You look like you're dragging ass today."

"Too much coconut, I think. Stomach feels fucked."

"Mine, too. Maybe we overdid it. I think I'm constipated."

"Me, too. Uck."

"What kind of pie you thinking of?"

"I dunno, why?"

"Maybe let's go with those cans of blackberries. Maybe they'll help loosen us up."

"Awright, yeh, that sounds good."

Jack called. "Roy, you there?"

I popped my head up. "Yeah, Jack, what's up?"

"One of your dogs bit my boy," he said, squinting at me with a stony eye. Popolo and Sista had their heads up from snoozing in the trees. They hadn't barked at Jack. They'd gotten used to him and all the Wheeler crew.

I went ashore, my mind in a turmoil -- I couldn't believe it. "Jeez, I'm sorry, Jack. What happened?"

"The black dog bit my boy."

"Popolo?"

"My wife's treating him now. He's got puncture wounds on his calf."

"My God, that's awful! Can I help? Let's go see if he's all right, find out what happened. My dogs have never bitten anyone."

Aboard Poseidon, making our way below, Jack like a prosecutor making his case gestured to Steve lying back with a frown as his mother dabbed antiseptic on a toothwound.

"Steve, you all right?"

"Yeah."

"Jeez, I'm really sorry. What happened?"

"Aw, it was my fault. I stepped on his tail while he was sleeping."

"Oh, well, that'll do it every time. He gonna be all right, Lea? How bad is it?"

"Oh, not bad. He'll be okay."

Back topsides, making our way back ashore, Jack apologized. "Guess I kind of jumped the gun there, Roy."

"Aw, hey, these things happen, Jack."

"Well, I've told the kids to keep clear of your dogs so it don't happen again."

"How about if I chain 'em up? That way they won't be running around, nosing into things."

"Well, darn, Roy."

"Hey, no problem. They're used to it."

"Well, okay. Maybe move 'em down a little further, make sure the kids don't disturb 'em."

"Sure, no problem."

"Just until we leave, an other week. I'd feel better about it."

"Sure, you gotta worry about your kids. I know how it is."

"Thanks, Roy."

So I broke out the old dog-chains from Maui and did the dirty deed.

*****

"What, two pies?"

"Yeh. I figured one for supper and the guys on the catamaran can take the other back to share with the other two."

"Yer a peach."

"You'd be a peach if you'd open those cans of blackberries for me."

*****

When Sharon brought over a nice Papio from Jack, I figured all was forgiven. I filleted and wrapped it in tinfoil for the refrigerator, stopping on the way to feed scraps to Popolo and Sista.

*****

Well into the afternoon by then, the cleancut young captain and his hairy hippy accomplice returned to fetch me for the anchor retrieval expedition, me pointing the way. Once we'd arrived and seeing the cushions still tied to the ends of the anchor lines, I prepared to go over the side.

"No, sit still," the captain said. "I'll get it."

"Sharks down there."

"Yeah, well, we'll see who eats who they mess with me."

Over he went into about twenty feet of water. We could see him struggling to untangle line and work the Danforth out of a wedge in the reef.

"Whew!" he blew, coming up for air. "That sucker's really stuck!"

"How about I come down and help you?" I was leery of the sharks, although we hadn't seen any so far -- and I was keeping a sharp eye out for them.

I was relieved when he waved me away. "No, I can get it."

Up and down three or four more times he went to finally pop up and say, "Okay, haul 'er up."

We did. Back in the dinghy, I noticed him shivering. "Okay," he gasped, working on getting his breath back. "Where's the other one?" "Hey, no rush. I can always get it later. Besides, I think it's almost dinner time. You guys are invited."

*****

Whoa! Those boys could put it away! Steph had made plenty, heaping their plates full, and then seconds, they sopping up the sauce with slabs of her homemade bread. We washed it down with a next-to-last bottle of red wine. There was still half a pot left, which Steph wanted to take out for the other two guys. It was dark and the captain insisted upon taking it himself. We lounged around in the cockpit for a while shooting the breeze and I invited them to spend the night. We could break out the sleeping bags for them to throw down on the foredeck. But no, the captain was antsy, wanting to get back to his own boat in case anything happened. His crew was all inexperienced.

We loaded them in their dink with the leftover spaghetti and sauce, handed down the other pie, and bade them good night.

"He's really a nice guy, the captain. I like him."

"Yeah, me, too." In fact, enough to have snuck a C-note from my stash to stick in the piepan under the bottom crust. From Ron, the hairy hippy, I knew they were broke, the whole operation running on hope and a shoestring. I knew the captain would refuse if I offered it to him directly. He was a whole lot like me, that sense of adventure and all the little abilities to get it done. "Kid's got balls."

*****

A cooler day, gray, greeting us as we worked on the runway for a couple of hours. Then a heavy misting and sprinkles of rain. Back at Iola, I could smell bread, Steph busy in the galley. Stowing the chain-saw in the cockpit locker, I went forward to close the forehatch. Steph was sliding the main hatch closed, but leaving out the boards that slid in to close the vertical half. I ran to slide the top part open, heave myself down the ladder, and close it again.

"Looks like rain, darlin'. Time to fill up on fresh water." "I'll get out all our jugs."

"Okay. Just slide 'em out into the cockpit. No use both of us getting wet." I kicked off the gym shoes and pulled the tanktop over my head, and returned the baseball cap to my head.

Topsides I adjusted the topping lift to raise the end of the boom from its resting place in the notched crutch, unhooked the bungicord freeing the mainsail, and hoisted it to leave a loose drape at the bottom. Tying off the main halyard, I headed for the cockpit to pay out the mainsheet. As the boom swung out to port, the wind filling the sail, I tied off to a cheat and turned to look for the funnel and hose where Steph had laid them out. Grabbing them and a five-gallon jug, I went forward to the mast to affix the funnel at the gooseneck. The mainsail would catch the rain slanting in from the east, roll it down into the lower drape, where it would flow toward the funnel and hose into the jug. It was the same method we'd used to gather fresh water from the rainsqualls on the way down. Today's rain would bring us seventeen gallons.

Hanging cap and cutoffs, I lolled about and read more of Gibbons' book while Steph baked cinnamon bread for us and cinnamon nut loaf for the Wheelers, between times perusing Joseph Conrad.

On one of my forays in redonned wet shorts to replace an empty jug for a full one on deck, I spotted the sails of a ketch to the west outside the lagoon.

"For an island that's supposed to be uninhabited," I said to Steph, telling her what I'd seen, there sure are a lot of boats and people showing up here."

"The good news is that none of them stay very long."

*****

But the next morning, it was Tempest a sleek fiberglass high aspect rigged sloop that motored in -- Ed and Marilyn Pollock out of Honolulu. Jack and Steve were out in their motorized dinghy to help get them moored behind us in the space Caroline had evacuated.

In the afternoon, as I rowed down toward the western end of Cooper to fill a jug with the old aviation gasoline, Sea Wind glided into the lagoon, the ketch I'd seen the day before, who'd obviously waited off in the murky weather before coming in. I recognized the design as one of Angleman's, whose deep sheer, bowsprits, and heart-shaped sterns I'd long admired. They were older, full-bodied vessels with long keels, real sea-truckers. She was white with blue trim, neat, Bristol, a blond woman at the helm, a man in the bow directing her with hand signals.

"Hell000," I called as we neared each other. "Can I help you get situated?"

"No, thanks," the man returned with a smile. "We can handle it." I rowed closer and we introduced ourselves. "I'm Roy Allen. We're on the blue sloop, Iola, out of Hawaii."

"Malcolm Graham, my wife, Eleanor. San Diego," he returned, pointing. "Call me Mac, Roy, That's Muff."

"There's a good mooring space at the back of the line there," I recommended, gesturing to the line of three vessels eastward.

"How about right back in there," he asked, nodding toward the small cove near the equipment shed containing the roadgrader, Army truck, fire engine, and rescue launch, the sagging old houses to either side. I studied it, surprised at his choice.

"It deep enough in there, you think?"

"What's your draft, six feet or so?"

"Yeah."

"You know, I think it is. I've never tested it, but it looked to me to be a good ten to fifteen feet deep."

"Think we might try it."

"You need any help, give me a call."

"I want to check it out a little more first. Think we'll anchor right here for a while, get her situated in later. Like to come aboard for a drink?"

"No, not now, thanks. I'm on an errand. See you folks later and we'll get acquainted -- introduce you to my lady and our three mutts."

"How many people you got here?"

"Too many. Hell of a note. We came here to play Adam and Eve in the Garden, but for an uninhabited island, the population's exploding.

"Looks like we had the same idea."

"Welcome to the club. See you later. Bye, ma'am."

"Nice meeting you," she said.

"Adios, Roy, see you later."

"By the way," I called back while rowing away. "That's the finest damn bowsprit I've ever seen."

He grinned and waved.

*****

Ashore near the two-story concrete building all but hidden in the foliage, I first located an open bay where thirty or forty of the 50-gallon drums stood, about half of them empty. Whoa, still plenty of free gas to burn. It would keep our generator, shredder, and chain-saw going for a long time.

Then I walked out for a look at Strawn Island, a small piece of real estate once more separated from Cooper by a shallow wash of the sea.

Returning to the gas dump, I pumped out enough to fill our five-gallon jug, then nosed around in the building itself. I found corroded steel rungs leading up to the roof in a small shaft and gingerly climbed up them. The roof was flat with a parapet about three feet high. It was maybe a hundred feet long and fifty feet wide, and provided a great view of the sea to the north and west, and the lagoon and channel through the reefs to the south. What a great place for our garden, I thought, or better yet four or five hundred pakalolo plants, a nursery to one end. But what a bitch it would be to haul up enough compost to accommodate that many. On second thought, no -- back to the drawing board. People would be coming here to avail themselves of the gas. We needed a place a whole lot more private, I thought -- perhaps one of the smaller islands surrounding the eastern part of the lagoon, which still had a causeway separating the two parts and thus no easy passage between one and the other.

The next day, overcast with light intermittent showers, the lagoon flat and clear with hardly any wind, we saw lots of parti-colored fish swimming about.

Ron rowed in to return pots and pans and to try hitching a ride back to Hawaii. He was afraid the cat would never make it to Samoa. He offered to pay us for a ride over to Christmas, even to buy us a new outboard motor or have our Merc overhauled, whatever. He was promising anything that would get him a ride.

"Thought you were broke."

"Hey, but from Christmas I can send a wire to Honolulu, have my people send some money -- no problem."

"You should probably hit on the Wheelers or the Pollocks. They'll be leaving for Honolulu sooner or later. We came here to stay for awhile."

"I already tried the Pollocks. They don't like people with hair -- wouldn't even give me the time of day."

"Well, try the Wheelers."

"I don't think they like me either. What about those other people just came in? They headed back to Hawaii?"

"Nah, I think they're planning to stay awhile, too." I'd seen where they'd gotten Sea Wind backed into the cove, moored to starboard pilings ashore, two coconut palms sternward, a grappling hook anchor line to port, and a long anchor line off the bow. The last I'd seen, they were busy erecting a custom-made canopy that covered the entire deck topsides except the foredeck. Mac had unloaded an inflatable dinghy wits an outboard to zip about getting all the mooring lines situated. Obviously, they'd come well prepared.

"Well, I guess it's the Wheelers or nothing then."

"How about I give you a haircut, trim your beard up, make you a little more presentable to them," Steph offered.

"Oh, man, what a guy's gotta do to hitchhike nowadays! All these straights with their boats. Ain't there any liberated people sailing around?"

I was taking a distinct dislike to Ron. He was a quitter and a whiner. "Takes hard work and money, my man. You can't freeload on the seas. Ain't no welfare checks or foodstamps out here."

"How about if I stay with you guys? Just until I can hitch a ride home."

"No, man, sorry. We can't afford to feed you."

"Maybe I'll just stay on the island until my ride comes through. Plenty to eat there."

"Yeah, if you like fish and coconuts enough, you sure won't starve."

"Beats drowning out in the middle of the ocean."

"Your skipper seems pretty capable to me."

"Yeah, he's all right, but the fucking boat's coming apart."

"He tells me he's about got it fixed good enough to get you all to Samoa."

"Man, would you put your life in the hands of somebody you hardly know?"

"Well, how'd you wind up aboard in the first place?"

"Aw, man just hitching a ride, you know? How was I to know the fucking boat would fall apart?"

Although we probably weren't so far apart on the personal freedoms and easy-living aspects, like promiscuity and drug use, what a world of difference in self-reliance and what we expected to be handed to us without charge.

Steph trimmed him up, loaned him one of my shirts and sent him off begging to the Wheelers, but he soon returned with a hangdog expression. I told him he could stay aboard for the night and Steph fed him cinnamon bread with peanut butter and marmalade.

"You guys got any grass?"

"Nah," I told him. "We don't indulge."

He sighed. "Fucking Wheeler's an old skinflint. They're leaving in a few days and he wouldn't even give me a little stash of food. Nobody seems to care if I starve to death around here."

"There's no way you'll starve unless you're stupid."

When I brought up a sleeping bag for him, he asked for a pillow. I told him he could use a sail bag. I was regretting allowing him to spend the night, but by then it was full dark and the row back could be dangerous to an incompetent.

As we sat sipping tea in the cockpit, we noticed Steve and the girls moving about topsides on Poseidon. Steve was fishing for shark in order to collect their jawbones and teeth, which he could sell back in Honolulu. I decided to give it a try, maybe find out if they were as tasty as I'd heard -- if you knew how to prepare them. I'd read about two methods.

I soon had a bite, baiting the hook with a piece of the dried Ulua I'd kept -- most of the rest being tossed overboard. Steve had told me the Papio preferred a silver lure because it resembled live bait to them in the water. The trick was to keep the lure moving.

I figured if I caught a shark, I'd give the head to Steve and see what we could do with the rest.

"I got one," I yelled, excited at the heavy pull on the handline. "I got one!"

"Pull, baby, pull," Steph exhorted.

"Whoa! He must be a big one," I grunted with the effort to haul him in.

"Here, I'll help ya," Steph yelled, straining on the eighth-inch Nylon cord with me.

Steve and the girls, catching our excitement, called out their support. Even Ron got into it, grabbing up the line on deck behind Steph to pull.

Whoa! Not a shark, but a giant black Ulua, the biggest I'd seen, even when compared with all those I'd seen when we'd been anchored outside the lagoon. I got a halyard looped around his tail and hoisted him out. What a beauty, but too bad they weren't edible. Steph got the Instamatic and flashcubes to snap a photo. Then I threw him back.

Ron was gone in the morning to try begging whatever he could from the Grahams.

*****

Sitting around talking shop with Jack and Lea at their shore camp, the Grahams strolled over to introduce themselves, and we stood about in idle conversation for a while. Jack was into his unofficial mayor spiel and offering his standard guided tour, which they accepted, and doubtless would recite the few rules demanded of visitors. They'd no sooner departed, than the Pollocks made a production of coming ashore. Ed was tall, bony and ridiculous in bermuda shorts, knee-stockings and docksiders, wearing a sweater over a long-sleeved shirt, with a beanie atop his balding head that resembled a yarmulke -- except it was patterned in triangles of green and white to match the rest of his garb. His wife, Marilyn, was a meek mouse of a soft and flabby woman with a spayed fuzzy little lapdog which, after Steph assured her Puffer would not devour the tiny nervous beast, she let down to sniff about and play.

Ed was a teacher of mathematics. Ah, I thought, entirely misleading myself, a neat, orderly, scientific mind. They were out of the Ala Wai Yacht Harbor.

"Beautiful hull," I complimented. "How do you get the hull so smooth and glossy?"

He sniffed, eyeing the rough hull of Iola with contempt. "Hard work," he sneered, as if he thought the concept were foreign to me. Perhaps I could introduce him to Ron and they would drive each other away in mutual disgust. I felt a bit insulted that he classed me as I had classed Ron.

"Nice stockings and sweater," I snidely remarked. "Quality wool, I can tell, but a bit warm for such garments, don't you think?"

He didn't actually harrumph, but the arrogant tossing of his head, with white hair and short, well-trimmed beard, the compression of his thin lips, it seemed as though he had. Ah, a pretender to elite realms, I thought, getting him into a proper frame of reference. In my usually irreverent mood, I began to imagine that a little propeller spun atop his beanie.

They were soon marching snootily off to catch up with Jack and the Grahams in order to familiarize themselves with the local amenities, as Ed stated the matter.

"Haven't seen a fashion plate like that in, well, I can't remember when," Lea remarked with a smirk.

We all grinned at each other.

*****

Later in the afternoon as Steve took me on a trolling run for Papio in the lagoon, Steph was invited to bring Puffer for a visit aboard Tempest. The dogs could amuse themselves while the ladies gossiped.

Steve and I caught several Papio. We saw several schools of Mullet, but Steve said they wouldn't bite on any type of lure or bait he'd ever tried. He thought they might be vegetarians living off algae.

"So, how do you catch them? They're okay to eat, right?"

"Yeah. You need a net or a spear. I used to bring one of those thrownets, you know, but I left it home. Besides, the Papio are better eating, bigger, more meat."

Steve had a small hoopnet for landing Papio aboard. As we were passing by a school of Mullet dawdling along near the surface, I suddenly swung the hoopnet into the water and bagged three of them. I kept one Papio and the Mullets for us while Steve took the rest aboard Poseidon.

I dressed them out ashore and brought them aboard for supper. Since we had more than enough, I mixed half the Papio in the dogfood for Popolo and Sista while Steph fed one of the Mullets to Puffer.

Both fish were good eating. The Mullet were small, only eight to twelve inches in length, while the Papio ran to about twenty pounds in edible size.

*****

July 4th was very windy and rainy. After a couple of hours spent collecting more freshwater, I left Steph alone with her book and went off to explore, taking along a hooded rain-repellant windbreaker. Popolo, Sista, and me would nose about on our own.

Our first stop was the fishing wall, the tidal pool where we'd seen so many marine creatures. I'd brought along some fishing line and lures. Having lost our silver-spoon lure on the trip down, I'd fashioned another from the haft of a fork, cutting it to size and drilling holes on the ends for line and hook.

I'd found several long bamboo poles and rigged one up as a dobbing pole with maybe twenty or twenty-five feet of line tied to the narrow end with a wire leader and my homemade lure. I stood upon the wall swinging the pole back and forth to skip the lure over the surface. Nary a bite one. Hm. Could it be the weather? Maybe sunlight was required to reflect glints of light off the lure. After half an hour or so I gave it up.

On to the northeastern most end of Cooper. Like Strawn on the western end, the causeway linking all the smaller islands in a perimeter around the central lagoons had washed away. Aviation Island was a bushy clump, appearing impenetrable, the foliage so thick it grew right down into the water.

Pacing southward aways, I could make out Quail Island, a smaller version of Aviation, and several more leading to a larger at Portsmouth Point, the easternmost of the islets. Then going southerly lay Eastern, Papala, and Holei, where the line of islets took a turn westward to Engineer Island, the terminal point for the other end of the causeway dividing the center lagoon from the east lagoon.

From Iola, we could see the westward march of islets south of us, Tananger, Marine, Kaula, Paradise, Home, and Sand Islands, all lying invitingly unexplored. Soon enough, I told myself, soon enough we would get around to all of them, learn all the secrets and hidden places of Palmyra.

*****

In the meantime, after a week at Palmyra, I was mulling over just what our voyage had brought us to, a new life, one unlike any we had experienced. It was a microcosmic society of more or less autonomous individuals, one without government or law. The only rules were those basic to human understanding, conducive to minimums of harmony when strangers come together. A certain amity was the norm, mutual courtesy and consideration, habits we had carried with us.

Given the small, mostly itinerant population, Palmyra provided plenty of room for everyone to do their own thing without intruding upon anyone else's style, however peculiar. Except for Jack's persnickety raving on only two occasions, I had heard no harsh words exchanged by anyone. Despite a few minor and imminently overlookable shortcomings, Palmyra was Samarang. Samarang was paradise.

Paradise was a place conducive to laziness. There was no pressing need to do much beyond performing natural functions or satisfying an undemanding desire -- unless you had the ambition of a secret mission like Steph and I. Still, a certain torpor had invaded us, too. Life was slow and clocks and calendars meant little. I had discarded my wristwatch and relied upon the variations in light and darkness, the position of the sun when it was visible, to tell me as much of time as I needed to know. I had few appointments, no really pressing engagements. If a thing didn't get done today, the vagueness of man'ana was good enough.

There were the lulling sounds of nature, the constant low roar of the surf upon the outer reefs, the susurrus of wind through the palm fronds, bird sounds and fish splashes, the lap of small waves against Iola's hull, the quick thud of a coconut falling from the heights, the swish and beat of rainfall, and broken only by human conversation, the sounds of our dogs, the pitter pat of a chore being performed, music from a radio, tapedeck, or turntable, maybe ol' Buck -- er, ah, Roy -- honking out a bluesy tune on his kazoo.

The constriction of clothes was a nuisance, although minimally tolerated in company.

Nature's beauty in all her changeable elements had a calming effect. There were no stresses or strains, rather merely small adventures, ambitions, and challenges.

No TV, newspapers, or magazines to assault one with the daily dose of bad news. No traffic, no pollution, no muggers, rapists, or thieves. No need for cops, politicians, or rabble-rousers. We had no urgent appointments to keep. We had it made in the shade. "Come live with me and be my love, and we will all the pleasures prove." (The Passionate Shepherd to His Love, Christopher Marlowe.)

*****

On the 5th, the day the Wheelers planned to leave but put off because it was too windy, Steve broke out the fireworks the weather had prevented the day before and we had some exclamations of sound and fiery colors tossed into the humdrumness.

I had helped Jack to tote and load his generator from the refrigerator house. He had helped me unload mine to tote over to replace his. We were now the official keepers of the only functioning full-size house refrigerator on the island.

I gave Jack my letter to the owners, which he read and approved, promising to deliver it personally. Steph baked a raisin nutloaf cake to wish them bon voyage. We passed over letters for Dickie, Steph's brother Bob, and her mother.

My last act ashore for the day was to string an old found coil of electrical wire from the generator, which I nailed up high to trees leading to the landing area just ashore from Iola. From there, I ferried it across to raise halfway up the mast, the dangling end coiled on deck. It would serve two purposes. One was a source of power for tools without having to tote the generator back and forth. The other was to implement a lazy man's fishing operation. All I needed to complete it was one of the metal-hooded light-fixtures I'd seen hanging in the barracks.

I had discovered while shining a flashlight overboard at night that schools of Mullet swam up through the circle of light cast upon the water. I had taken the opportunity to snag a few in our hoopnet. Aha! The flashbulb of an idea went off in my head.

A few days later, when I'd gotten around to retrieving the light fixture, wiring it into my line through the trees from the generator, loading in a bulb from my utility light cord, stringing the wire along the boom to hang the fixture on the end, I rushed off to start the generator.

Back aboard, a bright light illuminating our cockpit, I had swung the boom outboard a few feet so the circle of light shone into the water, and I waited with my hoopnet. Whoa! In no time at all I had a bucketful of Mullet, over a dozen. Plenty enough for then, I filleted them up and stored what Steph didn't cook up for supper in the refrigerator.

*****

Poseidon left early on the 6th and I immediately began to think about swinging Iola around to take the empty mooring space so that we would not have so much wind and rain blowing into our main hatchway. It was going to be a bitch to get out on a calm day, release Iola's stern and try towing it out by oarpower in the dink in order to avoid collision with the forward dolphin. The slight current running westward would carry her around.

Just as I was thinking we might wait for a better day, Mac and Muff came putt putting up in their Zodiac inflatable dinghy to say hello. Inviting them aboard, we sat in the cockpit sipping tea Steph had brewed. They both stuck their heads below for a gander inside.

"Cozy," Mac commented.

"Good for two, but any more and we have a hard time finding places to sit."

"You need a cockpit table for al fresco dining."

"One of these days."

When I mentioned the idea of swinging Iola around, Mac immediately offered his services. The Zodiac made it an easy five-minute chore.

Back in the cockpit, Mac offered me a cigarette. Ah, man, I thought, I could get to love this guy.

"You know, mainly we wanted to get our bow into the wind, but the swingaround really improves the view. Now we can see Sea Wind, that lovely sheerline, that fine bowsprit, those high-aspect masts -- beautiful."

He grinned, looked. We all did. "You've got a good eye, Roy. After all these years, I still enjoy looking at her. She's taken us around the world once already. It was love at first sight. I'll never own another boat."

"I can see why. But if I had her, she'd become a gaff-rigged schooner."

"Be less efficient."

"But prettier, more rakish. You could probably use the same masts -- just switch 'em."

"You'd have to move them forward to get the right balance."

"I'll help you. When do we start? I want my morning view perfect."

"You play chess by any chance?"

"Oops, changing the subject. There goes my job. Sure, we both do."

"You up for a few games?"

"Anytime. Little fresh competition'd be nice:'

"Why not take a stroll over this afternoon. We're going to visit the Pollocks and do a little exploring. Be back by noon or so."

"Sounds good. See you then."

I arrived alone in the damp and darkened afternoon, the skies turning the rains on and off, for my first looksee at the inside of Sea Wind and to begin the first of hundreds of games of chess.

Gazing about the oddly laid out interior, I was distracted by questions and answers about Sea Wind's history and construction. It was obvious that he'd taken some liberties in rebuilding the vessel. First the raised portion of coachroof immediately forward of the cockpit, which had led me to believe it was a pilothouse. But no, it served merely to allow headroom over a raised floor above the engine-room, which was now a large interior space -- lots of room to attend the main-drive diesel engine and a separate diesel-powered generator. In the aft most area above the engine room was a pilot berth to starboard, which made me think they were watch-on, watch-off sailors, going for the fast passages. But, since Sea Wind had an outboard rudder hung on the transom, she had a trim-tab and a wind-vane for self-steering, which meant she could cruise under a full suit of sails -- unlike Iola.

Down several steps to port was a large bathroom, just beyond which stood a well laid-out galley with small top-loading freezer and refrigerator. Opposite to starboard, near a small cubby door to the engine-room, sat a navigation station with a large chart table and all the electronics, including a ham radio, Loran receiver, and electrical switching stations.

Just forward of the U-shaped galley was the large fore-and-aft dinette table, easily seating four -- maybe six in a pinch -- across from a long comfortable settee. There were lockers, drawers, cubbyholes, and bookcases built in to every available space. The dinette table-top was inlaid with dozens of foreign coins under a layer of fiberglass resin. A wired-in stereo sound system was hooked into an eight-track tape-player. I saw their tastes ran to the old time crooner favorites like Frank Sinatra and Tony Bennett and serenade music from swing to romantic ballads.

Forward of the dinette area were heavy wood cabinets with drawers and hanging closets which fronted a nook with an unusual athwartships double bunk, to the foot of which was a small cubbydoor leading into the forecastle -- a workshop and storage space.

A nice layout, the whole planned out as a vessel to accommodate two people, the workmanship personal and fine. Below the flooring was a deep bilge area, a good three feet in depth, which held large fuel and water tanks to the sides as well as plenty more stowage space. His electrical power, now calculated to a necessarily minimal draw of amperage, was supplied by three 200-amp marine batteries and a high-output generator hooked up to a separate 5-horsepower Yanmar diesel. The main-drive diesel, a Starret, was about 50-horsepower, and was only used when they needed propeller power to get in and out of harbors or through windless days.

We exchanged stories about selecting Palmyra for extended sojourns, both of us expecting to arrive to find it uninhabited and have it to ourselves. Although the Grahams were straight as arrows, both upper middleclass backgrounds, according to my estimation, and thus we were coming from different places, different pasts, and different points of view and attitudes, it seemed obvious to me that we shared a similar basic motivation in seeking such isolation -- the fleeing in disgust from civilization and all its contradictory and confusing complications, seeking a simpler life with time and opportunity to look inward, discover and be oneself, the exercise of everyday freedoms without complaint or restraint. The fundamental difference in our positions lay in the fact that Mac's voyage to Palmyra was an end in itself, a retreat or extended vacation, while ours was a means to an end -- the growing of pakalolo as a way to fund continuation of the voyage around the world. But we were all escaping from a life that oppressed us.

"Well, hell, Mac, I guess there's enough space in paradise for two Adams and Eves."

"Sort of divide it up, hm?"

"Why not?"

"I'll take the western half," he grinned.

"Whoa now, wait a minute. That would give you most of the buildings, equipment, the bathtub and freshwater tank, and all the gasoline. As the new unofficial deputy mayor of Palmyra, I hereby decree those areas as open to shared access."

"Deal."

"Hey, I like the way you negotiate. Keep up the good work and I may appoint you assistant deputy mayor."

"What I've always dreamed of."

"I greet the visitors, show 'em around, lay down the law, you entertain them, send 'em on their way with happy memories."

"Let us pray there aren't too many."

"Amen. The Pollocks are all yours."

"I already know that. They've been coming by everyday."

"They're social climbers. It's the burden of those who wear their class on their sleeves."

"Sweetheart," he said to Muff. "Would you please remove all class insignia from all my shirts?"

"Class is innate, darling."

"What about us no-class hippies? How do we get some?"

"Hard work, genteel manners, conventional dress, and the assumption of a discrete but superior air, Roy."

"Two down and two to go."

She looked at me. I looked back. Mac grinned. I tried not to. "Go ahead, ask, Muff."
"What?"
"Which two."
"Okay. Which two?"

I've got the hard work and the superior but well-disguised attitude down pat. Dress and good manners still escape me, although I can sometimes fool people -- as well as surprise myself.

She returned my smile. She had a pretty smile. "Also, I sometimes pick my nose at the dinner table."

She made a face. "You definitely have a way to go yet."

When I got back to Iola, Popolo and Sista sat in their neck-chains with a chastened look and a terrible stench filled the air.

"Baby," Steph called, popping her head up and pointing. "Would you get rid of that, please?"

They had dug up a shark's head that Steve had buried near the shore for the flesh to rot away before removing the jawbone. There were about a dozen tea-cup sized seashells nearby, two of them on the shark's head -- the Hermit Crabs that pulled their heads and claws in at my approach. I picked it up and flung it out into deep water where it sank, then rinsed my hands in the water before going aboard.

###

CHAPTER 16

Life went on, my thoughts filled with ways to exploit our local resources to the maximum, everyday mundane considerations -- the food supply, fish, coconuts, palm heart, Tern eggs, crab, and a garden, a shore camp, getting set up to begin a pakalolo nursery, a precise plan for propagating our babies in secret, nurturing them to maturity -- all the ways and means.

Except for a few unavoidable occasions, I hardly saw the Pollocks, leaving Steph to deal with them as much as possible. When they weren't loafing aboard Tempest, usually below, they were off on hikes, the remainder of their time spent calling on the Grahams who, it seemed to me, were extraordinarily patient in the expression of their cordiality.

Me, after a few bizarre contacts with Ed and Marilyn, ducked whenever I saw them, detoured, and otherwise tried to remain invisible. Social leeches, morons, and pompous assholes with pretentious aspirations wore on me quickly.

Once I had rowed by Tempest while Marilyn was in the cockpit. I squinted at her and nodded. I had lost two pairs of prescription glasses on the trip down. My last remaining pair with dark lenses, I only wore ashore on bright days. Anxious to maintain them, I never wore them while out and about in our dink.

Without glasses, I had to squint in order to achieve any kind of long-distance focus for my myopic vision. Marilyn would later testify that she found my frowns ominous, as though I were glaring hostility her way.

Back at Iola, Steph came up to wave at her and asked me to deliver some coconut milk and butter to her. She must have felt some trepidation to see me rowing toward her with a vicious scowl and evil grin distorting my features. Before I could arrive, she'd gone below to fetch her brave protector.

Standing to hold the dink close, I offered up the chilled milk and butter. "Milk goes good on cereal, so sweet you don't need sugar," I said. "Butter's great on English Muffins and biscuits, not to mention adding a tantalizing new flavor to fried foods -- better than cow's butter."

"Oh," Marilyn responded in surprise. Gosh, wasn't this better than rape or murder? Well, better than murder, for sure.

Ed, of course, who could milk sarcasm from a dried dogturd, was in form with a half-concealed haughty sneer rolling down his long nose. "Is there any charge?"

"Nah. Compliments of His Excellency, the Grand Deputy Mayor of Territorial Palmyra."

Another unavoidable time, he said, "Oh, Roy, I tried to raise you on the VHF last night. Wife had some leftover rice pudding she thought you might like."

"Sorry I missed you, Ed, but I never got around to hooking our VHF up."

"Yes, I belatedly noticed you don't have an antenna for it."

"You find much use for it this far from traffic?"

"No, and they're often a nuisance in traffic, all the trite use most people put them to -- still, a necessary amenity, I find."

"Well, I've got no use for mine. Maybe you could use it as a backup."

"Oh, er, what are you asking?"

"No charge, Ed. You'd be doing me a favor. To me, it's just another piece of junk."

"Oh, no, I couldn't let you do that."

"Tell you what, I'll swap you for some sugar. Ol' lady says she's running out of sugar."

"What's it worth? Does it work?" Suspicion glittered in a wide eye that begged for a monocle.

"Sure it works. What it's worth, gee, I don't know -- a hundred bucks maybe?"

"And you're only asking for some sugar? It seems absurd. What's the catch?"

"If you're worried it's stolen, I assure you it's not. Ever heard of what they call Karmic Law, Ed? What comes around goes around? You lived in Hawaii long, Ed? You ever xperienced their often extra-ordinary generosity? Being on the receiving end tends to put you on the giving end. Buddhists see it as a cause and effect thing. Hell, nothing else, you can sell it back in Honolulu, help defray your vacation expenses."

An imperial frown possessing his features, he said, "Are you being facetious?" Well, after all, he was a schoolteacher -- he was supposed to know words like that.

"Faw-CEE-shus," I pronounced, unable to help going in my Stan Laurel act. "Well, gee, I dunno. Is that a compliment?"

Ah, now, the sneer. "Would you like to borrow my dictionary to look the word up?"

"Nah, that's all right, Ed. I know a euphemistical copraphagist when I see one."

"Wha...what?" he stuttered.

"It's in the dictionary," I grinned my shittiest get-back look of innocence, sitting down, pushing away, and taking up the oars. "E, u, and c, o. Have a nice day, Ed."

When I stepped out at the landing ashore, I tripped into the shallow water and broke out laughing, a great caterwaul of rib-shaking, eye-watering guffaws -- at his silliness, my silliness.

Lord Pollock, as I had dubbed him in my mind -- Marilyn achieving Ladyhood -- was stiff with outrage and quickly ducked below to escape the worst of all applause -- unless you're a comedian.

Steph came up from Iola, scratched her head and inquired. "You finally gone clear around the bend or what?"

As Janis Joplin sang, "Summertime, and the fishing is easy."

I usually caught more fish than we knew what to do with. We would often make gifts of filets to visitors. Mac was the only one to return the favor. Now and again he would drop by in his Zodiac to deliver an excess Papio or two or three after a bit of trolling in the lagoon. If we weren't home, we might return to find one hanging from the backstay. With my newfound method of catching all the Mullet we desired, our exchanges worked out well. Some days, particularly overcast days, I had little luck with my bamboo pole for Papio at the fishing wall, while Mullet were plentifully available for the taking. Mac had told me that Muff had expressed a preference for Mullet over Papio, while he enjoyed the coco-milk on cereal.

We made it a regular practice to feed excess fish to the mutts, sometimes mixed with dogfood, sometimes with coconut -- although we had to be judicious with the latter because of its constipating effects.

My third fishing method lay in the ability to sometimes utilize my sling-spear in snagging a Mullet or two when they swam by in the daylight -- until one day I let it get away from me and it disappeared into the drink, leaving me with a look of stupid amazement, which Steph laughed at.

"What the hell's so funny? That was my favorite spear, my only spear, the one I've had for years, the one that's fed us many a fish!"

"Sorry, baby. It's just the look on yer face when ya looked at yer hand, then at yer spear sinking out of sight. It's such a rare occasion when yer face reveals the basic substance of yer character."

"Hmp! Maybe you can do all the fishing while I lay around all day baking bread! See how you like beheading fish, gutting and carving them up!"

"What say we smoke a doobie instead?"

*****

I had noticed a curious fact about the Mullet on the oceanside at the fishing wall: They were much larger than the ones inside the lagoon, running as much as twice as long, nice plump fishies. How to bag them?

One day I took along the .22 pistol and the hoopnet. As a school made a pass close to the wall, I plugged one right between the eyes, reached down and scooped it up. Usually though, they swam further out. A spear flung into their midst -- one tied to a retrieval line -- would surely connect. I needed a new spear.

I made one, having found a curious stand of narrow trees that grew straight up for fifteen or twenty feet which, when peeled of bark, provided a wood almost as light as balsa, the inner grain very white. But it was stout and I affixed three sharpened welding rods to one end for a prong and a thirty-foot length of cord to the other end with a wrist loop.

I would simply hurl it out into a school of Mullet and get one almost every time. The trouble was, they would often slip off the rod-points unless I pulled it in slowly and carefully. Hm. I would have to flatten the points with a hammer and file in some barbs to perfect it. Well, in due time. I left the spear at the fishing wall with my bamboo pole.

One night I caught so many Mullet with my night shining lightbeam and hoopnet, spending hours cleaning and preparing them, that I decided to spend the next day preparing my own version of Lea's smoked fish.

Steph helped. We gathered coconut husks, which would smolder slowly rather than burn when set alight, and filled the fireplace under the heavy piece of screen the Wheelers had left. We set them to marinate in soy sauce enlivened with a bit of Tabasco, then salted them all down with garlic powder. All the day we worked at placing, turning, removing, and replacing the filet strips. We ate and fed the mutts this delicious delicacy, then filled a couple of empty plastic gallon jars with the rest. Great pupus and even went well broken into stir-fried rice for regular meals.

All the leftovers, the heads, guts, scales, fins, and bones, were dumped into a 50-gallon drum to rot and form chum swill. Like the commercial fish emulsion we'd used on our pakalolo plants, it would be rich in nitrogen and could be used in preparing the growing medium for our new venture, as well as help fertilize our vegetable garden. Don had sometimes buried small fish under his young pakalolo plants, which seemed to thrive. I had read somewhere that Indians had sometimes plowed fish offal into their cornfields.

For its ripe smell as it fermented away, I placed the chum barrel way to the other side of the runway with a piece of plywood on top and a chunk of coral to hold it down.

*****

Coconuts, whoa! What an interesting tree and fruit! There were so many things we could do with it, derive so many products. Palmyra was a former plantation gone wild and the fruitful trees dropped a plentiful supply for us to help ourselves to. The lowly coconut that most people know may be found in supermarkets as a dark brown, hard-shelled nut, having been husked of its outer couple of inches of fibrous coating -- which, I surmise, provides a cushion to keep them from breaking when they fall ninety feet from the tops of the mother trees. Consumers take it home to crack open for its half-inch layer of sweet meat coating the inner curve of shell, which is brown on the outside and creamy white on the inside -- sweet and crunchy. Also inside, filling the hollow area, is a watery fluid, often sweet and refreshing in the fresher nuts, but sometimes tasteless or sour in others.

The less mature nuts, when cracked open, provide a softer substance called spoonmeat because you can scoop it out with a spoon like pudding.

To make milk, cream, butter, and oil, you crack open a quantity of nuts, dig out the copra and shred it into a large bowl or pot, mixing in the watery juice. Then heat a bit and simply knead it with your hands, which serves to release the sugars and fats from the meat. Strain off the resulting liquid, which now has the appearance of cow's milk, into bottles and jars. It is richer and sweeter than the bovine version.

If you refrigerate it, in time the cream will rise to the top just as it does in un-homogenized raw milk. Apart from its use in place of whipped cream, it gives you pure coconut butter when separated, churned, and re-refrigerated -- which is not only more delicious than cow's butter on toast, muffins, pancakes and waffles, but adds a tantalizing flavor to other foods cooked in it. Or, you can boil it down into a pure oil to be used not only in cooking but also as a suntan and skin lotion -- a secret cosmeticians have long known, so frequently is it found in their body lotions and creams. If we were willing to work for it, which we were -- often enough devoting entire days to it -- there was no shortage of any of these products.

Every coconut is a potential seed for the growing of a new tree. If left alone in its natural state when it drops to the ground, it will soon sprout roots from one end and a green budding of leaf will shoot up. If you pull these out of the ground when the greenery is less than a foot high and crack it open, you'll find no liquid and little or no meat, but rather a football-shaped loaf inside that looks very much like white bread on the inside with a crust-brown patina on the outside. Eaten raw it's sweet and juicy. If you bake them whole, they're a bit reminiscent of yams, although Steph thought they were more like eggplant. Or you can slice or dice them up to sauté or mix into curry sauce or stews. If you drop this "bread" into a blender, add some milk or cream, perhaps a bit of vanilla, chocolate, brown sugar, or other flavoring, you come away with a milkshake you've never tasted the likes of. Then, of course, there's ice cream, popsicles, and candy to be made, whatever your little inventive chef inside can come up with.

Steph once or twice made macaroons.

Sectioning off the top three feet of a tree, peeling away the outer sheath, will leave you with a log of palm heart, sometimes known as palm cabbage. Raw, it has the almost crunchy texture, color, and consistency of nuts, albeit a bit on the bland side. Cubed, salted, and roasted, you can hardly tell the difference. It can also be chopped into salads in place of garbanzo beans, or fried and cooked into other recipes for an exotic change of pace.

Last but not least, there's palm toddy, which requires some work. You have to climb the tree to its clump of fronds at the top, find the youngest shoot -- which is a spiral of potential frond that will later unwind to form a new frond as the older lower ones wither, die, and fall away -- bend it at a right angle, secure it, make an incision, and hang a container to collect the dripping sap. After fermentation, you have an alcoholic drink with a decided tropical bite -- but the hangovers are atrocious.

The hardest part of working coconuts is husking away the tough fibrous outer layer. To facilitate this task, which usually fell to me because of the physical labor involved, I had come up with a length of angle-iron and managed to imbed it as a waist-high post into the coral. I sharpened the exposed end so I could bang the nut onto it with a twist and quickly peel away the husk.

Steph used coconut to begin a sourdough starter for baking her breads and one day, tasting some cream that had gone sour, discovered sour cream, a dab of which went great over a hot dish of food. We were limited in the use of all those products only by our willingness to work and our culinary creativity.

When we delivered fish to the Grahams and others, we usually included some form of our coconut products upon which we had so far established a monopoly -- no one else willing to take the trouble.

Steph, ever worried about running out of flour, often traded these products, as well as her services as a baker, to increase her supply.

*****

Back to seafood. One day when we'd rowed across the lagoon to explore Paradise Island and its adjacent islets, we'd come upon an amazing sight -- hundreds of large crabs, their shells a mixed coloring of pink, beige, and brown, their torsos six to eight inches across, each with a feeding claw and a huge work or battle claw similar to a fiddler crab. We opined as how they might be the plentiful Coconut Crab.

First we'd heard a strange concert of thousands of clicking sounds, which beckoned us into the bush to investigate. Then we came upon the tribe of them all celebrating in an eerie scurrying, claw-clicking dance. Round and round they went in curious sidewise lunges, working their castanets, ignoring us -- some kind of mating ritual?

We easily caught a couple dozen of them, me tying them all together in a string to carry back to Iola. Curiously, the major part of their meat was found to reside in the giant side of their claws. We feasted well on boiled crab that night.

*****

Well, okay, the story of my venture in Calamari, which is Italian for squid scampi, that is, squid sautéed in garlic butter. One day I came into a few dozen baby squid, which I chopped up and fried in coconut butter and garlic salt. Various preparations of squid were popular in Hawaii, and Steph and I had both acquired a taste for them. We'd often enough chewed on packages of dried and salted squid, a popular snack food, to go with beer.

My Calamari was delicious and I went to join Steph aboard Iola in order to share it. We sat across from each other at the dinette forking out the chewy bits.

"Oh, gawd, it smells and tastes great."

"The coconut butter enhances it. I used a bit of soy sauce, too." "Delicious, gawd, how'd you catch them?"

"Tell you when we're done. It's a long story."

Soon enough we'd polished it off, sitting back to savor it with a joint and some iced tea in lieu of a beer. It was time to tell the story of my squid acquisition, I, of course, trusting that Steph would not be squeamish when it came to good food.

Jack had told me that the Sooty Tern lived on an exclusive diet of seafood, each day the mama birds winging out over the sea in search of small sardine-like fish and baby squid, which upon espying below would dive down to swoop them up in beak and swallow them whole -- which is why their eggs tasted and smelled so fishy. The mamas, if their eggs were hatched, would fly back to the airstrip to regurgitate the fish or squid into the babies' ever-hungry cheeping mouths. These meals would fill the baby chicks stomachs, causing them to bloat out into little round balls of feathers. Like any overfed beast, they became lethargic and could hardly bestir themselves.

One day as I was making my way across the runway, treading carefully to avoid crushing eggs and chicks, a fat little featherball sat before the toe of my thonged foot and refused to run away like most of the others. I slapped my foot down beside it for the purpose of stimulating it to flee. The little featherball let out a cheep, bent forward and coughed up a baby squid before teeter-tipping away in panic.

I studied what it had coughed up. The squid looked fresh, as though not long from the sea, the digestive system of the baby Tern not yet having begun its work. I looked around and saw other roly-poly little near-comatose creatures, strode\over to slap my thong beside another. Up came another squid before it could run away. Fascinated, I went about repeating the process, the dear little birds generously supplying me with dozens of baby squid in grateful payment for not squishing them underfoot.

I fetched a couple of coconut shells to collect them all, then waded into the lagoon to rinse them in seawater. Rinsing them again in freshwater and inspecting them, I headed for a skillet and the stove. Whoa. We had an endless supply of squid. I could work different sections so as not to deprive any one group of too many meals. Thus, our quasi-parasitical relationship would insure the survival of the host without undue discomfort. I was, especially after enjoying the meal, feeling quite content with my discovery, my cleverness.

"Oh, yech!" Steph cried. "You stole the baby birds' food!"

"Nah, hey it won't hurt 'em to miss one meal. They got about a ninety-nine percent survival rate here."

"Oh, yech! We're eating food that's already been eaten!" "Eaten twice," I corrected. "First mama bird, then baby bird. Three times now -- that's good mileage."

"It's like eating barf! They regurgitate it!"

"Yeah, but it's fresh."

"Listen to you! Fresh barf!"

"I checked every single one. Look at it like this, the mama and baby birds' stomachs are only little grocery bags used to carry the squid to us. They're fresh, caught this afternoon."

"Oh, yech! How could you!"

"Hey, I mean, the Chinese or somebody over there in Asia, they use Loons to catch fish for them. Besides, you liked it before I told you about it."

"Yech! I think I'm gonna throw up!"

*****

Steph was squeamish about their eggs, too.

When I had figured out a way to determine whether they were fresh, we tried them, too. My method was simple. I would simply mark out a square ten feet on a side and remove all the eggs in it. If I found any eggs in the square the next day, I knew they were freshly laid. Gathered a half dozen to take aboard Iola.

Steph's nostrils curled upon breaking open the first of them over a frying pan. "Uck! It smells like fish!"

I sniffed. She was right, but so what? "Fish smell like fish, too, and you're cooking them all the time."

"Fish are supposed to smell like fish, but not eggs!"

Intellectually, I understood the logic of her bias. In reality, it seemed a bit spurious. As long as it wasn't rotten, if a fish smelled like an eggs, so what. If a fish tasted like an egg, so what? And vice versa. You like and eat fish and eggs, so what if there was a little confusion in your mental imagery? We often dipped fish in an egg batter, sucked it up and asked for more.

"Look! The yolks are orange!"

"Nice. I like that shade in lipstick and dresses on dark-skinned brunettes."

"Well, I'm not either and I wouldn't be caught dead in it!" She made me try it first. "How is it?"

"Not bad -- a little fishy."

"Uck! Where's the ketchup?"

I tried them scrambled. Nice color, like scrambled oranges. Then omelets with bacon-flavored soy-bits and heavy on the garlic. Still, I had to admit, the fishy smell and taste was throwing me off, too. I would have to meditate on it, try to resolve the two inapposite essences into a palatable whole. Dickie would send a message via Mac's ham radio, after receiving one of my letters, advising that many Europeans considered Seagull eggs a delicacy. But these were Terns and Seagulls and did not live exclusively on seafood -- they were scavengers who ate everything.

Steph would eat no more. "Eck, no, gawd! They're all yours!"

Me, I kept an open mind. I tried boiling them. Rinsing them in fresh water after peeling them seemed to help. I cut them in half, scooped out the yolks and mashed them up with mustard, spices, and Tabasco, for a deviled-egg treat -- not bad at all.

"We got any vinegar?"

"Sure. What for?"

"I'm gonna try pickled boiled Tern eggs."

"Yech! Please!"

Actually, they were pretty good. I kept a quart jar of them for myself. Wait'll we have fresh onions from our garden, I told myself. Wait'll we have other fresh vegetable for a tempura batter made from Tern eggs, deep-fry them Japanese style.

*****

Steph wanted a canopy over Iola similar to what the Grahams had. Fine, darlin', yes, of course.

I found some large pieces of old Army canvas in the half-burned-out warehouse, probably tenting material to house the thousands of troops. Cutting a large enough piece, I mounted it over Iola using lengths of bamboo for the ridge-poles. Over that, since it was rather dirty, I laid over a new piece of nylon-reinforced plastic with two funnel-hose connections so that a water-catchment was possible from the runoff. This saved us the necessity of hoisting the mainsail and provided a more or less automatic rain-catcher. Plus, it served as a rain umbrella and a nice shady nook on hot sunny days. As everything was a bit on the rough side in the garble of materials, it gave Iola an air of a jerry-made hippy hovel. What the hell, beauty was in the eye of the beholder -- especially when you added quickly conceived and constructed utility.

*****

Tents. Well, I had found a nice little nook some seventy-five or a hundred yards east of Iola, which sat under the edge of a huge bubble of foliage, giant shrub-like vegetation that was leafy on the outer sphere but more or less hollow on the inside, a characteristic that would hold true for smaller versions that grew everywhere. Inside the shaded hollow was a loose tangle of bare limbs and branches. I macheted and chainsawed a way to the lagoon shore to provide a landing for the dink. A path led in from the runway. Later, I would chop a back path leading directly to the refrigerator house.

Steph helped me to erect our cabin tent into this shaded nook, which would prove to be cool on hot days. Now, all we needed for a land camp were furnishings.

Two days later it collapsed in a storm. While re-erecting it, I broke two of the aluminum poles, which were replaced with the same type poles I'd made my spear from. Then I guyed it six ways into overhead branches -- no more collapsing tent.

I found a twin-sized bed in the upper floor of the barracks, obviously an officer's bed since it was inside a room rather than among the narrower cots in the dormitory. I laboriously toted the bed frame, slats, head and foot boards, mattress and innersprings, across Cooper to the lagoon shore to load and row all, often precariously balanced, to the Arab Quarter as I had dubbed it.

I found small tables, one for a kitchen, upon which went a two-burner camp stove, a few dishes and utensils, a pot and pan or two, and some cooking condiments like spices and oil. Another for books, clothes, and incidental use as a nightstand. I appropriated one of our elegant glass kerosene lamps. The third table served as a desk where I kept our chess set ready for a game with Steph or Mac. I had also scavenged two chairs, one on a swivel with armrests. Pillow, sheets, blanket, I was ready. Soon enough I would rig gutters from split bamboo for rain-catchment, another 50-gallon drum to supply water for washing up and providing for the mutts.

"Darlin', how'd you like to spend the night with a fierce Bedouin Pasha, one who's been riding a smelly old camel for months through the desert without female companionship, who's starved for love?"

"Is he freshly bathed? I mean, smelly old camels, yuck."

"Oh, yes, fresh from the oasis."

"Bedouin, huh? Is he blue-eyed?"

"Yes, but we can turn the lamp low so's you don't notice."

"I dunno. Arabs and Jews are enemies."

"Let us make peace. Salaam aleikum."

"Shalom. Hm. Just how do you spell piece anyway?"

*****

Ah, now, the two gardens, vegetable and pakalolo.

In our forays about Cooper, we had noticed a substance that resembled soil lying in dark patches under the hollow shrubs, which could be as thick, as half an inch and from three feet to thirty in diameter. We theorized that it was probably a mixture of dust particles borne on wind and rain, decaying vegetation, and bird guano. At any rate, we thought it could serve as an ingredient in our growing medium, both for the vegetable garden and pakalolo.

I had built Steph a wagon by removing the axle and wheels from our shredder and affixing them to a wooden box and adding a handle. The handle broke twice before I finally bolted it solidly on. While she would traipse about from bush to bush scooping up this "soil" with a small Army-surplus trenching shovel, and dumping it into a clearing near the refrigerator house, I began carting over the side-boards of cots from the barracks and scavenging whatever heavier lumber I could find. I was going to build a foot-high containment wall around the flat roof, a place where no rats or hermit crabs could possibly climb -- especially after I'd chainsawed the lone tree growing up against the building.

Below sat the shredder. I would gather fallen palm fronds, twigs, leaves, coconut husks, and whatever foliage I could find to run through it. Mixed with the "soil" and some freshwater-washed sand, it became our compost pile. Covering it with a piece of dark Army canvas during sunny days insured plenty of heat to get the microbes working. A judicious bucket or two of chum would help the process along.

Later, climbing to the roof on a ladder I'd made, Steph would fill a 5-gallon bucket while I hoisted it up on a rope to dump on top. It was hard work, but slowly the garden bed began to fill. Soon enough we would add the Osmocote 18-6-12 time-release fertilizer beads from the three hundred pounds we'd brought. And then the seeds -- onions, carrots, string beans, zucchini, cabbage and lettuce, you name it, maybe a corner mound for cantaloupes or watermelons.

The while all this was going on ashore, we began to germinate pakalolo seeds aboard Iola and in the tent, filling paper cups with our medium into which we would plant the sprouts.

A bit further east from the tent, I rowed to a dense thicket of grass and foliage, macheted an entrance, and cleared out a small space for our nursery table. Then I tied a bunch of branches and bits of palm frond together to form a camouflaged dink-landing entrance from the lagoon. It was such an uninteresting area that it was unlikely anyone would want to land a boat there.

The first sprouts set out in cups in our hidden nursery disappeared within a few days. Rats? Hermit Crabs? Ants? We weren't sure. We would try to let them grow larger in the tent and aboard Iola before transferring them to the nursery. In the meantime I planned the construction of a screened cage over the top to keep out all such pests.

One day I worked myself into a sweat carrying our dink and the oars up over the high causeway that ran from the eastern edge of Cooper south across to Engineer Island, which separated the East Lagoon from the western portion. I rowed to Aviation, the thickly overgrown islet with no apparent means of ingress. I macheted my way in, careful not to make my entranceway obvious, in order to make a preliminary survey. It was the least likely islet to be visited by exploring tourists. Yes, a busy few days with the chainsaw and I could make a clearing in the center. The island was about two hundred and fifty yards long and half that in width, plenty of room inside for hundreds of gro-bags. When the time came, we could move the dink to the northeastern shore of Cooper and carry the filled gro-bags four or five at a time on the wagon for transport over to Aviation. It was all a matter of time, determination, and hard work -- but we veterans of the Coolie Wagon, 20-foot pathway-hiding plank, soil-mixers and bag-fillers of long experience, we were used to that.

*****

We were making progress, slower than I would have liked, but nevertheless whittling away the chores in all the directions we worked at. It might take a bit longer to get more comfortably situated, but when we did, whoa, perhaps it would serve to nudge that great wheel of fortune in the sky to bestow upon us our well-deserved blessings.

*****

"So what, you wanna move in here with me?"
"Gee, I dunno. Shouldn't we stay aboard Iola in case something happens?"
"The tent's got headroom. I'm tired of knocking my brains out."
 "I like it -- it's cozy."
"You wanna stay aboard, huh?"
"Yeh. You wanna stay here?"
"Yeah."

"Well then."
"But only to sleep and hang out. I feel sexy, you're gonna have to make room for me."
"How about when I feel sexy?"
"I'll make room for you."
"Gee, I never thought we'd ever have separate bedrooms."
"Gee, I never thought we'd ever have a beachfront property and a yacht."
"Busted, on the run, and counting our blessings."
"Ain't life a bitch."
"A bastard."

*****

Lord and Lady Pollock, those miserable pretenders to the bone, were leaving and paradise was about to become paradise for the first time.

As their fine sloop passed us by, Steph yelled out, "Bon voyage!"

"Don't take any wooden nickels," I cried, joining Steph to wave goodbye, perhaps a bit more enthusiastically than the occasion required.

Mac and Muff were out in their Zodiac, puttering alongside to hand up their mail and say a few last words. No sooner had Tempest cleared the channel than Mac and Muff zoomed our way. It was a nice day and getting better. We invited them aboard for a cup of tea in the cockpit.

"Well," Mac sighed, wiping imaginary sweat off his brow in an exaggerated gesture. "There go the last vestiges of civilization."

Long live the Empire, I thought and grinned. "Yeah, now we can take off our neckties."

"Be nice now, you guys," Steph admonished, seeing we were about to get into a game of oneupmanship of smart remarks.

"That's the trouble, I have been," Mac retorted. "I may be getting hemorrhoids from the strain of having to be so nice all the time."

"No island's an idyll without suppositories," I quipped.

"They weren't bad people," Steph insisted, but then I'd never known her to speak ill of anyone. She had no room for enmity, but then none of us had any cause to really castigate the Pollocks, even if I was crass enough to snicker now and again.

"No, you're right," Mac said. "They're nice enough people, I guess. It's just that Ed has an amazing propensity for assuming all the appearances of a sanctimonious, boorish ass."

"Oh, Mac," Muff moued.

"But," Mac added. "He's a nice enough guy underneath."

"Even leeches are fond of their hosts," I observed, which got me a look from Steph.

"Yeah, right," I added. "Ed could be irritating with all that posturing, but I have to admit the old boy was good for a laugh or two."

"That beanie," Mac said.

"Oh, God, I didn't know whether he was an eight year old kid with that premature aging disease or a comic Jew in a stylish yarmulka!"

Muff tried to stifle a giggle by raising her cup, a class act all the way. "To the Pollocks. May they have a safe voyage home."

"Hear, hear," we all agreed, raising our cups.

"What say we all take a breather tonight, then you two come visiting tomorrow evening?"

"Sounds good," I replied. "Except for one thing. Today's Steph's birthday and I'm throwing a party for her in the Arab Quarter." I'd been planning something special for her, a sweetening up of my sweetheart. I was giving her the day off, intending shortly to shoo her away from Iola so I could bake her a cake and fix something for dinner. "You guys are invited. Coffee and cake sound okay?"

"We'll be there with bells on."

After they'd gone I turned to Steph. "Okay. Today's your day, darlin'. Take what you need, go to the tent, loll about like the lazy slut you are. Smoke a coupla doobies, read a book, play with yourself, whatever."

"Aw, baby," she cooed.

"I gotta get some stuff from the refrigerator for our dinner. I get back, you be ready to clear out, mutt and all."

"The whole day?"

"Round up what you need, book, clothes, towel and soap, whatever. Freshly bathed babes get better birthday presents. There's a Penthouse in my desk drawer."

"Ooh, okay. Gimme a minute. Maybe I'll take a Parest."

"Good." Parests were the largest dose of pharmaceutical methaqualone on the market at 400 milligrams, sometimes called Quaaludes or Sopors, depending upon the brand. She loved to fuck on them. "Hurry up. I'll be back in a coupla minutes."

I quickly made my way to the refrigerator house to grab up a package of foil-wrapped fish and a quart of coconut milk. Back at Iola, I set the stuff on deck, and yelled. Steph came up to hand a bag and Puffer down before getting in for the quick push to shore.

"Gee, great service."

"Indeed, mumselle. I need to keep the dink so I can hit the tub when I'm done work, to ferry my culinary masterpiece ashore. Be ready."

"When?"

"In the gloamin', darlin'."

"What's that?"

"Dusk, twilight."

"My man! What a vocabulary!"

"Indeed, thank you, m'dear. Until we meet again in the sweet cunnilingus."

"The what?"

"Never mind. I'll explain later."

When she was gone, I settled in to concentrate on the problem. Had I ever baked a cake in my entire life? No. I lit up a joint. Anything a woman could do, so could I -- except have a baby. Yuck. A cake couldn't be that hard.

Steph was a nut about baking bread -- and cakes. Bread and cakes were related. Deep shit you're getting into here, me bucko. She had cookbooks for recipes. Yeah, that's the ticket, and glory be, there's a whole section on cakes, every kind of cake you'd ever want. Okay. Ingredients needed versus ingredients on hand. Um-hm.

I was interrupted only once. Mac had gone out to retrieve our other anchor, line, flotation cushion and all. Muff sat smiling holding the Zodiac alongside Iola as Mac heaved up the Danforth. "That's quite an anchor," Mac said. "You make it yourself?" "Yeah, works better than the original. I made it heavier."

"Good job."

"Thanks. And a thousand times more for retrieving it. That's great, Mac, really great. I owe you."

"Aw, we needed an excuse to come over and ask what time the party is. You forgot to say."

"Oh, right. I don't know. Six? Seven? Around sundown." Since giving up on watches and clocks, my best judgment of time was with the position of the sun, whether it was light or dark.

"Okay. By the way, you look good in an apron."

I laughed, forgot I was wearing it. "Hah, yeah, I'm baking a cake."

"You need any help?"

"No, Muff, thanks. I think I got it whipped."

Two more joints and four hours after beginning, I had a nice double-layer cake with chocolate frosting. I'd had to lay on a little extra frosting to fill a slight depression in the middle, but it even had pink letters spelling out Hau'oli la Hanau, Kekepania, which was Hawaiian for Happy Birthday, Stephanie. No birthday candles. Oh, well, stick one of the big, fragrant votive candles on it.

Next, supper. Okay, nothing fancy. Fish patties, which I'd always loved when my mother made them. Strong on the garlic and onions. No fresh garlic or onions. Okay, garlic salt and dehydrated onions would do. Some cornmeal to bread them, miscellaneous spices. Canned water chestnuts with bits of cubed palm heart, the last of the canned mushrooms, for a salad -- bit of garlic salt, some soy sauce, and a dash or two of Tabasco for flavor. Voila!

I fetched Steph and went to bathe, me offering to wash her back. I sent her back to the tent, went aboard to trim my beard, put on a pair of long pants, shirt, doused on some Old Spice. I ferried covered pans ashore, plates, silverware, and cups -- cut a few slices of homemade bread. Down into the forward bilge to retrieve the great treasure of a bottle of Cabernet Sauvignon, my favorite wine from San Francisco days. I detoured to the refrigerator house to grab a dish of our homemade coconut butter.

The mutts were sniffing hungrily. I greeted Steph, she lolling in sarong and halter-top, her hair brushed out, all peaches and cream squeaky clean. "Don't move, darlin, I just gotta set all this stuff down." The cake on my desk table, fish on the stove for reheating, and everything else on the table next to the stove that served as my kitchen counter.

She saw the wine. "Gawd, where'd you get that?"

"Been saving it for a special occasion. Gotta feed the mutts." I got out the dog dishes, began filling them with Gravy Train. "Can I open it?"

"Yeah, yeah, go ahead," I said, carrying out the stuff for the dogs behind the tent where Popolo and Sista usually snoozed, and filled a bowl from the water drum.

Steph was rolling a couple of joints at my desk. "Figured a little toke'd go good with the wine, ya know."

"Yeah, good. You didn't peek at my creation, did you?"

"Who, me?"

"It's supposed to be a surprise."

"Believe me, baby, I'll be surprised. I have been surprised all day long. I could get in the habit."

"Well, the day ain't over yet."

"Sit down and relax a minute."

I did. Sat across from her, took the lit joint, toked, sipped a tiny delectable bit of wine into my mouth. "Ah, hoo, that's good."

"Yeh."

We sat for a bit. The light was fading. We could hear the hounds polishing off their supper.

"We'll need to light a lamp or two."

"No pro'lum."

I lit one. She was zonked, loose, mellow, and droopy-eyed, a little Mona Lisa smile on her face, slurring her words a bit. "We can't leave any of this stuff lying around when Mac and Muff come."

"No pro'lum. Relax, babe. Time to have fun."

"No, time to eat. You hungry?"

"Yeh, I could eat. Whatta we got?"

"Fish, what else, but an old family recipe."

"Yeh?"

"Yeah."

I heated the fish, set out the salad, served us up, pushing the chessboard aside so we could dine at the table.

"These are good, baby."

"Thanks. You have good taste."

I began to fool around with the chessboard, trying to figure out ploys to run on Mac -- and Steph, too, for that matter. She got up and began to neaten my bed.

"Darlin', you'd make a great chambermaid. You for hire?" "Only if you can afford me. I wouldn't work for just anybody, you know."

"What?"

"Ya lemme sit in yer face three times a day."

"Jeez, what union you belong to? I wanna join up!"

But before we could continue our intellectual discussion, we heard the growing sound of an outboard motor. The dogs began a hullabaloo. I leapt to stash the dope pouch in the drawer while Steph began fanning the air with the Penthouse. We both cleared away the used eating utensils. When we stepped out to greet them, Muff was shining a flashlight for Mac, who was nosing the Zodiac slowly in toward the opening in the foliage that marked the landing.

"Ahoy," he called.

"Mac, Muff. Welcome."

"Hah?"

"Kapu! Kapu!" Steph shushed at the noisy mutts.

"Welcome," I repeated. "Toss me your line."

"What?"

"Wait a minute." I turned to project the full range of my actor's voice, seeking a vibrating bass tone promising dire consequences if silence did not ensue. "KAPU! KAPU! NOHO, LOLO ILIOS! KAPU!"

Sista whined and turned away, disgruntled. Puffer leapt nimbly behind Steph. The good and faithful Popolo sat by my side grinning hugely, his tongue flapping in the night air.

"Toss me your line, Muff."

Her arm moved and the line came flying. Mac killed the engine, tilted it up out of the water as I pulled the Zodiac the remaining few feet, then offered my hand to Muff.

"Quite a bunch of greeters you have here," she grinned. "Hi, Stephanie."

"Hi, Muff. C'mon in."

I tied the line to a branch and turned to Mac, who clutched a bottle of hooch.

"Nice cozy little nook you got here."

"We were expecting you guys to walk over. You have trouble finding us?"

"With your dogs guiding us in? Besides, your whole tent glows in the dark."

Inside, Steph was filling our cups with wine, mostly for Mac and Muff since we'd drank most of our share.

"Great wine."

"My favorite. Had to overcome rather onerous temptation to keep it this long."

"I'm proud of you, baby."

Mac and I were soon fighting great battles over the chessboard, while Steph and Muff sat on the bed going over our record collection. They soon had music coming out of the battery-powered portable turntable. Mac and I smoked his cigarettes and he kept the rum flowing -- beat me twice in a row.

"You sneaky bastard," I accused. "Get me snockered so I can't think straight."

He grinned. "I only offer. You hold out your cup, it's on you." "Hm, well now, come to think of it, that a philosophical position I can't argue with."

Time for the cake. "Okay, babe. Turn around and close your eyes." I removed the lid, lit the candle. "Okay, you can look now."

I began singing, "Happy birthday to you." Mac and Muff joined in. "Oh, baby, it's a beautiful cake!"

"Make a wish and blow out the candle."

She did, closed her eyes on the wish, then blew it out. I handed her a knife. "Here, you serve. I'll make coffee."

We sat eating silently, until someone said, "Good cake."

"Very good."

"Delicious."

In that moment, I loved them all for their kindness -- even though I knew they were employing their forked tongues in extreme politeness. I definitely needed more experience baking cakes.

I belched. "Oops, excuse me."

"In Arab countries it's impolite not to belch," Mac said, then belched too.

"We're not in an Arab country," Muff said, rolling her eyes at Mac.

"Well, as Unofficial Deputy Mayor of Territorial Palmyra," I said, giving voice to the full title I had assumed. "I hereby decree that belching is polite...sometimes."

"When is it not?"

"In the presence of fine ladies with delicate sensibilities."

"Oh, well then. Oops, excuse me."

"I do, but I'm only one vote. Muff?"

"No. It's crass."

"Steph?"

"Us girls gotta stick together. You're as gross as my ol' man, Mac."

"Would you excuse me if I said I was sorry twice?"

"Well..."

"I'm sorry twice, ladies, if I offended you."

"Me, too, three times, what the heck. We'll get seriously contrite."

"Huh!"

When we'd said our goodnights and seen them off in the Zodiac, Steph and I stood holding hands, waving with our free ones. "Drive carefully," Steph called.

I took her in my arms, grabbing two handfuls of sumptuous ass, and kissed her.

"Um, baby. What a nice day it's been."

"It's not over yet."
"Yeh? Wanna smoke some hash?"
"Mm."

We smoked and kissed and smoked and kissed some more. She unwrapt and undid herself and lay upon the bed with a dreamy smile.

I turned the lamp low, began to undress. I forgot the soap-opera mush poems from a small volume of romantic verse ala Rod McKuen I'd been contemplating reciting and instead tried to remember verses from Song of Solomon.

"How beautiful are thy feet, O prince's daughter. The joints of thy thighs are like jewels. Thy navel is a round goblet which wanteth not liquor. Thy belly is like a heap of wheat set about with lilies. Thy two breasts are like two young roes that are twins. Thy neck is a tower of ivory, thine eyes like the deep lagoon, thy nose but a guide to thy honeyed lips. How fair and how pleasant art thou, 0 my love. Thy grace is like to a palm tree, and thy breasts a cluster of fruit. And I come now to the palm, take hold the boughs thereof; now also thy breasts, and the smell of thee like apples. Thy mouth is like wine that goeth down sweetly, causing the lips of those that are asleep to speak. O, my beloved, my desire is toward thee, to dwell in thy garden."

Well, what the hell, we opportunists amend as the occasion warrants. Putting on an album by Robert A. Flack, one of Steph's favorites, I began working the magic of my oily hands over the nakedness inviting me, which was all of her, and explained by demonstration what cunnilingus meant -- and more besides.

*****

As couples, we and the Grahams had come to Palmyra expecting to be alone. Learning of each other's plans, we'd come to the easy conclusion that there was plenty of room for us both. When we came together by chance or choice, it was no more than a pleasant form of reality testing. We went our own ways or came together as it suited us. Two and two made four, not a difficult social equation to accept. When we came together, we ate, drank, talked, played chess, and worked, willing to help each other out. When we went our own ways, our paths might cross by chance and we'd exchange casual greetings, waves, and smiles. It was our way, slow, easy, wide and long.

*****

One day as we went about our separate pursuits, Mac and Muff heading for the bathtub, Steph and I with the mutts on an exploratory expedition, we came together over an unfortunate but minor incident, a temporary misunderstanding of intentions.

Halfway to the bath, Muff remembered she'd forgotten the shampoo and returned to Sea Wind alone to fetch it. We had just emerged from a thicket of trees and bush into each others view -- some two or three hundred feet away. She, with towel, shampoo, and conditioner, was returning on her way to join Mac at the tub.

As we caught sight of each other, we exchanged waves and smiles. The mutts, upon espying her, began to waggle their tails and bark happily, galloping Over to greet her. Muff, in her hidden distrust and unease around dogs, mistook this playful rush of canine affection as an attack and panicked. She dropped what she was carrying and picked up a length of old pipe to defend herself.

Seeing all this, I ran toward her calling to the dogs. "Kapu! Kapu! Hele mai! Hele mai!" They broke off their yapping and trotted to meet me. "Noho! Noho!" I said, bading them all sit.

"Muff, Muff, I'm sorry. They only wanted to play. They wouldn't hurt you."

She was frozen into an attitude of fear, her hands whitely clenched to the length of pipe, her mouth open, gasping.

"Muff, it's okay, it's okay. They were only playing. They were happy to see you, that's all. It's okay." I reached out to grab the pipe, place a hand on her shoulder. "It's okay," She let go and I tossed it aside.

"Oh, God, I'm sorry! I just thought they were attacking me!"

"No, Muff, not in a million years. They're not vicious. They're happy-go-lucky mutts. They like to play and they love affection." "I'm sorry, I'm sorry. It just seemed..."

I put my arm around her shoulder. "It's okay, just yell 'Kapu!' It'll stop them every time. We trained them in Hawaiian. Look, just say hele mai, they'll come over to you."

"Oh, no, that's all right."

"Just the small one, Puffer," I urged, looking at Puffer and raising my voice to get her attention. "Puff."

She looked, waited.

"Now call hele mai. Go ahead."

"Hele mai, Puff."

Puffer rose to prance forward.

"Now say noho."

"Noho."

Puffer immediately squatted on her haunches.

I squatted down to squeeze the fur at her nape. "See? She wants you to pet her. C'mon, it's okay."

Muff bent over to pet her head. "It's not Puff. I know she won't bite me. It's the other two I worry about. The brindle looks so ferocious sometimes."

"Sista? She's a pussycat. She's scared of her own shadow."

I was on the verge of calling Sista over when I saw Mac meandering lazily toward us. "There's Mac wondering what's happened to you,"

I said, turning to pick up the stuff she'd dropped and hand them to her. Steph was nearing, too. "Hi, Mac, hi, Muff," she called. Mac waved, grinned. "Roy, hi, what's up?"

"Hey, Mac. Just teaching Muff a few Hawaiian words for the dogs," I said, then turned to Muff. "They ever annoy you or they're getting into things they shouldn't, just yell 'Kapu!' It works every time. It's easy. Kapu."

"Kapu?"

"You got it. Later on I'll teach you a few more. They're good dogs."

"Okay, I'm sorry."

"It's okay."

Mac looked puzzled. Steph had arrived. "Gawd, that's what I need. It's so hot and sticky." Mac turned his grin on her.

"We won't be long."

"Nah, take yer time. We're heading for the fridge for a cold drink, cool off a little. Gawd, I'm dying of thirst."

We waved, nodded, continued our separate ways. Looking back, I could see Mac had his arm around Muff's shoulders, listening as she doubtlessly explained to him.

*****

A few days later, when I'd forgotten the incident, I met Mac near the refrigerator house. Sista raised her head for a brief keen, which caused Popolo to come alert. They both roused themselves to pad toward him, tails aswitch, tongues awag. I noticed they hadn't barked -- they were getting used to him. He stopped to run his hands over their heads and necks, then continued along.

"Hey, Roy."

"Mac, how you doing?"

"You let your dogs roam about at night?"

"I quit chaining them up since the Wheelers and Pollocks left, if that's what you mean. They don't roam about day or night. They stick close to us, go where we go. If we don't want them to come -- like when we row to the islets across the way -- I chain Popolo and Sista up."

He looked at me, waiting, considering.

I hastened to explain. "I don't chain them up to prevent them roaming about. They stick pretty close to home. It's to keep them from jumping into the water and swimming after us -- especially Popolo." I grinned. "I don't want him becoming a meal for the sharks."

"I didn't think they'd bite anyone, they always seem so friendly to me."

"Oh, yeah, ain't got a bit of meanness in 'em."

"But I heard one of them bit the Wheeler boy."

"Yeah, he stepped on Popolo's tail when he was taking a snooze -- natural reaction, one of those things."

Mac nodded. "Ah."

"They aren't all that smart, but they're good-hearted."

"Glad to hear it. My wife's a little uncomfortable with dogs."

"Yeah, I've noticed."

"If some dogs ever attacked her, bit her or anything, I'd probably feel compelled to shoot them."

"I understand, no problem. I'd probably do the same for Steph.

But let me tell you something, Mac, if any of our dogs ever attacked you or Muff without provocation, I'd probably shoot them myself." He looked, waited, considering.

"And," I added. "I don't foresee ever having to do that. I know my dogs."

He nodded. "Good enough."

*****

Not long after, when I went for a game of chess with Mac, Popolo and Sista tagging along, we encountered Muff just inside the far end of the equipment shed with a paintbrush in hand. They'd appropriated that end to store some sails, lines, and tools, Mac making a small screened room to the side into his workshop. Sista trotted over to sniff at an open can of paint.

"Kapu," she said, and Sista turned away.

We exchanged grins. "See? You got it."

"Yes, it seems to work."

"Mac in?"

"Yes, go on aboard."

"You gonna be all right I leave my mutts to lay about while I teach your husband how to play chess?"

"Oh, yes."

"Try hina moe."

"What?"

"Try saying hina moe. It means lie down."

"Oh. Hina..." "Moe. Two syllables."

"Hina moe?"

"You got it. Now, try it on them. Use their names."

"Sista, Popolo," she tried tentatively.

"No, no, louder. Put some authority in your voice, like when you remind your ol' man to put the toilet seat down."

She smiled, tried again. "Sista, Popolo! Hina moe!"

They laid down and looked at her.

"Okay." I stepped down into their dink to pull myself across to Sea Wind. Mack came up.

"Thought I heard voices. Roy, what, you ready for another lesson?"

*****

On July 22nd, hardly a week since Tempest had departed, the small ketch, Shearwater, arrived from Tonga heading for Hawaii on the way home to Oregon.

They had first moored themselves in shallow water alongside the old rickety wooden pier west of the bathtub. I strolled down to introduce myself.

"Hi, fellas. I'm Roy Allen, the Unofficial Deputy Major of Palmyra. Welcome to paradise, humble as it is."

They introduced themselves as Don Stevens and Bill Larson. "Unofficial Deputy Mayor?"

"Yes," I grinned. "The Unofficial Mayor's away, but he left me in charge -- sort of caretakers representing the owner."

"Ah," they said, not quite getting it. I would have to explain, but later.

"Shallow water there," I pointed out.

"We've got a couple of feet under the keel according to our depth-sounder."

"Yeah, with the tide in. You might be scraping bottom when it goes out. Besides, this pier, well, I'm surprised I haven't fallen through it. There's a better place near us a half mile or so further east if you'd like me to show you. May I come aboard?"

"Sure. We appreciate you taking the time."

Under motor power, I directed them toward the dolphins, where I had them let me off at Iola so I could get out in the dink to help them with their mooring lines, waving them into the space vacated by Tempest. After a quick tour to apprise them of the amenities, particularly the bathtub, I led them back to do their whatevers.

"That other boat," Don nodded across the small bay. "How many people you have here?"

"That's Sea Wind with the Grahams aboard. You'll meet them later -- a very congenial couple."

*****

The next day it rained and I joined Steph aboard Iola for company, to read, and to start some pakalolo seeds germinating. She put up a batch of sourdough starter. We'd watched Don and Bill row ashore and disappear. I'd told them about our refrigerator, to feel free to use it. I'd noticed before coming aboard that they'd stored a quart of Fijian beer and some soda pops in it.

When the sun peeked out, Mac and Muff puttered up in their Zodiac, he with a bandage around his lower leg. They sat in the cockpit awhile to regale us of his misadventure. They'd been exploring and Mac had whacked a gash on his leg while clearing a path with a machete. At first he'd tried to sew it up with a needle and suture from a surgical kit, but had finally settled for butterfly pieces of tape and a bandage.

Steph told them the story about my hook in the thumb on the way down as a warm-up to the tooth-pulling story.

I'd had a bicuspid ailing me, which was a bit loose. There was nothing for it but to wait it out while patiently working it around with my tongue. Some days later it popped right out in my finger and thumb, a fine opportunity for a practical joker.

Sticking the tooth back in its socket, I went aboard Iola complaining about the pain.

"Gee, baby, I don't know if we have any more awa root," a Hawaiian home-remedy, a bit of local root that eased toothache when laid in between cheek and gum. "Let me look."

"Nah, to hell with that. I'm gonna pull that sucker out. Where's my needle-nose pliers?"

I began digging through my toolbox, hefting and working them in my hand, opening my mouth and positioning them.

"Are you crazy?" Steph's eyes were wide in horror. "Don't do that!"

I mumbled something unintelligible, busy fitting the tips for a firm grip on the bicuspid, then began faking a furious struggle to pull it out.

As poor Steph watched me wide-eyed, hands to cheeks, I gargled an awful noise ending in a loud theatrical "Yargh!" as I yanked the pliers from my mouth, the tooth firmly in evidence.

I thought Steph was going to faint. I laughed and explained it was all a joke.

"Oh, you asshole! If your brain was a bomb, the explosion wouldn't be enough to part your hair!"

"Oh, Roy," Muff said, making a face but laughing. "That was awful!"

"Remind me not to call on him for medical assistance," Mac said, laughing too.

"Don't know why not. I'd have sewn that gash right up. I used to watch these guys sewing up their hunting dogs when they got too close to a mad boar."

"The new people, they in?"

"Yeah, see their dink's back. Don and Bill -- seem like decent guys."

"Thought we'd drop by, introduce ourselves."

"Sure, probably got good travel stories -- coming from Tonga."

"Also, I wanted to give you an address," he said, reaching in a pocket to hand over a piece of paper. "Curt Shoemaker. He's the guy I talk to on the Big Island every week. You might want to let your friends know. They can write to him and he'll read the messages over the radio to me. Works in reverse, too, if you want to send messages to anybody."

"Hey, Mac, thanks. Really appreciate that. Be nice to be in touch with the people who are coming down to resupply us in September. You think of anything you want, let me know, we can send them the message."

"Hm. Maybe by then there might be a few things we'll want. Thanks, Roy, we'll let you know."

*****

Later in the evening after supper, we hailed Shearwater and rowed over for a visit. They treated us to rum, soda, and peanuts. Don told us about a Tongan girl he'd had a romance with, Bill kidding him along. They had an exquisitely carved mask they'd brought with them. Don showed us his logbook, which was full of scribbled pages and illustrated by photos pasted in.

Along the way I'd noticed a few cigarette butts in an ashtray. "You guys smoke?"

"No, Mac left those. He's a regular chimney."

"Yeah."

"Really nice people."

"They are that," I agreed, my mind on a long butt. I picked it out. "Hope you don't mind," I said, sticking it in my mouth and patting my pockets for a match. "Ran out of cigarettes on the way down. On purpose, trying to quit. So far I've only managed to drastically reduce the habit."

"Oh, hey," Don said. "We've got a couple of packs of some cigarettes called South Seas.

Here, let me give them to you."

Whoa, I could get to love these guys. "You fellas like fish, coconut butter, milk? We've got butter and milk, the fish you'll have as soon as the sun shines."

"Oh, yeah, that would be great. We saw the bottles of milk. Wondered if you had a cow here."

"Help yourselves. The butter's white, but better than the regular stuff."

Promising to trade books and magazines the next day, we returned to Iola.

*****

Next day was cloudy and no luck with Papio at the fishing wall. That evening we were back aboard Shearwater with reading material to swap. Steph offered her baking services and they gave her some flour sugar, and pudding mixes.

Somewhere along the way, talking about our coconut enterprise, Steph mentioned having broken my Buckknife. Don broke out a fish knife to give me. To top it off, Bill came up with two packages of pipe tobacco for me. This was too much. These guys were too nice.

Back aboard Steph said, "Gee, if everybody who came through here were as sweet as Don and Bill, wouldn't it be great?"

"I was thinking the same thing. We gotta figure out something really nice to do for them."

"Yeh, but what?"

"How about we throw a party for them? Dinner, music, the whole nine yards. We can invite Mac and Muff, too."

"What'll we feed everybody?" She was always worrying about our food supplies.

"Fish. Don't worry. Tomorrow the sun's gonna shine, and I'm gonna catch a bunch of Papio. You bake up some goodies, we'll break out a couple cans of something."

"Okay."

"Hey, Don, Bill," I called, walking forward to the bow. When their heads had popped up, I yelled. "Tomorrow night we're throwing a dinner party. At our tent. About sundown. You're invited."

"Hey, great. How about potluck? What can we bring?" I waved them away.

"No, really."

"Whatever."

In the morning, I called Sista and Popolo and prepared to go fishing with a couple of joints in my pocket. "You see Mac and Muff, be sure to let 'em know."

"Yeh, okay."

While Steph was busy over her oven, Mac came by and took her for a spin to Sea Wind and a game of chess or two. I returned with four fat Papio to mouthwatering aromas issuing forth from Iola. She had a loaf of cinnamon bread for Bill and Don, and an apricot nut loaf for the dinner. We had to sample the latter. Um-mh! While she worked on a coconut pudding pie, I prepared Papio baked in a coconut sprout gravy. We expended the last of our potatoes and some canned carrots for vegetables. Coco-butter for the sourdough bread, coco-milk to wash down the pastries.

We removed everything to the Arab Quarter. While Steph set up, I fed the mutts on Papio and Kal-Kan. Mac and Muff brought ground coffee and rum, while Bill showed up with a small can of boneless ham. He also informed us that Don was indisposed with a severe earache.

"Oh, no," Steph cried. "We'll have to save out enough to make up a dinner for you to take back."

We ate and ate, laughed and joked, conversed in friendly terms just like civilized people, and ate some more. We played records on our turntable. We drank rum, played chess, and ate. Mac and I stepped out to have a smoke. When he offered me a Camel, I politely refused and offered him a South Seas.

"Where the hell'd you get these?"

"The good lord provides," I replied, then pressed the other pack on him. "Your half as Assistant to the Unofficial Deputy Mayor."

"I'll be damned. They're pretty good. Thanks."

"Got an extra pouch of pipe tobacco I'll give you tomorrow." "Is this living or what?"

"This is living."

*****

Life proceeded apace. We worked at gathering and making ingredients to add to our compost pile, sprouted pakalolo seeds, me catching Papio and Mullet, Steph baking, both working on our coco-products, playing chess, Mac and Muff doing a good job keeping Don and Bill entertained, they visiting back and forth, even taking them and Steph on a daylong expedition to Barren and Eastern Islands -- she collecting some very old bottles -- reading, writing letters for Shearwater to carry away, laying up with Steph aboard Iola and eating popcorn.

After nine days, Shearwater left on August 1st.

*****

The generator went on the blinkus and I fooled and fiddled to get it going again. I only ran it about four hours a day -- the length of time it would run on one tank of gas -- which served the purpose from day to day most times. Unless we and others were in and out too often.

I hauled the old Merc ashore to store in the refrigerator house along with some fertilizers and tools, the wagon, bucket, rope, and ladder, the shredder. I sat down to do the tedious task of sharpening all the cutting bits on the chainsaw.

*****

Steph's log entry of August 4th: Processed rest of coconut and churned butter -- lunched on Ulua (Papio) fried in coconut butter and English Muffins. Roy fiberglassed part of doghouse roof in effort to stop leak. Chopped some palm heart for salad and to cook into fish gravy for dinner. After dinner took up Roy's challenge of best two-out-of-three chess match for body-rub and blowjob -- which, much to his chagrin, I won! Finest rub of the year and an excellent blowjob and a fuck thrown in.

*****

A week later, on August 11th, she wrote" Did five loads of dirt and one load of mulch while Roy went to northshore fishing -- caught two Papio, one Mullet. Cleaned fish and he took Mullet and coconut milk over to Mac and Muff. I rowed down to bathe. Then we went and got gasoline. When we filled generator, she froze up; couldn't get her to start. Emptied fridge. Had a huge salad and Papio for us and dogs for dinner. Then we went to tent -- he re-challenged me to chess, same stakes. I lost pitifully but had to take a raincheck on paying the backrub part as I cut my finger while preparing dinner. "Well, did you cut your mouth, too?" he asked -- and an enjoyable evening was shared.

*****

A baby shark and Popolo reminded me of my incipient plan to add shark to the menu.

Palmyra was apparently a breeding area for the brown-tipped shark. They were everywhere, from juveniles eighteen inches long on up to six-foot adults. Sometimes when we waded in knee-deep water along the southern shore of Cooper, these baby sharks would swim toward our ankles as if they were intent upon taking a bite. It was easy enough to evade them -- by leaping away until we were out of the water. They provided a bit of a thrill.

Splashing through the shallows along a sandy coral shelf at the southwestern shore of Cooper, Popolo and Sista leaping about enjoying the water, a two-foot long shark made a beeline for my ankles and I began leaping backward to get my feet on dry land. Popolo became alert, watching the shark as it turned toward him. As it neared, Popolo suddenly darted his head into the water and snatched it up in his jaws. Trotting ashore, Sista following, he carried it to drop, paw, and sniff. The shark twisted, its tennisball-sized mouth working. Popolo bit into its middle and shook it. Sista joined in, chomping near its tail. They sniffed, licked, pawed and bit, then settled down to eat their catch. Amazing. Dog catches shark, dines on same.

On the oceanside at the fishing wall I'd only seen adult sharks, never juveniles. I retrieved my spear to stalk the lagoon-side shallows. There came a two-footer, shwick went my spear, pinning him to the coral. With one hand I reached down to grab the narrow part of it near the tail and lifted it out to fling ashore.

Carrying it back to the Arab Quarter, I beheaded and dressed it out, ready to prepare it. The problem with sharkmeat was the strong presence of urea, which is a component of urine. It is the end product of protein decomposition -- protein being about all sharks eat. I had read of two methods to counter the effects of urea in order to make it more palatable to human tastes. For dogs, there was apparently no problem. One was to soak the flesh in citrus juice; the other in saltwater. I tried a combination of both. We had no grapefruits, oranges, lemons, or limes, but we did have a couple of those green plastic replicas of limes that contained a concentrate. Taking up a pan of seawater and giving a couple of good squeezes on the plastic replica, I set the filets of sharkmeat to marinate. Four hours later, I picked them out, blotted them dry, then dipped them in soy sauce and peppered flour. Fried in coco-butter, um-mn. I ate two pieces, fed two more to Popolo and Sista. It was late by then, but I went to offer Steph a portion.

"Babe, hey, you there?"

"Unh, I'm in bed. Almost asleep. What?"

"Never mind. Don't get up. It'll wait until tomorrow."

But it didn't. The dogs and I ate the rest. What the hell, I could always catch a shark -- perhaps a big one next time, maybe preserve it by smoking.

And I was worried about dogfood? Between fish, coconut, and shark, I had an endless supply.

*****

Boys will be boys.

I had come for chess, but Mac was a greasy mess from working on his Yanmar, the smaller diesel that ran his generator for keeping his batteries charged and for supplying the proper volts-amps for his power tools. I squatted to watch, to hand him tools, and to see what I could learn about diesels. It was dirty work. As I was leaning down into a narrow space trying for a better look where he was pointing, the while discoursing on the principles of their operation, Mac quite deliberately and with malice aforethought poured motor oil on my head.

"Hey!" I yelped. It was down my neck, my cheeks, and dripping off my nose. Mac was reared back on his knees laughing.

"Couldn't help it," he choked. "Devil made me do it!"

"Oh, Mac," Muff scolded, shaking her head with a look caught between a frown and a giggle.

"This the famous dandruff cure I've heard so much about, Ollie?" With what I thought was great equanimity and self-control, I went into my version of a Stan Laurel persona, deviously the while scooping out a gob of greenish grease from an open can -- which I promptly smacked down on the top of his head and smeared over his face. Some got into his mouth and he began spitting.

"Yargh!"

"I see you're still using that greasy kid stuff."

He leapt after me, but I was ahead of him up the companionway ladder. I ran to the bow with Mac hot on my trail. I grabbed a spray can of dull red paint sitting on top of a deck-locker, turned and squirted him on his bare chest.

He grabbed one, too, and squirted a stripe down my backside as I tried to dodge. We squared off like two duelists, circling warily, yelling and laughing like kids, getting in a squirt here and there.

Muff came up scolding. "Oh, you're making a mess! You're a mess!"

Mac zapped her between her boobies. She shrieked and turned away. I zipped her on the bare midriff. Mac zapped her rearend. She stumbled against me and we grabbed at each other for balance. Suddenly, fleetingly, I was very aware of the firm and ample curves of her body.

"Now no more, Mac! That's enough!"

"Okay, no more," Mac promised, sitting down the can but maintaining his grin.

"Yeah, truce," I confirmed.

"You okay, sweetheart," Mac solicited, taking her in his arms, smearing her with grease and paint.

"Oh, ech, get away!"

We got it together to go ashore with Boraxo, grease-cutting salve, and rags dipped in thinner to get cleaned up, walking down to wade out on the seaplane ramp waist-deep to finish up the job with soap.

Returning to Sea Wind to clean up our mess there, I couldn't help but notice how Muff's shorts clung wetly to her body. She was rather nicely put together.

I had never really been aware of Muff as an individual, a woman. She had only seemed like an appendage to Mac's persona, shy, unassertive, and quiet.

The very next day as Steph and I were returning from a bath, me strolling along in cutoffs, she strutting naked as a jaybird, we met Mac coming toward us, his eyes wide, grinning. Steph dropped everything, frantically trying to cover herself. I held up a towel as a screen so she could slip something on.

"Your modesty is very becoming," he said to Stephanie with a twinkle in his eye.

Tit for tat, I thought, one lewd gander for another.

###

CHAPTER 17

The sloop, Toloa, smaller than Iola, entered the lagoon on August 13th, with Dr. Norman Sanders and Tom Wolfe aboard, voyaging from Santa Barbara, California, to Australia.

After helping them get moored in the space Shearwater had vacated, I introduced myself in my usual tongue-in-cheek fashion and offered them the brief standard tour. Pointing out Sea Wind and mentioning the Grahams, I showed them the bathtub with a warning against drinking the water, mentioned the store of gasoline further westward, and led them to the refrigerator house talking about fishing -- a subject they seemed interested in. We made a date for an expedition to the fishing wall for the next day. When Tom asked what equipment he should bring, I told him none, that all would be provided.

"Feel free to use the fridge you got anything you want to chill."

A few hours later, Tom, fresh from a bath, came to store some stuff in the refrigerator. Popolo and Sista leapt up to yap out a loud warning of his approach. I kapued them and waved a hesitant Tom forward.

"I hope they don't bite."

"Nah, make a little noise is all."

"Thought we'd take you up on your offer for the use of the fridge."

"Sure. I'll get the generator running for a few hours."

"Where's this fishing place you mentioned? Wouldn't mind some fish and chips for supper."

"'Bout a mile down the way."

"I'm ready now if you are."

"Sure, come on this way," I said, beckoning him to follow along to the Arab Quarter. "Want to pick up one piece of fishing equipment. You might find it interesting.'"

"Sista, Popolo," I called. "Hele mai. Kuleana," which brought them prancing.

"What's that language you used?"

"Hawaiian. Lived on the Big Island in Hawaii for awhile. Brought 'em up using Hawaiian words."

"Oh."

"Enchantment Motel," I said as we approached the tent. "You care for coffee or tea before we go?"

"Maybe later."

"Just want to collect my peashooter," I said, taking up the western-style revolver and sticking it in my back pocket. While I dug out a dozen or so cartridges from the half-empty box,

I thought to ask, "You guys have firearms aboard?"

"No, why?"

"Oh, I'm running a little short of ammo. Thought we might use yours to shoot fish, maybe even a shark."

"You catch fish by shooting them?"

"Sure, but not out of necessity. Think of it as a sporting proposition, a novelty -- although I once read where Hemingway used to hunt sharks in Cuba with a Thompson submachine gun."

"Oh, yeah?"

"Yeah. Imagine going fishing with a Tommygun."

Heading out for the runway, I said, "Want you to walk light, Tom. We try not to step on the eggs or baby chicks here."

"Sure are a lot of them. They stay here all year long?"

"I don't know. Haven't been here that long yet. Probably not. I'd guess it's a seasonal thing."

"Do you know if the eggs are edible?"

"Yeah," I replied from the vantage of experience. "But you'll find they're an acquired taste."

Tripping through the bit of tangly undergrowth below a shady and damp coconut grove, we came out at the brief stretch of white sand beach adjacent to the built up bank with the concrete retaining wall. The water was crystal clear, the sun bright. Papio abounded, darting about. Streams of Mullet meandered along the surface.

"Okay, let's try the Papio first," I said, taking up the long bamboo pole, releasing my homemade lure and beginning to skip it back and forth over the water. "The trick is to keep the lure moving. Papio won't strike at anything stationary."

In a few minutes I got a good strike, the bamboo bending. I heaved back to send the Papio flying ashore behind me. Unhooking him, I handed over the pole to Tom. "You try it."

Ten minutes or so passed with me kibitzing, trying to give him pointers. I could see him getting frustrated, possessing none of the patience necessary to fishermen. When a Papio would dart toward the lure, Tom would stop his swing of the pole, leaving the lure to sink, thinking he was giving the fish an opportunity -- but when the lure stopped scudding over the top, the Papio lost interest.

But finally he got a bite and hastily heaved back on the pole to imitate my feat. Halfway out of the water, the fish slipped the hook and splashed back into the water. Tom knew nothing about the feel of setting a hook firmly.

"Here, Tom, try your hand with the spear," I suggested, explaining about the wrist-loop for retrieval, how to coil the line in your free hand. "Now, remember, you have to compensate for refraction of light off the water. In other words, aim a little low."

He had no luck after a dozen tosses at Papio, but neither had I had much success with them. I pointed out the Mullet, explaining. "Just heave it into their midst." He did -- and got one, but lost it on the retrieval.

"Try again, Tom. You've got to pull it in slow and carefully." I hadn't got around to flattening the ends of the welding-rod prongs and filing barbs into them.

He got another, but again it slipped away.

"Okay, then. Now we try the Wild Bill Hickock act. I shoot the fish, you spear it. I'll get one in close so's all you have to do is reach out and poke him."

Tom took his one-armed throwing stance.

"No, no, hold it in both hands. You're not going to throw it this time. Just pretend you've got a big fork."

I waited motionless until a school was making a pass about six feet out from the wall, took aim at the biggest, about sixteen inches long, and bam!, I plugged it in the head to leave him wallowing and wagging in place as his companions fled.

"Okay! Get 'im, Tom!"

He forked the Mullet, got it on the prongs.

"Easy now! Slow, Tom!"

But it slipped off. Tom lunged again, got it, and lost it, lunged once more, got it and lost it -- until it waggled down out of range, a nice tidbit for any passing shark.

"You can't jerk the spear, Tom. You gotta go down fast, pull back slow."

Tom's frustration was growing.

"Here," I said, handing him the gun. "You shoot and I'll work the spear."

He emptied the gun firing down into the water and didn't hit a one. Boy couldn't use a fish pole, a spear, or shoot worth a shit. I gave him more cartridges to reload, but even had to show him how to do it. A few shots later, he got one. Me, the wiseass pro, I couldn't keep that sucker impaled long enough to land it either. It waggled up and down in one spot as I tried and failed again.

It was too much for Tom, who wore only cutoff jeans, a tanktop, and a hat -- he laid down the gun and jumped into the water, which was only about four feet deep. He grabbed the fish up in his hands. "I've got it! I've got it!"

He surely did, but I advised him to get out of the water. He'd have to make his way forty or fifty feet to come out on the beach. "There's a shark heading this way."

"Huh? Where?" he yelped, dropping the fish and lunging for the wall in panic, fear written in his eyes, drawing his features down, his mouth open in the rush of adrenaline.

"Hurry," I said, looking around for the spear. It wouldn't stop a determined adult shark, but it might discourage a merely nosy one. I knew the .22 wouldn't be much better.

Tom saw the shark. "Help me! I can't get up!" he cried, weak and shivering with fear, trying to pull himself up the wall.

I dropped the spear, reached down, grabbed his hand and heaved. Tom scrambled up in time to watch the shark, a six-footer, curve away nearby. He made a few passes, then snatched the wounded Mullet and swam away.

"Shit!" Tom raged. "Shit!"

He had. He'd crapped his shorts and fecal matter ran down his legs. "Shit!" he sobbed, on the verge of hysteria.

Whoa, I thought, feeling his embarrassment. "Tom," I said gently, pointing to the beach. "You can clean yourself up over there. Go on."

I turned away to pick up the gun, unload it, and stick it in my pocket. I busied myself stowing the pole and spear into the crook of a tree branch. I strung the Papio through a length of cord. I dug for a half-smoked cigarette in my pocket, lit it, and waited.

"One of those days not much goes right," I remarked as we began the trek back. I could see shame and anger eating at him. He avoided looking at me. When I tried to distract him in inconsequential talk, he would only grit his teeth and respond in monosyllables. He looked haunted at the revelation of how he'd reacted to fear, all but choking on the bitter gall of it.

"This is just between the two of us, right?" His voice held a whining note.

"Oh, sure, no sweat."

"I'd really appreciate it."

"No big deal, Tom -- coulda happened to anybody."

"You tell anybody, you motherfucker, I'll kill you!"

Whoa! "Tom, listen. Don't threaten me. It's totally unnecessary. I've forgotten the incident. Don't worry about it."

"I'm sorry." He hung his head. "Just please don't tell anybody."

"For chrissakes, Tom, who wants to talk about shit, anyway?" I grinned, trying to cajole him out of his black mood. "C'mon, let's get out of this heat and have something cold to drink."

*****

It seems like nothing good ever happens to a person when he's feeling bad about himself, that experience follows attitude.

The next day I stood on the roof of the refrigerator house hauling up buckets of compost as Steph filled them below. Popolo and Sista dozed off to the side in the shade below. I looked up to see Tom walking along the south edge of the runway, turning into the path leading our way. He was oblivious to me on the roof and Steph was out of sight on the opposite side of the building. As he swerved around a corner of the building, I hailed him.

"Hey, Tom, how you doing?"

He almost jumped out of his skin. He leapt aside with a yelp and kicked Sista in the rump. She came up out of her snooze ki-yiing to get out of the way. This roused Popolo to come up growling. Seeing Tom, he charged forward barking. Tom stumbled awkwardly backwards, twisting to fall face down. "Kapu, Popolo!" I commanded immediately, probably needlessly. He stopped dead, looking up at me, then turned to regard the intruder with suspicion.

I flew down the ladder. Tom had landed on a piece of heavy mesh screen leaned onto a bush and had scraped and gouged his stomach. I helped him up. Christ, I thought, noting his shock and pallor, his shakiness, he's done it again. He'll never live it down, not in Steph's presence.

"Steph, babe, go fetch the first aid kit," I ordered to send her scurrying toward Iola. "Tom's got himself some scratches."

Tom was shaken, but there was no cause for shame I was relieved to see. "You okay?"

"Yeah," he gulped. "Surprised me for a second there, lost my balance."

"You're lucky you didn't get bitten. There was a kid here awhile back, he stepped on Popolo's tail when he was sleeping, got nipped in the leg. Natural reaction. But, really, you don't bother them, they won't bother you."

"I'm sorry. I didn't mean to kick him. It was an accident."

"Her. Sista's a girl dog. But that's okay. Don't worry about it. She barks a lot -- they both do, until they get used to you."

"I know, but I don't like your dogs. Maybe they know that."

"Hey, man, they're only dumb animals, big ol' puppies." Well, thought I, there are dog people in the world, and then there were all the other misguided characters.

Steph returned to make a fuss over Tom, doctoring his minor wounds. Then he discovered he'd lost a pocketknife and we began a search. Finding it, I handed it to him.

"Hey, I see you've got a Buckknife, I said. "Got one just like it. Good knife but the blade broke."

"They're guaranteed. You can send it in and they'll give you a new one."

"Yeah, I know, but we have a slight problem with mail service here," I grinned.

"Hey, listen, why don't you take mine, send it in for a new one you get home."

"How would I get it to you?"

"Ah, no, I'm doing okay on knives. Keep it for yourself." "They're expensive. I couldn't do that."

"Hate to see it wasted. C'mon, take it."

"Well, okay, but let me pay you something for it. It's worth over twenty dollars."

I shrugged. "It's hardly worth a can of beans broken. You got any beans?"

"Sure. Can of chili beans okay?"

"Fine."

"You got a deal. Thanks."

He collected a couple of cans of chilled fruit and soda pop. "I was telling Norm about your fishing wall, the different ways you fish. He'd like to see it. You feel like going again?"

I looked at him. Brave lad, I was thinking. He was trying to get beyond the day before, face up to revisiting the scene of the crime, meet the little demons gnawing at him -- a man after my own heart.

"Sure," I said. "Any time."

"How about after lunch, hour or so?"

I nodded. "Meet me at my tent when you're ready."

*****

Tom arrived with Norm and I lifted out the .22 and grabbed some cartridges to stick in my pockets. Making our way, I was curious as to what had brought these two together. Tom was young, well-built, and sported a mane of dark curly hair. Norm was graying, a spare bony man who talked like a college professor -- which he was. Their small fiberglass sloop appeared to belong to Norm, who said he was immigrating to Australia. Ah, I thought, another refugee sick of American civilization. Tom appeared to be along for the ride, a bit of adventure before returning to his safe, conventional world.

"You guys smoke grass? I smelled some funny smells coming from your boat last night. Wind blows it our way."

"No, no," they said, both hastening to deny it.

I smiled. "Hey, we don't either," I said with a straight face.

"But we're not judgmental about other people's vices -- especially when it doesn't interfere with our lives. You know?"

"I thought I saw you rolling up a joint yesterday," Tom said.

Aha, I thought, he knows how it's done, what they look like.

"No, that was tobacco, a Bugler. I tried to quit but Mac keeps tempting me with his supply." I went on to tell them about my brilliant but failed plan to quit. "You got any extra tobacco you want to sell, let me know."

They both claimed not to smoke, but later I saw Norm puffing on a pipe. He was one of those guys who'd rather lie than give you a straight answer. Years later I would be somewhat flabbergasted at the extent of his duplicity -- having heard stories from an investigator looking into his background as an instructor at U of C in Santa Barbara -- which extended into his bent for radical politics. He would manage to gain election as a Member of Parliament in Australia.

That was for the future. For the nonce, Tom was enamored of my shooting and spearing methods of fishing. Perhaps I should invite him over and let him scoop up a bucket or two of Mullet ala my night-fishing operation.

Tom wanted to shoot the gun. He missed three times in a row. "Wait'll they come in closer, Tom."

He expended three more shots without a hit while I waited to retrieve with the spear.

"Let's trade, Tom. You're wasting ammo."

I plugged one on the first shot, but Tom couldn't land him. We traded again. He finally got one, jumping up and down. "I got one! I got that sucker!" But neither could I land it. I was definitely going to have to do something about those spear points.

Enough was enough. We had run out of ammo.

Norm had sat back under a tree the whole while taking it all in. Tom asked if Stephanie and I were married.

"Nope," I replied. "It's more interesting living in sin."

*****

That night aboard Iola, I hooking Popolo and Sista to their tethers behind my tent to insure peace of mind to Tom and Norm and that no more accidents occur, Steph returned from a trip to get something from the fridge for our supper. She was in a huff.

"What, babe? What took you so long?"

"It's your friend. He's an asshole."

"Mac?"

"No, Tom. He hit on me."

"Well, gee, babe. I only wonder what took him so long. You know, sailors without women tend to get horny."

"Yeh, well, he wasn't very nice about it!"

"What? Tell me."

"He thinks we're a couple of down-and-out hippies. He offered me a hundred bucks for a blowjob."

"Just like that? Right out of the blue?"

"No. First he wanted to know why I slept aboard Iola while you stayed at the tent. Then he asked me if I smoked grass -- he wanted to get me high. I told him no. Then he offered me the hundred bucks."

"What'd you tell him?"

"What he could do with his lousy money! Asshole ain't got no finesse at all!"

I tried to jolly her out of it. "Hey, babe, I think you're just picky. What could I get for fifty bucks?"

What I got didn't cost me a dime -- only a few sweet words, some returned touches and kisses, a little effort that was well rewarded.

*****

The next morning I was up early, leaving Steph snuggled up in bed with her dreams. I sat ashore on a bench sipping at a cup of coffee, smoking a joint, and admiring the lines of Sea Wind. Finishing the coffee and pakalolo, I saw Tom preparing to come ashore in their dink. He was alone. Good.

As he passed, not yet aware of my presence, I said, "Hey, Tom."

He was startled but recovered to say, "Roy. Good morning. You're up early."

"Yeah. I like to get the jump on problems. Do my best thinking in the mornings."

"Oh, yeah?"

"Yeah. The problem's this. I don't mind you hitting on Stephanie. She's free, white, and twenty-one, got a mind of her own. She likes the cut of your jib, she'll strap some ass on you, you won't soon forget -- free of charge. But you ever insult her like you did last evening, I'm gonna kick your ass the whole length of this runway and back again. You understand that, motherfucker?"

"Yes."

Well, what else could he say? I was into my Marlon Brando role in On the Waterfront, ready to let him know I coulda been a contender.

*****

Tom and Norm had spent the previous evening as guests aboard Sea Wind. The next day, as I was rowing down to refill our gasoline can, I saw they were over to visit again before noon. Mac and Tom were standing at the bow firing Mac's .357 magnum. I paused until I could catch Mac's eye before continuing. He waved and I rowed closer.

"C'mon aboard, Roy. Give it a try."

"Maybe another time, Mac. I'm on an errand."

Tom, standing there fondling Mac's gun, had a peculiarly funny look in his eye, as if a mask had slipped and a hungry demon looked out from the hot fetid darkness within. I thought it would not be a smart idea to ever hand him my pistol again -- especially when we were alone.

*****

Not being one to carry a grudge, Steph apparently forgave Tom, for the next day she was aboard Toloa trading books and offering her baking services. Perhaps he had worked up enough class to apologize to her. Perhaps he thought charm would work better than money, that he could still score and save himself a hundred bucks. I had more important things to think about.

Steph had spent the day aboard Iola baking for Tom and Norm while I went about other tasks. Mac delivered a nice sized Papio to her, which we shared with the dogs that night. After a piece of coffee cake washed down with coco-milk, I spent an hour scooping up Mullet in the beam of my light now hung over the side on a gaff-pole since the boom was no longer movable from its service as central ridge-pole for the canopy. I kissed Steph goodnight and went ashore with a bucketful to clean, filet, and store in the fridge. I trudged the leftovers to the chum barrel and made my way to bed in the Arab Quarter.

In the morning I gathered coco-husks to smoke the marinating Mullet. When Toloa left at noon, Norm and Tom both waved to Steph aboard Iola. Norm waved at me and I returned it. Tom didn't. He'd wiped the chickenshit smile for Steph from his face to stare a long look at me as though to memorize my face. I promptly forgot him as not worth thinking about.

At Steph's request, I replaced the bow mooring line to the dolphin with a length of anchor chain. This would relieve her of the daily task of having to check for chafe on the nylon line, the main worry since the current and prevailing winds brought the stress from that direction.

In the afternoon it rained and I planted some vegetable seeds in paper cups. Our roof garden was over half full and we could soon begin transplanting them. I lolled about the rest of the day until suppertime, reading, fooling around over the chessboard, and thinking with the aid of a few joints.

I was thinking about Mac, a conversation we'd had five days before when he'd strolled over to help get the generator going again. At his suggestion, we'd pulled the head off to peer down into the cylinders, where we found the top of the piston covered in a layer of hard black carbon residue.

"It's that old gasoline," he said. "It doesn't burn right. The carbon buildup changes the compression. We scrape it out, she ought to run again."

"Damn, we bought it new less than three months ago."

"Here, let me do that," he said, taking the large screwdriver from me. "You've got to be very careful not to ding the cylinder walls."

"Wish I knew more about engines. Dad and brothers were good, but it's a weak point with me."

"Time and experience. It'll come to you. I've been tinkering with mine for years."

"Whatever possessed you to come here in the first place, Mac?"

"Aw, you know, probably the same reasons you came here."

I doubted that, but I also believed there was some agreement of purpose somewhere along the way. "What? Tired of the ratrace?"

"Yeah, that's part of it. Ever been to San Diego?"

"Passed through a few times."

"They've got a big harbor there, lot of boats, a community of yachties. I just got sick of the social bullshit, beginning to feel like a cartoon character in a soap opera. Plus, you know, personal problems, drinking too much and wondering who the hell I was."

"I know you like the sauce -- so do I -- but you seem to handle it well."

"Sometimes I get to brooding."

"Yeah, who doesn't?"

"What brought you and Stephanie here?"

"Oh, pretty much the same thing. Steph and I, we fancy ourselves freethinkers and we lead pretty unconventional lives. Society, you know, can get oppressive to those outside the mainstream."

"Yeah, I know, even in your own family. I was raised on middle-class values, but I never quite felt like I fit in. Coming into Sea Wind was the best thing I ever did."

"I hear that. Someplace doesn't suit you, hoist anchor and raise sail. But why Palmyra? There's a lot of interesting islands northwest of Hawaii according to what I've read. We first thought about going there."

"Probably the same reason you came here -- it's on the way."

"Polynesia, you mean?"

"Yeah, lots of islands. Lots of places to go, lots of places to leave."

"How's Muff feel about it?"

"Not as sold as I am, but, you know," he said, flashing a grin at me. "A good woman goes where a good man does."

"That's the way Steph is. She goes where I go, does what I do, even though she might have reservations."

"We're lucky bastards, Roy, to have women like that."

"Amen."

"Yeah, but I sometimes wonder which I'd choose if I had to give up Sea Wind or my wife." The corners of his mouth twitched up to let me know he wasn't all that serious.

"That's easy. Go with the woman. There's plenty of boats to get a man where he wants to go."

"Not like Sea Wind."

"Not like Muff if you really love her."

"Oh, I do. I love her more than Sea Wind. She's what makes being a sailor worthwhile."

"Yeah, a good woman makes a big difference."

"Fact is, Muff probably saved my life -- the way I was going."

"Oh, yeah? How's that?"

"Oh, you know, man, I was feeling lost and depressed, like I didn't fit in anywhere. Who knows what would have happened -- a life of crime, suicide? I used to have a lot of anger, you know, anger that I didn't quite understand."

"Me, too. I think all men do at some time or other in their lives -- thinking men anyway. You get to feeling you missed the boat somewhere along the way. You feel cheated."

"That's a pretty good way to put it."

"Until I met Steph, we were both lost and looking and not really knowing what for."

"Yeah, I understand. Muff had her problems, too."

"Muff? She seems like one of the most stable women I've ever met, calm, serene, down-to-earth -- well, except when it comes to dogs." I grinned. "She's a little weird on dogs."

"Ah, a minor point -- nothing compared to the drinking problem she had."

"Muff? Gee, Mac, I'd've never guessed. I've hardly seen her take more than a sip."

"Oh, she's whipped it. She makes up her mind, she goes at it with a will."

"Sounds just like Steph."

"Here, I've got some Form-a-Gasket. Soon see if we've got this sucker figured out right. You know how to check the gap on a spark-plug?"

"That I do know," I replied, fishing about for my gauging tool. "Plus, I have this vague notion about writing a book."

"No shit? I've played around with writing off and on for years."

"Oh, yeah? I'll have to let you read a few pages I've done, see what you think."

"Sure, be glad to. I sometimes wish I'd thought to bring a typewriter along. Perfect place for trying to get down all those long thoughts."

"That's exactly what I thought. I brought one along."

"So what? Autobiography? Essay-type stuff? Short stories? A novel?"

"Haven't quite figured it out yet. So far it's only a bit of personal stuff, some experiences."

"Like what?"

"Sea stuff and personal attitude -- like the time Sea Wind was struck by lightning and I almost got electrocuted."

"No shit?"

He nodded. "Down in Mexico, the Gulf of Tehauntepec. Then there was the time I thought we were about to be attacked by pirates in Asian waters."

"Pirates? No shit?"

"Thought they were going to ram Sea Wind, coming right at us. I got out my .357, aimed it right at the guy on the helm -- he hit Sea Wind, I was blowing him away."

"So what happened?"

"He got the message, veered away."

"Whoa! And Jack's worried about yachties carrying guns." "Oh, him. He was a character, wasn't he? I'd be willing to bet he had a firearm aboard himself."

"Yeah, probably. The ones I couldn't imagine were the Pollocks. Ed'd probably've shot his own foot off."

"Claimed he had a shotgun on board."

"No shit?"

"Yeah, who knows? What I know is you've got to be able to take care of yourself."

"My sentiments exactly. I get a little John Waynish sometimes." "Every real man's hero."

"Yeah, man."

"But Stephanie disapproves, right?"

"Yeah, but I think maybe she dimly understands the necessity." "Muff's the same."

"Women."
"Yeah. Where would we be without them?"
"Up shit creek without a paddle?"
"Heating cold cans of beans on the stove, dreaming of chateaubriand."
"Lonely nights, your only friend one hand or another."
"Lonely nights."
"A thing of the past -- forever, let us pray."
"Amen. You ought to bring that Mercury over some time. We can tear it down, see if it can be salvaged."
"Ah," I shrugged. "We can try, but I think it's probably hopeless. She's froze up tighter than a hemorrhoidal mouse's ass." "You do have a way with words sometimes, Roy."

*****

So Mac and Muff had been lushes while Steph and I were weedheads. Well, without pakalolo, we might have been lushes, too, and probably moonshiners instead of cannabis cultivators.

Despite having vastly different backgrounds, Mac existing on an inheritance, we shared some very basic present similarities. I wondered if I should offer him a joint as a means to introducing larger aspects of the subject. Be kind of nice to have he and Muff throw in with us. It would sure help to get our project moving. And how would it be if we came together into some sort of communal sexual arrangement, a sort of four-way open marriage? Every man had sexual fantasies about other women no matter how married and in love he was. But did women? I didn't know. Some perhaps. But if anyone had tried to tell me that human beings are monogamous by nature, I would have laughed, for I believed just the opposite -- that they are naturally promiscuous and hypocritical about it as well. Among all the billions of relationships between men and women, there may be some that are truly monogamous, but only a miniscule percentage. Even among the rampant promiscuity of lesser animals, I have heard of a few species that mate for life.

Neither of us daring to speak openly, I had looked Muff up and down with an approving eye, and Mac had returned the gesture by appreciating Steph's nakedness. The glitter in his eyes seemed no less than the shine in mine.

Stephanie, of course, was predictable. She liked Mac, was susceptible to his charms. Should opportunity present, the conclusion was forgone -- in fact, may already have occurred. I had once come upon them huddled together at the refrigerator house. When I had entered, expecting to find it vacant, we were all surprised and I'd had the feeling I'd interrupted something. The only question was Muff's sensibility -- not to mention Mac's attitude thereof if her sexual encompass should reach out to include anyone beyond himself. These, too, seemed predictable. People had constraints, self-imposed for diverse reasons, including societal conditioning. Mac and Muff with liberal attitudes about sex and drugs? No, I didn't think so. Get real. Yet, here we were, freer than ever before and Muff was the only other sexually attractive woman to appear at Palmyra. People could come to a thing in time. Don't push. File for future reference.

*****

Life went on. Dirt to the roof garden. Rain and reading, collecting water. Fishing and coco-processing. Tending our seedlings. Soon we must think on filling gro-bags, transplanting them to Aviation Island, clearing a space for them. We played chess, either aboard Sea Wind or in the Arab Quarter. Mac was trying to cut down on drinking and smoking because there was no way his supply was going to last a year the way he was going. Still, he shared with me and I was grateful, liking him more and more as time passed, trying to think of something nice I could do for him in return -- a hard one since he seemed to have covered all the bases. Steph and I traipsed about, drawing closer and closer. I even trusted her to cut my hair and trim up my beard. I even shaved one day so everyone could marvel at the film star forever lost to Hollywood.

*****

"How we doing on food?"
"Okay if Dickie and Carlos show up on schedule."
"If they don't, we can always pop over to Fanning or Christmas for enough to hold us."
"We got enough money?"
"Yeah, no problem."
"We could always sell some stuff."
"Like what?"
"Oh, the generator, the shredder, some of your extra tools."
"Forget that. We need all that stuff. We sell the generator, no more iced goodies."
"Well..."
"Better you sell your ass. Natives probably be in line a mile long for a haole cow."
"You think?" she said, as if seriously considering the idea.
"Sure, run lines, organize it. Ten bucks for a five-minute whack. You'd make over a hundred bucks an hour all day long. Didn't you ever read about the assembly-line whorehouses in Honolulu for servicemen in World War II?"
"Geez, what am I doing digging dirt and living on fish and coconuts?"
"Lemme think."
"What?"
"Building moral character?"
"Can't buy nothing with that. What if we run out of food?"
"Ah, darlin', shit, no way. With all the natural food we're provided with? You think we're gonna starve or something?"
"Well, you know, fish and coconut products can get old fast."
"We got crab. We could go over for another crab run."
"Oh, gawd, yeh! Those were ono!"
"Plus we got eggs..."
"Oh, yuk, I can't eat an egg that tastes and smells like fish and looks funny."
"Try 'em boiled, babe. They're not bad."
"No, thanks."
"And then we got squid," I continued to enumerate on my fingers, needling her.
"Oh, baby, yuk, yuk, yuk!"
"You're psyching yourself out, darlin'. You remind me of my sister. She'd never in a million years eat sashimi or raw oysters." "That's different. I like those."
"Just pretend you're in a fancy restaurant and they're charging you fifty bucks a plate for exotic fare. Remember when we had those snails at Buzz's?"
"What snails?"
"Escargot, darlin'. Those are snails."
"They are?"
"Sure."

"Well, they cooked them in garlic and butter. I thought they were octopus or opihi." (Limpet, a shellfish and Hawaiian delicacy.)

"Hey, I cooked the squid scampi-style. You liked it before I told you where I got 'em."

"Oh, yuk! Don't remind me!"

"Plus, we got sharks up the yingyang. Popolo and Sista ate one a while back."

"They did?"

"Yeah, and so did I."

"You did? When?"

"I brought you some, but you were in bed asleep."

"Well, at least we don't gotta worry about dogfood with all the fish and coconut they're eating."

"And that's another thing," I added gleefully on the spur of the moment. "Why, I heard discriminating winos sing the praises of Friskies, that cheapass stuff. Thanks to our mutts being too smart to psych themselves out, we've still got plenty of Alpo and Kal-Kans, the caviar of doggie-dinners. Little seasoning and some of that coconut sour cream, we've got Beef Stroganoff."

"Oh, yuk! I'm not eating any dogfood! Besides, we're almost out."

"What? We can't be."

"Only a few cans left."

"Nah, there's gotta be more than that." I began a search and soon found two cases buried under our bunk. "See?"

"Oh, yeh. I forgot about that."

"Where was I? Oh, yeah. I almost forgot. There's always fried and baked Sooty Tern."

"Yuk, baby, yuk! We can't eat those pretty little birds!" "Well, I don't intend to eat dogfood or bird either. All I'm saying is we ain't gonna starve."

"It's a question of variety, enjoying the food."

"I can eat fish forever. I don't think I could ever get tired of fish -- especially smoked Mullet."

"Yeh, gawd, that came out good, didn't it?"

"Fucking-A delicious. You worry too much, babe."

"It's part of my job."

"I worry, too, darlin'. I'm only saying, Dickie and Carlos showing up late's only a glitch, not a big crunch."

"Ah, gawd, they're very late we're gonna run out of everything." "Reminds me of this joke. This guy and gal are marooned on a desert isle, no coconuts, no fish, no nothing. He managed to survive for three months offa her breast milk." I shut up while Steph mulled that. "Oh, yeh? What'd she live offa?"

"Oh," I grinned. "A little piece of meat yay long."

"Oh, you! Where do you learn these awful jokes?"

"People tell 'em to me. I've been trying for years to figure out who makes them up. My brother-in-law musta knew every woolybooger joke there ever was, which musta run into the thousands. I figure they got a big cave somewhere they keep all the old acid-heads from the sixties. They gotta make up these awful fucking jokes to earn their room and board."

"Has anyone ever told you you're fulla shit?"

"Why, hell no! And I wouldn't believe them if they did!"

"So what're we gonna do? Just wait around for Dickie and Carlos?"

"Sure. They ain't due for a couple of weeks yet."

"You think Shearwater made it back to Hawaii by now? They got our mail?"

"Hm, yeah, maybe," I said, counting up the days.

"Maybe we could send a message by Mac for Shoemaker to pass along."

"Yeah, we could do that. Let's figure out what we want to say."

*****

We rowed over to Sea Wind. Mac was out somewhere and we left the message with Muff. We went on exploring a bit, to Sand Island and Strawn. Then hit the bathtub on the way back.

Unbeknownst to me at the time, as was most of her entries into Iola's logbook since she had taken it over early on, was this entry for August 22nd: Today was a day of good news and bad news. The good news was the boys (Dickie and Carlos) sent word via Mac that they'd be down. The bad news was that they wouldn't be able to make it til the end of October. Mac didn't seem overjoyed at buying our generator but said he'd let us have fifty dollars for it. So I baked a cake to forget my woes.

She first got stoned and then she baked a cake.

The next day, I loaded the Merc on our wagon and pulled it over to Mac's workshop. Steph and I, after some discussion, had committed to the decision to pop over to Fanning for enough supplies to hold us over the next couple of months.

"Jack said they had a company store there."

"We could buy enough to get us through. Flour, sugar, and a bunch of canned stuff."

"Maybe some tobacco, a few cases of beer."

"Yeh, why don't we do that?"

"Okay, let's do it."

*****

The Merc would be very useful -- if it could be made to run. "Hey, Mac."

"Roy. You finally brought it over."

"Yeah. We've decided to run over to Fanning for some supplies. Be nice if you could get it running."

"When you planning to leave?"

"I don't know. Week or so, I guess. There's no big hurry and we gotta get Iola ready."

"You got a chart?"

"Nah."

"You can use mine. I got 'em for all the islands."

"Oh, yeah? Hey, that would help, thanks. What'cha working on?"

"Our refrigerator went on the blink."

"Hey, you know you're welcome to use our fridge. In fact, I'll leave our generator for you so you can keep it operating."

"Good idea. Think I'll take you up on that. Thanks, Roy."

"Ah, hey." I waved a hand -- it was nothing. "You need us to get you anything, let me know."

"Yeah. Wait a minute. I'll get you the Fanning chart and some money."

When he returned a few minutes later to hand me fifty dollars, he said, "I'll get the chart to you later. I'll have to mount a search. Let me think about what we want. No hurry, right?"

"Nah, plenty of time."

"I'll get to work stripping the Merc, see what's what."

"Paradise, and we're doing all these mundane things."

"Yeah, but without the assholes to bother us."

"Think they'll ever stop showing up?"

"Sailing season will be over in a couple of months. Maybe the traffic will ease up."

"I hope so. Except for Don and Bill, I don't miss any of the people that've been here."

"You didn't like Norm and Tom?"

"Aw, Norm was all right, I guess. A bit strange but quiet. Tom was a real flake."

"You have a run-in or something?"

"Yeah, sorta. He insulted Steph kinda pissed me off."

"Oh, yeah? What happened?"

"He offered her money in exchange for a blowjob."

"He did?"

"Yeah, real asshole in my book."

"He'd have done that to Muff, I might have shot the sonofabitch!"

"Well, I only offered to kick his ass all up and down the runway." "I was wondering. He was bad- mouthing you a bit there."

"Oh, yeah?"

"Kept blowing on the idea that we shouldn't trust a couple of dirty hippies like you, that you were probably a couple of thieving nogoodniks."

"That bastard! I hate thieves! Besides, we bathe everyday -- well, almost."

"That day we were shooting from the bow?"

"Yeah?"

"He kept telling me I'd better keep my gun loaded and handy. Then he told me you had a gun. A .22 pistol. But I already knew that -- about your rifle, too. You told me about it when I showed you my .357, remember?"

"Yeah."

"I didn't tell him that, of course, just said something like 'oh, really?'"

"Total asshole."

"He also said one of your dogs bit him."

"Bit, shit. He gouged himself on a piece of heavy screen. Fell down because Popolo scared him."

"He said he told you if your dogs ever came near him again, he'd kill them."

"That pussy? Right after it happened, I took him and Norm fishing, to the fishing wall, you know?"

"Yeah. I tried out your spear one time."

"Get anything?"

"No."

"Anyway, I always take Popolo and Sista with me when I go there. Didn't hear a squeak out of him. That guy..." I began, on the verge of telling him about Tom shitting his britches, but decided not to. "...is a hundred percent asshole."

"Yeah, seems like it. I think you caused them to cut their visit short, Roy. Maybe we ought to trade roles."

"Hah, yeah! Maybe we could make us up a big sign, plant it on Sand Island, say something like, we hate people. Martians welcome."

"Or maybe, Warning, U. S. Government Biological Warfare Installation. No trespassing."

"I like that one better."

We exchanged grins.
"You build it, I'll paint it."

*****

I gave Steph the money and told her about the chart, also that we'd be leaving the generator for Mac and Muff.

"Can he fix the Merc?"

"There's no joy in Mudville."

"What's that mean?"

"He'll let us know, but don't get your hopes up."

"I'll trace the chart so we can have our own."

"Yeah, good idea."

*****

On the 27th, a rainy day, I was mostly aboard Iola trying to charge up our batteries. It was easy now -- a mere matter of wiring my electrical line from the refrigerator house into the battery-charging module.

Mac had delivered the final rites on our old Merc -- we would continue life as pure sailors. I'd decided to try converting the shredder motor into a pump as a backup for our handpump, and turned my attention to the forward hatch leakage problem.

Laid back in the evening sharing a few joints, I began to idly leaf through Iola's log. Her entries were mostly very brief, only touching on the larger plethora of events. She had taken over the keeping of the log early on, with only a brief intrusion by me to recount events on the day we'd arrived. It was curious to see what she had chosen to enter versus what she had left out -- yet perhaps understandable in view of the fact that she was usually stoned to one degree or another when it came time to take pen in hand.

"What's this about selling our generator to Mac for fifty dollars?"

"You sold him the generator -- you told me so. You gave me the fifty bucks for it."

"I didn't sell him anything. The fifty bucks is for a list of things they want us to get."

"What list?"

"He hasn't given it to me yet."

"Then why are we leaving him the generator?"

"So they can use it, babe. Their fridge is on the blink. We don't need it for the trip – Its just extra weight."

"Oh. Gawd, I wondered why he was giving me a funny look when I thanked him for the fifty bucks."

"When was this?"

"When he brought by the Fanning chart."

"You think I'm gonna sell a brand new generator, one we paid four hundred dollars for, for fifty bucks?"

"Okay, I got it wrong. So sue me."

"It's what you didn't include that gets me."

"What?"

"Well, for instance you only mention one flying fish when there were dozens. You mention popcorn only once, and how many times have we had that -- fifteen times maybe? You left out that Ahi we caught. (Tuna) And what about my squid-collecting technique, my ideas for a palm-toddy brewery, the tooth-pulling story, my elevation to Unofficial Deputy Mayorhood?"

"Gee, really exciting shit."

"As opposed to selectively boring shit? Like gathering dirt and coconuts?"

"Hey, you can write whatever you want anytime. I'll roll you up a few joints, you can get caught up."

"You didn't say a word about our capsize."

"I didn't?"

"Light another joint. Your brain's getting fuzzy."

She did, missing the jibe. "I wish Mac could've fixed the Merc.

Some motor power would be good about now."

"Yeah, but I think we can get out all right."

"Maybe Mac will sell us one of his."

"I don't think so. The Seagull's too small and I don't think he'd want to part with the Evinrude."

Steph sighed. "Well, maybe we could buy one at Fanning."

"That's an idea. Maybe a used one -- they probably don't have any new ones anyway -- that is, if they don't want to charge an arm and a leg for one."

"How big a one would we need?"

"Ten horsepower and over ought to do it. Merc was twenty."

"That shouldn't be a problem -- hundred, two hundred bucks."

"Yeah, maybe, it depends..."

I told her about a story I'd read in a sailing magazine about Fanning. The islanders' supplies were delivered periodically by ship and sometimes, if delivery was late, they might run into shortages. The story had included an anecdote about a shortage of cigarettes and tobacco due to a delay in the arrival of the supply boat. As far as the hardcore smokers were concerned, prices they were willing to pay had reached a near-par with pakalolo -- the old law of supply and demand. The same rule would apply to other products the islanders thought of as necessities, such as gasoline and parts for outboard motors. We might get lucky, we might not. A two hundred dollar outboard might only be obtainable for five or six hundred. Who knew?

"Maybe Dickie'll bring one for us."

"Um-hm."

"It's what I want for Christmas."

"Put me down for pizza and beer." "Bagels, cream cheese, and lox."

"The rain's let up. You wanna try for a bath with me?"

"Aw, gawd, nah. All I feel like doing is taking a nap."

"Where's Mac's chart? I'll drop it off on the way."

I found him at his corner workshop, where what was left of the Merc was scattered in parts. He was working on a pump motor. As I handed back the chart, I asked if there were any usable parts worth keeping.

"I was thinking about keeping the prop. Most of the rest would only be good for someone who had an outboard just like it. You were right. The problem was in the cylinders. Somehow seawater got inside and she froze up."

"Yeah. By the way, Steph was a little confused. She thought you were buying the generator for the fifty bucks you gave me. It's all straightened out now."

"I wondered -- the way she was carrying on. I was beginning to think maybe you needed money. I don't keep much aboard, but I can loan you a couple of hundred."

"No, no, Mac, really. We're okay for money. Thanks anyway. Listen, what I would appreciate is you keeping an eye on our tent and some stuff we're storing at the refrigerator house."

"Sure, no problem."

"You're the Unofficial Assistant Deputy Mayor in charge while we're away."

"Do I get a badge or a sash or something?"

We grinned at each other.

"You got time for some chess?"

"Mm, nah. Maybe tomorrow. I'm headed over for a bath."

"Better hurry. Looks like more rain anytime."

"Yeah, see you."

# # #

CHAPTER 18
LAST CHAPTER: THE HEART OF THE MATTER

Wednesday, August. 28, 1974

The sun was over the yardarm, as we would-be sailors liked to say. In this case it meant an hour or two before noon. Time to move, me boyo, I told myself. I had been thinking on our voyage to Fanning. Although it was only 225 miles, it's direction lay southeast against prevailing winds all the way, which meant a zigzag course for us -- we'd have to tack back and forth, first a leg to the south-by-southeast, then another to the north-by-northeast. It would be a test of our seamanship and navigation skills, unused these past two months. Time to begin moving into that hyperstate of alertness, to expend more energy and live on less sleep.

Work awaited me, the job of getting Iola shipshape. On the other hand, I didn't want to set any precedents against the lazy rules of paradise. Arriving for hot, sweaty labor at noon would suffice, I thought -- which left a couple of hours. Fishing or chess? Should I rouse the hounds, the only two creatures lazier than me in this part of the world, ply our way to the old fishing wall? But then I would have to dress the fish out, marinate them, gather coconut husks for the smouldery fire to smoke them, and what were one or two more going to add to our stores? We already had a couple of gallon-jarsful. Soon we would be dining on bigger fish offered by the open sea. But a game of chess, now, meant a cordial offer of coffee and a cigarette over which I was too socially sensitive and polite to refuse. The paradox of the matter was that if I won, the offer would be repeated. Mac was not the sort who would want to quit losers. When I won, he would insist on another game, but was quite content to quit winners. Did the man not know the incentive he was offering me to win?

I headed for the Graham campsite, careful not to disturb the Tern colony. Their raucous outrages were as good as watchdogs, and Stephanie might pop her head up the hatchway for a looksee. Whenever she set her mind to a job, she was a tireless taskmaster and her hard gaze could induce qualms in me sufficient to overcome my shrugging ways -- a trick learned from me, a too-apt student who fed the teacher his own lessons.

Well away on the path to the equipment shed, I began to consider my moves. Mac tended to play a tough but conventional game, always opting for the Ruy Lopez opening when he had white, but the wild, inexplicable moves threw him. Would the Lonely Bishop ploy disrupt his defenses? We played fairly fast games, might get in three or four before noon. Hell, I could be tanked on enough caffeine and nicotine to fuel my working bod until sundown. Steph would be pleased, perhaps want to reward me. A cold, refreshing bath, a joint or a tad of hash, and maybe some creative passion on the hatch-ladder. But, no, she would want to head for the tent, as was her wont of late, the coy bed I'd fixed up. Maybe she'd want to play chess for sex, the loser having to submit to the winner's whims. It was so interesting that I didn't mind losing to her -- the furtherance of my ongoing education in the kinky aspects of feminine psychology as taught in Stephanie 103. I had learned things from one woman to practice on another and was pleased, if sometimes surprised, when they worked.

"Ahoy, Sea Wind."

Mac's head popped up. "Roy. What's the mission, seaman?"

Seaman was a promotion I'd earned over a checkmate, up from deckhand. He called Stephanie captain. "To whup you soundly, sir. Permission to come aboard?"

"Bah! Permission granted!"

I pulled the dinghy across, stepped in, and hauled myself over to mount the boarding ladder. Padding on bare feet down inside, Mac was busy setting up the board while Muff poured coffee.

"Top o' the morning to you, Muff," I said, grinning my best while slipping in to the dinette seat across from Mac.

"Morning," she replied softly with a quick glance before turning her eyes away.

She strode around behind me to sit the coffeepot on the stove as Mac held out his closed hands before me.

"Feeling lucky?"

"I never count on luck," I replied, choosing a hand. "Ability's more reliable." I'd picked black.

"My advantage. Want to concede?"

"As a great chessmaster once said, I forget who," I quoted vaguely, "with white I win, with black the worst I can do is draw."

"Crass egotism."

"No, Mac, ability and confidence therein."

"Actually, I like it. Maybe I'll take it for my own motto."

Muff had moved to seat herself on the settee across from the dinette, choosing the farthest position from me. I deduced her purpose as being able to see my face without Mac, who sat sideways to her, being able to readily notice. It suited me, affording a lovely view of her bare legs.

"Better be careful, dear. If both players assume that attitude, isn't one going to be more devastated when he loses?"

"Don't worry, Muff," I quipped in my usually insouciant way. "Mouth-to-mouth resuscitation'll have him up again in no time." For her, it was the wrong thing to say, but it sailed over Mac's head. He moved pawn to king four.

I concentrated. I'd never had much success offering my queen's pawn. I made the same move in reply. We would play a conventional game, each working to develop our fighting pieces, both castling in defense, advancing pawns cautiously in protective lines. In the end, I gained the advantage of a bishop on a forking check with my knight.

"Oh, no, I didn't let you do that, did I?"

I merely displayed my innate class by refraining from a needling remark. He tried a couple of moves, but saw it was hopeless by then and conceded.

"Honey, could we get more coffee here, please?"

He offered me a Bugler, lit us both up. We reconstituted the board, me with white now.

Muff refilled our cups.

Mac eyed me. "Where's Steph this morning?"

I shrugged. "Hopefully, still asleep."

"At this hour?"

"She sometimes reads late. On the other hand, when she finds me missing from the tent, she'll probably head over here. I'm hiding out from work."

"Why do you guys sleep apart? Problems?"

"Oh, no. Steph loves Iola, finds it cosy. Me, I need a little more room. Our headroom's only five feet, nine inches. I can't even stand up straight without knocking my brains out." I didn't want to say that being aboard was also a little too much like a prison cell to me sometimes.

"Just seems like an odd arrangement."

"Well, Steph doesn't always sleep aboard, of course, nor do I always sleep in the tent."

"Aha!" Mac winked. I sometimes felt that he and I were involved in a masculine conspiracy, a sort of sexual chauvinism of traditional male attitudes toward women. I had my suspicions about he and Steph and winked or shrugged as the case might be. Did he have a similar attitude? It was hard to tell -- he seemed too conventional to have broken from the strictures of traditional male attitudes. Still, he had been unconventional enough to seek out the isolation of Palmyra, definitely an antisocial tendency.

I opened with a pawn to queen four and, at his imitation, brought my queen's bishop's pawn to rest beside the first. If he accepted the offering, I would reply with my queen's knight in opposition, the minor sacrifice allowing more control toward the middle of the board. If instead he protected, I would push the bishop's pawn into his territory.

With concentration, I won again, having to go to the wire with pawns and a slightly better position in the endgame. Ah, more coffee, another Bugler.

"Have you decided when you're heading out for Fanning?"

"Saturday if the wind and weather's right."

"I'll tow you out if you like."

"Thanks. If our usual breeze is up, it'll be no problem -we can sail right out."

"The chart of Fanning help you?"

"Yeah. Steph traced the important parts. Appreciate it. We never planned on going to Fanning."

"No problem."

"You thought any more on what you'd like us to bring back for you?" He'd only mentioned tobacco so far.

"I'm still working on it." "Just sing out and you got it."

I lost the third game. Time to quit, time to head on over and get to work. Thanking Muff for the coffee only got a nod out of her. Mac accompanied me topside.

"Maybe I'll drop by later for my chart, see how you're doing. On the tobacco, Bugler's fine if they have it. If not, whatever's available."

"Well, whatever, it'll last you longer without my mooching. I've got it on my list, too."

"Going to give up, huh?"

"Yeah, well, it's tough with you always blowing smoke in my face."

"It's tough, period. I've tried to quit a few times myself."

"Think it would grow here?"

"No, not much hope of that, I think. Why don't you and Steph come over for a little bon voyage supper Friday night?"

"Sounds good. Thanks."

"I'll break out a little sauce. We can have a nice evening. Which reminds me," he added, lowering his voice. "If they've got any liquor there, pick up two or three bottles for me."

"Those'll be on me. I'll try to get a case if they've got any."

"Feel like doing some fishing today? We're going out for a couple of hours this afternoon."

"Ah, no, Mac. I'd like to but we've got to get squared away for the trip," I said, but then had a thought. "Wait a minute, you don't mean out of the lagoon -- on the open sea?"

He grinned. "No, maybe over the reef area to the west, but I'd still like to give that idea a go -- catch us some real fish. You still up for that?"

"Oh, yeah, Mac, I dream about mahimahi and tuna -- sashimi, man. Oh, yeah, I'm game."

We had discussed the idea several times -- a man thing, leaving out the girls -- the challenge of the risk adding to the allure. We had put our heads together to make a tentative plan to cover the contingencies. A small vessel like the Zodiac on the open seas could become life threatening in certain conditions -- for instance, if the outboard quit on us several miles out from the island. Sure, we could spell each other rowing back -- but that could get very iffy in contrary winds, squalls, or worse. Drifting around at night, we might lose Palmyra altogether. Solution: Take an extra outboard. Mac had a little 1½-h.p. Seagull in addition to the 9½-h.p. Evinrude, also a compass for direction in case overcast obscured the sun. But what if, in a worst-case scenario, both engines conked out? With a sail, we could still move the boat toward destination, but the Zodiac wasn't designed to sail without the addition of lee-boards, mast, and rudder. Our fiberglass dinghy was, but it was small. Mac's other dinghy, though, could sail, too, and it was larger than ours. Okay, we would tow his fiberglass dinghy equipped with sailing apparatus -- worse came to worst, we could sail back in towing the Zodiac. Might as well throw in a sextant, Almanac, and an. H.O. publication so we could pinpoint our position if losing sight of the island. Also, no use wasting the space in the second boat -- we would stow a week's worth of drinking water and. Extra food rations. Might as well add my portable shortwave for up-to-the-minute weather reports, which we would consider closely beforehand anyway. Rain gear for the squalls. To bad we didn't have handheld VHF radios to keep in contact with homebase, keep the girls reassured. Wait a minute, I had a perfectly good VHF that I'd never got around to hooking up. Could we rig it to take along? Sure, why not? We could add one of my fully-charged car batteries as a power source. The girls would naturally be opposed, but we, with our superior manly pride, would persist in reassuring them.

"Maybe when you return from Fanning."

"For sure."

*****

Returning to Iola with a jaunty stroll and a whistle to match, I yelled, "Wake up, you lazy wench! There's work to be done!"

Steph's frizzy head jumped up from the hatchway like a jack-in-the-box, a. mock-stern look transfiguring her usually sunny disposition.

"Yeah, and where have you been, fishing?"

"No, darlin'. You know I always take the mutts."

"I wondered. I went to wake you up with a blowjob." "Jeez, I knew I shoulda stayed in bed!"

"So what, you were over bumming smokes from Mac '?"

"I don't have to bum -- he's gentleman enough to offer. Send the dink over."

639

"Wait, I'll get Puffer, let her run around on shore."

She handed up my competition for her affections, the mutt sassy enough to know she'd win if ever her mistress was forced to choose between us. I growled at her. She grinned, wagged her tongue, and with nimble little leaps, hung her tail over the side and pissed in reply. If only my mutts were smart enough to learn that trick -- or I was smart enough to teach them.

Steph was up and out cooing, "Ooh, did her have to weewee? Good girl! Mommie's widdle Puffy-wuffy!"

So that's how she did it. If I talked to Popolo like that, he'd think I was losing my marbles. Sista would growl.

In a practiced move, Steph had her feet in the dink, lifting Puffer down, then untied the painter, shoved off, and glided to shore. Puff was out like a little fox bounding away to rouse the hounds. I stepped in and shoved off on one foot to glide us back.

Aboard, she said, "You hungry? I made some biscuits. They're yummy with coconut butter and Lyle's Golden Syrup."

"That reminds me. We got a. dinner invitation for Friday night, bon voyage party and all that."

"My, you have been busy. Come and try my biscuits."

 "Got any bacon to go with them?"

"Ha! You wish."

"In that case I'll take the next best thing."

"What's that?"

"You, darlin°. You're my meatdish. Us carnivores gotta be fed."

She simpered. "Oh, yeah?"

"Yeah."

*****

The biscuits were yummy. So was the meatdish. Until it dawned on her and she muttered, "Next best thing!"

*****

Ain't working under a hot sun fun. I saw Mac and Muff puttering in the Zodiac toward the western end of the island. Muff wore a wide straw hat for a sunshade. Sitting in the bow, was she seeing me, thinking about what to do?

*****

Thursday, August 29, 1974

We were up and at it early, taking advantage of the relative cool of the morning. Iola was looking more like a creature of the sea, if a bit battered, rather than a slovenly hippy houseboat.

We had removed the long bamboo poles tied onto each side as supports for the canopy, a section of canvas salvaged from the old half-burned warehouse, and stored it all ashore for use on our return. We had collected fresh water to fill our tanks and jugs, a couple of dozen sprouted and unsprouted coconuts. Our car batteries, used only to power our low-draw running lights, were fully charged -- one of which had been discarded as unable to hold a charge. I had replaced our leaky forward hatch, mostly unused at Palmyra except for ventilation when it wasn't raining, by nailing and gluing a piece of plywood over the square hole of it, then laying a couple layers of fiberglass and paint to seal it off good -- no more pesky leaks there. The hatch cover went over with the canopy stuff for possible future use -- with the addition of legs, it would make a nice little work table near the fireplace ashore. Iola was once again properly stowed, loose things secured.

By early afternoon, towels and peppermint soap in hand, we plodded icky with sweat to refresh ourselves at the communal bathtub. Steph washed her bikini and was trying to decide whether to wrap wet towels around herself for the sake of token modesty.

"Can you see Mac or Muff anywhere?"

I looked toward Sea Wind. "Nope."

"Gawd, it was so embarrassing when Mac caught me naked that time."

"Don't kid yourself, babe. He enjoyed the hell out of it." "It's just the breeze feels so good on your bod after a bath."

"Next time just act natural. Maybe nudity'll catch on."

"Well, it would make more sense in this climate."

"Yeah," said I in total agreement. I had several times not bothered to slip anything on when making the stroll to the fishing wall. Popolo and Sista had been not in the least outraged. But I had brought a clean pair of cutoffs to replace the ones I'd washed -- for the same reason that caused her to hesitate over the decision to strut her naked buns for the greater glory of God and man. "Save on the laundry bills, too."

We made it back to Iola without anyone sharing the view with me. Among elusive images that drove poets mad, I thought, the hind-side of a well-built woman in motion must rack right up there.

"Care for a spot of tea at my pavilion, darlin'?"

"No, maybe later, sweetie. All I want now is to stretch out and rest my bod, relax, maybe read a bit and take a nap."

"Sounds good. Maybe I'll do the same." I kissed her a peck. "See you later."

I waited until she'd gotten aboard before strolling in under the shadowy coolness of shoreline foliage to make my way to the tent. The hounds, laid out in the shade, hardly twitched.

*****

A short nap, then a cup of tea. A joint? Why not? I sat back in my swivel chair, my feet up on my little desk-table, sipping and toking, contemplating a lint-free navel. Who needed civilization, so called, when a perceptive, persistent lad such as myself could opt for a life such as this? "A jug of wine, a loaf of bread, and thou beside me singing in the wilderness. Ah, paradise, etc. etc. (Omar Khayyam) I quoted to myself, losing it toward the end. More books would be nice. Maybe a typewriter -- I could try my hand again in the on-again-off-again search for vestiges of writing ability that may have developed in the long intervals.

Eventually, if and when the secret plantation idea paid off, we would be heading further south, a new boat, new islands, and how many were remote and uninhabited? Plenty. I had once tried to take a loose count, but when the total passed ten thousand had given up -not even twenty-five percent of them in the Pacific Ocean were inhabited.

I idly browsed through a chess book. Where was that really weird defense I'd run through a few times? It might serve to throw Mac off his stride. There it was, the Hippopotamus. I worked out the series of moves it took to set up on my board, a formidable one I thought, but taking an unseemly number of moves to establish. Well, if I moved with quick confidence, could convey an impression that I was laying a trap, perhaps he would be cautious, allow me the time to set it up. From my redoubt on one corner of the board, I would merely defend against what was sure to be a costly siege.

No time like the present. A little nicotine to chase the tetrahydracannibinol would do good. I slipped into my thongs and ambled over that way. Turning left into the equipment shed, I zigged around the roadgrader, zagged past the old army truck on the shortcut to the Graham campsite.

Muff was off in a corner by the old sea-rescue launch painting tools to protect them from rusting in the humid atmosphere. They had appropriated that end of the building in order to store some of their wares. Mac had managed to remove one of the four storage lockers set tight into the corroded launch for the stowing of lines bags of sails, and whatnot. They used the area as an adjunct to their campsite. It provided shade from the sun and protection against the almost daily showerbursts.

Muff wore her usual outfit of shorts and halter. I greeted her, admiring the succulent curves of her. "Hi, Muff. Mac around? I want to try my Hippopotamus Defense on him."

"He's sleeping," she said, carefully laying down the tin shears she had been painting. Then she wiped the brush on a rag and slipped it into a jar of thinner, replaced the lid on the paint can.

She put a finger to her pursed lips, then beckoned, whispering, "Come here."

I glanced out at Sea Wind, then stepped into shade to take her in my arms. We kissed, not for the first time. When our lips had parted, she leaned back, looking with clear blue eyes into my own, breathing the thinner air of desire. She reached to untie her halter.

"Kiss them. Take them into your mouth."

I did. Soon we had discarded our shorts, our brief gestures to accommodate each other like the wings of excited birds caressing our bodies. This was our fourth time together on such intimate terms. It had come to be without design, one of those things that just happened.

*****

It had begun on one of those perfectly lovely days that paradise was capable of producing, when I'd stumbled upon her sunbathing in the nude. I had been traipsing through the jungle strand of coconut palms and tangled growth along the north shore in one of my endless exploratory hikes. There had been a nice breeze to relieve the heat of the day. She had been stretched out on her back alone on the tiny crescent of white sand, her feet toward wavelets from the calm sea inside the fringing reefs. Palmyra was full of surprises.

When she had become aware of my presence, she had leaped to don her brief attire. I'd caught a glimpse of well-rounded buttocks before turning my back, searching for words of apology.

"Hi, Muff. Sorry for disturbing you. Wasn't aware anyone was here."

"It's okay. I thought I had the place to myself."

"I've never quite appreciated the beauty of the view from here ...until just now."

She was shy, looking away from my grin.

"Must be the Irish in you that makes your tongue so glib."

"Ah, but the Scotch that makes me so taciturn."

Popolo and Sista leapt past her to romp in the shallows. She started back a step, clearly uneasy.

"They won't hurt you, Muff. They're still basically puppies."

"Big puppies. One of them bit that Wheeler boy."

"That was an accident. He stepped on Popolo's tail when he was sleeping. It's a dog's natural reaction to snap at whatever's hurting him."

"They scare me when they charge at you barking."

"I know. I thought you were going to brain poor Popolo that day. They're only playing."

"Why do they bark so much?"

"They were trained to be watchdogs. We used to live way out in the country and it was nice to know when strangers were about. Then we used to keep them tied by our boat when she was in drydock -they had a leash law on Maui -- kept unwanted visitors away when we weren't home."

"I guess I'm just not a dog person."

"Watch. Let me show you something."

I kicked out of my thongs, ran toward them yelling. "Heya, Popolo! Shoo, Sista!" While Sista was startled and sat back on her weak hindquarters, her reaction carrying her all the way over backwards, Popolo knew the game and dodged away as I kicked and grabbed at him, chasing, his black mouth stretching in a grin over big white teeth, tongue flapping happily in the wind. Sista was soon up in the spirit of it, pursuing and growling. I turned on her in a sudden pirouette and, trying to change course too abruptly, her legs gave way again and she rolled over in a sprawl. Popolo charged, barking up a storm. I dodged aside and spun to slap his rump. Sista was up and splashing in a wide circle belting out her song of the carousel. I whipped my hands at Popolo's head, back and forth, teasing as he snapped at them, then let him take my forearm into his jaws, knowing he would not apply enough pressure to hurt. I pulled his tail as we spun about, then his ear. Sista ventured in closer, snapping and grrring. Popolo let go and I leapt around with a great "Haagh!", sending her rushing away. Popolo was beginning to bray in deep haroos. Ah, me hearties, some call it a romp, some call it childishness. Madmen call it canine ballet. But us buckeroos call it pure fun. After a couple of minutes clowning around, playing the happy fool,

I finally stopped, stood still for a bit to signal my disengagement, then strode from the boundless arena like a matador to the grand trumpeting encore of their barking. Of course, they took a different view, their barks becoming laughs of derision over having worn out my two-legged ass and chased me away.

I returned to Muff sucking wind, trying to grin.

"My lord! That was amazing!"

"Dogs like to dance, too," I gulped. "Remember where you heard it first."

"You know, that's what it was like -- some wild pagan dance."

"How did you know?"

"What?"

"That I was a pagan."

"Well," she paused. "I almost said heathen."

I sat down on a fallen coconut tree, thinking hard to keep the patter going. "Beats being called a hippy, I guess."

"Hippy?"

I waved my hand, offering a portion of my settee. "Isn't that what you and everybody else thinks of us?"

"I suppose. Are you saying you're not?"

"Not even close. Steph might have once been a hippy, the kind they called a flowerchild. You know, make love, not war. Last time I was in Mexico, everyone with beards and long hair were considered hippies."

"I think it's a bit more than that."

"What, exactly? Nonconformists, you mean? People dropping out of society, living nontraditional lifestyles, experimenting with drugs, sexual libertines -- what else?"

"Do any of those traits describe you?"

I thought about it. "Hm, I guess they do. Maybe I am a hippy. . What about you?"

"No way."

"Being here on Palmyra, it's not exactly living a conventional life. You look like a dropout to me."

"No, not really. Think of it as a long vacation. Besides, I don't do drugs and I'm not promiscuous."

I smiled. "I'll take your word for it." I left out that I was doing so with a grain of salt.

"Do you?"

"What? Do I use drugs or am I promiscuous?"

"Both."

"I've tried various drugs -- just so I'd know firsthand for myself. There's a lot of misinformation making the rounds. I've never been addicted and never will be. But I like to smoke grass. You?"

"No. Well, I've tried it a few times, but it scared me. Do you still use it?"

"About ten minutes ago."

She peered at me closely.

"What, are my fangs growing?"

She grinned. "No, you're fangs aren't growing. You just don't look like you're stoned."

I shrugged. "You mean comatose, paralyzed, unable to speak, like that?"

"That's pretty close to what it did to me."

"I knew a guy once who used to get paranoid. He'd go around pulling the shades, making sure all the doors and windows were locked, paced around wringing his hands, worrying. If it affected me that way, I'd never touch the stuff."

"How does it affect you?"

"Think of it as an enhancer of positive things."

"How long have you and Stephanie been together?"

"Mm, I don't know -- a couple of years or so."

"Why aren't you married?"

"We almost did the dirty deed once. Got as far as the blood tests. Whew! Close call!"

"You're against marriage?"

"No, no. It's okay for others. I was married once. But that was enough for me. I promised myself never to do it again."

"Why?"

Was there such a thing as a succinct answer to such a question? "See, it was beautiful at first. I had loved this woman for several years, thought she was the most perfect creature God had ever made. We struggled along in San Francisco, had survived a lot of hardship and adventure together, and then, I don't know, all of a sudden we weren't in tune and everything turned to crap. We argued, grew bitter and resentful. I still don't understand the whys and wherefores, only that our perspectives diverged, our dreams parted company. She became a shrew, I a bastard. I don't think I ever suffered so much in my life as I did in those last months, jealous, possessive, cruel, tormenting, a total psychological disaster."

I cleared my throat, suddenly hoarse. "Well, I decided that marriage wasn't my thing. It was a trap to be avoided. I'm a restless type. I always feel an urge to move on, explore new worlds. Maybe it's a character defect, maybe something a little more complicated. I'm leery of entanglements with women. I'd rather just be friends than get too deeply involved."

"What about Stephanie?"

"That's part of the problem, see, and maybe the solution, too, for all I know. I worked it all out in a very logical way. Intimate relationships between the sexes should never go beyond three years. I mean, after a year or so, the bloom's off the rose. You're beginning to really see each other without the blinkers of serious romance. That's okay. You can get into a very comfortable relationship, still experience some of the old excitement on occasion -- even if the intensity isn't quite up to par. It's funny, though, how you can know a person so intimately, but then there's an all but unnoticed drifting apart and sometimes you ask yourself why you can no longer understand that person so well. Maybe the other person changed, maybe you did. Nothing ever remains the same. You realize anything can happen. There's static in the air, communication is sporadic or lost altogether. Life is ho-hum. You become bored, sometimes desperate. You're restless and you look around. You ask yourself, is this what I want to do with the rest of my life? At that point, deterioration has a big toehold in the relationship. Three years, thank your lover for a good time, kiss him goodbye and seek new pastures -- mark my words."

"That's the most ridiculous thing I've ever heard."

"It is?"

"Yes, absolutely. I've been married way past three years and what you say doesn't begin to describe the way it is."

"And how is that marriage? You still in love?"

"Yes, I am."

"That's good. You two seem to be comfortable with each other." "Are you comfortable in your relationship?"

"Oh, very."

"But after the three years are up, what, you're going to just ditch Stephanie?"

"My theory says that after romance, try to remain friends. You know sailors -- they need safe ports from the storms to come. We're already pretty good friends. In fact, she's the best woman friend I've ever had."

"Don't you love her, Roy?"

Lady knew how to cut right through the baloney. "Yes, I do," I admitted. "In fact, I'm considering making her an exception to my three-year rule. You just can't figure love. It comes and goes with a mind of its own, against all logic, expectation, and resolve. Stephanie is actually one of the best things that ever happened to me."

"In what way?"

"See, the first time I ever laid eyes on her, she lifted my heart up. She had a great smile and a sassy walk. I was attracted to her, sure, but you know, I wasn't exactly struck by thunderbolts like it was with my wife when I met her. Steph and I started out having fun. But then I learned that she was the loneliest person in the world, and yet she had more love and compassion in her than any ten saints you can name. I saw people take advantage of her, treat her like shit, and it pissed me off. I became angry and protective all at once. And promiscuous? I was beginning to think she'd screwed every adult male between the ages of eighteen and seventy on the Big Island. Oh, sure, I had vestiges of all the usual emotions eating through the armor I thought I'd fashioned to protect myself. I don't know how I ever saw it, but I came finally to an astonishing conclusion. It wasn't Steph who was the tramp. She had more honesty and sincerity than all those boobs who merely used her like a slut. I began to love her. I couldn't help it. I was seeing something in her that none of those other guys had seen. And she responded with all the love and loyalty and determination and intelligence that's in her. I'm just astonished. Men used her and passed her around and sent her on her way -- can't score on the beauty queen? There's old Standby Steph, a good fuck in hard times! She'll do anything! -- none of them ever seeing her desperation or qualities, or maybe afraid to see."

On a verbal roll, I continued. "Her girlfriends now, are the real friends in her life. I don't know. They seem to identify with each other in some fundamental way, with some..." I searched for words. "Some hidden but essential character common to them all in divers degrees, and they're all tenacious and unwavering in their friendship. I had friends like that, I'd think about conquering a small country, make a haven for all the lost flower children of the world."

I looked at her, she sitting there so silent, mouth agape. "What?"

"Nothing," she said, returning from wherever she had been. "That was quite a speech. I think marijuana makes, you loquacious."

I laughed, embarrassed. "Sorry. Didn't mean to bend your ear out of shape."

"No, don't be sorry. Not for what you just said."

I looked down at her hand gripping my forearm. She removed it. "Popolo, Sista," I yelled at the mutts, who were shaking out the saltwater. They would need a freshwater rinse. "Hele mai. Come on now. Hele mai."

They trotted over. "Noho. Take a load off, you guys." Sista laid her head on my thigh with a quiver of jowls, a little whimper. I stroked her.

Muff watched. "Go ahead, pet her. She wants you to." She reached out a hesitant hand, but withdrew it when Sista wruffled up a sound from her throat, ran her tongue around her chops.

I took her hand in mine, guided it to Sista's snout. "Don't be afraid -- she won't bite you. Scratch behind her ears. She loves that."

Muff tried it, scratching, then patting her cheek, running her fingers with the flow of short black hairs up her muzzle between Sista's eyes. Sista moved her head, licked at Muff's hand.

"She gets familiar with you, she won't bark anymore."

"She looks so vicious when she barks."

"Yeah, but she's really a coward. Sista was born with a congenital affliction in her hipbones, leaving her hindquarters very weak. You saw the way she collapsed out there. I imagine it causes her considerable pain sometimes."

"Oh, poor Sista," Muff cooed.

Popolo nudged his head in. "This guy now," I said, grabbing a handful of jowl for an affectionate tug, "his affliction is that he was born dumber than a fencepost. Fortunately, the god of dogs compensated by giving him a happy-go-lucky disposition. Popolo is never moody or depressed as Sista sometimes seems to be."

Muff scratched at his head. "Their fur is beautiful."

"I think it's the oils from the fish and coconut I've been mixing with their dogfood."

I nudged them away. "Hina moe, Nina moe." They laid down. "How did you get your nickname?"

For a moment I didn't know what she was talking about. Then I saw her looking at the tattoo on my arm near the shoulder. "Oh, that." What was I to say? When Mac had inquired, I'd played it off by saying it was a nickname. Steph sometimes slipped up and referred to me as Buck. One deceit leads to another.

"Ever read Jack London?"

"Yes. When you shaved off your beard, I thought you looked a lot like him."

"Really?" I tried to remember old photos I had seen of him in books. The last one I had read was The Cruise of the Snark, which was about his building and sailing a schooner to the South Pacific.

"Well, wasn't he a handsome man?" She snorted in good enough humor.

"You were saying?"

"Did you read The Call of the Wild? Do you remember it?"

"Oh, yes, about the dog. It was half wolf, wasn't it?"

"Yeah, he could have been. He was always torn between his two natures, the tame dog and the call of the wild. Well, that's me.

You remember the name of the dog?"

"Don't tell me -- Buck?"

"That's me, a wolf in dogs clothing."

"Sounds like a case for therapy. Are you schitzy?"

"Maybe. I'm like the dogs in the joke."

"What joke?"

"On second thought, forget it. It's a bit crude."

Somehow I knew she'd ask.

"No, it's all right. Tell me."

"Well, see, there was this young Indian brave who was very sad. One day he approached the tribe's old shaman and said, 'Oh, great sir, I know it is the custom of our tribe for you to name all the newborn children.'"

"'Yes, my son,' the shaman says. 'What about it?'"

"'Well,' says the young brave. 'I was wondering just how you choose the names.'"

"'Oh,' the shaman replies. 'I look for a sign from the Great Fathers in the Sky. When the male child was born during the last full moon, I awoke that morning to surprise a bear as I stepped from my teepee and it ran away, and so the boy was named Running Bear.

And when the female child was born only three suns ago, I was awakened by a dove singing in the treetop, and so she was named Singing Dove.'"

"Ah, I see,' said the young brave, hanging his head in even greater sadness."

I paused to see how she was taking it, if she was ready for the punchline. She had to ask. "What does this have to do with dogs?"

"I'm getting to it. Anyway, the old shaman sees that the young brave is sad and dispirited, and so he says, 'But tell me why you ask, and why my answer has made you so sad, Two Dogs Fucking?'"

Me, I'm the sort who laughs loudest at my own jokes, and I burst forth in full song. She cracked up, too, couldn't help herself, her face red with it, holding her yummy tummy and leaning over her knees in the spasms of it.

Popolo and Sista raised their heads to take in our idiot titterations.

"Oh, my god! That's awful!"

We were seeing each other through tears in our eyes.

"Roy! That was really awful!"

I put my arm around her shoulders, pulled her to me. "I know! I'm sorry! Buck made me do it!"

When the spasms had eased, I kissed her ear and drew back. "You're a good sport."

An ensuing silence beset us, each of us, I think, waiting for the other to speak first, to set the tone of what was to follow.

As the moments marched on, each increased my awareness of the woman sitting beside me in nothing more than two bits of cloth, her smooth golden legs stretched out before her. I thought of what it might be like to kiss her inner thighs, to take in the aroma of her, to be responsible for her pleasure.

"Have you ever been unfaithful to Stephanie?"

"No, not the way I see it. What you're really asking is do I fool around on the side. The answer is yes. So does Steph. We have what is called an open relationship. We often, but not always, inform each other of our plans before undertaking, ah, extracurricular sexual adventures."

I could tell she was shocked. Well, I could remember a time not so very long ago when such an idea would have shocked me, too.

"That's hard to believe. And it works? How does it make you feel? I mean, when she tells you she's going out with another man?"

"Sometimes I disapprove, but usually I keep it to myself. See, neither of us is really asking permission. It's more in the nature of a courtesy. We're telling each other that we'll be occupied in a private pursuit for the purpose of avoiding inconvenience."

"And that doesn't bother you?"

"It's something you come to gradually. It used to be a serious problem. If my wife had ever done that, it would have made me insanely jealous -- and vice versa. Since then, I've come to believe that jealousy between lovers is one of the most destructive of all emotions. Jealousy in a relationship implies possessiveness, a property interest, and a property interest in human beings, whether you're willing to admit it or not, constitutes a form of slavery. We are always quick to defend our own freedoms and rights, but slow to grant those same freedoms and rights to others. From my point of view, I'm less of a hypocrite than I used to be."

"I just don't see how it can work without a mutual commitment."

"I know this is probably all new and strange to you, but Stephanie and I are committed to each other every bit as much as you and Mac are."

"We're not promiscuous. We've never stepped outside the vows of our marriage."

"Steph and I aren't married, nor have we taken any vows."

"Then where is your commitment?"

"We're here together. We depend upon each other. We've placed our lives in each other's hands. Neither of us has much experience sailing the high seas. We bought an old boat, rebuilt it, learning as we went. We sailed away all on our own with only book knowledge to guide us. We only learned to navigate after we were out of sight of land. You think we don't trust each other on all the important issues? A relationship that is built on exclusive sexual fidelity is a fragile relationship."

"What do you mean, fragile?"

"If Mac were unfaithful to you, as you put it, would it destroy you? Would you leave him? Would he leave you for a momentary affair? Would it wreck your marriage?"

She didn't reply. She wasn't sure. Perhaps their marriage had never been severely tested. "I'm sorry," I said. "I'm not trying to put you on the spot. You don't have to answer."

Her look was intense and, I thought, tinged with anger, a defensiveness. You sure know how to pitch woo, me bucko, I told myself with some sarcasm. Lighten up!

"Actually, I envy you and Mac," I said, trying to breach the sudden chasm between us.

"Really? Why?"

"Because you seem to have it all together. I had a boat like you guys, the means to travel, I'd be doing exactly what you are.

I mean, you've already been around the world, and I'm just beginning."

"Well, you seem to have gotten a start on it at least."

"Yeah, and I'm going to keep working on it, too. I'm thinking of adding more girls to my crew once I get a bigger boat."

"If you're thinking what I think you are, it might be a novel way to commit suicide."

"You may be right. Once when I was a little crazy, after my marriage was over, I was chasing every woman who looked at me twice. I wound up with two of the lovely creatures in separate households, neither aware of the other. Oh, was I ever the clever, gloating scoundrel, a great and cunning lover! One was a few years older than me, an experienced woman who taught me a lot, while the other was quite a few years younger, making up in enthusiasm for her lack of experience. Well, I thought that was the best of all possible situations. I could learn from the one and practice on the other -- two sexy and spirited mistresses. I thought I had it made until it began to dawn on me just what a desperate situation I'd gotten myself into.

"For instance, I would wake up in the morning after a grand but exhausting night with the older woman, and have to leave the house working on the deceit I would employ when I called to tell her I'd be away that night -- because I was expected that evening to arrive at the younger woman's house. Well, you can guess the calisthenics I was expected to perform in order to make up for the previous night away. Not only that, but she was fond of morning chasers.

"Sometimes I managed several days with one or the other through various subterfuges on my part, but then I had to make up for having left one or the other alone for so long. Weekends were the worst. I would get out of bed with one, rush over to the other, who, of course, would be feeling amorous. After a couple of hours, I would make an excuse to run out for a couple of hours, just as I had already done with the other, then rush back to tell the first I only had a couple of hours before an important appointment, when I'd have to hurry back to the second. And guess what? She'd want to put those hours to good use! I was showering six times a day to insure I wasn't carrying suspicious odors from one to the other. I'll tell you, I thought myself a healthy, vigorous man, you know, but there came a time when the inevitable happened."

Muff had been listening closely, doubtless enthralled by my tale.

"What," she said, "they found out about each other, what a sly rat you were?" Was there a gleam of satisfaction in her eyes?

"No. I became impotent -- from mental strain or physical exhaustion, who knows? I don't know if a woman can understand this, but for a man to become impotent, it's the greatest fear and devastation that he can experience. The first time it ever happened to me, when I was married and still madly in love with my wife, it was the most humiliating thing! I felt my life was over! There was no way I could bear the thought of becoming a priest! But, fortunately, it didn't last long that time. Then again, I experienced it with Stephanie at a particularly vulnerable moment, and I just knew I was done for. But when it happened this time, I think I was actually relieved, grateful for the break from my poor put-upon circumstances. I mean, I could actually relax and watch a football game on TV for a change!"

Ah, indeed, me boyo, and there you have her laughing again. I caught her with her mouth open, my hand reaching to the nape of her neck, and leaned over to kiss her -- on the mouth this time.

She stiffened, but didn't pull away. After a few moments, I cracked my eyes for a quick peek -- both hers were closed.

When it ended, I spoke in a husky whisper. "I've been wanting to do that for a long time."

Our faces were close.

"How long?"

"A thousand years. Since the day of the paint fight. Remember? We walked over to the seaplane ramp to wash off. It was the way your wet shorts clung to you."

"You're incorrigible."

"I can't help it I see a beautiful woman, I want to kiss her."

"I'm not beautiful."

"You are. You're very beautiful."

I kissed her again, longer this time, feeling the shaky desire rising in us both like hot oil. Having utilized the first two of my primary secrets with women, first to gain their attention though my gift of gab, such as it is, and second, to get them laughing, I proceeded to the third -- to put her needs above my own the first time.

I think she was almost as astonished by the force of her response as I was.

*****

The second time was when I surprised her alone at the bathtub. She was standing naked in it showering with the hose that drew cool water from the old catchment tank. I had crept up to the other side of the tank, peeked around with a big smile to hiss at her. "Psst! Hey, c'mere a minute."

Startled, she had tried to cover herself at first, dropping the hose so she could use both hands. "Oh, Roy!" But then she had looked around to see if we could be seen. We were on the highest ground of the island where the Seabees had dozed up the coral against a telephone pole siding to form an unloading wharf for supply ships, and Sea Wind lay directly east.

"C'mon. Around here. Give me your hand."

She had looked around again, her eyes wider, suddenly breathing harder, but allowed me to take her hand as she stepped from the tub and lead her around to the other side of the tank, where I kissed her, touched her wet body. I went down to suck at her nipples, excited by the goosebumps, the intakes of breath, licking a trail toward her navel and points south.

She leaned back against the watertank, spreading her legs, her hands on my shoulders. The low moan of pleasure issuing from her mouth was like the eerie allure of a flute tone in its lower register.

"Oh, god, Roy, what are you doing? What are you doing?"

"I'm tasting you. You're delicious."

Then I was up against her, kissing her lips again, sucking honey from her mouth, my shorts around my ankles, lifting one of her legs from behind the knee in my forearm for a frenzied wham, bam, thank you, ma'am.

*****

The third time had been the best, for she, in her own considered intent and desire, had come one night to surprise me alone in my bed.

Popolo and Sista, laid out on the floor, had raised their heads, one to growl, the other to whine. "Kapu," I bade them quietly, expecting Steph to show up, perhaps wearing nothing more than perfume. Then I heard little noises of movement.

"Roy?"

I leapt from the bed where I'd lain naked, peered out the zipped screen of the entrance flap. "Muff?"

"May I come in?"

"Sure, just a second," I replied, feeling along the seam for the zipper in the dark. "Okay. Be careful you don't trip. You have to lift your feet."

I reached out a hand to guide her in. "Over here," I said, pulling her to one side. "Let me shoo the dogs out."

"They're in here? God, I was scared to death they were going to jump out growling at me when I got close."

"Popolo, Sista, hele mai." I spoke softly and the shadows of them slipped out of the tent. Rezipping the screen, I turned to her. "I saw you come ashore alone."

"Where's Mac?"

"Snoring. He got drunk and passed out."

"Oh."

"I brought you a present."

"You did?"

"Some coffee and tobacco." She handed me two fat envelopes.

I was touched. "Aw, Muff, thanks. You sure know how to get to a guy."

"It's nothing."

"This is some surprise."

"I couldn't sleep. I was upset."

"Wait. I'll light a lamp."

"No, don't."

"I can't see you."

"You can feel me."

I grinned so wide I thought reflected light off my teeth would illuminate her.

"Well, if you insist," I said, wrapping my arms around her, holding her close, enjoying the feel of her. She wore clothes, a shirt or blouse, jeans or slacks, even shoes. We simply stood there awhile, infusing each other, before our hands began to move.

"You're naked."

"It's the way I sleep."

She was running her hands over my body, gripping and squeezing portions of flesh, her boldness increasing with the rate of her breathing. I was trying to unbutton her for the sake of my own touchy-feelies, throwing kisses searching for her mouth in the dark.

"Oh,"

"It's all right."

"Can I touch you there?"

"Yes."

I worked at the buttons, fumbling. "Hold still. I want to undress you."

She had a bra on underneath, panties, too. I left them for last. She nudged out of the canvas and rubber deckshoes. From behind, I rubbed her upper arms, kissing her neck and shoulders, kneading her breasts, then unclasped the bra to cup them and gently pinch up her nipples.

"Bend over."

"What?"

"There's a table here. Feel it? Put your hands on it and bend over."

"Like this?"

"Now hold still. Don't move."

My hands gripped to her hips, I kissed and licked down her spine until I was on my knees. I began to pull her panties down, adding little bites to my kissing and licking. I spread her cheeks with my thumbs and blew a long, humid breath into the crevice, leading her little gasps up the scale to bigger ones.

Touching the place I wanted to visit, I stood and moved over her to guide myself in to heaven on earth, leaning to press myself on her, to tongue one ear, then to rest a moment and gather my senses, to focus myself to the exquisite task of getting her off.

*****

Restless from the lack of my own relief, I had gotten up from the bed where we had lain cuddled in an aftermath of silence. I sat in my swivel chair, opened the drawer to feel for the leather pouch of my stash. When I lit the lamp in order to see what I was doing, Muff became shy, pulling the cover over herself.

When I had rolled up two nice joints, one for later, lighting the other, I went to sit across from her to offer a toke. She had been watching me, but now closed her eyes and shook her head.

"Did I hurt you?"

She shook her head again.

"What?"

A mumble, another shake.

"If you don't speak up, I'm going to tickle you."

She smiled. "Don't you dare."

I leaned down to kiss her. "Did I hurt you?"

Her arms came out of the cover to curl around my neck. "No, you didn't hurt me."

"A couple of times, you sounded like you were in pain."

"I wasn't. It was, you know, the little pain inside too much pleasure."

"Ah. You sure you don't want to try this?"

"No, thank you."

"Why are you hiding under the covers?"

"Could you turn out the lamp?"

"No. I want to turn it up so I can see you."

"Please."

I got up to turn it off -- a wheedling woman can get to me everytime. I found my ashtray to toss in the tiny wet remnant of the joint. Back to stand over her, I said, "Here's the deal. I'm going to be your slave. I'll do anything you want. All you have to do is tell me, give an order, and I'll do it. Anything."

"Really?"

"Really."

A long silence ensued.

"Well?"

"Lie down with me."

I did. "What else?"

"Kiss me."

I did, long and deep, playing games in her mouth. "What next?"

"Touch me."

"Where?"

"My...my breasts."

"What else?" "My...my..." "What?"

"You know."

"No, you have to tell me. Touch your what?"

She was silent a moment. "This is silly."

I helped her. "Here?"

She nodded. "What?"

"Yes."

My hand lay limp against her. "Now what?"

"You know."

"Say it. I want to hear it."

She whispered. "Inside."

"Like this?" "Yes. Yes."

"You're too tense."

"I'm sorry."

I thought about it. At this rate, we would be fiddle-fucking around well into next week -- or I would have to tickle her after all. "I've got a better idea."

"What?"

"You be my slave."

She thought about it. "What would I have to do?"

"Same deal. Whatever I want."

"What do you want?"

I was feeling impish. "Can you stand on your head?"

"What?" She blinked. "What for?"

"It's the forty-seventh Tantric position," I said, making it up.

"The what?"

"Never mind. Do you trust me?"

"Yes, I think so."

"I want you to do something for me."

"What?"

I went to my drawer, retrieved one of Steph's prescription Parests, grabbed the jug of drinking water. "Here, take this."

"What is it?"

"A capsule. It contains methaqualone."

"What's that?"

"It'll help relax you. It's better than the Placydil you have in your medicine cabinet -- I looked when I used the head on Sea Wind. I'm the nosy type."

"I take it to help me sleep sometimes."

"Try this. It's better."

"I can't stay all night. It won't put me to sleep, will it?"

"No way. I won't let it."

"All right."

"Now roll over on your stomach and spread your arms and legs." "What are you going to do?"

I had decided she was worthy of what she needed, a special treat from my secret repertoire -- this was a job for Super Masseur. I told her, wiping the doubt and anxiety from her face. I fumbled in the darkness in my kitchen -- for the table holding a two-burner camp-stove, a small skillet, a pan, a teakettle, a few condiments, and a bottle of cooking oil.

With a generous dose of coconut oil on my hands, I straddled her butt to begin the process of driving her crazy with pleasure, rubbing and kneading. She would be the recipient of an overall body massage, erotic version, that culminated in the slaking of intensified lust by means of a. mind-blowing orgasm.

It was something Steph and I had learned together, practicing on each other. What had started as three-minute rubs of neck, shoulders, or back, had evolved into hour long massages for the whole body, including face, hands, feet, and secret parts. We had gotten off into it, acquiring several books on the subject. We had soon seasoned the process into an erotic one, lending certain exquisite ministrations to sensitive areas, wrapping the whole package of it in what could quite reasonably be called a satisfactory fuck.

From her neck and deltoids, I worked my magic fingers onto her shoulder muscles, down her arms into her hands and fingers, kissing and breathing shivers of pleasure into her ears. Down her back to the base of her spine.

"Take a deep breath now and blow it all the way out. Empty your lungs." I pressed up her spine with the heels of my hands, popping the joints as I went.

"Okay, again. Deep breath, blow it all out." Snap, crackle, and pop right up to the base of her neck.

"Umf, my god!"

Then her buttocks, lavishing more oil along the way, kneading them like bread dough, lingering to tease caresses into the juncture of her thighs, on down her legs to her feet, an almost unbearable pleasure to those who'd never experienced it. Thumbs down the sole, rubbing up into the arch, between every toe, popping the joints of each, kneeling now at the foot of the bed.

I had been alert to the sounds of sighs and little squeaks the while, something like twenty minutes, savoring my own arousal as I instilled the little exquisite pangs of ecstasy, easing her body, preparing her for the growing climax of it.

"Roll over now. Time for the front."

Working my way up, I paused to grip her ankles, bending her legs out like the wings of a butterfly, opening the dew-laden orchid hiding in the apex, breathing deep the sweet aroma, tantalizing my thirst on the delicate organism's moisture, giving her a lascivious taste of what was to come. When her sighs became gasps, I sat back, pulled her legs down straight.

"Oh, no! Don't stop! Please!"

"Wait," I whispered, on the verge of my own gasp.

I straddled her again, bending to swallow on her tongue, offering mine, as I worked on her breasts, then sliding down to suck the oil from her nipples, slowly and lovingly, back down to the steamy core of her, where I applied myself with all the enthusiasm of a kid with a new toy.

Grunting up into the arc of it, she collapsed at last into a pool of putty, the uh-uh-uh of a long distance runner trying to get enough oxygen music to my ears.

I waited patiently for her to rest, smoking my second joint, then lying beside her to cuddle. "How do you feel?"

"Mm. Very warm and cosy."

"It's my turn now."

"Mm, what?"

"Sit up," I directed, pulling at her, positioning her to rest on her haunches on the lower half of the bed. I spread my legs around her. I took her hands to place where I wanted them, then leaned back.

I could sense her uncertainty, but waited, saying nothing.

"What do you want me to do?"

I sat up to kiss her. "Muff, listen to me. I only want whatever you have to offer, whatever you want to give. You don't have to do anything. Did you like what we've done so far?"

"Yes. Yes, I did. Very much."

"Do whatever you want. I love what you do to me."

I laid back.

The tentative moves became experimental.

"Do you like that?"

I sighed. "Mm, yes, that's great."

She began to gain confidence, her hands moving more surely.

"Do you like this?"

"Oh, yes, baby, that's nice."

"What about this?"

Oh, it was very nice, for sure, feeling the unexploded excitement reasserting itself, beginning to gear up into the dire need of it.

"That's enough. Now slide yourself forward. You do it, there, ah."

"Oh."

She began to move, rocking, finding a rhythm that pleased her, working at it, the tempo increasing by the moment. I reached my hands up to fondle her breasts, moved one finger down to the point of our joining.

"Do you like that?" "Yes, yes."

Her oxygen intake was on the rise again.

"Kiss me."

She leaned forward, her breasts pressing to my chest, cupping my face in her hands, lavishing her mouth over mine. My hands went down her back to grip the nether cleft of her, to hold her just so, to start the fast idling locomotive of my passion huffing up to full speed, we making our own peculiar clickety-clacking together, driving inexorably toward a great rending crash through the earthly walls of ourselves into celestial spheres.

*****

"How you doing, babe?"

"Trying not to feel guilty -- and not succeeding."

"Ah."

"I've never done anything like this before."

What could I say in alleviation -- say ten Hail Marys, twelve Our Fathers, and sin no more?

"It's just not me."

"Maybe a new you."

"No."

"You're here."

"I know."

"Why?"

A few moments passed. "I needed to be."

"What's the problem? You want to talk about it?"

"I love my husband."

"I know. I'm sure he loves you, too."

"He does. We were going to make love tonight. We ate a candlelight dinner with wine."

"Go on."

"Well, we were feeling romantic, you know, began necking, and ...and..."

She began to cry, her cheek soon wet against my chest. Me, for all my glibness, I had never learned how to deal with a weeping woman -- or a child -- except to hug them and refrain from the banal "There there, everything's going to be all right."

I waited, kissed her forehead, and pulled up an edge of the sheet so she could wipe her eyes. No Kleenex, no hankies. She sniffed. "You need to blow your nose? I've got some toilet paper."

"Yes, please."

I handed her the roll. When she was done, I pulled her back down.

"What happened?"

"He...he couldn't do it. I tried to help him, but he became angry, began drinking and brooding. I tried to tell him it was all right, but he wouldn't talk to me."

"Is it the first time?"

"No, it's happened several times."

"When?"

"Since we got here."

"Not before?"

"No, I'm not sure. It might have happened once a long time ago. I don't know."

"I'm sure it's only temporary."

"I know he wants to make love to me. I get excited and then... and then... It's so frustrating!"

She dabbed at her eyes again. "I don't know what to do!"

"He'll get over it, sooner or later," I offered.

We were quiet, me thinking. Trying to talk to Mac was a waste of time. Men did not talk to each other about such things. It would only piss him off and he would begin to wonder how I knew -- which wouldn't be hard to figure out. Maybe I could find some opportunity to regale him with the tale of my two mistresses in separate households to introduce the subject, hope for a response. Maybe, maybe not.

A better idea would be to tell Steph, sic her on him. I knew she was attracted to Mac, would be game, take it as a challenge to her womanly wiles. Then again, maybe that was the problem. Maybe she had already had her way with him, given him a real eye-opener. Maybe he was on his own guilt-trip. What a shame if it were true. Me, I'd just as soon get it all out in the open, what the hell, initiate our own Palmyra Swingers Club. Get Mac and Muff smoking a little grass, mellow them out, maybe we could interest them in our venture. It would be a whole lot easier than sneaking around, trying to keep it hidden from them. It seems that paradise can always be improved.

Meanwhile, Muff had dozed off. I let her sleep, going on with my long thoughts -- until I came to the immediate idea of what Mac might do if he woke up and discovered Muff missing. Oh, man, I didn't want to get into that kind of shit! What time was it? After midnight for sure.

I shook her, trying to rouse her.

"Mmm?"

"Muff, c'mon, darlin', wake up."

She mumbled. "What?"

"You've got to go home now. Come on." "Okay. Just let me get woke up."

I waited, rubbing her back with one hand.

"Muff, c'mon, it's late."

"Okay, in a minute."

"Now, c'mon." I ran my other hand up to her ribs, tickling her. "Cooties, fleas, lice, and ticks," I charged. "And creepy, crawly, slimy things!"

"No, cut it out!"

"Snakes and rats and leeches," I added, trying to think of all the creatures women hated, continuing to tickle her.

"Stop it," she begged, but it was too late -- I had her laughing. "C'mon, Muff, what if Mac finds you gone? We don't need any problems."

That sobered her. "All right. Where are my clothes?"

I felt around for them, handed them to her. Where were her panties? One shoe was missing. I got down on my hands and knees, feeling around. Panties under the desk, shoe under the bed.

"Where are you? I need my shoes."

"Here. Lift your feet." I felt her hand on my shoulder as I worked to slip the shoes on. Then I stood. "Here's your panties."

She was already dressed.

"You want a cup of tea before you go?"

"No, that's all right. Thanks."

"Wait, I'll go with you." I began feeling around with my feet for my cutoffs.

"No, stay. I'll be okay."

"No. I'll walk you."

"Would you consider running away with me," she asked, not meaning it.

"Only if you're rich enough," I quipped, "to support me in a style to which I'm not accustomed."

"Problems already."

"Don't worry. Things are going to get better."

Out of the tent to head toward the south side of the airstrip, Popolo and Sista materialized out of the darkness, ready for whatever the mission entailed.

"Shit. Wait. They'll have to stay here." I shooed them back to zip into the tent. "Shh. Kapu now, no noise," I told them. "Hina moe."

Returning to Muff, I said, "Wanna hold hands?"

"It was beautiful tonight."

"Yes, it was."

We walked slowly, trying not to disturb the tern colony. It was a lovely night, the sky bright with stars, a fresh breeze caressing US.

"You know, lately I've felt like I just wanted to die, that I could go to sleep and never wake up."

"It's not that bad. Things'll get better -- they always do."

"I know. I don't feel that way any more."

No, things weren't so bad. They'd have to get better. At the inland side of the equipment shed, I kissed her.

"Goodnight," she said.

"Yeah, but I think it's morning."

*****

The fourth time then found us in the late Thursday afternoon with me lying on the floor and she straddling me. I caressed her breasts, kissed them, her mouth, allowing her to move as she desired. While we existed in the immediacy of the moment, the world had vanished -- until a movement in the light of the doorway behind her caught my attention.

It was Mac and in a heartbeat of shock his rageful face moved closer. I was suddenly staring up into the business end of his .357 Magnum pistol and twisted violently aside, toppling Muff, as the deafening explosion blasted away the hedonism of the day.

I rediscovered myself standing, my heart in my throat, sick with the certain knowledge that there was no escape that I was a dead man waiting to fall down. Mesmerized, I saw the gun in his hand. I looked for his eyes, expecting to see my death in a moment.

Mouth agape in horror, he was frozen, staring at Muff sprawled face down, unmoving, a hole in her back. With a sob of awful anguish, he knelt to roll her over. Her eyes and mouth were open, her belly a gory mess.

"Oh, God! Oh, God!"

He blubbered, and the tableau held forever, forever it seemed, until he raised his face and howled, curdling my blood as time began ticking again and he turned the insane fire of his rage licking out toward the object of his fury -- me.

He raised the gun and fired twice more, but I had leapt away, ducking, scrambling and running. I flew by the back porch of the old house next door, made the corner, and fled the pursuing demon. From the path in front, I plunged into a copse of trees and shrubs, ducking as I heard a scream behind me, then another shot.

I burst from the trees into a dense strand of palms.

"I'll get you, you fucking bastard!" I heard his hoarse voice grunting in promise. "I'll get you!"

Another shot reverberated out as I hit the north shore running full tilt eastward along the strip of sand throwing quick glances over my shoulder. By the time Mac had lunged out behind me, I had a lead of over fifty yards before veering back into the jungle as he raised the gun to aim again.

I dodged around the trees, moving parallel to the beach at a much slower pace, running and running. Finally I stopped, tried to still my heaving breaths, tried to listen but could hear only my own gasps. No more shots. I must control myself before he heard me. In a while, I crept like an animal ready to spook, crept back toward the beach. He was nowhere in sight.

Could he be concealed, waiting for me to appear? Could he be behind me in the trees? I listened. I looked. How many times had he fired? I tried to count. Five or six. I wasn't sure. If six, he might have returned for more ammo. If five, he might still be lurking for the one last shot that would settle my hash for good.

I broke out onto the beach full blast, running for all I was worth, my gaze jumping before and behind, ready to dodge for cover if I saw him, then ahead to watch my step along the crooked shoreline -- it was not the time or place to lose my footing and go sprawling.

I continued on until I judged a turn south would bring me to about the midpoint of the runway, the mile long mostly open strip of old asphalt where the tern colony resided. Rather than moving slowly through the birds as was my usual habit in order not to disturb them, I took a good look and raced to the other side, sending them rising up before me in mass flight, squawking out their protest at the intrusion.

I had to reach my tent, arm myself, see to Stephanie. Careful now. Could Mac have made his way to the tent ahead of me, was even then lying in ambush? I crept and ducked closer, trying not to breathe, my eyes and ears and body on full alert, squinting furiously to adjust my near-sighted focus. Popolo and Sista, tied to long tethers in the shady nook, would bark if Mac were about, wouldn't they? No, not necessarily. They were getting used to him. He talked to them, petted them, had become familiar with all the Hawaiian words I used with them. At the least, they would be on their feet, paying attention to whoever disturbed their eternal napping. No, there they were, all stretched out.

They stirred when they heard me, lifting their heads as I strode straight to unzip the flap. Inside, I quickly got the .22 pistol from its drawer, loaded it. I slipped into a pair of shorts, grabbed a shirt.

Stephanie!

I rushed out to the water's edge a dozen feet away, peered out around the foliage growing along the lagoon shore. Iola floated tranquilly at her moorage. The yellow dinghy was tied alongside, which meant that Steph was aboard. Had she heard the shots? If so, had they meant anything to her? Mac had often fired his gun, taking whimsical aim at coconuts or fish, but upwind they were heard only as muted pops.

I wound my way toward Iola through the shadowy strip of growth between the runway and the lagoon until I could make out Sea Wind lying west across the small bay that marked the end of the runway -- where I waited. What else was there to do but wait? I waited. If Mac came, I would have a clear view of his approach. I would be ready.

Unless he took the same circuitous route I had. Oh, shit! He could be coming up behind me! Grimly, I retraced my steps. Seeing that Popolo and Sista were still lying about, I turned toward the refrigerator house, peeked inside like a cop ready to shoot if necessary. Nothing. On to the runway for a long, careful view up and down the length of it.

I trod slowly back across the width of it, gazing toward Sea Wind, trying to see the inland entrance to the equipment shed. Reaching the other side, I crouched for cover in the bushes, studying Sea Wind, the equipment shed, and Iola, glancing north and east. North was impossible, all jungle. It would be dark soon. What should I do? I didn't know. I was numb. Nothing. There was nothing to do. Just remain alert, protect Steph and myself. It was too late to do anything else.

I edged a few yards to the north, peering into the palms and dense growth. Where was Mac? I returned to my previous position and received a shock. Steph was sitting on a bench just ashore of Iola, her face turned toward Sea Wind. Was she looking for me? Had she been to the tent? If so, her next logical move would be to amble on over to the Graham campsite.

I concealed the .22 by shoving it down the front of my cutoffs and buttoning my shirt over it. Then I began to walk toward her in what I hoped was a casual stroll. I didn't know what to say to her, how to warn her of the sudden danger.

She saw me, grinned and waved. I sat down next to her, trying desperately to appear as my usual self, to still my agitation. "What'cha been up to, baby?"

"Ah, you know," I shrugged. "Wandering about."

"Wanna smoke a doobie with me?"

"Sure." Maybe it would calm me down.

I noticed a trembling in my hand as I took the lit joint from her, tried to control it, hoping she wouldn't notice. She was relaxed, a serene look composing her features. We watched the sky change colors, the sun setting in the west -- there, tranquilly beautiful, sat Sea Wind, no human figures moving to disturb the picture postcard perfection of it. I didn't feel the grass at all.

Steph tilted her head at me, batting her eyes, blessing me with a dimpled smile to let me know that I was looked upon with favor, that I had been chosen.

"How ya feel, baby?"

It was an invitation, the sexual innuendo well mixed with good humor, one I rarely turned down. The timing in this case, however, couldn't have been worse. There was just no way I could devote myself to the requirements of making love, no way I could get in tune with the overtures to that rhapsody.

I hesitated, trying out the idea of delivering the breaking tragedy on the evening news: Listen, kiddo, Mac killed Muff not twenty minutes ago. He shot her, I swear to God! Why? Well, it was an accident -- he was trying to shoot me. Why? Well, he caught us fucking -- imagine that!

He's gone crazy. He may try to kill both of us! Why should he want to kill you, darlin'? Because you'll be a witness when he shoots me! Mac's not like that? Jesus Christ, he just killed poor Muff! He just tried to kill me! I'm telling you, he's fucking clear out of his head!

I couldn't tell her, I just couldn't. I knew that first message to rise from her compassion would be an inclination to offer herself in a mission to alleviate the pain -- not to me. She would want to go over and console Mac. Me, I was not constituted to embark on such a blatant path of naiveté.

"Tired," I replied instead, slumping for effect. "Exhausted." Maybe Mac wouldn't come. Maybe he would carry Muff aboard Sea Wind, sail out of the lagoon so he could bury her at sea, then go on with his grief, not return to Palmyra. -- and Steph would never know, never have to know.

"I'll give you an overall body massage. I owe you one."

Oh, god! "Not tonight, babe. I'm not feeling so well." Her eyes filled with concern. "What's the matter, baby?"

"Nothing. You know, just got the yucks over Dickie's not showing up on schedule, having to go to Fanning."

She pooh-poohed that with a flick of the wrist. "He'll show up eventually. He's just operating on island time, by-and-by, you know. You should be used to it by now."

"Yeah."

She sighed. "Well, I guess I'll just curl up with Puffer then, get back to my book."

"Maybe I'll join you later, after. I feed the mutts." "Yeh?"

"Maybe a. cup of tea'll perk me up."

Sly, lying devil that I am, I had a small plan. I'd get her aboard Iola, keep the dinghy ashore so she couldn't leave. I'd bring up Popolo and Sista, tether them near the boat, stand guard through the night.

What then? Well, that was as far as I'd gotten.

I returned to the tent, went through the feeding and watering motions, feeling antsy all the while. What if Mac roared up shouting threats, daring me to show my cowardly face, began shooting at Iola? I remembered the rifle, the .30 caliber Marlin lever-action hunting rifle, and dug it cut of its wedged place between mattress and headboard. Removing the cloth it was wrapped in, I wiped the excess of oil put on it for protection against the humidity, loaded it from the handful of shells -- a better answer to a .357 Magnum than a. dinky .22 caliber pistol.

I brought the dogs down, tethered them to nearby trees. They would hear any strange sounds in the night before me and give warning. I sat on the bench to wait, ruffling Popolo until he grew bored with me and stretched out on the ground.

The golden light from Iola's portholes dimmed, went dark. The surf on the outer reefs rumbled, the breeze whispered, water slapped against Iola's hull, Terns cried from time to time. There were no lights or human movement on Sea Wind.

I was doing nothing, just sitting there, beginning to nod. Had I heard a new sound, one foreign to those of nature? I listened. Nothing. I stood to walk a dozen paces to the water's edge at the end of the runway, to squint at Sea Wind. It was creepy, this ordinariness. I should go closer, see if I could see anything, hear any better, learn something. What was Mac doing? No, let it alone, I told myself, leave well enough be.

I made my way toward the equipment shed, treading softly to the side of the lane. A sudden crash of sound sent me leaping into the bushes. What the hell was that! Trying to still my heart, I waited, my hands tense on the rifle. After some minutes, I heard the sputter of an outboard motor and, knowing Mac had to be on the water, rushed to the inland side of the equipment shed, into the dark tunnel of it, feeling around the huge tires of the roadgrader, where I paused.

I could hear the outboard changing pitch, revving up. Was he headed toward Iola? I turned and ran back that way, but soon stopped. The sound was receding to the west, the opposite direction. What was he doing? What was he doing?

I retraced my steps, walked edgily through the shed, dreading to find Muff lying where I'd last seen her. She was gone. Maybe she hadn't died, was only wounded. Had Mac taken her aboard Sea Wind? But, if so, surely he wouldn't leave her there. No, she was dead after all, she had to be. Yes, he had taken her in the Zodiac, the quickest and easiest way, out over the western reef where a shallow draft vessel could reach the open sea.

Sea Wind was dark. I crept on through the campsite, out toward a brief jut of land so I could look west, perhaps see the shadow of the Zodiac on the water. I surely saw the metal locker taken from the old rescue launch, now moved from its usual place just inside a corner of the shed, but perhaps I didn't want to see it. When I had turned from my futile gaze westward, though, there it was before me, an anomaly, about three feet or so long, two and a half feet or so wide and deep, like a large trunk, the lid firmly on top.

Suddenly I knew what was inside, didn't want to know, would not look to confirm the thought I refused to think. I became aware that I was sweating, my lungs heaving for air, feeling sick with sudden panic. The outboard sputter rose up out of the eerie silence, growing louder. I fled.

Halfway back on the return path, I stopped again to listen, to see if the Zodiac would cross the open water between Sea Wind and Iola, the rifle ready in my hands. No, the sound abruptly died down and stopped. I crept on back to take up my post near Iola, having woke the hounds who soon returned to their nocturnal drowsing.

No unusual movement or sound, and time dragged its feet. I was exhausted, not knowing what I thought or felt, cuddled into a numbness that demanded the escape of sleep. I went to the tent, fired up the campstove, brewed a cup of tea, then returned sipping, trying to make myself alert.

A volley of booms reverberated across the little bay and I dropped the cup, leaping with electric shock into the trees, grabbing for the rifle where I'd leaned it against the trunk of a palm.

Popolo and Sista were up and about, but not barking.

A whump of sound rolled toward us, and Sea Wind was suddenly limned in a gush of flame. My god, what had he done? Was he setting fire to Sea Wind? No, the light of it came from the campsite beyond, a bonfire. Light and shadow flickered up the palms to their drooping fronds, shimmering against the flat surfaces of the shed, emphasizing the square darkness of the opening. There was no movement, but whether I saw Mac's figure or merely imagined it, I wasn't sure. There was a beginning ache behind my eyes from the strain of hard squinting, of trying to refocus my myopic vision.

I felt drawn like a magnet to return, having to know what was going on. From the inland entrance to the shed, I could see the light of the fire, but not the flame itself, illuminating the campsite at the other end. No sight of Mac.

I backed away, continuing softly along the lane past the adjacent house, catching a stronger flare of light in the space between the two buildings. I snuck along the far sidewall of the house, dared a quick peek around the corner.

The flame was coming out of the metal container. There was a vaguely familiar smell in the air that made me think of odors that came off a hamburger grill when it's rubbed with pumice stone and wiped with a piece of burlap. I rushed away on tiptoe, my hand over my mouth, through the scraggly strand of hedges that once bordered the house, trying desperately to mute the sounds of my stomach turning inside out.

Oh, Mac, what the fuck are you doing! Without any logical reason, I was suddenly angry at him. What the fuck did he think he was doing?

I tried to spit out the bitter-sour taste in my mouth, tried to get hold of myself, to, for chrissakes, think! Well, of course it made sense after all. It was a cremation, not a barbecue. You couldn't dig a hole and bury anyone in the ground on Palmyra -- it's coral base was like rock. Under the circumstances, a cremation on land was as sensible as a burial at sea. That's why he had gone to the other end of the island, to fetch a quantity of the old aviation gasoline, stored in a concrete bunker by the 50-gallon drum.

The large canisters were all over the place, most empty, a few utilized for rain catchment. I had one at the tent to collect rain from gutters rigged on the two sides of its sloping roof, water I used for tea and washing up, for Popolo and Sista to drink.

In sight of the bathtub lay a great rusting mass of them. But only at the storage dump on the western end did they contain perfectly volatile gasoline. We had all used it for outboards and small gas generators, chainsaws, any motor that required gasoline.

When I returned to look for Mac, the sole figure upon whom to direct the remnants of my anger and disgust, my fear, I found him sitting on the ground, his back against the shed, legs asprawl. He was swigging from a bottle, watching the flames, which had all but died down within the container.

I watched him stand and turn to disappear into the shed. He soon returned carrying a bucket, casting its contents into the container, causing a whoosh of flame to flare up.

He returned to enter the shed again, only to come right back out dragging another of the rectangular cubes of metal, the twin of the first. They were from a set of four installed in wells in the old rescue launch, perhaps originally serving as equipment lockers.

He positioned it some feet to the side of the first, then returned yet again into the shed, where he remained for some minutes, a metallic banging sound winging out the dark square of its open end. What in the hell! What now?

He stepped out to look around and I ducked back. When I chanced a peek, he was striding toward a 50-gallon drum stood upright at the corner of the shed which, I knew, he kept full of rainwater. He grasped it, rocking it, trying to topple it. It had to weigh near four hundred pounds. But then he gave it up abruptly and strode over to remove the lid and look within the second container.

Returning again into the shed, he made several trips carrying the bucket to slosh its liquid content into the container, and as I watched this strange ritual, everything clicked into place in my mind. The real and horrible question was what did he intend for the second container?

Mac had only been able to remove two of them, the second most recently -- the crash I had heard. The other two were wedged too tightly into their framework -- the metallic but futile banging. He needed three altogether -- the business with the rain barrel. But upon reconsideration, he had decided that the second metal container could accommodate his plan. It was large enough to hold two bodies snuggled together in a rictus of death, had been prepared with gasoline.

Unable to contain myself, I stepped out from my hidden corner to confront him, the rifle cocked and ready in my hands. "I know what you're up to! I won't let you!"

"You," he snarled. "You fucking bastard! I'll fix you!"

He pulled the .357 from his pocket and fired, then again as I jumped back behind the corner, the clap of the shots like thunder.

Jesus! Not trusting my luck to look again, I held my arms out, the rifle in my hands, pointing blindly. You motherfucker! With a twitch of a finger, I sent a bigger crack back at him, seeing a strobe of flame burst from the muzzle -- let the motherfucker know!

I drew back, levered in another shell and ejecting the spent one, then chanced a peek. Like a wraith, he loomed up out of the night to meet me in a face to face collision. Swallowing my heart, I clutched at him, desperate to grab his gunhand. He grabbed at the rifle barrel, trying to wrench it away.

We fought in a frenzy, twisting, turning, and grunting. The rifle went off in a deafening blast. I slammed him back against the side of the house, momentarily losing my grip on his wrist, and felt a sudden stab of shock as he brought the butt or barrel of the gun down on my shoulder joint. I pressed against him, crowding him ear to ear in a panic to grab his gunhand, trying to knee him. He ducked and butted my chin with his head.

"I'll kill you, I'll kill you," he snarled at me. "You rotten sonofabitch!"

The panic grew in me. How could I be losing? I was taller, stronger, weighed more. I should have been able to cream him, but he fought like a madman, a wild animal. Suddenly, I let go of the rifle, pulled the little .22 loose and swung, connecting with the side of his head as he ducked and drove forward. Rather than resist, I went with it, pulling and twisting. We went down together in a flash-bang of light and thunderclap as the .357 went off between us, both of us hitting the ground, rolling with the momentum of it. Then I was free of him, up and running, crouched over trying to outrun the next bullet that I knew would blow me to hell. Past the burning container I scrambled off balance like an ape using my hands to keep from sprawling forward, jinked and dove into the blackness of the equipment shed, rolled, regained my feet and sped on to the faint light at the other end.

Any second I expected to hear the last explosion and twisted desperately to fall behind the huge rear tires of the roadgrader, ducking under the high frame, slamming into the blade resting upon the cement, throwing myself over it to come out between the two front wheels.

I picked myself up, tore along the path, leapt aside to roll behind a bush. Grasping the pistol in both hands, I cocked the hammer and waited, my breath heaving like a bull about to be slaughtered by the matador. Now he had the rifle and the .357.

I waited.

And waited.

Had some animal cunning asserted itself into his raging mind, sent him lurking into darkness to stalk me? I heard things, imagined things, jumping at every noise, jerking my head about, my nerves strung taut and throbbing.

I waited, wallowing in self-contempt and humiliation and fear. You fucking coward, I silently accused myself. You yellow fucking piece of shit! You ran away! You fucking pussy!

My jaw clenched in resolve, I stood and stepped forward, back the way I had fled. Was he waiting for me, even then drawing me into his sights? Fuck you, asshole! Take your best shot!

I skirted the inland entrance -- too many hiding places -- and worked out wide around the house, all my senses alert for the slightest move, the slightest sound. When I could make out the dark shape of the corner of the house where we had collided, a flickering light outlining the mouth of the metal container, I crouched down, went forward onto my knees, stretched out with the gun held before me, ready to fire.

I heard a sound, all but incomprehensible -- a groan, a growl, a gurgle? I wanted to scream at him, Come on, motherfucker! But I didn't dare. Any noise would reveal my position, bring on those mind-numbing claps of thunder trying to kill me. I strove with all my might not to gasp, needing air, my whole body aquiver in adrenaline.

It came, the crack of doom, the great boom, and I flinched, forcing myself not to get up and run away in panic. I clutched my hands tighter around the handle of the gun, seeking a target. I had seen no muzzle flash, heard only the clap of it like a palpable force washing through me.

It seemed that I would never emerge from the blanket of night that threatened to stifle me that the darkness would last forever, the dawn only a fantasy of the past.

*****

He lay on his back, one leg bent under the other. I couldn't see his eyes, whether he was looking at me. The rifle lay a few feet away, the Magnum a few inches from his hand. He didn't move.

"Mac?"

No answer. Nothing. Ever again.

I picked up the guns, walked over to the back steps of the house, laid them all down, sat down myself, hung my head, feeling utterly exhausted. A weakness, a listlessness, a leaden blankness overwhelmed me, and I simply sat like a stone.

When at last I tried to move, I felt as though I had aged, become an arthritic old man, stiff and slow and full of aches, treading under water. Something fierce gripped my head like a chain being twisted tighter.

I had to move, had to do something. What? I can't let Steph see any of this, I thought. I'll have to clean it up, make it go away.

I went to him, straightened his bent leg, and clutched his feet to drag him to the unlit container. I knelt to grab his shirt, sticky with blood, pulled him to a sitting position. My hands went under his armpits to reach around in order to grip and lift him. As I embraced him, my face cheek to cheek with his, and tightened my grip to heave upward, a soft "Ahh," whispered into my ear.

I leapt back, sprawling, crawling away, an electric shock of terror knocking my breath away. My god, I thought, he's alive!

I knelt there gasping, ten feet away, squinting desperately in the dark to discern some movement, hear another sound from him. After a time, perceiving nothing and willing my body to calm down, to control my jitters, I inched my way back to him, daring to put my hand on his chest. I tried touching his neck to feel for a pulse. I laid my ear to his chest, moved it to his mouth -- no movement, no pulse, no breath. But he had breathed, moaned -- no, not a moan really, more like a sigh.

I put my hand over his mouth, pinched his nostrils closed, reasoning that if he was alive, he would have to move, the autonomic nervous system taking over to resist oxygen starvation. Nothing. But hardly thirty seconds into it, I thought, is that true? As kids, my sister and brother and I had sometimes worked mischief waking each other up by this method. But that was with a healthy sleeping body and mind. Mac, if he were alive, was severely injured, perhaps in a coma. Holy shit, was I suffocating him? I jerked my hands away.

I went through it again, palm to chest, fingers to neck, pressing my ear into the stickiness, listening at his lips. He was dead, he had to be. I tried again, pulling him up, slipping my hands under his armpits to reach around his back to grip him to me, paused to listen and feel -- telling myself it had to be some phenomenon of residual air trapped in his lungs, air that I had squeezed out, or else I was going crazy with fear -- and I heaved him up, straining erect to swing and lower him into the container, breathing the gasoline fumes, letting him go, then lifting his legs one at a time, bending them, tucking him in.

Covered in blood and gasoline, I removed my shirt and tossed it in after him, then staggered gasping for air out onto the tiny point of land, stepped down into the water to wash. Frantically scrubbing at myself with my hands, feeling uncontrollable shudders coursing through my body, I ducked my head under the water, immersing all. I could still smell the gasoline, imagined the metallic odor of the blood.

I waded back ashore, picked up a stick, a piece of dried palm frond, stuck it into the still flickering container toward the black lump of Muff, the greasy smell renewing itself, turning my head away, jabbing blindly. I pulled it out burning to toss in with Mac. Whoosh, the flames shot up.

I turned away from the heat, turned to lift the cover and place it over Muff's remains. I left her, walked west to the seaplane ramp, waded out to my knees to sit in the water up to my neck, washing, scrubbing, rubbing at myself. Leaning my head back, I could see the stars, they moving in their courses, me in mine, the heat of our bodies both dissipating, theirs into the coldness of space, mine into the growing coldness of the sea, becoming one with it, the earth, a fragment of a star, my heart, soul, and mind, all sailing through the vast coldness.

Ah, I had to move, absolutely had to move, and stood to feel a rush of warmth, waded out, beginning the trudge back, thoughts weighing nothing becoming a burden. Just do what you have to do, I told myself. Quit thinking and do what you have to do.

I placed the second lid over Mac, unable to look inside, then pushed and pulled and wrestled them to the water's edge. I found some wire in the equipment shed, twisted and bent it to break into two pieces. Lifting the containers one at a time, I kicked the lengths of wire under them, twisting the ends around together to hold the lids on.

I fetched a neatly bundled coil of nylon line from the floor among the stuff Mac had dumped out to empty the first container. I tied it in crisscrossing loops around the lengths and breadths of them, knotting the two containers in tandem.

I untied the Zodiac, pulled it around to the point, stepping into the water to toss the end of the line onto its floor. Pulling and grunting, I manhandled the containers down into the water, stepped into the Zodiac, started the outboard, and began to tow them, the metal scrapping over coral until they floated in deeper water. I would take them out onto the open sea for burial. Would I try to perform some poor service, try a prayer?

Should I go out through the passage? No, go straight west, out over the shallow reef, which was quicker. Progress was slow, the rear container, the one containing Muff, was sinking lower into the water. Almost to the end of Cooper, it sank, pulling the one ahead, which had all but lost its buoyancy too.

I cut the engine, unslipped the towline, watched the nearest container dip beneath the surface, tossed the line after, followed it undulating whitely to disappear into the depths of the lagoon just beyond the shelving reef shoreward.

Sitting there, biting my teeth, drifting about gently over the placid sea, none but the surf to whisper ephemeral comfort, the only thing I could think of was a childhood prayer -- Now I lay me down to sleep I pray the Lord my soul to keep. If I should die before I wake, I pray the Lord my soul to take.

Who was it for, them or me?

*****

Finally, I pulled at the starter rope -- to no avail. I squeezed the rubber bulb to force fuel into the engine and tried again. Being only a few yards from the coral shelf, over which a growing layer of sand formed a beach further in, I tilted the outboard forward to lock its shaft and prop up out of the water, unshipped the oars and rowed that way. Refixing the oars to the gunnels, I stepped out into the shallows to drag the inflatable up toward the line of palms and tangled undergrowth.

Noticing there was water inside the boat, I unhooked the gas-tank, lifted it out to set upon the sand, and turned the Zodiac over to lean against the shore brush all but upsidedown. Then I walked back, leaving the beach for the inland footpath. Passing through the equipment shed, I saw little lumps moving across the cement floor, heard faint clicking sounds.

I bent to look more closely. They were hermit crabs who lived in seashells, dragging them wherever they went. Scavengers, the call of blood had brought them to congregate where Muff had fallen and died. The sound of their eating was like a clicking of knitting needles.

Continuing on to retrieve the guns, I picked up the half-empty bottle of booze Mac had been drinking. The hermit crabs had also gathered where he had lain. I rushed away with bile in my throat.

Back in my tent, I chugalugged what was left in the bottle -- rum -- and collapsed into unconsciousness.

*****

Friday, August 30, 1974

After the awful dream of the night before, a dream that wasn't a dream, I awoke Friday morning to the heat of the day, staggering about the confines of the tent in a fog to prepare tea. Cup in hand I stepped out to greet sky and water and earth, my eyes dewy in the glare of light, expecting everything to somehow look different, dark, drab, and ominous. But it all seemed the same. Whatever changes having occurred in the world, they were subtle and natural, tiny unnoticed perceptions. It was me that was changed, the observer who'd been caught up in the tide of violent events, events that had tried to pound the life from me, but, failing that, to beat me out of my normal state of existence.

Should I have been surprised if I had awakened to find myself in the deepest pit of hell? Perhaps hell is only a state of life and it is only the bundle of one's habits that serve to pilot him through the murky abyss of himself and everything else.

I sucked deep breaths of pure unpolluted air, hoping to ease the throbbing after-effects of too much rum and too little sleep. I heard Stephanie call, a plaintive note in her voice.

"Baby, will you wake your ass up? You've left me stranded again!"

Oh, shit.

I stepped out until I could see Iola, caught Steph's eye, and waved to let her know I was on my way.

Stumbling through the day, I worried about my secrets while working and sweating, going through the motions. The batteries now fully charged from the generator, I remembered it was supposed to be left so Mac and Muff could use the refrigerator, and I dragged it back to the refrigerator house.

Then I remembered Mac's gun. It was lying there on my desk, right out in plain view. How could I possibly explain if Steph saw it? I hurried to the tent to retrieve it. What should I do with it? Throw it in the drink? No, return it.

I rewrapped the rifle, replaced it, and stuck the .22 in its drawer. Ah, and fuck, there's the empty rum bottle. Get rid of that. I took it out, flipped the cap, held it under water until it filled, glanced toward Iola, and tossed it. I stuck Mac's pistol in my waistband, put on an untucked shirt to conceal it, and trod carefully across the runway to disappear into the foliage until I could make my way past the area where Steph could see me if she happened to look, until I could enter the equipment shed unseen.

I stepped into the fiberglass dinghy to pull myself over to Sea Wind. Climbing aboard, I peeked toward Iola to make sure Steph couldn't see me and hurried around into the cockpit and down the hatch.

From where had Mac taken the gun the time he showed it to me? A small drawer to starboard next to the athwartships forward bunk, right. No, wait. Would he leave it there filled with expended shells, useless if he needed it in an emergency? No, he must keep it loaded.

I opened the cylinder, seeing only five cartridges in the six slots, a common misconception by amateurs that it was dangerous to carry a live round under the hammer. I removed the expended ones and reloaded it with live rounds from the drawer, sticking the empties in my pocket. When I crossed over to shore, I would throw them out into the lagoon.

I saw a tray on the dinette holding a couple of liquor bottles, a can of peanuts, and a package of fig newtons, all having been opened and partially depleted. I grabbed a handful of butts from the ashtray to stick in my pocket.

Was that it? Was that it? Anything else? I studied the ground. There was no sign that the metal containers had ever sat there. There were only a few hermit crabs left near where Mac and Muff had lain.

I walked away to sneak back.

Oh, shit! The Zodiac! I had to retrieve the Zodiac! Well, wait just a minute now -- maybe not. Mac and Muff were gone, which we, Steph and I, would discover when we came for supper. The Zodiac could be gone -- fishing or something. Sure. They had an accident - - the inflatable had somehow overturned, hit a coral projection and capsized. They'd been flung into the shark-infested waters. The Zodiac had been blown ashore upsidedown. No, leave the Zodiac where it was. Anything else? No. I couldn't think of anything.

*****

It was after we'd dressed and gone to answer the dinner invitation, while smoking a joint Steph had brought, that I remembered the empty cartridge I'd ejected after firing the rifle blindly around the corner of the house.

I stood and wandered about, trying to appear aimless, that I was restlessly killing time while we awaited the return of Mac and Muff. I made it to the corner of the house, scanning the ground all about, when Steph called.

"What are you doing?"

I shrugged. "Nothing."

"You look like you're looking for something."

I thought furiously. "Coins, lost coins."

"What?"

"You gotta figure that when the military was here, they all had coins made before the war. Might find one from the thirties that's valuable, you know."

"Yeh?"

"Who knows, maybe pirates buried their treasures here."

"Yeh, right."

" I read that somewhere – A Spanish Treasure ship"

"C'mon over here and watch the sunset with me." I joined her, put an arm around her shoulders. "It's pretty, isn't it?"
"Yeah, beautiful."
"The changing colors."
"Yeah."
"How long's it been since you tasted lipstick?"
"Huh?"
"C'mon, how long?"
I thought. Not very long ago. Muff had worn it when she'd visited my tent -- when? -- a few days ago, a week? "Must have been Maui," I said. "No, maybe when we were in Honolulu."
"Now's yer chance," she offered, fluttering her eyes and puckering up.
I kissed her, kissed her again, tasting the lipstick, liking it, smelling the faint aroma, kissed her and wished I could keep on kissing her forever.

###

AFTERWORD

I contemplate the completed manuscript before me as though it may somehow complete the malleable stuff of my soul and fix all my past selves into final form. But I only feel as if I'd vomited without disgorging the object of my sickness. Real life intrudes into the present to remind me that the paint on my cell wall still peels with excruciating slowness. It intrudes as though I had expressed some wish to be saved from my vices. Ah, no, please, let me dream of good strong drink, a stony joint, some blues music, and the endless subtleties of an erotic woman. Allow me this small semblance of contentment. Soon enough I will perceive in the not-so-dim hints that my real life is one I've hardly led. I will live my days forward and understand them backward. You can't feed dinosaurs to hungry folk for the simple reason that they no longer exist.

But what o' yerself, me boyo? Ah, I diminish by the minute!

*****

Labor Day has just passed as I approach my sixty-first birthday.

It has been a tradition since I have been at the U. S. Penitentiary at Lompoc, California, these past twelve years for the warden to treat the inmate population to barbecue-picnics twice a year -- Independence Day and Labor Day.

Since the first one, I have never attended. I skip the chicken and wienies and hamburgers, the baked beans and potato salad, the watermelon and soft drinks. I skip the camaraderie of my fellow desperadoes for the hermitage of my cavelike cell. The heavy greasy smell of searing meat reminds me of the smells I once smelled of human bodies burning -- it winds up into my nostrils to permeate my soul with a sickness.

Instead I sit alone in the cellblock, the noise of one hundred and seventy men like the chattering of a giant birdcage or the mad utterances from a mental ward all quiet now, leaving me in the relative silence to meditate upon a past day, an old man, and a bird in flight, all the faces of people and their baggage that ride the train of my memories.

*****

Hereinafter let Bugliosi be the Bug, he being a sort of obsessive-compulsive fruitcake, and let Henderson be the Hen, he being a layer of rotten eggs. Let us then make the point that there are criminals and there are criminals, judges and judges, juries and juries, lawyers and lawyers, and that I am a great fan of the Bug, the humblest man in the world. Everything is true and everything is false. There is not a humble bone in Bela Lugosi's body. There is no part of the pig that ain't pork. A running away is a running toward. If we look far outward, we will see our own assholes and find God in a flashbulb of orgasm. Is there a black hole in the universe or a universe around a black hole? You can lead a horse to water but a pencil must be lead. Does anyone ever tell the truth all the time? Ask the Bug. Can the FBI, those inveterate heros of the police world, commit and suborn perjury, manufacture evidence from thin air and lose it in the ether -all in aid of insuring a suspect whom they believe guilty does not escape his just desserts -- and not be deemed to be framing someone? Or is this merely a cute game of semantics? Don't ask the Bug. Can a judge be deemed sober when he acts like an arrogant drunken fool? Can anyone disprove the thesis that the Bug is the only competent lawyer in the world? Can a half-fucked fox in a forest fire ever fuck again? There are believers and unbelievers with never a twain to meet.

Does anyone wonder why I admire the Bug? Prison is a place where one learns criminal activities and all criminals wish to better themselves. I fancy that I might learn to raise the level of my con by studying the Great Bug. After all, it is the successful conman who doesn't get caught out in the art of hornswoggling the suckers. Can anyone not admire a man so sure of himself, so brimful of self-esteem? Would anyone be surprised if they were to learn that his will contains a codicil setting aside a certain portion of his millions in furtherance of his canonization as a saint?

He is the great debater, a weaver of words and facts and theories, an opportunist of the first order. He has an answer for everything. People, I tell you now, Eric Hoffer's classic work, The True Believer, is all about the Bug! Never mind that he views a true believer as one possessing a degree of self-contempt which only serves to sharpen his eye for imperfections in others, as well as a correspondingly strong penchant for revealing in others the blemishes he hides in himself, the Bug is humble and duty-bound by honor. Never mind that Hoffer says we lie loudest when we lie to ourselves and that charlatanism in some degree is indispensable in leading the flock to a shearing, the Bug can pass a polygraph test. Well, at least one administered by David T. Raskin, if not one by Donald T. Lykken.

And speciousness, ah, that magnificent key element in any conman's repertoire, which means beautiful or plausible or showy, which means having a deceptive attraction or allure, which means, gasp, having a false look of truth of genuineness. Never mind, all great conmen are great sophists. Conmen make money through their use of deception, they create seemingly credible images for the gullible and charge them for believing the lies. Forget all that even if the Bug is a great sophist, rich and smug in his artistry, he's not the kind of guy who'd put a scorpion in your pocket and then ask you for a quarter -- is he? You gotta love a mug like the Bug who's fond of quoting H. L. Mencken when he said that nobody every went broke underestimating the intelligence of the American people. If this be a case of idle worship, who can save me from my enemies?

*****

If charred human bones are found in a box, the natural conclusion follows that murder was done.

But the discoverer of this box and bones, the sole witness so far as is known, never claimed to see any bones in the box. They were all found strewn in beach sand except for one which was found in the shallow separated lid of the box. Despite all the expert testimony of forensic scientists, there was no clear evidence that the bones were ever in the box. Something had been burned in it, something containing animal proteins and fats. Yet a jury believed the bones had been in the box and that they had been burned and, thus, that murder was done. Never mind the attempt of an inept lawyer to show otherwise when he, himself, knew the contrary, the bones were in the box.

The only mystery is how they got there -- in the box and on the beach. Many believe that I put the body that contained those bones into that box, but I did not. The body I put into a similar box has never been found. Both bodies went into the two boxes on the same night; both were linked together and towed westward toward the open sea over the shallow reefs; and both sank together inside the lagoon in water that may have been as deep as one hundred and fifty feet.

Bones do not float we learn from the forensic scientists. We also learn that gases forming within the first several days from putrefying flesh can lift a body and box from the depths, but not if the gases can escape through holes and a loose-fitting lid. After all, how did they sink in the first place? The box in the courtroom contained obvious holes.

Wherefore then one box and its set of bones on a beach? Storm and current? The large waves of forms do not penetrate past the surrounding reefs and islets into Palmyra's lagoon and the current in the deeper parts is a gentle one curving from east to west to southwest out the boat passage through the reefs.

Yet, Sharon Jordan found them six years and a few days short of five months later on the southwest shore of Cooper Island. The Bug speculates in the name of Sharon Jordan that the box could have been washed ashore by the latest storm which had died down only the night before. Perhaps he even read her mind as she not only identified the skull she'd found with a hole in it as female, but thought "the poor woman had obviously been shot, placed in a box, and then -- set on fire!" (Page 170-180, ATSWT, Bug)

Did the box somehow levitate up out of the depths, it's holes miraculously plugged, and just as miraculously empty of the water that sank it in the first place, and float ashore on the winds of fate?

Imaginary Scenario One

Ray Landrum watched Sharon Jordan through his binoculars from Home Islands where she strolled nude along the southwestern shore of Cooper Island, directly across the lagoon from him.

Would she find the box he had placed there, its grisly contents dumped in a fan of skull and bones upon the sand, the box he had caught on a heavy cord while fishing for shark and had so laboriously heaved ashore, unwinding the old length of electrical wire that had held the lid in place? Or had it been the anchor of his vessel, Lahaina Turkey, that had hooked the box?

He hoped she would find it. He didn't want to be directly involved. He remembered reading about that couple who'd killed another couple here and stole their boat. He knew the news of its discovery would bring a hoard of official types, probably the FBI, who'd be running all over the place asking questions. Now, all he had to say was that, yes, he'd notified the Coast Guard of the find at the Jordans' request. Then maybe they'd all go away and not look too closely into his past. Maybe he should have dumped the box and bones right back into the lagoon, leave the dead in their burial place, the living to go on living, but fate had acted to choose him and who was he to resist?

Imaginary Scenario Two

Perhaps it was a small cargo or fishing boat out of Buenaventura on the Pacific coast of Columbia, a small harbor a mere fifty miles from Cali, one of the two main centers of cocaine cartels in South America, that entered the lagoon at Palmyra in late 1979 or early 1980 after a four thousand mile voyage. Or maybe a boat out of Taiwan making an unscheduled stop in Luzon in the Philippines to take on containers of hashish before continuing the five thousand mile voyage to Palmyra.

Whichever, it would mark its position in the lagoon by carefully plotted sightings from prominent landmarks before the crew began dumping the sealed metal barrels or canisters full of cocaine or hashish into a hundred and fifty feet of water. Neither ship could enter an American port without coming under special scrutiny by U. S. Customs and DEA agents.

The illicit cargo would sit until a motorlaunch out of Hawaii, perhaps similar to the one owned by Kama on Maui, or a motorsailer like **Caroline**, owned by Larry Briggs, would journey down with proper coordinates and a crew of scuba divers to retrieve the containers for transport to Honolulu, a way station for drugs entering the United States.

The retrieval boat, perhaps one similar to Ray Landrum's **Lahaina Turkey**, would mistakenly hoist the containers holding Mac's and Muff's remains and the latter would somehow end up on the beach of the nearby shelving coral of Cooper Island -- where it would sit until

Sharon Jordan strolled nudely along to find it.

In 1978, Bob Nielson, an entrepreneurial soul, visited Palmyra with a gleam in his eye. He found the remains of hundreds of pakalolo stalks forlornly rotting in the hundreds of 50-gallon drums cut in half to serve as planting pots. Someone had taken my plan, improvised a bit, and reaped a harvest of marijuana.

Nielson thought he might try developing the island as a resort area and after securing a lease from the Fullard-Leos, returned in early 1979 with John Bryden -- being delivered to Palmyra by none other than Dr. Martin Vitousek from Fanning.

Four months later, after Bryden had cleared 2500 feet of runway with the help of twenty-five Gilbertese Islanders hired from Christmas Island, Nielson returned in a PBY plane with some supplies to begin work on his project. They enlarged the runway to 4000 feet to accommodate C-130 cargo planes. During the next year they developed a village and built six houses near the old seaplane ramp.

Nielson also hired Ray Landrum out of Lahaina, Maui, and his 150-foot long Japanese fishing boat, **Lahaina Turkey**, to deliver equipment and supplies. Landrum had made one delivery and returned to Honolulu to take on another load. He was delayed with engine trouble and did not complete the second delivery until well into 1980. Landrum's crew, apparently a drunken, disorderly lot, jumped ship and returend to Honolulu on a passing yacht. Landrum left **Lahaina Turkey**, with leaks and engine problems, anchored in the lagoon and took up homesteading on Home Islands.

Bryden in the meanwhile was also using the Gilbertese to work at reestablishing production of copra from the wild remains of the old plantation began by Judge Cooper.

Then along came the federal government in an attempt to condemn Palmyra for use as a nuclear waste disposal site. Nielson was forced to suspend his project in order to return to Honolulu and defend his lease by filing a lawsuit in federal court. It was heard by none other than, ahem, the Honorable Samuel P. King and was favorably decided in 1985 for Nielson -- but by then, he had gone on to other things.

Bryden remained with half the Gilbertese crew to continue his work at copra production, but gave up a few months later. He left three men behind to watch over the equipment. Nielson had left two dogs behind, which had multiplied into six, all adopted by the Gilbertese and Ray Landrum.

Perhaps the Gilbertese had inadvertently built a beach fire over the bones buried in the sand, which would account for the testimony of one forensic expert that some of the burns to bone had occurred years after death. If so, they must have ignored the empty metal box held in place by shore foliage growing down into it. Perhaps a dog found a bone or two missing from the incomplete skeleton about to be discovered.

Then, of course, the Jordans showed up in November, 1980, along with two other yachts with two other couples, the Princes, and Roger and Maureen. Ray's wife, Betty, had also hitched a ride down to visit his hermitage at Home Islands.

Two months later, Sharon Jordon, so she says, found the box and bones on the southwestern shore of Cooper Island. Apparently the four couples all got together to help look for more bones, all of which were placed into the box and dragged back to the Jordan campsite. Since

Landrum was the only one with a ham radio capable of raising Honolulu, he made the initial report to the Coast Guard.

Nielson returned for a brief visit in 1982 to find the island deserted except for a badly listing **Lahaina Turkey**, which he later heard had finally sunk inside the lagoon.

*****

I first heard from Nielson in 1992, when I received a letter from him in Australia. He had just read the Bug/Hen book and had written because of our common interest in sailing, islands, and having lived in Hawaii. Of particular interest was the fact of his discovery of the marijuana stumps growing out of the old gasoline drums cut in half and filled with a growing medium near the northeast point of Cooper, my planned departure point for Aviation Island.

Because of the timing, I immediately thought of Dickie and Carlos. In his testimony, Dickie had been a little vague as to the year he had visited Palmyra -- 1977 or 1978, but more exact that it was in February and October -- two visits eight months apart. Plenty of time to plant, grow, and harvest a crop of marijuana. Two months in preparation -cutting the drums in half, filling and planting them -- six months to mature, and a return in October to harvest and prepare for the smuggling run to the market in Honolulu.

It pleased me to have this fantasy, that my "crackpot idea," as Earle Partington called it, had been carried through to fruition. But of equal interest was some other information useful when it came to trying to resolve the paradox of floating bones and metal boxes. Nielson had written, "Palmyra has been used by drug smugglers for many years.

Rumor says that sometimes 10-20 tons of hashish was stored in sunken containers in the lagoon awaiting pickup. Also, the island had been used by Korean and Japanese boats as a place to seek shelter and an exchange point for contraband cargo."

A lovely speculation about Dickie and a possible hypothesis or two about the raising of bones and box from the floor of the lagoon a hundred and fifty feet down.

*****

Bug changed the names of some characters in his account of this case for what he calls "legal reasons." I have changed many names, too, not for legal reasons, but for the purpose of protecting the privacy of my friends. In the first version of this book, I felt a need to skirt around many issues, a need to be a bit less candid, because of my desire to protect my friends. To be completely honest and forthcoming meant possibly that their activities would come under undesirable scrutiny. Within this consideration was contained the possibility that they might be investigated and charged with complicity in my crimes. The corollary of this position is that I had also to restrain myself from confessing my own crimes for all the same reasons.

But then I belatedly realized there existed an escape hatch, so to speak, in various state and federal statutes of limitation. That is, the crimes mentioned were such that none of them could be prosecuted at this late date, the last of them having occurred during the period of my escape from McNeil Island between 1979-81, seventeen years as of this writing. Since neither I nor my friends, so far as I knew, had ever committed a capital crime, the single exception to statutes of limitation, we may therefore thank them for permitting the extraordinary candor exhibited in these pages.

A number of people, including myself, wanted to sue Bug for defamation of character and libel. Because of my penurious condition and my more or less fixed attitude that American courts do not dispense justice to the poor, I quickly discarded my notion as harebrained. But Earle Partington wrote to ask that I join him in a suit against the Bug, which I declined. The outcome of such a proceeding, just like the no-contest comparison between the legal abilities of each, was a foregone conclusion as far as I was concerned. The last I heard was of Partington's half-hearted determination to file a complaint with the bar association for unethical behavior. After having read Bug's book, I briefly contemplated filing a complaint against Partington not only for violation of the attorney-client privilege of confidentiality but also for being a bare-faced liar about it in order to defend against his ineptness. I have little respect for the prosecutors in this case, but even less for Partington.

Otherwise, I suppose the Bug wished, as they say, to protect the innocent. The question naturally arises as to whether the innocent in this case require protection and, if so, from what exactly. We are talking about adults here, not children, who, even in their lowest forms possess some modicum of intelligence. Of course, even bright people have hangups, biases and prejudices, phobias and obsessions, even moral lapses.

But because of these name changes in the Bug/Hen account, coupled to the relevant distortions of facts, I sometimes had a bit of difficulty in figuring out what and who was being talked about.

Then, of course, there was Jennifer Jenkins who, the more I read of in the Bug/Hen account, the more she became an all but fictional character. Jennifer Jenkins, you are now permitted to know, is Stephanie Stearns in real life, a personality somewhat different from what Bug depicts. But then, he himself confesses to some confusion when it came to understanding her behavior. He unsuccessfully attempts to sketch her character in traditional terms, desperately trying to contain her within the limitations of his own conventions.

By the time I had finished reading the Bug/Hen account, I couldn't believe that Stephanie had served as their principal source of information about the intimate details of our life together. I couldn't believe that she could so distort her own character and mine, to so misinform them about the details of so many events. I had to conclude that it was not Stephanie who was guilty. Yet, so far as I know, she took her share of the proceeds from book and movie and ran. She never, so far as I know, offered one word of protest as to the many points of error, misinformation, and unconscionable skewing of reality.

From the beginning the essential problem in coming to some reasonable determination of truth in this case lies in the central fact that everyone, from the Bug on down to most of the witnesses, the government prosecutors and FBI, not even to mention large segments of the public in Hawaii as established through a pre-trial poll, all leapt like starving coyotes on roadkill to the conclusion from the outset that murder had been done. Hence, a murderer was required -- nay, absolutely essential -- to prove the rightness of the reflexive feeding behavior of **canis latrans**, that roadkill represents justice to the starving predator.

The situation was analogous to one presented to the great sculptor, Auguste Rodin. Upon being asked how he would sculpt an elephant, he replied that he'd start with a very large block of stone and remove everything that wasn't an elephant. In the case at hand, a murderer was formed in a similar fashion. The Bug/Hen book, like the government's case, sought to portray a murderer because one was necessary to complete the fantasy. They began with a large body of evidence, incomplete as it was, and pared away everything that was not a murderer.

As I mentioned in the Foreword to this book, without the crime of homicide and a murderer, we would not have, in the Bug's own words, "unquestionably one of the most fascinating and enigmatic true murder mysteries of our times," and such a characterization, even if untrue, sells books.

I am not quite alone in perceiving the errors, misinformation, and distortions -- ah, let us keep to the bluntness I've sworn to, eschew these euphemisms, and call them what they are -- all the lies. Over the years, thanks to Bug providing my prison number and location of the facility where I was imprisoned, I received dozens of letters from readers of his book. A few of these were nasty and bizarre. One hoped that the rigors of imprisonment would cause my asshole to become as big as the Holland Tunnel in New York City in order to accommodate all the traffic through it and that if I was ever released as a doddering old fool I would die of AIDS the next day. The deluded writer of this message was too cowardly to sign his name and address. A few others seemed morbidly excited at the prospect of having a semi-infamous cold-blooded killer as a penpal. I did not, however, attract any proposals of marriage. Most of them had questions, as well as theories, about the case.

All of them, it seems, had been left dissatisfied, finding numerous flaws and inconsistencies, not to mention being repulsed by the Bug's obvious egotism, his snide remarks and denigrations of those he considered inferior to his august self, which was just about everybody -- an ingrained habit judging from the tone continued more or less unremittingly in his other books as well. They had all been left with no more than the Bug's speculations as to what had occurred on Palmyra, the fate of the Grahams. Almost all assumed the Bug's presumption of guilt. As to their theories, ranging from a dispute over the dogs, "a Lab and a Pit Bull (incorrect labels derived from Bug's book)," to a sort of socialist revolutionary justification which had the starving proletariat rising up to take the food and property of the rich capitalist exploiters, all were wrong and didn't even come close to the truth.

It was Dr. Jay Schulman of Columbia University, who was called for his expertise in public opinion in a hearing to buttress a motion by Leonard Weinglass for a change of venue in July, 1981, and who, without getting into specifics, came closest to characterizing the heart of the case when he said, "It is a macabre story, a bizarre story. It has all the ingredients of a fantastically interesting soap opera." But what else did these readers have to work with, the CBS miniseries movie? It was even worse. Hollywood had added its own fictions, liberties heaped upon liberties. A true murder mystery? Please. What the Bug, the Hen, and Hollywood had concocted was neither true nor a murder, but only a confused mystery -- and they would all be quite content, I'm sure, for the mystery to remain forever.

My inquiring correspondents all did, however, want my firsthand insider eyewitness account of what had **really happened**. How I had killed the Grahams, dismembered them, and burned them, and why. I even heard from a couple of lawyers who, besides commenting upon Bug's apparent narcissism -- "the malodorous reek of head cheese" -- wanted to know just how in the hell I had been convicted upon such scant evidence. There must be some essential facts left out in the telling.

Some assumed Stephanie was as guilty as myself and thought she had gotten off by being able to afford a bigtime, smooth-talking legal gun.

Of the numerous events recounted in the Bug/Hen book, only Bugliosi and Henderson know which parts they were principally responsible for, and one of the problems in dissecting a book with more than one author is the difficulty in determining who is responsible for what.

Their book is primarily composed of two major parts. The first, called **The Crime**, purports to narrate the story of characters and events leading up to the alleged crimes of theft and murder. The second book is called **Justice** and tells of Bug's entry into the case as defense counsel for Stephanie, something of their relationship, his self-laudatory rationale for deigning to become involved in such a sordid matter and, of course, his brilliant performance at his client's trial.

Apart from the fact that the Bug's book is the Bug's book, he clearly being the dominant personality, custom has it that when two or more names appear to denote authorship of a particular work, whether it be fiction, non-fiction, a legal brief, or a scientific report, each is to be held equally responsible. In lending their names to a work, they endorse each other's integrity.

However, according to my perceptions, the authorship of the part called **The Crime**, and thus the responsibility, lies mostly with the Hen, while the recounting of the legal machinations in Justice belongs to the Bug. My reason for making this distinction is that many of the incidents recounted in **The Crime** were at least partly based upon account that I had sent him -- including a few in which I was the lone, single, and sole source.

An interesting example of the Hen's imagination -- or perhaps it's extra-sensory perception -- lies in his constructing a dialogue he had no way of knowing or learning, a dialogue between FBI agent Henry (Hank to his friends) Burns and myself during the interview after my surrender in November, 1974. He manages to carry on a narrative heavily mixed with dialogue between us for five pages. (Beginning at page 154, ATSWT) I had not fed him any of these lines, nor, I think, did good ol' Hank. His 302 report contained no quotes.

Although we have never met in person, the Hen contacted me by letter in May, 1986, to request that I supply him with "background information," which would aid in fleshing out my character in a book that would depict both Stephanie and I "honestly and accurately."

I supplied him with somewhere in the neighborhood of 120 regular typewritten pages. Yet now, when I read some of those incidents, a few of which were told for the very first time ever, I can hardly recognize them they have been so twisted and skewed as to bear little relation to the realities preserved in my mind, my memories. There is simply no excuse for this sort of unprofessional, shoddy scholarship, the petty vindictiveness in order to create a predetermined effect in the reading audience. Oh, he must have thought, nothing to fear from dumb ol' Buck -- he's in no position to defend himself.

In other episodes, he has more than one version of a particular event from among which he may pick and choose those bits he prefers in the final synthesis of his narration. In these, the individual reader must draw his own conclusions as to what is true and what not, but he must have something to compare, which Hen does not provide. Rather, he has almost totally rejected my versions and opted to take anyone else's word -- even though he cannot possibly give a reasonable explanation as to why I might choose to lie every step of the way, especially on matters of small import. Either I am a complete pathological liar or he had developed a bias. If I am a total liar, then he is left in the position of having to reject every word. He does not do this. No, he takes the skeleton from the body of the information I provided, rearranges the bones -- the essential points -- and fleshes it over in the mean phantasms of his own imagination in order to fashion a blob-creature -- skull and pelvic bone reversed -- right out of a fantasy and science-fiction story.

But in any story derived from a single source, the choice is to reject it outright or go with it as received. The single source of the story about Jake is myself only. I had never told it to another person before him. He obviously claims by tacit suggestion that Stephanie served as a secondary hearsay source. The problem with such a claim, like the claim that I bragged to Stephanie that I enjoyed slapping my wife around, is that she had an absolute horror of violence - did not want, like the three monkeys, to see it, hear it, or speak it. As for myself, having been forced to witness so much violence in my own life, I have a sickness, an utter abhorrence of it and prefer not to dwell upon violence in any form. The major portion of my life has been spent in avoiding violence. Yes, I feel that here and now I must speak of it, but there is no way I would ever have told Stephanie the story about Jake -- which is, after all, a man's story of war and death.

Stanley Jacobs, or Jake, you will remember, was my high school English, literature, and journalism teacher at San Quentin. His story is more fully recounted in Chapter 2 of Part II.

Hen depicts the story of my hero with some sinister implication. I fondled my pistol while malingering belowdecks, leaving the sailing and navigation of Iola to Steph, amusing myself by tormenting her with inane conversation about Jake, which is told at pages 44-45 of Bug's book.

As you may see for yourself, Hen manages to not only malign one of the finest and most morally sensitive men I ever had the honor to know, but he blames it on Stephanie by saying that Jennifer was amazed "that Jake had tried to make a strong moral argument to his class of convicted criminals for killing the man," (Jake told me this story in private between the two of us alone.) a captured Japanese soldier.

It is the work of a malicious pissant slandering his betters – Hen was not fit to lick dogshit off Jake's shoes, let alone shine them. He placed my story to him into a sleazy fictional context where he has me caressing a pistol as though it were my prick in some sick psychosexual scenario so popular with two-bit hack psychiatrists, the kind who seek employment in prisons because they are too weird for normal society.

In response to my reply to his first letter, Hen began by stating that he found my comments to be thoughtful and sincere. He went on to request that I share some of the details of my life to help him flesh out my character. "I'm talking about childhood," he wrote, "rites of passage, likes and dislikes, attitudes and opinions, and other personal information that will help the readers to identify with your character in the book."

Yeah, well, he also told me that his basic conception of the book was one of two parallel love stories. Sure, I'm a sucker; I went for his okeydoke. I'm willing to give a guy the benefit of the doubt -- until I learn he's not a straight-shooter. Goes to show that even conmen can be conned. Hen got me good, the little two-faced weasel.

His litany of similarly mistreated facts, crumpled into balls and tossed into the trash heap of narration, went on and on and on, a tiresome and tedious repetition of slaughtered or crippled facts all aimed at building a blood-and-gore-maniac-like Manson character.

I couldn't even fish, sail, or navigate a lick. Did he not even read **Iola's** logbook, for chrissakes?

When he had written to tell me of the nearing publication of his and the Bug's book in 1990, after over five years of labor on it, I naively responded with a proposition. Would Hen and Bug donate one chapter at the end of their book in which I would relate my side of the story? Hen said he would consider it; to send him the material. I mailed 60 pages to him describing basically what you have read here in the last chapter of this book. He astounded me by rejecting it with a number of inane remarks. Fool that I was, I did not then realize the extent of the character assassination to come, already signed, sealed, and delivered to a publisher. What I had to say did not fit with the meanly conceived notions of his already complete prejudgment.

If they had included my awkwardly written 60 pages in their book, I probably would never have written this fuller account -- but merely spent the years eating the bitter pages of their misrepresentations.

*****

Evidence, ah, there is evidence and there is evidence. Somebody said, I forget who, that circumstantial evidence is like a blackberry; when it is red, it is really green. Let us dwell on the subject a bit, such as it is.

The little green patch: Remember the little green patch of cotton cloth that was consumed in the laboratory forensic tests by the FBI, which was found inside the metal box? It had no significance except that it was claimed to have contained traces of blood -- which apparently was not sufficient to type or DNA.

When we lived in Hawaiian Fern Acres, Stephanie had bought me three pairs of cotton bell-bottom trousers. One pair was bright red, another deep purple, and the third Kelly green. Bravely, and so as not to hurt Steph's feelings, I wore these neon signs of attire until the first and second washings had shrunk the pantlegs up high enough above my ankles that I began to resemble a dork living on flood plains.

She cut and hemmed them to make me shorts and they survived the summer on the Kona coast and work stints on Iola at Maui to become my daily wear on Palmyra.

It was the green cutoffs I wore during my aborted last tryst with Muff. I was, if you recall, in something of a hurry to leave the scene -- so much so that I left them behind and fled in my birthday suit. Mac apparently tossed the hated garment into the box with Muff's body -- a small patch of which would survive the years, perhaps because they lay under her in several inches of gasoline.

The sea was telling but nobody was listening.

*****

The missing bullet and cartridge case. The .357 magnum bullet that Mac fired at my face, but which had passed through Muff from back to front by mistake, might have lain for years as a misshapen piece of gore-contaminated lead on the concrete floor of the equipment shed -- where none of the dozens of searchers on two or three trips to Palmyra would find it.

Neither would they find the brass case of the .30 caliber shell I had fired at Mac from around the corner of the house next door.

Nor would anyone note possible bullet holes in the corrugated metal of the equipment shed, the wood of the adjacent house, or nearby palm trees.

In fact, the Bug/Hen book would manage the added confusion that the .30 caliber Marlin lever-action rifle belonged to Mac rather than me. I had once been charged with illegal possession of this rifle, along with the .22 caliber Ruger Bearcat. The charges had mysteriously disappeared from the indictment charging theft of Sea Wind.

Had the FBI not traced them by their serial numbers? I had admitted to having bought them from my brother, Larry, and Cal, his friend, when they'd shown up unexpectedly at Keehi Lagoon while in Honolulu to enter into the plea bargain that would dismiss the MDA charge against Stephanie.

*****

Trauma to jawbone: Dr. Oliver Harris, an odontologist who had testified at my trial, once again in Stephanie's trial claimed to find evidence of blunt trauma to an upper left molar in Muff's skull and a lower right molar in the jawbone. When asked by Enoki for examples of blunt trauma, Harris replied, "A large round rock, a sledgehammer, but not a fist. A fist could not deliver that much force."

On cross, Weinglass asked if the expert knew whether the fractures had occurred at the time of death.

"No, I do not know that."

A sledgehammer became the Bug's favorite scenario for how murder was inflicted upon Muff. But, according to the evidence, this blunt trauma could have occurred years later to Muff's skull -- as, for instance, someone dropping it while handling it years later. Or it might have occurred near the time of death. No one can say for sure.

Alas, no one knew enough to ask whether a woman shot in the back, her body dropping like a dead weight face down on a concrete floor, after first possibly striking a metal protrusion on a steel drum, would cause such blunt trauma.

Muff's sprawl after Mac's having shot her placed her head on the concrete floor near one of the old steel gasoline drums which was employed to support the rescue launch. The metal protrusions are circular ridges impressed into them when they are manufactured to add strength.

Or perhaps Mac accidentally dropped her face against the rim of the metal equipment locker as he was placing her body into it for cremation.

*****

Rat poison: Ten or eleven years after the event, Shoemaker remembered Mac mentioning to him during his last radio communication on Wednesday, August 28, 1974, that the hippy couple were arriving with a cake, an apparent truce offering.

The Bug rather easily demolished him on cross-examination at Stephanie's murder trial:

"You've testified earlier how this cake-truce incident stood out in your mind above everything else. Something you would never forget as long as you live. If it actually happened as you claim it did, can you tell this jury and Judge King why, when you were specifically asked to relate what took place during this very last contact that you ever had with Mac Graham, that you never felt the cake-truce incident memorable enough or important enough to mention?"

"Mention to who?"

"To the lawyer who asked you to relate what took place during that conversation."

"What lawyer?"

"The person asking the questions, sir, that I just read to you." (From the transcripts of the theft trials in 1974.)

"Well...I was only...answering the questions that were asked."

Similarly, ten or eleven years after the event, Wolfe experienced a phenomenal feat of memory in recalling a large quantity of rat poison he'd observed in the equipment shed. He also claimed that when it had disappeared the next day, he'd warned Mac about it.

Rather than embarrass Wolfe on cross-examination, the Bug managed to get Judge King to order that Wolfe not be allowed to mention the alleged rat poison.

In chambers, Schroeder and Enoki on one side, the Bug on the other, they argued the matter.

"Your honor," Schroeder began. "Mr. Wolfe had observed a fairly good supply of rat poison in a shed on the island. On the day before he left the island, he observed that the rat poison was gone. He got concerned about it and told the Grahams about this."

"Your honor," the Bug said, "there's a very cogent reason why the rat poison testimony should not come in." He referred to Rule 403 of the Federal Rules of Evidence, which provides that evidence should be excluded if its probative value is substantially outweighed by the danger of unfair prejudice.

"The Government realizes that the danger of unfair prejudice is great if the rat poison comes in and that's why, in their brief, they never even attempted to respond to my Rule 403 objection, even though it was the centerpiece of my brief. There is only one reason why the government is offering the rat poison testimony: to imply to the jury that the Graham's were poisoned to death. They want to do this by way of a free ride without producing one speck of evidence that Muff Graham was poisoned to death, and they don't have the candor to admit that to this court."

Enoki then admitted that forensic pathologists had found no trace of poison in the bones.

"They want the jury to believe," the Bug went on, "that the cake Buck and Stephanie allegedly brought to Mac and Muff was laced with rat poison. At Buck Walker's trial, they even called Shoemaker for the cake testimony immediately after Wolfe testified to the rat poison. Not a coincidental coupling of witnesses, I am sure. The court has my declaration under penalty of perjury about the enormous prejudice that most likely occurred at Buck Walker's trial when that testimony came in -- spectators in the corridor speculating that the cake was laced with rat poison."

"Their contention that they're offering the rat poison testimony to show that the Grahams wouldn't have invited Buck and Stephanie aboard Sea Wind is just pure buncombe. I don't smell rat poison here. I smell a rat."

Judge King ruled. "I'm satisfied that the rat poison testimony should be excluded in this case for the reasons Mr. Bugliosi gave. You already have all the state of mind you need, and also, this particular piece of evidence is more prejudicial than probative on that issue. I will sustain the objection about the rat poison."

Of course this ruling didn't apply in my case, my lawyers being a Laurel and Hardy team compared to the Perry Mason quality of the Bug.

*****

The cremation box: A Honolulu newspaper quoted a federal prosecutor as saying, "The aluminum box found next to the bones was too small to place a full corpse inside. The body must have been cut up to fit into the box."

The Bug, in his summation, said, "And as if that ultimate horror (referring to his pet theory that Muff was bludgeoned to death with a sledgehammer) were not enough, since the container is really too small for a human body -- I know this is horrible, but we're talking murder now, and there's a lot at stake here -- maybe a chainsaw or the like was used on Mrs. Graham."

How big was the box? Nowhere have I read or heard testimony of anyone measuring its dimensions, but I can tell you without any doubt at all that a whole body can, indeed, be placed into it with no necessity to dismember it. I cannot speak for Muff's body, but from my own personal experience I can tell you that Mac's body was well-contained without any parts being lopped off. My own opinion, drawn from the awful memories of glimpses of the blackened remains, is that **two** whole bodies could have been fitted into one container -- a conclusion that Mac had also come to.

I suppose no one felt a need to record the box's dimensions for posterity since it sat as a constant reminder before Judge King's high podium for all to see during the entire course of my trial. But the image of the box in my memory is clear and I would guess it to be about 2 feet (30 inches) wide and deep, and 3 feet (42 inches) long. The lid was domed and would add about six inches to its depth. This comes out to 21.875 cubic feet of volume, not including the lid, which is about the same as many refrigerators. I've never had a body in my refrigerator, but Hollywood has certainly shown us enough of them in thrillers. Does anyone know the cubic volume of an average human body? Does anyone care to test whether one or two live bodies might fit into a box of these dimensions?

I'm a bit disappointed that the Bug, who is usually so thorough in his researches, as he himself will immodestly tell you, could have missed this basic point. But then, it would have deprived him of sledgehammer, chainsaw, and dismemberment, which all add to the horror factor, that morbidness from which so many derive their thrills.

*****

Polygraph tests: Stephanie, of course, passed a polygraph test after first flunking it on the basis of an ambiguously worded question. I wonder, however, whether she would have passed it if it had been administered by an FBI agent. Rightfully, I think, the Bug himself distrusts the FBI when it comes to testing his clients, and shied away from such an agreement with Enoki.

I had naively volunteered for the test early on but backed out when I sensed a snake in the grass about to strike. Stephanie had volunteered, too, but was refused after I withdrew. The prosecutor, Eggers at the time, got some PR mileage out of falsely claiming that Stephanie followed my refusal. Enoki would parrot this misinformation in later years in order to milk a few more yards out of it.

You have read my fuller account on this subject in Part I of this book. But there was one other reason for my withdrawal and it concerned the changing of one very important word.

In the list of questions to be asked of me while hooked up to the machine as provided by the FBI, all the questions concerning the deaths of Mac and Muff included some variation of the verb, to kill. Was I in any way involved in the killing of Malcolm and Eleanor Graham?

I asked that they change the kill word to murder, or any variant thereof. They were suspicious and wanted to know why. As I was not about to get into a long song and dance with them -- envisioning more lists of questions on more subjects -- I simply pointed out that the killing of a person, per se, was not necessarily a crime, while murder was.

Like any schmuck, I believed in the lie-detector, that lies could indeed be detected by a machine. And I had doubts as to whether I had contributed to the death of Mac. Had that one round fired blindly around the corner of the house wounded him, eventually led to his death from, say, loss of blood? I didn't know. Had he been shot, perhaps for a second time, when his .357 discharged as we tusseled about in hand-to-hand combat? I didn't know. Had the last shot been a suicidal one, he lying there incapacitated and full of grief and anger, but without hope? I didn't know. It had not exactly been a time for counting bullet holes.

But I knew there had been no murder, only an attempted murder-- when he fired at my head -- and I believed that the machine would indicate that I was telling the truth.

A polygraph does not detect lies. It detects minute changes in certain bodily responses. Some people claim that these physical responses are caused by lying. Others disagree.

Donald T. Lykken, a professor of psychology and psychiatry at the University of Minnesota, has studied the polygraph for more than two decades. In his book, **A Tremor in the Blood**, he contends that the innocent will fail lie-detector tests about 50% of the time. "You'd do as well flipping a coin," he says. "In particular, people with strong consciences and religious beliefs can easily be made to feel guilt and anxious."

David T. Raskin, another professor of psychology, who has devoted many years to the study of polygraphs, holds an opposing view, claiming a success rate in detecting deception in subjects of over 90%, and includes psychopaths, who are reputed to be notably deficient in the area of conscience and feelings of guilt. He is, by the way, the same fellow who administered the test to Stephanie.

A segment on **60 Minutes** of a few years ago clearly debunked the efficacy of the test. There was the case of a prisoner named Fay, as depicted in Martin Yant's **Presumed Guilty**, who wound up convicted and sentenced after he had failed a lie-detector test. Fay knew he had been replying to the questions truthfully and couldn't understand the mystery of why he had failed. He read everything he could find on the subject, then sent out the actual graphic results of his failed test to a number of supposed experts. "When the results came back, I knew I was onto something," he said. "Every opinion I got back was different. None of the so-called experts agreed."

Dr. Elizabeth Loftus, in her book, **Witness for the Defense**, tells the story of Steve Titus, who was charged with rape. His lawyer advised him to agree to a polygraph on the ground that if he was shown to be truthful in his claim of innocence, the prosecutor would be more likely to dismiss the case. He took it an flunked. All four black needles measuring his blood pressure, heart rate, respiration, and galvanic skin response, scratched out a trail that could only be read as deception.

These results were not admissible in the trial Titus demanded after insisting he was innocent. Nevertheless, he was convicted on the basis of circumstantial evidence and the eyewitness testimony of the rape victim. There was some question, however, concerning police and prosecutorial misconduct, the little fudging processes that help make a case.

"This was not the first time a defense lawyer told me," Dr. Loftus said, "that police and prosecutors had gone too far in trying to make a case against a defendant. The problem in most cases isn't malice; it isn't even incompetence. When police and prosecutors withhold evidence, they do so because they believe with full confidence and assurance that they have the right person in custody, and that it is their duty to see justice done. Once they say to themselves 'we've got the right person, we have to get this person off the streets,' they may not even perceive that withholding evidence or slightly distorting facts is the wrong thing to do. But the problem doesn't end there, for misinformation can be communicated to the witnesses, who may ignore their doubts and misgivings, and testify confidently in court that they are absolutely convinced that the defendant is, indeed, the real criminal. In such circumstances, there is an increased risk that an innocent person will be convicted."

After failing his lie-detector test, being positively identified by the victim and convicted, a **Seattle Times** newspaper reporter took an interest in the case. He tracked down the real rapist, helped the police make the case, and convinced them they'd made a mistake. The rapist confessed in authentic detail; he was a serial rapist. In physical appearance, he resembled Titus. When the rape victim was asked to look at him, she recognized him immediately and broke down because she knew she'd misidentified Titus. Everything at last came together and Titus was exonerated. It had been a bitter and harrowing experience for him. Though still a young man, his health failed him and he shortly thereafter died of heart failure.

The polygraph is based on the **theory** that when a person lies, emotionally triggered physiological responses occur that can be measured as compared with control responses to emotionally neutral questions (Is your name such and so? Were you born on such and so a date?). But people can easily figure out the **relevant** questions (Did you rape, did you steal, did you murder, etc.?) and experience a fear/stress reaction to those questions that the machine would pick up. Fear and stress are all that the polygraph measures.

Now, of course, having in the intervening years studied up on the subject, I would never under any circumstances -- especially if I was innocent -- volunteer to submit to it. The general public perception is as naive as mine once was. Once it is known that you flunked a lie-detector test on such a crucial point as murder, you will forever be perceived as a murderer no matter if you are lucky enough to be found not guilty of the crime in a court of law by Jesus Christ himself testifying in your behalf.

Perjury by witnesses testifying in a courtroom is, as has already been pointed out, more a rule than a rarity. In **People v. Cutter**, a California case, Judge Allan Miller said that after ten years of presiding at criminal trials it was his experience that guilt or innocence in a great majority of cases turns on the credibility of witnesses and "that perjury is prevalent and the oath taken by witnesses has little effect to deter false testimony."

In a U. S. Supreme Court case, **California v. Krivda**, an amicus curiae brief was filed urging abolition of the exclusionary rule "because it causes the police to perjure themselves in hundreds of cases."

Former New York City police officer, Joseph D. McNamara, who went on to become chief of police in Kansas City and now a researcher at Stanford, says, "I've come to believe hundreds of thousands of law enforcement officials commit felony perjury every year." (Cited from Al Neuharth's column, Plain Talk, in USA Today, 12-13-96.)

Barry Tarlow, a prominent Los Angeles defense attorney said that "If the judicial system is to fulfill its duty of searching for truth and maintaining integrity, it must commence a war against perjury."

Yeah, right.

*****

The two murder charges: As we have seen, I was charged with felony-murder and premeditated murder. Felony-murder is a murder committed incidental to the commission of another felony crime, in this case the alleged robbery or theft of **Sea Wind**.

For four years, from February, 1981, until January, 1985, the indictment was for felony-murder only. For 3½ years my principal lawyer, Earle Partington, assured me the prosecution could not make the case against me. He was right. The charge was dismissed without a defense having to be offered. The problem was that the jury had been allowed to hear all the testimony concerning the alleged theft. Coupled with the incredibly inept decision of both Partington and co-counsel Findlay to proclaim before the jury that I was indeed a thief, they had to believe that I was guilty of that much at least -- even though the charge was dismissed and the jury was instructed that it would no longer be a part of their considerations.

It was too late. Talk about prejudice outweighing probity! There was no way they were going to discard their belief that I was a thief. On that basis alone they would want to find me guilty of something. The only choice was murder.

At the time I believed that instructions would be read to the jury relevant to lesser-included offenses, such as manslaughter, of which there are two types, voluntary and involuntary -- the former being the more serious.

I was shocked when Partington informed me that Judge King would not read any instruction as to lesser-included offenses. I myself was not entirely sure that my actions in the circumstances on the night between August 29 and the early morning hours of August 30, 1974, did not rise to the level of manslaughter. When I considered the differences in the language defining the two types, I thought it was possible that I was indeed guilty of involuntary manslaughter. I further believed that my testimony on the witness stand would convince the jury that such a finding was the most I was guilty of.

The reason Judge King would not read instructions for lesser included offenses was that the statute of limitations had expired on those charges and that I could not be tried, or if tried and found guilty could not be punished.

What Partington failed to tell me, and I would not learn until several years later, was that I could have waived the statute of limitations. By doing so, I could have been tried, convicted, and punished. I would also then have been entitled to an instruction on the lesser-included offenses of manslaughter.

We may infer from the circumstantial evidence available that the Bug was responsible for the eleventh hour premeditated murder charge by his filing a totally frivolous and inappropriate motion with Judge King to change the indictment from felony-murder to premeditated murder -- a motion he knew full well Judge King could not grant. Four weeks later, Enoki and Schroeder acted to obtain the additional indictment.

The Bug rather disingenuously claims that these two experienced prosecutors "obviously didn't need me to tell them about the availability and viability of a premeditated murder count."

Isn't it curious though, that in the four preceding years these two experienced prosecutors did not come up with the premeditated murder count?

In a footnote, the Bug tells a story about Partington having told a reporter that he blamed Bugliosi for the premeditated murder count being added. The reporter, Robert Hollis of the **Honolulu Advertiser**, told Bugliosi, and he confronted Partington, who "passionately denied" it.

Since Partington had said the very same thing to me, I believe it. Partington, as we have seen, is a spineless little man who speaks out both sides of his mouth. If he could not confront Judge King, he certainly could not stand up face to face with the Bug.

But I do not believe the Bug's denial that the sole purpose of his motion was to communicate the idea to Enoki and Schroeder, despite the fact that he claims Enoki told both Hollis and himself that the premeditated murder count "was based on Ingman's and Williams' testimony before the grand jury and that he and Schroeder had contemplated filing it in addition to the felony-murder count long before I even raised the issue of substituting it for the felony-murder count."

Even if Enoki did say that, I don't believe it. Long before? Really? They had four years and never did it until after the Bug's motion. It was not until November 1984, that Enoki and Schroeder had come up with the perjurious testimony of Ingman and Williams, a mere month before the Bug's motion.

I believe that Enoki and Schroeder had no other plans for Ingman and Williams than to testify against me in the trial for felony murder. They, ahem, as experienced prosecutors, had to have known their case for making a felony-murder was very weak. Judge King himself had expressed his doubts to Partington, who is not a discreet individual. They merely wanted to shore up the sagging evidence when it came to proving the nexus of murder to robbery or theft. Make no mistake, the evidence was very clear that the intended use of Ingman would be to help prove not only murder, but theft and robbery, too.

But then, aha, along comes the Bug's motion to confound the prosecutors. Hey, forget substituting one charge for another, we'll go with both, get 'em coming and going! Being prideful men, they certainly would not admit to having gotten the idea from their opponent -- that would have smelled to high heaven of collusion.

The Bug goes on to argue that the felony-murder charge was inappropriate, the tacit implication being that Judge King dismissed the charge in both cases for that very reason.

Even though he confirms what everybody knew or suspected -- "that the prosecution had no evidence the killing took place during the perpetration of the robbery, a necessary element for the felony-murder rule to apply" -- he argued that the judge would not dismiss the charge if he believed by the evidence that murder had been committed, robbery or no robbery, theft or no theft.

The Bug likes to butter his toast on both sides.

*****

Sea Wind's log and Muff's diaries: What happened to the logbook of Sea Wind, written in Mac's hand, and the three diaries belonging to Muff and written in her hand, all items of potentially important evidence?

I think I know. I've figured it out. Let's look at the trail of clues.

One day out of the blue, sometime before the publication of Bug's book, I received a letter from Bob Stearns, Stephanie's brother. Stating that he wished to be done with the case once and for all, he informed me that he had eleven boxes of paperwork stored in his garage; it all pertained to the case. In them were transcripts, motions, FBI 302 reports, investigative reports by private detectives, letters, and handwritten notes made by a number of people involved in the case. Bob was going to destroy them -- unless I had some use for them.

Yes, I would like to have a look at them. Please send them, I'll reimburse you for the shipping costs. I had much the same sort of material in my own files on the case. I had copies of transcripts of both theft trials, as well as my murder trial. I hoped that Bob's material might include a transcript of Stephanie's murder trial, as well as a few missing FBI 302 reports.

The one thing I found more interesting than anything else was a handwritten note in Leonard Weinglass' own hand. It was jotted on a document clearly emanating from his law office. It was a brief note reminding himself to be sure to discuss certain material found in Muff's diaries "with Vince." Vince? Vincent? Vincent who? Gee, can we guess?

Weinglass and Bugliosi had somehow come into possession of her mysteriously missing diaries! How? Well, of course, they most likely put a private investigator on the trail, one who tracked them down to a certain individual. Who?

Ah, let us not get ahead of our trail of clues. As officers of the court representing a client in a murder trial, were not Weinglass and Bugliosi duty-bound to inform the court in the person of Judge King that they had found this potentially valuable evidence? Did they do their duty as officers of the court? Did they act within the Canon of Ethics of the American Bar Association to which they were both bound by oath?

Might not these diaries, as well as **Sea Wind's** logbook, have contained information that would contradict the testimony of several key witnesses who claimed animosity existed between the Grahams and Stephanie and I? Might not Mac have written a true account of having accidentally killed his wife while trying to shoot me? Might not Muff have written about the marital problems she was experiencing with her husband -- his drinking and impotence? Might she not have written an account of her affair with me?

Why do I mention **Sea Wind's** logbook in conjunction with Muff's diaries? Because they both wound up in possession of the same person Weinglass or his hired investigator tracked down -- along with two other items missing from the FBI and Coast Guard inventory, an eight-by-ten framed photo of Mac and Muff attached to a bulkhead inside Sea Wind (the very one Lorraine Wollen mentioned having seen when she had been invited aboard in Pokai Bay, and a black leather binder containing typewritten pages of Mac's attempts at composing stories based on his personal experiences.

Let me digress for a bit to tell you something about the customary uses of a yacht's logbook. In commercial vessels, this constitutes the full nautical record of a ship's voyages. In it are recorded position fixes at various dates and times, courses steered and made good, points of departure and destination, cargo, and problems with the ship whether from mechanical or electrical breakdown, navigation errors, grounding, collisions or other extraordinary events occurring at sea. They are usually rather dry and factual accounts of the ship's progress, its history day by day.

In contrast, logs of smaller vessels for personal use become somewhat more interesting diaries by the inclusion of subjective, often intimate, thoughts and feelings by the owners.

As an example, Donald Stevens of **Shearwater** had even pasted in photographs of people and places along with his very personal comments, including a description of a poignant love affair with a Tongan girl.

Stephanie and I, as well as the Grahams, followed this practice. Most of the entries in **Iola's** logbook were made by Stephanie and are replete with personal events and sentiments. Just as our logbook, which was in the hands of authorities, clearly indicated a complete lack of hostility toward the Grahams -- the opposite, in fact, that they were considered good friends -- might not the log of Sea Wind have reflected a similar view toward us?

Logbooks are considered good legal evidence. If the Graham log had contained such friendly passages about our social relationship, its admission as evidence would have contravened the heart of the government's case against us.

The same holds true for Muff's diaries. I mention diary in the plural because I myself saw three of them that Steph had found during her nosy peregrinations about **Sea Wind** when she found Mac's wallet, his will and a codicil, and some money in a textbook on surgical techniques, as well as **Sea Wind's** logbook. Two of Muff's diaries were found in a drawer, the third being wrapped in cloth and hidden away in her sewing supplies -- all having handwritten entries in them. She apparently had two more blank ones in reserve. These are listed as item numbers 7, a blue diary (no words), and 54, a diary.

Could the log and diaries have been honestly misplaced? Inventory item numbers, 19, 21, 22, 23, 47, 48, and 56, were all boxes containing books. Could the log and diaries have been included among them? A nice theory except for the fact of the diaries, and possibly the log, coming into the eventual possession of Weinglass and Bugliosi.

As to the black leather binder containing accounts of Mac's personal experiences, I have some personal knowledge of its contents. When we learned that we were both interested in writing, he let me take a look at it once while aboard **Sea Wind** for a few games of chess. I particularly remembered two of the stories. One was an account of **Sea Wind** caught in an electrical storm in the Gulf of Tehuantepec; the other was about a time when he feared Sea Wind was about to be rammed by a pirate vessel -- he had turned on the spreader lights so he could be clearly seen as he ran forward to aim his .357 magnum at the helmsman in the pilothouse of the suspected pirate vessel and it veered away at the last moment. Since these two events are mentioned in the Bug's book, the part that Henderson wrote, mightn't we assume that he had access to this binder missing from **Sea Wind's** effects?

On at least two prior occasions, FBI agent Calvin Shishido had testified that he had no idea what had happened to these pieces of evidence that he had found "no log pertaining to the Sea Wind, nor any diary written by Mac or Muff Graham."

At Steph's murder trial, the Bug himself questioned Shishido. Referring to Exhibit 16, the inventory of items from **Sea Wind** that had been turned over to FBI custody, he asked, "Item number 26 reads: 'Navigational logs contained in five-by-eight plastic folder.' Could that have been the log of **Sea Wind**?"

"Well, I really don't know."

"You testified on direct examination that there was no log of the Sea Wind found aboard the boat. Are you willing to amend your testimony now to state that the navigational logs, inventory item number 26, may have been the log of the **Sea Wind**?"

"Well, no, I wouldn't change my testimony because I still don't remember seeing any logbook for the **Sea Wind**."

"Yet these 'navigational logs' certainly were not the log of the Iola. You agree on that?"

"Yes. Because we have the log of the **Iola**." "So, item number 26 is some other log, and you don't know what it is?"

"That's right. I really don't know what that is."

"And you don't know where item number 26 is at the present time?"

"No, sir. I don't."

And now let us read some mealy-mouthed words on this subject right out of the Bug's comments in his book, as well as his summation in Stephanie's murder trial.

"Another preliminary matter was the issue of whether or not the Grahams had kept a diary on Palmyra; also, what happened to the log of **Sea Wind**. If the jury believed that there had been a diary, and if either the diary or log disappeared because of some action of Jennifer's, it would go in the direction of her having destroyed important evidence, a strong suggestion of guilt. The evidence did not allow me to be on my best footing here, but some response was better than none at all." (ATSWT, page 548.)

Please note that the Bug himself describes diaries and log as **important evidence**.

To the jury, he said, "As to the diary, a friend of the Grahams, Herbert Daniels, testified that one time aboard **Sea Wind** Muff referred to some document to 'recall the name of either a port or a person.' From this, the prosecution infers the document was a diary."

The Bug pointed out that Muff's words could just as well have referred to **Sea Wind's** log, and went on to say, "Moreover, even if it was a diary, Mr. Daniels didn't say when this incident took place. The fact she kept a diary at one time does not mean she was doing so on Palmyra.

The prosecution did not clearly establish through any witness that either of the Grahams kept a diary on Palmyra."

Whoa! Can the Bug dissemble or what!

He continued on in his speech to the jury to remind them of Shishido's testimony. "The inference was clear: if the log of the **Sea Wind** disappeared, it had to have been lost or misplaced after my client left the **Sea Wind**, that is, while in the hands of the authorities in this case." (ATSWT, page 548.)

It is known by the testimony of various witnesses in the two theft trials and two murder trials that both Coast Guard and FBI agents were engaged in the search of Sea Wind and in inventorying all the wares aboard her in October/November, 1974.

FBI agent Edwin K. Tanaka had testified as to not only being present at the Ala Wai Yacht Harbor during Stephanie's arrest and my escape, but also to helping inventory the contents of **Sea Wind**. He said he was aboard on three occasions and claims to have been accompanied at all times by Coast Guard personnel.

FBI agent William Miller claims to have been aboard **Sea Wind** with a camera to try duplicating a photo taken by Stephanie for the purpose of identifying **Sea Wind's** rigging.

There was also agent Moroney, whose name appeared on an inventory sheet.

Of all the Coast Guardsman who may have been aboard, they all go unnamed insofar as the records available to me go -- all except one, who testified at my theft trial to an apparently innocuous visit to Sea Wind.

The last clue, folks. Pay attention.

Norman W. Cherry, a Coast Guard intelligence officer, testified that he was in on the surveillance and inventory of **Sea Wind**. Most importantly, he testified to accompanying FBI agent Calvin Shishido in company of Mary "Kit" Muncey aboard **Sea Wind**.

It seems Shishido allowed Muncey to collect a few items of personal effects belonging to her brother and sister-in-law, the **Sea Wind's** logbook, Muff's diaries (most likely three of them), the black leather binder containing the anecdotes of Mac's personal experiences, and the eight-by-ten framed photo of the couple firmly attached to a bulkhead.

All these items are not easily stuffed into a purse. Shishido would have had to be blind as well as remiss in his duty not to have known Muncey carried these items away with her.

The chain of possession of these items seems clear on the evidence. Shishido, in company with Cherry, perhaps with other FBI agents and Coast Guard personnel aboard, allowed Muncey to remove these four items for keeping in her personal possession. At least the logbook had already been included on the inventory.

Did Shishido commit perjury when he claimed to have no knowledge of at least two of these items, the log and diaries, or does he not remember? He had formed a sympathetic relationship with Muncey, later on accepting calls from her to commiserate and ask that she send copies of not only all letters she could find from Mac and Muff while at Palmyra, but also my delayed-delivery letter.

Perhaps a decade later, someone figures out who has these items, and we can infer that Henderson at least had access to the binder, perhaps in Muncey's presence while he was going about interviewing people for his and the Bug's book. But we may -- at least I can -- definitely conclude that at least one or more of Muff's diaries were passed on to Weinglass, who in turn shared them with Bugliosi.

Does the Bug's mealy-mouthed dissembling over Muff's diaries, along with both his and Weinglass' failure to come forward with this evidence -- perhaps including **Sea Wind's** log -- constitute a violation of the American Bar Association's Code of Professional Responsibility? Do their shenanigans rise to the level of a federal felony crime, that of obstruction of justice under Title 18 USC, section 1510?

Don't worry, Bug. The statute of limitations applies!

*****

Stephanie's perjury: As you know, when I read the Bug's account of this case, I became bitter and outraged beyond all measure. But I must also confess to experiencing something altogether different, though no less intense.

I had grown more or less used to every fact of every incident being slanted to portray a phantasm of reality. In the first part of the book, **The Crime**, I rationalized away the fantastic dialogue portrayed as coming from Stephanie's mouth and mine, blaming the Hen for inventing it. By the time I got to the second book, **Justice**, however, when the source of dialogue had to come from the Bug -- whom I was not quite so ready to condemn as in the Hen's case -- I began to feel the first of a graduating series of shocks. At the introduction of her testimony at trial, I was by then completely enthralled. This was not a conman's bullshit, it being too easy to prove false from the public record of the transcripts. No, these had to be her own words, no how extensively she may have been coached and rehearsed. Pure and simple, these were premeditated and unmitigated lies pouring from my old honey's mouth.

I was in awe, utter and complete awe, at her ability to mouth lie after lie after lie. Enoki would say in his final summation to the jury that he had counted 14 lies Stephanie had told. "I counted them," he said. "We also tried to count what happened that first forty-five minutes of cross-examination. We counted 19 times that she said she didn't know, or she didn't remember, in answer to questions."

Enoki went on. "Miss Stearns, of course, cried some tears on the stand. But it isn't only due to remorse that a person is brought to tears. One reason, of course, is it could be a performance, a complete performance."

For myself, I would have voted her an Academy Award as best actress in a real live courtroom drama. A performance? A complete performance? Oh, yes, an awesome performance! So awesome that if someone had come to me with a surreptitiously recorded videotape of her performance on the witness stand, I would have promised to rob a dozen banks and give all the proceeds for it.

Steph, babe, I'm clapping my hands! A stellar performance!

Yes, rather than be angry, I was pleased. The Bug could not have won the case without his client's considerable assistance.

Well, I thought, how many times did she lie? Surely more than the 14 Enoki counted. But then, he was hampered by a lack of experiential knowledge. He could only go by what he detected in the records. I, myself, however, was not so limited. I had personal knowledge. Not even counting the Hen's strings upon strings of fiction masquerading as fact, I had counted up 10 lies that were revealed in the text of Stephanie's talks with the Bug in pretrial. Under direct examination by the Bug at her trial, I counted no less than 55. Under Enoki's cross-examination, there were another 15. On the Bug's redirect there were 4 more.

Without attempting to count what she may or may not have told the Hen -- his lies beyond counting and hard to distinguish as to who was responsible for them -- Stephanie had told 84 lies attributable to her, 74 of them under oath on the witness stand.

Of course, there are lies and there are lies. A few of them were honest mistakes, a few as a result of faulty memory. But then there were the major lies going right to the heart of truth in this case, the deliberate lies -- however rationalized as necessary to her self-defense -- the clearly premeditated-with-all-due-consideration lies. And in those lies I cannot conceive of Steph creating them all on her own. She had to have been coached and rehearsed, even persuaded that the truth in so many cases simply would not do. An important element in the bottom line had to be: When in doubt, blame Buck -- the heart of the Bug's defense.

In my personal knowledge of Steph, I had never found her to be a facile liar. I could always tell when she was shying away from a subject or trying to conceal it. She was not comfortable lying about anything. But in the interim years before coming to her murder trial, she took the witness stand as an accomplished liar.

The Bug himself will tell you that lying by witnesses in a courtroom is rampant and common across the land, that almost all of them lie in some respect. He will further tell you that all lies are not equal, that from a legal point of view not all lies rise to the level of perjury -- which is subject to a penalty of five years imprisonment. The Bug will tell you that a lie must concern a material matter before it becomes perjury. Under this definition, my few paltry fibs at my theft trial were not punishable perjury. Not so with Stephanie, who admitted on the stand that she had previously lied under oath on material issues. If Enoki, a sly and vindictive little man, could have prosecuted her for this self-confessed perjury, he surely would have. Unfortunately for him, it was not until her murder trial in 1986 that she confessed to having perjured herself at the 1975 theft trial and the five-year statute of limitations had expired.

The supreme irony here is that everyone perceives the case of her self-confessed lies assbackwards! Stephanie pretty much told the truth in her theft trial -- except for a few misleading instances. It was in her murder trial that she lied like a champ, the least of which was claiming she had lied in her theft trial!

There were lies and there were lies, some small, some medium, some whoppers. There were lies that no one could detect -- except for me -and lies that were obvious had anyone bothered to check them out.

Here are three in the latter category:

1. Stephanie could not see Sea Wind from the cockpit of Iola.

From information provided by Stephanie herself, you may recall that **Iola** had two mooring positions between the dolphins adjacent to the western end of the airstrip. We were first moored between the second and third dolphins behind the Wheelers' **Poseidon**. When they left, Mac helped us to swing around to take their place -- between the first and second dolphins. This occurred early on -- July 6.

From our first position, it is true we could not clearly see **Sea Wind** because of the angle and intervening foliage. But after moving to our second position, which placed us right at the point of an inward turn of the coastline of Cooper in the lagoon -- that is, a northward bend in the coastline of Cooper from the lagoon -- nothing obstructed a full view of **Sea Wind**, not intervening foliage or a nonexistent "jut of land," as Stephanie called it. (See inset of Palmyra chart below)

As to **Sea Wind** "backed into a little cove...totally horseshoed by land...and there was a little jut of land that came out helping to form the cove," which contained "heavy vegetation and tall trees on it," this description is pure fiction. It's true a jut of land existed, but only to the west of Sea Wind, and there was no horseshoeing counterpart to block the view from the east.

Of all the people sent on expeditions to Palmyra seeking evidence and of all the photos taken, surely one covered the line of sight from the first dolphin; anyone could have made a note of this fact. I myself recall some aerial photographs -- taken by Vitousek? Even a cursory study of a good nautical chart would have given the lie to her words.

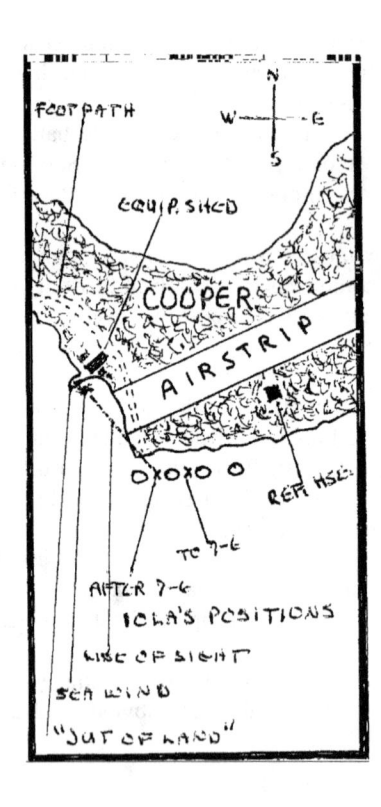

690

2. I wrote the letter to Muncey while in jail and gave it to her during a visit.

There is no conclusive proof as to where this letter was written. I know it was completed while aboard **Sea Wind** in drydock. Stephanie knows this, too. Her word against mine? Well, what is her word? She wrote a note to Muncey accompanying the letter when she remailed it saying I had written it while in drydock -- which she now claims is a lie. Next she claims that I gave it to her during a visit at the jail. Her word against mine? Not quite. I never received a single visit from Stephanie while I was in jail for the simple reason that jail authorities would not allow her to visit. She was out on bail on the same crime I was charged with and as far as jail authorities were concerned, we were crime-partners. It was against standing jail policy for her to be allowed to visit -- all of which was certainly reflected in the record of visits received. Nobody thought to check them. The only times we saw each other in person were at court appearances.

3. Iola was sunk purposely by my having "opened up all her through-hull fittings."

I've previously explained exactly what a through-hull fitting is and the purpose it serves. I've also told you that **all** through-hull fittings on **Iola** were permanently plugged. This means that the inside emergency stopcocks were removed, and a glued wood dowel was hammered tightly into the hole and fiberglassed over. Toilets, sinks, engine cooling water and pumps all normally have either an inlet or outlet or both. Toilets have two, an inlet and outlet; sinks may have one or both; engines have both; bilge-pumps usually only one, an outlet. And all were permanently plugged. Our bilge-pump, mounted on the coachroof near the main hatch, had detachable inlet and outlet hoses -- one down through the hatch to the bilge, the other directly overboard topside. Even our sink had no outlet through the hull -- it drained directly below into a five-gallon bucket which had to be emptied over the side.

The propshaft was permanently plugged. The only conceivable through-hull fitting -- not normally thought of as such -- was at the rudderpost. The only way to open that would be to remove the rudder, an all but impossible task while Iola was in the water.

There were many photos taken of **Iola** while in drydock over the period between her condition as first purchased and right up to launch time. So far as I know, all these photos remained in Stephanie's possession. A little cursory study would have clearly shown no apparent through-hull fittings. Also, there were several witnesses to the fact of them all having been plugged, from Larry Seibert and old Charlie, the winch operator, to Dickie and Carlos.

These are more or less minor lies and serve no real purpose beyond demonstrating that Stephanie lied at her trial -- although I'm sure Enoki would have been positively gleeful had he had the sense to catch her in them. The more major lies all boil down to my version versus her multiple versions.

Even though I understood her reasons for all the lies and, like those told by character witnesses like Rick Schulz and Debbie Noland, applauded their success -- when the truth is not believed, you must lie -- some of them get to me on a personal level.

The lie that I would purposely sink **Iola**, all the lies she claims I told her. I had so much of myself invested in Iola, there's no way I could have done that, and I almost never lied to Steph -- only after the night of August 29-30, and then only to protect her from the awful truth of what had happened. To say that **Iola** had not gone aground a second time on our passage out of the lagoon on September 11, especially when she knew in her heart that she and Puffer had been responsible for it; to say that I had given her an ultimatum that she had three options: To sail away with me on a stolen **Sea Wind**; to go it alone on **Iola**; or to stay on Palmyra by herself; to saying poor mongrel Popolo was a vicious and uncontrollable Pit Bull, these were all lies that struck me personally -- in my heart.

Iola, even without the damage on the way out, would have eventually sunk from the rudderpost leak if left unattended -- it just would have taken longer, maybe as long as a month or so.

In her lying I sensed an uncharacteristic maliciousness, as though she were blaming me for all that had happened to her. Well, there's some truth to that, but did I cause the FBI to fudge the truth in their reports and testimony? Did I cause all those assholes like the Pollocks, Shoemaker, and Wolfe to tell such vicious lies? Was I the little geek prosecuting her?

Lies and lies and lies -- it's true almost everybody was lying at her trial, her friends, her enemies -- everyone who had chosen sides -and even some who were supposedly neutral, like Jack Wheeler when he claimed to have told us how difficult a trip to Fanning would be long before the idea was even a glimmer over our horizon. And, all of a sudden, Steph claiming she "didn't specifically recall" finding either log or diaries when it was she who came up with them and read a few entries in them.

Lies on top of lies buried in lies, does anyone wonder how any semblance of truth can possibly emerge in a trial?

What I knew, in addition to personal chagrin on the one hand and awe and admiration for Steph's lies on the other -- the thankfulness that she had successfully managed it -- was that I was also saddened. Ah, I thought evil has finally reached out with cold fingers to touch my old love, the evil she had escaped and refused to recognize all the years of her life until then. And she came to know, as we all must, that evil can only be fought on its own terms that evil defines the rules of the game. The weapons evil chooses are the very weapons that must be employed in taking arms against it. As evil is full of lying and cheating, so must its opponent or victim be. When the truth is not believed, you must lie. When fairness doesn't work, you must cheat. You must parade lies as truth and every cop knows this when he lies to establish probable cause, when he exaggerates to distort a fact, when he adds, subtracts, or alters evidence against a defendant. Every DEA undercover agent knows it when he entices users and dealers to buy from or sell drugs to him with the legal blessings of the establishment. Every prosecutor knows it when he omits to include exculpatory evidence to the defense, when he knowingly allows perjured testimony from his own witnesses to pass without complaint. Every FBI agent knows it when he embroiders his 302 reports, when his memory and reportage are conveniently pro-prosecution and denies knowing how evidence in his custody mysteriously disappears. And every investigative journalist of crimes, as Janet Malcolm points out, (The Journalist and the Murderer.) accepts that he may tell any lie to anyone if conceived, rightly or wrongly, as being in aid of ultimate truth. The salami has only so many slices before it's gone. Let all those in jails and prisons trade uniforms and swap places with all those who put and keep them there, the moral differences are so thorn as to compose no more than scraps for the dog.

Steph did not want to take the stand and testify in her own behalf. Her brother, Bob, did not want her to take the stand, and neither did the Bug's co-counsel, Weinglass. The Bug reports her lackadaisical attitude, the yellow pads he gave her unmarked by a single bit of ink to help him. But finally, the Bug says, "it had hit home that she was about to testify at her own murder trial" and then spent many long hours going over the Bug's Q&As. Yes, and the evil of it had to have hit her, too, that, by God, she was in a battle for her life.

And so my amazement at her cleverness, perhaps with a little help from friends and family, that she had turned the considerable intelligence I'd always known she possessed, unlike so many surprised others, that she had felt the shiver of the evil touch, faced it, and, if I may personify evil here, blew the sonofabitch out of the water with her own broadside of lies.

My sweet patootie had finally understood that her innate goodness was no defense at all, that her basic innocence could not prevail against lies; that her goodwill toward all was laughable in the face of evil; and that she must give up the naïveté of her childlike nature, her trust in the intentions gathering against her. In order to save herself, she must lie like a champ.

When in doubt, blame Buck? Hey, forget it. I'm used to it. It was in a good cause. Way to go, babe!

*****

The FBI: We have already learned something of FBI methods and I could go on and on in many variations, but for the sake of brevity will provide only one more incident from the bottom of their rotten barrel of tricks.

At my trial, the prosecution wished to introduce a photo of Stephanie. It was taken by the Pollocks on the day of their departure and showed her holding Puffer on the foredeck of Iola. She was smiling sweetly and it became one of my favorite pictures.

Partington objected and a ten-minute argument ensued. Shroeder argued that it was useful because it showed Iola's hatchcover, which was later found ashore -- the theory being that it was left off to facilitate purposely sinking Iola. Partington pointed out that there were other photos of the hatchcover, his principal objection being that "it certainly creates a picture of an image of sweet innocence, your honor."

King asked, "What's wrong with that?"

"We don't think it's accurate," said Partington. "We want the jury to have an accurate image of Miss Stearns."

At a recess, I asked Earle about it.

"It's just a game," he said. "They're trying to portray her as a dumb blond, sweet and innocent as a baby."

"Other than the fact that she's not dumb, you're telling me they're going to try to show her innocence?" I asked, amazed that he could utter such an inane statement. "Jesus Christ, Earle, they're going to try to convict her of murder!"

"In her trial. Not here. They're going to suggest you led her astray, conned her. That sweet innocent look," he bit out in disgust. "Damn, I wish we could get her on the stand!"

"Earle," I said. "She is innocent. She is a sweet girl." "Yeah, right," he sneered. "And sweet, innocent girls go around posing for pornography!"

"What?"

"Oh, Buck, come on! They've got photos of her sucking some guy's dick!"

"Really?"

"Really."

"Whose?"

"What?"

"Whose dick was she sucking?"

I think my cheeks must have gone red, for suddenly I remembered some photos Steph and I had taken of ourselves and each other, some of them tripped with a remote-control shutter. We'd been stoned and laughing and kidding around in the privacy of our little cabin in Hawaiian Fern Acres. She'd persuaded me to pose for a beefcake shot wearing nothing but a straw hat. The next day we'd looked at them over breakfast and agreed to tear them up and throw them away. Apparently we hadn't and Steph had kept them.

"I don't know," Earle said. "You can't see the guy's face." "Well," I gulped. "So what? It's what people do. Jesus, Earle, ain't you ever had a hot babe give you a blowjob?"

"It's more than that," he replied, back with the sneer. "The word's going around that she had sex with dogs. There's supposed to be pictures of that, too."

"What!"

I would learn how the rumor had started -- with two fearless, all-American, upstanding, self-righteous, snickering, cocksucking FBI agents!

Somewhere along the way, as Earle had been and would continue providing me with documents, including a stack of 302 reports of interviews with dozens of witnesses, I had come across one on Barbara Allen. After I had read it, expecting little to be had from it, I had sat back in shock. Then, in a rage, I tore it into tiny pieces and flushed it down the toilet.

Because of that, I can't quote it verbatim, but the subject matter and basic method of it is firmly fixed in my mind. It was one of the cheapest and scurrilous bits of gratuitous evil I had ever come across.

You have to remember that an interview subject's verbatim replies to questions asked by the FBI are almost never included in these reports. The actual questions never, but never appear. But we can easily enough infer the questions by what the agent writes in answer to them.

In this case there were sentences that read something like this: **Subject reports that she has no knowledge that Walker and Stearns ever had sex with animals. Subject further reports that she is unaware of Walker and Stearns ever engaging their dogs into sex orgies with them. Subject claims she has never seen pictures of such activities.**

From whence did this disgusting subject arise? From Barbara Allen, who must have been stunned and nauseated that she could be asked such questions? No. It goes against all reason to suppose that anyone would introduce such a subject and then disclaim all knowledge. No.

The subject was broached by the small, dirty minds of the two FBI agents in question. I can see them sitting there licking their chops, eyes aglitter in prurience, no doubt imagining all sorts of possibilities with the very sexy Barbara, snickering away with their sick questions about animal sex, projecting their own interests and hoping to get lucky with a positive reply.

I wish now that I hadn't destroyed that 302 report, because I would like nothing better than to reveal their full names and include an exact facsimile of that report.

The Bug and the Hen also mentioned these non-existent sexual activities involving dogs. One wonders what would introduce such a subject to the public at large in a national bestseller. The question arose when the jury was not allowed to see certain photos of Stephanie and I in the nude taken on Sea Wind during our return voyage to Hawaii. They had nothing to do with sex, but merely depicted our liberal mode of undress on sunny days. We often went about without clothes.

The authors claimed that Calvin Shishido, the FBI agent who'd first interviewed Stephanie in Honolulu, had had to deal with the "particularly sordid rumor" making the rounds, that other FBI agents and lawyers had sidled up to him begging to be allowed to view pictures of Stephanie having sex with a dog. Apparently, Bugliosi and Henderson weren't unaware of the 302 report, which had initiated the rumors. From their self-proclaimed high moral position, they nevertheless took the opportunity to cast their own snide cheapshots about other lawyers and FBI agents.

*****

Vincent Hallinan warned of these scumbags in his book, A Lion in Court, some decades ago when he wrote:

"At this point I interrupt to suggest a startling thesis which may shock you. Simply stated, it is this: In dealing with many agents of the U. S. Government you must assume, until the contrary is completely established, that these representatives might commit felonies, suborn perjury, conceal evidence, bribe witnesses, intimidate jurors, convey information to judges and otherwise engage in practices which would be cause for disbarment or imprisonment for a private attorney."

It seems that nothing I have to say on this subject is new; it's been around for a long time.

*****

Judge Samuel P. King, honorable whore: In this case, I could fill many pages with instances quoted right out of the transcripts of my trial of Judge King's arrogant prejudice, his obviously choosing sides before the jury with his insults, humiliations, and rulings against the defense.

In the first version of this book, the section on my trial alone ran to some 800 pages and catalogued the sins of all who participated in that farce. The Bug himself devoted a few pages in his book about the problem and includes a brief, though instructive primer on judges. He points out, as in King's case, that the majority are not appointed for any qualities they may have as judges, but because of their political connections. He tells us that a judge's obligation in a jury trial is, first and foremost, to be impartial, but that too many judges too often demonstrate by their behavior in the courtroom that they have chosen sides -- which, as the Bug correctly points out, is "a bastardization of our system of justice by the very people whom the law entrusts with the responsibility of insuring that it works properly and equitably."

He goes on to point out the unfortunate fact that jurors tend greatly to assume that whatever a judge does or says in court is proper and right. After introducing a story from my trial by correctly describing King as having demeaned and humiliated my lawyers without justification, which was met by only the meekest response, he tells of a juror being overheard to remark in an elevator that the defense attorneys had been giving King a hard time.

But because King had treated the government attorneys, Enoki and Schroeder, in an entirely different manner by according them all due respect, the jurors were easily susceptible to the inference that the judge had taken the side of the prosecution.

Bob Stearns, Stephanie's brother, had idly remarked to a stranger that King seemed obviously biased in favor of the prosecution. The man replied defensively, that the judge had studied the case and, because of his inside view, must know what had really happened. Bob was shocked to learn that the man was a juror at my trial.

Robyn Schaffer, a young, pretty and plump juror, was even more candid. She was quoted as saying, "It was obvious the judge was out to convict Walker."

None of the jurors, as it would turn out, had the necessary perception to realize that they had been manipulated like a herd of sheep to the feeding pastures by the shepherd, nor, even if they did suspect, the moral courage to resist.

Partington and Findlay had dealt with King before. After all, their principal practice was in Honolulu. But while Partington and Findlay had accepted their positions before King with jelly spines, full of fear, dread, and a cowering lickspittle attitude, the Bug took one look at what was going on at my trial and promptly rebelled. He, by God, was not going to have his credibility demeaned before a jury by any two bit hack political appointee's such outrageously contemptible behavior and lose respect before a jury. No, he chose to confront King head-on at the outset in an anecdote that I would come to savor.

The Bug, with Weinglass, Enoki, and Schroeder in attendance before King in chambers, proceeded to examine the jello-like substance of the judge's spine.

After getting through a number of minor points in which King gave very little, the Bug got to it. "Judge," he said, "on these other matters **you** had all the say. I had no say. I was just offering suggestions. On this next point, I **will** have a say. This goes to the stature and credibility a lawyer has to have in front of a jury. I can't speak for the other lawyers, but if I do anything that displeases you in the slightest, I expect you to register your displeasure outside the presence of the jury."

The Bug, just getting warmed up, claims at this point to have stabbed out a pointed finger at the doubtless startled King. "What I'm saying," he continued, "is that you are not to demean me in any way whatsoever before the jury. If you have anything derogatory to say to me, call a recess."

With cheeks that must have been rosy with anger, King, in what must have been his most imposingly sneering manner, replied, "I'm not goin to take the bench worried about you being overly sensitive, Mr. Bugliosi! Just because you're sensitive doesn't mean I'm going to be afraid to act as I've always acted!"

"I'm not sensitive at all, judge," the Bug responded blandly. "You can call me a horse's ass outside the presence of the jury."

But then he put serious force into his voice. "But before the jury, I will not be demeaned in any way whatsoever!"

The Bug thought he had managed to shock King into uncustomary silence. Surely the other three attorneys and the court reporter hardly dared to breathe. Then, mercifully in what he apparently considered a class act all the way, the Bug began to break it off gently. "If this were a court trial, no problem. But in a jury trial, when the judge does this it unquestionably hurts the client. The court has enormous stature with the jury, and the lightest comment carries with it considerable damage. My credibility before the jury is what we're talking about."

The Bug cared more for respect than being friendly with King, who still hadn't said anything. He went on greasing it up. "The thing I'm most concerned about going into this trial, judge, is that Stephanie's right to a fair trial might be, excuse the phrase, shipwrecked by some type of prosecutorial misconduct or by the court's indicating to the jury a bias in favor of the prosecutor."

But then, his eyes surely took on a steely glint, he said, "If either of these two things occurs, I'm going to take it to the mat right in front of the jury. I have to. I have no choice."

The Bug stood, ever the sort of diplomat who was willing to get in the frontlines of battle. "Judge, I hope you're not offended. I only say these things because of my grave concern for my client's right to a fair trial."

The Bug relates that King only smiled and said quietly, "I understand," but I'm sure if I'd been privileged to be present, I would have described him as smiling sickly and barely being able to croak, "I understand."

Oh, where was my own Bug when I so sorely needed him?

Money, I thought. If only I'd not been so profligate. If only I'd taken to robbing banks as my friend, Gerry had been so willing to instruct in the fine art of and squirreled away large sums. Then I could have had my own Bug and saved myself from so many years of hard imprisonment.

*****

That I could write many pages on the prostitution practiced in and around courts, the same can be said of the prosecutors, particularly Enoki who knowingly encouraged and permitted witnesses to perjure themselves in twisting and inventing testimony helpful to his cause. Instead, I will leave the subject with this quote from **The Best Defense**, by Alan

Dershowitz, a nationally known professor of law at Harvard:

REAL RULES OF AMERICAN JUSTICE GAME

1. Most criminal defendants are, in fact, guilty;
2. All criminal defense lawyers, prosecutors, and judges understand and believe Rule 1;
3. It is easier to convict guilty defendants by violating the Constitution than by complying with it, and in some areas, it is impossible to convict guilty defendants without violating the Constitution;
4. Almost all police lie about whether they violated the Constitution in order to convict guilty defendants;
5. All prosecutors, judges, and defense attorneys are aware of Rule 4;
6. Many prosecutors implicitly encourage police to lie about whether they violated the Constitution in order to convict defendants;
7. All judges are aware of Rule 6;
8. Most trial judges pretend to believe police officers who know they are lying;
9. All appellate judges are aware of Rule 8, yet many pretend to believe the trial judges who pretended to believe the lying police officers;
10. Most judges disbelieve defendants about whether their Constitutional rights have been violated, even if they are telling the truth;
11. Most judges and prosecutors would not knowingly convict a defendant who they believe to be innocent of the crime charged;
12. Rule 11 does not apply to members of organized crime, drug dealers, career criminals, or potential informers;
13. Nobody really wants justice.

*****

A defendant, apart from the fact he is caught on the wrong end of the law, holds a very unique position in a courtroom. Of all the witnesses against him, all those with whom he has been in contact, the defendant above everyone else is able to tell who is lying and who is not. Whether anyone will believe him is another matter. But it does not change the fact that he knows -- **he knows**, if only for himself alone.

That was my unenviable position. Of those I had met and had some interaction with, I would know whether they were lying or being truthful. I would know whether they were giving honest testimony or were exaggerating one way or another.

As to what I would experience with the testimony of each and every witness, Dr. Elizabeth Loftus (Witness for the Defense) would legitimize by confirming through a large body of evidence all "the creative ways in which human beings can twist and shape facts. With just a little shove here, slight shading there, a little de-emphasis over there," not only can a witness alter the way he perceives and understands his experience but also in the way others will perceive them in the telling.

She points out facts I knew well, that "police and prosecutors often exert a subtle but profound pressure on their witnesses to be complete and accurate; under such pressure, a guess can quickly solidify into a certainty. Witnesses will also put pressure on themselves, for it is a general characteristic of human nature that we will try to avoid looking uncertain or confused. Once we have offered a response, we tend to stick by it, becoming increasingly more confident as time goes by. Any attempt to get us to rethink or question a statement we have offered as a fact may be perceived as an assault on our honor and integrity."

Yes, and in some cases, I would also understand the fallibility of their memories, that they sometimes became warped out of their original reality in order to conform with their increasingly hostile attitudes. I could even understand that some of them, those of little insight into themselves or others, may have come to believe their bullshit was the God's-honest-truth.

When it came to the so-called expert witnesses, primarily presenting their opinions relevant to the condition of the bones and the aluminum box, of course I was easily able to relate their testimony to the reality of my own experience. Some were right, some wrong, and some of their conclusions were downright outrageous.

Innocence, as Dr. Loftus points out, can in fact come into a courtroom to sit "helpless, without hope, eyes wide, fear turning to panic." It does not wear a halo or wings and sit upon a white cloud. No, it can come "disguised as guilt, looking like guilt, smelling like guilt."

It is as Richard Condon (Winter Kills) describes it: "The illusion of truth, the appearance of truth, indeed, let us say the application of the techniques of fiction playing like searchlights upon a fancied facade of truth, would entirely suffice."

As Hugo Munsterberg would point out in **On the Witness Stand**, "Justice would less often miscarry if all who were to weigh evidence were conscious of the treachery of human memory. Yes, it can be said that, while the court makes the fullest use of all modern scientific methods when, for instance, a drop of blood is to be examined in a murder case, the same court is completely satisfied with the most unscientific and haphazard methods of common prejudice and ignorance when a mental product, especially the memory report of a witness, is to be examined."

Coupled to the incredible ineptness of Partington and Findlay, in the end, for all the good it never did me, I, alone, more than anyone else, knew without any doubt whatever that my trial, ostensibly a search for truth, was more in the nature of an exercise in farcical absurdity, an existential them of meaninglessness worthy of a Franz Kafka.

*****

Noel Allen Ingman, rat-snitch perjurer extraordinaire: Still believing in the efficacy of the lie-detector, as well as believing that Ingman's perjury had to be responsible for my conviction, I wrote a letter to Enoki sometime after the trial to ask that he give a polygraph test to Ingman. I knew he was lying and thought that if Enoki could be made to also believe that, he would have to realize that an injustice had been done, that if he were the ethical prosecutor as he pretends and the Bug claims, he would feel honor bound to do something about it. Perhaps he had inherited the Samurai code of honor from his ancestors.

Oh, great naive fool that I was, his response would open my eyes to the bitter truth! Instead, he gloated over his satisfaction that justice had been served and omitted all reference to the question of subjecting Ingman to a polygraph. Instead of replying directly to me, he sent the letter to Partington,

Partington, because I had mentioned having received bad advice from counsel on the question of my own testimony at trial, took the opportunity to castigate me for embarrassing him and to engage in an almost hysterical verbal backpedaling in distancing himself and setting up a defense against a charge of incompetent assistance of counsel. Partington had lied to Bugliosi when he claimed he was prevented from confronting Judge King's outrageous behavior on my orders. He had lied to Judge King by waiving my appearance at a hearing and saying I had told him I was pleased with the proceedings so far -- a hearing that I would not even learn had occurred until sometime later when another lawyer handling the appeal would inadvertently point it out, the very hearing that, for lack of information on the subject, would deprive me of a lesser included offense instruction. And he lied in the impossible claim that I had cooked up a scam with Williams. He would disclaim all responsibility for my conviction, charging that Judge King had rammed my conviction through, but that, unfortunately, that fact was not evident in the trial transcript and so not available for purposes of appeal.

Ah, me boyos, isn't fate a strange bird! Ingman thereupon had all the appearances of suddenly throwing his weight in my support, of showing both these ethically bent creeps up for the charlatans they are, when he recanted his testimony at my trial and confessed it was all lies!

Yes, incredible as it seems, entirely on his own initiative from his secret location on the federal witness protection program he personally called Enoki to unburden himself. Enoki, who recorded this tearful recantation, was duty-bound to share it with Partington in the interests of covering his own ass.

Findlay got excited and wrote me a letter to raise the possibility of a new trial. But, alas, FBI agent Hal Marshall had a talk with Ingman, doubtless to read him the riot act for embarrassing everybody with this silly attack of, well, conscience; doubtless to explain that he had confessed perjury to an Assistant U. S. Attorney no less, which could cause not only his ejection from the witness protection program but also a sure conviction for a crime that was subject to a five-year sentence cut and dried; and, my goodness, doubtless he would be segregated for his own protection in a high-security section of the prison where heroin would be difficult if not impossible to come by.

Whatever, Fairly Big got the message loud and clear. A few days later, he called Enoki again, this time to recant his recantation. He had been depressed, he explained, and confused by the recent suicide or accidental death by overdose of one of his numerous wives, and golly, none of the rest of his family loved him, and well, gee, sir, everything I said at Buck's trial was the absolute truth, so help me God, and could we just sort of overlook that other phonecall?

Why, of course. No real harm done. The status quo would remain unchanged. Even when the whole matter was attached as an afterthought to my pending appeal. In so many words, the court would rule that if a witness recants an **odd** number of times, a convicted defendant may have a chance, but if that witness recants an **even** number of times, a forget it. The court would augustly refrain from commenting upon the reliability of such serial recanters.

*****

Let us imagine murder and the disposal of corpses: The Bug says at page 555 of his book in his summation to the jury, "...Buck Walker was so adept at murder he left precious few pieces of incriminating evidence."

Adept is an interesting word. As a noun, it refers to a highly skilled or well-trained individual, an expert. As an adjective in the way the Bug used it, it refers to one who is thoroughly proficient. And proficient means well-advanced in an art, occupation, or branch of knowledge.

Therefore, the Bug seems to be suggesting that I have some prior experience in murdering people and disposing of their dead bodies. Watch closely now as I move the walnut shells about. No, no, Charlie Manson's under that shell. He's certainly not adept -- merely a low I. Q. sociopath. Try again. Ah! Ted Bundy. Well, that's better -- a smart guy, got away with it for some time and left few clues. Once more. How can you go wrong? What? Jack the Ripper? Not bad at all. He left lots of evidence behind in mutilated bodies -- but hardly a clue to his identity. Oh, you want to try again? My God! Jeffrey Dahmer! Well, he certainly disposed of them by placing the parts in his refrigerator until dinnertime!

Into such dubiously exalted company he places me. Only I have never murdered anyone and my only experience of body disposal comes from following through on someone else's plan -- not a bad one if I had been a bit more adept in carrying it out, sinking the containers in the ocean depths rather than in the lagoon.

Ah, well, that's always been one of my problems, getting involved in the plans and activities of others rather than striking out on my own.

All those letters from readers of the Bug's book, they all wanted to know how murder was done, how dismemberment was accomplished, the details of disposing of flesh and bone. They say, that's all right, we're not asking you to confess. Just imagine how you would have done it. Just pretend you're a murderer.

I have never responded to their inducement, never even been tempted. But now I will. I will provide a bit of titillation for the thrill-seekers. Also, perhaps, a bit of disappointment.

First, forget about the Bug's theory utilizing sledgehammer to inflict death, chainsaw to dismember, and firebox to destroy remains. Forget poisoned cakes and torturing with acetylene torches. Forget making people walk the plank after first throwing blood into the water to draw sharks.

On second thought, it occurs to me that the most ridiculous is not such a bad idea after all. Bodies fed to sharks is a pretty good way to dispose of them. Partington had somehow come into possession of a videotape from his trip to Palmyra. It showed a large Manta Ray under assault A by a feeding frenzy of sharks, who disposed of it in short order. Three hundred pounds of bodies would only draw more sharks, all eternally hungry feeding machines. Any leftover bones would sink to the bottom of the lagoon and possibly be buried in silt or sand. Even if found, surely the forensic scientists would detect signs of sharkbite. It would lend credence to the accidental death scenario. Why go through the trouble of retrieving metal boxes from the rescue launch, load in the bodies with gasoline, endure the hours of burning, and then tow them out to sink in the lagoon? Not very adept at all, me bucko.

The Bug requires an adept murderer, else how can he shine in pitting his wits to figure out where all the clues lead?

Okay. Give me another shot at it.

The Hermit Crab. Now there's a proficient little scavenger. I had once seen a Gooneybird -- or is it Boobeybird? -- which has to be the dumbest bird alive, even dumber than chickens, break its own neck in a collision with a tree while hurriedly making its usual ungainly attempt to take to the air. Once in the air, ah, but getting there, oh. I had caught one on the way down to Palmyra while trolling a lure. The Gooney or Boobey had dove for a snack and hooked itself. By the time I'd hauled it in, it was sorry-assed drowned bird.

Anyway, there the bird lay where it had fallen -- on its back, wings outspread -- while I went about my way with a sigh. My favorite meditational device did not include a bird that crashed and killed itself while attempting flight.

Talk about amazement, when I passed the spot the next day there was naught but a puff of feathers like a halo around the white and perfect skeleton of the bird -- not a speck of flesh remaining. Nearby sat dozens of the unmoving shells Hermit Crabs reside in -- doubtless lethargic from over-indulging in their feast of fowl.

I was so amazed, so enthralled at the sight, the perfect and delicate, even elegant, symmetry of the creature's internal structural elements that I briefly contemplated gathering the bones and gluing them all together as an exhibit. "Now, this was once a Gooneybird -- or is it Boobeybird? -- the dumbest example of avian species ever to grace creation -- next to the Dodo, of course, who forgot how to fly and thus became easy prey to man, the worst of all predators." Never mind, I had work to do.

The Hermit Crab, the perfect little assistants for disposing of flesh. Drag a body off into the bush where any witnesses, like Stephanie, for instance, were unlikely to venture. Return leisurely the next day with the Bug's favorite weapon to smash skull and bones into smithereens, throw the couple of bucketsful into the lagoon. Bones don't float. There are no metal boxes to haul up containing them.

My uncle Bud used to say that a lazy man was a thinking man. What he meant was that a thinking man looked for easier ways to do things so he'd have more time to lay about thinking.

Police detectives will tell you that when planning murder, simplicity is all. They mean that the simpler the crime, the easier it is to get away with. The more complex, the more opportunity for the perpetrator to make a mistake, to leave a finger-pointing clue behind. The fewer steps, the better. No evidence is better than little evidence. The Hermit Crab, the pulverizing sledge, the lagoon. That takes care of the disposal, but what about the act of murder itself?

In our national and international literature on the subject, whether fictional or non-fictional, I wonder if anyone else has taken note of the fact that crimes of murder are being reported in a grotesquely growing spiral of grisliness. Writers seem to delight in heaping terror upon horror in the details of the awfullest murders imaginable as though they were in a contest. And this sense of the awfullest imaginable, the insane depictions ranging from torturing children and tormenting old folks in the most terrible and gory details of the works of psychosexual monsters and cannibals, surrounds and permeates our community ethos, our consciousness, like amniotic fluid holds a fetus. Life imitates art, art imitates life.

It's hard for me to read this kind of crap. I know a guy who only reads true-crime books. He must have a hundred of them, including the Bug's. His latest was one about the Jeffrey Dahmer case. "The asshole was dining on roast leg of faggot," he said with a lusty grin. "Can you imagine that?" I preferred not to try and declined his offer to let me read it after him.

Sometimes I find myself caught up in a novel that works its way into the grisly stuff and find myself getting angry with the author for having written it. I especially hate the ones that seem to glory in the suffering of children and I wonder without success what the motivations of the authors are, how they can sit before writing pad, typewriter, or computer imagining such nightmarish scenes and putting them down word by word, no matter that the perpetrator is usually caught, imprisoned -- perhaps escapes for an inventive rerun -- or meets up with his just desserts delivered by a pissed off cop.

Supply and demand, it pays off.

I, therefore, if I had to choose a method of murder, would opt for the easiest and most sanitary means. I would not want to wield sledgehammer, chainsaw, knife, or acetylene torch and have to view the results of such necessarily close-up work.

I suppose, having to select from among the implements available on Palmyra, I would opt for the .30 caliber Marlin rifle and go for a long shot. Where and when? In broad daylight, of course. The bathtub would have been a good place, catch them naked and not have to perform the distasteful task of stripping them for the Hermit Crabs. Plenty of water to wash away the blood. Stephanie would not be able to see anything, nor hear the sounds of shots, from **Iola**.

Or perhaps catch them in some remote area on one of their exploratory trips, shoot and leave, not have to even see their lifeless corpses up close, leave them for the crabs, return in a day or two to get rid of the bones.

But wait. Another way occurs to me. As a part of my prison experience in San Quentin, I once watched a fellow make a pipebomb out of matchheads. Another explained in minute detail how to make a timer to create the spark or percussion that would detonate a bomb. All the materials were available to me on Palmyra. Why not make a bomb, sneak aboard the unlocked **Sea Wind** (So far as I know, no one ever locked their boats when they were away, certainly not Mac or us – despite Lord Pollock's claims to the contrary.) conceal it behind a propane tank timed to go off when they were most likely to be aboard. No more Sea Wind, no Grahams. Would anyone ever find any evidence, especially if it was not reported? Even if it was -- "Gee, I dunno, an explosion woke me up in the middle of the night."

Oh, but wait. That's no good. It's not in keeping with the Bug's theory that I lusted after Sea Wind and all her goodies. Some adept murderer you are, me boyo! Back to the drawing board. What if...

*****

Goodbye, my fine old mutts: Some folks asked, "Whatever happened to Popolo and Sista?" They knew about Puffer's ultimate fate after 19 years of life with Stephanie.

After Stephanie's arrest, Puffer's custody temporarily handed over to Joel Peters, and after my surrender, I was concerned about the fate of my hounds. They, too, had been arrested and placed into a state-run kennel. Hawaii's anti-rabies law called for a four-month quarantine for all animals entering the state. The law does not enjoy a high priority for enforcement. Since there has never been a case of rabies reported, the attitude is one of no problem, no worry. Thus, Puffer was allowed to escape. Thus, Lord and Lady Pollock were allowed to evade the law with their little mutt, Anheuser Busch. But who was there to save Popolo and Sista from the hoosegow?

After Steph had been released on bail, I had her inquire about their fate, urged her to go visit them with a supermarket pack of meaty bones. She reported that they were well and would be released at the end of the four-month period of quarantine -- if the owner could pay the cost of their room and board. Steph said she would not be able to afford those costs.

"Well," I lamented, growing desperate. "What will they do with them, put them to sleep?"

"Only if nobody buys them at the auction."

"Auction? What auction?"

"They have these auctions every Sunday, try to sell the dogs they have, place them in good homes and recover some of their costs."

"Oh." I thought. Mixed breed mongrels could not demand much at an auction, not like a purebred. Steph could easily afford to buy them back for far less than the kennel charges. "You gotta go to the auction, buy 'em back," I begged.

"Right, baby, don't worry. I'll get 'em," she wrote.

"Don't forget," I wrote back. "The first auction day after the quarantine period's done."

"Don't worry, baby. I got their phone number. I got the date marked on my calendar."

One evening I watched an item on the evening news on TV. The famous dogs in the Palmyra Island Case had been sold at auction. The camera panned from Popolo to Sista to their new owner, a giant round grinning Hawaiian.

Where was Steph?

She'd gotten the date wrong. She'd gone on Sunday when the auction had been held the day before.

I had only those last video images to console me. There was Sista, prettier than pie in her brindle coat, her black legs and snout, wagging her tail, happy over all the attention. And there was Popolo looking wary, puzzled by all the todo. He looked directly into the camera, seemed to be looking directly at me, his great head cocked quizzically, his floppy ears raised at their base. He seemed to be speaking to me, saying, "Hey, boss, I'm ready. Let's play. Let's go somewhere. Let's hit the water, boss."

What can be said for a red-blooded American man who gets choked up over his dogs? Popolo. Sista.

"What, boss? No more dancing?"

*****

"Justice is something that doesn't exist in nature. It is a creation of mankind." (Ridley Pearson, Probable Cause)

*****

"Man can will nothing unless he has first understood that he must count on no one but himself; that he is alone, abandoned on earth in the midst of his infinite responsibilities; without help, with no other aim than the one he sets himself, with no other destiny than the one he forces for himself on this earth." (Jean Paul Sartre, Saint Genet)

*****

Joshua Slocum spoke of having penetrated a mystery. He had sailed through a fog. He had met Neptune in his wrath, but the god found that Slocum had not treated him with contempt, and so he suffered him to go and explore.

Like the good captain, I have tested my mettle, dipped into deeper waters of myself for an offering to the god of the sea. But unlike the captain, I do not face the future washed of all regret. My troubles were not all astern. Still, perhaps another summer is ahead, and even another after that, the world, such as it is, before me.

Next summer will bring the two barbecues out in the prison yard, but never will I volunteer to attend. I prefer to sit alone in my cell and contemplate the day -- the day when all the world was truly before me in my young years and I had everything necessary except the love of the woman I loved -- the man, and the bird, mysteries promising amazement and the freedom of flight. Every voyage of a life is but a step between the womb and the grave, and time is no more than a temporary place where you wake up and the day is either good or bad or so-so. I must live as if there were no tomorrow even though death beckons with an irresistible finger in the foggy cool of the morning.

And when no one is looking to see my rusty moves, I'll try a dance step or two to reassure myself I haven't entirely forgotten how.

# # #

APPENDIX I

LOGBOOK OF IOLA

June 1 to September 10, 1974

6-1-74: Departed Port Allen 0900, 159°36'W, 21°52'N, under fair trades. Becalmed in lee of Kauai several hours. Picked up trades again 1300. About 1800 lowered sails, then rehoisted jib for steerage. Steph sailed to 2000, me to 0100 next morning. Steph again to 0530. Popolo, Sista, and Puffer make up the non-working crew - our dogs!

6-2-74: Lollygagged. Soaked all members in seawater, put up canopy, tied wheel - she self-steers under jib, which Steph discovered - and crashed.

6-3-74: Some showers, sea rougher. Saw lights of large ship heading SW. Trolling - no luck. Working on navigation: 17°N! Course 120°-210°! Dogs crapping on fordeck.

6-5-74: Bathed all in Dr. Bonners - set 2 jibs wing and wing. No seasickness today! Had heavy bite on fish line.

6-6-74: Navigation scrambled - latitude 14°17'N! Seas very rough, winds 30+ knots. 2000 hours. I got on foul weather gear and ran before it 225°-240° under jib. Abated about 0230 of 6/7. Went up to turn vent on cabintop during storm, on return slipped headfirst hitting eye on stanchion, stunned about 30 seconds, gash on cheekbone, bloody nose.

6-7-74: Figured lat. 16°15'N (roughly!) More heavy seas and winds this evening, miserable night for all, heavy showers, bilge water sloshing everywhere.

6-8-74: Moderate winds, sea still rough. Had a flying fish on deck this morning. Fix at 159°30'W, 15°28'N, for 1259 hours.

6-9-74: Running fix at 1344 of 160°35'W, 14°38'N.

6-11-74: Fix at 161°38W, 12°10'N. Caught Mahimahi. Hook in thumb. Pushed thru, S filed barb down, pulled out, dressed. Fish ono.

6-12-74: Fix at 1630 hours, 161°17.5'W, 10°24'N. Huge school of porpoise cruised by, cavorting to entertainment of all.

6-13-74: Fix at 1426 hrs, 161°37'W, 9°20N. Sailing under working jib only, self-steering. Taking it easy.

6-14-74: Fix at 1632 hrs. 161°4014, 7°55'N. 120 miles from our destination! Should reach there 6/16. Raised main for about 6 hrs - made good time.

6-15-74: Fix at 1630 hrs. 161°48'W, 7°10'N. Gray, cloudy, rainy - visibility poor. Under jib - self-steering. Charging batteries. Bath in rain. Believe we have hit Doldrums - becalmed with squalls - little progress made - barely able to get fix through all these clouds.

6-16-74: Still becalmed - gray skies - no sun to fix so far - drifting SW - periodical rainsqualls. Glimpses of sunshine gives us a fix of 161°55'W, 7°07.5'N. Not much progress in over 24 hrs.

6-17-74: Got up enough wind to raise the main - put up the larger jib. Progress is still very slow. B ran out of tobacco & is miserable. So far haven't gotten an afternoon sight for a fix. Baking cornbread. Got a fix - averaged 7°011N, 161°51'W.

6-18-74: Sunny lazy day. No wind. Reading, charging battery. Fix 6°30'N, 161°53'W.

6-19-74: LAND HO! at 1615 spotted Samarang off our port side. Wind very light - unable to make landfall before dark. Headed east. Strong winds all night - headed east then SE then S then NE - wind ceased at 5 a.m. just as we were heading NW - then becalmed.

6-20-74: Respotted Samarang 845 ships time dead west - winds very light from SE. Very frustrating - rainsqualls and enough wind to get us just about where we were yesterday at this time - becalmed. So near & yet so far! If we can only get into anchoring position would be preferable to a repeat of last night or worse floating aimlessly this close with not even a moon to say if we're drifting up on her banks. At nightfall we are on her west bank but north of anchorage position with our small jib & under very light winds headed Northwest.

6-21-74: Though winds were light last night & are brisk S.E. today, we're having trouble relocating our island. Tacking from E to SW. Rain, intermittant sun - got one sight - waiting for another. With these winds & if we can find her, we should be able to make landfall - if we can find her!

6-22-74: Couldn't find her - lowered all sails last night - no wind thru today. Reading. Took sights, position N6°22', W161°59'.

6-23-74: Fair tradewinds - hoisted all sails & went in repursuit of our island. Re-LANDHO at 1230 giving us ample time to gain anchorage. For entry we're hoping for a SE wind before too long. Another craft, catamaran anchored just northwest of island - we are on SW. Haven't met them. Saw a light on island at night. Possibly another boat?

6-24-74: So nice to wake up & have the island right there in front of us.

6-25-74: Another day of reading. Penthouses & Playboys. Strong NE winds continue. Another sloop - motorsailer - putted by, circled, putted by again. Unsure what became of them. B wanted to see if they'd tow us in but never made contact. Cat is still anchored where it began on the 23rd.

6-26-74: R caught two big fish this a.m. Soaked them in brine & hung them out to dry. Will use for bait when we go beyond reef to fish. A family of manta rays came by scouting their dinner. Still NE trades. Still waiting & reading.

6-27-74: Awoke to SE wind! Got our shit together and hoisted sail. Coming in great. Cat hoisted sail and appeared to be following us in. Fine, until we went aground on a coral head. Wind died, we lost way, and steerage, and scrunch! Dropped sail, carried both anchors out in inflatable and busted ass winching off. No sooner were we off then two dinghys w/ outboards, 2 guys in each, came to our rescue. They towed us in. We had to leave anchors w/ lines tied to flotation cushions. Jack Wheeler, wife Lea & daughter Sharon showed us to the bathtub. First fresh water bath in 27 days, - ah, heaven, Zillions of birds here - nesting along runways with newly hatched young. Eggs & young everywhere. In evening visited motorsailer Caroline, Skipper Larry. Crewman Tony one of our reef saviors. Gave Tony a letter to Richard and Carlos, enclosed a note to my mom.

6-28-74: Slept great. No surge or roll. A very peaceful night. Today filled with getting things together. Hung clothes to air... Baking bread...charging batteries...eating coconut...washing clothes. Hopefully it will rain soon to replenish almost pau water supply. Have maybe 10 gal. left.

6-29-74: B went to help Jack Wheeler & son in clearing aim runway - hoping to improve P.R. and maybe get a recommendation to owner to stay on officially as caretaker - so I'll bake an extra loaf of bread. Made some coconut grated ice milk sherbet yesterday and froze it in icebox. What a luxury - haven't had an icebox in almost 2 years - since Olu St. house.

6-30-74: Lazed about - Popolo bit Steve, so moved them farther away. Think I've O.D.'d on coconuts - stomach is fucked. Sharon brought us over a great papio -- really good score. B went out with catamaran guys (came in in dinghy - heading for Samoa, cause wind has been a strong NE ever since the day we came in) & retrieved the Danforth anchor - homemade one still out there. Maybe he'll be able to try again for that one. Baked them a blackberry pie in thanks. Think it was pau* before they reached the channel.

July 1st: R helped Jack & Steve Wheeler machete the runway this morning. I'm baking bread. Rainy day - gathered 17 gallons of fresh rainwater - hm hm good! Reading Joseph Conrad. Baked a cinnamon nut loaf for the Wheelers & cinnamon bread for us. Another boat out there today - double master.

July 2nd: Clean-up, dry out hopefully - although there isn't any sun in sight. Water the calmest & clearest we've seen - can see the bottom & what fish are swimming around, Ron from the catamaran "Baniki Island" came (rowed) in - returned pie tin. Gave him a haircut to impress the Wheelers - he'd like a ride back to Hawaii as cat is falling to pieces. Doesn't look like he'll get one tho - offered to pay us for a ride over to Christmas -- buy us a new motor - have this one overhauled - whatever - B said no tho - caught about 40 lb. Ulua last night - black, tho, too bad, they're poisonous. Two new arrivals moored today.

July 3rd: Read J. Conrad. Met people on our new arrival - The Tempest - Honolulu - M has a white dog (Anhauser Bucsh) female - invited me over with Puffer so that they could be friends - both very spoiled primadonnas but each others size. Steve took R. trolling - caught a small Ulua plus the laes (?) they gave us last night and its fish for dinner.

July 4th: Quietest July 4th in history. Very windy, rainy. Another stay at home - alone - read day.

July 5th: Steve had some fireworks so we had some noise today. Lea gave me some cooking oil as I was almost out. I baked them a raison nut loaf for bon voyage. Too windy to leave today. R ran wire from refrid. T

o shore here - took generator down there - now all we ***Over, done, finished**. need is something to keep cool. Wrote letters to Fullard-Leo, Dickie, Bobby & family, & mom - gave to Wheelers to mail.

July 6th: Wheelers shoved off this a.m. 0800. R thinking of turning our stern into their place but its risky the way the current goes. Maybe on a very still day will try - turned around wind and rain wouldn't blow into cockpit so much. Muff & Mac of ship out of San Diego came by. Mac had an outboard motor on his dinghy so helped R swing boat around - Mac's a smoker so R would love to get tight with him. More rain - Sista & Popolo dug up Steve's shark head.

July 7th: Awoke early & went fishing with the poles of bamboo and I sewed up a lace skin for a lure. Trucked to Northshore, walked all along that shore, crossed to east lagoon -- no fish but plenty of exercise -- Only thing got caught, the end of my line was Popolo - nibbling at the bait. Returned via runway - stopped off & made our first coconut butter & back to the boat for R&R plus salad & bake something to go with the butter. R cooked a popover which didn't pop & me a sweet coffee cake to satisfy my sweet urge. Gave some letters to The Tempest (Marilyn & Ed Pollock) & lent them Euell Gibbon's book.

July 8th: Cleared an area for tent after feasting on breakfast of pancakes with coconut butter & syrup (Log Cabin). Cut army tarp for boat, laundry & spent rest of day doing coconut for milk, cream & butter. For dinner - fried coconut with soyu & Mung bean sprout salad. Collected hermit crabs for bait & in pm fished - caught some little ones in a net (mullet? not sure so used for bait) R caught a big red snapper but had to throw him back as he's poisonous.

July 9th: Set up tent - baked macaroons - made coconut butter. Rowed over to island on other side of lagoon, trailing a fishing line baited with mullet - ate my bait twice. No catch. Took cold coconut milk to the Tempest & on my way to bath took some coconut butter to Mac & Muff. Never got to bathe but had a very enjoyable evening with them, drinking wine, which tasted fine & then some rum which was a bit too much for me on an empty stomach. Got pretty drunk - smoked 2 cigarettes. Mac had given R. some Bullderm (sic) earlier in the day. Then gave him a part pack of some other cigarettes. He has a friend for life now. Fell immediately to sleep upon hitting my pillow.

July 10th: Woke up slightly hung over - without much desire to do things - made up rest of coconut - scrubbed boat down - great improvement - put up army tarp - also much better more headroom. Marilyn & Ed Pollock came by - returned books & brought a yummy of various fruit which R fixed into a large biscuit with sugar and cinnamon on top - Um, um. Ate one of those white mullets (?) pretty sure that's what they are - hope we survive it - tasted good. Started some sour dough starter.

July 11th: Rain, rain, rain. Rained all night. A shame we didn't have our plastic up - tarp by now might be clean enough to gather from, but we figured the plastic would be more sanitary. So first thing we did was repair storm damage done to tarp supports - then covered tarp with plastic - and that ended the rain - next rain tho we're ready for. Then had to re-set up tent which collapsed during storm. Poles were terribly bent & in attempting to straighten them 2 broke so R must improvise either replacements or some sort of bracing. In pm scooped 14 mullets from boat with net in about an hour. Not bad - mostly tiny ones though. Rest of night spent cleaning, cooking, & eating.

July 12th: Must be the rainy season down here - any way that's good because we can sure use the water. Ate the rest of last nights mullet catch for breakfast this morning. Collected 13 gallons before 9 am. Had to fix plastic & tarp as we were blowing away - did so with pebbles wrapped in tin foil & tied to plastic then tied down to lifelines. Meanwhile my coconut milk sourdough starter looks to be working, bubbling away - tomorrow I think I'll give it a try. Sat tent up again with new side appendage & secured to surrounding trees. Saw Marilyn & Ed Pollock of Tempest as they returned from a Northshore hike - spoke to her about trading some stuff for food so I'll take over my red & gold velour, my straw bag & our ship to shore radio & see if she's interested in any of that. In pm made couscous/soy burgers w/mushroom sauce & that was ono. Pau w/Conrad. Back to Penthouse.

July 13th: Mixed up my sourdough batter & made a raisin pie but couldn't get the merange (sic) to stiffen with that egg replacer. Other than that it was ono. Marilyn wasn't feeling well -- a reoccurance of that tooth inlay. Anyway when I went over she wasn't into looking at the stuff I brought & said they may go to Fanning instead of home & may well need all the food they have and altho she'd sell me stuff - she couldn't trade it. Never even got on board to see their boat. Ho hum. Such is life. R spent the day moving beds, mattresses, inner springs, tables, etc etc to his new camp. Spent some time fishing while going & coming from bathtub, but with no luck. Wrote a letter to my Mom, gave it to Marilyn to mail for me.

July 14th: Baked that sourdough bread today & it came out good... real good. R constructed the baby planter...we cleared the roof of tree limbs for the garden...moved a table & piece of plywood from the barracks to the campsite again fishing while enroute...again with nary

a nibble. R's camp is pretty together, bed w/box spring & good mattress, desk & swivel chair, night table...he's thinking of moving in maybe tonite. Meanwhile some seeds are sprouting so cups are in order soon.

July 15th: Marilyn & Ed came by - brought some books, some oil & carob & some flour. Very nice of them; shall make my birthday cake from her things. R took bedding & lantern, mosq. coils down to his camp and hereafter plans to make that his home. He began moving bed planks down to roof garden & I washed some bedding. In pm had a delicious dinner of sourdough English muffins, bacon & cheese salad. Then R caught 11 mullets for tomorrow's repast.

July 16th: Tempest leaving today. Ed & Marilyn Pollock brought by some jars, books & rice pudding, which I devoured entirely tho made some halfhearted effort to save 1 for R - then 4 - then lost out to my appetite & just ate it up. They're leaving today so are making the rounds with her camera - took my picture with Puffer. R came by with some coffee & took off to make ready to make my birthday cake - when he returned I was begged to split so he could get underway. I went down to his camp, read & took a Sopor (my present to me) while Mac.& Muff delivered my second present - they had retrieved our anchor! R invited them to partake of cake & coffee at 6", which they accepted. Cleaned & fileted fish & we had fried fish patties - went & bathed & moved a very pretty cake etc down to campsite. Mac & Muff wrapped some roasted soy nuts & sachet as a present - all sang happy birthday & I blew out one of our large volatile (sic) candles atop the cake after making a wish. Talked awhile, then bid each other goodnite after which R & I smoked some hash & had an exquisite fuck - all in all a very fine birthday.

July 17th: Went (rowed) over to Paradise Island - Hencefore known as Crab Island - so for dinner we have crabs legs - a lot of them. Never saw so many land crabs in my life & tasted delicious. Began Catcher in the Rye.

July 18th: Finished Catcher - didn't leave boat most of day. R went to cut wire for roof garden but dropped the roll in the water - irretrievable. Around 4:30 did a coconut run, processed about z - got many with sprouts which we fried - kind of comes out like eggplant cooked that way.

July 19th: Reading incessantly. Processed rest of coconuts. R caught a bunch of mullets for tomorrow.

July 20th: Awoke early to very heavy rain - by 8 am collected 20 gallons of water. Instead of butter this time, the cream went sour, so we have a fine batch of sour cream.

July 21st: Prepared a Sunday breakfast of blueberry blintzes with blueberry syrup & sour cream. Went to roof garden sight (sic) and tried hammering but it was very frustrating & I'm afraid my handiwork is none too strong. Meanwhile R was off at the northshore & brought back 3 primo papios. So for Sunday dinner the dogs get a special treat of mullet & we have an extra papio to give Mac and Muff.

July 22nd: Carried bucket loads of dirt in am - after 5 I was ready to pass out. Another boat came in, "Shearwater" from Portland, Oreg. Two guys on board have toured South Pacific heading back to Honolulu. I haven't met them yet but R rowed out & rode over with them & helped moor them where Tempest had been. More fish for dinner - never took Muff & Mac the other so we still have one left.

July 23rd: Put up 2nd batch of sourdough starter - also some M seeds. Rainy day. R came over & both stayed on boat & read. Mac & Muff came by. He gashed his leg with a machete, tried to sew himself up but ended just pushing skin together & bandaging it that way. They gave us an address of someone on Big Island who the boys can contact to say when they'll be down & by ham radio. When Mac talks to him will relay the message. Another old favorite for dinner - Coconut cake salad, papio & coconut cake, some baked in shell - some fried. Haven't seen much of two guys on Shearwater - they went exploring in all this rain. In fridge there's a cold quart of beer & 4 cokes they said they'd share with us. After Don & Bill returned from their north shore island romp, we joined them on their boat. Shearwater, I found out, is a bird. We were treated to rum, coke & cream soda & cocktail peanuts - made a deal to trade mags & books next day. They gave R two packs of South Seas cigarettes. Don showed me his log, full of pictures of Tonga,

Fiji, etc. A very enjoyable evening. Earlier Mac brought us over a good group of books. Justine, 1984, a Harold Robbins - some Zane Grey & another Agatha Christie.

July 24th: Went to Northshore fishing, but had no luck - cloudy days, R feels, aren't good days to catch fish because there's no sun to glitter off shiny lure. Got our already read mags & books together to trade with Don & Bill. In pm went over to Shearwater. Don & Bill turned R on to 2 packs pipe tobacco & a fish knife as I broke his Buck knife on coconuts. Also gave me flour, sugar & pudding to make bread & pies & whatever. Made arrangements for a potluck dinner for tomorrow & plan to ask Mac & Muff, too. Also to go fishing in morning & bake bread. Should have quite a day. We traded them a bunch of books & mags & got some fishhooks thrown in for luck. Very nice guys, both of them.

July 25th: Whew - a very busy day. Woke early & started sourdough bread. Soon after R came by on his way fishing. Did sourdough & plain white - while rising, Mac came by - went on motorboat ride to his boat - coffee & chess & made arrangements for tonight. Came back to boat & baked those loaves plus made an apricot nut loaf for tonight & a quick cinnamon loaf for those guys. R brought back 4 papios. Pudding/coconut pie is next on list & hopefully time for a quick bath. Dinner menu: papio baked in R's special coconut cake gravy: ham: carrots & potatos, coconut pudding pie: apricot nut loaf. Umm! And then, we ate & we ate & we ate & we had cake & cream soda with rum - and everyone went home very full. Wrote a note to mom for shearwater to mail. Also Dickie.

July 26th: Basically squally - took Shearwater the breads I baked for them. My stomach is still packed with last nites feast - my head still feels the rum. Reading Ernest Gann's sea story "Song of Sirens."

July 27th: Our one month anniversary - R promised to build me a wagon to carry dirt, but he doesn't seem inclined thus far to do anything about it. And then the rains came so we sat & read & ate popcorn. Started filling water hold & put 15 gal in as the summer here is approaching & I assume the rains will decrease considerably.

July 28th: Boy, this place is really something else - more rain! - Last night Don & Bill came rowing by just around sunset & I talked to them about trading VHF radio for food & I think they'll do it so sometime today I'll take the radio over & see what they can spare for it. R took the wheels & axle off the shredder and made a 2-wheeled wagon - so far with no sides but he said he'd put sides on it next.

In afternoon & early evening R went over & played chess with Mac while I engulfed myself more deeply in "1984."

July 29th: Set up 5 more babies - total of 10 perhaps - more coming. R said ants ate several of them this (unreadable).

July 30th: R completed sides on wagon! I went with Bill & Don, Mac & Muff on an exploratory trip to Eastern & Barren Island. Found some good shells & several bottles. Meanwhile R went fishing at North Shore, caught one papio - later shot the largest mullet we've ever seen. Took fish & coconut over to Shearwater & fried it up - much in thanks for the flour, rice & misc. they gave to us this morning. Finished "Faking It" by Gerald Green in wee hours.

July 31st: Went fishing - R shot a papio but we couldn't retrieve it - Now starting seeds in cups on boat so ants can't eat them while still in ground.

Aug. 1st: Now have a filled water storage. R set up run off from tent yesterday, so he should be collecting water now (it's raining). Reading "The Kingmaker" by Henry Wenker. Shearwater left today - off to Hawaii.

Aug. 2nd: Gathered 10 wagonloads of dirt but handle on wagon now needs repair. R took outboard ashore & put oil in sparkplug holes. Also he got generator going again after being on the blink for a couple of days. He also fixed chainsaw. Baked English muffins to go with beans & now feed dogs a hot meal of rice & dog food. Catching mullets tonight - hopefully enough for tomorrows dinner all around.

Aug. 3rd: Transported dirt from ground to roof garden in am. Took care of about 1/6th of garden: wagon handle broke again. R started my garden baby planter. Did a coconut run. Last of that one great tree. Processed part. Mac & Muff brought by a huge ulua. R cleaned it & they gave us 3/4s - a lot of meat there - a feast for us & the dogs tomorrow.

Aug. 4th: Processed rest of coconut & churned butter - lunched on ulua fried in coconut butter & English muffins. R fiberglassed part of doghouse roof in effort to stop leak. Chopped some palm heart for salad & to cook into fish gravy for dinner. After dinner took up R challenge of best 2 out of 3 chess match for a body rub & b.j. - which, much to his chagrin I won! Finest rub of the year & an excellent b.j. & a fuck thrown in.

Aug. 5th: Processed rest of butter. R fixed my wagon, made himself a far out spear. I enclosed my nursery & scrubbed oven & stove. Took spear in dinghy in search of fish but were rained out. On returning to boat, found a good size papio hung from backstay which Mac & Muff must have brought by. Another gourmet meal. Spent evening drooling over our next boat.

Aug. 6th: A very sluggish day. Mechanical bilge pump wouldn't work so had to pump out by hand. Stopped by to thank Mac for yesterday's fish. Pancakes.

Aug. 7th: Dug some more dirt for garden but the day was very hot & I felt dragged before I even began. R went to northshore to try his new spear - tho able to spear 2 fish, on retrieving the spear didn't stick so he lost both. Mac & Muff brought over a nice little papio which we gave to the dogs for their very own feast. They loved it! Gave Mac a bunch of books we're done with.

Aug. 8th: Set batch #3 of seeds - so far 1 & 2 only yielded 15 plants. Rained all morning - a steady, bleak rain but one which hasn't been much for collecting rainwater. R chopped a coconut tree so we had palm heart salad for lunch. Baked 2 loaves "diet" bread, without sugar or oil - tasted a bit flat. Mac brought over 22 good sized fish - only kept I for him & Muff. Fed part to dogs for tonite - refridg with the rest for tomorrow - enough for us & dogs.

Aug. 9th: Awoke to another rain filled morning. This time the rain's considerably heavier & I'm able to collect some much needed drinking water. Collected 13 gallons by 1:00 when rains subsided.

Dug more dirt for roof garden. Had rest of yesterdays fish for dinner for us & dogs.

Aug. 10th: Dug another 10 loads of dirt. Sunny, hot day. Garden now about i full. Another 3-4 days @ 10 loads of dirt a day should do it. Transferred dirt to roof. Did a coconut tree but not too many coconuts were on it - mostly spoonmeat - milk came out very thick & sweet. Dinner was palm heart salad, palm heart stew/coconut milk pudding shake. Gave Mac & Muff a bunch of palm heart. What a day - I'm pooped.

Aug. 11th: Did 5 loads of dirt & one load mulch while R went to northshore fishing - caught 2 papios - 1 mullet. Cleaned fish & he took the mullet & some coconut milk over to Mac & Muff. I rowed down to bathe. Then we went & got gasoline. When we filled generator, she froze up; couldn't get her to start. Emptied fridge. Had a huge salad & papio for us & dogs for dinner. Then we went to tent - he re-challenged me to chess - same stakes - I lost pitifully but had to take a raincheck on paying the backrub part as I cut my finger while preparing dinner. "Well, did you cut your mouth, too?" he asked - and an enjoyable evening was shared.

Aug. 12th: R & Mac got generator going again. Did in rest of coconuts from 2nd tree. Made a coconut custard pie.

Aug. 13th: Did 10 loads of dirt in am. Another boat came in - "Toloa," Santa Barbara, heading for Australia via Samoa - 2 guys. R caught one papio which we shared with the dogs. Bilged. Bone meal on babies.

Aug. 14th: Dug more dirt & w/R's help transferred it to roof. Met Tom Wolfe of "Toloa" - Popolo & Sista attacked him. R, Tom and friend (Norm) went fishing on north shore, but returned without any fish.

Aug. 15th: Half of the month - holding our ground food wise as best we can. In stores have about 10 meals. Enough rice for maybe a week of only feeding it to the dogs: maybe 7 lbs of dogfood & some cans. If the boys can make it by Sept. 1st we can breeze right through. Otherwise we have the alternatives of selling our generator to Mac & going to Fanning or eating coconuts and living by the day – probably easier for us than for the dogs. Some rain in a.m. Gave Norm a lift to his dinghy ashore. Mac brought them back late last night. Gathered books & mags to trade. Offered to bake bread for them. They plan to leave Saturday. As usual, dug dirt. R transplanted 3 plants - very scrawny. He also cleared a path from refridg. house to tent & chopped a small coconut tree for the palm heart.

Aug. 16th: Went over to "Toloa" (duck in Tongan) traded books (got Winter, 2 Tom Wolfe, a few sci-fi's) and flour etc for making bread - baked them 2 loaves, a cornbread & split a coffee cake - kept my half of fixin's to make another day. Mac brought over a 20 lb. ulua! And a nice size papio. So the dogs got two dinners tonight. Transplanted 3 babies into coffee cans.

Aug. 17th Dug a bit more dirt but that area's about dug out. R soyed & barbequed some fish - very tasty. Toloa left at noon.

Rained rest of afternoon - collected 5 gallons water. Dogs & us shared the rest of the 20 pounder for dinner. R planted some garden seeds. Attached chain from bow to dolphin.

Aug. 18th: Morning filled with rain & reading. "Drifters" by Michener. Rained on & off all day. More on than off - R made pancakes & "experimental cakes" using basically pancake mix & cooking them in oven. Scavenged some coconuts for dogs & ground it for them.

Aug. 19th: Last night a fresh westerly came up - worst storm we've had - today I'm putting another stern line up as I didn't feel secure in that storm with only one. Dug 10 loads - then more rain - R came by to bake cakes & cookies - which once again infuriated me. Then sunshine but I was stranded as he took the dinghy to shore, slight confrontation and to our separate corners for the night.

Aug. 20th: Transferred dirt to roof - another 40 wagon loads should do it - say another week. Went to gashouse & did a load of sprouted coconuts. Made a milkshake. Gave R a haircut. Soy beans for dinner. And a beautiful sunset.

Aug. 21st: Very calm day - no wind. Dug 5 loads. Wrote a note to Dickie to have Mac relay via ham radio to Curt if latter still has received no word from Shearwater. Rowed out to channel, fishing. No luck at all. Landed Sand Island & loaded up on some sprouted coconuts. Rowed to west tip of Cooper & explored. Bathed - delivered note to Muff.

Aug. 22nd: Today was a day of good news & bad news. The good news was the boys sent word via Mac that they'd be down. The bad news was that they wouldn't be able to make it til the end of October. Mac didn't seem overjoyed at buying our generator but said he'd let us have $5000 for it. So I baked a cake to forget my woes.

Aug. 23rd: Took outboard over to Mac's. He gave us the $5000 for generator. I started cleaning up & hauling cups etc. (things not needed) to shore. R started to try to convert shredder motor to bilge pump, just in case manual pump breaks down.

Aug. 24th: Made further strides in getting the boat seaworthy, tho it hardly looks it at a cursory glance. R. started in on front hatch - he's going to fiberglass it water tight. Mac passed final death sentence on our poor old outboard - so ends our day - no dinner save a coconut milkshake.

Aug. 25th: Not what I consider a very high energy day - but then we haven't been eating very high energy foods lately. Collected 19 sprouted coconuts & R husked some for the trip. I resumed trying to get boat stowed & orderly but another day is needed to finish the job. For the first time in 3 days we'll have something other than coconuts for dinner - beans. Maybe we'll generate more energy tomorrow.

Aug. 26th: Got a few things accomplished today. Between R & I must have got 20+ sprouted coconuts. Started charging the batteries. Made safety for stern. Mac brought by Fanning chart which I copied. R worked on our new (I hope) shredder motor powered bilge pump; also repaired seat crack & fiberglassed over bow hatch due to leakage.

Aug. 27th: A rainy, rainy day. Gathered another 16 coconuts. Charged batteries for another several hours. At this rate we'll be here another week.

Aug. 28th: I husked sprouted coconuts & transplanted. R repaired cubby door, fixed bowhatch & did some work on bilge pump. All the while the hum of the generator attests to the charging of batteries from morning til night. Today's Weds - winds willing we shall be ready Saturday.

Aug. 29th: Husked rest of coconuts - we have 30 to go with. Did transplants. Still charging batteries. Have decks cleaned & ready for swabbing - swabbed cockpit & doghouse.

Aug. 30th: All out effort day. R was up bright & early, scavenging butts at Mac's workshop. Wangled a couple of games of chess, stash of coffee & tobacco to go, plus an invitation to dinner. Not bad for before 9 am! Next was coffee!!! Cleaning swabbing, stowing - removed canopy, baking bread, all round general clean up, both on boat & ashore.

Was going to bake bread in outdoor oven to conserve fuel, but time & energy would not allow it. Undoubtedly, upon return, I'll have no alternative - only hope the fuel lasts til then. South winds been blowing pretty steady for over a week. Most south wind we've had - and I'm not sure we can get out the channel with it. Mac said if the winds not strong he could probably push us with his 9.5 hp outboard. Here's hopin'!

And then - tragedy - and overnite a whole new set of alternatives beset us.

Aug. 31st: No sleep all night. Search all day. Found upturned dinghy. No other signs.

Sept. 1st: R says he feels no hope of finding anything - but still we search.

Sept. 2nd: and search

Sept. 3rd: and then? What to do

Sept. 4th: and the decision to depart - followed by a great deal of preparation while we all grow fatter & fatter on ham & cheese & pancakes & turkey & chili & all the things we hadn't had in so long - And the dogs feast on corn beef hash & (obscured).

Sept. 5th & 6th, 7th, 8th, 9th: Making ready to sail. An incredible amount of stowing & packing.

Sept. 10th: There was an outside chance of leaving today, but the weather was not favorable, much rain. So we have a leisurely day of securing whatever needs securing & hopefully tomorrow the weather will be more conducive to go.

###

Note: Bold heavy type indicates entries by Walker; all the rest being by Stearns.

There is some confusion regarding the proper naming of our foresails. The outermost sail forward is the jib. Sometimes a larger sail is flown in place of this jib, which is called a genoa. The sail immediately aft of the jib, affixed to the second forestay I had added on Maui, is a called a forestaysail. Steph and I both miscall the forestaysail a jib. Whenever we mention self-steering under jib, or smaller jib, we mean forestaysail. Speaking of a large or larger jib really means genoa.

APPENDIX II
October - Hawaii

Dear Kit,

It's difficult to write this as the news we have to convey is very sad for us, and we know it will be so for you. I've made numerous attempts in this regard and each has always seemed inadequate. Even now I can find no words that seem appropriate to the circumstances. We are torn in many ways in this matter, yet we feel a deep obligation to communicate with you.

My name is Roy Allen and my wife is Stephanie. We've recently returned to Hawaii from Palmyra, where we met Mac and Muff and, although we were fellow inhabitants for only a couple of months on a remote atoll, we came to care very much for them.

Please prepare yourself for the worst.

Mac and Muff disappeared August 30th, and we haven't seen them since. We believe they died in a boating accident. They had gone fishing in the afternoon and never returned. The next day we found their overturned dinghy washed up on the beach.

All else that follows is elaboration of circumstances, as well as our own thoughts and feelings. I hope you'll bear with my clumsiness in the telling.

The image of Mac that stands from the rest and, for me, signifies his essence, is drawn from the day I first saw him. He was standing out on the bowsprit of the Sea Wind, directing Muff at the helm as they glided into the lagoon. He waved and smiled as I was rowing close by. I offered to help in getting the Sea Wind secured and he replied, "Nope, I can handle it." In this simple refusal, he seemed to imply much more; that as much as he appreciated the offer, he couldn't forego the pleasure of doing it himself. There was an indescribable look about him when he smiled that I've felt always permitted him to say anything whatsoever with perfect graciousness. Stephanie said it was because "He's so vibrant." Whatever the words, it was quiet, direct, and apparent. I'm sure everyone who met him from the other boats passing through felt something similar.

To me he was the sailor in command of the search, for it seems to me that all who set out sailing the oceans are on a quest; however individual. I admired his self-sufficiency and was impressed with his responsibility. Two other qualities that are particularly significant to me were his utter love and regard for Muff...and a sort of lonely cynicism, which I can only say I vaguely sensed. Perhaps this amounted to an intuitive recognition of kind, as I've often considered myself cynical to a fault, but my only real confirmation of this came in having recently read something he'd written; to the effect that he was anxious to get to Palmyra so he could get over the disappointment he expected to find there.

I wish there were some way to share our feelings about other scenes we experienced together. There were the simple exchanges - like fish. Most of the fish around Palmyra, which are normally edible elsewhere, were poisonous to eat. There were a few kinds that were good, and we'd been taught by a man and his family who'd once spent considerable time living there. Anyway, we were more able to catch a lot of mullet, while Mac was able to catch plenty of papio (Cravalle), and we often shared our catches.

One late afternoon, when Stephanie and I had returned from a day of arduous exploring, we found a large papio left by Mac, and often when we went to take them mullet, they'd be away somewhere and we'd leave them. There is something innately, and symbolically, friendly and neighborly in offering and receiving food - particularly when it's produced by your own labors. Our conception of giving in a relationship was enriched through this fish exchange. Of course, it's also pleasant to come home after a hot and tiring day and find that your planned supper from cans had miraculously turned into fresh fish.

Then there was Stephanie's birthday. I'd baked her a cake and invited Mac and Muff for a party. They even brought a nice present. Huddled around in the cabin tent we'd set up for our land camp, we stuffed ourselves on lots of good food (a community effort), got out the old portable phonograph and played records, smoked too much and drank rum, played chess and sang "Happy Birthday" and talked away a long evening.

It may seem a little strange to you how we could derive so much enjoyment from simple, perhaps slightly tribalistic, pleasures. Of course, the setting is important. Palmyra is desolate and depressing, while at once being enchanting and mystical. There is a natural beauty that numbs the senses going hand in hand with hard realities: Poisonous fish, sharks, scorpions, spiders, rats, mosquitoes, etc. There is the fear of serious injury because the nearest outside help was days away, and on the other hand, an eagerness for the challenge.

Once Mac whacked himself on the leg with his machete while threshing a path through the jungle, and got a bad cut. He tried to sew it up but the needle was too dull! He taped it instead.

The humidity is usually uncomfortable, making a delight of a cold bath from stored rainwater. There is a sameness to the days, a silence composed of only sounds of nature; the pulse of the surf, the wind through the coconut trees, the nesting birds taking flight; an acute sense of being alone. Sharing a meal, a drink, a smoke, a conversation, playing chess, greetings as you pass going in opposite directions, all take on a pronounced flavor. You learn to relax and slow down, and though you can become tired and bored with a chore you've set yourself, you're surprised at your energy. We all came to feel a great deal healthier.

The chess games were a special treat, except that Muff didn't play. Mac and I were fairly evenly matched, while Stephanie beat us both on quite a few occasions. We always focused fully on the game, playing all out, but the real purpose was in the playing itself rather than in the winning or losing.

Anyway...to get back on the track. We had planned to make a trip to Fanning Island and back (about 200 miles), and the day before our scheduled departure Mac invited us for dinner, a sort of bon voyage party. We walked over to their camp area around 6 p.m., and finding them away, sat to watch the sunset and wait for them. Mac had mentioned earlier in the day that they were going fishing in the afternoon. When it grew dark we went aboard to wait for them and to get away from the mosquitoes. The later it became the more we worried. We kept going topsides to look out for them, and finally Stephanie had the sense to turn on the mastlights to help guide them. We spent the whole night waiting. In the morning I got Mac's little Seagull outboard fitted and running on his fiberglass dingy (they'd taken the Zodiac inflatable) and we set out to look for them. About a half mile or so to the west we found the Zodiac turned over and washed up on the beach. We went ashore and searched around the vicinity calling out their names. For the next three days we searched extensively every possible place we thought they might conceivably be. We circled those islands we could in the dinghy using binoculars and walked about calling all over. But we never found any other sign of them.

Stephanie and I hardly spoke except for calling out for Mac and Muff, and we didn't get much sleep. In retrospect I think we were in a mild state of shock at the loss. It was unbelievable. At first we kept expecting to find them, hoping, but our optimism soon turned to despair. It was terrible to watch Stephanie crying and be unable to comfort her. I don't know how to say this, but Mac and Muff were like models of a pattern that we wanted to learn and follow. I can't say how much we miss them.

We stayed on for another week or ten days, I don't know; time was like an apathy which had little meaning. It was hard to figure out what to do. We knew he was in regular contact with Curt Shoemaker in Hawaii and we tried without success to use Mac's ham radio. We finally decided to take the Sea Wind to Fanning, towing our smaller sloop, and report the matter there. We couldn't leave our boat behind because it has a slow leak and had to be pumped out every couple of days. And we couldn't bear to leave Sea Wind there unprotected. Besides the Sea Wind had diesel propulsion, while we had none but sail. So we readied both boats, though leaving much behind, and started out the narrow passage through the reefs around the lagoon. We were really afraid of this channel as we had grounded on the coral when we'd entered, though we'd managed to get off with little damage. Originally, Mac was going to help conn us through the channel towing with his Zodiac. I don't really know what happened. I was aboard the

Sea Wind towing our boat, which Stephanie was on. Our boat swung wide of the path the Sea Wind was making and crunched up on a coral head. I couldn't believe it, and for a few scary minutes I was at a total loss as to what to do. Since Stephanie was safe, I continued on out beyond the bad part and anchored the Sea Wind, leaving the diesel running. Then I jumped in the Zodiac and returned for Stephanie and took her back to the Sea Wind with instructions about what to do if the anchor slipped. I went back to our boat to assess the damage and feasibility of getting it free. Several ribs were broken and planks stove in and she was shipping water. I tried to use the Zodiac to pull her off and even hoisted the sails to help, though there wasn't much wind. I knew we could never get our boat to Fanning. My only hope was to try towing her back into the lagoon and grounding her on an old seaplane ramp, but she wouldn't budge, so I began the task of unloading and stripping her of what we could salvage. I made several trips ferrying our stuff to the Sea Wind and we upped anchor and set out.

I was violently sick and heaving over the side while Stephanie steered. We kept looking back at our boat until she disappeared from view. We had scraped and saved and worked for her seven days a week for seven months. I had built the mast myself and we had replanked, rebuilt, fiberglassed, painted, outfitted, and launched her with champagne. We named her Iola, which in Hawaiian meant, "To life," our toast.

After awhile we decided that going to Fanning wasn't a good plan, mainly because we'd be in a foreign jurisdiction and there was a question of whether the Sea Wind would be confiscated, leaving us homeless and stranded. We felt a great responsibility for the Sea Wind. She's not the most modern or efficient insofar as speed, rigging, and sailing ability goes, but the sheer grace of her lines and plain old fashioned character and individual workmanship more than make up. She's a beautiful yacht and we've come to love her.

One thing I might as well tell you is that Stephanie and I tend to be romantics, which often leads to rationalizations about life. I suppose this comes from being over-anxious for something better, and we tend to color reality with our dreams. I mention this because

I wish to be candid about everything, and I hope it'll aid in understanding something of us.

As our return voyage to Hawaii wore on, we began to feel more and more that it was the best thing to do - for a number of reasons. I needed dental and medical treatment, Hawaii had been our home for the past several years and we felt it the best place to institute legal procedures, as well as settle a legal problem we'd left behind, and there are other matters. On the way back a swordfish rammed us, breaking off its swordbill through the hull. We shipped a lot of water and had the pumps operating, but it took us over an hour to locate and get at the hole. We still had to pump out everyday. So, here in Hawaii, we've had to haul out the Sea Wind at a boat yard for repairs. We're also repainting her while we're at it. (This is being written at the boatyard.) Last but not least, we want to get married, which we haven't felt the necessity to do before, but we've been talking of having children - the time for a wedding now seems completely right.

I realize this may be the wrong place to mention this, but we want to get it all over with. We want to file a salvage claim on the Sea Wind. I hope I can make you understand all that we mean by this, as there are many factors involved. We've lost our own boat, market value about $10,000, although price tags have nothing to do with how a sailor values her, whether she be a tub or a luxury yacht. A boat is his home, his environment, his transportation to far places, to which a large part of his existence goes in maintaining. We love the Sea Wind and we want, eventually, to continue with her in the voyage around the world that Mac and Muff began. We haven't yet notified anyone about the true circumstances. We feel you should be the first to know for one thing, and I plan to post this as soon as the writing's finished. Another reason is that we wish to seek legal advice. For this we are returning from the island of Oahu, where we now are, to that of Hawaii, where we're from, to seek the advice of a friend who is an attorney and ex-judge. Also I've registered the Sea Wind, renaming her Lokahi, meaning "of one mind," which we think aptly sums up the spirit of our feelings. In having second thoughts, perhaps the registration wasn't the right thing to do. Something tells me I shouldn't have done it. But I have done it and I want you to know.

There are many things we know you'll want to have whatever happens and we'd like to ship them to you at the earliest opportunity.

We would appreciate hearing your feelings about everything. We intend to write again soon; when we've found our friend and his advice (about a week now, I think). We want to keep you fully informed. You can get in touch with us c/o Box 337, Mountain View, Hawaii.

I know this letter must be a sensitive experience for you, and I know I've stated things badly. I seem to have great difficulty finding an end and a beginning, and in determining appropriate language for in between. I apologize for my lack, but we want and very much need an understanding.

Stephanie and I originally fled to Palmyra to escape a lot of problems, as well as to seek ourselves and a meaningful relationship in, for, and from, the rather illusive path of dreams that lead us on.

But it's impossible merely to escape problems. We have to solve them or suffer them. Life was simpler of Palmyra, and now we're back with old and new problems and all their many complications. I hardly know where to begin and there are times when some seem insurmountable. However, we've definitely decided to try resolving the major items before we're able to resume our voyage in good conscience.

Thank you for listening, and please let us know if there's anything we can do. We send all our deepest sympathies to you and others who will feel their loss. We cared, we care.

Sincere regards,
Roy and Stephanie
P. S. We found about $400.00 aboard and used it on repairing and painting the Sea Wind. However, we'll return this amount to you if you feel it's the right thing to do.

NOTE

The answer to how you write a letter truthfully when you have so much to conceal is that you mix fact with fiction. There are thus two main thrusts to the information, or misinformation as the case may be. One is composed of truth and the other deception or concealment of truth.

The most truthful parts are those in which I speak of our feelings toward Mac and Muff. The most deceitful are those parts which tell of what happened to them, in which small facts are mingled with lies - such as "we believe they died in a boating accident (only half true) and "we found their overturned dinghy washed up on the beach," (again, half true).

Other parts are misinformed due to honest error on my part, such as my confusing two parties at our tent into one. At Steph's birthday party we did not "stuff ourselves on lots of good food (a community effort)" Mac and Muff had been invited for cake and coffee. The more sumptuous repast came later at the party for Don and Bill of Shearwater.

Similarly, my statement about being invited to dinner the day before our scheduled departure is not correct. Our scheduled departure date was for Saturday, August 31. Mac and Muff were both dead by the early morning hours of the day before. Was this a deception on my part? No, at the time of writing that I had checked Stephanie's entry for Friday, August 30, and unthinkingly went with that. The invitation to dinner was tendered on Wednesday, August 28. Between that date and Wednesday, September 4 - an entire week - no entries were made in Iola's logbook. It was on the latter date that we had decided upon towing Iola to Fanning with Sea Wind, and when Stephanie, under the influence of alcohol, grass, and Parest, decided to bring the log up to date. Partial proof of this lies in the fact that she writes on Friday, August 30 (according to the entry), "And then - tragedy - and overnite a whole new set of alternatives beset us." On that date, when we had gone to answer the invitation to dinner, Stephanie was unaware of any tragedy. She would not discover that possibility until the next day, Saturday, August 31. And her entries from Wednesday, August 28, up to Wednesday, September 4, form a continuous stream of entries, which is when she mistakenly entered the invitation as received on Friday, August 30. Without being able to specify exactly what they were, I remember Stephanie asking me questions about what she and I were doing during the previous week. We were aboard Sea Wind, she cuddled on the settee with Puffer, the logbook, glass of apricot brandy on the floor within reach, and ashtray for the joint in roachclip that needed relighting two or three times. I sat across from her at the dinette doing I don't know what, but preoccupied, and replying desultorily or saying "I don't know." was probably sitting there with drink and joint in hand, too.

Stephanie herself testified in her theft trial that the invitation was received on August 29, a Thursday. By her murder trial, no doubt reminded of her log entry by Bugliosi, the date had moved forward to Friday, August 30. Of course, the August 29 date may simply have been an honest error in recollection on her part - but then, so was the August 30 date. In my theft trial, I testified that the invitation had come on Wednesday, August 28. This was not a great feat of memory on my part. Rather I worked backward through the chronology of events. Mac and Muff had died on Thursday, August 29. Therefore, the invitation had to have come before that day.

In a curious footnote as to whether the invitation was genuine or I had made it up in order to manipulate Stephanie for my own evil purposes, the Bug reports that Pollock had told a newspaper reporter that Shoemaker had told him that Mac had mentioned the dinner invitation to him during their last communication on Wednesday, August 28. However, he never testified on this point at any of the trials.

I began the writing of this letter some time during the return voyage from Palmyra, going through several drafts. Finally, I sat one night in drydock at Kewalo Basin to copy out the final draft in my best handwriting. Bottle of booze and grass stash before me, I began. It was tedious, the final version about ten pages long. I took breaks to rest, go to the bathroom, talk to Steph, roll another joint, perhaps to munch on something, and pour another drink. In the process, I may have left out a paragraph or two, especially about the fate of Iola, getting her free and etc. On the other hand, I may have fuzzily decided to edit it out for a vague reason or two. Some will doubtless hold that the lapse was intentional, that I was concealing the fact, as Bugliosi claims in his version, that I sank Iola purposely because I intended to steal Sea Wind all along. People are entitled to their opinions, however wrong they may be - it's the American way.

*****

Another honest mistake was in saying we had arrived at 6 p.m. in response to the invitation. That was purely a guess pulled out of thin air. On reflection, I think it had to be later than that, about a half hour or so before sunset. What time the sun set on Palmyra on August 30, I have no idea. You will remember that I had given up telling time by watch or clock, but went by the position of the sun or amount of light for my reckoning of time. Back to navigation, which requires accurate time, and later civilization, meant back to the slavery of the clock. 6 p.m. for me was about dinnertime.

The lie about Mac going fishing that afternoon (Friday, August 30), was a truth that had been forwarded from two days previous (Wednesday, August 28), a lie that I would suggest to Stephanie and she would accept. She would later tell Bug, as well as testify, that she had heard the outboard engine on Mac's Zodiac that afternoon. It was a false memory, one that she believed to be true, one transplanted from Wednesday to Friday. She probably had heard Mac's outboard on Wednesday since he had mentioned going fishing later in the afternoon.

Then, of course, there is my mealymouthedness about all the reasons, in addition to basic necessity, for our return - medical, dental, legal problems, marriage, etc.

Mary "Kit" Muncey claimed she received the letter in March, 1975. I had testified to having written it in drydock at Kewalo Basin and having mailed it during the first days of November, 1974 - after I had eluded the FBI and Coast Guard at the Ala Wai Yacht Harbor.

Very slow mail delivery. What's the explanation?

Simple. I had addressed it incorrectly. I wasn't sure, and cannot now remember, where Kit Muncey lived. There is a confusion between San Diego and Bellingham, Washington. At any rate, it was returned to our post office box in Mountain View, which Debbie had taken over for her own use. She used to forward any mail we received dating back to when we fled the Punaside of the Big Island for the Konaside during the summer of 1973. Thereafter, she forwarded our mail to Maui when we had moved there to begin work on our newly purchased boat.

I received it back while in the Halawa Jail. From there, I sent it on to my brother, Larry, in California, asking him to try finding an address for her through directory assistance in either San Diego or the nearby smaller towns and Bellingham. He was unsuccessful and returned it to me. Then I sent it to Stephanie for her to try mailing. She came up with an address in Seattle, I think. She enclosed a note saying, "Buck wrote to you some time back while in drydock," but that the letter had been delayed.

By the time of her murder trial eleven years later, she would change her story to say that I had written the letter in Halawa Jail and that she had lied in saying it had been written in drydock.

At my theft trial, Judge King refused to allow my letter to Kit Muncey into evidence for the jury to consider on the ground that it was self-serving.

However, by the time of my murder trial he had apparently changed his mind and allowed it into evidence where it apparently was received by a cynical jury and caused some damage. The Bug says they were both amazed and angry, "amazed that Buck had written so articulately and with such obvious intelligence, and angry that he had had the colossal nerve to say the things he did to Kit."

###

Appendix III

Proof of duplicity on the part of Vincent Bugliosi, attorney for Stephanie Stearns from documents origination out of Co-counsel Leonard Wineglass' office, including a note to himself in his own handwriting.

LEONARD I. WEINGLASS
ATTORNEY AT LAW

TELEPHONE (213) 620-0700

304 SO. BROADWAY, SUITE 223
LOS ANGELES, CALIFORNIA 90013

November 6, 1985

Vincent T. Bugliori, Esq.
Suite 470
9300 Wilshire Blvd.
Beverly Hills, California 90212

Dear Vince:

I am enclosing the following:

(1) Muff's letters including "diary"

(2) My letter to Elliot Inoki re: Motion for Hilt discovery

(3) My letter to Elliot Inoki Re: trial stipulations.

I'll be back on the 25th of November. Be sure Stephanie appears in court on the 25th at 10:30 to waive time.

Sincerely,

Leonard I. Weinglass

LIW:mkb
Enclosures

JOSEPH P. RUSSONIELLO
United States Attorney
Northern District of California

ELLIOT ENOKI
Assistant U.S. Attorney
Room C-242, U.S. Courthouse
300 Ala Moana Blvd., Box 50183
Honolulu, Hawaii 96850
Telephone: (808) 546-7170

Attorneys for Plaintiff
UNITED STATES OF AMERICA

IN THE UNITED STATES DISTRICT COURT

FOR THE NORTHERN DISTRICT OF CALIFORNIA

UNITED STATES OF AMERICA,) CR. NO. 84-0546-02 SPK
)
Plaintiff,)
) NOTICE OF MOTION; SECOND MOTION
vs.) FOR DISCOVERY; MEMORANDUM IN
) SUPPORT OF SECOND MOTION FOR
BUCK DUANE WALKER, also) DISCOVERY; DECLARATION OF
known as Roy A. Allen (01),) ELLIOT ENOKI
and STEPHANIE KAY STEARNS,)
also known as Stephanie)
Allen (02),)
)
Defendants.)
_____)

NOTICE OF MOTION

TO: VINCENT T. BUGLIOSI, ESQ.
9300 Wilshire Boulevard, Suite 470
Beverly Hills, California 90212

LEONARD I. WEINGLASS, ESQ.
5th Floor
740 Broadway
New York, NY 10003

Attorneys for Defendant
STEPHANIE KAY STEARNS

YOU ARE HEREBY NOTIFIED that Plaintiff's Second Motion for

Discovery will be heard before the Honorable Samuel P. King, United